CRITICAL SURVEY

OF

DRAMA

CRITICAL SURVEY

OF

DRAMA

Second Revised Edition

Volume 2
Minna Canth - Richard Foreman

Editor, Second Revised Edition
Carl Rollyson
Baruch College, City University of New York

Editor, First Editions, English and Foreign Language Series
Frank N. Magill

SALEM PRESS, INC.
Pasadena, California   Hackensack, New Jersey

Editor in Chief: Dawn P. Dawson

Managing Editor: Christina J. Moose

Developmental Editor: R. Kent Rasmussen

Project Editor: Rowena Wildin

Research Supervisor: Jeffry Jensen

Research Assistant: Michelle Murphy

Acquisitions Editor: Mark Rehn

Photograph Editor: Philip Bader

Manuscript Editor: Sarah Hilbert

Assistant Editor: Andrea E. Miller

Production Editor: Cynthia Beres

Layout: Eddie Murillo and William Zimmerman

Library of Congress Cataloging-in-Publication Data

Critical survey of drama / edited by Carl Rollyson.-- 2nd rev. ed.

    p. cm.

Previous edition edited by Frank Northen Magill in 1994.

"Combines, updates, and expands two earlier Salem Press reference sets: Critical survey of drama, revised edition, English language series, published in 1994, and Critical survey of drama, foreign language series, published in 1986"--Pref.

Includes bibliographical references and index.

ISBN 1-58765-102-5 (set : alk. paper) -- ISBN 1-58765-104-1 (vol. 2 : alk. paper) --

1. Drama--Dictionaries. 2. Drama--History and criticism--Dictionaries. 3. Drama--Bio-bibliography. 4. English drama--Dictionaries. 5. American drama--Dictionaries. 6. Commonwealth drama (English)--Dictionaries. 7. English drama--Bio-bibliography. 8. American drama--Bio-bibliography. 9. Commonwealth drama (English)--Bio-bibliography. I. Rollyson, Carl E. (Carl Edmund) II. Magill, Frank Northen, 1907-1997.

PN1625 .C68 2003

809.2'003—dc21

2003002190

Fourth Printing

PRINTED IN THE UNITED STATES OF AMERICA

CONTENTS

VOLUME 2

COMPLETE LIST OF CONTENTS

VOLUME 1

VOLUME 2

VOLUME 3

VOLUME 4

VOLUME 5

VOLUME 6

VOLUME 7

AMERICAN DRAMA

VOLUME 8

EUROPEAN DRAMA

WORLD DRAMA

DRAMATIC GENRES

DRAMA TECHNIQUES

RESOURCES

INDEXES

CRITICAL SURVEY
OF
DRAMA

MINNA CANTH

Born: Tampere, Finland; March 19, 1844
Died: Kuopio, Finland; May 12, 1897

PRINCIPAL DRAMA

Murtovarkaus, pr. 1882, pb. 1883
Roinilan talossa, pr. 1883, pb. 1885
Työmiehen vaimo, pr., pb. 1885
Kovan onnen lapsia, pb. 1888, pr. 1889
Papin perhe, pr., pb. 1891
Hän on Sysmästä, pb. 1893, pr. 1902
Sylvi, pr., pb. 1893
Spiritistinen istunto, pr., pb. 1894
Anna Liisa, pr., pb. 1895
Kotoa pois, pb. 1895

OTHER LITERARY FORMS

Minna Canth started her career as a journalist. In 1874, when her husband, J. F. Canth, took over the editorship of a weekly paper, *Keski-Suomi*, it was Minna who did most of the actual writing. With her forceful articles, she angered the owners of the paper, and subsequently, in 1878, the Canths switched over to another publication, *Päijänne*. Even as an acknowledged author, Canth pursued her journalistic writing mainly in the liberal periodical *Valvoja* and, from 1889 to 1890, in her own journal, *Vapaita aatteita*. Canth's first collection of short stories, *Novelleja ja kertomuksia*, was published in 1878 under the pseudonym Vilja. The stories are light, romantic tales written under the influence of the Norwegian Bjørnstjerne Bjørnson. The themes that Canth explored in her drama are the same as those in her short stories: social commitment, anger at society's neglect of its poor, and women's issues. Canth's dramatic talent and sharp ear for natural speech characterize her stories. Truly remarkable is the range of her female portraits; with equal veracity and sensitivity, she describes the gloomy existence of lowly maids, the strength of the women of the people, and the restricted lives of middle-class girls. Yet Canth's stories are uneven in quality: Many bear the imprint of haste,

written as they were during a spare moment and often lacking a final touch. Nevertheless, some of them, *Köyhää kansaa* (1886), *Hanna* (1886), *Kauppa-Lopo* (1889), and *Agnes* (1892), are among the most lasting artistic accomplishments of Canth's career.

ACHIEVEMENTS

Minna Canth has maintained her position as one of Finland's foremost playwrights. Her works belong to the living cultural heritage of Finnish Finland. Both professional theaters and amateur groups continue to stage her plays on a regular basis. As a daughter of the working class, she entered the country's cultural scene as an outsider and, propelled by her inner fire, introduced almost single-handedly the ideas of the "modern breakthrough" to Finland. Besides her literary accomplishments, her social significance cannot be overestimated. She championed the rights both of women and of the working class. Although active within the organized women's movement, she never slavishly followed its dictates. Unlike the majority of the participants in the movement, who came from the educated classes and primarily strove for equality with the men of their own class, Canth stressed the necessity for women of all classes to unite in a common struggle. She also realized that the initiative had to come from bourgeois women, who must be prepared for certain sacrifices in the beginning. As long as working-class women saw their families starve, their primary allegiance would not be with their sex but rather with their class in a fight for survival. Canth criticized the institutionalized Church, which supported the status quo by teaching the poor to accept their lot in life with humility and the upper classes to regard their privileges as theirs by the grace of God. To Canth, such views represented a ticking time bomb that would one day explode. As much as the most radical of her works shocked contemporary audiences, in equal measure they have inspired later generations of the working class. Canth spurred their cultural interests by providing them with "plays of their own" and thereby strengthening their self-confidence.

Canth's achievements were indeed remarkable, but they could have been even greater. She had the potential to become another August Strindberg or Henrik Ibsen had she the same opportunities. As it was, Canth never traveled outside Finland, and her exposure to theater was limited—a few visits to Helsinki and occasional guest performances in Kuopio by the Finnish theater. In addition to her writing, she managed a business and reared seven children.

BIOGRAPHY

The first nine years of her life, from 1844 to 1853, Minna Canth (born Ulrika Wilhelmina Johnsson) lived in Tampere, an industrial city in central Finland, where her father, Gustaf Wilhelm Johnsson, was employed in a textile mill. Although lacking in formal education, her father was highly regarded and advanced quickly in his job. In 1853, the family moved to Kuopio in eastern Finland, where Johnsson acquired a shop selling yarns manufactured by the Tampere factory. After graduating from a Swedish-language girls' school in Kuopio, Canth continued her education in a newly established teachers' college in Jyväskylä, which represented the highest level of education to which a young woman could aspire in Finland. In 1864, after only a year's studies, she fell in love with and married J. F. Canth, a teacher of natural sciences at the college. During the following years, until her husband's death in 1879, Canth devoted herself to their growing family. She did, however, find time to follow the major issues of the day, so that in 1874, when her husband took over the editorship of the paper *Keski-Suomi*, she was able to do most of the work. Canth translated foreign articles and wrote her own on topics familiar to audiences from her later artistic production: women's education and alcoholism and other social ills. It was also during these years in Jyväskylä that she first came in contact with the theater, when the young Finnish Theater from Helsinki, started in 1872, gave guest performances there. Also influential was her acquaintance with the directors of the theater, Emilie and Kaarlo Bergbom. This sister and brother pair were to remain Canth's mentors for years to come.

When Canth's husband died, leaving his wife with six children and expecting a seventh, she was forced to find some means of supporting her large family. Returning to Kuopio, she took over her parents' bankrupt yarn shop, and with skill and hard work, she managed to develop the business into a successful enterprise, which gave her and her family a solid living and enabled her to devote time to her writing and other cultural endeavors.

Although a small town and far from the country's capital, Kuopio had a bishop's seat, and the provincial governor resided there. A lively cultural life developed around the small circle of the town's intellectuals. Much of the credit goes, however, to Canth. Her house became the "salon" frequented by young intellectuals, the names of whom are today familiar to every Finnish schoolchild: the authors Juhani Aho and Heikki Kauppinen, the members of the gifted Järnefelt family, and the brothers Erkko, to mention a few. Books by European thinkers such as Georg Brandes, Charles Darwin, John Stuart Mill, Hippolyte-Adolphe Taine, Max Nordau, and the Scandinavian authors Ibsen and Strindberg were discussed. Canth translated some of their works and commented on them in her articles in *Valvoja* and in her own short-lived *Vapaita aatteita*. Under the guidance of the Bergboms, she also launched her dramatic career. Soon, however, it became apparent that the kinds of works desired by the theater did not always coincide with those that Canth felt compelled to write. Her first two plays, *Murtovarkaus* and *Roinilan talossa*, were public successes—harmless depictions of life in the Finnish countryside in the popular national Romantic style. By the third play, *Työmiehen vaimo*, the tone had changed. Brandes's thesis of literature, which emphasized the inclusion of issues of current interest, found a loyal follower in Canth, who increasingly attacked the hypocrisy of society, double morality, the Church, women's powerless position, and the economic plight of the working class.

In 1889, the performance of Canth's fourth major play, *Kovan onnen lapsia*, marked a turning point in her career and private life. Its radicalism shocked the audience, and the play was canceled after its opening night. More significantly, Canth's strongest supporters, the young intellectuals, thought that this time she had gone too far. The rift was further widened by their opposite stands in the so-called morality feud. Although both Canth and her young male supporters rejected the prevailing double standard of sexual morality, whereby men were allowed sexual freedom before and after marriage whereas women were expected to live by strict moral rules, they clashed over ways to remedy the situation. The men advocated free love for men and women but maintained that prostitution was a necessary evil in view of men's naturally stronger sex drive. Canth, on the other hand, called for the abolition of prostitution and demanded the same virtuous behavior from men and women. She was less motivated by idealistic morality than by her pragmatic concern for the women who became pregnant as a result of "free love" and the girls, mostly from the working class, who fell victim to prostitution. Worst of all, the men's attacks on Canth went beyond their differing points of view—they ridiculed her in public about her appearance, age, and lifestyle.

Before becoming an autonomous Grand Duchy of Russia in 1809, Finland had been an integral part of Sweden for centuries. As a result, Swedish was the language of administration, culture, and education. Yet the majority of the people spoke Finnish as their mother tongue. With the nationalistic movement that reached Finland around the middle of the 1800's, a strong, new interest was sparked in the Finnish language and culture. Both the Jyväskylä College and the Finnish Theater were products of the movement. Canth had always faithfully supported the Finnish cause and with her art contributed to its growth. Now in the 1890's, however, she found herself alienated from both the young Aho circle and the politically conservative Finns behind the Bergboms and the Finnish Theater. In Canth's view, a greater threat to Finland was posed by the nationalist groups in Russia than by the domestic language question. Furthermore, she encountered a more fertile soil for her ideas among such Swedish-language intellectuals as the author K. A. Tavaststjerna. That she wrote *Sylvi* in Swedish and offered it to the Swedish Theater did nothing to improve her relations with the Bergboms.

The times were changing, however, and new ideas were coming from abroad. The rational decade of the 1880's was yielding to the new currents of neo-Romanticism and Symbolism of the 1890's. Even Brandes, the father of realistic literature in Scandinavia, now espoused Friedrich Nietzsche-inspired radical aristocratism with stress on the exceptional individual. Instead of relying on the powers of reason, the new generation of writers and thinkers explored the secrets of the human mind, spiritism, and hypnotism. Canth did not remain unaffected by these ideas. Some personal tragedies, the death of three persons that had been close to her, a nineteen-year-old daughter among them, rendered her especially susceptible to the emotional appeal of the new "isms." More than any other thinker, the Russian author Leo Tolstoy had an impact on Canth. His ideas of pacifism, love, faith, and humility can be detected in *Papin perhe* and became the dominant force in her work by the time she wrote *Anna Liisa*. Canth was at the height of her creative powers and the mastery of her craft when in 1897, in her fifties, she died of heart failure.

ANALYSIS

In 1882, when Minna Canth began writing plays, she had few Finnish predecessors to emulate. After Aleksis Kivi in the 1870's, only some minor plays had appeared in Finnish. The lack of an established Finnish canon of drama was perhaps a blessing in disguise; it left the fledgling playwright with a greater sense of freedom.

MURTOVARKAUS

The plot of Canth's first play, *Murtovarkaus*, is conventional. The play ends happily with the well-to-do farmer's son, Niilo, marrying Helena, a poor but beautiful crofter's daughter. Before that, however, many a hurdle must be overcome. Niilo's father wants him to marry a wealthy neighbor's daughter, Loviisa, and she, quite aware of Niilo's financial strengths, eagerly accepts the offer. Therefore, Helena's appearance on the scene is most unwelcome. So that her rival will not pose a threat, Loviisa contracts the services of a village witch, who dutifully proceeds to arrange a break-in in Niilo's house and have Helena accused of it. Fearing her alcohol-prone father to be the real culprit, Helena compliantly accepts her imprisonment. Finally, Hoppulainen, a happy-go-lucky drunkard, Helena's other suitor, by chance comes on the true offender, the witch, and the innocent Helena regains freedom and fiancé. In the manner of the well-made play, the plot intrigue is built on unexpected happenings, misunderstandings, and overheard conversations. The characters are static, either entirely good or entirely bad, the most interesting of whom is Hoppulainen. Although irresponsible and saddled with many vices, he possesses a tender heart and a quick tongue. In him, Canth portrays the typical inhabitant of Savo province, known for his humor, carefree nature, and quick wit.

In spite of the play's many weaknesses, Canth's achievement in *Murtovarkaus* was notable, and the play has remained popular with audiences. It provides the theatergoer with light entertainment, events set in the Finnish countryside, and characters with whom audiences can identify. The dialogue flows effortlessly, and the cleverest lines are reserved for Hoppulainen, who is a virtual treasure house of Finnish proverbs and sayings. The melodious language, rich in parallelisms and alliteration, harks back to Finnish folk poetry.

Työmiehen vaimo

After one more play, *Roinilan talossa*, in the national Romantic style, Canth turned her attention to more serious issues, the women's question and the plight of the working class. In 1882, the Finnish diet had entertained a proposal that would have guaranteed married women the right to their own earnings. The defeat of the proposal provoked Canth's anger, and the defenseless position of the married woman constitutes the ideological core of Canth's next drama, *Työmiehen vaimo*. The play opens with Risto and Johanna's wedding. The bride, an industrious young woman, enters the marriage with sizable savings that now, in accordance with the law, are the property of her husband. In a year's time, all of her savings are gone, she has aged, and she is desperately struggling to support her ailing infant son. All her money, to the last penny, has gone to quench Risto's insatiable thirst. Risto strikes the ultimate blow when he steals Johanna's half-finished weaving from the loom, which causes Johanna to fall ill and die. Johanna's has not been

the only female life destroyed by Risto. With false promises, he has trapped and seduced the gypsy girl Homsantuu, a romantically wild and anarchistic child of nature. When Risto deserts Homsantuu, she shoots him. While being dragged away by the police, Homsantuu cries out the now famous lines: "Your law and justice. . . . These are what I ought to have shot." These words crystallized all of Canth's own resentment against the established social order.

Not only men but also bourgeois women and their lack of solidarity are chastised by Canth in *Työmiehen vaimo*. Two women, members of the local women's club, break into a tirade of accusations against Johanna without ever investigating the circumstances surrounding the theft. Because of Johanna's poverty and lack of social graces, the women regard her as a morally inferior being, unfit to be a mother and to receive their work consignments. Vappu, an independent and strong-willed person, is the only woman who supports Johanna, and after Johanna's death it is Vappu who adopts her son. Vappu realizes that marriage can be an ensnaring trap for a woman, and she steadfastly guards her freedom. In that, Vappu contrasts sharply with another female character in the play, a representative of the traditional woman, who regards marriage, set by God, as indissoluble, is always quoting from the Bible, and urges Johanna to surrender herself in humility to her husband's tyranny.

Kovan onnen lapsia

The tone of Canth's next drama, *Kovan onnen lapsia*, is sharper. The scene opens with a young boy about to die of hunger and lack of medical care. His mother, herself worn out prematurely by worry and deprivation, is a deeply religious woman who suffers in silence and accepts without protest her lot in life, regarding it as God's will. In contrast, a group of young workers, her husband among them, who have lost their jobs after openly challenging their employer, are determined to fight for a better future for their people. Their leader, Topra-Heikki, is a modern-day Robin Hood, generous but hot-blooded. With the intention of getting medicine for the sick child, Topra-Heikki sets the barn of a wealthy but miserly farmer on fire and then steals his money. When one of Topra-

Heikki's men, driven mad by a bad conscience, threatens to inform the authorities, Topra-Heikki feels forced to kill him. The police, however, catch up with Topra-Heikki and his friends. In the play's final scene, the police arrive at the cottage of the ailing boy. The father, who has had no part in the robbery, is arrested when he, at his pious wife's urging, admits to knowing about the stolen money. Topra-Heikki's good intentions have come to nothing; his help arrives too late, for the little boy has died. Now, only the mother and her two young daughters are left behind as the men are taken away to the accompaniment of the little girl's bitter cry. With their father, the family's breadwinner, gone, the child knows that only starvation and death await them.

Kovan onnen lapsia was performed only once at the Finnish theater in Helsinki. Strong public outcry was unleashed against Canth's alleged advocacy of violence on the part of the working class. From a modern-day vantage point, her message rings more like a warning to the establishment than a call to arms for the workers. Unfortunately, Canth's warnings went unnoticed. In 1918, a civil war broke out in Finland between the Socialist "Reds" and the bourgeois "Whites." The bourgeois won, Finland retained its newly gained independence, and democracy was given a chance to develop, but a lot of bloodshed and deep social divisions could have been avoided had soothsayers such as Canth been heeded. In *Kovan onnen lapsia*, Canth champions social reforms rather than revolution. Indeed, she does not sanction Topra-Heikki's behavior but clearly demonstrates how one criminal act leads to another. She understood, however, how bitterness can arise among poverty-stricken workers and lead to unintended violence.

Although the play contains genuinely touching scenes, it suffers from excessive didactic pathos and Robin Hood romanticism. Also, the extreme humbleness of the pious wife-mother dates the play. Such blind obedience and acceptance of life's hardships strike modern Scandinavian audiences as strangely unrealistic and antiquated.

PAPIN PERHE

The harsh public reaction to *Kovan onnen lapsia*, criticism from her supporters, and deaths in her inner circle of friends all contributed to the changed mood and mellower tone in Canth's next play, *Papin perhe*, one of her strongest. Although still addressing serious issues, such as women's subordination in family, Canth approaches her subject with more humor and less didacticism. Also evident is Canth's growth in terms of dramatic technique.

The plot intrigue evolves around the generational conflict between the repressive rule of a father, a pastor, and his progressive children. The battle lines are drawn when the son refuses to work for his father's conservative newspaper and is subsequently disowned by the father. In response, the son leaves for Helsinki and there joins the enemy camp, the competing liberal paper. The family's two other children, two daughters, follow their brother to Helsinki. Somewhat unexpectedly, the play ends in reconciliation. On the evening of the younger daughter's successful theater debut, the father arrives unannounced at his children's apartment. At the sight of her father, who was always vehemently opposed to his daughter's theater ambitions, the daughter becomes so frightened that she falls violently ill. This in turn shakes the father out of his self-satisfied complacency, making him realize not only that he drove his children away from home but also that he was about to kill one of them. Subsequently, father and children vow to respect one another's opinions, and the play ends as the older daughter recites Tolstoyan words of love: "Freedom is the most important thing. No it isn't. Love is."

Although many broken friendships were mended by *Papin perhe*, the harmonious relationship between Canth and the Finnish theater remained permanently damaged. Canth became increasingly alienated from the Bergboms' conservative Finnish nationalism, finding a more open-minded atmosphere in Swedish cultural circles. Her next play, *Sylvi*, which was originally written in Swedish, was first performed in the Swedish Theater.

SYLVI

Sylvi is the story of a childlike young woman married to a man many years her senior and her passionate love for Victor, a childhood friend. Considering her marriage an unfortunate mistake, Sylvi asks her husband for a divorce. When he categorically rejects all talk about it, Sylvi, in desperation, kills him with rat poison. Immediately afterward, in witnessing her husband's death agony, she bitterly regrets her act, but she never regrets or denies her love for Victor. Indeed, it is this love that sustains her in prison when she is tormented by remorse and a guilty conscience. In the end, when Victor announces that his feelings have changed and that he is engaged to another woman, Sylvi's emotional defenses collapse, and she loses her foothold on reality.

Sylvi resembles Ibsen's *Et dukkehjem* (pr., pb. 1879; *A Doll's House*, 1880) in many respects. Like Nora, Sylvi is her husband's cute plaything, his "kitty cat." Canth, like Ibsen, attacks the sanctity of marriage. For reasons of economy, lack of educational opportunities, and social prestige, young girls were often compelled to marry older men, thus passing from their fathers' patronage to that of their husbands. A clear conflict prevailed between the laws of nature and those of society. In the eyes of society, Sylvi is a woman of loose morals or even a hardened criminal. To Canth, she represents a victim of a hypocritical society. In fact, Canth's exaggerated emphasis of Sylvi's natural purity and childlike innocence detracts from her believability as a character.

Anna Liisa

Anna Liisa, Canth's masterpiece and last major play, shows the progress she made during her relatively short writing career, and it also reveals her changing outlook on life. Instead of social concerns, the focus lies on individual psychology. Anna Liisa and Johannes are in the midst of wedding preparations when their marriage plans are abruptly shattered by the arrival of Mikko, a former farmhand of Anna Liisa's father. In an effort to reclaim Anna Liisa, Mikko tells the family about the child Anna Liisa had borne four years earlier, when only fifteen, and her strangulation of the newborn. After the initial shock, the parents urge Anna Liisa to marry Mikko, father of the child, to keep the secret within the family. Not only does Anna Liisa refuse, but she also decides to confess everything in public. Only by accepting her rightful punishment, she believes, will she gain peace of mind. By surrendering herself voluntarily to the authorities, she rises in stature.

A clear indication of Canth's changed outlook is the fact that this time it is the village pastor, the villain of earlier Canth dramas, who comes to Anna Liisa's support and defense. Although led away in handcuffs, Anna Liisa appears at the end restored to her former greatness. She is, as Johannes puts it, at heart the same old Anna Liisa, a paragon of virtue and goodness, that he had planned to marry. Yet, the modern reader is likely to rebel against Canth's Tolstoyan doctrine of humility here. Has Anna Liisa not, as her mother wonders, suffered enough during the long years of lonely struggle with shame and guilt? Did she not deserve a chance for a new life with Johannes? Why is Mikko allowed to leave the stage unscathed? Admittedly he failed to win Anna Liisa back, but that hardly seems a sufficient punishment for his actions. The author of *Anna Liisa* is far removed from the indignant writer of *Kovan onnen lapsia* or even of *Sylvi*, written only two years earlier.

Other major works

SHORT FICTION: *Novelleja ja kertomuksia*, 1878; *Hanna*, 1886; *Köyhää kansaa*, 1886; *Salakari*, 1887; *Lain mukaan*, 1889; *Kauppa-Lopo*, 1889; *Agnes*, 1892; *Novelleja*, 1892 (2 volumes).

Bibliography

Marjormaa, Ulpu, ed. *One Hundred Faces from Finland: A Biographical Kaleidoscope*. Helsinki: FLS, 2000. An essay on Canth is included among the famous Finns covered in this volume.

Sinkkonen, Sirkka, and Aneneli Milén, eds. *Toward Equality: Proceedings of the American and Finnish Workshop on Minna Canth, June 19-20, 1985*. Kuopio: University of Kuopio, 1986. A collection of papers presented at the workshop on Canth held in Finland at the University of Kuopio in 1985. It examines her works as well as women's issues and feminism in Finland. Includes bibliography.

Wilmer, S. E., ed. *Portraits of Courage: Plays by Finnish Women*. Helsinki: Helsinki University Press, 1997. Examines the work of Canth and other Finnish women playwrights.

Virpi Zuck

KAREL ČAPEK

Born: Malé Svatoňovice, Bohemia, Austro-
Hungarian Empire (now in Czech Republic);
January 9, 1890
Died: Prague, Czechoslovakia (now Czech
Republic); December 25, 1938

PRINCIPAL DRAMA

Lásky hra osudná, wr. 1910, pb. 1916, pr. 1930
(with Josef Čapek)

Loupezník, pr., pb. 1920 (*The Robber*, 1931)

Ze života hmyzu, pb. 1920, pr. 1922 (with Josef
Čapek; *The Insect Play*, 1923; also known as
And So Infinituam: The Life of the Insects,
1923)

Věc Makropulos, pb. 1920, pr. 1922 (*The
Macropulos Secret*, 1925)

R.U.R.: Rossum's Universal Robots, pb. 1920, pr.
1921 (English translation, 1923)

Adam Stvořitel, pr., pb. 1927 (with Josef Čapek;
Adam the Creator, 1929)

Bílá nemoc, pr., pb. 1937 (*Power and Glory*, 1938;
also known as *The White Plague*, 1988)

Matka, pr., pb. 1938 (*The Mother*, 1939)

OTHER LITERARY FORMS

Karel Čapek was essentially a thinker who used a
variety of forms to express his philosophical and political ruminations. Aside from his dramatic writing,
Čapek's work falls into three categories: political and
philosophical writing, tales, and novels. Among his
political and philosophical publications are *Pragmatismus* (1918), a direct outgrowth of work he did
in his doctoral program at Charles University. This
was followed in 1920-1921 by *Musaion*, a collection
of essays on modern art, in part an outgrowth of
his doctoral dissertation, "Objective Methods in Aesthetics." In 1928, Čapek published the first of the
three volumes of *Hovory s T. G. Masarykem* (*President Masaryk Tells His Story*, 1934; also as *Masaryk
on Thought and Life*, 1938). This extensive work,
completed in 1935, grew out of Čapek's close friendship with his former university professor, Tomas G.

Masaryk, who served as Czechoslovakia's president
from 1918 until 1935. Out of this same period appeared a closely related collection of essays, *O věcech
obecných: Čili, Zóon politikon* (on public matters),
published in 1932. A posthumous collection of essays
Veci kolemnás (the things around us) was published
in 1954,.

Čapek, sometimes in collaboration with his brother
Josef, liked to write tales and sketches, often of the
fantastic. Many of these tales and sketches were collected and published, beginning with *Zářivé hlubiny*
(1916; *The Luminous Depths*, 1916), *Boží muka*
(1917; wayside crosses), and *Krakonošova zahrada*
(1918; the garden of Krakonoš)—all these pieces
written with Josef. In 1929, Čapek published on his
own two collections of tales, *Povídky z jedné kapsy*
(tales from one pocket) and *Povídky z druhé kapsy*
(tales from the other pocket), translated into English
and published together as *Tales from Two Pockets* in
1932.

Čapek's novels combine political philosophy with
a strong sense of the fantastic. The first, *Továrna na
absolutno*, appeared in 1922 and is variously known
in English as *The Absolute at Large* (1927), *Factory
for the Absolute*, and *Manufacture of the Absolute*.
Čapek then began the ambitious project of writing a
trilogy that consisted of *Hordubal* (1933; English
translation, 1934), *Povětroó* (1934; *Meteor*, 1935),
and *Obyčejný život* (1934; *An Ordinary Life*, 1936).
These three novels, coming just as Adolf Hitler's ascendancy in Germany was being noted widely, led to
Čapek's fifth novel, *Válka s mloky* (1936; *The War
with the Newts*, 1937), which was openly anti-Fascist
and specifically anti-Hitler. *První parta* (1937; *The
First Rescue Party*, 1939) continued to develop the
political philosophies found in the early novels.

ACHIEVEMENTS

Karel Čapek is remembered today for his popular-
ization of the word "robot," actually first used by his
brother Josef in his short story "Opilec" (1917) and
used by Karel in *R.U.R.: Rossum's Universal Robots*,

which was first produced in Prague in January, 1921. The word is from the Czech *robota*, meaning compulsory service or work. Popularizing this word, however, was certainly not Čapek's most notable professional achievement. A deeply philosophical man, professionally trained as a philosopher, Čapek was the first Czech writer to attract a broad international audience for his works, particularly for his expressionist drama, which has been translated into many languages and has been performed all over the world.

A versatile intellectual, Čapek, during his years on the staff of *Lidové noviny*, the most influential Czech newspaper, demonstrated by the excellence of his writing that journalism can be an art. He wrote on a broad range of subjects, from Persian rugs to gardening to drama and art. Čapek was also an incisive political thinker who wrote stirring political essays, but his political sentiments achieve a more universal expression in his plays and novels, particularly in such plays as *R.U.R.*, *The Insect Play*, and *Power and Glory* and in the novels of his trilogy comprising *Hordubal*, *Meteor*, and *An Ordinary Life*. His novel most familiar to English-speaking audiences is *The War with the Newts*, which builds directly on much of the social criticism found in *R.U.R.* and in *The Insect Play* and which presents one of the earliest direct literary attacks on Hitler. His trilogy has attracted considerable interest for its manner of dealing with the infinite diversity of the human personality.

Čapek, who was deeply involved in the arts and in the cultural life of Prague, served from 1921 to 1923 as director of Prague's City Theatre, where he directed thirteen plays. He was less comfortable as a playwright than he was as a journalist or a novelist because he believed that in drama the author has too little control over his own product: The actors and the director, by imposing their own interpretations on a play, wrest from it much of the authorial control that writers in other genres are able to preserve. It was perhaps this feeling that led him to directing for a short period of time.

Čapek's own plays show a concern with the man in the street, with the face in the crowd. He

was a champion of such people, and he wrote allegorically, particularly in *R.U.R.* and *The Insect Play*, about the relationship of such people to a modern, mechanized society. *The Insect Play* is particularly medieval in its conception, with each figure in the play representing some vice or virtue, clearly defined and unilaterally depicted. In a sense, this play was a prelude to the more fully expanded consideration of human personality that one finds in his later trilogy.

Čapek often wrote parody in his early work, attacking conventions indirectly but forcefully, taking the particular and turning it into an allegorical generalization, as he did even in his earliest play, *Lásky hra osudná* (the fateful game of love), written in collaboration with his brother, Josef, in 1910, though not staged until a decade and a half later, when a small company in Prague gave it a limited run. It was not given a professional performance until it was presented by Prague's National Theatre in 1930 along with a number of other short dramatic works by a variety of Czech playwrights.

Karel Čapek in 1938. (Hulton Archive by Getty Images)

Čapek, although not philosophically comfortable with the subjectivism of expressionism, used many of the conventions of expressionist drama in his writing. His staging was often expressionistic, as was his use of characters who performed like overgrown puppets, particularly the automatons of *R.U.R.* He also departed with considerable dexterity from his philosophical stance that literature should report on the basis of objective, virtually scientific observation rather than be subjective. Although he was a deliberate and indefatigable observer, as is made clear in his essays, he could not exclude from his writing the fruits of his own careful introspection.

From the time that Czechoslovakia was established as a separate political entity by the Treaty of Versailles in 1919, Čapek worked continually for the democratization of the country. Much influenced by Western culture, particularly that of France and England, Čapek believed firmly in representative government. His political views were much influenced by his extensive study of the pragmatism of William James during his days as a doctoral student at Charles University in Prague.

His close and early friendship with Tomas G. Masaryk grew steadily throughout Čapek's lifetime, and when Masaryk rose to the presidency of Czechoslovakia, he and Čapek were in weekly contact with each other. Through Masaryk, Čapek became an informal force in Czech politics and government. His political influence persisted until the end of his life, which was clearly shortened by his deep distress about Hitler's rise to power. It is speculated that Čapek's attack on Hitler in *The War with the Newts* was responsible for his not being awarded a Nobel Prize in Literature, for in the mid-1930's, Sweden was still trying to appease Hitler and was quite unwilling, presumably, to bring to Stockholm to receive the world's highest award in literature someone who had taken a political stand against the German tyrant.

BIOGRAPHY

Born on January 9, 1890, Karel Čapek was the youngest of three children. His sister, Helene, after whom a major character in *R.U.R.* is named, was born in 1886 and also became a writer. Josef, who was Karel's closest lifelong friend as well as his brother, was born in 1887. The Čapek family was living at that time in the idyllic country town of Malé Svatoňovice, close to what later became Czechoslovakia's border with Austria and Germany. The town, situated in the Krakonoše Mountains, was essentially bilingual, so that Čapek and his siblings grew up with equal fluency in German and Czech.

Čapek's father, Antonín, was a country doctor, but his interests encompassed a wide range of topics. Always intrigued by theater, he headed an amateur theatrical group in his town. He enjoyed painting, was a poet although he remained unpublished, and was an enthusiastic gardener who passed on this enthusiasm to both of his sons. Čapek's mother, Božena Čapková, was extremely cultivated, having a particular interest in the folklore of her area and in the music and tales that had grown out of this folklore. She told and read many tales to her children when they were very young, and she sang to them the songs of their region. The later work of both Čapek brothers reflects directly these early influences. Until his final days, Karel was more devoted to fairy tales than to any other form of literature, save, perhaps, mystery stories, to which he was addicted.

Božena Čapková was basically quite neurotic. Abused by her father, she quickly developed a resentment for and distrust of her husband. Their marriage was not a happy one. Her hypochondria manifested itself in an overconcern for the health of her children, particularly for the health of Karel, who was very small at birth and who suffered early from weak lungs, an affliction with which he lived throughout his life and which ultimately brought about his death in 1938.

Čapek was exposed to a broad range of people as he was growing up, partly because his father's patients came from all walks of life and levels of society and partly because his mother surrounded herself with the people who best knew the folklore of the region, the peasants who lived in the environs in which Čapek was reared.

The closeness that developed between Karel and his brother Josef is largely attributable to the fact that Josef was expected as a small child to look after his sickly brother. The two were virtually inseparable until 1910, at which time Karel went to Berlin to study and Josef went to Paris. By this time, Karel had studied at the gymnasium in Brno in the province of Moravia for two years, from 1905 to 1907; had completed secondary school in Prague, where his father, by then retired from his medical practice, had come with his wife to live; and had spent one year, 1909-1910, as a student of philosophy at Charles University, where he presumably first came under the strong influence of Tomas G. Masaryk, also a philosopher.

When Karel went to Berlin and his brother to Paris, the collaboration of their early days was interrupted. *Lásky hra osudná* had been completed, but it was still to be eight years before the two brothers published *Krakonošova zahrada*, a collection of their earlier sketches, and twelve years before they were to engage in the thoroughgoing collaboration of which *The Insect Play* was the product.

Čapek, who had an early interest in the writing of H. G. Wells, now developed a considerable and deep interest in the pragmatic and earlier philosophy of William James. During the summer of 1911, which he spent in France with his brother Josef, Čapek began to expand his interest in art and in aesthetics. He was introduced to the writing of Henri Bergson, whose concept of the *élan vital* was to become fundamental in the conscious vitalism found in much of Čapek's important writing. It was probably this exposure to Bergson that led Čapek in 1915 to complete a doctoral dissertation in the area of aesthetics. The title of his study, "Objective Methods in Aesthetics," clearly indicates the direction in which his thought was moving and suggests his philosophical, if not his actual, approach to art. From this period of his life, also, comes the seminar paper on pragmatism that was to result in the publication of *Pragmatismus* in 1918.

Čapek's spinal problems persisted, so that when he had completed his formal education he had to find a means of livelihood that would not overtax him. He suffered agonizing pain, which he is said to have borne with stoicism. In 1916, he found employment, which was to last for less than a year, as tutor to the son of Count Vladimír Lažanský. The count, on whose estate in western Bohemia Čapek resided during the term of his employment, was quite democratic in his outlook, and Čapek found his brief respite in residence with the count and his family congenial.

In 1917, however, Čapek returned to Prague to become a journalist, working for *Národní listy*, where he rose to the position of literary and art editor before resigning in 1921 to become a journalist for *Lidové noviny*. His brother Josef also worked as a member of the paper's staff. This work in journalism exposed Čapek to a broad variety of writing experiences and served to make him a sure and versatile writer.

It was at about this time that Čapek met Olga Scheinpflugová, an actress, who in 1920 played understudy to the lead in the Prague production of his play *The Robber*. Although their romance blossomed, Čapek believed that his health was not good enough for him to contemplate marriage, and it was not until 1935 that he and Olga, who was twelve years his junior, were finally married.

Meanwhile, Karel and Josef built a double house sharing a common wall in Prague. They lived in the close proximity that this house provided them from 1925 until Karel's death in 1938. In this house, they gardened together, worked together on their artistic endeavors, and held constant discussions. The "Friday Circle," established by Čapek in 1924, met weekly at this house and attracted the leading artistic and political figures of Prague, including President Masaryk, to its discussions.

In 1925, Čapek was elected president of Prague's PEN Club, but his tenure was short-lived because he did not wish to speak as an official. He resigned, craving the freedom and independence to speak as an individual artist rather than as the chief representative of a large group of writers. Again, in 1935, Čapek was drawn into PEN when, at H. G. Wells's prodding, he agreed to succeed Wells as international president of the organization. Čapek, however, was unable to attend the annual meeting of the international society, which that year was held in Latin America, so he was not to serve.

Politically, Čapek was a liberal of the Masaryk variety, deploring fascism and finding the representational governments of Great Britain and the United States far preferable to communism. He tried to solidify the Czech people, overcoming his inherent shyness in order to reach the citizenry by radio. If he succeeded at all politically, it must be said that he did so more fully through the indirect methods found in his literature than through his direct attempts to persuade his countrymen. His support of the presidency of Edvard Beneš brought livid outcries from many a Czech, as did his attempts to bring about some sort of peaceful concord between the Czechs and the southern Germans in the mid-1930's.

As the Nazi sphere of influence grew, Čapek became increasingly disheartened. The Munich agreement in 1938 between Germany and Great Britain in a way dealt Čapek a death blow. His disillusionment was ever with him for the remaining months of his life. His lungs, always weak, became inflamed, and on Christmas Day, 1938, less than a year before the beginning of World War II, he died. When Nazi troops entered Prague less than three months after his death, his widow, Olga, destroyed all his papers because she feared that his correspondence might incriminate the people named in it. The Nazis, apparently unaware of Čapek's death, came to this house with a warrant for his arrest. They succeeded in arresting Josef, who spent the rest of his life in the concentration camp at Bergen-Belsen, where he died shortly before the war ended.

ANALYSIS

Karel Čapek was concerned with the natural order of things, a theme that pervaded much of his work. His allegorical approach to expressionism linked his deep philosophical concerns to striking and often disturbing human situations. Artistically, politically, and socially, Čapek dealt with the human personality and with the fate of humankind. He attacked not only the conventions of the day but also human beings' general lack of awareness of their place in nature and in the continuum of events that demands their attention to foster the perpetuation of values and ideals as well as the survival of the human race itself.

LÁSKY HRA OSUDNÁ

Lásky hra osudná, Čapek's early dramatic collaboration with his brother Josef, is a one-act play that was not given a major premiere until twenty years af-

ter it was written, although it was produced by an amateur group in the mid-1920's. The play has neoclassical overtones, but only inasmuch as it establishes them to parody neoclassical form. The play is technically in the tradition of the *commedia dell'arte*, and it satirizes this tradition by its own artificial form. Each of the characters in the play is the clear representative of some single aspect of human character: Scaramouche, the obvious madman; Gilles, unwell and emotionally vulnerable, largely because of his own self-indulgence; Isabella, the agent of consternation, whose skirts are lifted by Brighella, thereby enflaming the emotions of the two rival suitors, Trivalin and Gilles. The two fight a duel over Isabella, thereby enabling the opportunistic Brighella to whisk Isabella away and to steal money from her rival suitors.

This is the stuff of which operas are made. The plot is thin and contrived. Still, the play is rescued from the banality that such a plot would suggest by the well-controlled wit of the brothers Čapek, who used the dialogue as a means of ridiculing and poking fun at the theater itself. Particularly engaging is a love scene in which Scaramouche announces that the theater is on fire, tacitly suggesting that the audience might flee and leave him alone with his ladylove, Isabella.

The play begins with a verse prologue that continues until Gilles interrupts in prose. He refuses to speak in verse, although reminded of his obligation to do so, and the play proceeds with an intermixture of versified dialogue and prose, as suits the satiric nature of the production. Although not a notable artistic achievement, this play shows two significant wits working harmoniously to produce a delightful entertainment with a cutting edge of irony throughout.

THE ROBBER

Čapek's first full-length play, *The Robber*, was begun in Paris in 1911, when the author was visiting his brother for the summer. The play apparently passed through a number of distinct versions before it was finally produced by the Prague National Theatre in 1920. The drama moves from realism to Symbolism and back again; it also moves from prose to verse, often without adequate preparation. The story is an old one: Mimi is dominated by her overly protective parents, who already have lost one daughter to an elopement with a man who quickly abandoned her. The father, a stuffy professor, and his wife have to go away on a trip, but the father fortifies the house against intruders and leaves Mimi in the capable hands of their trusted erstwhile servant, Fanka.

The robber is a rather typical hero: His background is unknown; he appears on the scene briefly, bringing about significant changes in the action; and he disappears almost as suddenly as he appeared in the first place. As soon as the parents have left, he makes his move. While Mimi tells him of her troubles, his understanding of and sympathy for her plight lead the hapless Mimi to lose her heart to him. He responds by instigating a fight with Mimi's suitor, a local bumpkin, who, being quicker on the draw than the robber, wounds him. The injured interloper leaves Mimi, promising to return, and being only slightly wounded, he returns that very night, meeting Mimi, who tiptoes past the sleeping Fanka, outside into the moonlight. The parents, who have premonitions of trouble, hurry home unexpectedly and send the robber off.

Mimi's parents exact from her a promise that she will never speak to the robber again, but as soon as he returns in the morning, she violates her promise. In a scene that is almost slapstick, Fanka and the parents come out to try to drive the robber away from outside the fortified dwelling, but he slips past them and into the house, locks the door, and takes to the balcony, gun in hand, ready to fight to the death if necessary to defend Mimi's right to make her own decision about whom she will marry. By this time, Mimi is hopelessly in love with the robber, although there is no suggestion that he reciprocates this love.

After one false start, the professor and his cohorts retake the house and the robber runs off to escape injury at the hands of Fanka, who is shooting at him. He does not leave, however, until the audience learns that Mimi's parents suffered through eight years of courtship before they married and that Mimi's father, the professor, assumes that such deprivation and suffering are what love is all about. Mimi's mother, though, questions the wisdom of their having been forced to wait so long. Mimi's sister returns, her face

covered with a veil, to tell Mimi her tale of being deceived by the man she loved.

Though the play is somewhat lacking in substance, it provided a pleasantly diverting evening for audiences. It presents essentially several faces of love and the contrast between youth and age in matters related to the heart. It attacks the question of the rights of the young over the rights of their elders and examines several sets of rights quite closely. The setting had about it certain gothic elements that were well suited to the romantic tone of the play.

THE INSECT PLAY

Čapek is often at his best dramatically when he is not writing about human beings, who often turn out to be unconvincing in his plays. In his collaboration with his brother Josef on *The Insect Play*, Čapek wrote a virtual medieval morality play. The insects are presented allegorically, and the whole action is unified by the tramp, who, in his role as stranger, serves the function of seer.

The play is divided into three acts, the first called "Butterflies," the second called "Creepers and Crawlers," and the last called "The Ants." Through these sets of characters, and through their notable characteristics, the brothers Čapek depicted a coherent and quite pessimistic view of human beings. Questions of family organization are central to each act, as are questions of greed, pride, vanity, and other deadly sins.

In the first act, two aging butterflies compete for the affections of the youthful poet, Felix, also a butterfly, who has the reputation of being a Lothario but who is really shy at heart. The butterflies, ethereal and lovely, are subject to the same whims as anyone else. They experience rivalry in love, and their actions are misinterpreted. They contrast sharply with the beetles in the next act, whose family exclusivity is limiting and ultimately cruel.

The natural order of things is presented without comment in the cricket scene, in which two crickets looking for shelter rejoice at finding the nest of another cricket who has fallen victim to a hungry bird that has gobbled him whole. Their good fortune is short-lived because they are barely installed in their new habitat before a cuckoo fly attacks and paralyzes them. The tramp ruminates on the cruelty and rapacity that he sees here. The cuckoo fly kills; the parasite eats the crickets and their larvae. In accord with Čapek's philosophy that drama should be objective rather than subjective, the authors present the facts of what has happened and leave the audience with these facts, although the tramp represents a subjective intrusion on the scene, somewhat in violation of Čapek's philosophy of objective realism in drama.

In *The Insect Play*, the brothers balance the actions of their three allegorical groups, using the tramp as a conscience, a representative of those who view the play. In the end, the tramp, begging for just a little more life, dies, his body left in a fen where slugs begin to feast on it. It finally is discovered by a woodcutter, and nearby, a group of schoolgirls on holiday, oblivious to the tramp's death, play in the lustrous sunshine. The natural order is irresistible. Life goes on, with all its cruelty and suffering.

R.U.R.: ROSSUM'S UNIVERSAL ROBOTS

Čapek's reputation as a dramatist of international stature was assured by *R.U.R.: Rossum's Universal Robots*, first performed in Prague early in 1921. The play was rapidly translated into many European and some Oriental languages. Foreign productions were staged as far away as the United States and Japan.

The play is concerned with the fate of humankind in the face of mechanization. The robots produced by the Rossum factory look and feel like human beings. They can experience pain, because were they not able to, they would soon be destroyed accidentally. They have no souls, not because souls are not manufacturable but because to give them souls would increase their price tremendously. They are good servants because they cannot feel fear, hatred, love, and sorrow, emotions that weaken human beings and divert them from their tasks.

Čapek's concerns in *R.U.R.* are broadly human and neither focus on any one nation nor point an accusing finger at the industrialized world; neither is *R.U.R.* a nostalgic looking back to more simple times. Rather, it is a quite objective statement of many of the problems brought on by industrialization, exaggerated just enough to make it seem slightly fantastic, yet based sufficiently in truth that its central message is not lost on audiences.

At first, the robots seem a great convenience. Soon there is no need for anyone to work. Robots do all the tasks, having been developed so successfully that they can perform in specialized, highly advanced occupations as well as in the menial occupations to which the early robots were consigned. Robots can typewrite and converse, and they provide specialized information in conversational tones. They are ever obedient, yet they have the ability finally to make discriminating responses.

Ultimately, however, the human race is threatened, first because it begins not to reproduce and then because the robots rebel and threaten to conquer the humans. The only advantage the humans have when the attack comes is that the robots do not know how to reproduce, how to make more robots, and their typical life span is only thirty years. This bargaining chip is lost, however, because Helena has burned the papers in which Rossum details how robots are made. With this act, all hope is lost.

R.U.R. harks back to the suggestion in *The Insect Play* of the specialized function of all creatures. In seeing the robots going about their specialized duties, one thinks back to the ants, beetles, and butterflies of the earlier play. Čapek is dealing conceptually with the whole question of purpose—not human purpose alone, but the purpose of all life. In *R.U.R.*, Čapek the philosopher achieved an ideal harmony with Čapek the dramatist. The play is filled with philosophical portents, yet it is good theater. If it avoids preaching, it probably does so because Čapek employed literary techniques that he learned as a child listening to fairy tales.

The fact that Helena Glory, when she appears early in the play, cannot distinguish between robots and humans suggests that Čapek thought the dehumanization of humankind was already well advanced. He sensed distant, indistinct rumblings on the international scene that were to spring full-blown on the world when Hitler began to take over Eastern Europe. It is not surprising that Čapek died shortly before the Nazi invasion of his own country. In some ways, the macabre fantasies that his plays had presented were now being acted out in ways more horrible than he could ever have imagined they would be. His spirit broken by the certainty of impending conflict, Čapek could no longer face the struggle, and his health, never very robust, failed utterly.

By the end of the second act, the robots in *R.U.R.* have killed all the humans except for Alquist, a construction engineer who may be their only hope. Alquist tries to unlock the secret of making robots, but he cannot. Finally, it is suggested that he dissect living robots to see how they are put together. He has trouble doing this. He then notes that two of the robots who serve him, Primus and Helena, have fallen in love, a contention he confirms by suggesting that he dissect one of them, only to have the other volunteer to be dissected instead. Alquist gives the two his blessing, and presumably there is some distant hope that a new race will come into being.

The play is structurally interesting. Its prologue is comic, while the rest of the play is solidly dramatic in a serious sense. The main action is over by the end of the first act. The two succeeding acts are anticlimactic and need dramatic alternatives.

THE MACROPULOS SECRET

In *The Macropulos Secret*, first produced in Prague in November, 1922, Čapek created perhaps his most memorable character, Emilia Marty. This protagonist is more than three hundred years old when the play opens, having been given a secret formula to ensure longevity by her father, physician to Emperor Rudolph II. This formula assures not only long life but also continuing youth, so that Emilia, who has now lived many lifetimes, all under different names, is not decrepit. She is merely bored at having been around too long. Life has lost all interest for her. The excitement is gone from it, and the audience is led to the inevitable conclusion that too long a life is far worse than death. Indeed, Čapek wrote, "A short life is better for mankind, for a long life would deprive man of his optimism."

As *The Macropulos Secret* develops, Emilia Marty tries to give the secret formula away. Various people want it, some for selfish and others for generous purposes. None, however, is to have it, because Kristina grabs the formula and burns it in a candle's flame, much as Helena in *R.U.R.* burns Rossum's formula for making robots.

ADAM THE CREATOR

In 1927, Karel and Josef Čapek again engaged in a collaboration, *Adam the Creator*, which, although promising dramatically, was not successful. The play's basic idea is an intriguing one. Adam, not pleased with the world as his God has made it, destroys it with the Cannon of Negation when humankind fails to listen to him. In his haste to do away with an unsatisfactory world, however, Adam has forgotten to include himself in the destruction, so that now he alone exists in a solipsistic state. God calls on Adam to rebuild the world he has destroyed, and he gives him a heap of dirt with which to accomplish his task.

Adam fails utterly to accomplish his deed and in desperation creates someone in his own likeness, Alter Ego. As similar as they first seem, the two are not compatible, and they quarrel bitterly and often. Alter Ego has an accountant's mentality. He wants his share of everything, including the Clay of Creation. When he and Adam set about remaking the world, Adam creates individuals, whereas Alter Ego creates nothing but hordes of undistinguished and undistinguishable beings, products of a mechanistic and materialistic mind. Alter Ego's creations are all the same; Adam's, on the other hand, are all different.

As might be predicted, the world that Adam and Alter Ego create is unbearable, and the two, now wholly discredited by their fellows, seek refuge in the hole from which the Clay of Creation originally came. Just a smidgen of earth remains in the hole. Alter Ego kicks it, and there being too little clay to make a whole man, the pile produces an unsightly dwarf, Zmeten, whose name means monster.

Adam and Alter Ego decide to destroy the world they have created, but Zmeten, who now has six children, will not hear of such a thing. He threatens them with their own Cannon of Negation, which he has now turned into a cookpot. As the play ends, a shrine marks the spot in which creation began, and the Cannon of Negation has been melted down and made into a bell. As the bell clangs, God speaks to Adam, who responds by saying that he will not tamper further with God's creation. In other words, he accepts things as they are, settling for the status quo.

The play leaves little cause for hope. In fact, it ends with the sort of encompassing ennui found in Emilia Marty in *The Macropulos Secret*, with the important difference that the people living in the world Adam and Alter Ego have created are mortal and are only serving a term. Nothing is perfect; life, rather than being good or bad, just is.

POWER AND GLORY

Power and Glory, written in 1937, was openly anti-Nazi in its original form. The Nazis had already infiltrated the Czech hierarchy by that time, and they refused to allow the play to be produced until it was made antiseptic by their standards. The title of the play refers to a horrible disease that decimates people past forty years of age by eating away at their flesh. Significantly, it is those over forty who conduct, but do not actively fight in, wars.

A brilliant physician, appropriately named Galén, has come up with a cure for the dreaded scourge, but he withholds his secret formula, demanding that in return for it the world must agree to live peacefully. The world is not ready to meet such a demand until the dictator, who, like Hitler, is preparing for an offensive war, develops the disease and is mortally ill with it. He concedes to Dr. Galén's demands, but as Dr. Galén is rushing with his cure to the dictator's bedside, he is waylaid by the mob and killed. The pessimism of the play presages the utter futility that was building in Čapek and in many other European intellectuals in the years of Hitler's rise to power.

THE MOTHER

Čapek's last play, which was his favorite, is an estimable one. *The Mother*, written in 1938, the year in which Čapek died, revolves around a mother, presented as the prototype of motherhood, who has stirred her five sons by telling them stories of their dead father's heroism in dying for his country. The father was the typical patriot, and the sons each represent a different category of person. One is a physician who loses his life in the practice of his profession. The twins are Petr, a liberal, and Kornel, a conservative, who fight in different armies in the same war and die on opposite sides. Another son is a pilot who dies while flying his plane to altitudes not previously reached. The youngest son, the only survivor, aspires to be a poet.

In the course of the play, each of the dead sons returns as a spirit and engages in dialogue with the mother. It is she who has made these youths, she who has shaped their values and ideals. Without her encomiums about the heroism of their father, her four dead sons might not have made the sacrifices they did and might still be alive. Her motherly love makes her wish that they were, and she cannot understand why they have sacrificed as each has. Having lost four sons, she first hides her youngest, trying to save him. Finally, however, she gives him a rifle and sends him off to fight. Čapek, never a pacifist, was not a warmonger either. The events through which he was living in Czechoslovakia in 1938 led him to the inevitable conclusion that under some sets of circumstances, people must fight.

Kornel and Petr seem like offshoots respectively of Alter Ego and Adam in *Adam the Creator*. Kornel, in rearranging a room, would keep everything as it had been, whereas Petr would arrange things as they should be. The mother represents the synthesis of these two opposing stands and would put things where they belong, where they can prosper.

OTHER MAJOR WORKS

LONG FICTION: *Továrna na absolutno*, 1922 (*The Absolute at Large*, 1927); *Krakatit*, 1924 (English translation, 1925); *Hordubal*, 1933 (English translation, 1934); *Povětroó*, 1934 (*Meteor*, 1935); *Obyčejný život*, 1934 (*An Ordinary Life*, 1936); *Válka s mloky*, 1936 (*The War with the Newts*, 1937); *První parta*, 1937 (*The First Rescue Party*, 1939); *Život a dílo skladatele Foltýna*, 1939 (*The Cheat*, 1941).

SHORT FICTION: *Zářivé hlubiny*, 1916 (with Josef Čapek; *The Luminous Depths*, 1916); *Boží muka*, 1917; *Krakonošova zahrada*, 1918 (with Josef Čapek); *Trapné povídky*, 1921 (*Money and Other Stories*, 1929); *Povídky z jedné kapsy* and *Povídky z druhé kapsy*, 1929 (*Tales from Two Pockets*, 1932); *Devatero pohádek*, 1931 (*Fairy Tales*, 1933); *Kniha apokryfů*, 1946 (*Apocryphal Stories*, 1949).

NONFICTION: *Pragmatismus*, 1918; *Kritika slov*, 1920; *O nejbližších vecech*, 1920 (*Intimate Things*, 1935); *Musaion*, 1920-1921; *Italské listy*, 1923 (*Letters from Italy*, 1929); *Anglické listy*, 1924 (*Letters from England*, 1925); *Hovory s T. G. Masarykem*, 1928-1935 (3 volumes; *President Masaryk Tells His Story*, 1934; also as *Masaryk on Thought and Life*, 1938); *Zahradníkův rok*, 1929 (*The Gardener's Year*, 1931); *Výlet do Španěl*, 1930 (*Letters from Spain*, 1931); *Marsyas*, 1931 (*In Praise of Newspapers*, 1951); *O věcech obecných: Čili, Zóon politikon*, 1932; *Obrázky z Holandska*, 1932 (*Letters from Holland*, 1933); *Dášeóka*, 1933 (*Dashenka*, 1940); *Cesta na sever*, 1936 (*Travels in the North*, 1939); *Měl jsem psa a kočku*, 1939 (*I Had a Dog and a Cat*, 1940); *Obrázky z domova*, 1953; *Veci kolemnás*, 1954; *Poznámky o tvorbě*, 1959; *Viktor Dyk-S. K. Neumann-bratří Č.: Korespondence z let 1905-1918*, 1962.

TRANSLATION: *Francouzská poesie nové doby*, 1920 (of French poetry).

BIBLIOGRAPHY

Bradbrook, Bohuslava R. *Karel Čapek: In Pursuit of Truth, Tolerance, and Trust*. Portland, Ore.: Sussex Academic Press, 1998. A critical analysis of the works of Čapek. Bibliography and index.

Makin, Michael, and Jindrich Toman, eds. *On Karel Čapek: A Michigan Slavic Colloquium*. Ann Arbor: Michigan Slavic Publications, 1992. A group of papers presented at a colloquium on Čapek. Bibliography.

Pynsent, R. B., ed. *Karel Matel Čapek-Chod: Proceedings of a Symposium Held at the School of Slavonic and East European Studies 18-20 September, 1984*. London: The School, 1985. A collection of papers presented at a symposium on Čapek. Index.

Schubert, Peter Z. *The Narratives of Čapek and Cexov: A Typological Comparison of the Authors' World Views*. Bethesda, Md.: International Scholars Publications, 1997. A comparison of the philosophical views of Čapek and Anton Chekhov as expressed in their works. Bibliography and index.

R. Baird Shuman

ION LUCA CARAGIALE

Born: Haimanale, Romania; January 30, 1852
Died: Berlin, Germany; June 9, 1912

PRINCIPAL DRAMA

O noapte furtunoasă: Sau, Numarul 9, pr., pb. 1879 (*A Stormy Night: Or, Number 9*, 1956)

Conul Leonida faţă cu reacţiunea, pb. 1880, pr. 1885 (*Mr. Leonida and the Reactionaries*, 1956)

Soacră-mea, Fifina, pr. 1883, pb. 1889

Hatmanul Baltag, pr. 1884, pb. 1889

O scrisoare pierdută, pr. 1884, pb. 1885 (*The Lost Letter*, 1956)

D'ale carnavalului, pr., pb. 1885 (*Carnival Scenes*, 1956)

Teatru, pb. 1889

Năpasta, pr., pb. 1890

Teatru: Opere complete, pb. 1908 (3 volumes)

Opere, pb. 1942, 1950, 1952 (7 volumes)

The Lost Letter and Other Plays, pb. 1956

Opere, pb. 1964 (4 volumes)

OTHER LITERARY FORMS

Ion Luca Caragiale is best known throughout the world as a playwright, but he was also a writer of short fiction, an active journalist and pamphleteer, and a poet.

ACHIEVEMENTS

From the time they were produced for the first time on the Romanian stage, Ion Luca Caragiale's plays have maintained a preeminent position in the Romanian national repertory and have become established in the repertory of many other European theaters. Indeed, Caragiale has been seen as the founder of the modern Romanian theater, a significant influence on such famous Romanian expatriates such as Marcel Iancu, Tristan Tzara, and Eugène Ionesco.

Caragiale was a fine observer of human nature; he aimed his wit at many aspects of society, hoping to improve it through laughter by causing the public to recognize itself in his characters: "In him," wrote Caragiale's contemporary, journalist Raicu Ionescu-Rion, "we see man stumbling toward light, man suffocated by the present, seeking something better." The poet Alexandru Vlahuţă, another contemporary, pointed out that one of the major sources for Caragiale's greatness was his ability to re-create on the stage a series of typical characters such as the eternal idealist, the venal bureaucrat, the cynical journalist, the innocent citizen, and the spoiled brat. Caragiale showed ignorance parading itself as seriousness, dishonesty trying to pass for wit, and cynicism trying to be mistaken for independence of mind. The playwright hoped that his reader, sensitized by the satire, would say with renewed conscience, "I want to be a different person."

Caragiale's social criticism made for him many powerful enemies. He had been introduced by the poet Mihail Eminescu and by Ion Slavici to Titu Maiorescu's influential circle, *Junimea* (the youth). He published many articles of drama criticism in the group's journal *Convorbiri literare*. Yet his constant criticism offended some of the group's members, and he was forced to break away from the circle after ten years. In spite of this disappointment, he did not change his independent attitude, staying away from ideologies and narrow nationalism. To dogmatic ideas, opinions, or systems, he was absolutely indifferent. From the beginning of his career to his last writings, he maintained a sharp eye, a pointed tongue, and an unfailing wit. His posthumous election to the Romanian Academy was a fitting tribute.

BIOGRAPHY

Ion Luca Caragiale's life and work were closely related. The writer did not shun publicity and enjoyed success while it lasted. When the envy and moral turpitude of his contemporaries forced him to leave his native land, Caragiale did not completely divorce himself from society but became more philosophical about his expectations.

Caragiale was born in Haimanale (now Caragiale), a small village near the Romanian city of Ploieşti, on January 30, 1852. He was the son of Luca Caragiale and Ecaterina Caragiale, née Karaba. Interest in the theater was a family tradition: Before becoming administrator of an estate, an attorney, and a magistrate, Ion Luca's father had been an actor. Two of his uncles, Costache Caragiale and Iorgu Caragiale, were actors, playwrights, and directors of their own theater companies.

Ion Luca Caragiale attended grammar school from 1860 to 1864, and the Ploieşti Gymnasium from 1864 to 1867. He also attended his uncle Costache's recitation and mime courses at the Bucharest Drama Conservatory. After graduation, he held a number of menial jobs, such as serving as a copyist for the Prahova County Court House and a prompter for the Bucharest National Theatre. In 1873, he wrote his first article in the satiric magazine, *Ghimpele* (the thorn). He also became administrator and chief editor for a variety of publications, alone or in cooperation with other writers: *Alegătorul liber* (the free voter), *Unirea democratică* (the democratic unity), *Claponul* (the capon), and *Naţiunea Română* (the Romanian nation). Between 1878 and 1882, he served on the editorial board of the newspaper *Timpul* (the time).

As noted above, the famous Romanian poet Mihail Eminescu, with the short-story writer Ion Slavici, introduced Caragiale to the prestigious literary circle *Junimea*. For this group, in 1879, he read for the first time his plays *A Stormy Night* and *Mr. Leonida and the Reactionaries*. After leaving *Timpul*, Caragiale became a school inspector. During this time, he wrote the farce *Soacră-mea, Fifina* (my mother-in-law, Fifina) and the comic opera *Hatmanul Baltag* (Chief Baltag). His best play, *The Lost Letter*, was written in 1884 and presented on the stage of the Bucharest National Theatre on November 13 of that same year. A year later, he presented *Carnival Scenes*. Caragiale became director of the Bucharest National Theatre in 1888, serving in this capacity for one year.

Also in 1888, he was married to Alexandrina Barelly. They had two children: Luca Ion, who became a writer, and Ecaterina. From an extramarital affair, he also had a legitimized son, Mateiu Caragiale, who became a very well-known writer in his own right.

After 1889, Caragiale became interested in tragedy and in psychological fiction. He wrote the short story "O făclie de Paște" (1892; "The Easter Torch," 1921). In it, he bitterly condemned anti-Semitism. He also wrote *Năpasta* (the curse), in 1890. In 1891, the Romanian Academy refused him an award for his work. Profoundly hurt by their decision and disillusioned, he moved away from the *Junimea* circle and began new literary associations. He finished *Moftul român* (the Romanian pretense) in 1893. During this period, he spent most of his time writing short fictional works: notes, literary fragments, sketches, and his famous *Momente* (1901; moments). These works were mostly published in the supplement to the newspaper *Universul* (the universe), between 1899 and 1901.

Publicly accused of plagiarism by an obscure newspaper reporter, Caragiale became the object of a campaign of calumny. Having inherited a large amount of money from one of his aunts and wanting to leave behind the bad feeling created by this unjustified charge, Caragiale became an expatriate in Germany, moving his entire family to Berlin in 1905. From Berlin, he continued to follow the events in his native country. Thus, during the violence of the peasant uprisings in 1907, Caragiale wrote a strong sociological commentary entitled *1907: Din primăvară până in toamna* (1907: from spring to fall). He published it in the German magazine *Die Zeit*.

Caragiale died in Berlin on June 9, 1912. Initially buried in Berlin, his body was exhumed and returned to his native Romania.

ANALYSIS

After a number of years spent publishing satiric pieces for various magazines, Ion Luca Caragiale asserted himself as an important playwright. He brought growth and innovation to the Romanian stage in the creation of characters, the development of themes, and the use of stylistic devices and sophisticated dramatic techniques. For example, Zița in *A Stormy Night* represents the end of a long line of evolution in the presentation of female characters in Romanian drama. Zița is also the culmination of a long line of medioc-

rities. Whereas in earlier Romanian plays the implications of the plays were mostly personal, the authors satirizing a bad marriage or a corrupt petty official, in Caragiale the author had become a surgeon whose work dissected society's mores: Adultery, graft, blackmail, falsified elections, violence, paternalism, and many other evils were examined.

By 1880, when Caragiale's plays were first performed, literary satire had already had a long tradition. In fables, vaudeville, and comic songs, playwrights amused audiences, poking fun at the 1848 bourgeoisie frightened by the threat of social unrest. The 1860's saw a strong reaction against the 1840's, especially among the more conservative audience that filled Bucharest's summer gardens. Parliamentary debates offered endless opportunities for a writer such as Caragiale to collect pearls of malapropism and ignorance: "Gentlemen, I find myself like the sea traveller, in an oasis" or "We shall dissect this government with the chemist's scalpel" did not escape him. Yet whereas before Caragiale, the humorous review and the amusing couplet had reflected social tendencies, Caragiale created a self-contained world of comic social types. Like Molière, he borrowed from a tradition in order to improve it.

Even allowing for potential discoveries of some new works—during the past ten years, for example, many articles by Caragiale have been discovered in old newspapers—the quantity of Caragiale's drama is relatively limited. His small body of work is distinguished by its thematic and formal unity; all his characters, for example, are closely related. Thus, Titircă (*A Stormy Night*) and Leonida (*Mr. Leonida and the Reactionaries*) share an obsessive passion for their favorite newspaper and become mesmerized by the malapropisms, misnomers, mixed metaphors, and generally sloppy jargon that they find in its pages. The same style will be picked up by the characters in *The Lost Letter*, especially when ordinary citizens must communicate with their party leaders and other officials. Even the world of *Carnival Scenes*, a world of pimps, kept women, hairdressers, and small-time employees, is not immune to jargon.

Two major tendencies can be found in Caragiale's plays: On one hand, his plays exhibit an almost classical propensity toward the unities of time, place, and action. All the misunderstandings in *Carnival Scenes*, for example, are created and solved during a single night. Events converge on the night preceding elections in *The Lost Letter*. In *Năpasta*, Dumitru's murder, Ion's mistrial, and Anca's marriage to the man whom she suspects of being the real killer all occur on a single day. Furthermore, each play features a relatively small number of characters. On the other hand, however, Caragiale's tendency toward classical concentration is opposed by the attention he pays to the process of individuation; the static vision stands against the historical vision. Hence, stage directions partake in characterization: In *A Stormy Night* the warden's sword is decorated by ribbons; in *Carnival Scenes*, a ballroom is ready for a lower-class costume party. Visible, well in evidence, is the men's room, in and out of which many events take place.

A STORMY NIGHT

In his first play, *A Stormy Night*, Caragiale focused on the liberal bourgeoisie of the 1860's. The central character, Dumitrache Titircă, is a carpenter, a man of property. A shrewd merchant, Titircă does not express his thoughts in public: "Well, as far as I can say, a businessman cannot wash his linen in public like a low life," he declares. As far as he is concerned, if one is not a man of property, one is nothing, only a "paper pusher." Only the masters of journalese impress him. He never ceases to be fascinated by the power of a jargon he cannot comprehend. One of the sources of the play's conflict, Titircă's jealousy, springs from his pride of ownership. He is vulgar and massive, but he acts with a certain gentleness toward his wife. Moreover, he never spells out his doubts to her. Even in his most doubting moments when he suspects that "his pride is gone," he protects Veta from the brutality of words. He extends the same type of courtesy to his wife's sister, Zița, the cause of the play's major misunderstandings.

Although Titircă has reached a certain position in society, he still has far to go. Right behind him, Chiriac, his handyman, follows closely: He shares Titircă's reverence for the newspaper *The Past and the Future*, saves money for his own business, makes love to Titircă's wife, and is a sergeant in the national guard in which Titircă is a captain. Another character is Rică Venturiano, a caricature of the aspiring poet: tall hat and glasses. An assistant clerk at the archives, a perennial law student, a beginning journalist, and a bad poet, Venturiano is a complete mediocrity. Nevertheless, he makes an impression on Veta's divorced sister, Zița, an "emancipated" young woman who is in love with the symbolism of romance and has learned to suffer.

MR. LEONIDA AND THE REACTIONARIES

Mr. Leonida and the Reactionaries is a one-act farce. Leonida, a retired bureaucrat, is a master at impressing his wife with his "ability" to interpret the news in the paper. After a heavy dinner, having spent too many hours reading the local paper, Leonida goes to bed but is soon awakened by the sound of repeated powerful explosions. Both he and his wife are convinced that the "reaction" is in the process of changing the government through a violent coup. Only in the morning, when the maid arrives with the milk, does Leonida discover that what he had taken for political violence had only been his neighbors celebrating a birthday and exploding firecrackers.

THE LOST LETTER

The plot in *The Lost Letter*, Caragiale's best-known play, is also very simple: Representatives of two opposing political camps are at odds with each other, fight each other, then are reconciled and live in peace through a compromise. Reminding one of Titircă and Chiriac, the two powerful male characters in *The Lost Letter*, Tipătescu, the commissioner of police, and Trahanache, the banker, are united through legal and illicit business interests. They also share the same political party and make love to the same woman, Trahanache's wife, Zoe. Like his friend Tipătescu, Trahanache identifies closely with his equals and looks down on those who have not yet made it to the top. When Cațavencu, the head of the opposition party, finds a love letter from Zoe to Tipătescu, he begins a campaign of blackmail and intimidation, requesting to be nominated commissioner in Tipătescu's place. Unfortunately for him, however, Cațavencu also loses the letter, and a candidate "from the center," Mr. Agamiță Dandanache, is chosen: The characters are only slightly surprised to hear that Dandanache himself had obtained his candidacy by using a certain "important" citizen's letter to another important citizen's wife. Found by the only honest person present at the elections, the Tipsy Citizen, Zoe's letter is finally returned to her, and with it normality returns.

Trahanache counteracts Tipătescu's arrogance with a sugarcoated benevolence behind which lies the shrewdness of an experienced politician. Apparently trusting, even indulgent regarding his wife's affair with Tipătescu, he seems to care more for his alliance with the latter than for his wife. Hence, he is the first to suggest that the letter is forged. A master of manipulation, Trahanache placates Cațavencu by using his own method: He blackmails him in turn.

Between the two, Zoe maintains a certain balance and at least the appearance of dignity. Through husband and lover, she literally owns the county; therefore, she wields much power. She is then entitled to offer Cațavencu the candidacy by guaranteeing him her vote and that of her husband. She can even afford to be merciful in the end when Cațavencu has lost. She knows the ropes, so she reminds him that this is not the last election in town. She also understandingly allows the petty arrangements of her lover's deputy: She knows that he has a large family; therefore, he is expected to steal or receive kickbacks.

Unlike all the other characters in the play, Cațavencu is not associated with any specific mannerism. The reason is evident: Had he been thus characterized, Cațavencu would have been less of a plastic man, flexible and ready to adapt to any situation. He can always protect himself through the use of bombast. Like a cat, Cațavencu always lands on his feet.

It is interesting to note that Caragiale intended to write a play that portrayed some of the characters of the preceding plays with the changes that might have occurred to them during a period of twenty-five years. All characters would have ascended the social scale: Titircă would now be a senator; Cațavencu, a secretary; Ionescu and Popescu, inspectors in the area of Romanian history. Titircă would no longer attend garden shows but rather would be invited to garden parties. Veta and Zița would become Tante Liza and Tante Zoe. Dumitrache would have made a fortune in oil, and his wife would now address him as "mon

cher." The ladies would speak only French, but take English lessons. They would be at home on Thursday afternoons and reserve the Romanian language only for the servants.

Caragiale considered the ending of *The Lost Letter* to be a good example of surprise denouement. The last in a long line of blackmailers, Dandanache is also the most abject. He obtains his desired candidacy through the use of the letter and, were he not to lose it, would use it over and over again as insurance against bad times. As for Ionescu and Popescu, two shadowy characters always in attendance on Cațavencu, they represent the faithful supporters, the blind allies without whom Cațavencu's successes would have been impossible.

A major source of humor in *The Lost Letter* is the lack of genuine commitment exhibited by all the characters. They are all survivors and masters of expedience. Thus, the politicians want the citizens to have their freedom, yet, if the citizens do not vote, they go to prison. At one moment, the representatives of the two parties insult each other and are ready to exchange blows; a moment later they are kissing and fraternizing. In fact, the ending of the play represents the quintessence of compromise: Cațavencu's courage regained, he prompts everyone to be happy and to celebrate the "honest" fights that have taken place during the elections, to celebrate "the progress" brought by these changes. Candidates, winners, losers, all embrace and join the triumphant parade that ends the play.

CARNIVAL SCENES

Although, in *Carnival Scenes*, Caragiale returns to the sordid world of the lower middle class, a class that slavishly imitates the manners and mores of the upper class, the play maintains the same sense of relativity. No one holds real principles. Everything is for sale or, at least, can be negotiated. Once again, anything that could threaten the status quo, compromise the equilibrium through which a hairdresser, Nae Girimea, has succeeded in keeping his two mistresses satisfied and, literally, out of each other's hair, is fought tooth and nail by Nae and his trusted apprentice, Jordache. The petty world in which Mița and Didina, the two principal female characters, succeed in misleading the older, wealthy men who support them, is placed under a microscope. Here, however, Caragiale's satire does not even reach the scope and complexity which he achieved in *A Stormy Night*.

NĂPASTA

Seeking a source of inspiration that would allow him to present more complex individuals, in *Năpasta*, Caragiale turned to the world of the countryside. Under the evident inspiration of the great Russian realists, Caragiale portrays the struggle of a simple peasant woman, Anca, to avenge the murder of her beloved husband. To attain her goal, Anca marries Dragomir, the killer, and she waits for the right moment for revenge. Often criticized for its lack of originality, *Năpasta* can offer a glimpse into Caragiale's tragic side, one that later became quite evident in short stories such as "The Easter Torch."

Caragiale spent the rest of his days writing short stories, sketches, and other short fiction. In them, he continued to create an unforgettable gallery of types, portraits of individuals who must have populated his world. He continued to characterize his personages in the same manner as he had done in his drama: He focused with intensity on each character's linguistic mannerisms or outstanding physical characteristics, seeking the telling detail. At the same time, however, his plays became increasingly popular and have long since become part of every Romanian citizen's national heritage.

OTHER MAJOR WORKS

SHORT FICTION: *Note şi schiţe*, 1892; *Păcat*, 1892; *Om cu noroc*, 1892; *Moftul român*, 1893; *Schiţe uşoare*, 1896; *Schiţe*, 1897; *Notiţe şi fragmente literare*, 1897; *Momente*, 1901; *Două bilete pierdute*, 1901; *1907: Din primăvară până in toamna*, 1907; *Novele, povestiri*, 1908; *Momente, schiţe, amintiri*, 1908; *Kir Ianulea*, 1909; *Schiţe nouă*, 1910; *Abu-Hasan*, 1915; *Reminiscenţe*, 1915; *Momente*, 1928 (2 volumes); *Sketches and Stories*, 1979.

POETRY: *Versuri*, 1922.

NONFICTION: *Culisele chestiunii naţionale*, 1896.

BIBLIOGRAPHY
"Ion Luca Caragiale." In *Playwrights*. Vol. 2 in *International Dictionary of Theatre*, edited by Mark Hawkins-Dady. Detroit, Mich.: St. James Press, 1994. A concise overview of the life and works of Caragiale.

Ionescu, Medeea. *A Concise History of Theatre in Romania*. Bucharest: Editura Stiintifica si Enciclopedica, 1981. This history of Romanian theater places Caragiale within the tradition.

Tappe, E. D. *Ion Luca Caragiale*. New York: Twayne, 1974. A basic biography of Caragiale that provides information on his life and works. Bibliography.

Liliana Zancu

MARINA CARR

Born: Dublin, Ireland; November 17, 1964

PRINCIPAL DRAMA
Low in the Dark, pr. 1989, pb. 1990
Deer's Surrender, pr. 1990
This Love Thing, pr. 1991
Ullaloo, pr. 1991
The Mai, pr. 1994, pb. 1995
Portia Coughlan, pr., pb. 1996
By the Bog of Cats, pr. 1997, pb. 1998
Plays: One, pb. 1999
On Raftery's Hill, pr. 2000, pb. 2000

OTHER LITERARY FORMS

Marina Carr is known most extensively for her work in drama, but she has also written a number of other works that have attracted critical attention. Her short story "Grow Mermaid" won the Hennessy Short

Story Prize. Another work, an essay entitled "Dealing with the Dead," was published in the *Irish University Review: A Journal of Irish Studies* (1998).

ACHIEVEMENTS

Although Marina Carr is a relatively recent arrival to the world of the theater, she has become very well known and widely celebrated for her work in Irish drama. *The Mai* won the Dublin Theatre Festival Best New Irish Play Award (1994-1995), and *Portia Coughlan* won the nineteenth Susan Smith Blackburn Prize (1996-1997). She has been offered several positions as writer-in-residence at Trinity College in Dublin (1998-1999) and Dublin City University (1999-2000). Her *Plays: One*, a collection, was published by Faber and Faber as part of their acclaimed Irish dramatist series. Carr also received the esteemed E. M. Forster Award from the American Academy of Arts and Letters.

BIOGRAPHY

Marina Carr was born on November 17, 1964, in Dublin, Ireland, but spent the majority of her childhood in Pallas Lake, County Offaly (the source of the dialect used in most of her plays). Daughter of Hugh Carr, a playwright and novelist, the young Carr was raised to have a keen interest in theater. She and her siblings wrote and presented plays filled with troubled families, robbers, and witches. After leaving public school, she attended the National University of Ireland, University College, Dublin, graduating in 1987 with a degree in English and philosophy.

Because of her consistent and excellent contributions to the Irish stage, Carr has served as a writer-in-residence at a number of colleges and other institutions, including the Abbey Theatre, Trinity College in Dublin, and Dublin City University. Her commitment to writing shows in the steady stream of awards she has received since her short story "Grow Mermaid" and her play *The Mai* both won major awards in 1994. Consequently, in 1996, Carr was inducted into Aosdána, an honorary and highly exclusive affiliation of artists engaged in literature, music, and visual arts who live and work in Ireland. In later years, Carr, along with her husband and two children, has contin-

ued to make the colorful history and folklore of Dublin the inspiration for her dramatic works and to embrace the beauties of the countryside and villas as her home.

ANALYSIS

Some critics have praised Marina Carr for her surreal depictions of Irish family life, describing her as one of the forefront voices in Irish dramatic literature. Some critics have noted Carr's adherence to the ancient form of tragedy and her reliance on sources of tragedy both ancient (Euripedes) and modern (Eugene O'Neill). Still others have praised her use of colloquial dialect, claiming it to be both authentic and moving. The fact that all these critics have found something unique to laud in Carr's work indicates the power and strength of her writing. As one of the most celebrated women writers in Ireland, Carr has made a lasting mark on the theater both inside and outside the British Isles for her unflinching examinations of dysfunctional family life, her modern reinterpretations of such classics as Euripides' *Mēdeia* (431 B.C.E.; *Medea*, 1781), and her presentation of Midlands Irish life, an area of Ireland hitherto ignored by Irish writers. In all Carr's dramas, women squarely face off against familial and personal weakness despite overwhelmingly negative consequences.

Carr began her dramatic writing career while studying English and philosophy at the University College of Dublin. She was particularly drawn to the works of Samuel Beckett and Tennessee Williams. Her absurdist comedy, *Ullaloo* (Gaelic for "death song"), has the same appeal as Beckett's *Fin de partie: Suivi de acte sans paroles* (pr., pb. 1957; *Endgame: A Play in One Act, Followed by Act Without Words: A Mime for One Player*, 1958). It presents the audience with two characters seeking laughably strange goals: a man trying to grow the longest toenails in the world and a woman trying to "achieve nothingness."

THE MAI

Although Beckett's influence is prominent in the works of most modern Irish writers, Carr sought out other spiritual ancestors in later years. She acknowledges the connection between her play, *The Mai*, and its literary forerunner, Tennessee Williams's *The Glass Menagerie* (pr. 1944). Millie, the narrator of Carr's moving familial drama, seeks, like Tom Wingfield, to free herself from her suffocating family and her mother (christened "Mary," but nicknamed "the Mai"), who has abandoned much of her good sense in favor of unattainable fantasy.

From the beginning of the play, the audience is informed of the difficulties the narrator and her family face. Millie tells the viewers that her parents' marriage is a sham because Robert, the Mai's husband, although only newly returned to his estranged wife after a separation of five years, has already begun another affair. The Mai, her name suggesting an impersonal title rather than a familiar name and a connection, familiar to Irish audiences, to the Virgin Mary (herself a distant, sad figure lacking a husband), has apparently been unable to defy the personal implications of her name (that she is, herself, distant and impersonal) and establish warm, intimate relationships. Although the Mai has had a house built in the countryside to entice her wandering husband home again, the attraction of the house ultimately cannot keep him home in the absence of personal feelings.

BY THE BOG OF CATS

In a panel discussion held as part of the Dublin Theatre Festival, Carr suggested that *Medea* was the literary antecedent for her seventh play, *By the Bog of Cats*. Like Medea, Carr's protagonist is a woman who not only has been discarded by her former lover (to whom she had taught the ways of love) in favor of a more socially acceptable "fiancée" but also has been threatened with the loss of their child. Hester Swane, the female outsider, kills her young daughter rather than surrender the girl to her father and his new, younger bride. Although Carr draws on the ancient Euripidean tragedy for the perusal of an audience that is presumed to know the story, Carr adds details and imagery that are strictly modern Irish.

By the Bog of Cats opens with Hester dragging the corpse of a black swan behind her. Taking a moment to rest and catch her breath, she is surprised by the appearance of a figure in formal dress and white gloves. Startled by the figure's archaic clothing, she asks him who he is. His casual, somewhat apologetic response, that he is a "ghost fancier," demonstrates the blending of supernatural horror and quiet humor

that is typical of a Carr drama. The Ghost Fancier, stating that he has a hard time distinguishing between sunset and sunrise because death has robbed him of a real sense of earthly time, is seeking out Hester's soul and, with a very gentlemanly air (he is far more civil than Hester's former beloved), apologizes for trying to take Hester with him before the day's end.

Unlike novelist Charles Dickens's horrific portrayals of spirits who cannot rest in their troubled graves, Carr's stage incarnations are essentially thoughtful and reflective. The Ghost Fancier is very gentle with the woman whose spirit he wants to take, giving Hester the opportunity to delay her ultimate departure. Even the Catwoman, an aged seer, instructs Hester early in the play that "Curses only have the power ya allow them." For all the mythic fatalism of its Medean antecedent, *By the Bog of Cats* gives Hester the ability and right to determine her fate. She, unlike Medea, is fully responsible for what happens to her. She decides to allow the Ghost Fancier to take her soul; she chooses to wear a wedding gown—denied her by her former lover—to disrupt that same lover's wedding; and she determines that only the murder of her child by her own hand will satisfy her need for revenge. Then, having scorched the local community's land and slaughtered their livestock for their complicity in her humiliation, Hester goes off to accept the Ghost Fancier's offer of death. The essentially Greek style of tragedy is transformed into a more Irish tale of self-determinism.

ON RAFTERY'S HILL

On Raftery's Hill, though occupied by three self-destructive generations of the Raftery family, is primarily dominated by the wickedness and weakness of one character. The monstrous Red Raftery, alternatively brutally vicious and disturbingly tender, is almost solely responsible for the degradation of his farm and family. In the years since he took the farm over from his parents, Red has hastened the death of his wife, sexually abused and raped both daughters (taking one as a kind of concubine), beaten his son into a stuporous, brain-damaged existence, and ruined his once-prosperous farm with his impatience and flights of temper. It is striking that a play that focuses on such an unpleasant person can be both compelling and, somehow, poetic.

Theater, both ancient and modern, has been composed of many monstrous fathers. Sophocles' *Oidipous Tyrannos* (c. 429 B.C.E.; *Oedipus Tyrannus*, 1715), William Shakespeare's *King Lear* (pr. c. 1605-1606), and Christopher Marlowe's *Tamburlaine the Great* (pr. c. 1587) are three stories concerning father figures famous for their lack of morality, but Red Raftery manages to hold his own among such notables for how he manages to reduce his family to such depths of misery—he is more of a beast than the animals he tortures and slaughters, once cutting the udder off a cow before killing it. His mother, Granny Shalome, has grown senile with advanced age and keeps trying to return to her childhood home, often failing to recognize her own son and grandchildren in the process. His only son, Ded, is half-witted from the severe physical beatings he suffered as a child and lives in the cowshed, and his daughter Dinah has only "lunatic drames [dreams] of somwan takin ya off a this Hill" to comfort herself with in the face of nearly thirty years of sexual abuse. Only Red's much younger daughter, Sorrel, has some hope of escape; she has acquired a fiancé, Dara Mood, who farms the land below the Hill. Even though her would-be husband is just a "scrubber" to Red, whose belligerent swaggering has made him unpopular with all his close neighbors, Sorrel is determined to leave the Hill and try to have some kind of normal life. Unfortunately, to her detriment, she refuses to take into account Red's suspicious nature and brutish desire to keep control of what he regards as his own. Sorrel's innocence blinds her to the unwholesome atmosphere surrounding her.

During the first act of the play, Red enters the stage with "two shot hares around his neck," a symbolic representation of his two daughters and an example of the play's animal imagery. He orders his younger daughter to gut them. Her refusal enrages him, causing him to see her at the forefront of a whole conspiracy within his own family and foreshadowing the end of act 1 when Red, raping Sorrel, accuses her and her fiancé of "tryin to steal me farm" and tells her that he'll "show [her] how to gut a hare."

This rape has devastating psychological effects on the young Sorrel. Although her sister Dinah has been raped by Red numerous times, eventually assuming a kind of surrogate wife status with him, she has no sympathy for Sorrel and blames her for the attack; "We're a respectable family, we love wan another and whahever happened ya happened ya be accident. D'ya honestly think we'd harm one another?" Red, too, shows astoundingly little remorse. His sole act of retribution, chucking a large check and the deeds to fifty acres of land at Sorrel's fiancé, Dara, without any friendly words or explanation, is singularly insulting and condescending to the young man. Dara, of course, refuses to accept what he regards as an "ungracious handout" even though he knows that Sorrel deeply desires the land and money to gain "standin in the community." Much as Red accused Sorrel of scheming to destroy their family, Sorrel blames Dara for "spoiling everything" and refuses to marry him. Red's desire for control and his brutality have once again condemned a daughter to a desolate life under the shadow of his perversity.

OTHER MAJOR WORKS

SHORT FICTION: "Grow Mermaid," 1994.

NONFICTION: "Dealing with the Dead," *Irish University Review: A Journal of Irish Studies*, 1998.

BIBLIOGRAPHY

Hurwitt, Robert. "The Healing Stage: Theater Offers Escape and Necessary Communion." *San Francisco Chronicle*, September 30, 2001. Hurwitt describes in detail the performance of Carr's *By the Bog of Cats* at San Jose Repertory Theatre. He sees Carr's play as a rural Irish *Medea* that imagines Euripedes' ancient tragedy in the context of the pain of the dispossessed outsider and deserted child. He particularly lauds Holly Hunter's portrayal of Carr's heroine, Hester Swane.

King, Robert L. "The Irish and Others." *North American Review* 285, no. 6 (November/December, 2000): 43-47. King reviews Carr's play, *On Raftery's Hill*, describing how the Irish dramatist, in particular, manages to gain prominence in the theater community by his or her portrayal of brutality and extravagance. He sees the typical Irish drama as relying on cultural symbols to maintain the empathy of Irish audiences while ensnaring foreign audiences with its sheer audacity of presentation. What makes this article particularly interesting is King's obvious familiarity with Carr's development as a dramatist.

_____. "Life in the Theater." *North American Review* 284, no. 2 (March/April, 1999): 45-48. King discusses the Dublin Theatre Festival of 1999, which featured such works as Carr's *By the Bog of Cats* and Jim Nolan's *The Salvage Shop*. King connects Carr's character Hester Swane with her Greek antecedent Medea to describe how modern Irish theater has found the most compelling modern drama to be the retelling of ancient mythology.

_____. "Premieres and Adaptations." *North American Review* 282, no. 2 (March/April, 1997): 48-52. King reviews several performances, including Carr's *The Mai*, at the McCarter Theatre in Princeton, New Jersey. He finds *The Mai* to be a highly symbolic play, embracing both Catholic and mythic imagery, that incorporates archetypes in both the names and attributes of its characters. He also studies the attitude of Irish and English playgoers to Carr's works, noting her reliance on icons and imagery familiar to Irish audiences.

Klein, Alvin. "Fatalism of the Greeks, Transplanted to Ireland." *The New York Times*, January 24, 1999, pp. 14-15. Klein compares Carr's *By the Bog of Cats* with Euripedes' *Medea*, examining each story's thematic reliance on the Greek understanding of fate. He makes comparisons between the plays' plots and characters, focusing particularly on the connection between Hester Swane and Medea.

McNulty, Charles. "Marina Carr: Unmotherly Feelings." *American Theatre* 18, no. 8 (October, 2001): 106-109. McNulty sees Carr as being typical of the blackly humorous Irish dramatist. He discusses her reliance on Tennessee Williams's *The Glass Menagerie* to achieve such a realistic portrayal of both the hysterical and smothering mother and rebellious, yet guiltily responsible daughter in *The Mai*.

Roche, Anthony. "Woman on the Threshold: J. M. Synge's *The Shadow of the Glen*, Teresa Deevy's *Katie Roche*, and Marina Carr's *The Mai*." *Irish University Review: A Journal of Irish Studies* 25, no. 1 (1995): 143-162. Roche examines not only the personal relationships within Carr's *The Mai* as a source of tension and conflict for the female heroine but also how each of the three plays relies on the actions and reactions of a single, focal character to advance the plot and develop the theme.

Julia M. Meyers

ALEJANDRO CASONA
Alejandro Rodríguez Álvarez

Born: Besullo, Spain; March 23, 1903
Died: Madrid, Spain; September 17, 1965

PRINCIPAL DRAMA

La sirena varada, pr., pb. 1934
Otra vez el diablo, pr., pb. 1935
Nuestra Natacha, pr. 1935, pb. 1936
Prohibido suicidarse en primavera, pr. 1937, pb. 1941 (*No Suicide Allowed in Spring*, 1950)
Las tres perfectas casadas, pr. 1941, pb. 1943

(based on Arthur Schnitzler's story "Der Tod des Junggesellen")
La dama del alba, pr., pb. 1944 (*The Lady of Dawn*, 1964)
La barca sin pescador, pr. 1945, pb. 1955 (*The Boat Without a Fisherman*, 1970)
Los árboles mueren de pie, pr. 1949, pb. 1950
Siete gritos en el mar, pr. 1952, pb. 1954
La tercera palabra, pr. 1953, pb. 1954
Obras completas, pb. 1954, 1959

OTHER LITERARY FORMS

Alejandro Casona began his career as a poet but published only two slim volumes, of no particular distinction. He earned the Premio Nacional de Literatura (national prize for literature) in 1932 for his collection of myths retold for children, *Flor de leyendas* (1933; flower of legends). Otherwise, aside from some desultory contributions to literary criticism and a few translations, Casona wrote only for the stage and screen. His film credits include versions of several of his own plays, an adaptation of Henrik Ibsen's *Et dukkehjem* (1879; *A Doll's House*, 1880), and original screenplays.

ACHIEVEMENTS

Alejandro Casona consistently enjoyed a rare combination of popular success and critical acclaim. His first performed drama, *La sirena varada* (the stranded mermaid), won for him the Lope de Vega Prize; moreover, Casona answered eighteen curtain calls at the premiere. *Nuestra Natacha* (our Natacha), a work of less artistic merit, had favorable reviews to go with its unbroken run of more than five hundred performances. Exiled during the Civil War, Casona took Latin America by storm. His old and new works played to packed houses from Havana to Buenos Aires, and he soon established himself as the most important dramatist in Argentina. His contemporaries hailed him for revitalizing the Spanish theater, and subsequent critics have confirmed that judgment. Casona, along with Federico García Lorca, deserves much credit for this dynamic resurgence, which continues to show its strength.

BIOGRAPHY

Alejandro Casona (Alejandro Rodríguez Álvarez) spent his entire life as an educator and a man of the theater. He was born in a tiny, remote village in Northern Spain to parents who taught in the local school. Casona trained for the same profession and worked regularly as a teacher and administrator until his exile. While stationed in the isolated Valle de Aráan, he began experimenting with drama, both as a teaching tool and for its own sake. After much initial frustration, he became an overnight success with the first performance of *La sirena varada* in 1934. Between 1931 and 1936, Casona combined his two callings as the director of Teatro del Pueblo (people's theater), an institution dedicated to bringing culture to rural districts. Besides writing several short pieces for performances and handling administrative duties, he took part in several tours. He fled Spain in 1937 and began a triumphant sweep through Latin America, giving lectures and directing productions in Puerto Rico, Cuba, Mexico, Colombia, Venezuela, Peru, Chile, and Argentina. In 1939, he settled in Buenos Aires, where he continued to compose new plays and began to write screenplays. After a long and productive residence in Argentina, he returned to Spain, where he died in 1965.

ANALYSIS

Alejandro Casona combined, in his best work, an enlightened didacticism with the grace of a born playwright. As a professional man of the theater, he experimented with various kinds of drama. *Nuestra Natacha*, for example, has its source in Casona's experience as a teacher and as director of Teatro del Pueblo. It conveys an overt and idealistic message and marks the only occasion on which Casona absolutely subordinated form to an idea. *Las tres perfectas casadas* (the three perfect wives), by contrast, is an uncharacteristically negative melodrama of betrayal and suicide, complete with an onstage shooting. In Casona's best work, however, he explored the problem of human unhappiness and examined some of the means commonly adopted to combat that problem.

The three plays to be considered all unfold according to this general pattern: An individual, usually a young man, attempts to find happiness by espousing an artificial system—by creating an institution of sorts—that is designed to shut out the pain and ugliness of life. A young woman, rescued from suicide, enters the picture; she brings about change, ultimately for the better. The system fails as unpleasant reality breaches its walls, but the young man and woman embark on a new, more promising quest for happiness: They acknowledge the potential ugliness of life but transcend it through love. Though Casona repeatedly employed these themes, devices, and characters, he imbued them with a striking freshness in each new version, so that he never seemed to be merely rehashing a formula.

The permutations of a single theme in these three plays should give some idea of Casona's command of his medium. Obliged by his values as an educator and a thinker to wrestle with the question of human happiness over and over again, he remained consistent without lapsing into monotony. His growth as a playwright kept pace with the increasing subtlety of his perceptions. In one sense, then, Casona's distinction as a dramatist is related to his integrity. He had the courage to write on any theme (the Fascist regime in Spain banned his writings for years) but the artistic sense not to degenerate into preachment. Perhaps as closely as any playwright of his time, he approached the ideal of *dulce et utile*: His plays teach ethical lessons, but that ethic includes an abiding love for the beautiful. His protagonists reject falsehood and ugliness in favor of truth and beauty—not as abstractions, but as active principles of life. Casona followed his own teachings; he stood up for truth and sweetened it with some of the most finely crafted plays of the twentieth century.

LA SIRENA VARADA

La sirena varada, the first of Casona's plays to be staged, establishes the pattern. Ricardo, the protagonist, falls into a well-intentioned error: He tries to attain happiness by fiat, by founding a republic of "orphans of common sense." Haunted by memories of an unhappy childhood, he strives for an irresponsible innocence, a life based on fantasy, into which no cold reason can intrude. A sign over the door—which somehow he never finds the time to put up—would read: "Let no one who knows geometry enter here." He has chosen his companions carefully; besides a tolerant servant and a painter who insists on going about blindfolded, Ricardo has rented a ghost with the house. He has also summoned a circus clown to act as president, and life seems to be going along very well.

For all its charm, Ricardo's grand scheme is unsound, even diseased. Even discounting the objections of the reasonable outsider, Don Florín, one cannot truly admire this republic: It is, simply, a despotism. Ricardo imposes his fantasy on the others with all the cruelty of youth. What seems at first to be romantic turns out to be merely decadent. Ricardo breakfasts in the middle of the night, as a puerile gesture of rebellion. They have run out of milk, so they subsist on coffee and rum. Rather than give up his rented ghost, the young despot convinces the timorous impostor that he is quite dead—the ghost of Napoleon Bonaparte—and obliges him to observe traditional haunting hours. He shows imagination, but no love.

The advent of Sirena, the putative mermaid, makes matters worse—though her presence will eventually help Ricardo to find a better answer. She delights his fancy with her faithful impersonation of a mermaid, but implicit in that identity is the image of death by drowning. As her role demands, she attempts to lure Ricardo into the depths. According to his own rules, he really ought to join her in her undersea palace. Indeed, to remain constant to his beliefs, he virtually must utter that other retort to unhappiness: suicide.

Fortunately, two factors impede this fatal misstep: the presence of Don Florín and Ricardo's core of health, intelligence, and goodness. Don Florín, like so many later characters in Casona's work, suffers the frustration of having found a way to live well without being able to impart it to the young people whom he loves. Despite Ricardo's gibes, the reader never questions the soundness of Don Florín. Unfortunately, he can only offer advice—much of it unheeded—and watch, as Ricardo blunders toward his own solution. With such help as he accepts, though, Ricardo does make progress: He never shows much enthusiasm for suicide, even under pressure from Sirena, and his subsequent decisions are always based on his love for her rather than allegiance to his system.

As always, when characters in a Casona play lock the front door against reality, it slips in through a side entrance. The circus clown, Papá Samy, finally arrives; he turns out to be Sirena's father and the bearer of a sorry truth: "Sirena" is quite insane. Ricardo once saved her from drowning—suicide—and she has been obsessed with him ever since. Even without such a tale to tell, Papá Samy would add little merriment to the place: He spends his time alternately getting drunk and reading the Bible.

This grim incursion comes almost as a relief to Ricardo. His love for the mysterious waif had already begun to change his values. Indeed, he had questioned her closely about her background, confessing that "this arbitrary life we've made for ourselves is starting to make me sick." The clown's revelations provide a pretext for abolishing most of the absurdities—and the cruelties—of the republic: The ghost becomes a gardener, the inhabitants adopt more regular habits, and Ricardo summons Don Florín back to restore Sirena—María—to her right mind.

Casona, however, does not permit Ricardo a facile turnaround. As Don Florín points out, the young dreamer has much to answer for, and merely behaving better does not excuse his earlier excesses. Nor has the falsehood of the establishment been completely exposed: Papá Samy has not told the whole truth, and Daniel, the so-called painter, continues to wear his blindfold. The third act of the play serves to reduce the remainder of Ricardo's little castle in the air to rubble and to force him to live in the world, not outside it.

Thus far, the truth has been unfortunate but still touching; reality has been saddening, but wanly beautiful. In the third act, there is a drastic turn for the worse. Daniel's blindfold, torn off at last by Ricardo, has covered eyes that were savaged by an explosion. Papá Samy, in his weakness, has bartered his daughter for beer. Ugliness on two legs enters, in the person of Pipo, circus owner and strongman. He has come to offer to sell Sirena to Ricardo, having had his fill of beating and raping her but reluctant to miss any chance of gouging some money.

This reeking embodiment of all that is sordid serves as a dragon to be routed. Improbably but inevitably, Ricardo puts the strongman to flight with a steely gaze and a calm threat. For all his muscles, Pipo functions primarily as a psychological menace. He leaves behind him the child in Sirena's womb and the horror of his memory. For a moment, all that has been accomplished seems in danger of crumbling. Ricardo once again turns his back on reality, having begun to comprehend its full potential for ugliness,

and urges a return to fantasy, to madness, to anything that will blot out the leering image of Pipo. This relapse sets up the ultimate victory: The poor little madwoman refuses to become a mermaid again, out of love for her unborn child and for Ricardo. He snaps out of his fit, and, as the play ends, "with infinite tenderness," he calls her by her real name, María. Thus, rather than surrendering to Pipo or fleeing from him, Ricardo and María have transcended him. They will make reality both beautiful and happy through love. The child, though sired by Pipo, will become theirs.

THE LADY OF DAWN

The Lady of Dawn, written some ten years later, bears the marks of the playwright's artistic maturity as well as of his exile. He avoids redundancy by changing the setting and by shifting the focus away from the young lovers. Ricardo founded his republic in a vague seaside house, sometime in the twentieth century. By contrast, *The Lady of Dawn* is set in Casona's native Asturias, and he evokes the spirit and the folklore of the region with loving accuracy. The horses, mills, and festivals to which he alludes belong to no specific era: They obey a rhythm of life as old as Christian Spain. In this setting, it seems appropriate that the young couple should share the spotlight with the personification of death. Though Casona will eventually make many of the same points, the presence of the Lady Pilgrim lends the play a profound dignity that is lacking in *La sirena varada*.

Just as Ricardo imposed fantasy and illogic, so the Mother demands grief, silence, and immobility. She chooses to nurture the memory of her lost daughter by brooding, and she expects the same of everyone else. On this, the fourth anniversary of the disaster, she wants no talking, no playing, no work. Like Ricardo, she bases her existence on an imagination gone astray, turned unhealthy. The Angélica she mourns never was; the memories she strives to preserve are, in a sense, fabrications. Also like Ricardo, she has the force of personality to impose her system on others—if not totally, at least enough to darken the lives of those around her.

Don Florín recurs in duplicate, as the Grandfather and as Telva, the servant. The Grandfather embodies the compassion and selflessness of his precursor. Telva inherits, in enhanced form, the good sense, garrulity, and spry strength of Don Florín. Each remonstrates with the Mother but to no avail; both are wise but unable to change the situation. Like Don Florín, they can accomplish nothing until some outside element disrupts the system.

In the earlier play, Sirena acted as that disruptive factor. Although at first she seemed to aggravate Ricardo's disease, she eventually drew him back to a real and healthy life. Similarly, Adela feeds the Mother's obsession by taking Angélica's place but subsequently cures the obsession by filling the void. Adela also resembles Sirena in her development: Rescued from drowning by her future husband, she makes the transition from would-be suicide to blissful beloved. Like Sirena, she takes over as the motivating force; the other characters discard the artificial and perverse ritual and do whatever they do for her sake.

Although Adela is the key to the plot, there can be no doubt that the Lady Pilgrim dominates the stage. She makes Death seem at once beautiful and tragic, incarnating as she does the tenderness of a woman and the implacability of doom. The Grandfather speaks for the audience in his hostile reception of the Lady Pilgrim and in his doubtful reflections as she begins to shake his prejudices. She has come for a life, as so often before—yet she leaves him wondering whether to resent or welcome her. Despite her role, she inspires compassion, even love. The children have no qualms; they accept her for her beauty and inveigle her into a game. In one of his most exquisite theatrical coups, Casona has her join in, laugh, and fall asleep, thus missing her dark appointment with Adela. Despite the error of the Mother—Casona frequently condemns parents who shut in their children—the power of life and joy persists and pulls off a miracle.

As in *La sirena varada*, the newcomer brings about a pervading but flawed bliss. Adela replaces Angélica and restores joy for everyone but Martín, the wifeless husband. He, alone, keeps her at a distance and continues to suffer. Eventually he reveals his plight: Angélica did not die, but rather fled with a lover, and so Martín is not free to follow his heart and begin a new life with Adela. He plans to flee the temptation. Not to be outdone in matters of self-sacrifice, she decides to drown herself to spare him this self-exile.

Angélica, oddly enough, functions in much the same way as Pipo. When Martín breaks down and tells the truth about her, the golden legend turns to mud. She compounds the ugliness by appearing in person, as a ragged and bitter floozy who threatens to drag virtually everyone down into the mire. Just as Sirena and Ricardo banished the gargoyle Pipo, however, so Death saves the situation here. Moved by compassion, she persuades Angélica to die in Adela's stead. Angélica drowns and is washed up with flowers in her hair, in full view of the assembled villagers. Instead of becoming a byword for betrayal, she will remain fixed in local lore as a saint of romance. Adela, Martín, and the Mother are all freed by the sacrifice and can truly begin to live. Death has confirmed the womanly side of her nature; she has replaced ugliness with beauty and has actually enhanced life.

Casona's nostalgia, as in the case of so many expatriates, lends a new depth of feeling to his work. Though he treats the same themes in both plays, *The Lady of Dawn* is the more moving and convincing. It depends on magic and ritual rather than whim and coincidence; it is anchored in the timeless reality of Asturias, not the private traumas of two little people. In short, the promise of *La sirena varada* is fulfilled in *The Lady of Dawn*: The brash innovator becomes an original craftsman, and Death enters to enrich the vision of life.

THE BOAT WITHOUT A FISHERMAN

In *The Boat Without a Fisherman*, Casona reworks his recurring themes into a starkly simple tale of sin and redemption. Ricardo Jordán, financier, speculator, and habitual exploiter of the widow and the orphan, has staked his happiness on success in the game of big business. As the scene opens, he is fuming dyspeptically in his office, with ruin staring him in the face. Right on cue, the Devil enters, resplendent in a business suit, to offer him a deal: Can he kill an unknown man, half a world away, with no risk of discovery? If so, his fortunes will be saved. Though already damned thrice over, Jordán hesitates; at last, simply by writing his name, he presumably kills Peter Anderson. To make his little experiment more interesting, however, the Devil lets Jordán hear Mrs. Anderson's scream of bereavement—perhaps the only thing capable of reaching Jordán's atrophied heart.

In this case, the playwright has chosen an artificial system known to all—the game of high finance. In consequence, he can dispose of it in the first act, without much ado. The wheeling and dealing that Jordán attempts to substitute for the natural activities of life has, at least on the stage, scant appeal. The underlings who scuttle in to fawn on Jordán after his Devil-aided coup serve to drive home an already obvious point: This is no way to live.

Estela Anderson, however, finds no better alternative. Like the Mother in *The Lady of Dawn*, she has allowed grief to take over; she clings to a grimly heroic pride and rules out the possibility of ever laughing or loving again. Even the presence of her mother—one of the most talkative, lively, and altogether delightful characters ever to grace a stage—cannot lighten the gloom she weaves about herself. To complicate matters, she suspects her sister's husband of the murder, which cuts off a major source of financial help and emotional support. There is no hope of change from within; only a wind from the outside world can clear the air.

Renewed light and joy come from an unlikely but obvious quarter. Estela has the remembered glimpse of her husband being pushed into the sea; Jordán has never stopped hearing the echoes of her scream. His advent will enable both to lay their ghosts to rest. The sun, with its flawless sense of timing, begins to shine. Jordán becomes the talk of the town, a precocious fisherman and tireless helper; everyone dreads his departure. As usual, the first change is not enough. Estela still clings to her suspicion, and Jordán to his secret. The change will remain superficial until each has dealt with the canker within.

From this point, coincidence—thematically justified—takes over. Just as Jordán gathers the resolve to confess, Estela's sister rushes in with the news that Cristián, the man whom Estela suspects, is dying. After some wavering, Estela goes to see him, accepts his confession, and forgives him, thus freeing herself from the burden of hatred. Jordán, meanwhile, learns that he has sinned only by intent; absolved of blood-guilt, he finds a loophole in his contract and foils the Devil by naming a new victim: the ruthless financier of the first act. By introducing Jordán to Estela, and thereby to love, the Devil has unwittingly set him on the road to salvation. The play ends with the reunion of Estela and Jordán, and the prospect of a hard-earned chance at happiness.

This play differs from Casona's earlier treatments of the same theme in several respects. First, he makes use of a wholesale change of scene: Ricardo has his office, Estela her net-festooned cottage. The synthesis is evident in the stage directions: The house remains the same, but Ricardo has brought the sun from the south to change its aspect. This in turn points up another difference: Unlike the homeless waifs of the earlier plays, Estela stays at home and devises her own system; the man comes to her. He saves her from drowning only in a metaphorical sense; her despair and her suicide are subtle and require more than expert swimming for their cure. Ricardo Jordán has no leering Pipo to combat, only himself; Estela's enemy is her own hatred, not the murderer. The self-defeating work of the Devil saves them both and gives yet another twist to the same enduring theme.

OTHER MAJOR WORKS

POETRY: *El peregrino de la barba florida*, 1928; *La flauta del sapo*, 1930.

SCREENPLAYS: *Veinte años y una noche*, 1940; *En el viejo Buenos Aires*, 1941; *La maestrita de los obreros*, 1941; *Concierto de almas*, 1942; *Cuando florezca el naranjo*, 1943; *Casa de muñecas*, 1943 (adaptation of Henrik Ibsen's play *A Doll's House*); *Nuestra Natacha*, 1943; *El María Celeste*, 1944; *Le Fruit mordu*, 1945 (with Jules Supervielle; adaptation of J. Jacques Bernard's *Martine*); *Margarita la tornera*, 1946; *El abuelo*, 1946 (adaptation of Benito Pérez Galdós's novel).

CHILDREN'S LITERATURE: *Flor de leyendas*, 1933.

BIBLIOGRAPHY

Díaz Castañón, Carmen. *Alejandro Casona*. Oviedo, Spain: Caja de Ahorros de Asturias, 1990. A biography of Casona, covering his writings and life. In Spanish.

Lima, Robert. *Dark Prisms: Occultism in Hispanic Drama*. Lexington: University Press of Kentucky, 1995. In his discussion of the demonic pact in Spanish drama, Lima examines Casona's plays *Otra vez el diablo* and *The Boat Without a Fisherman.*

Maio, Eugene A. "Mythopoesis in Casona's *La dama del alba.*" *Romance Notes* 22 (1981): 132-138. An examination of Casona's *The Lady of Dawn.*

Moon, Harold K. *Alejandro Casona*. Boston: Twayne, 1985. A basic biography of Casona that covers his life and works. Bibliography and index.

Philip Krummrich

MRS. SUSANNAH CENTLIVRE

Born: Whaplode(?), England; c. 1667
Died: London, England; December 1, 1723

PRINCIPAL DRAMA

The Perjur'd Husband: Or, The Adventures of Venice, pr., pb. 1700

The Beau's Duel: Or, A Soldier for the Ladies, pr., pb. 1702

The Stolen Heiress: Or, The Salamanca Doctor Outplotted, pr. 1702, pb. 1703

Love's Contrivance: Or, Le Medecin Malgré Lui, pr., pb. 1703

The Gamester, pr., pb. 1705

The Basset-Table, pr. 1705, pb. 1706

Love at a Venture, pr. 1706(?), pb. 1706

The Platonick Lady, pr. 1706, pb. 1707

The Busie Body, pr., pb. 1709

The Man's Bewitch'd: Or, The Devil to Do About Her, pr., pb. 1709

A Bickerstaff's Burying: Or, Work for the Upholders, pr., pb. 1710

Mar-Plot: Or, The Second Part of the Busie Body, pr. 1710, pb. 1711

The Perplex'd Lovers, pr., pb. 1712

The Wonder: A Woman Keeps a Secret, pr., pb. 1714

The Gotham Election, pb. 1715

A Wife Well Manag'd, pb. 1715, pr. 1724

The Cruel Gift: Or, The Royal Resentment, pr. 1716, pb. 1717

A Bold Stroke for a Wife, pr., pb. 1718

The Artifice, pr., pb. 1722

The Dramatic Works of the Celebrated Mrs. Centlivre, pb. 1872 (3 volumes)

The Plays of Susanna Centlivre, pb. 1982 (3 volumes)

OTHER LITERARY FORMS

In addition to her plays, Mrs. Susannah Centlivre published literary letters and some verse celebrating state occasions.

ACHIEVEMENTS

From 1700 until her death in 1723, Mrs. Susannah Centlivre was probably the most prolific and popular playwright in England. In her first ten years as a professional, she turned out a dozen plays for the stage; in the second half of her career, another seven.

Some of her plays closed after one or two nights, but others became exceptionally popular. *The Busie Body*, *The Wonder*, and *A Bold Stroke for a Wife* were major successes for Mrs. Centlivre, although these pieces had their longest runs after 1750. *The Busie Body*, her most popular play, was mounted at least 475 times between its premiere and 1800. David Garrick, the greatest actor of the century, gained at least part of his fame by his frequent portrayal of Marplot, the good-natured bungler in *The Busie Body*. For the last role of his career, Garrick chose Don Felix, a jealous lover in *The Wonder*. *The Busie*

Body and *The Wonder* even survived the doldrums of Victorian theater, becoming repertory pieces on the modern stage in Great Britain and the United States.

Mrs. Centlivre never became rich writing plays, but she did achieve some celebrity in literary circles. As a woman playwright, she was something of a novelty. Other women published plays, but very few. In her lifetime, Mrs. Centlivre had only two serious female rivals, Mary Manley and Mary Pix. Neither woman wrote so much or so well. Mrs. Centlivre also competed with male writers, becoming a friendly rival to such accomplished dramatists as George Farquhar, Nicholas Rowe, and Sir Richard Steele. Modern critics generally view Mrs. Centlivre as a competent professional whose plays make great theater, if not great literature.

BIOGRAPHY

The life of "celebrated Mrs. Centlivre," as she is commonly known to stage history, is poorly documented. A Susannah Freeman, born in Lincolnshire, probably to William and Ann Freeman of Whaplode, who had her baptized on November 20, 1669, is thought to have become Mrs. Susannah Centlivre. She was educated at home, but she left in her teens, evidently to escape a stern stepmother. Legend has it that she had some "gay adventures" during her early wanderings. One contemporary of Mrs. Centlivre related that when she left home, she stopped by the side of the road one day to rest, where she was spotted by a passing student from Cambridge University, Anthony Hammond, who—as the story goes—took pity on the fatigued and tearful girl and brought her to his quarters at the university. Disguised as Hammond's cousin Jack, Mrs. Centlivre is said to have studied at the university for two months, after which she left with Hammond's letter of recommendation. The story is probably apocryphal, but it exemplifies the kind of mythology that contemporaries used to explain Mrs. Centlivre's mysterious early years.

Mrs. Centlivre joined a company of strolling players around 1684. By most accounts she was always

Mrs. Susannah Centlivre (Courtesy of the New York Public Library)

attractive to men, including, some sources say, a Mr. Fox, who either married her or simply shared the same quarters with her for a while. Fox apparently died, and she seems to have married a Mr. Carroll, an army officer, in 1685. Carroll died within a year and a half from wounds sustained in a duel.

By 1700, Mrs. Centlivre had settled in London, where she began life as a professional playwright. Her early plays were not well received. Not until *The Gamester* was produced in 1705 did she have a genuine success.

After three more failures, Mrs. Centlivre enjoyed another success with *The Busie Body*, which, premiering in 1709, became her most popular play ever. Still, the kind of success that she enjoyed with *The Gamester* and *The Busie Body* did not provide an adequate living. For her income, Mrs. Centlivre, like most playwrights, depended on three sources: gifts from patrons of the arts, sales of play copies, and author benefit nights at the theater, during which she would receive all the ticket receipts, less the house's operating expenses. None of these sources was reliable, and there is evidence that between 1700 and 1707, Mrs. Centlivre spent some time as a strolling actor in the provinces, presumably supplementing the income she made from playwriting.

The burden of supporting herself was relieved considerably when, in 1707, she married the man with whom she would live for the rest of her life, Joseph Centlivre. As a cook for the Crown, Joseph could expect to make at least fifty-five pounds per annum, not a negligible income at the time.

After *The Busie Body*, Mrs. Centlivre was never to see another true success. She tried to take advantage of the play's popularity by writing the sequel, *Mar-Plot*, but like most sequels, it had a short run, lasting only six days during the 1710-1711 season. *The Wonder* in 1714 and *A Bold Stroke for a Wife* in 1718 had respectable runs, but they did not achieve real popularity until after 1750. Mrs. Centlivre died on December 1, 1723, in her house in London's Buckingham Court, where she had lived the last ten years of her life. She was buried in St. Paul's, Covent Garden.

ANALYSIS

If Mrs. Susannah Centlivre became the most popular playwright of her time, there was good reason for it. As a professional playwright, she wrote to eat, and thus to please. She gave the audience what they wanted, and she gave them plenty of it. Writing to please the audiences of the early eighteenth century was no easy task. In the preface to *Love's Contrivance*, Mrs. Centlivre complains that "Writing is a kind of Lottery in this fickle Age, and Dependence on the Stage as precarious as the Cast of a Die; the Chance may turn up, and a Man may write to please the Town, but 'tis uncertain, since we see our best Authors sometimes fail." If audiences were notoriously fickle, playwrights were careful also not to anger the moral reformers, who needed only the scantest traces of profanity or bawdy language to brand a play licentious.

Mrs. Centlivre's solution was to write entertaining plays that would offend very few theatergoers and, with any luck, please most of them. Thus, she avoided tough satiric material. Her plays may poke fun, but

they rarely abuse; they mock, but rarely malign. In English drama written between 1660 and 1685, so-called Restoration drama, comedy was often savagely satiric—and there was a good stock of comic butts: merchants, Puritans, fops, pedants, coquettes, and old lechers. Mrs. Centlivre adopted many of the comic types of the Restoration stage but treated them with a tolerance uncharacteristic of her models.

Indeed, the stock character is a major component of Mrs. Centlivre's drama and is usually found in formulaic plots, often variations on the boy-gets-girl theme. Mrs. Centlivre created characters not for the ages but for the Friday-afternoon show. She expected that her audience would recognize the character types and take delight in the predictable action, as the greedy merchant loses his money or the resourceful maid wins her beau. Indeed, in a play by Mrs. Centlivre, plot is often preeminent, featuring disguises, chance meetings, lovers' assignations, schemes, and counter-schemes—all the elements that could be expected from a busy play of intrigue. Centlivre's characters never stop to ponder aloud the ethics of their actions; rather, they pursue their aims until they are either fulfilled or frustrated. Much of Mrs. Centlivre's art, then, depended on giving new life to old characters and old plots, and in this she was very successful.

THE GAMESTER

In *The Gamester*, she wrote a didactic play showing the reformation of a compulsive gambler. The main action concerns Valere, who is in love with Angelica. Angelica returns his love but will not marry him unless he gives up gambling. Valere has another reason to forsake the dice when his father, Sir Thomas Valere, announces that he is tired of paying his son's debts and that he must marry Angelica or lose his inheritance. Therefore, Valere asks Angelica's forgiveness one more time, which she bestows, giving him a diamond-studded portrait of herself to seal the bargain.

Predictably, Valere still cannot resist the gaming tables, and he loses all his money to a pert young gentleman who turns out to be Angelica disguised in breeches; she has come to verify a rumor that Valere has broken his promise. Having won all his cash, Angelica convinces him to stake the precious portrait, which she also wins, and she dashes out before he has a chance to win it back.

When Valere goes to Angelica to claim her hand, she demands the portrait as proof of his faith. When he cannot produce it, she reveals it herself, making Valere believe that their relationship is over. Indeed, the situation looks desperate: When Sir Thomas enters the scene and learns what has happened, he disinherits his son. Sir Thomas's severity seems to shock Angelica, though, and she takes Valere back, recognizing, perhaps, her own hand in his downfall. Convinced that the couple will marry, Sir Thomas restores his son's fortune.

In writing *The Gamester*, Mrs. Centlivre was trying to capitalize on the vogue for didactic comedy that developed in the first decade of the eighteenth century. Didactic comedy, in which a character is reformed from vicious ways, never dominated the stage, but professionals such as Colley Cibber, Sir Richard Steele, and Sir John Vanbrugh all wrote plays of this type, with various degrees of success. Steele's *The Lying Lover: Or, The Lady's Friendship* (pr. 1703) was a failure, but as noted above, *The Gamester* enjoyed a successful run. Steele wrote a ponderous, preachy play; Mrs. Centlivre wrote something quite different.

Unlike *The Lying Lover*, *The Gamester* does not take itself too seriously. In his play, Steele works in a sermon on the evils of dueling, but Mrs. Centlivre never rails against gambling. Her prime interest is in the gamester, not in gaming itself. By reclaiming a gambler, she gives her play a moral pretext and a handy plot formula. Shocking people into giving up gambling was not her purpose; in fact, as a compulsive gambler, Valere does not have a bad life. He must occasionally avoid his creditors, and his dealings with Angelica and Sir Thomas are sometimes a bit awkward, but ultimately, his vice causes him relatively little hardship or distress. At the end of the play, he is a bit richer, and he has the girl.

In one sense, Valere's gaming works as Angelica's rival for his attentions. Because Mrs. Centlivre does not portray the life of a gamester as a difficult one, Valere's prime motive in giving up the dice is to win Angelica (and his inheritance). Mrs. Centlivre is, in

effect, giving us another version of the boy-gets-girl plot. As in many dramatic versions of this old story, the couple must overcome some difficult elders, represented by Sir Thomas, who threatens disinheritance, and his brother Dorante, a minor character with amorous designs on Angelica.

In keeping with the spirit of the play, Mrs. Centlivre makes neither her characters nor any of their fates very nasty. Perhaps she was worried that her play could be considered immoral if she portrayed vice too graphically. Valere is not Vice incarnate, nor is he even vicious—he simply has a vice, gaming. His habit is like a disease, and the audience is free to hate the disease while sympathizing with Valere himself. The audience forgives him and celebrates his happy end.

THE BUSIE BODY

In *The Busie Body*, a different kind of play, Mrs. Centlivre produced what some critics have called a romantic intrigue. Sir George Airy, a rich young gentleman, is in love with Miranda, who lives with her amorous old guardian, Sir Francis Gripe. Miranda wants no part of her guardian's romancing, but she is also rather coy with Sir George, whom she does fancy. The situation has a parallel in the plight of Isabinda, who is sequestered by her father, Sir Jealous Traffic. Traffic wants to save his daughter for a Spanish merchant, but Charles, the poor son of Sir Francis, provides some competition. The young lovers do eventually marry, but not before having many of their best-laid plans dashed by ill luck and by the good-natured but witless bungling of Marplot, the "busie body" of the title.

After viewing *The Gamester*, Mrs. Centlivre's audience could conceivably debate whether Valere deserved such good fortune at the end of the play. He does very little to earn it. *The Busie Body* does not pose the same kind of question. The play exhibits plot with a vengeance, and the characters are all familiar types, preventing the audience from taking any of them seriously. Sir Francis and Sir Jealous, for example, are typically stubborn, overbearing fathers who hinder true love by proposing and championing unsuitable matches for their children. In the rebellious lovers of *The Busie Body*, the audience recognizes more stock characters. Miranda is the familiar resourceful woman who seems to control much of the play's action and wins her man as much as he wins her. Miranda does not immediately express her love for Sir George: She keeps him dangling for a while. (The type is coy as well as cunning.) For all her schemes, though, the resourceful woman is generally a sympathetic character. So, too, is the sequestered maiden, the damsel in distress, of which Isabinda is a prime example. Locking up fair maidens for inevitable rescue was a staple of Spanish romance, but playwrights such as William Wycherley and Mrs. Centlivre put the device to good use on the English stage.

Mrs. Centlivre's rescuers, Sir George and Charles, would also have been familiar to the audience of 1709. As in many comedies with two pairs of lovers, the gentlemen are good friends. Both characters resemble the male component in Restoration comedy's "gay couple." Typically, the man and woman that make up the gay couple, while trying to outmaneuver scheming elders, engage in battles of wit as they guardedly measure the depth of each other's affection. Contests of wit were not Mrs. Centlivre's strong point, but there is a sparring match of sorts in the first meeting between Miranda and Sir George.

In Marplot, Mrs. Centlivre presented to her audience a character type less familiar than the others but still not entirely original. As the well-meaning bungler, Marplot has forebears in, for example, John Dryden's Sir Martin in *Sir Martin Mar-All: Or, The Feign'd Innocence* (pr. 1667). Of all the characters in *The Busie Body*, Marplot may be the most attractive. Although his mere presence is ruinous to the plans of the couples, his good heart and feeble wit keep one from really blaming him. In trying to delay Sir Jealous, Marplot succeeds only in confirming the father's suspicions that Charles is in his daughter's bedroom. At one point in the play, Sir George, to escape the eyes of Sir Francis, hides behind the chimney board. The fastidious Sir Francis wants to throw an orange peel in the chimney, so Miranda tells him that she is keeping a monkey there, a monkey that should be released only when the trainer is present. Sir Francis accepts this story and walks off, but Marplot cannot contain his curiosity and reveals George behind the board. Marplot yells out, and Sir George must bolt out of the room to remain undetected by the returning Sir Francis. Perhaps the audience never really becomes emotionally attached to Marplot—after all, he remains a type—but he is fresher than the other characters, charming and amusing.

No character, however, overshadows the action of *The Busie Body*. The play offers virtually a smorgasbord of comic plot devices. Secret meetings between lovers are interrupted by the unseasonable return of parents. Charles dispatches a letter to Isabinda, but the woman servant, Patch, accidentally drops it for Sir Jealous to find. Miranda gets rid of Sir Francis by telling him that he must attend the funeral of Squeezum the Usurer, but her guardian meets Squeezum on the street, hastening his return. There is little suspense—the audience knows that young love will conquer parental tyranny—but great pleasure in seeing the complex plot brought to a satisfactory conclusion.

A BOLD STROKE FOR A WIFE

Mrs. Centlivre's last great success, *A Bold Stroke for a Wife*, is a comedy with some scenes that border on pure farce. The business of the play is to get Colonel Fainwell, a soldier, married to his lover, Ann Lovely, whose dead father has left her the ward of four eccentric guardians: Sir Philip Modelove, an aging fop; Periwinkle, an antiquarian; Tradelove, a stockbroker; and Obadiah Prim, a Quaker. Ann cannot claim her fortune unless she marries a man agreed on by all four of her guardians—a requirement that, given their radically different dispositions, appears to be impossible to satisfy. The couple could not live on a soldier's wages; therefore, Fainwell must find a way to trick all four into accepting him as Ann's match. This he accomplishes through disguise and deception.

Unlike *The Busie Body*, *A Bold Stroke for a Wife* does not give the audience an endless series of comic devices. Fainwell uses one basic tactic throughout the play: impersonation. He appears as a fop to Sir Philip, as a collector of odd facts and curios to Periwinkle, as a Dutch trader to Tradelove, and as a Quaker to Prim. After winning the confidence of each guardian, he uses transparent tricks to gain their consent. For the most part, his ploys run smoothly, although there are some predictable complications. In general, the plot of *A Bold Stroke for a Wife* is not very compelling. The audience enjoys seeing the guardians duped, but its pleasure comes from the justice, not the methods.

The play works, in part, because some comic butts get their richly deserved rewards. Fops, stockbrokers, antiquarians, and puritans had long been targets of satire when Mrs. Centlivre wrote her play. Rarely, however, had so many types of butts appeared in one play. If tricking one kind of butt was funny, tricking four kinds would be even funnier—the more, the merrier.

The audience laughs because each of the butts, in his own way, is prideful and narrow-minded. Sir Philip affects French dress and the French language and disdains anything associated with his native England. Periwinkle is obsessed with the unauthentic artifacts of ancient history. The prime mover of Tradelove's existence is money, while Prim cares only for parading his piety and condemning the wicked ways of others.

In Restoration comedy, such figures would be abused and ridiculed. In contrast, Mrs. Centlivre does not treat her butts ruthlessly. Refusing to heap scorn on them, she laughs good-naturedly at their follies and invites us to do the same. She may have realized that there is a bit of Prim and Periwinkle in everyone.

OTHER MAJOR WORKS

POETRY: *The Masquerade*, 1713; *A Poem Humbly Presented to His Most Sacred Majesty George . . .*, 1714; *An Epistle to the King of Sweden from a Lady of Great Britain*, 1715.

BIBLIOGRAPHY

Bowyer, John Wilson. *The Celebrated Mrs. Centlivre*. Durham, N.C.: Duke University Press, 1952. The standard biography and literary analysis. Provides a thorough survey of Mrs. Centlivre's life and writings. Portrait, bibliography of Mrs. Centlivre's writings, and index.

Collins, Margo. "Centlivre v. Hardwicke: Susannah Centlivre's Plays and the Marriage Act of 1753." *Comparative Drama* 33, no. 2 (Summer, 1999): 179-198. An analysis of the social function of plays, focusing on *The Busie Body* and *A Bold Stroke for a Wife*.

Herrell, LuAnn Venden. "'Luck Be a Lady Tonight' or at Least Make Me a Gentleman: Economic Anxiety in Centlivre's *The Gamester.*" *Studies in the Literary Imagination* 32, no. 2 (Fall, 1999): 45-61. An examination of Mrs. Centlivre's moralizing against gambling as an attack on the wider social system. Provides an in-depth analysis of the play.

Kreis-Schinck, Annette. *Women, Writing, and the Theater in the Early Modern Period: The Plays of Aphra Behn and Suzanne Centlivre*. Cranbury, N.J.: Associated University Presses, 2001. An examination of the dramatic works of Mrs. Centlivre and Aphra Behn. Bibliography and index.

Lock, F. P. *Susannah Centlivre*. Boston: Twayne, 1979. Lock's focus on Mrs. Centlivre's plays is literary and critical as opposed to biographical and historical. He analyzes the plays in their historical context and concludes that her work fluctuates broadly. When at her best, she wrote amusing, light comedy of distinction. Chronology, bibliography, and index.

Rosenthal, Laura J. *Playwrights and Plagiarists in Early Modern England: Gender, Authorship, Literary Property*. Ithaca, N.Y.: Cornell University Press, 1996. Includes a discussion of Mrs. Centlivre in relation to her male critics.

Douglas R. Butler,
updated by Gerald S. Argetsinger

MIGUEL DE CERVANTES

Born: Alcalá de Henares, Spain; September 29, 1547
Died: Madrid, Spain; April 23, 1616

PRINCIPAL DRAMA

El trato de Argel, pr. 1585, pb. 1784 (*The Commerce of Algiers*, 1870)
El cerco de Numancia, wr. 1585, pb. 1784 (*The Siege of Numantia*, 1870)
Ocho comedias y ocho entremeses nuevos, pb. 1615 (includes *Pedro de Urdemalas* [*Pedro the Artful Dodger*, 1807], *El juez de los divorcios* [*The Divorce Court Judge*, 1919], *Los habladores* [*Two Chatterboxes*, 1930], *La cueva de Salamanca* [*The Cave of Salamanca*, 1933], *La elección de los alcaldes de Daganzo* [*Choosing a Councilman in Daganzo*, 1948], *La guarda cuidadosa* [*The Hawk-eyed Sentinel*, 1948], *El retablo de las maravillas* [*The Wonder Show*, 1948], *El rufián viudo llamada Trampagos* [*Trampagos the Pimp Who Lost His Moll*, 1948], *El viejo celoso* [*The Jealous Old Husband*, 1948], and *El vizcaíno fingido* [*The Basque Imposter*, 1948])
The Interludes of Cervantes, pb. 1948

OTHER LITERARY FORMS

Although Miguel de Cervantes longed for the popular success and financial rewards offered by the stage, he hoped to gain a more prestigious literary reputation as a great poet, as evidenced by the time and dedication that went into his long derivative poem *El viaje del Parnaso* (1614; *The Voyage of Parnassus*, 1870), as well as his numerous occasional poems, such as his songs addressed to the Invincible Armada. He believed that his reputation as a writer of narrative would rest on a work to which he devoted much of his energy during his last years, *Los trabajos de Persiles y Sigismunda* (1617; *The Travels of Persiles and Sigismunda: A Northern History*, 1619), a novel that he regarded as the best of all his works. It is no more remembered today and no more widely read than a lifeless pastoral novel written early in his career, *La Galatea* (1585; *Galatea: A Pastoral Romance*, 1833). His own age and subsequent generations have recognized his outstanding work to be *El ingenioso hidalgo don Quixote de la Mancha* (1605, 1615; *Don Quixote de la Mancha*, 1612-1620). In this long novel, Cervantes not only made a lasting contribution to the development of narrative form but also created two of the most memorable of all imaginary characters, the immortal knight-errant and his squire, Sancho Panza. Cervantes also played an important role in developing the short story as a genre.

ACHIEVEMENTS

Miguel de Cervantes contributed to the Spanish theater in two minor ways, by stirring critical debate and through some of his dramatic works, but he had relatively little impact on the drama of the Spanish Golden Age and does not rank as a playwright with the greatest names of the period, such as Lope de Vega Carpio, Tirso de Molina, and Pedro Calderón de la Barca. In the first part of *Don Quixote de la Mancha*, published in 1605, Cervantes included a lengthy and impressive attack on the drama of his day. In chapter 48, the canon and the priest exchange thoughts about the Spanish stage and the plays that were most popular. Using these characters as spokespeople for his own views, Cervantes particularly criticizes the violations of the classical unities, the alterations in historical facts, the neglect of moral lessons, and even the character of some of the playwrights. This attack prompted Lope de Vega to respond with the central critical work of the age, his *El arte nuevo de hacer comedias en este tiempo* (1609; *The New Art of Writing Plays*, 1914), in which he defended himself and his plays and explained that he wrote to please his audience and deliberately violated the rules to produce more entertaining drama. In prompting this remarkable essay in which the great playwright examined his own work and his own motives, Cervantes made a unique contribution to the theater of his time and to theater history.

In his attack in *Don Quixote de la Mancha*, Cervantes mentions by name his own play *The Siege of Numantia* as one of the few plays written in accord with the classical rules to have achieved a degree of popularity with the audience. Although the play did attain a degree of success on the stage in its own day, *The Siege of Numantia* has been more highly praised in later times by such men as Johann Wolfgang von Goethe, Percy Bysshe Shelley, Friedrich von Schlegel, and Arthur Schopenhauer. The play is in epic tragedy on a grand poetic scale, chronicling the demise in 134 B.C.E. of a Spanish town that refused to surrender to the Roman general Scipio. The stage is filled with heroic characters, grand gestures, and lofty speeches. Allegorical figures are used throughout, such as War, Pestilence, Hunger, Fame, the river Duero (complete with three tributaries), and even Spain herself. *The Siege of Numantia* is an odd kind of national epic, filled with patriotic dedication and an air of Spain's sense of its own illustrious destiny. Although it is almost oppressively solemn—indeed, it is the only work by Cervantes that is unrelieved by humor—the play is nevertheless a remarkable achievement and is unlike any other Spanish play.

Cervantes' greatest accomplishment in the genre of drama, however, is a series of short plays never performed in his lifetime. In 1615, he was forced to publish a volume of eight full-length plays and eight interludes that had all been refused for production by theater managers. The publication of the volume *Ocho comedias y ocho entremeses nuevos* (1615; eight new plays and interludes) at least got the works before the public. In a preface to the volume, Cervantes tried to gain for himself the recognition as a dramatist that had always eluded him. He complained that even though he had in his youth produced some plays that were received "without cucumbers," he had nevertheless put aside his pen when the playwriting crown was stolen by Lope de Vega. His plays, he asserted, had dared to reduce the number of acts for comedies from five to three (although other playwrights had done the same before Cervantes). He claimed to have represented the inner workings and secret thoughts of the soul on the stage for the first time and vowed that his plays set moral figures before the public and that his dramas were both didactic and entertaining. In fact, the comedies in the volume are failures as theater pieces—talky, lifeless, and badly constructed.

The interludes, however, are among his greatest achievements. Within this short form of the one-act farce, which would have been performed between the acts of a full-length play as an intermission piece, Cervantes' imagination took flight. Populated with characters that seem to have wandered into the interludes directly from the streets of Spanish cities, these plays are original, dynamic, and highly theatrical. They achieve a perfect balance between exaggerated farce and comic realism. The ruffians, students, drunkards, prostitutes, sacristans, soldiers, judges, yokels, con men, and magicians who come from the lower and middle classes are energetic, living figures. The brief comic interactions among them rank with the finest work in the one-act form by Anton Chekhov, August Strindberg, and Tennessee Williams.

Miguel de Cervantes (Library of Congress)

BIOGRAPHY

In the most interesting of the eight comedies by Miguel de Cervantes Saavedra published in 1615, *Pedro the Artful Dodger*, the title character dreams ambitiously of becoming all the great personages that a man can become—pope, prince, monarch, emperor, master of the world. After a career that is typical of a *picaro* or any other adventurous Spanish rogue of the time, Pedro finds his wishes realized when he becomes an actor and enters imaginatively into the ranks of the great. In much the same way, Cervantes' great ambitions in life were never realized, and the only satisfaction he found was in a world he himself created.

In one sense, Cervantes' greatest drama was his own life. Born in a small university city not far from Madrid, Cervantes traveled constantly with his family in his early years. His father, an impoverished and impractical man who attempted to earn a living as a surgeon, kept the family moving, from Valladolid to Córdoba, from Seville to Madrid. Cervantes learned the life of the road and the diversity of city life in Spain as a youth. The education he received was most likely from the Jesuits, and when he was in his twenties he journeyed to Italy. Perhaps fleeing from arrest as the result of a duel, he entered the service of Cardinal Aquaviva. In 1569, he enlisted in the Spanish army and went to sea. Cervantes was present at the sea battle of Lepanto in 1571. He served under the command of Don John of Austria in the famous victory against the Turks. Cervantes rose from his sickbed to join in the battle and was twice wounded, one wound leaving his left hand permanently crippled. With his brother Rodrigo, he embarked for Spain in 1575, but their ship was seized by Turkish pirates, and Cervantes spent five years in captivity as a slave. He later depicted those years in his play *The Commerce of Algiers*, which contains a self-portrait in a character named Saavedra, a man who gives aid and support to the other Christian captives.

Ransomed by Trinitarian monks, Cervantes returned to Spain, but not to glory and acclaim. With his military career at an end, Cervantes fell into poverty and moved from one failure to another, including an apparently unhappy marriage in 1584. Moving about Spain as in his youth, he again gained an education in the character and behavior of the Spanish lower classes, an education that continued when he was imprisoned twice in Seville, once in 1597 and again in 1602—both times, it is assumed, because of financial difficulties. Despite a life of bad luck, missed opportunities, and little reward for his talent, Cervantes did achieve popular success when the first part of *Don Quixote de la Mancha* was published in 1605, although his finances saw only minor improvement. In 1615, the second part of the novel appeared, to challenge the "false" sequels being produced by other writers seeking to capitalize on the book's success. Cervantes died in Madrid in 1616, at peace, having received the Sacraments.

ANALYSIS

Reading the drama of Miguel de Cervantes often results in a search for intimations or reminiscences of *Don Quixote de la Mancha*. The stature of this one work and the intensity of life conveyed in it nearly overwhelm the rest of Cervantes' artistic work. What is most interesting in examining Cervantes' drama is recognizing his obsession with certain themes and certain situations that eventually merge and metamorphose into the gigantic masterpiece. The dramas present these obsessions worked out onstage and in different, if not equally fascinating, guises.

THE SIEGE OF NUMANTIA

Perhaps the oddest source for one of the principal motivating themes of *Don Quixote de la Mancha* appears in *The Siege of Numantia*. It should come as no surprise that Cervantes, who always expressed pride in his accomplishments at the Battle of Lepanto, should have believed in the importance of the cultivation of heroism in human life. In *The Siege of Numantia*, that heroism is already inseparable from isolation and defeat. For Cervantes, heroism is not necessarily victory and glory; heroism may more naturally find expression and be more readily apparent in endurance, defiance, and failure. Greatness lies in the struggle itself, not in the outcome of that struggle. In the principal dramatic situation of the play, the town of Numantia has been completely isolated by the Roman general Scipio. His men have dug a trench around the city so that no food may enter it and no warriors leave it. Rather than losing his own men in battle, Scipio hopes to starve the town into submission. The people of the town stoically accept their fate, never turning on one another in their hungry desperation as Scipio anticipates, but rather using their remaining strength to strip the town of all vestiges of wealth that might interest the Roman conquerors. The townspeople die valiantly by their own hand or kill one another honorably and with goodwill, in fellowship and in defiance. The individual characters never assume personal identities, but the town itself becomes the hero, in a way that anticipates Lope de Vega's most famous play, *Fuenteovejuna* (wr. 1611-1618, pb. 1619; *The Sheep Well*, 1936), in which a town unites against an evil commander and, in doing so, becomes a kind of collective hero.

At the conclusion of the play, Cervantes brings on Fame, the last of the many allegorical figures who appear throughout the play. So that the moral of the play will not be misunderstood, Fame announces that in spite of the devastation and suffering witnessed by the audience, the play has a happy ending. The legend of the strength and determination of the citizens of Numantia will live for all time, proclaiming the greatness of the Spanish people, prompting future generations to follow the glorious path of honor shown by the city, and inspiring poets to praise the bravest of all unvanquished nations. Cervantes' sense of the mysterious ways in which defeat may be transformed into victory and failure inspire heroism found a home in the town of Numantia long before it traveled down the road in the person of a mad knight-errant.

A corollary to this theme is also present in many of the dramas: the resilience and recuperative powers of the human spirit. Cervantes certainly believed in the human capacity for rejuvenation. Failure, loss, and defeat do not necessarily mark an end, for the human spirit can always rekindle life and spark new energy and hope, even in the most unlikely places. In the second act of *The Siege of Numantia*, the magician Marquino raises a young man from the dead. He hopes to learn from the revived corpse secrets concerning the town's fate that the deceased might have

learned during his stay in the underworld. Even though the resulting news is tragic, the scene of the resurrection called forth theatrical magic from Cervantes that he too seldom displayed elsewhere. Made powerful and vivid with magic, ritual, incantations, fireworks, and thunder, the moment resonates with Cervantes' optimistic spirit.

TRAMPAGOS THE PIMP WHO LOST HIS MOLL

In an unusual manner, the same idea appears again in one of the strangest of the interludes, *Trampagos the Pimp Who Lost His Moll*, as Trampagos is mourning the death of his prostitute-companion. In a bizarre public display, he proclaims his life to be over. When other prostitutes accost him, he chooses a new favorite from among them. In a secondary movement in the same interlude, a famous criminal of the period, Escarramán, appears to bemoan his unhappy existence while exiled from Spain. To his delight, he learns that while exiled he has become a popular hero, a legend among young boys, a familiar figure onstage and in song; he has even had a dance named for him. His spirits revive and he is cheered as he dances at the pimp's "wedding." The play is filled with Cervantes' sense of rejuvenation and renewal, an optimism that is irrepressible and inspiring, even as he presents it in characters of dubious moral standing. There is also in the interlude a sense of the strange twists of fame and fortune, with a modest nod at his own failure ever quite to achieve the large recognition his genius deserved. The energy and life that inform this interlude combine with Cervantes' love of the Spanish people to produce an invigorating comic vignette out of the most unlikely of subjects.

THE JEALOUS OLD HUSBAND

Finally, many of the interludes turn on the nature of reality and illusion, the way in which people create their own worlds by the visions they choose to see. The idea is explored at magnificently humorous and marvelously moving lengths in the great novel. In the interludes, small dashes of illusion produce delightful comic twists. In *The Jealous Old Husband*, the title character guards his young wife to the point of suffocation because of his extreme jealousy, a passion so severe he even drives tomcats and dogs from his door because they are males. A neighbor woman takes pity on the young wife and devises a plan to fool the old man. She brings into the house a tapestry that presents a series of great heroes. One of the heroes is a living figure, a handsome young man who has been smuggled into the house for the young wife's amusement. The old man's worst fears are realized in this way. His own eyes are incapable of discerning the real figure from the painted heroes.

THE CAVE OF SALAMANCA

In *The Cave of Salamanca*, a husband who has just embarked on a journey returns unexpectedly because of a broken carriage wheel and interrupts a night of festivity planned by his wife and her maid with a sacristan and a barber. A student whom the wife has agreed to shelter for the night announces that he has learned magical arts in the mysterious "cave of Salamanca." To prove his skill, he "raises" two "devils"—the sacristan and the barber, who have been hiding. These "devils" proceed to party with the wife and maid while the credulous husband watches in amazement and requests to be taught these magical arts. As is the case so often in *Don Quixote de la Mancha*, magic exists here only in the eye of the beholder.

THE WONDER SHOW

The greatest of the interludes and perhaps Cervantes' single finest achievement in the drama also turns on this theme. *The Wonder Show* offers a variation on the delightful episode of Master Peter's puppet show in *Don Quixote de la Mancha*, with a touch of "The Emperor's New Clothes" added. A con man named Chanfalla arrives in a small town with his accomplices. Claiming to be renowned showmen, they announce that they will stage a marvelous pageant of glorious surprises for the mayor and townspeople. Because the pageant has been created by a magician, however, using magical incantations and mysterious devices, no one who is illegitimate or has a trace of Jewish blood can see the entertainment. The curtain goes up on a bare stage, and as Chanfalla and his men describe the stupendous stage visions, everyone in the audience pretends to see them. Samson appears in the temple, bulls and bears run through, some mice descended from those on Noah's ark frighten the ladies, and magical water from the river Jordan falls from the sky. The audience members begin creating their own visions of larks and dragons, lions and nightingales, and a young man of the town even dances with Herodias. When a real quartermaster arrives on the scene to announce that the town must prepare to billet approaching soldiers, the townspeople assume that he is a part of the pageant, an illusion like all the others. As the quartermaster in rage draws his sword and attacks the crowd, they turn on one another. Chaos ensues; Chanfalla and company bring down the curtain and leave the town.

The interlude is a magical piece of theater that examines reality and illusion, the nature of theater and theatrical illusion, and the trust that is necessary between artist and audience. In regard to the last idea, the interlude is similar to the hilarious moment in chapter 20 of the first part of *Don Quixote de la Mancha* when Sancho attempts to tell the knight the story of the goats. The interlude proves that Cervantes, while never realizing his own ambitions as a playwright, certainly understood the illusory nature of theatrical art and could explore his ideas through theatrical forms. If he never achieved mastery of the full-length and popular plays of his day, he left the world a number of small gems, bright, perfectly cut, and glistening with glimmers of the light that shines more brilliantly in *Don Quixote de la Mancha*.

OTHER MAJOR WORKS

LONG FICTION: *La Galatea*, 1585 (*Galatea: A Pastoral Romance*, 1833); *El ingenioso hidalgo don Quixote de la Mancha*, 1605, 1615 (*The History of the Valorous and Wittie Knight-Errant, Don Quixote of the Mancha*, 1612-1620; better known as *Don Quixote de la Mancha*); *Novelas ejemplares*, 1613 (*Exemplary Novels*, 1846); *Los trabajos de Persiles y Sigismunda*, 1617 (*The Travels of Persiles and Sigismunda: A Northern History*, 1619).

POETRY: *El Viaje del Parnaso*, 1614 (*The Voyage of Parnassus*, 1870).

BIBLIOGRAPHY

Castillo, David R. *(A)wry Views: Anamorphosis, Cervantes, and the Early Picaresque*. West Lafayette, Ind.: Purdue University Press, 2001. A look at anamorphosis (visual perception) in the works of Cervantes and an analysis of picaresque literature. Bibliography and index.

Close, A. J. *Cervantes and the Comic Mind of His Age.* New York: Oxford University Press, 2000. Relates Cervantes' ideas about comedy to those held by Spaniards of the Golden Age. Bibliography and index.

Cruz, Anne J., and Carroll B. Johnson, eds. *Cervantes and His Postmodern Constituencies.* New York: Garland, 1999. Essays on the literary works of Cervantes. Bibliography and index.

Finello, Dominick L. *Cervantes: Essays on Social and Literary Polemics.* Rochester, N.Y.: Tamesis, 1998. A look at Cervantes' work from the standpoint of social and literary issues. Bibliography and index.

Hutchinson, Steven D. *Cervantine Journeys.* Madison: University of Wisconsin Press, 1992. A look at the role that travel played in the writings of Cervantes. Bibliography and index.

La Rubia Prado, Francisco, ed. *Cervantes for the Twenty-first Century: Studies in Honor of Edward Dudley.* Newark, Del.: Juan de la Cuesta, 2000. A group of essays on Cervantes' life and works.

Reed, Croy A. *The Novelist as Playwright: Cervantes and the Entremés Nuevo.* New York: Peter Lang, 1993. A study of Cervantes' dramatic works. Bibliography and index.

David Allen White

AIMÉ CÉSAIRE

Born: Basse-Pointe, Martinique; June 25, 1913

PRINCIPAL DRAMA

Et les chiens se taisaient, pb. 1956, pr. 1960
La Tragédie du Roi Christophe, pb. 1963, pr. 1964 (*The Tragedy of King Christophe*, 1964)
Une Saison au Congo, pb. 1966, pr. 1967 (*A Season in the Congo*, 1968)
Une Tempête, d'après "La Tempête" de Shakespeare: Adaptation pour un théâtre nègre, pr., pb. 1969 (*The Tempest*, 1974)

OTHER LITERARY FORMS

Aimé Césaire has produced major works in a wide range of literary forms, including poetry (*Cahier d'un retour au pays natal*, 1939, 1947, 1956; *Memorandum on My Martinique*, 1947; also as *Return to My Native Land*, 1968), history (*Toussaint Louverture: La Révolution française et le problème coloniale*, 1960), treatises (*Discours sur le colonialisme*, 1950; *Discourse on Colonialism*, 1972), speeches (*Commemoration du centenaire de l'abolition de l'esclavage: Discours prononces à la Sorbonne le 27 avril 1948*, 1948), and numerous essays on poetry, politics, and culture in a wide variety of French, West Indian, and African publications. Césaire has delivered a large number of his speeches before the French National Assembly in his capacity as deputy of the Department of Martinique. As a consequence, much of his occasional work (telegrams, letters, interviews) has historical interest in its own right.

ACHIEVEMENTS

As poet, dramatist, politician, historian, and essayist, Aimé Césaire helped transform the French colonial world over a period of more than six decades. His reputation depends chiefly on his lengthy autobiographical poem *Return to My Native Land*, a passionate indictment of colonialism that the French poet and novelist André Breton hailed as "nothing less than the greatest lyrical monument of our time."

As a virtuoso performance and as a portrayal of the pain and anguish of Martinique's dispossessed, the poem burst on the literary scene, challenging the image of the French Antilles as the "happy isles" filled with inferior beings and unable to produce writers equal to those of Europe. Representing the culmination of almost a decade of intellectual dialogue among Africans and West Indians within the Parisian student community of the 1930's, the poem poignantly rejected assimilation for blacks, denounced the domination of the Western powers, and exalted the contributions of the black race. This sense of a unique black consciousness and common heritage—what Césaire himself described as "the awareness of being black . . . a taking charge of one's destiny as a black man, of one's history and culture"—was expressed in the term "negritude," first coined in the poem itself and later used to describe the movement led by Césaire, the French Guianan poet Léon Damas, and the Senegalese poet and statesman Léopold Senghor.

Césaire was instrumental in bringing African, Caribbean, and African American artists together in a common cultural front, whose various literary expressions in the 1920's and 1930's included the magazines with which he was directly involved—*L'Étudiant noir*, *Tropiques*, and *Présence africaine*. Negritude in this sense found evidence of black vitality and originality equally in the civilizations of ancient Africa and in the already distinctive cultural achievements of African American jazz, blues, dance, and literature of the Harlem Renaissance.

The most renowned French-speaking poet of the Caribbean, Césaire is at the same time an accomplished dramatist. Turning to theater in the 1960's in an effort to reach audiences that either could not read or could not understand his difficult poetry, Césaire composed three plays with conventional formats and easily discernible political themes. In *The Tragedy of King Christophe*, he treated the rise and fall of an early nineteenth century Haitian revolutionary. Moving from the Caribbean to Africa in *A Season in the Congo*, he considered the downfall of Congolese leader Patrice Lumumba. Finally, in 1969, using William Shakespeare's *The Tempest* (pr. 1611) as a source, he wrote an allegory of colonial conflict, *The Tempest*, which may have been modeled on the debates in the American black power movement between Malcolm X and Martin Luther King, Jr.. As a statesman, Césaire has been central in promoting the policies of autonomy in Martinique and has written extensively on governmental affairs.

Aimé Césaire in 1968. (AP/Wide World Photos)

BIOGRAPHY

Aimé Césaire was born on June 25, 1913, in Basse-Pointe, Martinique, in the French West Indies. Part of a large family, Césaire attended the Lycée Victor Schoelcher in Fort-de-France in 1924 and received a scholarship to study in France in 1931. In the years that immediately followed in Paris, Césaire met many of his major intellectual collaborators, including the future president of Senegal, Senghor, and the French Guianan poet, Damas.

In an environment marked by the popularity of the French Communist Party and the Surrealism of Breton, Césaire, Senghor, and Damas founded the journal *L'Étudiant noir* in 1934, calling for a "cultural revolution" and declaring themselves against the chains of logic and the "bourgeois ego." Following his admission to the prestigious École Normale Supérieure in 1935, Césaire began an intense period of poetic activity.

A few months after the publication of *Return to*

My Native Land in August of 1939, Césaire returned to Martinique to teach at the Lycée Victor Schoelcher, where one of his students was the future psychologist and theorist of decolonization, Frantz Fanon. Despite restrictions imposed by the Vichy regime during the war years, Césaire founded the journal *Tropiques* with his wife, Suzanne Roussy, and others. Deeply impressed by the journal's honesty and verve, Breton (who arrived in Martinique in 1941) wrote a preface to the 1944 edition of *Return to My Native Land* that contributed to Césaire's international reputation. Partly as an outcome of the invigorating effects of this meeting, Césaire published his next volume of poetry, declaring his embrace of the "miraculous weapons" of Surrealist poetic style, *Les Armes miraculeuses* (1946; *Miraculous Weapons*, 1983).

Inspired by a six-month tour of Haiti in 1944, Césaire came to pay homage to this site of the first successful slave rebellion in the early nineteenth century. Haiti's legacy plays an important role in his later work—particularly his drama *The Tragedy of King Christophe* and his history of the Haitian revolution, *Toussaint Louverture*.

In 1945, Césaire was elected mayor of Fort-de-France and deputy to the French assembly, positions to which he has been repeatedly reelected. In 1946, he voted for, and played a key role in promoting, controversial legislation demanding the assimilation of Guadeloupe and Martinique as departments of France. Still active in cultural affairs, in 1947, he helped create, with Alioune Diop, Paul Niger, and others, the influential journal *Présence africaine*, with the patronage of such French intellectuals as André Gide, Jean-Paul Sartre, and Albert Camus. Despite his other activities, he published another volume of poetry, *Soleil cou coupé* (1948; *Beheaded Sun*, 1983).

Outraged by the massacres of the Malgaches, the peoples of Madagascar, in 1947, he delivered a scathing attack on the "civilizing" mission of colonialism at the 1948 World Congress of Intellectuals for Peace in Poland, which would later be published as his *Discourse on Colonialism*, in the same year as his fourth volume of poetry, *Corps perdu* (1950; *Disembodied*, 1983). In 1956, as a result of the Soviet occupation of

Hungary, Césaire officially resigned from the Communist Party in a public letter to the party's general secretary, *Lettre à Maurice Thorez* (1956). As a result of leaving, he launched the Parti Progressiste Martiniquais.

Turning increasingly to the writing of drama in the 1960's, Césaire participated in the Festival of Black Arts in Dakar in 1966, where he presented his play *A Season in the Congo*. In 1972, he founded an annual Martinican cultural festival dedicated to the expression of West Indian culture.

ANALYSIS

Aimé Césaire's plays mark a conscious departure in style and artistic attitude from the main body of his poetry and are essential to a full understanding of his career—the career not only of a poet and historian but of a politician as well. With the exception of *Et les chiens se taisaient* (and the dogs grew silent), which was first included as a dramatic poem in *Miraculous Weapons* and only later revised in a special "theatrical arrangement" in 1956, all of Césaire's plays were composed and performed in the 1960's. In these years, the opportunities for decolonization had apparently increased abruptly. Several African states were for the first time winning their independence, and in the United States, the Civil Rights movement was at its height. As a longtime spokesperson for negritude, Césaire apparently wanted to reach audiences put off by the dense imagery of his Surrealist poetry—especially audiences from the largely illiterate countries in which decolonization was occurring. In the speeches of his characters, Césaire debates the entirely new set of problems created by independence: the problems of rebels in power, of former slaves who enslave others, and of anticolonialists who fight one another instead of the enemy.

As a group, Césaire's four plays can be said to touch on the principal concerns of his life's work. If *Et les chiens se taisaient* belongs to the world of *Return to My Native Land*, with its exotic invocations of revolt in a general or a metaphysical sense, the next three plays situate themselves in the history of the black movement: *The Tragedy of King Christophe* in the Caribbean of postindependence Haiti of the early nineteenth century, *A Season in the Congo* in the Congo of contemporary Africa, and *The Tempest* in the spiritual landscape of African American politics.

ET LES CHIENS SE TAISAIENT

Et les chiens se taisaient describes Césaire's journey from poetry to theater, and the play has been staged only in German translation. The play's hero, referred to simply as "the Rebel," carries on the obsessive interest in negritude from *Return to My Native Land*—at once enchained and wildly free, eloquent and mute, a descendant of slavery and of royalty. Although the play opens to a more-or-less conventional prison setting, where the Rebel has been condemned to death for killing his "master," the apparent order rapidly disintegrates into a series of hallucinatory tableaux representing various stages of colonization from Columbus to the present. Here, one finds sudden changes of scenery and quick jumps in time and place. The entire tapestry of characters and events therefore is located, fantastically, within what the play calls "a vast collective prison, peopled by black candidates for madness and death."

The play is a phantasmagoric record of rebellion and subjugation in their pure states, in which characters with emblematic titles such as "The Administrator" and "The Great Promoter" march before the reader hypocritically lamenting the "burden of civilization," while a Chorus representing the West Indian people admires the Rebel's example from a distance, without being able to follow it. "Bishops" and "High Commissioners" confront "Lovers"; statistics confront poetry. The play nevertheless establishes motifs that recur in Césaire's later dramatic work—particularly the image of the leader who contains perfectly within him the conscience of his race, who retains the memory of both the African royal splendor and its bondage, who employs beautifully the power of the word, but who (in spite of these things) remains isolated from a people who cannot attain his heights.

Césaire's next two plays, although emotionally and thematically linked to *Et les chiens se taisaient*, employ a very different theatrical strategy. Both *The Tragedy of King Christophe* and *A Season in the Congo*—the best-known and most widely performed

of his plays and among the few translated into English—are frankly historical and rooted in specific social situations. All three of his remaining plays, in fact, were deeply influenced by Jean-Marie Serreau, a follower of the German playwright Bertolt Brecht's "epic" school of theater, which sought to dramatize historical conflicts in such a way that the audience might participate in solving them. Serreau produced all three of these plays and commissioned *The Tempest*.

THE TRAGEDY OF KING CHRISTOPHE

The Tragedy of King Christophe is a tragedy of revolutionary decline. Based on an actual historical personage—one of the generals of Toussaint Louverture, who became ruler of Haiti in the early 1800's—the problem of power after independence is plainly meant to apply to the Third World leaders of the early 1960's: for example, Ben Bella of Algeria, Fidel Castro of Cuba, and Senghor of Senegal. The play's action revolves around the irony that Christophe, in order to outmaneuver his French colonial enemies, abolishes the republic and establishes himself as king. The question thus becomes: Can one defeat one's opponent by becoming like him? As portrayed in the play, the monarchy is a disturbing sight: Christophe conscripts workers to build a royal Citadel on the model of the pyramids, rants about there being "no freedom without labor," executes his own bishops and emissaries, and calls his people "niggers." The dramatic tension, however, is in no way one-sided. One is constantly reminded of Christophe's heroic defiance of the colonizer, his admirable ability to rely on "the will and the grace of [his] two fists."

The play is strikingly popular in its formal appeals. In an early monologue, for example, the Commentator explains the historical background needed to understand the action. Songs in dialect everywhere punctuate the longer speeches, a court jester entertains and instructs with his lyrical jabs and satirical jokes, and the number of crowd scenes underlines the communal (and not merely personal) significance of the tragic events.

A SEASON IN THE CONGO

A Season in the Congo is basically a repetition of *The Tragedy of King Christophe*, merely transplanted to the soil of the modern Congo. Here, the black revolutionary Patrice Lumumba is examined. The play has not generally been received as well as *The Tragedy of King Christophe*. It is packed with long monologues that are really declarations of positions and little more. Character itself becomes synonymous with a social position and is expressed typically in names such as "First Banker," "Second Banker," or "First Belgian Policeman" and "Second Belgian Policeman," and so on. The broad social nature of the drama is reflected also in the many fleeting glimpses of mass movements, demonstrations, strikes, appeals, and backroom negotiations, all of them contributing to a kind of pastiche of exemplary moments in the history of the Congo (modern Zaire).

THE TEMPEST

The Tempest, as indicated by its French title, calls attention to the unique concerns of "black theater" and seeks to illustrate them all the more clearly by adapting (and intentionally distorting) a well-known Shakespearean play. Prospero is the original colonial intruder, subjugating the black slave Caliban, in his own tropical home, while Ariel, a mulatto slave, makes his own deals with the master, often at Caliban's expense. As suggested here, the setting is neither the transhistorical mental realm of *Et les chiens se taisaient* nor the fixed locales of the historical plays but a symbolic model of Caribbean society as a whole, ruled by the dialectic of master and slave and complicated by the unequal status of the subjects themselves—a relationship already seen clearly in Basilio, Lumumba, and Kala Lubu of *A Season in the Congo*.

According to comments by Césaire, the play was intended to address problems within the Black Power movement of the United States; if it did, however, it did so indirectly. Given Césaire's intention, many have seen Martin Luther King in Césaire's Ariel and Malcolm X in his Caliban; evidence for this reading can be found in black power slogans such as "Freedom now," which appear in English in the original text.

In some respects, the play returns to Césaire's earlier lyricism. Described in Césaire's stage directions as having the "atmosphere of a psychodrama," the work plays up this unreality in at least two ways: by using anachronisms, usually with a satirical twist, as when the crew of the sinking ship in the first scene sings "Nearer My God to Thee"; and the stipulation in the stage notes that actors entering the stage may choose a mask at their discretion. Nevertheless, the specific Caribbean and North American motifs and the implicit challenge to Shakespeare's own imaginative vision make the play clearly political satire.

OTHER MAJOR WORKS

POETRY: *Cahier d'un retour au pays natal*, 1939, 1947, 1956 (*Memorandum on My Martinique*, 1947; better known as *Return to My Native Land*, 1968); *Les Armes miraculeuses*, 1946 (*Miraculous Weapons*, 1983); *Soleil cou coupé*, 1948 (*Beheaded Sun*, 1983); *Corps perdu*, 1950 (*Disembodied*, 1983); *Ferrements*, 1960 (*Shackles*, 1983); *Cadastre*, 1961 (*Cadastre: Poems*, 1973); *State of the Union*, 1966 (includes abridged translation of *Les Armes miraculeuses* and *Ferrements*); *Moi, Laminaire*, 1982; *Aimé Césaire: The Collected Poetry*, 1983; *Non-vicious Circle: Twenty Poems*, 1985; *Lyric and Dramatic Poetry, 1946-1982*, 1990; *La Poésie*, 1994.

NONFICTION: *Discours sur le colonialisme*, 1950 (*Discourse on Colonialism*, 1972); *Toussaint Louverture: La Révolution française et le problème coloniale*, 1960.

MISCELLANEOUS: *Œuvres complètes*, 1976.

BIBLIOGRAPHY

Arnold, A. James. *Modernism and Negritude: The Poetry and Poetics of Aimé Césaire*. Cambridge, Mass.: Harvard University Press, 1981. Arnold examines negritude and how it was expressed in the works of Aimé Césaire. Bibliography and index.

Bailey, Marianne Wichmann. *The Ritual Theater of Aimé Césaire: Mythic Structures of the Dramatic Imagination*. Tübingen, Germany: G. Narr, 1992. Bailey examines the works of Aimé Césaire, paying particular attention to their use of ritual and myth. Bibliography.

Davis, Gregson. *Aimé Césaire*. New York: Cambridge University Press, 1997. This work, part of a series on African and Caribbean literature, provides a look at the life and works of Césaire. Bibliography and index.

Munro, Martin. *Shaping and Reshaping the Caribbean: The Work of Aimé Césaire and René Depestre.* Leeds, England: Many Publishers for the Modern Humanities Research Association, 2000. Munro examines Caribbean literature through the works of Césaire and Depestre. Bibliography and index.

Pallister, Janis L. *Aimé Césaire.* New York: Twayne, 1991. A basic examination of the life and works of Césaire. Bibliography and index.

Suk, Jeannie. *Postcolonial Paradoxes in French Caribbean Writing: Césaire, Glissant, Condé.* Oxford, England: Clarendon, 2001. This study of Caribbean writing includes analysis and discussion of the works of Césaire.

Timothy Brennan

GEORGE CHAPMAN

Born: Near Hitchin, England; c. 1559
Died: London, England; May 12, 1634

PRINCIPAL DRAMA

The Blind Beggar of Alexandria, pr. 1596, pb. 1598 (fragment)

An Humourous Day's Mirth, pr. 1597, pb. 1599

All Fools, wr. 1599, pr. 1604, pb. 1605 (also known as *The World Runs on Wheels*)

Sir Giles Goosecap, pr. c. 1601 or 1603, pb. 1606

The Gentleman Usher, pr. c. 1602, pb. 1606

Bussy d'Ambois, pr. 1604, pb. 1607

Monsieur d'Olive, pr. 1604, pb. 1606

Eastward Ho!, pr., pb. 1605 (with John Marston and Ben Jonson)

The Widow's Tears, pr. c. 1605, pb. 1612

The Conspiracy and Tragedy of Charles, Duke of Byron, pr., pb. 1608

May Day, pr. c. 1609, pb. 1611

The Revenge of Bussy d'Ambois, pr. c. 1610, pb. 1613

The Masque of the Middle Temple and Lincoln's Inn, pr. 1613 (masque)

Caesar and Pompey, pr. c. 1613, pb. 1631

The Ball, pr. 1632, pb. 1639 (with James Shirley)

The Tragedy of Chabot, Admiral of France, pr. 1635, pb. 1639 (with Shirley)

OTHER LITERARY FORMS

George Chapman was a poet and scholar as well as a playwright. His literary career began with the publication of the poem *The Shadow of Night* in 1594 and included the completion of a poem begun by Christopher Marlowe, *Hero and Leander* (1598). Chapman seemed to have been proudest of his achievements as a self-taught scholar. He translated Homer's *Iliad* (c. 800 B.C.E.; part of book 18 appeared in 1598, and the entire work was published in 1611) and *Odyssey* (c. 800 B.C.E.; 1614). He also translated the lesser works of Homer (*The Crown of All Homer's Works*, 1624) and Hesiod's *Georgics* (c. 700 B.C.E.; 1618). Although a few of Chapman's plays enjoyed popularity into the eighteenth century, he was best known for his translations. His versions of Homer's works were read well into the nineteenth century and influenced poet John Keats, among others. Chapman regarded his work on Homer as his life's mission and believed that Homer's spirit had visited him and urged him on in his labors. His translation ends with the assertion, "The work that I was born to do, is done."

ACHIEVEMENTS

With the exception of *Chabot, Admiral of France*, George Chapman's plays were written and first produced over a seventeen-year span, from 1596 to 1613. Chapman regarded himself as a scholar and wrote plays simply to earn a living. In his own day, his plays enjoyed varying degrees of success, with his comedies and *Bussy d'Ambois* meeting with the greatest public favor. Today, Chapman's plays are seldom performed. They are generally well written, usually reflect his scholarly interests, and have dialogue that is sometimes difficult to speak. In his own day and in subsequent eras, Chapman's dialogue has been cited as the principal weakness of his plays. The syntax is sometimes so convoluted that actors would have difficulty speaking their lines. On the other hand, the good-natured wit of his best comedies, such as *All Fools*, makes them appealing even to modern audiences. Chapman lived when both William Shakespeare and Ben Jonson were writing some of the best plays written in any language. His plays suffer in comparison with theirs and thus are not performed as often as they might be. Nevertheless, his comedies have their own special qualities that make them interesting apart from the writings of his great contemporaries.

Chapman's dark and brutal tragedies lack the universal appeal of the comedies. They are interesting

George Chapman (Hulton Archive by Getty Images)

studies of character and moral issues and make for good reading. They are so seldom performed that one has difficulty ascertaining how they might be received by a modern audience.

Scholars place Chapman among the historically important English playwrights. He is credited with several innovations—such as the comedy of humors—that were later used by Ben Jonson and the Restoration dramatists. In overall achievement, he must rank behind Shakespeare and Jonson, but he might be fairly rated as ahead of his other contemporaries, although many of them, such as John Marston, Francis Beaumont, and John Fletcher, might be his superior in some aspects of drama. Having written in an era of great playwrights and great dramas, Chapman has the distinction of having been an innovator and of having created a style uniquely his own.

BIOGRAPHY

Little is known of George Chapman's life before the publication of *The Shadow of Night*. He was born near Hitchin, a town in rural Herfordshire, England, around 1559. His parents were Thomas and Joan Chapman. Thomas was wealthy, and Joan was the daughter of George Nodes, who had served Henry VIII. Chapman's older brother, Thomas, inherited nearly all the family estate, and Chapman was in financial straits for most of his adult life.

In about 1574, George Chapman may have attended a university, possibly Oxford. If he did so, he did not attend for long. He eventually joined Sir Ralph Sabler's household and was there until 1583 or 1585. From 1591 to 1592, he served in the battles against Spain in the Low Countries. After returning to England, Chapman fell under the influence of a group of prominent young men that included Christopher Marlowe and was nominally led by Sir Walter Raleigh. Their theories about philosophy and the occult provide much of the substance of Chapman's first poem, *The Shadow of Night*. With the publication of this poem and *Ovid's Banquet of Sense* (1595), Chapman became a prominent poet, but he remained poor.

Much of Chapman's adult life was marred by periodic imprisonment and battles with creditors. He had bad luck with his patrons, and his plays, even when successful, did not pay him enough to achieve permanent security. In 1600, he was jailed on fraudulent charges of failing to pay his debts. After certain passages of *Eastward Ho!* were perceived as insulting to the king, he was jailed in 1605 along with one of his coauthors, Ben Jonson. Chapman adamantly protested his innocence of intent to mock the king, and he and Jonson were eventually released. He was almost imprisoned again in 1608 for some offending scenes in *The Conspiracy and Tragedy of Charles, Duke of Byron*. This play angered the ambassador of France, whose protests resulted in heavy cutting of scenes by censors. In 1612, one of Chapman's few patrons, Prince Henry, died. King James did not fulfill Henry's pledge to support Chapman, and the playwright was again imprisoned for debt. Good fortune seemed his at last when the earl of Somerset became his patron and he gained favor in the royal court, but the earl was arrested for murder in 1615. Chapman remained loyal to Somerset, who was eventually pardoned (although he was not guilty) and released in 1622. During the intervening years, Chapman had to fight the old legal charges of debt until he was acquitted in 1621.

Chapman's public life was filled with difficulties, but what his private life was like is unclear. Certainly, his financial and legal problems must have clouded his personal relationships, but whether he was married or had a family is unknown. What little is known of his friendships indicates that he was loyal and formed long-lasting bonds. He seems to have been faithful to the memory of Christopher Marlowe. He was loyal to the earl of Somerset during the nobleman's most difficult moments, and he had a close friendship with Inigo Jones, the Jacobean court's chief architect and designer of sets for masques. His long friendship with Ben Jonson was stormy, particularly because of Jonson's bitter enmity with Jones.

Throughout debts, his imprisonment, and other setbacks, Chapman remained dedicated to an ideal. His life and achievements are colored by his determination to render in English the works of Homer. The classical structures of some of his plays reflect his research, his studies of the nature of power are informed by his classical readings, and his style is influenced by the classics of antiquity. He endured hardship, in part, because of his belief that he had a special purpose in life and because of his belief in the importance of literature.

ANALYSIS

George Chapman's plays are diverse in structure, topic, and style, yet they are united by his interests in learning and learned people, his dismay at the unfairness of human society, and his moral beliefs. Beginning with boisterous and exuberant comedy, moving through satire and tragicomedy, then through violently dynamic tragedies, and ending with philosophical tragedies, Chapman's plays reveal a remarkably coherent ethos and a mastery of poetry and prose that allows for wonderful diversity in the dramas.

THE BLIND BEGGAR OF ALEXANDRIA AND AN HUMOUROUS DAY'S MIRTH

The first extant play by Chapman, *The Blind Beggar of Alexandria*, exists only in a truncated version. It was very popular and was often performed, but only its subplot was printed in 1598. Its main plot can be interpolated only from fragments found in the subplot's story of Iris, the blind beggar. It shares with the play that followed it, *An Humourous Day's Mirth*, the distinction of being a comedy of humours—a play in which each of the characters represents an aspect of human nature, such as greed or sloth. Although Ben Jonson's *Every Man in His Humour* (pr. 1598) is sometimes credited with being the first comedy of humors, both of Chapman's plays predate it. Therefore, Chapman's first two plays have historical importance as the earliest extant examples of an important late Renaissance form of comedy, although the question of who actually invented the form is problematic. This form remained important for Jonson throughout his career, but it was abandoned by Chapman after 1602.

Neither *The Blind Beggar of Alexandria* nor *An Humourous Day's Mirth* is important for its artistry. Both are funny, and both have intricate plots typical of much of Chapman's comedy. The first shows his use of classical sources for inspiration, also typical of much of his dramatic writing. *The Blind Beggar of Alexandria* is peopled by Greek characters—King Ptolemy, Aegiale, Cleanthes, Prince Doricles, and others. The elements of Greek comedy, such as magic, are combined with Renaissance themes, such as comedy inspired by social manners. In his later plays, Chapman combined classical and contemporary forms to refresh stock ideas. *An Humourous Day's Mirth* is a weak play overcrowded with superfluous characters and is awkwardly constructed. Its significance for Chapman's later achievements is found in its scholarly heroine Florilla, whose true learning is contrasted with the pretenses of those around her. The assuming by characters of false humors, such as melancholy, in order to appear learned or sensitive, and the gulling of fools are reminiscent of the comedies of Jonson, but the concern for genuine learning, as personified by Florilla, distinguishes Chapman's work. Other playwrights of Chapman's day, including Jonson, mocked false learning and admired true scholarship, but none examined them as consistently as Chapman.

ALL FOOLS

An Humourous Day's Mirth was followed by a minor masterpiece of comedy, *All Fools*. The play is about Rinaldo, a schemer roughly related to the Vice of medieval morality plays and to the intriguing servant of classical drama; Valerio, Rinaldo's friend and favored son of Gostanzo; and Fortunio, Rinaldo's virtuous brother. Around these three young men revolve their fathers, a jealous husband, and the women— Gratiana and Bellanora—whom Valerio and Fortunio love. The intricate plot of the play is representative of comedies of its day. Rinaldo schemes to dupe various characters, and according to the weaknesses in their personalities, various characters are duped. Some, such as Gostanzo, think that they are gulling others even as they are gulled.

The plot of Chapman's *All Fools* comes mainly from Terence's comedy *Heautontimorumenos* (163 B.C.E.; *The Self-Tormentor*, 1598), although Chapman reworked it into a play that is more Elizabethan than classical in character and colored it with a strong moral point of view not found in Terence's play. Gostanzo is deluded about himself and his son Valerio; he believes himself to be wise and his son to be virtuous when, in fact, he is foolish and his son is a profligate gambler who is heavily in debt. Valerio marries Gratiana but keeps the marriage secret from Gostanzo because she is not wealthy enough for Gostanzo's approval and because he is supposed to be innocent of worldly matters such as male-female relationships. Gostanzo also has a daughter, Bellanora, who loves Fortunio, a modest and virtuous young man who also is not wealthy enough to satisfy Gostanzo. Once, when Valerio, Gratiana, Fortunio, and Rinaldo are together, they see Gostanzo approaching them, and all save Rinaldo flee. Rinaldo tells Gostanzo that Gratiana and Fortunio are secretly married and wish to keep the marriage secret from Fortunio's father, Marc Antonio. Gostanzo believes Rinaldo's story and tells it to Marc Antonio at the first opportunity, even though he had promised to keep the story secret. Under Rinaldo's influence, Gostanzo convinces Marc Antonio that Fortunio is in danger of becoming a dissolute young man and that Valerio might prove to be a good influence on him if Fortunio and Gratiana lived in Gostanzo's home. Thus, without his knowing it, Gostanzo arranges for Valerio and Gratiana to live together and leaves Fortunio free to court Bellanora.

All Fools might remain a funny but unexceptional comedy, but Chapman was enough of an artist to allow his characters to learn, grow, and change. The plot becomes increasingly complex as Gostanzo suspects that Valerio is having a love affair with Fortunio's wife (who is really Valerio's wife), and under Rinaldo's influence, he pretends to Marc Antonio that Gratiana is really Valerio's wife (which she is, but Gostanzo does not know it) and persuades Marc Antonio to take Gratiana into his house and to allow Valerio to visit her. Gostanzo, proud of his wisdom, believes he has gulled Marc Antonio. The plot expands to include Cornelio, a jealous husband, and Gazetta, his wife. Rinaldo tricks Cornelio into believing that Gazetta has a lover, and Cornelio attacks the supposed lover and arranges to divorce his wife. In the meantime, Gostanzo is tricked into giving his blessing to the marriage of Valerio and Gratiana, believing that he is tricking Marc Antonio because he thinks Fortunio is married to Gratiana. Cornelio learns of Rinaldo's deceit and decides to trick Rinaldo and Valerio. He tells Rinaldo that Valerio has finally been arrested for his debts and is held at the Half Moon Tavern. Rinaldo and Gostanzo rush to the tavern and find Valerio gaming and drinking. Gostanzo, learning of his son's profligacy and recognizing the trick that has been played on him, is at first enraged. He discovers that Fortunio and Bellanora have also married and that he is not as clever and wise as he thought. He has acquired enough wisdom to recognize his own limitations, however, and he accepts what has happened. With Cornelio's reconciliation with Gazetta, all parties are reconciled, and *All Fools* ends with its characters happy.

Although the play's ending seems a bit contrived, Gostanzo's growth is believable. His pride was immoral and helped to drive Valerio and Rinaldo to their deceitful behavior. Rinaldo is also proud; he takes pride in his ability to manipulate Gostanzo, Marc Antonio, and Cornelio. The comeuppance delivered by Cornelio is a necessary lesson for Rinaldo, who learns that he, too, can be tricked. Happiness is possible at the end of the play because the characters learn to accept themselves and others as they are. Pride and trickery had prevented such acceptance.

MAY DAY

All Fools has much charm and much good comedy; its mad plot can still entertain a modern audience. *May Day* also retains the ability to entertain, although it is not as strong a play as *All Fools*. In *May Day*, the schemer is Lodovico; other figures based on classical conventions appear in the play, including Quintiliano, a representative of the miles gloriosus (braggart soldier) commonly found in classical comedies. As in *All Fools*, conventions, classical or otherwise, serve as foundations for Chapman's development of complex characterizations and his sophisticated comedy. Like *All Fools*, *May Day* is a comedy of humors; Chapman wrote one more such play, *Sir Giles Goosecap*. Although still amusing, it lacks the spirited activity of the other plays. By 1602, Chapman was working on a new kind of comedy.

THE GENTLEMAN USHER

A tragicomedy is a play that has a plot like that of a tragedy but ends like a comedy. It is a genre that allows for much variety in plot and character, and one that can incorporate elements of other genres, such as romantic comedy. Shakespeare's *Measure for Measure* (pr. 1604), for example, could be classified as a tragicomedy because its plot focuses on the possible execution of an innocent man and the potential debauchment of a chaste woman. The potential tragic ending is averted only when the duke of Vienna reappears as himself. Of Chapman's tragicomedies, *The Gentleman Usher* is notable for its excellent characterizations and variety of action; it does not match Shakespeare's plays for depth of feeling or suspenseful plotting, but it compares well with any Elizabethan comedy in its richness of ideas and events. On the other hand, *Monsieur d'Olive* is a good play but not as well designed as its predecessor. It is notable more for its subplot than for its romantic central plot.

As in *All Fools*, notions of what constitutes virtuous conduct are called into question by *The Gentleman Usher* in the conflict between a father and his son. This time, the father and son both love the same woman. The son, Prince Vincentio, must, like Valerio, hide his intentions and behavior from his father, Duke Alphonso. Like Gostanzo, Alphonso is deluded about his own nature and that of his son. The rivalry of father and son is played out in a plot of treachery and danger. In *All Fools*, the scheming Rinaldo was mostly playful; he did some harm but was not inherently malicious. His counterpart in *The Gentleman Usher* is Medice, who is vengeful, ambitious, and willing to murder to get what he wants.

The malice of Medice is balanced by the pompous foolishness of Bassiolo, usher to Count Lasso, the father of Margaret, who is loved by Alphonso and Vincentio. Bassiolo fancies himself to be a schemer and agrees to be the go-between for Margaret and Vincentio after Vincentio flatters him. The bumbling Bassiolo provides much of the play's laughter, but even in his character, there is an element of menace. While Vincentio has been privately making fun of Bassiolo, he and his friend, Count Strozza, have also mocked Medice. Favorite of Alphonso, and ambitious, the proud Medice is angered by the two men. He graphically shows how the seemingly innocent conniving of Vincentio can be turned into tragedy. Alphonso has arranged for a boar hunt near the home of Count Lasso and Margaret; Strozza joins him in the hunt. Medice arranges for Strozza to be shot by an arrow, and Strozza barely lives. This near-tragedy is a prelude to a seemingly complete tragedy. The foolish Bassiolo comes to know that he has been tricked. Forced by Vincentio to continue as go-between, he overplays his role, and Alphonso and Medice discover that Vincentio has secretly courted Margaret. Vincentio flees, and Margaret, who has promised herself to Vincentio, covers her face with an ointment that disfigures it horribly; she hopes to repel Alphonso with her hideous looks. Only a doctor, acting as a *deus ex machina*, saves a comic ending by curing her disfigurement after Vincentio has shown that he loves her regardless of her looks. Medice is exiled and the other characters are reconciled.

The characters of *The Gentleman Usher* are well drawn, with the villain Medice comparing well even with the villains of Shakespeare's comedies. The play is full of activity, merriment, and suspense. Its main plot and subplot are well interwoven, and no event is without importance to the play as a whole. *The Gentleman Usher* ranks with *All Fools* as the best of Chapman's comedies and is representative of the best in English comedic traditions.

MONSIEUR D'OLIVE

On the other hand, *Monsieur d'Olive* is more satiric, with its subplot portraying the silliness of courtly ambassadorships. Its comic variety has been admired by such critics as Algernon Charles Swinburne. It, too, might be well received by a modern audience. Chapman would write only one more comedy, *The Widow's Tears*.

BUSSY D'AMBOIS

Chapman's first tragedies, *Bussy d'Ambois* and *The Conspiracy and Tragedy of Charles, Duke of Byron* (consisting of two mated plays, *The Conspiracy* and *The Tragedy*), feature angry and robust protagonists whose courage is offset by ignorance of human nature and misguided ambition. Both Bussy d'Ambois and the duke of Byron are betrayed and murdered. Although both plays are good and make for interesting reading, *Bussy d'Ambois* is superior in thematic construction and dramatic structure.

Bussy gains access to the court of Henry III, king of France, through Monsieur, the king's brother. A proud man, Bussy rapidly alienates the venal courtiers surrounding the king. He excites the jealousy of

the duke of Guise by making pleasant conversation with Guise's wife, Eleanor, and he persists even after Guise asks him to stop. Bussy also angers the courtiers Barrisor, l'Anou, and Pyrhot, who duel Bussy and two of Bussy's friends. All are killed save Bussy. Even though his blunt manner of speaking and proud demeanor have resulted in the deaths of five men and jeopardized his own life, Bussy learns little from his experiences. He receives a pardon for the killings from King Henry, who grants the pardon at Monsieur's behest, and he then begins a love affair with Tamyra, the wife of the count of Montsurry; she is also coveted by Monsieur. The play gains momentum and moves toward a seemingly inevitable conclusion. Bussy becomes the favorite of the king, and Monsieur grows envious of his status in the court.

A friar acts as go-between for Bussy and Tamyra and in a secret chamber invokes spirits to show them the future. They warn Bussy of the conspiracy of Monsieur, Guise, and Montsurry to murder him. Later, Montsurry stabs and then tortures Tamyra on the rack in order to force her to confess to her affair with Bussy. The friar is exposed as the go-between and is killed. His ghost warns Bussy of danger. Proud, headstrong, and not given to thoughtfulness, Bussy ignores all warnings and is tricked by Montsurry into walking into an ambush. He struggles mightily but is mortally wounded; in a gesture of defiance, he dies while leaning on his sword and speaking forgiveness of those who had betrayed him.

Bussy d'Ambois is one of the most popular of Chapman's plays. Its bloody scenes rival the most awful scenes of the revenge tragedies of the period, and its atmosphere is rank with the corruption and perversity characteristic of the Jacobean theater, but it is superior to most plays of its time in its intellectual themes and fully drawn characters. All Chapman's tragedies are concerned at least in part with knowledge and the lack of it, especially self-knowledge. None of the characters in *Bussy d'Ambois* truly understands his or her nature, even after that nature is exposed. Thus, these characters are unable to control events fully. King Henry cannot save his favorite, Monsieur cannot use Bussy to advantage, the friar cannot save himself, Tamyra cannot save her lover,

Montsurry is driven to murder, and Bussy walks into his own death trap. Bussy, like Byron in *The Conspiracy and Tragedy of Charles, Duke of Byron*, is a man of action and forthright in speech and behavior, but he lacks tact and thoughtfulness. Without intellectual substance, he is all bluster and blunder—a killing machine who cannot adequately battle lies, conspiracies, and corruption.

Bussy d'Ambois can be interpreted as an elaborate satire on the Renaissance individualist. Bussy's blunderings are unheroic and even silly. His loud manner of speaking is more offensive and egotistical than it is honest. The notion that he can reshape society is shown to be foolish by his susceptibility to the trickeries of those who are his moral inferiors. The horrible sufferings of his lover and the deaths of his friends are made to seem pointless by his empty gesture of standing and mouthing clichéd forgiveness as he succumbs to treachery he could easily have avoided if he had taken only a moment to think about what he was doing.

CAESAR AND POMPEY

Chapman's *Caesar and Pompey*, *The Revenge of Bussy d'Ambois*, and *The Tragedy of Chabot, Admiral of France* complete his study of character and knowledge and give his dramatic canon a well-rounded wholeness. These tragedies lack the dynamism of Chapman's other plays; they are static and devoted more to contemplation than to action. They make good reading and are moving in their portraits of good, thoughtful men trapped in insane events and corrupt societies.

Caesar and Pompey suffers from a corrupt text. It depicts Cato's efforts to save Rome from war and Pompey's downfall: The man of action, Pompey, and the thoughtful man, Cato, both die nobly, with Pompey having learned some wisdom and Cato having learned to act. Their deaths seem futile in terms of Rome's survival, but they both grow into better, more complete men than they were at the play's start.

THE REVENGE OF BUSSY D'AMBOIS

Clermont d'Ambois of *The Revenge of Bussy d'Ambois* is a thoughtful man like Cato, and he is typical of Chapman's introspective heroes. Scholarly, contemplative, and courageous, Clermont displays the potential weakness of the thoughtful person—he tends to hesitate and to accept evils he might change through well-considered action. A capable fighter, he nevertheless lacks the boldness of his recently murdered brother, Bussy. He does not believe that revenge is a worthy act, but the ghost of his brother exacts from him a promise to avenge his murder. Charlotte, the sister of Clermont and Bussy, shares Bussy's active and thoughtless nature. She exacts from her husband, Baligny, his promise to avenge Bussy's murder, and her foolish and poorly considered actions contrast with Clermont's caution.

Through Baligny, Clermont tries to challenge Montsurry to a duel, but Montsurry is frightened of him and avoids the challenge. Baligny is a malicious man who contrives to make trouble for those around him. He talks his way into King Henry III's confidence by arguing that crimes committed on behalf of a king are justified. The duke of Guise, who has atoned for his role in Bussy's death, has become Clermont's friend and a powerful member of the king's court. While behaving in a friendly manner toward Guise, Baligny encourages King Henry to fear and distrust the duke and the duke's friend Clermont. The flatteries and lies of Baligny do not sway Clermont one way or another because of his secure self-knowledge, but Clermont's insistence on not thinking ill of his brother-in-law makes him susceptible to trickery. When warned that Baligny has arranged his ambush, Clermont repeats his brother's error and ignores the warning. When ambushed, Clermont fights with great strength, drives away his attackers, and flees on foot until exhaustion forces him to stop. Once captured, he is surprisingly calm and accepting of his fate.

The duke of Guise persuades King Henry, who often vacillates under the influence of others, to release Clermont from prison, and Clermont goes to Guise's house. There, the ghost of Bussy again urges revenge. King Henry, angered by Guise's defense of Clermont, orders the duke's death. The king's men murder him as he comes to visit Henry.

Tamyra, wife of Montsurry and once Bussy's lover, helps Clermont enter Montsurry's house. Inside, his sister Charlotte has been stopped by Bussy's ghost in her own scheme to kill Montsurry. In a duel, Montsurry fights well but is slain by Clermont. A short time later, Clermont learns of the death of his close friend Guise, and in grief, he kills himself.

Clermont is a fine figure. The play is an exploration of his character and the nature of worldly knowledge and self-knowledge. The focus on Clermont's character, however, detracts from the action of the play. Some scenes are set pieces for expositions, and the action scenes come as bursts in the middle of a contemplative play. Clermont is like Shakespeare's Hamlet in his tendency to think rather than act, and like Hamlet, he is urged into revenge by a ghost. Unlike Hamlet, he exacts revenge not in an outburst forced by events but in a planned duel. In addition, Clermont is a man who does not worry about fate. Although introspective, he does not waffle in indecision; rather, he does not act because he does not want to act.

OTHER MAJOR WORKS

POETRY: *The Shadow of Night*, 1594; *Ovid's Banquet of Sense*, 1595; *Hero and Leander*, 1598 (completion of Christopher Marlowe's poem); *Euthymiae Raptus: Or, The Tears of Peace*, 1609; *An Epicede or Funerall Song on the Death of Henry Prince of Wales*, 1612; *Andromeda Liberata: Or, The Nuptials of Perseus and Andromeda*, 1614; *Pro Vere Autumni Lachrymae*, 1622.

TRANSLATIONS: *Iliad*, 1598, 1609, 1611 (of Homer); *Odyssey*, 1614 (of Homer); *Georgics*, 1618 (of Hesiod); *The Crown of All Homer's Works*, 1624 (of Homer's lesser-known works).

BIBLIOGRAPHY

Beach, Vincent W. *George Chapman: An Annotated Bibliography of Commentary and Criticism.* New York: G. K. Hall, 1995. A reference work providing extensive bibliographical information on Chapman. Index.

Bradbrook, Muriel C. *George Chapman.* London: Longman, 1977. This brief general overview of Chapman's life and work contains sections on the lyric poetry, including *Hero and Leander* and the translations of Homer and Hesiod. The individual chapters on the comedies and tragedies conclude that Chapman's modern reputation will have to be based on only the best of the lyrics plus two tragedies, *Bussy d'Ambois* and the two parts of the Byron play.

Braunmuller, A. R. *Natural Fictions: George Chapman's Major Tragedies.* Newark: University of Delaware Press, 1992. A study of Chapman's tragedies. Bibliography and index.

Florby, Gunilla. *The Painful Passage to Virtue: A Study of George Chapman's the Tragedy of "Bussy D'Ambois" and "The Revenge of Bussy d'Ambois."* Lund, Sweden: CWK Gleerup, 1982. An examination of the two Chapman tragedies about Bussy d'Ambois. Bibliography.

Hamlin, William M. "A Borrowing from Nashe in Chapman's *Bussy d'Ambois.*" *Notes and Queries* 48, no. 3 (September, 2001): 264-265. Hamlin raises the possibility that Chapman borrowed phrases from Thomas Nashe's *The Unfortunate Traveller* in his work *Bussy d'Ambois.*

Huntington, John. "Virtues Obscured: George Chapman's Social Strategy." *Criticism* 39, no. 2 (Spring, 1997): 161. Huntington discusses Chapman's use of obscurity, arguing that the dramatist and poet had an underlying theme of social consciousness. Although the essay focuses on his poetry, it provides insight into Chapman's other works.

Ide, Richard S. *Possessed with Greatness: The Heroic Tragedies of Chapman and Shakespeare.* Chapel Hill: University of North Carolina Press, 1980. A study of heroic characters in the dramas of Chapman and William Shakespeare. Bibliography and index.

Taunton, Nina. *Fifteen-nineties Drama and Militarism: Portrayals of War in Marlowe, Chapman, and Shakespeare's "Henry V."* Aldershot, England: Ashgate, 2001. An examination of war in the drama of Chapman and Christopher Marlowe as well as in William Shakespeare's *Henry V.* Bibliography and index.

Kirk H. Beetz,
updated by Howard L. Ford

MARY CHASE

Born: Denver, Colorado; February 25, 1907
Died: Denver, Colorado; October 20, 1981

PRINCIPAL DRAMA

Me, Third, pr. 1936 (revised as *Now You've Done It*)

Sorority House, pr., pb. 1939

Too Much Business, pb. 1940

A Slip of a Girl, pr. 1941

Harvey, pr., pb. 1944, pb. 1950

The Next Half Hour, pr. 1945

Mrs. McThing, pr., pb. 1952

Bernardine, pr. 1952, pb. 1953

Lolita, pr. 1954

The Prize Play, pr. 1959, pb. 1961

Midgie Purvis, pr. 1961, pb. 1963

The Dog Sitters, pb. 1963

Mickey, pb. 1969 (adaptation of her novel *Loretta Mason Potts*)

Cocktails with Mimi, pr. 1973, pb. 1974

OTHER LITERARY FORMS

Though best known for her stage comedies, Mary Chase also wrote two children's novels, *Loretta Mason Potts* (1958), of which her 1969 play *Mickey* is a dramatization, and *The Wicked Pigeon Ladies in the Garden* (1968). In addition, she wrote film adaptations of three of her plays, *Sorority House* (1939), *Harvey* (1950), and *Bernardine* (1957).

ACHIEVEMENTS

Mary Chase's most significant achievement on stage was *Harvey*, which also garnered her most significant award, the Pulitzer Prize in drama, 1945. *Harvey* played for more than four years in its first run on Broadway (1945-1949), and for seventy-nine performances in a 1970 revival. For four months during the 1952-1953 season, Chase had two plays running concurrently on Broadway, *Mrs. McThing* and *Bernardine*. She received the William MacLeod Raine award from the Colorado Authors League in 1944

and an honorary doctorate from the University of Denver in 1947.

BIOGRAPHY

Mary Coyle (later Chase) was born February 25, 1907, in Denver, Colorado, to Irish immigrant parents. The youngest of four children, she grew up in an environment rich with Irish folklore and mythology, which later influenced her plays and children's stories. A brilliant student, she was graduated from West Denver High School at the age of fifteen and studied classics at the University of Denver and later at the University of Colorado in Boulder.

On graduation, she began writing for the *Rocky Mountain News* and, in 1928, married fellow reporter Robert L. Chase. When a practical joke she devised got her fired, Chase concentrated on raising a family and writing plays for the regional theaters in Denver. In 1936, her first play, *Me, Third*, was produced in Denver, where it was such a success that producer Brock Pemberton was convinced it could succeed on Broadway. In March and April of 1937, retitled *Now You've Done It*, it played forty-three performances at the Henry Miller Theatre in New York—not a hit by Broadway standards. Her next play, *Sorority House*, did not tempt Broadway but interested Hollywood: It was filmed by RKO-Radio in 1939, starring Veronica Lake. After two more Chase comedies did not play beyond Boulder, Chase and Pemberton tried Broadway once more with *Harvey* and hit it big.

Not only was *Harvey* one of the biggest hits of the 1944-1945 season, but also it won the 1945 Pulitzer Prize in drama. The original production ran 1,775 performances, was revived on Broadway in 1970 for another 79, and has been in constant production on the regional, academic, and community theater stage ever since its close in New York in 1949. Enjoying her fame from *Harvey*, Chase decided to try her hand at serious drama. *The Next Half Hour* was even a bigger Broadway flop than her first, running only 8 performances in 1945. This experience, coupled with the emotional trauma of sudden fame and wealth, brought on a depression only momentarily assuaged by the success of the 1950 film version of *Harvey* starring Jimmy Stewart.

Riding the crest of the film's success, Chase was able to put the finishing touches on two scripts in 1952, *Mrs. McThing*, which opened in New York in February, and *Bernardine*, which opened eight months later. Although neither would reach the iconic status of *Harvey*, both were modest hits, both at the box office and with the critics, and *Bernardine* was filmed by Twentieth Century-Fox in 1957.

The following year, Chase produced a children's novel, *Loretta Mason Potts*. In 1961, her last original Broadway production, *Midgie Purvis*, ran for only twenty-one performances. In the next decade, Chase published three more plays, including a stage adaptation of her children's novel, but none of them received significant theatrical production. The 1970 New York revival of *Harvey* was followed in 1972 by the Hallmark Hall of Fame televised version, and in 1975 by the London Stage revival. In 1981, Chase died of a heart attack in Denver.

ANALYSIS

Mary Chase's comedies are not only composed of fantasy: They are also *about* fantasy, its importance in refreshing the human spirit. In *Harvey*, Elwood P. Dowd is graced with visions of a giant white rabbit named Harvey, but in the end it is clear that other people—his sister Veta and psychiatrist Dr. Chumley—need Harvey more than Elwood does. *Mrs. McThing* presents two sets of fantasies: Mrs. Larue's idealization of the well-behaved child she wishes her son Howay to be and Howay's daydream of his ideal life of adventure. In *Bernardine*, the fantasy is the erotic wish-fulfillment of teenage boys in 1950's America: The title character is the ideal woman created by a gang of boys.

In addition to fantasy, all three plays deal with the theme of respect for nonconformity. It might be more precise to say that in all three plays, a major character comes to realize that the only thing to which the supposed eccentric does not conform is other people's

expectations. In *Harvey*, Elwood drinks too much to suit his sister, who also wishes he would not rave about his giant rabbit friend. In *Mrs. McThing*, Mrs. Larue expects her son to behave like a "normal" boy who does as he is told, without realizing that her son's behavior is normal and that her idealization is a fantasy. In *Bernardine*, the mother of an older child, this time a teenager, similarly expects her son to be her best friend and ridicules the gang with which he finds a more liberating self-identity.

HARVEY

An incident from Chase's childhood may have inspired the character of Elwood P. Dowd, the protagonist of *Harvey*, and her mother's admonishment supplied a major theme. Chase's mother stopped a group of boys from throwing snowballs at an old woman. The playwright's mother shooed away the hooligans and told her daughter never to be unkind to a person others say is crazy because "crazy" people often have a deep wisdom. That lesson stuck with young Mary, and she turned it into a Pulitzer Prize-winning comedy. The audience's sympathies in the comedy are tilted heavily in Elwood's favor, and theatergoers half believe that the giant rabbit Elwood sees is real—especially when doors open and close when no one is on stage.

Chase has been accused of satirizing modern psychiatry in *Harvey*, but the actual target of the satire—if barbs as blunt and soft as hers can be called satire—is a tendency for twentieth century America to confuse respectability and conformity with sanity. Even if Elwood's visions of a rabbit named Harvey are delusional (and the action of the play suggests they are not), the only thing threatened by the delusion is his sister's social status. Virtually every character in the play except for Elwood exhibits a manic energy: his niece Myrtle, in her search for a husband; his sister, in her quest for acceptance in high society; the psychiatrists, in pursuit of acceptance of their theories (as well as what turns out to be a rather unhealthy desire to control people); and the strong-arm orderly, in his attempt to find a chance to turn his verbal threats into physical violence. In the midst of all this turmoil, Elwood's calm suggests to the audience, subconsciously, even before the idea is corroborated by dialogue, that this supposed madman is the most rational character in the play.

However, the one irrational force that dominates the play is not fantasy but love—both in the romantic sense (though that is minor incident) and in the philosophical sense of self-giving. Elwood encourages young love wherever he finds it, particularly between the young psychiatrist Dr. Sanderson and Nurse Kelly. His sister Veta, on the other hand, suspects the sanitarium staff of having designs on her person. Both Dr. Chumley and his orderly Wilson have a well-developed eye for the ladies. Finally, Elwood is very fond of his invisible companion, but he is willing to give up Harvey to please his sister Veta.

MRS. McTHING

The fantasy in *Mrs. McThing* is effected in a way different from how it is brought about in Chase's other plays, though it is most closely related perhaps to *Harvey*. Just as theatergoers are made to partake in Elwood's delusion (if it is that) when they see doors open, presumably to accommodate a giant rabbit, in *Mrs. McThing*, they see everything from the point of the youngster Howay Larue. The ringleader of a crime mob seems to be at the top of the heap until his mother appears and slaps him for staying out late the night before. When the police search the gang for weapons, they discover only comic books, cereal, and bubble gum. The world of the play is the real world but seen through a child's eyes, suggesting a further point about Chase's fantasy: It is fantastic only if people hold certain presuppositions about the nature of reality, which Chase's Celtic imagination does not automatically grant.

A more serious point to the fantasy, however, involves Howay's mother. In the opening scene, she is amazed and delighted to find Howay behaving exactly as she always wanted: polite, obedient, and anticipating and fulfilling her every wish. However, the delight turns sour as she realizes that the "Howay" who seems to be her maternal wish-fulfillment is a hollow construct—in the language of the play, a "stick." The fantasy logic of the play asserts that the real Howay has been replaced by a stick-Howay by the magic of a witch named Mrs. McThing. However, the magic is very realistic, because if a real little boy

began to act out his mother's image of how the ideal little boy should act, behaviorists would use the same sort of language: The boy, in acting out his mother's needs rather than his own, becomes hollow, less real, a stick figure standing in for the "real" boy.

Part of the impossible ideal that Mrs. Larue wants to create for Howay is a matter of class—something that she has in common with Veta in *Harvey* and Mrs. Weldy in *Bernardine*. The cartoonish gangsters, like Wilson the orderly in *Harvey* or the teenage gang in *Bernardine*, are the supposedly undesirable element that the maternal figure—Mrs. Larue, Veta, and Mrs. Weldy—must learn to embrace or at least not to fear. To Howay, the gangsters represent the untidiness and avoidance of authority that is part of being a boy.

BERNARDINE

The teenage boys in *Bernardine* struggle in the same conflict as Howay in *Mrs. McThing*, though further along the continuum. They, too, are pressured to conform to their mothers' expectations, and their gang behavior is in a large part a reactionary refusal to do so, much like Howay's idyll with gangsters. One minor character, Vernon Kinswood, represents the filial ideal of the only mother who appears in the play, Mrs. Ruth Weldy. Her son Buford, or "Wormy" as he is known to the gang, is pressured to be more like Kinswood, every mother's dream. Instead he wants to be more like Beaumont, the leader of the gang, particularly when it comes to women. Yet Mrs. Weldy keeps her son on such a short leash that he feels he has no time for the rituals of courtship and so gains a reputation—both in the gang and among the girls of his high school—as a lecher.

The plot of *Bernardine* demonstrates a painful paradox about the nature of fantasy—that the more it becomes embodied in a real human being, the less real it becomes. Wormy's friend Kinswood embodies the maternal ideal of Mrs. Weldy and her circle of friends. Yet when Kinswood rather sycophantically insinuates himself into adult conversation with the ladies, their delight wears off: His eagerness to please their parental expectations is too much for them to take. Similarly, for Wormy, Kinswood is merely tolerated as a cover. The more central fantasy, however, the adolescent male erotic dream that the boys call

Bernardine, follows the same process of disillusionment on being embodied in Enid Lacy.

Wormy, tired of rejection by high school girls, vows to pick up an older, sophisticated woman in the lobby of the swankiest hotel in town. When the boys, who have come along to watch Wormy in his attempt, see the beautiful Enid, who so perfectly matches their made-up ideal, they instinctively proclaim her Bernardine. Yet when Wormy almost triumphs, getting into her hotel room, he discovers that the joy in a fantasy is precisely its unreality. Enid, who is going along with the pickup to feed her own fantasy, discovers the same lesson, underscored when she discovers that Wormy's mother is one of her adult friends. Yet in exploring the limits of fantasy, *Bernardine* affirms the value of fantasy in helping people cope with the world.

OTHER MAJOR WORKS

SCREENPLAYS: *Sorority House,* 1939; *Harvey,* 1950; *Bernardine,* 1957.

CHILDREN'S LITERATURE: *Loretta Mason Potts,* 1958; *The Wicked Pigeon Ladies in the Garden;* 1968.

BIBLIOGRAPHY

Kerr, Walter. "Remembrances of Things Past." In the *God on the Gymnasium Floor,* edited by Walter Kerr. New York: Simon and Schuster, 1971. In light of James Stewart's 1970 Broadway revival of *Harvey,* Kerr observes how the play has held up over a quarter century and that its immense popularity threatens to obscure its technical brilliance. The greatest contributor to its success, however, is its simplicity.

Miller, Jordan Y. "Harvey." In *American Dramatic Literature: Ten Modern Plays in Historical Perspective,* edited by Jordan Y. Miller. New York: McGraw Hill, 1961. Faults apparent structural weaknesses in *Harvey*—a lopsided first act, too slow a pace, a love affair that goes nowhere—then admires the play for succeeding despite these difficulties because of its triumphant characterization of the protagonist, Elwood P. Dowd.

Nathan, George Jean. "American Playwrights Old and New." In *Theatre in the Fifties,* edited by George Jean Nathan. New York: Alfred A. Knopf, 1953. Admires Chase's craft but denies the consensus of the critics that *Bernardine* and *Mrs. McThing* are successful in treating fantasy on stage.

Sievers, W. David. "New Freudian Blood." In *Freud on Broadway: A History of Psychoanalysis and the American Drama,* edited by W. David Sievers. New York: Hermitage House, 1955. Considers Chase's flop *The Next Half Hour* a botched attempt at realism but values both *Mrs. McThing* and *Bernardine* as contributions to the psychology of fantasy on stage.

John R. Holmes

ANTON CHEKHOV

Born: Taganrog, Russia; January 29, 1860
Died: Badenweiler, Germany; July 15, 1904

PRINCIPAL DRAMA

Platonov, wr. 1878-1881, pb. 1923 (English translation, 1930)
Ivanov, pr., pb. 1887, revised pr. 1889 (English translation, 1912)
Medved, pr., pb. 1888 (*A Bear,* 1909)
Predlozheniye, pb. 1889, pr. 1890 (*A Marriage Proposal,* 1914)
Leshy, pr. 1889 (*The Wood Demon,* 1925)
Svadba, pb. 1889, pr. 1890 (*The Wedding,* 1916)
Yubiley, pb. 1892 (*The Jubilee,* 1916)
Chayka, pr. 1896, pb. 1897, revised pr. 1898, pb. 1904 (*The Seagull,* 1909)
Dyadya Vanya, pb. 1897, pr. 1899 (based on his play *The Wood Demon; Uncle Vanya,* 1914)

Tri sestry, pr., pb. 1901, revised pb. 1904 (*The Three Sisters*, 1920)

Vishnyovy sad, pr., pb. 1904 (*The Cherry Orchard*, 1908)

The Plays of Chekhov, pb. 1923-1924 (2 volumes)

Nine Plays, pb. 1959

OTHER LITERARY FORMS

Within the ten-volume edition of his works published in 1901, Anton Chekhov included 240 of the hundreds of stories he had written for dozens of newspapers and magazines. Many of these stories were collected and published in hardcover form as Chekhov progressed in his career: *Pystrye rasskazy* (1886; motley stories), *Nevinnye rechi* (1887; innocent tales), *V sumerkakh* (1887; in the twilight), and *Rasskazy* (1888; stories). Some of his most famous stories are "Gore" ("Sorrow"), "Toska" ("Misery"), "Step'" ("The Steppe"), "Skuchnaya isoriya" ("A Dreary Story"), "Palata No. 6" ("Ward No. 6"), "Chorny monakh" ("The Black Monk"), "Tri goda" ("Three Years"), "Muzhiki" ("Peasants"), "Kryzhovnik" ("Gooseberries"), "Dushechka" ("The Darling"), "Dama s sobachkoi" ("The Lady with the Dog"), and "Nevesta" ("The Betrothed"). In addition, Chekhov wrote a work of reportage on conditions on the island penal colony of Sakhalin: *Ostrov Sakhalin* (1893-1894).

ACHIEVEMENTS

Anton Chekhov began writing as a means of earning an income, and in doing so he built up a large audience for his comic tales, which he wrote at a rate of more than one per week. At the same time, he attracted the attention and approval of a broad range of writers and critics. As his career progressed and his literary efforts grew more serious, his appeal never wavered, and his popularity and reputation continued to grow as he expanded into drama. In 1900, he became one of the first ten literary members of the Russian Academy of Sciences, inducted at the same time as Leo Tolstoy, and during his life he influenced many younger writers, including Maxim Gorky. Since his death, his reputation has grown steadily, and now he is universally recognized as one of the

Anton Chekhov (Library of Congress)

founders of modern drama and one of the greatest of short-story writers.

BIOGRAPHY

Anton Pavlovich Chekhov was born in the provincial town of Taganrog, Russia, on January 29, 1860. The grandson of a serf, Chekhov was the third of seven children. Chekhov said of his early days, "There was no childhood in my childhood," largely because of his father, Pavel, who frequently forced Chekhov to tend the family's unheated food and hardware store until late at night. Chekhov's father beat his children and taught them how to cheat customers, yet he was in his own eyes a religious man. He forced his children into a religious choir that rehearsed frequently and sang at various churches. Chekhov disliked these duties. It is not surprising that in later life he was not a religious man, that he spent his life trying to "burn the slave" out of himself and become a man of culture, and that he became convinced that work was useless unless it improved humankind's lot.

Chekhov's home life was disrupted in 1876 when his father's business went into bankruptcy and his father fled to Moscow to escape debtors' prison. His mother sold the house, took the younger children, and joined her husband. Chekhov stayed behind to finish his schooling and became, at sixteen, the main support of the family, providing income by tutoring. He finished school in 1879, rejoined his family, and tried to provide material and moral support, lecturing at times on the need to avoid lies, affirm human worth, and be fair, all values that would be of great importance in his later work.

In Moscow, Chekhov studied medicine and supported the family by writing stories in humorous magazines under the name Antosha Chekhonte. His first story was published in 1880 in the magazine *Strekoza* (dragonfly), and in 1881, he finished his first full-length play, *Platonov*, though it was not performed or published in his lifetime. In October of 1882, he met Nicolai Leikin, the owner of the weekly magazine *Oskolki* (fragments); they became friends, and soon scarcely a week went by without a Chekhov story appearing in the magazine. These early ventures saw him through medical school, and in 1884, Chekhov finished his medical studies and took up practice. By December 10 of that year, however, Chekhov became ill, coughing up blood, his first attack of tuberculosis, the disease that would kill him twenty years later. For the rest of his life, no year would go by without similar attacks.

Chekhov recovered rapidly and managed to ignore the implications of his symptoms, resuming his normal life. In December, 1885, he accompanied Leikin to St. Petersburg, the literary center of Russia at the time, meeting Aleksei Suvorin, owner of the powerful daily newspaper *Novoye vremya* (new times), and Dimitry Grigorovich, a noted novelist. After his return to Moscow, he received a letter from Grigorovich urging him to respect his talent and write seriously; Chekhov responded that Grigorovich's letter was "like a thunderbolt," making him believe in his talent for the first time. Suvorin also wrote, inviting Chekhov to contribute to *Novoye vremya*. Chekhov accepted, beginning a long relationship with the newspaper and with Suvorin.

In 1887, Chekhov completed the full-length play *Ivanov*, which was a popular success. In 1888, he experimented with longer prose forms and produced the much-acclaimed novella "The Steppe"; he was also awarded the Pushkin Prize for the best literary work of the year for his collection of stories *V sumerkakh*. In drama, he achieved financial success with two popular one-act comedies, *A Bear* and *A Marriage Proposal*.

In June, 1889, Chekhov's brother Nicolai died of tuberculosis as Chekhov tended him, and late in the year, his full-length play *The Wood Demon*, at first rejected as "too tedious," was finally performed but was an almost complete failure. Chekhov began to doubt his dramatic ability, and, except for the one-act comedy *The Jubilee*, he abandoned drama until 1896. Indeed, Chekhov underwent a crisis of self-examination in 1889, doubting his literary and medical abilities and even his own worth.

Until this time, Chekhov's writing had been extraordinarily fluent. He wrote quickly, and almost everything he wrote was successful. Critics had begun to complain, however, that he had no purpose, no aim, and Chekhov was troubled with the same thought. Tolstoy's moral philosophy, advocating an ascetic search for self-perfection, influenced him for a time. In 1890, Chekhov startled his friends but lifted himself out of what he described as a "spiritual stagnation" by undertaking a long and arduous trip to the prison colony of Sakhalin, located on an island off the eastern coast of Russia, to make study of conditions there. It may be that this trip crystallized Chekhov's belief that a person must not be content merely to see everything; he must also do something about what he sees.

There is ample evidence of Chekhov's activity after he returned from Sakhalin. In 1891, a famine year, he devoted himself to collecting food and money for starving farmers. In 1892, he bought Melikhovo, an estate of 675 neglected acres, and poured his efforts into planting, pruning, and improving. He planted thousands of trees, including an apple and a cherry orchard. At Melikhovo, he led medical efforts to forestall threatened cholera epidemics. He also took on the tasks of constructing rural schools, stocking the Taganrog library, and providing constructive criticism for many aspiring writers, displaying the energy and purpose lacking in so many of his dramatic creations.

By 1896, Chekhov was again tempted by the theater, and *The Seagull* opened on October 17 of that year. *The Seagull* failed, and its author vowed never again to write drama. In 1898, however, Vladimir Nemirovich-Danchenko and Konstantin Stanislavsky created the Moscow Art Theater and received permission to use *The Seagull* in its repertory. The theater's first few productions failed, and by the time that the company was ready to stage *The Seagull*, it needed a success. The opening on December 17, 1898, exceeded everyone's hopes; it was an enormous success, and the theater adopted the seagull as its permanent emblem.

The success of *The Seagull* was shadowed by a deterioration in Chekhov's health. A severe pulmonary hemorrhage in 1897 forced him away from Moscow to temperate Nice during the winter of 1897-1898, and in 1898, he settled outside Yalta and gave up the practice of medicine.

On October 26, 1899, the Moscow Art Theater performed the second of Chekhov's great plays, *Uncle Vanya*. This play was followed by *The Three Sisters* on January 31, 1901, and then by *The Cherry Orchard* on January 17, 1904. All three plays were only moderate successes at first but gained in favor as audiences and actors grew to understand them.

Chekhov met Olga Knipper, an actress, through the Moscow Art Theater. They were married on May 25, 1901, but most of their married life was spent apart, Olga's career demanding that she live in Moscow and Chekhov's health preventing him from living there except during the summer. Chekhov's belief in purposeful work made him content with this situation.

Throughout 1903 and 1904, Chekhov's health declined steadily, and in June of 1904, he went with Olga to a German health resort in Badenweiler. He seemed to respond to treatment at first, but he died early in the morning on July 15. He was buried a week later in Moscow.

ANALYSIS

Anton Chekhov was talking about other writers when he said, "The best of them are realists and de-pict life as it is, but because every line they write is permeated, as with a juice, by a consciousness of an aim, you feel in addition to life as it is, also life as it should be, and it is that that delights you." These very qualities that Chekhov praises in other great writers are the qualities in his greatest plays, *The Seagull*, *Uncle Vanya*, *The Three Sisters*, and *The Cherry Orchard*, plays that continue to delight audiences throughout the world, though that delight is sometimes expressed in tears.

Chekhov has been called a depressing writer, one who bring tears to an audience's eyes, but he rejected that view adamantly, saying that he had never wanted tears: "I wanted something else. I wanted to tell people honestly: 'Look at yourselves. See how badly you live and how tiresome you are.' The main thing is that people should understand this. When they do, they will surely create a new and better life for themselves." Audiences will continue to be moved to tears by Chekhov's plays, but his words give his audience a way of understanding the main ingredients of his greatness. His powers of observation and his honesty permitted him to create characters readily recognizable as human, characters sharply individualized yet representative. He was convinced of the need for unceasing striving, a belief that pervaded his life and work; and he had a faith that the future would bring a better life for humankind.

Chekhov's exceptional powers of observation, no doubt sharpened by his scientific training, enabled him to bring to the stage living characters. This was the single guiding purpose of Chekhov's early writing, to show "life as it is." This purpose, however, could not sustain him for long, and especially after his crises in 1889 and his trip to Sakhalin in 1890, he came to believe that "A work of art should express a great idea." If Chekhov's plays can be said to have a great idea, it must be that human beings must work ceaselessly and that their labor must be accompanied by a faith in the usefulness of that work, a faith in the future. In all his best plays, the themes of work, faith, and purpose are present, and in all there is a stab of pain and pity at the recognition of how often humans are idle, how many there are who do no work, how many who work to no end, how few who possess faith, how difficult it is to persevere in one's faith, how often dreams are not fulfilled, and how transient is all human happiness. Chekhov's purpose, however, went beyond the pain of recognition. He hoped that when people recognized themselves in his characters, they would go on to "create a new and better life."

Chekhov did not begin his dramatic career with the happy mixture of observation, purpose, and knowledge of the stage that was to characterize his later work. His earliest play, untitled by Chekhov but commonly referred to as *Platonov*, is a long and rambling work, full of dramatic stereotypes and heightened, exaggerated scenes, with little of the flavor of his later works. His next full-length play, *Ivanov*, was staged and was a popular success, but Chekhov was not satisfied with it, for good reason. It, too, was stilted and did not in Chekhov's view reflect the truth about human life. By the end of the 1880's, Chekhov had already formed the opinion that "A play ought to be written in which people come and go, dine, talk of the weather, or play cards . . . because that is what happens in real life. Life on the stage should be as it really is and the people, too, should be as they are and not stilted." Chekhov would need a new kind of drama to embody such perceptions, and he was not successful at creating it until 1896. His first attempt at a new drama, *The Wood Demon*, first performed in 1889, failed so badly that Chekhov turned away from drama for six years. During this time, he achieved fame for his fiction. As fame brought more money and therefore allowed him more time to work on each piece, he wrote longer and longer pieces, and so was gradually led back to full-length drama.

Ultimately, Chekhov found a way to fulfill his dream of capturing real life on the stage by rejecting the dramatic conventions of his time. Although the drama of his contemporaries focused on action, often melodramatic action, Chekhov's last plays are primarily works of inaction, works in which the needed action takes place offstage. Chekhov prevents the audience from being distracted by activity, focusing attention on the inner lives of his characters.

These inner lives are often both painful and ridiculous. It has long been a difficulty for critics that

Chekhov called *The Seagull* and *The Cherry Orchard* comedies and insisted that they were not tragic. In truth, many of the characters in his plays are absurd: Their concerns are ridiculous, and the detached observer must confess that they are silly. It is a rare viewer, however, who can be detached about Chekhov's characters. The audience simultaneously recognizes the foolishness and the humanity of the characters, touched by the recognition of how real the characters' problems are to them, how impossible the characters find it to extricate themselves from their problems. Some of their dreams are absurd, but they do not know how to help themselves, and so their lives pass them by without teaching them how to live. Chekhov shows convincingly "what fools these mortals be," but the audience, being mortal, is moved to pity, not laughter.

THE SEAGULL

The Seagull was partially inspired by events in Chekhov's life. Chekhov had for years known a woman named Lydia, or "Lika," Mizinova, who was apparently in love with him; he was seemingly less in love with her. They were very close, but Chekhov was not interested in marriage, and Lika turned her attention to another man, I. N. Potapenko, a married friend of Chekhov. The two had an affair that resulted in Lika's pregnancy and her abandonment by Potapenko. She went to Europe to deliver the baby, but the baby died soon after Lika's return to Russia. The episode no doubt disturbed Chekhov, and there is some indication that he felt a degree of guilt in the matter. Nina, a central character in the play and the only one who finds an answer for her life, is based on Lika, whose true experience provides the central theme of *The Seagull*.

The play opens at the country estate of Sorin, a retired justice. His sister, Arkadina, an actress, is making a visit to her brother's home with her lover, the writer Trigorin. Living with Sorin is Arkadina's twenty-five-year-old son, Konstantin Trepliov, who, as the play begins, is about to stage a play that he has written for the benefit of his mother and the other guests on the estate. The play features Nina, whom Trepliov loves. Also attending the performance are Dorn, a doctor; Medvedenko, a schoolmaster; Shamrayev, Sorin's bailiff; his wife, Polena, and their daughter

Masha. Masha sets the tone of Chekhov's play with her first lines. When Medvedenko asks her why she always wears black, she replies that she is "in mourning for my life." Medvedenko loves Masha and wants to marry her, but Masha feels nothing for him and loves Trepliov instead. In turn, Trepliov cares nothing for Masha and focuses all his dreams on Nina. As Trepliov's play gets under way, strain is plainly seen in the relationship between Arkadina and her son. Trepliov wants very much to impress his mother with the play, but she interrupts it several times with her comments. Arkadina claims that her son has no talent, but Dorn sees some power in the play, though he thinks it lacks a "definite idea." Nina complains that the play has no living characters, but the novice playwright defends himself by claiming that plays ought not to show things as they are, or as they ought to be, but rather as they appear to us in our dreams, an attitude that would get little sympathy from Chekhov.

Chekhov would certainly sympathize, however, with the most prevalent problem in the play: unrequited love. Trepliov yearns for the love of his mother but does not receive it, Nina becomes enamored of Trigorin and ends up running off to meet him in Moscow, and Arkadina also wants the love of Trigorin but must settle for dominance over him: He loves no one. Dorn comments on the situation at the end of act 1 with the lines, "How distraught they all are! And what a quantity of love about! . . . But what can I do, my child?" One can almost hear Chekhov directing these words to Lika Mizinova.

Acts 2 and 3 develop Nina's infatuation with Trigorin and the relationship between Arkadina and Trepliov. Nina is impressed by Trigorin's fame and occupation and thinks only of him. Trepliov sees that he has lost his mother to Trigorin and that he is losing Nina as well. He is wrought up enough to kill a seagull and present it to Nina, telling her that he will soon kill himself as well. Trigorin comes on the scene shortly after Trepliov leaves, and the scene gives him an idea for a story, as he tells Nina in a speech that foreshadows their future affair: "A young girl, like you, has lived beside a lake since childhood. She loves the lake as a seagull does . . . but a man comes along, sees her, and having nothing better to do, de-

stroys her, just like this seagull here." This "idea" is of great symbolic importance because it is the first example of a perspective that will come up again and again in Chekhov: The greatest destruction is casual, ignorant, rooted in idleness. Nina understands nothing of the implications of the speech and, by the end of act 3, the affair is arranged.

Trepliov, true to his word, shoots himself but suffers only a grazed head. Nina is "casual" about the injury, and Arkadina, though maternal for a few moments, soon begins to argue with her son again.

In act 4, which opens two years later, Trigorin and Arkadina return to visit Sorin, who is ill. In the two-year interval, Masha has married Medvedenko in an attempt to put Trepliov out of her mind, and they now have a child but essentially nothing has changed: Medvedenko still spends all his time worrying, either about his daughter or about money, and Masha, still yearning for Trepliov, is cruel to her husband and has virtually abandoned her child. Trepliov has succeeded in publishing but has found no contentment. Nina, after running away with Trigorin, became pregnant. He abandoned her, she lost her child, and her acting career is floundering.

While the rest of the company go to a late supper, Nina comes on the scene, drawn by the news that Arkadina and Trigorin have returned. She converses with Trepliov, and clearly he still loves her. Of all the characters in the play, only Nina has changed. She has suffered greatly, but she has learned from her trials; as she tells Trepliov, "what really matters is not fame, or glamour . . . but knowing how to endure things." Nina then leaves to pursue her acting career in an obscure village; she still loves Trigorin, but that does not stop her from living. Trepliov, however, does not have Nina's faith. With the final realization that she is gone from his life and that his mother has no need of him, he has no use for himself, and he goes offstage and shoots himself. The rest of the characters, playing cards as they hear the shot, send Dorn out to investigate. They accept his explanation that the noise was just a bottle of ether exploding; as the curtain falls, Dorn takes Trigorin aside to give him the news of the shooting and to tell him to take Arkadina back to the city lest she find out. Thus the audience hears of the shooting as the card game continues, and really nothing is changed.

The play ends on the same note on which it began. If Masha started the play mourning her life, she has not stopped mourning during the two years of the play's action, and though she has a husband and a child, she cannot be said to live. Trepliov, too, has spent his time mourning rather than living, and if his death brings about no change, that is not surprising, for his death is no different from his life. Arkadina starts the play wrapped in her idleness, incapable of feeling or understanding her son's misery, and it is not at all surprising that she plays cards as he shoots himself. Change can be seen only in Nina, who has learned not to fear life, and who works toward a future goal with faith and dedication.

UNCLE VANYA

The exact date of composition of *Uncle Vanya* is unknown, but it is known that it had been performed for some time in rural theaters before it was performed by the Moscow Art Theater. In fact, though Chekhov claimed that it was a totally new play, acts 2 and 3 are taken almost completely from his earlier failure, *The Wood Demon*. Although *Uncle Vanya* had its beginnings in *The Wood Demon*, it is in fact a very different play. While the earlier play was a failure, *Uncle Vanya* is a convincing, deeply moving work, perhaps Chekhov's most touching play.

Uncle Vanya is subtitled "Scenes from Country Life in Four Acts," and all the action of the play takes place on the estate of Serebryakov, who has recently come there to live with his young, beautiful second wife, Yelena, after retiring from his university position. Their arrival proves a disturbance to those who have been living on or about the estate, especially Sonya, Serebryakov's daughter; Vanya, Sonya's uncle, the brother of Serebryakov's first wife; and Astrov, a doctor who is Vanya's friend. Both Serebryakov and Yelena have a hand in the crisis.

Vanya and Sonya have devoted their lives to managing the estate, saving and scrimping to send every spare ruble to Serebryakov, thinking him talented, even brilliant. When he arrives on the estate, however, he is seen to be another sort of man. He suffers from gout, is perpetually in a bad mood, thinks of no

one but himself, and disturbs the routine of the estate, staying up late at night writing and then not rising until late in the day. For Vanya, Serebryakov's arrival is even more disturbing; his routine and his illusions are shattered. He realizes that all of Serebryakov's work has been shallow, commonplace, and that his writing will not outlive him. Vanya believes he has lost his life and has worked for the last twenty-five years for nothing.

More disturbing yet is the presence of Yelena, for she is young, beautiful, and idle. She draws the attention of all who see her. Vanya falls in love with her, and his love is made more painful by his jealousy of Serebryakov. Astrov, hardworking and idealistic, has been a friend of the family for years and has paid monthly visits to the estate; his work as a doctor and his efforts to preserve the ecology of the region have exhausted him, and while his intelligence is still sharp, he complains that his feelings have become deadened, leaving him incapable of love. Even he, however, is susceptible to Yelena's charms, and before long he is ignoring his work and making daily visits to the estate. Sonya, a good-hearted, hardworking, but plain woman, has been cherishing a love for Astrov for some time, and it is agony for her to see him attracted to Yelena instead.

The crisis comes to a head when Serebryakov calls a family meeting, expresses his discontent with life on the estate, and presents his plan to sell the estate so that he can live more comfortably. Vanya goes into a rage because Serebryakov's plan would leave Vanya and Sonya homeless, and Serebryakov backs down from his plan, after which Vanya twice tries to shoot him, missing both times. He gives up in disgust, and the third act ends. In act 4, Serebryakov and Yelena return to the city, where they will be mailed money by Vanya and Sonya. In short, things return to their original state, except that illusions have been stripped away. Vanya knows that his efforts have been wasted, and Sonya knows that her love for Astrov has been in vain. Astrov leaves also, and while he will return, his visits will be less frequent than before. In the final scene, Sonya and Vanya sit down to their work again, and while Vanya might not be able to endure on his own, Sonya's strength and faith in the future enable them to continue. In the long closing monologue, she voices her resolve to endure: "Well, what can we do? We must go on living. We shall go on living. . . . We shall live through a long, long succession of days and tedious evenings."

It is not difficult to see the resemblance between Sonya and Nina in *The Seagull*. Both possess what Chekhov called "iron in the blood," a strength that keeps them living and working, a strength born of faith in the future. There are also resemblances among other characters in the two plays. The idleness of Yelena and selfishness of Serebryakov have their parallels in Arkadina, Masha, and Trigorin. Indeed, the general atmosphere of the two plays is similar: Life is hard, and work and faith are needed to endure it well. Few have such faith, and thus, few are able to endure and still live vitally. As Vanya says, "When people have no real life, they live on their illusions."

In Astrov, the audience sees Chekhov's complex human vision. In many ways, Astrov is like Chekhov: He is a dedicated doctor and takes delight in the planting of trees. He suffers, however, for his efforts; they exhaust and deaden him, and his exhaustion threatens him with loss of faith and leaves him incapable of love. Yet he is a man of ideals, respected by all in the play except the self-centered Serebryakov. Yelena sees his excellence clearly and speaks movingly when she says, "He plants a tree and wonders what will come of it in a thousand years' time, and speculates on the future happiness of mankind. Such people are rare, and we must love them." The symbol of tree planting is particularly apt in communicating Chekhov's vision, for it is an act which yields no instant gratification. Astrov sees that the casual destruction of forests will create a dismal future, but deliberate efforts to restore them will bring hope for a better life.

In contrast, Yelena is an object of present beauty. She represents a human physical ideal, less than ideal in other ways. She does no work, has no thoughts of the future, and lives her life in idleness and boredom. Her threat is that she infects others with her ennui and self-indulgence. If there is no work for the future, Chekhov asks in this play, how is human life to improve?

THE THREE SISTERS

Chekhov had always prided himself on the speed and ease with which he wrote, but *The Three Sisters* was different. Numerous letters testify to the difficulty with which the play progressed; it was pulled out of him slowly, no doubt a result in part of his declining health, but probably also because it is his most searching, introspective play. It looks long and deeply at its characters, and it is no accident that it is the only one of his major works that he referred to as a "drama." Chekhov might have claimed that *The Seagull* and *The Cherry Orchard* were comic in their vision, but in *The Three Sisters*, his sympathy for the plight of his characters outweighs all other considerations: The play is a choral lament over the loss of life.

At the center of the chorus are the three Prozorov sisters: Olga, an unmarried teacher; Masha, married to Kuligin; and Irina, the youngest sister, who is twenty as the play begins. These characters are supplemented by a considerable supporting cast. Of greatest importance are Andrey, the brother of the three sisters; Vershinin, the battery commander of the military garrison in the provincial town where the sisters live; and Tuzenbakh, a lieutenant who is in love with Irina. Others are Chebutykin, an army doctor; Natalya, Andrey's fiancée and then his wife; Kuligin, a teacher; and Solyony, a suitor for Irina. Each of the characters takes on a life of his or her own, all come together in the complex harmony that makes the work so compelling.

The three sisters, though the details of their dreams are different, sing the same refrain: "To Moscow." Eleven years before the action of the play, the family lived in Moscow, and each of the sisters yearns for Moscow as the fulfillment of her dream. Olga thinks that she would be happy if she were married, and Masha thinks that she would be happy if she were not. Irina thinks that happiness lies in working, but when she goes out to work she resents it. Andrey thinks that he would be happy if he were a professor in Moscow, but he does nothing to realize that dream; he spends his time making picture frames and playing the violin.

The play's action spans four years, beginning on the celebration of Irina's name day, at which Vershinin, the new battery commander, presents himself. He is from Moscow and was a friend of the sisters' late father; the sisters immediately are interested in him. They envy his recent life in Moscow, though he claims to prefer the provincial town. Masha takes a special interest in him, and, though both are married, an affair develops as the play proceeds. Also in the first act, Andrey proposes to Natalya; they are married by the time act 2 begins, and by the play's end, they have two children, though by then, Natalya (not, like the other characters, part of the aristocracy, but rather a member of the rising middle class of Chekhov's time) is having an affair with the head of the local council and has virtually driven the Prozorovs from their home. Another love theme concerns Irina. Tuzenbakh is in love with her and remains devoted to her throughout the four-year span of the play. Irina gives him little encouragement, for he is not handsome, and she has always dreamed of meeting her husband in Moscow. Tuzenbakh has a dangerous rival in Solyony, an eccentric, morbid character who insults everyone but Irina and is determined that he will have "no happy rivals."

The dream of going to Moscow remains unfulfilled. As the play ends, Vershinin and his men are transferred to another city, ending his affair with Masha, who returns in misery to her spineless but kind husband. Irina, finally convinced that her dream of going to Moscow will never be realized, consents to marry Tuzenbakh, though she does not love him. Before they marry, however, Solyony kills Tuzenbakh in a duel, and Irina is left alone. Olga has gone through the play hoping for some change in her burdensome life, a husband perhaps, or a rest from the constant demands of her teaching, but no husband is forthcoming, and by the end of the play her teaching chores are multiplied, because she has been made headmistress. Andrey has spent four years regretting his marriage and dreaming of great academic triumphs in Moscow, yet by the play's end, he is reduced to baby-sitting while his wife entertains her lover. All the dreams of the sisters have been crushed, four years of life have been lost, and the play ends with the courageous but tragic spectacle of the sisters trying to cope, trying to live, though they suffer and

do not know why. While Sonya in *Uncle Vanya* believes that the future will bring her rest, the three sisters try to believe that the future will bring them life.

Though the sisters arrive at no answers, the questions of happiness and the future are raised often in the play. These questions are debated by Vershinin and Tuzenbakh several times; the most important of the debates takes place in act 2, when Masha joins in. Vershinin poses the question, "What will life be like in two or three hundred years?" and leaves the floor open for speculation. Tuzenbakh responds that the superficial details of people's life will change, but their essential situation will not: ". . . man will be sighing much the same as before, 'Ah, how difficult life is.' And yet he will be afraid of death and as unwilling to die as he is nowadays." Vershinin's views are different; he believes that somewhere in the future "a new, happy life will appear." He believes that the present generation sacrifices happiness now so that future generations can be happy—indeed, that such altruism is the meaning of life—but Tuzenbakh denies that people know anything about meaning. At this point, Masha breaks in, claiming that "man must have faith, or he must look for faith. Otherwise, his life is empty, empty. . . . Either you know the reason why you are living, or else everything is nonsense." In this debate lies all the suffering of humankind. Masha seeks to know why she exists, but who is to tell her? While she waits for an answer, life passes her by. Tuzenbakh denies that there is an answer or rather denies that there is any way to find the answer and so does not trouble himself overmuch with the question. Vershinin defines his own answer, his own explanation for his sufferings, one very similar to Chekhov's own beliefs, and it helps him to carry on. What makes the difference, Chekhov suggests, is faith in the future. Faith is belief without proof, and only such faith can enable a person to work with confidence for the future happiness of the race while recognizing its present misery. This was Chekhov's situation. He could see that most people were miserable and dissatisfied, that they frittered their lives away on trivial concerns, and so he postulated a movement toward perfection and tried with his plays to contribute to it. Though many around him did nothing, he viewed them more with pity than with disdain, as Tuzenbakh views Solyony: "I'm both sorry for him and annoyed, but I'm more sorry."

THE CHERRY ORCHARD

The Cherry Orchard, Chekhov's last play, caused considerable disagreement between Chekhov and Stanislavsky over questions of staging, for Chekhov contended that it was a comedy while Stanislavsky claimed it was a tragedy. One must feel sympathy for Stanislavsky, for, despite many farcical elements in the play, it moves the audience to a complex sadness rather than to laughter. Most of the characters, though silly, even hilariously so, fail to understand their lives, fail to live meaningfully, and therefore lose their lives. Still, Chekhov was at least partially right, for, in the character of Anya, who at seventeen is the youngest character in the play, the audience can see some hope for the future, for a new life beginning, as in the character of Nina in *The Seagull*.

The action of the play takes place on the estate of Madame Lyubov Ranevsky. She has been absent from her estate for some time, having run off to Paris with her lover to escape the grief she felt over the loss of her young son. She returns virtually penniless, confronted with the problem of what to do to save the estate and its beautiful cherry orchard. With her on the estate are her brother Gaev; Varya, her adopted daughter; Anya, her natural daughter; and their servants Sharlotta, Yepihodov, Dunyasha, Firs, and Yasha. This group is supplemented by Trofimov, a young student who keeps getting expelled from the university for his revolutionary views, and Lopakhin, a wealthy merchant and former peasant. As the action opens, the problem to be solved is how to pay all the money owed on the estate; this question remains unresolved throughout the play. Indeed, Lyubov and her clan seem incapable of any kind of action. She and her kind, like the Prozorovs, are a dying breed. Although they recognize the fact, they seem helpless to do anything about it. They are fast being replaced by the rising merchant class, Lopakhin and his kind, as the Prozorovs were gradually replaced by Natalya and her lover in *The Three Sisters*.

The play is full of comic touches: Yepihodov's shoes squeak, Trofimov falls down a flight of stairs (without hurting himself), Varya gives Lopakhin a swat on the head meant for Yepihodov, Lopakhin teases Varya, Gaev speaks nonsense and talks to bookcases, and Sharlotta gives demonstrations of parlor magic. The play is kept from farce, however, by Chekhov's delineation of character. The audience comes to know the characters too well to laugh at them, instead feeling a sense of profound pity for their pain and helplessness.

Only Lopakhin has a plan to "save" the estate, but his plan is to destroy the orchard, build little villas on the property, and rent them out, thus providing a steady income. He suggests this solution to Lyubov, but she has lived on the estate since she was a child; she loves the orchard and does not seriously consider Lopakhin's plan. Instead, the family debates grand schemes and hopes for aid from distant relations but proves incapable of taking any action. Lyubov has grown so used to squandering her money that she cannot stop, and during the play, she gives gold to a beggar, though Varya is forced to feed the servants nothing but soup. The audience waits for the inevitable to happen, as it does when the estate is sold at auction, bought by Lopakhin, who proceeds with his original plan. The final act shows the Ranevsky family leaving their beloved home with the sound of axes in the background as their cherry orchard becomes a thing of the past.

The play's plot is simple; there are no surprises. Chekhov brings forth the inner lives of his characters so that the audience can understand them, see their foolishness, and yet pity them. Gaev is an excellent example. He has deep feelings and the urge to express them, but no one wants to listen to him. No one protests when he speaks in meaningless billiard terms, but when he speaks what is really in his heart, everyone protests. Perhaps it would be better for Gaev to remain silent, as Anya suggests he should, for no one listens to him; he does not even listen to himself, for though he hears the "call" to work, he has never heeded it.

Therein lies the problem of the play: No one combines the qualities necessary for a meaningful life. Some, such as Varya and Lopakhin, are workers, and some—such as Trofimov, Lyubov, and Gaev—have beautiful ideas, but no one works in behalf of worthy ideas. Lopakhin labors only for money, without any vision of the future, so he is able to destroy the orchard without even recognizing what he is doing, what is being lost. Trofimov makes compelling speeches about the need for work, the need to build for the future, but he only listens to the sound of his voice; he does not work. Varya spends every moment working, caring for the estate, but she labors only so that she will not have time to lament her fate. She hates her work but cannot bear idle time, for when idle, she weeps. Lyubov herself has compelling ideas, centering on her love for the man in Paris and for the orchard, but she does not know what to do for the things she loves. She loves the cherry orchard and idly watches it pass from her hands.

Each of the characters speaks of his or her innermost anxieties, and yet each remains alone, for while they speak their anguish the others go about their lives, never listening, caught up only in their own struggles. This failure to listen, this obliviousness, is the most distinctive element of the play, for it isolates the characters from one another and makes any individual effort fruitless.

The final image of the play is that of Firs, the oldest character, who is left behind, forgotten by the family he has served all his life. Left alone after his years of service, he comments to himself that "Life has slipped by as though I hadn't lived." The last sounds of the play are the mournful sound of a breaking string and the sound of an ax chopping down a tree in the orchard. Much that is beautiful goes to waste and is destroyed in this play, and the orchard stands as a symbol for all. It was beautiful, but it had no purpose, and so it must be reduced to nothing. The same can be said of Lyubov, Gaev, and others. The one bright spot is Anya, still young enough to put her life to some purpose, as she plans to do as the play ends. She does not mourn the loss of the orchard, for she plans to make all Russia her orchard, a plan of which Chekhov would approve.

In this last play, Chekhov included a bit of dialogue that goes a long way toward explaining his purpose in writing for the theater. Lopakhin tells Lyubov that he went to see a play (a conventional comedy)

the day before that was very funny. Lyubov answers with a speech that could not have defended Chekhov's drama more eloquently: "And most likely there was nothing funny in it. You shouldn't look at plays, you should look at yourselves a little oftener. How gray your lives are. How much nonsense you talk." That is why Chekhov has, and will continue to have, so secure a place in the world of drama: He shows his audiences the triviality, the grayness of their lives, so that they will change themselves, working with faith toward a greater future for humankind.

OTHER MAJOR WORKS

SHORT FICTION: *Skazki Melpomeny*, 1884; *Pystrye rasskazy*, 1886; *Nevinnye rechi*, 1887; *V sumerkakh*, 1887; *Rasskazy*, 1888; *The Tales of Tchehov*, 1916-1922 (13 volumes); *The Undiscovered Chekhov: Forty-three New Stories*, 1999.

NONFICTION: *Ostrov Sakhalin*, 1893-1894; *Letters on the Short Story, the Drama, and Other Literary Topics*, 1924; *The Selected Letters of Anton Chekhov*, 1955.

MISCELLANEOUS: *The Works of Anton Chekhov*, 1929; *Polnoye sobraniye sochineniy i pisem A. P. Chekhova*, 1944-1951 (20 volumes); *The Portable Chekhov*, 1947; *The Oxford Chekhov*, 1964-1980 (9 volumes).

BIBLIOGRAPHY

Allen, David. *Performing Chekhov*. New York: Routledge, 2000. A look at the production of Chekhov's dramatic works on the stage. Bibliography and index.

Bloom, Harold, ed. *Anton Chekhov*. Philadelphia, Pa.: Chelsea House, 1999. A critical assessment of the literary works of Chekhov. Bibliography and index.

Callow, Philip. *Chekhov, the Hidden Ground: A Biography*. Chicago: Ivan R. Dee, 1998. A biography of Chekhov that covers his life and works. Bibliography and index.

Gilman, Richard. *Chekhov's Plays: An Opening into Eternity*. New Haven, Conn.: Yale University Press, 1995. A scholarly study of the dramas of Chekhov. Bibliography and index.

Gottlieb, Vera, and Paul Allain, eds. *The Cambridge Companion to Chekhov.* New York: Cambridge University Press, 2000. A guide to the life and works of the playwright.

Malcolm, Janet. *Reading Chekhov: A Critical Journey.* New York: Random House, 2001. A critical analysis of the works of Chekhov. Bibliography.

Rayfield, Donald. *Anton Chekhov: A Life.* 1998. Reprint. Evanston, Ill.: Northwestern University Press, 2000. A detailed biography of Anton Chekhov including material about his relationship with various members of his family and his antecedents, his literary friendships, and the literary environment of prerevolutionary Russia. Index.

_____. *Understanding Chekhov: A Critical Study of Chekhov's Prose and Drama.* Madison: University of Wisconsin Press, 1999. A critical examination of the writings of Chekhov. Index.

Senelick, Laurence. *The Chekhov Theatre: A Century of the Plays in Performance.* New York: Cambridge University Press, 1997. A look at the stage history and production of Chekhov's works.

Hugh Short

LUIGI CHIARELLI

Born: Trani, Italy; July 7, 1880
Died: Rome, Italy; December 20, 1947

PRINCIPAL DRAMA

Una notte d'amore, pr. 1912
Er gendarme, pr. 1912 (with Gino Monaldi)
Extra Dry, pr. 1914, pb. 1926
La maschera e il volto, pr. 1916, pb. 1917 (*The Mask and the Face*, 1927)
La scala di seta, pr. 1917, pb. 1922
Le lacrime e le stelle, pr., pb. 1918
Chimere, pr. 1920, pb. 1921
La morte degli amanti, pr. 1921, pb. 1924
Fuochi d'artificio, pr., pb. 1923 (*Money, Money!*, 1927)
Les Trips à la mode de Caen, pr., pb. 1925
La providente Lucilla, pb. 1928
Jolly, pr. 1928, pb. 1929
Don Juan, pb. 1929
K. 41, pr. 1929, pb. 1930
L'anello di Teodosio, pr., pb. 1929 (radio play)
La reginetta, pb. 1929, pr. 1931
Leggere e scrivere, pb. 1929, pr. 1931
L.E.F., pb. 1930
L'errore necessario, pb. 1930
Scaramanzia, pr., pb. 1931
Un uomo da rifare, pr., pb. 1932
Clara ha ragione, pb. 1932
Carne bianca, pb. 1934
La follia dell'oro, pb. 1935
Una più due, pr., pb. 1935
Il cerchio magico, pr., pb. 1937
Enea come oggi, pb. 1938
Pulcinella, pb. 1939
Ninon, pb. 1940
Enrico VIII, pb. 1941, pr. 1948
Il teatro in fiamme, pr. 1945
Essere, wr. 1946, pr., pb. 1953

OTHER LITERARY FORMS

Although Luigi Chiarelli is best known for his work in the theater, he enjoyed a distinguished career as a journalist as well, later in life becoming a theater and film critic. He also published three volumes of short stories.

ACHIEVEMENTS

Luigi Chiarelli is remembered today as the progenitor of an important concept of theater—*teatro del grottesco,* or Theater of the Grotesque—rather than for his individual plays themselves. Indeed, only one of his plays, *The Mask and the Face*, has attained longevity among theatergoers, critics, and historians of drama, enjoying worldwide acclaim soon after its first performance in May, 1916. Nevertheless, with this play Chiarelli inaugurated the Theater of the Grotesque (the term actually derives from a line in the play), a movement that heralded the twentieth century reaction against the traditional nineteenth century bourgeois drama and had a significant impact on such innovative playwrights as Luigi Pirandello. Along with other plays by Chiarelli that can be classified as "grotesque," *The Mask and the Face* both questioned traditional bourgeois values and awakened anxiety over those values in those who were not yet conscious of their artificiality—hence opening the search in theater for new foundations on which to build a more genuine life, one that could be lived with one's own face instead of a social mask. Chiarelli thus was instrumental in changing the conventional dramatic manifestations of the bourgeois worldview that had dominated the stage for decades, paving the way to a new attitude toward the purpose and practice of theater.

BIOGRAPHY

Born in Trani in the province of Bari in 1880, Luigi Chiarelli soon moved with his family to Rome, where he completed his secondary education. He could not afford to attend a university after his father died, and being the oldest of five children, he went to work in a government office. During this period (1895-1910), he began his youthful attempts at playwriting, composing eight plays that he later disavowed. He also contributed regularly to *L'Alfieri* and *La patria*.

In 1911, Chiarelli left his job to have more time for writing and to become a freelance reporter for the Milanese newspaper *Il secolo*, soon becoming its editor. In Milan, he became acquainted with some of the most prominent Italian dramatic companies, directors, and actors. He continued to write, and finally, in 1912, his two one-act plays *Una notte d'amore* (a night of love) and *Er gendarme* (the policeman) were performed in Bologna and Milan, respectively.

They were well received, although not great successes.

In the summer of the next year, Chiarelli wrote in twenty days his masterpiece, *The Mask and the Face*, which was rejected more than once before its first performance. In 1914, he was editing *Armi e politica* in Turin when he was drafted. He continued to contribute to Italian newspapers during the war, and in May, 1916, he managed to get a pass to go to Rome, where *The Mask and the Face* was premiering with the Compagnia Drammatica di Roma. Three months later, Virgilio Talli, one of the most famous actor-directors of his time, who had previously refused to stage the play, produced it in Milan. The success of *The Mask and the Face* was instantaneous, both with theatergoers and with most critics. Still a soldier, Chiarelli married in the same year.

After the war, Chiarelli continued to write for the theater, but he also translated plays from Latin, Spanish, French, and English, in 1918 starting his own company, Ars Italica. In 1923, he became drama critic for the Rome paper *Corriere italiano*, and in 1924, he presented a project for a national theater at the First National Congress of the Theater. He was twice (in 1925 and in 1945) elected president of the Playwrights Guild and vice president (1929-1930) of the International Authors Association. He often traveled outside Italy to participate in congresses of the International Authors Association and to be present at various productions of *The Mask and the Face*.

In 1928, Chiarelli started painting small landscapes in oils, which he showed in Milan and Geneva in 1930 and in London in 1931. During the last years of his life, he wrote film criticism for the newspaper *Il tempo*, as well as continuing to write plays. He died in Rome, his home since 1937, on December 20, 1947.

ANALYSIS

Among the forty-odd plays that Luigi Chiarelli wrote, there are farces, comedies, political satires, serious bourgeois dramas, melodramas, reworkings of ancient myths, symbolic pieces, and the grotesque plays for which he is best known. Although his efforts at straight comedy and straight drama were less than successful, one can find some dialogue, certain scenes, or entire acts written with flair, distinction, and engaging liveliness. On the whole, however, these works (some of them performed a few times, others unpublished or unperformed) do not succeed in communicating a universal truth or a new artistic vision, and are remembered primarily by students and historians of drama.

Chiarelli's particular talent revealed itself in the plays he wrote at the beginning of his career and on which his reputation as a playwright therefore rests. These plays inaugurated and are an integral part of that Italian dramatic mode known as the Theater of the Grotesque.

Although *The Mask and the Face* is immediately associated with the Theater of the Grotesque—indeed, it has been labeled its manifesto—Chiarelli was neither the most famous nor the most talented among the group of playwrights employing this style in the years surrounding World War I: Pirandello, to name only the most illustrious of several, also wrote in the grotesque style; other dramatists commonly associated with the style Chiarelli inaugurated include Rosso di San Secondo, Luigi Antonelli, and Enrico Cavacchioli. While the giant Pirandello went beyond this style to challenge fundamental concepts of the theater, the others continued for the most part to work within the limits established by Chiarelli.

The circumstances that gave rise to the new dramatic expression in general and to Chiarelli's expression in particular are to be found (as new trends in art often are) in a situation of crisis. This artistic phenomenon was both the response to that crisis and an attempt to overcome it. The crisis was twofold: spiritual and artistic. During World War I and the period immediately preceding it, thoughtful people in Italy and Europe as a whole were experiencing intellectual and moral disorientation. Old institutions remained in force, but they represented old ideals that had lost their authority; the human relationships permitted by the old mores did not fulfill the individual's needs. Indeed, those relationships appeared mechanical and meaningless, and the individual often felt caught in a stagnant daily routine without challenge, growth, or

sense. The artistic crisis consisted of the impasse at which the theater found itself at the beginning of the twentieth century. The dominant dramatic works were in the tradition of Romantic drama, a mimetic theater that for decades had mirrored and mimicked the life of the dominant class, the bourgeoisie. While the realistic theater in France challenged the Romantic tradition by deliberately representing the experience of the lower classes, the revolt in Italy was more extreme, challenging the mimetic element itself: The new playwrights continued to construct "traditional" plots centering on honor, love, and money, with the usual complications and subplots and the traditional characters—husband, wife, and lover—but portrayed these situations and characters with a new, contorted, bizarre twist, rendering plots that confounded theatergoers' expectations. The new plays appeared strange, proportionless, unnatural, unreal—grotesque. This new use of traditional plot situations and characters to evoke unexpected reactions and outcomes was the essence of the new theater and its aim: to raise questions in the minds of theatergoers concerning accepted, but no longer valid, bourgeois values.

Another important influence on the new Italian drama was the centuries-old *commedia dell'arte*. The characters of the new dramatists are at times exaggerated to the point of parody and act in an unrealistic, puppetlike fashion reminiscent of the types of the *commedia dell'arte*. The new drama employed such caricatures to expose the barrenness and rigidity of bourgeois mores.

THE MASK AND THE FACE

Chiarelli's appropriate description of *The Mask and the Face* as a "grotesque" drama gave the name to the new movement. He knew that his play was neither tragedy nor comedy and was aware of the originality of his experiment. His chosen label alludes to the definition of the grotesque in painting used as far back as the sixteenth century by the Renaissance art critic Giorgio Vasari: "monsters deformed by a freak of nature or by the whim and fancy of the workers, who . . . made things outside of any rule." Chiarelli saw the deformation of the traditional play that his own play signified, and so did the critics and audiences in Italy and abroad. The play seemed a "small revolution at home."

The Mask and the Face is a freakish, whimsical, and fanciful mixture: tragedy bordering on the comedic, tears on the brink of laughter. The characters (a count, a magistrate, a lawyer, an artist, and beautiful wives and women), the setting (a rich villa on Lake Como), the situation (a romantic triangle), and the fatuous conversation—all hark back to the traditional bourgeois drama at the play's outset, but toward the end of the first act, the action takes on a less familiar form, one that is both familiar and a caricature of the familiar. The plot clearly shows the double distortion. Count Paolo Grazia discovers that his wife, Savina, has taken a lover on the same evening that he has vowed to his friends (in adherence to the traditional code of honor) that he would kill his wife were she ever to take a lover. Having made this discovery, he finds himself honor-bound to commit murder.

The melodrama requires a death. At this early point in the drama, the coordinates of duty and feeling, ideals and reality, beliefs and impulses, and reason and spontaneity are set at odds. Paolo seizes Savina by the throat but cannot bring himself to kill her. Savina, intuiting his feelings, responds: "Paolo, for heaven's sake, drop this mask. Be sincere with yourself. Look into your heart. Don't be a slave to your words and to your conventional ideas." Paolo is confronted with the fact that he cannot act on his cruel (and stupid) words, which came not from his heart but from the common coin of his culture. Realizing that he has been living according to societal convention, that he has taken his mask at "face" value, he rebels against his acculturation and sends Savina abroad, telling everyone that he has shot her and dumped her in the lake. He then turns himself in to the police. The obvious irony consists of a situation that does not allow for authenticity: Paolo has unknowingly and unconsciously lied to himself and to his friends and neighbors through his mask. Now he is forced to lie to the others again, after he has taken it off.

Act 2 begins when Paolo returns home from his trial, where he has been acquitted owing to a clever

defense by his lawyer friend Luciano Spina, who, unknown to him, is Savina's lover. A crowd of friends (including those who were present on the fatal evening) enthusiastically congratulate him for having avenged the besmirchment of his honor. Some of their wives offer themselves to him. There are also flowers and letters from distant, unknown women who offer him virginal and faithful love and marriage. Paolo is disgusted by the grotesque buffoonery and ridiculousness of it all. The situation becomes even more grotesque when a decomposed body is found in the lake; everyone assumes it is Savina's, and it is brought into the house. Paolo has to acknowledge the corpse and go through the masquerade of his wife's funeral. To this *coup de théâtre* another is added, intensifying the grotesquerie: Savina arrives all the way from London. She has returned to her husband, whom she loves and without whom, she confesses to him, she cannot go on living—it would be better to die. Paolo tries to reject her, but, by the end of act 2, he asks her to wait for him in their former bedroom while he attends to her "funeral." Although Paolo loves his wife and, at the beginning of the act, declares that "men should have more courage, they should cast off the conventionalities which in their pride and vanity they have erected. They should forget all the lies they have uttered, so that finally they can be honest and sincere with themselves," he is not prepared to renounce entirely the role of the implacable husband.

In act 3, on the day after the funeral, Paolo still resists: "The situation is always the same." Savina goads him: "It is only for us to change it. . . . What do all those people matter to you? Why do you still think of subordinating your feelings, your life, your happiness to them?" He is not convinced: "But our life is not made up of ourselves alone." Savina counters by suggesting that in order to become his authentic self, he must throw away his mask and be willing to risk the ridicule of the others: "Above all, we must be ourselves."

Later, while insincere and ceremonious friends are pretending sorrow for the presumedly dead Savina, the live Savina is recognized by Luciano, her former lover, for whom she now feels only contempt. In order to avoid jail for the simulation of a crime, Paolo must run away; he does not want to pay the price for reentering a society in which he does not believe: "I have no longer the slightest desire to render an account of my life to anyone, neither to society, nor to my friends, nor to the law, nor to anyone; I have had enough of it, I want to become. . . ." Here, at the end of the play, Chiarelli adds a last macabre touch: Paolo cannot finish his sentence; he is silenced by "the solemn and measured notes of Chopin's Funeral March" accompanying the funeral procession as it slowly passes by. Is Chiarelli suggesting that Paolo will be able to reenter society only as corpse? Or that only corpses—masks—belong to it? Or that the only thing in life that is worthwhile is the fleeting moment of a kiss, the kiss Paolo gives Savina after the interrupted sentence and just before the curtain falls?

Although some critics claim that the play ends optimistically, it ends neither optimistically nor pessimistically; it ends grotesquely. Seriousness and comedy are so densely and tensely intertwined that the reader and spectator are not able to react in a simple and clear way. Chiarelli himself, who like many authors annotated his own text, stated through Cirillo, his mouthpiece character: "In life next to the most grotesque buffoonery burns the most terrible tragedy; the grin of the most obscene mask covers the most searing passions!"

The mixture of the tragic and the comic in *The Mask and the Face* is well balanced; nowhere does one cancel the other. The audience's interest is always sustained at that thin line that divides tears and laughter. For this reason, the play is difficult to perform, requiring the actors not to identify with the characters; the recitation should be stylized in both the serious and comic lines. That the audience is to identify with neither the serious nor the comic is emphasized by the device of inserting into the play a character who functions as the author's mouthpiece, a device used by all the playwrights of the Theater of the Grotesque. This technique has the effect of continually distancing the audience, preventing it from becoming involved in the emotional content of the action. It was the forerunner of Bertolt Brecht's alienation effect in his epic theater.

PIRANDELLO

It is perhaps too daring, if not simply wrong, to call Chiarelli, as some critics do, Pirandello's spiritual father; nevertheless, it is almost obligatory, when speaking of the Theater of the Grotesque, to consider as well the theater of the great Sicilian, who judged Chiarelli's play a "transcendental farce." In the same year in which *The Mask and the Face* premiered, Pirandello wrote *Pensaci, Giacomino!* (pr. 1916), and in the following year *Il berretto a sonagli* (pr. 1917; *Caps and Bells*, 1957) and *Il piacere dell'onestà* (pr. 1917; *The Pleasure of Honesty*, 1923) were premiered. These plays share some concerns and some devices of the Theater of the Grotesque: All three deal with the conflict between the individual and deadening social duties; the point of reference of the plays is the triangle of husband-wife-lover, and the author inserts himself in the lines of the play; the characters must shed their imposed or self-imposed masks in order to discover their faces. Although Chiarelli and the other playwrights of the new mode always dealt with a struggle against society in the belief that a face—a real self—did, after all, exist, Pirandello took a different route, his interests not aimed at the confrontation between the individual and society but at the division in the individual himself. In Pirandello's mature vision, there are not necessarily faces under the masks but simply "naked masks"—the title he gave to his entire theatrical œuvre. In fact, he suggests that there is no self. In the works of Chiarelli and the other new Italian dramatists, humankind confronts human emptiness and social disorder; in Pirandello, humankind confronts sheer chaos and void.

CHIMERE AND LA MORTE DEGLI AMANTI

Chiarelli composed four other plays which follow closely the spirit of the new Theater of the Grotesque, but he never again achieved that felicitous moment of inspiration, that equilibrium of opposites that enlivened his original and successful drama. These also deal with the interplay of mask and face. *Chimere* (chimeras) and *La morte degli amanti* (the lovers' death) present the usual triangle, but while Paolo and Savina, in their epiphany, come to know a self nobler than a mask, the protagonists of these two plays undergo degradation. Claudio and Marina, the couple in *Chimere*, discover that the ideals of virtue and honor by which they thought they were living are only chimeras. *La morte degli amanti* is a caricature of romantic love and death. The lovers, whose operatic names are Alfredo and Eleonora, want to kill themselves to give a grandiose ending to their grand passion, now that her husband knows. When the husband arrives at the suicide scene, all ends in ridicule: The wife goes back to him and the lover finds someone else to love.

LA SCALA DI SETA

La scala di seta (the silken ladder) depicts moral corruption. The mask is represented by the superficial and silly Désiré, a dancer who climbs the "silken ladder" of success. He marries the wealthy daughter of a minister of the government and, entering politics himself, also becomes a minister. His gentle and honest antagonist Roberto is a failure.

MONEY, MONEY!

Money, Money! is a better comedy, second only to *The Mask and the Face*. Count Gerardo, back from the United States without an American fortune, confides to his friend Scaramanzia, who is accompanying him, that he is thinking of suicide. Scaramanzia is able to make people believe the count is a millionaire and, by means of clever trickery, makes a real fortune for him. Thus, appearance becomes reality.

SCARAMANZIA

Chiarelli wrote in other dramatic modes, from farcical to symbolic. Perhaps reminded of past success, he entitled a one-act play *Scaramanzia*, but the former trickster is now a pathetic hunchback who secretly and hopelessly writes love letters to beautiful Nuccia, signing them with the name of her handsome fiancé. She does not know that her beloved is in jail— he has told her that he is at the university. The ugly hunchback, who cannot bear to see Nuccia ruin her

life for a criminal, kills him when he comes out of jail, then writes her a farewell letter, signing it, as he has signed the others, with her lover's name.

ESSERE

Chiarelli's last play, *Essere*, seems vaguely and strangely to recall Pirandello's *Sei personaggi in cerca d'autore* (pr., pb. 1921; *Six Characters in Search of an Author*, 1922). Six travelers at a station are eager and anxious to take a train for the capital; they are not human beings but ghostlike creatures— instincts, subconscious impulses—and they want to live. The stationmaster is the father of them all. Trains pass in vain—they cannot embark. Only a foolish common man was once able to escape. When he now comes back and tells the other six he is disillusioned by the experience of his life, they nevertheless retain their desire "to be."

OTHER MAJOR WORKS

SHORT FICTION: *La mano di Venere*, 1935; *La figlia dell'aria*, 1939; *Karakè*, 1944.

BIBLIOGRAPHY

Berghaus, Günter. *Italian Futurist Theatre, 1909-1944*. Oxford, England: Clarendon Press, 1998. A look at Italian theater during the time in which Chiarelli was active. Bibliography and index.

Vena, Michael. *Italian Grotesque Theater*. Cranbury, N.J.: Associated University Presses, 2001. Contains an introduction to and translation of Chiarelli's *The Mask and the Face*, along with two other plays from the Italian grotesque theater. Bibliography and index.

_____. "Luigi Chiarelli (1880-1947): Profile of a Playwright." *Connecticut Review 7* (1974): 59-63. A concise presentation of Chiarelli's life and works.

Emanuele Licastro

CHIKAMATSU MONZAEMON
Sugimori Nobumori

Born: Fukui, Echizen Province, Japan; 1653
Died: Sakai, Japan; January 6, 1725

PRINCIPAL DRAMA

Yotsugi Soga, pr. 1683, pb. 1896

Shusse Kagekiyo, pr. 1686, pb. 1890

Semimaru, pr. 1686 (English translation, 1978)

Sonezaki shinjū, pr. 1703 (*The Love Suicides at Sonezaki*, 1961)

Yōmei Tennō Shokunin Kagami, pr. 1705

Horikawa nami no tsuzumi, pr. 1706 (*The Drum of the Waves of Horikawa*, 1961)

Shinjū Kasaneizutsu, pr. 1707

Tamba Yosaku, pr. 1708 (*Yosaku from Tamba*, 1961)

Shinjū Mannensō, pr. 1708 (*The Love Suicides in the Women's Temple*, 1961)

Keisei Hangokō, pr. 1708

Meido no hikyaku, pr. 1711 (*The Courier for Hell*, 1961)

Yugiri Awa no Naruto, pr. 1712

Kokusenya kassen, pr. 1715 (*The Battles of Coxinga*, 1951)

Yari no Gonza, pr. 1717 (*Gonza the Lancer*, 1961)

Nebiki no kadomatsu, pr. 1718 (*The Uprooted Pine*, 1961)

Soga kaikeizan, pr. 1718 (*The Soga Revenge*, 1929)

Heike nyogo no shima, pr. 1719 (English translation, 1979)

Hakata Kojorō Namimakura, pr. 1719 (*The Girl from Hakata: Or, Love at Sea*, 1961)

Futago sumidagawa, pr. 1720 (*Twins at the Sumida River*, 1982)

Tsu no kuni meoto-ike, pr. 1721 (*Lovers Pond in Settsu Province*, 1992)

Shinsu kawa-nakajima kassen, pr. 1721 (*Battles at Kawa-nakajima*, 1992)

Shinjū ten no Amijima, pr. 1721 (*The Love Suicides at Amijima*, 1953)

Onnagoroshi: Abura jigoku, pr. 1721 (*The Woman-Killer and the Hell of Oil*, 1961)

Shuju Yoigoshin, pr. 1722 (*Love Suicides on the Eve of the Koshin Festival*, 1992)

Kanhasshu tsunagi-uma, pr. 1724 (*Tethered Steed and the Eight Provinces of Kanto*, 1992)

Major Plays of Chikamatsu, pb. 1961

Chikamatsu: Five Late Plays, pb. 2001

OTHER LITERARY FORMS

Chikamatsu Monzaemon is known primarily for his plays.

ACHIEVEMENTS

Chikamatsu Monzaemon took the *jōruri* puppet theater, the leading popular theatrical form of his day, and through his own dramatic and poetic skill lifted a plebeian art form to the heights of serious drama. In this accomplishment, he brought changes to the theater of his age as significant as those achieved by Zeami Motokiyo in the medieval Nō theater several centuries earlier. The range of his writing, from political dramas on Chinese and Japanese themes to intimate stories about the domestic life of his contemporary society, has given him the nickname of the Japanese William Shakespeare. The two societies were sufficiently different that the appellation cannot hold; nevertheless, the comparison does suggest the power of Chikamatsu's theatrical creations to hold the attention of audiences down to the present day. Widely admired and often copied, Chikamatsu remains the most important figure in the Japanese theater from the seventeenth century to modern times, when his works have been adapted for the modern stage and for films as well with great success.

BIOGRAPHY

Despite Chikamatsu Monzaemon's enormous popularity, few details about his life are clear that do not relate directly to his theatrical activities. Born Sugimori Nobumori, his exact place and date of birth and death are still contested, and little is known of his early education, except from the internal evidence of the plays, which reveals his real familiarity with Chinese philosophical writings and Japanese Buddhist texts, as well as a love of Japanese classical prose and poetry. Chikamatsu began writing plays for both the puppet theater and then later for live actors (in Kabuki), but he spent the major part of his career working in the puppet theater, particularly at the Takemotoza in Osaka; a number of his great plays were written for that performing group. When his patron Takemoto Gidayū died in 1714, Chikamatsu, by then an experienced writer of sixty-one, decided to help the new head of the troupe to continue and, putting forth his best efforts, wrote a half dozen of his greatest plays in the next and final decade of his active life. The exact circumstances of his last years are unknown, and details about his domestic life are few and contradictory. What is known of the man is derived from his art.

ANALYSIS

Although Western writers tend to use the world "play" or "drama" in describing the work of Chikamatsu Monzaemon, some explanation of the word *jōruri* will be helpful in understanding Chikamatsu's accomplishments, as well as his inevitable limitations. When Chikamatsu began his career, there were no troupes of live actors performing any kind of real dramatic spectacle. Rather, chanters of various sorts of stories, usually historical accounts of the Japanese medieval wars, considerably embellished, began to use musical accompaniment, simple puppets (worked by multiple handlers from below), and scenery to illustrate their accounts. The very name *jōruri*, which defines the genre, is taken from the name of one of those historical embellishments, a fictional princess who supposedly fell in love with Yoshitsune, the celebrated general who died during the civil wars in 1185 and who remained one of the great cultural heroes of the Japanese tradition. During the period prior to Chikamatsu's ascendancy, various chanters (all of whom wrote their own texts) tried adapting certain features from the elegant medieval Nō theater in order to give their popular stories more shape and substance. When Takemoto Gidayū himself decided to commission the young Chikamatsu to compose a

text for him to perform, a new tradition was begun, for up until that time, no "playwright" as such had ever been used. This new division of labor helped increase enormously the potential for literary expression.

Reading a translation of a Chikamatsu play, Westerners will find the structure of dialogue plus narrator relatively familiar, yet it must be remembered that in Chikamatsu's time, one performer chanted all the roles and created all the voices. This bravura aspect of the performance was an important consideration in the planning and organization of the texts and gives *jōruri* a resemblance to Western opera, where certain conventions are also embedded in the text. This is one limitation placed on Chikamatsu's art, and yet, on the whole, it was one with which he could live comfortably as he was in control of the script. Chikamatsu also experimented at various points in his career with writing for Kabuki actors, theatrical groups that had begun to perform dramas in the large cities. The actors had a tendency to change Chikamatsu's lines, however, and so he returned to writing for the puppet theater and continued to do so for most of his career. The Kabuki theater, indeed, grew up in the shadow of the *jōruri* puppet theater and imitated its style in many important respects, including the stylization of physical movement. By the middle of the eighteenth century, the Kabuki had become more popular than the *jōruri*; efforts were made in the early nineteenth century to win back audiences to the puppet theater (by then called Bunraku), but the actor's theater continued in its ascendancy. By that time, the actors often performed Chikamatsu's dramas as though they had been written for them, but, in fact, virtually all of Chikamatsu's great works were composed for the puppet stage.

During the early years of his career, Chikamatsu tended to write dramas on historical themes, adapted from various chronicles or from medieval Nō dramas. In 1703, he wrote a play about contemporary life, *The Love Suicides at Sonezaki*, and after the success of that experiment, his writings began to encompass both styles.

Chikamatsu's audiences in his mature years were almost completely made up of the merchant class in

Osaka, the center of protobourgeois culture in Japan during that period. Because of strict social class barriers imposed by the Tokugawa shoguns since shortly after 1600, the merchants were cut off from higher forms of culture, yet came to have the money, the leisure, and, eventually, the cultivation to pursue artistic interests and pastimes. Therefore, both types of plays written by Chikamatsu appealed greatly to them: The history plays (*jidaimono*) served as a means to teach them about the glories and complexities of the Japanese past, both in the court and in military circles, and the domestic dramas (*sewamono*) provided them with a powerful glimpse into the intimacies of the world that they themselves inhabited. For modern audiences, these domestic dramas, which deal with the vicissitudes of the personal lives of the townspeople, still possess an emotional reality that is compelling. For all the differences between the urban society at the time of Chikamatsu and now, there are certain powerful similarities, which make the domestic dramas both appealing and poignant even today. In fact, Chikamatsu may have been the first major dramatist to make ordinary men and women, with all their foibles and weaknesses, the protagonists of tragic drama. A dramatist such as George Lillo in eighteenth century England attempted to do the same sort of thing in his play *The London Merchant: Or, The History of George Barnwell* (pr., pb. 1731), but it was not until much later that such characters were regularly portrayed in a sympathetic fashion on the European stage. For a modern reader, Chikamatsu may often seem closer to an Arthur Miller than to a Shakespeare.

As the historical dramas of Chikamatsu were always drawn from actual events in the past, so the domestic dramas, too, were taken from real events in Japanese society, often dramatized as soon after the fact as possible. In a special way, these domestic plays served as living newspapers, which presented accounts of lurid or sensational events adapted for their theatrical effectiveness. The attraction for the audience of such plays thus lay far less in the "plot" of the events portrayed, which they knew at least in outline, than in experiencing the art with which Chikamatsu reworked his material. Much ink has been

spilled over the question as to whether Chikamatsu was a "realist," in a contemporary sense of the world. The playwright himself put these questions to rest in an eloquent statement he made during the course of an interview that was published after his death. When asked about the need to create an art that would resemble reality closely, he replied that art and reality were not the same. Pure realism "does not take into account the real methods of art. Art is something which lies in the slender margin between the real and the unreal . . . and entertainment lies between the two." To a modern reader, it is clear that both the artifice of the puppets and the beauty of Chikamatsu's language (and here he most resembles Shakespeare) could lift the most banal, even sordid, "reality" to great heights of genuine pathos.

THE BATTLES OF COXINGA

Of the history plays, the only drama available in full translation is Chikamatsu's most successful effort, *The Battles of Coxinga*, first performed in 1715 and undoubtedly his most popular work. The play concerns the exploits of Coxinga, a famous hero in Japanese history who was involved in the battles surrounding the fall of the Ming Dynasty in China, about a century or so before the composition of the play. His exploits had become legendary, and the play contains a number of incidents from his complex career juxtaposed and embellished to make as brilliant a series of effects as possible. Read on the page, the text seems full of bombast and arbitrary confrontations, but seen in performance, *The Battles of Coxinga* provides a series of striking vignettes that exploit the possibilities of the puppet stage to their fullest. It has often been said that audiences were particularly excited by *The Battles of Coxinga* because it dealt with the exotic Chinese scenes at a time when, because of the policies of the Tokugawa shogunate, the Japanese themselves were no longer allowed to travel abroad. Whatever the reason, the scenes of China and Chinese life presented make up in color and fantasy what they may lack in historical veracity.

The play opens at the court of the Ming emperor in Nanking. He is portrayed as a weak man, surrounded by corrupt ministers; only one, Go Sankei, argues for justice, but he cannot stop the rout of the imperial forces by the enemy Tartars. The emperor is murdered. Go Sankei manages to escape with the empress, who is pregnant with the child who will carry on the imperial line; when she in turn is killed, he exchanges his own newborn child for hers, so that the imperial line may continue. Go Sankei then sends the imperial princess off on a boat so that she can escape the battle and, he hopes, reach Japan. This first act, like the rest of the play, is filled with devices that call to mind the most outrageous Jacobean tragedies: Eyes are gouged out; babies are torn from the womb. With actors, the effect would be merely grotesque; with puppets, the results seem larger than life and quite heroic.

In the second act, Coxinga (who is half Japanese and half Chinese) is quietly fishing and thinking on the fate of the Ming court, where his father had been a high-ranking minister. When the princess drifts to shore in her boat, Coxinga and his Japanese wife decide that he should travel to China to attempt to keep the Ming Dynasty from collapse. In this section of the play, Coxinga's speeches are a model of powerful eloquence, indeed, grandiloquence. The subsequent scenes contain a combination of battles and adventures, including a fight with a tiger that must have taxed the original producers considerably. Coxinga now begins to gather around him brave Chinese who wish to fight the Tartars as well.

In act 3, Coxinga meets his half sister, and after a complex series of maneuvers, he manages to win both her and her husband, a general, to his side. Again, the actions are, like the language employed, far larger than life. In act 4, Go Sankei, still attempting to escape the Tartar soldiers, leads the young imperial prince to a mystical mountain summit where the Nine Immortals of China look out over the destinies of the nation. Coxinga appears, and the two unite for a final victory, helped by the Immortals, who build a sort of rainbow bridge to help them escape from the attacking enemy. When the villainous soldiers rush across, the bridge dissolves and they are crushed below at the foot of the mountain. The final act of the play brings all the contending forces together. The evil minister is captured, and Coxinga and his allies are triumphant.

Described in such a fashion, the play may seem merely bombastic, but it possesses a beauty and excitement in the original that in some fashion may call to mind the effect of a play such as Christopher Marlowe's *Tamburlaine the Great* (pr. c. 1587). As noted above, the play is meant to be larger than life, both in its language and as a theatrical event. At the same time, even within this heroic framework, Chikamatsu manages moments of humor and whimsy that are on a wholly human scale. In terms of high entertainment, the play is unsurpassed. Indeed, Chikamatsu's formula for success—a mixture of the nationalistic, the exotic, and the poetic—is one that has succeeded in most cultures.

OTHER HISTORICAL DRAMAS

Most of Chikamatsu's other historical dramas deal with events in earlier Japanese history, with stories taken either from the world of the Heian court in the eleventh century or from the medieval war period that followed. Again, bombastic generals and sophisticated courtiers are brought to life in complicated plots that allow for a full range of fantasy in setting, action, and language. Some plays use earlier dramas and expand on them. A notable case in point is that of Chikamatsu's *Semimaru*, which uses the Nō drama of Zeami by the same title as a centerpiece and then extends the story backward and forward until a full evening of intrigue and adventure is created. Again the audience, doubtless familiar with the original drama, took pleasure less from the tale of the blind prince than from the variations that Chikamatsu played on a legend already known. Modern audiences often find these historical dramas somewhat unsatisfying because of their general and diffuse nature, in which plots and subplots often relate to each other in only the most general way. Then too, the cultural knowledge on the part of spectators that could bind these elements together has been lost, so that modern Japanese audiences are practically at as much of a loss as Western spectators or readers in catching the subtle implications of Chikamatsu's juxtapositions.

DOMESTIC DRAMAS

It is perhaps for reasons such as these that, in the twentieth century at least, Chikamatsu's reputation has shifted from his historical to his domestic plays, which now have taken on new value. Original audiences could take much for granted in these plays. Now, because of Chikamatsu's faithful renderings of certain details of Tokugawa life and culture, modern viewers can savor the atmosphere of a quite different time through the means of these dramas, which, although often melodramatic and arbitrary in plot structure, contain the kind of elegant language and emotional commitment on the part of the author that make the situations powerfully touching.

THE LOVE SUICIDES AT SONEZAKI

The first of the domestic plays, *The Love Suicides at Sonezaki*, was written twelve years before *The Battles of Coxinga*. The play was evidently written to serve as a kind of interlude for a longer historical drama, and in its three brief scenes, Chikamatsu portrayed a highly poetic version of the suicide of the two young lovers. In Tokubei, the shop attendant, Chikamatsu created what may be the first modern hero—weak, vacillating, yet capable of being aroused to righteous fury. He is in love with a courtesan from the licensed quarters, Ohatsu, who works in a teahouse, actually a kind of elegant brothel sanctioned by the Tokugawa authorities. Forced to part from her by the machinations of the evil Kuheiji, Tokubei decides to "show all Osaka the purity at the bottom of my heart," and the couple vow to commit suicide together. Their parting moments in the teahouse, filled with little touches of realism provided by the minor servants and other characters, are nicely portrayed, and the final scene, when the lovers journey to their death at the Sonezaki Shrine, is one of the most sustained examples of lyric writing in the Japanese theater. Through the device of the narrator, Chikamatsu solves the problem that has plagued all writers of realistic theater who have sought for a way for characters of limited education and insight to speak with eloquence. The great poetry is here provided by the narrator, who takes the audience both inside the thoughts of the characters (who actually say very little) and then back into the realm of philosophical, in particular Buddhist, speculation. The death of the lovers is both touching and convincing. With this play, Chikamatsu successfully created a new genre of drama, and, at least in the final scene, achieved a

standard of poetic excellence that he later equaled, but never surpassed.

As his career continued, Chikamatsu went on to develop the genre of the domestic play, adding new elements and more complex plots, so that, rather than serving as interludes during longer performances of historical dramas, the domestic plays came to stand as independent and complete works in themselves. Quite often the plays were written about incidents that took place in the licensed quarters, such as *The Uprooted Pine*, but others dealt with adultery, murder, and piracy, even life in a Buddhist monastery.

THE LOVE SUICIDES AT AMIJIMA

Chikamatsu's greatest achievement in this genre, however, is surely his play *The Love Suicides at Amijima*, written in 1721, just at the end of his career. Performed countless times by puppet troupes and by Kabuki companies as well, the play has both been adapted for the modern stage and made the subject of a famous film. *The Love Suicides at Amijima* is often considered to be the greatest single work written for the traditional Japanese stage. Like Chikamatsu's first domestic play, *The Love Suicides at Sonezaki*, *The Love Suicides at Amijima* builds its complex plot on a simple story of a weak but good-hearted man who falls in love with a courtesan and decides to die with her. In the later play, however, which is in three acts, the playwright has provided a whole network of minor characters and situations that flesh out the action and render the outcome all the more moving and inevitable. As with the other plays of this sort, Chikamatsu based his drama on a series of actual events and evidently went to considerable trouble to learn certain details of the incident before composing his text.

The earlier play, *The Love Suicides at Sonezaki*, shows poetic excellence, but *The Love Suicides at Amijima* is graced as well with a certain elegiac tonality that can only be described as religious. Even the title itself in the original Japanese contains a hint of Buddhist salvation, since the place-name Amijima can be rendered as the "island of nets," a reference to the image that depicts Buddha catching the innocent and the sinful alike in his nets to haul them up to paradise.

In the first act, Jihei, the paper merchant, is in love with the courtesan Koharu, in defiance of his wife and her relatives. There is also a villain who vies for Koharu's affections, Tahei. Within this simple basic structure, Chikamatsu weaves a number of new elements to add emotional complexity. A mysterious samurai, who remonstrates with Jihei about his debauchery, later turns out to be his brother. Later, in the second act, Jihei learns that his wife, Osan, has been instrumental in attempting to separate him from Koharu, but in a stunning twist, he manages to persuade his wife to allow him to ransom Koharu to save her from the advances of Tahei. Jihei's parents-in-law suddenly arrive and, shocked by his behavior, decide to take their daughter Osan back home with them. In the final act, Jihei decides to commit suicide with Koharu. He pays his debts and leads her away. As in *The Love Suicides at Sonezaki*, the language of this last act is particularly powerful. The lovers lament their fate, and, by implication, the power of the society that has forced them to part. Through the power of his language and imagery, Chikamatsu allows the pair to make a kind of transcendental spiritual pilgrimage to a realm where obligations can be cast aside, and where the two can live as Buddhist priest and nun, "to escape the inconstant world." As the priests at a nearby temple begin their chant at dawn, Jihei puts Koharu to death, then does away with himself. His body, washed out to sea, is picked up by the fishermen in their nets.

In terms of consistency of characterization and power of imagery, *The Love Suicides at Amijima* remains a superb example of the possibilities of *jōruri*. For a modern reader, the form certainly has limitations. Characters are seldom ambiguous, since the heads used for the puppets have fixed expressions which reveal the general nature of the character being portrayed. Then too, since the puppets are lifeless, the text prepared for the chanter must be strong, even strident, in order to make up for the lack of interior life in the dolls themselves. The social mores of the time, particularly those pertaining to the licensed quarters, are sufficiently removed from those of modern life to make the passions of the various characters seem overwrought and, occasionally, downright out-

landish. Nevertheless, a play like *The Love Suicides at Amijima* still rings true, whatever the problems of historical distance, because of the power of Chikamatsu's language and his commitment to an understanding of what were, for him, situations of genuine dignity and pathos within the context of his own society.

BIBLIOGRAPHY

Brazell, Karen, ed. *Traditional Japanese Theater: An Anthology of Plays*. New York: Columbia University Press, 1998. Includes one of Chikamatsu's love suicide plays as well as introductions describing the genre and the specific play.

Gerstle, C. Andrew. *Circles of Fantasy: Convention in the Plays of Chikamatsu*. Cambridge, Mass.: Harvard University Press, 1986. A study of the plays of Chikamatsu, focusing on literary conventions. Bibliography and index.

_____. "Heroic Honor: Chikamatsu and the Samurai Ideal." *Harvard Journal of Asiatic Studies* 57, no. 2 (December, 1997): 307-381. A look at the samurai in the play *Kanhasshu tsunagi-uma* (*Tethered Steed and the Eight Provinces of Kanto*).

Heine, Steve. "Tragedy and Salvation in the Floating World: Chikamatsu's Double Suicide Drama as Millenarian Discourse." *The Journal of Asian Studies* 53, no. 2 (May, 1994): 367. Chikamatsu's dramas are examined in the light of Buddhist and Confucian theology regarding double suicide.

Kominz, Laurence R. *Avatars of Vengeance: Japanese Drama and the Soga Literary Tradition*. Ann Arbor: Center for Japanese Studies, University of Michigan, 1995. An examination of the story of the Soga brothers' failed vendetta through its retelling in Nō, Kabuki, and Bunraku. Chikamatsu wrote thirteen plays about the Soga brothers.

Pringle, Patricia, ed. *An Interpretive Guide to Bunraku*. Honolulu: University of Hawaii at Manoa, 1992. Essays examine various aspects of the puppet theater, particularly Chikamatsu's *The Love Suicides at Sonezaki*.

Sakamoto, Edward. "The Ancient Artistry of Bunraku: A Japanese Puppet Theater Keeps a Four-

Hundred-Year-Old Tradition Alive." *Los Angeles Times*, September 25, 1988, p. 3. An introduction to Bunraku and Chikamatsu written on the occasion of the Bunraku Puppet Theatre of Osaka performing one of Chikamatsu's works in Los Angeles.

Sasayama, Takashi, J. R. Mulryne, and Margaret Shewring, eds. *Shakespeare and the Japanese Stage*. New York: Cambridge University Press, 1999. Contains a comparison of Chikamatsu and William Shakespeare.

J. Thomas Rimer

ALICE CHILDRESS

Born: Charleston, South Carolina; October 12, 1916
Died: Queens, New York; August 14, 1994

PRINCIPAL DRAMA

Florence, pr. 1949, pb. 1950
Just a Little Simple, pr. 1950
Gold Through the Trees, pr. 1952
Trouble in Mind, pr. 1955, pb. 1971
Wedding Band: A Love/Hate Story in Black and White, pr. 1966 (staged), pr. 1973 (televised), pb. 1973
The World on a Hill, pb. 1968
Wine in the Wilderness, pr. 1969 (televised), pb. 1969, pr. 1976 (staged)
String, pr. 1969 (staged), pb. 1971, pr. 1979 (televised; adaptation of a Guy de Maupassant story)
The Freedom Drum, pr. 1969 (music by Nathan Woodard, retitled *Young Martin Luther King*)
Mojo: A Black Love Story, pr. 1970, pb. 1971
When the Rattlesnake Sounds, pb. 1975 (for children)
Let's Hear It for the Queen, pb. 1976 (for children)
Sea Island Song, pr. 1979 (with Woodward; pr. 1984 as *Gullah*)
Moms: A Praise Play for a Black Comedienne, pr. 1987 (with Woodard)

OTHER LITERARY FORMS

Although she wrote many plays, Alice Childress is perhaps better known for her young adult novels, especially *A Hero Ain't Nothin' but a Sandwich* (1973). Childress wrote the screenplay for the film based on this book, which premiered in 1978. Her other novels include *Rainbow Jordan* (1981) and *Those Other People* (1989), both for young adults, and *A Short Walk* (1979).

ACHIEVEMENTS

Alice Childress's *Gold Through the Trees* was the first play by an African American woman to be produced professionally with union actors. In 1956 Childress became the first woman to receive an Obie Award, for *Trouble in Mind*. She was appointed to the Radcliffe Institute (now the Mary Ingraham Bunting Institute) for Independent Study (1966-1968) and was awarded a graduate medal for writing produced there. Her novel *A Hero Ain't Nothin' but a Sandwich* was named the ALA Best Young Adult Book of 1975, and it received the Jane Addams Award for a young adult novel in 1974.

BIOGRAPHY

Alice Childress was five years old when her parents separated and she was sent to live with her maternal grandmother, who had seven children of her own. Although Grandmother Eliza was a poverty-stricken former slave with only a fifth-grade education, she was intellectually curious and self-educated. Childress credited her grandmother with teaching her how to observe and encouraging her to write. Her grandmother also took her to Salem Church in Harlem, where Alice learned storytelling from the Wednesday night testimonials. Childress was educated in New York public schools, leaving before she graduated from high school. She encountered racial prejudice at school but recalled several teachers who made a difference, encouraging her to read and introducing her to the library.

Childress revealed little about her private life, but it is known that she married and divorced Alvin Childress, who played Amos on television's *Amos 'n' Andy Show*. The couple had a daughter, Jean, born on November 1, 1935, who was raised by her mother. To support herself and her child while she tried to establish her writing and acting career, Childress held a variety of jobs, including domestic servant, salesperson, and insurance agent. Through these jobs, she became acquainted with numerous working-class people, whose lives became the basis of characters in her later plays and novels.

In 1941 Childress joined the American Negro Theatre (ANT), which met in the Schomburg Library in Harlem. Like all ANT members, Childress participated in all aspects of theater, though her main interest was acting. She stayed with ANT for eleven years but was frustrated by the emphasis on issues important to black men and the consequent neglect of black women's issues and roles. When she tried to act in the theater at large, she ran into problems because she was considered too light-skinned to play black roles but not fair enough to play whites. Although she starred in the Broadway production of *Anna Lucasta* (1944-1946) and did some work in radio and television, Childress finally concluded that she would be better able to express herself as a writer.

Interested in creating complex and realistic black female characters, Childress wrote *Florence*, a one-act play that she hoped would show that African American drama did not have to be sensational to be significant. This drama, about a working-class black woman on her way to New York to rescue her daughter from a failed career in the theater, opened new areas to African American theater, eventually influencing Amiri Baraka's Black Revolutionary Theater and woman-centered African American dramatists such as Ntozake Shange. Childress's next plays did not focus on women, however. One was a reworking of Langston Hughes's serialized articles, *Simple Speaks His Mind*, published in the *Chicago Defender*, as a musical review titled *Just a Little Simple*.

In 1955, Childress returned to her controversial subjects and assertive black women characters with *Trouble in Mind*, a play about a black actress trying to maintain her dignity while playing menial roles. The play was well received Off-Broadway, but Broadway options were abandoned because producers considered it too risky for the commercial theater. It was presented twice by the British Broadcasting Corporation (BBC), however. Childress received the Obie Award for *Trouble in Mind* in 1956, becoming the first woman to receive the award.

Also in 1956, Childress published *Like One of the Family: Conversations from a Domestic's Life*, a series of vignettes or monologues that incorporated sketches from her *Baltimore Afro-American* column "Here's Mildred," which she would write through 1958. The column and book centered on Mildred, a domestic servant modeled on Childress's aunt. On July 17, 1957, she married a musician named Nathan Woodward. She and Woodward collaborated on a number of projects; he wrote music for her play *Sea Island Song*, later produced as *Gullah*.

During the 1960's, Childress focused on writing plays. She chose to ignore white audiences and focused on controversial topics, which made production difficult. During this period, she wrote *Wedding Band: A Love/Hate Story in Black and White*, which focused on interracial lovers; *The Freedom Drum* (later retitled *Young Martin Luther King*); *String*, an adaptation of Guy de Maupassant's story "A Piece of String"; and *Wine in the Wilderness*, on revolution and black males' problematic attitudes toward black women.

Also during this period, Childress participated in a variety of communities of writers and scholars. In 1965 she was part of a BBC panel discussion, "The Negro in American Theater," which also included James Baldwin, LeRoi Jones (Amiri Baraka), and Langston Hughes. The writer Tillie Olsen recommended Childress for an appointment at the Radcliffe Institute for Independent Study, where she worked on her writing from 1966 to 1968.

During the 1970's Childress traveled extensively to study drama and other arts: to the Soviet Union in 1971; to Beijing and Shanghai, China, in 1973; and to

Alice Childress in 1991. (Ray Grist)

Ghana, West Africa, in 1974. She also shifted the focus of her own writing at this time, producing a young adult novel, *A Hero Ain't Nothin' but a Sandwich* and its screenplay; two plays for children, *When the Rattlesnake Sounds*, about a summer in the life of escaped slave Harriet Tubman, and *Let's Hear It for the Queen*; and *A Short Walk*, a novel. Also in 1979, Childress's play *Sea Island Song*, which had been commissioned by the South Carolina Arts Commission, was presented in Columbia and Charleston, South Carolina, during the observance of Alice Childress Week.

In the 1980's, Childress continued to write and speak out. She wrote her second young adult novel, *Rainbow Jordan*, in 1981. She was artist-in-residence at the University of Massachusetts, Amherst, in 1984. Her final works were *Moms: A Praise Play for a Black Comedienne*, based on the life of comedienne "Moms" Mabley, and a novel, *Those Other People*. Her daughter Jean died of cancer in May, 1990. Four years later, Childress died of cancer, in Queens.

ANALYSIS

Alice Childress's playwriting career spanned four decades, an achievement in itself. Even more impor-

tant, she broke with tradition followed by both male and female playwrights, which held that significant African American drama dealt with sensational topics such as lynching and focused on male concerns such as the disenfranchisement of the black man. Childress chose instead to write about the concerns of black women. A major theme is the female psychological journey; it applies equally to her domestics such as Mildred in *Like One of the Family* and disappointed artists such as Wiletta Mayer in *Trouble in Mind*.

Childress addressed issues of gender and race through her black female characters. She worked against stereotypes prevalent in both black and white American literature to present ordinary women—strong, searching for their identities, and standing up to prejudices based on class, gender, and race. Even when she wrote about controversial topics such as miscegenation, her characters and the situations mere realistic and believable. Her explorations laid the groundwork for later African American women playwrights such as Ntozake Shange and Sonia Sanchez.

Childress's unwillingness to compromise her principles or play to white audience cost her in terms of production and visibility. However, she attracted the attention of feminist scholars in the 1980's and 1990's, and she has always had the attention of African American theater people. Elizabeth Brown-Guillory calls her the mother of African American professional theater, and the debt that those who followed her owe to her pioneering work in presenting realistic and complex black women characters supports that title.

TROUBLE IN MIND

Childress uses two tried and true theatrical devices in *Trouble in Mind*—a play-within-a-play and metadrama, focusing on an examination of theater itself. Placed in the larger context of the Civil Rights movement, with allusions to Rosa Parks and Martin

Luther King, Jr., the play features Wiletta Mayer, a veteran actress who has been cast in an antilynching drama written by a white playwright. Although Wiletta and the other veteran black actors have been conditioned to accept the denigrating conditions of working in white-controlled theater, she cannot justify her character's advising her son to give himself up to a lynch mob. When she argues against the play and its portrayal of blacks, the cast is dismissed with the clear implication that Wiletta will not be called for the next rehearsal. The play-within-the-play, however, has made clear the problems of stereotypes of African Americans.

WEDDING BAND

This play about the ten-year romantic relationship of a black seamstress, Julia, and a white baker, Herman, was not well received either by blacks, who saw it as integrationist, or whites, who were offended by the topic of miscegenation. In the world of the play, Julia receives little support from her black neighbors, who do not see her relationship with Herman as positive in any way, or from Herman's mother and sister, who make racist comments and try to sabotage the relationship. When Herman develops influenza, collapsing in Julia's home, the situation is serious because the same laws that have prevented Julia and Herman's marriage will result in their prosecution if the relationship is discovered. Julia calls in Herman's mother, but instead of help, she gets abuse. She does stand up to her, though, claiming her place as her daughter-in-law. The play examines problematic relationships between black and white women and between black women themselves, as well as the interracial love relationship.

WINE IN THE WILDERNESS

Wine in the Wilderness is set in the apartment of a middle-class black artist during a 1960's Harlem riot. Childress depicts the arrogance and ignorance of the black middle class in the artist's treatment of a young lower-class black woman, Tommy (Tomorrow Marie). The artist, Bill, has been working on a triptych dedicated to black womanhood—as Bill understands it. He has completed two of the panels, one depicting "innocent" black girlhood, the second a beautiful, regal woman representing an idealized Mother Africa.

He has been looking for a model for the third panel—the "lost" black woman of his imagination, rude and vulgar, the antithesis of the African queen. His neighbors find Tommy during the riot, and she, believing that she is to be the model for an ideal woman in the artist's work, goes with them to his apartment. When she realizes the truth, she confronts the group. Finally Bill understands his shortsightedness and persuades "his" Tomorrow to pose for the new center panel as woman of the future. The middle-class assimilationists learn to value an assertive black woman.

OTHER MAJOR WORKS

LONG FICTION: *A Short Walk*, 1979.

SHORT FICTION: *Like One of the Family: Conversations from a Domestic's Life*, 1956.

SCREENPLAY: *A Hero Ain't Nothin' but a Sandwich*, 1978 (adaptation of her novel).

CHILDREN'S LITERATURE: *A Hero Ain't Nothin' but a Sandwich*, 1973; *Rainbow Jordan*, 1981; *Those Other People*, 1989.

EDITED TEXT: *Black Scenes: Collection of Scenes from Plays Written by Black People About Black Experience*, 1971.

BIBLIOGRAPHY

Austin, Gayle. "Alice Childress: Black Woman Playwright as Feminist Critic." *Southern Quarterly* 25 (Spring, 1987): 53-62. Focuses on Childress as social critic and transformer of images of black women. Discusses *Trouble in Mind* and *Wine in the Wilderness* in the context of Elizabeth Abel's three stages of feminist criticism.

Brown-Guillory, Elizabeth. "Black Women Playwrights Exorcizing Myths." *Phylon* 48 (Fall, 1997): 229-239. Examines the work of Childress, Lorraine Hansberry, and Ntozake Shange in dispelling stereotypical myths of African American characters, such as the tragic mulatto and the comic Negro, and in presenting new constructions, such as the black militant and the evolving black woman.

_____. *Their Place on the Stage: Black Women Playwrights in America*. Westport, Conn.: Greenwood Press, 1988. Contains summaries and comparisons of the work of Alice Childress, Lorraine Hansberry, and Ntozake Shange.

Dugan, Olga. "Telling the Truth: Alice Childress as Theorist and Playwright." *The Journal of Negro History* 81 (Annual, 1996): 123-137. Examines Alice Childress's essays as a reflection of her theory of a black self-determinist theater, in which individual black playwrights should use black culture and history in plays that demonstrate black self-determination. Childress believed such plays should focus on realistic situations and conditions under which African Americans live.

Jennings, LaVinia Delois. *Alice Childress.* New York: Twayne Publishers, 1995. A comprehensive and accessible critical introduction to Childress's life and work. Contains a discussion of Childress's life and career in theater as well as summaries and critiques of individual works. Especially helpful are a succinct chronology of Childress's life and work and a bibliography, which is divided into primary sources—Childress's novels, plays, productions in other media, and her articles, essays, and interviews—and secondary sources.

Elsie Galbreath Haley

FRANK CHIN

Born: Berkeley, California; February 25, 1940

PRINCIPAL DRAMA

The Chickencoop Chinaman, pr. 1972, pb. 1981
The Year of the Dragon, pr. 1974, pb. 1981

OTHER LITERARY FORMS

In addition to his plays, Frank Chin has published a collection of short stories, the novels *Donald Duk* (1991) and *Gunga Din Highway* (1994), and numerous articles on Asian American literature and culture, some of which have been collected in *Bulletproof Bandits and Other Essays* (1998). He also co-edited a pioneering anthology of Asian American writing titled *Aiiieeeee! An Anthology of Asian American Writers* (1974), substantially revised in 1991 as *The Big Aiiieeeee!*

ACHIEVEMENTS

Frank Chin is the first Chinese American playwright to have had serious drama produced on the New York stage (at the American Place Theater) and on national television (by the Public Broadcasting Service). Having come into prominence in the 1960's and 1970's, he represents the consciousness of Americans of Chinese descent—those born and reared in the United States, who thus have only tenuous ties to the language and culture of China.

In addition to his achievements as a playwright, Chin has garnered attention as an editor of Asian American literature, a fiction writer, and an essayist. His work has been recognized with many awards, among them the American Book Award for lifetime achievement, and several prizes and grants from organizations such as the Rockefeller Foundation, the American Place Theater (New York), and the National Endowment for the Arts.

BIOGRAPHY

Frank Chew Chin, Jr., was born a fifth-generation Californian of Chinese American parentage on February 25, 1940, in Berkeley, California, near Oakland, where his parents lived and worked. During his infancy, his family sent him to the sierra, where he was cared for by a retired vaudeville acrobat and a silent-film bit player. After World War II, he rejoined his family and grew up in the Chinatowns of Oakland and San Francisco, attending Chinese as well as English schools. During these years, he identified closely with his father, who was prominent in Chinatown governance and who became the president of the Six Companies (roughly the Chinatown equivalent of being elected mayor). Chin was graduated from the University of California at Berkeley, where he won several prizes for fiction writing; during his student years, he undertook the adventure of traveling to Fidel Castro's Cuba. In 1961, he was awarded a fellowship at the Writers' Workshop at the University of Iowa.

After leaving Iowa, Chin spent some time with the Southern Pacific Railroad, becoming the first Chinese American to work as a brakeman on the rails laid by his forefathers. Chin left the railroad company to become a writer-producer for KING-TV in Seattle, and several of his shows were aired by the Public Broadcasting Service (PBS) and on *Sesame Street*.

Chin left Seattle to teach Asian American studies at San Francisco State University and the University of California, Davis. With a group of scholars, he organized the Combined Asian American Resources Project (CARP), which collected literary, documentary, and oral history materials now kept in the Bancroft Library of the University of California, Berkeley. CARP has since been responsible for the publication of key Asian American texts by the University of Washington Press. In 1972, Chin founded the Asian American Theater Workshop in San Francisco with the support of the American Conservatory Theater (where he has been a writer-in-residence). In 1971, Chin married Kathleen Chang, daughter of a prominent intellectual Chinese family; the marriage ended in divorce after five years, and Chang later became haunted by visions that drove her to commit suicide in 1996 on the campus of the University of Pennsylvania. In the last decades of the twentieth century, Chin maintained his residence in the Los Angeles area (living with his third wife and third child), where he channeled his energies toward the writing of fiction, essays, and children's literature rather than drama. Meanwhile, his continuing research in Asian American folklore and history has been supported by several grants (including a Rockefeller Fellowship at the University of California, Los Angeles) and has borne fruit in several important exhibitions.

ANALYSIS

It may be said that Frank Chin has pioneered in the field of Asian American literature. His daring and verbally exuberant theater has asserted the presence of the richly unique and deeply human complexities of Chinese American life, and his work has brought this presence to the attention of the American public. Chin has sometimes been considered the John Osborne, or the angry young man, of his generation of Chinese Americans. His plays turn on themes of identity— anguished and indignant probings into ethnic identity, gender identity, and self-identity. In them, Chin mirrors the issues and realities of Chinese American life and history as lived in Chinatown ghettos; they seek to expose and explode generally held stereotypes of Chinese Americans as an emasculated model minority with a quaintly exotic culture. Painful truths told with exuberant verbal pyrotechnics are trademarks of Chin's theater, and the characteristic gamut of his language ranges from black ghetto dialect to hipster talk

Frank Chin (Corky Lee)

to authentic Chinatown Cantonese (not Hollywood's "Charlie Chan-ese"). He has criticized the false myths and the deadening stereotypes of self and ethnicity held by Asians and whites alike. At a time when it was ripe and necessary to do so, Chin proclaimed and proved that there is such an entity as Asian American literature. American literary history must henceforth reckon with that claim if it is to be true to itself.

Since the initial mark made by his two plays written in the 1970's, Chin has not had any new plays published or staged. Chin has instead turned his very considerable creative literary energies toward writing novels, short fiction, juvenile literature, and essays of cultural criticism. Chin's turn away from drama is in part due to a disappointment that an authentic Asian American theater (as he sees it) has not emerged. When he wrote his first plays, he had hoped that a genuinely Asian American theater would come into being, a theater that would resemble Dublin's Abbey Theater of the early 1900's and that would nurture genuinely Asian American dramatic talents just as the Abbey nurtured a crop of distinctively Irish playwrights such as Sean O'Casey, John Millington Synge, and William Butler Yeats. Chin's two plays, nevertheless, are considered classics of Asian American literature, and they continue to be studied in the academy and to attract analytical commentary and debate. There have been many revivals of these plays, especially in Los Angeles and San Francisco.

Chin's plays center on a protagonist's confrontation with the problematics of identity. *The Chickencoop Chinaman* is the more experimental in technique, with an almost cinematic use of montage, flashbacks, symbolic stage sets, and surrealistic, dreamlike sequences. *The Year of the Dragon* is more conventional, a drama of family and psychological conflict set in a San Francisco Chinatown apartment.

THE CHICKENCOOP CHINAMAN

The Chickencoop Chinaman is a play that treats the theme of identity through dispelling stereotypes and myths. The play is divided into two acts. Each act has a scene in Limbo (a surreal transitional time-space located between realistic time-spaces), a sequence recollecting a past obsession with a mythic figure (for example, the miracle-working Helen Kel-

ler in act 1, the popular-culture hero the Lone Ranger in act 2), and scenes set in the realistic location of 1960's Pittsburgh, where the problem of the protagonist's identity is worked out.

The play's action centers on Tam Lum, a Chinese American filmmaker who is making a documentary about a black boxing champion named Ovaltine Jack Dancer, a boyhood idol with whom he once shared a moment of mystic brotherhood urinating in unison in a roadside bush. Tam comes to Pittsburgh from San Francisco in search of Dancer's father, Charley Popcorn, who was a quintessential formative figure for Dancer and who now runs a Pittsburgh theater. Allegorically, Tam's creation of a film about Dancer is an effort to express an identity for himself, and his search for Charley is his search for a father figure.

Before arriving in Pittsburgh, Tam is introduced in a Limbo scene on his airliner from San Francisco. The flight attendant is transformed into a Hong Kong Dream Girl clad in a drill team uniform and twirling a baton (hence an American dream girl, too). Indeed, the woman represents the American stereotype of Asian women—attractive, compliant, trained to give pleasure. Although Tam scoffs at the Hong Kong Dream Girl's stereotypical identity, it becomes apparent that his own identity is problematic. For example, when asked what his mother tongue is, Tam can speak no Chinese, but instead begins speaking in tongues, using a startling array of American dialects. Tam also points out that Chinese American identity is not one ordained by nature; Chinese Americans are not born to an identity but must synthesize one out of the diverse experiences of living in crowded Chinatown tenements, metaphorical chicken coops. This opening sequence, then, poses the play's central theme: the problem of stereotyping and identity.

In Pittsburgh, Tam stays with a boyhood friend, a Japanese American dentist named "Blackjap" Kenji. Kenji's apartment in Pittsburgh's black ghetto, Oakland, ironically underlines the circularity of Tam's search (since San Francisco has its Oakland too), and its location within carshot of a railroad yard is a symbolic reminder of the Chinese American contribution to American history. Tam and Kenji, who grew up in the black ghetto of Oakland, California, talk in exuberant black dialect and express themselves by slapping skin; they have, to a great degree, adopted the style and expressiveness of a black identity.

Kenji's ménage includes Lee, a part-Chinese woman who is passing for white. She has a young son, Robbie, by a previous liaison or marriage. Lee has a love-hate relationship with men of color, men whom she collects and then uses her whiteness and sexuality to dominate and intimidate. Thus, Lee lives platonically and parasitically with Kenji, in fact reducing him to a sexless host.

During their reunion scene in act 1, Tam and Kenji reenact a past obsession that they had with the figure of Helen Keller, imitating and parodying her. This may seem pointlessly cruel until one realizes that, in Chin's play, Keller symbolizes the myth of the disadvantaged person who overcomes all handicaps and pulls herself up by her own bootstraps. In other words, she epitomizes what American society fondly thinks that every disadvantaged minority group can do for itself. When Tam and Kenji mock and demythologize the figure of Helen Keller, they are, in particular, rejecting the popular American myth that Asian Americans are a model minority capable of miracles of self-help.

Act 2 opens with another scene in which Tam and Kenji again recollect a mythic figure, this time the Lone Ranger. As a boy, Tam had fantasized that, behind his mask, the Lone Ranger was Chinese, and Tam had therefore identified with him as a heroic role model who represented the possibility that a Chinese American could become an idol of the American public. As Tam reenacts his past fantasy in his adulthood, however, he realizes that the Lone Ranger is a racist, as is clear in his treatment of Tonto, and that he is not by any means a Chinese. In fact, the Lone Ranger is an obese white man who sadistically shoots Tam in the hand (symbolically handicapping him physically), then lays on him the curse of being an honorary white (handicapping him psychologically with this false identity). This episode, then, demythologizes the private fantasies of any Chinese American who might believe that he can easily achieve heroic status in the American imagination; it also shows the wounding consequences of the Chinese

American fantasy that they can be accepted as honorary whites.

Tam and Kenji then track down Charley Popcorn. They are crushed, however, when Charley reveals that he is not, in fact, Dancer's father—that Dancer had constructed a myth around his memories of their association. Thus Tam's search for a surrogate and idolized father figure in a black man ends in disillusionment.

Returning to the apartment, Tam and Kenji undergo another identity crisis, this time precipitated by Lee's former husband, Tom. His name suggests the stereotype of the subservient minority, "Uncle Tom," and he is the very model of the minority that has attained middle-class success. Tom has heard of Kenji's decent but sexless relationship with Lee and wants to take Lee and Robbie back. Yet, now Kenji authoritatively stands his ground, sends Robbie to bed, and asserts that he wants Lee to stay and that he will father children with her.

Tam, too, appears to recover from his shattering disillusionment with Charley. In the surrealistic penultimate scene, he is shown being borne to Kenji's apartment on Charley's back, and in this position, Tam recalls the unmanning events when his wife left him on his birthday. In the play's last scene, however, Tam makes a great effort and stumbles into Kenji's apartment carrying Charley on his back. This reversal of position symbolically denotes Tam's freedom from his past reliance on an identity borrowed from the blacks and a new determination to find the wherewithal for a future identity from sources within himself. He is thus able to keep his integrity despite the needling of Lee and the allurement of Tom's imitation whiteness. Just as Kenji and Lee are united in a new relationship, so Tam is shown coming to terms with an identity grounded on his own ethnicity. Before the curtain falls, Tam is shown in the kitchen unashamedly practicing the craft of his ethnic group *par excellence*. As he prepares the food, he reminisces about the Chinese American legend of the Iron Moonhunter, a mythic train that the Chinese railroaders supposedly created out of parts stolen from the railroad companies, and which wanders the West searching out the souls of dead Chinese to bear them home to their families. Chin seems to understand that people need myths, and in the end, his protagonist, disillusioned with the black myth that is unavailable to him and rejecting a white myth that he finds contemptible, shapes his own myth of identity in the heroism and craft of Chinese America.

THE YEAR OF THE DRAGON

Chin's second play, *The Year of the Dragon*, is more conventionally structured than its predecessor and was accorded a national audience in a television production on the Public Broadcasting Service's "PBS Theatre in America" in 1975. This play also treats the theme of identity, but it focuses more sharply and poignantly on the question of self-worth: the worth of an individual self to loved ones (family) and the worth of a minority ethnic group to the majority society (white-dominated America). Again, stereotypes form the chief factor that obscures individual worth and identity—stereotypes about family relationships, stereotypes about ethnicity. These thematic strands are worked out in the exposition of the many psychological conflicts and confrontations in the well-established Eng family of San Francisco's Chinatown.

The exposition, and exposé, of ethnic stereotypes is presented chiefly through two elements of the play: the family business of providing tours of Chinatown and the new Anglo son-in-law whom their daughter has brought from Boston. The family owns Eng's Chinatown Tour and Travel agency, and the eldest son, forty-year-old Fred, conducts tours of San Francisco's Chinatown. For the sake of business, however, Fred cannot show Chinatown as it really is; rather, he must pander to the stereotypes of Chinatown held by the American public—that it is an exotic place of delicious foods, mysterious (but safe) goings on, and incomprehensible (but happy) inhabitants composed of attractively available women, complaisant men, and harmonious families with above-average children. Fred knows that he is being false to himself and his people when he gives his happy tour-guide's spiel, and he mutters curses at his customers under his breath beneath his patter. In reality, Fred would like to tell the truths of Chinatown, which he sets down in short stories, but no one will publish his work.

Through Fred's situation, then, Chin portrays the stifling effects of ethnic stereotypes.

The other element in the play that deals with ethnic stereotypes is presented through the character Ross, the Eng family's Boston-bred son-in-law on a honeymoon visit from the East. He is portrayed as a well-meaning but oafish Sinophile who has studied Chinese (although in a dialect different from the Eng family's), admires Chinese culture and customs, and thinks of Chinese Americans as the only minority group that does not dislike white dominance. Such stereotypes prevent him from seeing the Chinese American realities that trip him up constantly. His type of cultural voyeurism is subtly captured in the play's final scene, in which he is appointed photographer to take posed pictures of the Eng family. In this technically effective scene, Chin uses spatial form as adroitly as did Gustave Flaubert in the "agricultural fair" scene of *Madame Bovary* (1857; English translation, 1886). Through a kind of auditory montage, Chin creates an ironic counterpoint commenting on Ross's photography by interspersing the scene with the sounds and spiel of a tour guide describing a Chinese New Year's parade offstage. Just as the tourists are gawking at the Chinatown parade, so is Ross ogling his new Chinese American family.

In probing the stereotypes of familial relationships, Chin makes a painful but necessary criticism of stereotypes held by his own ethnic group. He also dispels the Charlie Chan-esque stereotype held by many Americans, that Chinese families are uniformly harmonious and hierarchical.

Much of the conflict in the family swirls around its patriarch, Pa Eng, who came to the United States in 1935 accompanied only by his infant son Fred, for he was forced to leave his wife in China because United States immigration laws excluded Chinese women from entering America. Pa Eng soon married a fifteen-year-old American-born Chinese girl (Ma Eng), who risked losing her American citizenship by marrying the man she loved (her citizenship was at risk not because she married a bigamist but because another American anti-Chinese law forbade American-born women to marry Chinese men on pain of forfeiting their citizenship). Ma Eng bore and reared two children, meanwhile pampering Pa Eng in his stereotypical Chinese view of the patriarch as a kind of semidivinity.

When the play opens, Pa Eng has prospered, to the point that he has been elected mayor of Chinatown. Yet he is now old and ill, and he believes that his days are numbered. He wants to die in the bosom of his family, so he has sent for his first wife (China Mama). This he has done without communicating his intent to his family. (In fact, throughout the play, the family members can hardly be said to communicate; they never bother to listen to what others have to say.) China Mama's arrival, as can be expected, precipitates several crises during which Pa Eng appears an inconsiderate, uncomprehending, ego-bound patriarch. He commands Ma Eng, who is unnerved by this presence in her household, either to relinquish her home or to be subservient to China Mama and begin teaching her English. It is in his relationship with Fred, however, that Pa Eng's authoritarian role becomes most apparent.

Pa Eng's patriarchal dominance and his Chinese values have acted as longstanding denials of Fred's identity and self-worth. Fred had aspired to be a writer, but his father scoffed at this: According to stereotypes he holds, if one is not a doctor or a lawyer, one is nothing at all. Pa Eng gives his mayoral speech to Ross to edit, not to Fred, who majored in English. Nevertheless, Fred is a dutiful son, nursing his father when he spits blood and even going through a daily ritual of accompanying him to the toilet and wiping him after a defecation, a viscerally affecting scene to stage. Fred has also sacrificed his own college career to work and provide for his sister's college expenses, but his father does not appreciate that, probably because his stereotypical values do not accord much importance to daughters. Fred also is aware that his younger brother, Johnny, is deteriorating into a gun-wielding Chinatown mobster and wants him to leave his environment and go to college in the East. This Johnny resists. Fred knows that Johnny will comply if Pa Eng orders him to go, but Pa Eng refuses. Instead, Pa Eng wants Fred to accompany him as he delivers his mayoral speech. In this speech, he plans to acknowledge Fred as his heir, but he will do it in such a way that Fred will always be fitted with the stereotypical identity of a Number One Son, a person who has no self-worth beyond that which derives from his father. This is unacceptable to Fred, who refuses to go with his father as long as he refuses to order Johnny to leave Chinatown. In attempting to impose his will on his son, Pa Eng resorts to violence and slaps him repeatedly. Yet the physical exertion is too much for the sick old man, and he dies in this pitiable moment of futile tyranny. Tragically, Pa Eng's death does not free Fred. The closing tableau of the play shows Fred being submerged by his milieu as he slips into the spiel of the Chinatown tour guide, and as the spotlight singles him out, Fred is shown dressed glaringly in white, the Chinese symbol of death.

OTHER MAJOR WORKS

LONG FICTION: *Donald Duk*, 1991; *Gunga Din Highway*, 1994.

SHORT FICTION: *The Chinaman Pacific and Frisco R.R. Co.*, 1988.

TELEPLAYS: *S.R.T., Act Two*, 1966; *The Bel Canto Carols*, 1966; *A Man and His Music*, 1967; *Ed Sierer's New Zealand*, 1967; *Seafair Preview*, 1967; *The Year of the Ram*, 1967; *And Still Champion . . .*, 1967; *The Report*, 1967; *Mary*, 1969; *Rainlight Rainvision*, 1969; *Chinaman's Chance*, 1971.

NONFICTION: *Bulletproof Buddhists and Other Essays*, 1998.

EDITED TEXTS: *Aiiieeeee! An Anthology of Asian American Writers*, 1974 (with others; Asian American writing); *The Big Aiiieeeee!*, 1991.

BIBLIOGRAPHY

Barnes, Clive. "Theater: Culture Study." *The New York Times*, June 3, 1974, p. 39. A balanced review of *The Year of the Dragon* in performance at the American Place Theater in New York City. Barnes notes that the play has "gaps" and "lacks energy at times" but is still "interesting." He praises the "absolutely fascinating . . . insights" that Chin provides while dispelling stereotypes about Chinese Americans, investigating Chinese American identity, and exploring generational differences.

Chua, C. L. "*The Year of the Dragon*, by Frank Chin." In *A Resource Guide to Asian American Literature*, edited by Sau-ling Wong and Stephen Sumida. New York: Modern Language Association, 2001. Intended for students and teachers, this essay provides an overview of the play, historical contexts, pedagogical suggestions, and intertextual linkages.

Kim, Elaine H. *Asian American Literature: An Introduction to the Writings and Their Social Context*. Philadelphia: Temple University Press, 1982. In chapter 6 of this essential and pioneering study of Asian American literature, Kim discusses Chin together with other writers of his generation. Kim's focus is on Chin's short fiction and *The Chickencoop Chinaman*. She analyzes the play as a forum for Chin's ideas on Chinese American culture, identity, and manhood, ideas that are darkened by a pervading sense of futility, decadence, and alienation. Kim also faults Chin for the use of "unbalanced" dialogue (that is, monologic lectures) and stereotyped women characters.

_____. "Frank Chin: The Chinatown Cowboy and His Backtalk." *Midwest Quarterly* 20 (Autumn, 1978): 78-91. This essay by the doyenne of Asian American literary critics is an earlier version of the previous bibliographic entry. The essay, however, is more acerbic than the book chapter; it finds that *The Chickencoop Chinaman* conveys "contempt for the Asian American identity" and portrays the "pathetic futility of the male protagonist."

Kroll, Jack. "Primary Color." *Newsweek*, June 19, 1972, 55. Extolls *The Chickencoop Chinaman* as "the most interesting play of the American Place Theater" that year. Compares Chin with John Osborne and Chin's protagonist to Lenny Bruce, sees Chin's thematic concerns as his generation's search for identity, and characterizes Chin's language as "rogue poetry of deracination" enlivened by the "beat and brass, the runs and rim-shots of jazz."

Ling, Jinqi. *Narrating Nationalisms: Ideology and Form in Asian American Literature*. New York: Oxford University Press, 1998. This book devotes a complete chapter to the plays of Frank Chin, discussing their ethics and poetics. It also comments on issues of masculinity, the effects of commercialization, and the postmodern nature of Chin's theatrical art.

McDonald, Dorothy Ritsuko. Introduction to *"The Chickencoop Chinaman" and "The Year of the Dragon": Two Plays by Frank Chin*. Seattle: University of Washington Press, 1981. This extensive introduction provides information on Chin's background and his views on Chinese American history. Makes an intelligent thematic commentary on Chin's plays. Sees Chin's intent as attempting to dispel stereotypes about Chinese Americans and to recover mythic archetypes (such as Kwan Kung, patron deity of war and letters) to validate the Chinese American male. A valuable essay marred by some errors of detail.

Oliver, Edith. "Off Broadway." *The New Yorker* 48 (June 24, 1972): 46. An enthusiastic response to *The Chickencoop Chinaman* that hails its historical importance for bringing "the first news (theatrically speaking) of the Chinese Americans in our midst." Characterizes the play as "moving, funny, pain-filled, sarcastic, bitter, ironic . . . in a furious and dazzling eruption of verbal legerdemain." Notices a "few paltry things that are wrong" with it but finds that these "hardly matter," given the play's theatrical inventiveness.

Wong, Sau-ling. *Reading Asian American Literature: From Necessity to Extravagance*. Princeton, N.J.: Princeton University Press, 1993. Contains a brilliant chapter analyzing theme and imagery in Chin's drama.

Yin, Xiao-huang. *Chinese American Literature Since the 1850's*. Urbana: University of Illinois Press, 2000. This study contains a section dealing with the debate between Maxine Hong Kingston and Frank Chin when Chin had accused her of inauthenticity.

C. L. Chua

CARYL CHURCHILL

Born: London, England; September 3, 1938

PRINCIPAL DRAMA

Downstairs, pr. 1958
Easy Death, pr. 1962
Owners, pr. 1972, pb. 1973
Moving Clocks Go Slow, pr. 1975
Objections to Sex and Violence, pr. 1975, pb. 1985
Light Shining in Buckinghamshire, pr. 1976, pb.
    1978
Vinegar Tom, pr. 1976, pb. 1978
Traps, pr. 1977, pb. 1978
Cloud Nine, pr., pb. 1979
Three More Sleepless Nights, pr. 1980, pb. 1990
Top Girls, pr., pb. 1982
Fen, pr., pb. 1983
Softcops, pr., pb. 1984
Plays: One, pb. 1985
A Mouthful of Birds, pr., pb. 1986 (with David Lan)
Serious Money, pr., pb. 1987
Ice Cream, pr., pb. 1989
Hot Fudge, pr. 1989, pb. 1990
Mad Forest: A Play from Romania, pr., pb. 1990
Churchill Shorts: Short Plays, pb. 1990
Plays: Two, pb. 1990
Skriker, pr. 1993
Blue Heart, pr., pb. 1997
This Is a Chair, pr. 1997, pb. 1999
Plays: Three, pb. 1998
Far Away, pr. 2000, pb. 2001

OTHER LITERARY FORMS

Although Caryl Churchill is known primarily as a playwright, her writing career actually began with radio plays in the early 1960's, when *The Ants* was broadcast in 1962. *The Ants* was followed by other radio plays, including *Lovesick* (1967), *Identical Twins* (1968), *Abortive* (1971), *Not, Not, Not, Not, Not Enough Oxygen* (1971), *Schreber's Nervous Illness* (1972), *Henry's Past* (1972), and *Perfect Happiness* (1973). Churchill has also written several teleplays: *The Judge's Wife* (1972), *Turkish Delight* (1974), *The*

After-Dinner Joke (1978), *The Legion Hall Bombing* (1978), and *Crimes* (1981).

ACHIEVEMENTS

Caryl Churchill is claimed by several political and artistic constituencies: She is hailed as a major voice for English socialists; is cited frequently by feminists; is the darling of proponents of workshops, or group construction, of plays; and is clearly a postmodern voice. Certainly, Churchill is each of these things, but, above all, she is a writer of the human presence and a champion of the individual choice. Her particular achievement is not to experiment but to experiment with a difference. Her unusual use of theatrical structure always aims to reveal the value of the eccentric individual over the concentricities of an exploitive social order. She is an established playwright whose work, though highly unusual in structure, is widely and well received in the English-speaking world, having been successfully produced both in London and in New York. Churchill won the Obie Award for best Off-Broadway play in 1982, 1983, and 1988. In 1988, she also won London's Society of West End Theatre Award.

BIOGRAPHY

Caryl Churchill was born in London, England, on September 3, 1938. She lived in Montreal, Canada, from 1948 to 1955, and there attended the Trafalgar School. From 1957 to 1960, she studied English literature at the University of Oxford and took her bachelor of arts degree from that institution in 1960. Her first dramatic works were produced at the University of Oxford, but many of her early plays remain unpublished. In 1961, she married David Harter; she is the mother of three sons. As his wife's career developed, Harter gave up his lucrative private law practice so that his wife could spend more time writing. A prolific playwright, Churchill received her first professional stage production in 1972 when *Owners* was performed at the Royal Court Theatre. From that point on, she became closely associated with that theater. She has been a member of the Joint Stock Theatre Group, an organization dedicated to collective creation of theatrical work, and has worked with the Monstrous Regiment, a feminist theater union. Churchill has contributed frequently to the British Broadcasting Corporation's (BBC) radio and television broadcasts. In an incident now notorious, she and her director, David Lan, insisted that their names be left off the credits of the BBC's 1978 television production of *The Legion Hall Bombing* because the producers had censored the work. As her reputation spread, Churchill's works were brought to the United States and were staged by Joseph Papp in New York. She is a playwright of considerable international importance.

ANALYSIS

Caryl Churchill has become well known for her willingness to experiment with dramatic structure. Her innovations in this regard are sometimes so startling and compelling that reviewers tend to focus on the novelty of her works to the exclusion of her ideas. Churchill, however, is a playwright of ideas, ideas that are often difficult and, despite her bold theatricality, surprisingly subtle and elusive. Her principal concern is with the issues attendant on the individual's struggle to emerge from the ensnarements of culture, class, economic systems, and the imperatives of the past. Each of these impediments to the development and happiness of the individual is explored in her works. Not surprisingly for a contemporary female writer, many times she makes use of female characters to explore such themes.

Churchill has openly proclaimed herself a feminist and a socialist. She is also emphatic in her position that the two are not one and the same. Indeed, her plays do not attempt to confound the two issues, although *Top Girls* does investigate the influence that capitalism can have on women and their willingness to forsake their humanity for economic gain. Churchill has examined with great sympathy, in works such as *Fen* and *Light Shining in Buckinghamshire*, the plight of the male, or of both genders, caught up in the destructiveness of inhuman economic forces. Churchill herself has argued that both issues are so important to her—the plight of women and the need for a socialist

world—that she could not choose between them and would not have one problem alleviated without a concurrent solution to the other. In another sense, Churchill is interested in the greater issues of gender and the games of power played with gender at stake. Just so, she is equally committed to considering the individual and the power drained from that individual by the forces of modern economic and social systems.

Whatever her politics and philosophy, Churchill brings a fire and an energy, a special eye and ear, to the postmodern English drama. She is an inspiration to the feminist movement and to women intellectuals around the world. She remains a force crying out for the release of the individual of either gender from the oppressive imperatives of past practices and present expectations. To her art, she contributes an inventive mind and a willingness to invest great energies in wedding the play to the performance. She has continuously rejected linear structure and the use of the master narratives of socialist realism to present her themes. She has also rejected the Brechtean epic theater in favor of using "found objects," such as various couples in a hotel room or snatches of everyday speech, and recontextualizing these found objects into new situations that emphasize new meanings. In this way she is much like the famous avant-garde artist Gaston Duchamp who made a fountain of a toilet bowl.

An important factor in Churchill's proclivity for structural experimentation is her long and close association with workshop groups, whose aim is the collective creation of theater pieces through the interaction of actors, writers, directors, choreographers, and other artists. Two such groups have been especially influential on Churchill's artistic development: The first is the Monstrous Regiment, a feminist theater union that helped Churchill create *Vinegar Tom*; the other is the Joint Stock Theatre Group, with whose help she fashioned several important works, including *Cloud Nine*, *Fen*, and *A Mouthful of Birds*.

The Joint Stock Theatre Group, with directors such as Max Stafford-Clark, Les Waters, and David Lan, and choreographer Ian Fink, operates with suggestions that come from any group member. For example, *Light Shining in Buckinghamshire*, Churchill's first venture with the group, began with a member's suggestion concerning the motives for the mass immigration of villagers in seventeenth century England. After the initial proposal of the idea, the group set out to research the topic, following it with a theatrical workshop in which the group improvised scenes based on that research. These workshop scenes were interrupted by a "writing gap" during which Churchill wrote the script. Rehearsals came next, with more group interaction and improvisation on the script. *Fen* followed virtually the same process and was based on a suggestion to explore what it must have been like, in a rural English village, to have the social and agricultural habits of centuries suddenly overturned by the intrusion of modern capitalism, brought in the persona of a Japanese businessman who buys all the village's farmland. In another example, the group's director, Lan, was interested in the politics of possession, while Churchill was interested in the theme of women becoming violent and rebellious rather than submitting to their traditionally assigned, passive role. The Joint Stock Theatre Group went to work with these ideas, and *A Mouthful of Birds* was born. This creative method, which gives a privilege to experimentation and outright and frank theatricalism, seems to serve Churchill well.

Churchill also has a special relationship with London's Royal Court Theatre, where she was resident dramatist in 1974-1975 and where she has had many of her plays performed in the main playhouse and the experimental Upstairs Theatre. Churchill's radio and television works are often broadcast by the BBC, and her plays are frequently staged outside Great Britain, especially in the United States, where she was first introduced by Joseph Papp at the Public Theatre of New York City.

Churchill has also worked with educational institutions such as the Central School of Speech and Drama in London. She and school director Mark Wing-Davey took a group of ten graduate students to Bucharest where they worked with students at the Romanian Institute of Theatre and Cinema on the creation of *Mad Forest*.

WOMAN AS CULTURAL CONCEPT

In four of her best-known works—*Cloud Nine*, *Top Girls*, *A Mouthful of Birds*, and *Vinegar Tom*—

Churchill presents woman as a cultural concept and displays the power of that concept to submerge and smother the individual female. In *Cloud Nine*, a parallel is suggested between Western colonial oppression and Western sexual oppression. This oppression is seen first in the family organization and then in the power of the past to demand obligations from the present. Although her characters use geographical distance and literally run away from the past, no one in *Cloud Nine* can exorcize the ghosts of established practices and traditions.

Top Girls is a depiction of the exploitation of women by women, a technique well learned through generations of women being exploited by men. The play portrays a group of friends, all successful women in the fields of literature and the arts, who gather for a dinner to celebrate Marlene's promotion to an executive position in the Top Girls employment agency. Viewers are introduced to scenes of Marlene's workplace and to her working-class sister and niece, Angie. In a painful end to *Top Girls*, Churchill reveals how one woman character is willing to sacrifice her very motherhood to maintain her position in the world of business, a world that the play shows to be created by and for men. Following a bitter argument between Marlene and her lower-class sister, it is also revealed that Marlene's "niece" is actually her illegitimate daughter.

The issues in *Top Girls* and *Cloud Nine*, however startlingly presented, are ones commonly addressed in modern culture, even if usually addressed with an attitude different from that of Churchill. *A Mouthful of Birds*, however, is altogether different, for it addresses the most sensitive and most taboo of all matters concerning women: sex and violence. Furthermore, in *A Mouthful of Birds*, Churchill turns the tables and considers sex and violence as perpetrated not by men on women but by women on men, thereby taking one more step into the forbidden matters of gender.

The theme of society's oppressed females is perhaps most powerfully presented in one of Churchill's earlier works, *Vinegar Tom*, a piece created especially for the Monstrous Regiment. *Vinegar Tom* is a play about witches, but there are no witches in it, only four women accused of being witches. Set in seventeenth century England, the play depicts four women accused by society of the vaguest of crimes: sorcery. Their only crime, however, has been to follow an individual impulse. Joan Nokes is simply poor and old, two conditions that are not supposed to happen simultaneously to Western women. Her daughter, Alice, understands sex as an individual matter and is inclined to enjoy a man if he suits her fancy. When Alice asserts her right to have an illegitimate child, she is labeled a "whore," since she is neither a virgin nor a wife. Betty, the play's third woman, is called a witch for refusing to marry the man picked out for her, and Susan, the fourth, is seen as a witch for choosing life over death: When put to the water test (witches float, the innocent sink), Susan elects to swim, thus saving herself but forcing society to find a way to kill her. All four women are emerging, strong-willed individuals whose only crime is to be themselves in an oppressive and conservative society. Because they will not carry out their assigned female roles, they are cast as witches and hanged as a logical consequence of their chosen lifestyles.

UNIQUE DRAMATIC STRUCTURE

It is virtually impossible to discuss thematic issues in Churchill's work without simultaneously considering her special treatment of dramatic structure. Each of her pieces is a unique construction, innovatively assembled and using unconventional and highly theatrical devices. Furthermore, Churchill's plays remain compelling, mysterious, and, at the same time, refreshingly accessible.

Cloud Nine presents, in part 1, an English family living in colonial Africa. The father, Clive, though far from home, "serves the Queen." He is father not only to his children but to the natives as well. Churchill has a special device for underscoring this male-dominated world. She calls for Billy, Clive's wife and the mother of the children, to be played by a male. To reinforce her statement, Churchill asks that the black servant, Joshua, be played by a white performer. Thus both characters, despite the race and gender of the performers, become whatever the white father wishes them to be. When a lesbian nanny, Ellen, appears, homosexual orientation is suspected in the children and the "perfect" family is created.

Part 2 has additional surprises. The colonial family returns to England without the father. In England, the grown-up children seek to realize their separate identities, but the freedom to be fully choosing individuals still eludes them. They fret over not having the father to tell them what to do, and the traditions of the past weigh heavily on them, keeping them in their assigned roles. One of the daughters, Lin, a diminutive for Ellen, the lesbian nanny of part 1, had married to fulfill social expectations. Now divorced and having custody of her child, she openly lives with a female lover. Even that important change in sexual orientation, however, is not sufficiently liberating, for as Lin remarks, she can change whom she sleeps with but she cannot change everything. In a wistful scene, she attempts to conjure up a goddess, one she knows will never materialize, begging the deity to give her the history she never had, make her the woman she cannot be. In *Cloud Nine*, Churchill reverses the traditional immigration pattern. Often parents settle in a new land but bring the past and its old ways with them; in *Cloud Nine*, however, the children flee their past by returning to the old land, but they are still smothered by ancient habits, expectations, and icons. This preoccupation with the ghosts and hauntings of the past, indeed with the very nature of time itself, is further explored by Churchill in the unusual pieces *Traps* and *Moving Clocks Go Slow*.

A recurring structural device in Churchill's dramaturgy is to have one actor play several roles. Most of her better-known works—*Serious Money, Top Girls, Light Shining in Buckinghamshire,* and *Cloud Nine*—make use of multiple role playing. Although the device may be considered merely idiomatic with her, Churchill usually has a point to make in employing multiple role playing. In *Serious Money*, for example, the actors are assigned a series of roles that may be summed up in a single universal type, so that one actor, for example, plays a stockbroker or a financier while another plays various women who pander their bodies or their souls to men of high finance.

Even more idiosyncratic in structure is the powerful *A Mouthful of Birds*, in which the stories of seven contemporary personas are interwoven with the ancient ritualistic events of Euripides' *Bakchai* (405 B.C.E.; *The Bacchae*, 1781). Dionysus, the Greek God of wine, appears throughout the piece dancing in a modern woman's petticoat. Amid ancient scenes of ecstasy and emotional and physical violence, the modern characters appear in their normal daily activities. They each present a monologue in which they attempt to explain why they have failed to meet their obligations. Secret and mysterious problems of possession emerge. The atmosphere of the play is charged with the sensuality of accepted violence, violence intermingled with the irresistible quality of sex. One woman character, for example, who is stereotypically squeamish about skinning a dead rabbit for supper, calmly tells her husband to go to the bathroom, where he will find their baby drowned. Churchill juxtaposes this modern violence against the culminating terror of *The Bacchae*, the gruesome moment when Agave, in a Dionysian ecstasy, tears apart the body of her son Pentheus.

Hotel represents yet another structural experimentation for Churchill. It is an opera, with music by Orlando Gough, set in two hotel rooms simultaneously with actors playing multiple roles. A number of different couples occupy the rooms at one time or another, including a couple having an adulterous affair and another couple who are homosexual. A television set also figures as a major character. By doubling and tripling the actors in various roles, Churchill subtly emphasizes the commonality of human oppression and pain. Typical of Churchill, the story is not linear, but rather occurs in fragments. The dialogue is also presented in fragments. As Churchill points out in the introduction to the play, she has constructed the work in the way we perceive opera in performance, especially classic opera in languages other than English. We hear snatches of dialogue, but the requirements of the music often overshadow the entire line. The use of fragmented dialogue and non-linear story development is also found in plays such as *This Is a Chair*, where a series of domestic scenes is compared to events about the world through the use of placards naming each scene. Churchill's use of fragments of dialogue suggests that language can often fail as a means of communication, especially when those us-

ing language take little care in its employment. This suggestion is further emphasized in that the fragments are always realistic bits of everyday conversation used in a surrealistic manner.

OTHER MAJOR WORKS

TELEPLAYS: *The Judge's Wife*, 1972; *Turkish Delight*, 1974; *The After-Dinner Joke*, 1978; *The Legion Hall Bombing*, 1978; *Crimes*, 1981.

RADIO PLAYS: *The Ants*, 1962; *Lovesick*, 1967; *Identical Twins*, 1968; *Abortive*, 1971; *Not, Not, Not, Not, Not Enough Oxygen*, 1971; *Schreber's Nervous Illness*, 1972; *Henry's Past*, 1972; *Perfect Happiness*, 1973.

TRANSLATION: *Thyestes*, 1994 (of Seneca).

BIBLIOGRAPHY

Betsko, Kathleen, and Rachel Koenig, comps. *Interviews with Contemporary Playwrights*. New York: Beech Tree Books, 1987. In this provocative interview, the playwright discusses her concept of feminism and compares the London and New York productions of *Cloud Nine*.

Bigsby, C. W. E., ed. *Contemporary English Drama*. London: Edward Arnold, 1981. This collection of essays about the British theater provides a key to locating Churchill among her contemporaries. The essay by Christian W. Thomsen, "Three Socialist Playwrights: John McGrath, Caryl Churchill, Trevor Griffiths," is informative about contemporary socialist thought in England and the way in which it is revealed in the plays of Churchill and her peers.

Cousin, Geraldine. *Churchill, the Playwright*. London: Methuen Drama, 1989. An excellent general study of Churchill's drama. All the issues present in Churchill's work are examined as they are found in the plays themselves.

Fitzsimmons, Linda, comp. *File on Churchill*. London: Methuen Drama, 1989. This brief volume is a compilation of "file material" on Churchill, including lists of sources to consult, quotations from articles about the playwright, biographical data, production information, and reviews of productions. An excellent and dependable source book.

Kaysser, Helen, ed. *Feminism and the Theatre.* Basingstoke, England: Macmillan, 1988. As the title suggests, this volume is a collection of essays on feminists in theater, and includes an excellent essay on Churchill by a leading feminist critic in the United States, Sue Ellen Case. The volume is useful not only for the Case essay but also for aiding those interested in placing Churchill in the context of contemporary feminist thinking. It is also instructive in the uses of feminist thinking in Churchill's work.

Kieburzinka, Christine Olga. *Intertextual Loops in Modern Drama.* Madison, N.J.: Farleigh Dickinson University Press, 2001. Contains excellent chapter on the construction of *Mad Forest*, revealing how Churchill cooperated with various workshop groups in the writing and structuring of her plays, in this case a group of students from London and Romania.

Randall, Phyllis, ed. *Caryl Churchill: A Casebook.* New York: Garland, 1989. A collection of essays pertaining to Churchill as a working dramatist.

August W. Staub

COLLEY CIBBER

Born: London, England; November 6, 1671
Died: London, England; December 11, 1757

PRINCIPAL DRAMA

Love's Last Shift: Or, The Fool in Fashion, pr., pb. 1696

Woman's Wit: Or, The Lady in Fashion, pb. 1697, pr. 1699

The Tragical History of King Richard III, pr. 1699, pb. 1700 (adaptation of William Shakespeare's play)

Xerxes, pr., pb. 1699

Love Makes a Man: Or, The Fop's Fortune, pr. 1700, pb. 1701

The School Boy: Or, The Comical Rivals, pr. 1702, pb. 1707

She Wou'd and She Wou'd Not: Or, The Kind Imposter, pr. 1702, pb. 1703

The Careless Husband, pr. 1704, pb. 1705

Perolla and Izadora, pr. 1705, pb. 1706

The Comical Lovers, pr., pb. 1707

The Double Gallant: Or, The Sick Lady's Cure, pr., pb. 1707

The Lady's Last Stake: Or, The Wife's Resentment, pr. 1707, pb. 1708

The Rival Fools, pr., pb. 1709

The Rival Queens, pr. 1710, pb. 1729 (burlesque)

Ximena: Or, The Heroic Daughter, pr. 1712, pb. 1719

Myrtillo, pr., pb. 1715 (masque)

Venus and Adonis, pr., pb. 1715 (masque)

The Non-Juror, pr. 1717, pb. 1718

The Refusal: Or, The Ladies' Philosophy, pr., pb. 1721

The Plays of Colley Cibber, pb. 1721 (2 volumes), pb. 1980 (reprint)

Caesar in Aegypt, pr. 1724, pb. 1725

The Provok'd Husband: Or, A Journey to London, pr., pb. 1728 (completion of Sir John Vanbrugh's play)

Damon and Phillida, pr., pb. 1729 (ballad opera)

Love in a Riddle, pr., pb. 1729 (ballad opera)

Papal Tyranny in the Reign of King John, pr., pb. 1745

The Lady's Lecture, pb. 1748

The Dramatic Works of Colley Cibber, pb. 1777 (5 volumes)

OTHER LITERARY FORMS

Colley Cibber wrote a number of nonfiction works in his later years: *An Apology for the Life of Colley Cibber* (1740), *A Letter from Mr. Cibber to Mr. Pope* (1742), *The Egoist: Or, Colley upon Cibber* (1743), *A Second Letter from Mr. Cibber to Mr. Pope* (1743),

Another Occasional Letter from Mr. Cibber to Mr. Pope (1744), *The Character and Conduct of Cicero* (1747), and *A Rhapsody upon the Marvellous* (1751). In addition, having been made poet laureate in 1730, he wrote a series of annual New Year's and birthday odes celebrating the virtues of George II.

ACHIEVEMENTS

Colley Cibber's reputation rests on his career as an actor, manager, and playwright. As an actor, he was one of the principal comedians of his time, winning fame for his portrayals of a particular character type, the foppish fool. As one of several actor-managers, he was the reader for Drury Lane and determined which new plays were performed and which were rejected. As a playwright, he wrote a series of successful dramas, including the first sentimental comedy, *Love's Last Shift*. Today, his plays have chiefly historical interest, but a good half dozen became staples of the theatrical repertory during the eighteenth century. In his autobiography, *An Apology for the Life of Colley Cibber*, Cibber likened his plays to his children: "I think we had about a dozen of each sort [that is, children and plays] between us; of both which Kinds, some dy'd in their Infancy, and near an equal number of each were alive, when I quitted the Theatre." Cibber's autobiography provides not only a record of his life but also a theatrical history of London during the Restoration and early eighteenth century. Today, it is Cibber's most widely read work.

BIOGRAPHY

Colley Cibber was the son of Jane Colley and Caius Gabriel Cibber, a master sculptor from Flensburg, Schleswig. Cibber's father had intended his son for the Church, but Cibber became stagestruck at an early age and in 1689 joined the Theatre Royal as an unsalaried apprentice. Even though his early years were not marked by financial success, in 1693, Cibber married Katherine Shore, the daughter of Matthias Shore, who held the post of Sergeant Trumpet at court.

Discouraged by the poor roles he was assigned, Cibber wrote a play (*Love's Last Shift*) with a role for himself. Sir Novelty Fashion was not the main char-

acter in the play, but the part gave Cibber a chance to demonstrate his comic abilities. Shortly after the play's premiere in 1696, Sir John Vanbrugh wrote *The Relapse: Or, Virtue in Danger* as a sequel to *Love's Last Shift*. Cibber's performance as Lord Foppington (the new title for Sir Novelty) in Vanbrugh's play confirmed his success in *Love's Last Shift* and established him as one of the leading comedians of his day. As a playwright and an actor, Cibber did not limit himself to comedy, but it was in this genre that he enjoyed his greatest successes. In addition to writing and acting, Cibber became increasingly involved in the administration of Drury Lane, eventually becoming one of the triumvirate of actor-managers who ran the company.

The 1720's were marked for Colley Cibber by well-publicized quarrels with Alexander Pope, Henry Fielding, John Dennis, and Nathaniel Mist. Cibber's popularity also declined during this decade; there appeared to be a permanent claque in the audience that disapproved of everything Cibber did. As reader for Drury Lane, Cibber was the most influential of the three actor-managers. Many of his problems stemmed

Colley Cibber (Library of Congress)

from his cavalier treatment of new works that were submitted to the company for possible performance.

In 1730, Cibber was named poet laureate. This new post proved a source of both pleasure and aggravation for Cibber. It gave him an entry into the highest levels of society but also made him the target of new volleys of ridicule, since he was not a skilled poet.

In 1733, Cibber retired from the stage, but he continued to make guest appearances until 1745, when his play *Papal Tyranny in the Reign of King John* was presented, with the author playing Cardinal Pandulph. Neither the play nor Cibber's performance was well received; it marked his last appearance on the stage.

In 1740, his autobiography appeared and became an immediate success, quickly going through several editions. In 1743, Pope immortalized Cibber as the King of the Dunces in *The Dunciad* (1728-1743), thus bringing to a head their long-standing feud. Despite the attacks by Pope and other men of letters, Cibber enjoyed his final years, for he had achieved the status of a celebrity and was accorded preferential treatment by the finest families of England.

ANALYSIS

As the reader for Drury Lane, Colley Cibber was widely hated for his many rejections of plays on the basis of their lack of theatricality. According to Richard Hindry Barker in *Mr. Cibber of Drury Lane* (1939), for Cibber, theatricality meant "effective situations, plenty of opportunities for stage business, good acting parts suitable for [Robert] Wilks, [Barton] Booth, Mrs. [Anne] Oldfield, and himself." These criteria are surely the outstanding characteristics of his own dramas. He knew what worked on the stage, and he fashioned his plays accordingly.

Today, Cibber is remembered as the creator of the first eighteenth century sentimental comedy; this accomplishment can best be understood in terms of the theatricality of his plays. Cibber did not set out to write a new kind of comedy. Rather, he set out to write a play that would show off the skills of his actors and that would leave his audience pleased and satisfied at the end of the evening. In his first play, he discovered a number of formulas that worked well on the stage. In a Cibber comedy, there are two plots involving a series of deceptions that lead up to discovery scenes in acts 4 and 5, in which the complications of the evening are resolved in a moral, decorous way. Usually, a leading character in the main plot comes to recognize that he has been living according to a false set of values. When he sees the errors of his ways, the problems of the evening are resolved. What makes Cibber a less than compelling dramatist is that this reversal usually does not grow out of characterization. Cibber's heroes and heroines perform a mental about-face in act 5, brought about by manipulations in the plot rather than by a process of self-discovery. The action in the secondary plot usually resembles the action in the main plot, but it does not depend on a character's sudden transformation for its resolution.

Cibber's plays are well crafted. No matter how complicated the plots become, they are always easy to follow, and all conflicts are neatly resolved by the end of the performance. Cibber gave his audiences the satisfaction of seeing virtue rewarded and lovers correctly matched. His characters are, by and large, stock figures taken from the world of the Restoration comedy of manners. Many of the situations and plot complications also are part of the stock-in-trade of the Restoration stage. Nevertheless, his plays do represent a quite significant departure from the dramatic world of William Wycherley, Sir George Etherege, and William Congreve, in whose plays the endings are rarely so neat and uncomplicated.

LOVE'S LAST SHIFT

Love's Last Shift was Cibber's first play and immediately established him as an important playwright. The main plot involves the reconciliation of a debauchee with the wife he had abandoned eight years before: Loveless "grew weary of his Wife in six Months; left her, and the Town, for Debts he did not care to pay; and having spent the last part of his Estate beyond Sea, returns to *England* in a very mean Condition." He thinks his wife Amanda is dead, but she in fact is alive, having remained faithful to him and come into an estate of her own with the death of a rich uncle. Amanda is not the witty heroine of Restoration comedy but a precursor of the noble heroine of eighteenth century drama, a model of fidelity and moral strength as she sets herself an all but impossible task:

> Oh! to reclaim the Man I'm bound by Heaven to Love, to expose the Folly of a roving Mind, in pleasing him with what he seem'd to loath, were such a sweet Revenge for slighted Love, so vast a Triumph of rewarded Constancy, as might persuade the looser part of Womankind ev'n to forsake themselves, and fall in Love with Virtue.

Loveless is a more familiar figure from the world of Restoration comedy, a rake who has lived according to a delusion of his sex and class about marriage: "an affectation of being fashionably Vicious, than any reasonable Dislike he cou'd either find in" his wife's "Mind or Person." Amanda, who has been altered (but not for the worse) by smallpox since Loveless last saw her, is persuaded by Young Worthy to trick her husband into her bed. This plot involves two transformation scenes. In act 4, the audience has the titillating experience of seeing the apparently virtuous Amanda abandon herself to the pleasures of "a lawless Love: I own my self a Libertine, a mortal Foe to that dull Thing call'd Virtue, that mere Disease of sickly Nature." In act 5, when Loveless discovers the mistake he has made, he admits the errors of his ways and returns to his faithful wife, a scene that reportedly brought tears to the eyes of the first-night audience.

These characters are one-dimensional figures committed to particular moral points of view, but the clash between these opposing views gives their scenes dramatic tension. Cibber also managed to leaven their scenes with laughter by introducing a subplot involving Loveless's servant Snap and Amanda's maid. Snap is placed under a table throughout Loveless's assignation with Amanda. After Loveless and Amanda retire, Snap sneaks up on Amanda's maid, who is listening at her mistress's door, and begins to take advantage of her. When she gets a chance, the maid tricks him into falling into the cellar, but Snap pulls her down with him and they spend the night together. Their brief scenes form an appropriate low-comedy contrast to the more serious affairs of their master and mistress.

The secondary plot ostensibly involves the correct mating of the Worthy brothers. Young Worthy loves Narcissa, who is betrothed to Elder Worthy, who loves Hillaria, Narcissa's cousin. At the end of the play, the couples are correctly matched, but Cibber's working out of this plot was perfunctory, since his real interest in this part of the play was Sir Novelty Fashion, the role that helped to establish him as an actor. One might expect Sir Novelty, a stock figure from Restoration drama modeled after Sir Fopling Flutter in Etherege's *The Man of Mode: Or, Sir Fopling Flutter* (pr., pb. 1676), to function as possible rival for the hands of Narcissa and Hillaria, but he is so obviously a fool that no one, save himself, takes him seriously. Rather than using Sir Novelty to add complications to the secondary plot, Cibber used the plot as an occasion to display Sir Novelty. As a prank, the four young lovers lure Sir Novelty to St. James's Park with the promise of a rendezvous with Narcissa, whom he assumes must be enamored of his charms. Instead, he meets Mrs. Flareit, a used mistress he wants to get rid of. The scene, like so many of Cibber's big comic scenes, is filled with physical action. At its climax, the emotional Mrs. Flareit attempts to run Sir Novelty through with a sword. Occurring at the beginning of act 4, this scene with its broad humor balances the almost melodramatic meeting between Loveless and Amanda at the end of the act. In addition, the scenes thematically resemble each other, since both involve tricks played on male characters who are overly concerned with following the false dictates of fashion. Unlike Loveless, Sir Novelty experiences no moral reformation. He is simply exposed as the fool he is, to the general amusement of all.

THE CARELESS HUSBAND

In *The Careless Husband*, written eight years later, Cibber used more artfully many of the elements that had worked so well in *Love's Last Shift*. Sir Novelty reappears as Sir Foppington, but now he furthers the plot. He is still a fantastic fool, but not so ludicrous that he cannot make a devoted lover jealous when he ogles the lover's mistress. The double plot once again involves a similar situation played out with two couples, but here the characters in both plots are from the same genteel level of society and interact with one another. In the main plot, Sir Charles Easy is married to a faithful woman who sincerely loves him. Only at the end of the play does he learn to value her devotion and cast off the conventional role of jaded husband who must look outside his home for pleasure. In the secondary plot, Lady Betty Modish is pursued by a faithful suitor, Lord Morelove, who sincerely loves her. Only at the end of the play is she able to come to grips with her true feelings for him and to cast off her conventional role of the desirable beauty who delights in exercising her power over men and in keeping them on a string.

These characters neatly complement one another. Lady Easy is a model of virtue. Even when she discovers her husband sleeping with her maid, she suppresses her anger and thinks instead of his needs by placing a scarf "gently over his head" so he will not catch cold. Her only concern is that he should not wake and be irritated: "And if he should wake offended at my too-busy care, let my heart-breaking patience, duty, and my fond affection plead my pardon." Lady Betty Modish is a flirt. She cannot resist engaging in battle with the opposite sex and is satisfied with nothing less than victory: "Let me but live to see him once more within my power, and I'll forgive the rest of fortune." Sir Charles Easy is a man of the world, careless in his affairs, weary of the complicated games lovers play: "I am of late grown so very lazy in my pleasures that I had rather lose a woman than go through the plague and trouble of having or keeping her." Lord Morelove is so timid that he would never even attempt such an affair: "The shame or scandal of a repulse always made me afraid of attempting a woman of condition."

The reconciliations in act 5 are better prepared for here than in *Love's Last Shift*. Sir Charles Easy and Lady Betty Modish may not be in touch with their true feelings, but the audience is well aware of them. In this context Lady Easy is extremely useful. To a modern reader, she may appear impossibly prim and virtuous, but she is aware of the true feelings of Sir Charles and Lady Betty, and she helps expose what the characters themselves do not know. Here, for example, Lady Easy probes the feelings of Lady Betty:

LADY BETTY MODISH: But still, to marry before one's heartily in love—

LADY EASY: Is not half so formidable a calamity. But if I have any eyes, my dear, you'll run no great hazard of that in venturing upon my Lord Morelove. You don't know, perhaps, that within this half hour the tone of your voice is strangely softened to him, ha! ha! ha! ha!

At the end, the reader does not feel that the reconciliations have been imposed by the law of happy endings; they are rather the natural consequence of character in action.

THE PROVOK'D HUSBAND

Cibber's last successful play, *The Provok'd Husband*, was presented twenty-four years after *The Careless Husband*. Like so many of Cibber's works, it is not a completely original play. In this instance, Cibber revised an unfinished play that came into his hands after the death of its author, Sir John Vanbrugh. The changes Cibber made give a good indication of his theatrical interests. Vanbrugh's play consisted of two plots and was entitled *A Journey to London*. The main plot involved a well-to-do family from the country, the Headpieces, who come to London only to fall easy victims to the lures of the big city. The secondary plot involved the battling Loverules, who fight over Lady Loverule's extravagances. Peter Dixon suggests in his edition of the play that if Vanbrugh had finished the work, the Loverule plot would have issued "in an angry separation, without hope of reconciliation, but also without the possibility of divorce." Cibber, who had a reputation as the dramatist of genteel society, reversed the importance of the two plots. The disputes between the Townlys (the new name for the Loverules) became the primary plot, while the misadventures of the Wrongheads (the new name for the Headpieces) became the secondary plot. In act 5, Cibber provided a moral conclusion with the reconciliation of the Townlys.

The theme of a wife's financial excesses dominates the Townly plot. Lady Townly is addicted to gambling. Her fault is not simply a matter of extravagant expenditures, for she virtually abandons her husband for the pleasures of the hazard table, associating with the least reputable people in polite society and sleeping until five in the afternoon.

In act 5, however, Lady Townly reforms when she is threatened with the possibility of being cut off from her husband's wealth and her position as his wife. Her reformation is as unprepared for as Loveless's in *Love's Last Shift*. Both characters renounce their wicked ways after having spent a whole play demonstrating how committed they are to their profligate habits. In her recantation, Lady Townly sounds suspiciously like another Cibber character, Lady Betty Modish in *The Careless Husband*. Both ladies are great beauties who use their allure to gain power over men. Not surprisingly, both of these parts were written for Cibber's favorite actress, Anne Oldfield.

The secondary plot is also dominated by a conflict between spouses. Lady Wronghead quickly learns the main vice of the married lady in town—to spend money. She starts with knickknacks and fripperies, since the greatest distinction of a fine lady in this town is in the variety of pretty things that she has no occasion for, but soon moves on to the pleasures of the hazard table, to which she is introduced by Lady Townly. At the end of the play, there is no recantation scene for Lady Wronghead. Rather, she is whisked back to the country, where she belongs and where she will do herself and others no harm. The Wrongheads, like Sir Novelty Fashion, exist to amuse the audience; moral reform is not possible for them.

In this late comedy, Cibber once more manipulated the character types and situations with which he had worked for thirty years. Cibber's career as a dramatist does not reveal growth; rather, it reveals an early mastery of the requirements of the stage that sustained him for the rest of his career and made him the most important writer of comedies in the early eighteenth century.

OTHER MAJOR WORKS

NONFICTION: *An Apology for the Life of Colley Cibber*, 1740; *A Letter from Mr. Cibber to Mr. Pope*, 1742; *The Egoist: Or, Colley upon Cibber*, 1743; *A Second Letter from Mr. Cibber to Mr. Pope*, 1743; *Another Occasional Letter from Mr. Cibber to Mr. Pope*, 1744; *The Character and Conduct of Cicero*, 1747; *A Rhapsody upon the Marvellous*, 1751.

BIBLIOGRAPHY

Ashley, Leonard R. N. *Colley Cibber*. Rev. ed. Boston: Twayne, 1989. Ashley devotes one chapter to Cibber's youth and then gives an account of him as an actor, listing the various roles he played and counting his performances at 2,936. One chapter judges Cibber's work as a dramatist, and three chapters deal with his life in the theater. His quarrel with Alexander Pope is also summarized. A good bibliography completes this study.

Barker, Richard Hindry. *Mr. Cibber of Drury Lane*. New York: Columbia University Press, 1939. Reprint. New York: AMS Press, 1966. A well-written and comprehensive biography, especially good for the discussions of the rise of the actors-managers and their last years. The chapter entitled "The Struggle with Lincoln's Inn Fields" is an informative account of the theater at that location.

Koon, Helene. *Colley Cibber: A Biography*. Lexington: University Press of Kentucky, 1986. Besides offering an authoritative biography, Koon includes invaluable appendices entitled "The Genealogy of the Cibber Family," "Cibber's Second Letter to Alexander Pope," "Colley Cibber's Will," and "Chronological List of Cibber's Roles." The notes and bibliography are excellent sources for further information.

Szilagyi, Stephen. "The Importance of Being Easy: Desire and Cibber's *The Careless Husband.*" *Texas Studies in Literature and Language* 41, no. 2 (Summer, 1999): 142-159. This discussion of *The Careless Husband* examines the desires of its characters and their longing for ease.

Wallace, Beth Kowaleski. "Reading the Surfaces of Colley Cibber's *The Careless Husband.*" *Studies in English Literature, 1500-1900* 40, no. 3 (summer, 2000): 473-489. Wallace argues that although at first reading *The Careless Husband* appears to be a conventional sentimental comedy, it actually makes a deeper statement.

Edward V. Geist,
updated by Frank Day

JOHN PEPPER CLARK-BEKEDEREMO

Born: Kiagbodo, Nigeria; April 6, 1935

PRINCIPAL DRAMA

Song of a Goat, pr., pb. 1961

The Masquerade, pb. 1964, pr. 1965

The Raft, pb. 1964, pr. 1966 (radio play), revised pr. 1978

Three Plays, pb. 1964

Ozidi, pb. 1966

The Boat, pr. 1981, pb. 1985

The Bikoroa Plays, pr. 1981, pb. 1985 (includes *The Boat*, *The Return Home*, and *Full Circle*)

Collected Plays, 1964-1988, pb. 1991 (includes *Song of a Goat*, *The Masquerade*, *The Raft*, *Ozidi*, *The Boat*, *The Return Home*, and *Full Circle*)

The Wives' Revolt, pb. 1991

All for Oil, pr., pb. 2000

OTHER LITERARY FORMS

John Pepper Clark-Bekederemo is recognized as a major poet for his collections *Poems* (1962), *A Reed in the Tide: A Selection of Poems* (1965), *Casualties: Poems, 1966-1968* (1970), and *A Decade of Tongues* (1981). He has also published literary criticism with *The Example of Shakespeare: Critical Essays on African Literature* (1970) and a travel diary, *America, Their America* (1964).

ACHIEVEMENTS

John Pepper Clark-Bekederemo was a member of an extraordinary group of creative young Nigerian writers and artists who began their careers in the early 1960's with publication in the legendary magazine *Black Orpheus*. Contributors besides Clark-Bekederemo included Chinua Achebe, the Nobel Prize winner Wole Soyinka, and Christopher Okigbo. The nature of this publication defined Clark-Bekederemo's subsequent work. He wished to establish and confirm the importance and dignity of his Ijaw inheritance in the river delta of Nigeria and yet communicate these roots through publication in En-

glish. Both in his poetry and in his drama, he presented his ancestry with affectionate sensibility. Yet because he had become an academic within the formal university system that the British had exported to West Africa, he was committed to linking this antecedence with the wider concept of international, universal human issues. His major works draw from the specific environment of his birth. He uses English to make profound statements about the conditions of humanity in the contemporary world, but an English skillfully adapted to express its African context.

BIOGRAPHY

John Pepper Clark-Bekederemo was born in the Western Rivers area of Nigeria in Kiagbodo, Warri Province, on April 6, 1935. His father, Clark Fuludu Bekederemo, was a chief. He attended several local schools, the most important being Government College in Ughelli. In 1954, he spent a year as a clerk in a government office before earning entrance to a college in Ibadan that would subsequently become the University of Ibadan. At the university, he rapidly entered the literary milieu and became editor first of *Beacon* and later of *Horn*, student magazines that offered early opportunities for publication to several writers who would become the first generation of Nigerian authors. In 1960, he was graduated with a B.A. in English, worked briefly as information officer with the Ministry of Information at Ibadan, and then was appointed an editorial writer for the *Express*, a Lagos newspaper. It was this position that permitted his appointment as Parvin Fellow at Princeton during the 1962-1963 academic year. For various reasons, this opportunity occasioned mutual dissatisfaction, and for Clark-Bekederemo, it provided the basis for a rather bad-tempered diary of that year, *America, Their America*. On his return to Nigeria, he spent a year as Research Fellow at Ibadan and began the field research that produced the *Ozidi* saga. In 1964, he married a Yoruba woman, Ebun Odutola, a talented actress. They had three children: two daughters,

Ebiere and Imoyadue, and a son, Ambekederemo. That same year, he joined the faculty of the University of Lagos and in 1972 was appointed professor of English. The years 1975 and 1976 saw him as Distinguished Fellow at Wesleyan University in Connecticut. In 1979, however, he chose to give up an academic career in order to concentrate on writing. He returned to his birthplace at Kiagbodo. He became influential in Nigerian theater, and in 1982, he formed the PEC Repertory in Lagos. After his return to Kiagbodo, he preferred to add his father's name, Bekederemo, to his own in formal matters, as demonstrated in his collection of plays and poems published in 1991.

ANALYSIS

John Pepper Clark-Bekederemo's first play was *Song of a Goat*. Its title indicates the multiple cultural elements he integrates into his drama. There is obvious reference to classic Greek in that the very term "tragedy" translates as "goat song" (*tragos* meaning "goat," and *oide* meaning "song"). There is also a parallel tradition from Africa. By Ijaw custom, a goat is the appropriate sacrifice—in the manner of the Hebraic concept of scapegoat. Similarities with the Irish playwright John Millington Synge are also apparent. Clark-Bekederemo accepts Synge's view of the tragic dignity of humble people.

SONG OF A GOAT

The plot of *Song of a Goat* presents a conflict between traditional and modern beliefs, though this does not seem to be the central element. The tragedy itself derives from urgent human responses. Zifa's wife, Ebiere, consults a "masseur," who is both doctor and priest, concerning her infertility. From her diffident explanations, it becomes clear that the husband has become impotent: "I keep my house/ Open by night and day/ But my lord will not come in." The doctor argues that "some one has to go in, or they will take rust." He advises the tribal custom that someone within the family, such as Tonye, his younger brother, substitute for the husband. "That'll be a retying of knots," and there will be continuity of issue. Clark-Bekederemo presents a curious psychological ambivalence in response to this advice. Even

though presumably the practice is legalized by long-term custom ("What I suggested our fathers did not forbid"), Ebiere is as horrified as any Western wife would be. "I'll not stay here longer to hear this kind of talk," she says. With ominous perception, she answers, "That will be an act of death." Her husband Zifa is also violently shocked by the suggestion. He prefers to wait: "The thing may come back any day." He is shamed that he will receive public scorn for his impotence. "Everybody will be saying, there/ Goes the cock. . . ." There are continuing hints that his problem is imposed by the gods as punishment for some very vaguely defined and unpurged offense committed by his father.

After some months of barrenness, Ebiere, bitter against her husband and lusting with thwarted passion, teases Tonye into seducing her. He resists at first, for the deed is wicked, but he embraces her with such ardor that there is no possible pretense that he is simply obeying the decrees of custom. This is naked adultery passionately performed. Zifa finds his incestuous brother in his bed and berates him: "I can't believe it. . . . My own brother who I have looked after." Zifa decides that he will kill the adulterer, but before he can do this, in shame Tonye goes and hangs himself. It seems there is nobility in this decision, for he takes on himself the crime of suicide and frees Zifa from the penalty for committing the most heinous crime conceivable in Ijaw life: A deed that offends the gods. Zifa recognizes this sacrifice. "I thought to kill/ You but in that office you have again performed my part." Only now does his self-condemnation confirm the possible justice of the act. "He went to my wife. . . . Was that not a brotherly act?" Ebiere is said to have miscarried his brother's son. Despairing at the disaster his own anguish and jealousy have wrought, Zifa commits suicide by drowning himself in the sea, yielding to the power of the gods whom in his life he has opposed. The masseur concludes by attempting words of comfort and reconciliation, rather than blame, in the face of tragedy that reduces men to misery and defeat. "It is enough/ You know now that each day we live/ Hints at why we cried at birth." Here is the moral essence of the tragic condition. The urgency in this play does not rest with the external cultural conflict, though this is often mentioned. The conflict between human passion and moral duty provides the trigger for the inescapable disaster constantly prophesied by an old woman who leads the neighbors in the role of Chorus. Cassandra-like, she issues warnings that are perceived but not heeded. This makes for absorbing drama in the classic tradition.

The richness of the language more than sustains the tension of the events. Clark-Bekederemo enjoys the long, extended poetic metaphor. Ebiere's unpregnant womb is compared to a "piece of fertile land— run fallow with elephant grass," an analogy he carries through to extreme development. This technique connects with the Ijaw preference for the riddle when matters are too intimate to be spoken of directly. There is the almost William Shakespearean invective: "You lame thing, you crawling piece/ Of withered flesh." Clark-Bekederemo also employs the profoundest declamatory poetry. "You may well cry. But this is nothing/ To beat your breast. It was how/ We all began and will end." Here is something rare on the contemporary stage—a modern tragedy, a form that Western playwrights have only rarely achieved in the twentieth century.

THE MASQUERADE

The Masquerade is closely linked with the earlier play. It is essentially similar in mood and structure. One of the chief characters derives from *Song of a Goat*. It is now determined that Ebiere died giving birth to Tonye's son, Tufa. The earlier play spoke of her surviving a miscarriage. That minor point indicates that the two plays were not conceived originally as part of a single cycle. Tufa grows up and travels from his home, hoping like Oedipus to escape from the curse of his illegitimate origin. The play begins with a sense of foreboding. Without knowing the reason ("as far as I know no feasts have been left out," says one), the villagers see ominous signs: "The tilt [of the moon] is prominent,/ It is never so but there is disaster."

Into this situation comes Tufa. Titi is the local belle. A neighbor's description of her almost parodies the famous report of Cleopatra by Enobarbus: "Her head high in that silver tiara so/ Brilliant it was blind-

ness trying to tell/ Its characters." Tufa immediately falls for her, and at first the affair seems blessed. The couple make love in lyric poetry: "Your flesh under flush/ Of cam flashes many times lovelier than gold/ Or pearls." Soon, however, gossip informs of the tragic but polluting events of Tufa's past: "His father/ Usurped the bed of his elder brother, yes,/ Brazenly in his lifetime, and for shame/ Of it hanged himself." Titi's father, Diribi, immediately condemns Tufa and forbids the marriage: "Consider the taint." He fears that the curse Tufa bears will spread among the entire family. If they associate with him, the gods will threaten them, too. The mother is equally dismissive, saying, "the man is no more your husband now happily/ His past and back are in full view." Tufa is told "leave my daughter alone, . . . and go your curse-laden way." To her father's horror, Titi defies him and argues that she will marry Tufa in spite of "this prospect of pollution." Her father curses Titi, calling her "this witch and bitch/ Who has quite infected her breed." Tufa, however, is touched by the generosity of her love and recognizes her devotion. Titi "called herself my wife, my bride ready to go with me/ In spite of my shame." Her father, in spite of his great affection, is more concerned with his consequent family shame and determines to kill her. Though "she tried tears, tried prayers," he shoots her with the very gun Tufa had given him as a present. He turns the gun on Tufa and wounds him mortally. Tufa staggers out to join Titi, after confessing, "I am that unmentionable beast/ Born of woman to brother." Borrowing from Greek, Clark-Bekederemo has the priests observe, "Who/ The gods love they visit with calamity." No action need be taken against the father. In this situation, no human punishment can add to the misfortune imposed. He has destroyed himself. He "who was so tall and strong/ Before. . . . Now at one stroke/ See him splintered to the ground." The tragedy that began with *Song of a Goat* has now worked itself out, purging the crime from which it originated in the manner of the great Greek tragedies.

Again, one should observe the controlled poetry that Clark-Bekederemo employs. Like that of Shakespeare, it can range without any apparent contradiction between colloquial conversation and great poetic feeling. Beautiful are the lines: "It is the time/ Of night. There is a catch in the air/ Will not hold. Not a rustle of leaves,/ Not a cry of a bird, nor the sudden charge/ Of sheep or goats. . . ."

THE RAFT

The Raft explores a new topic, a circumstance reminiscent of Stephen Crane's famous short story "The Open Boat." It describes four workers: Olotu, the educated townsman; Kengide, the cynic; Ogro, the traditionalist, and Ibobo, the priest figure. They are camping on a huge raft of hard wood logs, sailing it down river to the port. Owing to mischance or carelessness, the ropes tying it during the night come away and they drift helplessly down the river, unable to control direction or to determine where they are because of the heavy fog. This danger frightens them, and one by one these men are brought to the breaking point and die. The raft itself would seem to be a general symbol of individuals' inability to be masters of their environment, indicating their weakness when pitted against the superior power of circumstance. Some critics have argued that because this was written when Nigerian political events seemed to be equally drifting before the resolution of an army coup, direct reference must be intended. The times may conceivably have been in Clark-Bekederemo's mind when he invented this plot, but the play is certainly far more universal in its concept than any political tract would be. The characters in the play do not represent public persons, even obliquely, nor are they conceived as representing generalized attitudes of the time. They are individuals battling fierce problems in a highly realistic setting. The play succeeds on the stage because the potential allegory is never allowed to intrude into the actual events.

The raft begins to drift when by some inexplicable means its mooring ropes break. "What I can't understand is how all/ The seven gave way. . . . Some madman/ Came aboard and cut us loose?/ Some ghost or evil god." The speculations indicate the cosmic nature of their plight. They find that they are being carried out to sea on the ebb tide. Desperately they apply all of their skill. As they contemplate the prospect of death, they agonize and discuss their chances, reminisce about their pasts, their families, their jobs, their

hopes. Yet disaster cannot be avoided. First, Olotu is taken away when a part of the raft breaks off and he is unable to swim back. "He's adrift and lost!" is the cry. The greater truth comes in the responsive observation, "We are all adrift and lost!" Then they hear a ship coming. Ogro decides his best chance is to swim to it and be hauled aboard. The sailors see him and beat him away until he becomes entwined in the stern wheel and is killed. None will assist in escape. Now only Ibobo and Kengide remain. Ibobo thinks that he recognizes a small town they are passing and decides to jump overboard. Kengide holds him back, warning him of sharks, but Ibobo asks, "are/ You afraid to be alone?" With a more generalized recognition that typically links actual event to universality, Kengide says, "Aren't you afraid to be left alone/ In this world, aren't you?" They decide to shout in the hope of attracting attention. The last lines of the play are their forlorn and feeble voices crying "Ee-ee-eee!" which, in a stage direction, Clark-Bekederemo reminds his readers is "the long squeal as used when women go wood-gathering and by nightfall have still not found their way home." In a sense, the tragedy here is less personal, more cosmic. The suffering is not imposed on the characters because there is some taint in their past, some evil to be assuaged. Here is the more pessimistic conclusion that all persons are doomed to suffer in a universe that is implacably indifferent to their fate. This view does not allow the note of hope that occurs in the final resolution of many tragedies when even death can be seen as a kind of liberation from the pains of enduring the arrows of life. Here, death is an end without purpose and without meaning imposed by powers beyond human beings' control and indifferent to their fate.

OZIDI

Ozidi brings a major change in the direction of Clark-Bekederemo's work. The original *Ozidi* is a traditional poetic saga of the Ijaw people. The playwright affirms its epic status, calling it "an old story, truly heroic in proportion, arising out of a people's sense of their past." In its original form, its performance lasts seven days and is embellished with dance, music, ritual masks, and costumes. In drawing on the historical event, Clark-Bekederemo has departed from the universalist ideas of his earlier plays and immersed himself deeply in his African inheritance. This involvement makes it difficult for him to extract a sequence of action that will be appropriate for a formal theatrical presentation, inevitably restricted both in time span and area.

Clark-Bekederemo's concern for *Ozidi* has an extended history. He first heard the tale when Afoluwa of Ofonibenga recited it to an eager school audience. It had such an impact that he worked for ten years as a researcher to record permanently this oral, public event. The results were a film, a record of the music, and, in 1977, an Ijaw/English side-by-side transcription of nearly four hundred pages. While continuing this long-term study, in 1966, he attempted to distill the extensive epic into an English-language dramatized version. The result presents barriers to the non-African reader. The fullest comprehension may seem to require anthropological knowledge. Nevertheless, the play has moments of dramatic intensity and the basic plot is clear enough, even though compression requires external explication.

The story spans two generations. A new king must be selected, this time from the house of Ozidi. He refuses the honor and is amazed when his younger brother, Temugedege, a discreditable and feeble figure "dribbling with drink," demands his rights to the throne. He greedily imagines his power, intending to become "terror of all our/ Territories." The populace consider his pretensions ridiculous. Ozidi agrees with their judgments but insists that, as his brother has been made king, all the normal honors are due him, including lavish gifts: "A god is/ A god once you make him so," he says. His subjects have no intention of gratifying so feeble a monarch, for "nobody is going to serve Temugedege; he is an idiot." When Ozidi insists that the traditional generosities are required no matter how inadequate the recipient, there are murmurs of revolt. Rather than tax themselves for safety from the ruthless Ozidi, they prefer to plan his death. Because one of the expectations of a new king is a symbolic skull, they attack Ozidi, cunningly destroy his magic security, and send his head to his brother. "There is our tribute to you, King." He is too weak to do other than flee. Ozidi's grandmother Oreame escapes with his pregnant wife, Orea, who delivers a child also called Ozidi.

The second section deals with young Ozidi's upbringing largely at the hands of his grandmother, who uses her skills in magic to develop his courage so that he will be the means of revenge for his father's murder. She intends that he "must go forth and scatter death among/ His father's enemies." He returns to his father's home and reinstates himself: "Let's raise again the compound of my fathers." Urged by his grandmother and protected by her magic, he seeks out his enemies and throws down a challenge by shamefully and publicly stripping their wives. He singles out his opponents and fights them one by one. Though they confront him boldly, "Ozidi, I am going to eat you up today," he is always victorious. Others seeking to avenge their friends are equally eliminated, their magic brought to nothing against Oreame's spells. The sequence of deaths affects Ozidi, until a woman can ask, "Is there nothing else you can do except kill?" Finally blinded by herbs, he kills both enemy and grandmother, for she has not thought to protect herself from her own grandson. He is attacked by fever and nursed by his mother. He wins that bodily battle and thus defeats King Smallpox, the ultimate enemy of the people, who will not "set foot again on this shore." The end is somewhat surprising, but it is clear that some general victory other than satisfied revenge is required to achieve Ozidi's full heroic status.

The events in this play are repetitive and sometimes confusing. The language, seeming sometimes close to Ijaw, makes for difficult interpretaion. At other times, it has the familiar Clark-Bekederemo lyrical conviction. "What need have/ We to stand up when silk cotton trees lie prostrate/ We are reeds only, mere reeds in the storm, and must/ Stretch our broken backs on the ground." *Ozidi* is less immediately accessible to a non-Nigerian reader, but it has the same tragic power and evocative language found in the earlier plays and exhibits Clark-Bekederemo's determination to draw ever more deeply from his African experience and culture.

ALL FOR OIL

For many years after his writing of *Ozidi*, Clark-Bekederemo seems to have preferred to concentrate on poetry, and perhaps his reputation in this genre is higher than his reputation as a dramatist. However, his contribution to the theater continued with production of *The Bikoroa Plays*, *The Wives' Revolt*, and *All for Oil*.

The production of Clark-Bekederemo's *All for Oil* coincided with the celebration of Nigeria's fortieth anniversary of independence. The play is a biographical drama that draws on Nigeria's historical background involving the trade of palm oil and the present plight over oil in Nigeria and the Niger Delta. *All for Oil* is a literary testament to Clark-Bekederemo's belief that "we should sit together and decide the conditions of our living together."

OTHER MAJOR WORKS

POETRY: *Poems*, 1962; *A Reed in the Tide: A Selection of Poems*, 1965; *Casualties: Poems, 1966-1968*, 1970; *Urhobo Poetry*, 1980; *A Decade of Tongues*, 1981; *Mandela, and Other Poems*, 1988; *Collected Poems, 1958-1988*, 1991; *A Lot from Paradise*, 1997.

NONFICTION: *America, Their America*, 1964; *The Example of Shakespeare: Critical Essays on African Literature*, 1970; *The Philosophical Anarchism of William Godwin*, 1977; *State of the Union*, 1985.

EDITED TEXT: *The Ozidi Saga*, 1977.

BIBLIOGRAPHY

Cartey, Wilfred. *Whispers from a Continent: The Literature of Contemporary Black Africa*. New York: Vintage Books, 1969. Clark-Bekederemo's *Song of a Goat*, *The Masquerade*, and *The Raft* are analyzed in considerable detail, toward Cartey's thesis that in Clark-Bekederemo's plays "man is indeed adrift and his actions to escape the drift are futile."

Egudu, Romanus. *Four Modern West African Poets*. New York: NOK Publishers, 1977. Only indirectly dealing with his drama, the chapter on Clark-Bekederemo nevertheless makes the point that, like his poetry, his drama takes on "the theme of calamity, of the tragic 'reality' of existence." Characters are victims of punishment, often undeserved, from society and the gods.

Esslin, Martin. "Two Nigerian Playwrights." In *Introduction to African Literature: An Anthology of Critical Writing from "Black Orpheus,"* edited by Ulli Beier. Evanston, Ill.: Northwestern University Press, 1967. Clark-Bekederemo is compared with Wole Soyinka, but with more theatrical authority than African expertise. This article first appeared in Clark-Bekederemo's own magazine. Particularly informative on the question of English-language theater for African writers.

Fearn, Marianne. *Modern Drama of Africa, Form and Content: A Study of Four Playwrights*. Ann Arbor, Mich.: University Microfilms International, 1978. A section of chapter 3 deals with the verse theater of Clark-Bekederemo and his use of traditional music, dance, and folk characters. Strong bibliography on African drama.

Graham-White, Anthony. *The Drama of Black Africa*. New York: Samuel French, 1974. Chapter 5 gives a brief biography, then discusses the plays, from *Song of a Goat* to *Ozidi* (based on Ijaw traditional drama), in terms of Greek tragedy, cursed houses, and fallen heroes. Contrasts Clark's pessimism with Wole Soyinka's more positive views. Index and valuable chronology.

Irele, Abiola. Introduction to *Collected Plays and Poems, 1958-1988*. Washington, D.C.: Howard University Press, 1991. A substantial introduction to Clark-Bekederemo's dramatic and poetic work, discussing his debt to European theatrical tradition, especially the Theater of the Absurd. *Ozidi* is cited as his "most fully realized play."

Povey, John. "Two Hands a Man Has." In *African Literature Today: A Journal of Explanatory Criticism*, edited by Eldred D. Jones. Vol. 1. London: Heinemann, 1972. An analysis of Clark-Bekederemo's poetry, which he himself refused to separate from his drama; T. S. Eliot's influence is noted. The title refers to Clark's recurring theme of the fundamental contradiction in individuals as a result of their dual parentage.

John Povey,
updated by Thomas J. Taylor
and Andrea E. Miller

AUSTIN CLARKE

Born: Dublin, Ireland; May 9, 1896
Died: Dublin, Ireland; March 19, 1974

PRINCIPAL DRAMA

The Son of Learning, pr., pb. 1927, pr. 1930 (as
    The Hunger Demon)
The Flame, pb. 1930, pr. 1932
Sister Eucharia, pr., pb. 1939
Black Fast, pb. 1941, pr. 1942
As the Crow Flies, pr. 1942 (radio play), pb. 1943,
    pr. 1948 (staged)
The Kiss, pr. 1942, pb. 1944
The Plot Is Ready, pr. 1943, pb. 1944
The Viscount of Blarney, pr., pb. 1944
The Second Kiss, pr., pb. 1946
The Plot Succeeds, pr., pb. 1950
The Moment Next to Nothing, pr., pb. 1953
Collected Plays, pb. 1963
The Student from Salamanca, pr. 1966, pb. 1968
*Two Interludes Adapted from Cervantes: "The
    Student from Salamanca" and "The Silent
    Lover,"* pb. 1968
*The Impuritans: A Play in One Act Freely Adapted
    from the Short Story "Young Goodman Brown"
    by Nathaniel Hawthorne*, pb. 1972
The Visitation, pb. 1974
The Third Kiss, pb. 1976
Liberty Lane, pb. 1978

OTHER LITERARY FORMS

Austin Clarke was most prolific as a poet; all his
dramatic writings are also in verse form. Between
1917, when his first major poem, the narrative epic
The Vengeance of Fionn, was issued by Maunsel in
Dublin and London, and 1974, when his *Collected
Poems* appeared just before his death, Clarke published numerous books of nondramatic verse as well
as many individual poems. *Selected Poems*, edited
and introduced by Thomas Kinsella, was published
posthumously in 1976.

In addition to his dramatic verse, Clarke wrote in a
variety of poetic genres—narrative epic poems, sat-

ires and epigrams, religious poems, confessional and
meditative works, and erotic and love poetry. He also
translated poems from the Gaelic. The subjects of his
poetry—though diverse in some ways—are all related to aspects of Irish life and Irish culture, past and
present.

Clarke wrote three novels, *The Bright Temptation*
(1932), *The Singing Men at Cashel* (1936), and *The
Sun Dances at Easter* (1952). Although these works
are in the form of prose romance, full of adventure
and fantasy, they also express Clarke's preoccupation with the problems of the development of the individual within the limits imposed by society, specifically Irish society. All three novels were banned at
publication by the Irish Free State government. *The
Bright Temptation* was reissued in 1973, but copies of
Clarke's other two novels have virtually disappeared.

Besides poetry and novels, Clarke produced three
book-length memoirs: *First Visit to England and
Other Memories* (1945), *Twice 'Round the Black
Church: Early Memories of Ireland and England*
(1962), and *A Penny in the Clouds: More Memories
of Ireland and England* (1968). These books offer important insight into Clarke's development as a major
writer in twentieth century Ireland.

Finally, Clarke was a prolific journalist, a frequent
contributor of essays, reviews, and criticism to several major publications: *The Daily News and Leader*
(London; which later became *The News Chronicle*),
The Spectator, and *The Irish Times*. Between 1940
and 1973, he contributed more than a thousand articles on both narrowly literary as well as wide-ranging
nonliterary topics to *The Irish Times*. Clarke also
wrote longer prose pieces for *The Dublin Magazine*
and *The Bell*.

ACHIEVEMENTS

In the judgment of many critics of Irish literature,
Austin Clarke was the most important of the poets of
the generation of Irish writers after William Butler
Yeats. As a poet, Clarke's achievements are impressive. He wrote almost exclusively of Irish themes,

myth, tradition, and history, and his own experience of Irish life and culture. Indeed, he has been called the "arch poet of Dublin," and his commitment to Gaelic poetic forms and prosody—assonantal patterns, vowel rhymes, tonic words—helped revise and preserve that poetic tradition.

Clarke was also a significant force in the revival of verse drama in Ireland. In 1941, partly as a vehicle for performance of his own dramatic writings, Clarke, with Robert Farren, founded the Dublin Verse-Speaking Society, which performed on Radio Éireann and at the Abbey Theatre. In 1944, he and Farren founded the Lyric Theatre Company, which presented plays in verse form at the Abbey until the disastrous fire there in 1951.

Clarke was a prolific man of letters, publishing a large amount of nonfiction and criticism for more than four decades in such respected outlets as *The Bell*, *The Dublin Magazine*, and *The Irish Times*. Clarke's founding of a private small press, the Bridge Press, inspired other Irish writers to found small presses of their own that were later influential in the resurgence of Irish writing in the 1960's and 1970's. For thirteen years, Clarke presented a weekly broadcast on Radio Éireann on Irish poetry. He was president of the Irish branch of the International Association of Poets, Playwrights, Editors, Essayists, and Novelists (PEN) for six years, and in 1952, he became president of the Irish Academy of Letters.

Clarke received many awards and prizes in recognition of his achievements as a writer. For his early lyric poetry, he was honored with the National Award for Poetry at the Tailteann Games in 1928. In 1964, for *Flight to Africa and Other Poems* (1963), Clarke won the Denis Devlin Memorial Award for Poetry from the Arts Council of Ireland. Like the best of his later poetry, the poems in *Flight to Africa and Other Poems* depart from the themes in his earlier works, dealing with issues of universal significance and exhibiting a more mature style. The next year, Clarke was awarded a prize by the Arts Council of Britain.

In 1966, on the occasion of his seventieth birthday, Clarke was presented with a festschrift containing poems and tributes by major Irish literary figures. That same year, an honorary degree was conferred on him by Trinity College. In the closing years of his impressive career, Clarke was awarded the Irish Academy of Letters's highest award for literature, the Gregory Medal. He also received the American Irish Foundation's Literary Award. In 1972, Irish PEN nominated him for the Nobel Prize. A special issue of the *Irish University Review* was devoted to Clarke shortly before his death in 1974.

Clarke's commitment to a literature that spoke most directly to the Irish themselves, within Irish literary and social traditions, about Irish themes, issues, and conflicts, has exerted unfortunate limitations on his general appeal, despite the fact that much of his work ultimately transcends its Irish context to deal with universals in human experience. The increasing critical focus on Clarke's works may help extend his reputation beyond the confines of Ireland.

BIOGRAPHY

Augustine Joseph Clarke was born in Dublin, Ireland, on May 9, 1896. His parents, Augustine Clarke and Ellen Patten Browne Clarke, produced twelve children; three daughters and one son, Austin, survived. The young Clarke was educated at Belvedere College (1903-1912) and then at University College of the National University of Ireland on a three-year scholarship of forty pounds a year. At University College, Clarke studied with such prominent figures in Irish literary life as Douglas Hyde and Thomas MacDonagh, and he read Yeats, George Russell (Æ), George Moore, and other English and Anglo-Irish writers. Clarke began to immerse himself in Irish culture and the Celtic Twilight and to explore the literary movements of the time.

Clarke received his bachelor of arts degree with first class honors in English language and literature in 1916, the year of the Easter Rising, and the next year, his master of arts degree, again with first class honors in English. He was then appointed assistant lecturer in English at University College, to replace his teacher, MacDonagh, who had been executed by the British after the Easter Rising.

Clarke published his first significant poem, *The Vengeance of Fionn*, an epic in the Irish mythic tradition, in 1917. The poem was much praised and Clarke was hailed as a "new Yeats." For the next several years, Clarke devoted himself to the study of Gaelic prosody and Irish myth and folklore. In 1920, Clarke married for the first time, but the marriage was to last only ten days. He married again in 1930. In 1921, he was appointed assistant examiner in matriculation, National University of Ireland, a post he held until 1970.

By the mid-1920's, Clarke had shifted his attention away from early Irish themes and had turned instead to the Celtic-Romanesque medieval period as a source of poetic inspiration. The poems in Clarke's *Pilgrimage and Other Poems* (1929) deal with themes from this period and illustrate his commitment to Gaelic prosody.

In 1927, Clarke completed his first verse drama, *The Son of Learning*, and saw it produced at the Cambridge Festival Theatre in October of that year. Between 1922 and 1937, Clarke lived in England. During this period of "exile," he wrote several more verse plays. In 1932, Clarke's first novel, *The Bright Temptation*, was banned by the Irish Free State government. That same year, Clarke was made a member of the Irish Academy of Letters at the invitation of Yeats and George Bernard Shaw.

Between 1933 and 1937, Clarke served as a judge for the annual Oxford Festival of Spoken Poetry. In 1936, when he turned forty, his *The Collected Poems of Austin Clarke* was published with an introduction by Padraic Colum, and his second novel, *The Singing Men at Cashel*, was banned in Ireland.

In 1937, Clarke returned to take up permanent residence in Ireland and to become engaged in all aspects of Irish literary life. Clarke's next book of verse, *Night and Morning* (1938), marked another turn in his poetic career, from medieval Irish traditions to more complex themes dealing with the struggle between the individual conscience and constituted authority, between personal faith and belief and the Catholic Church in Ireland.

Though he would produce no more poetry for many years, Clarke engaged in a variety of literary activities during the time of his poetic silence. He began to offer literary broadcasts on Radio Éireann and made regular contributions to newspapers and literary magazines. He set up his own private press, the Bridge Press, and held regular literary evenings at home on Sundays. He established the Dublin Verse-Speaking Society and the Lyric Theatre Company in cooperation with Robert Farren and worked with dramatic productions by these groups. During this period, Clarke also continued to write verse plays, and he completed his third novel, *The Sun Dances at Easter*, in 1952.

In 1955, Clarke published *Ancient Lights: Poems and Satires*, his first book of verse in nearly two decades. After a period of ill health, Clarke published his *Collected Later Poems* (1961), a volume that helped establish his reputation as a modern Irish poet. This was followed in 1963 by the publication of his *Collected Plays*, which contained all the plays he had written up to that time. During the 1960's, Clarke published two memoirs, *Twice 'Round the Black Church* and *A Penny in the Clouds*.

Clarke died in 1974, only a few months after the publication of his *Collected Poems*. Several of his plays were published posthumously, and a volume of his verse, *Selected Poems*, edited by Thomas Kinsella, appeared in 1976.

ANALYSIS

Austin Clarke began his literary career as a poet. His first published works were several simple poems that appeared in 1916 and 1917 in a Dublin weekly, *New Ireland*. His first significant published poem was *The Vengeance of Fionn*. This epic poem and the other poems Clarke wrote early in his career drew heavily on Irish myth and the legends of pre-Christian Ireland. During the 1920's, Clarke turned from these themes to medieval Ireland and the monastic tradition as a source of poetic inspiration. In the 1930's, he abandoned these influences to write what could be called confessional poetry, particularly on subjects concerning the conflict between human intellect and the limits imposed by religious dogma. His own Catholic upbringing and subsequent difficulties with the Irish Catholic Church served as an important source of inspiration during this period.

After a self-imposed exile in England that began in 1922, Clarke returned to Ireland in 1937. Between

1937 and 1955, there was a long silence in Clarke's poetic output. Instead, he turned to the writing of verse drama and worked actively for the support of the production of his own verse plays and those of other Irish verse playwrights, including Yeats. Clarke's first two verse plays had been written in England: *The Son of Learning* and *The Flame*. All his subsequent dramas were written in Ireland between 1939 and 1974. Two plays, *The Third Kiss* and *Liberty Lane*, were published posthumously.

None of the major writers of drama in post-Revival Ireland—Sean O'Casey, Lennox Robinson, George Shiels, Paul Vincent Carroll, the collaborators Frank O'Connor and Hugh Hunt—wrote verse plays. Clarke was essentially alone in his continued commitment to this dramatic form. At the Abbey Theatre, the only verse plays to have been presented in the first third of the twentieth century were those of Yeats.

Clarke's first play, *The Son of Learning*, was written in 1927 while he was in England. Although Yeats rejected it on behalf of the Abbey, it was performed at the Cambridge Festival Theatre in October, 1927. The performance was repeated by the Lyric Theatre Company at the Abbey in 1945.

Clarke's poetic drama drew, like the poetry of his early and middle career, on Irish myth, the folklore and legends of pre-Christian Ireland, and medieval Ireland and its monastic traditions. Although Clarke followed Yeats as a writer of verse drama, and although his own verse drama company performed Yeats's plays, the tenor of Clarke's own verse plays differs significantly from the austerity, formality, and symbolic structures Yeats favored. Like his own later poetry, Clarke's verse dramas focus on human conflicts and dilemmas, on the problems of individual freedom in the face of religious dogmatism. They blend, in an essentially satisfying way, comedy and tragedy. A comic view of life and a well-developed sense of the absurdity of the human condition motivate many of the major and minor characters in Clarke's dramas.

The plays in Clarke's dramatic canon are clearly uneven in quality. Although critics have varied in the rigor with which they have addressed and judged Clarke's drama, there is general agreement that a good part of the dramatic writing will today sustain the interest of only the most serious student of modern Irish literature. The best writing in Clarke's verse plays emphasizes his range and versatility as both poet and dramatist. Even in the least successful of his plays, Clarke's effects are neither entirely unsatisfactory nor entirely frivolous. Nearly every one of his plays is, at heart, a study of the conflict between the individual and the community—more specifically, between the Irish Church and Irish society, and the natural instincts of the common Irishman and Irishwoman. Clarke recast this basic conflict in settings as wide-ranging as those of his nondramatic poetry.

MINOR PLAYS

Some of the less successful plays, such as *Black Fast*, *Sister Eucharia*, and *The Plot Is Ready*, are of interest mainly because of the intellectual questions and conflicts of conscience they present and the ambiguity in which the "resolution" in each play leaves the reader/viewer. *The Moment Next to Nothing* was simply an unsuccessful attempt to translate into dramatic form Clarke's last novel, *The Sun Dances at Easter*, which had been banned in Ireland.

Seven short, minor plays on various themes are of little dramatic consequence, except that they often display Clarke's fine sense of language and his ability to work within such earlier dramatic traditions as masque and farce. *The Kiss* and *The Second Kiss*, both written in couplets, are light, short pieces that deal amusingly with the amorous adventures of Pierrot and his love, Columbine. Two short plays drawn from the works of Miguel de Cervantes, *The Student from Salamanca* and *The Silent Lover*, are bawdy little farces written in the form of the interlude, the brief diversions typically presented between medieval morality plays. Clarke's other minor plays are *The Impuritans, The Third Kiss*, and *Liberty Lane*. *The Visitation* appeared in a special issue of *Irish University Review* (1974) devoted to Clarke.

At least one critic has observed that several of the later minor plays, especially *The Impuritans* and the interludes from Cervantes, might most properly be considered along with the poems of Clarke's old age, which focus happily on erotic themes and celebrate human sexuality.

Clarke's remaining five plays, which will be considered briefly here, offer a sense of the kind of dramatic achievement in verse of which Clarke was clearly capable and also indicate the wide range of types and styles of verse drama he undertook.

THE SON OF LEARNING

The Son of Learning, as Clarke himself recalled, found its inspiration in a translation by Kuno Meyer of an Irish legend about King Cathal of Munster, who falls in love with Ligach, a noblewoman whose brother disapproves of the match. The brother causes Cathal to be cursed with a hunger demon. The unfortunate king is taken to the monastery in Cork to be rid of the demon. The play's central character, a wandering scholar, also arrives at the monastery, enrages the monks because of his audacious lack of piety, and is condemned to death. By virtue of his skill with words, however, it is the scholar, not the monks, who lures the demon out of Cathal and packs him off to Hell.

Within this simple framework, particularly in the conversations between the scholar and the monks, the scholar and the demon, Clarke explores the effects of religious dogmatism, the traditional discord between scholar and monk, intellect and faith. The overall tone is comic, based on exaggerated character, action, and speech. In the end, which is characteristically ambiguous, the king is cured—but by what agency, exactly, Clarke is cunningly silent. Audience members are left to decide for themselves.

This first play shows how Clarke's verse dramas differ from the verse dramas of Yeats. They are less solemn, more comic. The speeches of the characters, while expressed in verse, are more human and idiomatic. In all, Clarke's plays are peopled not only by distant, legendary heroes but also by real people who have real foibles and who are faced with truly human dilemmas and choices.

THE FLAME

Clarke's next play, *The Flame*, takes place in a convent and explores the conflict between the individual and the religious community. In *The Flame*, a young medieval nun secretly violates her order's rules by permitting her once luxuriant hair to grow again. Her preoccupation with herself causes her to neglect her duty—to tend the flame of Saint Brigid, which has burned at the convent for centuries. She is brought before the abbess for punishment. At the end of the play, the young nun is vindicated by an event one might call "miraculous." About its actual dimensions, the author is once again ambiguous.

AS THE CROW FLIES

As the Crow Flies is Clarke's most fully mature dramatic work in verse, written especially for presentation on radio. In it, he confronts all the challenges posed by an art form that must rely for effect almost entirely on voices, and he is particularly successful.

The play has a seemingly simple plot. Three monks, waiting out a terrible storm, take refuge in a cliffside cave that may have once been the dwelling of an ancient holy hermit. Over the din of the storm, they hear the voices of animals from Irish myth. In an eagle's nest on the top of the cliff, the Crow of Achill, who has wrought evil for centuries, tells tales to the eaglet nestlings. When the eaglets wonder whether the storm that crashes about them is the worst storm there ever was, the Crow prompts the mother eagle to ask first the Stag of Leiterlone and then the Blackbird of Derrycairn. When they cannot answer her, the Crow urges the mother eagle to fly off to question Fintan, the Salmon of Assaroe, the wisest of all creatures. Fintan tells the eagle that he can recall the Deluge, surely the worst storm in history. He also tells her that through his endless existence, he has found no explanation for the violence, war, greed, and slaughter that seem to be the "unchanging misery of mankind." The eagle's joy in her newly found knowledge is dreadfully quenched: She returns to her nest to find that the evil Crow of Achill has devoured her babies.

All through the night, the three monks have listened to the conversations of the animals and, except for Aengus, seem to have comprehended their meaning only partially. After the storm subsides, the monks, who have returned to their boat, watch the eagle hurl herself against the cliff where her babies perished. As he watches, Aengus shivers. He tells the others, "I know/ The ancient thought that men endure at night/ What wall or cave can hide us from that knowledge?"

As the Crow Flies is very probably Clarke's most fully realized verse drama. The dialogue is rich, vital, and evocative. The verse forms are intricate and challenging. The sound effects implied in the text suggest that a well-mounted production would be particularly haunting and memorable. Clarke effectively uses the voices of the blackbird and the other animals—creatures he has taken from Irish myth—to present and explore the theme of the duality of nature that is at the heart of this play. The responses of the three monks to the conversations they overhear convincingly represent three different ways of dealing with reality.

Overall, *As the Crow Flies* is a satisfying, if unsettling, presentation of Clarke's own inner conflicts, themes he had explored in earlier works and continued to probe until his death: the problems of good and evil in the world, of the clash between faith and reason, of the continuing tension between the rational and the irrational in human existence.

THE VISCOUNT OF BLARNEY

The Viscount of Blarney was written for performance on either stage or radio; it illustrates particularly well Clarke's depth and versatility in the creation of meaning-laden dialogue in verse. This play, the only one of Clarke's major works to be set more or less in the present, concerns the personal development of Cauth Morrissey, who has been reared in an orphanage and who is naïve in her interpretation of the world she encounters as a young adult. Some critics have suggested that the play is about the situation of youth in modern Ireland, caught between the oppressive teachings of the Catholic Church and their own natural desires, interests, and inclinations. Cauth is confronted by a variety of phantoms and demons, a pooka, and various primordial fears. She is finally rescued from her terrors and ignorance by a schoolmaster who coolly and methodically helps her get at the irrational roots of her fear.

THE PLOT SUCCEEDS

Finally, there is *The Plot Succeeds*, not to be confused with the earlier, lesser work, *The Plot Is Ready*, mentioned above. The former is a poetic pantomime, a frankly easygoing work in which the comedic elements eclipse the weightier themes typical of most of Clarke's other verse plays. The play is a pleasant mélange of mistaken identities, magic spells, and clowning. The basic action turns on the attempt of the main character, Mongan, to "win back" his wife, Dulaca, whom he has lost in a card game. *The Plot Succeeds* demonstrates that Clarke had a genuine gift for comedy, had he chosen to develop it.

OTHER MAJOR WORKS

LONG FICTION: *The Bright Temptation*, 1932, 1973; *The Singing Men at Cashel*, 1936; *The Sun Dances at Easter*, 1952.

POETRY: *The Vengeance of Fionn*, 1917 (based on the Irish Saga "Pursuit of Diarmid and Grainne"); *The Fires of Baal*, 1921; *The Sword of the West*, 1921; *The Cattledrive in Connaught and Other Poems*, 1925 (based on the prologue to *Tain bo Cuailnge*); *Pilgrimage and Other Poems*, 1929; *The Collected Poems of Austin Clarke*, 1936; *Night and Morning*, 1938; *Ancient Lights*, 1955; *Too Great a Vine: Poems and Satires*, 1957; *The Horse-Eaters: Poems and Satires*, 1960; *Collected Later Poems*, 1961; *Forget-Me-Not*, 1962; *Flight to Africa and Other Poems*, 1963; *Mnemosyne Lay in Dust*, 1966; *Old-Fashioned Pilgrimage and Other Poems*, 1967; *The Echo at Coole and Other Poems*, 1968; *Orphide and Other Poems*, 1970; *Tiresias: A Poem*, 1971; *The Wooing of Becfolay*, 1973; *Collected Poems*, 1974; *Selected Poems*, 1976.

NONFICTION: *First Visit to England and Other Memories*, 1945; *Poetry in Modern Ireland*, 1951; *Twice 'Round the Black Church: Early Memories of Ireland and England*, 1962; *A Penny in the Clouds: More Memories of Ireland and England*, 1968; *The Celtic Twilight and the Nineties*, 1969; *Growing Up Stupid Under the Union Jack: A Memoir*, 1980.

BIBLIOGRAPHY

Corcoran, Neil. *Poets of Modern Ireland*. Carbondale: Southern Illinois University Press, 1999. Contains an essay on Clarke, which while focusing on his poetic achievements, provides insight into his verse plays.

Halpern, Susan. *Austin Clarke: His Life and Work*. Dublin: Dolmen Press, 1974. While this survey of Clarke's prolific output in prose and verse concentrates on the verse, Halpern does devote a chapter to Clarke's theory and practice of drama. She discusses all Clarke's plays and places them in the context of Clarke's work as a whole. Substantial bibliography.

Harmon, Maurice. *Austin Clarke: A Critical Introduction*. Dublin: Wolfhound Press, 1989. A comprehensive introduction to the life and work of Clarke. Drawing on a wide variety of sources, this study provides much background information and focuses on Clarke's verse. Devotes a substantial chapter to Clarke's drama. Exhaustive bibliography.

Ricigliano, Lorraine. *Austin Clarke: A Reference Guide*. New York: G. K. Hall, 1993. A bibliography of Clarke's works and articles and books on the poet and dramatist. Index.

Schirmer, Gregory A. *The Poetry of Austin Clarke*. Notre Dame, Ind.: University of Notre Dame Press, 1983. This critique of Clarke's poetry sheds light on his dramatic works, which were verse plays. Bibliography and index.

Patricia A. Farrant,
updated by George O'Brien

MARTHA CLARKE

Born: Baltimore, Maryland; June 3, 1944

PRINCIPAL DRAMA

A Metamorphosis in Miniature, pr. 1982
The Garden of Earthly Delights, pr. 1984 (music by Richard Peaslee)
Vienna: Lusthaus, pr. 1986, pb. 1987 (text by Charles Mee, Jr., music by Peaslee)
The Hunger Artist, pr. 1987 (text by Richard Greenberg, music by Peaslee, set by Robert Israel; adaptation of Franz Kafka's story and diaries)
Miracolo d'Amore, pr. 1988
Endangered Species, pr. 1990
Alice's Adventures Under Ground, pr., pb. 1994 (with Christopher Hampton)

OTHER LITERARY FORMS

Martha Clarke is known for her extensive work as a choreographer and performer for the dance companies of Pilobolus and Crowsnest. Her dramatic works do not fall easily into any one genre. They incorporate elements of dance, music, and visual arts, as well as use of text, and involve collaborations with other artists.

ACHIEVEMENTS

Martha Clarke was already a highly acclaimed dramatic modern dancer performing in a world-renowned dance company, Pilobolus Dance Theater, when she crossed over into creating theatrical works. Her contributions as a choreographer include, with Pilobolus, *Ciona*, *Monkshood's Farewell*, and *Untitled*. These dances remain in the repertory of Pilobolus and are also presented by other major dance companies. Clarke has been compared to other experimental theater directors such as Robert Wilson, Ping Chong, and Meredith Monk for her ability to create multimedia theater pieces. Clarke's are noted for their visual beauty and a characteristic use of movement and timing. Clarke's innovative approach to her work encourages dancers, actors, designers, composers, and writers to work in a highly collaborative way toward a complex and richly textured performance-art object. Her first major theatrical production, *The Garden of Earthly Delights*, won a Village Voice Obie Award for Richard Peaslee's lush musical score. In 1988, she received a Guggenheim Fellowship intended for travel in Europe following the run of *Miracolo d'Amore*. Two years later, while rehearsing *Endangered Species*, Clarke was awarded a prestigious MacArthur

Martha Clarke in 1988. (AP/Wide World Photos)

Foundation Fellowship of $285,000 over the next five years. She is regarded as one of the most original directors in theater and one of the foremost innovators in American performance art.

BIOGRAPHY

Martha Clarke was born in Baltimore, Maryland, on June 3, 1944. As the second child and only daughter in a financially secure and artistically inclined family, she was encouraged to pursue her creative interests at an early age. Her father was a lawyer who had been a jazz musician and songwriter. Her mother played the piano, and her mother's father, a businessman, presented string quartets at his home on Tuesday nights and collected antique musical instruments. Shirley Clarke, the avant-garde filmmaker, was Martha's aunt, on whose suggestion her niece was named after dancer/choreographer Martha Graham.

Clarke's childhood was spent in Pikesville, Maryland. She attended a small private school in Baltimore, whose board of trustees included her father. At

age six, she began studying dance at the Peabody Conservatory of Music and taking drawing lessons on Tuesday afternoons at the Baltimore Museum. Horseback riding was another favorite activity and one she pursued in the summers at the Perry-Mansfield Camp in Colorado. There, in 1957, she met Helen Tamiris, who cast her, at age thirteen, as a child in *Ode to Walt Whitman*. Clarke says that she was hooked on dancing from the first time she worked with Tamiris.

When Clarke was fifteen, Tamiris and Daniel Nagrin asked her to attend their first summer workshop in Maine. Nagrin hoped to make Clarke an apprentice in the new company they were forming. Instead, Clarke chose to attend the American Dance Festival in Connecticut, where she first met Louis Horst, Merce Cunningham, Martha Graham, José Limón, Charles Weidman, and Alvin Ailey, and where she first saw the work of Anna Sokolow, whose dramatic dances greatly impressed her.

The next year, when she applied to the Juilliard School, Horst was on her jury, and he encouraged her to begin classes immediately and skip her senior year in high school. At Juilliard, she studied dance composition with Horst, who inspired and intimidated her. Horst's class in modern forms, in which dance studies are composed based on medieval and primitive art and Impressionist painting, was instrumental in developing her theatrical style.

Although Clarke was a Graham major and Horst was Graham's associate, it was the work of Sokolow and Anthony Tudor to which the young student was attracted. For two years, she studied with Tudor and as a sophomore danced a large part in a small ballet that he choreographed. She admired Tudor's work and its musicality. Also at Juilliard, she danced in the companies of Ethel Winter and Lucas Hoving, performing *Suite for a Summer Day* by the latter in 1962. She was in the first Dance Theater Workshop production with Jeff Duncan, after which she joined Sokolow's company. During her three years with the company she appeared in *Session for Six* (at Juilliard), *Lyric Suite, Time + 7*, and *Dreams*. Clarke left the company because she found the work bleak and believed that she was becoming artistically limited.

Shortly after she was graduated from Juilliard, she married sculptor Philip Grausman, a Prix de Rome winner. For the first five years of their fifteen-year marriage (they were divorced in 1980), Clarke stopped dancing. The couple lived in Italy for part of this time, immersing themselves in the art world. Shortly after their return to the United States, their son David was born. Grausman was named artist-in-residence at Dartmouth College, but Clarke saw herself as a twenty-seven-year-old mother and retired Anna Sokolow dancer. She and her husband moved into a large farmhouse, which resembled her childhood home, and built a dance studio for Clarke.

By this time, the four men who started Pilobolus were already touring. Clarke met Alison Chase, the Pilobolus men's dance teacher at Dartmouth, and the two became close friends. One of the members of Pilobolus, Robert Morgan Barnett, was an art major at Dartmouth and an assistant to Grausman. Barnett and Clarke began improvising dances in her studio after Barnett was forced to return early from a tour because of an injury. Clarke and Chase soon joined the previously all-male company. What drew her to Pilobolus was the company's irreverence and its rediscovery of the body. She believed that the inclusion of women in the company would allow the possibility of romance, gentleness, and delicacy to the male-oriented humor and gymnastics that were the company's trademarks. As a member of Pilobolus, she developed and performed *Ciona*, *Monkshood's Farewell*, and *Untitled*. In the seven years she was with Pilobolus, from 1972 through 1979, she created six solos, *Pagliaccio*, *Fallen Angel*, *Vagabond*, *Grey Room*, *Nachturn*, and *Wakefield*.

Her years with Pilobolus identified her as a clown and as a serious dramatic performer, but she wearied of the company's hectic touring schedule. Encouraged by Charles Reinhart, director of the American Dance Festival, and Lyn Austin, producer/director of the Music-Theater Group, Clarke left Pilobolus to start her own company, Crowsnest. Clarke joined with Felix Blaska, the French dancer and choreographer, whom she had met in Paris during her touring years with Pilobolus, and Pilobolus dancer Barnett. The trio worked collaboratively, and their work was described as a form of imagist movement-art when they first appeared at the American Dance Festival. Clarke and Blaska created *La Marquese de Solana*, and, with Barnett, *Haiku, The Garden of Villandry*, and *Fromage dangeureux*.

Clarke's first step into theater from dance was as choreographer for the Long Wharf Theater's production of Igor Stravinsky's *L'Histoire du soldat* in New Haven. For Austin, who first suggested that she direct, Clarke and Linda Hunt created a two-woman dance-drama collage for the company's season in Stockbridge, Massachusetts. This work was followed by a production of *Elizabeth Dead*, a play by the humorist for *The New Yorker*, George W. S. Trow. Clarke's debut as a New York theater director came with the production of *A Metamorphosis in Miniature*. The late David Rounds and Hunt performed Clarke's dramatization of the Kafka story with a ten-page script and much physicalization.

In 1984, under the auspices of Music-Theater Group/Lenox Arts Center, Clarke created *The Garden of Earthly Delights*. The hourlong work, based on the painting of Hieronymus Bosch, was a collaboration with Crowsnest and other dancers, with composer Peaslee and musicians, and with lighting designer Paul Gallo. After a successful engagement at St. Clement's in New York, *The Garden of Earthly Delights* toured the United States and Europe.

By this time, Clarke was working on *Vienna: Lusthaus*. Like the Bosch piece, *Vienna: Lusthaus* began with visual images, initially inspired by an exhibition about *fin de siècle* Vienna that Clarke had seen in Venice. Once again, the project was a collaboration with dancers, musicians, composer Peaslee, set and costume designer Robert Israel, lighting designer Gallo, and with a text written by historian and playwright Charles Mee, Jr. Music-Theater Group/Lenox Arts Center again produced the work, which opened at St. Clement's for a two-week run before moving to The Public Theatre on June 4, 1986.

Like the works before it, Clarke's next project was a collaborative creation. Clarke returned to the literary inspiration of Franz Kafka's writings to begin *The Hunger Artist*. This time, she used not only the story "A Hunger Artist" but also the writer's own life in letters and diaries for inspiration. The company of dancers, actors, and musicians, along with Clarke, designer Israel, composer Peaslee, and playwright Richard Greenberg, focused on the themes of starvation and death, physical, emotional, and artistic. *The Hunger Artist* was also produced by the Music-Theater Group and opened at St. Clement's Theater on February 26, 1987.

The 1988 New York Shakespeare Festival in association with the Spoleto Festival produced Clarke's next work, *Miracolo d'Amore*. Clarke continued collaborating with the eminent team of Peaslee, Gallo, and Israel to produce a work closer to opera but with no plot and no actual text. *Miracolo d'Amore* opened at the Spoleto Festival in Charleston, South Carolina, amid an uproar over the nudity in the piece, though Clarke thought the real controversy was over the violence, especially toward women, depicted in this work. Nevertheless, when *Miracolo d'Amore* moved to New York, audiences and critics praised the visual beauty of the stage images, the evocative operatic score, and Clarke's idiosyncratic movement vocabulary used to expose the so-called miracle of love. Not all the criticism, however, was favorable. Some critics noted that though meticulously crafted and expertly produced, *Miracolo d'Amore* failed to provide any fresh perspectives on Clarke's favorite themes of men and women in love and conflict.

Clarke explained that the negative criticism of *Miracolo d'Amore* probably had something to do with her choice of subjects for her subsequent project, *Endangered Species*, produced in 1990 after nearly two years of preparation. The cast consisted of eleven actors and seven animals, among them an elephant from the Circus Flora who befriended Clarke when both were performing at the 1988 Spoleto Festival and whose trainer, one of the co-owners of the circus, talked at length with Clarke about the problems of animal poaching. Then, as Clarke describes it, ideas about animal rights, human slavery and racism, the American Civil War, and the Holocaust seemed to come together for her, with ideas for the text drawn from Walt Whitman's *Leaves of Grass* (1855). Clarke again gathered her collaborative team of stage designers (Gallo, Israel, and composer Peaslee) and brought

in Robert Coe to adapt the text, but *Endangered Species* opened the Next Wave Festival at the Brooklyn Academy of Music to cool notices and closed after playing only fourteen of its scheduled thirty-five performances. Nevertheless, critics have not wavered in their belief that Clarke is an uncompromisingly precise theater director with a unique creative sensibility and artistic vision.

ANALYSIS

Martha Clarke's works are in a performance genre that as yet has no name. It is a blending and fusion of dance, drama, music, gesture, light, scenic design, and text into performance pieces that mirror her unique artistic vision. Clarke is in a group of experimental performance artists that include Robert Wilson, Ping Chong, Meredith Monk, and Peter Brook. Clarke's work as a conceptual director is distinguished from that of her peers by its painstaking use of movement and its density in a typically brief (usually one-hour) performance. Clarke achieves this synthesis of mediums by a collaborative, collagelike approach to composition.

Collaboration begins when rehearsals begin. Each performer, musician, composer, or designer is free to offer suggestions for the assemblage of fragments that will grow into a finished object of art. A long trial-and-error period ensues, during which the director develops movement phrases out of gestures and begins to keep a notebook of the ideas that work in rehearsal. She begins to distill the images and to dovetail the events while she looks for the contradictory images that will give the work texture and solidity. Clarke looks for a through-line that will unify her ideas, and she arranges and rearranges the scenes until they are compressed into their final form. She searches in works of art and writings for ideas that can be interpolated into the work. The final product is the result of the creativity of many people, but Clarke is responsible for the ultimate examination, selection, adaptation, and direction of all the elements.

Traces of Clarke's earlier work with Pilobolus Dance Theater can be seen in her theatrical direction and in her use of movement within the new works. In one of Pilobolus's best-known dances, *Monkshood's*

Farewell, the members of the company, for the first time, began to organize the material with a dramatic logic instead of simply from an abstract point of view. The piece is reportedly based on the work of James Thurber, Hieronymus Bosch (for whose painting Clarke's work is named), Breughel the Elder, Geoffrey Chaucer's *The Canterbury Tales* (1387-1400), Sir Thomas Malory's *Le Morte d'Arthur* (1485), and a Craig Claiborne soup recipe, among other things. The four male members of the company joust, using the women as lancers, but later all six appear as the cretinous characters from the Bosch and Breughel paintings.

THE GARDEN OF EARTHLY DELIGHTS

In *The Garden of Earthly Delights*, Clarke uses the Bosch painting as a point of departure for her own exploration and animation of the depicted world. She was attracted to the extremes of human emotion and behavior evident in the painting. The work is conceived as a left-to-right reading of the triptych, beginning in the Garden of Eden. The Garden of Earthly Delights and Hell are interrupted by an interpolation of the Seven Deadly Sins, the subject of another Bosch painting.

The director attempts to extract the qualities of the painting and condense its crowded, bustling panorama by giving Bosch's figures kinetic life. Though Clarke consulted science-fiction/fantasy writer Peter Beagle, who wrote a book on the painting in 1982, for an interpretation of the qualities in the painting, her approach to the creation of *The Garden of Earthly Delights* is primarily choreographic. Each vignette in the work has some characteristic movement idea repeated rhythmically until it dissolves to make way for the next image.

In Clarke's hourlong enactment, seven dancers and three musicians are incorporated into a series of *tableaux vivants*. The vignettes include scenes of Eve wrapping her long hair around Adam, a serpent who produces the apple from between her thighs, performers who appear as musical instruments and trees, bawdy peasants, putti flying overhead, and angels falling through the heavens, transformed into demons, crashing in midair, and plummeting into Hell. Clarke summons the entire Bosch landscape, from the dreamlike Garden of Eden to medieval poverty to a nightmarish eternity.

The grotesque, acrobatic, and allegorical use of the human body always interested Clarke and the other members of Pilobolus. Clarke's exploration of metaphorical dance imagery developed differently, however, in the solo works she choreographed for Pilobolus and Crowsnest. Her work is characterized by its use of movement repetition, its languid, deliberate pacing, and the eroticism of the movement images. She believes that the slow pace allows the audience members time to respond to the complete scope of visual and textual associations with their own, more personal set of references.

VIENNA: LUSTHAUS

The pleasure-garden idea returns in Clarke's *Vienna: Lusthaus*, but this time, the director has chosen an entire city and culture, turn-of-the-century Vienna, as her point of departure. Clarke had worked at least twice before on a similar theme. One of the first dances by Alison Chase and Clarke, *Cameo*, was a study of the relationship between two Victorian women. In Pilobolus's *Untitled*, two nine-foot women dance about the stage in flowing Victorian dresses until two nude men appear from beneath their skirts. *Vienna: Lusthaus* conjures an entire world, a dreamlike world of images that gradually shifts from a sensuous dream to an intensely disturbing nightmare, similar to the progression in *The Garden of Earthly Delights*.

Clarke's *Vienna: Lusthaus* was inspired by the art of the period, particularly that of Gustav Klimt and Egon Schiele, and by the political and social atmosphere at the traumatic beginning of the twentieth century in Vienna. The suicide of Prince Rudolf at Mayerling and the assassination of Archduke Ferdinand in 1914 provide the margins between which Clarke's surrealistic series of vignettes is set. Clarke was interested in a closer study of the veneer of graciousness, civility, and manners in Vienna that concealed the dark beginnings of twentieth century psychosis and warfare.

On this work, Clarke enlisted playwright Mee to help develop a performance text. Mee used material from Sigmund Freud's *The Interpretation of Dreams*

(1900), historical sources, and his own dreams to produce a text consisting of reminiscences spoken as monologue. These spoken memories, whose themes are primarily love and death, have an unashamed directness that makes them sound like dreams. Clarke and the performers worked to distill the text into vignettes, which are connected thematically rather than dramatically. Clarke thinks of this as an instinctual process rather than an intellectual one, and one that evokes the internal world of actors and audience.

The walls of the set are slanted, and a scrim is placed between the stage and the audience to distort the view. Although some of the images are quite beautiful, others are ominous. A young couple caress and embrace each other on the floor in an erotic scene until the young woman is replaced by an old woman, whom the young man continues to kiss. Most of the men are dressed as soldiers, and the women are dressed in Victorian petticoats and long slips. Beautiful nudes pose as artists' models. Actors read fragments of Freud's letters. Skaters in plumed hats and waltzing soldiers and girls glide through the moonlight to fragments of the music of Richard Strauss. A booted man with a riding crop flicks it menacingly across a girl's face and then over her body.

A woman recalls her mother carrying an armful of flowers through the house on a summer day but then says that when her mother's mind began to wander, she walked through an open window and fell to her death. A half-dressed soldier appears with a girl in a petticoat, who sits in his lap and acts like a puppet. A clarinetist and accordion player begin tuneless renditions of carnival music. The waltzing young soldiers begin marching to a resounding martial drumbeat. At the end, snow begins to fall. A woman embraces the body of a dying soldier. She raises his dead body and bangs it against the floor. Eventually, she stops. The snow keeps falling as the dead man speaks. He asks, "What colors does the body pass through in death?" Another man answers dispassionately, "First pink, then red, light blue, dark blue, and finally purple-red." Until this ending, these images are not presented linearly, but with amplifications, double meanings, contradictions, and a definite dramatic progression from the frivolous to the sinister.

Throughout, there is a sensuality and a surreal lack of logic. More than half the scenes are wordless but incorporate movements based on the same themes as those in the text. Clarke, once again, uses her characteristic technique of condensing, slowing down, and sharp-focusing the movement. Clarke finds that in working with actors and texts there is a natural sense of timing that corresponds to music. The speed and variation of certain phrases have a musical sense. She is interested in the slow development of a scene on stage which can mesmerize and stimulate the viewer's imagination. One of the actors turns into a horse, demonstrating the movements of the horse's arched legs and completing the transformation in one gesture. His foot becomes a hoof, and the man becomes an animal. Throughout *Vienna: Lusthaus*, the performers conjure scenes of the elegance and the decadence of this city of contradictions.

THE HUNGER ARTIST

Following this work, Clarke began the process of researching, discussing, probing, and distilling new material once again. *The Hunger Artist* is not a revival of her earlier *A Metamorphosis in Miniature*, but a complete reworking of the Kafka material. Letters and diaries, as well as Kafka's body of fictional work, were consulted. Playwright Greenberg worked with the actors to bring the letters to life. Scenic designer Israel created a set that outlines a triangular house with striped walls, and he placed a large box filled with earth onstage. Bentwood chairs were planted in the earth bed along with Dresden china and silverware, a nineteenth century rocking horse and cabbages. Peaslee's musical score contains phrases of Czech folk songs.

Clarke found a through-line in the theme of starvation and dying. In Kafka's famous story "A Hunger Artist," the main character earns his living by fasting and eventually starves himself to death. In Kafka's personal life, Clarke found evidence of emotional starvation in his relationships with his father and his fiancée Felice, and in his hunger for a normal life. One performer in *The Hunger Artist* resembles a Kafka insect when seen behind a World War II gas mask. Another performer poses in a small doorway, holding a hatchet, while one of the women performs a lyrical dance movement with a cabbage on her head.

MIRACOLO D'AMORE

Unlike her three previous theater works, Clarke's inspiration for *Miracolo d'Amore* was eclectic rather than drawn from one particular artistic, historical, or biographical source. Italo Calvino's *Fiabe italiane* (1956; *Italian Folktales*, 1975), Charles Darwin's *The Expression of the Emotions in Man and Animals* (1872), Giovanni Battista Tiepolo's paintings of *commedia dell'arte* characters (especially the Pulcinellas), French artist Grandville's nineteenth century illustrations of women as flowers from *The Court of Love*, as well as poetry by Dante and Petrarch, provided the wide range of sources from which Clarke began her process of sifting, extracting, and then creating the images that finally composed the fifty-five-minute piece with a cast of eight men and seven women.

In the opening moments of *Miracolo d'Amore*, an essentially indistinguishable hunched character, whose face and body are covered by ill-fitting sackcloth, slowly drags a stick across the stage. The set—composed of titled walls, skewed doors, and angled windows and columns—is dimly lit but resembles a Venetian piazza in russet and ocher colors. Four nude women appear bathed in the golden light of a doorway, holding hands and tiptoeing into the first of several round dances with precise articulation but cool detachment. The group joins together, revolves in the space, then separates, and the figures dissolve one by one into the shadows of the set. The individual segments that compose *Miracolo d'Amore* are enacted between these slow and quiet round dances and seem to be complete and self-contained though they arrive at no particular narrative conclusion.

The vocal score for *Miracolo d'Amore* combines Peaslee's operatic songs of Italian love poetry sung by mostly soprano and countertenor voices with sounds of nature, the ocean and the wind, bird calls and cries, laughter and screams, and an inarticulate gibberish-Italian pseudolanguage that Clarke often uses in juxtaposition with an accompanying image of beauty or cruelty. The men, sometimes dressed as Pulcinellas, other times naked, masked, or otherwise

disguised, approach the women with various intentions. At times they can be tender admirers, drawn to the beauty of the women dressed as flowers. Alternately, they portray predators whose fear or repulsion of the women turns to violence and commonly sends them back to the safety of the other men.

In one scene, a man slowly lifts a woman's skirt as she lies on the floor and puts his head between her legs; when his face reemerges, he lets out a great roar. Another man portrays a Christlike figure on a cross who is fed spaghetti from a bowl and who then transforms himself into an awkward bird looking for food and then a club-footed peasant limping offstage. A woman reaches between the legs of another woman and brings forth a seashell. A naked man, lying downstage, transforms himself into a fish. In the most climactic segment, if one could be described as such, the clownish men seem to woo the flowerlike women, engaging in tender caresses and embraces that gradually shift from lovemaking to gang rape and beating. The final moments of the piece set the gun-carrying men against one another in a shootout, yet the women reprise their silent, aloof handheld dance off the stage.

Miracolo d'Amore may have been less successful than previous Clarke works in its attempt to illuminate the provocative subject of love, desire, and violence between women and men, but there seemed to be no question that Clarke succeeded once again in integrating theater, movement, art, and music with the haunting images of her imagination.

ENDANGERED SPECIES

Clarke's next work, *Endangered Species* is, like *Miracolo d'Amore* and its predecessors, essentially a nonnarrative series of vignettes for actors, singers, and dancers but with the addition of four horses, a monkey, a goat named Bert, and an elephant named Flora. Clarke described the roles of these animals as equal to those of the human company members in the creation and performance of this sixty-five-minute examination of animal and human oppression. The stage is covered with a plot of dirt and wood chips, an iron bed on the left, and a chair set in an otherwise empty space. Upstage, two oversized white doors are lit to reveal the shadows of the deftly moving actors or occasionally open for a glimpse of an elephant strolling back and forth. The score combines often loud recorded sound effects of bombings, a Nazi rally, and children screaming with a capella musical fragments, and the spoken snippets of Walt Whitman's *Leaves of Grass* text.

Endangered Species has a nightmarish quality in its scenes of violence and cruelty, yet the entire piece is, like Clarke's previous works, visually sensuous and deceptively beautiful. In one sequence, a woman writhes suggestively on the back of a horse that stands perfectly still. Sometimes the horses circle the stage, at times with riders standing on their backs. In one scene, a white woman sits in a black man's lap while he caresses her, yet another woman is sexually abused by one of the men. A white man beats one of the black men. A horse ambles through, then a naked man runs past and is shot. His limp body hangs overhead until the end of the piece, when the others are all shot to the sounds of a massacre and bombing. In the closing moments, a man walks through reciting Whitman's words "I think I could turn and live with animals."

Ultimately, criticism of *Endangered Species* centered on what Frank Rich of *The New York Times* considered Clarke's inability to contribute to the audiences' knowledge or sense of urgency about the horrors of violence and oppression. Clarke herself considered this a very personal and risky project in both her choice of material and her choice of casts, but *Endangered Species* may have proven to be too thematically varied for the kind of treatment Clarke envisioned.

BIBLIOGRAPHY

Clarke, Martha. Interview by Arthur Bartow. In *The Director's Voice*. New York: Theatre Communications Group, 1988. An interview with Clarke made during the development of *Miracolo d'Amore*. Bartow says that audiences respond to Clarke's "images in the same manner as they are created— viscerally." The interview is concerned with the intricacies of Clarke's creative process from the moment she conceives a work through its collaborative creation. Clarke discusses her transition to

the theater from dance and each of the projects she has produced since beginning work with the Music-Theater Group.

Gussow, Mel. "Clarke Work." *The New York Times Magazine*, January 18, 1987, 30-34. Gussow provides extensive biographical information and discusses Clarke's major theatrical works, collaborations, and artistic vision. He says that "Clarke's work is distinctive in its passion, its use of movement, its brevity and its concern with art and culture." Also contains photographs from productions of *The Garden of Earthly Delights* and *Vienna: Lusthaus*.

Kaufman, Sarah. "Choreographer Martha Clarke, Back on Her Feet: After a Flamboyant Rise and Fall, a Daring Leap at Simplicity." *The Washington Post*, October 17, 1999, G01. Kaufman interviews Clarke regarding the opening of *Vers la flamme*, Clarke's dance interpretation of five stories by Anton Chekhov. Also contains discussion of *Endangered Species*.

Nadotti, Maria. "What Becomes of the Brokenhearted?" *Artforum* 27 (September, 1988): 117-121. A thorough critical analysis of *Miracolo d'Amore* that examines the various literary and artistic sources for the work and provides clear descriptions of the visual effects and stage designs. Nadotti also offers a brief overview of Clarke's previous theater projects in order to place this piece in context.

Osterle, Hilary. "Alas, No Giraffe." *Dance Magazine* 64 (October, 1990): 46-49. Osterle provides background information on the creation of *Endangered Species*, speaks with Clarke and the performers about this unusual theatrical adventure, and discusses the various ideas and concerns that shaped this piece over its two-year formation.

Rothstein, Mervyn. "Martha Clarke's Thorny Garden." *The New York Times*, July 12, 1988, pp. 1, 26. A feature article on Clarke following the opening of *Miracolo d'Amore* at the Spoleto Festival. Rothstein provides insightful glimpses at this work in particular, as well as a substantial interview with Clarke.

Diane Quinn

PAUL CLAUDEL

Born: Villeneuve-sur-Fère, France; August 6, 1868
Died: Paris, France; February 23, 1955

PRINCIPAL DRAMA

L'Endormie, wr. 1886-1888, pb. 1925

Tête d'or, first version pb. 1890, second version wr. 1895, pb. 1901, pr. 1919 (English translation, 1919)

Fragment d'un drame, pb. 1892

La Jeune Fille Violaine, first version wr. 1892, pb. 1926, second version pb. 1901

La Ville, first version pb. 1893, second version pb. 1901, pr. in Dutch 1926, pr. in French 1955 (*The City*, 1920)

L'Échange, first version wr. 1893-1894, pb. 1901, pr. 1914, second version pr. 1951, pb. 1954

Le Repos du septième jour, wr. 1896, pb. 1901, pr. 1965

Partage de midi, first version pb. 1906, second version pr., pb. 1948 (*Break of Noon*, 1960)

L'Otage, pb. 1911, pr. 1914 (*The Hostage*, 1917)

L'Annonce faite à Marie, first version pr., pb. 1912, second version pr. 1948 (revision of *La Jeune Fille Violaine*; *The Tidings Brought to Mary*, 1916)

Le Pain dur, wr. 1913-1914, pb. 1918, pr. 1949 (*The Crusts*, 1945)

Protée, first version pb. 1914, second version pb. 1927, pr. 1955 (*Proteus*, 1921)

La Nuit de Noël, pb. 1915, pr. 1917

Le Père humilié, wr. 1915-1916, pb. 1920, pr. 1946 (*The Humiliation of the Father*, 1945)

L'Ours et la lune, pb. 1919, pr. 1948

Le Soulier de satin: Ou, Le Pire n'est pas toujours sûr, wr. 1919-1924, pb. 1928-1929, pr. 1943 (*The Satin Slipper: Or, The Worst Is Not the Surest*, 1931)

L'Homme et son désir, pr., pb. 1921

La Femme et son ombre, pr. in Japanese 1923, pb. 1927, pr. in French 1948

Le Peuple des hommes cassés, wr. 1927, pb. 1952

Sous le rempart d'Athènes, pr., pb. 1927

Le Livre de Christophe Colomb, pb. 1929, pr. in German 1930, pr. in French 1953 (libretto; music by Darius Milhaud; *The Book of Christopher Columbus*, 1930)

Le Festin de la sagesse, wr. 1934, pb. 1939, pr. 1950

Le Jet de Pierre, wr. 1937, pb. 1949

Jeanne d'Arc au bûcher, pr. in German 1938, pb. 1938, pr. in French 1940 (English translation, 1939)

L'Histoire de Tobie et de Sara, pb. 1942, pr. 1947 (music by Milhaud)

Le Ravissement de Scapin, wr. 1949, pb. 1958

OTHER LITERARY FORMS

Although Paul Claudel's reputation rests primarily on his drama, he also wrote a substantial amount of poetry and a wide variety of nonfiction works. One of Claudel's most important poetic works is his *Cinq Grandes Odes* (1910; *Five Great Odes*, 1967), a five-part poem whose content was inspired by Claudel's reflection on a sarcophagus. Other important works of poetry include *Corona Benignitatis Anni Dei* (1915; *Coronal*, 1943), *Poèmes de guerre* (1922), and *Cent Phrases pour éventails* (1927; *A Hundred Movements for a Fan*, 1992). His nonfiction consists of essays, journals, and correspondence with such personages as Jacques Rivière, André Gide, André Suarès, and Darius Milhaud. His twenty-seven-volume *Œuvres complètes* was published between 1950 and 1967.

ACHIEVEMENTS

Paul Claudel's literary fame did not come with the publication of his first works. Even when the late nineteenth century critics were willing to accept the Symbolist theater of Maurice Maeterlinck, Claudel's masterpieces were generally ignored. Except for the encouragement he received from friends, he found approval only with the post-World War II generation in his country. His lack of success was partly because he was away from France on diplomatic missions and was hardly in a position to make himself known. Further, he was too religious for the secular Third Republic of France, and his poetry lacked the Alexandrine meter and other conventional forms; most of the time it omitted rhyme. His drama is both a soul-searching and a soul-saving adventure in which the eternal destiny of humanity takes priority over other aspects of life. Some critics have observed that Claudel did not use the kind of literary language that most Frenchmen cherished: They accused him of writing French literature in German. These criticisms contain a bit of truth. Certainly, there is nothing classical in the form that Claudel adopted for his theater, and it is true, too, that the staging of *The Tidings Brought to Mary* in Hellerau, Germany, in 1913, was considered one of the major events in Claudel's career as a dramatist: Germany thus understood and appreciated Claudel before France did. In a way, German theatergoers opened the eyes of Frenchmen to their forgotten dramatist. Late in life, however, he achieved the recognition he deserved.

Paul Claudel (Library of Congress)

BIOGRAPHY

Paul-Louis-Charles-Marie Claudel was born in Villeneuve-sur-Fère (Tardenois), France, on August 6, 1868, the youngest of three children. His father, Louis-Prosper Claudel, was a civil servant who came to Villeneuve-sur-Fère from La Bresse, a small town in the Vosges region. By nature he was an unsociable and taciturn person whose profession turned him into a nomad, and he had little time for his children. Claudel's mother, Louise Cerveaux, came from a family that had its origins in Villeneuve-sur-Fère. The family moved often, following the transfers of the father from Villeneuve-sur-Fère, Bar-le-Duc, Nogent-sur-Seine, Wassy, Rambouillet, and Compiègne, until the mother finally agreed to move and settle with her children in Paris. Paul Claudel was fourteen at the time.

Contrary to what one might expect, Paris did not fascinate the young Claudel, nor did Paris bring a respite to the endless family quarrels that were a part of Claudel's childhood. The pressure of Claudel's anarchist instincts, which the restless atmosphere of the capital exacerbated, led him to thoughts of suicide. As he grew into adulthood, however, he also saw the positive side of Parisian life. He discovered the "mystical" beauty of Richard Wagner's music; he joined the group that gathered around Stéphan Mallarmé; and he enjoyed the company of classmates and colleagues who later became well-known personalities in the first half of the twentieth century. In 1886, Claudel discovered the works of Arthur Rimbaud, in the June issue of *La Vogue* magazine, where he first read *Les Illuminations* (1886; *Illuminations and Other Prose Poems*, 1932) and *Une Saison en enfer* (1873; *A Season in Hell*, 1932).

On December 25, 1886, Claudel went to Notre-Dame Cathedral in Paris, where, during the early afternoon Office of Vespers, he experienced the stirrings of faith that would change the course of his life and work. His life and his obvious talent took on purpose. He was to remain forever a poet committed to God and humankind.

After passing the examination for the Ministry of Foreign Affairs, Claudel entered into a diplomatic career that continued until 1935. His first consular assignment took him to New York and Boston in 1893. By this time, he was the author of *Tête d'or* and *The City*. His first encounter with American life inspired in him the *L'Échange*, a masterpiece that presents a realistic image of late nineteenth century American life and civilization. His diplomatic life took him next to China. Between 1895 and 1900, Claudel held posts in Fuchou, Shanghai, and Hankou. During this period, he began writing poetry. On his return to France in 1900, he thought of abandoning poetry and becoming a monk but changed his mind. He then decided to pursue his diplomatic career, which led him back to China.

On his return to China in 1900, he met "Ysé" (Rose Vetch), with whom he shared an adulterous relationship for four years. This experience was another turning point for the man and the artist. The idea of woman as at once temptress and the source of salvation for man, a theme that can be found in many of his works, was conceived out of this episode. This theme is especially pronounced in such works as *Break of Noon*, *The Tidings Brought to Mary*, and *The Satin Slipper*, in which the dichotomy between the two aspects of woman is transformed and transcended.

In 1906, Claudel married Reine Sainte-Marie-Perrin, daughter of the architect of the Basilica of Fourvière in Lyons. Three days after his marriage, Claudel returned to China, accompanied by his wife. From that time until his death in 1955, Claudel's professional life never knew an eclipse.

ANALYSIS

Jean Giraudoux, who hardly ever agreed with Paul Claudel in aesthetic matters, believed that Claudel was one of the prophets who come to visit Earth once every three or four hundred years. The post-World War II generation of France concurred with these sentiments of Giraudoux. Thanks to the initiative onstage of Jean-Louis Barrault, the aging Claudel found attentive ears among the youngest of the French intelligentsia. The literary destiny of Claudel had suddenly changed: The writer whom some critics had accused of not writing in French was now recognized as one of the greatest masters of the French language, although his theater serves neither the rules of classicism nor the revolution of the Romantics: Claudel set his own rules from the beginning and proved that art meets the needs of new times only when it renews itself. In his dramas, he broke away from psychological analysis and sought to teach that the grandeur of human beings lies not so much in their intricate nature as in their destiny, which carries them into eternity. Because the world of humans is universal because it is religious, the horizontal dimension of life calls for its complementary and vertical dimension. It is this latter dimension that serves the soul as its natural atmosphere. No doubt, the journey of the soul is tragic, for every visible thing constitutes an obstacle to the soul on its way to salvation. The tragic hero in Claudel's drama must learn that temporal existence is a means of redemption: It passes, but not without opening the doors to another existence. The tragic sense of life is thus accompanied by a deeper joy. By placing life into its proper perspective, Claudel reaffirms the age-old wisdom that, just as happiness is the result of healthy relationships between human beings, joy consists for man and woman in recognizing their relationship with God. The destiny or fatality of the ancient world of the Greeks has been replaced in Claudel's drama by a providential and loving God who directs and attracts humanity.

L'ENDORMIE

Claudel began to write in his early youth. He wrote *L'Endormie*, his first drama, between 1886 and 1888, although he claims to have written it earlier, perhaps in 1882-1883. Its sources may be traced to the myth of beauty and the beast, to *Roman de Renart* (c. 1175-1205), to William Shakespeare's *A Midsummer Night's Dream* (pr. c. 1595-1596), or even to John Keats's *Endymion* (1818). The subject matter is rather simple: The young playwright has been infatuated in his dream by Galaxaure, a beautiful woman whom he follows into a forest. There, some fauns lead him to a cave, where he finds Galaxaure asleep; she has been waiting for some time for the poet to awaken her. When the poet penetrates the cave, he finds not the beautiful woman but an ugly, snoring being, a huge "paunch." In his fright and disappointment, the young poet runs away from the scene, pursuing now in his anger Volpilla, one of the fauns, who makes fun of his adventure.

With this early play, Claudel reveals two major aspects of his theater: first, the ever present comic atmosphere that runs parallel to his most dramatic interpretation of life, and second, the idea of the impossibility of love that opposes Claudel to the Romantics. Yet Claudel has been called a Romantic by Henri Peyre. André Malraux, in his *Les Voix du silence* (1951; *The Voices of Silence*, 1953), affirms that *The Tidings Brought to Mary* responds to the dream that Victor Hugo had about the perfect drama, described in his preface to *Cromwell* (1827; English translation, 1896). Claudel, however, was a Symbolist who never betrayed reality and who always respected the two faces of life: the grotesque and the sublime.

The extraordinary phenomenon in Claudel's theater is that his personal life animates it so much that the evolution of his drama is identical with his personal spiritual growth. Although the supernatural is always present in it, the movement progresses from revolt and destruction, through suffering, toward reconciliation and peace. Under a faithful autobiography, the spectator discovers the universal man; as Antoine Vitez writes, Claudel "has given of his own life an entirely mythological reading."

TÊTE D'OR

The giant figure of Cébès rises from the very first scene of *Tête d'or*, as a "new man" in front of "unknown things," one who is fundamentally "ignorant," wondering about the meaning of life and death, love and hatred, salvation and redemption. He is endowed with an immense desire to know, to live, to act, and with a strong will not to die. Simon Agnel is returning from a long exile, carrying on his shoulders the dead body of his wife. While he is burying the dead woman, his old friend, Cébès, who loved the same woman, recognizes him. Cébès himself, as Agnel later discovers, is marked with the sign of death. On the one hand, then, there is Agnel, who promises a future in which he intends to rebuild the world; on the other hand, there is the dying Cébès to tell about the

joy of the last hour: "It is joy," he says, "that you find in your last hour, and I am this very joy and the secret which cannot be told." On hearing the word "joy," Agnel would like to know its origin, meaning, and purpose, but death prevents Cébès from answering. It is, then, up to Agnel to find joy in his own way. It will not take very long for him to find out that the road to joy leads through suffering and transfiguration. He renounces love, assumes a new identity (he is now called Tête d'or), eliminates the vestiges of the past, and, after his victory over the enemy, murders the Old King. He then sends the Princess into exile and takes into his power the destiny of the Empire. "I want everything," he exclaims. This exclamation startles the Tribune of the People, who, like a Greek god, warns him, "Listen to me, young man, your success made you lose the sense of measure." The superhuman efforts did not, indeed, suffice for Tête d'or to reach all of his lofty goals, and the second time he must face the same enemy, his army suffers a crushing defeat, and he is mortally wounded.

At this point, however, the drama reaches a turning point. The failure of Tête d'or does not mark the denouement; on the contrary, he is given the opportunity to find his complete identity. Before the hour of his death, Tête d'or could be considered as an old brother of those existential heroes of André Malraux or Antoine de Saint-Exupéry, who, in order to experience the meaning of their existence, plunge themselves into fulfilling action. Mere action, however, cannot stretch existence beyond its temporal dimensions: The last act always demands the meaning, or the conclusion, of death. Tête d'or has never been able to answer the question he raised to himself: "Who am I?" That is why he is a pagan.

The drama is saved from its pessimistic conclusion by the mysterious presence of the Princess. She is a living symbol, standing "behind" Tête d'or to explain her fidelity to the present, hope in the future, and love for the life hereafter. She knows that she must die for the other: "I will not let you die in despair," she tells Tête d'or. From a purely existential point of view, one could say that the life of the Princess grazes the limits of the absurd. "I was born to love," she says. "And I die for. . . ." With the unfinished sentence, she turns the spectator's attention from a philosophical level to the realm of theological truth: "No one dies for himself." The Princess changes her role and name from one play of Claudel to another: At times she is the Church, at another time she is Wisdom, or Love; in *Tête d'Or*, it is she who opens the eyes of the hero to the source of light and teaches him that the quality of death illumines the whole of life.

Death as a major theme—"The evil of death, the knowing of death"—appears from the very first plays of Claudel and continues its presence throughout his whole body of work. This consciousness of death had its genesis in Claudel's childhood. He often recalled the shock he experienced during the long-lasting suffering of his grandfather, who died of cancer. He was similarly marked by the great number of suicides that plagued his small native town of Villeneuve-sur-Fère. During his own unhappy childhood, he thought many times of suicide. Finally, the exile he had to embrace in his professional life was a constant reminder of Rimbaud's warning that "the real life is absent."

THE CITY

Tête d'or measures the worth of life through the kind of death by which the hero draws his ambitious life to conclusion. *The City* widens the scope of the playwright's interest and proposes to explore the destiny of the city. This play can be best understood if studied within the framework of present-day ecological concerns. Malraux summed up the essence of this consciousness when he said that the present epoch "learned that even civilizations are mortal." Cities, like human beings, are born and die. The city that Claudel proposes to study does not possess an existence that is independent from people, for people are the city. "Pollution" and "renewal" reflect the quality of life and the health of the human spirit. Claudel believed that the visible city stands for human creativity; it is a work of art: "The city is the form of humanity."

The poet, aware of his creative power and sensing the heart of the city, is called on to envisage the "renewal" of the city at large. As Lambert de Besme and Avare contemplate the city from the high ground of Besme's garden, they tell in a few words what they think the city is: For Besme, it is the space where two individuals cannot join each other; the closer they come, the farther they find themselves from each other. Avare sees in the city a place that merely "glitters with a fabricated light." He does not hide his disgust for the people who populate this "habitat of corruption," nor does he hide his intention to destroy it all. A revolution that tears down the whole city will answer his wishes.

The poet stands in the middle of all these events. His name, Cœuvre (which combines *cœur*, heart, and *œuvre*, work), symbolizes the nature of the work of reconstruction to be performed. The poet's role is threefold. His first role, as Besme explains, is through "his song without music" and his "word without voice," which tunes humanity to the "melody of this world. . . . You explain nothing . . . but all things become explicable by you." His second role is to give to the city of after-revolution a king, his own son Ivors, who was born of Lala. This son-king is the fruit of his love for the woman. By the time of the "reconstruction" of the city, Cœuvre has become a bishop, and, as such, through his divine-poetic word, he leads the city to God. This third and theological role of Cœuvre is coupled with the political program that Ivors has already outlined. The new prince, says Ivors, should assure his "unimpeachable authority," while knowing that "prince" does not mean "principle"; no one is the principle or goal of his own existence. His conversion to the faith of his father, however, is not given as the denouement of the drama: That is found in a prophetic vision that predicts a universal breakdown in human society. When Ivors recognizes in Lala his mother, he calls her "the Mother of Folly, the Mother of this aberrant people, the Nymph of the human forest, the promiser of the peace of sustenance." Although he holds her responsible for the "city laid waste," it is obvious that she (or the being she symbolizes) is the one who can make the renaissance happen. Because she is "the truth with the face of error," and a "promise which cannot be kept," Claudel will not cease to ask her to explain the origin of evil, the meaning of human love, the love of God, the meaning of history, and love and redemption.

LE REPOS DU SEPTIÈME JOUR

The "heavenly voice" that Claudel heard in the poems of Rimbaud was but the voice of the nostalgia that the child-poet, caught in the evil of his time, felt for the absence of good. Charles Baudelaire's *Les Fleurs du mal* (1857, 1861, 1868; *Flowers of Evil*, 1909) was another reminder for Claudel of the power of evil in the world. In *Le Repos du septième jour*, having recognized the "troubles of his people" and "the calamity of fear" that the unnecessary visits of the spirits cause in the kingdom of the living, the Emperor descends to Hell to discover the reason for these untimely visits. After obtaining the consent of the Spectre of the Emperor Hoang-Ti, he departs on his mission. In Hell, he speaks with the spirit of his mother, with the Demon, and with the Angel of the Empire. He hears from his mother that, in Hell, justice exists for eternity and that while life was a short span of existence on earth, here "they" are exposed for all eternity to the "abominable furor" of the Beast, whose heart is as empty as a tomb where "the very dead is dead." By speaking of the Demon, as though she had named him, she causes the Demon to appear and takes the place of the interlocutor.

What is evil? According to the Demon, evil consists in the fact that the creature to whom existence has been entrusted seizes it as if it were his proper purpose and goal; that is why "they" are joined to themselves. The Angel of the Empire is more explicit and lucid about the nature of evil. He says, "Just as the saint creature attaches himself to God as to his goal, Satan enjoys Him as his cause." Because the essence of God is existence, the created being who takes his existence from Him cannot turn the essence of God into his own goal. Everything that exists is good; evil, then, is that which does not exist. The created being is good because he was created by God; if there is evil in him, evil is found in the way the contingent being turns himself away from the goal for which he was created. Egoism has a reality of its own, but it never exists on its own. Yet it plays a major role in the drama of the world. Claudel explains this role of evil in a more elaborate manner in *The Satin Slipper*; in *Le Repos du septième jour*, he makes the returning Emperor summarize his findings in the

following way: "The Evil in the world is like a slave who makes the water mount." The Emperor understands that the real lesson is a question of wisdom: In order to avoid evil, man must make "a donation of everything," including himself.

BREAK OF NOON

Making a "donation" in this spirit is generally associated with the concept of religious vocation. Four years after he wrote these lines, Claudel asked for admission to the monastery of Ligugé. His decision to become a monk was certainly not made lightly, yet in spite of the serious thought he had given this question, his request was turned down by the Superior of Ligugé, and Claudel returned to China to resume his diplomatic career. On the voyage back to China, he met "Ysé" of *Break of Noon*. The first edition of the drama in 1906 was limited to two hundred copies, and it was not until 1948 that the general public was given access to it. The plot of the drama is simple: Mesa and Ysé meet on an ocean voyage and fall in love, and for their love they sacrifice everything: she, her family and children; he, his career and God. De Ciz, the husband of Ysé, has been an unsuccessful engineer; Amalric, in his last business adventure, lost his entire fortune. Ysé is the unhappy but faithful wife who has never experienced the joy of being loved. Mesa, having tried to make a "donation" of his life to God, received silence for an answer, which he took as a categorical refusal. God refused him, while the other three seem to have been refused by life itself. They share, however, the same destiny: They meet on an ocean liner, at "midday," in the middle of their lives, in the middle of the Indian Ocean, halfway between Europe and Asia, between the known past and the unknown future.

The sadness of Mesa is greater than that of the others: He believes that God has forgotten him and left his place empty. Should he not do something to fill the emptiness of his life? There is indeed a woman, called Ysé, who has been placed on the same ship—call it Providence or fatality—who could fill the emptiness in Mesa's life and even make him forget God. After all, he has confessed that, having tried the monastic life, he lost "all sense of purpose," and that unhappiness became his only lot. Mesa begins to judge the whole universe by dividing it into two: "on one side Ysé"; on the other side, "everything, less Ysé."

The joy of the "donation of everything and of oneself" has no possible place in *Break of Noon*, because Mesa and Ysé give themselves to each other, excluding everything else. At this point, the Claudelian logic closes on Mesa and Ysé: Just as Mesa confesses that the only object of knowledge he retained was Ysé herself, Ysé, in turn, relinquishes eternity in the name of love. Like the characters in *Le Repos du septième jour*, the Claudelian heroes must relearn that by giving absolute preference to a created being, humanity commits the greatest evil, that evil that is synonymous with death. The experience of evil in *Le Repos du septième jour* is "fictitious," while that in *Break of Noon* was real and personal; therefore, Claudel could not plunge Mesa and Ysé into eternal damnation.

To Claudel, human love, however it may have degraded itself, remains always an image of Divine Love. The most logical course for the playwright would be to have the lovers share the graces of midnight, for they have already shared the splendor of midday. Claudel, however, avoids anything that may give his play the impression of providing an easy thesis. Instead of forcing on them an artificial "conversion" to God, he makes them turn to their own love to make them believe that God can punish each "with the frightening love of the other." Thus, Claudel liberates himself and his characters from the romantic love that places itself above all judgments. The myth of Tristan and Iseult cannot be applied here: Although Mesa and Ysé die, they do not expect to reawaken to the reality of their own love, but rather to the splendor of God's eternal love, which is the *raison d'être* of all love.

The experience that inspired *Break of Noon* was so immense and rich in its emotional impact that Claudel could hardly have prevented it from erupting into his work. It was his first encounter with the love of a woman, and it happened at the noon of his life, only a few weeks after his intention to become a monk was denied. From a literary point of view, *Break of Noon* proclaims the *felix culpa*: From a moral point of view, the experience changed Claudel's interior life.

THE TIDINGS BROUGHT TO MARY

Albert Camus relates in *La Peste* (1947; *The Plague*, 1948) that a would-be novelist spent all his life revising the first sentence of his novel. The American, he says, calls it "absurd," but the Frenchman thinks that it is "grotesque." Claudel, without being either, spent his life revising *The Tidings Brought to Mary*. It is Claudel's most frequently staged drama. Yet, however popular, the drama did not reach the stage of the Comédie Française during the lifetime of its author.

The plot of the drama is based on four major events: First, Violaine forgives Pierre de Craon, who has attempted to rape her, and as a sign of forgiveness, she kisses him on the cheek. By that gesture, she assumes the leprosy with which he was struck at the time of his offense. Violaine's sister Mara has witnessed the scene. Second, by becoming a leper, she is rejected by her fiancé, Jacques Hury, who instead of marrying Violaine, marries Mara. Third, spending eight years in seclusion, Violaine offers her life to God, for the whole Church, France, and her family: At the end, she raises Mara's child from the dead. Fourth, Mara, being jealous of Violaine's sanctity, on her way home, after the scene of a miracle on Christmas Eve, kills Violaine. Anne Vercors, the father, returning from his pilgrimage to Jerusalem, finds the dying Violaine under a pile of sand; he takes her into his arms and carries her home.

The old man, Anne Vercors, can be imagined as a sort of *deus ex machina*, whose role is to elucidate the meaning of past events. He is not, however, an outsider to these events. At the beginning of his call, which prompted his journey to the Holy Land, there was a revelation: He had become conscious that, while "they were too happy," there were others who were not happy enough. He offered, then, his happiness for that of the rest of the world. The reason Violaine kissed Pierre de Craon was that his despair demanded compassion, understanding, and love. When Anne Vercors returns the dying Violaine, Jacques Hury sees in her only the "reprobate," the leper who failed because she loved "another." Not so, says the father: "Jacques, my child! the same call the father heard, also the daughter listened to it." The sacrifice that is demanded of the Christian cannot be measured in mathematical terms: At the end, Violaine resuscitates Mara's child; how could she "refuse to be a saint" when a "miserable being" such as Mara is begging for it? This is how Claudel imagines the Christian vocation: The Christian must step out of himself in order to find in the other the object of happiness and joy. On the one hand, Claudel recognizes that Christianity, by its very nature, involves a principle of contradiction. On the other hand, he believes that the religious act, par excellence, is prayer in which one makes "donation" of oneself. Prayer is a gratuitous act that serves another and expects nothing in return.

Drama itself—in its Claudelian interpretation—glorifies because prayer constitutes its very action. Ultimately, both Anne Vercors and his daughter Violaine testify to the fact that happiness is found neither in the idea of well-being cherished by the bourgeois society nor in the dream of materialism: It is, rather, a part of the joy of creation that humanity must live in its plenitude.

THE SATIN SLIPPER

Of Claudel's remaining plays, the most important is *The Satin Slipper*. This unorthodox drama is divided into four *journées*, the fourth one having been the first to be written, and each *journée* has the length of a complete play. The drama does not follow the classical unities, yet its focus on a central action creates the impression of unity: the story of the forbidden love of Don Rodrigue and of Dona Prouhèze. *The Satin Slipper* repeats none of Claudel's previous dramas, yet it is not alien to them. Indeed, many critics regard it as the summation of his artistic creation and of his thought.

Don Rodrigue and Dona Prouhèze fall in love at their first encounter, which lasts only a few minutes. For the rest of their lives, their love will teach them separation rather than union. They can never fulfill their love; they cannot marry each other. When they meet for the first time, Dona Prouhèze is married. When she becomes free, after the death of her husband (Don Pélage), Don Rodrigue is in South Amer-

ica, and Dona Prouhèze is forced by circumstances to marry Don Camille, a man whom she hates. This is a marriage of interest: Don Camille has some "African" blood, and if he remains faithful to the Spanish crown, the Spanish Empire will greatly profit from his services. Don Camille does not live up to the expectations of his king, and Dona Prouhèze, in her desperation, calls for Don Rodrigue's military help. The aid, however, does not come soon, as it takes ten years for the letter to reach Don Rodrigue. Don Rodrigue arrives in Mogador, the African fortress, only in time to save Dona Prouhèze's daughter, Dona of Seven-Sorrows. Once they reach safety on Don Rodrigue's boat, Dona Prouhèze blows up Mogador with herself and Don Camille in it. Don Rodrigue later loses the good graces of the Spanish monarch and is exiled, ultimately to be sold as a slave.

One of the merits of the drama is that it responded to the question that Mesa raised in *Break of Noon*: "Why this woman, why suddenly this woman on the ship?" Mesa's question could thus be rephrased: What is the meaning of love? Claudel recognizes that love, contrary to the doctrines of Romanticism, is not an immanent value and should not be taken as a goal in itself. Rather, love should be regarded as a sign for a higher good than itself, a force that leads the lovers to the authentic object of their love. The joy of the person who loves is situated outside the visible sphere of things. "How should we enjoy life," asks Claudel, "while our love is absent?"

Without denying the reality of the love between Don Rodrigue and Dona Prouhèze, Claudel places it into the service of their redemption. Because, in the Claudelian system, woman stands for the Church, wisdom, the Blessed Virgin, or the anima (soul), it is her duty to reveal the absolute beauty that makes all desire for created beings or things vain and foolish. The whole life of Don Rodrigue is guided by the prayers of his Jesuit brother, who offers his martyrdom for him. In the same way, Dona Prouhèze predestines herself to live according to the spirit, and thus she offers one of her "satin slippers" to the Blessed Virgin so that, in case she might want to run away from her, she may do so only on a crippled foot. The price that they both must pay for joy is immense, because they are not allowed to follow their hearts. For Claudel, this price of renunciation is exactly what love is seeking: a liberation from the conditions of earthly life.

OTHER MAJOR WORKS

POETRY: *Connaissance de l'est*, 1900, 1952 (*The East I Know*, 1914); *Art poétique*, 1907 (*Poetic Art*, 1948); *Cinq Grandes Odes*, 1910 (*Five Great Odes*, 1967); *Vers d'exil*, 1912; *Corona Benignitatis Anni Dei*, 1915 (*Coronal*, 1943); *La Messe là-bas*, 1921; *Poèmes de guerre*, 1922 (partial translation *Three Poems of the War*, 1919); *Feuilles de saints*, 1925; *Cent Phrases pour éventails*, 1927 (*A Hundred Movements for a Fan*, 1992); *La Cantate à trois voix*, 1931; *Dodoitzu*, 1945; *Poèmes et paroles durant la guerre de trente ans*, 1945; *Visages radieux*, 1947; *Premiers Vers*, 1950; *Poésies diverses*, 1957; *Autres Poèmes d'après le chinois*, 1957; *Petits Poèmes d'après le chinois*, 1957; *Traductions de poèmes*, 1957; *Œuvre poétique*, 1957; *Poèmes retrouvés*, 1967.

NONFICTION: *Jacques Rivière et Paul Claudel*, 1926 (*Letters to a Doubter: Correspondence of Jacque Rivière and Paul Claudel*, 1929); *Positions et propositions I*, 1928; *L'Oiseau noir dans le soleil levant*, 1929; *Écoute, ma fille*, 1934; *Positions et propositions II*, 1934 (*Ways and Crossways*, 1933); *Conversations dans le Loir-et-Cher*, 1935; *Un Poète regarde la Croix*, 1935 (*A Poet Before the Cross*, 1958); *Figures et paraboles*, 1936; *Toi, qui es-tu?*, 1936; *Les Aventures de Sophie*, 1937; *L'Épée et le miroir*, 1939; *Contacts et circonstances*, 1940; *Présence et prophétie*, 1942; *Seigneur, apprenez-nous à prier*, 1942 (*Lord, Teach Us to Pray*, 1948); *Le Livre de Job*, 1946; *L'Oeil écoute*, 1946 (*The Eye Listens*, 1950); *Discours et remerciements*, 1947; *Du côté de chez Ramuz*, 1947; *La Rose et le rosaire*, 1947; *Paul Claudel interroge le Cantique des Cantiques*, 1948; *Sous le signe du dragon*, 1948; *Accompagnements*, 1949; *André Gide et Paul Claudel, 1899-1926*, 1949 (*The Correspondence, 1899-1926, Between Paul Claudel and André Gide*, 1952); *Emmaüs*, 1949; *Une voix sur Israël*, 1950; *André Suarès et Paul Claudel*, 1951; *L'Évangile d'Isaïe*, 1951; *Francis Jammes-Gabriel Frizeau et Paul Claudel*, 1952; *Introduction au Livre de Ruth*, 1952; *Paul Claudel interroge l'Apocalypse*, 1952; *Le Symbolism de la Salette*, 1952; *J'aime la Bible*, 1955 (*The Essence of the Bible*, 1957); *Conversation sur Jean Racine*, 1956; *Qui ne souffre pas? Reflexions sur le problème social*, 1958; *Darius Milhaud et Paul Claudel*, 1961; *Aurélien Lugné-Poe et Paul Claudel*, 1964; *Au milieu des vitraux de l'Apocalypse*, 1966; *Jacques Copeau-Charles Dullin-Louis Jouvet et Paul Claudel*, 1966; *Journal I*, 1968; *Journal II*, 1969; *Mémoires improvisés*, 1969.

MISCELLANEOUS: *Œuvres complètes*, 1950-1967 (27 volumes).

BIBLIOGRAPHY

Bugliani, Ann. *Women and the Feminine Principle in the Works of Paul Claudel*. Madrid: J. Porrúa Turanzas, 1977. This study focuses on the portrayal of women in Claudel's works. Bibliography.

Caranfa, Angelo. *Claudel: Beauty and Grace*. Lewisburg, Pa.: Bucknell University Press, 1989. A critical study of Claudel's writings, with particular emphasis on his sense of aesthetics. Bibliography and index.

Killiam, Marie-Thérèse. *The Art Criticism of Paul Claudel*. New York: Peter Lang, 1990. A look at Claudel's critiques of art, which reflected his aesthetic sensibilities, which also found expression in his writings. Bibliography and index.

Knapp, Bettina Liebowitz. *Paul Claudel*. New York: Ungar, 1982. A biographical examination of Claudel that also provides critical analysis of his dramatic works.

Lambert, Carole J. *The Empty Cross: Medieval Hopes, Modern Futility in the Theater of Maurice Maeterlinck, Paul Claudel, August Strindberg, and Georg Kaiser*. New York: Garland, 1990. The works of Maeterlinck, Claudel, Strindberg, and Kaiser are compared and contrasted. Bibliography.

Longstaffe, Moya. *Metamorphoses of Passion and the Heroic in French Literature: Corneille, Stendhal, Claudel*. Lewiston, N.Y.: Edwin Mellen, 1999. A comparison of heroes and passion in the works of Claudel, Stendhal, and Pierre Corneille. Bibliography and index.

Paliyaenko, Adrianna M. *Mis-reading the Creative Impulse: The Poetic Subject in Rimbaud and Claudel, Restaged*. Carbondale: Southern Illinois University Press, 1997. A comparison and contrast of the works of Claudel and Arthur Rimbaud. Bibliography and index.

Moses M. Nagy

JEAN COCTEAU

Born: Maisons-Laffitte, France; July 5, 1889
Died: Milly-la-Forêt, France; October 11, 1963

PRINCIPAL DRAMA

Antigone, pr. 1922, pb. 1928 (libretto; English translation, 1961)

Orphée, pr. 1926, pb. 1927 (*Orpheus*, 1933)

Oedipus-Rex, pr. 1927, pb. 1928 (libretto; English translation, 1961)

La Voix humaine, pr., pb. 1930 (*The Human Voice*, 1951)

La Machine infernale, pr., pb. 1934 (*The Infernal Machine*, 1936)

L'École des veuves, pr., pb. 1936

Les Chevaliers de la table ronde, pr., pb. 1937 (*The Knights of the Round Table*, 1955)

Les Parents terribles, pr., pb. 1938 (*Intimate Relations*, 1952)

Les Monstres sacrés, pr., pb. 1940 (*The Holy Terrors*, 1953)

La Machine à écrire, pr., pb. 1941 (*The Typewriter*, 1948)

Renaud et Armide, pr., pb. 1943

L'Aigle à deux têtes, pr., pb. 1946 (*The Eagle Has Two Heads*, 1946)

Bacchus, pr. 1951, pb. 1952 (English translation, 1955)

Théâtre complet, pb. 1957 (2 volumes)

Five Plays, pb. 1961

L'Impromptu du Palais-Royal, pr., pb. 1962

The Infernal Machine and Other Plays, pb. 1964

OTHER LITERARY FORMS

Jean Cocteau took considerable delight in working on the borderlines separating various literary genres and those traditionally dividing literature from the other arts. As a result, his artistic output is both extraordinary and difficult to classify. *Le Potomak* (1919), his first important work, moves freely among verse, prose, dialogue, and drawing. His novel *Les Enfants terribles* (1929; *Children of the Game*, 1955), generally considered to be his masterpiece, is as much autobiography as fiction. He wrote magnificent poems, such as *La Crucifixion* (1946), but he also insisted that his novels, his criticism, in fact, all his works, are poetry. Many of his works for the stage can be called drama in only the broadest sense of the term: An example of such works is the scandalous ballet scenario *Parade* (1917), created in collaboration with Eric Satie and Pablo Picasso, and performed by Sergei Diaghilev's Ballets Russes. In 1921, Cocteau collaborated with six composers of the group known as "Les Six" (they included Louis Durey, Arthur Honegger, Darius Milhaud, Germaine Tailleferre, Georges Auric, and Francis Poulenc) and the Swedish Ballet Company in creating *Les Mariés de la tour Eiffel* (1921; *The Wedding on the Eiffel Tower*, 1937), this time contributing to the choreography as well as the dialogue. Cocteau also created a number of original and highly regarded films, beginning with *La Sang d'un poète* (1930; *The Blood of a Poet*, 1932), and including, among others, *La Belle et la bête* (1946; *Beauty and the Beast*, 1947) and *Orphée* (1950; *Orpheus*, 1950). Cocteau also wrote many witty, incisive nonfiction works, often autobiographical in nature; *Opium: Journal d'une désintoxication* (1930; *Opium: Diary of a Cure*, 1932) and *La Belle et la bête: Journal d'un film* (1946; *Beauty and the Beast: Journal of a Film*, 1950) are examples of his work in this area. Much of his work was experimental and often designed to shock, to break new ground and redefine the old.

ACHIEVEMENTS

Neal Oxenhandler eloquently sums up the current image of Jean Cocteau by entitling a study of the latter's theater *Scandal and Parade*: Only time and cautious scholarship will be able to reveal the worth of the artist and his work buried beneath the "scandal and parade." There can be little doubt that he was an important innovator on the stage. If one judges by what has frequently been the twentieth century artist's basis for self-evaluation—that is, if one judges Cocteau as experimenter and innovator—then one can consider him a leader in the arts of his time. That he reveals in his dramas dark corners of the human condition, particularly that of the twentieth century, is an aspect of his work that is too little understood. Because Cocteau was not a partisan, as were George Bernard Shaw or Bertolt Brecht, critics have too often overlooked the importance of his social and, in the broad sense, political worldview. Indeed, Cocteau shows throughout his best works the uncanny and incisive perception of an outsider.

BIOGRAPHY

It could be argued that Jean Maurice Eugène Clement Cocteau was born and bred to be an outsider. Reared by a family of stockbrokers, diplomats, and admirals, he was a product of the *grande bourgeoisie française*, neither entirely of the middle class nor entirely of the aristocracy. His parents, Georges and Eugénie Lecomte Cocteau, a couple who were no strangers to the arts, introduced Jean, his brother Paul, and his sister Marthe to music, theater, architecture, indeed, all the fine arts. Georges died when Jean was nine years old, and his mother, with whom he had a long and close relationship, had difficulty keeping the boy at the Petit Lycée Condorcet, where he was a poor student. Instead, Cocteau preferred to fol-

low his own interests at home and to attend the theater regularly.

His birthplace, Maisons-Laffitte, allowed Cocteau easy access to Paris, where he involved himself in the various avant-garde movements that followed hard on one another in the early part of the twentieth century, finding comradeship in unconventional undertakings with fellow outsiders. His friends included such writers as Edmond Rostand, Catulle Mendès, Leon Daudet, Marcel Proust, and the Comtesse Anna de Noailles. By 1909, he had published his first book of poems, *La Lampe d'Aladin*.

Soon afterward, he met the director of the Ballets Russes, Sergei Diaghilev, a man who influenced Cocteau immensely, inspiring him to write a number of ballet scenarios. Diaghilev's remonstrance to "Astonish me!" is claimed to have set Cocteau on his life-long aesthetic course to surprise and shock his audiences.

Cocteau's homosexuality was another factor that contributed to his outsider's perspective, placing him outside conventionality and impressing itself on his life, outlook, and art. He formed pivotal mentor-

Jean Cocteau (National Archives)

student-love relationships that would shape his artistic endeavors. His friendship with Raymond Radiguet, which had much to do with Cocteau's movement toward a more simple, classical style, and that with actor Jean Marais were two such important unions.

With the outbreak of World War I, Cocteau, rejected for active service because of his poor health, joined a civilian ambulance unit on the Belgian front. His experiences during this time formed the basis for his novel *Thomas l'imposteur* (1923; *Thomas the Impostor*, 1925), which was later made into a film. Toward the end of the war, Cocteau began his association with Pablo Picasso. Along with Satie and Diaghilev, they collaborated to create the ballet *Parade*, whose atonal music and radical set and costumes caused a sensation. (This production marked Cocteau's break with Igor Stravinsky, with whom he had been closely associated, and his alignment with Les Six.) With Radiguet's death in 1923 from typhoid fever, Cocteau, inconsolable, became addicted to opium yet continued his prodigious artistic production. During this period, *Orpheus* and *Oedipus-Rex*, an opera-oratorio, were produced.

In the 1930's, Cocteau turned his attention to film, creating a number of highly original works in that medium. The late 1930's marked the beginning of Cocteau's long collaboration with Jean Marais, during which he designed many roles especially for the young actor; the result was a series of masterpieces for screen and stage.

Cocteau took a pacifist stand during World War II, and his nonconformity during the German Occupation nearly cost him his life. Several of his stage works were banned for being "immoral," and he was beaten by members of a French Fascist group for refusing to salute their flag. Somewhat later, he braved official disapproval by testifying on behalf of criminal-turned-novelist Jean Genet. Cocteau continued to write, paint murals, direct films, design fabrics, and travel until 1953, when his health began to fail. In 1955, he was elected to the Académie Française and the Royal Belgian Academy. In 1956, he was awarded an honorary doctorate of letters from Oxford University. Cocteau died at Milly-la-Forêt, outside Paris, on October 11, 1963.

ANALYSIS

Early in his career, during and after World War I, Jean Cocteau wrote scenarios for ballets and adaptations of Greek myths. His plays of the late 1920's and early 1930's were highly original and brought him much attention. Cocteau gave the Oedipus legend a lasting form in his opera-oratorio *Oedipus-Rex*, and *Antigone* bears historical significance beyond its considerable intrinsic merits. In the late 1930's and the 1940's, under the influence of Jean Marais, Cocteau turned to contemporary problems, creating taut psychological dramas in the style of Boulevard drama; *Intimate Relations* is the most highly regarded of these middle works. Cocteau's later plays reflect his interest in reaching back into the past for both subject and form. *Renaud et Armide* and *L'Impromptu du Palais-Royal* appeal, respectively, to Jean Racine and Molière for models. *The Eagle Has Two Heads* returns to the nineteenth century romantic melodrama for conventions and to the period's history for plot elements. *Bacchus* combines historical drama and the Erasmian colloquy to create a mood-picture of the early Reformation. In these plays of his final years, Cocteau created works of transcendent stature. Of these, *The Eagle Has Two Heads* is the most beautifully crafted and most often performed.

Although it can be claimed that Cocteau's plays fall into distinct groups, or periods, the essential unity of all of Cocteau's plays must be noted. That he consistently chose a perverse or inverted vantage point, in order to astonish his audience with the unexpected, reflects the essential relation of his art to society. Cocteau added immensely to the arsenal of modern stage techniques; he had a keen ability to pick a subject to pieces and, in the process, demonstrate the absurdity of the whole. Always ready to draw out those elements that another playwright might have omitted, Cocteau, at his best, could also pare down to a minimum what was to be included.

In *Bacchus*, a dramatic masterpiece from Cocteau's late period, the playwright has a character speak a line that might be taken as a summation of the standard view of critics that he had produced too many works: "You speak too much to say one memorable word." Yet while it is true that Cocteau poured forth so many volumes of plays, as well as so many other works, brevity and conciseness are the hallmarks of the works just treated. Moreover, in these plays, Cocteau combines the quality of a subtle artist who exclusively moves by indirection with that of the "astonisher" of the bourgeoisie—that of the social and political satirist completely without partisan dogma. Few twentieth century writers have succeeded in being scandalous to the extent of being persecuted, even beaten, and having their works banned, and yet without ever having taken a clear partisan position. In this trait Cocteau recalls an earlier French iconoclast: Voltaire succeeded in fighting the Church without being an atheist; Cocteau, in lambasting the establishment without being a Marxist.

ANTIGONE

Antigone clearly demonstrates this capacity, at once, to draw out and to pare down the elements of the original drama, so much so that Sophocles would have found Cocteau's version, if not unrecognizable, at least, un-Sophoclean and un-Greek. The play was a significant contribution to the neoclassical movement in the arts of the 1920's. Igor Stravinsky and Les Six were setting forth the aesthetic of the pared-down and the streamlined in music. Picasso, who did the scenery for *Antigone*, was making thin-lined sketches of classical subjects; indeed, it is commonly believed that he adopted this style under the direct inspiration of Cocteau's own drawing style. Cocteau's thin single line in ink, which captures the essentials of form and meaning, graphically embodies, not only the style of Cocteau's neoclassical works, but also the aesthetic underlying all his works. In all the arts of this avant-garde neoclassicism, Greco-Roman subjects are used wherever possible; they are rendered, however, with a style and for a purpose that is modern. Sometimes a small touch in the dialogue of *Antigone*, more often, in the stage directions, makes it clear that the work is about modern France, indeed, about the modern experience.

Cocteau heavily underlines those elements in Creon the Tyrant that would be found in any twentieth century ruler. Like his modern counterparts, he lives in constant fear that the opposition is secretly plotting his downfall. Above all, Creon mistakenly believes that money is the wellspring of everyone's deeds. He even accuses the obviously irreproachable seer Tiresias of taking foreign bribes. Money, which is but one element among many in the work by Sophocles, is heavily underscored by Cocteau in his delineation of Creon. The supreme irony of Creon's tragedy is that his downfall results not from a group of paid subversives, motivated by worldly considerations of money and power; rather, he receives justice from someone who is inspired by moral sanctions.

Yet the agent of Creon's undoing has a further irony—it is a young woman, Antigone. When Antigone tells her sister that they must jointly act according to higher ethical demands and bury their brother in spite of Creon's law forbidding it, Ismene replies that she cannot, because women are helpless in the face of male power. Although Ismene proves unable to take action with her sister, she desires, in accordance with her conception of women, to partake of the martyr role that grows out of Antigone's act. Female submission in the face of male domination is the essence of Creon's conception of political power in the largest sense. He says that disorder is his greatest fear and that nothing would strike at the primal basis of his order with more certainty than the revolt of the women. "City," "family," and even the army depend on keeping women in their place within the patriarchal structure, and consequently, nothing is more deadly than should it happen that "the anarchist is a woman." Creon puts the matter even more brutally to his son Haemon, saying that the city is but a wife to its leader. In a patriarchal structuring of both family and city, both a wife and the people must be kept subordinate to the male in power. Cocteau's choice of lines for Creon cuts even deeper: As he believes that money is the motivating force of those who resist power, so, too, does he believe that women are instruments of propagation and nothing more. Concerning Haemon's deep love for Antigone, his intended wife, Creon says that "he will find another womb." These elements are in Sophocles' play, but Cocteau has selected them out from other elements, brought them to the fore, and underscored them in a way that renders them modern.

Cocteau's *Antigone* was the first in a series of

Greek dramas adapted by twentieth century French writers to shed light on the modern human situation—a series culminating in Jean Anouilh's *Antigone* (pr. 1944; English translation, 1946) and Jean-Paul Sartre's *Les Mouches* (pr., pb. 1943; *The Flies*, 1946). Cocteau constantly reminds the viewer through subtle touches in the *mise en scène* that he is viewing the present indirectly through the past. He instructs the actors to speak in very high-pitched voices as though they were reciting from a newspaper article. In another stage direction, he tells the actors playing the guards to stand on either side of Antigone and hold each end of a spear before her so that she will resemble a prisoner in a courtroom dock between two policemen.

Cocteau's *Antigone* represents the eternal spirit of disorder that eats away at the social structure on all levels—a structure that Cocteau finds inevitably repressive of the best in the human spirit. The fact that Antigone is a woman gives an added impact to the symbol: She has the capacity to deconstruct not only the obvious political system at the top but also the institution of the family. Cocteau's drama presents an outsider who gives her life to reveal the hypocrisy and rottenness of the social fabric. *Antigone*, although possibly influenced by the first wave of the feminist movement as it broke around Cocteau at the time he was writing the play, is not a tract for the stage as is George Bernard Shaw's *Mrs. Warren's Profession* (wr. 1893, pb. 1898), but it is still no less important socially or politically, and it is in some ways, perhaps, more profound.

Intimate Relations

In his second dramatic period, Cocteau set out to grapple with modern situations directly. *Intimate Relations* is the most highly valued and frequently performed of Cocteau's dramas about contemporary life. This play is most remarkable for its objective, detached view of the family as a structure of emotional relations and the neuroses stemming from them. One might term it a sociopolitical work even though, on the one hand, it avoids the underlying support of middle-class morality of the Boulevard dramas and the overt left-wing preachments of the *pièce a thèse*, on the other.

Although it could be argued that the family relations of the characters in *Intimate Relations* are unusual, the truths revealed in the play still have general relevance. Cocteau has structured the characters and their relations in what might be described as a pentangle: A mother inordinately loves a son, who loves a young woman, who was the mistress of the son's father, who, in his turn, is loved by the sister of his wife. Cocteau has made the family an unusual one for the purpose of making the dynamics of such a group all the more painfully apparent.

The two sisters, Yvonne, the wife, and Lèo, the unmarried sister, form the symbolic crux of the play. Lèo's presence has a certain ambiguity. It is she who saves Yvonne's life in act 1, but it is her series of attempts to salvage the family from shipwreck that leads to Yvonne being emotionally jettisoned from the family, resulting, then, in her suicide. At first, Lèo hatches a plot to separate the young couple (Madeleine and Michel); then, growing to like Madeleine, she hatches another plot to bring the young people back together again, thereby separating mother and son (Yvonne and Michel). Lèo's will to rule is a double-edged sword that saves and kills. The stage directions for *Intimate Relations* make clear the polarity between Lèo, on the one hand, and Yvonne and Madeleine, on the other: Cocteau observes that Yvonne's room represents chaos and Madeleine's, cosmos.

It is one of the beautiful subtleties of *Intimate Relations* that Cocteau does not make it emphatically apparent that his sympathies are with the figure of disorder, Yvonne. It is only by viewing *Intimate Relations* in the context of Cocteau's other plays that this attitude becomes clear. Antigone, the emblem of disorder, must die to bring tragic self-awareness to Creon, the emblem of order. Yvonne must also die a martyr's death. Yet, in *Intimate Relations*, the martyrdom has little effect because, at the play's end, a sinister order has been restored: Michel has found a new and more solid mother figure in Madeleine. This inevitability moves toward its tragic end in a real *coup de théâtre*.

The Eagle Has Two Heads

Equally exciting in dramatic structure is *The Eagle Has Two Heads*, which is perhaps the most theatrically viable of all the plays of Cocteau's last period, during which he experimented with past forms and conventions. Indeed, considered formalistically, this play is both a literary and a theatrical tour de force. Cocteau has compared the three-act structuring of this drama to a fugue: The first act, he says, is devoted to the queen; the second act, to Stanislas. In the last act, the two themes jointly culminate in a double suicide. This literary structure, however, had less a musical than a theatrical inspiration: Marais requested from Cocteau a play in which he could remain mute in the first act, have moments of ecstatic vocalizing in the second, and mime a melodramatic death in the third act. Cocteau set out to write an actor's play much like the singer's opera of the bel canto style and, then, to combine this style with elements of the romantic dramas of Victor Hugo. The miracle is that Cocteau succeeded in creating a complexly formulated, but no less moving, drama.

In essence, the play is a carefully concerted interchange between the queen and Stanislas, the would-be assassin, then her lover, and, finally, her assassin in fact. The first act is pervaded by the queen's monologues: The first of these is addressed to the imagined presence of her husband, an assassinated king; later, when Stanislas, the king's *Doppelgänger*, appears, she addresses him—mute as he is with exhaustion and defiance. From his appearance up to the finale of the play, however, Stanislas, and not the queen, is the motive force of the action—the poet-playwright, as it were. Indeed, in a moment of authorial reflexivity, Cocteau has the queen say that Stanislas has been the "author" of the three-act structure, "the drama." In act 1, he is the assassin who breaks into her stuffy existence like a romantic storm; in act 2, he inspires her to true queenship; finally, he poisons himself in order not to stand in the way of the queen's new will to power. The queen then becomes the author of her own destiny, paradoxically, by rejecting temporal power and by driving the poet mad with anger so that he will carry through with her assassination. Within the realm of the drama, then, the tragic finale is the queen's creation—in the end, she plays poet-playwright.

The play is also structured around symbols of contradiction and paradox. Ten years before the action of

the play, the assassin of the king used a dagger concealed in a bouquet of flowers. In act 1, the queen saves the life of her own would-be assassin; but, in act 2, the assassin, paradoxically, brings her back to life, at least for a temporary respite, from the living death of her ten-year state of mourning for the king. The double-headed eagle of the title represents contradiction and tension; yet, as the queen says, if one of the heads is cut off, the eagle dies. By means of this emblem, Cocteau seems to be saying that contradiction is needed if the spirit of a ruler, of a poet, or of a lover is to soar beyond the mundane. As Stanislas, the poet and lover, tells the queen, he does not offer her banal "happiness," but rather a joint alliance—"an eagle with two heads." During a dangerous horseback ride she takes in the mountains, the queen comes to realize that without the tension of life and death, there can be no beauty, no poetry in living. Only by loving her would-be assassin does she become a ruling queen; only by ruling does she discover the tragic desperation of life; only by discovering this desperation does she prepare herself for death.

Few directors have ever shown the keen sense for the psychological aptness of *mise en scène* that Cocteau does in this play—particularly in act 1. This play draws heavily on the *Hamlet, Prince of Denmark* (pr. c. 1600-1601) archetype; the relationship between Stanislas, who looks like the dead king, and the queen corresponds to that between Hamlet and his mother. The queen even describes Stanislas's sudden appearance through the open windows with poetic images used in William Shakespeare's scenes involving the ghost of Hamlet's father. To add point to the subtext, Cocteau has Stanislas, in his newly acquired capacity as court reader, recite the scene between Hamlet and his mother, the queen. It is no surprise, then, that the first act of the play is to be staged exactly like the traditional bedroom setting for *Hamlet*—complete even to the portrait of the king on the wall (an important touch in productions of *Hamlet* into the twentieth century, when it was replaced by a miniature in a locket). The stage directions call for the queen to make her first entrance from beyond the portrait, which pivots around; Cocteau thereby creates a concise metaphor for the ten years of the queen's life of mourning before the time of the play.

The queen is a strange composite of Elizabeth of Austria, Ludwig II of Bavaria, and Queen Victoria. In creating the queen and her environment, Cocteau has admirably captured the sense of the hothouse atmosphere of *fin de siècle* Europe, the country waiting for a great war to cut through the oppressiveness of emperors, kings, and aristocrats. The queen, as much as Stanislas, is an anarchist. She is an amateur of storms: She speaks of lightning that will destroy her genealogical tree and of the storm that will scatter the leaves of the book of court etiquette; she calls on Stanislas to destroy—to be a storm. In the end, she (herself) must be the anarchistic agent of the queen's (her own) assassination: Thereby, she becomes Cocteau's most complete symbol of self-sacrifice in celebration of disorder.

OTHER MAJOR WORKS

LONG FICTION: *Le Potomak*, 1919; *Le Grand Écart*, 1923 (*The Grand Écart*, 1925); *Thomas l'imposteur*, 1923 (*Thomas the Impostor*, 1925); *Le Livre blanc*, 1928 (*The White Paper*, 1957); *Les Enfants terribles*, 1929 (*Enfants Terribles*, 1930; also known as *Children of the Game*); *Le Fantôme de Marseille*, 1933; *La Fin du Potomak*, 1939.

POETRY: *La Lampe d'Aladin*, 1909; *Le Prince frivole*, 1910; *La Danse de Sophocle*, 1912; *Le Cap de Bonne-Espérance*, 1919; *L'Ode à Picasso*, 1919; *Poésies, 1917-1920*, 1920; *Escales*, 1920; *Discours du grand sommeil*, 1922; *Vocabulaire*, 1922; *Plain-Chant*, 1923; *Poésie, 1916-1923*, 1924; *Cri écrit*, 1925; *Prière mutilée*, 1925; *L'Ange Heurtebise*, 1925; *Opéra*, 1927; *Morceaux choisis*, 1932; *Mythologie*, 1934; *Allégories*, 1941; *Léone*, 1945; *Poèmes*, 1945; *La Crucifixion*, 1946; *Anthologie poétique*, 1951; *Le Chiffre sept*, 1952; *Appogiatures*, 1953; *Clair-obscur*, 1954; *Poèmes, 1916-1955*, 1956; *Gondole des morts*, 1959; *Cérémonial espagnol du phénix*, 1961; *Le Requiem*, 1962.

SCREENPLAYS: *Le Sang d'un poète*, 1932 (*The Blood of a Poet*, 1949); *Le Baron fantôme*, 1943; *L'Éternel retour*, 1943 (*The Eternal Return*, 1948); *La Belle et la bête*, 1946 (*Beauty and the Beast*, 1947); *L'Aigle à deux têtes*, 1946; *Ruy Blas*, 1947; *Les Parents terribles*, 1948 (*Intimate Relations*, 1952); *Les Enfants terribles*, 1950; *Orphée*, 1950 (*Orpheus*, 1950); *Le Testament d'Orphée*, 1959 (*The Testament of Orpheus*, 1968); *Thomas l'Imposteur*, 1965.

BALLET SCENARIOS: *Le Dieu bleu*, 1912 (with Frédéric de Madrazo); *Parade*, 1917 (music by Erik Satie, scenery by Pablo Picasso); *Le Boeuf sur le toit*, 1920 (music by Darius Milhaud, scenery by Raoul Dufy); *Le Gendarme incompris*, 1921 (with Raymond Radiguet; music by Francis Poulenc); *Les Mariés de la tour Eiffel*, 1921 (music by Les Six; *The Wedding on the Eiffel Tower*, 1937); *Les Biches*, 1924 (music by Poulenc); *Les Fâcheux*, 1924 (music by George Auric); *Le Jeune Homme et la mort*, 1946 (music by Johann Sebastian Bach); *Phèdre*, 1950 (music by Auric).

NONFICTION: *Le Coq et l'Arlequin*, 1918 (*Cock and Harlequin*, 1921); *Le Secret professionnel*, 1922; *Lettre à Jacques Maritain*, 1926 (*Art and Faith*, 1948); *Le Rappel à l'ordré*, 1926 (*A Call to Order*, 1926); *Opium: Journal d'une désintoxication*, 1930 (*Opium: Diary of a Cure*, 1932); *Essai de la critique indirecte*, 1932 (*The Lais Mystery: An Essay of Indirect Criticism*, 1936); *Portraits-souvenir, 1900-1914*, 1935 (*Paris Album*, 1956); *La Belle et la bête: Journal d'un film*, 1946 (*Beauty and the Beast: Journal of a Film*, 1950); *La Difficulté d'être*, 1947 (*The Difficulty of Being*, 1966); *The Journals of Jean Cocteau*, 1956; *Poésie critique*, 1960.

TRANSLATION: *Roméo et Juliette*, 1926 (of William Shakespeare's play).

BIBLIOGRAPHY

Griffith, Alison Guest. *Jean Cocteau and the Performing Arts*. Irvine, Calif.: Severin Wunderman Museum, 1992. This museum catalog includes critical analysis of Cocteau's work as well as information on his contribution to the performing arts. Bibliography.

Lowe, Romana. *The Fictional Female: Sacrificial Rituals and Spectacles of Writing in Baudelaire, Zola, and Cocteau*. New York: Peter Lang, 1997. Lowe compares and contrasts the works of Cocteau, Charles Baudelaire, and Émile Zola, especially their treatment of women. Bibliography and indexes.

Mauriès, Patrick. *Jean Cocteau.* London: Thames and Hudson, 1998. A biography of Cocteau that covers his life and works, including details of his work in films.

Saul, Julie, ed. *Jean Cocteau: The Mirror and the Mask: A Photo-Biography.* Boston: D. R. Godine, 1992. This compilation from an exhibit celebrating the one-hundred year anniversary of his birth,

with an essay by Francis Steegmuller, provides insights into the life of Cocteau.

Tsakiridou, Cornelia A. *Reviewing "Orpheus": Essays on the Cinema and Art of Jean Cocteau.* Lewisburg, Pa.: Bucknell University Press, 1997. Although this work focuses on the screenplays and film work of Cocteau, it also sheds light on his dramatic works.

Rodney Farnsworth

PADRAIC COLUM

Born: County Longford, Ireland; December 8, 1881
Died: Enfield, Connecticut; January 11, 1972

PRINCIPAL DRAMA

The Children of Lir, pb. 1901 (one act)
Broken Soil, pr. 1903 (revised as *The Fiddler's House*, pr., pb. 1907)
The Land, pr., pb. 1905
The Miracle of the Corn, pr. 1908
The Destruction of the Hostel, pr. 1910
Thomas Muskerry, pr., pb. 1910
The Desert, pb. 1912 (revised as *Mogu the Wanderer: Or, The Desert*, pb. 1917, pr. 1932)
The Betrayal, pr. 1914
Three Plays, pb. 1916, revised 1925, revised 1963 (includes *The Land*, *The Fiddler's House*, and *Thomas Muskerry*)
The Grasshopper, pr. 1917 (adaptation of Eduard Keyserling's play *Ein Frühlingsofer*)
Balloon, pb. 1929, pr. 1946
Moytura: A Play for Dancers, pr., pb. 1963
The Challengers, pr. 1966 (3 one-act plays: *Monasterboice*, *Glendalough*, and *Cloughoughter*)
Carricknabauna, pr. 1967 (also as *The Road Round Ireland*)
Selected Plays of Padraic Colum, pb. 1986 (includes *The Land*, *The Betrayal*, *Glendalough*, and *Monasterboice*; Sanford Sternlicht, editor)

OTHER LITERARY FORMS

Padraic Colum's career as a writer spanned nearly three-quarters of a century. His first one-act play was published in 1901, and he continued to write poetry until his death in 1972. For most of his life, his living was made largely from his children's books, many of which have become classics. Like all truly good books of their kind, they are readable and engaging for adults as well as for children. Such works as *A Boy in Eirinn* (1913), *The King of Ireland's Son* (1916), *The Adventures of Odysseus* (1918), *The Children of Odin* (1920), *The Golden Fleece and the Heroes Who Lived Before Achilles* (1921), and *Legends of Hawaii* (1937) won for him respect both as a children's writer and as an expert on folklore and mythology. "The storyteller," he wrote, "must have respect for the child's mind and the child's conception of the world, knowing it for a complete mind and a complete conception. If a storyteller has that respect, he need not be childish in his language. . . . If children are to will out of the imagination and create out of the will, we must see to it that their imaginations are not clipped or made trivial."

Colum's literary output also included two novels, *Castle Conquer* (1923) and *The Flying Swans* (1957), several travel books, a literary recollection of James Joyce (written with Mary Colum), and a biography of Arthur Griffith, one of his earliest friends and the first president of the Irish Free State. A bibliography of

Colum's separately published books would run to more than seventy titles. If miscellaneous works were added to this—books he edited, prefaces, introductions, and periodical publications of poems, stories, and essays—the number would be in the thousands.

In all Colum's prose works, his style is direct, lucid, and graceful, but his literary reputation rests most securely on his poetry, which has been widely anthologized and warmly praised by writers and critics since his poems first began to appear in the opening years of the twentieth century. The poet George Russell (Æ), one of Colum's earliest and most enthusiastic admirers, wrote in 1902 that he had "discovered a new Irish genius: . . . only just twenty, born an agricultural labourer's son, laboured himself, came to Dublin two years ago and educated himself, writes astonishingly well, poems and dramas with a real originality. . . . I prophesy about him." By 1904, Colum's poems had begun to appear in anthologies in Ireland and the United States, and since then every major collection of Irish poetry has included his work. Critics have consistently placed his name high on lists of the best Irish poets, but his poems have inspired few detailed scholarly studies. His poetry, in fact, resists such treatment: It is not easily identified with any particular school or movement, and it contains no esoteric philosophy to be glossed or obscure passages and patterns of symbolism to be unraveled. Indeed, its most distinguishing characteristics are simplicity and clarity. Often the poems are dramatic lyrics spoken by Irish peasants. Many are acutely accurate observations of commonplaces, as are those in his *Creatures* (1927) and *The Vegetable Kingdom* (1954).

ACHIEVEMENTS

Although few scholars have written about Padraic Colum's poetry, scholars and poets have been generous in honoring him. He was elected president of the Poetry Society of America in 1938 and won its medal in 1940. He also received honorary doctorates from the University of Ireland and Columbia University and awards from the Academy of Irish Letters and the American Academy of Poets. Critic Edmund Wilson, after reading a collection of Colum's poems, wrote to

Padraic Colum (Library of Congress)

him that "I wept while reading . . . some of them—not for sentiment, which doesn't often make me weep, but for the beauty of the lines. If everybody in Ireland hadn't been so overshadowed by Yeats, you would certainly have stood out as one of the best poets in English of your time."

Colum's reputation as a poet was well deserved, but it was one that did not altogether please him. He did not disown the title of poet, but he frequently objected to the exclusiveness of the label when it overshadowed his accomplishments in the theater. On one occasion, while discussing with a friend how future generations would remember him, he insisted that the popular notion that he was primarily a poet was a misconception. "I am primarily a man of the theatre," he argued, "and always have been." Colum repeated this judgment several times toward the end of his life. A few weeks before his death at the age of ninety, he told a reporter from *The New York Times* that he was often prouder of his plays than of anything else he had written. Whenever he was in a position to influence the shaping of his public identity, he was careful to point out the close connection between his poetry and his plays. One such opportunity came when he was being interviewed by a writer who was preparing an introductory study of his works. "In the early part," Colum directed, "put my poems and plays together. The sort of plays I was writing for the theatre and the sort of poems I was writing are about the same sort of people and treat them in the same sort of way." Referring to such early poems as "The Plougher" and "An Old Woman of the Roads," he suggested that "you would put it best by saying that they were dramatizations. They're really characters in a play that hadn't been written." He was given another opportunity when Irish Radio invited him to sketch a prose portrait of himself. "Anything I have written, whether verse or narrative," he said during the broadcast, "goes back to my first literary discipline, the discipline of the theatre."

BIOGRAPHY

Padraic Colum wrote his first play when he was nineteen and his last when he was eighty-five. In all, he wrote about two dozen plays of varying lengths, many in several different versions. His plays have been produced at the Abbey and Gate theaters in Dublin, on Broadway by David Belasco and Iden Payne, Off-Broadway, at the Dublin Theatre Festival, on Irish television, in the little theaters that flourished in Dublin in the 1960's, and by amateur groups in Ireland, England, the United States, the Middle East, and Australia.

There was little in Colum's family background to suggest a career as a playwright. Unlike William Butler Yeats, John Millington Synge, Lady Augusta Gregory, and most of the other playwrights of the Irish Literary Renaissance with whom he became associated, his background was rural, Catholic, and working-class. His mother was the daughter of a gardener, and his father the son of a tenant farmer. Colum's father seems to have been temperamentally unsuited to handle the responsibilities of a growing

family and, according to Colum, "was always unlucky looking for jobs." He worked first as a teacher in a national school and later taught the children of paupers at Longford Workhouse in the Irish midlands; he eventually became master of the workhouse but had to resign the position because of his drinking and mishandling of funds. He left Ireland for a few years to work at various jobs in the United States but returned when Colum was nine and moved the family to Sandycove outside Dublin, where he had found a job as a clerk in the railway station. Padraic entered the local national school, though his attendance became irregular when he was old enough to take a part-time job. He and his brother Fred worked as delivery boys for the railroad and took turns attending school, one going one day, the other the next. When he was seventeen, Colum left school after passing his examinations and began work as a clerk at the Railway Clearing House on Kildare Street in Dublin.

Colum soon became interested in drama, though all he knew about plays and playwriting was what he had learned from the national school curriculum, from books he found in the local library, and from rare visits to the theater in Dublin, where the fare tended to be a mixture of music-hall variety shows and popular English comedies. He recalled later that when he began writing his first play, he "knew nothing whatever about the theatre. I had seen [Dion Boucicault's] *The Colleen Bawn*, *The Shaughraun*, and some shows put on by amateurs, and I had gone to the Gaicty Theatre, and spent a whole shilling for a seat in the pit . . . to see Mr. and Mrs. Kendall in a play called *The Elder Miss Blossom*." This was in 1899, and there was as yet no such thing as a native Irish drama, apart from the melodramas of Boucicault. The Abbey Theatre, which would provide models for the next generation of playwrights, was still six years from being founded, and the Irish Literary Theatre, which Yeats, Lady Gregory, and Edward Martyn had established with the aim of creating a native drama, was only in its first year of production. Colum saw none of the Irish Literary Theatre's plays that year and, in fact, saw none of its subsequent productions except the final one on October 21, 1901. This was a double bill featuring *Diarmuid and Grania* by Yeats and George Moore and *Casad-an-Sugan* (*The Twisting of the Rope*), Douglas Hyde's play in Irish.

Colum's first effort at playwriting was, instead, a result of his attendance at the *tableaux vivants* that the patriotic Daughters of Ireland were staging to promote nationalistic sentiment. "They were statuesque groups introduced by some familiar piece of music, and holding their pose for some minutes—an elementary show in which costume, music and striking appearance were ingredients," Colum later wrote. "I was in an audience that witnessed 'Silent, O Moyle, Be the Roar of Thy Waters.' I felt there should be words to give life to the pathos of children transformed by an enchantress stepmother; my mind was already on plays. I began a one act play in verse, *The Children of Lir*, and sent it to [the Daughters of Ireland]." Although they did not produce the play, Colum succeeded in getting it published in *The Irish Independent* on September 14, 1901. It was his first published work. During the next three years—what Colum called his apprentice period—he published several more one-act plays, including plays based on Irish history and mythology, Ibsen-like problem plays, a dramatic monologue, and a melodramatic propaganda play, written to discourage enlistments in the British Army. As might be expected, these early plays are, for the most part, awkward and immature, and Colum made no later effort to revise or republish them. They do, however, show a precocious grasp of dramatic techniques and a rapidly developing skill.

Colum's full-length play *Broken Soil* was produced by the Irish National Theatre Society in 1903, the same year it produced the first plays of Synge and Lady Gregory. Almost immediately Colum was recognized as a playwright of great promise and sound dramatic judgment. When he was only twenty-three, he was selected by the National Theatre Society to be a member of its first reading committee, a role he shared with Yeats and Æ. Yeats was particularly impressed by Colum's work, describing him in 1904 as "a man of genius in the first dark gropings of his thought" and noting that "some here think he will become our strongest dramatic talent." Colum's plays and poems also won for him the patronage

of Thomas Hughes Kelly, an American millionaire living near Dublin, who awarded him a five-year grant—beginning at seventy pounds and increasing by ten pounds per year—to support his literary work. With this subsidy, Colum was able to quit his job as a railway clerk in 1904 and devote his full time to writing. He quickly developed into an accomplished playwright, and the popularity of his next play, *The Land*, helped to confirm Yeats's prediction. Produced in 1905 after the Irish National Theatre Society was reorganized as the Abbey Theatre, it gave the Abbey what it much needed when many were criticizing it for being something less than the national theater it purported to be—a play that was both a critical and a popular success. Irish and English critics hailed it as "the best play yet given us by the dramatic movement" and "one of the most important plays which have appeared in English for a long time." Although this praise was perhaps extravagant, the play did add a new dimension to the dramatic movement. As one reviewer explained: "What we have been waiting for is a play that should be at once good and popular. Mr. Yeats has proved a little too abstruse, and Mr. Synge a little too bizarre to get fully down to the hearts of the people."

The Land was the first of a series of three plays dealing with life in the Irish midlands that firmly established Colum's reputation as a major playwright and a pioneering figure in the realistic movement. The second in the series was a thorough reworking of *Broken Soil*, which he retitled *The Fiddler's House*. It was performed in 1907 by the Theatre of Ireland, a splinter group formed after Colum and others had left the Abbey in a dispute over theater policy a year earlier. By all accounts, the Theatre of Ireland production was inept. As a result, the play did not receive the public exposure it deserved, even though most critics thought it a much better play than *The Land*. Andrew E. Malone, for example, described it as "in every respect Colum's best play" and considered it "equal to the greatest in the Irish theatre." After Colum left the Abbey Theatre, he never fully reestablished his association with it. He did, however, give it *Thomas Muskerry*, the third of his realistic Irish plays, for production in 1910. The public reception of this play was mixed, with opinions turning on the harshness of its characterization of small-town merchants. While some reviewers found the play brilliant, others damned it as libeling the Irish national character. The issues raised by *Thomas Muskerry* were debated for several weeks in the columns of Dublin's newspapers. Like Synge's *The Playboy of the Western World* (pr., pb. 1907) and Sean O'Casey's *The Plough and the Stars* (pr., pb. 1926), however, the play survived the controversy it aroused and is now generally considered to be Colum's masterpiece.

In 1912, Colum married Mary Catherine Gunning Maguire, whom he had met while she was a student at University College, Dublin. By then, his five-year grant had expired, and his income was now dependent on his freelance writing. He and Mary supplemented this by teaching in a private school but soon decided that if Colum was to earn a living as a writer, he would have to find a wider market than Dublin offered. When his aunt in Pittsburgh offered to pay their fare to the United States, they accepted, hoping to make careers for themselves there as writers. They left for the United States in 1914, and both subsequently succeeded in their goals, Colum by his voluminous output of books, essays, and literary journalism, and Mary by becoming a highly respected literary critic, writing reviews for *The New York Times* and several other major newspapers and literary journals and serving as literary editor of *Forum*.

In the ten years between the end of his apprenticeship in 1904 and his emigration to the United States, Colum wrote a number of other plays. None was in the manner of his three major realistic plays, and none was given a successful production until several years after he left Ireland. *The Miracle of the Corn*, written for the Irish National Theatre Society, was accepted and put into rehearsal in 1904 but for some reason was not performed. The Theatre of Ireland staged it in 1908 in a production that seems to have been less competent than that of *The Fiddler's House*. One critic in the opening-night audience commented that the actors spoke their lines so softly that they could not be heard in the first row. Colum wrote an adaptation of the medieval miracle play *Secunda Pastorum* (fifteenth century; commonly known as *The Second*

Shepherds' Play) at Yeats's suggestion in 1911, but the Abbey did not produce it. Of the other plays, only *The Destruction of the Hostel* was staged while Colum still lived in Ireland, and this was in an amateur production by the boys' acting class of St. Enda's School. After leaving the Abbey, Colum hoped to make a name for himself in the London theater and wrote three plays for production there. He was unable, however, to find a producer for *The Desert* or "Theodora of Byzantium," and a London production of *The Betrayal* was canceled after Lady Gregory refused to grant permission for a group of actors under contract with the Abbey to act in it.

Colum's interest in the theater continued after his arrival in the United States. His first job there was at the Carnegie Institute in Pittsburgh, where he was hired to assist in the production of a series of Irish plays. His *The Betrayal* was given its first production as part of the series. In 1915, Colum moved to New York, where he lectured on Irish drama and announced his intention of joining John P. Campbell, a former artistic director of the Ulster Literary Theatre, in establishing the Irish Theatre of America, to be modeled after the Abbey Theatre. Colum and Campbell held an organizational meeting, issued a statement of plans to the press, and produced their first play in February, 1915, but the group failed to gather momentum and disbanded soon afterward. Over the next forty-five years, Colum's contacts with the theater became less frequent. *The Grasshopper*, his adaptation of Eduard Keyserling's *Ein Frühlingsofer*, was produced on Broadway in 1917 and at the Abbey in 1922. *The Fiddler's House* received its first Abbey Theatre production in 1919 and was revived in New York in 1941. *Mogu the Wanderer*, a revised version of *The Desert*, was produced at Dublin's Gate Theatre in 1932 with a young Orson Welles in a leading role. Michael Myerberg, who had successfully produced Thornton Wilder's *The Skin of Our Teeth* (pr., pb. 1942), bought the option on *Balloon*, an experimental play modeled partly on the Italian *commedia dell'arte* and partly on American comic strips, published by Colum in 1929, and tried it out for two weeks in 1946 in Ogunquit, Maine, but did not take it into New York. Myerberg also commissioned Colum to write the screenplay for a 1954 adaptation of Engelbert Humperdinck's opera *Hansel and Gretel* (pr. 1893), in which the actors were animated dolls. Also in 1954, Colum assisted Marjorie Borkenstein in adapting James Joyce to the stage in *Ulysses in Nighttown*.

Such activities kept Colum sporadically in touch with the theater but were not enough to keep alive the reputation as a playwright he had established decades earlier in Dublin. Although his notebooks for these years show that the theater was rarely far from his mind, most of his writing efforts for the stage went into adaptations of other people's work and seemingly endless revisions of plays he had written years before. He produced only one wholly new play between 1912 and 1961. This was *Balloon*, and an anecdote about it reveals how difficult it was for Colum to keep alive his reputation as a man of the theater. His friend Charles Burgess tells of an encounter with him in New York during the 1950's. "You are talking to a dead man," Colum said, and Burgess recalls:

> That afternoon he had called on a producer to whom he had recently sent a play. . . . As they had discussed the possibility of a production, the producer had said to him, off-handedly, that of course they'd have to use a different name. Colum, rising to his work's defense, had replied, "Well, I don't know. . . . Most of the people who know the play tell me that *Balloon* is a very good name for it." "Oh, I don't mean the title of the play," the producer had countered, "it's the name Padraic Colum I'm referring to. There was another playwright by that name at the turn of the century and I think we'd be criticized if we used his name."

In the last ten years of his life, Colum stepped up his efforts in the drama and succeeded to some degree in bringing his name again before the playgoing public. In 1960, he began work on a cycle of Yeatsian Nō plays, the first of which, *Moytura*, was published in 1963. Also in 1963, he published a significantly revised edition of his realistic *Three Plays*. The revisions demonstrated a good sense of dramatic structure and revealed that Colum's mastery of dialogue was better than it had ever been. *Moytura* was performed at the Pike Theatre in Dublin in 1963, and productions of it and of other Nō plays followed on Irish radio and

television. Three of the plays, *Monasterboice*, *Glendalough*, and *Cloughoughter*, were gathered together under the title *The Challengers* and staged in 1966 at Dublin's Lantern Theatre. The following year, *Carricknabauna*, a dramatic adaptation of some of Colum's poems, was performed Off-Broadway and, as *The Road Round Ireland*, at the Lantern.

Despite Colum's final flurry of activity, his dramatic efforts, spaced over a period of more than sixty years, do not add up to a distinguished career in the theater and hardly seem to justify his insistence that "if I am not a playwright, I am nothing." There is clearly an element of exaggeration in such a statement, but if there is, Colum's need to exaggerate is at least partially understandable as a protest against premature burial by literary historians who persisted in reporting that he had abandoned the stage for good in 1910 and Broadway producers who thought him long dead. There is also a temptation to dismiss Colum's repeated assertions that he was primarily a playwright as the wishful thinking of an old man who had never quite got over his first flush of success on the stage. Such an attitude does not do Colum justice, for his plays have never been fully evaluated, and the importance of their position in his identity as an artist has never been acknowledged.

ANALYSIS

Padraic Colum was a major figure in the Irish Literary Renaissance both because he was the first to deal realistically with the Irish peasant farmer and because of the influence his plays had on the playwrights who followed him. Something of the pervasiveness and power of his influence comes through in the open letter that Yeats wrote to Lady Gregory in 1919, in which he announced that he was giving up public theater for a more private theater of the drawing room. Yeats wrote that while he had sought to create a poetic drama, the Abbey playwrights, following Colum's lead, had instead succeeded in "the making articulate of all the dumb classes each with its own knowledge of the world, its own dignity, but all objective with the objectivity of the office and the workshop, of the newspaper and the street, of mechanism and of politics." It was, nevertheless, the realistic drama of peasant life that won for the Abbey Theatre its international recognition.

Colum himself did not claim to have been the inventor of the peasant play; he said that he shared the distinction with Synge. "My *Broken Soil* and Synge's *In the Shadow of the Glen* were produced within a month of each other," he wrote. "These two plays inaugurated the drama of peasant life. Yeats's *Cathleen ni Houlihan*, in which the characters are peasants, was produced first, but *Cathleen ni Houlihan* is symbolic and not a play of actual peasant life." "A play of actual peasant life" aptly describes what Colum sought to write, and it was with this type of play, in his view, that Ireland began to have a truly native drama—plays he described as being "authentic in idiom and character" and expressing "the sum of instincts, traditions, sympathies that made the Irish mind distinctive." Probably the most important concept in Colum's view of drama was that plays should *express* Irish life. Synge and others poeticized the life of the peasant; Colum saw a poetry within that life and expressed it realistically. In doing so, he saw his work as being distinctly "democratic, not only because it deals with the folk of the country and the town, but because it is written out of recognition of the fact that in every life there are moments of intensity and beauty." Other Irish playwrights wrote about peasants, but none accepted them on their own terms. They saw them as outsiders would see them: Yeats's peasants are romantic idealizations, Lady Gregory's are caricatures—only slightly less broad than the nineteenth century "stage Irishmen"—and Synge's, for all the richness and beauty of their language, are exaggerations of the Irish peasant. Of all the early Abbey Theatre playwrights, only Colum, who grew up among peasant farmers and small-town merchants, accurately reflected their character, their language, and their concerns.

Because of their realistic portrayal of Irish life, Colum considered *The Land*, *The Fiddler's House*, and *Thomas Muskerry* to be his most important and most influential plays. Most literary historians agree with this judgment. What gives each of the plays its dramatic vigor and depth of characterization is the tension inherent in Colum's view of Ireland. Each presents a pair of characters whose energy or imagination is too strong to be held back by the dreary inertia of Irish country life. Matt Cosgar and Ellen Douras in *The Land*, Maire Hourican and her father, Conn, in *The Fiddler's House*, and Muskerry and Myles Gorman in *Thomas Muskerry* all experience a conflict between their feelings of responsibility to something in this spiritually cramped existence and a deeper need to rise above it. The attention that Colum gives to realistic detail in the plays is a means of emphasizing the part in the conflict played by everyday life in Ireland. Permeating the three plays as a motivating force and linking them thematically is the struggle for freedom that is resolved in *Thomas Muskerry*'s final triumphant symbol, Myles Gorman, whom Colum described as "a man of energy set free on the roads."

THE LAND

Because he considered these plays so central to his reputation as a playwright, Colum revised them frequently throughout his life. He first gathered them together as *Three Plays* in 1916 and later published revised editions of the collection in 1925 and 1963. With the exception of *The Land*, which received only light revision, the plays in the 1963 edition differ significantly from the versions that were staged nearly a half a century earlier. *The Land* was inspired, Colum said, by the Land Act of 1903, which enabled Irish tenant farmers to purchase their land. The play's central conflict is between two generations: the farmers, who have fought to win their land, and their children, who are tempted by the call of the larger world outside. The younger generation prevails in the end, with Matt Cosgar and Ellen Douras departing for the United States and leaving their claims to their fathers' farms to Ellen's less imaginative brother Cornelius and Matt's slow-witted sister Sally.

Although Colum referred to it in 1910 as only "a sketch for a play" and wrote in 1963 that "if staged these days *The Land* would have to be played as an historical piece and for character parts," the play is notable for its strong characterization of Sally and the two fathers, Murtagh Cosgar and Martin Douras. It also has a strongly unified plot and a clean story line. By unfolding his plot against the larger historical backdrop of the farmers' progress from tenants to landowners, Colum managed to reinforce the irony of the exodus of Ireland's most gifted young people at the very time when the country had something to offer them.

The Land plays well on the stage—when the Dublin International Theatre Festival was inaugurated in 1957, it was the only early full-length Abbey Theatre play selected—but it is inferior to Colum's other two realistic dramas. The plot is perhaps too neatly constructed and the characters too conveniently paired off; the son and daughter of Murtagh Cosgar wed the son and daughter of Martin Douras, and six young emigrants to the United States in act 2 are balanced against six farmers who commit themselves to the land in act 1. Matt and Ellen, moreover, are too thinly characterized for the parts they play, and Cornelius's curtain speech is too obviously propagandistic. Nevertheless, because of both the popular support it won for the Abbey and its value as a commentary on social and political changes, the play has undeniable historical importance. *The Land*, in fact, is the only one of the three plays about which it can be said with any justice that historical value outweighs literary worth.

THE FIDDLER'S HOUSE

The Fiddler's House is similar to *The Land* in both theme and plot: An aging fiddler, Conn Hourican, leaves the farm that his daughter Maire has inherited to follow the roads, playing at festivals and in public houses. Maire, whose increasing sense of affinity with her father is matched by a growing aversion to Brian McConnell, the man whom she had intended to marry, decides to follow her father on the roads and deeds the farm to her younger sister, Anne. *The Fiddler's House* was probably Colum's most frequently revised play, and through several revisions, the focus switched back and forth between the two main characters. In a letter to his patron, Kelly, in 1910, Colum revealed his fascination with the characters of Conn and Maire and suggested that Maire dominated the unpublished *Broken Soil*. "Now that I read the plays," he wrote, "Conn Hourican and [Maire] Hourican in *The Fiddler's House* are more vivid to me than any of the people in *The Land*. I know that you prefer *Bro-*

ken Soil to *The Fiddler's House*, the play that has taken its place. . . . But I thought Conn Hourican worth a play, and I tried to make a new one for him." Conn dominated both the 1907 and 1925 versions of the play. Later, however, Maire began to grow in Colum's imagination. In the preface of the 1963 edition of *Three Plays*, he says:

> The motive in its early version was simply "the call of the road." It became *The Fiddler's House* when a real conflict was seen as developing in it, the conflict between father and daughter in which reconciliation came when Maire Hourican becomes aware that she, too, has the vagrant in her. Later, when produced in New York by Augustin Duncan, something else in her character was made explicit. Her recoil from her lover is due to her fear of masculine possessiveness—a recoil not extraordinary in a girl brought up in the Irish countryside.

In the 1963 revision of the play, Maire regained the ground that she had lost in the versions of 1907 and 1925, and the characters settled into a state of equilibrium, each interesting for different reasons. While the divided focus of the play kept it from greatness, it also gave the Irish stage two memorable characters. The complexly motivated Maire is particularly well drawn. When Brian tries to dominate her and threatens to carry her off by force to marry him, she begins to realize that, more than marriage, she wants freedom. When she leaves to follow her father at the play's close, the possibility of reconciliation with Brian is more remote than it had been in the earlier plays. Through the various revisions, Colum gradually transformed her from a girl who wants only a home and a husband to a woman who wants to shape her own life.

THOMAS MUSKERRY

Thomas Muskerry went through a similar evolutionary process of revision, and by the time he completed the process, Colum had transformed his weakest play into his strongest. Andrew E. Malone, writing about the early Abbey Theatre version of the play, termed it "in every respect inferior to *The Land* and *The Fiddler's House*"; Robert Hogan, writing in 1967 about the final revision, called it Colum's "masterpiece." Most critics concur with Hogan's judgment. In writing the play, Colum drew on his earliest childhood experiences at the Longford Workhouse. As the play begins, Muskerry, master of a workhouse in the Irish midlands, is at the end of a successful career and looking forward to a pleasant retirement in the cottage he plans to buy with his life savings. By the play's end, he lies dead in a pauper's bed at the workhouse. In the intervening scenes, it is discovered that he had accidentally mismanaged the workhouse's funds, and the Crilly family, into which his daughter had married, persuades him to resign as master to save the family's reputation in the village. They also persuade him to give up his plan of buying a cottage and to live with them behind their shop. Once he abdicates his power to the Crillys, however, they become increasingly neglectful of him, even as he uses his savings to keep their shop from foundering. At the end of the play, he is penniless and spiritually broken by the ingratitude of his daughter and her in-laws and by the humiliating taunts of Felix Tournour, the workhouse porter. The only person who shows him any sympathy is Christy Clarke, an orphan whom he had befriended.

The 1910 version of *Thomas Muskerry* was little more than the bare bones of a play and had succeeded only on the merits of an unusually moving final act; it had little else to recommend it. The first act did scarcely more than lay an Ibsen-like foundation of complex exposition and introduce a large cast of sparsely drawn characters—each arriving and departing at too obviously opportune moments. The succession of events necessary for the play's later developments was more mechanical than dramatic and too rapid to be credible. The second act moved along at the same quick pace, carrying Muskerry mechanically through the events that led finally to his death. Muskerry in the closing scenes achieved—in his mixture of pathos and tragedy, failure and triumph—a grandeur reminiscent of Lear. The play, in fact, resembled William Shakespeare's tragedy in many ways and gained strength from the underlying but unspoken allusion to *King Lear* (pr. c. 1605-1606) that reverberated through the unfolding pattern of filial ingratitude.

The later version of *Thomas Muskerry* more than compensates for the artistic deficiencies of the early version. Structurally, Colum's innovations slow the pace and allow the play to build more powerfully to its climax. What was merely a mechanical succession of events in the first version takes on an aura of inevitability in the revision. In rewriting the play, Colum divided the first act into two scenes by reshuffling the exposition and spreading the action over two evenings instead of one. He also suggests early in the first scene that Felix Tournour has information that may later damage Muskerry's reputation and jeopardize his pension. In the earlier version, Tournour's knowledge had come as a surprise late in the play and had no real effect on the action. With this small change, Colum was able to foreshadow the most important turning point in Muskerry's fortunes and to orchestrate Tournour into a nemesis who lurks through four acts before he finally strikes.

Between the original first and second acts, Colum inserted a new act that accomplishes several things. It begins with the senile bantering of two elderly inmates who reflect on the change in masters and, in the process, reveal to the audience the old master's record of humane kindliness. Their reverential comments continue in choric counterpoint behind the main action, in which Muskerry is quietly shunted aside to make room for his successor. Like the early slights of Goneril and Regan in *King Lear*, the early shifts in the way his daughter and her in-laws treat the retired Muskerry provide the first glancing blows at his dignity and prefigure the larger insults that follow. Into the new second act Colum also introduced a traveling photographer whose uncertainty about whether Muskerry is still master of the workhouse helps to bring into focus the other characters' attitudes toward the protagonist.

The third act of the 1963 play is the original second act; in the revision, Colum polished and augmented the dialogue to improve characterization and made the act a third again as long by the introduction of another character, Peter Macnabo, who, like Muskerry, is a former workhouse master fallen into disgrace. The addition of Macnabo alone would have been enough to improve the overall quality of the play. His indomitability, industrious self-sufficiency, and rising fortunes as he begins a new life for himself provide a strong contrast to Muskerry's decline. The positioning of his visit between the petty quarrels of the Crilly family and examples of Tournour's growing arrogance gives the new version's third act a dramatic intensity almost equal to that of act 4, and the combination of naïveté and shrewdness that prompts Macnabo at the age of sixty to attempt a new career manufacturing traditional Irish clay pipes makes him one of the play's most finely drawn characters.

The fourth act differs little from the strong concluding act of the original. Colum's major change was to expand the part of Muskerry's young ward, Christy Clarke, so that in the closing scenes he functions as something of an adopted Cordelia in ironic contrast to the Goneril and Regan of Muskerry's daughter and the Crilly family. Colum's changes in the play involved more than simply improving its structure and adding new characterization and dialogue. While the 1910 version presented an array of broadly sketched characters, the revision contains a gallery of fully delineated personalities. Muskerry, already a powerfully conceived protagonist in the original, is a truly memorable one in the final version. The revised play also features three unusually strong supporting characters in Christy Clarke, Peter Macnabo, and Felix Tournour. The remaining characters in the revised version all have the fullness and clearly defined identities that they lacked in the original. The dialogue, moreover, shows the sure hand of an artist with more than fifty years of experience as both a poet and a playwright.

Despite the high quality of his art and the glowing predictions of fellow writers such as Yeats and Æ, Colum never became truly famous. His emigration to the United States probably had much to do with this. His best plays were the early Abbey Theatre works about rural Irish life; when he left Ireland, he lost the stimulus of a convenient stage and an appreciative audience. Though he had been famous as a poet and playwright in Dublin, he was virtually unknown in New York and had to begin again to make a name for himself while expending much of his creative energy on the children's books and literary journalism that provided his income. Perhaps he was partially a vic-

tim of his own personality and of his ability to do many things well. If he had been flamboyant, irascible, or conspicuously tormented, he might have become a literary personality, as have many writers of less talent. Instead, he was a quiet, good-natured, and apparently happy man. If anything, he was conspicuously unflappable. "Every serious Irish writer has a pain in his belly," Æ once chided Frank O'Connor, who was complaining of indigestion. "Yeats has a pain in his belly; Joyce has a terrible pain in his belly; now you have a pain in your belly. Padraic Colum is the only Irish writer who never had a pain at all."

OTHER MAJOR WORKS

LONG FICTION: *Castle Conquer*, 1923; *The Flying Swans*, 1957.

SHORT FICTION: *Selected Short Stories of Padraic Colum*, 1985 (Sanford Sternlicht, editor).

POETRY: *Wild Earth: A Book of Verse*, 1907; *Dramatic Legends, and Other Poems*, 1922; *Creatures*, 1927; *Way of the Cross*, 1927; *Old Pastures*, 1930; *Poems*, 1932; *Flower Pieces: New Poems*, 1938; *The Collected Poems of Padraic Colum*, 1953; *The Vegetable Kingdom*, 1954; *Ten Poems*, 1957; *Irish Elegies*, 1958; *The Poet's Circuits: Collected Poems of Ireland*, 1960; *Images of Departure*, 1969; *Selected Poems of Padraic Colum*, 1989 (Sanford Sternlicht, editor).

SCREENPLAY: *Hansel and Gretel*, 1954 (adaptation of Engelbert Humperdinck's opera).

NONFICTION: *My Irish Year*, 1912; *The Road Round Ireland*, 1926; *Cross Roads in Ireland*, 1930; *A Half-Day's Ride: Or, Estates in Corsica*, 1932; *Our Friend James Joyce*, 1958 (with Mary Colum); *Ourselves Alone: The Story of Arthur Griffith and the Origin of the Irish Free State*, 1959.

CHILDREN'S LITERATURE: *A Boy in Eirinn*, 1913; *The King of Ireland's Son*, 1916; *The Adventures of Odysseus*, 1918; *The Boy Who Knew What the Birds Said*, 1918; *The Girl Who Sat by the Ashes*, 1919; *The Boy Apprenticed to an Enchanter*, 1920; *The Children of Odin*, 1920; *The Golden Fleece and the Heroes Who Lived Before Achilles*, 1921; *The Children Who Followed the Piper*, 1922; *At the Gateways of the Day*, 1924; *The Island of the Mighty: Be-*

ing the Hero Stories of Celtic Britain Retold from the *Mabinogion*, 1924; *Six Who Were Left in a Shoe*, 1924; *The Bright Islands*, 1925; *The Forge in the Forest*, 1925; *The Voyagers: Being Legends and Romances of Atlantic Discovery*, 1925; *The Fountain of Youth: Stories to Be Told*, 1927; *Orpheus: Myths of the World*, 1930; *The Big Tree of Bunlahy: Stories of My Own Countryside*, 1933; *The White Sparrow*, 1933; *The Legend of Saint Columba*, 1935; *Legends of Hawaii*, 1937; *Where the Winds Never Blew and the Cocks Never Crew*, 1940; *The Frenzied Prince: Being Heroic Stories of Ancient Ireland*, 1943; *A Treasury of Irish Folklore*, 1954; *Story Telling, New and Old*, 1961; *The Stone of Victory, and Other Tales of Padraic Colum*, 1966.

BIBLIOGRAPHY

Bowen, Zack R. *Padraic Colum: A Biographical-Critical Introduction*. Carbondale: Southern Illinois University Press, 1970. A comprehensive critical review of Colum's prolific output in various genres. Beginning with a biographical introduction and a consideration of the historical context of Colum's work, the study goes on to deal in turn with Colum's poetry, drama, fictional and nonfictional prose, and children's literature. Extensive bibliography.

Journal of Irish Literature 2 (January, 1973). This special issue on Colum contains a miscellany of Colum material, including tributes from a number of Irish scholars, a substantial interview, and articles surveying Colum's achievements. Also included is a portfolio of work by Colum, including two plays, poems for children and other verse, and various prose pieces, one of which is a self-portrait.

Sternlicht, Sanford. *Padraic Colum*. Boston: Twayne, 1985. An introductory study of Colum's long life and various literary achievements. Much attention is given to Colum's poems. Also contains a detailed chapter on the prose and another on Colum's works of mythology, which are associated with his children's writing. Includes a chronology and a bibliography.

Gordon Henderson,
updated by George O'Brien

WILLIAM CONGREVE

Born: Bardsey, Yorkshire, England; January 24, 1670
Died: London, England; January 19, 1729

PRINCIPAL DRAMA

The Old Bachelor, pr., pb. 1693
The Double-Dealer, pr. 1693, pb. 1694
Love for Love, pr., pb. 1695
The Mourning Bride, pr., pb. 1697
The Way of the World, pr., pb. 1700
The Judgement of Paris, pr., pb. 1701 (masque)
Squire Trelooby, pr., pb. 1704 (with Sir John Vanbrugh and William Walsh; adaptation of Molière's *Monsieur de Pourceaugnac*)
Semele, pb. 1710 (libretto), pr. 1744 (modified version)
The Complete Plays of William Congreve, pb. 1967 (Herbert Davis, editor)

OTHER LITERARY FORMS

Although William Congreve is remembered today as a dramatist, his first publication was a novella, *Incognita: Or, Love and Duty Reconcil'd*, which appeared in 1692. He also published a translation of Juvenal's eleventh satire and commendatory verses "To Mr. Dryden on His Translation of Persius" in John Dryden's edition of *The Satires of Juvenal and Persius* (1693), as well as two songs and three odes in Charles Gildon's *Miscellany of Original Poems* (1692). Later, Congreve reprinted these odes, together with translations from Homer's *Iliad* (c. 800 B.C.E.; English translation, 1616), in *Examen Poeticum* (1693).

His other translations from the classics include Book III of Ovid's *Ars amatoria* (c. 2 B.C.E.; *Art of Love*, 1612) in 1709 and two stories from Ovid in the 1717 edition of *Ovid's Metamorphoses*. His original poetry was first collected with his other writings in *The Works of Mr. William Congreve* (1710) and frequently reprinted throughout the eighteenth century. After 1700, Congreve abandoned serious drama in favor of social and political interests, although he did write a masque and an opera after that date and collaborated with Sir John Vanbrugh and William Walsh on a farce. In response to Jeremy Collier's attacks on Restoration playwrights, Congreve wrote a short volume of dramatic criticism, *Amendments of Mr. Collier's False and Imperfect Citations* (1698). Congreve's letters have been edited by John C. Hodges and are available in *William Congreve: Letters and Documents* (1964).

ACHIEVEMENTS

William Congreve's first play, *The Old Bachelor*, was an instant success; its initial run of fourteen days made it the most popular play since Thomas Otway's *Venice Preserved* (pr., pb. 1682). *The Double-Dealer* was not as instantly successful, but *Love for Love* was so popular that Congreve was made a manager of the theater. *The Mourning Bride* was still more successful; in 1699, Gildon said of the work that "this play had the greatest Success, not only of all Mr. Congreve's, but indeed of all the Plays that ever I can remember on the English Stage." Congreve's last comedy, *The Way of the World*, though now universally regarded as his best and arguably the best Restoration comedy as well, met with little support at the time, and its cool reception drove Congreve from serious drama.

Throughout the eighteenth century, Congreve's reputation remained high, both for his poetry and his plays. Edward Howard, in his *Essay upon Pastoral* (1695), said that Congreve possessed the talent of ten Vergils. Dryden, who equated Congreve to Wil-

liam Shakespeare on the stage, declared that in his translations from the *Iliad*, Congreve surpassed Homer in pathos. Alexander Pope's translation of the *Iliad* (1715-1720) was dedicated to Congreve, as were Sir Richard Steele's *Poetical Miscellanies* (1714) and his 1722 edition of Joseph Addison's *The Drummer: Or, The Haunted House*. In the nineteenth century, Congreve's reputation declined, along with the public's regard for Restoration comedy in general, because of the sexual licentiousness depicted in the plays. With the twentieth century, however, came a reevaluation. When *The Way of the World* was revived at Cherry Lane Theatre in New York in 1924, it ran for 120 performances. That work and *Love for Love* remain among the most frequently acted of Restoration plays, and Congreve's other two comedies are also occasionally staged. Although Congreve's one trag-

William Congreve (Library of Congress)

edy has not worn as well, he may be today the most popular and most highly regarded English dramatist between William Shakespeare and George Bernard Shaw.

BIOGRAPHY

William Congreve was born on January 24, 1670, at Bardsey, Yorkshire, England. In 1674, his father, also named William, received a lieutenant's commission to serve in Ireland, and the family moved to the garrison of Youghal. In 1678, the elder William was transferred to Carrickfergus, another Irish port, and again, the family accompanied him. Congreve's knowledge of port life may have contributed to his depiction of the sailor, Ben, in *Love for Love*; Ben's use of nautical terms demonstrates the playwright's familiarity with this jargon. When the elder Congreve joined the regiment of the duke of Ormond at Kilkenny in 1681, his son was able to enroll in Kilkenny College, which was free to all families who served the duke. Here, Congreve received his first formal education and his first exposure to the high society that gathered around the wealthy duke of Ormond. After spending four and a half years at Kilkenny, Congreve entered Trinity College, Dublin (April 5, 1686), where he had the same tutor as Jonathan Swift, Saint George Ashe. The theater in Smock Alley, Dublin, was at this period being run by Joseph Ashbury, who, like Congreve's father, served under the duke of Ormond. Congreve may already have known Ashbury before coming to Trinity College, and Congreve's frequent absences from college on Saturday afternoons suggest that he was spending his time at the theater. Here, he would have seen a fine sampling of contemporary drama and could have begun to learn those dramatic conventions that he perfected in his own works.

In 1688, James II fled to Ireland. Perhaps fearing a massacre of Protestants in retaliation for their support of William of Orange against the Catholic Stuart king, the Congreves left Ireland for their family home in England. Congreve went first to Staffordshire to visit his grandfather at Stretton Manor; there, he wrote a draft of *The Old Bachelor* before coming to London to enroll in the Middle Temple to study law.

Congreve was not, however, an ideal law student. Like Steele's literary Templar in *The Spectator*, he frequented the Theatre Royal in nearby Drury Lane and Will's Coffee House rather than the Inns of Court.

At Will's, Dryden held literary court; by 1692, Congreve had become sufficiently friendly with the former laureate that he was asked to contribute a translation of Juvenal's eleventh satire to Dryden's forthcoming edition of the satires of Juvenal and Persius. Together with Arthur Manwayring and Thomas Southerne, Dryden was helpful to Congreve in revising *The Old Bachelor*. (In 1717, Congreve partially returned the favor, editing and writing an introduction to a posthumous edition of Dryden's *Dramatick Works*.) The play opened at the Theatre Royal in Drury Lane on March 9, 1693, with a brilliant cast, including Anne Bracegirdle as Araminta. Congreve was soon in love with Bracegirdle, who would play the heroine in each of his succeeding works and who may have been his mistress. In December, 1693, Congreve's second comedy, *The Double-Dealer*, was performed. Though Dryden praised it profusely, the play was not initially well received. After Queen Mary requested a special performance, however, its popularity increased.

Love for Love needed no royal sponsorship for its success. The first play to be performed in the restored Lincoln's Inn Fields Theatre (April 30, 1695), it ran for thirteen nights. Congreve was made one of the managers of the theater in return for a promise of a play a year, if his health permitted. Congreve needed two years to complete *The Mourning Bride*, which opened on February 27, 1697. The tragedy was worth the wait, for it was eminently successful. Three more years elapsed before Congreve's next play. Meanwhile, in 1698, Jeremy Collier attacked the Restoration stage in general, and Congreve in particular, for immorality. Congreve replied with his *Amendments of Mr. Collier's False and Imperfect Citations*. Between ill-health and the controversy with Collier, Congreve was unable to stage *The Way of the World* until March, 1700. Dryden recognized its genius, writing to Mrs. Steward on March 12, "Congreve's new play has had but moderate success, though it deserves much better." Coupled with Collier's attacks, the poor reception of *The Way of the World* convinced Congreve to abandon serious drama, but he continued to write and remain interested in the theater.

On March 21, 1701, *The Judgement of Paris*, an elaborate masque, opened at Dorset Garden with Bracegirdle as Venus. With Vanbrugh and Walsh, Congreve adapted Molière's *Monsieur de Pourceaugnac* as *Squire Trelooby*, which was performed in March, 1704. He also wrote the libretto to an opera, *Semele*, which was not performed in his lifetime. For a brief time, too, Congreve, Vanbrugh, and Walsh managed a theater in the Haymarket.

Although Congreve held a variety of government posts throughout his life—the type of minor posts with which men of letters were often rewarded in that era—he did not have a lucrative position until 1705, when he was made a commissioner of wines, with an annual salary of two hundred pounds. Congreve was an ardent Whig, but he had so agreeable a personality that when the Tories came to power, Jonathan Swift and Lord Halifax (to whom Congreve had dedicated *The Double-Dealer*) intervened to help him retain this income. Dryden was not merely flattering when he wrote, "So much the sweetness of your manners move,/ We cannot envy you, because we love." Not until almost a decade later, when the Hanoverians came to power, did Congreve enjoy a substantial income, receiving the post of secretary of the Island of Jamaica. He discharged his duties by a deputy, continuing to lead a placid, retired life in London during the winter and in various country houses during the summer. As he wrote to Joseph Keally, "Ease and quiet is what I hunt after. If I have not ambition, I have other passions more easily gratified."

One passion was for Henrietta, duchess of Marlborough, whom he met in 1703. In 1722, Congreve went to Bath for his health, and Henrietta accompanied him, even though she was married to the son of Lord Treasurer Godolphin. The following year, when she gave birth to her second daughter, Mary, it was assumed that Congreve was the child's father. Henrietta was by his side when he died on January 19, 1729, and when she died four years later, she was buried near him in Westminster Abbey.

ANALYSIS

William Congreve began writing some thirty years after the Restoration, yet his plays retain many of the concerns of those written in the 1660's and 1670's. Foremost among these concerns is what constitutes a gentleman; that is, how one should act in society. The seventeenth century, particularly after 1660, was very interested in this matter; some five hundred conduct books were published during the century, the majority of them after the Restoration.

The response that Congreve gives, which is identical to that of Sir George Etherege, William Wycherley, and other Restoration dramatists, may be summed up in a single word: wit. This wit encompasses far more than mere verbal facility. By the time Sir Richard Blackmore attacked wit as suitable "only to please with Jests at Dinner" ("A Satyr Against Wit," 1700), the term had lost much of its significance. For Congreve, Dryden's definition is more relevant than Blackmore's: "a propriety of thoughts and words"—and, he might have added, of conduct. As Rose Snider wrote in *Satire in the Comedies of Congreve, Sheridan, Wilde, and Coward* (1937), "Decorum (true wit) might be defined simply as a natural elegance of thought and conduct, based on respect for sound judgment, fidelity to nature, and a due regard for beauty."

What constitutes propriety and fidelity to nature is subject to varying interpretation. To the nineteenth century, Restoration comedy was at best "the Utopia of gallantry, where pleasure is duty, and the manners perfect freedom" (Charles Lamb, "On the Artificial Comedy of the Last Century"), at worst the height of immorality. Chastity was not a requirement for the late seventeenth century gentleman, though it was for the lady. Charles de Saint-Denis de Saint-Évremond expressed well the age's sexual ethics: "As for the Hatred of villainous Actions, it ought to continue so long as the World does, but give leave to Gentlemen of refin'd Palates to call that Pleasure, which gross and ill-bred People call Vice, and don't place your Virtue in old musty Notions which the primitive Mortals derived from their natural Savageness."

In keeping with this genial libertinism is a rejection of prudence, financial as well as sexual. Money is not to be saved but spent, and spent on pleasure.

Business is rejected as an improper pursuit. In the first scene of *The Old Bachelor*, Congreve presents in the dialogue between Bellmour and Vainlove a catalog of unworthy occupations for the genteel and indicates that the proper pursuits are witty conversation and love.

To a certain extent, this hedonism was a reaction to the restraints imposed by the Puritan Protectorate. After the Restoration, playwrights, who had lost their occupation under Cromwell, continued to portray the final victory of Cavalier over Roundhead. The Puritan cleric is a standard butt of Restoration satire. So, too, is the "cit," the merchant—not only because he was likely to be a Dissenter rather than an Anglican but also because mercantile London supported Cromwell while in general the country squires remained loyal to the Crown. Those who suffered the most under the Protectorate, the Court party, took their revenge in their plays when they returned to power.

Restoration comedy does not, however, restrict itself to negatives, nor to rejecting conventional morality and ridiculing its followers. The Truewit is indeed a libertine and often a spendthrift and free-thinker, but he espouses positive values that offset these signs of youthful exuberance. Bravery, for example, is highly prized. The wit will not tolerate an insult; a sign of wit is a willingness to defend one's honor. A character such as Captain Bluffe (in *The Old Bachelor*), who draws his sword only when all danger is past, or Fainall (in *The Way of the World*), who draws his sword on a woman, shows himself to be no true wit.

Urbanity is another attribute of the Truewit. He must be able to engage in brilliant repartee; his conversation must never be dull, vulgar, overly serious, or abstruse. A wit must never lose his temper, for reason should always control emotion. He must be aware of the latest fashions and observe them. Excesses in dress, manner, or speech are scorned, as are rusticity and bad taste. Because the wit must fit into polite society, the rustic is a butt of humor on the stage even though his political views probably harmonized with those of the playwrights who were mocking him.

Yet another virtue is intelligence, of which one outward sign is again brilliant conversation. A further indication is the ability to outsmart those who would thwart the wit's desires—generally comic villains who try to prevent his attaining a suitable wife and estate. Although these villains make a pretense of being clever and urbane, their speeches and action expose their flawed nature, which leads to their punishment at the end of the play.

Selflessness is also a Restoration ideal. Prodigality is not a vice but rather a manifestation of generosity. Fondlewife (*The Old Bachelor*) leaves his wife to secure five hundred pounds and is almost cuckolded during his absence. By contrast, Valentine (*Love for Love*) is willing to give money to a discarded mistress (though not to a creditor). When wits scheme, they are trying to secure what should rightfully be theirs; when fools and Witwouds plot, they are trying to secure what should belong to another. The latter are greedy and so are frustrated.

Restoration comedy is thus moral in its intent, punishing those who deviate from societal values and rewarding those who are faithful to those norms. These values are not Victorian, nor are they the values of religious fanatics, Puritans, or nonjurors such as Jeremy Collier—hence the repeated charges of immorality brought against Congreve and his contemporaries. In emphasizing intelligence, generosity, urbanity, and bravery, though, these dramatists were drawing on a tradition that went back to Aristotle's *Ethica Nicomachea* (335-323 B.C.E.; *Nicomachean Ethics*, 1797), and their view of comedy is Aristotle's as well. Defending himself against Collier, Congreve conceded that he portrayed vice on the stage, but he did so because comedy, according to Aristotle, depicts "the worst sort of people." It portrayed such people, Congreve continued, because "men are to be laugh'd out of their Vices in Comedy; the Business of Comedy is to delight, as well as to instruct: And as vicious People are made asham'd of their Follies or Faults, by seeing them expos'd in a ridiculous manner, so are good People at once both warn'd and diverted at their Expense." Collier and his successors did not find this response persuasive; they saw little to choose between Bellmour and Heartwell (*The Old Bachelor*) or between Mirabell and Fainall (*The Way of the World*). On the other hand, Congreve's appreciative audiences have always understood the important distinction.

At the same time that Congreve's plays are the artistic consummation of the traditions of Restoration comedy, they also reveal a breaking away from those traditions. Though these plays accept societal norms, and though the hero and heroine must be able to conform to societal expectations, they recognize the flaws of society also. Instead of trying simply to blend into society, the true wits seek to establish a private world beyond it. They recognize that beneath the glittering costumes and language lurk hypocrisy and brutality. Marriages are more often made in countinghouses than in heaven; a wedding is often the beginning of a domestic tragedy rather than the end of a social comedy. Life does not always proceed smoothly, and even when it does, it leads to a loss of youth, beauty, and attractiveness. Congreve reaffirms the *carpe diem* spirit—eat, drink, and be merry—but he does not blink from the rest of the refrain—for tomorrow we die.

The sadness beneath the surface of Congreve's plays also derives from his refusal to dehumanize the targets of ridicule. Restoration comedy is social rather than psychological, and Congreve's plays are primarily concerned with how one should act in society. For the first time in the period, though, those who do not conform are not simply dismissed as fools. In fact, Pope wondered whether Congreve actually portrayed any fools, and in his dedication of *The Way of the World*, Congreve noted that audiences had difficulty distinguishing "betwixt the character of a Witwoud and a Truewit" in that work. Congreve probes beneath action to motivation to reveal what Heartwell, Fondlewife, Lord Plyant, and Lady Wishfort are thinking. These characters recognize their weaknesses; they are not merely two-dimensional types but three-dimensional people capable of suffering. By granting humanity to would-be wits and fools, Congreve was unconsciously moving away from the purely satiric toward sentimental comedy.

His one tragedy, which is actually a tragicomedy, similarly uses many of the conventions of the period while showing significant variations. The diction is inflated, as is typical of heroic tragedy. The action is remote in time and place, the characters of noble birth and larger than life, the conflict Hobbesian as rivals ruthlessly contend. Unlike earlier heroic tragedy, however, the resolution to the conflict comes not through a Leviathan, not through some divinely ordained ruler, but rather through a Glorious Revolution that overthrows unjust, though otherwise legitimate, authority in favor of a benign, popularly proclaimed monarch as exponents of power yield to advocates of love. The influence of John Locke and the deposition of James II echo in the play, especially when contrasted with Dryden's tragedies, which espouse the divine right of kings.

THE OLD BACHELOR

Congreve may have begun *The Old Bachelor* as early as 1689, at the age of nineteen. Although Dryden proclaimed it the best first comedy he had ever seen, it shows in many ways evidence of being an apprentice piece. It is the only one of Congreve's comedies that lacks dramatic tension. There is no reason why Bellmour and Belinda could not marry in the first scene because there are no blocking characters to prevent the match. Another flaw is Congreve's ambiguous attitude toward Belinda. In the *dramatis personae*, he describes her as "an affected Lady," and in his *Amendments of Mr. Collier's False and Imperfect Citations*, he indicates that she is not intended to be admirable. Anne Bracegirdle, who always played the heroine in Congreve's works, took the role of Araminta; Belinda was played by Susanah Mountfort, who performed as the obviously foolish Lady Froth in *The Double-Dealer*. Because role and performer blended with each other in Restoration drama, audiences would expect that Belinda/Mountfort was intended as a butt of ridicule for her affectation and that Araminta would be the ideal to be admired. Yet at the end of the piece, Belinda is rewarded with marriage, while Araminta remains single.

The Old Bachelor also suggests its author's youth in its close adherence to the conventions of Restoration drama. It is, for example, the only one of Congreve's comedies that has for its hero a practicing, rather than a reformed, rake. It introduces, somewhat gratuitously, standard butts of Restoration satire: a rustic boor (Sir Joseph Wittol), a pretender to valor who is in fact a coward (Captain Bluffe), a Puritan merchant (Fondlewife), and an old man who, according to the *dramatis personae*, while "pretending to slight Women, [is] secretly in love."

Aside from the treatment of Belinda, the play does show a sure hand in exposing these various pretenders and in providing suitable punishment for them. Sir Joseph Wittol is tricked out of one hundred pounds and married to Vainlove's discarded mistress. Captain Bluffe is shown to be aptly named; he is valorous only in the absence of danger. He is beaten and kicked by Sharper and married off to Silvia's maid, Lucy, who had been Setter's mistress. Heartwell, who pretends to misogyny and candor, is punished by being made to believe that he has married Silvia and then being informed that she is not as chaste as he had assumed. Though he is again unmarried, he is tormented and mocked for his folly. Fondlewife has married a woman too young and sprightly for his years; additionally, he devotes himself to business, which Bellmour calls "the rub of life [that] perverts our aim, casts off the bias, and leaves us wide and short of the intended mark." Fondlewife narrowly escapes cuckolding, and one senses that the escape is only temporary. As Vainlove notes, "If the spirit of cuckoldom be once raised up in a woman, the devil can't lay it, 'till she has done 't."

Congreve shows great skill in handling the dialogue. Bellmour and Belinda exemplify the witty couple of Restoration comedy; as is typical of duels between the witty man and woman, Belinda has the better of their exchanges. Vainlove and Araminta, too, engage in witty debate, and again the woman proves the wittier; in one dialogue, Araminta reduces Vainlove to a defeated "O madam!," at which point she dismisses the conversation—and her suitor—with a call for music. The men and women also engage in repartee among themselves, deftly leaping from one topic to another, devising fresh and apt similes, coining paradoxes, brilliantly sketching a character in a line. The play abounds in the sheer joy of words, as when Barnaby tells Fondlewife, "Comfort will send Tribulation hither." Restoration audiences attended comedies less for their plots than for their wit, and

the success of *The Old Bachelor* shows that Congreve did not disappoint them in this regard.

While Congreve was offering largely conventional fare in his first comedy, even here one finds hints of sadness beneath the comic surface. John King McComb argues (in his essay "Congreve's *The Old Bachelor*: A Satiric Anatomy") that Bellmour, Vainlove, Heartwell, Fondlewife, and Spintext are stages in the rise and fall of the lover—from rake, to fop, to gull, and finally, to cuckold. The "cormorant in love," as Bellmour describes himself in the first scene, admits that "I must take up or I shall never hold out; flesh and blood cannot bear it always." Vainlove has been a cormorant in love, too, but now contents himself with arousing desire and leaving to others the task of satisfying it. Heartwell, too, was a rake in his youth, but his passion has ebbed; unlike Vainlove, he no longer can excite women at those rare instances when he wishes to and so must attempt to purchase love. At the last stage are Fondlewife and Spintext; the latter never appears in the play but is mentioned as being a cuckold, while the audience sees Fondlewife first almost suffering the same fate and then refusing to believe the ocular proof. Bellmour, too, will age, Congreve seems to suggest; he will lose his looks and gaiety and perhaps be reduced to the state of a Heartwell or Fondlewife. The last speech of the play, which Congreve gives to Heartwell, projects such a fate for the youth.

Restoration satire is also muted in the play through the humanization of Heartwell and Fondlewife, both of whom show more sense than the typical comic butt. Heartwell's pretended aversion to "the drudgery of loving" must be exposed, since love is the chief concern of the Truewit and thus not to be slighted. Neither can pretense go unpunished. Yet Heartwell himself understands his dilemma as he is caught between reason and desire. Standing before Silvia's house he declares, "I will recover my reason, and begone." He is, however, fixed to the spot; his feet will not move: "I'm caught! There stands my north, and thither my needle points.—Now could I curse myself, yet cannot repent." After Heartwell is caught and exposed, Congreve does not mask his real anguish. In a speech reminiscent of Shylock's "Hath not a Jew eyes," Heartwell turns on his mockers: "How have I deserved this of you? any of ye?" Vainlove urges Bellmour to stop ridiculing Heartwell—"You vex him too much; 'tis all serious to him"—and Belinda agrees: "I begin to pity him myself."

Similarly, Fondlewife, Puritan, banker, old man that he is—and any one of these characteristics would suffice in itself to render him ridiculous in a Restoration comedy—has moments of self-knowledge that grant him a touch of humanity. When he discovers Bellmour with his wife, he, too, speaks with dignity. Though Bellmour kisses Laetitia's hand at the very moment she is being reconciled to her husband, Fondlewife's tears and professions of kindness take some of the edge off the satire. If one must choose between the world of Bellmour and that of Fondlewife, one will certainly prefer the former; even so, Congreve understands that with all its admirable qualities, its wit, grace, youth, and intelligence, that world, too, is not devoid of faults.

THE DOUBLE-DEALER

Congreve's second play, *The Double-Dealer*, demonstrates much greater control over his material; it also contains a more fully developed negative portrayal of society. In *A Short View of the Profaneness and Immorality of the English Stage* (1698), Jeremy Collier noted, "There are but Four Ladys in this Play, and Three of the biggest of them are Whores. A Great Compliment to Quality to tell them there is not above a quarter of them Honest!" Despite Congreve's efforts to dismiss Collier's observation, Congreve does indeed indict the fashionable world, and his epigram from Horace—"Sometimes even comedy raises her voice"—suggests that he intended to go beyond the conventional butts of Restoration satire. Small wonder that fashionable society returned the favor with a cool reception of the piece.

Artistically, *The Double-Dealer* is much more coherent than *The Old Bachelor*. As Congreve wrote in the dedication, "I made the plot as strong as I could, because it was single; and I made it single, because I would avoid confusion." This single plot revolves around the love between Cynthia and Mellefont, who wish to marry, and the efforts of Maskwell and Lady Touchwood to prevent the match. The intrigues of these blocking figures, though conventional in comedies of the period, provide dramatic tension lacking in Congreve's earlier piece.

Congreve's handling of this central conflict, however, is less conventional. Typically, the Truewit defeats the Witwoud through his greater intelligence and so proves himself worthy of the witty heroine. When Mellefont proposes that he and Cynthia elope and thereby end the plotting and counterplotting, she rejects so simple a solution, demanding "a very evident demonstration of" her lover's wit. Until Maskwell overreaches and betrays himself, though, Mellefont is powerless to direct the action of the play; instead, he acts as Maskwell directs.

The conversation is not as sprightly as in Congreve's other plays or in Restoration comedy generally. Mellefont and Cynthia are too good-natured to take verbal advantage of the follies of those around them. While their benevolence makes them likable, it also tends to make them dull. They seem to anticipate the comedies of Steele rather than looking back to those of Etherege and Wycherley. Like Maskwell, the Witwouds are left to expose themselves: Lady Froth attempts a heroic poem on "Syllabub," for which Brisk provides inane commentary; Lord Froth claims that the height of wit is refraining from laughing at a joke, yet he laughs incessantly; Lady Plyant thinks herself a mistress of language but contrives such convoluted sentences that her lover, Careless, is driven to exclaim, "O Heavens, madam, you confound me!"

These Witwouds are as vain as they are foolish. In a telling piece of byplay, Lord Froth takes out a mirror to look at himself; Brisk takes it from him to admire himself. This sign of vanity is repeated when Lady Froth hands her husband a mirror, asking him to pretend it is her picture. Lord Froth becomes so enamored of the image he sees that his wife declares, "Nay, my lord, you shan't kiss it so much, I shall grow jealous, I vow now." Like false wit, vanity is left to mock itself.

Even sex, treated so cavalierly in other comedies of the period, is here largely a disruptive rather than a regenerative force. Each of the married women in the play is false to her husband. Lord Froth and Sir Paul Plyant are old and foolish and so "deserve" to be cuckolded, but the same cannot be said of Lord Touchwood. Lady Touchwood's passion for her nephew Mellefont threatens to upset Cynthia's marriage as well as her own and to subvert, through incest, proper familial relationships. Her passion for Maskwell, meanwhile, threatens to allow a member of the servant class to become a lord, as she contrives to have Maskwell supplant Mellefont as her husband's heir. The seriousness of this sexual promiscuity is manifest at the end of the play; Lady Touchwood is to be divorced and so lose her position in society.

Surrounded by vanity, infidelity, folly, and knavery, Cynthia has good reason to wonder whether she and Mellefont should continue to participate in the social charade. "'Tis an odd game we are going to play at; what think you of drawing stakes, and giving over in time?" she asks Mellefont. She understands that marriage is not a great improver: "I'm thinking, though marriage makes man and wife one flesh, it leaves them still two fools." The song that concludes this conversation with Mellefont warns of yet another threat: "Prithee, Cynthia, look behind you,/ Age and wrinkles will o'ertake you;/ Then, too late, desire will find you,/ When the power must forsake you." To become like her stepmother, Lady Plyant, or Mellefont's aunt, Lady Touchwood, may be the fate reserved for Cynthia. The melancholy implicit in *The Old Bachelor* here rises to the surface. Mellefont remains cheerful, but his optimism seems misplaced. He has grossly misjudged Maskwell; he may be misjudging all of reality. Though the true lovers marry, and though Maskwell and Lady Touchwood are banished at the end of the play, Congreve had not yet found, as he did in his last play, a way to reconcile the private world of virtue with the public world of folly, sham, and pretense. Cynthia and Mellefont remain apart from society; they do not control their actions, nor do they appear much in the play. The implication is that one can preserve one's innocence only by avoiding the fashionable world. The play thus foreshadows the gloom of the Tory satirists as well as the sentimental comedy of the next age.

LOVE FOR LOVE

Congreve was stung by the cool reception of his bitingly satiric *The Double-Dealer*. Although he believed that satire is the aim of comedy, in his next play, *Love for Love*, he disguised his attacks on fashionable society and offered a more traditional Restoration comedy. As he notes in the prologue: "We hope there's something that may please each taste." Much of the satire of *Love for Love* is confined to Valentine's mad scenes in the fourth act. By putting these comments into the mouth of a seeming madman, Congreve can be harsh without offending; it is as if he were stepping outside the world of the play to deliver these observations. Valentine in his madness is utterly Juvenalian, railing against all aspects of the fashionable world. There is more truth than wit in such observations as, "Dost thou know what will happen to-morrow?—answer me not—for I will tell thee. Tomorrow, knaves will thrive through craft, and fools through fortune, and honesty will go as it did, frostnipped in a summer suit." Scandal, Valentine's friend, is also harsh in his analysis of society: "I can shew you pride, folly, affection, wantonness, inconstancy, covetousness, dissimulation, malice, and ignorance, all in one piece. Then I can shew you lying, foppery, vanity, cowardice, bragging, lechery, impotence and ugliness in another piece; and yet one of these is a celebrated beauty, and t'other a professed beau." Beneath the surface, the way of the world is vicious and foul.

By the end of the play, though, Valentine abandons his feigned madness, and Scandal is willing to take a kinder view of the world than that expressed in the song: "He alone won't betray in whom none will confide;/ And the nymph may be chaste that has never been tried." Although society in *Love for Love* has its faults, these spring more from folly than from vice; the world here is closer to that of *The Old Bachelor* than to that of *The Double-Dealer*. There are no villains such as Maskwell or Lady Touchwood, no divorce, no banishment from society.

As in *The Old Bachelor*, there *is* considerable pretense that must be exposed and, to an extent, punished. Tattle pretends to be a great rake, a keeper of secrets, and a wit. Foresight pretends to be wise, to be able to foretell the future, and to be a suitable husband for a "young and sanguine" wife. Sir Sampson Legend pretends to be a good father and a fit husband for Angelica. Each of these pretenders is exposed and punished. Tattle is married off in secret to Mrs. Frail, a woman of the town. Fondlewife is cuckolded. Sir Sampson's plan to cheat his son of his inheritance and his fiancée is frustrated. These characters are Witwouds because they fail to adhere to the ideals of Restoration society. Sir Sampson is greedy; Foresight has failed to acquire wisdom with age; Tattle seeks a fortune rather than pleasure. They all want to be Truewits, but they are unable or unwilling to conform to the demands of wit.

Below them are Ben and Miss Prue, respectively a "sea-beast" and a "land monster." Neither has had the opportunity to learn good manners, Ben because he has spent his life at sea and Prue because she has been reared in the country rather than the town. They are no match for even the pretended wits. Tattle quickly seduces Prue; Mrs. Frail seduces Ben. Society has no place for these characters, who return to their element at the end of the play.

Above the fools and would-be wits are Valentine and Angelica. She is the typical Restoration witty lady, able to manipulate Foresight and Sir Sampson and control Valentine to attain her goal, which is a suitable marriage. Valentine has many of the characteristics of the wit—he is generous, he prefers pleasure to prudence, he is a clever conversationalist—but Angelica will not marry him until she is certain that he really is a proper husband.

At the beginning of the play, there is some question as to his suitability, not because he has been a rake, not because he has spent money recklessly—these are actually commendable activities—but because he has been trying to buy Angelica's love. Valentine's lavish entertaining has been to impress her; he seems to regard her as mercenary and must learn her true character. Having failed to purchase her with his wealth, Valentine next tries to shame her with his poverty; here, again, he fails. Then he tries to trick her into expressing her love by feigning to be mad. As a Truewit, Angelica is able to penetrate this disguise also. Only when Valentine abandons all of his tricks and agrees that Angelica should have free choice of a husband does she accept him. Marriage for her is a serious business; she must be certain she

is not submitting to tyranny or being pursued solely for her large fortune.

The blocking figure in *Love for Love* is, then, Valentine himself, and the plot of the play concerns his learning how to interact in society. Ben and Miss Prue do not learn how to do so, in part because of their previous experiences, in part because their teachers are would-be instead of true wits, in part because they lack intelligence and so are easily deceived. Foresight, Tattle, and Sir Sampson fail to learn because their characters are flawed. Foresight thinks he will learn from astrology, while Sir Sampson and Tattle think so highly of themselves that they are not even aware that they need to be taught anything.

Congreve indicates in *Love for Love* that one must live within a society that is less than perfect but that one can do so pleasantly enough if one adheres to the ideals of Restoration comedy. The despair in *The Double-Dealer* yields here to a happier vision. Valentine and Angelica, unlike Mellefont and Cynthia, understand their society and have shown their ability to survive in it.

Because Congreve recognizes the limitations of the fashionable world, he is sympathetic to characters who do not quite fit in. Ben is not simply a butt of ridicule because he is an outsider. Whereas Tattle is punished with Mrs. Frail, Ben escapes that fate. Because he does not share society's viewpoint, Ben is also able to make some telling comments. He speaks his mind, shuns pretense, is generous, and understands that he will be happier at sea than in London. Prue, too, is honest; though she is Tattle's willing pupil, she does escape marrying him. The innocent fools suffer less than do the Witwouds.

With *Love for Love*, Congreve has found his true voice—a combination of satire, compassion, and wit. His hero and heroine understand both the attractions and faults of society and therefore are able to skate deftly on the surface of their world without succumbing to its folly, as Bellmour and Belinda may, or being overwhelmed by its viciousness, as Mellefont and Cynthia may be. It is a shorter step from *Love for Love* to *The Way of the World* than from *The Old Bachelor* to this comedy.

THE MOURNING BRIDE

Before making that step, however, Congreve turned to tragedy, though *The Mourning Bride* resembles Congreve's other plays, for, like the comedies, it explores the questions of how the individual should act in society and what constitutes a proper marriage. On the one hand are Zara and Manuel, who rely on royal birth and power. They believe that power can command even love; Manuel wants to compel his daughter to marry Garcia, the son of the king's favorite, and Zara seeks to force Osmyn to marry her. Manuel is therefore another version of Sir Sampson Legend, who would have his child act as he himself wishes, regardless of the child's desires. Zara is a tragic rendition of Lady Touchwood, who would rather murder the man she loves than see a rival marry him. Significantly, Elizabeth Barry played both Lady Touchwood and Zara. Zara and Manuel serve as blocking figures, much like Maskwell and Lady Touchwood, but with more power to do evil.

Contrasted to these two are Osmyn and Almeria. They, too, are of royal birth, but instead of using power to create love, they use love to get power. They are generous, brave, intelligent, like their comic counterparts. Like them, too, they are young, confronting a harsh world controlled by their elders. As in the comedies, the values of the young triumph, but in the process the villains are not simply exposed but, as befits a tragedy, killed. The true lovers wed; Zara and Manuel also "marry"—at the end of the play, Zara drinks to her love from a poisoned bowl, embraces him, and dies by his side exclaiming, "This to our mutual bliss when joined above." Like Tattle and Mrs. Frail, the unworthy characters are joined. The analogy is strengthened by the masked wedding each undergoes. Just as Tattle and Mrs. Frail do not recognize their partners until it is too late, so Zara believes she is dying beside Osmyn rather than Manuel.

The deposition of the old by the young marks a triumph of love over power. It also addresses the question of what constitutes legitimate power. The older generation believes that birth and rank alone are sufficient; Manuel and Zara sense no obligation to anyone but themselves. Theirs is the belief in the divine right of kings to govern wrongly. Osmyn and Almeria have a different view. Though of royal birth, Osmyn is elevated to the throne by the people, who rebel against Manuel's tyranny. Congreve, staunch Whig, is portraying the Glorious Revolution, in which the hereditary monarch, because he has abused his power, loses his crown to a more worthy, because more benevolent, successor.

THE WAY OF THE WORLD

In the first scene of the fourth act of *The Way of the World*, Congreve directly addresses the issue of how two people can live harmoniously with each other while retaining personal autonomy and dignity on the one hand and remaining part of the social world on the other. This famous "Proviso" scene has a long theatrical history. A scene that first gained prominence in Honoré d'Urfé's *L'Astrée* (1607-1628, 1925; *Astrea*, 1657-1658), versions appear in four of Dryden's comedies—*The Wild Gallant* (pr. 1663), *Secret Love: Or, The Maiden Queen* (pr. 1667), *Marriage à la Mode* (pr. 1672, pb. 1673) and *Amphitryon: Or, The Two Socia's* (pr., pb. 1690)—in James Howard's *All Mistaken: Or, The Mad Couple* (pr. 1667), and Edward Ravenscroft's *The Careless Lovers* (pr. 1673) and *The Canterbury Guests* (pr. 1694). As he did so often, Congreve used a well-established convention but invested it with new significance and luster. The proviso in *The Way of the World* is not only the wittiest of such scenes but also the most brilliantly integrated into the theme of the play. Indeed, the scene illuminates the plight of every witty heroine who had appeared on the Restoration stage and summarized the hopes and fears of all fashionable couples to that time.

Millamant does not want to "dwindle into a wife"; Mirabell does not want to "be beyond measure enlarged into a husband." She wishes to be "made sure of my will and pleasure"; he wants to be certain that his wife's liberty will not degenerate into license. In the Hobbesian world of self-love, rivalry, and conflicting passions, these two therefore devise a Lockean compact, creating a peaceful and reasonable accommodation between their individual and mutual needs. They will not act like other fashionable couples, "proud of one another the first week, and ashamed of one another ever after." They will act more like strangers in public, that they may act more like lovers in private. Millamant will remain autonomous in her sphere of the tea table, but she will not "encroach upon the men's prerogative." She will not sacrifice her health or natural beauty to fashion or whim; otherwise, she may dress as she likes. Together the lovers create a private world divorced from the follies and vices of the society around them while retaining the freedom to interact with that society when they must.

In contrast to this witty couple are Fainall and Marwood. As the names suggest, Fainall is a pretender to wit, and his consort, Marwood, seeks to mar the match between Mirabell and Millamant because of her love—and then hate—for Mirabell. She, too, is a pretender, a seeming prude who in fact is having an affair with Fainall. Whereas the witty couple seek to preserve their private world inviolate, Fainall and Marwood attempt to exploit private relationships. Fainall has married for money, not love, and once he has secured his wife's fortune, he intends to divorce her, marry Marwood, and flee society. Later, he and Marwood conspire to secure half of Millamant's and all of Lady Wishfort's estate by threatening to expose Mrs. Fainall's earlier affair with Mirabell, hoping that Lady Wishfort will pay to keep secret her daughter's indiscretion and prevent a public divorce.

On yet another level are Lady Wishfort, Petulant, and Witwoud, who have no private life at all. Lady Wishfort cannot smile because she will ruin her carefully applied makeup; the face she presents to society must not be disturbed by any unexpected emotion. All of her efforts are directed to appearing fashionable—hence her fear of Mrs. Fainall's exposure. Hence, too, her inflated rhetoric when she tries to impress the supposed Sir Rowland. Petulant wishes to appear the true Restoration wit and so hires women to ask for him at public places. He will even disguise himself and then "call for himself, wait for himself; nay, and what's more, not finding himself, sometimes [leave] a letter for himself." Witwoud, as his name indicates, seeks to pass himself off as a wit but must rely on his memory rather than his invention to maintain a conversation. His cowardice or stupidity prevents his understanding an insult, and he mistakes

"impudence and malice" for wit. He will not acknowledge his own brother because he believes it unfashionable to know one's own relations, thus surrendering private ties to public show. Sir Willful, Witwoud's half brother, is the typical rustic. Like Ben and Prue in *Love for Love*, he has no place in society. He withdraws from social interaction first by getting drunk and then by returning to his element, leaving the urban world entirely.

Congreve thus offers four ways of coping with the demands of society. One may flee completely, as Sir Willful does and as Marwood, Fainall, and Lady Wishfort talk of doing. Mirabell and Millamant could adopt this solution, too. If they elope, Millamant will retain half of her fortune, enough to allow the couple a comfortable life together, but they would lose the pleasures of the tea table, of the theater, of social intercourse—of all the benefits, in short, that society can offer. One can also submit one's personality completely to society and abandon any privacy (Petulant and Witwoud). One can use private life only to serve one's social ends (Fainall and Marwood), or one can find a suitable balance between them. Presented with these choices, Mirabell and Millamant wisely choose the last.

The question posed here is not only one of surfaces, of how best to enjoy life, although that element is important. Additionally, Congreve here explores differing ethical stances. The opening conversation between Mirabell and Fainall establishes the moral distinction between them. Fainall states, "I'd no more play with a man that slighted his ill fortune than I'd make love to a woman who undervalued the loss of her reputation." Mirabell replies, "You have a taste extremely delicate, and are for refining on your pleasures." Fainall's may be the wittier comment, but it is also the more malicious. True wit in *The Way of the World* embraces morality as well as intelligence. Mirabell does prove more intelligent than Fainall, outwitting him "by anticipation" just as he has cuckolded Fainall by anticipation. Even so, in their conversations the difference in cleverness is not as apparent as it is between Witwoud or Mirabell or Lady Wishfort and Millamant. Congreve once more is moving toward sentimental comedy by creating an intelligent hero who is also sententious. He is fore-shadowing Addison's attempt in the *Spectator* "to enliven Morality with Wit, and to temper Wit with Morality."

The tone is bittersweet—another anticipation of the next age. Like Belinda in Pope's *The Rape of the Lock* (1712, 1714), Millamant must grow up. Just as she cannot be a coquette forever, so Mirabell must put aside his rakish past. One has a sense of time's passing. Even amid the witty repartee of the proviso scene, Mirabell looks ahead to Millamant's pregnancy, and to the time beyond that when she will be tempted, as Lady Wishfort is now, to hide her wrinkles. Her maid will one day say to her what Foible tells her lady: "I warrant you, madam, a little art once made your picture like you; and now a little of the same art must make you like your picture."

With this new sense of the future coexists a new sense of the past, a sense that one's earlier actions have consequences. Valentine is able to dismiss a former mistress with a gift of money and to redeem his earlier extravagances through an inheritance and a good marriage. Mirabell is not so fortunate. His previous affair with Mrs. Fainall is not immoral—no one condemns Mirabell for it—but neither is it a trifle to be quickly forgotten. Because of that affair, Mrs. Fainall has had to marry a man she dislikes and who hates her; she is not merely asking for information when she inquires of Mirabell, "Why did you make me marry this man?" Nor has Mirabell escaped all consequences, for this affair gives Fainall the opportunity to seize half of Millamant's—and thus half of Mirabell's—estate.

The artificial world and golden dreams of *The Old Bachelor* have essentially vanished in *The Way of the World*. The form remains—the witty couple contending successfully against the Witwouds and the fools; the young struggling against the old; the flawed but brilliant urbane society opposing vulgarity and rusticity. Congreve has elevated this form to its highest point; there is no more lovable coquette than Millamant, no Restoration wit more in control of his milieu than Mirabell. Yet the substance, the sense of passing time, of the sadness of real life, is undermining the comedy of wit. Alexander Pope called

Congreve *ultimus Romanorum* (the ultimate Roman). He is truly the greatest of the Restoration dramatists, but he is *ultimus* in its other sense as well—the last.

OTHER MAJOR WORKS

LONG FICTION: *Incognita: Or, Love and Duty Reconcil'd*, 1692 (novella).

POETRY: "To Mr. Dryden on His Translation of Persius," 1693; *Poems upon Several Occasions*, 1710.

NONFICTION: *Amendments of Mr. Collier's False and Imperfect Citations*, 1698; *William Congreve: Letters and Documents*, 1964 (John C. Hodges, editor).

TRANSLATIONS: *Ovid's Art of Love, Book III*, 1709; *Ovid's Metamorphoses*, 1717 (with John Dryden and Joseph Addison).

MISCELLANEOUS: *Examen Poeticum*, 1693; *The Works of Mr. William Congreve*, 1710; *The Complete Works of William Congreve*, 1923, reprint 1964 (Montague Summers, editor; 4 volumes).

BIBLIOGRAPHY

Bartlett, Laurence. *William Congreve: An Annotated Bibliography, 1978-1994*. Lanham, Md.: Scarecrow Press, 1996. A bibliography of works concerning Congreve. Index.

Hoffman, Arthur W. *Congreve's Comedies*. Victoria, B.C.: University of Victoria, 1993. A critical study of Congreve's comedic dramas. Bibliography.

Lindsay, Alexander, and Howard Erskine-Hill, eds. *William Congreve: The Critical Heritage*. New York: Routledge, 1989. These essays trace Congreve's critical reception from the immediate acclaim that greeted his first comedy to the emergence of modern academic criticism in the twentieth century. The editors include a generous selection of dramatic reviews, particularly from the eighteenth century, when all five of his plays were a standard part of the repertory. Bibliography.

Sieber, Anita. *Character Portrayal in Congreve's Comedies: "The Old Batchelor," "Love for Love," and "The Way of the World."* Lewiston, N.Y.: Edwin Mellen Press, 1996. An examination of the characters in three of Congreve's best-known comedies. Bibliography.

Thomas, David. *William Congreve*. New York: St. Martin's Press, 1992. A critical analysis of the works of Congreve, along with details of his life. Bibliography and index.

Young, Douglas M. *The Feminist Voices in Restoration Comedy: The Virtuous Women in the Play-worlds of Etherege, Wycherley, and Congreve*. Lanham, Md.: University Press of America, 1997. A look at female characters in the Restoration comedies of Congreve, George Etherege, and William Wycherley. Bibliography and index.

Joseph Rosenblum,
updated by Genevieve Slomski

MARC CONNELLY

Born: McKeesport, Pennsylvania; December 13, 1890

Died: New York, New York; December 21, 1980

PRINCIPAL DRAMA

Dulcy, pr., pb. 1921 (with George S. Kaufman)

To the Ladies, pr. 1922, pb. 1923 (with Kaufman)

Merton of the Movies, pr. 1922, pb. 1925 (with Kaufman; adaptation of Harry Leon Wilson's story)

The Deep Tangled Wildwood, pr. 1923 (with Kaufman; originally as *West of Pittsburgh*, pr. 1922)

Helen of Troy, N.Y., pr. 1923 (with Kaufman; music and lyrics by Bert Kalmer and Harry Ruby)

Beggar on Horseback, pr. 1924, pb. 1925 (with Kaufman; based on Paul Apel's play *Hans Sonnenstössers Höllenfahrt*)

Be Yourself, pr. 1924 (with Kaufman; music by Kalmer, lyrics by Ruby)

The Wisdom Tooth, pr., pb. 1926

The Wild Man of Borneo, pr. 1927 (with Herman J. Mankiewicz)

The Green Pastures: A Fable, pb. 1929, pr. 1930 (adaptation of Roark Bradford's sketches in *Ol' Man Adam an' His Chillun*)

The Farmer Takes a Wife, pr., pb. 1934 (with Frank B. Elser; adaptation of Walter D. Edmond's novel *Rome Haul*)

Everywhere I Roam, pr. 1938 (with Arnold Sundgaard)

The Flowers of Virtue, pr. 1942

A Story for Strangers, pr. 1948

Hunter's Moon, pr. 1958

The Portable Yenberry, pr. 1962

OTHER LITERARY FORMS

Marc Connelly is known primarily for his plays, but he also wrote many short humorous stories for *The New Yorker* and other magazines, a number of essays, a novel (*A Souvenir from Qam*, 1965), and an autobiography (*Voices Offstage*, 1968).

ACHIEVEMENTS

Marc Connelly is known mainly as a writer of polite farce of a conventional stamp. He enjoyed the partnership of a first-rate collaborator (George S. Kaufman) in his early years, the services of the stars of Broadway to speak his words, and one enduring artistic and commercial success, *The Green Pastures*, which won the 1930 Pulitzer Prize in Drama and made him a millionaire. He broke new ground in wedding his romantic views to expressionistic techniques in a way that was suitable for the popular audience of the day. Although his early successes were generally predictable comedies of manners, he was never content to restrict his plays to a single type, freely using features of the progressive theater of the time. His greatest work, *The Green Pastures*, which may seem condescending and simplistic to present-day readers, represented a breakthrough for the theater of 1930: an all-black cast in a recasting of the Bible, set in the rural South. Connelly's dreams of an earthly paradise in which the common person can find fulfillment despite self-doubts and the burden of anxiety about the world are realized most completely in this play, set far from New York with characters different from the often fatuous urban types he had drawn so successfully. When audiences of the mid-1920's wanted someone to celebrate their heady exuberance and make them laugh, Connelly provided the gags and the situations to which they could respond; when the audiences of the Depression era wanted to find some hope in the future, Connelly responded again with a worldview pure in its simplicity, self-assured in its happy resolutions of misfortune, and delightful in its crackling wit.

Four of Connelly's collaborations with Kaufman in the years before *The Green Pastures* were successful: *Dulcy* and *To the Ladies* arose from a character already popular in a New York newspaper column; *Merton of the Movies*, one of the earliest satires on Hollywood, adapted cinematic techniques to the stage; and *Beggar on Horseback* introduced expressionism to Broadway. Later, *The Wisdom Tooth*, written by Connelly alone and chosen by Burns Mantle for *Best Plays of 1925-1926*, once more employed two realistic scenes flanking a fantasy.

Connelly's good taste, solidly American values, and ready wit made him a successful writer in other areas as well, from his radio play, *The Mole on Lincoln's Cheek* (1941), to his fiction, both long and short. In the same year that *The Green Pastures* won the Pulitzer Prize, Connelly also won the O. Henry Award for the 1930 short story "Coroner's Inquest." He was given honorary degrees by Bowdoin College (1952) and Baldwin-Wallace College (1962).

Connelly's plays have rarely been revived in recent years, and except for *The Green Pastures*, his works are read only by historians of the stage. Nevertheless, his lasting achievement, *The Green Pastures*, is a monument of the American theater, distinguished by the purity of its sentiment, the richness of its language, and the charm of its imagination and humor.

Marc Connelly in 1937. (Library of Congress)

BIOGRAPHY

Marcus Cook Connelly was born December 13, 1890. The year before, his parents, Patrick Joseph and Mabel Louise Fowler (Cook) Connelly, two touring actors, had settled in McKeesport, Pennsylvania, blaming the death of their first child on the hardships of the touring life. His father managed the White Hotel, a favorite stop for traveling circus troupes and theatrical companies, who imbued young Marc with what he later described as "the early feeling that going to the theatre is like going to an unusual church, where the spirit is nourished in mysterious ways, and pure magic may occur at any moment."

Connelly's father died of pneumonia when his son was twelve, and following the failure of the White Hotel in 1908, Connelly's hopes for college were dashed. When he and his mother moved to Pittsburgh, Connelly began a career with local newspapers, finally becoming second-string drama critic and author of a humorous weekly column, "Jots and Tittles," for the Pittsburgh *Gazette Times*. He also spent his evenings writing, directing, and stage-managing skits for the Pittsburgh Athletic Association. In 1913, Connelly wrote the lyrics for Alfred Ward Birdsall's

The Lady of Luzon, which so impressed local steel magnate Joseph Riter that Connelly was commissioned to write the lyrics and libretto for a play that Riter was producing on Broadway, *The Amber Princess*. The play, which after two years of rewriting finally contained only Connelly's title and the lyrics to one song, failed, and the hopeful young playwright was forced to return to newspaper work, this time far from home.

While covering the theater district for the New York *Morning Telegraph* in 1917, Connelly met George S. Kaufman, who was then second-string drama critic for *The New York Times*. At the suggestion of the producer George C. Tyler, Connelly and Kaufman collaborated on a vehicle for Lynn Fontanne entitled *Dulcy*, which opened August 13, 1921, and was so popular (running for 246 performances) that they immediately created a sequel as a vehicle for another young star, Helen Hayes, entitled *To the Ladies* (which ran for 128 performances). The team again collaborated on a misguided effort, *The Deep Tangled Wildwood*, which was shelved following a disastrous out-of-town tryout in May, 1922, and later reworked and produced on Broadway on November 5, 1923, running for only sixteen performances. Their greatest success as a team came with *Merton of the Movies*, the story of an innocent shop clerk who seeks stardom in Hollywood. It opened in November 13, 1922, and played for 398 performances.

At this same time, Connelly was firmly entrenched as a member of that group of literary and theatrical wits who lunched together at the Algonquin Hotel. In addition to the charter members, Franklin P. Adams, Jane Grant, Harold Ross, and Alexander Woolcott, the group included Robert Benchley, Dorothy Parker, Ring Lardner, Heywood Broun, Robert E. Sherwood, and others. In 1925, Grant, Ross, Woollcott, Kaufman, Connelly, and others founded *The New Yorker*, to which Connelly contributed numerous essays and pieces of short fiction between 1927 and 1930.

Kaufman and Connelly collaborated on three more plays, two of them musicals: *Helen of Troy, N.Y.*, with songs by Bert Kalmer and Harry Ruby, and *Be Yourself*, which starred Queenie Smith; the third was the fantasy *Beggar on Horseback*. When *Be Yourself* closed, the partnership was effectively over, although the two remained friends and were said to have been working on a musical about a union boss at the time of Kaufman's death.

Connelly went to Hollywood in 1925 to write the screenplay of a Beatrice Lillie vehicle, *Exit Smiling* (1926), returning to Broadway for his directorial debut in his play *The Wisdom Tooth*, a showcase for the actor Thomas Mitchell, which ran for 160 performances. Connelly next collaborated with Herman J. Mankiewicz on a failed production, *The Wild Man of Borneo*, which closed after fifteen nights. For the next two years, Connelly avoided the theater and concentrated his efforts on *The New Yorker*.

In the fall of 1928, Connelly's cartoonist friend Rollin Kirby recommended that he read a book by a New Orleans newspaperman, Roark Bradford, entitled *Ol' Man Adam an' His Chillun*, a series of stories from the Old Testament told in the language of a black Southern preacher. Connelly immediately took to the book and visited Bradford in Louisiana, where he refined his knowledge of the dialect and found the spirituals a chorus would sing between the scenes. Once the play was written, Connelly spent the better part of a year seeking financial backing, as most producers feared offending both blacks and whites, the religious and the nonreligious. Finally, a broker, Rowland Stebbins, put up the necessary money, and on February 26, 1930, *The Green Pastures* had the first of its more than sixteen hundred performances. This play, for which he derived not only great financial rewards but also the deepest sense of fulfillment, formed the summary moment of his long career in the theater, a moment he never approached later in his life.

In 1930, Connelly married the actress Madeline Hurlock; they were divorced in 1935. It was during this period that Connelly wrote his last hit, *The Farmer Takes a Wife*, written with Frank B. Elser from his play *Rome Haul* (based on Walter D. Edmond's novel) and starring Henry Fonda. None of Connelly's remaining plays—*Everywhere I Roam* (written with Arnold Sundgaard), *The Flowers of Virtue*, *A Story for Strangers*, *Hunter's Moon*, and *The Portable Yenberry*—played more than fifteen performances. During this time, Connelly became involved in projects outside the theater. He directed his own adaptation of *The Green Pastures* for film (1936) and wrote several other screenplays as well, including *Captains Courageous* (1937). He also wrote a successful radio play, *The Mole on Lincoln's Cheek*, and, much later, a humorous novel, *A Souvenir from Qam*, as well as his autobiography, *Voices Offstage*, all the while contributing numerous pieces, mostly on his travels, to popular magazines. He occasionally acted, playing the Stage Manager in a 1944 production of Thornton Wilder's *Our Town*, and Professor Charles Osnan in Russel Crouse and Howard Lindsay's *The Tall Story*, both on Broadway (1959) and in the film (1960). He also served as the Narrator for the Off-Broadway revue *The Beast in Me* (1963), drawn from the writings of James Thurber. A founder of the Dramatists Guild, past president of the Authors' League of America, he was president of the National Institute of Arts and Letters from 1953 to 1956. From 1946 to 1950, he taught playwriting at Yale and frequently conducted seminars in the years following. Connelly's quiet humor remained keen to the end. On his ninetieth birthday, after receiving a certificate of appreciation from Mayor Ed Koch of New York, he said, "Some days I feel like an old man of 137, and other days like a mere boy of 136."

ANALYSIS

Marc Connelly's early plays were highly successful largely because they adequately fulfilled audience expectations. He chose his collaborators well, as he did the books and plays that he adapted. Although not a man of surpassing originality, he nevertheless brought a distinctive tone of gentility and sweet romanticism to his humor, tempering the brusque manner of Kaufman or the cynicism of Paul Apel. Throughout his work runs an implicit faith in people's ability to act for the good of themselves and of humankind. For Connelly, humor brings forth all the elements of an earthly paradise: happiness, laughter, freedom from care, and harmony with others.

DULCY

After a brief friendship, Connelly and Kaufman began their collaboration with *Dulcy*. A popular char-

acter in Franklin P. Adams's New York *World* column "The Conning Tower," Dulcinea was a chic suburban wife given to wearing fashionable clothes and uttering fashionable platitudes. A kind of satiric weather vane of the rising New York social set, she was ripe for appropriation for the stage, and she was taken by Connelly and Kaufman with Adams's full support. Characteristically, they did not make her an object of satiric attack; rather, they made her language and that of her friends a vehicle for laughter. The play centers on Dulcy Smith, who in her Westchester home hosts a weekend party for her husband Gordon's new business partner, C. Roger Forbes. Forbes wants to acquire Gordon's jewelry business for only a fraction of its real value. Dulcy sets out to get more money from Forbes, a fairer price, and the action of the play turns on her efforts.

The other houseguests provide the heroine with a sufficient variety of difficulties to resolve before the final curtain. Dulcy's brother, William Parker, falls in love with Forbes's daughter Angela, who is already loved by another guest, screenwriter Vincent Leach. Schuyler Van Dyck is an otherwise attractive man who continually talks about the fortune he does not have, while Henry is a reformed forger whom Dulcy has converted into a butler.

Leach is supposed to encourage Mrs. Forbes's desire to write for the movies, but Forbes is antagonized by Dulcy's ploy, for he does not want his wife to become involved in the movie business. Dulcy further angers Forbes by helping his daughter Angela, who plans to elope with Leach. Indeed, Forbes becomes so angry that he threatens to leave at once, canceling his offer to buy Gordon's business.

Dulcy is "a clever woman," however, and in the third act, all the complications are resolved. Forbes agrees to pay 25 percent for Gordon's business, rather than the 16 2/3 percent initially offered. Instead of eloping with Leach, Angela is married off to Dulcy's stockbroker brother, William, pleasing her father no end. Schuyler Van Dyck is taken by Forbes for what he pretends to be, and Henry is exonerated of the charge of having stolen a pearl necklace.

If the action is uninspired, the *au courant* dialogue charmed contemporary audiences. Dulcy's trite expressions are played off against those of the clever characters, the most clever of whom is her brother, who is rewarded with the girl of his dreams. The jargon of various professions is exquisitely mocked: Leach speaks the language of Hollywood (particularly in his account of his movie *Sin*, the play's finest satiric set piece); Forbes speaks the language of Wall Street; and an incidental character, Tom Sterrett, an "advertising engineer," speaks the lingo of Madison Avenue. Broadway found itself laughing at this congenial burlesque of jargon, for the authors never make their satire sting but rather invite one to pardon these amiably foolish types.

MERTON OF THE MOVIES

Franklin Adams provided the impetus for another Connelly-Kaufman collaboration when he recommended in his column of February 3, 1922, *Merton of the Movies*, a novel by Harry Leon Wilson. The producer George C. Tyler then suggested it to the team, and the play opened November 13, 1922. Wilson's novel is a biting attack on the hypocrisy and meretriciousness of Hollywood and its reflection of the pervasive lack of culture in the United States; Connelly and Kaufman viewed Hollywood with an air of such superior amusement that they could not feel themselves threatened enough to knot the lash of their satire any more than they had with *Dulcy*. Instead, they made the play a story of one man realizing his dream to be a Hollywood star, ultimately becoming as vapid and cynical as those he had so long worshiped on the screen. The play was a critical and popular success, running for 398 performances.

Merton Gill is a clerk in a general store in Simsbury, Illinois, who gains stardom in Hollywood. His knowledge and interest in the "art" of the movies is limited to the fan magazines and public relations interviews he devours, and so at the beginning of the play he is as easy a butt for jokes as is the movie industry itself. The summation of all his dreams is Beulah Baxter, the lead in the popular *Hazards of Hortense* serials to which Merton became addicted back in Simsbury. When he finally meets her, he finds not the sweet and simple ingenue she portrays but an oft-married, selfish starlet whose concerns about her art are as limited as her vocabulary. Tricked into

appearing in a parody of his cinematic idol, Harold Parmalee, Merton becomes an overnight star. His gimmick is playing amusing roles seriously, which leads everyone (including the audience) to imagine that poor Merton is being used. In his final speech, however, which endeared him (and the play) to the Broadway audiences, Morton claims that he was not unwittingly used but that he had known what he was doing all along: He was creating satire so clever that most of his fans did not understand it.

Merton of the Movies was not the first parody of Hollywood, but it was one of the first stage productions to attempt the rapid scene shifts common to the medium it was satirizing. There are four acts and six scenes in this play, where *Dulcy* had three acts and one set only. Moreover, the action of the play unfolds before the audience as if they were watching a film in the process of being shot.

This play also presents the typical Connelly-Kaufman character: the innocent but honest man whose dreams are often compromised or negated by his own unwillingness or inability to act properly. Despite Connelly's dreamily romantic views of life, his leads tend to gain only ironic successes, as here, when Merton's very lack of talent makes him a star; the meaning of what he has learned about Hollywood (that is, that lack of talent does not make bad entertainment in the eyes of the moguls, but is perceived as "satire") is lost on him. Still, Connelly and Kaufman could not be accused of writing satire in *Merton of the Movies*, for the message of the play is too light and the attacks too gentle.

BEGGAR ON HORSEBACK

Beggar on Horseback declared itself more forcefully on the subject of the worthwhile in art and also represented a further advance in the team's stagecraft. Suggested by the German expressionist Paul Apel's play *Hans Sonnenstössers Höllenfahrt* (pr. 1911), the play nevertheless is essentially Connelly and Kaufman's own, as Alexander Woollcott pointed out in his introduction to the printed version.

Beggar on Horseback develops the old chestnut, "Put a beggar on horseback and he'll outride the devil," by depicting, in Connelly's words, "a fantasy in which a young musician would go through a maze of kaleidoscopic experiences, the basic theme of which would be the ancient conflict of art and materialism." Neil McRae is a good composer but an improvident man who compromises his talent by writing cheap orchestrations of the sort that periodically drift in his window from the street. His wealthy neighbors are the Cady family: Mr. Cady is a businessman from Neil's hometown. Mrs. Cady is a society volunteer for worthy causes. Their daughter, Gladys, is a ray of sunshine who brings Neil candy for his tea, and Homer, the son, is perpetually morose. Neil's friend, Dr. Albert Rice, suggests to Gladys that she marry Neil to give him the emotional and financial support he needs to get on with his writing. To calm his nerves, Neil takes a sleeping pill, and as he drifts off to sleep, Cynthia, to whom Neil has proposed, turns him down because she cannot support him as well as Gladys can.

The dream sequence that follows was remarkable for the Broadway stage of 1924: As Neil's future life is played out, he watches himself marry Gladys, whose bouquet is made of dollar bills, in a ceremony accompanied by the kind of sporty music he had heard in his apartment. The hectic pace of their social life prevents Neil from composing, and when he takes a job in Cady's widget business he begins to amass a fortune by day, which he and Gladys will spend at jazz clubs by night. He finally sells his symphony, but Gladys destroys the manuscript, and Neil in a rage kills all four Cadys.

Neil comes to trial with Mr. Cady as the judge; the chief witness is Mrs. Cady, the prosecutor is Homer, and the members of the jury are all dance instructors. Neil loses his case after presenting as evidence on his behalf a ballet composed by himself and Cynthia, and he is sentenced by the jury to write popular songs for the rest of his life. Bent on suicide, he takes another pill, and Cynthia promises to stand by him forever.

The dream sequence ends with Cynthia knocking on the real door of Neil's apartment. Gladys breaks the engagement when she realizes that Neil's true love is Cynthia, and the lovers remain together.

Here, for the first time, Connelly and Kaufman do more than merely ridicule: They state clearly what is valuable for the artist both objectively (in the realistic sequences) and subjectively (in the dream sequence). The realistic sections are portrayals (in the manner of *Dulcy* and *Merton of the Movies*) of the lovable innocents and the mendicant fools of 1920's society. When in the dream one butler becomes two and those two become four, and so on, until the stage is literally filled with hustling butlers, the audience sees a dramatic representation of wealth overrunning the individual who possesses it. The play is also remarkable for the integral role that music plays in it. The authors were not afraid to follow their own artistic prescriptions, involving the music of Connelly's friend (and for a time, roommate), the composer and critic Deems Taylor, as an essential part of rather than accompaniment to the dramatic movement of the play, both in the realistic and in the dream sequences. While many more revolutionary developments were taking place in the 1920's in American experimental theaters—as well as in Europe—*Beggar on Horseback* introduced expressionism to Broadway, and for this alone the play deserves a place in American theatrical history.

THE GREEN PASTURES

The Green Pastures marked a significant advance in Connelly's ambitions as a dramatist. In his previous plays, he had focused on a limited area of modern life: society life, Hollywood, business. In *The Green Pastures*, he attempted a unified retelling of the principal document of our culture within the context and language of rural Southern blacks. He was interested not in theological exactitude but rather in the humanistic message that even "De Lawd" comes to accept through his suffering: Humankind's essential imperfection must be accepted, for people's nature is to sin without regard to De Lawd's praise or damnation; this is the cross both humanity and God, as symbolized by Jesus on the cross at the end of the play, must bear. Suffering ennobles the sufferer, human or divine, and the anguish of the realization of humankind's nature is, in the closing words of the play, "a terrible burden for one man to carry."

The first part of the play covers events from Creation to the Flood. These ten episodes begin with a Sunday school lesson presided over by Mr. Deshee, who tells his children about Heaven, Creation, Adam and Eve, Cain and Abel, and Noah, showing how humankind fell from grace and how, with the Flood, it must begin again. Here is where *Dulcy*, *Merton of the Movies*, and *Beggar on Horseback* would have ended, full of promise, but Connelly was no longer satisfied to end on such a note. The end of part 1 finds De Lawd merely hopeful of the success of his new start and Gabriel downright uncertain.

Part 2 begins with two Heavenly Cleaners in De Lawd's office complaining that a little speck on De Lawd's horizon, Earth, is taking up too much of his time; Gabriel reports that the supply of thunderbolts is depleting without sufficient benefit for their use. De Lawd resolves to try once again with humankind, and he shows Moses how to trick Pharoah into letting his people out of Egypt. Joshua finally gets them to the Promised Land, but soon, in the words of Mr. Deshee, "dey went to de dogs again." The scene changes to a Harlem-style nightclub with golden idols and money-changing priests that bring De Lawd to renounce his creation and declare that he will not save humankind again.

In scene 6 of part 2, the fall of Jerusalem is played out. De Lawd is so moved by the statement of faith in the God of Hosea given by Hezdrel—a character created without biblical authority and in certain respects morally superior to even De Lawd—that he turns to a dialogue with Gabriel on the nature of humankind, which can be so evil, yet so noble and courageous in the face of suffering. De Lawd realizes that he, too, must suffer for each new thing he learns about humankind, and the joint suffering of God and humanity is made manifest in the Crucifixion, seen in shadow on De Lawd's wall. With this scene witnessed, the severe, noble black Lawd, now given hope in his creation for the first time, smiles broadly as the chorus sings "Hallelujah, King Jesus."

The play was received with overwhelming critical and popular praise, even from African Americans, who, if they were offended by the stereotypical poverty and near-illiteracy of Mr. Deshee and his charges, were nevertheless elated at the acceptance Broadway audiences gave this all-African-American cast, behaving, with the exception of the Harlem-speakeasy Babylon scene, in a good and proper way. To what extent the simplistic figures of De Lawd and

his minions and the hot-tempered, immoral, and occasionally violent characters such as Cain, Zeba, the Children of Noah, and the Children of Israel represented caricature with which the New York audience could feel comfortable, and to what extent they represented behavioral archetypes that transcend race, is an open question. Connelly himself left no doubt about how he viewed them:

> I never saw my play—and I certainly don't now—as part of any civil rights movement, as for or against *any* movement. It was no more simply about a race of people than [Gerhart Hauptmann's] *The Weavers* say, or [Maxim Gorky's] *The Lower Depths* was simply about one particular class of people. My play had little to do with Negroes—or, rather, it had as much to do with yellow and white and red as it did with black. *Green Pastures* was, at heart, about humanity, but maybe that's a little hard to explain today.

This play of simple faith in humankind came at the right time, as the United States was sinking into the Depression; with confusion and despair all around, Connelly brought hope and laughter to a darkening country.

OTHER MAJOR WORKS

LONG FICTION: *A Souvenir from Qam*, 1965.

SHORT FICTION: "Luncheon at Sea," 1927; "Gentlemen Returning from a Party," 1927; "Barmecide's Feast," 1927; "The Committee: A Study of Contemporary New York Life," 1928; "The Guest," 1929; "Coroner's Inquest," 1930.

SCREENPLAYS: *Whispers*, 1920; *Exit Smiling*, 1926; *The Suitor*, 1928 (short); *The Bridegroom*, 1929 (short); *The Uncle*, 1929 (short); *The Green Pastures*, 1936; *I Married a Witch*, 1936; *Captains Courageous*, 1937 (with others); *Crowded Paradise*, 1956.

RADIO PLAY: *The Mole on Lincoln's Cheek*, 1941.

NONFICTION: *Voices Offstage: A Book of Memoirs*, 1968.

BIBLIOGRAPHY

Brown, John Mason. *Dramatis Personae: A Retrospective Show*. New York: Viking Press, 1963. This comprehensive history of the American theater in the twentieth century also covers the long career of Connelly in theater, radio, and Hollywood.

Daniel, Walter C. *"De Lawd": Richard B. Harrison and "The Green Pastures."* New York: Greenwood Press, 1986. In this volume, Daniel reviews African American contributions to the American theater and the role of Connelly in stage history.

Nolan, Paul T. *Marc Connelly.* New York: Twayne, 1969. Nolan provides a concise but useful study of

the colorful author and supplements his book with a useful bibliography.

Wainscott, Ronald H. *The Emergence of the Modern American Theater, 1914-1929.* New Haven, Conn.: Yale University Press, 1997. This wide-ranging study of American theater looks at topics such as American expressionism and examines George Kaufman and Connelly's *Beggar on Horseback.*

Ward W. Briggs,
updated by Peter C. Holloran

PIERRE CORNEILLE

Born: Rouen, France; June 6, 1606
Died: Paris, France; September 30, 1684

PRINCIPAL DRAMA

Mélite: Ou, Les Fausses Lettres, pr. 1630, pb. 1633 (English translation, 1776)

Clitandre, pr. 1631, pb. 1632

La Veuve: Ou, Le Traître trahi, pr. 1631, pb. 1634

La Galerie du palais: Ou, L'Amie rivale, pr. 1632, pb. 1637

La Suivante, pr. 1633, pb. 1637

La Place royale: Ou, L'Amoureux extravagant, pr. 1634, pb. 1637

Médée, pr. 1635, pb. 1639

L'Illusion comique, pr. 1636, pb. 1639 (*The Illusion*, 1989)

Le Cid, pr., pb. 1637 (*The Cid*, 1637)

Horace, pr. 1640, pb. 1641 (English translation, 1656)

Cinna: Ou, La Clémence d'Auguste, pr. 1640, pb. 1643 (*Cinna*, 1713)

Polyeucte, pr. 1642, pb. 1643 (English translation, 1655)

La Mort de Pompée, pr. 1643, pb. 1644 (*The Death of Pompey*, 1663)

Le Menteur, pr. 1643, pb. 1644 (*The Liar*, 1671)

La Suite du menteur, pr. 1644, pb. 1645

Rodogune, princesse des Parthes, pr. 1645, pb. 1647 (*Rodogune*, 1765)

Théodore, vierge et martyre, pr. 1645, pb. 1646

Héraclius, pr., pb. 1647 (English translation, 1664)

Don Sanche d'Aragon, pr. 1649, pb. 1650 (*The Conflict*, 1798)

Andromède, pr., pb. 1650

Nicomède, pr., pb. 1651 (English translation, 1671)

Pertharite, roi des Lombards, pr. 1651, pb. 1653

Œdipe, pr., pb. 1659

La Toison d'or, pr. 1660, pb. 1661

Théâtre, pb. 1660 (3 volumes)

Sertorius, pr., pb. 1662 (English translation, 1960)

Sophonisbe, pr., pb. 1663

Othon, pr. 1664, pb. 1665 (English translation, 1960)

Agésilas, pr., pb. 1666

Attila, pr., pb. 1667 (English translation, 1960)

Tite et Bérénice, pr. 1670, pb. 1671

Pulchérie, pr. 1672, pb. 1673 (English translation, 1960)

Suréna, pr. 1674, pb. 1675 (English translation, 1960)

The Chief Plays of Corneille, pb. 1952, 1956

Moot Plays, pb. 1960

OTHER LITERARY FORMS

Although Pierre Corneille is known principally for his plays, he wrote a number of poems and at least one ballet libretto. Of his poetry there remain approximately one hundred pieces in French and a small number in Latin. Outside the theater, however, his best-known literary work is a long religious poem of thirteen thousand lines, the *Imitation de Jésus-Christ*, published in its entirety in 1656. A free translation of Saint Thomas à Kempis's Latin work, it enjoyed an immediate success; four editions were published in 1656 alone. Another adaptation of a Latin religious work into a lengthy French verse, *Office de la Sainte Vierge*, published in 1670, was a relative failure, for it was not reedited. To accompany a three-volume edition of his plays, Corneille published in 1660 a series of essays in which he formally presented his critical theories: three *Discours* and the *Examens* (one for each play). While some critics refer to Corneille's theory of drama as evidence that he misunderstood his own plays, the *Discours* and *Examens* can nevertheless be very helpful in understanding French classical theater. There exist twenty-four letters by Corneille, of little general interest.

ACHIEVEMENTS

Generally hailed as the originator of French classical tragedy, Pierre Corneille is recognized as a master dramatist whose work founded a theater admired and envied by the rest of Europe throughout the seventeenth and eighteenth centuries. Ever the innovator, Corneille attempted many types of drama during his long career. Although he is known mainly as a tragedian, his thirty-three plays include heroic comedy, comedy of manners, comedy of intrigue, sacred plays, machine plays, and ballet librettos. His career met with both dazzling success and abysmal failure. He was praised as the greatest French dramatist during the first half of his career, but the changing tastes of the Parisian audience and the popularity of Corneille's younger rival Jean Racine marred the latter part of his life. Although his later plays were for the most part critical and financial failures, recent critics have rehabilitated a number of these mature works.

Corneille's lasting influence on the French theater is perhaps his most noteworthy achievement. Most commentators agree that he fixed the genre of tragedy, separating it from its Greek origins and giving it an entirely new character. With Corneille, tragedy presents to its audience a precise moral and emotional conflict which is thoroughly analyzed and finally resolved through the interactions of a limited number of characters. Many have noted that Corneille's drama is not tragic in the Aristotelian sense. It was in essence a modern conception based not on the emotions of terror and pity but rather on admiration. Although destiny plays a role in Corneillian tragedy, the Greek tragic hero, a plaything of fate, becomes for Corneille a being confronted by an apparently irresolvable—and thus tragic—conflict, but who prevails, guided by an essential freedom enlightened by sound judgment and supported by will. Derived from tragicomedy, Corneille's tragedies, with the exception perhaps of his last play, *Suréna*, end on a note of hope and even joy. In general terms, it is a theater of optimism.

BIOGRAPHY

Pierre Corneille was born to a prosperous bourgeois family. His father and grandfather were lawyers in the parliament of Rouen, and, after studying Latin at the local Jesuit school (where he won prizes for Latin verse composi-

Pierre Cornielle (Library of Congress)

tion), Corneille took a law degree in 1624. In 1628, his parents bought for him a position as king's counselor in the Rouen office of the departments of waterways and forests and of the admiralty, posts that he conscientiously filled until 1650. Corneille lived for many years in Rouen, moving to Paris only in 1662 in order, perhaps, to satisfy a promise made to the French Academy on his election in 1647, which required that its members reside in Paris. His younger brother Thomas, also a popular dramatist, with whom Corneille had a long and close relationship, may also have influenced the decision to move to the capital. Corneille had six children with Marie de Lampérière, whom he married in 1641 and whose family background was similar to his own.

Corneille met with immediate success as a dramatist. His first play, the comedy *Mélite*, submitted to the famous actor Montdory while his theatrical troupe was performing in Rouen in 1629, was a triumph when Montdory performed it in Paris in the following year. Seven more plays (of which six were comedies) made Corneille a well-known young author when, in early 1637, probably the most significant play in the history of French drama, *The Cid*, scored an unheard of popular success. Historians have made much of the three-year silence following *The Cid* (pique at the critics who condemned the play? or pressing legal burdens in Rouen?), yet three more resounding successes followed: *Horace*, *Cinna*, and *Polyeucte*. During the "Corneillian decade," the 1640's, Corneille consolidated his status as the premier French playwright. In 1651, the dismal failure of *Pertharite, roi des Lombards* precipitated a second "silence." From 1651 to 1656, Corneille devoted most of his time to the *Imitation de Jésus-Christ*. Finally, encouraged by the powerful financial secretary Nicolas Fouquet, Corneille returned to the theater with *Œdipe*, presented in 1659 to a delighted Parisian audience. The remainder of his productions did not equal the popular acclaim of the earlier plays. Although he continued to write, Corneille's inability to adapt to changing tastes most likely explains his decline. Almost unnoticed by the public, *Suréna*, produced in 1674, marks his definitive retirement. Corneille was considered passé, although the performance

of six of his tragedies at Versailles in 1676 is evidence of the dramatist's continuing reputation.

Very little is known of Corneille's private life. Literary historians have emphasized, however, the duality of his life. The creator of heroic and majestic characters designed to elicit the public's admiration, a dramatist with worldwide fame, Corneille was apparently a good bourgeois family man, a minor magistrate who led an uneventful life. Contemporary accounts indicate that he was a shy, retiring man who cut a very poor figure in Parisian society. As a writer, nevertheless, Corneille was a proud man, very conscious of his merit.

ANALYSIS

The concept of the Corneillian hero, although it is somewhat misleading because it tends to oversimplify a vast and varied body of plays, has fired the imagination of generations. Seen in purest form in the earlier plays, this hero, torn between the dictates of duty, honor, and patriotism and the demands of love, achieves, through the strength of reason and will, an absolute realization of self. Often surrounded by mediocrity or by relative values, the hero is concerned solely for his *gloire*, which might be defined as an extreme form of aristocratic honor and self-respect, providing self-definition. Love in the hero is not an irrational, all-consuming emotion but rather is based on reason and respect for the beloved's merit, or *gloire*. It is not surprising that Pierre Corneille has historically enjoyed periods of popularity before and during wars: His work has been the source of heroic inspiration and energy in France's spiritual heritage.

L'ILLUSION COMIQUE

Corneille's first eight plays, all but one of them comedies, combine obvious influences from contemporary drama with the playwright's search for greater independence. The most remarkable of his early plays is *L'Illusion comique*, which Corneille in 1660 called a "strange monster." It is clear that he wrote the play without the slightest regard for the dramatic unities then being promulgated by literary theorists. Called a Baroque drama because of its emphasis on illusion, instability, and metamorphosis, the play is the culmination of Corneille's early period and contains an effective apology of the theater, and, perhaps, of the career that Corneille had chosen for himself.

Act 1 is a kind of prologue: Pridamant has spent years searching for his son Clindor, who was alienated from his father ten years earlier. Having found no trace of his son, Pridamant is brought by his friend Dorante to the grotto of the magician Alcandre. With a sweep of his magic wand, Alcandre shows to Pridamant some of his son's varied adventures during the last ten years. Thus, in act 2 a play-within-a-play begins in which Clindor is valet to the cowardly military captain Matamore, a farcical character who boasts of fantastic military and amorous exploits. Both men love Isabelle, who in turn loves Clindor. Adraste, another rival for the love of Isabelle, fights Clindor, who, though wounded, kills Adraste. Clindor is condemned to execution for murder. Isabelle's servant, Lyse, who is loved by Clindor's jailor, succeeds in freeing Clindor. He, Lyse, and the beloved Isabelle flee. At the end of each act, there is a brief return to the grotto, where Pridamant records his reactions to his son's adventures. At the end of act 4, Pridamant breathes easily after his son's escape, but Alcandre promises him more tense moments. Suddenly, in act 5, a transformation in Alcandre's show occurs: Clindor, richly dressed, courts another woman. He has forsaken Isabelle, who, dressed as a princess, complains of Clindor's infidelities to Lyse. The jealous husband of the woman whom Clindor is courting, Prince Florilame, has Clindor killed and kidnaps Isabelle. Pridamant, who believes that he has witnessed the murder of his son, is inconsolable until Alcandre reveals yet another scene: Clindor, Isabelle, and the others are counting and dividing money. It turns out that they are actors, and the last scene was a fragment of a tragedy that they had just performed. Pridamant, relieved but scandalized by the idea that his son has chosen such a "degrading" profession, is finally convinced by Alcandre's eloquent defense of the theater and of Clindor's honorable profession.

Built on levels of illusion, *L'Illusion comique* contains a play-within-a-play-*within*-a-play. The notion of theatricality is central to the play. The magician Alcandre takes on the role of director and author while Pridamant represents the dazzled and deceived audience. Within the levels of illusion, there is a hierarchy. On the lowest and least effective level, Matamore and his swashbuckling boasts create "illusions" that fool no one. On the highest level, Alcandre creates superbly effective, magical, supernatural illusions that occur in a secret place (the grotto) and are inaccessible to the vast majority of people. Between these two extremes lies the theater, a remarkable source of illusion accessible to all, a "magical" place presided over by "magicians"—actors, directors, and, above all, playwrights. *L'Illusion comique* reflects the generally high esteem in which the theater was held in the period. In 1641, a royal decree affirmed the dignity of the actor's profession; only toward the end of the century did the prestige of the stage begin to decline. The extraordinary renown of Corneille's next play attests the popularity of drama in the 1630's.

THE CID

For *The Cid*, by far his most successful and well-known play, Corneille drew his inspiration from a contemporary Spanish work, Guillèn de Castro y Bellvís's *Las mocedades del Cid* (1621). It was necessary to adapt this long and diffuse foreign play to the tastes of the French audience. Corneille simplified and condensed, keeping the essential Romanesque theme of an aristocratic hero who accepts the tragic burden of opposing moral obligations and thus transcends the contingencies of the human condition. The two major characters are Rodrigue and Chimène, who are betrothed at the beginning of the play. The rivalry between Rodrigue's aging father, Don Diègue, and Don Gomès, father of Chimène, initiates the conflict. Furious after the king's appointment of Don Diègue as tutor to the prince, the younger Don Gomès slaps and thus mortally insults Rodrigue's father. Too old to avenge this affront, Don Diègue asks his son to preserve the family honor. Rodrigue must choose between his family and his love, and in a famous soliloquy (the "Stances du Cid," act 1 scene 6), decides to challenge the more experienced Don Gomès. In arriving at this decision, Rodrigue realizes that failure to uphold the family honor would inevitably result in the loss of Chimène because inaction would make him unworthy of her. Though steeped in emotion, the decision is thus both logical and necessary. In act 2, Rodrigue kills Don Gomès in a duel. The act's last scene stages a confrontation before the king between Chimène, who demands that her father's murderer be punished, and Don Diègue, who justifies his son's honorable action. Chimène thus undergoes a conflict similar to that of Rodrigue: She is torn between two passions, family honor and love, and she chooses honor.

Act 3 contains the poignant scene in which Rodrigue confronts Chimène, asking that she personally end his life and thereby avenge her father. This she cannot do: She demands that he leave her house yet gives him to understand that she loves him still. Her true feelings are expressed with marvelous economy in a famous line often cited as an example of Corneille's use of *litotes* (a figure of speech in which an affirmative is expressed by the negation of its contrary): "*Va, je ne te hais point*" ("Go, I do not hate you"). This emotional duel is said to have provoked great admiration and emotion in contemporary audiences. This scene of interior conflict accompanies an exterior threat: The infidel Moors are massing to attack the city of Seville. Exhorted again by his father, Rodrigue leads a force that, in the course of a nocturnal battle, defeats the Moors and saves the realm. Now a great hero, the right arm of the king, Rodrigue receives the title of le Cid, or Lord, from his vanquished foes. This turn of events obliges Chimène to assert an even greater force of will: For honor's sake, she must persist in seeking vengeance on the new and acclaimed hero of Spain. Although knowing that Chimène still loves Rodrigue, the king allows her to choose a champion. Don Sanche, rejected lover of Chimène, will uphold her cause in single combat with Rodrigue, after which Chimène will marry the victor.

In the last act, Rodrigue bids farewell to Chimène: He is resigned to his death. After the duel, Don Sanche enters the scene, and Chimène believes that he has triumphed. Cursing Don Sanche, she admits publicly her undying love for Rodrigue. The king reveals the truth: that Rodrigue had won, spared his adversary, and sent him to Chimène as messenger. Asking that she forgive Rodrigue, the king declares that a year's delay will temper Chimène's desire for

revenge, after which she and Rodrigue will marry. During this time, Rodrigue will be able to accomplish greater exploits, thus increasing his *gloire* and making him even worthier of Chimène's noble hand.

The concept of rivalry informs the action of *The Cid*. The king's decision at the outset exacerbates the rivalry between the proud fathers. The inevitable conflict then falls on the children: Both Rodrigue and Chimène must equal the aristocratic resolve of the other. Products of a feudal ethic that places honor above all else, the young couple are heroic yet sensitive. Each suffers, yet neither's strength of will weakens. The seemingly irresolvable conflict is reconciled by the couple's submission to higher authority. The king, who has the last words in the play, imposes his will on a younger generation, which accepts the idea of monarchical order. Represented by the fathers, the less-sympathetic older generation exhibits the intransigent feudal mentality of kill or die. Corneille's emphasis on youth, on young lovers who provoke the pity but above all the admiration of the audience, is a keystone in his drama. It is important to note that the play traces the development of Corneillian heroism in Rodrigue. An inexperienced young man at the opening of the play, albeit with much potential because of his illustrious blood, Rodrigue becomes the "Cid." There is an upward movement in which Rodrigue and Chimène are apotheosized. *The Cid* remains perhaps the best example of the ethical values of Corneillian drama: a noble idealism oriented toward the glorification of the passions and the self.

The huge popularity of *The Cid* touched off a debate famous in French literary history—"la querelle du *Cid*." This quarrel is significant, reflecting a period in which the "baroque" and the "classical" styles were at odds. One of Corneille's major rivals, Georges de Scudéry, wrote in 1637 *Observations sur le Cid*, in which he condemned the choice of subject as being inappropriate in a genre whose subjects should have ancient sources; he also attacked Corneille's "plagiarism," the play's stylistic defects, and its inattention to the rules of drama. The last criticism is perhaps the most interesting. Scudéry declared that *The Cid*'s many plot elements could never occur within the prescribed twenty-four-hour time limit; the play's action is therefore not verisimilar. The concept of *vraisemblance*—verisimilitude—was a fundamental tenet of the classical theoreticians. Scudéry also complained of the play's apparently unnecessary characters, in particular the Infante, the princess who also loves Rodrigue. Much emphasis was placed on act 1 scene 3, in which the overweening Don Gomès insults and slaps the older Don Diègue onstage. Critics condemned the incident as shocking: It violated the dictum of *bienséance*—decorum—a moral and social principle that required propriety of representation and satisfaction of the tastes and mores of the public. The debate became so bitter that the powerful minister Cardinal Richelieu, wishing to establish the authority of the newly formed French Academy, ordered it to arbitrate the dispute. The *Sentiments de l'Académie sur Le Cid*, issued in October, 1637, praised the playwright yet confirmed Scudéry's criticisms concerning Corneille's neglect of the rules. Disturbed by the Academy's judgment, Corneille corrected certain verses condemned by his critics; not until the author's preface in the 1648 edition and in the play's *Examen*, published in 1660, did Corneille attempt detailed self-justification. At any rate, the public acclaim accorded the play must have mitigated Corneille's chagrin.

HORACE

That Corneille was affected by academic criticism seems to be confirmed in his next play, *Horace*, first performed in 1640. After the depiction of Castilian honor, Corneille chose a subject taken from Roman history, thus apparently bowing to one of Scudéry's criticisms of *The Cid*. Although Corneille is still somewhat cramped by the unities of time, place, and action—there are many incidents and a complex plot structure in *Horace*—they are well observed, and many critics regard the play as the first true French classical tragedy.

The action opens on the eve of the decisive battle between Alba and Rome, two historically linked cities engaged in fratricidal war. These links are manifest in the play's major characters. The Roman hero Horace is married to Sabine, from Alba, while Horace's sister Camille is fiancée to Curiace, brother of Sabine. The atmosphere of foreboding before the bat-

tle yields to hope when, to limit bloodshed, Curiace announces the decision to allow three champions from each side to determine the war's outcome. This initial hope, however, is disappointed when Rome reveals its choice. Horace and his two brothers are designated to champion their city's cause. Fate strikes another blow when Alba reveals its choice: Curiace and his two brothers will defend Alba's honor and independence. An intimate conversation between Horace and Curiace, who are friends, discloses their characters. Horace demonstrates an inhuman resolve, renouncing all former ties of love and friendship, while Curiace tempers his patriotism with emotion and regret.

The two armies share Curiace's sentiments, for the play's fourth *coup de théâtre* offers renewed hope. Each side refuses to allow the two families to destroy each other, and a decision to consult the gods is made. Destiny is irresistible: The gods confirm the initial choice. Act 3 concludes with the outcome of the battle seemingly decided, for the news from the field of combat is that Horace's two brothers are dead and that he has fled. Another dramatic surprise ensues in act 4: A messenger reveals that Horace's flight was simply a ruse to separate his opponents, a trick that has given him the victory. Despite the death of two sons, Horace's father is ecstatic at his news, while Camille, overcome with grief, curses both Rome and her brother when he returns, glorious, from the field. Provoked beyond endurance, Horace kills his sister. Act 5 presents the trial of Horace, presided over by King Tulle. Although Valère, who loved Camille, pleads passionately for swift and harsh punishment of the fratricide, Old Horace eloquently declares that his son's act was virtuous, for he punished a traitor, and that Horace should be permitted to continue to uphold the strength and honor of Rome. Tulle pronounces judgment: Horace will live to serve the state, but he must submit to an expiatory ceremony. Curiace and Camille will be interred in the same tomb.

Like *The Cid*, *Horace* presents a hero who overcomes an emotional conflict and accepts a painful obligation. His victory, like that of Rodrigue, accords him the status of national hero, but whereas Rodrigue's star continues to rise at the play's close, Horace's *gloire* is apparently overshadowed by his crime. For him, his act is reasonable. Just before dispatching his sister, he declares: ". . . *ma patience à la raison fait place*" ("my patience yields to reason"), yet his wife, Sabine, Valère, and Tulle consider it a brutal, inhuman act. Perhaps not a Corneillian ideal, Horace fails to maintain the balance of tender sentiments and an impulse to heroic action that Rodrigue attained. Critics hold divided opinions concerning Horace's culpability. The traditional view sees him as a "ferocious brute," an unrepentant fanatic. This judgment, however, ignores Corneille's idea, expressed in the third *Discours*, that Horace is indeed a hero. Under Horace's apparent insensitivity is a young man who suffers a cruel destiny. His barbarous yet necessary act reveals his strength of will. As a Roman conscious of Rome's destiny, Horace believes that his act is patriotic and religious: He destroys an individual, his own sister, who has refused to accept the gods' decree of Roman supremacy. His blind acceptance of this fateful decree isolates him and thus constitutes a tragic situation *par excellence*. Despite differing interpretations of *Horace*, the Corneillian formula obtains in this play: a series of ordeals that the hero must overcome at the peril of his life, reputation, and personal happiness.

The political overtones of *Horace* should not be ignored. The play was produced in a time of an almost fratricidal war between France and Spain and was dedicated to Cardinal Richelieu. In addition, its themes corresponded to a governmental policy based on authority and national unity. Horace is the hero of a totalitarian regime at war. The play seems to acknowledge a political doctrine supporting unquestioned submission to the public interest in a time of national danger, a doctrine promulgated by Richelieu. Corneille's vision of Roman history is thus reflected in and supported by the political realities of 1640. A modern viewpoint has seen in *Horace* a powerful message: In a totalitarian state, in which total obedience is demanded, war dehumanizes. Horace, at the beginning of the play a sympathetic, humane young man, becomes, in his loyalty to the state, a fanatic who will destroy all dissenters.

CINNA

Corneille's interest in the political becomes more apparent in his next play, *Cinna*, produced also in 1640. A play of vengeance pursued and clemency achieved, *Cinna*, set in ancient Rome, pits the young couple Emilie and Cinna, in league with a coconspirator, Maxime, against the emperor Auguste. Emilie, whose father was murdered by Auguste, has promised to marry Cinna if he succeeds in assassinating the emperor. Just as Cinna and Emilie exult in the conspirators' well-conceived plans for the assassination set for the following day, Auguste summons Cinna and Maxime. This occurs at the end of act 1, thus creating great suspense, a trademark of Corneille's dramaturgy. Act 1 immediately reveals Auguste's purpose. Tired of maintaining his power, he asks for advice: Should he continue to rule or step down? Cinna, fearful of losing the opportunity to assassinate Auguste and thus lose Emilie, advises the emperor to keep his power, advice that dumbfounds Maxime, who had counseled the alternative. After this fateful interview, Cinna confides to Maxime the true reason for the plot: It is merely a means by which he will win Emilie. Maxime, a secret lover of Emilie, is devastated, and he arranges for Auguste to discover the plot. Meanwhile, Cinna's initial resolution yields to doubt. He is torn between his love for Emilie and his rekindled loyalty to a trusting Auguste. However he acts, he will lose self-esteem, a major component of Corneillian *gloire*. In act 4, Auguste learns of the conspiracy. He too is torn: Should he punish severely those whom he trusted, or—his political lassitude comes into play here—should he forgive? Auguste's wife, Livie, advises clemency. While clemency appears to be the most expedient political solution, Auguste vacillates, thus increasing suspense. Isolated and insecure, wishing to be free of the burden of rule yet conscious of his duty to Rome, Auguste grants forgiveness to the plotters. This heroic change from the murderous tyrant described in the beginning of the play to a magnanimous ruler effects a change in the others; it appears that the seemingly endless cycle of revenge and suppression has ended. Demonstrating his ability to overcome personal feelings of anger and revenge, Auguste, inspired by the gods, has abandoned a rule based on fear and founded a new order of justice and humanity.

Many commentators have seen in *Cinna* echoes of the political climate in France in 1640. Numerous plots had sprung up against Richelieu, who was consolidating the central authority of the crown against the threatened and powerful nobility. The play has been judged an appeal to both the Cardinal and the French people: National interest demanded a renunciation of revenge for past wrongs. To accomplish this, both sides must exercise the heroic restraint exemplified in the play. He who reigns must take the initiative. It would be wrong, however, to insist on this aspect of the play. Contemporary audiences appeared to have been moved more by the love of Cinna and Emilie than by Auguste's clemency. To see the play as a study of the motives and behavior of conspirators in general is perhaps a more valid political interpretation.

POLYEUCTE

Whereas *Horace* depicted monarchical Rome at the beginning of its ascent to world power, and *Cinna* treated a restless Rome under its first emperor, *Polyeucte*, Corneille's next play, focuses on Rome later in its history, when mystical Christianity began to make inroads into pagan Rome's supremacy. Here Corneille deals with the psychology of the early Christians, ready and willing to endure martyrdom for their faith. The drama is played out on three broad levels: sentimental and familial, political, and religious. Polyeucte, an Armenian prince, is married to Pauline, the daughter of the ambitious Roman governor of Armenia, Félix, who has forced this marriage for political ends. Polyeucte's friend Néarque has convinced him to be baptized, but Polyeucte hesitates because of Pauline's protests. In act 1 scene 3, Pauline reveals to her confidante a dream in which she has seen her husband killed among a group of Christians and in the presence of Sévère, a Roman hero whom she loved and whom she believes dead. The play thus opens with Pauline's fears of impending disaster made manifest in a dream. In the following scene, a key piece of information emerges: Sévère, very much alive, is on his way to Armenia to celebrate his recent victories; Pauline is extremely disturbed by this news.

Pauline and Polyeucte are each torn by an emotional conflict: Polyeucte's love for Pauline competes with his love for God, while Pauline's emotions are divided between Sévère and her husband. This rivalry produces not jealousy and revenge but rather sacrifice and ultimate reconciliation. In an interview with Sévère, Pauline recalls her love for him but affirms her fidelity to Polyeucte. During a public ceremony in honor of Sévère, the recently baptized Polyeucte has resolved to break the pagan idols, thereby demonstrating his new faith and assuring martyrdom. The effect of divine grace after his baptism explains this sudden transformation from the fearful and hesitant Polyeucte of act 1. Between acts 2 and 3, Polyeucte commits this daring act; unrepentant, he is immediately imprisoned, while Néarque is summarily executed by order of Félix.

There follows a series of entreaties to Polyeucte, who refuses to recant. Pauline's feelings for her husband grow as she realizes the strength of his will and his faith. Still somewhat hesitant when he thinks of his beloved Pauline, Polyeucte finally sacrifices his terrestrial love, entrusting Pauline to Sévère. Although Félix is torn between fear of Rome, whose policy is to put to death Christian dissidents, and his affection for his daughter, who implores her father to forgive Polyeucte, Polyeucte is, indeed, executed. Before his death, Polyeucte declared that he would "obtain" divine grace for Pauline and Félix when he sees God face to face. This wish is granted after his death: Pauline, then Félix, miraculously convert to Christianity at the end of the play. Sévère marvels at this sudden turnabout and promises to do his utmost to prevent further persecutions.

Polyeucte resembles the archetypal Corneillian hero: He undergoes and overcomes a series of ordeals in which friendship, love, and passion combat a higher ideal. He attains genuine apotheosis; his death not only has brought about the blessed conversion of his wife and father-in-law but also has benefited many other converts. This is confirmed by Sévère's reaction at the play's close. Polyeucte, however, does not aim for worldly glory as do Rodrigue, Horace, and Auguste. He strives for an otherworldly glory that far transcends the heroism of other plays. As in other plays, reconciliation and union reign at the end. On the sentimental level, the marriage of Polyeucte and Pauline, never truly united in life, has been transformed into a union divinely consecrated through Polyeucte's martyrdom. Politically, the conversion of Félix marks the end of the ancient pagan order and inaugurates the rise of the Christian era of the Roman Empire. Finally, on the religious level, divine grace has proven its efficacy; Polyeucte's militant faith will serve as an illustrious example to others.

THE DEATH OF POMPEY

With *Polyeucte*, Corneille had reached the summit of his success. The tragedies written and produced between 1643 and 1651 bear witness to his ambition to produce plays that were at once innovative and entertaining. *The Death of Pompey*, in which Pompée does not appear (although Corneille called him the "principal actor), is a political play that opposes two sets of characters: César and Pompée's widow, Cornélie, who strive to be worthy of the heroic Pompée's memory; and the youthful Egyptian king Ptolomée and his Machiavellian advisers. Unlike the protagonists of earlier plays, however, no character here undergoes a heroic ascension.

THE LIAR

Also during the 1643 theatrical season, Corneille returned to comedy with *The Liar*, considered by some scholars a self-parody. A complex comedy of intrigue, *The Liar* presents Dorante, who, after confusing the names of two young ladies, finds himself in an amusing imbroglio. Parodic elements are occasionally quite specific: Dorante's father, Géronte, chiding his dishonest son in act 5 scene 3, for example, parodies Don Diègue challenging Rodrigue in act 1 scene 5 of *The Cid*. The liar's constant self-transformations also recall the heroic metamorphoses of the tragedies. Motivated no doubt by the success of the play, Corneille composed a sequel, *La Suite du menteur*, his last true comedy, presented in 1644.

NICOMÈDE

Corneille's last great success before the failure of *Pertharite, roi des Lombards* and his subsequent retreat from the theater in the 1650's was *Nicomède*. After exploiting the Romanesque and the melodramatic in *Rodogune*, *Héraclius*, and *The Conflict*, Corneille returned to political and familial tragedy in *Nicomède*. Arisonoé, the stepmother of Nicomède, who is the son of King Prusias of Bithynia, plots to destroy her proud and courageous stepson. Encouraging Nicomède to defy the Roman conquerors of Bithynia, she hopes that Rome will kill him, leaving the throne empty for her own son, the docile Attale, whom the Romans favor as the next king. Nicomède scorns the political machinations of his weak father and of Rome's ambassador, Flaminius, who use Laodice, loved by both Nicomède and Attale, as political blackmail. After Nicomède's arrest for refusing with disdain and contempt Prusias's ultimatum, Attale is named king, but he immediately realizes that the Romans will never permit him to marry Laodice. In a sudden turnabout, Attale, aided by a popular uprising in support of Nicomède, saves his half brother. Nicomède, ever generous and strong, returns the throne (which the populace wished for him) to Prusias. Touched by Nicomède's magnanimity, all are reconciled at the play's close. Inasmuch as the hero in *Nicomède* suffers no true inner conflict, the play differs fundamentally from the earlier tragedies. The "happy" denouement does not project an optimistic vision of an ever more glorious future for the hero but suggests rather the political reality of a dominant Rome which has the power and the will to control the individual liberty so essential to Corneillian *gloire*. Personal choice is thus limited, for Nicomède succeeds only temporarily in safeguarding his own independence and that of the state. The last words in the play belong to the politically astute Prusias: "Let us ask the gods . . . for the friendship of the Romans."

ŒDIPE

Corneille ended his retirement in 1659 with *Œdipe*, a popular success, the subject of which had been suggested to the author by the influential finance minister Fouquet. There followed a series of plays that did not enjoy the success of the earlier works. It is apparent that Corneille's continued emphasis on the political and his appeal to the intellect did not meet with favor among a new generation of theatergoers who craved, according to a contemporary observer, only "sorrow and tears." Although Corneille attempted to respond to the public's changing tastes, his theater continued to depict large historical and political tableaux; they had become anachronisms.

SURÉNA

His last play, *Suréna*, met the same fate as most of the later plays. Recent critics have rehabilitated this unjustly ignored masterpiece. Eurydice, the daughter of the king of Armenia, is betrothed to Pacorus, the son of Orode, king of Parthis. Although she dutifully accepts this political engagement, she loves Suréna, a famous Parthian general who has defeated the Romans and who returns Eurydice's affection. Orode, fearful of Suréna's reputation and power, offers his daughter Mandane to Suréna in order to assure his loyalty. Suréna, having made a vow of fidelity to Eurydice, refuses to marry Mandane. In vain, Suréna attempts to conceal the true reason for his refusal. After discovering that Suréna loves Eurydice, Orode gives an ultimatum: Suréna will either marry Mandane or die. The unshakable Suréna refuses to yield despite the entreaties of his sister Palmis. Just as Eurydice has decided to prevail on Suréna as well, grave news arrives: He has been assassinated. On hearing the news, Eurydice collapses, dying of grief.

Some commentators have judged this play a substantial modification of Corneille's earlier heroic manner: They emphasize that Suréna sacrifices all to love, that he is indifferent to *gloire*, thus in a mold different from Rodrigue, and so on. Despite his assertion that worldly fame does not equal one moment of happiness, Suréna does, however, demonstrate a strength of character not unlike that of earlier Corneillian heroes. He affirms his essential liberty and individual rights by not submitting to Orode's ultimatum. Moreover, the political situation, in which a king feels threatened by a more noble subject, recalls other plays, most notably *Nicomède* and *Agésilas*. Like other Corneillian heroes, Suréna is the right arm of the king and a courageous warrior. That Eurydice— a princess—loves him bears witness to his inherent merit. Suréna elicits pity by his unjust death and admiration, the touchstone of Corneille's drama, by the grandeur of his resolve. Corneillian glory, for Suréna a "cold and vain eternity," is opposed to an inner freedom that provides protection against the vagaries of

destiny. Suréna dies faithful to himself: He is perhaps the supreme expression of Corneillian psychology.

OTHER MAJOR WORKS

NONFICTION: *Discours*, 1660; *Examens*, 1660.

TRANSLATIONS: *Imitation de Jésus-Christ*, 1656; *Office de la Sainte Vierge*, 1670.

BIBLIOGRAPHY

Auchincloss, Louis. *La Gloire: The Roman Empire of Corneille and Racine*. Columbia: University of South Carolina Press, 1996. A study of the dramas of Corneille and Jean Racine that dealt with the Roman Empire.

Carlin, Claire L. *Pierre Corneille Revisited*. New York: Twayne, 1998. A basic biography of Corneille that examines his life and works. Bibliography and index.

_____. *Women Reading Corneille: Feminist Psychocriticisms of "Le Cid."* New York: Peter Lang, 2000. Corneille's *The Cid* from a feminist perspective. Bibliography and index.

Clarke, David. *Pierre Corneille: Poetics and Political Drama Under Louis XIII*. New York: Cambridge University Press, 1992. An examination of the political aspects of Corneille's dramatic works. Bibliography and index.

Goodkin, Richard E. *Birth Marks: The Tragedy of Primogeniture in Pierre Corneille, Thomas Corneille, and Jean Racine*. Philadelphia: University of Pennsylvania Press, 2000. A study of the tragedies of Pierre Corneille, Thomas Corneille, and Jean Racine with emphasis on primogeniture. Bibliography and index.

Longstaffe, Moya. *Metamorphoses of Passion and the Heroic in French Literature: Corneille, Stendhal, Claudel*. Lewiston, N.Y.: Edwin Mellen, 1999. An examination of the hero as portrayed in the works of Corneille, then Stendhal and Paul Claudel. Bibliography and index.

Lyons, John D. *The Tragedy of Origins: Pierre Corneille and Historical Perspective*. Stanford, Calif.: Stanford University Press, 1996. A look at history in the tragedies of Corneille. Bibliography and index.

Robert T. Corum, Jr.

NOËL COWARD

Born: Teddington, England; December 16, 1899
Died: Port Royal, Jamaica; March 26, 1973

PRINCIPAL DRAMA

I'll Leave It to You, pr. 1919, pb. 1920
Sirocco, wr. 1921, pr., pb. 1927
The Better Half, pr. 1922 (one act)
The Young Idea, pr. 1922, pb. 1924
London Calling, pr. 1923 (music and lyrics by Noël Coward and Ronald Jeans)
Weatherwise, wr. 1923, pb. 1931, pr. 1932
Fallen Angels, pb. 1924, pr. 1925
The Rat Trap, pb. 1924, pr. 1926
The Vortex, pr. 1924, pb. 1925
Easy Virtue, pr. 1925, pb. 1926
Hay Fever, pr., pb. 1925
On with the Dance, pr. 1925
The Queen Was in the Parlour, pr., pb. 1926
This Was a Man, pr., pb. 1926
Home Chat, pr., pb. 1927
The Marquise, pr., pb. 1927
This Year of Grace!, pr., pb. 1928 (musical)
Bitter Sweet, pr., pb. 1929 (operetta)
Private Lives, pr., pb. 1930
Some Other Private Lives, pr. 1930, pb. 1931 (one act)
Cavalcade, pr. 1931, pb. 1932
Post-Mortem, pb. 1931
Words and Music, pr. 1932, pb. 1939 (musical)
Design for Living, pr., pb. 1933
Conversation Piece, pr., pb. 1934
Point Valaine, pr., pb. 1936
Tonight at 8:30, pb. 1936 (3 volumes; a collective title for the following nine plays, which were designed to be presented in various combinations of three bills of three plays: *We Were Dancing*, pr. 1935; *The Astonished Heart*, pr. 1935; *Red Peppers*, pr. 1935; *Hands Across the Sea*, pr. 1935; *Fumed Oak*, pr. 1935; *Shadow Play*, pr. 1935; *Family Album*, pr. 1935; *Ways and Means*, pr. 1936; and *Still Life*, pr. 1936)
Operette, pr., pb. 1938

Set to Music, pr. 1939, pb. 1940 (musical)
Blithe Spirit, pr., pb. 1941
Present Laughter, pr. 1942, pb. 1943
This Happy Breed, pr. 1942, pb. 1943
Sigh No More, pr. 1945 (musical)
Pacific 1860, pr. 1946, pb. 1958 (musical)
Peace in Our Time, pr., pb. 1947
Ace of Clubs, pr. 1950, pb. 1962
Island Fling, pr. 1951, pb. 1956
Relative Values, pr. 1951, pb. 1952
Quadrille, pr., pb. 1952
After the Ball, pr., pb. 1954 (musical; based on Oscar Wilde's play *Lady Windermere's Fan*)
Nude with Violin, pr. 1956, pb. 1957
South Sea Bubble, pr., pb. 1956
Look After Lulu, pr., pb. 1959
Waiting in the Wings, pr., pb. 1960
High Spirits, pr. 1961 (musical; based on his play *Blithe Spirit*)
Sail Away, pr. 1961 (musical)
The Girl Who Came to Supper, pr. 1963 (musical; based on Terence Rattigan's play *The Sleeping Prince*)
Suite in Three Keys: Come into the Garden Maude; Shadows of the Evening; A Song at Twilight, pr., pb. 1966
Cowardy Custard, pr. 1972, pb. 1973 (also as *Cowardy Custard: The World of Noël Coward*)
Oh! Coward, pr. 1972, pb. 1974 (also as *Oh Coward! A Musical Comedy Revue*)
Plays: One, pb. 1979
Plays: Two, pb. 1979
Plays: Three, pb. 1979
Plays: Four, pb. 1979
Plays: Five, pb. 1983

OTHER LITERARY FORMS

Noël Coward was an extraordinarily prolific playwright, lyricist, and composer, writing more than fifty plays and musicals during his lifetime. He did not limit his literary endeavors solely to drama but ventured into other genres as well. These diversions into the realm of fiction, nonfiction, and poetry proved equally successful for him. In addition to his plays, Coward wrote three novels (two unpublished), several collections of short stories, satires, a book of verse, and several autobiographical works, *Present Indicative* (1937), *Middle East Diary* (1944), and *Future Indefinite* (1954).

Coward's versatility is also apparent in his original scripts for five films, his screenplays and adaptations of his hit plays, and his several essays on the modern theater that appeared in popular journals and in *The Times* of London and *The New York Times*. Like his plays, Coward's other works reveal his distinctive satiric style, sharp wit, and clever wordplay.

ACHIEVEMENTS

In 1970, Noël Coward was knighted by Queen Elizabeth II for "services rendered to the arts." The succinct phrasing of this commendation is as understated as some of Coward's best dialogue, considering his long and brilliant career in the theater. Coward wrote plays specifically designed to entertain the popular audience and to provide an amusing evening in the theater. Few of his plays champion a cause or promote a social issue. His most noteworthy achievement came in the writing of scores of fashionable comedies, revues, and "operettes" that were resounding successes on the English, American, and Continental stages and continue to enjoy success today. For this insistence on writing light comedy, he received substantial criticism, and several of his works were brusquely dismissed as "fluff" by critics. These same plays, however, never wanted for an audience, even during the most turbulent, politically restless years.

Coward came to be associated with the 1920's in England in much the same way that F. Scott Fitzgerald was identified with the Jazz Age in the United States. Whereas Fitzgerald seriously examined the moral failings of his prosperous characters, however, Coward treated them lightly. His plays chronicle the foibles, fashions, and affairs of the English upper class and provide satirical vignettes of the social elite. Coward's life and work reflect the same urbane persona; indeed, he wrote his best parts for himself. Coward's world was that of the idle rich, of cocktails, repartee, and a

tinge of modern decadence; this image was one he enjoyed and actively promoted until his death.

For all their popularity, most of Coward's plays are not memorable, save for *Private Lives*, *Blithe Spirit*, *Design for Living*, and possibly one or two others, yet his song lyrics have become part of the English cultural heritage. "Mad Dogs and Englishmen," from *Words and Music*, achieved immortality when its famous line "Mad dogs and Englishmen go out in the mid-day sun" was included in *The Oxford Dictionary of Quotations*.

Coward's reputation rests less on the literary merits of his works and more on the man, who as an accomplished actor, entertainer, and raconteur displayed enormous resilience during his five decades in the public eye. One of the obvious difficulties in producing a Coward play is finding actors who are able to handle the dialogue with the aplomb of "the master." What made Coward's plays successful was not

Noël Coward (Library of Congress)

so much a strong text, but virtuoso performances by Gertrude Lawrence, Jane Cowl, Alfred Lunt and Lynn Fontanne, and Coward himself. The public continues to be amused by his works in revivals, especially when performed by actors, such as Maggie Smith, who can transmit Coward's urbane humor to today's audiences.

BIOGRAPHY

Noël Pierce Coward was born December 16, 1899. He was the child of Arthur Sabin Coward and Violet Agnes Veitch, who married late in life after meeting in a church choir. Coward's family on his father's side was very talented musically. They helped nurture the natural virtuosity of the child, instilling in him a lifelong love of music.

Because his birthday was so close to Christmas, Coward always received one present to satisfy both occasions, but on December 16, his mother would take him to the theater as a special treat. He first attended a matinee at the age of four, never realizing he would spend the next seventy years of his life in service to the dramatic muse. As he grew older, he found these junkets to the theater more and more fascinating, and after returning home would rush to the piano and play by ear the songs from the production he had just seen.

Coward made his first public appearance, singing and accompanying himself on the piano, at a concert held at Miss Willington's School. Though obviously a very talented child, Coward's precocity did not carry over to his formal education. At best, his schooling was sporadic. For a time, he attended the Chapel Royal School at Clapham in hopes of becoming a member of the prestigious Chapel Royal Choir. Failing his audition as a choir member, he was taken from school and did not attend any educational institution for six months, at which time he was sent to school in London. He was ten years old.

Coward was an incorrigible, strong-willed child, given to tantrums when he did not get his way. These traits, inherited from both sides of his argumentative family, are evident in his characters, and each of his plays contains a rousing altercation scene. He was indulged by his mother, who became the stereotypical stage mother during his early years, and it was at his mother's insistence that he began attending Miss Janet Thomas's Dancing Academy in addition to his regular school in London. Soon, Miss Thomas's school usurped the position of importance held by traditional academic fare, and Coward became a child performer.

Coward's first professional engagement, and that which launched his long career, was on January 28, 1911, in a children's play, *The Goldfish*. After this appearance, he was sought after for children's roles by other professional theaters. He was featured in several productions with Sir Charles Hawtrey, a light comedian, whom Coward idolized and to whom he virtually apprenticed himself until he was twenty. It was from Hawtrey that Coward learned comic acting techniques and playwriting. He worked in everything from ballets to music halls and made it a point to study the more experienced performers to learn to "catch" the audience quickly. This skill was one he actively drew on in the writing of his plays.

At the tender age of twelve, Coward met one of the actresses who would help contribute to his overwhelming success, Gertrude Lawrence; she was then fifteen and a child performer as well. The occasional acting team of Coward and Lawrence would become synonymous with polished, sophisticated comedy during the 1920's, 1930's, and 1940's.

When he was fifteen, Coward was invited to stay at the country estate of Mrs. Astley Cooper. This stay, and subsequent visits, influenced his life markedly in two ways: He grew to know intimately the manners and mores of the upper class, and through Mrs. Cooper, he came to meet Gladys Calthrop, who was to become his lifelong friend and the designer for his productions.

Coward began his writing career when he was sixteen by writing songs and selling them for distribution. He turned his hand to playwriting when he was seventeen and found that he was very good at writing dialogue. Success came quite early to Coward. He was already accepted as an accomplished actor on the London stage when he began writing. By 1919, his play *I'll Leave It to You* was produced in the West End with Coward in the leading role. One of the idiosyncrasies of Coward's writing is that often he wrote "whacking good parts" for himself or for people he knew. Some of his best plays are essentially vehicles for his own talents or those of Gertrude Lawrence and later of the Lunts.

I'll Leave It to You met with moderate success, and Coward received great praise from critics for his playwriting abilities, although Sir Neville Cardus, writing in the *Manchester Guardian*, faulted the play for its narrow focus on the world of the idle rich. This criticism dogged Coward throughout his career.

Coward went to New York for the first time in 1921 and arrived virtually penniless. He sold three satires to *Vanity Fair* in order to support himself. Though he may have begun the 1920's in penury, Coward's position as the most popular playwright in the English theater became secure during this decade. In 1924, *The Vortex* was produced in London. Coward's most important serious play, *The Vortex* broke with English theatrical tradition in its choice of subject matter: drug addiction. This Ibsenesque approach to a problem created quite a sensation. It was hailed by many critics as an important play but also found dissenters who labeled it "filth" and "dustbin drama."

In late 1927, Coward purchased 139 acres in Kent called Goldenhurst Farm. This was the first residence he used as a retreat to escape the glitter of the stage. Eventually, he would own others in Jamaica, Paris, Geneva, and London. The years from 1928 to 1934 are regarded by many as Coward's "golden years." His string of successes during this period include some of his best and most famous plays and revues: *This Year of Grace!*, *Bitter Sweet*, *Private Lives*, *Cavalcade*, *Words and Music*, *Design for Living*, and *Conversation Piece*. According to Coward in a letter written to his mother, *Bitter Sweet* was the only show that played to capacity houses in New York during the stock market crash of 1929. By the 1930's, the opening of a Coward play in London was regularly attended by royalty and other prominent socialites.

Coward took his success and the responsibility of fame seriously. When asked to aid the Actors' Orphanage, he did so willingly and subsequently became president of the organization, a position he retained from 1934 to 1956.

After World War II, Coward fell from grace with many critics, who regarded him as being past his literary prime. The year 1949-1950 proved the lowest point in his career as he received poor reviews for his plays and scathing reviews for his film *The Astonished Heart*. The drama was changing during these restless years that would produce playwrights such as John Osborne, and Coward was momentarily out of step with the times. He turned to the writing of fiction and produced several short stories and his autobiographical work *Future Indefinite*.

By the late 1950's, audiences were once again in love with Coward. His plays, revues, and nightclub appearances were extremely successful. The critics, however, remained vitriolic, but their rancor failed to dim the enthusiasm of the general theatergoing public, who clamored for more Coward plays. In 1969, there was a seventieth birthday tribute to Coward in London that lasted a full week. On January 1, 1970, Coward's name appeared on the Queen's New Year's list as a Knight Bachelor, for services rendered to the arts. For the remaining years of his life, he was Sir Noël Coward. In the same year, he was awarded a special Tony Award by the American theater for Distinguished Achievement in the Theatre. In 1972, he received an honorary Doctor of Letters from the University of Sussex.

Coward died of a heart attack in Jamaica on March 26, 1973, bringing to an end a career of more than sixty years in the theater. The most lasting tribute awarded to Coward is the continued success that meets revivals of his plays and musicals. Coward created a mystique about himself during his lifetime, and this intangible quality of wit and sophistication has become part of the Coward legend, which has become a part of the colorful heritage of the theater.

ANALYSIS

As a playwright, composer, lyricist, producer, director, author, and actor, Noël Coward spent his life entertaining the public. This he did with a flair, sophistication, and polish that are not readily found in twentieth century drama. He wrote farce, high comedy, domestic and patriotic melodramas, musical comedies, and revues. His plays were popular fare in

England and the United States for years because Coward recognized that the "great public" for which he wrote his plays wanted, above all, to be entertained.

All of Coward's plays fall into easily recognizable stylized patterns. Essentially, Coward wrote modern comedies of manners that are as reflective of twentieth century mores and sentiments as their Restoration forebears were of those in the seventeenth century. For the most part, his plays are set in drawing rooms and usually have a couple involved in a love relationship as the central characters. He draws heavily on his theatrical background and populates his plays with theatrical and artistic characters. These temperamental personages allow Coward to involve them easily in the constant bickering and verbal fencing that came to be the trademarks of a Coward play. Each of his characters vies to get the upper hand over the others. Arguments are central to his work, and much of his humor relies on sophisticated insults. Coward's dialogue bitingly exposes hypocrites and the petty games played by the upper class; his plays parody Mayfair society mercilessly. Unfortunately, his plays involve little else. There is little motivation of character, less development of theme, and what thin remnant of plot remains is swept along in the incessant bantering of the characters. Robert Greacen, referring to *Fumed Oak*, remarked that "an observant foreigner might sit through the entire play . . . and simply hear people talking and believe that no action was taking place at all." Such statements apply to most of Coward's plays.

This criticism reveals both the strongest and the weakest aspects of Coward's theater. He was capable of writing brilliant, naturalistic dialogue with an astonishing economy. In spite of this enormous talent for writing dialogue, however, little happens in his plays to advance the plot. Most of his plays remain structurally flawed, relying heavily on the use of *deus ex machina* and coincidence for plot resolutions.

Thematically, Coward's comedies examine true love, adulterous affairs, and domestic upheavals. His more serious plays focus on a variety of topics, including drug addiction, infidelity, and patriotism. The few patriotic plays he attempted strongly support solid middle-class values and promote a stereotyped image of the stoical Englishman.

Though his works appear to have identifiable themes, they lack a thesis. Coward's plays realistically depict modern characters in absorbing situations, but the characters are not as fully developed as the situations in which they find themselves. Their motivations remain obscure. Even in the serious plays, his position on his subject is never clearly revealed. Most of his serious dramas fail because he never brings the moment to a crisis, and so his plays end anticlimactically. According to Milton Levin, Coward's plays "raise no questions, they provide few critical footholds, they simply ask to be praised for what they are, sparkling caprices."

Generally, the success of Coward's plays depended on the ability of the actors to carry his rapier-sharp dialogue. He freely admitted tailoring choice roles to his talents and those of his friends. Coward and Gertrude Lawrence in *Private Lives*, Coward and the Lunts in *Design for Living*, Coward with Beatrice Lillie in *Blithe Spirit* mark legendary moments in theatrical history that cannot be replicated. When criticizing drama, one must consider the text in production. It is this consideration that elevates the relatively weak scripts of Coward's plays to modern classics.

Embodied in Coward is a theatrical trinity of actor, playwright, and producer. The inability to separate completely one from the other in studying his works contributes to the mystique that surrounds the man. Rarely are his works found in academic anthologies of the genre, but the imprint of his productions is still discernible in the theater today.

Coward was a highly developed product of the 1920's and the 1930's and of the social milieu he frequented, and, to a not inconsiderable extent, the current popularity of his work originates in the nostalgic hunger of contemporary audiences for an age more verbally sophisticated and carefree than their own. Nevertheless, at their best, Coward's plays continue to sparkle with their author's lively sense of wit, talent for dramatic dialogue and construction, and genius for the neat twist in dramatic action. These significant talents make Coward's theater instructive as well as delightful.

DESIGN FOR LIVING

Design for Living was the end result of a plan by Coward, Alfred Lunt, and Lynn Fontanne to act in a play together, written specifically for them. They originally conceived of this idea in the early 1920's, and the gestation period required for Coward actually to write and produce the play lasted eleven years. *Design for Living* scrutinizes a free-spirited and occasionally painful *ménage à trois* comprising Gilda, an interior decorator, Otto, a painter, and Leo, a playwright. The most striking quality of the play is its completely amoral stance on marriage, fidelity, friendship, and sexual relations. Pangs of conscience are fleeting in these characters as their relationships as friends and lovers become apparent to one another and to the audience.

It is the amorality of the characters, rather than a perceived immorality, that has provoked criticism of this play. Coward forms no conclusions and passes no judgment: The play ends with the three characters embracing and laughing wildly on a sofa, and the audience is provided no clue as to how they should judge these amorous individuals. They are asked to watch and accept without being given a resolution to the plot. Most of the criticism directed at the production resulted from a misunderstanding of the title on the part of the critics. Coward intended his title to be ironic. It was taken to be an admonition that the Bohemian lifestyle depicted onstage was not merely acceptable but was actually preferable to conventional ways as a "design for living."

Design for Living was a vehicle for the formidable talents of Coward and the Lunts. The dialogue is quick and sharp as the three characters alternately pair off, argue, and reunite. The theme stressed most strongly in this play, and the one that offers its most redemptive qualities, is that of friendship. Gilda, Otto, and Leo value their mutual companionship, but their active libidos complicate their relationships. *Design for Living* was judged to be "unpleasant" by the critics, but it enjoyed a phenomenal success with audiences in England and the United States.

PRIVATE LIVES

Private Lives, considered one of Coward's best plays, "leaves a lot to be desired," by the author's own admission. The protagonists, Amanda and Elyot, are divorced and meet again while both are honeymooning with their new spouses. Their former affection for each other is rekindled, and they abandon their unsuspecting spouses and escape to Paris. Here, they are reminded of what it was in their personalities that prompted them to seek a divorce. The scene is complicated by the arrival of the jilted spouses, who come seeking reconciliation, but who eventually are spurned as Amanda and Elyot, after arguing violently, leave together, presumably to lead a life of adversarial bliss.

Amanda and Elyot are interesting, fairly well-drawn characters; these roles were written with Gertrude Lawrence and Coward in mind. The secondary characters, the spouses, Victor and Sibyl, are two-dimensional and only provide a surface off which to bounce the stinging repartee of the reunited couple. Coward himself has described *Private Lives* as a "reasonably well-constructed duologue for two performers with a couple of extra puppets thrown in to assist the plot and to provide contrast."

OTHER MAJOR WORKS

LONG FICTION: *Pomp and Circumstance*, 1960.

SHORT FICTION: *Terribly Intimate Portraits*, 1922; *Chelsea Buns*, 1925; *Spangled Unicorn*, 1932; *To Step Aside*, 1939; *Star Quality: Six Stories*, 1951; *The Collected Short Stories*, 1962; *Pretty Polly Barlow and Other Stories*, 1964; *Bon Voyage and Other Stories*, 1967; *The Complete Stories of Noël Coward*, 1985.

POETRY: *Not Yet the Dodo*, 1967; *Noël Coward: Collected Verse*, 1984.

SCREENPLAYS: *Bitter Sweet*, 1933; *In Which We Serve*, 1942; *This Happy Breed*, 1944; *Blithe Spirit*, 1946; *Brief Encounter*, 1946; *The Astonished Heart*, 1949.

NONFICTION: *Present Indicative*, 1937; *Australia Visited*, 1941; *Middle East Diary*, 1944; *Future Indefinite*, 1954; *The Noël Coward Diaries*, 1982; *Autobiography*, 1986.

MISCELLANEOUS: *The Lyrics of Noël Coward*, 1965; *The Noël Coward Song Book*, 1980; *Out in the Midday Sun: The Paintings of Noël Coward*, 1988.

BIBLIOGRAPHY

Briers, Richard. *Coward and Company*. London: Robson Books, 1987. A short, well-illustrated biography of the English actor, playwright, composer, director, producer, and bon vivant.

Castle, Terry. *Noël Coward and Radclyffe Hall: Kindred Spirits*. New York: Columbia University Press, 1996. Contains a comparison of Coward and Hall as well as of homosexuality and literature. Bibliography and index.

Citron, Stephen. *Noël and Cole: The Sophisticates*. New York: Oxford University Press, 1993. A comparison of Coward and Cole Porter as composers. Bibliography and index.

Fisher, Clive. *Noël Coward*. New York: St. Martin's Press, 1992. A biography of the multitalented Coward. Bibliography and index.

Hoare, Philip. *Noël Coward: A Biography*. New York: Simon and Schuster, 1996. A biography of the dramatist that covers his life and works. Bibliography and index.

Kaplan, Joel, and Sheila Stowell, eds. *Look Back in Pleasure: Noël Coward Reconsidered*. London: Methuen, 2000. A study of the dramatic works of Coward and his influence. Bibliography and index.

Levin, Milton. *Noël Coward*. Boston: Twayne, 1989. This short but updated biography of the playwright contains a useful bibliography.

Morella, Joe. *Genius and Lust: The Creative and Sexual Lives of Noël Coward and Cole Porter*. New York: Carroll and Graf, 1995. Morella compares and contrasts Coward and Porter, examining their works and lives. Index.

Susan Duffy,
updated by Peter C. Holloran

MICHAEL CRISTOFER
Michael Procaccino

Born: Trenton, New Jersey; January 22, 1945

PRINCIPAL DRAMA

The Mandala, pr. 1968
Plot Counter Plot, pr. 1971
Americomedia, pr. 1973
The Shadow Box, pr. 1975, pb. 1977
Ice, pr. 1976
Black Angel, pr. 1978, pb. 1984
C. C. Pyle and the Bunyon Derby, pr. 1978
The Lady and the Clarinet, pr. 1980, pb. 1985
Amazing Grace, pr. 1996
Breaking Up, pr. 1997, pb. 1999

OTHER LITERARY FORMS

Michael Cristofer is said to be a man of many talents who loves drama in all of its varied forms: He has been an actor, a screenwriter, a playwright, a producer, and a director. Although he got his start writing plays such as *The Shadow Box* in the 1970's and returned to the theatre with *Amazing Grace* and *Breaking Up* in the 1990's, Cristofer never ignored the "big screen"—the motion picture industry—because of any single-minded devotion to theater. Although writing for the stage is his preferred pursuit, Cristofer's love for dramatic writing has led him also to write screenplays. Sometimes he has rewritten his own plays, as his 1999 screenplay version of *Breaking Up*, but he created other screenplays, including his adaptation of John Updike's *The Witches of Eastwick* (1987), solely for the motion picture industry.

ACHIEVEMENTS

After he spent ten largely unremarkable years as an actor, Michael Cristofer's fortunes changed when he took his play *The Shadow Box* and produced it Off-Broadway. With this character piece about three patients at a hospice for the terminally ill, Cristofer won the 1977 Pulitzer Prize in Drama and a 1977

Tony Award. This was not the last time *The Shadow Box* would receive praise: In 1980, when he rewrote *The Shadow Box* for television, the play again was lauded—this time with the 1981 Humanitas Prize for Best Screenplay and a nomination for both a Golden Globe (Best Screenplay) and an Emmy (Best Television Drama). These accomplishments seemed to spur Cristofer on to success in his previously uncelebrated acting career; he received an Obie Award in 1979 (for his performance in *Chinchilla* at the Phoenix Theatre) and a Theater World Award (for his role Trofimov in Andre Serban's production of *The Cherry Orchard* at Lincoln Center) even though his interest in acting was waning in favor of the greater promise of success at writing. *Amazing Grace* was granted the American Theatre Critics Association's Best New Play Award in 1996. The 1998 teleplay *Gia* further demonstrated Cristofer's ability to write convincing drama: He won the Director's Guild of America Outstanding Directorial Achievement in Movies for Television Award (1998), was nominated the same year for the Writer's Guild of America Television Award (1998), and even managed to receive a nomination for an Emmy (Outstanding Writing for a Miniseries or a Movie, 1999).

BIOGRAPHY

Michael Cristofer, born Michael Procaccino, was born on January 22, 1945, to working-class parents in White Horse, New Jersey (described by Cristofer as being between Philadelphia, Pennsylvania, and Trenton, New Jersey). Deciding to pursue an acting career, Cristofer joined Washington, D.C.'s prestigious Arena Stage Company for the 1967-1968 season but was disenchanted with the roles he received. He lived in Philadelphia during the early 1970's, becoming part of the Theater of The Living Arts acting company but again felt himself stirred to go further away from home in search of fame. He briefly appeared in a repertory company in Beirut, Lebanon, served stints in a variety of Philadelphia acting troupes, and made it to Broadway in 1977, cast as Trofimov in the Lincoln Center revival of *The Cherry Orchard*.

Comparing his own experiences in New York to those of his tragic heroine in his teleplay *Gia*,

Cristofer states that he knows what life was like for an "Italian kid" who wants to leave a stifling hometown and become successful. Until *The Shadow Box* was produced on Broadway in 1977, Cristofer had met with limited success as an actor. He had had a role in the unaired pilot of *Crime Club* (Columbia Broadcasting System, 1975) and the 1976 National Broadcasting Company (NBC) remake of *The Entertainer* and had acquired two motion picture credits for his roles in *The Crazy World of Julius Vrooder* (1974) and *An Enemy of the People* (1978), but his acting had not attracted much in the way of either critical attention or financial stability. Then, in 1977, Cristofer began to receive critical praise for his work not just as an actor, but also as a writer. *The Shadow Box* was a huge critical success, garnering three major awards in four years of production.

Before *The Shadow Box*'s Broadway run, Cristofer had had a few plays produced (*The Mandala*, *Plot Counter Plot*, and *Americomedia*) but had been relatively uninterested in changing his focus from acting to writing. After *The Shadow Box*, however, Cristofer found that his writing skills (at least in terms of their critical success) overshadowed his abilities as an actor. Cristofer's last screen role was as an Arab in *The Little Drummer Girl* (1984), allowing him to turn his attention fully to the writing of dramatic works. Between 1984 and 2001, Cristofer wrote no fewer than fourteen plays and screenplays. An early produced script was *Falling in Love* (1984), a loose remake of *Brief Encounter* (1946) with Robert De Niro and Meryl Streep as married commuters who fall in love. His adaptation of John Updike's novel *The Witches of Eastwick*, starring Jack Nicholson as the creator of a modern-day coven (featuring Cher, Michelle Pfeiffer, and Susan Sarandon as modern-day witches), even proved to be as financially successful as it was critically acclaimed.

ANALYSIS

One of the most fascinating aspects of reading the theatrical works of Michael Cristofer is how often one encounters Elizabeth Kubler-Ross's five stages of dying: denial, anger, bargaining, acceptance, and, finally, transcendence. *The Shadow Box*, presenting the stories and opinions of Steven, Brian, and Felicity, three terminally ill patients, and *Amazing Grace*, describing the final days of a female serial killer on death row, deal directly (and obviously) with the issue of death, but *Breaking Up* also seems to rely thematically on Kubler-Ross's five stages for its overarching plot. In a metaphorical sense, the emotions and thought processes inherent in the ending of a relationship echo the same concerns, negotiations, and pain inherent in the termination of life. Given the parallel nature of love and life, Cristofer seems most interested in finding out how his characters handle endings—the end of love, life, and happiness.

THE SHADOW BOX

The Shadow Box depicts poignantly the struggle that the three terminally ill people and their most valued loved ones face as they try to cope with impending death in different ways: intellectualization, fantasy, and direct confrontation. The three families explore the complexity of their separate relationships as death approaches, but through clever staging the audience sees how their issues and struggles overlap. Even the conversations within each of the three "cottages" blend audibly together: one conversation, between the cancer-ridden Steven and his timid wife, Maggie, leads directly into another conversation between the intellectual Brian and his sexually daring former wife Beverly. That conversation, in turn, takes the bitterness of Brian's gay lover, Mark (who feels unappreciated), and thematically compares it to the bitterness that a mother, Felicity, feels as she waits, interminably, for the arrival of an absent daughter. The families are radically different in their methods: Steven hasn't been able to break through Maggie's steadfast denial of his terminal illness, Felicity remains alive (in spite of severe pain) through sheer force of will, and Brian, Mark, and Beverly (who all accept Brian's death with varying levels of grace) are haunted by their inability to connect emotionally with one another. Nevertheless, they remain identical in their purposes: They all seek to come to terms with their respective imminent separations.

Perhaps the most interesting aspect of *The Shadow Box*, however, is its use of an unseen Interviewer to pry open the internal thoughts of the dying. Instead of leaving the task of revealing inner thoughts to lengthy monologic passages (a common method for revealing the internal deliberation of characters), Cristofer introduces an unseen voice that spends the beginning of each scene questioning and comforting Brian, Steven, and Felicity. It is these characters' reactions to the Interviewer that help define personalities and motivations that might otherwise remain vague.

AMAZING GRACE

Cristofer's story of a woman on death row also suggests Kubler-Ross's five stages of death. *Amazing Grace* is based on the true-life story of Velma Barfield, the first woman to be executed in North Carolina since the overturning of the ban on the death penalty. Barfield, convicted of killing several elderly relatives under her care, faced the death penalty in 1984 and claimed, during her imprisonment, to have found religion in prison. Whether or not Barfield's assertion was true, Cristofer apparently found the idea of "jailhouse redemption" to be a compelling basis for a play—particularly since the jailhouse redemption in question involved the most unlikely of serial killers—a middle-aged woman.

Selena Goodall, Cristofer's character, is an emotionally disturbed woman whose frustration at her low station in life and her unsatisfactory relationships causes her, in a fit of almost uncontrollable rage, to kill her nagging, abusive mother. The feelings of power and satisfaction that wash through Goodall after killing the woman who abused her as a child are so strong that she kills several more times in an effort to recapture the feelings of self-empowerment and relief. The play describes a personal evolution that transforms her from a submissive caretaker who has only barely survived childhood abuse, to a cunning manipulator, to a death row inmate. Cheerfully engrossed in a needlepoint canvas she will not have time to finish, Goodall has found peace with herself and her death because she has accepted the "Amazing Grace" of religion. Although viewers may find it difficult to sympathize with Goodall's cheerfulness and impossible to understand her calm assurance of having been "saved," one cannot help but to wonder if Goodall has, in fact, transcended the fear and anger that her impending execution must engender in her.

BREAKING UP

Although the first two of Cristofer's plays dealt with the end of human life, it is equally fascinating to see Cristofer's contemplation of Kubler-Ross's five stages in the context of a failing relationship. His closed, two-character study of a relationship's end is almost clinical in its appraisal of the lovers' denial, anger, bargaining, acceptance, and transcendence. *Breaking Up* is rich in both comic asides and scathing, emotional tirades. Photographer Steve is shallow, evincing only the slightest interest in his schoolteacher lover's thoughts and emotions. Monica, on the other hand, constantly talks in circles around the internal tensions of her two-year love affair without managing to address any of the real issues that the two of them face. Initially denying that they have any communication problems at all, they come to realize that whatever sparks or affection they might have had for one another during their first few months together, the couple's passion has long since burned out, and they have, for all intents and purposes, lost interest in one another. Only their stubborn defiance in the face of stark reality keeps them together—a turn of affairs that makes for sharp arguments in which Steve's flippant indifference intensifies Monica's implacable fury. Although there is always the dim hope that the two could reconcile and regain their love for one another (Steve suggests on several occasions that, deep down, he still feels the sparks that originally brought them together), the possibility of such a rebirth seems too "difficult" for the emotionally lazy pair to even attempt.

The stark reality of the play and its breathtakingly accurate (and painful) portrayals of Steven and Monica's violent clashes suggest that real-life breakups, whether those of Cristofer or of his associates, are the source material for this dramatic work. If so, *Breaking Up* seems to suggest that the death of a relationship can be nearly as painful as the death of a loved one.

OTHER MAJOR WORKS

SCREENPLAYS: *Falling in Love*, 1984; *The Witches of Eastwick*, 1987 (adaptation of John Updike's novel); *Bonfire of the Vanities*, 1990 (adaptation of Tom Wolfe's novel); *Mr. Jones*, 1993; *Breaking Up*, 1997 (adaptation of his play); *Original Sin*, 2001.

TELEPLAYS: *The Shadow Box*, 1980 (adaptation of his play); *Gia*, 1998.

BIBLIOGRAPHY

Abele, Elizabeth. "Michael Cristofer." *Images: A Journal of Film and Popular Culture* 10 (March, 2001). Abele's discussion of Cristofer's treatment of the dying process (Kubler-Ross's five stages) seems particularly useful in understanding the basic themes behind many, if not most, of Cristofer's theatrical dramas. According to Abele, Cristofer seems to be constantly working through images of death and rebirth, denial and transcendence, and the processes that make living and dying so diffcult.

Amorosi, A. D. "Twenty Questions: Michael Cristofer." *City Paper* (January 29-February 5, 1998): 86-87. Amorosi's article, one of a relative handful dealing with Cristofer's theatrical writings, allows Cristofer to draw connections between his personal history and his written works. Amorosi points out how closely Cristofer associates with his focal characters, even to the point of descending into sentimentality or bathos. The success of *The Witches of Eastwick* versus the failure of *Mr. Jones* seems to describe Cristofer's overly intense preoccupation with character identification.

Rawson, Chris. "Legit Reviews: *Amazing Grace*." Review of *Amazing Grace* by Michael Cristofer. *Variety* 360, no. 13 (October 30, 1995): 18. A favorable review of a performance of *Amazing Grace* by the Pittsburgh Public Theatre.

Savlov, Mark. "*Breaking Up*." *Austin Chronicle*, October 20, 1997, pp. 62-65. Savlov interviews Australian actor Russell Crowe on the difficulties of portraying Steven, the stolid photographer in the film version of Cristofer's 1997 play *Breaking Up*. Savlov reports that Crowe found the character to be particularly difficult to play because of his uncommunicative nature and also found Cristofer's script itself to be very complex and challenging. He contrasts the differing goals of Cristofer and director Greenberg.

Julia M. Meyers

MART CROWLEY

Born: Vicksburg, Mississippi; August 21, 1935

PRINCIPAL DRAMA

The Boys in the Band, pr., pb. 1968
Remote Asylum, pr. 1970
A Breeze from the Gulf, pr. 1973, pb. 1974
Avec Schmaltz, pr. 1984
For Reasons That Remain Unclear, pr. 1993,
    pb. 1996
Three Plays, pb. 1996

OTHER LITERARY FORMS

Mart Crowley is known primarily for his plays. He wrote the screenplay for a 1970 film adaptation of *The Boys in the Band*. He is also the screenwriter of *Cassandra at the Wedding* and co-author of *Fade-in* (neither screenplay released), and has several teleplays to his credit.

ACHIEVEMENTS

Mart Crowley brought the subject of male homosexuality into the open in the American theater with his 1968 comedy-drama *The Boys in the Band*. His plays are characterized by a clashing mix of personality types and a keen comic sense for one-liners. The significance of Crowley's work rests entirely on his first play and its introduction of a once-taboo subject. The play and the subsequent film adaptation of it are important milestones in the history of gay activism in the United States. Unlike Tennessee Williams, William Inge, and Edward Albee, who kept the topic of homosexual passions on the periphery of their work, Crowley made the initial leap that openly established gay drama and unapologetically linked his own life with his writing. The playwright's outrageously comical dialogue and his daring display of his own emotional failures are the most impressive and perhaps the most enduring of his contributions to the stage. A 1996 revival of *Boys in the Band* at the WPA Theatre in New York City received critical and audience substantiation of its durability, relevance, and historical importance twenty-eight years after its first production.

BIOGRAPHY

Martino Crowley was born in Vicksburg, Mississippi, on August 21, 1935. Crowley's parents were conservative and religious, and they scrupulously brought up Mart, their only child, in the teachings of the Roman Catholic Church, enrolling him in a parochial high school in Vicksburg. His father, an Irishman from the Midwest, owned a pool hall called Crowley's Smokehouse, which bore the motto "Where all good fellows meet." As a child, Crowley was asthmatic and sickly, a condition that changed, he claims, immediately after his departure from Vicksburg. An avid filmgoer and starstruck reader of Hollywood gossip magazines since early childhood, he left home in the early 1950's, moving to Los Angeles, where he took a number of low-paying jobs in order to be near the motion-picture studios. His father, who had cherished the hope that his only son should attend Notre Dame, finally compromised and convinced Mart to attend Catholic University of America in Washington, D.C., where he won awards for costume and scene design. After two years there, Crowley, unhappy with the conservative social atmosphere in Washington, returned to Hollywood and began working on a degree in art at the University of California, Los Angeles, hoping to become a scenic designer in films. Crowley returned to Catholic University not long afterward and worked in the university theater. At one point, he collaborated with fellow collegian James Rado, later one of the writers of the rock musical *Hair* (which ran concurrently in New York with Crowley's hit *The Boys in the Band* in 1968), and the two of them produced a revue sketch. Crowley also worked in summer-stock theater in Vermont.

After his graduation from Catholic University in 1957, Crowley briefly considered joining the Foreign Service but moved back to Southern California instead, where he wrote a number of unproduced scripts for motion pictures and television. He took jobs with various film production companies, working on such films as *Butterfield* 8 (1960) and *Splendor in the*

Grass (1961). He also worked as a script-writer in the early 1960's for several television production companies. The popular film star Natalie Wood, whom Crowley met while both were working on *Splendor in the Grass*, hired him as a private secretary in 1964, a position he held until 1966. During this time, he wrote a screen adaptation of Dorothy Baker's novel *Cassandra at the Wedding* (1962) expressly for Wood and French director Serge Bourguignon. The film was never produced. Ridden with anxiety and depression, Crowley moved to Rome for a winter, staying with film star Robert Wagner and his wife, Marion.

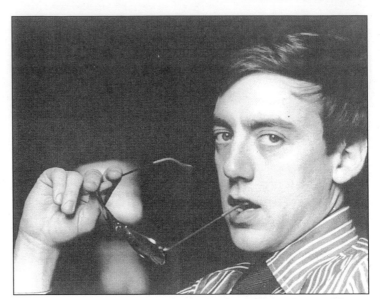

Mart Crowley in 1968. (AP/Wide World Photos)

In 1967, Paramount Studios completed a film from an original screenplay by Crowley entitled *Fade-in*. The project was a hectic and disappointing experience for the young writer, and after all of his effort, the studio did not release the film. After six months of rest and psychoanalysis to cope with this ego-flattening experience, Crowley got the idea to write a play about homosexual friends at a birthday party. (His notes on the theme of homosexuality, including fragments of dialogue and character sketches, were begun as early as 1959.) Crowley finished the play, *The Boys in the Band*, in five weeks during the summer of 1967 while he was house-sitting in the Beverly Hills home of performer Diana Lynn. The agent he subsequently contacted about the script replied that although the play was very good, she did not believe the American stage was ready for a drama almost exclusively about homosexual men. She nevertheless sent a copy of the play to producer Richard Barr, who liked it and decided to produce it at his Playwrights Unit workshop. Robert Moore, an actor who had known Crowley at Catholic University and in summer stock, expressed interest in making his debut as a stage director with the play. More difficult, however, was the task of finding performers willing to be cast in the play. A number of actors read the play and liked it but refused to risk their professional images by performing homosexual characters onstage. The play was finally

cast with an ensemble of largely unknown performers. Gay civil rights agitation began to make news in the years shortly preceding his play, but Crowley remained detached from being an activist, and asserted that he did not write *The Boys in the Band* with revolutionary intention.

The Boys in the Band first appeared at the Vandam Theatre in January of 1968. Three months later, the play made its debut on the New York stage at Theatre Four. It was a success both at the box office and with most of the theater reviewers. Apart from viciously homophobic reviews from critics such as Martin Duberman and John Simon, the reviewers judged the play for its composition and production, rather than for its subject matter. Surprisingly, the play became controversial not so much in the heterosexual as in the homosexual community. The source of the contention may be inferred from the emphasis and wording of some of the favorable mainstream reviews, which commented on the play's portrayal of the "tragic" or even "freakish" aspects of the "homosexual life-style." Such generalizations were not, however, necessarily invited by the play. The production ran for more than one thousand performances in New York and was produced with great success in London, in regional theaters across the United States well into the 1970's, and as a 1970 film featuring the original

Off-Broadway cast directed by William Friedkin. The play's director, Robert Moore, won a Drama Desk Award, and Cliff Gorman, who played the role of Emory, received an Obie Award (for performances in Off-Broadway theaters). The play was also included in several lists and anthologies of "best plays" of the 1960's. Many persons accounted for the play's success by observing that it offered the homosexual community a chance to see and hear itself represented onstage and the heterosexual community a chance to eavesdrop on the former. By the time the play had been made into a motion picture, however, a considerable portion of the gay public objected to the play on the grounds that it made homosexuality seem like a form of neurosis characterized by religious guilt, loneliness, and self-loathing. However, the 1996 WPA Theatre production brought about some amelioration of this attitude. Crowley has stated that by 1990 *The Boys in the Band* "was beginning to be politically correct again."

The year the film adaptation of *The Boys in the Band* was released, an earlier play by Crowley, *Remote Asylum*, was produced in California to universally unfavorable reviews. Opening at the end of 1970 at the Ahmanson Theatre in Los Angeles, *Remote Asylum* was not subsequently produced in New York. A third play, *A Breeze from the Gulf*, opened at the Eastside Playhouse in New York in October of 1973 to a somewhat better response. The writer's most intimate play, *A Breeze from the Gulf*, though praised for its competent writing and acting, lacked the audience appeal and the ability to stir up controversy that had made his first play a success. Its run was scarcely longer than *Remote Asylum*'s, but it took second place for a New York Drama Critics Circle Award. Crowley thereafter retired from playwriting and returned to television.

During the 1979-1980 television season, he was executive script consultant, then producer, for the ABC series *Hart to Hart*. In 1993, his latest play, *For Reasons That Remain Unclear*, was produced at the Olney Theatre Center for the Arts in Maryland and received further regional theater productions in Nebraska, Ohio, Oregon and elsewhere. Co-incidental with the 1996 New York revival of *Boys in the Band*,

an anthology of three of Crowley's plays, including *For Reasons That Remain Unclear*, was published.

In 1986, he began writing and adapting novels, such as James Kirkwood's *There Must Be a Pony* (1986), for television. He also appeared in the film adaptation of Vito Russo's book *The Celluloid Closet* (1995). He is working on *The Men from the Boys*, a sequel to *The Boys in the Band* that unites all but two of the original characters. According to interviews, he has also explored some areas for new theatrical productions.

The success of Crowley's work signaled a social change that allowed artistic discussion of the gay personality in the hands of more competent playwrights, as with Michael Cristofer's *Shadow Box* (pr. 1975, pb. 1978), Lanford Wilson's *Fifth of July* (pr., pb. 1978), and Martin Sherman's *Bent* (pr., pb. 1979). Contemporary plays dealing more directly with the gay experience, such as Harvey Fierstein's *Torch Song Trilogy* (pb. 1978-1979, pb. 1979) and Larry Kramer's *The Normal Heart* (pr., pb. 1985), about the AIDS (acquired immunodeficiency syndrome) epidemic, owe much to Crowley's groundbreaking achievement.

ANALYSIS

Mart Crowley's plays are not entirely autobiographical, but, as the playwright points out in an interview with Mel Gussow, "Any fool knows you have to live through something to write about it." As a device for giving his plays immediacy, however, each play contains a character named Michael, whom the audience is invited to let stand for the playwright himself. Crowley's persona is spared little in the psychological flayings that are characteristic of the writer's work. Contrary to what one might expect of an autobiographical protagonist, Michael/Mart does not embody positive, ideal, or necessarily healthy outlooks on life. In all of Crowley's plays, but especially in *The Boys in the Band*, Michael is characterized as self-pitying, debt-ridden, guilt-stricken, and vindictive; a failure as a friend, son, lover, and artist; a victim of excessive, intense self-scrutiny. The other characters stand in contrast to this negative image, or, to be more accurate perhaps, their personalities are in tension with his, caught in a web that alternately feeds and falls prey to Michael's repression, egotism, and anger.

Each play divulges a different part of the author's life, and consequently each play presents a separate but related galaxy of affection and social belonging. As they were produced, the plays run in reverse chronological order. *The Boys in the Band* presents a thirtyish Michael in the company of his homosexual friends and former lovers in his rented lower-Manhattan apartment. The setting for *Remote Asylum* is a run-down mansion in Acapulco, and its *dramatis personae* include a bizarre assortment of misfits and outcasts surrounding an aging female film star. The characters abuse one another in a sort of shark frenzy of emotions, and the result is a more vicious, bleaker version of Lanford Wilson's multicharactered comedies, with Crowley's emphasis falling more definitely on decadence.

A BREEZE FROM THE GULF

A Breeze from the Gulf presents Michael from age fifteen to age twenty-five. It is the most intimate of the three plays. Its only characters are Michael, his mother, Loraine, and his father, Teddy. Most of the dramatic action occurs in their family home in Mississippi, though the stage setting is only suggestive, avoiding naturalism or a sense of definite place. The play is not a simple exercise in nostalgia. The Connelly family is pathogenic; each of the three members is both victim and abuser of the other two. The play does not idealize bygone times. Its focus, which becomes gradually evident in the first act, is the painful psychological interdependency of son, father, and mother. The second act portrays a scene out of the playwright's life to which Crowley's previous two plays had only referred: the father's dying confession in the arms of his son on the floor of a hospital ward. The impact of this scene in the context of all the others is to assert that family relationships can be, and often are, morbidly corruptive to the individual human spirit.

FOR REASONS THAT REMAIN UNCLEAR

By the playwright's admission, a now older Michael appears in the character of the screenwriter Patrick in *For Reasons That Remain Unclear*. Crowley's 1993 play concerns a forty-five-year-old Hollywood writer who spends the day in Rome with an elderly American priest (Conrad) from Los Angeles whom he has encountered by chance. Retiring to Patrick's hotel room, the play's setting, the two engage in a long evening discussion that ultimately reveals that they share a disturbing past. Patrick has recognized the unsuspecting priest as one who molested him as a child. During the evening, the writer, whose character scarcely masks a cynical nature, playfully but progressively baits the priest and eventually confronts him with the latter's shameful past. When finally naming Conrad's crime to his face, Patrick is less offended by its nature than devastated that he once admired being loved by a man who withdrew his love and called it a sin. Bereft of the priest's attention, the young Patrick has been left hollow with nothing left inside but indifference and a detachment toward everything that is given any emotional credence. The experience has caused him to fill his emptiness with expensive, inanimate possessions and has blocked him for many years from writing a play. The once sunny but now shamed priest begs his former student for absolution. Patrick ultimately forgives him but his inability to love endures. Crowley, who had suffered sexual abuse as a child and had not written a play in nine years until this one, gives the drama a self-reflexive quality by making Patrick a writer. He admits that he had written the play as a kind of exorcism that helped him to purge the childhood sexual abuse he suffered. Baltimore and Washington, D.C., critics essentially praised the play and its 1993 production, calling it strong stuff that was "particularly good and gutsy." Crowley's principal plays feature protagonists grappling with low esteem stemming from homophobia, family breakdown, and child abuse.

THE BOYS IN THE BAND

Of the five plays Crowley produced within half a decade, only one, *The Boys in the Band*, earned a reputation for its writer. Twenty years after its New York opening, the play was still regarded as a landmark (historical, if not ideological) of gay drama. Its chronological proximity to the Stonewall Riots of June, 1969, lends added significance to its first production. Critic James W. Carlsen made the play the dividing point in the dramatic representation of gay men on the stage, his subtitles demarcating "Pre-*The Boys in the Band* Perceptions" and "Post-*The Boys in the Band* Portraits." The changing attitudes toward homosexuality that the play helped to inspire turned eventually against the neurotic and self-demeaning "boys" in the drama. Without making an undue claim to "literary greatness" for the play, it is possible to defend it against its detractors, whose objections are primarily ideological, by asserting its social importance as a vehicle for making gay men more visible, and thus more vocal and politically viable, in American society. While the play does reinforce certain stereotypes of male homosexuality in the characters of Michael and Emory, *The Boys in the Band* also includes a number of other "types" that were hitherto unrepresented on the stage: The gay man as athletic, virile, capable of both fidelity and promiscuity, self-knowing, "ordinary," or "masculine" appeared in this play for the first time. The play also debunked a number of flattering truisms about homosexuals, such as that all gay men are more sensitive, tasteful, or witty than heterosexual men.

The focus of most of the criticism the play has received is its central character, Michael, who experiences more than his share of self-loathing and bitterness because of his homosexuality. As his friend Harold points out to him at the end of the play, Michael's problem is not his homosexual nature but his failure to accept himself as he is. Psychologists call this type of homosexuality "ego-dystonic," and the condition is considered a treatable psychological problem. It is thus possible to interpret Michael's personality as indicative of a real psychological disorder and not as symbolic of an inherent or typical maladjustment of the homosexual mind. That it is not the latter is evident in that other characters, such as Harold, Hank, and Larry, do not appear to suffer from the same self-hatred and in that Michael's identity problem is explicitly compared to Bernard's, who struggles with feelings of inferiority because he is black. The charge that the play reinforces the prejudice that all gay men are really unhappy and that homosexual relationships are spurious is largely accurate, but it fails to take into account the tremendous step that

was taken by the playwright in presenting even a somewhat compromising portrait of gay culture.

The Boys in the Band falls into a category of mid-twentieth century American drama sometimes labeled "comedy of exacerbation": An assortment of characters reveal themselves to themselves and to one another through some sort of excruciating ordeal, often, ironically, a party game. Whatever device is used, the veneer of each participant is stripped in order to bare the fact that the basis for much of his existence is rationalization, repression, or fantasy. The characters' relationships with one another flicker between love and loathing, and the repartee is savagely witty and unnervingly accurate. The epitome of this style of drama is Edward Albee's comedy-drama *Who's Afraid of Virginia Woolf?* (pr., pb. 1962), to which *The Boys in the Band* is often compared. Albee's "Get-the-Guests" scene is structurally similar to Crowley's second act. In both, the device of a game is used to trick one of the participants into making a painful admission. Yet Michael's obsessive attempt to make his college friend Alan admit that he had a homosexual affair with a mutual friend fails and, like George and Martha's "game," backfires on him, revealing his own vulnerability and sadness.

The 1996 revival at New York's WPA Theatre had critics and theater colleagues continuing to support the play and pointing out that its portrait did not suggest that all gay relationships were as ill fated. Actor-playwright David Greenspan, to cite one example, who played the role of Harold in the 1996 production and is quoted in a review of Gerard Raymond, commented that the play was about "a specific group of people who are not conscious. . . . You see how twisted these guys have gotten from whatever experience they've had. It's like a bad Christmas dinner." Greenspan further observed that a 1990's audience still had much to learn from the drama whose less than admirable characters are all carrying torches for unavailable people and looking for love in just the wrong places, which is "still a relevant issue, and it's what makes the play so powerful."

The least that can be said for Crowley's contribution to the American theater is, sadly, also the most that can be said for it: His play *The Boys in the Band* opened up the subject of homosexuality to dramatic treatment. Though less positive than its successors, the play is no less forthright, and dramas such as Harvey Fierstein's *Torch Song Trilogy* (pb. 1978-1979, pb. 1979) and Jane Chambers's *Last Summer at Bluefish Cove* (pr. 1981, pb. 1982) would perhaps have never been were it not for Crowley's timely and trailblazing effort.

OTHER MAJOR WORKS

TELEPLAYS: *There Must Be a Pony*, 1986 (based on James Kirkwood's novel); *Bluegrass*, 1988; *People Like Us*, 1990.

BIBLIOGRAPHY

Carlsen, James W. "Images of the Gay Male in Contemporary Drama." In *Gayspeak: Gay Male and Lesbian Communication*, edited by James W. Chesebro. New York: Pilgrim Press, 1981. A serious examination of the effects of Crowley's play on social perceptions of homosexuals in the early 1970's, and of subsequent changes in the dramatic interpretations of gay characters, such as in Lanford Wilson's *Fifth of July* (pr., pb. 1978) and Martin Sherman's *Bent* (pr., pb. 1979).

DeGaetani, John L. *A Search for a Postmodern Theater: Interviews with Contemporary Playwrights*. New York: Greenwood Press, 1991. Discusses *The Boys in the Band*, especially Michael's Catholicism; Crowley notes that the "Catholic Church still [1991] teaches that homosexual practices are a sin." Good update on Crowley's views on gay rights, homophobia, Cardinal John Joseph O'Connor, and AIDS.

Epstein, Hap. Review of *For Reasons That Remain Unclear* by Mart Crowley. *Washington, D.C., Times*, November 15, 1993. Epstein points out that whether or not the play holds autobiographical clues, the playwright's drought is over. Citing the play as "particularly good and gutsy," he commends Crowley's treatment of the issue of child molestation and the Catholic priesthood.

Feingold, Michael. "Queerly Beloved." *Village Voice* 27 (July 2, 1996): 82. Includes a review of *The Boys in the Band*. Feingold dismisses as minor flaws the drama's plot contrivances and datedness of 1968 gay types held up for comparison with 1996. He praises Crowley as the first and most effective anthologist of gay urban behavior.

Kroll, Gerry. "And the Band Played On." *Advocate* 708 (July 28, 1996): 47. Kroll profiles Crowley's career leading up to the success of *The Boys in the Band* and his thoughts of writing a sequel. Crowley's reaction to the 1968 performance is discussed; the playwright felt the play was unfairly criticized as being pessimistic and cited the characters of Hank and Larry as reflecting a positive relationship.

Raymond, Gerard. "Boys Will Be Boys: Crowley's Characters Get a Second Opinion." *Village Voice* 25 (July 2, 1996): 83. Discusses the 1996 revival, its actors and their opinions about their characters, the drama's issues, and the audience's reaction.

Rouseck, J. Wynn. "*Reasons* Finds Mystery Outside the Confessional." *Baltimore Sun*, November 16, 1993. Cites that the play is Crowley's first in nine years, and deals courageously with controversial issues within the Catholic Church. Rouseck notes that on the same day the play opened, and the day after, two scandals concerning Catholic clergy and sexual abuse occurred.

Scheie, Timothy. "Acting Gay in the Age of Queer: Pondering the Revival of *Boys in the Band*." *Modern Drama* 42, Spring, 1999: 1-15. Scheie defines the attitude and persona of the gay spectator, the queer spectator, and the humanist spectator. He notes that all three audience types will come together to watch *The Boys in the Band* in a shared recognition of history, desire, and constraint.

Joseph Marohl,
updated by Thomas J. Taylor
and Christian H. Moe

JOHN CROWNE

Born: Shropshire, England; c. 1640
Died: London, England; April, 1712

PRINCIPAL DRAMA

Juliana: Or, The Princess of Poland, pr., pb. 1671
*The History of Charles the Eighth of France: Or,
    The Invasion of Naples by the French*, pr. 1671,
    pb. 1672
Calisto: Or, The Chaste Nymph, pr., pb. 1675
    (music by Nicholas Staggins)
The Country Wit, pb. 1675, pr. 1676
*The Destruction of Jerusalem by Titus Vespasian,
    Parts I and II*, pr., pb. 1677
The Ambitious Statesman: Or, The Loyal Favorite,
    pr., pb. 1679
Thyestes, pr., pb. 1681
City Politiques, pr., pb. 1683
Sir Courtly Nice: Or, It Cannot Be, pr., pb. 1685
    (adaptation of Agustín Moreto y Cabaña's
    comedy *No puede ser: O, No puede ser guardar
    una mujer*)
Darius, King of Persia, pr., pb. 1688
The English Friar: Or, The Town Sparks, pr., pb. 1690
Regulus, pr. 1692, pb. 1694
The Married Beau: Or, The Curious Impertinent,
    pr., pb. 1694
Caligula, pr., pb. 1698
The Dramatic Works of John Crowne, pb. 1872-
    1874 (4 volumes; James Maidment and W. H.
    Logan, editors)
The Comedies of John Crowne, pb. 1984 (B. J.
    McMullin, editor)

OTHER LITERARY FORMS

John Crowne is remembered primarily for his
plays, although he also wrote some verse and a novel,
*Pandion and Amphigenia: Or, The History of the Coy
Lady of Thessalis* (1665).

ACHIEVEMENTS

John Crowne was one of many playwrights who
flourished in the small but intense theatrical world of
Restoration London. In some ways, he is the archetypal dramatist of the time. He wrote to gain royal
favor and to advance socially; he wrote in several
genres to satisfy the taste of his aristocratic audience: court masques, historical tragedy, heroic tragedy, comedy of wit, and tragicomedy. Crowne's plays
commented, directly and indirectly, on contemporary
political and social issues. Despite the attention to
relevance, Crowne patterned his plays on the best
models: Seneca, William Shakespeare, and Jean Racine in tragedy; Lope de Vega Carpio and Molière in
comedy. That Crowne's career spanned a quarter of a
century suggests that he was popular and skillful and
an important playwright.

From the dramatic variety of the time, two genres
emerge as characteristically Restoration. The first is
heroic tragedy. John Dryden was the preeminent
practitioner of the form in plays such as *All for Love:
Or, The World Well Lost* (pr. 1677) and *The Conquest
of Granada by the Spaniards* (part I, pr. 1670, part II,
pr. 1671). Crowne is somewhat beneath Dryden's
level of achievement. Lacking Dryden's skill in poetry and subtlety in psychological conflict, Crowne
successfully created larger-than-life heroes and
placed them amid spectacular action.

The second genre is the comedy of wit. Here again,
Crowne ranks immediately below the best writers,
such as Sir George Etherege and William Wycherley.
Though somewhat weak in plotting, Crowne excelled
in creating ingenious situations, introducing farcical stage business, and portraying eccentric *dramatis
personae*—the sort that good character actors very
much like to play.

Though his tragedies are badly outdated by their
idealism about monarchy and their relevance to Restoration politics, his comedies are less so. Several
were revived occasionally in the 1700's. The gem
among them is *Sir Courtly Nice*, which remained a
staple of the eighteenth century theater and is refreshingly amusing still.

BIOGRAPHY

John Crowne was the son of William Crowne, who fought on the Parliamentary side in the English Civil War. In 1657, he accompanied his father to America, and while the elder Crowne established a proprietorship in Nova Scotia province, young Crowne enrolled in Harvard College. William Crowne's claim to Nova Scotia was made doubtful by a partner's perfidy and by the restoration of Charles II; therefore, in 1660 John Crowne accompanied his father to London, where they sought royal protection for the proprietorship. In the meantime, Crowne earned a living by becoming a gentleman-usher to an elderly lady and by writing a prose romance in the style of Sir Philip Sidney's *Arcadia* (1590). The family's hopes for reclaiming the proprietorship ended in 1667 when Charles II ceded Nova Scotia to the French.

Most scholars agree that Crowne wrote plays in order to provide an income and to secure Charles II's royal favor so that he might compensate the family for its lost lands. Crowne succeeded in the first goal but not in the second. For fourteen years (1671-1685), Crowne strove mightily to please Charles and his court. He wrote plays virtually on command, often following the king's advice for themes, characters, or Continental models to imitate. Crowne's dramas in these years are clearly Royalist in sentiment. They articulate aristocratic values and defend Charles against his enemies. Unfortunately for Crowne, Charles had more people who sought favors than he had resources with which to favor them.

After Charles's death in 1685, Crowne continued to support himself by his pen. He wrote, saw produced, and had published six plays in the next thirteen years. By the late 1690's, however, his health was failing; he was plagued by what he described as "a distemper, which seated itself in my head, and threatened me with an epilepsy." Crowne secured an annual pension from Queen Anne, which lasted until 1706. After that, it is unclear how he was able to live; presumably, he resided in poverty and went unremarked by a new generation. In 1712, he died.

ANALYSIS

John Crowne wrote seven tragedies and five com-edies, frequently repeating character types, plot devices, and thematic concerns from play to play. His method and his achievement can be best understood by a close analysis of three plays. *The Destruction of Jerusalem by Titus Vespasian* was his most popular tragedy and remains a good example of the peculiar type of Restoration tragedy called heroic drama. In *Sir Courtly Nice*, Crowne's most successful comedy of wit, clever men and women of fashion compete with one another in wordplay and intriguing. *City Politiques* is unlike Crowne's other comedies; it relies on farce and on the ridicule of specific contemporary personalities for its impact, but even the modern reader who does not understand the political allusions can appreciate Crowne's ability to keep the stage filled with interesting characters and action.

THE DESTRUCTION OF JERUSALEM BY TITUS VESPASIAN

Like Restoration tragedies in general, *The Destruction of Jerusalem by Titus Vespasian* interweaves complex love plots and complicated political plots. The complexities of love Crowne borrowed from the same source that all of his fellow dramatists used: French romances and tragedies of the early and middle 1600's. The political complications Crowne took from the world around him. The restoration of the monarchy in 1660 had neither ended the competition for power between the king and Parliament nor stilled the loud debate over whether the English throne should be occupied by a Protestant or a Catholic monarch.

Crowne's *The Destruction of Jerusalem by Titus Vespasian* was patterned after John Dryden's *The Conquest of Granada by the Spaniards*, which had been a great success in the early 1670's. Like Dryden, Crowne wrote his play in rhyming couplets (imitating the French tragedies that Charles II loved) and doubled the normal length to ten acts. In both plays, the action centers on several monarchs who are caught in a maze of political and romantic obligations. Finally, Crowne followed Dryden in using special stage effects to heighten the tension. If Crowne had lived three centuries later, he could have easily written scripts for cinema epics.

The action of *The Destruction of Jerusalem by Titus Vespasian, Part I* commences on the eve of Passover, 72 C.E. The city of Jerusalem awaits the arrival of a Roman army under Titus Vespasian. The city's high priest and governor, Matthias, works to prepare the defenses, but he faces insubordination from John, leader of the Pharisee party, who believes that Matthias is secretly in the Romans' pay. Matthias governs in place of the Jewish king, recently killed under mysterious circumstances. The dead monarch's sister Berenice, appointed by the Romans to rule, has returned to the city in the hope of preventing resistance to the imperial army. Berenice's heart, however, is not in her mission, because she is in love with Titus, the son of the Emperor Vespasian.

Also present in the city are two exiled monarchs, Phraartes and Monobazus, who have fallen in love with Jewish noblewomen. Phraartes, who believes that religion is a myth supporting the divine right of kings, loves Matthias's daughter Clarona, a vestal virgin of the temple. Clarona is attracted to Phraartes but refuses to violate her vow of eternal virginity. Monobazus loves Berenice, but his ability to woo is inhibited by his secret knowledge that he is her brother's murderer. Berenice, smitten by Titus, hardly notices Monobazus.

Though neither king makes progress in courting his beloved, both use their swords effectively. First they fight off the Edomites, a neighboring tribe invited by John to invade the city on the pretext of forestalling the Romans. Next they rescue Matthias when John leads the Pharisees in open rebellion and captures the temple. Phraartes demands from Matthias Clarona's hand in marriage as his reward. The high priest is willing if a legal loophole can be found that would release Clarona from her vows. As they deliberate his daughter's fate, a messenger announces that the Roman army has made camp on nearby hills. On this ominous note, part I ends.

Part II opens with Titus pacing in his tent, torn between his love for Berenice and his duty to the empire. Titus's second-in-command convinces him that duty is superior to love, and two allied kings convince Titus to conquer before the Jews can rally under a new leader. Berenice arrives at the Roman camp soon afterward, but after a long and passionate interview, Titus pushes her away.

Inside Jerusalem, conditions worsen as food supplies dwindle. John continues his efforts to kill or capture Matthias. Phraartes is wounded in a second skirmish against the Pharisees. As Clarona binds his wound, she admits her love and hints that if the two of them can save the city, she might renounce her vow. In the meantime, the Jews lose an ally: Monobazus follows Berenice to the Roman camp.

Phraartes departs in search of food supplies. Returning with some provisions, he finds Matthias again in the hands of the Pharisees and once more rescues him. Phraartes now promises Clarona that he will bring in his own Parthian troops to save the city. Titus acts to counter Phraartes' plans even though Berenice attempts to distract the Roman general by threatening to kill herself if her love is not requited. With a heavy heart, Titus chooses duty over love. Berenice fails to carry out her threat.

Monobazus, now ashamed of his beloved and his love, returns to join Phraartes in the city's defense. The two kings find the temple desecrated by John's forces and discover Matthias and Clarona mortally wounded. After his beloved dies in his arms, Phraartes decides to give up his life fighting the invaders. Monobazus decides to do the same after passing up the chance to flee the doomed city. They die like brothers, side by side in combat.

Titus enters the city in triumph and spares the survivors. Berenice visits him one last time, and when he again refuses to return her love, she goes into permanent and secret exile. As the play ends, Titus stands alone onstage, still agonizing over whether duty can be worth such a sacrifice.

It is easy to discern political themes in the play in which the Restoration audience could see their own concerns reflected. The Jews face aggression from the greatest power in the world, Rome, just as England feared domination by neighboring France, which, under Louis XIV, was Europe's most powerful nation. The Jewish resistance against the invader is hampered by internal dissension, just as Charles's policies were hampered by opposition from anti-Royalist groups.

The most important political theme centers on the rulers in the play: Phraartes, Monobazus, Matthias, and Titus. The hero is not any of these but rather the institution of kingship itself. The four represent facets of Charles II, his life, his obligations, and his privileges. Phraartes and Monobazus are kings in exile, echoes of the Charles who was in exile in the 1650's. Although they have no kingdoms that obey them, Phraartes and Monobazus speak and act with a natural and convincing authority; clearly, they believe that the authority of kingship flows from divine approbation rather than from popular will. Matthias represents the besieged ruler who struggles bravely against the odds when domestic rebels join foreign enemies in threatening the state. Titus shows the personal sacrifice that kingship demands: For the good of the state, he must deny the longings of his own soul and reject the woman he loves. There is not a consistent political allegory in the play; rather, Crowne presents several vantage points from which to survey the character of a king.

All of the rulers speak eloquently about political obligation: Their diction is elegant and their imagery rich in metaphor. Phraartes and Titus speak with the same poetic force about love. Phraartes with Clarona and Titus with Berenice engage in lengthy debates that reveal the depth of their commitment. What makes the lovers' anguish such good stage business is that each pair is caught in an inescapable dilemma: Clarona has made eternal vows to a religion Phraartes despises; Berenice and Titus must be traitors in order to be lovers. As Crowne devises the situations, lifelong doubt, exile, or death are the only solutions.

Spectacular staging heightens the emotional impact of the play's political themes and romantic dilemmas. An angel appears against the ceiling of the temple to prophesy the doom of the city, and the ghost of Herod walks abroad to do the same. The laments of enslaved citizens and dying warriors are heard offstage, and there is an abundance of swordplay, chases, and stabbings onstage. In the tenth act, the temple catches fire, and Phraartes and Monobazus (seen in silhouette) fall from a prominent battlement as they are fighting Romans. The stage itself is an ambitious multilevel setting from which Matthias can look down at rebel Pharisees, the exiled kings can glare down at invaders, and the nightdress-clad Clarona can gaze down at her lover. No wonder *The Destruc-*

tion of Jerusalem by Titus Vespasian was Crowne's greatest success in the 1670's.

SIR COURTLY NICE

Among his comedies, *Sir Courtly Nice* was Crowne's most popular play, and it has retained its reputation as his best. Like other Restoration comedies of wit, it combines a love plot with social commentary. Its themes are love, marriage, and independence: *Sir Courtly Nice*'s dual heroines struggle to achieve the third without sacrificing the first two.

Violante, in love with Lord Bellguard, hesitates to marry him because of his treatment of his unmarried sister Leonora. Bellguard has set a maiden aunt and two eccentric kinsmen (the religious fanatic Testimony and the antireligious zealot Hothead) to watch over the girl. These three sentinels hinder Leonora's romance with Farewel, the son of a rival noble family. Bellguard is cautious because he thinks that all women are promiscuous by nature. Violante and Leonora decide to teach Bellguard a lesson.

Violante asks Farewel to help, and he suggests that they employ Crack, a poor but ingenious scholar expelled from the university for studying magic. Their first victim is Surly, a cynical and unpleasant man in love with Violante. She promises to respond to Surly's awkward advances if he chases away Bellguard's choice of suitor for Leonora, Sir Courtly Nice. Meanwhile, Crack, disguised as a traitor, gains access to Leonora and gives her a locket containing Farewel's picture.

Surly visits Sir Courtly, a man of elegant, even fastidious, manners. Arriving drunk, Surly annoys Sir Courtly by announcing his intention to woo Leonora. Surly annoys him to an even greater extent when he exhales his foul-smelling breath.

Bellguard meanwhile finds Farewel's picture in Leonora's possession and accuses her of being a wanton. With the sentinels in an uproar over the accusation, Crack enters in a new guise and manages to right the situation. Pretending to be Bellguard's crazy but rich cousin, Sir Thomas Calico, he provides Leonora with an absurd alibi. Bellguard, deferring to the wisdom of the wealthy, accepts the lame excuse. Crack tells Leonora that Farewel will visit her that night.

Sir Courtly comes courting. Leonora's aunt wishes to remain behind to supervise the lovers, but Bellguard escorts her out of the room. Leonora listens to Courtly's smug and silly avowals of love and responds mockingly. Surly interrupts to woo Leonora himself and to taunt Courtly. Against his will, Courtly timorously challenges Surly to a duel in order to save face.

Meanwhile, Crack sneaks Farewel into Leonora's room. Her aunt discovers his presence, and an alarmed Bellguard hunts for the intruder throughout the house. Crack comes to the rescue again by declaring that it was he who let Farewel, whom he identifies as his future brother-in-law, into the house. Bellguard is willing to forgo suspicion if Leonora promises to listen once more to Courtly's proposal. She tries, but she indignantly leaves the room as Courtly professes love and offers marriage as he stands gazing fondly at himself in a mirror. The aunt, entering the room and seeing no other woman, takes Courtly's words as applying to herself. When she loudly accepts, Courtly is too preoccupied to notice her misinterpretation.

Leonora takes her fate into her own hands, leaving Bellguard's house to marry Farewel. Violante praises her friend's love and brave spirit, contrasting it with the aunt's betrayal of trust at the first opportunity. Bellguard is finally convinced that not all women need close supervision. As a final test, Violante teases Bellguard by flirting with Surly. When Bellguard responds with passionate declarations rather than jealous accusations, Violante knows she has a man on her terms. No longer afraid that Bellguard will try to control her as he did Leonora, Violante agrees to become his wife.

Crowne wrote *Sir Courtly Nice* as an adaptation of a Spanish comedy, *No puede ser: O, No puede ser guardar una mujer* (1661), by Agustín Moreto y Cabaña. Charles II himself suggested the adaptation to Crowne, who revised the original to suit an English audience and his own dramatic skills. The Spanish play had used the framing device of a debate about the nature of women that leads to a wager. Crowne abandoned that device and began his comedy *in medias res*. One of Crowne's favorite techniques was to multiply character types. In *Sir Courtly Nice*, he

uses not one eccentric kinsman but two and has Crack appear in a variety of disguises. The effect is a more lively play; more characters enter and leave the stage than in most comedies.

Crowne's strength was not in the creation of memorable leading characters but in forming a cast with several strong roles. Indeed, the enduring popularity of *Sir Courtly Nice* can in part be attributed to its appeal to acting companies. There are numerous good parts, and even the smaller roles add distinctively to the whole. The play depends for success not on one or two stars but on the successful interaction of the company. Crowne worked closely with actors and actresses, often tutoring them about the way he imagined his characters being played. *Sir Courtly Nice* is an actor's play as much as it is the author's play.

All of Crowne's characters are strong. Violante and Leonora are atypical Restoration heroines who possess more initiative and spirit than women—real or fictitious—were allowed in the seventeenth century. Testimony and Hothead are bold caricatures of mentalities that were powerful and respected in the age. Sir Courtly is a magnificent fop whose folly is not exposed by others so much as it is revealed by his own actions; his every mannerism betrays the narcissism that leads to his comeuppance in the mirror scene. Surly is a delightful foil to Courtly—one of the crudest of numerous ill-mannered Restoration rakes. These characters interact in a comedy that is always funny, though not always kind. Their story is one that does not pale, the perennially interesting tale of young lovers who must use ingenuity to circumvent the objections of the older generation—or of their peers who prematurely think like the older generation.

CITY POLITIQUES

Crowne's other important play, *City Politiques*, does not fit into any established genre of comedy. It is too politically oriented to be a romantic comedy; it has too many scenes of farce to be a comedy of wit or a comedy of manners. It is a play of its time, when a playwright employed his dramatic skills on behalf of his patron or of his party. The years from 1678 to 1682 were a time of serious political crisis in England, and when King Charles emerged victorious from that crisis, Crowne celebrated the triumph with a satiric production that ridiculed the Whigs, the enemies of royal rule. *City Politiques* laughs at the issues and personalities of the Popish Plot from the safe vantage of hindsight.

The Popish Plot crisis began in 1678 when a former clergyman, Titus Oates, claimed that he had uncovered a plan by which English Catholics, the pope, and the French king intended to assassinate the Protestant Charles II and replace him with his Catholic brother, James. On the sworn testimony of Oates and several others, thousands of Catholics were implicated and arrested; two dozen were put to death. Charles's opponents united to campaign for the Exclusion Bill, which would remove the incentive for a plot by barring James from the succession. Charles opposed the measure, but for the next two years, both Parliament and the city of London were dominated by the bill's supporters. With many of his nobility and the country's major city hostilely disposed, Charles's reign became difficult. In 1681, after much of Oates's testimony had been discredited, the king dissolved the Whig-dominated Parliament. By 1682, the Whig control of London had collapsed, and many leaders of the party fled the country. Except for the emotional scars, the crisis was over.

City Politiques, a series of connected sketches more than a coherent play, ridicules the assumptions and practices of the Whigs during the Popish Plot. It shows ambitious statesmen relying on false oaths to gain selfish ends, citizens defying authority under the cover of respectability but actually motivated by mere whimsy, and lawyers using the laws against the source of all law, the king. Contemporaries delighted in drawing connections between the characters Crowne put on the stage and the actual persons who had important roles in the plot. Modern readers do not enjoy such identifications long after the fact, but they can enjoy Crowne's clever dramatization of humankind's less respectable motives for action.

The action of *City Politiques* occurs in Naples, where the rakish nobleman Florio plans to seduce Rosaura, the young second wife of the newly elected Podesta (mayor of the city). To attain his goal Florio pretends to be a supporter of the Podesta; he also pre-

tends to be incapacitated by venereal disease. In the course of his scheme, Florio befriends the Podesta's son, Craffy, who confides one day that he is in love with his stepmother. When Florio threatens to tell the Podesta, Craffy replies that he will get a dozen paid informants to swear that Florio is the woman's lover.

The Podesta and his followers, openly called Whigs, celebrate his election by acting rudely to the royal governor. When the governor refuses their request to have the Podesta knighted, the mayor vows to gain revenge by fomenting rebellion. One of his supporters is the lawyer Bartoline, who has recently married a much younger woman, Lucinda. Her beauty immediately attracts the eye of another rake, Artall, who disguises himself as Florio. Thinking "Florio" a dying man, Bartoline leaves Lucinda with him while he goes about the Podesta's business. Artall uses the opportunity to teach her the difference between a virile nobleman and an impotent lawyer.

The Podesta continues to harass the governor. He calls the citizens to arms by spreading rumors that a foreign army is poised to invade, and he hires Bartoline to prepare a false indictment against the governor. Bartoline, however, is playing a double game: At the same time he helps the Podesta indict the governor, he is helping the governor press charges against the Podesta and his followers. Florio meanwhile harasses the Whigs by publishing a mock proclamation against them.

Florio goes to Rosaura's apartment. A drunken Craffy interrupts their assignation, attempting to seduce Rosaura while Florio pretends to be the Podesta asleep on the couch. When the real Podesta enters the house, Rosaura tricks Craffy into attacking his father while Florio escapes. Father and son wrestle each other to the ground before realizing their mistake.

Later, Artall again tricks Bartoline. Hoping that the dying Florio (Artall in disguise) will include Lucinda in his will, Bartoline allows his wife to visit Florio's bedroom. At the same time, Craffy discovers the real Florio making love to Rosaura in a nearby room. Craffy calls the Podesta, but the mayor is assured by Bartoline that Florio is with Lucinda and must not be disturbed. Thus, the two rakes complete the double cuckolding while Craffy is deemed mad. Afterward, "Florio" brazenly carries Lucinda from her husband's house while Bartoline watches helplessly.

Florio plays one more trick on the Podesta. His servant Pietro pretends to be a Spanish nobleman with influence on the governor. Pietro promises to help the Podesta become lord treasurer if he will betray his followers, and the Podesta enthusiastically agrees. When the governor arrives at the mayor's house, however, it is with a warrant, not a knighthood, in hand. The Podesta is under arrest for causing false alarms among the citizens. Bartoline, too, is under arrest: To gain revenge on "Florio," he paid several informants to accuse him of treason. When he identifies Artall as Florio, Bartoline is arrested for harassing an innocent bystander. The governor concludes the play by warning everyone to leave politics to those properly in authority.

City Politiques shows that once a citizen has broken faith with his legitimate ruler, he can expect no one to keep faith with him. After the Podesta begins to plot against the governor, his son attempts to steal his wife, his best friend succeeds in seducing her, and his lawyer tries to frame him. Likewise, if a man has betrayed his ruler, he will betray anyone, as the Podesta plans to betray his followers. Political rebellion leads to the loss of fidelity at all levels of society.

Phrased this way, the theme of *City Politiques* is indeed serious, but its onstage execution is humorous. Florio and Artall are witty seducers, as anxious to puncture the husband's pomposity as to enjoy the wife. Craffy is a zany and incompetent would-be rake, so infatuated with Rosaura that he talks to himself about his passion even in his father's presence. Bartoline lisps peculiarly and gratingly, making numerous inadvertent puns. The stage business is as inventive as the characters' speaking habits. Craffy's wrestling match with his father wrecks the entire room; the dual cuckolding unfolds daringly and rapidly.

Proof that Crowne's satire struck home was his fate after the play opened: Outraged Whigs assaulted him on the street. Whatever pains Crowne suffered on that occasion must have been eased by his knowledge that the play was a success. London audiences relished his satiric depiction of those who, only months before, had been powerful and feared enemies.

OTHER MAJOR WORKS

LONG FICTION: *Pandion and Amphigenia: Or, The History of the Coy Lady of Thessalis*, 1665.

POETRY: "A Poem on the Death of King Charles," 1685; "The History of a Love Between a Parisian Lady and a Young Singing Man," 1692.

BIBLIOGRAPHY

Canfield, J. Douglas. "*Regulus and Cleomenes* and 1688: From Royalism to Self-Reliance." *Eighteenth Century Life* 12 (November, 1988): 67-75. Crowne's tragedy *Regulus* shows a Royalist perspective on the Revolution of 1688. The play draws a parallel between Great Britain and ancient Carthage, suggesting that by banishing warriors loyal to the rightful rulers, rebel leaders invite divine vengeance on the kingdom. Crowne argues dramatically that faithfulness is the most important virtue in a nation's political life.

_____. *Tricksters and Estates: On the Ideology of Restoration Comedy*. Lexington: University Press of Kentucky, 1997. Canfield includes considerable discussion of lesser Restoration comedy dramatists such as Crowne, as well as the masters.

Cordner, Michael. "Marriage Comedy After the 1688 Revolution: Southerne to VanBrugh." *Modern Language Review* 85 (April, 1990): 273-289. Crowne's *The Married Beau* is one of many comedies of the time whose plot concerns the marital disharmony following a wife's discovery of her husband's real or supposed adultery. Unlike Restoration wives who repaid infidelity with infidelity, postrevolutionary wives remained determinedly virtuous. In a new age, dramatists unhesitatingly changed the convention of Restoration comedy.

Kaufman, Anthony. "Civil Politics—Sexual Politics in John Crowne's *City Politiques*." *Restoration: Studies in English Literary Culture, 1660-1700* 6 (Fall, 1982): 72-80. Kaufman examines how the games of seduction and sexual competitiveness that form the plot of Crowne's most famous comedy are a metaphor for the political struggle between Whigs and Tories during the Popish Plot and Exclusion crisis of 1678-1682.

Murrie, Eleanor Boswell. *The Restoration Court Stage, 1660-1702, with a Particular Account of the Production of "Calisto."* 1932. Reprint. New York: Barnes and Noble, 1966. Part 3 of this study of plays performed at Charles II's court focuses on the production of Crowne's masque *Calisto*. It reports in fascinating detail the information that has survived about the performance: the lists of ladies and gentlemen of the court who performed in minor roles and in the chorus, the cost of the elaborate sets, the ushers' instructions for seating the audience, and the costumes worn by the royal princesses who took the leading roles.

Owen, Susan J. *Restoration Theatre and Crisis*. Oxford, England: Clarendon Press, 1996. Owen examines the connection between politics and drama, devoting a chapter to Crowne and discussing *The Ambitious Statesman*.

White, Arthur Franklin. *John Crowne: His Life and Dramatic Works.* Cleveland, Ohio: Western Reserve University Press, 1922. This classic study examines the life and works of Crowne.

Robert M. Otten

SOR JUANA INÉS DE LA CRUZ
Juana Inés de Asbaje y Ramírez de Santillana

Born: San Miguel Nepantla, Mexico; November, 1648 (baptized December 2, 1648)
Died: Mexico City, Mexico; April 17, 1695

PRINCIPAL DRAMA

Amor es más laberinto, wr. 1668, pr. 1689 (with Juan de Guevara)

El divino Narciso, pr. c. 1680, pb. 1690 (*The Divine Narcissus*, 1945)

Los empeños de una casa, pr. c. 1680, pb. 1692 (based on Lope de Vega Carpio's play *La discreta enamorada*; *A Household Plagued by Love*, 1942)

El mártir del Sacramento, San Hermenegildo, pr. c. 1692, pb. 1692

El cetro de José, pb. 1692

The Three Secular Plays of Sor Juana Inés de la Cruz, pb. 2000

OTHER LITERARY FORMS

Sor Juana Inés de la Cruz is better known for her poetry and one celebrated prose work than for her dramatic output. Though Sor Juana wrote more than four hundred poems—including sonnets, *romances* (eight-syllable lines with assonance in even lines), *redondillas* (four eight-syllable line verses with an *abba* rhyme pattern), *décimas* (ten eight-syllable line verses rhymed *abba-ac-cddc*), and *villancicos* (church carols)—her fame rests on a relatively small number of poems; she is probably best known for her sonnets. Although her poems are Baroque in style, many of them are beautifully lyric and clear; they frequently treat the subjects of love and disillusionment.

Primero Sueño (first dream), her long poem of almost one thousand lines, is in imitation of Luis de Góngora y Argote's *Soledad primera* (1613; *First Solitude*, 1964). In this dream narrative, her soul ascends to heavenly exaltation, but then descends to devote itself to scholarly pursuits and methodical knowledge. It has been described by the critic Francisco López Camara as "a hymn to the awakening of the spirit of investigation or research, and an unsuspected forerunner of the poetry of the eighteenth century Enlightenment."

Her most famous prose work, *Respuesta de la poetisa a la muy ilustre Sor Filotea de la Cruz* (1700; reply of the poetess to the illustrious Sister Filotea de la Cruz), written March 1, 1691, is invaluable for the light it throws on Sor Juana's life. In 1690, she had written a criticism of a sermon by the famous Portuguese Jesuit priest Antonio de Vieyra. The Bishop of Puebla was so impressed by it that he had it printed and then wrote her praising the work but suggesting that she limit herself to theological discussions and avoid secular matters; he signed the letter "Sor Filotea de la Cruz." Sor Juana's lengthy prose reply provides a wealth of biographical information concerning her material existence as well as her mentally tortured life.

ACHIEVEMENTS

Sor Juana Inés de la Cruz is regarded as the most important writer of colonial Latin America. Daughter of a Basque father and Creole mother, she inherited physically from both continents. This heritage was enhanced by broad religious and secular study and development, so that she was a literary fusion of Spain and her native Mexico.

Seventeenth century Spain was the heyday of the Baroque, and it is in this vein that most of Sor Juana's writings were couched. Yet her style is not stilted, nor even as intricate in many cases as that of her master, Góngora, nor of the dramatic author Pedro Calderón de la Barca, many of whose writings she imitated. She demonstrated extraordinary skill in handling Baroque conventions, infusing her delicate language with feminine vision and sensitivity. This sensitivity and poetic beauty won for her the title among her contemporaries of "the tenth muse"; she is considered the last great lyric poet of Spain and the first great poet of America. Many of her sonnets and shorter lyric poems are distinguished by their transparent clarity and exquisite beauty; she stands out as the supreme poet of her time in Castilian Spanish.

Sor Juana spent most of her life within the confines of the convent, although the nun had previously enjoyed courtly life in the viceroyalty of Mexico. Her yearning for knowledge and her acute interest in secular matters did not, however, discourage her devotion to the religious life; she was neither a reformer nor a critic. Her writings display a spirit in conflict: an awareness of, and attraction to, both the religious and the secular. Both her poetic and dramatic works

Sor Juana Inés de la Cruz (Library of Congress)

frequently express *encontradas correspondencias* (triangular antitheses) wherein A loves B, but B does not reciprocate; C loves A, but A does not love C. This structure is exemplified in her famous *romance* in which the poetess loves Fabio, who does not love her; and Silvio loves her, but she does not reciprocate his love. At times her penchant for logical structures and argumentation dominates her verse: Her preoccupation with ideas may seem greater than her concern for artistic creation.

As a poet of the New World, Sor Juana was aware of native culture and sympathetic to it, while being basically and deeply Christian. Native culture is interwoven into her writings, especially the dramatic works. This characteristic can be seen in *Loa* for *The Divine Narcissus*. Occident, when urged to become Christian, explains that the native Indians have their Communion just as the Christians do. Her empathy for the indigenous peoples of America appears elsewhere as well.

Sor Juana was a passionate scholar as well as a poet. Her scholarly pursuits were always within the bosom of the Church; her works show a deep familiarity with the Christian Scriptures and Catholic canon, while revealing a scholarly cognizance of history. They demonstrate her awareness of new discoveries and scientific thinking and include praise for scientific knowledge and method. This is exemplified in Echo's observation in *The Divine Narcissus* that the darkening of Earth at the time of Narciso's (Christ's) death could not be the result of a real eclipse, since neither sun nor moon was in proper position for this to occur.

Some critics consider Sor Juana's drama to be superior even to her poetry, although her drama is far less well known, doubtless because it falls outside the bloodlines of modern drama: Her secular plays are modeled on the seventeenth century cape and sword genre, while her religious plays combine the allegorical intent of medieval drama with the rhetorical extravagance of the Baroque.

BIOGRAPHY

Juana de Asbaje y Ramírez de Santillana was born November 12, 1651, in San Miguel Nepantla, Mexico. Southeast of Mexico City and within view of two of its most impressive volcanoes, Popocatepetl and Ixtaccihuatl, this sleepy town produced one of Mexico's greatest lyric poets. Juana's baptism took place in the equally beautifully situated town of Amecameca.

Juana entered religious life at an early age and thus is best known by the name of Sor Juana Inés de la Cruz. She was a precocious child, learning to read at the age of three. She was born of a Spanish father and a Creole mother and registered on the rolls of the church as "a daughter of the Church" because her parents were not formally married.

A desire for learning nudged her early; she yearned to know Latin and, after twenty lessons, continued studying on her own so that she was later even able to write verses in Latin. She stopped eating cheese because it was said that it made one stupid. Living with her maternal grandparents, she eagerly read her grandfather's library. In her eagerness to learn, she would cut off a few inches of her hair, and if she had not reached her learning goal by the time

her hair regained its previous length, she cut it again. She believed that a head so devoid of learning should also be devoid of hair.

She begged her mother to let her go to Mexico City, dress as a boy, and enter the university. At eight, she did go to Mexico City to live with relatives. About the same time, she wrote a dramatic poem to the Eucharist. In the capital, this child prodigy caught the eye of the vicereine, the Marquesa de la Laguna, who brought her to live as her lady-in-waiting in the luxurious viceregal palace. Her wit and knowledge caused the viceroy to invite professors from the University of Mexico to examine her in various areas of knowledge; they marveled at her composure and learning. She was envied by the women and courted by the men because of her beauty and worldly wisdom.

In the seventeenth century, a woman had a choice of either marriage or the convent. Sor Juana announced herself completely disinterested in marriage. Fortunately for her, at that time in most sisterhoods, discipline was not severe and within the walls one could find many of the comforts and amenities of secular life. Thus Sor Juana's choice at sixteen years of age to take her religious vows may not have been so much her desire for an ascetic life, as for an opportunity to continue unhampered in her search for knowledge. Urged by a zealous confessor, she decided to leave the ease and stimulating activities of the viceregal palace.

On August 14, 1667, she entered the Convent of the Discalced Carmelites of Saint Joseph. The strict life there and her inner conflict resulted in ill health, however, and she withdrew on November 18 of that year. On February 24, 1669, she took the first vows in the Convent of the Order of Saint Jerome. This was a less severe and strict life—a virtual haven of calm and culture, a social and literary center. Here she had the occasional companionship of the Manceras, Paredes, and Galves, and in the interlocutory of the convent could visit with the learned Don Carlos de Sigüenza y Góngora, professor of mathematics in the University of Mexico, who could inform her about many of the scientific advances of the time. By this date, many of the European ideas of the early 1600's were reaching Mexico; there was even comparatively free circulation of nontheological books in Mexico during this period. Sor Juana voraciously sought and exploited all this learning. In addition, she wrote her poems and plays and carried on an extensive correspondence. In this convent she spent the rest of her life, surrounded by her extensive library, until a few years before her death.

The religious institution she had entered, however, was basically identified with the old ways of thinking and concern was felt about her salvation. Sor Juana had hoped that entrance into the convent might slake her thirst for material knowledge, but when she sought to become more ascetic by depriving herself of her books, her mind became even more active. She thrived on experimentation. She became torn between reason and passion, and was instilled with guilt. Toward the end of her life, this guilt became severe. Mexico was suffering from both natural and political problems: rain, flood, famine, pestilence, a total solar eclipse, and riots that almost ended Spanish authority.

At the same time, Sor Juana's supportive confessor withdrew, and she was harassed by his successor. In 1693, the second edition of a volume of her poems appeared in Spain, and copies soon appeared in Mexico. These circumstances worked against her spiritual life, causing her, on February 8, 1694, to pen a reaffirmation of her faith, written in her own blood, and renew her vows. Her library, said to number some four thousand volumes, and her other personal possessions were sold for charity. Mortification of the flesh became part of her life in the ensuing months. A pestilence struck the city, and as a result of her ministrations to her sick sisters in the community, she met her death on April 17, 1695. The "Muse of Mexico" had ceased to sing. Her passing must have been some satisfaction to her, for her last years were tormented by the mental conflict and turmoil caused by her passion for religion and secular matters, and she yearned to die.

ANALYSIS

In the exaltation of reason, clarity, and decorum that dominated the eighteenth century, there was a strong reaction against the Baroque, and indeed Baroque literature fell into virtual oblivion. Toward the beginning of the twentieth century, however, interest in the Baroque began to stir, and it is thus that not only the literature of the Baroque Spanish masters but also Sor Juana Inés de la Cruz's contribution to the field have again been brought to light and appreciated.

All of Sor Juana's drama is written in verse. She used a multiplicity of verse forms, exploiting them in order to set an effective tone for a particular character or scene. Relative to content, it is important to note that at the end of the seventeenth century, the Catholic Church and Sor Juana, especially through her theater, tried to make the dogma of the Eucharist dynamic. Sor Juana sought to unveil the Mysteries of Christ; obviously the most difficult part was how to make the invisible visible. She attempted to achieve this through allegory, myth, and metaphor; her intent was didacticism through entertainment, and even her secular plays reveal the influence of religious drama. Like Calderón, she used carts to represent different scenes, and her dramas include music and singing, as well as one or more choruses—which, as in Greek literature, serve to emphasize ideas presented through the plays.

Sor Juana used the dramatic props of her time for her writings. For the reader who can enter imaginatively into that distant period, her plays will come alive. Further, her variation in verse form not only displays her skill in handling many types but also provides interest and dispels monotony. Finally, one must marvel at her knowledge of both biblical and historical events as she weaves these into her plots. The combination of history, mythology, and religion must have produced a wonderfully exhilarating effect on audiences in her day, and it is still capable of engaging readers centuries later.

The collected dramatic output of Sor Juana consists of two comedies of intrigue, *A Household Plagued by Love* and *Amor es más laberinto* (love is a greater labyrinth); three *autos sacramentales*, *The Divine Narcissus*, *El mártir del Sacramento, San Hermenegildo* (the martyr of the Sacrament, Saint Hermenegildo), and *El cetro de José* (Joseph's scepter); two *sainetes*; and eighteen *loas*.

An *auto sacramental* is a one-act play concerning the Sacrament; a *loa* is a one-act play, usually quite short, which is generally allegorical and supports the Eucharist. A *loa* preceded each of Sor Juana's *autos*. Her sacramental plays and *comedias* are similar in form and style to those of the Calderón school. In fact, one of Calderón's plays is entitled "Los empeños de un acaso" (wr. 1639), and a few lines are identical to those that Sor Juana penned in her *A Household Plagued by Love*. This does not mean that Sor Juana was a plagiarist. Her independent attitude and thirst for knowledge caused her to read voraciously, and she synthesized what she learned into her own expression. Religion was the basis for what she wrote; her prime topics throughout her works were love and the Eucharist.

A HOUSEHOLD PLAGUED BY LOVE AND AMOR ES MÁS LABERINTO

The longer plays of Sor Juana can be divided into two types: the secular and religious. Her two secular plays, *A Household Plagued by Love* and *Amor es más laberinto*, are probably the most appealing to present-day audiences. Each of these three-act plays formed the greater part of a *festejo*, an evening of entertainment. A *festejo* usually honored one or more noted individuals.

The *festejo* of *A Household Plagued by Love* consisted of the three-act play, preceded by a *loa*. Intercalated between the acts were two *sainetes* and three songs praising the honored guests. The play concluded with a *sarao*, a brief play praising the viceroy and his family in music and dancing. The *sainetes*, or farces in this *festejo*, end in song, or song and hisses. The first of these poked fun at women; the second made jest of the play being staged. The entire *festejo* of *A Household Plagued by Love* required more than two hours to be performed.

Amor es más laberinto was also a three-act play; act 2, however, was written by Juan de Guevara, a well-known figure who had come from the Royal Court of Madrid to Mexico City and may have been Sor Juana's cousin. This play is also preceded by a *loa*.

These two plays have similar themes: noble people in love, disguised characters who appear or hide in inhospitable surroundings, mistaken identity, and repetition of situations. This mix-up of identities in semidarkness may seem improbable to present-day readers; this type of plot, however, was customary in seventeenth century drama. As usual during this period, the protagonists will marry happily—"All's well that ends well."

The locale of *A Household Plagued by Love* is Toledo, Spain. Pedro loves Leonor, and Pedro's sister Ana loves Carlos; Leonor and Carlos, however, love each other—thus the familiar triangle. After a series of intertwined events—an attempt at eloping, a sword fight, sanctuary requested and granted in the "enemy's" house, and mistaken identity because of disguised characters in the night—Leonor and Carlos are allowed to marry, and Ana will marry her promised lover, Juan. Each is happy with the marriage partner designated for him or her; the servants also marry.

The theme of *Amor es más laberinto* is based on the legend of Theseus and the Minotaur of Crete; the setting is Crete. Again, unrequited love enters when Theseus, who was brought as a captive to Crete to die by being sacrificed to the Minotaur in the Labyrinth, falls in love with Fedra, not with her sister Ariadne, who loved him and had also saved his life. Various intrigues surface among the characters, assisted by the servants, but again in the end the lovers, as well as two pairs of servants, are promised to each other in harmonious union. The title of the play derives from the conceit that the labyrinth of love is greater than that of Crete. As noted previously, the second act of this play was not written by Sor Juana; one wonders why.

In these two plays, Sor Juana portrays various types of love, but never does improper or immoral love enter. She carries out the Golden Age principle of honor in a delightful manner; no woman's honor is sacrificed. *Amor es más laberinto* has an added dimension because of its basis in mythology, which allows Sor Juana to demonstrate her knowledge of Greek legend.

THE DIVINE NARCISSUS

All three of Sor Juana's *autos* center on the Eucharist. Of the three, *The Divine Narcissus* is by far the best known and is considered the best of the many mythological *autos* written during this period. Divine Narcissus (Christ) is enamored of Human Nature and is dying of love for her. Echo is envious of this love and is filled with hate. Narcissus looks into the water—Christ seeking his image in Human Nature—and becomes the flower that bears his name; Christ's presence in the flower is the Host. Echo is an important figure, at times almost lovable. There are long speeches of familiar biblical stories, including Christ's temptation and passion. Echo and others echo, repeating only the last word of Narcissus's speeches; the composite of these words, repeated together, results in fascinating Baroque verses. The play is acknowledged as an unrivaled metamorphosis of the mythological to the theological. There are many carts with elaborate decor. Biblical events are paraded by almost endlessly, especially those of Christ's crucifixion and the ensuing natural events.

EL CETRO DE JOSÉ

El cetro de José is also an allegory. Joseph's story as told in the Old Testament is recounted: his being sold into slavery, the temptation with Potiphar's wife, supplying grain to his family through his brothers, the interpretation of Pharaoh's dream, and so on. The brothers' reference to bread clearly means the Bread of Christ. Joseph is Christ; the bread and wheat refer to the Eucharist. Prophecy has an important role throughout the play, and at the end when the Chalice and Host are displayed, the Sacrament is praised while two choruses sing joyfully.

EL MÁRTIR DEL SACRAMENTO, SAN HERMENEGILDO

El mártir del Sacramento, San Hermenegildo is religious but has an interwoven secular vein. It is based on the historical conflict between adherents of the Arian heresy and the orthodoxy of the established Church. Hermenegildo, now an orthodox believer, is the son of a committed heretic. He is captured by his father, and although his brother (who would inherit the throne should Hermenegildo be put to death) pleads for him, the father decides that he must at least test him: A heretical bishop offers Hermenegildo the Sacrament. When Hermenegildo refuses to accept it, his father has him executed, and the play ends. Sor

Juana, incidentally, has been criticized for this ending, because, according to Catholic canon law, Hermenegildo could have accepted Communion from this bishop, despite the bishop's heresy, and thus could have avoided death.

THE LOAS

Each of the three *autos* described above has an introductory *loa*. That of *The Divine Narcissus* is noteworthy because it combines Aztec religious rites with Christian dogma. America and Occident, who represent the Aztec religion, inform Religion that they have a ritual similar to the Christian Eucharist; they make reference to a custom that does not appear in detail in the *loa*. In this rite, a statue of Huitzilopochtli (the Mexican god of war) was made of grain mixed with blood, which represented the death of their god. This mixture was distributed in a ceremony resembling the communal meal of the Eucharist. In the *loa*, Religion hopes to convince them that they should turn to the True Religion; she plans to do this through the *auto* which follows.

The *loa* which introduces *El cetro de José* is similar in theme to that of *The Divine Narcissus*. It is considered better than those of Calderón for it has no unjustified fantasies. Faith and the Law of Grace have convinced Natural Law and Nature of the superiority of the Eucharist over indigenous human sacrifice. Idolatry enters and provides through her speeches the depth of native reasoning for their ritual. Faith argues for the Christian belief until Idolatry eagerly awaits the forthcoming play to see the proof. It is a twin of the *loa* introducing *The Divine Narcissus*.

The *loa* preceding *El mártir del Sacramento, San Hermenegildo* introduces a discussion among two students and their teacher concerning the *finezas* (favors) of Christ—which is the greatest. Unique to this *loa* is a play-within-a-play. Hercules plants his famous pillars and then declares: "Non plus ultra," but Columbus sets out into the deep, finds the New World and returns with his *plus ultra*. The *loa* concludes that the death of Christ may seem unsurpassable, but in the elements of the Last Supper, Christ exceeds that love, and the Eucharist triumphs.

Of the other thirteen *loas*, all of which are independent, one is sacred, while the remaining are secular. Five of the secular ones are written in praise of Carlos II, the inglorious Spanish king reigning in the latter half of the seventeenth century. There is a delightful and happy mixture of the elements of earth, fire, air, and water with time, celestial bodies, and so on. They all create hymns praising him. There is one *loa* each to the queen and queen mother, and the Marqueses de Laguna (the viceroy of Mexico and his wife), who were such faithful patrons for Sor Juana, as well as their family, are celebrated in *loas* presented on their birthdays or other occasions.

OTHER MAJOR WORKS

POETRY: *Inundación castálida*, 1689; *Segundo volumen de las obras*, 1692 (the long poem *Primero sueño* is translated as *First Dream*, 1983); *Fama y obras póstumas*, 1700; *The Sonnets of Sor Juana Ines de la Cruz in English Verse*, 2001.

NONFICTION: *Respuesta de la poetisa a la muy ilustre Sor Filotea de la Cruz*, 1700.

MISCELLANEOUS: *Obras completas de sor Juana Inés de la Cruz*, 1951-1957 (4 volumes: I, *Lírica personal*, poetry; II, *Villancicos y letras sacras*, poetry; III, *Autos y loas*, drama; IV, *Comedias sainetes y prosa*, drama and prose; Méndez Plancarte, editor); *A Sor Juana Anthology*, 1988.

BIBLIOGRAPHY

Flynn, Gerald C. *Sor Juana Inés de la Cruz*. New York: Twyane, 1971. A general biography of Sor Juana that examines her life and works. Bibliography.

Kirk, Pamela. *Sor Juana Inés de la Cruz: Religion, Art, and Feminism*. New York: Continuum, 1998. An examination of Sor Juana's role in the church as well as her literary efforts. Bibliography and index.

Merrim, Stephanie. *Early Modern Women's Writing and Sor Juana Inés de la Cruz*. Nashville, Tenn.: Vanderbilt University Press, 1999. An examination of Sor Juana as an early woman writer and comparison with other women writers. Bibliography and index.

_____, ed. *Feminist Perspectives on Sor Juana Inés de la Cruz*. Detroit, Mich.: Wayne State University Press, 1999. A feminist interpretation of the life and works of Sor Juana. Bibliography and index.

Paz, Octavio. *Sor Juana Inés de la Cruz*. Cambridge, Mass.: Harvard University Press, 1988. A biography of Sor Juana, the seventeenth century nun. Bibliography and index.

Evelyn Uhrhan Irving

FRANZ THEODOR CSOKOR

Born: Vienna, Austro-Hungarian Empire; September 6, 1885
Died: Vienna, Austria; January 5, 1969

PRINCIPAL DRAMA

Thermidor, pr., pb. 1912
Der grosse Kampf, pb. 1914
Die Sünde wider den Geist, pb. 1917, pr. 1919
Der Baum der Erkenntnis, pb. 1917, pr. 1924
Die rote Strasse, pb. 1918, pr. 1921
Gesellschaft der Menschenrechte, pr., pb. 1929
Besetztes Gebiet, pr. 1930, pb. 1932 (*Occupied Territory*, 1995)
Gewesene Menschen, pb. 1932, pr. 1936
3. November 1918, pb. 1936, pr. 1937 (*The Army of No Return*, 1960; also as *November 3, 1918*, 1995)
Gottes General, pr., pb. 1939
Kalypso, pr., pb. 1946
Der verlorene Sohn, pr. 1946, pb. 1947 (*The Prodigal Son*, 1995)
Medea Postbellica, pr. 1950
Europäische Trilogie, pb. 1952 (includes *Occupied Territory*, *November 3, 1918*, and *The Prodigal Son*)
Pilatus, pr. 1952, pb. 1954

Olymp und Golgatha, pb. 1954 (includes *Kalypso*,
    Caesars Witwe, and *Pilatus*)
Caesars Witwe, pb. 1954, pr. 1955
Hebt den Stein ab!, pb. 1957, pr. 1958
Treibholz, pb., pr. 1959
Das Zeichen an der Wand, pb., pr. 1962
Die Kaiser zwischen den Zeiten, pb. 1965
Alexander, pb. 1969

OTHER LITERARY FORMS

Franz Theodor Csokor is best known for his plays,
but he published some well-received volumes of poetry, notably *Der Dolch und die Wunde* (1917; the
dagger and the wound) and *Immer ist Anfang* (1952;
there is always a new beginning). In addition to a few
collections of short fiction, he also wrote a novel
about the Anabaptist movement, *Der Schlüssel zum
Abgrund* (1955; the key to the abyss). His most
widely read prose works are his autobiographical narratives, combined in *Auf fremden Strassen* (1955; on
foreign roads), which deal with his continual flight
from the Nazis before and during World War II.

ACHIEVEMENTS

Franz Theodor Csokor first attracted public attention in 1933 when he vehemently opposed the beginning persecution of German Jewish writers at the PEN
International Congress in Ragusa. This courageous
stance led to his eventually being forced into exile.
After his return to Austria after World War II, he became the president of the Austrian PEN club in 1947
and received numerous prizes and awards, among
them the Literature Prize of Vienna in 1927 and 1953,
the Grillparzer Prize in 1937, and the Austrian National Literature Prize in 1955, the highest honor the
Austrian government gives to a writer. Csokor and
Fritz Hochwälder are considered the two most influential Austrian dramatists of the post-World War II
era. Csokor was also nominated for the Nobel Prize.

BIOGRAPHY

Franz Theodor Csokor was born on September 6,
1885, into an affluent middle-class family. His family
tree includes members of almost all ethnic and national groups in the Austro-Hungarian Empire—he

called himself a "true Austrian blend"—and therefore
he is a true representative of that multinational social
order that appeared at the height of its glory but was
already doomed at the time of his birth.

After his high school graduation, Csokor studied
art history at the University of Vienna but soon abandoned his studies to pursue his true vocation: literature, particularly drama. In 1912 his first play, *Eine
Partie Schach* (a game of chess), later published as
Thermidor, was performed in Budapest in Hungarian.
Csokor, who attended the premiere, did not understand a single word of his own play. The success of
the play confirmed his determination to devote his
life to the theater.

During World War I, Csokor was at first an infantry soldier but was later transferred to the imperial
war archives, where Rainer Maria Rilke and Stefan
Zweig were among his colleagues. His elder brother
was killed in the war, an event that Csokor had difficulty coping with and that led him to ally himself
closely with the pacifist expressionist writers of the
postwar period. The plays *Der Baum der Erkenntnis*
(the tree of insight) and *Die rote Strasse* (the red
road) as well as some volumes of expressionist poetry
stem from this time.

In the years after the war, Csokor worked as
dramaturge and director at several Viennese theaters
and studied subjects related to classical antiquity and
Christianity. He became fascinated with the nineteenth century dramatist Georg Büchner, for whose
stark *Woyzeck* (wr. 1836, pb. 1879; English translation,
1927) he wrote a conciliatory conclusion. Büchner
is also the protagonist of his play *Gesellschaft der
Menschenrechte* (society of human rights), which was
performed on all important German stages until 1933
when the Nazis' rise to power led to a drastic change
of fortune in Csokor's dramatic career. From Büchner,
Csokor adopted the notion that art and political activism are compatible activities.

Because he spoke out against the book burnings of
the Adolf Hitler regime while he attended the PEN
congress in 1933, further performances of his plays
in Germany were prohibited, and as he has stated, he
lived with his suitcases packed from 1933 to 1938, all
the while witnessing the growing strength of the Nazi

movement in his native Austria. Despite his misgivings about the political developments, he considered it his duty to continue to write and remain in Austria. His reputation as a dramatist was firmly established with the production of his most famous and popular play, *November 3, 1918*, his dramatic requiem for the Austro-Hungarian Empire.

While Csokor was working on *Gottes General* (god's general), his play about the founder of the Jesuit order, Ignatius of Loyola, Hitler annexed Austria, and Csokor finally went into exile in Poland. It became the beginning of a long odyssey, as Csokor had to continue to retreat from the advancing German troops, first from Poland to Romania, from there to Belgrade, and finally to the Adriatic island of Korcula. After Allied troops landed in southern Italy, Csokor worked as a propaganda officer for the British and finally returned to Vienna in 1946. This ordeal is described in his autobiographical narratives *Als Zivilist im Polenkrieg* (1940; a civilian in the Polish war) and *Als Zivilist im Balkankrieg* (1947; a civilian in the Balkan war), which were later combined under the title *Auf fremden Strassen* (1955, on foreign roads).

From his return to Austria in 1946 to his death in 1969, Csokor produced a large number of plays and reworked some of his earlier work into thematically grouped collections, including *European Trilogy* (*November 3, 1918*; *Occupied Territory*; *The Prodigal Son*). At the time of his death, on January 5, 1969, he was working on a play about Alexander the Great. He was to the last a fixture in the literary coffeehouses of Vienna and much revered by the Viennese for whom he represented a nostalgic memory of the great days of the Austro-Hungarian Empire, as well as a shining example of principled resistance against a more unpleasant regime of the immediate past.

ANALYSIS

With a dramatic career spanning both world wars, Franz Theodor Csokor and his dramatic work provide a panorama of the main developments in twentieth century Austrian drama and of the social and political upheavals that shook this era. In contrast to the resignation and ironic distancing so typical of many of the

Austrian *fin de siècle* writers, Csokor always stressed the importance of political activism and the strident defense of humanist ideals in a world rapidly abandoning such principles. Even his early plays written under the influence of Strindberg and the early expressionists not only urge an examination of an increasingly materialistic world (*Die rote Strasse*) and the battle of the sexes (*Der Baum der Erkenntnis*) but also advocate strong personal engagement to bring about a change in traditional values and attitudes. In his plays of the 1920's and 1930's, Csokor tries to come to terms not only with the catastrophic consequences of World War I, in particular the death of his only brother, but also with the disintegration of the Austro-Hungarian multination empire and the resulting rise of increasingly aggressive chauvinist nation states in Europe. His plays of that period are often based on historical events in which the main theme is the defense of individual freedom against totalitarian ideologies, both religious and secular, and the responsibility of the individual to fight for the preservation of humanist ideals threatened by these ideologies. Like many of his protagonists, notably Ignatius of Loyala in *Gottes General* and Stipe in *The Prodigal Son*, Csokor lived his own life according to the principles he advocated, even when they endangered his life and his economic well-being.

Csokor's post-World War II plays continue this examination of individual responsibility and the moral dilemmas confronting people in modern society, notably in the play *Das Zeichen an der Wand*, inspired by the Adolf Eichmann trial. Although the themes of his plays transcend specifically Austrian problems, only a few have been translated into English, probably because of his extensive use of dated Austrian vernacular and his attachment to expressionist characters and structures, even in the representational plays of his later life. However, a good translation of the three plays in the critical edition of his *European Trilogy* has been available since 1995 and allows the English-speaking reader access to his most often performed and most highly praised plays. The plays in the trilogy appeared individually and were gathered under this title in 1952 to reflect a thematic rather than a chronological sequence.

NOVEMBER 3, 1918

November 3, 1918 is a quasi-historical drama taking place mainly during and after the signing of the armistice between Austria-Hungary and the Entente. The action takes place in a military convalescent home high on a snowbound mountain in southern Austria. Eight officers and men representing all the national and ethnic groups of the empire coexist there in relative harmony, bonded by their service in the imperial army and their fight against a common foe. Kaczuk, a Polish Marxist sailor, enters to bring them the news of the armistice and the subsequent dissolution of the monarchy. Immediately the men begin to draw apart and to see themselves as members of distinct national groups with territorial and political conflicts of interest. Colonel Radosin, the commanding officer, refuses to accept the disintegration of the old system, which had united so many different nationalities, and appeals to the others to uphold the supranational ideals of the defunct empire in spite of the present political situation. When his appeals prove fruitless, he commits suicide. His funeral is the last common action to which the men agree; then they go their separate ways, despite the fact that some of them will not survive the journey home without the support of the others. As the curtain falls, the Slovenian officer Zierowitz and the German nationalist Ludoltz begin their armed struggle for dominance over Carinthia, the area in which the convalescent home is located. This is a historically accurate representation of the so-called "after war," fought between Austrian and Slovenian nationalists immediately after World War I over the territory that is now one of the Austrian states.

November 3, 1918 was written eighteen years after the historical events it portrays. It is Csokor's requiem for an admittedly less than perfect political idea, the multinational Austro-Hungarian Empire, which had nevertheless provided political stability in Central Europe for many years. At the same time, it is an attempt to give an explanation for the disastrous rise of chauvinist fascist movements in Europe after World War I. Csokor was convinced that extreme nationalism was the equivalent of egotism and self-centeredness in individuals; he considered dedication to higher ideals individually and to a supranational political structure as essential for the survival of humankind. He would have looked at the disintegration of the former Yugoslavia as confirmation of these beliefs and would surely have been gratified by the gradual development of a European Union. Indeed, even at the end of *November 3, 1918* there is a brief glimpse of hope for such a future development when the nurse, left alone with Ludoltz who is willing to kill and to die for his proto-Nazist ideas, indicates that Colonel Radosin might rise from the grave again in years to come.

OCCUPIED TERRITORY

This play, though written six years before *November 3, 1918*, is set against the background of the French occupation of the German Ruhr territory in 1923. The Treaty of Versailles had constrained Germany to pay huge reparations to the victorious nations, and when Germany refused to live up to the conditions of the treaty, French troops invaded the main industrial area in Germany to exact the reparations by force. In the play, a group of radical German nationalists instigates violence against the occupation forces, mainly to further its own political goals. Significantly, the French occupiers never appear on the stage: The conflict plays out mainly between Monk, the pacifist humanist mayor of Kaiserborn, and Schlern, the leader of the militant nationalists who stir up patriotic fervor amongst the population by provoking violence from the occupiers. Monk, who sees the looming catastrophe and does not want these nationalist hoodlums to come to power, is faced with a dilemma: He can keep the peace and prevent the rise to power of the radicals only by delivering them to the sworn enemy, thus appearing to become a traitor to his own people. Nevertheless, he sees this course of action as the lesser of two evils and hands Schlern over to the authorities for instant execution; he himself is lynched by the "patriotic" mob in retaliation.

Occupied Territory logically continues the theme of *November 3, 1918* by showing the moral corruption and selfishness of extreme nationalism. Schlern and his group are single-mindedly determined to bring their chauvinist, racist ideology to power in

Germany. They are no longer bound by any individual ethos but subordinate everything, including their own life, to their misguided cause. Csokor finds this lack of morals and the abandonment of individual responsibility abhorrent, but he is well aware of the fatal attraction of such "patriotic" slogans. He also makes it clear that it is the duty of morally intact individuals to fight this development, even at the cost of their own lives.

THE PRODIGAL SON

In *The Prodigal Son*, this thematic trend is brought to its logical conclusion by showing the obligation to fight such inhumane ideologies, even by extreme measures. Stipe, the young partisan, returns home to warn his family of an impending threat from the fascists whom he is fighting and asks his to brothers to join him. When they refuse, his father Otac must choose between saving Stipe or himself and his two other sons. He chooses Stipe and is executed by the fascists while Stipe kills his own brothers, taking the wife and child of one of them into the hills. *The Prodigal Son* is therefore the fitting conclusion to this trilogy, which is, as a whole, a refutation of and a call to resistance against chauvinism and fascism and which insists on the duty of moral individuals to resist such movements and ideologies at any cost.

OTHER MAJOR WORKS

LONG FICTION: *Der Schlüssel zum Abgrund*, 1955.

SHORT FICTION: *Über die Schwelle*, 1937; *Der zweite Hahnenshrei*, 1959; *Ein paar Schaufeln Erde*, 1965.

POETRY: *Die Gewalten*, 1912; *Der Dolch und die Wunde*, 1917; *Immer ist Anfang*, 1952.

NONFICTION: *Auf fremden Strassen*, 1955; *Zeuge einer Zeit*, 1964.

BIBLIOGRAPHY

Brandys, Brygida. "Das dramatische Werk von Franz Theodor Csokor." *Kwartalnik Neofilologiczny* 28 (1981), 407-427. A comprehensive survey of Csokor's dramatic opus, with detailed analyses of the major plays. Less idolatrous and more scholarly than Wimmer. In German.

Lichliter, Katherine McHugh, ed. *A Critical Edition and Translation of Franz Theodor Csokor's "European Trilogy."* New York: Peter Lang, 1995. Contains *November 3, 1918, Occupied Territory*, and *The Prodigal Son*. Apart from modernized, readable translation of the plays, there is ample historical and critical material in the introduction to each play, as well as a good general cultural-biographical essay.

Wimmer, Paul. *Der Dramatiker Franz Theodor Csokor*. Innsbruck: Wagner, 1981. The only comprehensive study of Csokor's complete dramatic works, by a friend and admirer. Good plot synopses and analyses of all plays, even some unpublished ones. In German.

Franz G. Blaha

RICHARD CUMBERLAND

Born: Cambridge, England; February 19, 1732
Died: Tunbridge Wells, England; May 7, 1811

PRINCIPAL DRAMA

The Banishment of Cicero, pb. 1761
The Summer's Tale, pr., pb. 1765
The Clandestine Marriage, pr. 1766
The Brothers, pr. 1769, pb. 1770
The West Indian, pr., pb. 1771
The Fashionable Lover, pr., pb. 1772
The Choleric Man, pr. 1774, pb. 1775
The Walloons, pr. 1782, pb. 1813
The Mysterious Husband, pr., pb. 1783
The Carmelite, pr., pb. 1784
The Natural Son, pr. 1784, pb. 1785
The Box-Lobby Challenge, pr., pb. 1794
The Jew, pr., pb. 1794
The Wheel of Fortune, pr., pb. 1795

First Love, pr., pb. 1795

Don Pedro, pr. 1797, pb. 1831

False Impressions, pr., pb. 1797

The Unpublished Plays of Richard Cumberland,
   pb. 1991 (Richard J. Dircks, editor)

OTHER LITERARY FORMS

Richard Cumberland is remarkable for the volume and variety of his literary output. Experimenting in several different genres, he earned a reputation in his day as a distinguished man of letters. Most of his works, however, have not survived.

Cumberland had early ambitions as a poet, his first publication being an imitation of Thomas Gray, *An Elegy Written on St. Mark's Eve* (1754). He was to publish *Odes* in 1776, and a volume entitled *Miscellaneous Poems* two years later. A religious epic, *Calvary: Or, The Death of Christ* (1792) sold well, which encouraged him to collaborate with Sir James Bland Burgess in *The Exodiad* (1807). Cumberland rendered some fifty psalms into English meter in *A Poetical Version of Certain Psalms of David* (1801) and reflected on his life in verse in *Retrospection* (1811).

Cumberland also won renown as an essayist for his multivolume work *The Observer*, which first appeared in 1785, with editions following in 1788 and in 1798. It featured a discussion of the early Greek drama with some original translations (notably Aristophanes' *Nephelai* (423 B.C.E.; *The Clouds*, 1708). Cumberland wrote pamphlets—defending his grandfather's reputation, among other causes—and a religious tract. He entered the realm of art history with his *Anecdotes of Eminent Painters in Spain During the Sixteenth and Seventeenth Centuries* (1782) and published the first catalog of the paintings housed in the royal palace at Madrid.

The pathetic scenes that mark Cumberland's drama are also found in his fiction: *Arundel* (1789), an epistolary novel of the form popularized by Samuel Richardson, and *Henry* (1795), a conscious imitation of Henry Fielding. Cumberland's active involvement in the theater resulted in numerous prologues and epilogues as well as an edition of *The British Drama* with biographical and critical comments, published posthumously in 1817. In 1809, Cumberland also founded *The London Review*, which invited signed articles from contributors; it appeared only twice. His *Memoirs of Richard Cumberland, Written by Himself* (1806-1807), perhaps the most lasting of his nondramatic productions, preserved for posterity the record of his long and productive career.

ACHIEVEMENTS

Richard Cumberland is remarkable for his long and varied contribution to the theater. During his career, which spanned forty years, he wrote some fifty dramatic pieces, including musical comedies and operas, a masque, classical historical and domestic tragedies, translations and adaptations, farces, and occasional pieces. The genre in which he excelled was sentimental comedy, and for years he was the most successful writer in the field. His sentimental comedies held the stage against the masterpieces of Oliver Goldsmith and Richard Brinsley Sheridan. His very preeminence, however, made him vulnerable to attack, and unfortunately he has been handed down to posterity, through the eyes of his opponents, as "the Terence of England, the mender of hearts," according to Goldsmith in "Retaliation" (1774).

Indeed, Cumberland is remembered primarily for his place in the debate between sentimental and laughing comedy. The issues were hotly contested: What is the primary purpose of the stage? Should comedy be realistic or idealistic? Should it ridicule vices and follies or present models worthy of imitation? Should playwrights appeal to the intellect or to the emotions? Should they aim to provoke superior laughter or sympathetic tears? Stated in these terms, the answers seem obvious, with the common verdict in favor of "true," or laughing, comedy. One should not forget, however, the response of Cumberland's contemporaries. In his day, he was enormously popular as well as influential. Many imitators followed Cumberland's lead, ensuring the dominance of the sentimental school to the end of the century.

Cumberland was convinced of the moral utility of the drama and took his role seriously as reformer of the age. He created characters specifically to combat national prejudices, and he attacked fashionable vices. This was done both by means of admonitory examples (the ruined gambler in *The Wheel of Fortune*) and by direct statement. Aphorisms are to be found throughout Cumberland's plays, and a useful lesson is often expounded at the end.

Cumberland was unusual as a "gentleman" playwright and was considered a credit to the profession. He was well educated in classical as well as English stage tradition and drew on his knowledge for his works. His writing was admired for its elegance and accurate portrayal of high life. The refined sensibility of his heroines and the tearful pathos they inspired were highly commended.

Cumberland was superior to other writers in this genre in that he was able to blend humor with sentiment. In almost all his plays, one finds "low" characters, included for comic relief, as well as sprightly ladies, amorous spinsters, and henpecked husbands. Strongly patriotic, he liked homegrown English characters and created some memorable types, such as the Irishman Major O'Flaherty. He could also employ local color to advantage, as he did in the seaside scenes in *The Brothers*.

Through his long acquaintance with the theater, Cumberland developed a good sense of what would work onstage. It was often remarked that his plays performed better than they read. He was able to use all the resources at his disposal (scenery, costumes, and so on) to enhance his plays. He also knew the abilities of the performers and could write parts that would exploit their talents. Some of these roles—Penruddock or Belcour, for example—were favorite acting parts. Famous in his own time, Cumberland was the last and the best of the sentimental dramatists. Of his many plays, *The West Indian* survives as a classic.

BIOGRAPHY

Richard Cumberland was born on February 19, 1732, in the Master's Lodge at Trinity College, Cambridge, into a family of clergymen and scholars of whom he was justly proud. His father, Denison Cumberland, later bishop of Clonfert and Kilmore, was descended from the bishop of Peterborough, who wrote an influential treatise in refutation of Thomas Hobbes, *De Legibus Naturae, Disquisito Philosoph-*

ica (1672). Cumberland's mother, Joanna, was the daughter of the famous classics scholar Richard Bentley. Cumberland cherished fond memories of this learned man and upheld Bentley's reputation all his life.

At the age of six, Cumberland was sent to school at Bury St. Edmunds, where, encouraged by headmaster Arthur Kinsman, he stood first in his class. In 1744, he entered Westminster School contemporaneously with Warren Hastings, George Colman, and William Cowper. In Cumberland's school days, an interest in the drama was awakened by his mother's reading of William Shakespeare; on an early trip to the theater, he was much impressed by the innovative acting of the young David Garrick.

In 1747, Cumberland was admitted to Trinity College, Cambridge, where he enjoyed the quiet life of study and intellectual exertion. He took his bachelor of arts degree in 1751 with high honors and was elected to a fellowship two years later. He felt drawn to an academic or clerical career and relinquished his calling with some regret when more worldly prospects presented themselves.

The great Whig Sir George Montagu Dunk, second earl of Halifax, out of gratitude to Cumberland's father, offered to take Cumberland as his private secretary. Cumberland moved to London to take up the post, which gave him the opportunity to move in political circles. In 1759, he married Elizabeth Ridge, with whom he was to have four sons and three daughters. Fortunately for his growing family, he was appointed the Crown Agent for Nova Scotia and Provost Marshal of South Carolina, which added to his income.

Cumberland accompanied Lord Halifax to Ireland in 1761 as Ulster secretary. This experience was later to bear fruit in Cumberland's drama, when he brought original Irish characters to the stage. The relationship with his patron cooled on Cumberland's refusal of a baronetcy, and when Halifax became secretary of state in 1762, he appointed a rival as under secretary. Cumberland was forced to accept a minor position as clerk of reports on the Board of Trade.

With little to do and in need of money, Cumberland began in earnest his career as a dramatist. His first play, *The Banishment of Cicero*, was refused, but in 1765, *The Summer's Tale* was produced, a musical comedy imitative of Isaac Bickerstaffe. This provoked a charge from which Cumberland was often to suffer, that of plagiarism, and he turned his efforts to a genre more conducive to his talents, that of sentimental comedy. In 1769, *The Brothers* played at Covent Garden to great applause.

An unexpected compliment to Garrick in the epilogue won Garrick's friendship and led to a very productive association between the two. As actor-manager of Drury Lane Theatre until 1776, Garrick produced several of Cumberland's plays, which benefited from Garrick's expert knowledge of stagecraft. Their first effort was also the most successful: *The West Indian*, which appeared in 1771, enjoyed an extraordinary first run of twenty-eight nights, was frequently revived and held the stage to the end of the century. When his third comedy, *The Fashionable Lover*, also won favor, in 1772, Cumberland was established as the leading dramatist of the sentimental school.

Cumberland's preeminence in the theater won for him his entrée into the leading social and literary circles of the time. At the British Coffee House, he met Samuel Johnson, Sir Joshua Reynolds, Edmund Burke, and Samuel Foote. He patronized the painter George Romney. He dined at Elizabeth Montagu's ("Queen of the Blues"); he knew Hester Thrale and irritated Horace Walpole. As to the latter, although Cumberland moved in society with ease, proud of his dignified position as "gentleman playwright," he had a temperament that provoked as much enmity as friendship.

Most unsatisfactory were his relationships with fellow dramatists, for Cumberland was reputed to be envious of all merit but his own. His discomfiture at the success of Sheridan's *The School for Scandal* (pr. 1777) was widely reported. As the most popular exponent of sentimental comedy, Cumberland was vulnerable to attack by those who preferred laughing comedy, and when Goldsmith's famous essay on the subject, "An Essay on the Theatre," appeared in 1773, Cumberland took it as a personal affront. He replied in a vitriolic preface to his (appropriately entitled)

play *The Choleric Man*. Proud of his accomplishments though professing humility and sensitive to criticism though pretending to lofty indifference, he exasperated even Garrick, who called him a "man without a skin." Cumberland was identified by contemporaries as the original of Sheridan's caricature in *The Critic* (pr. 1779) and was known as Sir Fretful Plagiary.

Cumberland's literary career was interrupted in 1780 by involvement in political affairs. He had been appointed Secretary to the Board of Trade in 1775 through the interest of his patron and friend Lord George Germain. For this nobleman, then colonial secretary, Cumberland undertook a secret mission to Spain to arrange a separate peace treaty. When negotiations failed in 1781, Cumberland was recalled and was treated ungratefully by the government, which refused to reimburse him for his expenses. Moreover, he lost his post when the Board of Trade was abolished in 1782. Disappointed and in need of money, Cumberland retired to Tunbridge Wells, where he tried through unceasing literary activity to recoup his fortunes.

The first work produced after Cumberland's return, *The Walloons*, a play with a strong Spanish flavor, failed to please, but he had more success with a domestic tragedy, *The Mysterious Husband*, in 1783. *The Carmelite*, staged in 1784 with an impressive gothic setting, displayed the extraordinary talents of actress Sarah Siddons as the heroine. Cumberland won little approval for his next few ventures, and it was not until 1794 that he again found his audience.

The Box-Lobby Challenge, produced early that year, was amusing fare, and a few months later *The Jew* was widely acclaimed. For the title role of the latter, Cumberland created a sympathetic character whose apparent avarice cloaked benevolent actions. Another powerful figure animated *The Wheel of Fortune* in 1795, giving actor John Philip Kemble one of his favorite roles. *First Love*, in the old vein of sentimental comedy, also won favor. These plays briefly restored Cumberland to his former popularity, but in the years to come, he was unable to match their success. He continued to write prolifically up to his death but for the most part failed to suit the taste of the audience and complained of the degeneracy of the stage.

Perhaps for this reason, Cumberland turned to other channels, and the years of his retirement saw a tremendous outpouring of fiction, poetry, and prose. This unremitting literary activity was at least partly a result of financial pressure. Toward the end of his life, his unfortunate situation attracted notice as one unworthy of a venerable man of letters.

By 1800, Cumberland had outlived his own generation and was viewed by his younger contemporaries as a figure from another era. He enjoyed his position as elder statesman and was accorded respect for his age and accomplishments. He liked to encourage young writers of talent, entertaining them with anecdotes of his own younger days. Always staunchly patriotic, he raised a corps of volunteers to meet the threat of a Napoleonic invasion; two of his sons died serving their country. At his death, at the age of seventy-nine, Cumberland left a modest estate to his youngest daughter. He lies buried in the Poets' Corner of Westminster Abbey.

ANALYSIS

Richard Cumberland took seriously his role as moralist and reformer and set himself a novel didactic task: "I thereupon looked into society for the purpose of discovering such as were the victims of its national, professional or religious prejudices; . . . and out of these I meditated to select and form heroes for my future dramas."

THE WEST INDIAN

In his popular play *The West Indian*, he defends the character of a Creole. The basic plot is a familiar testing device, set up in the opening scene. Stockwell awaits the arrival from Jamaica of his unacknowledged son; he decides to defer acknowledgment of their relationship until he has had an opportunity to evaluate the young man's behavior. Should his son, Belcour, satisfy this scrutiny, Stockwell will reward him with legitimacy, a fortune, and a place in English society.

Interest in Belcour is awakened before his entrance and increased by the parade of black porters. Nor is he likely to disappoint expectations; he enters breezily, complaining of the rapacious mob at the waterside. As a stranger to English society, he is able to view it objectively and provide satiric commentary. Moreover, as a "child of nature," his viewpoint should be a healthy corrective. Generous and honorable himself, he does not suspect duplicity in others; while this makes him an easy dupe of the scheming Fulmers, it redounds to his credit as a proof of his innocence.

Belcour's lack of guile is an endearing trait: The candor with which he acknowledges his faults to Stockwell disarms reproof, and his ingenuous confession to Charlotte of the loss of her jewels wins an easy forgiveness. This West Indian shows the human heart in its natural state—impulsive, mercurial, and uncontrolled. He himself bemoans the violence of his passions, blaming them on his tropical constitution. He is driven by his powerful urges. Inflamed by the beauty of Louisa Dudley, he sacrifices every other tie to possess her. Plunging headlong into error, he is chastened by the mischief that ensues. Like so many other libertines, Belcour is reclaimed by a virtuous woman. Kneeling at her feet, he pledges his love, grounded now on principle. In their union, the ideal of a feeling heart tempered with reason will be achieved.

Belcour is valued above all for his benevolence. A creature of instinct, his first impulse on hearing of distress is to relieve it. His follies and virtues proceed from the same source—a warm heart. He reflects the fundamental belief of sentimental drama in the natural goodness of people and contradicts the orthodox Christian view of human beings' sinfulness. Sympathy with one's fellow creatures is the moral touchstone for all the characters in the play—a quality conspicuously lacking in Lady Rusport, who represents the Puritan position. She was taught never to laugh; she abhors the playhouses; and she upholds the letter of the law over the spirit of charity. She is rightfully excluded from the happy ending.

Cumberland's fallible but generous hero, who would not be out of place in a laughing comedy, resembles Henry Fielding's Tom Jones and Richard Brinsley Sheridan's Charles Surface. The play abounds with high spirits; besides the amusing peccadilloes of Belcour, there is a subplot involving the lively Charlotte Rusport. She is unexpectedly forthright, avowing her love for Charles although uncertain of its return. This reversal of roles, in which a lady takes the active part in the wooing, is frequently seen in Cumberland's plays. Charlotte's witty repartee, directed even at the sentimental heroine, prevents Louisa's distresses from appearing too pathetic.

A similar defusing of sentiment is accomplished by Major O'Flaherty. He is a stage Irishman with a difference; while retaining some national traits, he has many admirable qualities, showing courage, loyalty, and generosity. It is he, after all, who discovers and delivers the will that brings about the happy reversal of fortune. His joyful exuberance animates this otherwise tearful scene. He punctures the Dudleys' formal rhetoric with irreverent comments, undercuts Lady Rusport's tirade, and interrupts the highly emotional father-son reunion.

In *The West Indian*, Cumberland skillfully blends comic and sentimental elements. It is unique in this regard; more often, his plays are thoroughly imbued with sentiment. *The Fashionable Lover*, for example, shows more clearly what is meant by the "tearful Muse."

THE FASHIONABLE LOVER

The opening of *The Fashionable Lover* is reminiscent of a comedy of humors, in which each character appears onstage to exhibit his or her particular foible. A Scotsman complains of extravagance to a foppish French valet; a railing misanthrope irritates a dissolute aristocrat; and a musty Welsh antiquary squares off with a vulgar merchant. The tone is one of satire until the introduction of the sentimental plot. This involves a poor orphan, surprised by the rakish lord into a compromising situation. Wherever Miss Augusta Aubrey turns in her hapless state, tears are sure to follow.

Cumberland aims to inspire pity through the picture of virtue in distress. He presents characters in a middle walk of life, with whose problems the audience can identify. The appeal to the heart is beneficial and instructive; it enlarges one's sympathies and strengthens one's affections. To evoke this response, Augusta is cast on the world bemoaning her hard lot.

Nor is she likely to minimize her sorrows: "I have no house, no home, no father, friend, or refuge, in this world." The smallest problems are magnified in her eyes; the awesome prospect of independence overwhelms her. Preoccupied as she is with her troubles, it is difficult to rouse her from self-pity. Even when informed of her good fortune, Augusta weeps, reflecting how unaccustomed she is to happiness.

Just as Augusta is unlikely to show stoic fortitude, she is also incapable of acting spiritedly on her own behalf. Her most likely resource at this critical pass would be her fiancé, but rather than appeal for his aid, she advises him to forget her. When he demands an explanation, she replies ambiguously that she accepts her fate. It is not surprising that Mr. Tyrrel concludes that she is guilty, for she makes no effort to deny it.

The heroine's extraordinary passivity is the result of her extreme sensibility; she is tremblingly alive to every sensation and fearful of aggression. Ushered into the presence of a man who eyes her keenly, Augusta complains, "his eyes oppress me." She is delicate of body as well as of spirit, and the least exertion exhausts her. Reunited with her long-lost father, she weeps, faints, and has to be carried away. Her feminine frailty endears her to the hero because she so evidently depends on his protection.

Such a pathetic heroine requires a rescuer. A conventional figure is an elderly gentleman somewhat removed from the action who wanders through the play doing good. He appears at propitious moments to solve difficulties, remove obstacles, and shower benefits on the needy. In *The Fashionable Lover*, there are at least three rescuers. Colin MacLeod is the most colorful of these and the linchpin of the plot. He is on hand at every critical juncture: He meets Augusta in the street and later saves her from rape, and he intercepts her father on his return and masterminds the final discovery. An attractive character with his homely, forceful dialect and blunt humor, he was intended by Cumberland to combat prejudice against the Scots. It is clear that Colin is economical on principle and not parsimonious. He disapproves of wasteful expenditure and lives frugally that he may be the more generous to others. He is the mouthpiece for several moral maxims that serve the playwright's didactic purpose.

Colin's confederate is a stock type, not quite so original. Like Tobias Smollett's Matthew Bramble, Mortimer cloaks his charitable deeds under an affected cynicism. Extremely susceptible to human suffering, he hides his soft heart within a crusty shell. He succors the afflicted, expecting no reward but his own gratification. He proves that one acts benevolently for purely selfish reasons and calls himself a voluptuary in virtue. Besides protecting Augusta, he is determined to extricate Lord Abberville from the snares of evil. The return of the prodigal is a familiar motif in Cumberland. He frequently attacks fashionable vice in his plays: Dueling is discussed in *The West Indian* and condemned as ignoble murder. Gambling is another favorite topic and is treated as a serious crime; typically, it leads to other follies. Lord Abberville, for example, comes to realize that "gaming has made a monster of me"; grateful for his reprieve on the brink of ruin, he promises to reform.

The ending is conventional: The dishonest are chastised, the wicked repent, and the chaste lovers, blissfully united, are lavishly endowed with fortune. This is the "tin money" of which Goldsmith complained; the conclusion demonstrates the sentimentalist's rather simplistic view of poetic justice. Virtue need not wait for the hereafter; Cumberland himself takes on the role of Providence, distributing appropriate rewards and punishments before the curtain falls.

THE WHEEL OF FORTUNE

Romantic love is often at the center of Cumberland's plots, which typically revolve around a young couple who encounter difficulties in bringing their attachment to fruition. The obstacles they face recur: parental opposition, difference of class or fortune, misleading appearances, or the waywardness of one of the parties. A conventional pair of star-crossed lovers appears in *The Wheel of Fortune*. What is surprising is that their affair is secondary, significant only for its effect on the protagonist.

Roderick Penruddock is an unusual hero for a Cumberland play in that he is well past the age of courtship. In his youth, he was cruelly betrayed by his friend and robbed of his beloved. Bitter and disillusioned, he has withdrawn into gloomy seclusion. The play opens on his inheritance of a vast estate, to which the property of his enemy has been mortgaged. His accession to wealth gives him the power to destroy his foe and rouses in him long-suppressed emotion. The conflict of the play is internal, as he is tempted by, contends with, and eventually vanquishes the spirit of revenge.

In this brooding figure, the play shows signs of the taste for melodrama that was to dominate the English stage in the nineteenth century. There are also certain Romantic tendencies that link it to a later era. Immediately striking is the setting; the first scene takes place in a wild and remote landscape, extremely picturesque. The character of the misanthrope is well adapted to his environment: Penruddock is not only an isolated but also an alienated man. Deeply passionate, he has never forgiven his injuries. Inexorable in anger, he is equally tenacious in love. Though rejected and forgotten by his betrothed, he retains her image fresh in his mind and is haunted by her voice. The anguish of his loss has driven him close to madness.

The turbulence of Penruddock's mind is shown by the intemperance of his language. He rails at the beguiling world that entices only to destroy: "Away with all such snares! There's whore upon the face of them." At home in a stormy wasteland, he is out of place in London. In a gaily festooned ballroom, he looks "like a gloomy nightpiece in a gilded frame." In the streets, the beggars shrink away from his grim visage, which bears the "mark of Cain." He is almost Byronic in his role as a man set apart by a fateful destiny.

Penruddock also shows the Romantic need to escape the corrupting influence of society. He is more content in a simple cottage than in the splendid mansions of the city. He is loath to leave his humble abode and anxious to return. When he has won his battle of conscience, he looks forward to the solace of a self-approving conscience in his rural retreat.

This is a familiar notion in a sentimental play, that good deeds are also pleasurable. One finds an increasingly greater emphasis as the century progresses on sensual gratification, on luxuriating in emotions for their own sake. Penruddock shows signs of this preoccupation; he is completely engrossed by his own subjective experience. Wandering the streets of London, he considers the tumult outside as a reflection of his own state of mind. At every stage of the action, he feels his own mental pulse. Moreover, he deliberately seeks out potentially stimulating situations. He rereads Mrs. Woodville's letter for the tender melancholy it produces, which he indulges to the full. His self-consciousness is characteristically Romantic.

Despite these innovative features, Penruddock is contained within the structure of a sentimental play, and in the end he is reclaimed. The change begins in the third act, when he abandons his aloof and ironic pose to defend his actions. He sympathizes strongly with Henry and is finally able to forgive his debtor. Consonant with Cumberland's philosophy, the spirit of vengeance has been a brief aberration in an otherwise benevolent soul. Apparently, Penruddock's former state of alienation has also been a distortion of his true nature, to which he is now restored. By the end of the play, he has grown remarkably sociable. He compares his heart, overflowing with sympathy, to a river flooding its banks. The bonds have been reestablished, and Penruddock has been accepted back into society.

In *The Wheel of Fortune*, enormously popular in its day, Cumberland demonstrated his ability to adapt to the latest literary trends; however, later he fell back on his old recipes for success, despite the fact that these outmoded forms failed to please. In his last years, he complained of the deterioration of standards, to which he would not accommodate himself, and pleaded for tolerance. Cumberland's influence on the theater effectively ended in 1795.

OTHER MAJOR WORKS

LONG FICTION: *Arundel*, 1789; *Henry*, 1795.

POETRY: *An Elegy Written on St. Mark's Eve*, 1754; *Odes*, 1776; *Miscellaneous Poems*, 1778; *Calvary: Or, The Death of Christ*, 1792; *A Poetical Version of Certain Psalms of David*, 1801; *The Exodiad*, 1807 (with Sir James Bland Burgess); *Retrospection*, 1811.

NONFICTION: *Anecdotes of Eminent Painters in Spain During the Sixteenth and Seventeenth Cen-* turies, 1782; *The Observer*, 1785; *Memoirs of Richard Cumberland, Written by Himself*, 1806-1807; *The Letters of Richard Cumberland*, 1988 (Richard J. Dircks, editor).

TRANSLATION: *The Clouds*, 1798 (of Aristophanes' play).

MISCELLANEOUS: *The London Review*, 1809 (editor); *The British Drama*, 1817.

BIBLIOGRAPHY

Bevis, Richard. *The Laughing Tradition.* Athens: University of Georgia Press, 1980. Focusing on the varieties of comic theater in the age of actor David Garrick, Bevis investigates the traditional critical dichotomy between an entrenched, uninspired sentimental mode and an upstart, imaginative laughing mode. He discusses Cumberland's major comedies as a response to audience demands for "clean fun" and morally uplifting themes.

Campbell, Thomas J. "Richard Cumberland's *The Wheel of Fortune*: An Unpublished Scene." *Nineteenth Century Theatre Research* 11 (1983): 1-11. This article demonstrates what can happen to a play as it passes from text to performance. The omitted scene was probably cut by John Kemble, who played the comic lead of Penruddock in the first performance.

Detish, Robert. "The Synthesis of Laughing and Sentimental Comedy." *Educational Theatre Journal* 20 (1970): 291-300. Detish argues that a proper reading of Cumberland's most important play, *The West Indian*, requires a recognition of the tension between laughing comedy aggressively espoused by Oliver Goldsmith in the 1770's and sentimental comedy dominant since the days of Richard Steele.

Dircks, Richard J. *Richard Cumberland.* Boston: Twayne, 1976. This full-length critical study of Cumberland's life and works evaluates Cumberland's little remembered novels and poems, as well as the more important plays, to present a complete picture of a writer who produced literature popular with contemporary audiences but uninspiring to, and not influential on, the next generation of authors.

Traugott, John. "Heart and Mask and Genre in Sentimental Comedy." *Eighteenth Century Life* 10 (1986): 122-144. The author considers Cumberland's *The Jew* among the worst sentimental comedies of the eighteenth century for its "genteel vulgarity." In contrast to the plays of Oliver Goldsmith and Richard Brinsley Sheridan, Cumberland's work coyly courts a sense of worldliness that it affects to scorn. Traugott offers on thematic grounds an explanation for the lack of reputation of Cumberland's later plays.

Lorna Clarke,
updated by Robert M. Otten

FRANÇOIS DE CUREL

Born: Metz, France; June 10, 1854
Died: Paris, France; April 26, 1928

PRINCIPAL DRAMA

L'Envers d'une sainte, pr., pb. 1892 (revision of *L'Ortie*; *A False Saint*, 1916)

Les Fossiles, pr., pb. 1892, revised pr. 1900 (*The Fossils*, 1915)

L'Invitée, pr., pb. 1893

L'Amour brode, pr., pb. 1893 (revision of *Sauvé des eaux*)

La Nouvelle Idole, pb. 1895, pr. 1899

La Figurante, pr., pb. 1896

Le Repas du lion, pr. 1897, pb. 1919, revised pr. 1920 (*The Lion's Meal*, 1942)

La Fille sauvage, pb. 1902, pr. 1906

Le Coup d'aile, pr., pb. 1906 (*The Beat of the Wing*, 1909)

La Danse devant le miroir, pr., pb. 1914 (revision of *Sauvé des eaux*)

La Comédie du génie, pb. 1918, pr. 1921

L'Âme en folie, pr. 1919, pb. 1920

Théâtre complet, pb. 1919-1924 (6 volumes)

L'Ivresse du sage, pr., pb. 1922

Terre inhumaine, pr. 1922, pb. 1923

La Viveuse et le moribond, pr., pb. 1926

Orage mystique, pr., pb. 1927

OTHER LITERARY FORMS

Before becoming a playwright, François de Curel attempted for several years to write fiction. Three of his short stories appeared in French magazines between 1886 and 1894, and he published three novels: *L'Été des fruits secs* (1885; the summer of withered fruits), *L'Orphelinat de Gaëtan* (1888; the orphanage of Gaëtan), and *Le Sauvetage du gran-duc* (1889; the rescue of the grand duke). Charles Maurras, in reviewing the last novel, urged Curel to try writing for the theater instead—a bit of advice that Curel promptly followed.

ACHIEVEMENTS

François de Curel was perhaps the most important new French playwright introduced by André Antoine's Théâtre Libre, which between 1887 and 1896 freed French drama from the rigid form and trivial themes of the "well-made play" popularized by Eugène Scribe and Victorien Sardou. Produced at the Théâtre Libre in 1892, Curel's *A False Saint* and *The Fossils* failed with audiences but were praised by critics—a pattern that followed him throughout his career until the last decade or so, when he finally achieved some popular success. The critical praise did gain for him entry into the more conventional Parisian theaters, where most of his subsequent plays were produced, though the spirit of the Théâtre Libre remained his chief inspiration (and indeed, Antoine acted key roles in some of his later plays). Curel viewed the theater as a place for airing serious concerns rather than for offering mere entertainment. His part in educating the French public to this view is indicated by the public acceptance of his work in the last stage of his career, when two of his plays had impressive runs and most of his earlier plays were revived.

Aside from his brief vogue and his undoubted historical significance, Curel's achievement is problematical. He is reminiscent of a less talented Henrik Ibsen. Like the mature Ibsen, Curel presents a surface realism that is broken through by symbolism and poetic passages. Like Ibsen, Curel tends to center his plays on strong central characters. Unfortunately, Curel lacked Ibsen's knowledge of the theater and skill in dramaturgy. Curel's clumsiness surfaces, for example, in improbable plots, in occasionally long-winded speeches and debates, and in the way his characters sometimes announce the exposition or analyze themselves. Despite strenuous efforts to revise most of his plays after he gained experience, Curel never overcame his awkwardness. This awkwardness, combined with his shaky public reception for so long, apparently limited the dissemination of Curel's plays outside France.

It seems unlikely that Curel's plays will ever be revived, except possibly as camp. He wrote a drama of ideas, and his ideas are now outdated or at best quaint (he was an aristocrat and a chauvinist, both French and male). If some of Curel's plays are ever brought to the modern stage, it will be those that best present an enduring theme: the efforts of individuals to cope with change. Among such plays are *A False Saint*, *The Lion's Meal*, and *The Beat of the Wing*, but Curel's little masterpiece on this theme is, as the title suggests, *The Fossils*. Generally speaking, Curel's best plays are those in which he closely engages, either openly or in disguise, the circumstances of his own life.

BIOGRAPHY

The facts of François de Curel's life have an enormous bearing on his work, explaining not only why he became a playwright but also, in many instances, his choice of themes. Curel presents the unhappy spectacle of a person caught both between two times and between two countries. As so often seems the case with artists, Curel's art flowed out of his unhappiness. By and large, his life is a story of frustration, especially frustrated pride.

Curel would seem initially to have had little reason for frustration. On his father's side, he was a viscount, tracing his aristocratic roots all the way back to the Crusader Gaulthier de Curel. By the time of Curel's birth, however, the aristocracy was under attack: After repeated revolutions, republican sentiment ran high in France, serving not only to restrict the aristocracy's actual power but also to hold the ancient privileges up to scorn.

Still, his mother's side of the family seemed to offer ample scope for a young man's energies: His mother's family, the de Wendels, were rich and powerful ironmakers in Alsace-Lorraine, and it was this family industry that Curel was educated to enter. After attending the College of the Jesuits in Metz, he took a degree in metallurgical engineering from the École Centrale des Arts et Manufactures at Nancy in 1876. Meanwhile, following the Franco-Prussian War (1870-1871), the Germans had annexed the territory of Alsace-Lorraine. Before they would let him help manage the family industry, the German authorities demanded that Curel renounce his French citizenship and become an official German subject. This Curel indignantly refused to do.

Thereafter, the young French engineer with the proud heritage retreated to his estate and settled into a daily round of reading, hunting, and "living." It seems only natural that this brooding existence would eventually lead to literary efforts, first in fiction, then in drama. Here, too, Curel seemed doomed to frustration, until after years of struggle, he submitted three plays under three different names to André Antoine at the Théâtre Libre. Antoine accepted all three (though he produced only one after he learned Curel's stratagem), and Curel was ecstatic. Later, Curel wrote that going to Paris to help with the productions of his plays at the Théâtre Libre was among the happiest experiences of his life. Moreover, he found in Antoine a strong advocate to whom he was always thankful.

The details of Curel's personal life are scanty. He remained a bachelor all his life. There is some evidence that Curel, a spiffy, energetic little man with almost a military bearing, was exceptionally single-minded in his pursuit of *la gloire*, which he finally attained in 1918 when he was elected to the French

Academy. He died ten years later, after writing several more plays and seeing his complete works for the theater published between 1919 and 1924.

ANALYSIS

The term "drama of ideas" provides a convenient starting point for understanding François de Curel's work. Curel's interests ranged over most of the burning issues of his day: science versus morality (*La Nouvelle Idole*), capital versus labor (*The Lion's Meal*), savagery versus civilization (*La Fille sauvage*), love versus war (*Terre inhumaine*), patriotism and the pursuit of glory (*The Beat of the Wing*), the springs of artistic achievement (*La Comédie du génie*), and the nature and power of love (several plays).

Behind all this miscellany, however, is a strong singleness of purpose. Just as Curel became an artist to justify his existence, so the art he created strives to achieve the same aim. The issues about which Curel chose to write generally bore some relationship to his personal circumstances, and he did not so much empathize with the characters he created as create characters to express some aspect of his personality. In itself, the wide range of issues on which he focused represents the attempt of an outmoded aristocrat to cope with change, to join the life of his time, yet he did not so much join it as fight it. At heart he remained a first-class reactionary, using a since-perfected technique: While seeming to accept the new ideas, he co-opted them to serve the old order.

What enabled Curel to absorb new ideas but maintain an essentially reactionary stance was his acceptance of the theory of vitalism, which was gaining ascendancy in his time over the impotent and outmoded Victorian fashion of moralizing. Encouraged by such thinkers as Friedrich Nietzsche and Henri Bergson, reflected in the drama of Henrik Ibsen and George Bernard Shaw and the psychological theories of Sigmund Freud and Carl Jung, vitalism was an amalgam of Romanticism and the new science that proved to be consistent with literary naturalism. Instead of God, vitalism posited some vague "life force" at work in the universe. In human beings, the life force expressed itself through the instincts, which were the real mainsprings of human behavior beneath all the polite and effete forms. Living right meant discovering one's real nature and being true to it (as does Nora in Ibsen's *Et dukkehjem*, pr., pb. 1879; *A Doll's House*, 1880). Thus, Curel's version of true love is rough-and-ready procreation; romance is a hindrance that delays, distracts, and dissipates the life force (sometimes fatally). More important, being true to one's own nature means that a savage will return to savagery, that civilized beings will recognize the French flag as their greatest symbol, and that the cream of society—that is, the aristocracy—will rise to the top (and peasants will be peasants).

In technique, also, Curel was not as avant-garde as his initial association with the Théâtre Libre suggests. He does not indulge in the naturalistic excesses of the "slice of life" (*tranche de vie*); instead, his technique is a mix of the old and new that is again reminiscent of Ibsen. Like Ibsen, Curel offers a realism that is propelled by the well-oiled devices of the well-made play. In attempting to appeal to audiences who preferred not to be taxed intellectually, Curel continued to use the current tricks of the trade while aiming at raising the moral and intellectual standards of the day.

A FALSE SAINT

A False Saint was Curel's first play to be produced. One of the three plays that the aspiring playwright submitted to Antoine at the Théâtre Libre, its 1892 production favorably impressed the critics in the audience but not the audience itself, which stamped and tried to interrupt the performance. The audience's displeasure is understandable, because *A False Saint* is dominated by the powerfully negative figure of Julie Renaudin, whose character could be considered a precursor to the Nazi mentality. The play, however, did not serve as a warning of the dangers inherent in amoral vitalism when it is thwarted and perverted; instead, Julie's destructive instincts are merely a negative testimony to the elemental power of the life force. It is a force not to be denied, one way or another.

The play begins when Julie leaves the Order of the Sacred Heart and returns home after eighteen years. A conversation between Julie and her old confidante, Aunt Noémie, reveals that Julie can now safely return, since Henri, Julie's cousin and onetime fiancé, died three months before. Henri had jilted her and married a smart Parisian, Jeanne. In retaliation, Julie had pushed Jeanne into a ravine, causing her to give birth prematurely and almost causing the death of both mother and daughter. Still, Jeanne had not blamed Julie, nor had she betrayed her. Thereupon, Julie had entered the convent, ostensibly to expiate her guilt but in actuality, through her symbolic act of self-immolation, to stir Henri's guilt. She succeeded, as Jeanne now tells her. Julie is pleased, but not for long. Left unable to bear another child, Jeanne told Henri of Julie's criminal behavior. Maddened to learn this, Julie returns to her quest for revenge, this time picking on Christine, Jeanne and Henri's daughter. Gaining the admiring girl's confidence, Julie tries to destroy Christine's engagement to young Georges Piérrard. Julie runs Georges off, persuades Christine that the fellow is unworthy, and causes Christine to enter the convent. Only when Christine discloses that her father's deathbed thoughts had been full of Julie, to whom he had urged Christine to be kind, like a daughter, does Julie relent. Confessing her vengeful aims, Julie determines to reenter the convent, and Christine and Georges are left to patch things up.

Curel also patches things up somewhat with the ending of *A False Saint*. Combined with the play's title and some pointed comments of young Piérrard, the perfunctory ending finally makes a muted moral judgment on Julie's behavior. Otherwise, the play focuses too sympathetically on Julie's bitter destructiveness, still improbably strong after eighteen years of convent life. Perhaps Curel embodied some of his own bitterness in Julie. He was also no doubt enlightened by his audience's reception of Julie, whose essential nastiness is symbolized at the end when she squeezes a baby bird to death onstage.

THE FOSSILS

A much more attractive work than *A False Saint* is *The Fossils*, also produced at the Théâtre Libre in 1892. Again the production failed, but this time because of poor acting; again the critics hailed Curel as a powerful new talent. Several years later, *The Fossils* was successfully produced by the prestigious Comédie-Française, where the play entered the repertory. Of all Curel's plays, *The Fossils* is most likely to

appeal to a modern audience. More tightly plotted than his usual work, *The Fossils* again shows Curel dealing with material close to his heart, but openly and honestly. Indeed, *The Fossils* dramatizes Curel's most intense personal concern: the decline of the aristocracy.

The Fossils centers on the Duke of Chantemelle's family, but it is clear that the Chantemelles represent a class of sociological "fossils." Decadent and of no use to society, the Chantemelles are in danger of dying out. The only son, Robert, is dying of consumption, leaving no one to carry on the family name. Robert, however, discloses one last remaining hope: He has an illegitimate son, the result of an affair with Hélène Vatrin, his sister's former companion. His mother, the duchess, had ejected Hélène from the family circle under mysterious circumstances, but now there is a reconciliation, an arrangement, and a marriage whereby Robert assumes paternity. After the marriage, however, Hélène's earlier rejection comes to light. Before Robert, his father the duke had been Hélène's lover. As the duke says, the child is "ours" in more ways than one. The tensions aroused by these family disclosures and the efforts to keep the family from crumbling not only suggest the tenuous existence of the aristocracy but also make for strong drama in the manner of Greek tragedy. Some of the tensions are relieved when the family comes together around Robert's coffin in a powerful final scene: The family's instinct to survive triumphs over its terrible knowledge.

In his will, read in the final scene, Robert proposes a formula whereby the aristocracy will not merely survive but will again be a force in national life. Just as Robert's marriage with the commoner Hélène represents a compromise, so his formula represents a compromise with democratic principles. Earlier in some key imagery, Robert had expressed his preference for the Northern forest—where the tall oaks shading and protecting the undergrowth suggest the aristocracy—over the dull Riviera, where the sameness of the waves rolling in suggests the leveling effects of democracy. In his formula, Robert proposes that the hereditary aristocracy educate itself to be an aristocracy of merit so that it might survive as the big oaks do, shading and protecting the scrawny undergrowth. After all, the aristocracy might as well make itself useful, and what better way than to go on doing what comes naturally? Such was the formula that Curel also proposed in *The Lion's Meal*, as an alternative to socialism, and such was apparently the formula on which he based his own life.

THE BEAT OF THE WING

Produced at the Théâtre Antoine (the former Théâtre Libre) in 1906, with Antoine in the lead role, *The Beat of the Wing* was scheduled for revival in 1915 but prohibited by the wartime French censor. As a play concerning a French officer who turns against the French flag, written by a native of Alsace-Lorraine who was waiting out the war in neutral Switzerland, *The Beat of the Wing* did perhaps raise a few questions. Still, if the play is properly understood, the censor's prohibition seems ludicrous. *The Beat of the Wing* must be one of the most fervent paeans to patriotism ever written; indeed, the patriotism expressed here might better be described as old-style chauvinism. The play is about the search for glory—which, when attained, lifts one above common humanity like an eagle carrying one aloft—but glory is narrowly defined as distinguished service to France.

At the beginning of the play, Bernard Prinson's search for glory, as a leading French politician, is compromised by the sudden appearance of his renegade brother, Michel. A former army officer and explorer, Michel had experienced the fluttering wings of glory himself when he was hailed for conquering a rich Central African kingdom for France. Upon returning to the African kingdom, Michel promptly installed himself as dictator, committing such atrocities as those of Kurtz in Joseph Conrad's *Heart of Darkness* (1902). His greatest atrocity, however, was to have wiped out a French expeditionary force sent to quell him. He knew that he was dead to all hope of French glory as soon as he fired on the French flag. The natives eventually rebelled, mutilated Michel, and left him for dead. Somehow he survived and made his way to London, where he lived under an assumed identity. Now, with his horribly disfigured face and uncaring reprobate manner, Michel shows up at his brother's home just in time to embarrass Bernard politically. The outcome, however, is anticlimactic.

Michel flinches every time he sees the French flag, which is often (military maneuvers are going on). All that he wants is to be accepted into humanity again. Michel gains acceptance in the person of his illegitimate daughter, Hélène, a fellow family outcast who has spent most of her life stuck away in a boarding school. They run off together at the end of the play.

Like Curel's other works, *The Beat of the Wing* is notable for what it suggests, almost painfully, about its author. Again, the central figure, the jolly pariah Michel, seems to reflect Curel himself, scarred and unregenerate but still seeking acceptance and even glory. The idea of glory through service to France is consistent with Curel's notion of an aristocracy of merit. Curel's ideas here, however, are not sufficiently embodied in dramatic form. Too much of the play is taken up with the lengthy relation of Michel's improbable past, and after that not much happens except for a considerable amount of discussion about glory and the flag. This diffuse form is unhappily only too typical of Curel's dramaturgy.

VITALISM PLAYS

Many of Curel's plays—and many of his weakest—center on the theme of love; of his other remaining plays, most treat issues that are related to his vitalism. *La Fille sauvage* (the wild girl), for example, illustrates the enduring power of natural instincts through the story of an African maiden who is rescued out of savagery, tries to adapt to civilization, and eventually chooses to return to her savage origins. Three other plays, however, suggest the sublimation of elemental instincts into higher, refined forms. *La Nouvelle Idole* concerns a doctor who injects with a cancer virus a girl who is dying of tuberculosis. The experiment backfires when the girl recovers from her tuberculosis; thereupon the doctor also injects himself with the deadly cancer virus. Their willing sacrifice of themselves to scientific study, submerging the individual life instinct into a concern for humanity, shows a new avenue to nobility and glory. Similar themes are developed in *La Comédie du génie* (the comedy of genius) and *Terre inhumaine* (inhuman land). Exploring the wellsprings of artistic achievement, in the person of a playwright resembling Curel himself, *La Comédie du génie* recommends, instead of paternity, the channeling of the love instinct into a love for humanity. *Terre inhumaine* treats the chance encounter, in wartime Lorraine, of a German officer's highly born wife and a French spy who are drawn both to love and to kill each other; while deploring the ravages of war and their effect on the instinct to love, the play also demonstrates the sublimation of that instinct into a higher form: patriotism. These four plays are of mixed quality, though generally better than the plays about love. *La Fille sauvage* and *La Comédie du génie* are rambling structures, but *La Nouvelle Idole* and *Terre inhumaine* embody truly dramatic tensions.

THE LION'S MEAL

Of Curel's remaining plays, perhaps the one that is of greatest interest, and the highest quality, is *The Lion's Meal*. Here the political results of Curel's thinking are dramatized through the development of his central character, the aristocrat and industrialist Jean de Miremont. To atone for his unintentional killing of a workman, the young Jean dedicates his life to helping the workers' cause. At first he attempts to minister to the workers with the softening influence of religion but to little avail. Nor is socialism the answer: The workers are like children, too undisciplined and irresponsible to create their own social order. Instead, Jean matures to see enlightened self-interest and paternalism as the answer. By following his natural instincts to lead and to amass profit, Jean thereby creates the industrial order whereby the workers also benefit, even if he gets the lion's share.

The Lion's Meal sums up Curel's thinking nicely, spelling out the political implications only hinted at in *The Fossils*. Like *The Fossils*, *The Lion's Meal* shows Curel responding directly to his own situation, trying to cope personally with the changes of his time. Whatever the merits of Curel's solutions, it is in these plays, in which he directly engages the parameters of his own existence, that Curel is still interesting today.

OTHER MAJOR WORKS

LONG FICTION: *L'Été des fruits secs*, 1885; *L'Orphelinat de Gaëtan*, 1888; *Le Sauvetage du gran-duc*, 1889.

BIBLIOGRAPHY

Cardy, Michael, and Derek Connon, eds. *Aspects of Twentieth Century Theatre in French*. New York: Peter Lang, 2000. In its description of French theater in the twentieth century, this work provides context in which to understand Curel's later works.

SantaVicca, Edmund F., comp. *Four French Dramatists: A Bibliography of Criticism of the Works of Eugène Brieux, François de Curel, Émile Fabre, Paul Hervieu*. Metuchen, N.J., Scarecrow Press, 1974. A bibliography of the criticism that has been written about Curel and three other French dramatists.

Waxman, Samuel M. *Antoine and the Théâtre Libre*. 1926. Reprint. New York: B. Blom, 1968. This examination of Antoine and the Théâtre Libre looks at the influence that this theater had on Curel.

Harold Branam

D

GABRIELE D'ANNUNZIO

Born: Pescara, Italy; March 12, 1863
Died: Gardone, Italy; March 1, 1938

OTHER LITERARY FORMS

Gabriele D'Annunzio is more famous as a poet and novelist than as a dramatist. His first book of poems, *Primo vere* (1879, 1880), was assembled when he was a teenager, and he was very prolific thereafter, following with *Canto novo* (1882, 1896; new song) and *Intermezzo di rime* (1884, 1896; an interlude of verses). *Alcyone* (1904; English translation, 1977) was intended to be the third book in a heptalogy called *Laudi del cielo del mare della terra e degli eroi* (1899). The project was not completed, but the 1899 work was expanded to create *Alcyone*, as well as *Maia* (1903), *Elettra* (1904), *Merope* (1912), and *Canti della guerra latina* (1914-1918). D'Annunzio was also renowned, and sometimes notorious, for his novels; *Il piacere* (1889; *The Child of Pleasure*, 1898), his first, caused a scandal. *Giovanni Episcopo* (1892; *Episcopo and Company*, 1896) and *L'inno-cente* (1892; *The Intruder*, 1898) exhibit a Dostoevskian influence, while *Il trionfo della morte* (1894; *The Triumph of Death*, 1896) and *Le vergini della rocce* (1896; *The Maidens of the Rocks*, 1898) show the influence of Friedrich Nietzsche, Arthur Schopenhauer, and Richard Wagner. *Il fuoco* (1900; *The Flame of Life*, 1900), inspired by his affair with the well-known Italian actress Eleonora Duse, caused another scandal. Throughout his career, he published collections of prose, including short stories, sketches, and meditations, such as *Terra vergine* (1882, 1884; the virgin land), *Il libro della vergini* (1884; the book of the virgins), and *San Pantaleone* (1886), later republished as *Le novelle della Pescara* (1902; *Tales from My Native Town*, 1920). Later, D'Annunzio also wrote *Contemplazione della morte* (1912; contemplation of death), *Vite di uomini illustri e di uomini oscuri* (1913), *La Leda senza cigno* (1916; *Leda without swan*, 1988), *La musica di Wagner e la genesi del "Parsifal"* (1914), and *Il notturno* (1921; nocturne). He wrote the screenplay for the film *Cabiria* (1914), as well.

ACHIEVEMENTS

Gabriele D'Annunzio's plays contain some of the most poetically beautiful passages in Italian drama.

The early works, such as *The Dream of a Spring Morning* and *The Dream of an Autumn Sunset*, are lush, decadent, lyric, and effusive, very much in the *fin de siècle* style, shifting from the realism of Giovanni Verga, Luigi Capuana, and Guy de Maupassant (early influences) into the sensuality and eroticism of Oscar Wilde's *Salomé* (pb. 1893). Although D'Annunzio's reputation has suffered because of his overtly fascist politics and because modern literature has moved toward a starker mode of expression, he has been called the greatest lyric talent in Italy in the twentieth century. *The Daughter of Jorio* represents D'Annunzio at his best, combining realistic details of folklore and peasant life in the Abruzzi region with passionate dialogue and intense emotion. It is usually called D'Annunzio's masterpiece and has often been revived.

BIOGRAPHY

Gabriele D'Annunzio was born on the Adriatic coast in the main town of the Abruzzi region, Pescara, to Francesco Paolo D'Annunzio and Luisa De Benedictis of the "pure Sabellian race." His mother is reported to have said, "My son, you are born on a Friday and in March. Who knows what great things you will do in the world!" The prediction was borne out as he manifested his literary talent at an early age. A brilliant, precocious student at one of the best schools in Italy, the Liceo Cicognini in Prato, he published his first poem, "Ode a Re Umberto" (ode to King Umberto), in 1879. His first book of poems, *Primo vere*, followed that year. These works exhibited the influence of poet Giosuè Carducci's *Odi barbare* (1877; *Barbarian Odes*, 1939); Carducci had attempted to bring Italian poetry from Romanticism back to its classical roots by experimenting with the rhythmic structure of Greek and Latin verse forms, while intensifying certain Romantic elements.

When he moved to Rome in 1881 to attend the university, D'Annunzio was already well known, having been praised by Giuseppe Chiarini in an enthusiastic article in *Fanfulla della*

Domenica. D'Annunzio further increased his nascent fame by spreading a rumor of his death, showing the flamboyance that would mark his entire life. He became part of the literary and intellectual life of Rome and contributed to newspapers and reviews such as *La cronaca bizantina*, *Il capitan Fracassa*, and *La tribuna*. His second book of poetry, *Canto novo*, was praised; his third, however, *Intermezzo di rime*, aroused a fire storm of controversy, the first of many in his life. Considered too sensual, the book provoked a debate on decorum in literature and even drew sharp criticism from Chiarini, who believed that D'Annunzio had betrayed his promise with an im-

Gabriele D'Annunzio (Library of Congress)

moral work. All this criticism merely made D'Annunzio more famous.

In 1884, his *Il libro della vergini* aroused another controversy, not only because of its contents but also because of a disagreement between author and publisher concerning the cover design. In 1885, D'Annunzio was wounded in the head in his second duel but went on with his writing, a year later publishing *San Pantaleone*, a collection of naturalistic sketches and stories influenced by Verga and de Maupassant. It, too, provoked the predictable culture shock, by now a trademark of D'Annunzio's career. As if literary disputes were not enough, he became involved in politics, publishing *L'armata d'Italia* (1888; the Italian fleet), calling for Italy to build up its naval power.

His first novel, *The Child of Pleasure*, remains his most famous and once again whirled him into controversy. Written at the house of painter Francesco Paolo Michetti, it focused on the sensual pleasures of Roman life and has been called a "breviary of decadence," the hero confusing art with life. D'Annunzio would later recognize his hero as a type of Superman, as defined by Nietzsche. Trying to live out this role made D'Annunzio the greatest of the decadents and resulted in numerous scandals, duels, and his divorce in 1891 from his wife of eight years, Maria Hardouin di Gallese, by whom he had three sons.

During his year of military service, D'Annunzio wrote *Episcopo and Company*, which shows the influence of Dostoevski. *Poema paradisiaco* (1893) shows the corresponding influence in poetic form. In 1891, he moved to Naples and continued to waver between the Dostoevskian influence (*The Intruder*) and the Nietzschean (*The Triumph of Death*), in which one can perceive a desire to escape decadent sensuality by death. Inspired by Nietzsche's *Die Geburt der Tragödie aus dem Geiste der Musik* (1872; *The Birth of Tragedy*, 1968), D'Annunzio set sail in 1895 for the Aegean Islands, a trip that would push him toward the writing of drama and that inspired *Maia*, a collection of poetry flowing in free rhythms, evoking the heroic glory of ancient Greece.

On his return, D'Annunzio met the great tragic actress Eleonora Duse and began his scandalous affair with her, as well as one of the most productive periods of his life. Duse agreed to act only in his plays, and, settling into a villa in Settignano, near Florence, they worked together in productions of such plays as *The Dream of a Spring Morning*, *The Dead City*, *Gioconda*, and *La gloria*. He also became more deeply involved in politics during this period, having been elected to the Italian Parliament in 1897 for a three-year term. Called the "representative of Beauty" in some quarters, D'Annunzio switched from ultra-conservative to liberal politics with the words "I choose life!" He was not reelected.

His novel *The Flame of Life* made obvious reference to his ongoing affair with Duse and caused yet another scandal. During the affair, he also wrote his best poetry, in the collection *Alcyone*, celebrating summer on the Tuscan coast. By 1910, the costs of living "like a Renaissance prince" forced him to flee his creditors. He moved to Paris and wrote several works in French, including *Le Martyre de Saint Sébastien*, which was performed with music by Claude Debussy and dances by Ida Rubinstein.

In 1915, D'Annunzio, after offering his services to France, was given twenty-five thousand francs to pay off his debts and was sent home to Italy to call for Italian intervention against Germany. He made several speeches that were wildly received by those supporting him and on May 24, war was declared. Seeing himself in a heroic role, he immediately left for the front, serving in the cavalry, infantry, and navy. On one occasion, he invaded an Austrian port in a small motorboat. He also flew over Vienna, dropping anti-Central Powers leaflets. Fearless, he was wounded in the wrist and lost an eye.

At the war's end, D'Annunzio was commander of an air squadron in Venice. When the Treaty of Versailles severed Dalmatia from Austria, he, like many Italians, expected it to become part of Italy. He seized control of Fiume, Dalmatia's capital, with the proclamation, "Citizens, Gabriele D'Annunzio is here. Not a word. Weep for joy." Having occupied the city, he established a temporary government, soon dissolved under pressure from the Italian military. Though clearly guilty of treason, he was received as a hero and retired to his home, Villa Cargnacco, on Lake Garda at the foot of the Alps.

Although D'Annunzio's relationship to fascism is still a matter of debate, there is no question that he publicly supported the regime. He lived as a recluse after 1936, sleeping in a coffin (to get accustomed to it) and thinking of various ways to die flamboyantly, such as being blown from a cannon. He died of a brain hemorrhage in 1938 at his desk, writing with an old-fashioned quill.

ANALYSIS

As if to match the fervor with which Gabriele D'Annunzio lived, the passion with which a variety of his writings have been discussed is virtually unprecedented. Few writers have been so provocative in so many genres over such a long period, and, as a result, the measure of his literary achievement has been obscured. Oscar Wilde, playing a similar role in Britain, has drawn sympathy over the tragedy of his later life. However, D'Annunzio, the eccentric fascist hero in his villa, draws no such sympathy, and often it is difficult to tell whether critics object more to his life or his writings. In 1901, Francis Thompson criticized D'Annunzio's obsession with his role as artist and called it his greatest defect. Benedetto Croce called him a dilettante, while Henry James attributed D'Annunzio's success to the strange mingling of the aristocratic with the vulgar, which strikes the reader or viewer as odd, and extraordinarily interesting. Clifton Fadiman argued that D'Annunzio's vulgarity coincided with and enhanced the vulgarity of his epoch.

On the other hand, Arnold Bennett called the sexuality of his works "adult," "subtle," and "refined." Joseph Hergesheimer called him a genius, and Federico Nardelli called him the "only truly great Romantic." Even after he had cast the great Duse aside and violated much of her privacy with *The Flame of Life*, she seems to have thought of her lover as the dramatic equivalent to Wagner. She limited much of her repertory to his works and spent enormous efforts on creating the equivalent, for D'Annunzio, to the Wagner festival hall at Bayreuth.

A more balanced appraisal came from Ashley Dukes in 1911. He asserted that D'Annunzio had discovered his gift for word painting to be merely decorative and, therefore, had propped up his dramatic works with "two unsteady supports, a gross form of theatrical sensation" and "a bastard symbolism." Yet, he added, there was something more to D'Annunzio's drama than his words. He was a dramatist concerned with the problem of sex. He portrayed "conditions of high nervous tension without the skill to make them develop convincingly." He commented that D'Annunzio was "meteoric, productive of much dust and little drama," then added, "But there is grace in his flight. . . . The conjurer is sometimes a magician. He has the will to illusion. Let us be grateful." Dukes seemed to know that by most standards of dramatic art, D'Annunzio is odd, histrionic, and unconvincing. Yet this makes his often awkward dramas somehow arresting. Opera is often odd, histrionic, and unconvincing, yet arresting because of its music. D'Annunzio's drama can be seen in this operatic tradition. There is so much "music" in his lush writing that one is often willing to overlook whatever other faults it may contain.

By the time that he had begun writing drama, D'Annunzio was a whole-hearted enthusiast for the concept of the Superman. He had been developing the idea even before his reading of Nietzsche and had never completely conformed his perception of the Superman to that of the German philosopher. D'Annunzio saw himself in the Superman role, and his own courage (or madness) in the face of real danger cannot be doubted. He also found no need to be constrained by conventional moral ideas in his relationships with women, creditors, and the theatergoing public. He has been accused, not without justice, of having only this one idea woven through his entire œuvre.

THE DEAD CITY

After *The Dream of a Spring Morning* and *The Dream of an Autumn Sunset*, D'Annunzio wrote his second most successful play, *The Dead City*, which clearly reveals the Superman theme. An archaeologist named Leonardo is excavating the tombs of the Atrides in Mycenae. Somehow, this site, permeated with the bloodshed and horror familiar to readers of Aeschylus and other ancient Greeks, seizes control over Leonardo. He falls in love with his sister Bianca Maria, and when a great poet, Alessandro, falls in love with her, Leonardo kills her. Leonardo, in saying that he has done for her what no one else can do, reveals himself to be a Superman, unrestrained by the ordinary morality and conventional passions of other human beings.

Gioconda and Francesca da Rimini

Gioconda has its Superman in the form of a sculptor, Lucio Settala, who cannot create his art without the adulterous love of Gioconda. The Superman in *La gloria* is a political schemer of imperialistic and nationalistic beliefs, Ruggero Flamma. He becomes the lover of Anna Commena, the former mistress of Cesare Bronte, a liberal. After establishing an aristocratic dictatorship, Ruggero is assassinated by Anna.

In *Francesca da Rimini*, Francesca is portrayed with a bit more human sensitivity than D'Annunzio's usual heroes, and the reconstruction of the historical setting has often been praised, along with many exquisitely beautiful passages.

The Daughter of Jorio

The Daughter of Jorio has often been called D'Annunzio's dramatic masterpiece. He has often drawn from his childhood in the Abruzzi region for his short stories and sketches in the mode of Verga and de Maupassant, especially in the collections *San Pantaleone* and *Tales from My Native Town*. The play is set among superstitious peasants, and the details of their lives and the sense of place manifested in the play are often cited as the elements that make it so much better than many of his other works. In it, the shepherd Aligi and the daughter of a sorcerer, Mila di Codra, are lovers. Aligi's father comes to the lovers' cave and demands that his son return to the village and his betrothed. Tensions mount and Aligi strikes his father, killing him. To save Aligi, Mila assumes the guilt, claiming that she used sorcery to make it seem as though Aligi had done it. Eventually, even Aligi comes to believe her account, as Mila is carried away to be burned at the stake.

It is clear, even from this brief outline, how intense a play it is. The plot, though not beyond the realm of probability, is highly melodramatic—operatic—with high emotion: son killing father, woman dying to save the man she loves. The eloquent writing comes dangerously close to dragging down the play. Yet its unabashed emotionalism and eloquence seem appropriate to the story. Though some critics have interpreted the play as being about the good, yet fettered, passions of nature that are unchained and then destroyed by the greed and limited vision of ordinary people, most have accepted it for its surface value: the story of a heroic woman who sacrifices herself for love. On the play's American tour in 1909, the *Boston Transcript* summed up the favorable response: "There is no doubting the play's beauty as poetry, its power as drama, its vividness, . . . its insistent horror—and its insistent fascination." It was widely performed between its premiere and D'Annunzio's death.

La fiaccola sotto il moggio

La fiaccola sotto il moggio (the torch under the bushel) presents its theme of love more realistically than *The Daughter of Jorio* as it reveals the decadence of the family Sangros. *La fiaccola sotto il moggio*, *The Daughter of Jorio*, and *Francesca da Rimini* are often called D'Annunzio's most beautiful plays.

Più che l'amore

Più che l'amore (more than love) created another scandal at its premiere in Rome, even though it merely reworked the Superman theme. The hero, Corrado Branda, is an explorer in the Italian colonies of Africa who brags about killing a lion single-handedly and leading native troops against the enemy. He is also portrayed as a person beyond ordinary morality, as he cheats at cards and seduces his best friend's sister.

La nave and Fedra

La nave (the ship) combines the Superman theme with Italian imperialism, but, as Domenico Vittorini has observed, the love of the main character, Marco Gradico, for Basiola gradually obscures D'Annunzio's call to make the Adriatic an Italian sea. Love, or lust, becomes the major occupation of D'Annunzio's Superman, and all other ideals become secondary. The same is true of Phaedra's love for Hippolytus in *Fedra* (Phaedra), inspired by the ancient Greek myths, Seneca's tragedy, and Jean Racine's *Phèdre* (pr., pb. 1677; *Phaedra*, 1701).

Le Martyre de Saint Sébastien

After going into voluntary exile in France, D'Annunzio wrote several plays in French. The first, *Le*

Martyre de Saint Sébastien, created yet another scandal as the sexual overtones overpowered whatever religious emotion was contained in the piece. Its chief interest today is in the music written for it by Claude Debussy. D'Annunzio's career in drama ended at the outset of World War I. After the war, perhaps he sensed that whatever he had wished to say on the stage had long since been exhausted.

OTHER MAJOR WORKS

LONG FICTION: *Il piacere*, 1889 (*The Child of Pleasure*, 1898); *Giovanni Episcopo*, 1892 (*Episcopo and Company*, 1896); *L'innocente*, 1892 (*The Intruder*, 1898); *Il trionfo della morte*, 1894 (*The Triumph of Death*, 1896); *Le vergini della rocce*, 1896 (*The Maidens of the Rocks*, 1898); *Il fuoco*, 1900 (*The Flame of Life*, 1900); *Forse che si forse che no*, 1910; *La Leda senza cigno*, 1916 (*Leda Without Swan*, 1988).

SHORT FICTION: *Terra vergine*, 1882, 1884; *Il libro della vergini*, 1884; *San Pantaleone*, 1886; *Le novelle della Pescara*, 1902 (*Tales from My Native Town*, 1920); *Le faville del maglio*, 1924, 1928 (2 volumes).

POETRY: *Primo vere*, 1879, 1880; *Canto novo*, 1882, 1896; *Intermezzo di rime*, 1884, 1896; *Isaotta Gùttadauro ed altre poesie*, 1886, 1890; *San Pantaleone*, 1886; *Elegie romane*, 1892; *Poema paradisiaco—Odi navali*, 1893; *Laudi del cielo del mare della terra e degli eroi*, 1899; *Maia*, 1903; *Elettra*, 1904; *Alcyone*, 1904 (English translation, 1977); *Merope*, 1912; *Canti della guerra latina*, 1914-1918; *Asterope*, 1949; *Le laudi*, 1949 (expanded version of 1899 title, also includes *Maia*, *Elettra*, *Alcyone*, *Merope*, and *Asterope*).

SCREENPLAY: *Cabiria*, 1914.

NONFICTION: *L'armata d'Italia*, 1888; *L'allegoria dell'autunno*, 1895; *Contemplazione della morte*, 1912; *Vite di uomini illustri e di uomini oscuri*, 1913; *La musica di Wagner e la genesi del "Parsifal,"* 1914; *Per la più grande Italia*, 1915; *La penultima ventura*, 1919, 1931 (2 volumes); *Il notturno*, 1921; *Il libro ascetico della giovane Itali*, 1926; *Le cento e cento e cento pagine del libro segreto di Gabriele D'Annunzio tentato di morire*, 1935; *Teneo te, Africa*, 1936; *Solus ad solam*, 1939.

MISCELLANEOUS: *Opera omnia*, 1927-1936; *Tutte le opere*, 1930-1965; *Tutte le opere*, 1931-1937; *Opera complete*, 1941-1943 (41 volumes); *Nocturne, and Five Tales of Love and Death*, 1988.

BIBLIOGRAPHY

Becker, Jared. *Nationalism and Culture: Gabriele D'Annunzio and Italy After the Reisorgimento*. New York: Peter Lang, 1994. A look at D'Annunzio and his links to Italian fascism that places his works within the history of his time. Bibliography and index.

Bonadeo, Alfredo. *D'Annunzio and the Great War*. Cranbury, N.J.: Associated University Presses, 1995. A scholarly examination of D'Annunzio's role and stance in World War I. Bibliography and index.

Ledeen, Michael Arthur. *D'Annunzio: The First Duce*. 1977. Rev. ed. New Brunswick: Transaction, 2002. An examination of the political beliefs and activity of D'Annunzio. Bibliography and index.

Valesio, Paolo. *Gabriele D'Annunzio: The Dark Flame*. New Haven, Conn.: Yale University Press, 1992. A critical examination of the works of D'Annunzio. Bibliography and index.

Woodhouse J. R. *Gabriele D'Annunzio: Defiant Archangel*. 1998. Reprint. Oxford, England: Oxford University Press, 2001. A good basic biography of D'Annunzio that covers his life and works. Bibliography and index.

J. Madison Davis

SIR WILLIAM DAVENANT

Born: Oxford, England; February, 1606
Died: London, England; April 7, 1668

PRINCIPAL DRAMA

The Cruell Brother, pr. 1627, pb. 1630

The Tragedy of Albovine, King of the Lombards,
   pb. 1629

The Just Italian, pr. 1629, pb. 1630

The Siege: Or, The Collonell, pr. 1629, pb. 1673

Love and Honour, pr. 1634, pb. 1649

The Witts, pr. 1634, pb. 1636

News from Plimouth, pr. 1635, pb. 1673

The Temple of Love, pr., pb. 1635 (masque)

The Platonick Lovers, pr. 1635, pb. 1636

The Triumphs of the Prince d'Amour, pr., pb.
   1636 (masque)

Britannia Triumphans, pr., pb. 1638 (masque)

The Fair Favorite, pr. 1638, pb. 1673

Luminalia: Or, The Festival of Light, pr., pb.
   1638

The Unfortunate Lovers, pr. 1638, pb. 1643

The Distresses, pr. 1639, pb. 1673 (also as *The
   Spanish Lovers*)

Salmacida Spolia, pr., pb. 1640 (masque)

The First Days Entertainment at Rutland House,
   pr. 1656, pb. 1657 (music by Henry Lawes)

The Siege of Rhodes, Part I, pr., pb. 1656, *Part II*,
   pr. 1659, pb. 1663

The Cruelty of the Spaniards in Peru, pr., pb.
   1658

The History of Sir Francis Drake, pr., pb. 1659

Hamlet, pr. 1661, pb. 1676 (adaptation of William
   Shakespeare's play)

Twelfth Night, pr. 1661 (adaptation of
   Shakespeare's play)

The Law Against Lovers, pr. 1662, pb. 1673

Romeo and Juliet, pr. 1662 (adaptation of Shakespeare's play)

Henry VIII, pr. 1663 (adaptation of Shakespeare's
   play)

Macbeth, pr. 1663, pb. 1674 (adaptation of Shakespeare's play)

The Playhouse to Be Lett, pr. 1663, pb. 1673

The Rivals, pr. 1664, pb. 1668

The Tempest: Or, The Enchanted Island, pr. 1667,
   pb. 1670 (with John Dryden; adaptation of
   Shakespeare's play)

The Man's the Master, pr. 1668, pb. 1669

OTHER LITERARY FORMS

Apart from his plays, Sir William Davenant is best known for his unfinished heroic poem, *Gondibert* (1651).

ACHIEVEMENTS

Sir William Davenant began his career as a playwright in the age of Ben Jonson and ended it in the age of John Dryden. Already a well-established playwright and poet laureate before the closing of the playhouses at the beginning of the English Civil War in 1642, Davenant managed a limited revival of theatrical entertainments toward the end of the interregnum. Despite the Puritan prohibition against staging plays, Davenant succeeded in obtaining government consent to present "entertainments" at Rutland House in London in 1656. These "entertainments" were musical rather than strictly dramatic, with set declamations instead of plots and entries instead of acts and scenes, but their popularity kept the theater from vanishing entirely during the protectorate of Oliver Cromwell and kept it poised for a revival after the restoration of Charles II in 1660.

Davenant may be credited with having introduced the first actress on the English stage, when Mrs. Edward Coleman sang the role of the heroine Ianthe during the production of his "opera" *The Siege of Rhodes* at Rutland House in the fall of 1656. This production also made use of the changeable scenery that until this time had been restricted to private theaters and court masques. After the Restoration, Davenant retained and expanded his use of changeable scenery, designing his new theater in Lincoln's Inn Fields to take advantage of its possibilities and spurring imitation by his competitors. Thus, the staging of almost every kind of drama was radically altered.

Davenant operated his theater under a patent that was granted to him by Charles II. In need of plays to produce, he revived some of Ben Jonson's and adapted several of William Shakespeare's. Indeed, Davenant's adaptation of *Macbeth* held the stage well into the eighteenth century, and his adaptation of *The Tempest* well into the nineteenth. As an innovator and an impresario, Davenant changed the course of English theatrical history and extended his influence well beyond his own age.

BIOGRAPHY

Sir William Davenant (or D'Avenant), son of John Davenant, a vintner, was born at Oxford, England, near the end of February, in 1606. As a young man, he wrote his first plays while living in the household of Sir Fulke Greville, and by 1638, he was sufficiently established as a poet and playwright to suc-

Sir William Davenant (Courtesy of the New York Public Library)

ceed Ben Jonson as poet laureate. When civil war broke out in 1642, Davenant, a staunch Royalist, risked his life for the Stuart cause. He fled to the Continent for a time, and in 1650 he was on his way to America to become lieutenant governor of Maryland when his ship was intercepted and he was captured and imprisoned in the Tower of London. It was there that he wrote most of his unfinished heroic poem *Gondibert*. Influential friends finally secured his release from the Tower, after which Davenant managed to live on good terms with the Puritan government. He eventually secured official permission to stage operatic entertainments at Rutland House in London, beginning in May of 1656.

Four years later, when the monarchy was restored, Davenant expected court preferment on the basis of his past service to the Stuarts. Although Charles II did grant him a patent to operate a theater, Davenant never regained the favor he had enjoyed under Charles I. Therefore, instead of relying on the patronage of the court, he busied himself with writing and staging plays for the Duke's Company, which he managed at Lincoln's Inn Fields in the public playhouse that he himself built to accommodate the changeable scenery that had been the prerogative of the earlier private theaters. His post-Restoration career lasted only seven years, but during that time, he managed to establish actresses on the English stage, to change play production radically, and to create a new appreciation of Shakespeare's plays, even if in a greatly altered version.

Davenant was married three times. In 1632, he wed a still unidentified woman to whom he was reputed to have been unfaithful. After her death (the date of which is unknown), Davenant married Dame Anne Cademan in 1652. She died in 1655; in that same year, he married Henrietta-Maria du Tremblay, who had four sons by previous marriages. They subsequently had nine sons. He had only one daughter, with one of his first wives. After Davenant's death in 1668, Henrietta-Maria helped prepare an edition of his works. Davenant was buried in Westminster Abbey. His epitaph epitomizes his achievements: "O rare Sir Will. Davenant."

Analysis

Thematically and technically, Sir William Davenant's plays link the theater of Charles I with that of Charles II. For example, the seeds of Restoration comedy are embedded in *The Witts*, in which Davenant explores the subject of wit, using heroes and heroines who prefigure those of Sir George Etherege, William Wycherley, and William Congreve. His early tragedies and tragicomedies, such as *Love and Honour*, explore the love and honor conflicts that later dominate Restoration heroic drama, beginning with Davenant's own *The Siege of Rhodes*. His court masques for Charles I and his queen, Henrietta Maria, used the movable scenery that he would popularize in the public theater after the Restoration. His revivals of the plays of Ben Jonson and his adaptations of Shakespeare's plays preserved and advanced the reputations of those writers during the reign of Charles II.

Davenant's plays as a whole reveal the "imagination" of two ages—that of Charles I and that of Charles II. The heroes and heroines of Restoration tragedy and comedy are nascent in Davenant's early plays and reach their maturity in his later plays, reflecting the heroic ideals and pragmatic cynicism of the age of Charles II. Indeed, the unpleasantness of the English Civil War and the uncertainties of the restored monarchy seem both to have enhanced expectations for a new heroic age and to have tempered those expectations with the wisdom of the recent past.

However well Davenant may have reflected his world, he also dared to try to shape it, both politically and theatrically. He was no mere spectator during the English Civil War but risked his life in the service of the Crown. In the theater, he risked Puritan opposition to present his entertainments at Rutland House, and he risked introducing actresses and innovative staging in the public playhouse. Like Young Pallatine in *The Witts*, Davenant had wit; like Alphonso in *The Siege of Rhodes*, he had heroic ideals; but above all, like the player and the housekeeper, he had a "playhouse to be lett." To his credit, he filled its stage with exceptional entertainments.

The Witts

The Witts is perhaps the best of Davenant's early comedies. During the seventeenth century, the term "wit" came to have multiple meanings. It could mean verbal cleverness expressed in appropriate and sustained repartee, the synthetic faculty of the mind that could see similarities in apparently dissimilar things, the ornamentation of discourse, or gamesmanship, implying a superior understanding of "the way of the world."

Gamesmanship comes closest to the meaning that concerns Davenant in *The Witts*. Most of the characters in this work are concerned with outmaneuvering their opponents in games of love and legacy. The contest is between the Truewits—those who truly have wit—and the Witwouds—those who think they have wit but do not. Davenant represents the first in the characters of Young Pallatine and Lady Ample; the second, in the characters of the Elder Pallatine and his companion, Sir Morglay Thwack, a country squire.

These last two characters come to London to live by their wits, which to them means seducing rich women who will afterward support them lavishly. Young Pallatine, already in London, has been successful at this game, having gone so far as to persuade his mistress Lucy to sell her belongings to pay for his indulgences. When the brothers Pallatine meet in London, the elder rejects his younger brother's plea for money, and Young Pallatine plots how he may reap both revenge and reward at his brother's expense.

Young Pallatine enlists Lucy in his plot. When Lucy's aunt finally turns her out of her house, she seeks aid from a friend, the wealthy Lady Ample, who, of all the play's characters, turns out to be the wittiest because she can best understand and control her own and others' actions. Lady Ample eventually uses that wit to foil her guardian, Sir Tirant Thrifty, who has picked out an inappropriate husband for her.

In one of the play's key scenes, Lady Ample discusses her wit with Lucy, whom she first takes to task for being so dull-witted and traitorous to her sex as to support a man. Lady Ample, who says she draws her wit from nature, argues instead for tempting "the Fowl" until it can be "caught" and "plume[d]." She then proceeds to demonstrate the application of this principle by acquiring complete mastery over the Elder Pallatine.

After a series of twists, turns, and deceits, engineered by Young Pallatine, Lucy, and Lady Ample herself, the Witwouds are totally humiliated. Sir Morglay Thwack resolves to return to the country while the Elder Pallatine is forced to recant his pretensions to wit. Surprisingly, however, Lady Ample, eager to escape the match arranged by her miserly guardian, agrees to marry the Elder Pallatine because she likes being able to dominate one who has so much money and so little wit.

Lady Ample further demonstrates her mastery over him by forcing him to sign certain bonds without him knowing what it is he is signing. It turns out to be a deed to part of his estate that he has unwittingly signed over to his younger brother. This generous settlement allows Young Pallatine and Lucy to marry. That done, Lady Ample confirms her intention to marry the Elder Pallatine, whom she "has the wit to govern." This scene, in which an independent woman sets the terms on which she will be married, is a forerunner of the famous "proviso" scenes of Restoration comedy in which like-minded heroines set forth the terms on which they will consent to marry. Thus, Lady Ample clearly proves to be the best gamester, and therefore the greatest wit, among all the characters. With the addition of more polished repartee and a worthier adversary, Congreve at the end of the seventeenth century would refine a charming Lady Ample into the brilliant Millamant of his *The Way of the World* (pr., pb. 1700).

THE FIRST DAYS ENTERTAINMENT AT RUTLAND HOUSE

The English Civil War temporarily halted Davenant's playwriting career, but toward the end of the interregnum, Davenant succeeded in convincing the Puritan government that theatrical entertainments could be useful in teaching morality. Davenant was granted permission to set up a semiprivate stage at Rutland House, his London residence, and to present *The First Days Entertainment at Rutland House* on May 23, 1656. Carefully avoiding even the semblance of drama, Davenant's entertainment was little more than two debates, interspersed with musical interludes. The first debate concerned the usefulness and morality of public entertainments. Indeed, *The*

First Days Entertainment at Rutland House was itself designed to demonstrate that public entertainments need not threaten either public morals or the Puritan government. The second debate concerned the relative merits of Paris and London, with, of course, English nationalism triumphant.

THE SIEGE OF RHODES

Encouraged by the success of this initial enterprise, Davenant again used Rutland House to present his "opera" *The Siege of Rhodes* in the fall of 1656. This time Davenant was more daring, moving his entertainment a step closer to drama by giving it a thin plot and characters developed beyond those of the debaters in *The First Days Entertainment at Rutland House*. In fact, Edward J. Dent in his *Foundations of English Opera* (1928) argues persuasively that *The Siege of Rhodes* was originally written as a play but altered to include instrumental and vocal music to circumvent the Puritan prohibition against the staging of plays. Nevertheless, Davenant was careful to call his work neither drama nor opera, but *The Siege of Rhodes: Made a Representation by the Art of Prospective in Scenes, and the Story Sung in Recitative Musick*. He even avoided the designation "act" by borrowing the term "entry" from the court masques, which he had composed during the reign of Charles I. Thus, *The Siege of Rhodes* has five "entries" instead of five "acts."

From the court masque, Davenant also borrowed the idea of using changeable scenery in his entertainments at Rutland House. Scenes were changed in full view of the audience and indeed were themselves sometimes the most important part of the entertainment. In his preface to *The Siege of Rhodes*, Davenant complains that the narrowness and shallowness of the stage at Rutland House greatly limited his use of spectacle. To create his effects, Davenant used a proscenium arch to frame movable backflats and wings. No attempt at realism was made; instead, the various scenes merely suggested an appropriate atmosphere (though not without inevitable incongruities). Generally, the actors played on the stage apron in front of the proscenium rather than close to the scenery behind it.

Women had long taken part in the court masques.

Usually the queen and some of her ladies-in-waiting would appear as goddesses, often accompanied by spectacular scenic effects. On the English public stage, however, men customarily acted women's roles. The closing of the theaters in 1642 meant that by 1656 Davenant had no readily available young actors specifically trained to interpret female roles. Furthermore, Davenant's exile in France had accustomed him to seeing actresses rather than actors in women's roles. Thus, his first production of *The Siege of Rhodes* also marked the first appearance of an actress on the English public stage, when Mrs. Edward Coleman sang the role of the heroine, Ianthe.

After the Restoration, Davenant converted this work into a heroic play. The essence of this genre was the conflict between love and honor. Its heroes and heroines either were exemplary in virtue or were Herculean figures not subject to customary moral niceties. Its verse form was the heroic couplet—the rhymed iambic pentameter closed couplet—deemed most suitable for the expression of heroic ideals. Finally, it emphasized spectacle, sometimes at the expense of sense, as George Villiers, duke of Buckingham, was to point out in *The Rehearsal* (pr. 1671, pb. 1672), which burlesqued the conventions of the genre.

The Siege of Rhodes is a quasi-historical drama. In 1522, the Ottoman Turks besieged Rhodes, garrisoned by the Knights of Saint John, under the command of Villiers de L'Isle-Adam. The knights fought valiantly and, though defeated, won the respect of the Turks and safe conduct from the island. Into this story Davenant inserts his hero, Alphonso, and his heroine, Ianthe. Alphonso is one of the defenders of Rhodes; Ianthe, his bride, having sold her jewels in Sicily to procure arms for the garrison, sets sail for Rhodes but is intercepted by the Turkish Fleet and taken prisoner by its commander, the sultan Solyman. Ianthe conquers the sultan by her virtue, and he grants her safe passage to Rhodes. Alphonso is less than happy to see her, since he assumes her safe conduct has been granted because Solyman has enjoyed her favors. Overcareful of his honor, Alphonso fails to recognize honor in others. His resultant jealousy momentarily overwhelms his love, but

when the siege resumes and both he and Ianthe are wounded, he at last realizes his folly, and the pair are reconciled, though the outcome of the siege is left in doubt.

To balance Alphonso's jealousy, Davenant introduces Roxolana, Solyman's wife, who is jealous of her husband's appreciation of and attention to Ianthe. Their marital discord is less definitely and happily reconciled because their marital peace is achieved not by love or trust but by the watchfulness of Roxolana's waiting-women, who have been charged to report any infidelity of Solyman.

Indeed, the notion of reconciliation is crucial to an understanding of *The Siege of Rhodes* because much of the play's structure seeks a creative rather than a destructive tension between opposites, especially between love and honor. Therefore, antitheses abound. For example, West and East are represented by the Rhodians and the Turks respectively, Christian and Muslim by Alphonso and Ianthe and by Solyman and Roxolana; the play's diction is liberally sprinkled with references to order and chaos, public and private worlds, harmony and discord, passion and reason, and light and darkness.

Viewed from this perspective, the marital discords of Alphonso and Ianthe and of Solyman and Roxolana take on new meaning. The former resolve their discord through the creative power of love and thereby reach a new harmony; the latter achieve only the appearance of a resolution, since the destructive power of jealousy still mars their relationship. These private reconciliations, however, are played out against the backdrop of a larger and much more public discord—the siege itself, which is left unresolved.

This larger conflict was not resolved until Davenant wrote part 2 of *The Siege of Rhodes*. Always the impresario, he staged parts 1 and 2 on alternate days at Lincoln's Inn Fields Theatre. Part 2 continues Davenant's theme of love and honor. This time, the defenders of Rhodes, threatened by famine and by the inevitability of a direct Turkish assault, must choose either an honorable death or an ignoble surrender. Ianthe is sent to negotiate with Solyman, who once again treats her honorably. Alphonso's jealousy is reawakened but eventually subordinated to his fear for

Ianthe's safety. Roxolana's jealousy, also rekindled, is somewhat assuaged by her awe of Ianthe's virtue, which lies not so much in Ianthe's reputation as in a sense of personal integrity that allows her to risk her reputation by returning to Solyman's camp. Similarly impressed, Solyman allows Ianthe to set honorable conditions for the surrender of Rhodes. Thus, Ianthe's virtue reconciles both private and public tensions—a happy ending indeed for an England still struggling with the destructiveness of its civil war and the uncertainties of its restored monarchy.

THE PLAYHOUSE TO BE LETT

A different sort of reconciliation must be effected in Davenant's *The Playhouse to Be Lett*. The prologue likens this work to a new-fashioned "monster" whose disproportionate limbs "are disjoyn'd and yet united too." Davenant, the successful theater manager, takes his audience behind the scenes to observe the workings of a Restoration playhouse, empty for the summer but about to be rented for various entertainments. The housekeeper and a player must choose among such prospective tenants as a dancing master, a musician, a gentleman, and a poet.

Four entertainments are selected, three of which are by Davenant himself. The French farce presented in act 2 is Davenant's own translation of Molière's *Sganarelle: Ou, Le Cocu imaginaire* (pb. 1872). Acts 3 and 4 revive two of Davenant's Rutland House entertainments: *The History of Sir Francis Drake* and *The Cruelty of the Spaniards in Peru*. Act 5 is a travesty of Katherine Philips's tragedy *The Death of Pompey* (1663), a translation of Pierre Corneille's *La Mort de Pompée* (pr. 1643).

Interesting as each of these entertainments may be, it is the action of the frame story that is of most importance, for *The Playhouse to Be Lett* is really a play about the problems of managing a playhouse. Together with plays about the problems of producing a play, it belongs to the sizable group of Restoration plays concerned with theatrical self-consciousness. Many of these plays use a frame story in which a playwright and one or more critics attend the rehearsal of a play, whose action is often interrupted by their comments or by those of the actors themselves, who step out of character momentarily. The epitome of this genre was *The Rehearsal*, which satirized John Dryden and poked fun at the absurdities of heroic drama.

Davenant, whose work preceded *The Rehearsal*, uses a rehearsal framework only in the loosest sense of that word. There is a rehearsal of what will be presented for the summer season, but there is no attempt to interrupt or to correct the individual presentations. In fact, the player and the housekeeper are not even the final judges of what is to be presented. Near the end of the first act, a crowd is gathering outside the theater in order to "see strange things for nothing." The player sends a dozen laundry maids with "tough hands" to keep them out. Nevertheless, at the end of *The Playhouse to Be Lett*, this imaginary audience is revealed to be, in reality, the actual theater audience that has been watching Davenant's entertainment. The player observes that somehow their neighbors have been let in; if they elect to stay, they are likely to hear "An Epilogue, since they have seen a Play." Thus, Davenant's audience is suddenly brought into the action of *The Playhouse to Be Lett*, and the frame characters' awareness of the audience is responsible for the abrupt ending of Davenant's entertainment with no judgments among the prospective renters having been made by the player and the housekeeper. Instead, those judgments will be made by the spectators themselves—a process Dryden was later to term the law of "pit, box, and gallery." The audience alone will determine the profitability of an entertainment. Indeed, throughout act 1, the housekeeper and the player discuss possible audience responses to the kinds of entertainments proposed by the prospective renters and even discuss packing the audience with favorable critics, including a one-handed man who claps by striking his hand against his cheek. Therefore, in giving the audience a look behind the curtain of the playhouse, Davenant also gives the audience a look at itself. His parading before them of the popular entertainments of the town, generated by his audience's insatiable appetite for novelty, would later be enlarged on by Henry Fielding in the third act of *The Author's Farce* (pr., pb. 1730), in which emblematic representations of the "pleasures of the town" vie for a chaplet to be awarded by the Goddess of Nonsense to her favorite devotee—an honor that eventually goes to Signior Opera.

Davenant's jest at the expense of his playhouse audience illustrates his capacity to play with the paradoxes of the imagination. One of the primary meanings of "imagination" in Davenant's day was the capacity to form images. As the player and the housekeeper in the first act of *The Playhouse to Be Lett* discuss the anticipated responses of their projected audience, they create the image of an early Restoration audience eager for novel entertainments. At the end of act 5, this image fuses with its underlying reality when this imaginary audience is identified with the audience present at Davenant's play. In turn, *The Playhouse to Be Lett*, termed a dramatic "monster" in its prologue, becomes an image of the audience because it reflects their tastes.

OTHER MAJOR WORKS

POETRY: *Madagascar: With Other Poems*, 1638; *Gondibert*, 1651 (unfinished); *The Seventh and Last Canto of the Third Book of Gondibert*, 1685; *The Shorter Poems and Songs from the Plays and Masques*, 1972 (A. M. Gibbs, editor).

NONFICTION: *The Preface to Gondibert with an Answer by Mr. Hobbes*, 1650 (with Thomas Hobbes).

MISCELLANEOUS: *Works*, 1673, 1968 (reprint); *Dramatic Works*, 1872-1874 (5 volumes, James Madiment and W. H. Logan, editors).

BIBLIOGRAPHY

Bordinat, Philip, and Sophia B. Blaydes. *Sir William Davenant*. Boston: Twayne, 1981. This volume begins with a chapter on Davenant's life and times and then surveys the early plays, the masques, and the Restoration plays. The bibliography is excellent, including even dissertations and theses as well as the usual primary and secondary sources.

Canfield, Douglas J. *Heroes and States: On the Ideology of Restoration Tragedy*. Lexington: University Press of Kentucky, 2000. This general study of Restoration tragedy contains an analysis of Davenant's *The Siege of Rhodes*.

Edmond, Mary. *Rare Sir William Davenant*. New York: St. Martin's Press, 1987. A scholarly study, with rich notes, that treats the whole career. Davenant as man of the theater is considered in chapters treating the early plays and masques, *Gondibert*, the opera, the formation of the "Davenant/Killigrew stage monopoly," and Davenant as theater manager and stage director. Helpful bibliography.

Wiseman, Susan. *Drama and Politics in the English Civil War*. Cambridge, England: Cambridge University Press, 1998. This study on what happened after the theaters were closed includes a chapter on Davenant and covers many lesser known figures.

Valerie C. Rudolph,
updated by Frank Day

ROBERTSON DAVIES

Born: Thamesville, Ontario, Canada; August 28, 1913
Died: Toronto, Ontario, Canada; December 2, 1995

PRINCIPAL DRAMA

Overlaid, pr. 1947, pb. 1949 (one act)
At the Gates of the Righteous, pr. 1948, pb. 1949
Eros at Breakfast, pr. 1948, pb. 1949
Hope Deferred, pr. 1948, pb. 1949
The Voice of the People, pr. 1948, pb. 1949
Eros at Breakfast and Other Plays, pb. 1949 (includes *Hope Deferred*, *Overlaid*, *At the Gates of the Righteous*, *The Voice of the People*)
At My Heart's Core, pr., pb. 1950
King Phoenix, pr. 1950, pb. 1972
A Masque of Aesop, pr., pb. 1952
A Jig for the Gypsy, pr. 1954 (broadcast and staged), pb. 1954

Robertson Davies (Jerry Bauer)

Hunting Stuart, pr. 1955, pb. 1972
*Love and Libel: Or, The Ogre of the Provincial
    World*, pr., pb. 1960 (adaptation of his novel
    Leaven of Malice, 1954)
A Masque of Mr. Punch, pr. 1962, pb. 1963
Hunting Stuart and Other Plays, pb. 1972 (includes
    King Phoenix and *General Confession*)
Question Time, pr., pb. 1975

OTHER LITERARY FORMS

Robertson Davies is known primarily as a novelist. His most highly acclaimed novels form the Deptford Trilogy: *Fifth Business* (1970), *The Manticore* (1972), and *World of Wonders* (1975). These three novels were preceded by another trilogy, set in the fictional community of Salterton: *Tempest-Tost* (1951), *Leaven of Malice* (1954), and *A Mixture of Frailties* (1958). Another trilogy consists of *The Rebel Angels* (1981), *What's Bred in the Bone* (1985), and *The Lyre of Or-*

pheus (1988). His novel *Murther and Walking Spirits* (1991) continued his interest in reconstructing the main character's past by means of supernatural devices. His earliest success was the publication of three books based on a newspaper column, "The Diary of Samuel Marchbanks," in which he offered witty observations on the social pretensions of a small Ontario town: *The Diary of Samuel Marchbanks* (1947), *The Table Talk of Samuel Marchbanks* (1949), and *Marchbanks' Almanack* (1967).

Davies also wrote a teleplay, *Fortune, My Foe* (1948), and he enjoyed a considerable reputation as a critic. His articles, essays, and observations have been collected in several books, including *A Voice from the Attic* (1960), *One Half of Robertson Davies* (1977), *The Enthusiasms of Robertson Davies* (1979), and *The Well-Tempered Critic* (1981). Subjects to which he turned his sharp pen included contemporary Canadian theater, the manners and mores of small-town residents, the humor of Stephen Leacock, the history of the Stratford Shakespearean Festival, and the Canadian national identity. His scholarly writing centered on theater history and dramatic literature, particularly of the nineteenth century.

ACHIEVEMENTS

Robertson Davies is recognized as one of Canada's foremost writers, and, although his influence was predominately in fiction, his impact on the emergence of drama and theater uniquely Canadian has been widely appreciated. The source of this influence was divided between his position as a respected critic and scholar and his original and striking dramatic writing. As Master of Massey College, a position he held from 1962 to 1981, and as founder and senior scholar of the Graduate Centre for the Study of Drama, Davies influenced two generations of students at the University of Toronto.

The period immediately following World War II was of great significance to the development of indigenous Canadian drama. A spirit of nationalism, arising in large part from the important contribution of Canadian regiments to the victory in Europe, fueled a renewed interest in plays about the Canadian experience. At the same time, there was a sharp increase in the number of plays being performed in theatrical centers such as Toronto. The new professional theater companies were looking for new plays that would appeal to local audiences and with which they could make their reputations. One such company was the Crest Theatre, and several of Davies' plays were written for this group. Other influential plays by Davies were written for amateur companies and became staples of the amateur repertoire in Canada. As a result, between 1945 and 1965 Davies was the dominant English-Canadian playwright.

Davies was awarded the Leacock medal for humor in 1955, the Lorne Pierce medal for contribution to Canadian literature in 1961, and, in 1973, the Governor-General's Award for Fiction. He was a fellow of the Royal Society of Canada, the recipient of honorary degrees from more than ten universities, an honorary member of the American Academy (the first Canadian to be so honored), and a Companion of the Order of Canada.

BIOGRAPHY

William Robertson Davies was born on August 28, 1913, in Thamesville, Ontario, to William Rupert Davies, editor of the *Thamesville Herald*, and Florence Sheppard McKay Davies. In 1926, the Davies family moved to Kingston, where William Rupert Davies became owner and editor of the Kingston *Whig* and later, when the two local papers merged, of the Kingston *Whig Standard*. The fictional town of Salterton, which provides the environment for three of Davies' novels, bears a remarkable resemblance to the town of Kingston.

Davies was greatly influenced by the literary and dramatic activities of his parents, both of whom had a lively interest in music and theater. At that time, there was little professional theater in the small towns of Ontario, but the family traveled regularly to Toronto, Ottawa, and Detroit to see productions touring out of New York or London. The influence of the great masters of the art of acting is felt in much of Davies' work, but most notably in *World of Wonders*, which is a fictional treatment of the Canadian tour of John Martin-Harvey, one of the last proponents of the nineteenth century school of Romantic acting.

Davies' love of theater was evident throughout his academic career. As a schoolboy, he dramatized classic novels for his fellow students to perform. He acted in local amateur theater productions in the community and at school. At Balliol College, Oxford, he was active in the Oxford University Dramatic Society as an actor, stage manager, and director. He also did his bachelor of literature thesis on Shakespeare's boy actors, publishing it in 1939.

The young Davies determined to make his career in theater, and, as there was virtually no professional theater in Canada at the time, he remained in England and found employment at the Old Vic Repertory Company. He performed only minor roles and proved more valuable in teaching theater history in the company school and doing literary work for the director, Tyrone Guthrie, an old school friend from Oxford. It was there that he met Brenda Mathews, a young Australian actress and stage manager, whom he married in 1940.

The theaters in London closed with the outbreak of World War II, and the Davies returned to Canada, where Davies became literary editor of *Saturday Night*, a monthly cultural magazine. In 1942, they moved to Peterborough, and Davies became the editor and publisher of the *Peterborough Examiner*, a position he held until 1962. In 1943, he began the syndicated column "The Diary of Samuel Marchbanks," featuring satiric observations and anecdotes about fictional characters, situations, and attitudes in a small Ontario town, as seen through the eyes of a thinly disguised Robertson Davies. Selections from this column were collected in three books: *The Diary of Samuel Marchbanks, The Table Talk of Samuel Marchbanks*, and *Marchbanks' Almanack*.

It was also at this time that Davies and his wife became active in local amateur theatricals. He began to write full-length and short plays, submitting one of them, *Overlaid*, to a play competition in Ottawa in 1947. As the winning play, it was produced by the Ottawa Drama League. The same group produced his next short comedy, *Eros at Breakfast*, the following year, and entered their production in the national amateur dramatic competition, the Dominion Drama Festival. The production won a trophy for best production of a Canadian play and Davies won the prize for author of the best Canadian play. Moreover, the production was selected to represent Canada at the Edinburgh Festival in Glasgow in 1949.

With this encouraging beginning, Davies went on to write, in quick succession, *Fortune, My Foe* (which carried off the same prizes as *Eros at Breakfast*), *At My Heart's Core*, and *King Phoenix*. By 1948, Davies had become the most produced English-Canadian playwright, with amateur groups across Canada performing his plays

Nevertheless, at this time, Davies' energies were being directed more and more toward the writing of full-length fiction. *Tempest-Tost, Leaven of Malice*, and *A Mixture of Frailties* were published in the 1950's, and in 1953, Davies discontinued the Marchbanks column. He did not, however, entirely turn his back on the theater; on the contrary, his writing benefited from two exciting new developments in Canadian drama. In 1953, the Stratford Shakespearean Festival was founded, and Davies became a member of the board of directors, a position he held until 1971. From 1953 to 1955, he published an annual record of the history of the festival, which was then under the leadership of his friend Tyrone Guthrie. These volumes were published as *Renown at Stratford*: *A Record of the Shakespeare Festival in Canada, 1953* (1953), *Twice Have the Trumpets Sounded*: *A Record of the Shakespeare Festival in Canada, 1954* (1954), and *Thrice the Brinded Cat Hath Mew'd: A Record of the Shakespeare Festival in Canada, 1955* (1955). The second development was the emergence of a fully professional theater company in Toronto, the Crest Theatre, for which Davies wrote several plays. The company produced his *A Jig for the Gypsy* in 1954 and *Hunting Stuart* in 1955. *General Confession* was written in 1956 for the same group but was never performed.

Davies' considerable energies were further diverted when, in 1962, he was appointed by Vincent Massey to be the first Master of Massey College, a college for graduate students at the University of Toronto. In 1960, Davies had been appointed a professor of English and began his teaching career. He remained a member of the academic community for

twenty years but was always skeptical about his adopted world, as is evident in the pointed satire in his novel *The Rebel Angels*.

In 1960, Davies attempted a dramatization of his novel *Leaven of Malice*, titled *Love and Libel*, which Tyrone Guthrie directed for the New York Theatre Guild. Reviews were mixed; the production closed after four days, and Davies himself was dissatisfied with his adaptation. He consented to rework the script for an amateur production at Hart House Theatre at the University of Toronto in 1973 under the same title as the novel, and it was this version that was produced at the Shaw Festival in 1975. In 1975, Davies wrote *Question Time* for Toronto Arts Productions, a leading Toronto professional company. Again, the results were not entirely positive. The reviews were mixed, and audiences were puzzled by the play's nonrealistic style. Davies was more comfortable writing for amateur groups, including the theater group at his old school Upper Canada College, which produced *A Masque of Aesop* in 1952 and *A Masque of Mr. Punch* in 1962. In 1967, the year of the centennial celebrations in Canada, he contributed one segment to *The Centennial Play*, which was written expressly for amateur audiences. It was given its first full-scale production by a group with which Davies had been associated at the beginning of his writing career, the Ottawa Little Theatre.

In 1981, Davies retired from his duties as Master of Massey College to dedicate himself full-time to his writing. Thereafter, he continued to contribute to scholarly and popular periodicals on a regular basis but concentrated on his novel writing. He contributed regularly to *The New York Times Book Review*, *Maclean's*, *Harper's*, and other literary periodicals in the last decades of his life. A television documentary on Davies, "The Magic Season of Robertson Davies," was aired in 1990.

ANALYSIS

In all of his nondramatic writing, Robertson Davies demonstrated a keen sense of the absurdity of social pretension, an awareness of the dark world of the unconscious, and a love of magic. In many of his fictional works, the theater plays an important part, whether it be the amateur production of William Shakespeare's *The Tempest* (pr. 1611), which sets the stage for *Tempest-Tost*, or the flamboyant actor-manager of the melodramatic school who holds center stage in *World of Wonders*. Regardless of genre, Davies' perspective is that of the ironic, detached, urbane, yet sensitive observer, a reporter of the quirks of fortune that act on human existence and that serve to reveal the inner workings of the heart.

The dramatic writing of Davies stands far removed from the mainstream of mid-twentieth century drama. The majority of modern drama is realistic in language and characterization, if not in form. Davies rejected this trend for older and blatantly theatrical models such as medieval masques and morality play and nineteenth century Romantic comedies and melodramas. In his commentary on his own plays, Davies confirmed his commitment to alternatives to realism. He rejected the naturalistic school of drama, which seeks to reproduce daily life on the stage, for, as Davies noted, it is the paradox of the theater that plays are sometimes most like life when they are least like a photograph of reality.

Davies' love for some of the older forms of drama sprang from his conviction that these forms were closer in spirit to the original, primal function of all art. He sought theater that would fill audiences with a sense of wonder. The theater, in Davies' view, should be a place of spiritual refreshment, and this is particularly the case, he suggested, in melodrama and in the earliest forms of drama. Theater began, he reminded his audience, as a temple, a place where people expected to experience the full range of human emotion—the glorification of the godlike in man as well as his invigorating wickedness.

Davies readily admitted to being an old-fashioned playwright longing for a theater that had perhaps entirely disappeared. He wrote plays that call for acting in the classic Romantic style he remembered so fondly from visits to the theater during his youth. His plays necessitate this larger-than-life manner because they deal with fundamental conflicts between archetypal forces.

Davies was equally unfashionable in the strongly didactic tone of his plays. He defined himself as a moralist, one who perceives several insidious diseases of the spirit and seeks to cure them with the powerful antidote of laughter. So strong were Davies' opinions that he eschewed subtlety in favor of direct statement, as well as a decidedly oracular tone thinly disguised with a sugary coating of wit.

Davies recognized that his attitudes ran against the *Zeitgeist*, but he remained true to his original commitment to the magical rather than the ordinary. As a result, his dramatic writing is remarkably unified in style.

The predominant identifying feature of Davies' plays is their language. Modern fashion leans toward dramatic dialogue that is colloquial, filled with slang and expletives, and minimal. Davies chose the opposite extreme, and his plays are linguistic feasts of wit, flights of fancy, and lucidity. Davies defended his style by pointing out that, for those with intelligence, style, sensitivity, and the wit to give form to random human discourse, conversation is an art. Davies' attitude toward conversation is expressed in *Fortune, My Foe* by Professor Rowlands, who describes himself as having a gift for something that is undervalued: good talk. Rowlands claims to be an artist, a master of poetry that is verbal and extempore but that is still poetry. Indeed, in general, the characters in the plays of Robertson Davies speak in a manner remarkably reminiscent of that of the playwright himself.

Davies' carefully constructed sentences are the perfect vehicle for another dominant attribute of his writing, his satire and parody of Canadian institutions and attitudes. There is nothing oblique about this element of Davies' dramas: The incorporation of the satiric element is very much a part of the moral thrust of the plays. Virtually every character in every play is given at least one well-constructed aphorism, and characters have a decided tendency to address one another in short moral lectures. At times these digressions threaten to slow the dramatic movement of the plot to a standstill, but the sheer pleasure of Davies' language retains the goodwill of the audience.

The witty repartee characteristic of a Davies play is generally given plausible motivation, given the setting and the intellectual attributes of the speakers. Chilly Jim and Idris Rowlands, who exchange quips and aphorisms in *Fortune, My Foe*, are two such plausible moral wits. Rowlands, as noted above, is a university professor who describes himself as a professional talker, a poet of conversation, while Chilly confesses that language is his hobby. Their conversations, which are filled with the most carefully crafted language, are entirely believable. Modern audiences are used to fast-paced and tightly edited forms of entertainment, but Davies crafts his plays for a pre-modern, slow-moving dramatic form and for audiences who prefer to savor *bons mots*.

In dramatic structure, Davies' plays are also strongly influenced by archaic forms. Several of his plays, most notably *Question Time*, take the form of a morality play, with a central character representing humankind interacting with personifications of the human psyche on a journey toward self-discovery. In *Question Time*, Peter MacAdam is a representative of humanity (his name means "son of Adam") and of all Canadians (as Prime Minister of Canada) who is launched on a journey into his unconscious mind after a plane crash in the Arctic. While he lies in a coma, his mind is freed to explore his inner landscape in search of his true identity. He encounters personifications of his own attributes—totem animals—and finally convenes the Parliament of the Irrational, wherein two versions of himself lead the debate as to whether he should live or die.

Debate is another traditional element of the morality play, and Davies' characters frequently engage in such contests. Many of his plays focus on two essential forces in conflict, with the balance clearly weighted toward one of the two parties. This is the case in *Overlaid*, where Pop represents life-affirming forces (Eros), and Ethel, life-denying forces (Thanatos).

In drawing on an archaic form such as the morality play, Davies did not stifle audiences with dusty scholarship. Rather, he adapted the model to realize the potential of the modern stage to become a forum for an exploration of those deep concerns humanity shares. Davies replaced the absolute Christian moral doctrines espoused by the medieval morality plays with a standard of judgment that is not external but internal. Davies was concerned with individuals'

judgment of themselves, their perception of their soul in its entirety, and their recognition of the unlived lives that, if unattended, are sure to have their revenge.

In characterization, Davies also rejected the expected naturalistic layering of details or the question-filled outlines of the contemporary theater. Instead, he relied on character-types as symbolic vehicles for his morality lessons. He generally structured a play around a single protagonist whom he presented in the most exciting and positive manner. He surrounds this character with a variety of less fully developed creations, all of whom exist to fulfill a thematic function, to embody a force against which the hero reacts. Minor characters are given single and striking identifying characteristics and then allowed to interact within situations that are crafted to bring essential conflicts to the surface.

Davies' heroes share the attributes of the artist, and those characters who stand in opposition embody those forces that seek to destroy or limit the artistic function. Davies' sharp juxtapositions of these forces indicate his condemnation of certain attitudes. Ranged against the positive force of art, which is linked with spiritual enrichment, intuition, sensitivity, perception, and wonder, are narrow materialism, ignorant respectability, cultural philistinism, dogmatic religion, science, modern impatience, insufficient education, and the absence of laughter. Those characters who lack a sense of humor are perhaps the most barren, pretentious, and emotionally undernourished (as well as the least appealing to the audience). Their grim devotion to principle—whether it be religious, social, or scientific—is the most effective force against the joyful spirit of the healthy soul.

In his most successful novels and plays, Davies explored the relationship between human consciousness, trapped as it is in the perceptions of daily reality and blinded by the limitations of sensibility, and the unconscious, that vast, uncharted, terrifying world whence springs all art, all vitality, and all meaning. From Davies' perspective, the conflicts of the unconscious mind are more real than the trivial, day-to-day concerns of observable reality.

Davies' fascination with the internal workings of

an individual dates, he reported, from the health dialogues in which he acted as a child. These little skits were set in such locales as the stomach and featured naughty foods as well as the angelic Miss Milk and Mr. Apple. In one of his earliest plays, *Eros at Breakfast*, Davies returns to this idea and shows us a young man's soul when he first experiences love. With this fantasy, Davies is able to teach a few lessons about the inner workings of the mind: Love comes, we learn, not from the mind, but is initiated by sentiment, enhanced by the liver, and finally affects the soul. In his later plays, Davies took on increasingly complex aspects of human experience, until he came to grips with the nature of identity and strove to define more clearly the soul itself. En route, Davies' expert knowledge of and defiant admiration for melodrama was transferred to the interior landscape, so that striking character-types merge with psychological allegory.

JUNGIAN INFLUENCE

Davies' psychological allegory approach was greatly influenced by the theories of Carl Jung, in particular the definition of the three attributes of the personality: the persona, the anima, and the shadow. In his scholarly writing, Davies explored the relationship between Jungian archetypes and melodramatic character-types, and scholars have traced a similar correspondence in Davies' fiction. In melodrama, they appear as the hero, the heroine, and the villain; in Davies' plays, they emerge in a variety of forms as he experimented with the dramatic presentation of this theory.

An early, unproduced experiment is *General Confession*, which Davies singled out as his favorite play. An elderly Casanova entertains two young lovers with three conjured figures: the philosopher Voltaire, the evil magician Cagliostro, and an unnamed beautiful woman. The figures act out scenes from Casanova's past, and in the last act, Casanova is put on trial for his sins, with the philosopher as adviser, the woman as defender, and the magician as accuser. Finally, Davies gives these last three figures allegorical titles: they are, respectively, Casanova's Wisdom, his Ideal of Womanhood, and his Contrary Destiny. Casanova and his two young friends learn an impor-

tant lesson in identity: Everyone has within him a wise adviser; an ideal, to provide direction; and an enemy, against which to test himself.

This dramatization of Jung's theory of the personality injected Davies' writing with an atmosphere of the mystical, which underlies the surface narrative he presents. In *Question Time*, he jettisons the external reality within which he tried to work in *General Confession*, using the patterns of dreams for his dramatic form and the images of Jungian theory for characters and setting. The *terra incognita* into which Peter MacAdam journeys in *Question Time* is the world of the unconscious, here made remarkably theatrical by Davies' image of the Arctic as the last unchartered realm of our world and so the perfect metaphor for the unchartered territory of the mind. His description of the stage presentation indicates the mystical atmosphere he wished to evoke; he asked for music that is not the conventional movie sound track, but something truly mysterious, embracing, alive. The set, he suggested, should create the effect of a landscape that, although unfriendly, is of transporting beauty.

DEPICTIONS OF CLASS DIVISIONS

Along with his old-fashioned dramatic form, Davies often alienated audiences by expressing attitudes that are unfashionable to state publicly, though they may be widely held. In two areas, in particular, he incurred the wrath of sectors of the public. Davies had strong feelings about class divisions, as is evident in the characterization in his plays. In *Question Time*, the representatives of the working classes are Madge and Tim, and the portrait is not at all flattering. Crude language, cruder vision, and the most narrow-minded selfishness characterize these figures. Tim is much given to simplistic, clichéd pronouncements against the rich, and he makes several references to his union. He is particularly irritating in the second half of the play, where he disrupts the formal rituals with obnoxious and ignorant objections. Davies seemed to be implying that the common people are easily led, uneducated, brutish, and totally lacking in any sensitivity to the world of the spirit. Regardless of the veracity of this portrait, it is in sharp contrast to the egalitarian ideals mouthed by most contemporary playwrights.

Davies was openly elitist about the world of art and espoused an aristocracy of the soul: Some people are open to its magic, and some are closed. This capacity is not always tied to class and education, for some of Davies' most obtuse and closed characters suffer from an excess of money and schooling. More often than not, however, the most appealing, witty, sensitive, and attractive of Davies' characters are members of the social elite. Davies described repeatedly the natural grace and acquired good taste of the ladies in *At My Heart's Core*, qualities that are very much part of their breeding as gentlewomen. Contrast is provided by Sally and Honour, the first an Indian servant whom Davies describes as giggling at the most inopportune moments or brandishing a skillet, and the second an uneducated Irish settler who has just borne a child to her foster father. In a telling scene, Mrs. Frances Stewart, whom Davies portrays as the most beautiful and gracious of the ladies, suggests that, if Honour does not wish to stay in bed to recover from the birth of her child, she might just as well go out into the kitchen and help Sally. Frances means no insult here, nor does Davies. Honour is more comfortable serving Frances, and both women accept the responsibilities and privileges of their different positions. There is no hint of these two having been born equal.

EXPLORATIONS OF GENDER

Another issue on which Davies expressed decided and unpopular ideas is gender. In direct statement as well as by implication, Davies communicated his belief that women and men are different and that the world runs most smoothly when both sexes know their strengths and limitations and do not attempt to shatter the natural order. For Davies, women are the more sensitive, the givers, the supporters. This does not mean that they are incapable of intelligence, of spirit, or of strength, but theirs is a distinctly feminine intelligence, spirit, and strength. Frances Stewart in *At My Heart's Core* is a woman witty enough to match swords with the devilish tempter Edmund Cantwell, intelligent enough to admit his success and attempt to deal with the dissatisfaction with which he attempts to poison her life, and strong enough to deliver a baby, outface a drunken settler, and remain

alone in the forest eight miles from her closest neighbor. When her husband returns, however, she bows to his masculine wit, intelligence, and strength and allows him to solve the social entanglement in which she finds herself. It is Thomas Stewart who hands out justice to the erring settler, who gets to the bottom of the plotting of Edmund Cantwell and who embodies the most vital and theatrical love of life, exemplified by his mimicry of the music-hall clown Grimaldi.

The explanation for Davies' attitude toward his female characters rests partially in his personal Victorian sensibilities but also in his use of the female gender to embody the values of the spirit. The most striking example of this occurs in *Question Time*, in the figure of La Sorcière des Montagnes de Glace. In the final moments of the play, Davies explicates her symbolic function: She is the ultimate authority in the world of the soul, the final reality, the life force, a power so old that she "makes all monarchies seem like passing shadows on her face, and all forms of power like games children tire of." Women cannot complain that Davies disliked their sex, but they are perhaps correct when they say that he did not portray them realistically on the stage.

PERENNIAL THEMES

Given Davies' concern with the interior of the human mind, it is no surprise to discover two perennial themes in his dramatic writing: the quest for personal identity and the magic of art. These are not new themes, and Davies' treatment of the importance of self-knowledge and the unique properties of art and artists was not new. What is striking is the way in which he united these two themes with a third concern that figured largely in his dramatic writing: the relationship between art, personal identity, and the national identity of Canadians. When asked to describe the theme of *Question Time*, Davies' reply was brief and to the point; he stated that the play was about the relationship of the Canadian people to their soil and about the relationship of a man to his soul, both of which we neglect at our peril.

These relationships, and the parallels between the two, form the thematic content of many of Davies' plays. Canada, he suggested, suffers from a lack of emotional stimulation, from a denigration of the arts that might have been appropriate in a pioneer society but was sadly out of place in the twentieth century. By evoking the magic and power of art, Davies hoped to awaken his audiences to the need for the life-giving spirit of art in their lives.

FORTUNE, MY FOE

Nowhere is the pure magic of the performing arts more powerfully evoked than in *Fortune, My Foe*. Here the art form is puppetry, and the artist is Franz Szabo, a refugee who has brought to Canada a European artistic discipline and awareness. Franz gives voice to Davies' view of artistic creation when he describes his profession. It takes sixteen years to acquire the skill of a marionette master, but once acquired, it allows the puppet master to infuse his creation with a part of his own soul, so that the figure is more real, more truly alive, than the puppet master himself. Although his new Canadian friends warn him that Canada is a cold country, inhospitable to artists, Franz is determined to remain and find an audience for his puppets. In the course of the play, he is partially successful in this quest.

The individual most deeply affected by his encounter with the artist Szabo is Nicholas, a young university professor on the brink of leaving Canada for a more lucrative career in the United States. Nicholas has despaired of ever achieving a decent income in Canada, a country where the questions he asks meet only with blank incomprehension and where the yearnings he feels find no understanding. He realizes the importance of art to the health of the soul: Art fills a need in the heart; it provides brilliant color, the warmth and gaiety that people crave. Others who come in contact with Franz Szabo respond less favorably. Vanessa Medway is enchanted and eager to become involved, but her impatience bars her from partaking of an artistic experience that requires a minimum of two years' training. Vanessa exemplifies a worldview that Davies labels as distinctively modern: detached, unemotional, fast-moving, quickly tiring of things and people, yet capable of perception and honesty. Ursula Simonds wants to alter Szabo's art to pure didacticism; she claims that art without a message is worthless, while Szabo argues that art is not to be trusted unless it is in the hands of artists, not educators or revolutionaries.

The least appealing response comes from Mrs. E.C. Philpott and Orville Tapscott, representatives from the local recreation board, whom Davies uses to satirize certain educational theories that emphasize the scientific approach. Tapscott and Mrs. Philpott regard puppets as ideal for instruction in oral hygiene and for developing manual dexterity in young girls. Their belief in their power to do good is so powerful that it blinds them to the simple, pure message of Szabo's little theater. They are, Davies suggests, the half-educated, who are the least likely to appreciate art. They find Szabo's dramatization of the story of Don Quixote immoral, offensive, and antisocial. Terrified of any art that ventures into the area of deep personal concerns, they are blind to their own need for art to save them from emotional starvation.

Szabo has the strength to survive the condemnation of the emotionally barren and the impatience of the modern. He reminds his friends that a real artist is tough; as long as he keeps the image of his work clear in his heart, he will not fail. Canada is his country now, and though he foresees struggle, he will continue his search for an audience. His optimism tips the balance for Nicholas, and the play ends with the young man's announcement that he, too, will stay in Canada.

It is the cynical Chilly Jim, however, who voices Davies' most powerful evocation of the potential of the theater. Chilly has seen three murders, but nothing has moved him like Szabo's puppets. The theater makes him feel something he has not experienced since he was a boy, a kind of religious wonder:

> You've always suspected that something existed, and you've wished and prayed that it did exist, and in your dreams you've seen little bits of it, but to save your life you couldn't describe it or put a name to it. Then, all of a sudden, there it is, and you feel grateful, and humble, and wonder how you ever doubted it. That little stage makes me feel like that—quiet and excited at the same time.

This is the power of the theater that Robertson Davies celebrated in his writing.

OTHER MAJOR WORKS

LONG FICTION: *Tempest-Tost*, 1951(with *Leaven of Malice* and *A Mixture of Frailties* known as the Salterton Trilogy); *Leaven of Malice*, 1954; *A Mixture of Frailties*, 1958; *Fifth Business*, 1970 (with *The Manticore* and *World of Wonders* known as the Deptford Trilogy); *The Manticore*, 1972; *World of Wonders*, 1975; *The Rebel Angels*, 1981 (with *What's Bred in the Bone* and *The Lyre of Orpheus* known as the Cornish Trilogy); *What's Bred in the Bone*, 1985; *The Lyre of Orpheus*, 1988; *Murther and Walking Spirits*, 1991; *The Cunning Man*, 1994.

SHORT FICTION: *High Spirits*, 1982.

TELEPLAY: *Fortune, My Foe*, 1948.

NONFICTION: *Shakespeare's Boy Actors*, 1939; *Shakespeare for Younger Players: A Junior Course*, 1942; *The Diary of Samuel Marchbanks*, 1947; *The Table Talk of Samuel Marchbanks*, 1949; *Renown at Stratford: A Record of the Shakespeare Festival in Canada, 1953*, 1953 (with Tyrone Guthrie); *Twice Have the Trumpets Sounded: A Record of the Stratford Shakespearean Festival in Canada, 1954*, 1954 (with Guthrie); *Thrice the Brinded Cat Hath Mew'd: A Record of the Stratford Shakespearean Festival in Canada, 1955*, 1955 (with Guthrie); *A Voice from the Attic*, 1960; *The Personal Art: Reading to Good Purpose*, 1961; *Marchbanks' Almanack*, 1967; *Stephen Leacock: Feast of Stephen*, 1970; *One Half of Robertson Davies*, 1977; *The Enthusiasms of Robertson Davies*, 1979; *The Well-Tempered Critic*, 1981; *Reading and Writing*, 1993; *The Merry Heart: Reflections on Reading, Writing, and the World of Books*, 1997; *"For Your Eyes Alone": Letters, 1976-1995*, 1999.

BIBLIOGRAPHY

Cameron, Elspeth, ed. *Robertson Davies: An Appreciation.* New York: Broadview Press, 1991. Provides criticism and interpretations of Davies' life and works. Bibliography.

Cheaney, J. B. "Bred in the Bone: The Fiction of Canadian Author Robertson Davies." *The World & I* 16, no. 8 (August 2001): 247-255. Profiles the life and works of Davies.

Davies, Robertson. "Robertson Davies: An Interview." Interview by Michael Hulse. *Journal of Commonwealth Literature* 22, no. 1 (1987): 119-135. A warmhearted chat by the fireside, mainly on Davies' novel characters, but touching at several points on his writing methods. Briefly mentions *Question Time* and Davies' process for revising drafts.

_____. *The Well-Tempered Critic: One Man's View of Theatre and Letters in Canada.* Toronto: McClelland and Stewart, 1981. The first half of this volume is a collection of essays on the theater, spiced with Davies' own acerbic wit but revealing his benevolent attitude toward traditional, even medieval, dramatic forms. Contains many reviews of the festival seasons at Stratford, Ontario.

La Bossière, Camille R., and Linda Morra, eds. *Robertson Davies: A Mingling of Contrarieties.* Ottawa: University of Ottawa Press, 2001. Examines, among other topics, Davies' humor, "masks," and postmodern elements in his works. Bibliography.

MacLulich, T. D. *Between Europe and America: The Canadian Tradition in Fiction.* Toronto: ECW Press, 1988. Despite its title, this study deals with Davies' earliest plays, *Hope Deferred* and *Overlaid*, before a brief synopsis of *Fortune, My Foe* and *At My Heart's Core*. Much on Davies' prose work as well. Helpful index.

Peterman, Michael. *Robertson Davies.* Boston: Twayne, 1986. A general study of Davies' novels and essays, as well as two chapters on his plays, early and late. Contains a chronology, a bibliography, and an interesting discussion of his first, unpublished play, *The King Who Could Not Dream*. Index.

Steinberg, M. W. "Don Quixote and the Puppets: Theme and Structure in Robertson Davies' Drama." In *Dramatists in Canada: Selected Essays*, edited by William H. New. Vancouver: University of British Columbia Press, 1972. Offers a structural analysis of Davies' early plays, notably *Fortune, My Foe, At My Heart's Core*, and *A Jig for the Gypsy*. "Eminently stageworthy and . . . a valuable contribution to a genre that Canadian talent has unfortunately neglected," Steinberg notes.

Woodcock, George. "A Cycle Completed: The Nine Novels of Robertson Davies." *Canadian Literature: A Quarterly of Criticism and Review* 126 (Autumn, 1990): 33-48. A good overview of Davies' major literary contribution, as a backdrop for his dramatic output. Woodcock sees Davies' "traditional" forms as "calming and comforting" in an otherwise "permissive" literary world.

Leslie O'Dell,
updated by Thomas J. Taylor

OWEN DAVIS

Born: Portland, Maine; January 29, 1874
Died: New York, New York; October 14, 1956

PRINCIPAL DRAMA

For the White Rose, pr. 1898
Through the Breakers, pr. 1899
The Confessions of a Wife, pr., pb. 1905
The Family Cupboard, pr. 1913, pb. 1914
The Detour, pr. 1921, pb. 1922
Icebound, pr., pb. 1923
The Nervous Wreck, pr. 1923, pb. 1926
The Haunted House, pr. 1924, pb. 1926
The Good Earth, pr., pb. 1932 (with Donald Davis; adaptation of Pearl Buck's novel)
Jezebel, pr., pb. 1933
Ethan Frome, pr., pb. 1936 (with Davis; adaptation of Edith Wharton's novel)
Mr. and Mrs. North, pr., pb. 1941 (adaptation of Frances and Richard Lockridge's novel)

OTHER LITERARY FORMS

In addition to more than three hundred plays, Owen Davis wrote a radio series entitled *The Gibson Family* (1934), which lasted for thirty-nine weeks. He was also a screenwriter in Hollywood, where his work included *Icebound* (1924), *How Baxter Butted In* (1925), *Frozen Justice* (1929), and *Hearts in Exile* (1929).

In 1930, dissatisfied with Hollywood and its exploitation of the writer, Davis returned to writing for the stage. In 1931, he published a volume of autobiography, *I'd Like to Do It Again*; he updated his life story in 1950 with *My First Fifty Years in the Theatre*.

ACHIEVEMENTS

Owen Davis's career spanned almost sixty years, and during that period, he wrote more than three hundred plays, most of which were performed professionally. Inasmuch as his work was produced in New York for thirty-seven consecutive seasons, and twenty of his plays were produced in Hollywood as movies, he was, from 1900 to 1950, America's most prolific playwright. Drama critic George Jean Nathan called Davis "the Lope de Vega of the American Theatre."

Davis began his career as a writer of Ten-Twent'-Thirt' melodramas, and by 1910, he achieved recognition as the dominant writer in this dramatic form. Motivated to be a serious writer, Davis wrote *The Family Cupboard*, which enabled him to move from the visually dominated melodramas to comedy. Always seeking to grow as an artist, Davis shifted from situation comedy to psychological melodrama; perhaps his finest work in this form was the 1923 play *Icebound*, for which he received the Pulitzer Prize and for which he was inducted into the National Institute of Arts and Letters. Later, he would serve on the Pulitzer Prize selection committee.

In addition to his work as a dramatist, Davis sought to free the writer from managerial abuse and plagiarism. Therefore, he became actively involved in founding the Dramatists' Guild, serving as its president in 1922. As president, he addressed himself to such issues as film rights, actors' homes, loans, and other issues germane to the theater profession. Davis had a gift for organization and administration and was continually drafted into leadership positions.

BIOGRAPHY

Born in 1874, Owen Davis was one of eight children of Abbie Gould Davis and Owen Warren Davis. His father, a graduate of Bowdoin College and a Civil War veteran, was primarily in the iron business, owning the Kathodin Iron Works and serving one term as president of the Society of American Iron Manufacturers. Later, he operated a photography studio on New York's Forty-second Street. He died in 1920 of a heart attack.

Davis went to school in Bangor, Maine, and at the age of nine wrote his first play *Diamond Cut Diamond: Or, The Rival Detectives*. At the age of fourteen, he enrolled as a subfreshman at the University of Tennessee. To satisfy his father, Davis left after one year and attended Harvard. Because Harvard did not have a theater and drama department, Davis first majored in business and then transferred, in 1893, to the sciences to become a mining engineer. While at Harvard, Davis participated in football and track and organized the Society of Arts, under the auspices of which he produced his verse dramas. In 1893, he left Harvard without a degree and followed his family to Southern Kentucky, where he was hired by the Cumberland Valley Kentucky Railroad as a mining engineer. Dissatisfied, Davis decided that he wanted to become a playwright or an actor. In 1895, with twelve dollars in his pocket, he quit his job and went to New York City. Meeting with continual discouragement, Davis was finally aided by theater manger A. M. Palmer, whose influence helped Davis get work as a utility actor, stage manager, press agent, advance man, company manager, and in some instances assistant director for the Fanny Janauschek Troupe. Davis left the company in 1896, committed to becoming a writer.

Giving full attention to writing, Davis tried to sell his first play, *For the White Rose*. Meeting with rejection after rejection, he became determined to figure out a formula for the then-running successful plays. After studying the melodramas and the audiences, Davis discovered that he needed to write for the "eye rather than the ear"—that is, he needed to emphasize scenic elements. Davis also concluded that the successful melodramas depended on such common fea-

tures as a strong love interest, the triumph of good over evil, and stock comic characters. Although *For the White Rose* was finally produced in 1898, *Through the Breakers* was to be Davis's first successful play.

In January, 1901, Davis met Elizabeth Drury "Iza" Breyer, whom he married on April 23, 1902. They remained married for fifty-five years and had two sons. In 1902, Davis and Al "Sweetheart" Woods signed an agreement that led in 1905 to the well-known "Owen Davis-Al Woods Melodrama Factory," from which fifty-nine plays were produced, the first being *The Confessions of a Wife* in 1905. While pouring out "Davidrama" after "Davidrama," as his particular brand of melodrama was labeled, at a rate of eight or more per year, Davis began using such pseudonyms as Arthur Lamb, Martin Hurly, Walter Lawrence, George Walker, and John Oliver.

Not satisfied with his success as a popular playwright, Davis struggled to write serious drama. In 1918, he moved from the melodrama of the Ten-

Owen Davis (Courtesy of the New York Public Library)

Twent'-Thirt' theaters to try his luck on Broadway. Success on Broadway was not easy to achieve, and Davis again studied the work of other successful writers (such as Clyde Fitch) to ascertain the necessary formula. Besides writing plays, he published articles on the theater in *The New York Times* and other periodicals.

Disturbed and sobered by World War I, Davis read works by Henrik Ibsen, Maxim Gorky, Gerhart Hauptmann, and other serious dramatists whose naturalistic emphasis on the influence of heredity and environment is apparent in such Davis plays of the early 1920's as *The Detour* and *Icebound*. Another departure in Davis's work occurred with his farce *The Nervous Wreck*, which Davis called "the terrible play which made us all rich." Whereas his Pulitzer Prize drama, *Icebound*, made one thousand dollars weekly, *The Nervous Wreck* brought in twenty-one thousand dollars a week. Made into the musical *Whoopee* (1928), remade as *Up in Arms* (1944), and later adapted for the screen (Davis was not involved in these projects), *The Nervous Wreck* was Davis's most popular and most lucrative work. From 1924 to 1941, Davis worked on movies, on radio, and on drama at the Lakewood Theatre in Skowhegan, Maine (known as "Broadway in Maine"), as well as on Broadway. His play *Jezebel* failed in New York, but as a 1938 movie, it earned for Bette Davis an Academy Award. Davis's last major achievement was his adaptation of Edith Wharton's *Ethan Frome* (1911). Failing eyesight and bad health slowed his output, and his last substantial work was *Mr. and Mrs. North*. Davis died in New York City on October 14, 1956.

ANALYSIS

Writing plays like "a freshman writes home for money—as frequently and with as little effort," Owen Davis became the United States' most prolific dramatist. He began with melodramas, then moved on to comedy, and psychological drama.

THE DETOUR

While under the influence of naturalistic drama, Davis wrote one of his finest plays, *The Detour*. Still using the melodramatic form, Davis varied his approach with a realistic style. The characters are there-fore depicted as products of heredity and environment, placed in circumstances in which they struggle physically and psychologically against these forces. Despite their efforts to circumvent their fate, the destiny that shapes their ends prevails.

The central character, Helen Hardy, exemplifies this determination in the face of hardship. For ten years, Helen has scrimped and sacrificed for the sake of her daughter, Kate, who aspires to be a painter. Helen's dream for Kate is in reality her own unfulfilled dream "to get away and go to New York, or somewheres where bein' born and bein' dead wasn't the only things that ever happened." Her efforts to escape her environment, however, fail when fate intercedes in the guise of Stephen Hardy. Helen admits that, in her loneliness, "somehow I got to loving him before I knew it." Married and feeling trapped, Helen doggedly tells Kate, "Your life isn't going to be like this." Helen's struggle against destiny becomes the central conflict of the play.

The struggle focuses on Kate's suitor, Tom Lane, and takes on larger proportions when Tom, echoing a widely held viewpoint, affirms that "women ought to just cook, and clean, and sew, and maybe chop a little wood, and have the babies. . . . And if a woman sometimes gets to thinkin it ain't quite fair" and decides to alter the situation, "she's flyin' in the face of Providence." To expedite Kate's departure to New York, Helen sells her bedroom wardrobe and with the additional money plans for Kate to leave immediately. Again, Stephen Hardy intercedes. Obsessed with owning land, and needing money to buy what he considers a prime section, Stephen takes the money intended for Kate. This makes the men happy: Stephen will get his land, and Tom will get Kate. Stephen's act is a villainous one, and inasmuch as Tom supports Stephen, he must share that guilt. Thus, the men in *The Detour* symbolize society and its failure to guarantee equal rights for women. The play ends with the forces of tradition victorious: An art critic seriously questions Kate's talent, and Kate decides to remain with her family and Tom. Despite this defeat, Helen is undaunted; "she stands, her face glorified, looking out into the future, her heart swelling with eternal hope."

ICEBOUND

The influence of naturalism is also apparent in Davis's prizewinning play *Icebound*. In this work, despite his intention to move away from melodrama, Davis retained many of the basic elements of that form. Unlike tragedy, which contains highly serious action that probes the nature of good and evil, melodrama generally lacks moral complexity; in melodrama, good and evil are clearly defined. Although the plot of *Icebound* is essentially melodramatic, the play also features an element of psychological complexity that distinguishes it from straight melodrama.

Jane Crosby is an adopted second cousin to the Jordan family. Taken in by the family's matriarch, Jane is considered an outcast by the rest of the family, especially as the mother is dying and the Jordan wealth is to be inherited. Responding to her enemies, Jane asserts her "hate" for the Jordans and her plans "to get away from them." As for the dying mother, "She was the only one of you worth loving, and she didn't want it." When the mother dies, fate intervenes in the guise of the dead woman's will: Jane is left the Jordan home and money. When the will's contents are revealed, the Jordan family's sentiments are summed up: "We'll go to the law, that's what we'll do." Thus, Jane is pitted against the greedy and vengeful Jordan clan. The conflict is clearly defined, and the audience is sympathetic to Jane.

Had Davis kept the focus solely on the conflict between Jane and the Jordans, the play would be a simple melodrama; instead, he chose to emphasize the role of Mrs. Jordan's son Ben, the black sheep of the family. Ben is a "wild, selfish, arrogant fellow, handsome but sulky and defiant." Indicted by the grand jury for his "drunken devilment," he has run away to avoid state prison. While he is still a fugitive, Ben, risking capture, returns to see his dying mother, and after her death, he is arrested. Alone and without money, Ben is befriended by Jane, in whose custody the court places him. Four months later, Ben comes to grips with his past. Ashamed and feeling remorse about his past behavior, Ben struggles to express his repressed emotions. Admitting love for his mother and for Jane, Ben beseeches Jane to "help me to be fit." With Ben's reformation, society's positive values emerge triumphant over the baneful influence of the Jordan family. No longer emotionally icebound, Ben marries Jane, who gives him his rightful inheritance.

ETHAN FROME

Davis was active as a playwright for many years after the appearance of *Icebound*, but the only significant work of this later period was his adaptation, with Donald Davis, of *Ethan Frome*, Edith Wharton's short novel set in a harsh New England landscape. Ethan "lives in a depth of moral isolation too remote for casual access." He is married to Zenobia, whom Davis characterizes as cruel, harsh, impersonal, and drab, like the play's New England winter setting. In that she represents those forces that seek to enslave Ethan's body and soul, and in that she drives the action to catastrophe, Zenobia (or Zeena) is the villain.

Despite her sickly appearance, Zeena is a forceful personality, and on issues of importance to her, her strength surfaces. For example, she demands that her cousin Mattie Silver be allowed to come and live with them as a hired girl. Citing a complete lack of money, Ethan protests against this demand, but Zeena settles the issue by curtly asserting, "Well—she's comin' just the same, Ethan!" The consequences, however, are not what Zeena intended: Mattie's presence "thaws" Ethan, and eventually, the two fall in love. Jealousy rages within Zeena, who conspires to get rid of Mattie. For years, Ethan has felt trapped by the farm that he inherited, and with Mattie leaving, Ethan's "desire for change and freedom" are resurrected. Ethan tells Zeena that he plans to go West for a fresh start and that Zeena may have the farm. Zeena, however, wishes to keep Ethan enslaved, and, playing on his strong sense of duty, she makes Ethan realize that he is a "poor man, the husband of a sickly woman, whom his desertion would leave alone and destitute." Ethan and Mattie decide to kill themselves by sledding at high speed "into that big elm . . . so't we'd never have to leave each other any more." Their decision gives the play an element of high seriousness; it is a tragic action rather than a melodramatic one. The act of crashing into the elm is also symbolic in that it dramatizes the perennial conflict between human beings and nature. Typical of characters in tragedy whose decisions cause their undoing, Ethan and Mattie survive. Not only does their survival create a reversal in the action, but also it suggests nature's superior force. Although crippled, Ethan can walk, but Mattie is partially paralyzed and is confined to a wheelchair. Ethan and Zeena are tied down to a daily existence of caring for the farm and for Mattie. Nature has demonstrated its mastery over human destiny.

OTHER MAJOR WORKS

NONFICTION: *I'd Like to Do It Again*, 1931; *My First Fifty Years in the Theatre*, 1950.

SCREENPLAYS: *Icebound*, 1924; *How Baxter Butted In*, 1925; *Frozen Justice*, 1929; *Hearts in Exile*, 1929.

RADIO PLAY: *The Gibson Family*, 1934 (series).

BIBLIOGRAPHY

Goff, Lewin. "The Owen Davis-Al Woods Melodrama Factory." *Educational Theatre Journal* 11 (October, 1959): 200-207. One of the first major scholarly articles on Davis. Goff examines the unique, exclusive contract between Davis and controversial theatrical producer Al Woods, whereby the writer turned out fifty-eight plays over a five-year period.

Middleton, George. *Owen Davis, January 29, 1874-October 14, 1956.* New York: Dramatist Guild of the Authors League of America, 1957. A brief remembrance of the writer and his work.

Moses, Montrose J. *The American Dramatist.* 1925. Reprint. New York: B. Blom, 1964. Moses describes the development of Davis in the context of the many forms of American melodrama. He includes many quotations from an interview with the author.

Rahill, Frank. "When Heaven Protected the Working Girl." *Theatre Arts* 38 (October, 1954): 78-92. This piece reviews Davis's work in the Ten-Twent'-Thirt' drama, with specific examples of how popularly priced plays were created. It focuses on some of the social and political events that became the subjects of many of the melodramas.

Witham, Barry B. "Owen Davis: America's Forgotten Playwright." *Players* 46 (October/November, 1970): 30-35. Witham's article is a complete synopsis of Davis's dramaturgy from the melodramas to the award-winning later plays. It also reviews Davis's accomplishments outside the theater, such as his pioneering work on behalf of the Dramatist's Guild and the Authors' League of America.

Loren Ruff,
updated by Barry B. Witham
and Michael L. Quinn

EDUARDO DE FILIPPO

Born: Naples, Italy; May 24, 1900
Died: Rome, Italy; October 31, 1984

PRINCIPAL DRAMA

Farmacia di turno, wr. 1920, pr. 1931, pb. 1959
Uomo e galantuomo, wr. 1922, pr. 1933, pb. 1959
Filosoficamente, wr. 1928, pb. 1959
Sik-Sik, l'artefice magico, pr. 1929, pb. 1932 (*Sik-Sik, the Masterful Magician*, 1967)
Chi è cchiù felice 'e me!, pb. 1929, pr. 1932
Quei figuri di trent'anni fa, pr. 1929, pb. 1932
Natale in casa Cupiello, pr., pb. 1931 (*The Nativity Scene*, 1997)
Gennariello, pr., pb. 1932
Ditegli sempre di sì, pr. 1932, pb. 1959
Io l'erede, wr. 1932, pr., pb. 1942
Quinto piano ti saluto!, pb. 1934, pr. 1936
Uno coi capelli bianchi, pb. 1935, pr. 1938
L'abito nuovo, pb. 1936, pr. 1937 (based on a scenario by Luigi Pirandello)
Pericolosamente, pb. 1938, pr. 1947
La parte di Amleto, pr., pb. 1940
Non ti pago!, pr., pb. 1940
Napoli milionaria!, pr., pb. 1945 (English translation, 1996)
Occhiali neri, pr., pb. 1945

Questi fantasmi!, pr., pb. 1946 (*Oh, These Ghosts!*, 1964)

Filumena Marturano, pr. 1946, pb. 1947 (*The Best House in Naples*, 1956; also as *Filumena*, 1978)

Le bugie con le gambe lunghe, pr., pb. 1948

Le voci di dentro, pr. 1948, pb. 1949 (*Inner Voices*, 1983)

La grande magia, pr. 1949, pb. 1950 (*The Grand Magic*, 1976)

La paura numero uno, pr. 1950, pb. 1951

I morti non fanno paura, pr. 1952, pb. 1956

Amicizia, pr. 1952, pb. 1956

Mia famiglia, pr., pb. 1955

Bene mio e core mio, pr. 1955, pb. 1956

De Pretore Vincenzo, pr., pb. 1957

Sabato, domenica e lunedì, pr. 1959, pb. 1960 (*Saturday, Sunday, Monday*, 1973)

Cantata dei giorni pari, pb. 1959

Il sindaco del Rione Sanità, pr. 1960, pb. 1961 (*The Local Authority*, 1976)

Il figlio di Pulcinella, pr. 1962, pb. 1966

Tommaso d'Amalfi, pr. 1963, pb. 1966

Dolore sotto chiave, pb. 1965, pr. 1969

Il cilindro, pr., pb. 1966

Il contratto, pr., pb. 1967

Il monumento, pr. 1970, pb. 1971

Cantata dei giorni dispari, pb. 1971 (3 volumes)

Gli esami non finiscono mai, pr., pb. 1973

I capolavori di Eduardo de Filippo, pb. 1973 (2 volumes)

Three Plays, pb. 1976

OTHER LITERARY FORMS

Eduardo De Filippo published poetry, wrote several screenplays, and contributed several articles on the theater and acting to major Italian newspapers.

ACHIEVEMENTS

It took many years for Eduardo De Filippo to achieve the national and international success of the other famous Italian playwrights, Luigi Pirandello and Ugo Betti, despite his extraordinary dramatic output and despite the continuous and astounding success of his plays, which were performed in the major cities of Italy and elsewhere in Europe. In large part, this relative critical neglect was a consequence of De Filippo's decision to employ the Neapolitan dialect.

In 1932, however, the De Filippo Company presented *Chi è cchiù felice 'e me!* (who is happier than I?) at one of the most prestigious theaters of Naples, the Sannazzaro, and this, coupled with the backing of the well-known Renato Simoni, Massimo Bontempelli, and Luigi Pirandello, the 1934 Nobel Prize-winner in literature, began to shape De Filippo's place in the history of Italian literature. By 1938, he was receiving wide critical acclaim. *The Best House in Naples*, published in 1947, was the dramatic vehicle that propelled De Filippo into stardom; with it, he struck at the very heart of the problem of contemporary living.

Perhaps De Filippo's greatest contribution to the dramatic theater was the reestablishment of communication between the stage and the audience. De Filippo believed that audiences want the author to tell them about things that happen in their own lives—things with which they can identify. De Filippo said that when the author does this, he enters the theater from the stage door but leaves it arm in arm with the audience. To be successful in this endeavor, the author must prepare a script that is always an instrument that is mobile, flexible, and malleable for the public.

A second important contribution was De Filippo's refinement of some of the elements of the *commedia dell'arte* as they existed in the Neapolitan dialect theater. His Pulcinella and other *commedia dell'arte* characters resembled the original, but they were changed to become more dramatic, more capable of conveying their real suffering and sadness within the comic nature of their prescribed roles.

On December 18, 1972, De Filippo was awarded the prestigious Feltrinelli Prize for Drama, and on December 16, 1975, he received the Pirandello Prize for Drama. On July 15, 1977, he was awarded an honorary degree, Doctor of Letters, by the University of Birmingham, England, and in November, 1980, he received the same degree from the University of Rome. In September, 1981, he was made a senator for life in the Italian Parliament.

BIOGRAPHY

Eduardo De Filippo was born in Naples in 1900, the illegitimate son of Eduardo Scarpetta and Luisa De Filippo, the niece of his legitimate wife. It can be said that De Filippo was born into the theater, since his father was an actor and playwright who also owned a theatrical company.

De Filippo made his acting debut at the age of four, performing the part of a small Japanese child in his father's play, *The Geisha*, and then played minor roles for the next five years. His father taught him assiduously the art of acting, especially the techniques of working within the framework of the improvised script and the understanding and projection of the characters of the *commedia dell'arte*, particularly that of Pulcinella.

De Filippo did go to school, but he found school to be boring and stultifying. He looked forward to the summers, when he would work and perform in the theater. When he was fourteen, he joined the acting troupe of Enrico Altieri, a popular comic actor in Neapolitan plays. It was from Altieri that De Filippo learned to portray the character Pulcinella and to capture the spirit of the Neapolitan theater, which was to be the cornerstone of his own plays—that is, the sadness of the people and the bitter reality of life in Naples. In 1911, De Filippo joined the Vincenzo Scarpetta troupe, staying with that group until called for military service in 1920. After his military service, he joined the Francesco Corbinci troupe, then the Peppino Villani troupe, and finally he rejoined Vincenzo Scarpetta in 1923. His father died in 1925.

Having already written a one-act play, *Farmacia di turno* (pharmacy on duty), he moved to his first three-act play, *Uomo e galantuomo* (man and gentleman). He continued acting with several troupes, including those of Pasquale Molinari and Luigi Carini, but he dedicated as much time as possible to playwriting. The success of his plays prompted him to propose to his brother, Peppino, and his sister, Titina, that they should form their own company. In 1931, they formed the Compagnia del Teatro umoristico: I De Filippo. The company performed in Naples and Rome and, in 1932, it opened at the Sannazzaro Theater in Naples with *Chi è cchiù felice 'e me!*, to great acclaim. The troupe weathered the difficult war years and the death of their mother in 1944, but widening disagreement between Peppino and Eduardo on what course their theater should follow led to the group's dissolution. Peppino wanted to continue performing the traditional Neapolitan farces, whereas Eduardo leaned quite heavily toward plays that expressed his concern for the social realities of his time. As a result of the breakup, Eduardo bought the old San Ferdinando theater, renovated it, and opened it with the express purpose of providing the public with contemporary plays that focused on real political and social problems. Thus, his success in the world of drama was assured.

De Filippo had married Dorothy Pennington in 1928, but the marriage was to last only a few months (it was annulled in the Republic of San Marino in 1952). In 1956, he married Thea Prandi, a former actress, with whom he had been living for some time and with whom he had had two children, Luca and Luisella. The couple separated in 1959, and Thea died in 1961. In 1977, he married an old friend, Isabella Quarantotti. De Filippo died on October 31, 1984.

ANALYSIS

Eduardo De Filippo's early, intensive training in the Neapolitan theater led him to believe in the importance of strong characterization rather than of plot; thus, his plays revolve around the everyday life of the people of Naples—their language, customs, beliefs, superstitions, mannerisms, habits. He made it a point to show the seamier side of life, and so he filled his plays with those types who lived on the fringes of acceptable social behavior and who were either victims of social injustices or who perpetrated injustices on others.

Indeed, in De Filippo's plays, there is a continuous examination of the concept of justice—or, if one wishes, the concept of injustice. He primarily focuses on the oppression of the disenfranchised because it is they who have been beaten, reviled, and abused. The guilty are those who have the power, who rule, who command, and they, in turn, are morally corrupt. Their corruption engenders a disrespect for the law, a lack of faith in social mores, and an invalidation of all the rules of living within a social order. The only avenue left for the weak is to fight back, to rebel, to take the law into their own hands, to seek vengeance—in short, to create their own laws. The end result can be, and often is, an anarchic way of life that strengthens the power of the corrupt and weakens the victims of corruption. Consequently, distrust, threats, thievery, ransom, and lies become an integral part of the lives of the masses. Even when those who have suffered injustices at the hands of corrupt leaders become a part of the middle class and seem to have what they need to live well, they care only for their own well-being and they will do anything—illegal and corrupt, if necessary—to maintain their newly found social position.

De Filippo dedicated his life to combating injustice and corruption, and his plays were the vehicle with which the battle was fought. He realized that people had to defend themselves constantly from the onslaught of those evils. Yet if the common people could not find justice and purity in the laws of the land nor in those who upheld the laws of the land, what were they to do? To whom could they turn for help and guidance? The countervailing force should have been the nuclear family, according to De Filippo. Unfortunately, the family was, in effect, simply a microcosm of life, of reality, so that the family in his plays reflects those difficulties and problems that face all members of society: a lack of communication between people (in the family it would be a lack of communication between husband and wife and/or between parents and children), a distrust of one another, the experiences of jealousy, hate, bitterness, greed, treachery, and oppression, and the agony of illness and death. The conclusion is that when the family is no longer a haven from the evil in the world, people can find solace only by isolating themselves from everyone. In their isolation, they create an ideal, fantasy world in which the ugly and repulsive modes of living are nonexistent. It is here that De Filippo is a master as he skillfully plays illusion against reality. Many critics see the influence of Luigi Pirandello, with whom De Filippo had collaborated on a stage presentation of Pirandello's *Liolà* (pr. 1916; English

translation, 1952) and *Il berretto a sonagli* (pr. 1917; *Caps and Bells*, 1957), and his own *L'abito nuovo*.

It is clear that De Filippo wants one to believe that people need illusions when they no longer can face the harsh realities of life, and his characters tend to create those illusions when they have reached the breaking point. De Filippo, however, also conveys the belief that people cannot shut out reality forever; they must struggle to face it, to grasp it firmly, to wrestle with it, and eventually to change it. This is the challenge that De Filippo makes his characters face; this is the challenge that he offers to all his public. Corruption and injustice can be destroyed if one is willing to fight them and to reestablish true moral values, especially if those values revolve around the traditional one of family unity. The metamorphosis of the isolated individual into a caring, loving member of the family unit is not an easy or rapid one; rather, it is extremely difficult and gradual, for those who surround the isolated individual constantly erect barriers that hamper the transformation. What the individual must do is recognize that there are barriers, identify them, hurdle them, and then be prepared to defend his newly found moral stance against the derisive jeers of the other members of the family. He must pronounce convincingly the importance of the essential values of family unity.

De Filippo divided his plays into two groups: *Cantata dei giorni pari* (cantata of the even days) and *Cantata dei giorni dispari* (cantata of the odd days). The former encompasses all the plays written up to the beginning of World War II and the latter all the plays written after 1940. The "plays of the even days" generally reflect De Filippo's fascination with the farcical Neapolitan theater. They have been characterized by critics as the least important of his works, yet they show, in some fashion, his preoccupation with the ideas and the themes that dominate his "plays of the odd days." The farcical may be the most evident aspect of those early plays, but underneath the farcical there already is a satiric current that probes the social injustices of society.

FARMACIA DI TURNO

De Filippo's first play, *Farmacia di turno*, lacks the nuance and the bite of his later plays. This one-act play, however, anticipates, in modest form, the characterizations, the realistic locales in Naples, and the themes of his mature works. The story takes place in a pharmacy owned by Saverio, a setting filled with people who are seeking medicines that will alleviate their suffering. The play suggests that some of their ills are spiritual rather than physical and that their pain cannot be alleviated by medicines. Saverio's wife has deserted him, but this does not bother him because he never did think highly of marriage. One of the clients has asked for rat poison, which he then inadvertently leaves on the counter. In the meantime, Saverio's former wife's servant comes in to get some medicine for her mistress, picks up the wrong parcel—the rat poison—and goes home. The obvious conclusion is that Saverio's former wife will die and that he will be falsely accused of murder. Thus, the fickle hand of fate has struck once again. Although the story sounds implausible, there is enough truth in it to make the play believable.

UOMO E GALANTUOMO

De Filippo's first three-act play, *Uomo e galantuomo*, has none of the sadness and cynicism of *Farmacia di turno*. It is filled with comic dialogue and slapstick humor in the vein of the *commedia dell'arte*. Even so, it does touch on the Pirandellian theme of sanity versus insanity. Alberto, impresario of a penniless theatrical troupe, falls in love with a young girl, Bice, about whom he knows nothing. Gennaro, the lead comic of the troupe, is chosen to find out where she lives, which he does. Alberto goes to Bice's mother to announce his intentions to marry her but learns that Bice already is married. In order to save face, he feigns insanity. Bice's husband requests that Alberto be committed to an asylum, but the authorities rule that he is sane; Bice's husband insists that Alberto continue acting insane to save his own honor. Learning that Bice has had an affair and that Bice knows about his own extramarital affairs, the husband also feigns insanity, and when the innkeeper presents the bill to Gennaro, he too "becomes insane" in order not to pay the bill. The weakness of the play is that the farcical humor overshadows a potentially significant theme: the plight of people who must resort to such devious means in order to survive.

SIK-SIK, THE MASTERFUL MAGICIAN

The jewel of De Filippo's even-day plays is *Sik-Sik, The Masterful Magician*. Sik-Sik is a clearly defined and fully developed character. As De Filippo describes him, he is a "typical traditional strolling actor: poor, tormented, and . . . a philosopher." Sik-Sik struggles to survive in a society that does not seem to have a place for him. His life is meaningless, and yet his will to survive is strong. He lives in a world of illusion and dreams: He is the master of his art, and he will be acclaimed by all as such, or so he believes. He hungers for applause, the food that will sustain him. (These are the same factors that are a part of the lives of the characters in De Filippo's post-World War II plays.)

Sik-Sik usually has a *compare* (assistant) who is planted in the audience to participate in Sik-Sik's magical tricks. One night, the regular assistant, Nicola, does not show up, and so Sik-Sik gives the job to Rafele, who is well-meaning but somewhat incompetent. When Nicola appears at curtain time to do his usual job, Rafele does not want to relinquish his new position. A scuffle ensues between the two, and during the course of the performance, when Sik-Sik asks for a volunteer from the audience, both Nicola and Rafele respond, and Sik-Sik's magical, illusionary world begins to crumble. To the audience's great amusement, the secrets behind the trunk escape and the disappearing doves are revealed. In the confusion, a real padlock instead of a fake one is used to lock Sik-Sik's pregnant wife in a trunk, and when she cannot escape, as she usually does, Sik-Sik is forced to break the lock with a hammer to free her. Finally, a chicken instead of a pigeon comes out of Rafele's hat, but Sik-Sik saves at least a small part of his magical "mastery" by telling the audience that through his magic he has turned the pigeon into a chicken.

NAPOLI MILIONARIA!

Napoli milionaria! initiated the second phase of De Filippo's plays, the plays of the odd days, in which the emphasis is on specific themes. *Napoli milionaria!* is a bittersweet comedy that lashes out at the war, the government and its leaders, corruption, and ill-gotten wealth. The war envelops the people with the destruction and killing that accompany it, but the true sadness is the effect of the war on the behavior of the people. War seems to bring out all the worst elements, and destroy all the good, of human conduct. The story revolves around the Iovine family. Gennaro Iovine, unemployed because of the war, becomes involved in the black market, an activity he abhors but in which he feels he must engage to survive. On the other hand, his wife, Donna Amalia, is not bothered by it; what must be done, must be done, she contends. When one day the police arrive to verify their suspicions about the Iovine family, Gennaro hides the merchandise under the bed, lies on it pretending that he is dead, and is surrounded by crying women. An aerial bombardment causes alarm and disrupts the mourning. The investigating officer is moved by the fact that Gennaro keeps on playing dead in the face of real danger and decides not to take any action against him. Later the audience learns that Gennaro has been deported to Germany and that Donna Amalia has become rich. On his return home, Gennaro finds that he is an outsider; he is ignored by his wife. He also learns that his oldest daughter is pregnant by an American soldier who has deserted her, his son is a thief, and another daughter is critically ill. Donna Amalia realizes the ugliness of the black market when she cannot get medicine for her daughter because other black marketeers have it all. Finally, the accountant, Riccardo, a victim of Donna Amalia's oppressive black-market prices, provides the medicine to help cure the daughter. The moral is that unity extends beyond the family to society as a whole.

THE BEST HOUSE IN NAPLES

The most famous De Filippo play is perhaps *The Best House in Naples*, also known as *Filumena*; it was certainly his most successful. It is a play that focuses on the overpowering authority of the nuclear family and the moral demands that it places on each member of the family. Filumena is the very essence of the woman who believes in God, in religious faith, in sacrifice, in patience, and she also is a passionate woman subject to moments of violent jealousy. Filumena, born into poverty and forced by poverty to become a prostitute in her youth, has been the kept woman of the well-to-do Domenico for more than twenty years. She perceives the injustice of life, however, when Domenico shifts his affections to a younger woman. With a fierce determination to establish her dignity as a woman, a true wife, and a mother (she has had three sons by unknown fathers), she devises a plan to force Domenico to marry her. She feigns a serious illness, and on her "deathbed" she asks Domenico to grant her one last wish—to marry her. He does so believing she will die very soon. Instead, Filumena leaps from the bed, asserts herself as a wife should, and takes over the running of the house. Domenico wants to have the marriage annulled on the grounds that he was tricked into marriage, but when Filumena tells him that one of the sons is his, refusing to reveal which one it is, he accepts the situation and adopts all three. Thus the traditional family has been established, family unity prevails, and Filumena and Domenico have achieved a sense of dignity.

The Best House in Naples symbolically deals with the social truism of the brotherhood of man: Love knows no social barriers. All members of society are equal and all are entitled to justice. In its use of the conventional materials of farce and comic theater to make a serious point, it is characteristic of De Filippo's drama.

OTHER MAJOR WORKS

POETRY: *Il paese di Pulcinella*, 1951; *'O canisto*, 1971; *Le poesie*, 1975.

SCREENPLAYS: *Sono stato io!*, 1937; "Adelina," episode of *Ieri, oggi e domani*, 1963 (with Isabella Quarantotti; *Yesterday, Today, and Tomorrow*, 1964); *Matrimonió all'italiana*, 1964 (*Marriage Italian Style*, 1964); *Spara forte, più forte . . . non capisco*, 1966 (with Suso Cecchi D'Amico; *Shoot Loud, Louder . . . I Don't Understand*, 1967).

TELEPLAYS: *Peppino Girella*, 1963 (with Isabella Quarantotti); *Li nepute de lu sinneco*, 1975 (based on work by Eduardo Scarpetta); *'O Tuono 'e marzo*, 1975 (based on work by Scarpetta).

NONFICTION: *L'arte della commedia*, 1964.

BIBLIOGRAPHY

Ardito, Carlo. Introduction to *Four Plays*, by Eduardo De Filippo. London: Methuen Drama, 1992. In his introduction to his translations of four major plays by De Filippo, Ardito presents information on Filippo's life and works.

Ciolli, Marco. *The Theatre of Eduardo De Filippo: An Introductory Study*. New York: Vantage Press, 1993. A critical study of the drama of De Filippo. Bibliography.

Hampton, Wilborn. "A Popular Italian Playwright and a Wartime Family." Review of *Napoli milionaria!*, by Eduardo De Filippo. *New York Times Current Events Edition*, February 13, 1995, p. C15. A review of De Filippo's *Napoli milionaria!*, per-

formed by the Jean Cocteau Repertory at the Bouwerie Lane Theater in New York.

Mignone, Mario B. *Eduardo De Filippo*. Boston: Twayne, 1984. A biography of De Filippo that covers his life and works. Bibliography and index.

Stokes, John. "Priceless Tears." Review of *Filumena*, by Eduardo De Filippo. *Times Literary Supplement*, October 23, 1998, p. 22. Stokes reviews a production of De Filippo's *Filumena* (*The Best House in Naples*), directed by Peter Hall and starring Judi Dench at the Piccadilly Theatre in London.

Joseph E. Laggini

THOMAS DEKKER

Born: London, England; c. 1572
Died: London, England; August, 1632

PRINCIPAL DRAMA

The Whole History of Fortunatus, pr. 1599, pb. 1600 (commonly known as *Old Fortunatus*)

The Shoemaker's Holiday: Or, The Gentle Craft, pr., pb. 1600 (based on Thomas Deloney's narrative *The Gentle Craft*)

Patient Grissell, pr. 1600, pb. 1603 (with Henry Chettle and William Haughton)

Satiromastix: Or, The Untrussing of the Humourous Poet, pr. 1601, pb. 1602

Sir Thomas Wyatt, pr. 1602 (as *Lady Jane*), pb. 1607

The Honest Whore, Part I, pr., pb. 1604 (with Thomas Middleton)

Westward Ho!, pr. 1604, pb. 1607 (with John Webster)

The Honest Whore, Part II, pr. c. 1605, pb. 1630

Northward Ho!, pr. 1605, pb. 1607 (with Webster)

The Whore of Babylon, pr. c. 1606-1607, pb. 1607

The Roaring Girl: Or, Moll Cutpurse, pr. c. 1610, pb. 1611 (with Middleton)

If This Be Not a Good Play, the Devil Is in It, pr. c. 1610-1612, pb. 1612 (as *If It Be Not Good, the Devil Is in It*)

Match Me in London, pr. c. 1611-1612, pb. 1631

The Virgin Martyr, pr. c. 1620, pb. 1622 (with Philip Massinger)

The Witch of Edmonton, pr. 1621, pb. 1658 (with William Rowley and John Ford)

The Noble Soldier: Or, A Contract Broken, Justly Revenged, pr. c. 1622-1631, pb. 1634 (with John Day; thought to be the same as *The Spanish Fig*, 1602)

The Wonder of a Kingdom, pr. c. 1623, pb. 1636

The Sun's Darling, pr. 1624, pb. 1656 (with Ford)

The Welsh Embassador: Or, A Comedy in Disguises, pr. c. 1624 (revision of *The Noble Soldier*)

The Dramatic Works of Thomas Dekker, pb. 1953-1961 (4 volumes; Fredson Bowers, editor)

OTHER LITERARY FORMS

Thomas Dekker was also known in his time as a prolific pamphleteer. His pamphlets are characterized not by a failure of moral judgment, as some critics have charged, but by a deliberate strategy of refraining from gratuitous finger-pointing. *The Wonderful Year* (1603), for example, presents two long poems that are supposed to be the prologue to a play and a summary of its action and, in a prose section, that action—stories of English reaction to the death of Eliz-

Thomas Dekker (Hulton Archive by Getty Images)

abeth I; Dekker leaves the reader to decide whether there is a thematic relationship in the tripartite struc ture of the work, which links the death of Elizabeth and the devastating plague of 1603, whether these di sasters are to be regarded as retribution for England's sins, and whether the accession of James represents God's gift of unmerited grace. Such implications are there, but the author draws no final conclusions. In this and other pamphlets, Dekker typically adopts the role of observer-reporter, who, like the Bellman of London, carries his lantern into the darkest corners of his dystopian world to reveal the deepest degrada tions of the human spirit. In this regard, like modern social critics, he is content to "tell it like it is"; the se lection of specific detail furnishes the didactic under pinning of his vision. In works such as *The Bellman of London* (1608) and the different versions of *Lan thorn and Candlelight* (1608, 1609; revised as *O per se O*, 1612; *Villanies Discovered*, 1616, 1620; and *English Villanies*, 1632, 1638, 1648), the reader dis covers an alarming truth: The social and political or ganization of the underworld is a grotesque parody of

polite society and the Jacobean establishment. Thus, rogues and thieves have their own laws, codes of eth ics, and standards of "scholarship," which hold a wide currency in both town and country. As demon strated in *The Gull's Hornbook* (1609), they have even developed their own professional language. In this world, God is not an immediate presence, al though he may work out his providential purposes in the hearts and minds of human beings; Dekker, how ever, is chiefly interested in sociological rather than theological sins, as seen in *The Seven Deadly Sins of London* (1606), in which he carefully adapts the traditional medieval framework to fit his own expe rience of life in the city of London. Even in his nu merous descriptions of Hell, Dekker presents an es sentially secular view of the afterlife, designed to show that the community of rogues is an integral part of the Jacobean commonwealth.

Another significant feature of the pamphlets— significant for an understanding of the plays—is the evidence they give of Dekker's familiarity with and manipulation of a wide range of literary forms and conventions. *The Wonderful Year* combines elements of narrative journalism, the frametale, the morality play, and the jestbook. *The Seven Deadly Sins of Lon don* involves some knowledge not only of the medi eval tradition of the sins but also of morality drama, estates satire, and pageants. *The Bellman of London* parodies the Utopian travelogue, while *The Gull's Hornbook* should be read in the tradition of education books such as Baldassare Castiglione's *The Courtier* (1528). Such a review only scratches the surface of Dekker's diverse reading and interests; it is only in works such as *Four Birds of Noah's Ark* (1609), mod eled on contemporary prayer books, that the author maintains a relatively simple structure. An awareness of Dekker's breadth is of the first importance for a reading of his plays, which also draw on a multi plicity of forms. To some extent, the plays also repre sent a necessary thematic balance to the moral vision of the pamphlets, for in his drama, Dekker provides the role models usually missing in his prose works— protagonists such as Moll in *The Roaring Girl*, the saintly Dorothea in *The Virgin Martyr*, and the Subprior in *If This Be Not a Good Play, the Devil Is in It*, who rise above worldly temptations. Such characters suggest that, while it is often impossible to make clear moral distinctions in a world in which knaves and politicians are easily confused, one can successfully rely on one's own moral intelligence. The key to this steadfast vision might well be summarized by a brief passage from *The Seven Deadly Sins of London*: "Wee are moste like to God that made us, when wee shew love to another, and doe most looke like the Divell that would destroy us, when wee are one anothers tormentors."

ACHIEVEMENTS

Although he had a hand in some aspect of the creation of at least seventy plays, it is unfair to dismiss Thomas Dekker as a mere refurbisher of old plays, for there is no question that his frequent collaboration with lesser dramatists was a necessity forced on him in his constant struggle against bankruptcy. His equally frequent collaborations with such outstanding dramatists as Thomas Middleton, John Webster, and John Ford indicate that he was held in high esteem as a playwright. In fact, a fair estimate of his achievement may never be possible, since at least forty-five of his plays have not survived, and much of the work attributed to him remains a matter of critical conjecture. On the other hand, extant plays, such as *Old Fortunatus* and *Satiromastix*, that are attributed solely to Dekker reveal little sense of moral, thematic, or structural unity. The playwright's handful of genuine masterpieces, including *The Shoemaker's Holiday*, the two parts of *The Honest Whore*, and *If This Be Not a Good Play, the Devil Is in It*, conclusively prove, however, that he was capable of transcending the difficulties that mar his lesser works.

At his best, Dekker was an excellent lyric poet, as illustrated in the pastoral scenes of *The Sun's Darling* and the poignant love songs and laments that appear throughout his works. He was also the master of lively and racy dialogue, particularly in the characterization of clowns, rogues, citizens' wives, and old men. Owing to his creation of such memorable characters as the voluble Eyre and his uppity wife Margery (*The Shoemaker's Holiday*), Orlando Friscobaldo and the scoundrel Matheo (*The Honest Whore*),

Scumbroth and the devils (*If This Be Not a Good Play, the Devil Is in It*), and Elizabeth Sawyer (*The Witch of Edmonton*), Dekker has gained a reputation as a "realist." Although it is true that he is at his best among the shops and stalls of London, it is more accurate to recognize Dekker as a dramatist who breathed new life into essentially old forms and conventions, for the roots of his invention lie in the chronicle play, folklore, the mystery plays, and moral interludes of the previous age. His dramatic preferences are clearly revealed in his typical choice of subject, such as legendary biography (in *The Shoemaker's Holiday*), Prudentian psychomachia (in *Old Fortunatus*), medieval hagiography (in *Patient Grissell* and *The Virgin Martyr*), anti-Catholic polemic (in *The Whore of Babylon*), and the use of diabolical temptation similar to that found in such old plays as Christopher Marlowe's *Doctor Faustus* (in *If This Be Not a Good Play, the Devil Is in It*). Dekker's drama, more fully than that of any of his contemporaries, demonstrates the continuing vitality of medieval themes and conventions in Renaissance theater. His greatest achievement was to re-create these traditions on the Jacobean stage with moral force and perspicuity.

BIOGRAPHY

The phrase "my three-score years" in the dedicatory epistle to the 1632 edition of *English Villanies* suggests that Thomas Dekker was born in 1572, probably in the City of London. His broad knowledge of Latin literature suggests that he received a grammar school education, although all such speculation about his early years is mere conjecture. Because he was ranked by Francis Meres, in 1598, among the best English writers of tragedy, he must have begun writing plays as early as 1595; his name first appears in Philip Henslowe's diary in 1598 as the author of the lost play *Phaeton*, and he may also have collaborated with Anthony Munday, Henry Chettle, Thomas Heywood, and William Shakespeare in *The Booke of Sir Thomas More* (c. 1595-1596). Numerous other references in Henslowe's papers and on the title pages of published plays show that Dekker remained extremely busy from 1598 to 1613, writing for the Lord Admiral's Men and occasionally for the Children of Paul's. He was also constantly in debt during this period and was forced to supplement his income by the publication of pamphlets. In 1613, he was imprisoned for debt for the third time and remained in the King's Bench prison until his eventual release in 1619. During his last years, Dekker wrote several plays for the Palsgrave's Men and published several more pamphlets. He apparently refused to attend church from 1626 to 1629 in order to avoid being arrested for debt and was consequently indicted for recusancy. It is believed that he was buried in the parish of St. James, Clerkenwell, on August 25, 1632. The fact that his widow, Elizabeth, refused administration of his will suggests that Dekker had no estate to administer and that death came as his final release from the specter of debtors' prison.

ANALYSIS

Critical condemnation of Thomas Dekker as "a moral sloven" or as a hack with a marginal understanding of dramatic structure is chiefly based on unsympathetic readings of such early plays as *Old Fortunatus*, *Patient Grissell*, and *Satiromastix*. To some extent, the adverse assessments are justified, for these plays are quite severely lacking in structural coherence. Part of the problem, however, may lie in the sheer intransigence of Dekker's sources. The fact that Dekker did possess a keen sense of dramatic structure and moral integrity can easily be demonstrated by an analysis of two of his finest works, *The Shoemaker's Holiday* and *The Honest Whore, Part II*.

THE SHOEMAKER'S HOLIDAY

Based on Thomas Deloney's prose narrative *The Gentle Craft* (1597-c. 1598), *The Shoemaker's Holiday* reveals its structural strategy in the opening scene, in which a discussion between Sir Roger Otley, Lord Mayor of London, and Sir Hugh Lacy, the powerful Earl of Lincoln, is animated by the latent hostility that divides the landed nobility and the wealthy, self-made citizenry of London. Both men fear an elopement between the earl's nephew, Rowland Lacy, and Rose, the Mayor's daughter. Rather than expose his treasury to the frivolous exploitation of a courtly son-in-law, Sir Roger has ordered his daughter into rustic banishment. The earl, to avoid besmirching the fam-

ily dignity and turn his nephew's attention elsewhere, has arranged to have his nephew lead one of the regiments about to invade France. Lacy, however, leaves his command in charge of his cousin Askew, but before he can escape, he is temporarily interrupted by a shoemaker, Simon Eyre, and his men, who try, unsuccessfully, to intercede for the newly married journeyman Rafe, who has been pressed for service in France. Realizing the futility of his plea, Eyre then encourages Rafe to fight for the honor of the gentle craft of shoemakers. The poignant departure scene is highlighted by the generous monetary gifts showered on Rafe and by Rafe's gift of a pair of monogrammed shoes he has made for Jane, his bride. Rafe's obedience provides a stark contrast to the irresponsibility of Lacy, who, though he insists on Rafe's loyalty, has no intention of fulfilling his own patriotic duty. Meanwhile, Jane's distress is reflected in a parallel scene in which Rose learns of Lacy's orders to leave for France. Lacy, however, has decided to use his knowledge of the shoemaker's trade learned on an earlier trip to Germany, to find work with Eyre, who will be shorthanded without Rafe's services. In the following scene, the audience is entertained by the lively bustle of Eyre's shop as he drives his men into honest industry and heaps torrents of loving abuse on his wife, Margery, when she tries to exert a little domestic authority over his employees. Lacy, now posing as Hans Meulter, a Dutchman who speaks only broken English, appears to apply for a job but is hired only because of the strong support of Hodge and Firke, Simon's other workmen. This scene reinforces the central theme of class conflict, because it demonstrates both that true love knows no social barriers and that a resourceful courtier can humble himself to the level of mere apprentice.

By stark contrast, in act 2, Dekker introduces the character of Hammon, an upstart citizen who, in the hope of impressing the exiled Rose, dresses in the height of fashion and ludicrously affects the language of courtly love. Even though his suit is favored by Sir Roger, Hammon is sternly rebuffed when he proposes marriage to Rose. Ironically, Sir Roger is far more impressed by the citizen who apes courtly manners and speech than by the true nobility of Lacy, who is willing to sacrifice all, including social status, for the sake of love. In the third scene, Lacy repays his employer's kindness by introducing him to a Dutch captain who sells Eyre a cargo of valuable merchandise at a great bargain. In order to impress the captain and effect the deal, Simon disguises himself as an alderman, a post he later achieves.

The first scene of act 3 renews Sir Roger's entertainment of Hammon as a suitable husband for Rose, but once again Rose firmly rejects the proposal, much to her father's disgust, and when he learns of Lacy's desertion, Sir Roger's suspicions are highly aroused. In the second scene, Simon's men play on Margery's vanity by suggesting how she should respond to the news that Simon has been elected High Sheriff of London. The festivities are dampened by the unexpected return of Rafe, who has suffered the amputation of a leg. His grief is doubled when he discovers that Jane has secretly left the Eyre household. His distress, however, is swept aside by the triumphal entrance of Eyre, wearing the sheriff's chain of office. The third scene, in which Sir Roger honors Eyre at a banquet, is pivotal to the main plot, for it provides an opportunity, when Simon's men perform a morris dance, for Lacy to reveal his identity to Rose. This scene also reinforces the striking contrast between the pretentious gravity of Sir Roger and the bluff good nature of Simon Eyre. Margery's amusing efforts at courtly decorum also provide an ironic commentary on citizen snobbery. Having been unsuccessful in his pursuit of Rose, Hammon subsequently proposes to Jane, now working as a seamstress, and when she rejects him on the grounds that she is still married, Hammon concocts a false report of Rafe's death in battle. In spite of her evident grief, Hammon relentlessly presses his case until Jane agrees to marry him.

Act 4 begins with excited speculation that Simon will become the next Lord Mayor, but the shoptalk is interrupted by Rose's maid, Sybil, who has been sent to arrange a secret meeting between Rose and Lacy. In the following scene, Rafe learns that Jane is going to marry Hammon when Hammon's servant is dispatched to Eyre's shop to have a pair of shoes made after the exact model of those which Rafe had

given Jane. The wily Firke promises to devise a scheme to prevent the marriage. In scene 3, Lacy is surprised during his secret assignation with Rose by Sir Roger, yet he eludes detection by pretending, in the character of Hans, to measure Rose for shoes. When, shortly after, Sir Hugh is announced, Hans and Rose manage to slip away undetected. When Sybil eventually reveals their elopement, Sir Hugh, fully aware of his nephew's experience as a shoemaker in Wittenberg, realizes how he has been duped. At this point, Firke enters with the shoes that Rose had actually ordered and, seeing the danger to Hans, manufactures a story that misdirects the two enraged elders to St. Faith's, where a marriage, but that of Hammon and Jane, is scheduled. It is important to note that Dekker uses pairs of shoes throughout act 4, in both the main plot and the subplot, to effect the union or reunion of souls.

In the opening scene of act 5, Simon Eyre, who has been elevated to the office of Lord Mayor, agrees to intercede on behalf of Rose and Lacy to the king himself, who has accepted an invitation to dine with him that same day. Simon undertakes this potentially dangerous mission because he will not "forget his fine Dutch journeyman." In the scene following, Rafe, Firke, and Hodge intercept Hammon and his men who are escorting Jane to St. Faith's. Realizing that her husband still lives, Jane immediately rejects Hammon, while the shoemakers give his men a sound thrashing. Sir Hugh and Sir Roger appear at this moment, only to discover that Firke has deceived them, for Rose and Lacy have already been married at the Savoy. Finally, Eyre and his men entertain the king at a great banquet, dedicating the day to their gentle craft and their patron Saint Hugh. This saint's association with the city of London suggests good fortune not only for shoemakers but also for Lacy, who as the Earl of Lincoln's heir and as a shoemaker himself, embodies the best of both worlds. In spite of the earl's vigorous objections, the king, responding graciously to Eyre's humble petition, pardons Lacy's desertion. The shoemaker-mayor, "one of the merriest madcaps" in the land, carries the day, and the king reconciles Sir Roger and Sir Hugh to the marriage of Lacy and Rose.

In adapting Deloney's novel for the stage, Dekker drastically revised the character of Simon Eyre, who in Deloney's work seems much more like Dekker's Sir Roger Otley, a ceremoniously grave and ambitious man who plots his rise to power. Thus, Dekker suppresses the darker side of the bargaining for the Dutch merchandise and creates in Simon an irrepressible force for good. Furthermore, although Deloney's Eyre believes in thrift and hard work, Dekker's Eyre is less motivated by purely economic considerations than he is by an exhilarating sense of the value of work *as* work. It is also important to note that *The Shoemaker's Holiday* is not a dynamic play, for Dekker's treatment of his main characters permits no internal conflict, no self-discovery, and no essential growth. Simon, Lacy, Rose, and the shoemakers remain, throughout, perfectly secure in the holiness of their hearts' affections, and their knowledge is instinctive rather than based on systems of moral philosophy or codes of social behavior. In the very integrity of their words and actions, their lives exemplify the theme of the comedy: that love and nobility transcend such considerations as wealth, class consciousness, or political status. Although Simon Eyre achieves all the social distinctions that mean most to men such as Sir Roger and Sir Hugh, he remains completely oblivious to them. His love of life, his concern for his men, and his innate patriotism are never corrupted. From beginning to end, he remains "the merriest madcap" in the land, whose triumphs are based on goodwill and honest industry. It is also significant that his victory over class prejudice is realized through the royal intervention of the legendary King Henry V, who recognizes in Eyre's raucous good humor a strain of genuine nobility that escapes the pettier understanding of such men as Sir Hugh and Sir Roger. In fact, it is tempting to see in Eyre and his men a group of individuals who represent the exact social obverse of Shakespeare's Falstaff and his predatory followers.

Throughout the play, Dekker skillfully interweaves the various strands of plot to achieve both a structural and thematic unity, not only in the resolution of the romantic intrigues but also in the establishment of a new social order that sweeps aside the trivial differences that divide courtiers and citizens. Beginning with the class conflict developed in the initial debate between Sir Roger and Sir Hugh, each consecutive scene either opposes or reinforces the class harmony that must eventually prevail in the final scene. Lacy's decision to work as a tradesman and the friendship and loyalty he finds in the assistance of Hodge and Firke counterpoise the noble pride of the Earl of Lincoln. The truth of Lacy's love for Rose, for which he risks all, is neatly balanced against the unscrupulous conduct of Hammon, whose romantic affections and courtly love language are offset by Lacy's true nobility and Rafe's simple devotion to Jane. Rose and Jane suffer the anguish of forced separation from their lovers, and both are reunited in scenes that involve the manufacture and delivery of shoes from Eyre's premises. Sir Roger's preference for Hammon provides a ludicrous commentary on the blindness of class snobbery, as do Margery's feeble attempts at gentility and decorum. The one flaw in Lacy's behavior, his desertion from patriotic duty, is structurally necessary to justify his employment in Eyre's shop and thematically essential to provide the reason for the king's intervention against the feuding parents. The act of royal clemency, in turn, affirms the primacy of love and resolves the theme of class conflicts, and the royal pardon itself is based on the king's affirmation of Simon Eyre as the exemplar of social and political harmony.

THE HONEST WHORE, PART II

Dekker's greatest work, however, is *The Honest Whore, Part II*, a tragicomedy using most of the characters from the first part (written in collaboration with Thomas Middleton), in which is dramatized the moral conversion of the whore Bellafronte by Hippolito, the son-in-law of the Duke of Milan. In the resolution of *The Honest Whore, Part I*, the scoundrel Matheo has been forced to marry Bellafronte because he had been initially responsible for leading her into a life of sin. The subplot of the first part features the tempting of Candido, a patient man who triumphs over the constant humiliations heaped on him by his shrewish wife Viola.

The second part of *The Honest Whore* begins with Bellafronte and an unnamed scholar waiting to make petitions to Hippolito. His summary dismissal of the scholar is ominous, for the clear implication is that the scholar is willing to sell his genius for money. The suggestion that the scholar is an intellectual prostitute, however, may be more a reflection on the prince's mind than on the scholar's integrity. On the other hand, Hippolito does listen to Bellafronte's request that he intercede on behalf of the profligate Matheo, who has been condemned for killing a man in a duel. At the same time, finding himself strangely attracted to the fallen woman whom he had once redeemed, he also promises to reconcile her, if he can, to her estranged father Orlando Friscobaldo, who had abandoned his support when she resorted to prostitution. Hippolito makes good his promise in the following scene when he intercepts Orlando and urges him to forgive his daughter, who has turned away from sin. The old man appears totally intransigent in his repugnance for Bellafronte and rebukes Hippolito for disturbing his peace, although secretly he resolves to keep an alert watch over Bellafronte and her disreputable husband. In the third scene, a number of gallants visit the linen-draper Candido, who has remarried after Viola's unexpected death. Urging him to subdue the pettish whims of his new bride, lest she too turn into an untamable shrew, they together devise a scheme in which Ludovico Sforza, in the role of an apprentice, will test her mettle.

Act 2 begins with Matheo's return from prison, although it is immediately apparent that he has not changed his ways, a fact that sorely distresses Bellafronte, who has now been reduced to virtual destitution. Their quarreling is interrupted by Orlando, who has disguised himself as his own servingman, Pacheco. When he and Matheo exchange disparaging remarks about her father's honesty, Bellafronte will not tolerate their insults, even though the old man has abandoned her to humiliation and direst poverty. Reassured by this successful testing of his daughter's virtue, Orlando offers his services to Matheo and gives him money for safekeeping. When Hippolito visits Bellafronte, Orlando quickly discerns the drift of the prince's interest in his daughter and watches anxiously to see how she will react to even greater temptations. Later, however, she dispatches Pacheco

with a letter and a diamond she wishes to return to Hippolito. She also gives the old man a cryptic message that rejects the prince's lecherous designs. In the following scene, Candido reduces his new wife to submission after challenging her to a duel with yardsticks. This scene highlights the virtue of a wife's loyalty and obedience to her husband in a test that clearly parallels Bellafronte's support for a far less worthy husband.

Act 3 opens with Orlando's delivery of Bellafronte's letter not to Hippolito but to Infelice, who subsequently confronts her husband with positive proof of his treachery. Hippolito feigns contrition but nevertheless resolves to give full rein to his lust. With "armed Devils staring in [his] face," like Angelo in William Shakespeare's *Measure for Measure* (pr. 1604), the young prince is less captivated by Bellafronte's beauty than by her persevering virtue. In the meantime, Orlando returns to find that Matheo has squandered all the money he had entrusted to him and has even robbed his wife of her gown, which he intends to sell to satisfy his desire for a cloak and rapier. Matheo even urges her to return to her profession in order to keep him supplied with ready cash. After the husband's angry departure, Orlando consoles his daughter and plots an appropriate revenge. Bellafronte's trial is further reflected in the following scene, in which Candido's wife is tested by the gallants who lure the husband into a protracted discussion of his wares while Lieutenant Bots, a denizen of the local stews, tries unsuccessfully to lure her into prostitution.

Orlando appears in his own person, in the first scene of act 4, to accuse Matheo and Bellafronte of maintaining a bawdy house, but his daughter disclaims her past and pleads with the old man not to leave her destitute, since poverty may drive her back into a life of sin. After engaging in a shouting match with Matheo, Orlando storms out of the house, only to return moments later in the guise of Pacheco, who commiserates with Matheo and promises to help him burglarize his father-in-law's house. After the husband's departure, Hippolito appears and argues with Bellafronte in the hope of making her turn "whore/ By force of strong perswasion." His argument, however, is unconvincing, because he merely reverses the claims he had presented in his earlier conversion speech in *Part I*; Bellafronte triumphs because her arguments are firmly based on the real shame and degradation she has actually experienced as a whore. Though soundly defeated in this exchange, the prince swears to press his case "even to Hell's brazen doores." In scene 2, Orlando enlists the duke's aid in having Matheo arrested for theft committed against two peddlers who are actually Orlando's own men in disguise. Aware of Hippolito's infidelity to Infelice, the duke also orders the arrest of all harlots and bawds, including Bellafronte. In the third scene, the gallants, including Matheo, entertain Bots and Mistress Horsleach and lure the unsuspecting Candido into drinking their health while Orlando delivers the stolen goods for their appraisal. When the trap is set, the constables arrive, first to arrest the bawdy-house keepers and Candido, and second to apprehend Matheo for theft and possession of stolen goods.

The final act begins with Ludovico informing Hippolito of Bellafronte's arrest, the news of which drives the prince into a frenzy of rage. He races off to storm the Bridewell, where the duke and Infelice lie in wait for him. All the interwoven threads of intrigue are carefully drawn together in the long final scene as Orlando and the duke confront Matheo and Hippolito with the enormity of their behavior. Still disguised as Pacheco, Orlando orchestrates the arraignment of Matheo, who first tries to pin the blame on Bellafronte and then on Pacheco himself. He even accuses Hippolito and Bellafronte of whoring, claiming to have caught them together in bed. When Infelice demands justice against the bewildered Bellafronte, Hippolito confesses his miserable failure in trying to tempt Bellafronte; at this moment, Orlando casts off his disguise to exonerate his daughter of Matheo's malicious accusation, while at the same time certifying the veracity of the prince's confession. Matheo is saved from the charge of theft because the men he had robbed are Orlando's own servants. Matheo is not pardoned for his merits, or even in the hope that he will reform, but as a reward for Bellafronte's patient loyalty to him. Similarly, Candido, who remains the soul of patience, is elevated to the rank of "king's

counselor." Hippolito is ignored but is doubtless restored to Infelice's good graces.

It was a stroke of realistic genius on Dekker's part to leave Matheo only grudgingly repentant at the end of the play, for his insolent prodigality and his cruelty toward Bellafronte make it impossible for his crimes merely to be whitewashed. The main point of the resolution is to demonstrate how completely the "whore" has overcome the obstacles that have constantly threatened her progress. In *Part I*, Bellafronte's conversion becomes the continuing butt of scurrilous jests and innuendos, which partly suggest that she will be unable to sustain her penitence and purity of moral purpose. Her final victory in *Part II* is earned against almost insuperable odds, in spite of the seemingly mitigating fact that her father has been watching over her, for there is no question that Orlando undertakes his role with a view to testing fully her reformed character. The implication is clearly that he will once again abandon Bellafronte if she suffers a relapse. In fact, her conversion to chastity in *Part I* would ultimately have proven unconvincing had not Dekker submitted her to the protracted trials and grief of *Part II*, for which Matheo's thorough, unrelenting evil is thematically essential.

It seems likely that Dekker was attracted to a reexamination of the temptation theme after his less than successful effort at reworking the legend of patient Griselda. Unlike the saintly Grissell, who has never experienced the pleasures of forbidden life and who is never seriously threatened by Gwalter's cruelty, Bellafronte undergoes a series of much more realistic temptations. Her chastity is severely tested not because her resolution is weak but because she faces the constant fear of degrading poverty and starvation. In this light, Hippolito's importunate lust represents no serious threat because her resistance is firmly based on the clear recollection of the disgust and shame she has actually experienced as a prostitute. On the other hand, Matheo's repulsive suggestion that she return to her "profession" poses a genuine threat because it represents a terrifying dilemma: She must choose between a return to prostitution or continued resistance to her husband's will. The stripping away of her self-respect reaches its nadir with Matheo's theft of her gown, which is sold to feed his uncontrollable greed. It is at this point that Orlando knows he must intervene to uncloak Matheo's villainy, but he only makes this decision when he is thoroughly convinced that her steadfast resistance to temptation is genuine.

Structurally, the subplot provides consistently strong reinforcement of the trial theme in the main plot, particularly since it involves not only the enduring patience of Candido, whose unassailable virtue reminds one of Grissell's, but also the successful resistance of Candido's new wife to the schemes of Bots, Horseleach, and Ludovico. The duke's Milan, plagued as it seems by all the seven deadly sins, is Dekker's re-creation of the Jacobean London so vividly depicted in the rogue pamphlets. In such a world, Hippolito, Matheo, the bawds, prostitutes, and gallants "doe most looke like the Divell that would destroy us, when wee are one anothers tormentors," and they are frequently described in terms of diabolic imagery. Furthermore, true to Dekker's basically Arian moral thought, Bellafronte demonstrates that love, obedience, and perseverance are the constant virtues of a distinctly possible reformation. In this play and in *The Shoemaker's Holiday*, Dekker left at least two works that demonstrate architectonic unity and a keen sense of moral values. For this achievement, he deserves to be ranked among the excellent second-rank dramatists of the Elizabethan-Jacobean stage.

OTHER MAJOR WORKS

NONFICTION: *The Seven Deadly Sins*, 1606; *News from Hell*, 1606; *The Bellman of London*, 1608; *Four Birds of Noah's Ark*, 1609; *The Gull's Hornbook*, 1609; *A Work for Armourers*, 1609; *Penny-Wise, Pound-Foolish*, 1631; *The Plague Pamphlets of Thomas Dekker*, 1925 (F. P. Wilson, editor).

MISCELLANEOUS: *The Wonderful Year*, 1603 (prose and poetry); *The Double PP*, 1606 (prose and poetry); *Lanthorn and Candlelight*, 1608, 1609 (prose and poetry; revised as *O per se O*, 1612; *Villanies Discovered*, 1616, 1620; *English Villanies*,

1632, 1638, 1648) *Dekker, His Dream*, 1620 (prose and poetry); *The Non-Dramatic Works of Thomas Dekker*, 1884-1886 (4 volumes; Alexander B. Grosart, editor); *Thomas Dekker: Selected Prose Writings*, 1968 (E. D. Pendry, editor).

BIBLIOGRAPHY

Adler, Doris Ray. *Thomas Dekker: A Reference Guide*. Boston: G. K. Hall, 1983. An annotated bibliography of works on Dekker. Index.

Champion, Larry S. *Thomas Dekker and the Traditions of English Drama*. 2d ed. New York: Peter Lang, 1987. A study of Dekker and his place in the English drama tradition. Bibliography and index.

Correll, Barbara. *The End of Conduct: Grobianus and the Renaissance Text of the Subject*. Ithaca, N.Y.: Cornell University Press, 1996. In her scholarly study of Renaissance literature, Correll examines Dekker's *The Gull's Hornbook*. Bibliography and index.

Gasper, Julia. *The Dragon and the Dove: The Plays of Thomas Dekker*. New York: Oxford University Press, 1990. A critical analysis of Dekker's plays that focuses on his treatment of kings and rulers as well as of Protestantism. Bibliography and index.

McLuskie, Kathleen. *Dekker and Heywood: Professional Dramatists*. New York: St. Martin's Press, 1993. A comparison of Dekker and Thomas Heywood, as well as a description of the theater of England during their lives. Bibliography and index.

Twyning, John. *London Dispossessed: Literature and Social Space in the Early Modern City*. New York: St. Martin's Press, 1998. This study focuses on Dekker's descriptions of London and of city and town life in England during his lifetime, including how they were portrayed in his literary works. Bibliography and index.

E. F. J. Tucker,
updated by Frank Day

SHELAGH DELANEY

Born: Salford, Lancashire, England; November 25, 1939

PRINCIPAL DRAMA

A Taste of Honey, pr. 1958, pb. 1959

The Lion in Love, pr. 1960, pb. 1961

The House That Jack Built, pb. 1977, revised pr. 1979

Don't Worry About Matilda, pr. 1983 (radio play), pr. 1987 (staged)

OTHER LITERARY FORMS

Three of Shelagh Delaney's screenplays have become successful films: *A Taste of Honey* (1961, with Tony Richardson), based on her stage play of the same title; *Charlie Bubbles* (1968), based on one of her short stories; and *Dance with a Stranger* (1985), based on a celebrated murder case and trial in the mid-1950's. Two other screenplays were not as successful: *The White Bus* (1966), from a Delaney short story, filmed but never released, and *The Raging Moon* (1970). Delaney has done several teleplays, including *St. Martin's Summer* (1974), *Did Your Nanny Come from Bergen?* (1970), and *Find Me First* (1979). She has one television series to her credit, *The House That Jack Built* (1977), adapted for stage performance in New York in 1979. She has also written two radio plays, *So Does the Nightingale* (1980) and *Don't Worry About Matilda* (1983), which was very favorably reviewed. In 1963, a collection of semiautobiographical short stories appeared: *Sweetly Sings the Donkey*. A number of her essays appeared in the 1960's in *The New York Times Magazine* and *Cosmopolitan*.

ACHIEVEMENTS

Shelagh Delaney is highly regarded for her ability to create working-class characters and to express the difficulties of their lives in industrial northern England. She is a playwright of a particular region and social class. Both *A Taste of Honey* (which won the New York Drama Critics citation as best foreign play

of 1961) and *The Lion in Love* employ such settings and characters. Her focus on the domestic tensions in the lives of working-class families is especially sympathetic to women, though never sentimental. Delaney's early work for the stage and her later television, film, and radio plays seem to revolve around the dreams and frustrations of women in contemporary society. While she was at first mistaken as an "Angry Young Woman," her focus has generally not been on large social issues but on individuals confronting their economic and social limitations and dealing with their illusions. *A Taste of Honey*, *The Lion in Love*, and several of her works in other media study characters who belong to families yet who are isolated even from those closest to them. That her characters face their difficulties with humor and wit sets her apart from many of her contemporaries, such as John Osborne.

BIOGRAPHY

Shelagh Delaney was born on November 25, 1939, in Salford, Lancashire, England. She remembers her father, Joseph, a bus inspector, as a great storyteller and reader. Delaney's education was erratic, marked by attendance at three primary schools and her failure of the eleven-plus qualifying examinations for grammar school. She was admitted to the Broughton Secondary School and, after a fair record of achievement, was transferred to the more academic local grammar school. At fifteen, she took her General Certificate of Education, passing in five subjects, and at age seventeen, she left school. She held a number of jobs in succession, working as a shop assistant, as a milk depot clerk, as an usher, and finally as an assistant researcher in the photography department of a large industrial firm.

The encouragement Delaney received at Broughton School led her to continue her writing later. She had already begun a novel when she saw a performance of Terence Rattigan's *Variation on a Theme* (pr., pb. 1958), which she disliked and which she thought she could better. This experience served as a catalyst for reshaping her novel into the play that became *A Taste of Honey*. She sent the revision to Joan Littlewood, leader of a radical London group called Theatre Workshop, who began rehearsals immediately. Its initial run began May 27, 1958, at the Theatre Royal, Stratford East, and lasted a month. Restaged six months later at the Theatre Royal, it eventually opened in London, on February 10, 1959. When it opened in New York, in October, 1960, it was very well received and ran for 391 performances.

Delaney's second play, *The Lion in Love*, was heavily criticized on its opening in Coventry in September, 1960. Attacked as verbose, without unity and focus, its London run was brief. After *The Lion in Love*, Delaney turned her efforts to television and film, adapting her short stories to create some of the works. In 1961, she worked with director Tony Richardson to produce a successful film version of *A Taste of Honey*, one which differed markedly from the stage version in its realism. The production won for her a British Film Academy award. Her 1963 collection of short stories, *Sweetly Sings the Donkey*, also contains a version of "The White Bus," later filmed but never released. Her successful screenplay for *Charlie Bubbles*, reportedly based on a short story, won for her a Writers' Guild Award. Throughout the 1970's, most of her work was in television, including a series, *The House That Jack Built*, which she adapted for an Off-Off-Broadway production in 1979. Her 1985 screenplay *Dance with a Stranger*, her first work based on historical, rather than imagined, characters and situations, was a notable success; in the same year, she was made a Fellow of the Royal Society of Literature.

ANALYSIS

Shelagh Delaney's stage plays *A Taste of Honey* and *The Lion in Love*, though very different in style, share several themes and emphases. Despite early critics' comments that the plays have "no ideas" and nearly no plot, both communicate effectively the loneliness of their working-class characters and their dreams and frustrations as they deal with the realities of love. In both plays, families are portrayed who, except by accident of birth and location, are strangers. Cut off from security and stability by education, social class, and economics, these characters are further isolated by a peculiar stubbornness and pride, in part a defense against the vulnerability love brings.

Delaney has been applauded for her realism, especially in her language and her treatment of relationships. She deserves, however, equal praise for her creation of a mythic world, filled with powerful symbols of brokenness. When the plays appeared, critics recognized her regionalism, humor, and vivid women characters. Yet Delaney's early critics frequently assumed that the plays should be closed, climactic, showing issues resolved and measurable growth. Neither *The Lion in Love* nor *A Taste of Honey* fulfills such expectations. Instead, Delaney's world is one in which change is slight and in which circularity is common: Sons behave like fathers, and daughters follow their mothers. This world is, despite Delaney's humor, a difficult one. Her characters fear and hurt too much to become vulnerable, and they are ultimately detached from one another save for brief moments of consolation followed by antagonism.

A TASTE OF HONEY

A Taste of Honey is briefly told in two acts. As the play opens, Helen, a "semi-whore," and her sixteen-

Shelagh Delaney (Hulton Archive by Getty Images)

year-old daughter Josephine, or Jo, are moving into a desolate two-room flat in Manchester. Helen soon decides to marry Peter, a raffish one-eyed car salesperson, and the two abandon Jo. Jo, too, has a love interest, in a black sailor, who proposes to her and consoles her as Helen and Peter leave. The second act, set six months later, introduces Geof, a homosexual art student, who moves in with Jo, now pregnant from her Christmas affair. He fixes up the apartment, attempts to help Jo accept the child, and eventually offers to marry her. In Jo's last month of pregnancy, Helen returns, her marriage having broken down. She bullies Geof into leaving and takes over as Jo goes into labor. When she discovers that the baby may be black, she leaves, ostensibly for a drink, promising to return. Jo's last lines are from a nursery rhyme of Geof's, holding out the promise of a benefactor who will care for her.

A Taste of Honey succeeded in part because of its daring plot, but primarily because of the strength of its characterizations, especially of Jo. Delaney's realistic dialogue creates a sense of authenticity of character that masks considerable implausibility. Particularly in the opening scenes with Helen and Jo, the rhythm of attack and defense, the revelation of past failures, the barely concealed insults, the self-deprecation, the sharpness and sustained talk tantalize the audience. Out of fragments of conversation, partial revelations, and even asides to the audience, Delaney creates individuals with deep and universal human needs. Out of this battle of words, partially revealing Jo's hope for love and her need for affirmation from her mother, come the forces that propel her into her love affair.

Delaney's male characters are significantly weaker than her women. Peter is more a caricature, some of his mannerisms suggesting a middle-class dropout now slumming with Helen. His villainy is stereotypical: Complete with eyepatch for a war wound, he carries a walletful of pictures of other girlfriends, though courting Helen. Geof is equally vague, in part because of his homosexuality. He is clearly the more sympathetic, in that he makes no demands on Jo, but is an easy and deferential target for Helen when she returns.

Although it may be said that little happens in the play, its physical and verbal compression makes the interaction of the characters overwhelming. Jo and Helen's two-room flat reflects a world lacking intellectual and physical privacy, in which the characters literally lack room to grow and develop. Similarly, the play's allusiveness contributes to a sense of the mythic nature of the action: References to other works of literature ranging from nursery rhymes to Sophocles' *Oidipous Tyrannos* (c. 429 B.C.E.; *Oedipus Tyrannus*, 1715) are embedded in the dialogue. That they are suggested, rather than developed fully, may reflect Delaney's youthfulness.

The play's style, a result of the production techniques of the Theatre Workshop, makes it a mixture of gritty realism and dreams. Both the dialogue and the situation seem realistic: The language has the distinct flavor of a region and a class, and the characters' reactions to their situation seem authentic. Yet the text also seems stylized and Brechtian in its rapid pacing, asides in the third person to the audience, and a music-hall style of humor, including insults and songs. A small jazz band plays between scenes and provides music to which the characters enter and exit, many times dancing as they do. Significantly, the play never becomes abstract or allegorical, as do Bertolt Brecht's *Der kaukasische Kreidekreis* (1944-1945; *The Caucasian Chalk Circle*, 1948) and *Der gute Mensch von Sezuan* (1938-1940; *The Good Woman of Setzuan*, 1948), dealing with similar situations.

The collaboration of the Theatre Workshop is important, for *A Taste of Honey* was significantly reshaped from the original text. John Russell Taylor studied the original text of the play as it went to the Theatre Workshop and the final printed version. Aside from minor cutting to tighten dialogue, two major changes in the performance version are evident. First, the character of Peter is much weakened in performance, and he becomes a much more sinister figure. His marriage to Helen, successful in the original draft, now fails. The original draft employs his marriage to Helen as the basis for a more radical plot change from performance: He offers to take in both Jo and the baby. As the play ends, Jo seems destined to return to her mother. Geof is left alone onstage, holding the doll that he had given Jo, all that he will have of the relationship. This seems to suggest much greater optimism in the original text than in performance and also a significant focus on and greater sympathy for Geof.

A Taste of Honey, by structure and characterization, indicates both the intense needs of its characters for love and affirmation and the likelihood of their failure to meet those needs. Most of the characters voice a longing for affection and love, but nearly all are defensive and uneasy in relationships with others. Although Jo is the most fully realized character, Geof, though shadowy, is more sympathetic because of his willingness to become what Jo needs. Yet his love for her leads to his willingness to leave when Helen pushes him out. Despite Helen and Jo's reunion at the play's end, the inability of the characters to adapt their personal needs to those of others leaves only guarded optimism about the future.

THE LION IN LOVE

The Lion in Love, a three-act play set in the north of England, is both more compressed and more diverse than *A Taste of Honey*. Delaney has extended her range of characters with an entire family, the Freskos: grandfather Jesse, his daughter Kit and her husband Frank, and their children, Banner and Peg. She further includes minor characters: Nora, who is having an affair with Frank; Loll, Peg's boyfriend and fiancé; and Andy and Nell, the former character an injured acrobat and pimp for the latter.

Instead of nine months' action, as in her previous play, Delaney dramatizes three days several weeks apart, yet this does not tighten the structure of the play. Although characters confront opportunities for fulfillment, through hesitation or fear, most of them lose their chance. The action consequently seems either directionless or circular, with little external change. Frank, who sells toys from a suitcase stand in the marketplace, spends most of his time with Kit arguing and being insulted. Either a permanent booth or Nora's offer to set up a shop with him would mean personal and economic security. In the end, Frank gains neither, and he remains trapped in his complex and antagonistic relationship with Kit. Peg and Loll,

though able to see what has happened to the older generation, seem no wiser or better able to govern their emotions, and Peg apparently elopes with Loll. Only Banner, in his departure for Australia, is able to escape the limitations of marriage but at the cost of abandoning his family and any support it may offer. Even Nell and Andy and their dreams of a new act for performance are blighted: He is not as good a dancer as she thought.

The title of the play is from an Aesopian fable in which a lion permits a forester to remove his claws and teeth as preconditions for marrying the forester's daughter. Once he submits, the forester kills him. The moral, "Nothing can be more fatal to peace than the ill-assorted marriages into which rash love may lead," applies to both the parents and children of the Fresko family. Both Kit and Frank seem to have lost by their marriage, and Loll and Peg may do the same. The banter of the partners back and forth, the attempt at friendship and intimacy, the defensiveness and caution are the same in both the younger and older lovers.

Once again, Delaney focuses more on the women of the play than the men. Although Kit does not enter immediately, she dominates the action and provides the center of interest. In a sense, the other members of her family exist only in their reaction to her. Her love of life and excitement, her determination not to behave as an adult and accept adult limitations, her chosen independence from children, husband, and father, make her a dynamic figure in an otherwise unchanging situation. She seems always to transcend the limitations of situation, class, and economic factors. Yet her "liveliness" is in fact destructive, provoking her husband's affairs and her daughter's disillusionment and eventual elopement. Although Peg is much less developed than Kit, her history will probably be the same. She has the wit, insight, and longings of her mother.

Delaney's men are, once again, shadowy or insufficient figures. Although each has plans and dreams, none seems able to realize them or even develop commitment to them. They wander aimlessly, which may communicate a psychological truth but which confuses audiences. Jesse, the grandfather, the garrulous commentator on life, the link with the past, seems, despite his history, to have little to offer. Frank is much more fully realized, but his motives are still confused, and he is unable to confront his motives for returning to Kit. Banner and Loll are undeveloped, each with a dream that necessitates leaving and has only vague longings to support it.

The Lion in Love has a quite different production style from that of *A Taste of Honey*. Gone are the Brechtian elements, the asides, the jazz band in the wings, the dancing entrances and exits. Although the stage directions indicate that the set is "suggested rather than real," with a backdrop which is "a fantastic panorama" of the city and "the local bombed-site" at the back, the play is much more conventionally realistic. Although the stage action is at points quite lively, as at the opening of act 2, set on market day, the pacing throughout is measured. The biting humor of *A Taste of Honey* remains, but not the mixture of fantasy and reality.

OTHER MAJOR WORKS

SHORT FICTION: *Sweetly Sings the Donkey*, 1963.

SCREENPLAYS: *A Taste of Honey*, 1961 (with Tony Richardson); *The White Bus*, 1966; *Charlie Bubbles*, 1968; *The Raging Moon*, 1970; *Dance with a Stranger*, 1985.

TELEPLAYS: *Did Your Nanny Come from Bergen?*, 1970; *St. Martin's Summer*, 1974; *The House That Jack Built*, 1977 (series); *Find Me First*, 1979; *The Railway Station Man*, 1992.

RADIO PLAY: *So Does the Nightingale*, 1980.

BIBLIOGRAPHY

Delaney, Shelagh. "How Imagination Retraced a Murder." *The New York Times*, August 4, 1985, p. B15. Delaney discusses how she came to write the screenplay for the first nonfiction drama she wrote, *Dance with a Stranger*. Relates briefly the facts of the life of the protagonist, Ruth Ellis, then argues for the validity of Delaney's imaginative reconstruction of the character, criticized by people who knew Ellis. Delaney uses the wildly differing opinions of others to argue that her reconstruction is adequate, because "we are all figments of each other's imaginations" and cannot really know or understand one another.

Gillett, Eric. "Regional Realism: Shelagh Delaney, Alun Owen, Keith Waterhouse, and Willis Hall." In *Experimental Drama*, edited by W. A. Armstrong. London: G. Bell and Sons, 1963. Compares Delaney and three other "regional" playwrights, discussing their authentic handling of characterization and dialogue. Notes the weakness in plotting, but general improvement in characterization, in Delaney's second play.

Kitchin, Laurence. *Mid-Century Drama*. 2d ed. London: Faber and Faber, 1969. A brief interview with Delaney, suggesting elements that went into her style in *A Taste of Honey*: a storytelling tradition from her father, a welfare state upbringing that left her disenchanted with socialism, and popular cinema.

Oberg, Arthur K. "*A Taste of Honey* and the Popular Play." *Wisconsin Studies in Contemporary Literature* 7 (Summer, 1966): 160-167. Studies Delaney's first play as a product of collaboration between the playwright and the radical Theatre Workshop. Delaney's stylistic borrowings from music-hall theater and Victorian melodrama create much of the vitality of the play, but Oberg believes that they ultimately inhibit the play's aspiration to rise to serious drama.

Taylor, John Russell. *The Angry Theatre: New British Drama*. Rev. ed. New York: Hill and Wang, 1969. Presents the first careful analysis of the original script of *A Taste of Honey* and its adaptation by the Theatre Workshop and further contrasts several major features of the play with the film version, done in a realistic mode, in 1961. Major changes in production included tightening of dialogue, revision of the roles of two of the male characters, and a significant change in the play's ending. Taylor continues with an examination of *The Lion in Love*, the short-story collection *Sweetly Sings the Donkey*, and the screenplay for *Charlie Bubbles*.

Wellwarth, G. E. *The Theatre of Protest and Paradox*. Rev. ed. New York: New York University Press,

1971. Links Delaney's first play, in its examination of the problems of loneliness and failed communication, to Samuel Beckett, Eugène Ionesco, Jean Genet, and Arthur Adamov. Points out that the asides to the audience in *A Taste of Honey* conceal the characters' ability to communicate to the audience but not with one another.

Richard J. Sherry

GIAMBATTISTA DELLA PORTA

Born: Naples (now in Italy); 1535
Died: Naples (now in Italy); February 4, 1615

PRINCIPAL DRAMA

L'Olimpia, wr. 1550, pr. 1588, pb. 1589
L'astrologo, wr. 1570, pb. 1606 (*The Astrologer*, 1615)
La turca, wr. 1572, pb. 1606
La sorella, pr. 1589, pb. 1604 (*The Sister*, 1610)
Penelope, pb. 1591
La fantesca, pb. 1592
La Cintia, pb. 1592
La trappolaria, pb. 1596, pr. 1614
La furiosa, pb. 1600
I due fratelli rivali, pb. 1601 (*The Two Rival Brothers*, 1980)
I due fratelli simili, pb. 1604
La carbonaria, pb. 1606
Il moro, pb. 1607
La chiappinaria, pb. 1609
Il Georgio, pr., pb. 1611 (verse play)
La tabernaria, pb. 1612
L'Ulisse, pb. 1614
Le commedie, pb. 1910-1911 (2 volumes)

OTHER LITERARY FORMS

Although Giambattista Della Porta's dramatic output was both vast and significant, and although it continued through almost the entire span of his life, the author himself often dismissed it as "youthful trifles." Indeed, during his lifetime, the Neapolitan's reputation derived mainly from his esoteric and multifaceted scientific pursuits. His interests in this field ranged widely, from mnemonics, cryptography, and astrology to meteorology, agriculture, mathematics, astronomy, alchemy, and various other forms of conventional and unconventional research. His most celebrated scientific works, such as *Magiae naturalis* (1558, 1589; *Natural Magick*, 1658)—a medley of serious scientific research and fanciful probing into the occult and the exotic—and *De humana physiognomonia* (1586; *Of Human Physiognomy*, 1829)—a work propounding the idea that certain animal-like features of people's physical appearance correspond to specific traits of their character, thus making it possible to judge people's dispositions by their physical appearance—made Della Porta a celebrity and are remembered today. Ironically, however, and despite the fact that some modern scientists see in Della Porta's scientific work the presage of such scientific inventions as photography (through his rediscovery of the camera obscura) and of criminal anthropology, today Della Porta's fame rests primarily on the seventeen plays that have survived.

ACHIEVEMENTS

The surviving fourteen comedies and three tragedies of the doubtless more than thirty dramatic works written by Giambattista Della Porta constitute one of the most imposing monuments of sixteenth century Italian theater. In mere numerical terms, these plays place Della Porta among the most significant playwrights of the late Renaissance period. Della Porta's various other eclectic interests, however, prompted the author himself to dismiss his plays as secondary. Nevertheless, Della Porta's theater, with its sense of life that is both facetious and sentimental, seems a deliberate and conscious effort to mitigate the popularity of the *commedia dell'arte* by incorporating some of its elements into the erudite dramatic tradition.

In the light of the fact that the Counter-Reformers often attempted to ban theatrical performances, especially of comedies, with the intention of cleansing drama of immorality and paganism, it is quite remarkable that a man such as Della Porta managed to publish such a large number of plays. Employing complicated plots ending in improbable denouements, Della Porta succeeded in the difficult task of reconciling belief in the Christian God with the pagan concept of fate by converting the latter into Divine Providence. In post-Tridentine Italy, his plight was a common one. Playwrights were confronted with a difficult task: that of not allowing a Peripatetic, providential solution—which would wholly adhere to theatrical tradition and to Aristotelian precepts—to contradict one's expression of the Christian precept of free will.

Despite their often scurrilous language and ever-present sensual overtones, the general atmosphere in Della Porta's plays is that of a *commedia grave*, with all the hyperboles and metaphors peculiar to the serious and sentimental pre-Baroque theater. The earliest and latest of Della Porta's comedies, however, manage somewhat to escape this evident didactic and moral intent with their at times unwonted licentiousness. Because of their inner balance and well-developed mixture of sentimentalism and pathos, Della Porta's plays exercised a surprising influence on other playwrights, both Italian and foreign. William Shakespeare himself may well have been influenced by Della Porta's *The Two Rival Brothers* while writing *Much Ado About Nothing* (pr. c. 1598-1599); certainly Della Porta's comedies found other ready imitators in England in a number of early dramatists, such as Walter Hawkesworth, Samuel Brooke, George Ruggle, Thomas Tomkis, and Thomas Middleton. In other countries, especially in France, Della Porta's works were soon known either directly or through adaptations of the *commedia dell'arte*, and several of his comedies were imitated or freely translated by such writers as Tristan L'Hermite, Jean de Rotrou, and Molière. In Italy, Della Porta's influence was widely and immediately felt, and although it was particularly evident in Neapolitan erudite comedy, it also gave rise to a plethora of disciples and imitators all over the peninsula, much later affecting even the work of Carlo Goldoni.

BIOGRAPHY

Giambattista Della Porta, the third of four sons, was born in the fall of 1535 in the municipality of Naples. As his father, Antonio, was a nobleman greatly interested in humanistic learning who surrounded himself with poets, artists, mathematicians, and philosophers, Della Porta was tutored in these disciplines by the most learned doctors Naples could offer. It seems probable that he also attended some of the lectures delivered by the neo-Pythagorean philosopher Girolamo Cardano during Cardano's brief stay in Naples, for Della Porta's work reflects traces of Cardano's teaching of a sort of natural magic in which both doctrine and casuistry played a part.

Although it is not known exactly when Della Porta became interested in theater, he was no doubt stimulated by the frequent dramatic performances given in Naples, not only by numerous professional troupes but also by patrician dilettantes, who often performed the works of contemporary Neapolitan playwrights and poets such as Bernardino Rota, Angelo di Costanzo, and Gianni Domenico di Lega. Yet Della Porta's initial endeavors, which won for him an early reputation as a scientist and a cryptographer, were mostly in the area of scientific research. His *Natural Magick*, first published when he was twenty-three years old, though he claimed to have written it when he was fifteen, and *De furtivis literarum notis: Vulgo de ziferis* (of secret writing), published in 1563, brought him immediate fame. After extensive traveling in Italy, France, and Spain—where he was received by Philip II—Della Porta returned to Naples to publish yet another scientific work, his *Arte del ricordare* (1566; mnemonic art), which added to his growing reputation. This work was also relevant to the theatrical arts, as Della Porta stressed the importance of cultivating memory through the application of the proper methods, most particularly in the case of actors.

Despite the fact that by 1566 Della Porta had published only these three scientific works, he had already written several dramatic works, and only a few years later one of his contemporaries, Giovanni Matteo Toscano, included him among the most representative living men of letters. Indeed, Della Porta stated that he wrote his first comedy, *L'Olimpia* (Olympia), "at an early age," probably in 1550.

Della Porta wrote in a time, however, in which free philosophical and scientific speculation in Italy was crippled by the Counter-Reformation, and as a "naturalist," Della Porta could not easily have escaped investigation. Further, the character of soothsayer and sorcerer had begun to be ascribed to him via popular lore. Although no record has survived, Della Porta must have been denounced to the Inquisition sometime before 1578, for there remains an entry from 1580 that refers to his reexamination before the Inquisition's tribunal. The actual trial, which conditionally cleared him, probably had taken place the year before. The judge, perhaps mockingly, perhaps paternally, advised him against writing on illicit subjects and suggested that he limit himself to comedy. Frightened, Della Porta complied, shortly after going to the length of joining a Jesuit lay congregation and taking active part in works of piety and charity.

In November, 1579, Della Porta's lot improved when Cardinal Luigi D'Este, a famous patron of the arts and learning, issued an invitation to join his household in Rome. Seeing an opportunity to restore his reputation, Della Porta readily accepted the invitation and commenced many literary and scientific projects, inclusive of some theatrical works, which he sent to his patron. Invited by Cardinal D'Este to join him in Venice, Della Porta arrived there in December, 1580, and began immediately to experiment with parabolic mirrors and an "occhiale" (eyeglass), which later led him to contest Galileo's priority in the invention of the telescope. Even after Jean Bodin in his *De la Démonomanie des sorciers* (1580; of the demoniac mania of sorcerers) accused Della Porta of being a sorcerer and of having shown witches how to use secret unguents, Della Porta did not lose the cardinal's protection. In fact, in the early part of 1581, Della Porta left Venice at the cardinal's urging, joining his patron in Ferrara, where he most likely met Torquato Tasso and Giambattista Guarini, among

other celebrated poets of the time. That same year, he wrote a treatise on palmistry, *Della chirofisonomia* (of chirophysiognomy), which did not see publication until 1677, almost a century later. The year following his move to Ferrara, Della Porta's scientific experiments met with some success when he perfected a method for the extraction of beechnut oil; his patron was further delighted with the news that he was on the brink of the discovery of the greatest secret of alchemy: the philosopher's stone, with which base metals could be transmuted into gold.

Della Porta began publishing again in 1583 and 1584, releasing to the presses a two-volume work on agriculture: *Villae* (1583; the orchard of his country house, and 1584; the olive grove of his country house). By the end of 1583, he had also completed the manuscript of one of his best-known works, *Of Human Physiognomy*, which was to appear in 1586 notwithstanding the fact that the Roman Index of 1559 had specifically banned all treatises on physiognomy. In 1583, Della Porta had also completed *Phytognonomica* (the physiognomy of plants), which was published that year, as well as the manuscript of the second, greatly expanded edition, in twenty parts, of *Natural Magick* (which reappeared in the form of a sort of encyclopedia in 1589) and in which Della Porta proudly announced that the human mind could never surpass the inventions therein to be found, ranging from the rediscovery of the camera obscura to chapters on such disparate topics as cosmetics and love potions.

In 1588, Della Porta's first comedy, *L'Olimpia*, was staged (probably in Rome), though it did not appear in print until 1589, in Naples. This work was followed by others; in 1591, the tragicomedy *Penelope* (Penelope) appeared, the introduction of which contained the announcement of imminent publication of several other comedies. Of these, however, only *La fantesca* (the maidservant) and *La Cintia* were published, in Venice, in 1592. Della Porta's dramatic productivity was probably the result of religious censorship. Several years earlier, the Inquisition, suspicious of Della Porta's probing into the secrets of nature in conjunction with such questionable acquaintances as Tommaso Campanella and Paolo Sarpi—the latter of whom was to write *Istoria del concilio Tridentino* (1619; *The Historie of the Council of Trent*, 1620)—forbade Della Porta to publish *Of Human Physiognomy*. The death of Cardinal D'Este in 1587 had deprived Della Porta of the cardinal's powerful protection, and in 1592—the same year in which Giordano Bruno had been arrested by the Inquisition—the Venetian Inquisitors advised Della Porta that publication of anything without securing permission previously from the Roman High Tribunal would have serious repercussions. Nevertheless, less than one year later, while in Padua, he renewed his acquaintance with Campanella and Sarpi and there, for the first time, met the young Galileo. Since Della Porta published that same year a work on optics, *De refractione, optices parte* (1593; of refraction), discussion of this subject must have certainly followed the meeting with Galileo.

Very little is known of Della Porta's whereabouts in the last years of the century. It is probable that the severe penalties that the Inquisition meted out to Bruno, Campanella, and other freethinkers induced Della Porta to keep as low a profile as possible. Scarcely any new work appeared: merely the comedy *La trappolaria*, published in 1596, to be followed five years later by the publication of *The Two Rival Brothers*. Also in 1601, after almost a decade of silence, Della Porta again published scientific works: *Caelestis physiognomoniae* (celestial physiognomy), in which he attempted a reconciliation between free will, the divinatory arts, and astrology, and several works on hydrology and mathematics. In 1604, two years after the publication of a Latin translation of his work on mnemonics, Della Porta wrote another treatise on chemistry and alchemy, *De distillatione* (of distillation), which was published four years later in 1609, bearing a dedication to Prince Federigo Cesi, founder of the prestigious and still active Accademia dei Lincei. Della Porta became a member of the Accademia dei Lincei in 1610, the same year in which he dedicated another work (now lost) on natural secrets, the "Taumatologia," to the Holy Roman Emperor Rudolph II in a fruitless effort to obtain the Inquisition's permission to publish. Less controversial works, in particular his comedies, fared better.

Between 1604 and 1609, Della Porta published *The Sister*, *The Astrologer*, *La turca*, *La carbonaria* (the coal ruse), *Il moro* (the Moor), and *La chiappinaria* (the bear trick).

Shortly after Della Porta's admission to the Accademia dei Lincei, a small dispute arose over who had, in actuality, first invented the telescope. The aged Della Porta, perhaps with some merit but with very little proof, claimed to have been the original inventor, preceding Galileo and others. To strengthen his claim, Della Porta wrote a treatise, *De telescopio* (of the telescope), which remained unpublished until 1940. In 1611, he published a sacred tragedy in verse, *Il Georgio*, and a year later published *La tabernaria* (the tavern play). In 1614, Della Porta published his last play to appear during his lifetime, the tragedy *L'Ulisse* (Ulysses).

Named by Prince Cesi to direct the Neapolitan branch of the Accademia dei Lincei, in the last years of his life, Della Porta busied himself with this and with the academy of the "Oziosi" whose leader was the famous Baroque poet Giambattista Marino. Having attempted the construction of a telescope that, as he wrote Galileo, would have been able to penetrate the highest heavens, and pursuing to the last his search for the philosopher's stone, the old and ailing writer died in Naples on February 4, 1615.

ANALYSIS

Clearly influenced by Plautus, whose works Giambattista Della Porta translated and adapted, the playwright and author of the no longer extant "De arte componendi comoedias" (the art of writing comedies) deftly melded to classical motifs the many elements of regional storytelling tradition. Though his declared intention was to restore the traditional classical theater, the language and spirit of Della Porta's characters, as well as numerous references to daily life, unmistakably point to the writer's personal experience within the historical framework of sixteenth century Italy.

The second half of the sixteenth century was a turning point in the development of Italian drama. This had been marked by the emergence of the *commedia dell'arte*, which, in turn, signaled the crisis of the "erudite" drama. Because they were timely, Della Porta's comedies were often adapted as *canovacci* by the professional actors of the *commedia dell'arte*, though it seems unlikely that Della Porta himself wrote *scenari* for them. Della Porta's comedies do not encompass revolutionary innovations in content or technique; they are rather a consummate reelaboration of the Renaissance comic theater. His range extended by classical and Boccaccean themes, distinctly anticipating the controlled hyperbole of pre-Baroque theater, Della Porta was one of the first Italian playwrights to blend romantic and pathetic elements into the comic situation, in a manner that would soon become established in the new genre of tragicomedy.

Della Porta's comic effects are heightened by a colorful and vigorous language. The speech of his characters is devoid of complex nuances and overly sophisticated literary allusions. Indeed, Della Porta employs a language that can produce the maximum reaction from an average, not particularly learned audience: a kind of bourgeois speech to be enjoyed by anyone possessing an average education, occasionally punctuated by expressions peculiar to a character that serve to define or reinforce that character. Even when, as frequently occurs, Della Porta borrows directly from the classical tradition, he does so in such a way as to isolate the lines and situations from their original context, emphasizing them in a contemporary manner rather than through the traditional interpretative modes.

There is scant information available regarding precisely when and where Della Porta produced his theatrical works, the number of which makes him the most prolific dramatic writer of the time after Giovanni Maria Cecchi. He began writing his comedies at an early age, and his first comedy, *L'Olimpia*, is introduced by a virginal and shy young girl—possibly an allusion to the fact that this was Della Porta's first dramatic work—who declares that she would have not appeared in public if the Prologue had not forced her to do so. Of the more than thirty dramatic works probably written by Della Porta, only fourteen comedies and three tragedies have survived. Of the comedies, the majority of them share an obvious Plautine

derivation as well as a resemblance to their more contemporary models—such as the works of Ludovico Ariosto, Bibbiena, or Niccolò Machiavelli. The emphasis, however, is on the plot rather than on characters: on the *ingenium* and *maraviglia* of fantastic complex twists and intrigues, *burle* and countertricks. Character development is not totally neglected, but though Della Porta's characters do not wear the masks of the *commedia dell'arte*, they belong nevertheless to the large reservoir of traditional stock types. Wicked pedants, deceitful gluttonous servants, old and young lovers, boastful Spanish captains and other braggarts, witty wives outsmarting their unfaithful husbands—all are clearly recognizable, utterly stylized characters who permitted Della Porta to concentrate freely on the structural quality of his works, on the expressive language and situations clearly aimed at achieving the maximum, at times farcical, comic effect.

La fantesca

La fantesca, one of the most successful and representative of Della Porta's comedies, encompasses both the Plautine and the novelesque tradition in its skillful manipulation of the many elements present in sixteenth century comic theater. Della Porta's lively use of Neapolitan dialect and boastful Spanish, double entendres and boutades, as well as proverbs and popular sayings, is unrivaled. The plot is typically complicated by implausible disguises and coincidences, elaborate subterfuges, and amorous rivalries between fathers and sons, all of which are enriched by the spicy dialogue. Young Essandro has fallen in love with Cleria, daughter of the rich Neapolitan physician Gerasto. Disguised as a maidservant named Fioretta, Essandro enters Gerasto's household and persuades Cleria to reciprocate the love of "her" twin brother, whom he will naturally impersonate. Gerasto, however, falls in love with Fioretta (Essandro), arousing the jealousy of his wife, Santina, and of the housekeeper Nepita. Matters are further complicated with the arrival from Rome of the pedant Narticoforo and his son Cintio, to whom Cleria had been previously betrothed. Essandro's alert and faithful servant, Panurgo, intervenes to help his master stave off the danger. Because Narticoforo and Gerasto have not yet met, Panurgo and the parasite Morfeo success-fully impersonate both Gerasto and Cleria to Narti-coforo, and Narticoforo and Cintio to Gerasto, sow-ing at each instance discord. Panurgo and Morfeo, who behave as idiotically as possible, ultimately man-age to inflame Narticoforo to such a degree that the Roman pedant hires a Spanish braggart, Capitan Dante, to teach Gerasto a lesson. Gerasto, in turn, hires another Spaniard, Pantaleone, "matador de panteras y leones" (killer of panthers and lions), to defend him-self against Narticoforo. The two Spanish captains, however, rather than fighting, become friends in cowardice and together run away in the face of the abuse showered on them by the exasperated prospec-tive fathers-in-law. After a failed attempt by Gerasto to meet with Fioretta (at the rendezvous he finds in-stead his angry wife, Santina), Essandro and Panurgo's deceit is revealed. Things are about to become worse when Essandro's uncle Apollione arrives, recogniz-ing in Panurgo his long-lost brother, the father of Essandro. All ends well with Essandro's betrothal to Cleria and that of Cleria's sister to Cintio, while Gerasto promises from this point on to lead a more honest life.

OTHER PLAYS

Although equally indebted to the heterogenous sources regularly used by Della Porta, *The Astrologer* and *La turca* differ from *La fantesca* and Della Porta's other comedies. A bitterly realistic and criti-cal view of the world and, in particular, of Naples here is made manifest. In *The Astrologer*, the title character, Albumazar, speaks of Naples as a city of thieves and rogues. These comedies are also unique in that Della Porta adds to the recurrent Renais-sance theme of romantic rivalry between fathers and sons a biting criticism of the sensual and often bru-tal behavior of the older men. In *The Astrologer* and in *La turca*, as in most of Della Porta's comic the-ater, despite the exuberant and at times farcical use of the *lazzi* of the *commedia dell'arte*, a sentimental

vein is accompanied by a judgmental, almost moral-istic tone. Plays such as *Il moro*, *La furiosa*, and *The Two Rival Brothers*—which are often favorably com-pared to Lope de Vega Carpio's comedies—all be-long to a new tragicomic phase by means of which Della Porta succeeded in modernizing the genre, maintaining the lively tone of popular comedy while adapting to the stricter atmosphere of the Counter-Reformation.

OTHER MAJOR WORKS

NONFICTION: *Magiae naturalis*, 1558 (4 vol-umes), 1589 (20 volumes; *Natural Magick*, 1658); *De furtivis literarum notis: Vulgo de ziferis*, 1563; *Arte del ricordare*, 1566; *Phytognonomica*, 1583; *Villae*, 1583-1592; *De humana physiognomia*, 1586 (*Of Human Physiognomy*, 1829); *De refractione, optices parte*, 1593; *Pneumaticorum*, 1601; *Caelestis physiognomoniae*, 1601; *De distillatione*, 1609; *Della chirofisonomia*, 1677; *De telescopio*, 1940.

BIBLIOGRAPHY

Clubb, Louise George. *Giambattista Della Porta, Dramatist*. Princeton, N. J.: Princeton University Press, 1965. Clubb examines the life and works of Della Porta, paying particular attention to his plays.

Eamon, William. *Science and the Secrets of Nature: Books of Secrets in Medieval and Early Modern Culture*. Princeton, N.J.: Princeton University Press, 1994. Eamon's examination of the scien-tific side of Della Porta, among others, sheds light on his literary work.

Herrick, Marvin Theodore. *Italian Comedy in the Re-naissance*. 1960. Reprint. Freeport, N.Y.: Books for Libraries, 1970. This work on Italian comedies produced during the Renaissance describes how Della Porta's dramatic works fit into the larger picture.

Roberto Severino

MERRILL DENISON

Born: Detroit, Michigan; June 23, 1893
Died: Bon Echo, Ontario, Canada; June 13, 1975

PRINCIPAL DRAMA

Brothers in Arms, pr. 1921, pb. 1923 (one act)
From Their Own Place, pr. 1922, pb. 1923 (one act)
Balm, pr. 1923, pb. 1926
Marsh Hay, pb. 1923, pr. 1974
The Weather Breeder, pb. 1923, pr. 1924 (one act)
The Unheroic North, pb. 1923 (includes *Brothers in Arms*, *From Their Own Place*, *Marsh Hay*, *The Weather Breeder*)
The Prizewinner, pr., pb. 1928
Contract, pr. 1929
Haven of the Spirit, pb. 1929 (one act)
The U.S. vs. Susan B. Anthony, pb. 1941 (one act)

OTHER LITERARY FORMS

Merrill Denison not only contributed to the emergence of indigenous Canadian drama for the stage but also was involved in the establishment of radio as a medium for drama. On the invitation of the radio department of the Canadian National Railways, Denison wrote a series of radio dramas based on incidents from Canadian history, which were broadcast as the *Romance of Canada* series in the winter of 1930-1931. He produced a similar series for American radio, entitled *Great Moments in History*, broadcast during 1932 and 1933. He continued to write original radio dramas and adaptations until 1944. Denison's historical writing also took the form of company biographies, histories of large corporations that were more than mere self-serving eulogies or lists of directors. The first of these was *Harvest Triumphant* (1948), about Massey-Harris Company, the farm equipment manufacturer. He also wrote about Canada's largest brewery in *The Barley and the Stream: The Molson Story* (1955) and about the Royal Bank, in *Canada's First Bank: A History of the Bank of Montreal* (1966-1967). Denison's major prose works are *Boobs in the Woods* (1927), a series of comic anecdotes about

tourists and residents of the backwoods of Ontario, and *Klondike Mike* (1943), a biography of the Yukon Gold Rush prospector Michael Ambrose Mahoney. Both books have been praised as essentially accurate accounts freed from the restrictions of factual documentation. Denison also regularly contributed both fiction and nonfiction to newspapers and magazines. His collected papers are housed at Queen's University in Kingston, Ontario.

ACHIEVEMENTS

Merrill Denison was the first and most successful of a group of writers in the 1920's who sought a truly indigenous Canadian dramatic literature. He has been called Canada's first nationalist dramatist and the founder of modern Canadian drama. This reputation is based on four short comedies and one full-length drama. When these plays were first presented to the public, critics agreed that Denison showed great promise. Edith Isaacs, editor of *Theatre Arts Monthly*, in reviewing the publication of *The Unheroic North*, a collection of Denison's plays, called him a Canadian Eugene O'Neill. Ironically, this praise appeared at the same time Denison was turning his back on the theater and beginning his exploration of radio as a forum for his writing. It was not until 1971, on the fiftieth anniversary of the production of *Brothers in Arms*, that the Canadian literary community attested unequivocally Denison's contribution to the evolutionary growth of Canadian literature. Also, it was not until 1974, one year before his death, that his best play, *Marsh Hay*, received a public performance. Given the small quantity of his contributions to theater and the admittedly flawed nature of his dramatic writing, how can it be that Denison holds such a significant position in the history of Canadian drama?

The answer to that question lies only partly in the barren nature of Canadian dramatic literature before the 1960's. W. S. Milne, in reviewing *The Unheroic North* for *Canadian Forum* in 1932, commented with bitter sarcasm, "Some half dozen plays, mostly of one act; four of them dealing with the same restricted milieu; not a bit of imagination in one of them, unless by accident. A small thing almost perfectly done. That is the dramatic achievement of Merrill Denison, and he is Canada's greatest dramatist." At that time, Denison was one of the very few playwrights exploring issues of interest to Canadians and presenting a realistic picture of life in Canada. As a leading member of the first wave, his position in history books is assured; however, the achievement of his dramatic writing is not limited to its historical significance.

A close examination of the plays allows for a rebuttal to Milne's condemnation of "not a bit of imagination in one of them" and supports the praise given by those dramatists who followed Denison's leadership and innovation. In his attitude toward contemporary social issues, Denison provided a model for the social realism that became the mainstay of several of Canada's leading playwrights and theater companies. The same is true of Denison's commitment to historical subjects. His influence was apparent in the lively theater scene in Toronto in the 1960's, which was dominated by plays that bore a remarkable resemblance, in form, content, and impact, to Denison's work. In particular, the docudramas of this period, based on incidents from history or observation of real-life situations and people, followed Denison's commitment to dramatizing only those situations that he himself had observed.

In retrospect, Denison is worthy of the title Father of Canadian Drama not only because he was the first but also because his plays demonstrate all the potential of a great dramatist as well as all of the flaws of a young writer. The tragedy is that Denison, for whatever reasons, turned his back on playwriting before the promise of his first works could be fulfilled. He needed an ongoing relationship with professional actors and directors and a sympathetic public to grow as a writer, and in Canada at that time, he was cut off from these. One can only speculate that he might indeed have become the Canadian O'Neill—if only he had had a Canadian Provincetown Players.

BIOGRAPHY

Merrill Denison was born in Detroit, Michigan, on June 23, 1893. That he was born an American rather than a Canadian resulted from the fact that his mother wanted her child not to be a subject of the British Crown. Shortly before the birth, she had traveled from her home in Toronto to Detroit in order to accomplish this. A well-known feminist, Flora MacDonald Denison was a descendant of Nathaniel Merrill, who had left Connecticut in 1774 to settle in Kingston as part of the second exodus of United Empire Loyalists. Flora continued the family tradition of outspoken individualism. In 1905, after five years as a manager of the women's wear department of a large department store, Flora refused to punch in on the newly installed time clock, on the grounds that the newfangled system fostered class distinctions.

Merrill Denison was an only child, and the influence of his mother on his private and public life was strong. He supported her stand on women's issues, and he was president of the University Men's League for Women's Suffrage in Canada. By contrast, Denison's father, Howard, had little influence. A commercial traveler, he was at home only irregularly, although his son remembers him as a friend. Flora was responsible for Merrill's literary bent as well as his social awareness. She contributed a regular column on women's suffrage to the *Sunday World* of Toronto and took every opportunity to speak and write about religious, social, and political controversies. Another enduring love that passed from mother to son was of the Bon Echo resort on Lake Mazinaw in northern Ontario. This backwoods area not only became Denison's holiday and retirement home but also provided the setting and characters for his most significant dramatic writing. Flora first took the eight-year-old Denison to Bon Echo in 1901; in 1910, she bought the twelve-hundred-acre resort; Denison managed a summer hotel there from 1921 to 1929; and in 1959 he turned the property over to the Ontario government for use as a provincial park.

As a young man, Denison studied at the University of Toronto for one semester and then departed "by mutual consent." After a series of odd jobs, including work as a journalist, drama critic, advertising agent, and timekeeper in a steelworks plant, he returned to the University of Toronto to study architecture. In 1916, he departed to serve two years with the American Ambulance Field Service in France. In 1919 and 1920, he worked as an architectural draftsman in Boston and New York, but architecture was not to be his career. In fact, he wrote a critique of his architectural education, which appeared in 1922 in *The American Architect*. The magazine's publishers reportedly offered him the editorship, which he refused. After he returned to the family home in Toronto, he was approached by Roy Mitchell, the dynamic and forward-looking director of Hart House Theatre at the University of Toronto, to become the theater's art director. His first stage designs were for a production of Euripides' *Alkēstis* (438 B.C.E.; *Alcestis*, 1781) in February of 1921. He also tried his hand at acting and became a playwright by the end of the season.

Denison tells an amusing story of how this came about. Mitchell had planned an evening of three Canadian plays for April, but only two, both tragedies, had been found. Five weeks before the opening, Denison and Mitchell were joking about where to find a true Canadian. Denison claimed that the only untainted Canadians he had known were the backwoodsmen near Bon Echo, the subject of so many of the amusing stories with which he had regaled his friends. The result: He was locked in the director's room and told to turn out a play based on his famous story of the Upper Canada College principal trying to acquire the use of a boat from a backwoodsman. As Denison reports, "Well, with no inhibitions and a deadline, I was able to accomplish the feat in about four and a quarter hours."

Brothers in Arms, as this play was called, enjoyed remarkable popularity, appearing in ten editions from 1923 to 1975, and was performed an estimated fifteen hundred times from 1921 to 1971. The initial response, however, was not undivided. Hart House was governed by a theater committee that had to give approval to all scripts. This group, shocked by the ungrammatical language of backwoodsmen and by the satire of patriotism that fuels the comedy, rejected Denison's script. After Mitchell threatened to resign, however, the play was added to the program, and theater history was made.

Denison continued with Mitchell at Hart House Theatre and saw productions of *The Weather Breeder* on April 21, 1924, and *The Prizewinner* on February 27, 1928. The one-act format was necessitated by Mitchell's commitment to an evening of short plays by three different writers, but in 1929, Denison was given a chance to provide an entire evening's entertainment. He wrote *Contract*, described by the Toronto *Star* as "good-natured satire . . . charged with local allusions . . . convincing and clever." Other reviews were equally positive, but this was to be Denison's last major stage production. The first twentieth century English-Canadian playwright to attempt to make a living from his writing in Canada was forced to abandon the stage in order to earn enough money to survive.

In 1929, Denison was approached by Austin Weir, who was then in charge of radio programs for the Canadian National Railways, with the idea of presenting episodes from Canadian history over the air. At first, Denison was dubious about the potential of such a venture, having an ambivalent regard for the medium and questioning, as he later admitted, anyone's ability to discover in Canadian history the material out of which half a dozen, let alone twenty-five, romantic dramas could be written. He soon warmed to the task, however, and became fascinated with the potential of radio for dramatic presentation. The result was the radio series known as *Romance of Canada* directed by Tyrone Guthrie and broadcast in the winter of 1930-1931 over a transcontinental chain by Canadian National Railways' Radio Department. Six of the scripts were published in 1931 under the title *Henry Hudson and Other Plays*. So successful was this series with both audiences and critics that Denison was commissioned by the J. Walter Thompson Company to write a similar series dealing with U.S. history. Denison produced a forty-week series of half-hour programs, broadcast during 1932 and 1933, entitled *Great Moments in History*, and he continued to earn his living writing for American radio networks through World War II. He was best known for his ability to dramatize historical events in a manner both educational and entertaining. During the war, he wrote for U.S., British, and Canadian radio, including the British Broadcasting Corporation's *Home Hour*, for which he produced dramatized commentaries explaining the U.S. war effort to United Kingdom listeners.

Denison's storytelling skills led him to several prose treatments in both short and full-length form. *Klondike Mike*, a biography of Michael Ambrose Mahoney, a survivor of the Klondike Gold Rush, was a best-seller within weeks of its publication and was a Book-of-the-Month Club selection. It was reprinted in 1965 and received the accolades of another generation of Canadians. Nevertheless, playwriting and storytelling were insufficient sources of income, and Denison's attempt at resort management was also not a financial success. His alternative career was in journalism. As a regular contributor to leading daily newspapers and monthly magazines, Denison spoke out on cultural and social issues that concerned him deeply. These included the state of drama in Canada, the potential of radio as a social and cultural force, the hardships endured by those trying to survive in the less developed regions of Canada, and the need for a strong conservationist policy to protect the natural beauty of the unspoiled north.

In 1922 and 1923, Denison was a contributing editor of *The Bookman*, from which position he analyzed the causes of the slow emergence of indigenous Canadian literature. His theory, that Canadians suffer from an inferiority complex—or "an intellectual timidity born of a false feeling of inadequacy or inability"—has profoundly influenced subsequent theories and later practitioners. Being an American by birth and citizenship and a Canadian by choice of residence, Denison was also able to comment insightfully on relations between these neighbors. Though he opposed nationalism as a divisive international force, Dension remained throughout his life an ardent advocate of Canadian nationalism because of his sense of the feelings of inferiority suffered by Canadians, despite prodigious accomplishments in many areas. "You will have to find out about yourselves and know and appreciate yourselves before you can expect other people to know and understand you," he advised in 1949. In 1967, the year of the Canadian Centennial, his message had altered as little as the problem he ad-

dressed: the ignorance of Canadians about their own past achievements.

An interest in history, biography, and journalism made Denison a logical choice for the Massey-Harris Company when it celebrated its one hundredth birthday in 1947 with a booklet outlining its history. Denison admitted that "farm implements had never been numbered among my irrepressible enthusiasms," but he soon became fascinated with the technological advancements pioneered by the firm, as well as the position of the company in the social, economic, and international history of Canada. He received permission to prepare a full-length biography, which was published in 1948 as *Harvest Triumphant*. Company biographies usually are of little interest save to those members of past and present management who receive the praise that seems to be the sole motive for their production, but in this case, Denison's book not only was an overwhelming commercial success but also set a creative precedent for the company biographies that followed.

Denison was much in demand following the success of *Harvest Triumphant* to record the achievements of other companies. The most respected of these biographies were *The Barley and the Stream*, a history of the powerful Molson brewery empire; *The People's Power: The History of Ontario Hydro* (1960); and *Canada's First Bank*. In each of these company biographies, which involved several years of historical research and for which Denison demanded freedom from interference by company management, Denison remained true to his commitment to the importance of the country's history for an understanding of what it meant to be a Canadian. He did not limit his definition of history to political events. History, he said,

is to be found in the nature of the land itself, dominated by the Laurentian Shield. It is to be found in the struggles of a tiny population to subdue that and other regions, in the long wait for the tools with which to master the Prairies and the Far North, the Shield and its inaccessible forests and once-useless water power. It is linked to canals, railroads, hydro-electric power, diamond drills, airplanes and caterpillar tractors, far more than it is to fluctuating fortunes of political parties or the decisions of the Privy Council. The story is to be found in the mineshafts and the lumber camps and the holds of the Great Lakes Freighters; in the tellers' cages of banks from Canso to the Yukon; in the custom brokers' records of a hundred ports around the world.

Master storyteller Denison dedicated his life to transmitting, in a variety of forms, incidents from real life, contemporary and historical, that would hold a mirror up to the Canadian people, in which they might more clearly see themselves. He tried to battle the inferiority complex that he saw around him in order to give the citizens of his adopted country the same love for the land and its people that he so fervently felt.

ANALYSIS

Merrill Denison was one of the group of Canadian writers who, in the 1920's, first attempted to dramatize the uniquely Canadian aspects of their national experience. If this were his only achievement, he would be a provincial writer of interest only to his immediate contemporaries and to theater historians. It is his unique attitude to the Canadian experience that marks his contribution to dramatic literature and gives it enduring value.

Three aspects of Denison's dramatic writings distinguish his work. His plays are first and foremost realistic, based entirely on personal experience and observation and written with careful attention to believable dialogue, setting, action, and characterization. Second, he is both antiheroic and antiromantic, dedicated to debunking the false image of Canada as the home of Mounties and noble, simple hunters—natural heroes of the virgin wilderness. Finally, he brings to his writing a sense of comedy tempered with commitment to justice—a commitment that leads him to explore social problems objectively and in defiance of contemporary morality. The result is a group of plays that have not become dated with the passage of time.

FROM THEIR OWN PLACE

In his short comedies, Denison uses character types, two-dimensional creations that function within a limited plot line. The plays turn on a single narra-

tive device, usually a reversal. In *From Their Own Place*, city dweller Larry Stedman turns the tables on the backwoodsmen who have attempted to sell him the furs from illegally trapped animals for an inflated price (while arguing over who is the rightful owner of the furs) by calling in the game warden to witness all three men deny ownership. The tricksters are tricked into parting with the furs, and the naïve city dweller pays only for the cost of the trapping license.

Even within the limitations of the one-act structure, Denison creates evocative and well-crafted explorations of life in the northern areas of Ontario. His attention to language demonstrates the fine ear of a raconteur adept at mimicry. The ungrammatical utterances of the locals might offend university committees, but this language provides authenticity and a rich comic texture. Denison does not use foul language, but he still manages to capture the flavor of backwoods speech. When Alec, one of the tricksters, swears that half of the furs are his, he vows, "If they aint will the Lord strike me down right here where I'm stanin and send me to burnin hell for ten thousand years wiv a cup of cold water just beyond my lips and me not able to reach it."

Denison does not incorporate these vivid colloquialisms for mere comic effect; language is always tied to the characters and to their social environment. Sandy, caretaker for the Stedmans, and Cline, who habitually sells them worthless objects, debate the relative morality of their positions: Sandy attacks first, saying, "You've sold him enough trash now to satisfy anybody but a MacUnch." Cline indignantly defends his family name with "That's a fine thing for you to say, and you married to a MacUnch yourself and had three children by her. And the hull of you half starved till you got a job from the old lad. It aint everyone can get a job caretakin and not have nothin to do." Sandy retorts, "No, there aint but one can get it and that's me and it wouldn't matter if Emmy had twelve children and all of them twins, I wouldn't be like yous MacUnches trying to sponge off'n the only friend the backwoods has." Buried in this amusing exchange is the presentation of a serious socioeconomic situation. The duplicity of Sandy and Cline evolves into a hilarious farce of entrance and exit, lie and counterlie, as they conspire to cheat Stedman and then betray each other, but their convoluted relationship also points to a condition of inbreeding that Denison had observed and on which he had commented in his letters and articles, and their actions are motivated by a poverty that is tragic. "It's a hopeless country to try and make a living in. Even if it is the most beautiful spot in the world," comments Harriet Stedman, in an effort to excuse the stealing and lying of Sandy, Cline, and Alec.

BROTHERS IN ARMS

Brothers in Arms, like *From Their Own Place*, features two-dimensional characters, simple plot devices, comic exchanges, and serious social commentary. J. Altrus Browne, a businessman, and his wife, Dorothea, have ventured to a hunting camp in the backwoods. Dorothea exhibits all of the romanticism of an outsiders' view of Canada; she wants to meet a *coureur de bois* (a French or half-breed trapper), one of the romantic figures of whom she had read in books or seen in movies about Canada. Her husband is presented even less sympathetically, as an impatient, insensitive, and pompous fool. Having received word of a business deal worth twenty-five thousand dollars, he is determined to catch the next train to Toronto but must wait for Charlie to drive them out in the only car. Dorothea views her environment through a glaze of romanticism: "I think your camp is adorable. It's so simple, and direct. So natural." Browne judges by a different standard: "I should never have come up into this God-forsaken hole at all." Syd, an authentic *coureur de bois*, unrecognized by Dorothea, and a fellow veteran (a brother-in-arms), unrecognized by Browne, sees his surroundings with the clear vision of a man who is resigned to the reality of survival in a "wild, virgin country," where there are a few deer left, although most have been scared off by the neighbor's hounds. Although Syd lives far from civilization, that "keeps folks outa here in the summer. City folks is a kinda bother. . . . They's always tryin to get a feller to work. One way and another they figger they's doin a feller a favour to let him work for em." Dorothea tries to fit Syd into her preconceived notions, suggesting to him that he wants to be left alone to lead his own simple life, but Syd de-

fies romanticism. His relaxed manner and unconventional attitudes might entice audience sympathy, but Denison undercuts this by also presenting his laziness and destructive shortsightedness. The hunters tear up the floorboards rather than split firewood, so the abandoned farmhouse they use for their camp is slowly being destroyed.

Denison has some pointed comments to make about the army. Syd and Browne were both soldiers, but their experiences in the war were quite different. Syd's view of "their war" is "they wasn't no sense to it to my way of thinkin." Syd's version of sentry duty—"They wasn't a German this side of the ocean and they wasn't no sense hangin around in the cold. So I went in and went to bed"—horrifies Browne but arouses in Dorothea continued romanticism: "Don't you love his sturdy independence? It's so Canadian." Denison tempers this satire with a bitter image when Syd voices his most pointed criticism of officers and businessmen: "Perhaps you ain't used to listenin much in your business. We got a feller up here that got his eyes blew out in France can hear most a mile away." Finally, Denison, having created a vehicle for his satiric portrait of romanticism and the army, ends the piece with the comic reversal. Charlie arrives at last, only to inform the Brownes that Syd, with whom they have been talking all along, could just as well have driven them to the train, being half owner of the car. Browne explodes with the question, "Why didn't you say you could drive us?" to which Syd replies, "You never ast me."

THE WEATHER BREEDER

In *The Weather Breeder*, Denison explores a theme that plays a part in all of his dramatic writing: the relationship between character and natural environment. Old John, a backwoods farmer, is gloomy when the weather is glorious because he is certain that a storm is blowing. When the storm arrives, he is overjoyed because his sour predictions have come true; when the storm passes by and causes minimal damage to the vulnerable crops, he becomes gloomy again. Old John's attitude toward the weather becomes a metaphor for his pessimistic outlook: "It aint natural to have three weeks without a storm and the longer she waits the worse she'll be. We'll have to pay for it." As Jim, John's young helper, notes, John makes life miserable for everybody with his sour prophesying of inevitable doom. Even the most perfect of days becomes merely an excuse to prophesy that an entire summer's worth of bad weather is building up, waiting to descend on them all at once.

Denison based *The Weather Breeder*, like all of his plays, on attitudes that he had observed in the communities around Bon Echo. For the bare subsistence farming such an environment provides, weather can destroy the hopes of a lifetime. Old John expects a certain amount of hardship every year, and, when it holds off for a time, he expects his share of disaster to occur in one huge cataclysm. This bleak outlook, ingrained in Old John's personality, is largely played for comic effect, and the serious implications of his pessimism are further undermined by a rather mundane motivation for his sour spirits: Old John has been laid up with a serious injury; his foot was caught in a thresher.

MARSH HAY

Thus, in his short plays, Denison did not give full expression to his harsh vision of Canadian life. In his full-length drama *Marsh Hay*, however, he directly addressed the devastated state of the northern backwoods, where, as a result of unrestricted lumbering from 1850 to 1890 and ravaging forest fires, the land had been transformed. As Barnood, a struggling farmer in *Marsh Hay*, recalls, "I can remember when a man could drive a team through a stand of white pine for days . . . but the lumber companies and the fire gouged her clean. Turned it into so much bare rock and scrub popple." The farms of the area were abandoned by those with the resources and vision to escape. Those who remained were forced into a cruel, grasping search for survival. Outsiders such as Thompson, the city lawyer (a less satiric portrait than Browne), might call them lazy and shiftless, but Barnood defends his fellow survivors: "I don't know as you call a man that works fourteen or sixteen hours a day, lazy. They don't make much of a livin, Mr. Thompson. Pick up a few dollars from the city people that summers on the lakes back here . . . do a little trappin . . . kill a deer or two . . . raise a few potatoes between the rocks and cut marsh hay."

Marsh Hay tells the story of the Serang family. John, the father, like the John in *The Weather Breeder*, is a sour, bitter man, so broken by the desperation of his effort to scratch a living in this desolate region that he is incapable of any positive feeling. He summarizes his life thus: "Twenty years of a man's life gone into workin fifty acres of grey stone . . . cuttin marsh hay to keep a couple of sows and a half dead horse alive. Cuttin marsh hay because the land won't raise enough fodder to winter a rat. A dozen scrawny chickens . . . twelve children. Five dead, thank God. Twenty years of a man's life." There is an alternative, to travel west to the fertile land of the prairies, but for John Serang, this is the bitterest twist of fate he must endure: When he was young enough to go, he could not break free, and now he is too worn out to summon the energy and too poor to finance the trip. As he ironically notes, "If we'd lived in England they'd a paid our fare."

John sees no hope for change in his situation and expects no help from a change in government. As he says to his neighbor Barnood, "Andy, the only thing a change in government ever changes, Andy, is the government." A government cannot make the weather good or make the hay stand shoulder high in the marshes, nor is the government even likely to build railroads all through the back country, a more realistic hope at which John also sneers.

John's wife, Lena, shares this desolation, so reflective of the barren environment. Their marriage is one of continued accusation and bitterness. John calls her a damned sow, and she replies, "It's a wonder I aint killed you before this John. Callin me . . . look at me! Look at me! Worn out before my time . . . bearin your children. And you call me that. It's a wonder I aint killed you." Denison's stage direction notes, "Lena comes slowly to John, vehemence and heat forgotten and nothing but cold, bitter rage left her." John replies, indifferently, "I wish you had."

In this sort of home, it is not surprising to find that the children are dispirited, cruel, and desperate for any means of escape. John's bitterness has been passed on like a disease to his surviving offspring. Sarilin, fifteen years old, says, "Paw don't like us to do nothin. It don't make no difference to him but he won't let nobody have no fun. He never has done hisself and he don't know what it is." Her solution is to follow in the path of her sister Tessie, who runs off with a boy at the beginning of the play. The result is that Sarilin finds herself pregnant. Walt, who is the father of the child, tries to escape an forced marriage, which, as even old John admits, would be a cruel trap. This has been John's own experience, but Denison does not wholly doom the next generation to this horrible cycle. Pete, John's youngest, is determined to continue to attend school despite the eight-mile walk each way. "I want to get some learnin so's I can get out a this back country and go out front. I aint goin to spend my life workin this farm."

The most profound hope for the family comes from an unlikely source. Sarilin's pregnancy, which is viewed by the community as a shameful and tragic event and by the minister as a heinous sin, is for Lena an inspiration for dignity and renewed caring. This comes about through a chance meeting with a city woman (based on Denison's mother), who shares with Lena the unconventional philosophy that no child is illegitimate. As Lena reports it, "She said it was natural . . . she told me people is ruled by laws . . . just like a tree is . . . and she says no one was to blame." Lena resolves to follow unflinchingly the woman's recommendation never to let Sarilin feel ashamed, and to give the baby the best chance they can. The strength of her conviction has a profound effect on the family. The two boys, Jo and Pete, share in her caring for Sarilin, and even John finds himself half believing her. The house itself reflects the transformation. In his stage direction, Denison says, "Where before was a feeling of extreme squalor, poverty, tragic futility, there is a feeling of regeneration. The place lacked self-respect before . . . all echo the evident attempt to make the place decent to live in."

The regeneration, however, is short-lived. Tessie infects her younger sister with a cynical realism that arises naturally out of being reared in hatred. Children are only another mouth to feed, another link on the chain of entrapment. She suggests a self-induced abortion, and Sarilin complies. The final act of the play brings us full circle, to a scene of abject misery. The despair is palpable, made all the more bitter by John's

begrudging respect for Sarilin's decision: "I don't know but what she showed pretty good sense, too." The same recriminations are voiced by John and Lena, and even Lena's last residue of gentle feeling, "We must've been kinda fond of each other to stick together all these years, John?" is shattered by John's brutal and uncompromising reply, "Fond? Fond be damned. We stuck together because we couldn't get away from each other. That's why we stuck. We're chained here. That's what we are. Just like them stones outside the door, there. Fond? Bah!"

The dramatic writings of Denison exhibit many of the weaknesses of any young dramatist. He has been criticized for simplistic characterization, particularly of the women in his short plays, who have a tendency to utter the most inane superficialities. Even *Marsh Hay*, his most ambitious work, suffers from a lack of complexity in the delineation of the relationships and emotions of the central characters. In dramatic structure, his plays rely on twists of plot that are at times difficult to believe, and his language, though vigorous and amusing, is also repetitive, particularly in the longer drama, which is weighted with so many references to "fifty acres of grey stone" that it begins to read as though it were "fifty acres of grey prose."

These flaws, however, do not outweigh Denison's real achievement. It is his unflinching commitment to the recording of events, attitudes, and problems he observed in the area around his beloved Bon Echo that merits most praise. Unfortunately, his most exciting attribute as a dramatist may well have been a factor in Denison's unwillingness to write another play after *Marsh Hay*. The documentation of observed social phenomenon was fine when it was sugarcoated with comedy, but in a serious form it was unpalatable to audiences. Denison was passionately committed to the social message he wished to convey, but the public was not ready to hear it. It is to be regretted that this gifted playwright did not find the environment within which to fulfill his early promise.

OTHER MAJOR WORKS
SHORT FICTION: *Boobs in the Woods*, 1927.
RADIO PLAYS: *Henry Hudson and Other Plays*, 1931 (6 plays from the *Romance of Canada* series).

NONFICTION: *Klondike Mike*, 1943, 1965; *Harvest Triumphant*, 1948; *The Barley and the Stream: The Molson Story*, 1955; *The People's Power: The History of Ontario Hydro*, 1960; *Canada's First Bank: A History of the Bank of Montreal*, 1966-1967 (2 volumes).

BIBLIOGRAPHY

Fink, Howard. "Beyond Naturalism: Tyrone Guthrie's Radio Theatre and the Stage Production of Shakespeare." *Theatre History in Canada/Histoire du Théâtre au Canada* 2 (Spring, 1981): 19-32. Denison wrote scripts for Tyrone Guthrie when he came to Canada in 1931 to produce radio plays. Guthrie returned to Canada in 1952 to found the Stratford Shakespeare Festival. Fink traces the influence of Denison and radio on Guthrie's staging of Shakespeare's plays.

Guthrie, Tyrone. *A Life in the Theatre*. London: Hamilton, 1961. Guthrie's autobiographical reminiscences cover his time with Denison producing the radio series *Romance of Canada* in the early 1930's. Denison wrote all the scripts for that series, and Guthrie remembers that the playwright gradually grew exhausted and drained of new ideas.

Savigny, Mary. *Bon Echo: The Denison Years*. Toronto: Natural Heritage, 1997. A historical examination of Denison, his mother, and Bon Echo, the backwoods area that was at the heart of Denison's plays. Includes bibliography and index.

Wagner, Anton. Introduction to *Canada's Lost Plays*. Vol. 3 in *The Developing Mosaic: English-Canadian Drama to Mid-Century*, edited by Anton Wagner. Toronto: Canadian Theatre Review Publications, 1980. Wagner describes the Canadian theatrical scene in the early twentieth century and Denison's place in it. He says that Denison could have been the Eugene O'Neill of Canada except that he was not connected to a theater troupe, so many of his plays were not produced. This volume contains Denison's play *The Weather Breeder*.

*Leslie O'Dell,
updated by Pamela Canal*

DENIS DIDEROT

Born: Langres, France; October 5, 1713
Died: Paris, France; July 31, 1784

PRINCIPAL DRAMA

Le Fils naturel: Ou, Les Épreuves de la vertu, pr., pb. 1757 (*Dorval: Or, The Test of Virtue*, 1767)
Le Père de famille, pb. 1758, pr. 1761 (*The Father of the Family*, 1770; also as *The Family Picture*, 1871)
Est'il bon? Est'il méchant? pr. 1781, pb. 1834

OTHER LITERARY FORMS

In his own day, Denis Diderot was best known for his numerous unsigned contributions to the *Encyclopédie* (1751-1772; *Encyclopedia*, 1965), his reviews of the biennial art exhibitions in Paris (*Salons*, 1845, 1857), and his philosophical writings. Diderot also wrote extensively on the theater, and he produced a number of fictional works, beginning with the erotic Les Bijoux indiscrets (1748; *The Indiscreet Toys*, 1749). The best of his novels, however, appeared only posthumously: *La Religieuse* (1796; *The Nun*, 1797), *Jacques le fataliste et son maître* (1796; *Jacques the Fatalist and His Master*, 1797), and *Le Neveu de Rameau* (1821, 1891; *Rameau's Nephew*, 1897). His letters were edited by Georges Roth and Jean Varloot and have been published in sixteen volumes (*Correspondance*, 1955-1970).

ACHIEVEMENTS

To his contemporaries, Denis Diderot was known as "Monsieur le Philosophe." As coeditor and then sole editor of the *Encyclopédie*, he guided that masterpiece to its completion despite the desertion of col-

Denis Diderot (Library of Congress)

twenty-five in France alone by 1800. *The Father of the Family* was even more successful: thirty-two editions in French before 1800 as well as ten in German, three in English and Dutch, two in Russian, Danish, Polish, and Italian, and one in Spanish. As with his fiction, though, Diderot's most enduring work in this genre appeared posthumously. *Est'il bon? Est'il méchant?* has not been absent from the theater for long since the amateur theater Équipe began performing the piece in Paris in 1951. More significant for the eighteenth century stage were the essays that Diderot wrote about the theater, challenging the rule-bound attitudes of playwrights and actors and impelling the stage toward more natural presentations in both content and manner.

BIOGRAPHY

Denis Diderot was born in Langres, France, on October 5, 1713. His father, Didier Diderot, was a master cutler; his mother, Angélique Vigneron, was the daughter of a tanner. The family was therefore decidedly bourgeois. Although Diderot was to quarrel with his family's religious values, he remained true to his middle-class origins in the plays he wrote in the 1750's. Destined by his father for the priesthood, Diderot was enrolled in the local Jesuit college. In 1728, he went to Paris to continue his religious studies; four years later, he received a master of arts degree from the University of Paris. By then, he had lost all interest in a clerical career, so for two years he studied law under Clément de Ris. This occupation also failed to suit him, and for the next decade he earned a precarious living as tutor and hack writer.

Following his secret marriage in 1743 to Anne-Toinette Champion, the daughter of a lower-middle-class widow who owned a linen shop, Diderot sought a more stable income. Therefore, he began to translate into French a series of English works that would help shape his thinking and culminate in the monumental *Encyclopédie*. In 1745, Diderot published *Principes de la philosophie morale: Ou, Essai de M. S.*** sur le mérite et la vertu, avec réflexions.* The "M. S.***" of the subtitle was Anthony Ashley Cooper, third earl of Shaftesbury, whose *An Inquiry Concerning Virtue and Merit* (1699) formed the basis

laborators and censorship by the government. This work, along with his philosophical writings, set forth the fundamental ideas of the French Enlightenment and challenged the old regime's politics and thoughts. Although the fiction that appeared in his own lifetime—*The Indiscreet Toys*, "Les Deux Amis de Bourbonne" (1773; "The Two Friends from Bourbonne," 1964), *Entretien d'un père avec ses enfants: Ou, Le Danger de se mettre au-dessus des lois* (1773; *Conversations Between Father and Children,* 1964)—was not well received, his posthumously published works have established him as a leading prose writer of the eighteenth century, a worthy contemporary of Samuel Richardson and Laurence Sterne in England. Similarly, as a dramatist he was known in his own day as the author of two relatively unsuccessful plays. After two performances in 1757, *Dorval* did not appear onstage again for fourteen years. *The Father of the Family* fared better. The King of Naples requested it four nights in a row, and it was frequently revived throughout the eighteenth and early nineteenth centuries. Both were popular in book form, *Dorval* going through four editions in its first year and some of this modified translation. The work introduced Diderot to the optimistic, natural morality of Shaftesbury, a view that would color Diderot's writings for the rest of his life. Further translations followed, making Diderot a logical choice to work on a French version of Ephraim Chambers' *Cyclopaedia: Or, Universal Dictionary of the Arts and Sciences* (1728).

Although Diderot was not initially named editor, he eventually assumed this post, first with Jean Le Rond d'Alembert and then, in 1758, by himself. In addition, he contributed many articles to this work. Though such responsibilities might have been sufficient to occupy his time, he wrote prolifically during these years, producing numerous philosophical essays, an erotic novel, and two plays.

His early writings led Diderot into conflict with the government. *Pensées philosophiques* (1746; *Philosophical Thoughts*, 1916) was condemned by the Parlement of Paris in July, 1746, shortly after it was published. In 1747, the manuscript of *La Promenade du sceptique* (1830), an attack on Christianity, was seized before publication. For his speculations on the origins of the universe, he was imprisoned in the fortress of Vincennes outside Paris for three months in 1749. These experiences, coupled with the official suppression of the *Encyclopédie* a decade later, made Diderot cautious about exposing his manuscripts even to friends. Consequently, the works for which he is best known did not appear in his own lifetime, and his reputation in the eighteenth century did not rival that of contemporaries he has come to overshadow in the twentieth.

He did, however, have his admirers in his own time. Among them was Catherine the Great of Russia, who in 1765 engaged in a clever bit of patronage. She bought Diderot's library and made him curator for life, agreeing to take possession only after Diderot's death. This generosity guaranteed Diderot's financial security. To thank her, he traveled to Russia in 1773, where he frequently discussed political reforms with his patron. After returning to France in 1774, he continued to send advice to Catherine, who kept her fondness for Enlightenment ideas limited to the theoretical. Until his death on July 31, 1784, Diderot continued writing for posterity. His final treatise on moral philosophy, *Essai sur les règnes de Claude et de Néron* (1782), is a fitting capstone for his work, revealing his bitterness about the past but also his hopes for a future that he did so much to shape.

ANALYSIS

Although Denis Diderot was in his mid-forties before he wrote his first play, his interest in drama was long-standing. Later in life, he commented that, "I myself, when I was young, hesitated between the Sorbonne and the Comédie. In winter, in the worst sort of weather, I used to recite roles from Molière and [Pierre] Corneille out loud in the solitary walks of the Luxembourg [Gardens]." In his *Lettre sur les sourds et muets* (1751; *Letter on the Deaf and Dumb*, 1916), he again recalled his early fondness for and knowledge of drama: "Formerly I used to visit the theater very often, and I knew most of our good plays by heart." He would astonish those sitting around him by putting his fingers in his ears—a way of testing his memory—and surprise them even more by weeping at the tragic parts even though he apparently could not hear anything being said onstage.

This interest in the theater is also evident in his early writing. *The Indiscreet Toys* criticizes the artificiality of the theater. Diderot imagines someone being told that he is going to witness the intrigues and actions at court; instead, he is led to a spot overlooking a stage. According to Diderot, the spectator would not be fooled for an instant because contemporary stagecraft lacked realism. Another of Diderot's concerns emerges from a contribution of his to the third volume of the *Encyclopédie*. Under the heading "Comédiens," he defends actors by stressing their ability to incite in audiences a love of virtue and a dread of vice.

DORVAL

By the time he wrote *Dorval*, then, Diderot had acquainted himself with the great French theatrical tradition of the seventeenth century as well as contemporary drama, and he had spent at least a decade thinking about the kind of plays he thought most appropriate for the stage. *Dorval* was the first of his two attempts to create an example that would illustrate his precepts. Thus, the play rejects the rigid distinction between comedy and tragedy. The piece ends happily, with the appropriate people marrying each other and a supposedly lost fortune recovered. Before this cheerful resolution, however, Dorval several times contemplates fleeing society and comes close to marrying his half sister, Rosalie. Also, Clairville narrowly escapes death in a duel and almost loses the woman he loves.

This serious treatment of middle-class characters was unconventional, though not unprecedented. It represented a new genre of serious comedy, which Diderot called *drame*, and it declared that the bourgeoisie was no longer to serve only as the butt of satire. Indeed, through Clairville, Diderot praises the commercial class, observing, "Commerce is almost the only endeavor in which great fortunes are proportional to the effort, the industry, and the dangers that render them honest." Constance adds, "Our birth is given to us, but our virtues are truly ours," suggesting that the only distinctions worth making among people derive from their behavior, not their inherited rank in society. A century earlier, the very title of Molière's *Le Bourgeois Gentilhomme* (pr. 1670; *The Would-Be Gentleman*, 1675) would have made it clear to an audience that the play mocked middle-class pretensions. By the mid-eighteenth century, though, Diderot, the son of middle-class parents, portrays the middle class as dignified. Alexis de Tocqueville, in *De la démocratie en Amérique* (1835-1840; *Democracy in America*, 1835-1840), would observe that "the tastes and propensities natural to democratic nations, in respect to literature, will . . . first be discernible in the drama." Diderot's plays, along with those of his contemporaries, such as Pierre-Claude Nivelle de La Chaussée, Philippe Néricault Destouches, and Paul Landois, herald the ascendancy of the French middle class.

Dorval also puts into practice Diderot's belief in the power of the stage to reform society. Although Dorval observes that people speak of virtue too much, none of the characters, Dorval included, tires of moralizing. The piece's subtitle, "The Test of Virtue," indicates the play's moral theme, and Constance expresses Diderot's view on the potential of the theater as a moral agency when she tells Dorval, "The effect of virtue on our soul is no less necessary, no less powerful, than that of beauty on our senses. There is in the heart of man a yearning for order . . . which makes us sensible of shame. . . . Imitation is natural to us, and there is no example that compels us more forcefully than that of virtue."

This virtue that Diderot preaches in his play is less personal than social. Dorval is not condemned for being born out of wedlock, and the danger that Dorval escapes in renouncing Rosalie is less the union with his half sister than the betrayal of his best friend. Constance, his first love, persuades Dorval that personal inclinations must yield to duty, and Dorval agrees before he learns of his relationship to Rosalie. Constance repeats Diderot's views about people's social obligations when Dorval proposes to resolve his dilemma of loving both Constance and Rosalie by fleeing society completely. In a speech that ended a fifteen-year friendship between Diderot and the reclusive Jean-Jacques Rousseau, Constance tells Dorval, "You have received rare talents, and you must give an account of them to society. . . . I appeal to your heart. Ask it, and it will tell you that the good man belongs in society, and only the wicked person remains alone."

Dorval was intended to instruct not only Diderot's audiences but also the play's performers. According to a preface that Diderot included in the published version of the work, all the actors are supposedly the people they are representing, and they are reenacting events that actually befell them. Moreover, the production is intended only for themselves; they are performing in a salon without an audience. Dorval does allow Diderot to observe, but no one else knows he is present. This elaborate fictional frame emphasizes Diderot's belief that actors were paying too much attention to their audiences and so not behaving naturally. The result was a loss of realism, for the performers who were supposedly interacting with one another or meditating in private were always addressing the spectators. Hence, Diderot banished all asides from the play and included elaborate stage directions to encourage the players to behave as if the curtain had not risen. He wanted them to imagine an impenetrable barrier between themselves and the viewers, for Diderot believed that, paradoxically, only by ignoring the audience would an actor be able to please it.

A short time after its completion, the play was produced twice at Saint-Germaine-en-Laye, twelve miles west of Paris, where the action of the piece supposedly occurred. The first performance was well attended; on October 1, 1757, Alexandre Deleyre, a minor contributor to the *Encyclopédie*, wrote to Rousseau that he had been at "the first performance, where I wept copiously, although not intending to." According to Élie-Catherine Fréron, though, no one came to the second performance, and the Comédie-Française refused to produce the play until 1771.

THE FATHER OF THE FAMILY

Despite Diderot's disappointment over this poor reception, he quickly penned a second, similar work, *The Father of the Family*. Like *Dorval*, this play revolves around a dual courtship: Saint-Albin woos the poor Sophie while the poor Germeuil pursues Saint-Albin's sister, Cécile. Whereas in the first piece, the only obstacle to the marriages is the characters' divided love—Dorval loves both Rosalie and Constance, and Rosalie loves both Clairville and Dorval—here, the Père de famille and his imperious brother, the Commander, object to the matches as unsuitable. Diderot draws on his own experiences for the plot, for his own father opposed his marriage to Anne-Toinette Champion precisely because she, like Sophie, was poor. Moreover, just as the Commander tries to use a *lettre de cachet* to separate the lovers by imprisoning Sophie, so Diderot was briefly locked in a monastery by his father.

Because Diderot portrays himself in Saint-Albin, one might expect that his sympathies would lie with the son rather than with the father. Instead, Diderot remains neutral, casting the play as a battle between parental prudence and youthful impetuosity. The Père is generous—he gives money to the poor and has willingly supported Germeuil; he is reasonable—he agrees to see Sophie before reaching any decision and then patiently explains his objections. He is also honest, dismissing a servant who lies to him. These good qualities become even more evident as Diderot contrasts the Père with his brother, who would achieve his ends by force rather than reason and who

exhibits all the prejudices of the old regime. The Père opposes the marriage because of what he foresees as its negative social consequences, "the disorder of society, the confusion of blood and rank, the degradation of families." In other words, the Père upholds solid bourgeois values. Happily, Sophie proves to be sufficiently wellborn to deserve Saint-Albin; in fact, she is his first cousin.

Like Constance in *Dorval*, the Père has urged that personal considerations yield to social responsibility. When Cécile says that she wants to enter a convent, again he places society ahead of the individual, asking her, "Who will repopulate society with virtuous citizens, if the women the most worthy of being mothers of families refuse that role?"

Once more, Diderot used the theater as a vehicle for demonstrating his critical as well as his social theories. The middle-class characters are treated seriously, and the piece emphasizes their station in life rather than their peculiarities. Diderot had objected to the tradition, dating from Roman times, of portraying such types as the miser, the braggart soldier, or the wily servant. Instead, he urged that actors present the father, the lawyer, and the tradesman as they should ideally behave, thus heightening realism and morality in the play.

Another dramatic concern evident in this play is the tableau. Believing that the theater should present a series of "living pictures," Diderot provided numerous examples in this piece. His stage directions are so extensive as to remind the reader of George Bernard Shaw's lengthy instructions. Diderot thought that French actors were so concerned with speaking that they did not perform, so he tried to introduce elements of the pantomime to redress the imbalance.

Although more successful than its predecessor, *The Father of the Family* still did not meet as favorable a reception as Diderot had hoped; it was the last play Diderot offered his contemporaries. Nevertheless, his interest in the theater did not diminish. In 1760, he worked on translating Edward Moore's middle-class tragedy *The Gamester* (pr. 1753) and circulated the manuscript among his friends; the translation was finally published in 1819. He continued to write about the stage if not for it, and he used dramatic devices such as dialogue in his fiction. A number of these pieces have been successfully produced in this century: *The Nun* was made into a motion picture, and *Rameau's Nephew* was staged in Paris in 1963 to warm reviews.

EST'IL BON? EST'IL MÉCHANT?

The work that has won for Diderot the most respect as a dramatist, however, is *Est'il bon? Est'il méchant?*, which began in 1775 as *Plan d'un divertissement*, progressed to *La Pièce et le prologue* in 1777, and in 1781 emerged as a four-act play. Unknown in his own lifetime and rejected repeatedly by the Comédie-Française in the nineteenth century, it is the only one of Diderot's plays to be revived repeatedly in the twentieth. In this piece, Diderot made no attempt to instruct, no effort to implement his dramatic theories. Instead, he created a highly entertaining, fast-paced, witty comedy built around the crafty, semiautobiographical Hardouin.

Everyone asks favors of this person, and he obliges them, but in such a way as to raise the questions of the play's title. Madame Bertrand wants to be able to transfer her pension to her son and turns to Hardouin to use his influence on her behalf. He succeeds by persuading his friend Poultier that Madame Bertrand's son is also his (Hardouin's) own, thus making Madame Bertrand appear to be an adultress and her son a bastard. De Crancy wants to marry Mademoiselle de Vertillac, and when the girl's mother objects, he asks Hardouin to intercede. Hardouin does; he forges letters that convince the girl's mother that Mademoiselle is pregnant and so should marry even De Crancy to avoid disgrace. Hardouin is involved in so many plots and deals with each so ingeniously that the audience constantly marvels at his cleverness. At the same time, one wonders how long the charade can continue. Eventually, everyone learns of the humiliating ways in which Hardouin has secured for them what they wanted, but in the climactic trial scene (act 4, scene 4), he is pardoned without being totally exonerated. Hence, the play's title questions remain unanswered; each spectator must decide for himself whether Hardouin is good or wicked.

Absent from this play are the long, moralizing speeches and the tearful resolutions that mar Dide-

rot's earlier pieces. He had at last discovered that the true end of the theater is to entertain and to ask questions, not to answer them. Not that his other works are unimportant in the history of French theater. In 1759, for example, the Comédie-Française banished audiences from the stage for precisely the reason Diderot had given for ending the practice: It detracted from the realism of the performance. The genre of serious comedy that he advocated enjoyed some decades of popularity both on the Continent and in England, and his views on the didactic power of the stage remained influential well into the nineteenth century. One sees such ideas reflected even in the works of Henrik Ibsen and Shaw. Yet only when he abandoned theory in *Est'il bon? Est'il méchant?* could he himself create a work of sufficient stature to grant him his wish to be remembered as a first-rate dramatist.

OTHER MAJOR WORKS

LONG FICTION: *Les Bijoux indiscrets*, 1748 (*The Indiscreet Toys*, 1749); *Jacques le fataliste et son maître*, 1796 (wr. c. 1771; *Jacques the Fatalist and His Master*, 1797); *La Religieuse*, 1796 (*The Nun*, 1797); *Le Neveu de Rameau*, 1821, 1891 (*Rameau's Nephew*, 1897).

SHORT FICTION: "L'Oiseau blanc," 1748; "Les Deux Amis de Bourbonne," 1773 ("The Two Friends from Bourbonne," 1964); *Supplément au voyage de Bougainville*, 1796 (*Supplément to Bougainville's Voyage*, 1926); "Ceci n'est pas un conte," 1798 ("This Is Not a Story," 1960); "Madame de la Carlière: Ou, Sur l'inconséquence du jugement public de nos actions particulières," 1798; *Rameau's Nephew and Other Works*, 1964.

NONFICTION: *Pensées philosophiques*, 1746 (English translation, 1819; also as *Philosophical Thoughts*, 1916); *Lettre sur les aveugles*, 1749 (*An Essay on Blindness*, 1750; also as *Letter on the Blind*, 1916); *Notes et commentaires*, 1749; *Lettre sur les sourds et muets*, 1751 (*Letter on the Deaf and Dumb*, 1916); *Pensées sur l'interprétation de la nature*, 1754; *Entretiens sur "Le Fils naturel,"* 1757; *Discours sur la poésie dramatique*, 1758 (English translation of chapters 1-5 in *Dramatic Essays of the Neo-Classical*

Age, 1950); *Les Salons*, 1759-1781 (serial; 9 volumes), 1845, 1857 (book); *De la suffisance de la religion naturelle*, 1770 (wr. 1747); *Entretien d'un père avec ses enfants: Ou, Le Danger de se mettre au-dessus des lois*, 1773 (*Conversations Between Father and Children*, 1964); *Essai sur Sénèque*, 1778 (revised and expanded as *Essai sur les règnes de Claude et de Néron*, 1782); *Essais sur la peinture*, 1796 (wr. c. 1765); *Pensées détachées sur la peinture*, 1798; *Plan d'une université pour le gouvernement de Russie*, 1813-1814 (wr. c. 1775-1776); *Paradoxe sur le comédien*, 1830 (wr. 1773; *The Paradox of Acting*, 1883); *La promenade du sceptique*, 1830 (wr. 1747); *Le Rêve de d'Alembert*, 1830 (wr. 1769; *D'Alembert's Dream*, 1927); *Diderot's Early Philosophical Works*, 1916 (includes *Letter on the Blind*, *Letter on the Deaf and Dumb*, *Philosophical Thoughts*); *Concerning the Education of a Prince*, 1941 (wr. 1758); *Correspondance*, 1955-1970 (16 volumes); *Œuvres philosophiques*, 1956; *Œuvres esthétiques*, 1959; *Œuvres politiques*, 1962.

TRANSLATIONS: *L'Histoire de Grèce*, 1743 (of Temple Stanyan's *Grecian History*); *Principes de la philosophie morale: Ou, Essai de M. S.*** sur le mérite et la vertu, avec réflexions*, 1745 (of the earl of Shaftesbury's *An Inquiry Concerning Virtue and Merit*); *Dictionnaire universel de médecine*, 1746-1748 (of Robert James's *A Medical Dictionary*).

EDITED TEXT: *Encyclopédie: Ou, Dictionnaire raisonné des sciences, des arts, et des métiers*, 1751-1772 (17 volumes of text, 11 volumes of plates; partial translation *Selected Essays from the Encyclopedy*, 1772; complete translation *Encyclopedia*, 1965).

MISCELLANEOUS: *Œuvres*, 1798 (15 volumes); *Œuvres complètes*, 1875-1877 (20 volumes); *Diderot, Interpreter of Nature: Selected Writings*, 1937 (includes short fiction); *Selected Writings*, 1966.

BIBLIOGRAPHY

Brewer, Daniel. *The Discourse of Enlightenment in Eighteenth Century France: Diderot and the Art of Philosophizing*. New York: Cambridge University Press, 1993. This work focuses on Diderot as a member of the Enlightenment in France. Bibliography and index.

Curran, Andrew. *Sublime Disorder: Physical Monstrosity in Diderot's Universe*. Oxford, England: Voltaire Foundation, 2001. An examination of physical monstrosity in Diderot's writings. Bibliography and index.

Furbank, Philip Nicholas. *Diderot: A Critical Biography*. New York: Alfred A. Knopf, 1992. A biography of Diderot that covers his life and works. Bibliography and index.

Goodden, Angelica. *Diderot and the Body*. Oxford, England: Legenda, 2001. A study of Diderot that focuses on his portrayal of the body.

Kaufman, Peter H. *The Solidarity of a Philosophe: Diderot, Russia, and the Soviet Union*. New York: Peter Lang, 1994. This study examines Diderot's philosophy and its lingering influence. Bibliography and index.

Pucci, Suzanne L. *Sites of the Spectator: Emerging Literary and Cultural Practice in Eighteenth Century France*. Oxford, England: Voltaire Foundation, 2001. This work looks at the literary world in eighteenth century France, focusing on Diderot's *Les Salons* and Marivaux's *Le spectateur français*. Bibliography and index.

Rex, Walter E. *Diderot's Counterpoints: The Dynamics of Contrariety in His Major Works*. Oxford, England: Voltaire Foundation, 1998. A scholarly study that examines polarity in Diderot's works. Bibliography and index.

Joseph Rosenblum

STEVEN DIETZ

Born: Denver, Colorado; June 23, 1958

PRINCIPAL DRAMA

Brothers and Sisters, pr. 1982 (music by Roberta
    Carlson)
Railroad Tales, pr. 1983
Random Acts, pr. 1983
Carry On, pr. 1984
Wanderlust, pr. 1984
Catch Me a Z, pr. 1985 (music by Greg
    Thiesen)
More Fun than Bowling, pr. 1986, pb. 1990
Painting It Red, pr. 1986, pb. 1990 (music by
    Gary Rue, lyrics by Leslie Ball)
Burning Desire, pr. 1987
Foolin' Around with Infinity, pr. 1987, pb. 1990
Ten November, pr., pb. 1987 (music by Eric Bain
    Peltoniemi)
God's Country, pr. 1989, pb. 1990
Happenstance, pr. 1989 (music by Eric Bain
    Peltoniemi)
After You, pr. 1990, pb. 1992
Halcyon Days, pr., pb. 1991
To the Nines, pr., pb. 1991
Trust, pr. 1991, pb. 1992
Lonely Planet, pr. 1992, pb. 1994
The Rememberer, pb. 1993, pr. 1994 (based on the
    memoirs of Joyce Simmons Cheeka)
Boomtown, pr. 1994
Silence, pr. 1995 (adaptation of Shusaku Endo's
    novel)
Dracula, pr. 1995, pb. 1996 (adaptation of Bram
    Stoker's novel)
Handing Down the Names, pr. 1995
The Nina Variations, pr. 1996
Private Eyes, pr. 1996, pb. 1998
Still Life with Iris, pr. 1997, pb. 1998
Rocket Man, pr. 1998
Force of Nature, pr. 1999 (based on Johann
    Wolfgang von Goethe's *Elective Affinities*)
Paragon Springs, pr. 2000 (based on Henrik
    Ibsen's *An Enemy of the People*)
Inventing Van Gogh, pr. 2001
Leaves, pr. 2001 (a radio play)

OTHER LITERARY FORMS

Steven Dietz is a writer who has built his reputation exclusively on his plays. He has published several articles about the theater and writing in *American Theatre Magazine* and the *Los Angeles Times*. Several of his plays have been translated into other languages: *Private Eyes* into French, German, and Slavic; *Dracula* into Japanese; *Handing Down the Names* into German; and *Lonely Planet* into Japanese, Spanish, Portuguese, and French. Motion picture rights for *Trust* were optioned in 1993 by True Pictures, New York, and rights for *Still Life with Iris* were optioned by Flatiron Films in 1999.

ACHIEVEMENTS

Steven Dietz's plays, produced at more than eighty regional theaters across the country, on Off-Broadway, and in Japan and South Africa, have won numerous awards. *Lonely Planet*, for example, garnered for Dietz the PEN Center USA West Award in Drama and was selected as One of the Best Off-Broadway plays of 1995. *Still Life with Iris* won the Kennedy Center Fund for New American Plays Award in 1996 and three years later the American Alliance for Theatre and Education Distinguished Play Award. Dietz has been named to playwriting fellowships from the McKnight and Jerome foundations and the National Endowment for the Arts, as well as to directing fellowships from McKnight and Theatre Communications Group. He received both a National Endowment for the Arts playwriting fellowship and a Theatre Communications Group fellowship in directing in 1987. In 1988 he received a Society of Midland Authors award. A Creative Achievement Award from the University of Northern Colorado Alumni Association was conferred on him in 1996, and he received a $10,000 Emerging Artist Award from the Bagley Wright Fund (Seattle) for Artistic Excellence in 1999.

BIOGRAPHY

Steven Dietz was born in Denver, Colorado, on June 23, 1958. His father, John, a conductor on Burlington Northern, was a railroad man for forty-three years; his mother, Irene, was a homemaker. Growing up, Dietz had very little theater in his upbringing—he occupied himself playing sports, mainly baseball and tennis. He fell in with a group of theater friends in high school, where he saw his first play. At the University of Northern Colorado, he majored in theater, graduating with a B.A. in 1980.

Dietz then moved to Minneapolis, where he lived and worked for eleven years. This was a formative and productive period in his artistic development. With the Playwrights' Center as his artistic home, he worked as playwright and director at many of the local theaters. He cofounded Quicksilver Stage (1983-1986), was artistic director of Midwest PlayLabs (1987-1989), and even directed an opera, *Saint Erik's Crown*, in St. Peter, Minnesota (1989). During this period, Dietz directed world premier productions of early plays by (then) up-and-coming writers, such as John Olive's *The Voice of the Prairie*, Kevin Kling's *21-A* and *Lloyd's Prayer*, and Jon Klein's *T Bone N Weasel*.

Dietz has been resident director of Sundance Institute, Utah (1990), and an associate artist at A Contemporary Theatre, Seattle (1990-1991). He moved to Seattle in 1991 and in 1996 married playwright Allison Gregory, with whom he had a daughter, Ruby Clementine. He constantly works at his craft, keeping a notebook handy to jot down snippets of conversations, signs in storefronts, and anything else that captures his attention.

Dietz has served as artist-in-residence or faculty member at Arizona State University (1993), Whitman College (1997), Mercer University (2000), and Seattle University (2002). In 2002, he received two commissions: from A Contemporary Theatre (Seattle) to do a new play called *Fiction* and from Purple Rose Theatre (Michigan) to do *The Ride Inside*. He has also received play commissions from Milwaukee Repertory Theater, Actors Theatre of Louisville, Arizona Theatre Company, San Jose Repertory Theatre, and the Seattle Children's Theatre.

Steven Dietz in 1996. (AP/Wide World Photos)

ANALYSIS

Steven Dietz is a versatile playwright who uses an impressive array of subjects and styles and whose plays are seen in theaters across the United States. The language of his plays is direct, the structure is intricate, and the character relationships are honest. He is prolific, establishing a respected body of work rather than producing a single, defining dramatic work. Dietz has said that a driving motivation behind his plays is to get his audience interested in the world. He therefore uses facts liberally in his writing—historical events, family history, and literary allusions. *God's Country*, *Handing Down the Names*, and *Ten November* are examples of plays based on factual events. Plays that begin with literary epigrams include *Private Eyes* (a quotation from Anne Sexton), *Rocket Man* (Philip Levine), *Trust* (Andre Dubus), *Halcyon Days* (Lance Morrow), and *Force of Nature*, which is based on Goethe's novel *Die Wahlverwandt-schaften* (1809; *Elective Affinities*, 1849).

Dietz has also commented that he sees theater as a public forum in which people can gather to consider and discuss things that confront them, including politics and social and humanitarian issues. He uses the U.S. invasion of Grenada as backdrop for *Halcyon Days*, which includes as characters a broad section of humanity: medical students, senators, shop clerks, and presidential speechwriters. No matter how grim the theme or plot becomes, Dietz regularly intersperses wit, irony, and outright humor into his plays. *Lonely Planet*, a play about men dying of AIDS (acquired immunodeficiency syndrome), for example, is relieved with light-heartedness and warmth. Especially in the later plays, Dietz often employs direct address of the audience, signifying that he does not wish his readers or viewers to remain passive during and after they experience his work.

TEN NOVEMBER

Dietz wrote this play while living and working in Minneapolis. Most Minnesotans are familiar with the Lake Superior tragedy of the ore freighter that disappeared with all hands on board in a storm on November 11, 1975, an event Gordon Lightfoot memorialized in his ballad "The Wreck of the *Edmund Fitzgerald*." Commissioned by the Actors Theater of St. Paul to create a theater piece on a topic of his choosing, Dietz collaborated with composer Eric Bain Peltoniemi to focus on this maritime tragedy, gathering extensive historical information about the vessel and studying the Coast Guard report about its sinking.

Dietz's approach was not an attempt to present individual stories of the twenty-nine men who perished aboard the freighter. Nor did he seek to determine an ultimate cause for the accident or to assign blame. Instead, the play presents his and his collaborator's response to the event, focusing on "the myth of invincibility in our culture and our attempts to deal with loss." He begins both acts of the play with epigrams that are lines from the American poet Emily Dickinson, who writes about the universal loss of human love through parting. Dietz dedicates his play to the men of the *Edmund Fitzgerald*.

Using nine actors and three singers, the play's compelling narrative blends several discourses: myths of other vessels lost on the Great Lakes; transcripts from radio communications between the *Fitzgerald* and the *Arthur M. Anderson*, a steel ore carrier proceeding along a similar route; hypothetical shipboard conversations among the *Fitzgerald*'s crew; fictionalized recollections of last conversations between survivors and their loved ones; testimony from the Coast Guard hearing following the tragedy; and excerpts from the final report of the Marine Board of Investigation. The play ends with actors chanting in turn the names and ranks of each of the twenty-nine men who perished aboard the *Fitzgerald*.

GOD'S COUNTRY

This powerful 1989 play about the white supremacist movement has been produced more than two hundred times, on both college stages and international venues in Johannesburg and Pretoria, South Africa. Dietz adds to the historical focus of *God's Country* by using literary epigrams to introduce the two acts. He quotes Voltaire in act 1: "Anyone who has the power to make you believe absurdities has the power to make you commit injustices." Act 2 begins with a passage from Santayana: "Fanaticism consists in redoubling your efforts when you have forgotten the aim." These two quotations suggest the volatile themes and the mounting danger and aggression of the play. Three women and seven men play multiple roles; a preteen boy rounds out the cast.

Dietz dedicated his play to the memory of Alan Berg, a bright and outspoken Jewish radio talk-show host murdered in Denver in 1984 by neo-Nazis. Berg, labeled in the play as a "bleeding heart with an acid tongue," appears as a character in a play that details the anger and bigotry leading to both his Mafia-style execution as well as crimes before and after his murder. The radical right was incensed with Berg's penchant for questioning certain beliefs and considered his murder to be a type of salvation. The play pits Berg's frank rationality against the madness and rage of the neo-Nazis who stalk him. Much of this complicated tour de force, which opens and closes simply, with a young boy pledging allegiance, is a courtroom docudrama that depends on direct address to the audience. It conveys the history and beliefs, the promotion and demise of the movement known as The Order, which was built on such ultra-right-wing organizations as the Ku Klux Klan, the Aryan Nations, and the American Nazi Party. On a more universal level, the play demonstrates how bigotry in adults fosters bigotry in their children and how crowd mentality, both mindless and destructive, can transform into a crime spree and ultimately into devastating, incendiary revolution.

Lonely Planet

This play has been produced Off-Broadway and at numerous regional theaters throughout the country, including the Circle Repertory Company (New York). It departs from Dietz's other works in that the cast is so small and in that truth and illusion are equally critical. Cast for two male friends and set in the map store owned by one of them in an unspecified American city, the play begins with an epigram by absurdist playwright Eugène Ionesco, "We will leave some traces, for we are people and not cities," a line repeated in the play's final scene. Broadly stated, the play is a compassionate comedy about friendship and loss in the age of AIDS, though the disease is not named in the play. As in Ionesco's play titled *Les Chaises* (pr. 1952; *The Chairs*, 1958), *Lonely Planet* gradually assembles onstage for symbolic purposes a room full of various chairs—in Dietz's play each chair represents a particular friend who has died of AIDS. The other important symbol in the play is a huge photograph of planet Earth hanging on a wall in the map shop. The photo, taken by astronauts of Apollo 17 and now a defining image of the planet, suggests vulnerable humanity threatened by darkness and the void. The play is an extended conversation between Jody and his younger friend Carl about their friendship, about dreams and memories that may or may not be true, and about the frustrations of living in today's world. Jody, the agoraphobic map store owner, exits at one point to be tested for the human immunodeficiency virus (HIV). The play ends with Carl on stage with "his" unique, turquoise-and-silver kitchen chair, signifying that he

has joined the ranks of their friends who have succumbed to AIDS.

The reminiscences between the men, at times interrupted with a telephone that is ringing in the map shop, conjure past dates they have had with other men and name particular friends who have died. They discuss their individual place and significance in a world in which they continue to exist after their friends have departed, and they honor the memories of those departed friends.

In the "Author's Note" to the play, Dietz says that "history . . . is not the story of grand acts and masterpieces . . . [but] the inexorable accumulation of tiny events" affecting ordinary people. Therefore, "our legacy is our friends" and nurturing friendship is the best way to exist in the world.

Other major work

screenplay: *The Blueprint*, 1992.

Bibliography

Istel, John. "Risking Sentiment." *American Theatre* 12, no. 10 (December, 1995): 38. This interview with Dietz focuses on his award-winning play *Lonely Planet*. Dietz discusses the play as an homage to friendship, as a literary riff on themes and intentions central to Ionesco's absurdist play *The Chairs*, and as a vehicle for comparing a particular convention of mapping (the Greenland problem of transferring three-dimensional geography to a two-dimensional illustration) to the distortion of reality. Dietz concludes with a statement about the importance of sentiment in his drama.

Tu, Janet I-Chin. "Playwright Steven Dietz Juggles Many Projects." *Seattle Times*, February 1, 1998, p. M1. The author shows Dietz at work in his Queen Anne home in Seattle with twenty assorted boxes of his plays and script notes in his basement. She discusses how prolific Dietz is both in print and on stage; highlights awards, work habits, and other biographical details; and includes testimony and tributes from his friends.

Jill Barnum Gidmark

OWEN DODSON

Born: Brooklyn, New York; November 28, 1914
Died: New York, New York; June 21, 1983

PRINCIPAL DRAMA

Deep in Your Heart, pr. 1935

Including Laughter, pr. 1936

The Shining Town, wr. 1937, pb. 1991

Divine Comedy, pr. 1938, pb. 1974 (music by Morris Mamorsky)

The Garden of Time, pr. 1939 (music by Shirley Graham)

Everybody Join Hands, pb. 1943

New World A-Coming, pr. 1943, pb. 1944

The Third Fourth of July, pb. 1946 (with Countée Cullen)

Bayou Legend, pr. 1948, pb. 1971 (adaptation of Henrik Ibsen's *Peer Gynt*)

Till Victory Is Won, pr. 1965 (opera; with Mark Fax)

Freedom, the Banner, pb. 1984

OTHER LITERARY FORMS

During Owen Dodson's undergraduate years at Bates College, his poetry appeared in such publications as *Opportunity*, *New Masses*, and the *New York Herald Tribune*. Over the decades, numerous periodicals and anthologies have published his verse. His three volumes of verse are *Powerful Long Ladder* (1946), which includes excerpts from his *Divine Comedy* verse play; *The Confession Stone* (1968), which was revised and enlarged as *The Confession Stone: Song Cycles* (1970); and *The Harlem Book of the Dead* (1978), which features Dodson's poetry and James Van Der Zee's photographs.

Dodson also wrote two novels. *Boy at the Window* (1951) is an autobiographical novel about Coin Foreman, a nine-year-old Brooklyn boy. When the novel was published in paperback in 1967, the title was changed to *When Trees Were Green*. In his second novel, *Come Home Early, Child* (1977), Foreman is now an adult. Although his novels received favorable commentary from critics, his poetry and drama earned him greater acclaim.

ACHIEVEMENTS

Owen Dodson's writing talents garnered diverse honors. He was the recipient of various writing grants including the General Education Board (1937), Rosenwald Fellowship (1943), Guggenheim Fellowship (1953), and Rockefeller (1968). In 1942 *The Garden of Time* earned Stanford University's Maxwell Anderson Verse Drama Award (second prize). In 1956 "The Summer Fire," the first chapter from *Come Home Early, Child*, placed second in the *Paris Review*'s 1956 short-story contest and was included in *Best Short Stories from the Paris Review* (1959). Bates College bestowed additional honors on its distinguished alumnus; he was elected to Phi Beta Kappa in 1951 and was awarded an honorary doctorate of letters in 1967. Dodson also received an honorary doctorate from Missouri's Lincoln University in 1978.

Owen Dodson (Courtesy of the New York Public Library)

Paying tribute to Dodson's literary legacy, Glenda Dickerson and Mike Malone created *Owen's Song*, a collage of his plays and poems. *Owen's Song* was performed in 1974 at the Last Colony Theater, Washington, D.C.; the Harlem Cultural Center, New York; and the Eisenhower Theater in the John F. Kennedy Center for the Performing Arts, Washington, D.C. One year later, Dodson received the New York Black Theater Alliance's AUDELCO (Audience Development Company) Outstanding Pioneer Award in recognition of his contributions to the growth and development of African American theater.

BIOGRAPHY

Owen Vincent Dodson, the grandson of former slaves and the ninth child of Nathaniel and Sarah Dodson, was born on November 28, 1914, in Brooklyn, New York. His father was a syndicated columnist and director of the National Negro Press. Before Owen's thirteenth birthday, death claimed four siblings and both parents; as a result, Owen and the other Dodson children lived with their older sister Lillian, an elementary school teacher. Dodson graduated from Thomas Jefferson High School in 1932, earned a B.A. from Bates College in 1936 and a M.F.A. degree from the Yale School of Fine Arts, School of Drama in 1939.

At Bates, Dodson's passion for poetry and drama was evident. In response to his criticism of a sonnet by John Keats, his professor directed him to write sonnets himself, which Dodson did at the rate of four sonnets a week during his undergraduate years. This output enabled him to become a published poet while still an undergraduate. Also at Bates, he wrote and directed plays, and during his senior year, he staged *The Trojan Women*.

At Yale, two of Dodson's best known plays, *Divine Comedy* and *The Garden of Time*, were first produced. Dodson, recognized as a promising poet, soon gained attention as an up and coming dramatist. Talladega College commissioned him to write a play *Amistad*, commemorating the hundredth anniversary of the slave-ship mutiny led by Joseph Cinque.

After Dodson received his graduate degree from Yale, he began his career as an educator. He was em-ployed by Spelman College and later at Hampton University. Dodson was one of the founders of the Negro Playwright Company in 1940. In 1942, during World War II, he enlisted in the Navy. While stationed at the Great Lakes Naval Training Center in Illinois, Dodson wrote and directed *Heroes on Parade*, a series of plays, including *Robert Smalls*, *John P. Jones*, *Booker T. Washington*, *Lord Nelson*, *Dorrie Miller*, *Everybody Join Hands*, *Old Ironsides*, *Don't Give Up the Ship*, *Freedom, the Banner*, and *Tropical Fable*. Some of these plays were performed by other military drama groups in the United States and abroad. Dodson received a medical discharge in 1943.

On June 26, 1944, twenty-five thousand people saw *New World A-Coming* at Madison Square Garden. Based on the production's success, Dodson was appointed executive secretary of the American Film Center's Committee for Mass Education in Race Relations. Other prominent committee members were Arna Bontemps, Langston Hughes, and Richard Wright. Dodson was a prolific dramatist. He collaborated with the well-known Harlem Renaissance poet Countée Cullen and wrote *The Third Fourth of July* and *Medea in Africa*, an adaptation of Euripides' *Mēdeia* (431 B.C.E.; *Medea*, 1781) that was based on Cullen's play *Medea* (pr., pb. 1935) and Dodson's *The Garden of Time*. Dodson also collaborated with composer Mark Fax and wrote two operas: *A Christmas Miracle* and *Till Victory Is Won*.

In 1947 Dodson joined the faculty of Howard University, and a decade later, he was appointed chair of the drama department. He taught during the day and directed during the night. Indeed during his long career, he directed more than one hundred plays. In the fall of 1949, Dodson, Anne Cooke, and James Butcher led the Howard Players on a three-month tour of northwestern Europe. After the group's return to Washington, D.C., the United States government presented Howard University with the American Public Relations Award. During the 1954-1955 season, Dodson directed the premier performance of James Baldwin's *The Amen Corner* nine years before its Broadway debut. He also staged productions of plays by former Howard students, including Amiri Baraka (then known as LeRoi Jones).

In 1970 Dodson retired from Howard. However, his passion for the theater and poetry remained steadfast. He continued to direct plays and write poetry, including *The Confession Stone* and *The Harlem Book of the Dead*. Dodson taught at City College of New York and at York College in Queens. He died on June 21, 1983, in New York. Memorial services were held in Washington, D.C., and New York.

ANALYSIS

Although Owen Dodson—teacher, director, and critic—made many valuable contributions to African American drama as he encouraged and trained actors and playwrights, his plays remain his most significant theatrical accomplishment. Dodson, the author of at least thirty-seven plays and a dominant director in African American university theater for more than thirty years, was not the first black dramatist; however, he was one of the first black playwrights to consistently write and direct serious African American plays. Therefore, he is a literary forefather of younger generations of black playwrights such as Lorraine Hansberry and August Wilson as well as black directors, including Lloyd Richards. He has been hailed as the dean of African American drama.

In Dodson's plays, themes, plot, and characters are upstaged by language. His most widely known theatrical works are verse plays. He was one of the first playwrights, white or black, to effectively use verse drama. Even when Dodson wrote other types of plays, language remains, more often than not, the most potent element.

The epigraph ("It takes a powerful long ladder to climb to the sky/ An catch the bird of freedom for the dark") for Dodson's first volume of verse, *Powerful Long Ladder*, has relevance for his plays. The ladder is a metaphor for whatever individuals need, and the bird of freedom represents goals and desires. In *The Shining Town*, black women need to endure in order to reach financial stability. In *Divine Comedy*, the churchgoers need to turn away from a con man and empower themselves to obtain life's basic necessities. In *The Garden of Time*, the characters must realize that racism affects love. In *Bayou Legend*, Dodson's second full-length play, which critics have described

as a fantasy and an allegorical poetic legend, Reve Grant fails to learn until it is too late that to compromise one's life is to compromise one's soul. He "chose the kingdom of compromise, of nothing, of mediocrity" as he longed for wealth and power.

THE SHINING TOWN

The setting of this one-act play is a subway station in the Bronx during the Depression. New York is no "shining town" for the women who participate in a twentieth century version of a slave auction. African American domestic workers compete with each other for daily jobs offered by white women who offer extremely low wages. As the black women wait for their potential employers to arrive at the station, the atmosphere of gloom increases. The dark station corresponds with the women's despair. Dodson suggests that Abby, a little girl who accompanies her mother on her quest for employment, is doomed to the same fate. Dodson completed this play at Yale, but it was not produced there. One scholar, James V. Hatch, speculates that Dodson's less than flattering images of white women may be the reason *The Shining Town* was not produced at Yale.

DIVINE COMEDY

Divine Comedy is another drama that Dodson completed at Yale. It premiered at Yale, was reviewed favorably in *Variety*, and remains one of his best-known plays. This verse play in two acts portrays a character based on Father Divine, the self-proclaimed religious leader. Dodson boldly focuses on an infamous black character at a time when a number of African American writers and scholars advocated positive images only. *The Shining Town*'s Depression era time period is repeated here, and despair is also prevalent in this play. For example, a mother realizes she is rocking a dead baby. However, unlike *The Shining Town*, *Divine Comedy* does not have a pessimistic ending. The characters eventually realize they have to make their own lives better instead of depending on a religious charlatan. At the end, the characters proclaim: "We need no prophets./ This Winter is Autumn./ We need no miracles./ We *are* the miracle." Love is also an important factor in this play, as Cyril Jackson demonstrates the extremes to which a son will go to protect his mother.

THE GARDEN OF TIME

This three-act verse play, completed and produced at Yale, is Dodson's interpretation of Euripides' *Medea*. *The Garden of Time*, a drama of interracial relationships, begins in ancient Greece, and midway through the play, the characters are in Georgia and Haiti. Concurrent with the shift in settings is the transformation of characters. Medea becomes Miranda, a Haitian, and Jason becomes John, a plantation owner's son. When *The Garden of Time* was staged at Yale, Shirley Graham was the play's only black actor. Graham, who was also enrolled in Yale's School of Drama, wrote the music for the play. *The Garden of Time* is one of Dodson's best-known plays and the winner of the Maxwell Anderson Verse Drama Award (second place) at Stanford University in 1942, yet ironically, it remains unpublished.

Dodson's plays provide insight into African American life, yet they are not limited to the black experience. Achieving universality in his writing was of primary importance to Dodson. His plays transcend cultures and time. *The Garden of Time*'s choral refrain, which was later titled "Circle One" and published in Dodson's *Powerful Long Ladder*, applies to the universality of life found in his plays: "Nothing happens only once,/ Nothing happens only here,/ . . . All the lands repeat themselves,/ Shore for shore and men for men."

OTHER MAJOR WORKS

LONG FICTION: *Boy at the Window*, 1951 (also published as *When Trees Were Green*, 1967); *Come Home Early, Child*, 1977.

SHORT FICTION: "The Summer Fire," 1956.

POETRY: *Powerful Long Ladder*, 1946; *The Confession Stone*, 1968 (revised and enlarged as *The Confession Stone: Song Cycles*, 1970); *The Harlem Book of the Dead*, 1978 (with Camille Billops and James Van Der Zee).

SCREENPLAY: *They Seek a City*, 1945.

RADIO PLAYS: *Old Ironsides*, 1942; *Robert Smalls*, 1942; *The Midwest Mobilizes*, 1943; *Dorrie Miller*, 1944; *New World A-Coming*, 1945; *St. Louis Woman*, c. 1945 (adaptation of Countée Cullen and Arna Bontemps's play); *The Dream Awake*, 1969.

NONFICTION: "Twice a Year," 1946-1947; "College Troopers Abroad," 1950; "Playwrights in Dark Glasses," 1968; "Who Has Seen the Wind? Playwrights and the Black Experience," 1977; "Who Has Seen the Wind?: Part II," 1980.

BIBLIOGRAPHY

Hatch, James V. *Sorrow Is the Only Faithful One: The Life of Owen Dodson*. Urbana: University of Illinois Press, 1993. Authorized biography by the preeminent Dodson scholar. Contains a chronology of Dodson's involvement in the theater as writer, director, set designer, and actor.

Hatch, James V., and Omanii Abdullah, eds. *Black Playwrights, 1823-1977: An Annotated Bibliography of Plays*. New York: R. R. Bowker, 1977. Categorizes and provides production information for Dodson's plays. Contains entries for more than thirty of Dodson's plays.

Peterson, Bernard L., Jr. *Contemporary Black American Playwrights and Their Plays: A Biographical Directory and Dramatic Index*. New York: Greenwood Press, 1988. Contains production information for Dodson's plays written, produced, or published after 1950.

_____. "The Legendary Owen Dodson of Howard University: His Contributions to the American Theatre." *The Crisis* 86 (1979): 373-378. Contains biographical and critical commentary. Speculates that Dodson's greatest literary legacy will be his drama rather than his poems

_____. "Owen Dodson." *Early Black American Playwrights and Dramatic Writers: A Biographical Directory and Catalog of Plays, Films, and Broadcasting Scripts*. Westport, Conn.: Greenwood Press, 1990. Contains a brief biographical entry. Categorizes and provides production information for Dodson's plays written, produced or published before 1950.

Linda M. Carter

TANKRED DORST

Born: Oberlind, Germany; December 19, 1925

PRINCIPAL DRAMA

Gesellschaft im Herbst, pr. 1960, pb. 1961

Die Kurve, pr. 1960, pb. 1962 (*The Curve*, 1963)

Freiheit für Clemens, pr. 1960, pb. 1962 (*Freedom for Clemens*, 1967)

Grosse Schmährede an der Stadtmauer, pr., pb. 1961 (*Great Tirade at the Town-Wall*, 1961)

Die Mohrin, pr., pb. 1964

Toller: Szenen aus einer deutschen Revolution, pr., pb. 1968

Eiszeit, pr., pb. 1973 (with Ursula Ehler)

Auf dem Chimborazo, pb. 1974, pr. 1975 (with Ehler)

Three Plays, pb. 1976

Die Villa, pr., pb. 1980 (with Ehler)

Merlin: Oder, Das wüste Land, pb. 1980, pr. 1981 (with Ehler)

Der verbotene Garten, pb. 1983, pr. 1984 (with Ehler)

Heinrich: Oder, Die Schmerzen der Phantasie, pb. 1984, pr. 1985

Werkausgabe, pb. 1985-2001 (7 volumes)

Ich, Feuerbach, pr., pb. 1986 (with Ehler)

Parzival: Ein Szenarium, pr. 1987, pb. 1990 (with Ehler and Robert Wilson)

Korbes, pr., pb. 1988 (with Ehler)

Karlos, pr. 1989, pb. 1990 (with Ehler)

Fernando Krapp hat mir diesen Brief geschrieben, pr., pb. 1992 (with Ehler; *Fernando Krapp Wrote Me This Letter: An Assaying of Truth*, 1996)

Herr Paul, pb. 1993, pr. 1994 (with Ehler)

Die Schattenlinie, pb. 1994, pr. 1995

Nach Jerusalem, pr., pb. 1994 (with Ehler)

Die Geschichte der Pfeile, pr., pb. 1996

Die Legende vom armen Heinrich, pb. 1996

Harrys Kopf, pr., pb. 1997 (with Ehler)

Wegen Reichtum geschlossen, pr., pb. 1998 (with Ehler)

Grosse Szene am Fluss, pb. 1999, pr. 2000 (with Ehler)

Die Freude am Leben, pb. 2001, pr. 2002 (with Ehler)

OTHER LITERARY FORMS

Although Tankred Dorst is known primarily as a dramatist, he has written essays and other prose works that he often used as springboards for his plays. In addition to serious drama, he has extensively written and produced plays for children and fables for grownups, some of which were performed in puppet theaters. Dorst is also known for his radio plays and scripts for television, and in the 1970's and 1980's, he distinguished himself in the German film industry by writing and directing motion pictures. Dorst has supplied libretti for several operas and ballets and translated several plays from the French and English. His 1962 article "Die Bühne ist der absolut Ort" (the stage is the unequivocal place) contains Dorst's views of the theater, its role, its relationship to reality, and the theatrical devices he employs.

ACHIEVEMENTS

At a time when only a handful of German dramatists were able to contribute anything original for the stage, Tankred Dorst—though inspired by already established German (Bertolt Brecht) as well as by some foreign, especially French, models (Jean Giraudoux, Jean Anouilh, and Eugène Ionesco)—appeared in the German theater as a fresh and independent voice endowed with an innate sense of theater and stage technique. Unflinchingly, Dorst persevered in cultivating his vision, often in face of critical or political pressure to "take sides," especially in plays dealing with controversial figures or issues. That he was quite successful in his pursuit is demonstrated by prizes and awards received not only in Germany but also abroad. His theater debut, *Gesellschaft im Herbst* (autumn party), won for him the prize of the city of Mannheim (in 1959), which was followed by the Villa Massimo stipend for a sojourn in Rome. Other awards came almost yearly: the Gerhart Hauptmann Prize in 1964, the prize of the city of Munich in the same year and again in 1969, the prize of the city of Florence and the Theater Prize of Lisbon in 1970, the Bavarian Academy of Fine Arts Prize for Literature in 1983, and the Royal Film Institute of Belgium's L'Age d'Or award in 1984.

BIOGRAPHY

Tankred Dorst was born on December 19, 1925, in Oberlind near Sonneberg in Thuringia. His father was an engineer and manufacturer. As a teenager, Dorst became fascinated with the theater and dreamed of becoming a theater dramaturge. In 1942, as a seventeen-year-old high school student, he was drafted into the army. He was taken prisoner of war and placed in various English and American camps in Belgium, Great Britain, and the United States. Released in 1947, he finished his interrupted high school studies (*Abitur*) in 1950 and then studied literature, art history, and drama at the Universities of Bamberg and Munich, without getting a degree. After 1952, he resided in Munich.

Dorst went through his theater apprenticeship while working with a students' puppet theater (*Das kleine Spiel*, the little play) in Schwabing, a bohemian section in Munich. He detailed his experiences there in a collection of essays, *Geheimnis der Marionette* (1957; the secret of the puppet), and in *Auf kleiner Bühne: Versuche mit Marionetten* (1959; on a small stage: experiments with puppets).

Soon, however, Dorst was acclaimed as a new talent in the German postwar theater, first gaining attention through a prize given by the city of Mannheim for his draft of *Gesellschaft im Herbst* and then by having the play produced almost simultaneously in several German theaters. Even more successful were his one-act plays: *Freedom for Clemens*, *The Curve*, and *Great Tirade at the Town-Wall*, all three performed in more than 150 theaters as well as translated into various languages. His new versions of some old plays (Ludwig Tieck's *Der gestiefelte Kater*, 1797, pr. 1844; *Puss-in-Boots*, 1913-1914) and legends such as the old French love story of Aucassin and Nicolette (*Die Mohrin*) gave Dorst an opportunity to display his mastery of the stage by intermingling the most diverse theatrical techniques and devices, from play-within-a-play to masks and variety-show sketches and interludes. *Die Mohrin* (the Saracen girl) he also revised as a libretto for an opera.

In 1967, at the time of widespread student unrest in Germany and elsewhere, Dorst became a center of controversy with his new play, *Toller: Szenen aus einer deutschen Revolution* (Toller: scenes from a German revolution). Ernst Toller (1893-1939), a great German poet and dramatist of expressionism, took part in a short-lived but violent revolution at the end of World War I and was elected president of the Bavarian Soviet Republic, which was soon suppressed by the right-wing militarists. Condemned to prison for a relatively short term (unlike other revolutionaries, who were summarily executed), Toller, after the rise of the Nazis, became a refugee in the United States, where he committed suicide in 1939. Based partly on Toller's autobiographical memoirs, Dorst portrays Toller as a sincere but muddle-headed idealist who plays a role of a revolutionary as if he were an actor on the stage; with such a leader, the revolution was bound to fail. The widow of another prominent revolutionary presented in the play accused Dorst of having falsified the facts to suit his theatrical idea, and students and the leftist press claimed that he had exposed to ridicule the whole concept of revolution. In spite of, or because of, the controversy, the play was staged by numerous theaters in Germany and abroad, and a version of it ran on German television. Dorst proved that he was not afraid to create social and political debate by creating other semidocumentary plays, among which *Eiszeit* (ice age) was just as contentious. It treats Knut Hamsun (1859-1952), Norwegian novelist and dramatist, the winner of the Nobel Prize for Literature (1920), who, when Germans occupied Norway during World War II, sided with the collaborationist government of Vidkun Quisling and after the war was locked in an old people's home.

In 1970, Dorst was invited to spend some time as a writer-in-residence at Oberlin College in Ohio, and in 1973 he lectured at universities in Australia and New Zealand. Starting in 1974, Dorst worked together with his life companion, Ursula Ehler, on a long history of an upper-class German family that is in part rooted in the experiences of his own family. This family chronicle yielded several self-contained plays as well as prose works, television dramas, and films.

In the 1970's and 1980's, Dorst achieved a considerable success as a film director, his films gaining honors at various festivals. He has been elected to a number of German academies and is a prominent member of the writers' association, PEN. In 1990, Dorst was awarded the prestigious Büchner Prize. In 1994, he was conferred the title Dramatist of the Year by German drama critics.

ANALYSIS

Tankred Dorst's plays are distinguished above all by their craftsmanship and theatrical sensibility, which arise no doubt from Dorst's early preoccupation with puppet theater and his conviction that the stage is an instrument through which a dramatist can filter his creative ideas. With his first performed play, *Gesellschaft im Herbst*, Dorst exhibited his talent for presenting not only the characters of his play but also the setting and situations in which they find themselves as a theatrical artifice. Only rarely does he allow "the truth of life" or "the tragic sense of disillusionment" to be sensed from behind the scrim that he intentionally places between his play and the audience. Although this first play may remind one of Jean Giraudoux's *La Folle de Chaillot* (pr., pb. 1945; *The Madwoman of Chaillot*, 1947) in its effete, aristocratically seedy milieu as well as its burlesquing of the material greed of the aggressive commercial class, Dorst's play fundamentally differs from the older model. His play seems to be concerned less with the conflict between old values and twentieth century avariciousness and barbarism than it is with the prevalent human tendency to prefer illusion to reality, the ease with which people are ready to believe in the most preposterous suggestions—in this case, that an enormous treasure lies buried in the foundations of a castle. Thus, from the very beginning, Dorst was less interested in psychological realism than in playing out universal themes by way of theatrical magic.

Dorst's next performed dramas reiterate some of his basic ideas, which are expertly developed in three one-act plays that immediately followed. In *Freedom for Clemens*, he subtly manipulates the conceit that human beings can readily be convinced by others to accept the conditions of slavery as being those of freedom; in *The Curve*, the common assumption of social order and purpose in the world is quickly turned upside down to reveal a vision of frightening absurdity; and in *Great Tirade at the Town-Wall*, the authorities toy with ordinary citizens until they are reduced to ranters lamenting their fate with no one to hear them.

Dorst's dramas, however, should not be reduced to a few overriding ideas, for this would deny his virtuosity, the skill with which he constructs his plays. The Countess de Villars-Brancas in *Gesellschaft im Herbst* appears at first to be easy prey for unscrupulous treasure diggers and other social vultures and hangers-on. Soon, however, she is revealed as a metaphor for an "autumn society" that has outlived its usefulness and is ready to decamp, but not before the rest of society's dregs and their frenzied "dance around the Golden Calf" are exposed. In *Freedom for Clemens*, Dorst underscores the Everyman features of Clemens, who is imprisoned for an undisclosed transgression, by giving him and other actors in the play puppetlike movements. They are supposed, however, to possess the agility of jugglers and acrobats.

Although Dorst borrows from the French absurdist theater, the techniques employed in several of his plays hark back to the old Italian *commedia dell'arte* and beyond, including masks and plays-within-plays. The absence of seriousness on the surface of his plays is contradicted, however, by disturbing thoughts at their core. Thus in *Freedom for Clemens*, the question arises as to the meaning of freedom in general: If one is nestled comfortably in any one place, protected from viewing the outside world—like Clemens in his cell—and thus voluntarily relinquishing the freedom of often precarious commitment outside, preferring the safe containment within the four walls, is one then free or captive? Can one avoid seeing, by extension, parallel examples in the world at large? Is the word "freedom" merely a slogan to be placed on banners, a cliché without any deeper meaning?

THE CURVE

The grotesque one-act play *The Curve* is similarly disturbing. It presents two symbiotic brothers (one works with his hands, the other with his head, like Gogo and Didi in Samuel Beckett's *En attendant Godot*, pb. 1952, pr. 1953; *Waiting for Godot*, 1954) who exist in an almost idyllic way at a dangerous bend in the road. They are creatures of ordinary, even cozy, domesticity who make their living from accidents that regularly happen at the curve. Their absurd profession—fashioning coffins for victims, burying them with proper ritual, repairing and then selling the victims' cars—parodies respectable and industrious ways of making a living. The latest victim, a highly placed government official who ignored the brothers' letters to him in reference to the dangerous curve, while appearing dead, suddenly recovers from the accident and pledges to remove the fatal hazard. At the prospect of losing their livelihood, the brothers murder the official and he is solemnly buried like the rest. The conditions whereby some people die and others benefit from their death are thus perpetuated. The farcical tone and the absurdity of the plot are underscored by the hypocritical rhetoric, the contrast between those who have "our best interests at heart," on one hand, and the gruesomeness of the underlying reality, on the other.

GREAT TIRADE AT THE TOWN-WALL

Great Tirade at the Town-Wall, which has as its source an ancient Chinese shadow play, immediately impresses the spectator with its simple but powerful setting, which recalls the Chinese costume plays by Bertolt Brecht. A fisher-woman beats against an enormous wall guarded by the imperial army, pleading that her soldier-husband be returned to her. Because he is dead, another soldier feigns to be her husband, and the imperial officers decide to have fun at the expense of the unfortunate woman. She is to prove that the man who claims to be the missing soldier is indeed her husband, for she is quite prepared—though knowing the truth—to take him as such. She fails, not because she cannot pretend, which she masterfully does, but because the passion

with which she pursues her cause frightens the soldier away. Having lost, she laments her fate before the silent city wall.

Although some critics have seen in the play the metaphor of an ever-present barrier dividing those in power, who toy with other people's lives, and the abject supplicants, who are always losers in their quest, other critics consider the central play-within-a-play representative of the perennial difficulty of establishing a mutual understanding between a man and a woman. The man flees from the all-embracing protectiveness of a strong, articulate woman to the more adventurous, albeit more dangerous, life of a soldier.

TOLLER

Dorst's semidocumentary plays, based on politically engaged historical figures, made him a celebrated if controversial dramatist. Toller, as noted above, appeared at a critical point in the political and social life of Germany. After more than two decades of apparently acquiescing to the idea of "not shaking the boat," accepting as normal the utter commercialization and even militarization of one Germany and the collectivization and Sovietization of the other, German young radicals clamored against all authority, proclaiming the necessity of wholesale social revolution. When Dorst branded Toller as a self-dramatizing idealist who plays roles from his own plays—notably *Masse-Mensch* (pr. 1920, pb. 1921; *Masses and Man*, 1924)—thus belying the bloody political as well as human reality of the revolution, that was more than the rebellious youth or liberal intellectual press could take. Students especially felt betrayed by a member of the intelligentsia from whom they would have expected support for their struggle for a more just society. When Dorst, in *Toller*, presented both sides of the uprising, showing the revolutionaries as well as the right-wing militarists to be contemptuous of human lives, the leftists charged that Dorst's play had distorted the truth, advocating the bourgeois view of revolution as an aberration of normal social behavior.

Aside from its questionable political import, *Toller* succeeds as an effective though disconcerting spectacle: Scenes of political caucusing are placed against scenes of private life; impassioned humanitarian appeals against macabre scenes of anti-Semitic students masked with clownishly exaggerated Jewish noses chanting and dancing; and the servant girl's indifference to her student lover's attempt of raising her social conscience against executions and trials that in themselves mock justice and humanity. All these scenes, independently arranged in the Brechtian manner, dramatically reinforced with films, placards and oversized puppets, present a show of shattered dreams and painful nightmares.

EISZEIT

Dorst's disdain for all preconceived political opinions and his disregard for the prevalent ideological pressure were made even more explicit in *Eiszeit*. The subject, a Quisling collaborator, was provocative, especially when the man in question was Knut Hamsun, an acknowledged giant of Norwegian and world literature. That there was no outright condemnation of the traitor was, to the majority, altogether appalling. Though Hamsun's arrogance and contempt for democracy and his shameless recalcitrance and political perversity were in no way concealed in the play, there was at least a tinge of admiration for his "being true to himself," for not yielding to this or that suggestion of what he should do or think. Dorst is interested in questions of morality, human decency, and integrity, but he loads the questions when he posits them in such a way that they appear somewhat blunted: Why, he asks, should a writer have deeper political insights than other citizens? Does literary fame have anything to do with a writer's political and moral integrity? *Eiszeit*, however, is not as effective theater as *Toller* is. The young partisan, who is filled with hatred for the old writer and mopes around the old people's home where Hamsun is kept under investigation, is supposed to be Hamsun's antagonist and counterweight in the scale of social values and political morality. His enmity, however, is inadequately articulated, and his challenges in no way balance out the old man's arguments; moreover, his suicide—an admission of defeat in the face of Hamsun's fascinating impenetrability—is dramatically unconvincing. Ultimately, Dorst's portrayal of Hamsun does not add much to the audience's understanding of a man whose only regret is that he is now old and helpless, frozen in his "ice age."

DER VERBOTENE GARTEN

Another play that centers on a famous writer—one who, like Hamsun, evoked as much denunciation and ridicule as he did admiration—is *Der verbotene Garten* (the forbidden garden), which was first produced as a radio play and then, in 1984, as a stage drama. The work revolves around Gabriele D'Annunzio, the Italian poet, novelist, dramatist, and aviator. Physically unprepossessing, he cleverly cultivated his image as a great lover (his liaison with the famous actress Eleonora Duse was well publicized in his novel *Il fuoco* (1900; *The Flame of Life*, 1900) and a great national hero (based on his Fiume expedition in 1919). D'Annunzio's "patriotic" exploits and his intimate friendship with Benito Mussolini contributed to the general rise of chauvinistic and fascistic sentiments in Italy after World War I.

THE FAMILY PLAYS

In the late 1970's, Dorst, in cooperation with Ehler, wrote a number of plays dealing with a German family that were in part based on autobiographical details. The comedy *Auf dem Chimborazo* (on the Chimborazo) and his subsequent plays *Die Villa* (the villa) and *Heinrich: Oder, Die Schmerzen der Phantasie* (Henry: or, the pain of fantasy), in addition to his prose and television works, represent various stages in a long family chronicle, which depicts a well-to-do German family caught in the historical upheaval and catastrophic events of the crucial years between the 1920's and the 1950's. The destiny of Germany is juxtaposed to the fortunes of the family members, each with different political as well as social loyalties, biases, hopes, and preconceptions. Although Dorst continued to avoid making any judgments, political or otherwise, the underlying tone of these plays is darker, and a sense of pessimistic disillusionment has crept in. The characters in the family chronicle cannot learn from their painful experience but continue clinging to their self-deluding images until they perish, which seemingly they must. The chance to begin anew, either on a personal or a national level, has been frittered away, often through stubborn foolishness and a false sense of pride.

MERLIN

What remains is an individual as well as a national wasteland, as Dorst makes clear in the subtitle to his monumental Arthurian spectacle, *Merlin*. *Merlin* is the story of the modern world: the bankruptcy of all utopian ideals. Consisting of ninety-seven scenes covering 375 pages, *Merlin* is a kaleidoscope composed with most diverse elements: fairy tales and comic-strip-like scenes, myth and farce, bits of dialogue and colorful but loose episodes, history and legend. Merlin, the Celtic magician, is the central character and at the same time the master of ceremonies who puts into motion this spectacular vision. To give the play its proper cosmic significance, Dorst introjects a Faustian bet that concerns nothing less than the destiny of humankind. The outcome is never in doubt, as the subtitle indicates. The human beings will senselessly destroy themselves in a chimerical ideological battle and leave this earth a wasteland.

That Dorst would gravitate toward television and cinema seemed natural. His dramatic flair, his large theatrical visions, are perhaps constrained by the physical confines of the stage. In whatever medium Dorst chooses to create, however, he will continue to astound his audiences with his inventiveness and theatrical mastery.

LATER PLAYS

Dorst's later plays turned minimalist in terms of plot and language. He based his play *Korbes* on a Grimm fairy tale, using it to convey a feminist message against male bullying. Korbes mistreats his housekeeper to such a degree that she finally leaves him, although he has gone blind. Korbes's daughter replaces the housekeeper, but his bullying becomes even worse than before. The play does not offer any redemption. As the curtain falls, the male protagonist is thrashing around with his stick, while his daughter avoids getting hit.

His *Herr Paul* is based on the slogan "Who lives, irritates." The protagonist, Mr. Paul, does not want to irritate and lives a totally passive life in an old soap factory that Mr. Helm wants to renovate and convert into a coin-operated laundry. Helm and his business partner want to evict Mr. Paul from his residence, but their rantings are in vain. Mr. Paul's passive aggres-

siveness wins out against modern enterprise.

Die Schattenlinie (the shadow line) deals with neo-nationalism and racism in modern Germany: The liberal protagonist Malthus is confronted by the fact that his son Jens has murdered a black man from Sierra Leone. Malthus defends his liberal philosophy that has been defeated by his own son. In *Nach Jerusalem* (travel to Jerusalem), a group of outcasts from society living in the basement of a hotel under construction show through their insane actions and demonstrations that they will reach their "New Jerusalem," a place of redemption and happiness. *Die Legende vom armen Heinrich* (the legend of poor Henry) is an anachronistic reenactment of the legend of a medieval knight who is cured of leprosy by the love of a pure young girl. Although often dealing with issues of public concern, such as neo-nationalism and racism, Dorst's late plays have become increasingly private and mystic in subject matter and dramatic representation.

OTHER MAJOR WORKS

NONFICTION: *Geheimnis der Marionette*, 1957; *Auf kleiner Bühne: Versuche mit Marionetten*, 1959; "Die Bühne ist der absolut Ort," 1962; *Was sollen wir tun: Variationen über ein Thema von Leo Tolstoi*, 1996 (with Ursula Ehler).

BIBLIOGRAPHY

Giles, Steve. "The Anxiety of Influence of Tankred Dorst's *Deutsche Stücke*." In *A Radical Stage: Theatre in Germany in the 1970's and 1980's*, edited by W. G. Sebald. New York: Berg, 1988. Deals with Dorst's political commitment and the politicization of the West German stage in the 1970's and 1980's.

Hayman, Ronald, ed. *The German Theater: A Symposium*. New York: Barnes & Noble, 1975. Symposium proceedings dealing with German theater of the 1970's.

Innes, Christopher D. *Modern German Drama: A Study in Form*. Cambridge, England: Cambridge University Press, 1979. A monograph that devotes approximately eight pages to Tankred Dorst.

Frank S. Lambasa,
updated by Ehrhard Bahr

JOHN DRINKWATER

Born: Leytonstone, England; June 1, 1882
Died: London, England; March 25, 1937

PRINCIPAL DRAMA

Ser Taldo's Bride, pr. 1911 (one act; adaptation of
   Barry Jackson's play)
Cophetua, pr., pb. 1911
An English Medley, pr., pb. 1911 (masque; music
   by Ruthland Boughton)
Puss in Boots, pr., pb. 1911
The Pied Piper: A Tale of Hamelin City, pr., pb.
   1912 (masque; music by S. W. Sylvester)
*The Only Legend: A Masque of the Scarlet
   Pierrot*, pr., pb. 1913 (masque; music by
   J. Brier)
Rebellion, pr., pb. 1914
Robin Hood and the Pedlar, pr., pb. 1914 (masque;
   music by Brier)
The Storm, pr. 1914, pb. 1915 (one act)
The God of Quiet, pr., pb. 1916 (one act)
The Wounded, pr. 1917
X = O: A Night of the Trojan War, pr., pb. 1917
   (one act)
Abraham Lincoln, pr., pb. 1918
Oliver Cromwell, pb. 1921, pr. 1923
Mary Stuart, pr., pb. 1921
Robert E. Lee, pr., pb. 1923
Robert Burns, pb. 1924
The Collected Plays of John Drinkwater, pb. 1925
   (2 volumes)
The Mayor of Casterbridge, pr., pb. 1926
   (adaptation of Thomas Hardy's novel)
Bird in Hand, pr., pb. 1927
John Bull Calling: A Political Parable in One Act,
   pr., pb. 1928
A Man's House, pr. 1931, pb. 1934
Napoleon: The Hundred Days, pr., pb. 1932
   (adaptation of Giovacchino Forzano and Benito
   Mussolini's play *Campo di Maggio*)
Laying the Devil, pr., pb. 1933
*Garibaldi: A Chronicle Play of Italian Freedom in
   Ten Scenes*, pb. 1936

OTHER LITERARY FORMS

Starting in 1903 with *Poems*, John Drinkwater published a number of volumes of poetry, the most significant of which are *Poems, 1908-1914* (1917), *Poems, 1908-1919* (1919), *Selected Poems* (1922), *New Poems* (1925), and *The Collected Poems of John Drinkwater* (in three volumes, two published in 1923 and one in 1937). His most important critical and biographical studies are *William Morris: A Critical Study* (1912), *Swinburne: An Estimate* (1913), *Lincoln, The World Emancipator* (1920), *The Pilgrim of Eternity: Byron—A Conflict* (1925), *Mr. Charles, King of England* (1926), *Cromwell: A Character Study* (1927), *Charles James Fox* (1928), *Pepys: His Life and Character* (1930), and *Shakespeare* (1933). His autobiographical volumes are *Inheritance* (1931) and *Discovery* (1932); they cover only the period to 1913.

ACHIEVEMENTS

For three decades, from early in the twentieth century until he died in 1937, John Drinkwater was a consummate man of the theater—a playwright, actor, producer, director, and critic. Foremost among his achievements was his role in the organization and development of the Birmingham Repertory Theatre, one of Great Britain's most innovative and influential companies. In addition, the popular success of his verse dramas encouraged other playwrights to work in the same genre, and his prose play *Abraham Lincoln* was the most notable historical-biographical play of its time. Both it and the earlier verse drama *X = O* were important expressions of antiwar sentiment, to which audiences responded enthusiastically, and *Abraham Lincoln* enjoyed long runs in London and New York. Active as he was in the theater, Drinkwater was also a prolific man of letters. He wrote critical studies of Algernon Charles Swinburne, William Morris, and William Shakespeare; biographies of such famous men as Abraham Lincoln, King Charles I, Oliver Cromwell, Samuel Pepys, and Lord Byron; a novel; essays; and film scripts. He also was a major poet in the Georgian movement. Although he

John Drinkwater (Hulton Archive by Getty Images)

was a popular poet, critics did not regard his poetry favorably, labeling it derivative, unimaginative, and sentimental.

Though public and critical interest in him had faded by the time of his death, and he and his work have been largely ignored in the decades that followed, Drinkwater merits at least a footnote in studies of modern English drama for his attempts to revitalize poetic drama in the twentieth century and to develop the chronicle play into a viable modern dramatic form. More than most playwrights, he brought to his craft (as Arnold Bennett put it) "a deep, practical knowledge of the stage."

BIOGRAPHY

John Drinkwater was born on June 1, 1882, in Leytonstone, Essex, England, to Albert Edwin and Annie Beck Brown Drinkwater. His father, headmaster of the Coburn Foundation School at Bow, in East London, had been active in amateur theatricals and, in 1886, embarked on a career in the theater as an ac-

tor, playwright, and manager (setting a pattern for his son to follow years later). Because his mother was terminally ill, young Drinkwater was sent to live with his maternal grandfather in Oxford when he was nine. An indifferent student, he left Oxford High School in 1897 for Nottingham, where he worked for the Northern Assurance Company and did some acting in amateur productions. His transfer in 1901 to the Birmingham branch of the firm was a fortuitous move, for there he met Barry Jackson, a well-to-do theater enthusiast (two years older than Drinkwater) who presented plays at his father's palatial home. When Jackson's group went public as the Pilgrim Players, Drinkwater joined them, and, in 1909, he gave up his career in insurance to work for the Players, becoming general manager in 1913 (by which time the Pilgrim Players had become the Birmingham Repertory Theatre and had a theater). By the time he left Jackson's employ in 1918, Drinkwater had directed more than sixty productions, had appeared (under the name of John Darnley) in about forty roles, and had written a number of plays, including *X = O* and *Abraham Lincoln*. His wife, Kathleen Walpole, whom he had married in 1906, also acted in the company (as Cathleen Orford).

The presentation of *Abraham Lincoln* at Sir Nigel Playfair's theater, the Lyric, in a London suburb, starting on February 19, 1919 (it had a run of four hundred performances), and its subsequent New York production made Drinkwater a celebrity on two continents. Birmingham gave him an M.A. in 1919, and he was in demand for lecture tours of the United States. On his return home, in 1921, from his second trip to the United States, Drinkwater met and fell in love with the violinist Daisy Kennedy. This shipboard romance led to an affair that culminated in the breakup of Drinkwater's marriage to Kathleen Walpole and of Kennedy's to Russian pianist Benno Moiseiwitsch. Drinkwater and Kennedy married in 1924 and during the next decade traveled widely on concert, lecture, and stage tours in the United States, on the Continent, and in Britain. They also became major figures on the London social circuit. Through this entire period, Drinkwater wrote for the stage; wrote articles, poems, and biographical and critical studies; did screenplays as well as lyrics for films; wrote two volumes of autobiography; and edited anthologies. He also continued to act, and shortly before he died—at his London home on March 25, 1937—appeared in the role of Prospero in a Regent's Park, London, production of Shakespeare's *The Tempest*.

ANALYSIS

In an early essay, "The Nature of Drama," John Drinkwater says that a person chooses to write drama "quite definitely with the response of a theatre audience in his mind, and it is for this, and not because of any inherent virtue which he finds in this form and in no other, that his choice is made." The public reaction to at least three of his plays—*X = O*, *Abraham Lincoln*, and *Bird in Hand*—suggests that he chose well.

COPHETUA

In the preface to his collected plays, Drinkwater says that his "affections have never been divided between poetry and drama," and he recalls that he hoped "to help as far as one could towards the restoration of the two upon the stage in union." Despite John Galsworthy's admonition to him that "the shadow of the man Shakespeare is across the path of all who should attempt verse drama in these days," Drinkwater was not deterred, and his first solo venture as a playwright (he previously had put a Barry Jackson sentimental comedy, *Ser Taldo's Bride*, into rhymed verse) was *Cophetua*, a one-act play in verse about a stubborn king who resists the demands of his mother and counselors that he wed but then decides to marry a beggar-maid, whose beauty and purity win over the aghast mother and counselors. Though the play has neither literary nor dramatic merit, it is of some interest, for the independent-minded Cophetua is a character type that reemerges in later Drinkwater plays. Drinkwater wrote the play as a conscious experiment: "I used a variety of measures for the purpose of seeing whether a rapid and changing movement of rhyme might not to some extent produce the same effect on the stage as physical action." The effort failed, but Drinkwater concluded: "The experiment, I think, showed that there were exciting possibilities in the method, and if I had been born into a theatre that took kindly to verse as a medium I be-

lieve that interesting things might have been done in its development."

REBELLION

Drinkwater's only full-length poetic drama, *Rebellion*, also was a failure, in large part because of its overly rhetorical blank verse (which Drinkwater "stripped . . . of a little of its rhetoric" in the printed version). Nevertheless, it remains interesting because it recalls William Butler Yeats's *The King's Threshold* (pr. 1904), also about a struggle between a king and a poet, and foreshadows later Drinkwater plays that focus on war and the conflict between liberty and tyranny.

THE STORM

Little more than a curtain raiser, *The Storm* also has an Irish connection, for it is a contemporary rural tragedy that echoes John Millington Synge's *Riders to the Sea* (pb. 1903). The only one of Drinkwater's poetic dramas with a contemporary setting, *The Storm* is about women vainly awaiting the return of the man of the house, who is lost in a storm. The conflict centers on the boundless optimism of the young wife and the insistent pessimism of an old neighbor. Though blank verse is too stately a measure for the occasion, the play does possess tragic intensity, primarily because of the fully developed character of the wife, Alice, who is Drinkwater's most memorable creation.

THE GOD OF QUIET

The death in 1915 of poet Rupert Brooke, who was serving in the Royal Naval Division, heightened Drinkwater's antipathy toward war. He had met Brooke through Sir Edward Marsh, editor of *Georgian Poetry* (1912-1922), in which both were represented, and the two had become close friends. Drinkwater's last verse plays, *The God of Quiet* and *X = O*, are complementary works that reflect both sorrow over Brooke's death and disdain for war. The earlier of these one-act plays is the lesser of the two.

In *The God of Quiet*, war-weary people (young and old beggars, a citizen, and a soldier) meet at a life-size statue of their god, a Buddha-like figure, where they are joined by their king, who also has tired of the lengthy conflict and now preaches humility and love. The enemy king comes in prepared to resume the battle, denounces the God of Quiet for having "slacked the heat" and turned the people against war, and drives his dagger into the god's heart. The effigy comes to life, cries out "Not one of you in all the world to know me," and collapses. The first king is angered ("Why did you do it? He was a friendly god,/ Smiling upon our faults, a great for-giver . . ./ He gave us quietness—"), curses his en-emy, draws his sword, and vows "to requite the hon-our of this god." The din of war is heard as the curtain falls. Although the message is clear, the play lacks impact because the generalized characters are merely two-dimensional (not at all universal types), the dia-logue is stilted, and the setting lacks precision.

X = O

On the other hand, $X = O$, the theme of which is the same, is a play of enduring sensitivity and impact. Briefer even than *The God of Quiet*, $X = O$ was a crit-ical and popular success when first presented, and the passage of time has not dimmed its luster. Its struc-ture is simple: Set during the ninth year of the Trojan War, the parallel scenes of the play show a pair of Greek soldiers and then two Trojan warriors lament-ing what they consider a futile war, regretting the need to kill their adversaries, and yearning to return home. Each man is named and distinctively individu-alized, and all share an appreciation of the beauty and promise of life; as the mathematical equation in the title suggests, the erstwhile enemies are portrayed as sharing character traits and aspirations.

One of the youths in each camp must leave for his daily chore of killing an enemy soldier. The Greek who remains, a poet, is killed by the Trojan who is a would-be statesman with a dream of "Troy regener-ate." The Trojan who stays behind, a sculptor, is killed by the Greek who wants to become a politician. On each side, then, an artist is slain by an aspiring politician, a representative of the state, a detail that surely has its genesis in the deaths of Brooke and other young poets of Drinkwater's generation in World War I, which was at its height when Drinkwater wrote the play.

In writing his five verse plays, Drinkwater at-tempted "to find some other constructional idiom whereby verse might be accepted as a natural thing

by a modern audience." By 1917, however, despite the popular success of $X = O$, Drinkwater had (as he reports in his autobiography) "a growing conviction that if I was to take any effective part in the practical theatre of my time, I should have to abandon verse for prose. Full of reforming ideas as we all were, I soon began to realise that in this fundamental matter of expression it would be futile, and indeed pointless, to try to alter the habit of an age." Somewhat defen-sive about his decision, he says in the preface to the collected plays:

The transition from verse to prose, from $X = O$, that is, to *Abraham Lincoln*, was not a surrender, but a recog-nition that any chance of development in one's dra-matic technique depends upon an acceptance of the fact that if one insists on staying in the theatre at all one may be anything one likes so long as one is not doctrinaire. The problem to be solved was how to keep in the sparest prose idiom something of the enthusiasm and poignancy of verse. In the days when verse was the natural speech of the theatre, its beauty, like the beauty of all fine style, reached the audience without any insistence upon itself. The guiding principle of the speech of these plays later than $X = O$ has been, so far as I could manage it, to make it beautiful without let-ting anybody know about it.

ABRAHAM LINCOLN

Abraham Lincoln was a transitional work for Drinkwater; although it was his first prose play, the dramatic tableaux that dominate this chronicle are linked by choral odes in verse. The play was closely tied to its immediate predecessors by its theme as well, for it is as obviously an antiwar drama as is $X = O$. It also set the pattern for Drinkwater's plays *Oliver Cromwell* and *Robert E. Lee*; all three of these histori-cal plays dramatize the problem of leadership, and each is developed in a series of episodes that chrono-logically traces the development of the hero and cumu-latively delineates his personality. Indeed, Drinkwater said that he conceived of the three plays as a unit and according to "a more or less definite plan."

In a note included in the first edition of *Abraham Lincoln*, Drinkwater says that his "purpose is not that of the historian but of the dramatist . . . of the drama-tist, not that of the political philosopher," and that his "concern is with the profoundly dramatic interest of [Lincoln's] character, and with the inspiring example of a man who handled war nobly and with imagination." Given his primary aim, he has "freely telescoped [historical] events, and imposed invention upon [their] movement, in such ways as I needed to shape the dramatic significance of my subject."

Abraham Lincoln begins in Springfield, Illinois, with townsmen talking of their neighbor's nomination for the presidency; it concludes with the assassination of the president at Ford's Theatre. Lincoln is portrayed as a peace-loving man who endures the agonies of war for the sake of lasting freedom. His last speech, given to the theater audience immediately before his assassination, epitomizes his character; he concludes: "With malice toward none, with charity for all, it is for us to resolve that this nation, under God, shall have a new birth of freedom; and that government of the people, by the people, for the people, shall not perish from the earth." Drinkwater's use of Lincoln's words in this context typifies the dramatic license that he exercises throughout the play.

When originally produced at the Birmingham Repertory Theatre on October 12, 1918, the play was a great hit. This provincial success did not assure a West End opening, however. In fact, managers either ignored or rejected it, and the London production was at Hammersmith, a suburb. Enlightened by its popularity there, West End managers tried unsuccessfully to convince Sir Nigel Playfair to bring it to the city. Finally, the city came to the play. The public loved it, for *Abraham Lincoln* was timely and obviously touched a responsive chord, a pervasive concern among people living with war and desiring peace, and brought admiration for a strong, principled leader who could guide his country through a dangerous period. Another determining factor in the popular success of the play was that the United States and Great Britain had jointly fought in a common cause, and the British, who had become increasingly interested in American history, saw in the play a reflection of their own sufferings and triumphs. In like manner, when *Abraham Lincoln* was produced in New York (for which production Drinkwater made his first trip to the United States, appearing in the play as a chroni-

cler), Americans responded favorably to the patriotic theme and noted the intended parallels between Lincoln and Woodrow Wilson. In sum, it matters not that today, *Abraham Lincoln* seems closer to melodrama than it is to tragedy; it was the right play for its time.

BIRD IN HAND

Among Drinkwater's other plays (and masques, a form of which he was fond), *Bird in Hand* merits attention, in part because it is an atypical light comedy in the tradition of Oliver Goldsmith's *She Stoops to Conquer* (pr. 1773), but also because it shows Drinkwater's skill at orchestrating a varied group of well-developed characters in a realistic Midlands setting. His familiarity with the Cotswolds, where he rented a cottage for a time and about which he wrote in *Cotswold Characters* (1921), is apparent. The plot revolves about the reluctance of an innkeeper to permit his daughter to marry the son of a local baronet as he believes that people should keep to their station in life. The efforts of his daughter, wife, and assorted guests fail to persuade him to renounce his prejudices, and he is moved to consent only through trickery. Although the plot is not very original, the play succeeds because Drinkwater gave his characters—stereotypical though they are—a measure of individuality, and he had them speak realistic dialogue. Further, the frivolity of the complications and the lightness of style and tone do not obscure the serious dimension of the play: an examination of the perennial problem of the generation gap. Coming almost ten years after the success of *Abraham Lincoln*, which prompted him to move to London, *Bird in Hand* marked Drinkwater's triumphant return to the Birmingham Repertory Theatre. The play was first produced there, with Drinkwater directing and including Peggy Ashcroft and Laurence Olivier as the young lovers. Its subsequent popularity in London and New York rivaled that of *Abraham Lincoln*, and reviewers on both sides of the Atlantic were generally more enthusiastic than they had been about any of Drinkwater's other plays.

OTHER MAJOR WORKS
POETRY: *Poems*, 1903; *Poems, 1908-1914*, 1917; *Poems, 1908-1919*, 1919; *Selected Poems*, 1922; *New*

Poems, 1925; *The Collected Poems of John Drink-water*, 1923-1937 (3 volumes).

NONFICTION: *William Morris: A Critical Study*, 1912; *Swinburne: An Estimate*, 1913; *Lincoln, The World Emancipator*, 1920; *Cotswold Characters*, 1921; *The Pilgrim of Eternity: Byron—A Conflict*, 1925; *Mr. Charles, King of England*, 1926; *Cromwell: A Character Study*, 1927; *Charles James Fox*, 1928; *Pepys: His Life and Character*, 1930; *Inheritance*, 1931; *Discovery*, 1932; *Shakespeare*, 1933.

BIBLIOGRAPHY

Abercrombie, Lascelles. "The Drama of John Drinkwater." *Four Decades of Poetry, 1890-1930* 1, no. 4 (1977): 271-281. Abercrombie was a fellow dramatist who also wrote one-act verse plays in the 1920's. This article, an edited version of a previously unpublished 1934 lecture, contains a discussion of verse drama and the possibilities for its acceptance by twentieth century audiences and analyses of Drinkwater's plays.

Berven, Peter. "John Drinkwater: An Annotated Bibliography of Writings About Him." *English Literature in Transition: 1880-1920* 21 (1978): 9-66. Introduced by a two-page biographical-critical statement, this comprehensive work contains almost five hundred annotated entries, covering the full range of Drinkwater's career as playwright, poet, critic, biographer, and anthologist.

Clark, Keith. *The Muse Colony: Rupert Brooks, Edward Thomas, Robert Frost, and Friends: Dymock, 1914*. Bristol, England: Redcliffe, 1992. A look at the Dymock group of poets, to which Drinkwater belonged. Bibliography and index.

Gale, Steve H. "John Drinkwater." In *Late Nineteenth and Early Twentieth Century British Literary Biographers*, edited by Steven Serafin. Vol. 149 in *Dictionary of Literary Biography*. Detroit, Mich.: The Gale Group, 1995. A concise overview of the life and works of Drinkwater.

Parker, Rennie. *The Georgian Poets: Abercrombie, Brooke, Drinkwater, Gibson, and Thomas*. Plymouth, England: Northcote House in association with the British Council, 1999. A look at the poets Drinkwater, Lascelles Abercrombie, Rupert Brooke, Wilfrid Wilson Gibson, and Edward Thomas. Provides insight into Drinkwater's dramatic works. Bibliography and index.

Gerald H. Strauss

JOHN DRYDEN

Born: Aldwinckle, England; August 19, 1631
Died: London, England; May 1, 1700

PRINCIPAL DRAMA

The Wild Gallant, pr. 1663, pb. 1669
The Indian Queen, pr. 1664, pb. 1665
The Rival Ladies, pr., pb. 1664
The Indian Emperor: Or, The Conquest of Mexico by the Spaniards, pr. 1665, pb. 1667
Secret Love: Or, The Maiden Queen, pr. 1667, pb. 1668

Sir Martin Mar-All: Or, The Feign'd Innocence, pr. 1667, pb. 1668 (adaptation of Molière's *L'Étourdi*; with William Cavendish, duke of Newcastle)
The Tempest: Or, The Enchanted Island, pr. 1667, pb. 1670 (adaptation of William Shakespeare's play; with Sir William Davenant)
An Evening's `Love: Or, The Mock Astrologer, pr. 1668, pb. 1671 (adaptation of Thomas Corneille's *Le Feint Astrologue*)
Tyrannic Love: Or, The Royal Martyr, pr. 1669, pb. 1670

The Conquest of Granada by the Spaniards, Part I,
    pr. 1670, pb. 1672

The Conquest of Granada by the Spaniards, Part II,
    pr. 1671, pb. 1672

Marriage à la Mode, pr. 1672, pb. 1673

The Assignation: Or, Love in a Nunnery, pr. 1672,
    pb. 1673

*Amboyna: Or, The Cruelties of the Dutch to the
    English Merchants*, pr., pb. 1673

Aureng-Zebe, pr. 1675, pb. 1676

The State of Innocence, and Fall of Man, pb. 1677
    (libretto; dramatic version of John Milton's
    Paradise Lost)

All for Love: Or, The World Well Lost, pr. 1677, pb.
    1678

The Kind Keeper: Or, Mr. Limberham, pr. 1678, pb.
    1680

Oedipus, pr. 1678, pb. 1679 (with Nathaniel Lee)

Troilus and Cressida: Or, Truth Found Too Late,
    pr., pb. 1679

The Spanish Friar: Or, The Double Discovery, pr.
    1680, pb. 1681

The Duke of Guise, pr. 1682, pb. 1683 (with Lee)

Albion and Albanius, pr., pb. 1685 (libretto; music
    by Louis Grabu)

Don Sebastian, King of Portugal, pr. 1689, pb.
    1690

Amphitryon: Or, the Two Socia's, pr., pb. 1690

King Arthur: Or, The British Worthy, pr., pb. 1691
    (libretto; music by Henry Purcell)

Cleomenes, the Spartan Hero, pr., pb. 1692

Love Triumphant: Or, Nature Will Prevail, pr., pb.
    1694

The Secular Masque, pr., pb. 1700 (masque)

Dramatick Works, pb. 1717

The Works of John Dryden, pb. 1808 (18 volumes)

OTHER LITERARY FORMS

If one follows the practice of literary historians
and assigns John Milton to an earlier age, then John
Dryden stands as the greatest literary artist in England between 1660 and 1700, a period sometimes
designated "the Age of Dryden." In addition to his
achievements in drama, he excelled in poetry, translation, and literary criticism. He wrote some two hun-

John Dryden (Library of Congress)

dred original English poems over a period of more
than forty years, including the best poetic satires of
his age, memorable odes, and a variety of verse epistles, elegies, religious poems, panegyrics, and lyrics.
His prologues and epilogues, attached to his dramas
and those of his contemporaries, stand as the highest
achievements in English in that minor poetic genre.

For every verse of original poetry Dryden wrote,
he translated two from another poet. Moreover, he
translated two long volumes of prose from French
originals—in 1684, Louis Maimbourg's *Histoire de
la Ligue* (1684) and, in 1688, Dominique Bouhours's
La Vie de Saint François Xavier (1683)—and he had
a hand in the five-volume translation of Plutarch's
Bioi paralleloi (c. 105-115; *Parallel Lives*, 1579)
published by Jacob Tonson in 1683. The translations
were usually well received, especially the editions of
Juvenal and Persius (1693) and Vergil (1697).

Dryden's literary criticism consists largely of
prefaces and dedications published throughout his ca-

reer and attached to other works. His only critical work that was published alone was *An Essay of Dramatic Poesy* (1668). As a critic, Dryden appears at his best when he evaluates an earlier poet or dramatist (Homer, Vergil, Ovid, Geoffrey Chaucer, William Shakespeare, Ben Jonson, John Fletcher), when he seeks to define a genre, or when he breaks new critical ground, as, for example, in providing definitions of "wit" or a theory of translation.

ACHIEVEMENTS

In a period of just over thirty years (1663-1694), John Dryden wrote or coauthored twenty-eight plays, an output that made him the most prolific dramatist of his day. His amplitude remains even more remarkable when one considers the amount of poetry, criticism, and translation he produced during the same period. This prolific production is equaled by the variety of the plays: heroic plays, political plays, operas, heroic tragedies, comedies, and tragicomedies. In his prefaces and other prose works, Dryden commented at some length on the various types of plays, seeking to define and to clarify the dramatic forms in which he wrote.

Yet Dryden himself recognized that his dramas were not likely to wear well, and his literary reputation today rests largely on his poetry and criticism. The operas *King Arthur* and *The State of Innocence* (which was not produced during his lifetime) survive primarily in their lyrics. Like other operas of the time, they were somewhat primitive, judged by modern standards, with relatively little music—something more akin to the masque or to modern musical comedy than to grand opera. The heroic plays are too artificial to appeal to any but the most devoted scholars of the period, and Dryden's comedies and tragicomedies suffer in comparison with those of his contemporaries, Sir George Etherege, William Wycherley, and William Congreve, not to mention his predecessors in English drama. As an index to the taste of the Restoration, however, the plays remain valuable and instructive, reflecting the levels of achievement and prevalent values of dramatic art of the time. Further, a study of Dryden reveals much about both aesthetic and intellectual influences on the drama of his period and the development of the dramatic genres of his age.

BIOGRAPHY

John Dryden was the eldest of fourteen children in a landed family of modest means whose sympathies were Puritan on both sides. Little is known of his youth in Northamptonshire, for Dryden, seldom hesitant about expressing his opinions, was reticent about details of his personal life. At about age fifteen, he was enrolled in Westminster School, then under the headmastership of Dr. Richard Busby, a school notable for its production of poets and bishops. Having attained at Westminster a thorough grounding in Latin, he proceeded to Cambridge, taking the B.A. in 1654. After the death of his father brought him a modest inheritance in the form of rents from family land, Dryden left the university and settled in London. Though little is known of his early years there, he served briefly in Oliver Cromwell's government in a minor position and may have worked for the publisher Henry Herringman. He produced an elegy on the death of Cromwell, yet when Charles II ascended the throne, Dryden greeted the new ruler with a congratulatory poem, *Astraea Redux* (1660). After the Restoration, he turned his main interest to the drama, producing an insignificant comedy, *The Wild Gallant*, and collaborating with Sir Robert Howard on a heroic play, *The Indian Queen*. He married Lady Elizabeth Howard, Sir Robert's sister, a marriage that brought him a generous dowry and, eventually, three sons in whom he took pride.

Throughout his career, Dryden was no stranger to controversy, whether literary, political, or religious; in fact, he seemed all too eager to seize an occasion for polemics. In literature, he challenged Sir Robert Howard's views on drama, Thomas Rymer's on criticism, and the earl of Rochester's and Thomas Shadwell's on questions of literary merit and taste. After receiving encouragement from Charles II, Dryden entered the political controversy over succession to the throne with *Absalom and Achitophel* (part 1, 1681; part 2, with Nahum Tate, 1682). Later, he explained his religious views by attacking Deists, Catholics, and Dissenters in *Religio Laici: Or, A Lay-*

man's Faith (1682); then, he shifted his ground and defended Catholicism in *The Hind and the Panther* (1687).

For a variety of reasons, Dryden was the most often assailed among major poets in his time, a fact attributable in some measure to envy. In an age when almost everyone prized his own wit, Dryden attained eminence without obviously possessing more of that quality than many others. Yet his willingness to plunge into controversy won him a host of enemies, and his changes of opinions and beliefs—literary, religious, political—made him vulnerable to criticism. Examining Dryden's changes of allegiance and point of view one by one, a biographer or critic can provide a logical explanation for each. This task is perhaps most difficult in literary criticism, where Dryden defended a position with enthusiasm only to abandon it later for another, which he advocated with an equal enthusiasm. To his contemporaries, some of his changes were to be explained by self-interest, and, rightly or wrongly, the charge of timeserving became a potent weapon in the hands of his critics.

In 1668, Dryden was appointed poet laureate, a position he held for twenty years, and he also signed a lucrative contract with the Theatre Royal to produce three new plays each year. Though he was unable to produce this stipulated number over the decade of the contract, he nevertheless received his share of theater revenues. During his term as laureate, he received a two-hundred-pound annual stipend, an amount that was later increased to three hundred pounds when he became historiographer royal, but irregularly paid. He was active as a dramatist throughout the 1670's, though he gradually turned his interest to poetic satire, beginning with *Mac Flecknoe: Or, A Satyre upon the True-Blew-Protestant Poet, T. S.* (1682).

With events surrounding the Popist Plot (1678) posing a threat to the government of Charles II, Dryden all but abandoned the theater, writing instead satires, translations, and then his religious poems. Initially, he carried the field for the king, but after the fall of James II and the loss of his political cause, he also lost the laureateship and its accompanying pension.

During the final period of his life, 1688-1700, Dryden made a brief return to the theater, producing an additional five dramas, but he devoted most of his considerable energy and talent to translations of poetry, achieving success with his patrons and public.

Analysis

John Dryden was a prolific playwright, creating heroic plays, political plays, operas, heroic tragedies, comedies, and tragicomedies; however, he is best remembered for his poetry and criticism, as many of his plays did not stand the test of time.

Marriage à la Mode

Dryden's best comedy is generally considered to be *Marriage à la Mode*. His others rely heavily on farcical situations and double entendre and, at times, inept licentiousness that makes comedies such as *The Assignation* and *The Kind Keeper* seem unnecessarily coarse even by the standards of his time. *Marriage à la Mode* combines in its two distinct plot lines the conventions of the romantic tragicomedy and the Restoration comedy of manners, a genre not fully established when Dryden produced his play.

The tragicomic plot involves the theme of succession, perhaps Dryden's most frequent dramatic theme after love and honor. Polydamas, having usurped the throne of Sicily, discovers two young persons of gentle birth but unknown parentage who have been living among fisher folk under the care of Hermogenes, a former courtier. When Hermogenes tells the usurper that Leonidas is his son, born after his wife had fled from him, the king accepts this as correct, even though Leonidas is actually the son of the king he had deposed. When Polydamas insists that Leonidas marry the daughter of his friend, Leonidas refuses because of his love for Palmyra, the girl with whom he had been discovered. To frustrate this passion, Polydamas seeks to banish her, whereupon Hermogenes declares that Palmyra is the king's daughter and claims Leonidas as his own son, for he cannot risk revealing the truth about Leonidas, in reality the rightful successor. Polydamas than seeks to have Palmyra marry his favorite, Argaleon, and banishes Leonidas, later changing the sentence to death. Facing execution, Leonidas manages to proclaim his right to the throne, to bring his captors over to his side, and to oust Polydamas, whom he generously forgives as the father of his beloved Palmyra.

The tragicomic characteristics are all present—the unusual setting; the usurper; the long-lost noble youth; the faithful servant; the idealization of romantic love, struggling successfully against the odds and triumphing. To heighten the tone, Dryden uses blank verse rather than prose and, in the most serious passages, employs rhymed heroic couplets. The tragicomic plot, in the manner of John Fletcher, reveals a significant debt to Elizabethan and Jacobean tragicomedies.

Whereas in the main plot, the attitude toward love is idealistic, the subplot represents a sharp contrast in the value placed on both love and marriage. Dryden creates two witty couples—Rhodophil and Doralice, Palamede and Melantha—the first pair married and the second engaged by arrangement of their parents. Their attitudes toward marriage and love are as cynical and sophisticated as is standard in the comedy of manners. Palamede hopes before marriage to carry off an affair with his friend Rhodophil's wife, while Rhodophil hopes to make Melantha his mistress. They freely satirize Puritans and country folk, and the prevailing attitude of society toward marriage is indicated by Rhodophil when he speaks of his wife, "Yet I loved her a whole half year, double the natural term of any mistress; and I think, in my conscience, I could have held out another quarter, but then the world began to laugh at me, and a certain shame, of being out of fashion, seized me." Disguises, masked balls, and assignations keep the plot lively and suspenseful, though the couples' goals are never realized because all plans either are intercepted or go awry, and at the end, they part still friends. Throughout, the dialogue sparkles with repartee unequaled in any of Dryden's other plays. It includes Melantha's affected French expressions along with much double entendre and innuendo, yet it is never brutally licentious in tone, as is true of dialogue in comedies such as *The Kind Keeper.*

Though the two plots are loosely connected, Rhodophil does bring the newly found gentlefolk to the court, and both he and Palamede unite to support Leonidas in the final act. Further, the attitudes of parents who arrange marriages are condemned in both plot lines. For the most part, however, the plots occur in two separate worlds—the witty and sophisticated world of the comedy of manners and the idealistic and sentimental world of tragicomedy.

HEROIC PLAYS

During the period from 1663 to 1680, Dryden wrote, entirely or in part, twenty-one plays. His initial success came with his heroic plays from *The Indian Queen* to *Aureng-Zebe*, by which time the genre had almost run its course. The heroic play was influenced by a variety of sources, including the English dramas of John Fletcher, the French tragedies of Pierre Corneille, and the French poetic romances of Madeleine de Scudéry and Gautier de Costes de La Calprenède. The most prominent feature that set the genre apart from the usual tragedy was the dialogue in heroic couplets, attributed to the playwrights' efforts to please Charles II, who, it was said, had come to enjoy the rhymed French drama he saw during his years in exile. Dryden defended the artificiality of rhymed dialogue on the grounds that the plays dealt with conflicts and characters above the commonplace; thus, the stylistic elevation provided by rhyme was appropriate. The characters, however, engage in lengthy rhymed speeches, usually with two characters confronting each other, and the result has seemed in a later time excessively artificial.

The plays frequently employ spectacle, enhanced by songs, dances, and elaborate costumes. The settings are usually exotic rather than English, thus heightening their romantic appeal. *The Indian Queen* and *The Indian Emperor*, for example, are set in Mexico, whereas both parts of Dryden's *The Conquest of Granada by the Spaniards* are set in Spain. Warfare, conquest, and striving dominate the plays.

The characters belong to a set of types that include as the protagonist the love-honor hero, who finds himself involved in intrigues and power struggles that put those virtues to the test. Like the other characters, he does not change; the tests the characters encounter are intended to show the strength of their virtue or the depth of their depravity. The hero is surrounded by such Fletcherian types as the sentimental maiden, whom he loves; the evil woman, who shamelessly attempts to gain him for herself; the weak king, whom others are attempting to topple from the throne; the faithful friend; and an antagonist who is almost but not quite a Machiavellian villain motivated solely by ambition. The hero is sometimes fortunate and prevails over all of the obstacles he encounters; at other times, he dies without any success other than preserving his love and honor.

The romantic excesses of heroic plays were satirized by George Villiers, duke of Buckingham, in his burlesque *The Rehearsal* (pr., pb. 1672), which has as its major character John Bayes, a brilliant satiric depiction of Dryden. Villiers parodies many of the absurd and inflated lines of Dryden and others who wrote in the form, yet *The Rehearsal* failed to drive the heroic drama from the stage. The genre remained viable for nearly two decades, until the late 1670's, when the playwrights began shifting their efforts to a less flamboyant form of tragedy.

AURENG-ZEBE

Aureng-Zebe, the last of Dryden's heroic plays, was judged by him to be his best, though in the prologue he announced that he had grown weary of rhyme, an indication of his imminent shift to blank verse as the appropriate meter for serious drama. By comparison to Dryden's earlier heroic dramas, *Aureng-Zebe* makes less use of song and dance and includes less rant and bombast, yet it clearly preserves the major elements of the genre.

Set in India at the time of the Mogul Empire, it derives events and characters from history, though Dryden freely alters the sources. The aging emperor, a stereotypical weak king, finds his throne challenged by several of his sons, the loyal Aureng-Zebe being an exception. Aureng-Zebe is depicted by his friend Arimant, governor of Agra, as "by no strong person swayed/ Except his love," a hero of unshakable loyalty who hopes that he will attain the hand of the captive queen Indamora for his support of the emperor.

While *Aureng-Zebe* is tame by earlier standards of the heroic play, echoes of the swashbuckling, superhuman hero remain. In armed conflict, the hero defeats two rebellious brothers, Darah being the first, "Darah from loyal Aureng-Zebe is fled,/ And forty thousand of his men lie dead." The threat represented by Morat, the ambitious villain of the play, is not so easily parried, for he has raised an immense force thus described by Abbas: "The neighb'ring plain with arms is coverd o'er;/ The vale an iron harvest seems to yield/ Of thick-sprung lances in a waving field." The hyperboles, typical of the genre, suggest the physical threat posed by Morat; his character also serves as a foil to that of Aureng-Zebe, for he does not properly control his passions. Primarily motivated by a desire for power, he also wishes to abandon his faithful wife, Melesinda, for Aureng-Zebe's beloved Indamora, who finds him repulsive. Further complications arise when the emperor falls passionately in love with Indamora, and the Empress Nourmahal, Aureng-Zebe's stepmother and the "evil woman" of the play, conceives a strong passion for her stepson. Confronted with news of his father's love for Indamora and his placing her under arrest, the hero accepts the challenge involving both his love and honor.

Aureng-Zebe finds himself threatened from many directions when he intercedes with the emperor and attempts to prevent the emperor's petulant imprisonment of Nourmahal. No sooner has the emperor seen Nourmahal taken away than he summons the rebellious Morat with the intent of making him his heir, all because of Aureng-Zebe's love for Indamora. Boldly entering unannounced, Aureng-Zebe attempts to end the alliance between the emperor and Morat by offering to disband his army if Morat will withdraw his forces from the city, leaving the emperor in control. Despite these peace-making efforts, the emperor orders Aureng-Zebe's arrest when he will not renounce his love for Indamora. When Indamora pleads for Morat to spare the life of Aureng-Zebe, he demands her love in exchange, which she curtly refuses. The alliance between the emperor and Morat is broken when the emperor learns of Morat's passion for Indamora. After Aureng-Zebe has been released through the efforts of Indamora and Arimant, Indamora finds great difficulty in convincing the jealous hero that she has remained faithful and has not betrayed him with Morat. Meanwhile, having lost the favor of the emperor, Morat rebels against him.

The outcome is obscured when Arimant, in a disguise that results in his being mistaken for Aureng-Zebe, is killed and Morat has to break off a long seductive speech to Indamora to quell an uprising. In the final battle, Aureng-Zebe leads the emperor's forces to victory, and Morat, mortally wounded, manages to prevent his mother from murdering Indamora. Her violent passion frustrated, Nourmahal poisons herself, and the Emperor grants Aureng-Zebe both the state and Indamora.

In *Aureng-Zebe*, the characters who retain their honor reap the rewards of both love and honor, whereas those who do not control their passions and ambition encounter misfortune. The abruptness and violence of passions are appropriately accompanied by abrupt and violent actions in the plays. A major difference between good and evil characters becomes the measure of control over passions, not the violence of the passion itself. Dryden's characters, both the good and the bad, express themselves blatantly where sexual passions are concerned, a phenomenon not limited to the characters of the heroic plays.

ALL FOR LOVE

Of *All for Love*, his tragedy based on Shakespeare's earlier great work *Antony and Cleopatra* (pr. c. 1606-1607), Dryden himself commented that he had never written anything "for myself but *Antony and Cleopatra*." The drama reflects Dryden's vision of tragedy, sometimes designated by critics as "heroic tragedy" to indicate certain similarities to the heroic play. The chief among Dryden's works in the type include *Oedipus, Troilus and Cressida, Don Sebastian, King of Portugal* and *Cleomenes, the Spartan Hero*. Unlike the heroic plays, these are written in blank verse and their sources are Shakespearean or classical. They demonstrate fewer of the epic dimensions of the heroic play, and the heroes are more nearly realistic characters. Although Dryden succeeds more fully in presenting human emotions in these dramas, in part because the medium of blank verse is more suited to emotional expression, he achieves the effects of pathos and sentiment rather than pity and fear.

In *All for Love*, Dryden follows the dramatic unities of time, place, and action, which he regarded as ornaments of tragedy, though not indispensable. The hero, Antony, is presented on the final day of his life, which happens to be his birthday. Facing imminent defeat at the hands of Octavius, he encounters temptations to abandon the great passion of his life, Cleopatra, in order to prolong the contest or to minimize the consequences of the loss. Restrictions inherent in the dramatic unities result in characters that are not nearly so complex as those of the source, Shakespeare's *Antony and Cleopatra*. Cleopatra neither wavers in her devotion to Antony nor reflects at length on her role as queen, as she does in Shakespeare's tragedy. Dryden's Ventidius shares qualities drawn from Shakespeare's character of the same name but also from Shakespeare's Enobarbus, the devoted adviser who abandons Antony. Ventidius strives to deliver Antony from his passion for Cleopatra, while, at the same time, her servant Alexas is scheming with Cleopatra to keep Antony's devotion. Caught in the struggle between love and duty, Antony appears a weak hero. Ventidius first offers Antony, then under attack by Octavius, the support of twelve legions if he will abandon Cleopatra, pointing to this as a necessary condition since the legionnaires refuse to come to Egypt and insist that Antony join them to assume command. Seizing on this chance for victory, Antony agrees, only to change his mind when he receives a parting gift, a bracelet, from Cleopatra, who unexpectedly arrives to put her gift on his arm.

Ventidius next arranges for Antony to make an honorable peace with Caesar, leaving him with limited power, if he will return to his wife Octavia. When Octavia appears with their two daughters, Antony is unable to withstand their pleas and agrees to return to her, dispatching Dolabella to deliver a farewell to Cleopatra. This episode reveals the flaws in Alexas's and Ventidius's calculations. Alexas reasons that Cleopatra may win Antony back by arousing his jealousy through Dolabella, whereas Ventidius assumes that jealousy will convince Antony that Cleopatra was worthless. Thus, both adversaries steer Antony in the same direction for different ends. The result is that Octavia becomes so distressed at Antony's obvious jealousy over their reports that she leaves him. In return for Antony's hostility and anger and after the loss of a battle at sea, Cleopatra sends word of her death, which Antony cannot bear. Following his self-inflicted mortal wound, he is taken to Cleopatra, whose death following his brings a sense of triumph.

Although scenes such as that between Antony and Octavia involve a generous amount of sentimentality, Dryden achieves in *All for Love* an intensity that is lacking in most of his plays, one whose emotional effects are not dissipated through digressions or loosely related subplots. The play reveals a tightly unified plot line in which characters' motives and actions are influenced primarily by strong romantic love.

DON SEBASTIAN, KING OF PORTUGAL

Dryden's tragedy *Don Sebastian, King of Portugal*, written after the Glorious Revolution, is his longest drama and, in the view of critics from Sir Walter Scott to Bruce King, his finest dramatic achievement. In the play's preface, Dryden acknowledges that the players cut more than twelve hundred lines from the acted version. Though the play's themes are universally appropriate for tragedy, it includes a closely related comic subplot, and it ends not with the death of the hero or heroine but with their retirement from the world of affairs. The play incorporates numerous qualities and dramatic techniques that Dryden employs elsewhere in his work and may be the most fruitful play to examine for clarifying his dramatic art.

The play is set in North Africa, where Don Sebastian, king of Portugal, and his allies have been defeated and captured after warring against the Moors. Sebastian's chief desire is to marry the woman he loves, Almeyda, Christian queen of Barbary, also held captive. This he manages to do after the emperor Muley-Moluch has given him a measure of freedom so that Sebastian can attempt to win Almeyda's hand for the emperor. Sebastian and Almeyda escape the emperor's retribution for their marriage, because he is slain in a rebellion, but they do not escape fate. In the final act, they learn from the old counselor Alvarez, who has just been freed from captivity, that they are half brother and sister, having had the same father. The incestuousness of their relationship, unknowing though it was, forces them to part, with each retiring to a separate religious house.

The Moors are portrayed throughout the play as riven by factions, the chief threat being the effort of the emperor's favorite, Benducar, to topple him from the throne, ostensibly in favor of the emperor's brother, Muley-Zeydan, but in reality for himself. In this attempt, he involves the populace, the religious leader Mufti Abdalla, and Dorax, a Christian who has turned against Sebastian and has joined the Moors. Dorax later joins Sebastian, after the fall of the emperor, to defeat the uprising and restore worthy leaders to their places. A comic subplot involves the efforts of the Christian captive Don Antonio to flee the household of the Mufti with his daughter Morayma and his treasure, in much the same way that Lorenzo and Jessica flee Shylock in Shakespeare's *The Merchant of Venice* (pr. 1604).

The exotic setting, the theme of heroic love, the stock characters, and the broils and warfare represent familiar themes and situations of Dryden's dramas. Occasionally, one also finds in the dramas some exceptional improbabilities. In this play, for example, Dorax, having lost the confidence of the Moors, is poisoned by two of them, Benducar and the Mufti, but survives because each poison neutralizes the effect of the other. Yet *Don Sebastian, King of Portugal* illustrates other characteristics of Dryden's dramatic art that are less obvious but more influential and significant: the theme of incest, actual or suppressed; anticlericalism; political satire and allusions; and scenes of reconciliation. In *Don Sebastian, King of Portugal*, unwitting incest occurs between Sebastian and Almeyda after they are married, and such is their consternation when they discover they have violated the taboo that Sebastian believes suicide the only escape until Dorax dissuades him. The situation resembles somewhat that of Oedipus in the version of the old Greek drama that Dryden and Nathaniel Lee produced for the Restoration stage. It is as though love in Dryden is so exalted, wrought up to such a pitch, that introduction of the taboo acts to heighten it and make the plight of the lovers more poignant. In *Don Sebastian, King of Portugal*, the theme is counterbalanced by the story of Violante, who denied affection to the husband Sebastian had chosen for her and awaited for many years her beloved Dorax.

It is unclear why anticlericalism becomes such a prominent theme in the works of Dryden, though it seems plausible that his profound distrust and dislike of Puritan influence on political affairs may in part explain it. The Mufti represents the typical clergyman in Dryden, usually the object of satire in both the poems and the plays. He is ambitious, avaricious, sensual, officious, and usually hypocritical. The Mufti appears ridiculous in both political and personal affairs, becoming the object of humor and scorn. Dryden does not, of course, ridicule clergymen of the Church of England, but wherever he introduces a pagan, a Muslim, or a Catholic religious figure, the character becomes the object of satire.

In its political theme, the play concerns betrayal and misappropriation of power. The emperor, having usurped the throne, discovers that he can trust no one, least of all Benducar, his closest adviser. Benducar incites the mob to rebellion, and they manage to defeat and kill the emperor, barbarously showing his head on a pike as that of a tyrant. Like a true Machiavellian, Benducar muses on the thesis that might makes right: "And I can sin but once to seize the throne; all after-acts are sanctified by power." Such passages as this in Dryden's plays, poems, and translations following the Glorious Revolution usually serve as oblique satire of the new monarchs, and his distrust of the judgment of the common people where political affairs are concerned is a recurring theme throughout his work.

A final characteristic of Dryden's theater is evident in act 4, scene 3, often considered the most successful scene of the play. It depicts the intense quarrel of the two friends, Dorax and Sebastian, and their reconciliation. Dryden may have based this scene on the quarrel of Brutus and Cassius in Shakespeare's *Julius Caesar* (pr. c. 1599-1600); similar scenes occur in other works of Dryden, notably in *Troilus and Cressida* and *Cleomenes, the Spartan Hero*. Although Dorax has fought on the side of the Moors, he defends and spares the life of Sebastian—so that he can kill him to exact his own revenge. He holds a powerful grudge because Sebastian did not adequately reward him for his prior service and awarded the hand of Violante to another courtier, Henriquez. Facing an imminent fight to the death with Dorax, Sebastian explains that Henriquez had sought the hand of Violante first, that Henriquez had died defending Sebastian, and that Violante now waits for Dorax. Accepting Sebastian's explanation, Dorax submits, is restored to favor, and promises that he will serve Sebastian as faithfully as Henriquez had done. In the final act, Dorax helps Sebastian bear manfully his sense of guilt and loss. Scenes of intense confrontation permit the dramatist to display a range of emotions in a brief space, as well as a heightening and diminution of passions. Dryden's ability to capture such a range of tones compensates to a degree for his lack of a greater gift as a dramatist—the ability to show growth and development of his characters.

OTHER MAJOR WORKS

POETRY: *Heroic Stanzas*, 1659; *Astraea Redux*, 1660; "To My Lord Chancellor," 1662; *Prologues and Epilogues*, 1664-1700; *Annus Mirabilis*, 1667; *Absalom and Achitophel, Part I*, 1681; *Absalom and Achitophel, Part II*, 1682 (with Nahum Tate); *The Medall: A Satyre Against Sedition*, 1682; *Mac Flecknoe: Or, A Satyre upon the True-Blew-Protestant Poet, T. S.*, 1682; *Religio Laici: Or, A Layman's Faith*, 1682; *Threnodia Augustalis*, 1685; *The Hind and the Panther*, 1687; "A Song for St. Cecilia's Day," 1687; *Britannia Rediviva*, 1688; *Eleonora*, 1692; "To My Dear Friend Mr. Congreve," 1694; *Alexander's Feast: Or, The Power of Music, an Ode in Honor of St. Cecilia's Day*, 1697; "To My Honour'd Kinsman, John Driden," 1700.

NONFICTION: *Of Dramatic Poesie: An Essay*, 1668; "A Defence of *An Essay of Dramatic Poesy*," 1668; "Preface to *An Evening's Love: Or, The Mock Astrologer*," 1671; "Of Heroic Plays: An Essay," 1672; "The Author's Apology for Heroic Poetry and Poetic License," 1677; "Preface to *All for Love*," 1678; "The Grounds of Criticism in Tragedy," 1679; "Preface to *Sylvae*," 1685; *A Discourse Concerning the Original and Progress of Satire*, 1693; "Dedication of *Examen Poeticum*," 1693; "A Parallel of Poetry and Painting," 1695; "Dedication of the *Aeneis*," 1697; "Preface to *Fables Ancient and Modern*," 1700; "Heads of an Answer to Rymer," 1711.

TRANSLATIONS: *Ovid's Epistles*, 1680; *The History of the League*, 1684 (of Louis Maimbourg's *Histoire de la Ligue*); *The Life of St. Francis Xavier*, 1688 (of Dominique Bouhours's *La Vie de Saint François Xavier*); *The Satires of Juvenal and Persius*, 1693; *The Works of Vergil*, 1697.

BIBLIOGRAPHY

Archer, John Michael. *Old Worlds: Egypt, Southwest Asia, India, and Russia in Early Modern English Writing*. Stanford, Calif.: Stanford University Press, 2001. Contains a scholarly examination of Dryden's *Aureng-Zebe*, along with Shakespeare's *Antony and Cleopatra* and the works of John Milton. Bibliography and index.

Bywaters, David. *Dryden in Revolutionary England*. Berkeley: University of California Press, 1991. This book describes the rhetorical stages by which Dryden, in his published works between 1687 and 1700, sought to define contemporary politics and to stake out for himself a tenable place within them. The study reveals much about the relationship between Dryden's politics, polemics, and art. Contains an epilogue and extensive notes.

Hammond, Paul. *John Dryden: A Literary Life*. New York: St. Martin's Press, 1991. This study of Dryden's life examines the texts that he produced and the relationship of these texts to the society they reflect. The work consists of chapters on different aspects of Dryden's works. They are arranged approximately chronologically to suggest the shape of his career and to explore his own developing sense of his role as the premier writer of Restoration England, both dominating and detached from the world in which he moved. Select bibliography and extensive notes.

Hammond, Paul, and David Hopkins, eds. *John Dryden: Tercentenary Essays*. Oxford, England: Oxford, 2000. A collection of twelve essays that place Dryden in the context of his time and suggest a more elevated place for the poet in literary history.

Owen, Susan J. *Restoration Theatre and Crisis*. New York: Clarendon Press, 1996. A look at theater in England in the seventeenth century, focusing on Dryden and Aphra Behn. Bibliography and index.

Winn, James Anderson. *John Dryden and His World*. New Haven, Conn.: Yale University Press, 1987. Examines the man, his work, and the world in which he lived. Considers the subtle relations linking this world's religious beliefs, its political alliances, and the literary styles it favored. Views Dryden's work as a product of his particular historical situation. Includes illustrations and appendices on Dryden's family history.

_____, ed. *Critical Essays on John Dryden*. New York: G. K. Hall, 1997. A collection of essays on the literary works of Dryden. Bibliography and index.

Stanley Archer,
updated by Genevieve Slomski

ALEXANDRE DUMAS, *FILS*

Born: Paris, France; July 27, 1824
Died: Marly-le-Roi, France; November 27, 1895

PRINCIPAL DRAMA
Le Bijou de la reine, wr. 1845, pr. 1855, pb. 1868
La Dame aux camélias, pr., pb. 1852 (*Camille*, 1856)
Diane de Lys, pb. 1852, pr. 1853
Le Demi-monde, pr., pb. 1855 (*The Demi-Monde*, 1858)
La Question d'argent, pr., pb. 1857 (*The Money-Question*, 1915)
Le Fils naturel, pr., pb. 1858 (*The Natural Son*, 1879)

Un Père prodigue, pr., pb. 1859

L'Ami des femmes, pr., pb. 1864 (*The Woman's Friend*, 1928)

Les Idées de Madame Aubray, pr., pb. 1867 (*Madame Aubray's Ideas*, 1931)

Théâtre complet, pb. 1868-1898 (8 volumes)

Une Visite de noces, pr., pb. 1871

La Princesse Georges, pr. 1871, pb. 1872 (*Princess George*, 1881)

La Femme de Claude, pr., pb. 1873 (*The Wife of Claude*, 1905)

Monsieur Alphonse, pr. 1873, pb. 1874 (English translation, 1886)

L'Étrangère, pr. 1876, pb. 1877 (*The Foreigner*, 1881)

La Princesse de Baghdad, pr., pb. 1881

Denise, pr., pb. 1885 (English translation, 1885)

Francillon, pr., pb. 1887 (English translation, 1893)

Théâtre complet: Théâtre des autres, pb. 1894-1895 (2 volumes)

OTHER LITERARY FORMS

Most of the works of Alexandre Dumas, *fils*, were published in the late nineteenth century by Calmann-Levy. In addition to his theatrical works, Dumas wrote twelve novels, two of which, *La Dame aux camélias* (1848; *Camille*, 1857) and *Diane de Lys* (1851), he later dramatized. The others are prosaic and pretentious, including the best known and most successful, *L'Affaire Clémenceau: Mémoire de l'accusé* (1866; *The Clemenceau Case*, 1890), a sort of autobiographical *roman à thèse* in which the author, at length, attacks societal prejudices against illegitimate children. In his later years, Dumas was himself embarrassed by his youthful prolixity and withdrew most of the novels from publication. As a result of restrictions in his will, almost none of Dumas's correspondence has been published.

ACHIEVEMENTS

The career of Alexandre Dumas, *fils*, is one of the most intriguing in nineteenth century French letters. Although easily the most popular dramatist of his time, he has today but two claims to notoriety. First,

he was the illegitimate son of one of the most illustrious men of the time, Alexandre Dumas, *père*, author of *Les Trois Mousquetaires* (1844; *The Three Musketeers*, 1846); second, he wrote what was without doubt the most successful play of the nineteenth century, *Camille*, which set the model for French drama for fifty years. Beyond these two distinctions, Dumas's life and literary work is largely ignored by modern scholars, despite the fact that he was one of the most prolific, successful, and influential dramatists of his day.

Between 1852 and his death in 1895, Dumas penned a nonstop series of novels, plays, and social treatises all aimed at instructing and edifying the general public on the necessity of strengthening and preserving the traditional family structure. Therefore, the terms often applied to his theater—*le théâtre utile* (useful theater, a term Dumas himself coined) or *le théâtre à thèse* (thesis theater)—serve to describe an artistic perspective that is intentionally didactic and therefore usually (unintentionally) devoid of subtlety and replete with sentimentality.

Alexandre Dumas, fils (Hulton Archive by Getty Images)

Often overlooked but of particular historical interest today are Dumas's pamphlets and long memorandums defending the rights and privileges of women. Notable among these are *L'Homme-femme* (1872; *Man-Woman: Or, The Hearth, the Street*, 1873) and *Les Femmes qui tuent et les femmes qui votent* (1880; the women who kill and the women who vote), which argue for women's suffrage, for the election of women to governmental posts, for reform of the divorce law, and against traditional evils (such as prostitution and adultery) that threaten the stability of the family unit.

Most experts also agree that 1852, the year of the appearance of *Camille*, marks one of the most significant moments in the history of French theater. While Victor Hugo in his earlier work *Marion de Lorme* (1831; English translation, 1895) and Émile Augier in *L'Aventurière* (1848) had treated the same subject as that of Dumas's play (an innocent young man falling in love with a fashionable courtesan), each had distanced the action from the contemporary scene by creating elaborate costume dramas. In contrast, the youthful Dumas chose to represent his own place and age, Paris in 1848, an idea revolutionary in its simplicity. In so doing, he fundamentally changed the course of French drama. For some fifty years after the appearance of *Camille*, the best French theater concerned itself primarily with the presentation of social themes of universal concern at the time, such as the plight of the disenfranchised, the ease with which wealth corrupts people, and the vulnerability of women and children. In short, Dumas's work introduced realism to the French stage, albeit a stylized realism by modern standards. With the creation of Marguerite Gautier, the heroine of *Camille*, a new age of French drama began. Marguerite is one of the great female roles of all time and attracted all the most talented actresses of the day, including Sarah Bernhardt. The story itself has proved to be ageless. Within a year of its appearance, Giuseppe Verdi had adapted the play as an opera, *La Traviata*, and some twenty films have been based on the work, the most famous being *Camille* (1937), starring Greta Garbo and Robert Taylor.

The present-day lack of interest in Dumas's thesis plays may be explained partially by the fact that he was never able to focus his attention beyond a singular concern for preserving, through the dramatic mode, the sanctity of family life. His well-known motto, "*L'action morale et social par la littérature dramatique*" (moral and social action through dramatic literature), testifies to this *idée fixe*. Many critics have faulted Dumas for his limited thematic range; he persisted in doing often what he did well—instructing the public on the importance to society of a secure family unit.

Although many of Dumas's contemporaries found his pessimistic social prognostications more humorous than sobering, his perception of the decay underlying the gilded façade of the Second Empire was both just and acute. He spoke out unsuccessfully yet indefatigably on such complex social issues as prostitution, adultery, divorce, abortion, and the importance of "real love" in safeguarding traditional domestic life. Several of Dumas's pamphlets, including *La Question du divorce* (1880; the question of divorce) and *La Recherche de la paternité* (1883; the search for paternity), were influential in setting the stage for much-needed legislation.

Dumas was elected to the French Academy in 1874, an honor never bestowed on his *bon vivant* father. This official recognition of Dumas, *fils*, coming some twenty-two years after his first literary triumph, indicates the degree of popular and critical success that he attained during his lifetime.

BIOGRAPHY

Relatively few details of the private life of Alexandre Dumas, *fils*, are known. Typical of the discretion that he maintained in later life is the stipulation in his will prohibiting the publication of his correspondence. Most of what is known of Dumas's youth comes from his admittedly autobiographical works, particularly *The Clemenceau Case*, which recalls the author's pubescent years fairly accurately.

Perhaps the most significant event in Dumas's life was his birth, for the questions of parentage and the importance of the family became constant if not strident themes of his later work. Alexandre Dumas, *père*, while working as a clerk for the Duc d'Orléans in Paris, met a young seamstress, Marie Catherine

Lebay, living in his apartment building. In 1824, she bore him a son. Although Dumas, *père*, would later become his son's most ardent supporter and most lovingly biased critic, it is some indication of the elder author's preoccupations during these early years that he did not "recognize" his son until 1831, well after his financial success had been assured with the play *Henri III et sa cour* (pr., pb. 1829; *Henry III and His Court*, 1832). At this time, Dumas, *père*, attempted to bring his son into his home, but Mlle Lebay (Dumas never married her), a devoted mother, refused to relinquish her son. A lawsuit followed, and, as was the custom of the time, the father received custody of the son. The younger Dumas later related to friends that he had to be forcibly removed from under his bed when his father came to get him.

Many of the details of these early years are recounted in the novel *The Clemenceau Case*. The primary character is an illegitimate son, Pierre Clemenceau, who suffers a painful existence as a youth, constantly persecuted by his peers at school because of the circumstances of his birth. (Unlike Dumas, however, Pierre later becomes a successful artist, only to have his happiness shattered by his wife's infidelity, which he ultimately avenges by killing her.) The childhood traumas associated with his illegitimacy no doubt provided a firm base for Dumas's later social crusades. When he attacked the laws preventing illegitimate children from learning their paternity and the laws that discriminated against unwed mothers, Dumas spoke most passionately, for he spoke from personal experience.

As a result of these early experiences, Dumas's youth seemed to him inordinately painful. He spent six miserable years in school at the Pension Saint-Victor, a rigorous institution where Jules de Goncourt was also educated. Here his peers reveled in ridiculing his illegitimate birth. Dumas's formal education ended at the age of seventeen after two years at the Collège Bourbon, from which he was never graduated. At this time, he went to live with the elder Dumas, adopting many of his father's worst habits; by the age of twenty-four, he confessed to being fifty thousand francs in debt. Without any strong parental guidance, enchanted by his newfound freedom, and,

as a result of his father's reputation, surrounded by all manner of glittering luminaries, the young Dumas plunged headlong into the treacherous currents of Parisian bohemian life. The cafés, the dancing halls, the nightlife of the grand boulevards where wealthy young men moved freely among the most famous courtesans of the day—this was Dumas's world, a world he came to know largely to the exclusion of all others and which provided primary source material for almost all his later work. It was Dumas, *fils*, who coined the term *demi-monde* to describe this world, where licentious decadence took on a certain respectability.

Amid this *demi-monde*, Dumas met his first love, Marie Duplessis (née Alphonsine Plessis). This encounter was of paramount importance for French drama, for Marie would become, in 1848, "the lady of the camellias," Marguerite Gautier, lover of Armand Duval. Although much has been made of this real-life affair, evidence now indicates that it was only a youthful infatuation. Dumas was twenty when he met Marie; he was prepared to give himself totally to her, but she was unable to abandon the security that her dependable, wealthy clientele afforded her. The affair continued, hot and cold, until 1845, when Dumas, unable to accept the fact that Marie would not voluntarily abandon her lifestyle in his favor, ended it almost resolutely. "I'm neither rich enough to love you like I'd want to," he wrote in his famous final letter to her, "nor poor enough to be loved as you would like." Unlike the play, Dumas's story ended definitively here: He went happily off to Spain with his father; Marie died in Paris of consumption two years later.

About this time, Dumas fell in love with a young Russian woman, the countess of Nesselrode, wife of the Russian ambassador to Paris. Annoyed by Dumas's impetuous advances toward his wife, the ambassador decided to return to Russia, his wife safely at his side. Undaunted, Dumas set out in pursuit, only to be stopped at the Polish border. There, the real-life tale ended, but again Dumas would adapt reality to art. From this adventure, he drew the outline for the plot of his novel *Diane de Lys*, which he dramatized in 1853 under the same title. Shortly after this affair, Dumas began a liaison with Nadejda

Naryschkine (née Knorring), the wife of a Russian prince. Only the bare outline exists of the events that followed. The princess bore Dumas a daughter, Marie-Alexandre Henriette (called Colette), in 1860. In May, 1864, Prince Naryschkine died, and on December 31, 1864, the princess and Dumas were married. Dumas recognized Colette the same day. A second daughter, Marie-Olga Jeanne, was born in 1867. If Dumas's early experiences furnished him material for his later literary work, they certainly had little effect on how he managed his personal life, although, in all fairness to him, such maneuverings seem fairly tame in comparison with those of many of his contemporaries.

While Dumas sorted out his various affairs, he continued to write a series of generally successful plays. His ability to work hard and to separate his professional commitments from his social commitments was one of the more admirable qualities inherited from his father. In 1876, *The Foreigner* was presented at the Théâtre Français, marking his entry into the elite group of dramatists whose work was accepted by the Comédie-Française. In the ensuing years, Dumas continued to write pamphlets calling for various fundamental changes in the paternity and divorce laws and supporting the rights of women. His drama, too, assumed a more pessimistic and messianic tone as he became more and more disturbed by the decadence of Parisian life under the Third Republic. Yet, despite his fierce dramatic defenses of the family, Dumas found it difficult to practice what he preached; in 1887, he took a mistress, Henriette Escalier, the wife of the painter Félix Escalier.

Dumas's last play, *Francillon*, appeared in 1887, after which he wrote virtually nothing. His time had passed him by; the "useful theater," for all its realism, was not in tune with the demanding tenets of the naturalists (such as Émile Zola and Henry Becque), who sought to present "a slice of life." For the aged Dumas, this disinterested presentation of "life as it really is," rather than as interpreted through the eyes of the artist, was particularly disappointing. Such a view was, to Dumas, implicitly amoral, and thus valueless. In these last years, he felt acutely at odds with his age and chose to live an insular, bourgeois existence, wintering in Paris, and traveling to his country

homes at other times. Eventually, Mme Dumas, ill and unable to bear her husband's infidelity, left home to live with her daughter Colette, while Dumas took an apartment close to Henriette. In April, 1895, Mme Dumas died; at the end of June of the same year, Dumas married Henriette. In November, Dumas died of an embolism and was buried in the Montparnasse cemetery, not too far from Marie Duplessis.

ANALYSIS

The plays of Alexandre Dumas, *fils*, can be easily divided into three thematic groups or periods. His early *comédies de mœurs* (comedies of manners), written between 1852 and 1855, include three of his best-known works: *Camille*, *Diane de Lys*, and *The Demi-Monde*. These first and best works are concerned with presenting a realistic picture of a certain side of Parisian life in the early years of the Second Empire. The second group, the *pièces à thèse* (thesis plays), includes those plays written between 1857 (*The Money-Question*) and 1871 (*Princess George*); as their appellation suggests, each of these plays contains a single, clearly focused thesis that offers a solution to some troubling social evil. From 1873 (*The Wife of Claude*) through 1881 (*La Princesse de Baghdad*), the playwright entered a mystical-symbolic period in which he attempted to create, not the real-life characters of his earlier work, but, as he said, "essences of beings." These works proved to be so esoteric that the public recoiled from them in absolute rejection. In an attempt to recapture his audience, Dumas conceived two final works, *Denise* in 1885 and *Francillon* in 1887, in which he reverted to the earlier, successful *pièce à thèse* formula. Even though both works were enthusiastically received by the public, the author's will to produce had weakened. He wrote no dramatic works after 1887.

Of these three periods, only the first two are of general interest to the modern student, Dumas's symbolic period having been such a complete failure. His early work, although rarely produced today, offers the reader some interesting material, including a variety of realistic and entertaining depictions of the earthier side of Parisian life during the Second Empire. Of Dumas's many plays, *Camille* (a comedy of manners) and *Madame Aubray's Ideas* (perhaps his most representative *pièce à thèse*) are of particular interest, for they provide an introduction to the most important elements of the author's work. In order to appreciate Dumas's contributions to the development of French drama through these works, it is helpful to recall the state of the theater in Paris in the 1840's and 1850's.

In retrospect, the theatrical scene into which Dumas's work came was rather dismal. With only a few exceptions, the dramatic offerings of the 1840's and the early 1850's are among the most banal in nineteenth century French letters. The contemporary theater was dominated by the dramatic artifices of Eugène Scribe (he wrote more than three hundred plays between 1815 and his death in 1861) and by those who rigorously adhered to Scribe's doctrine of the well-made play. For Scribe and his collaborators, the success of a play depended primarily on the unwinding of a plot of labyrinthine complexity through the ingenious use of intellectual legerdemain and *coups de théâtre* that would bewilder and enchant the audience. Such fare was immensely popular among a theater audience composed largely of nouveaux riches, whose thirst for pure diversion and entertainment well reflected the general social tenor of the times. The year 1843 marked, with the production of Hugo's *Les Burgraves* (pr., pb. 1843; *The Burgraves*, 1896), the death of Romanticism on the stage. That same year, François Ponsard's reworking of the classical tragedy *Lucrèce* was met with great success by a public long overwhelmed by the excesses of the Romantic theater; the *école du bon sens* (the school of good sense) had been inaugurated. The best work of this group of reactionaries against the Romantics, however, would not appear until 1854, with Émile Augier's *Le Gendre de M. Poirier* (*Monsieur Poirier's Son-in-Law*, 1915), and again in 1855 with *Le mariage d'Olympe* (*Olympe's Marriage*, 1915), the latter being an undisguised reply to Dumas's *Camille*, in which the author presents the thesis that a scarlet woman can never be redeemed by true love.

Camille

Within this setting, *Camille* appeared like a thunderbolt, cleansing the stale air that had surrounded the Romantic theater and, with one electric jolt, rend-

ing nineteenth century French theater into two parts, before and after Dumas, *fils*. If one is to believe the critics of the period, this is no overstatement. The play appeared startlingly revolutionary and refreshing to a tired theater public; words such as "original," "unique," and "new" appear over and over in the reviews of the time. Almost all the tenets of Scribe, and particularly the doctrine of the sublimation of life to artifice, fell before Dumas's art. The theme, that of an honest young man falling in love with a courtesan, was also intriguingly controversial, even though Hugo and Augier had presented somewhat similar circumstances in earlier works. What was most welcome, however, was the fact that on almost every count, the play diverged from the accepted theatrical formulas of the day. The work is almost completely devoid of artifice. There are no startling unveilings of concealed identities, no fortuitous discovery of a revealing letter, no attempts whatsoever to conceal any element of the plot from the audience. The work shocked audiences by its sheer simplicity. What Dumas presents here is an unencumbered love story, the success of which depends largely on the dynamics of dialogue and the verisimilitude of the relationship between Marguerite and Armand. As might be imagined, the author had great difficulty in getting his play produced.

It was not only the originality of the work but also the attention given to a courtesan that initially threatened to prevent the production of the play. In 1847, Dumas had written a romanticized account in novel form of his affair with Marie Duplessis. The work was an instant success and brought the author his much desired notoriety. As was the vogue of the period, Dumas hastened to adapt his work to the stage, the great arena for intellectual combat under the Second Empire. Real literary success meant success in the theater. Working night and day for a week, Dumas completed his play in the summer of 1849.

The story of how the play finally came to the stage is a drama in itself. At first, Dumas hoped that his father's theater, the Théâtre Historique, would produce the work, but a series of unfortunate circumstances led to the closing of the theater at the end of 1849. Over the course of several months, all the major theaters in Paris rejected the work, either for moral reasons or because it lacked the Scribian elements popular at the time. Finally, in mid-1850, the Vaudeville Theater accepted the work, but when the play was submitted to the government censors, it was banned as an affront to public morality. Not until after the *coup d'état* of December, 1851, was production of the play approved. The first performance was at the Vaudeville Theater on February 2, 1852, the fifth anniversary, to the day, of the death of Marie Duplessis. Despite numerous expressions of fear, even among the actors, that the play was too revolutionary in style and structure for Parisian audiences, opening night was an unqualified success; two hundred performances to packed houses followed. The modern comedy of manners was firmly established.

The plot of *Camille* is refreshingly simple when compared with those of other plays of the period. In the first act, there is essentially no action in the traditional sense. The opening scene takes place in Marguerite's Parisian boudoir, where, during the course of an evening, the audience is introduced to all the fluttering characters who hover around Marguerite, who is known to all as the lady of the camellias because of her singular love for this delicately scented flower. (The scents of all other flowers, she contends, make her ill.) Marguerite's collection of friends, all of whom have arrived for dinner after an evening at the opera, constitutes an odd, but fairly accurate menagerie of Second Empire types, although Dumas has given each a distinctively individual character. Arthur de Varville is a tireless young dandy who, despite Marguerite's constant rejection of him, returns night after night to be near her, submitting to her unyielding abuse ("You are monotone," she tells him); his destiny, Varville maintains, is simply to await his love. Varville is everything that Armand is not—rich, self-confident, and titled. He is not, however, loved. Prudence, one of Dumas's most vivid creations, is an aged courtesan who has passed the point where she can survive by her trade. In order to live, she attaches herself to Marguerite, procuring for her friend and basking in the reflected glory of Marguerite's salon. Her fate is a harsh and constant reminder of the inevitably cruel end that awaits such women. In contrast

with Prudence, for whom age is a curse, the enchanting old Saint-Gaudens has learned to enjoy the privileges that come with age. His natural good humor, his willingness to be the subject of good-natured ribbing about his age, and his honest, robust approach to love and life contrast with the almost frantic deportment of his younger friends. In the youthful world of Marguerite, where age and the loss of beauty are the most cruel enemies, Saint-Gaudens reminds the viewer of the fun one can have in growing old gracefully, unconcerned about the passage of time. In one of her many ironic statements, Marguerite says in reference to Saint-Gaudens, "It is only the old who do not grow old." Also introduced in the first act are the young couple Nichette and Gustave, whose happy marriage at the end of the drama provides a foil for the tragic ending of Marguerite and Armand.

These fully developed secondary characters, appearing so early in the play, assist in the rapid unraveling of the complex character of Marguerite and of the youthful, almost irrational devotion of her admirer, Armand Duval. Marguerite is one of the great roles of the French stage because her character elicits such complex emotions from the audience. She is the quintessential scarlet woman with a heart of gold. One may recoil before her morality, but one is, like her many admirers, irresistibly drawn toward her fundamental goodness, her sincerity and warmth. She can be tender and unselfish, yet she is not easily duped, nor is she unaware of the dangers of allowing anyone, such as Varville, to get too close to her. She has worked too hard to achieve her current standard of living to commit herself to any one man, which would necessitate rejecting that life. In the early moments of the play, she makes no excuses for the life she has chosen. She is real, she knows what and who she is, and she is happy in that knowledge.

Her feverish lifestyle, however, has also taken its toll. While attempting a spirited polka with Saint-Gaudens, Marguerite collapses, an indication that she continues to suffer from some debilitating illness and a foreboding of things to come. Profiting from the moment, Armand dashes to her aid and within minutes reveals his love to her. He has spent two years loving Marguerite from afar, inquiring about her to her friends, too timid to approach her for fear of rejection. Armand treats Marguerite not as a courtesan but as a woman, and his interest in her begins to shake her usually implacable self-confidence. She momentarily rebuffs him; however, Armand's obvious sincerity and his declaration of "profound and eternal love" cause Marguerite to drop her defenses. Act 1 ends with Marguerite symbolically giving her heart to Armand in the form of a camellia. He may return to see her, she tells him, when the flower has faded, "the length of an evening or a morning."

From this point, events move rather quickly. Within a week, Marguerite has committed herself to Armand and, despite premonitions that her happiness may only be leading her toward an unhappy end, she makes arrangements to secure a house on the outskirts of Paris for them. Suddenly, Marguerite questions her present lifestyle; she sees in her old life only "decay, shame, and lies," and in Armand, her young knight, "ardent, and happy," all that she needs to satisfy her. They will be off together, unmindful of the odds against their happiness; as Armand declares, "Let's not be led by reason . . . let's follow our love."

In the country, Marguerite regains her health. Her former concern for material comfort has completely disappeared; now she is willing to sell all her possessions, unbeknown to Armand, to be able to continue this idyllic life. In similar fashion, Armand goes to Paris to make secret arrangements to borrow money for the same purpose. In Armand's absence, his father, Monsieur Duval, arrives to see Marguerite. He explains to her that he has arranged an advantageous marriage for his daughter but that the prospective groom's family has heard troubling rumors about Armand's involvement with a less than respectable woman. He pleads with Marguerite to abandon Armand so that his daughter's happiness can be assured. Furthermore, he adds, Armand can have no future if he continues on his present course. Marguerite's love for Armand gives her strength to agree to Duval's request. When Armand returns, she has left him a letter containing a fabricated story that, during their entire stay in the country, she has been seeing another man. Armand returns to his father; Marguerite returns to Paris where, without funds, she succumbs to the advances of Varville.

Some weeks later, Armand encounters Marguerite, on the arm of Varville, at an elegant soiree of dancing and gambling at the home of Olympe, one of Marguerite's courtesan friends. Their encounter is certainly one of the most dramatic scenes ever written for the French stage. After some scathing repartee, Armand manages to engage Varville in a series of extravagant bets, all of which Armand wins. Then, while the other guests exit for dinner, Armand confronts Marguerite, accuses her of never having loved him, throws her to the floor and flings his money in her face. Varville, having witnessed the scene from the wings, challenges Armand to a duel, which takes place offstage with a predictable conclusion—Varville is only wounded. All this proves to be too much for Marguerite. She becomes increasingly ill. As she nears death, she receives a letter from Monsieur Duval in which he recognizes her courage and noble character and asks her pardon. He promises to tell Armand the whole truth, but the truth comes too late. When Armand returns to reclaim his love, only moments of life remain for Marguerite. At least, she maintains, she can die happy, for she did the right thing for the right reasons. She has no regrets: "I lived for love," she says, "and I shall die for it." Surrounded by her friends, she dies in Armand's arms.

Despite the obvious sentimentality of the final act and some lines that strain belief (for example, when Marguerite finally has reason to live, she says to Armand, "Death is necessary, and I love it, since it waited for your return before taking me"), there is an irresistible charm about the whole play. Marguerite is a living character, capable of great love, tired of her hollow existence, ready for the security of the love of a single man. She has seen in Prudence and Olympe the results of a life abandoned to pleasure and materialism, and her love for Armand is selfless and genuinely noble. Armand is as attractive and lifelike as Marguerite. Impetuous, prone to irrational jealousy, prepared to abandon everything, even family, for Marguerite, Armand suffers through the conflicting emotions experienced by many young men on first encountering love.

The question of the morality of the play is still debated by critics today. Many have believed that Marguerite's final lines, in which she essentially praises her own strength of will for having done the right thing by Armand, "in the name of love," are an attempt by Dumas to excuse Marguerite's past. Such a conclusion would suggest that Dumas supported the thesis that love can rehabilitate even the most experienced courtesan and that Marguerite's past should be forgiven because of her noble sacrifices. Other critics, however, have pointed out that Marguerite does in fact die, while Monsieur Duval, the symbol of the conventional family, is never criticized. In fact, Marguerite seems honored that Monsieur Duval has recognized, even at this late date, the depth of her character, for she reads his letter over and over "for strength." The weight of the evidence seems to be on the side of Monsieur Duval and traditional morality. Had Dumas wished to absolve Marguerite, it would have been a small matter to permit her to live, but for Dumas this would not have been realistic or logical.

THE NATURAL SON

Such concern for presenting a logical denouement to his work became even more important as Dumas developed his thesis plays. The first of these works, *The Natural Son*, left no doubt about the author's views on the subject of the rights of illegitimate children. In several long scenes, the legal technicalities of the issue are presented in full detail while the characters go to great lengths to consider the problem from all angles. The plot itself is quite involved, but the outcome is simple, direct, and unambiguous: The illegitimate son succeeds on his own despite the odds against him. In the final act, in a moment of poetic, but seemingly harsh, justice, the son resolutely refuses to be recognized by his father because the father seeks not the son's love but his fortune. In his preface to the play, Dumas recounts how his director, Montigny, pleaded with him to change the ending to permit the father and son to unite. Dumas refused, maintaining that, given the events of the play, any son would react in a similar fashion. He must have been at least partially correct, for the play was successful, spurring him on to write six more *pièces à thèse*, each intentionally didactic and aimed at resolving some

social evil. *The Money-Question* demonstrates how a virtuous family can be momentarily overcome by the attraction of money. *The Wife of Claude* considers the question of divorce when a husband and wife prove to be entirely incompatible. Perhaps the most characteristic of these plays is *Madame Aubray's Ideas*.

MADAME AUBRAY'S IDEAS

The plot of the drama is, like all those of Dumas's best plays, straightforward. Madame Aubray is a widow left to rear an only child, Camille. Modeling the drama on the parable of the lost sheep (as stated in the preface), Dumas created in Madame Aubray the most devout and charitable of shepherdesses. Her life's mission is to take into her home and nurture those in greater need than she. One of them, Jeannine, is an unwed mother with a small child. The principal action of the play (there are several complementary subplots) involves Madame Aubray's attempts to rehabilitate Jeannine (who has become pregnant more as the result of ignorance than of sensuality) by finding her a suitable husband. Also central is the developing love between Camille and Jeannine. When Madame Aubray's attempts at matchmaking fail, Camille is delighted and quickly asks his mother's permission to marry Jeannine. To her son's great surprise, Madame Aubray refuses to give her consent. Camille is desperate, but his mother stands firm. Jeannine, in an attempt to deal with her own pain and to spare Camille further hurt, informs Madame Aubray that she will lie to Camille; she will admit to having had more than one illicit affair. This she does, but Madame Aubray, suddenly aware of the Christian dilemma before her and unable to participate in such a bold lie, stops Jeannine and cries out to her son, "She lies! . . . Marry her!" In the light of her beliefs, Madame Aubray has no choice but to consent to her son's marriage. The thesis is clear enough, but what strikes the reader is the logical way in which Dumas leads the audience toward the only possible conclusion. There are no artificial attempts to avoid the final decision. Despite the pressures of the age to abandon the fallen woman, the audience has no choice but to accept the logic of the denouement.

Many of Dumas's most cherished themes are developed in *Madame Aubray's Ideas*. Camille speaks at some length of society's need to protect women by educating them, and in one famous scene, Madame Aubray eloquently defends the rights of unwed mothers by reminding her listeners that all are guilty of some equivalent sin. Although the work often assumes the manner of a homily, one cannot deny the power of the character of Madame Aubray. She clearly reveals the difficulty of reconciling Christian teaching with personal reality. If one accepts a certain doctrine (or law, or social convention) as truth, then, Dumas maintains, one must be willing to live by that truth, no matter the consequences. The role of the thesis play—to provoke discussion on social issues—is clearly revealed here.

With *Madame Aubray's Ideas*, Dumas firmly established the model for the thesis play. The focus on a single, controversial issue, the simplicity of the setting and the plot (there is no action in the traditional sense), and the dependence on thesis rather than on the characters to sustain interest, were all new elements for the French stage. The fatal weakness of thesis plays in general, however, is that they treat issues of immediate importance to their contemporary public. Most of the problems that Dumas addressed are no longer vital social issues; therefore, most of his later work has little attraction for the modern audience.

OTHER MAJOR WORKS

LONG FICTION: *Aventures de quatre femmes et d'un perroquet*, 1846-1847 (6 volumes); *Césarine*, 1848; *La Dame aux camélias*, 1848 (2 volumes; Ca-mille, 1857); *Le Docteur Servans*, 1848-1849 (2 volumes); *Antoine*, 1849 (2 volumes); *Trois Hommes forts*, 1850 (4 volumes; *Three Strong Men*, 1878); *Diane de Lys*, 1851 (3 volumes); *Le Régent Mustel*, 1852 (2 volumes); *La Dame aux perles*, 1853 (4 volumes; *Annette: Or, The Lady of the Pearls*, 1891); *Un Cas de rupture*, 1854; *L'Affaire Clémenceau: Mémoire de l'accusé*, 1866 (*The Clemenceau Case*, 1890).

SHORT FICTION: *Contes et nouvelles*, 1853.

POETRY: *Péchés de jeunesse*, 1847.

NONFICTION: *L'Homme-femme*, 1872 (*Man-Woman: Or, The Hearth, the Street*, 1873); *Entr'actes*, 1878-1879 (3 volumes); *Les Femmes qui tuent et les femmes qui votent*, 1880; *Noveau entr'-actes*, 1890.

BIBLIOGRAPHY

Garrett-Groag, Lillian. *The Ladies of the Camellias.* New York: Dramatists Play Service, 1996. An examination of Dumas's *Camille* and the actresses who starred in this play.

Maurois, André. *Three Musketeers: A Study of the Dumas Family.* London: Cape, 1957. A biography that covers Alexandre Dumas *fils* as well as his father and grandfather. Bibliography.

Schwarz, Henry Stanley. *Alexandre Dumas, fils, Dramatist.* 1927. Reprint. New York: B. Bloom, 1971. A classic biography of Dumas, covering his life and works.

William C. Griffin

ALEXANDRE DUMAS, *PÈRE*

Born: Villers-Cotterêts, France; July 24, 1802
Died: Puys, France; December 5, 1870

PRINCIPAL DRAMA

La Chasse et l'amour, pr., pb. 1825 (with Adolphe de Leuven and P.-J. Rousseau)

La Noce et l'enterrement, pr., pb. 1826
Henri III et sa cour, pr., pb. 1829 (*Catherine of Cleves*, 1831; also known as *Henry III and His Court*, 1904)
Christine: Ou, Stockholm, Fontainebleau, et Rome, pr., pb. 1830

Napoléon Bonaparte: Ou, Trente Ans dans l'histoire de France, pr., pb. 1831

Antony, pr., pb. 1831 (English translation, 1904)

Charles VII chez ses grands vassaux, pr., pb. 1831

Richard Darlington, pr. 1831, pb. 1832

Teresa, pr., pb. 1832 (based on a draft by Auguste Anicet-Bourgeois)

Le Mari de la veuve, pr., pb. 1832

La Tour de Nesle, pr., pb. 1832 (redrafted from a manuscript by Frédéric Gaillardet; English translation, 1906)

Le Fils de l'émigré: Ou, Le Peuple, pr. 1832, selections pb. 1902

Angèle, pr. 1833, pb. 1834

La Vénitienne, pr., pb. 1834

Catherine Howard, pr., pb. 1834 (English translation, 1859)

Cromwell et Charles 1, pr., pb. 1835 (with E.-C.-H. Cordellier-Delanoue)

Don Juan de Marana: Ou, La Chute d'un ange, pr., pb. 1836

Kean: Ou, Désordre et génie, pr., pb. 1836 (with Théaulon de Lambert and Frédéric de Courcy; *Edmund Kean: Or, The Genius and the Libertine*, 1847)

Piquillo, pr., pb. 1837 (libretto; with Gérard de Nerval)

Caligula, pr. 1837, pb. 1838

Le Bourgeois de Gand: Ou, Le Secrétaire du duc d'Albe, pr., pb. 1838 (with Hippolyte Romand)

Paul Jones, pr., pb. 1838

Bathilde, pr., pb. 1839 (with Auguste Maquet)

Mademoiselle de Belle-Isle, pr., pb. 1839 (English translation, 1855)

L'Alchimiste, pr., pb. 1839 (with Nerval)

Léo Burckart, pr., pb. 1839 (with Nerval)

Jarvis l'honnête homme: Ou, Le Marchand de Londres, pr., pb. 1840 (originally credited to Charles Lafont)

Un Mariage sous Louis XV, pr., pb. 1841 (*A Marriage of Convenience*, 1899)

Jeannic le Breton: Ou, Le Gérant responsable, pr. 1841, pb. 1842 (with Eugène Bourgeois)

Lorenzino, pr., pb. 1842

Le Séducteur et le mari, pr., pb. 1842 (with Lafont)

Halifax, pr. 1842, pb. 1843 (with Adolphe D'Ennery?)

Le Mariage au tambour, pr., pb. 1843 (with Leuven and Léon Lhérie)

Les Demoiselles de Saint-Cyr, pr., pb. 1843 (*The Ladies of Saint-Cyr*, 1870)

L'École des princes, pr. 1843, pb. 1844 (with Louis Lefèvre)

Louise Bernard, pr., pb. 1843 (with Leuven and Lhérie)

Le Garde forestier, pr., pb. 1845 (with Leuven and Lhérie)

Un Conte des fées, pr., pb. 1845 (with Leuven and Lhérie)

Sylvandire, pr., pb. 1845 (with Leuven and Louis-Émile Vanderburch)

Les Mousquetaires, pr., pb. 1845 (with Maquet; adaptation of Dumas's novel *Vingt ans aprés*)

Une Fille du Régent, pr., pb. 1846

Échec et mat, pr., pb. 1846 (with Octave Feuillet and Paul Bocage)

La Reine Margot, pr., pb. 1847 (with Maquet; based on Dumas's novel)

Intrigue et amour, pr., pb. 1847 (adaptation of Friedrich Schiller's play *Kabale und Liebe*)

Le Chevalier de Maison-Rouge, pr., pb. 1847 (with Maquet; *The Chevalier de Maison-Rouge*, 1859)

Hamlet, prince de Danemark, pr. 1847, pb. 1848 (with Paul Meurice; adaptation of William Shakespeare's play)

Monte-Cristo, parts 1 and 2, pr., pb. 1848 (with Maquet; *Monte-Cristo*, part 1, 1850)

Catilina, pr., pb. 1848 (with Maquet)

La Jeunesse des mousquetaires, pr., pb. 1849 (with Maquet; based on Dumas's novel *Les Trois Mousquetaires*; *The Musketeers*, 1850)

Le Chevalier d'Harmental, pr., pb. 1849 (with Maquet; based on Dumas's novel)

La Guerre des femmes, pr., pb. 1849 (with Maquet; based on Dumas's novel)

Le Connétable de Bourbon: Ou, L'Italie au seizième siècle, pr., pb. 1849 (with Eugène Grangé and Xavier de Montépin)

Le Testament de César, pr., pb. 1849 (with Jules Lacroix)

Le Comte Hermann, pr., pb. 1849

Le Cachemire vert, pr., pb. 1849 (with Eugène Nus)

Urbain Grandier, pr., pb. 1850 (with Maquet)

Le Vingt-quatre février, pr., pb. 1850 (adapted from Zacharias Werner's play *Der 24 Februar*)

Les Chevaliers du Lansquenet, pr., pb. 1850 (with Grangé and Montépin)

Pauline, pr., pb. 1850 (with Grangé and Montépin; based on Dumas's novel)

La Chasse au chastre, pr., pb. 1850 (with Maquet?; based on Dumas's story)

Le Comte de Morcerf, pr., pb. 1851 (with Maquet; part 3 of *Monte-Cristo*)

Villefort, pr., pb. 1851 (with Maquet; part 4 of *Monte-Cristo*)

Romulus, pr., pb. 1854

L'Orestie, pr., pb. 1856

L'Invitation à la valse, pr., pb. 1857 (adapted in English as *Childhood Dreams*, 1881)

Le Roman d'Elvire, pr., pb. 1860 (with Leuven)

L'Envers d'une conspiration, pr., pb. 1860

La Veillée allemande, pr. 1863, pb. 1864 (with Bernard Lopez)

Madame de Chamblay, pr. 1868, pb. 1869

Les Blancs et les bleus, pr., pb. 1869 (adaptation of part of his novel)

Théâtre complet, pb. 1873-1876 (25 volumes)

The Great Lover and Other Plays, pb. 1979

OTHER LITERARY FORMS

Alexandre Dumas, *père*, wrote a large number of historical novels, achieving great fame in 1844 with the publication of *Les Trois Mousquetaires* (*The Three Musketeers*, 1846) and the beginning episodes of the serialized *Le Comte de Monte-Cristo* (*The Count of Monte-Cristo*, 1846). The novels grew out of his great interest in the history of France; throughout his career he published historical accounts, beginning with a few *scènes historiques* in 1831 and including two larger historical compilations, *Gaule et France* in 1833 (*The Progress of Democracy*, 1841) and the important *Chroniques de France* (chronicles of France), which began in 1836.

Dumas enjoyed travel, and he produced numerous travelogues. Many of these appeared in the various newspapers and magazines that he published and edited and for which he frequently wrote much of the material. He also published his memoirs, and in 1837 he and Gérard de Nerval collaborated on a comic opera, *Piquillo*, for which the music was composed by Hippolyte Monpou. At the time of Dumas's death, he was writing a cookbook, *Grand Dictionnaire de cuisine*, which was completed for him by Anatole France.

ACHIEVEMENTS

Alexandre Dumas, *père*, was the most prolific author and the most popular author of his time. He wrote more than one hundred plays, succeeding notably in both drama and comedy; he also wrote many major fictional works, including two of the most famous novels in history. At the height of his success he was called "the uncrowned King of Paris."

His dramatic career was meteoric. While still in his twenties he wrote two plays that helped to revolutionize the drama of Paris, and within a few more years, he produced some of the most popular plays of the entire century. Before he wrote *Henry III and His Court* in 1829, Dumas was virtually unknown; within hours of the final curtain of this *drame historique*, France's first historical drama, he was the sensation of Paris and was being lauded as the champion of the French Romantics. Although Victor Hugo's *Hernani* (pr., pb. 1830; English translation, 1830) is generally considered the play that issued the Romantics' challenge to French classicists, Dumas's romantic drama of adultery, revenge, and political hatred came a year before *Hernani*.

Two years later, Dumas duplicated his previous success and inspired new controversy with *Antony*, the first *drame moderne* (modern drama). In this story of adulterous passions, period costuming was replaced by modern dress, and the setting, language, and characterization were all contemporary. *Antony* was a dramatic triumph for Dumas, but its attack on the social values of the age caused furious controversy that lasted for years.

The astounding success of *La Tour de Nesle*, staged in 1832, gives clear evidence of Dumas's gift

Alexandre Dumas, père (Library of Congress)

for drama. Two other writers had worked on this melodrama of lust, incest, and murder without satisfying their producer. The piece was then brought to Dumas, who immediately saw its possibilities. He rewrote the opening to define situation and characterizations, added several scenes, created new dialogue, and produced a terrifying story that evidently had some eight hundred performances within three years. Dumas had created the most successful melodrama of the age.

Toward the end of the 1830's, Dumas decided to venture into comedy, and in 1839 he produced a full five-act comedy, *The Lady of Belle Isle*. None of his plays except *La Tour de Nesle* enjoyed more performances; this story of a young lady's virtue threatened by but saved from a seducer was still in the repertory of the Comédie-Française at the turn of the century.

Dumas's popularity in the 1830's and 1840's was immense. In some years, four or five of his plays were produced, and in April of 1839 he actually had three premieres at three different theaters within fourteen days. His plays had a powerful influence on the direction French drama would take for years to come.

Dumas added greatly to his fame through his novels, and it is as a novelist rather than as a playwright that he will be remembered most. *The Three Musketeers* has thrilled generations of readers since its first appearance in 1844. The account of the friendship of the young d'Artagnan with the three musketeers, Athos, Porthos, and Aramis, and of their combined efforts to thwart the schemes of the malevolent Cardinal Richelieu and his cruel subordinate, Milady, is one of the best-known adventure tales of the past two centuries.

The only rival to *The Three Musketeers* in popularity among Dumas's novels is *The Count of Monte-Cristo*. The story of Edmond Dantès' revenge against the men whose lies had caused him to be unjustly imprisoned first appeared as a *roman-feuilleton*, a serial novel. Readers eagerly followed each installment as Dantès, now escaped from prison and known as the Count of Monte-Cristo, implacably pursued and caused the destruction of his enemies.

BIOGRAPHY

Alexandre Dumas, *père*, was born on July 24, 1802, in Villers-Cotterêts, a small village northeast of Paris. He was the son of one of Napoleon Bonaparte's generals, Thomas-Alexandre Dumas, and Marie-Louise-Elisabeth Labouret, daughter of an innkeeper in Villers-Cotterêts; he was the grandson of a French marquis, Antoine-Alexandre Davy de la Pailleterie, and a black slave girl, Marie-Cessette Dumas.

When General Dumas was returning to his wife and daughter from Bonaparte's campaign in Egypt, a violent storm in the Mediterranean led to his capture by enemy forces; he spent about twenty months as a prisoner in Naples, suffering much abuse and perhaps even a poisoning attempt. He was not able to return to his family until May of 1801. His only son, the dramatist, was born the following year. The general, never in good health after his captivity, died in 1804, leaving his family with limited financial means.

In his boyhood Dumas showed little interest in studies, preferring to spend his time hunting in the forests near Villers-Cotterêts. His attitude toward books was eventually changed by two new arrivals in the village. Amédée de la Ponce, a hussar officer, taught him Italian and some German, and introduced him to Johann Wolfgang von Goethe's *Die Leiden des jungen Werthers* (1774; *The Sorrows of Young Werther*, 1779) and to the works of Friedrich Schiller—the European Romantic movement thus reached Villers-Cotterêts. A Swedish nobleman, Vicomte Adolphe de Leuven, thrilled the young romantic with stories of Paris—and the Parisian theater in particular. The two decided to collaborate in writing comedy, finishing one play in 1820. Although this light comedy was not of interest to producers, the collaborators were not deterred from writing two additional plays before the end of 1821. It was Leuven who introduced Dumas to the novels of Sir Walter Scott and the riches of romance and history that they contained. Dumas was enthralled; as soon as he had read *Ivanhoe* (1819), he immediately started writing a play based on it, and he made plans to move to Paris to pursue a literary career.

In 1823 in Paris, Dumas was made painfully aware of the deficiencies in his education; he evidently secured a job as copyist for the duke of Orleans (later King Louis-Philippe) only by virtue of his beautiful handwriting. Luckily, one of the other workers in the office advised Dumas on what to read to improve himself and to prepare for a writing career. The suggested works included the great epic poets, French historians, and such moderns as George Gordon, Lord Byron; Victor Hugo; and Alphonse de Lamartine.

Shortly after his arrival in Paris, Dumas began an affair with Marie-Catherine-Laure Labay, a seamstress, who bore him a son on July 27, 1824 (the son was also to become a famous writer, Alexandre Dumas, *fils*). In 1830, Dumas began an affair with an actress, Bell Krelsamer, who bore him a daughter, Marie-Alexandrine, in 1831. By this time Dumas had become a famous playwright.

A minor theatrical success in 1825 had given Dumas all the encouragement he needed to pursue a career in the theater. With Leuven and P.-J. Rousseau he wrote *La Chasse et l'amour* (hunting and love), and this piece was produced on September 22 at the Théâtre de l'Ambigu-Comique. Before the end of 1826, he had another work on the stage, *La Noce et l'enterrement* (the wedding and the burial), which had a run of forty performances.

In the next two years, Dumas staged nothing, but he learned much. He thrilled to the performances of plays by William Shakespeare given in 1827-1828 by a traveling troupe of English actors, including Edmund Kean (whom Dumas would later make the hero of one of his plays). Also, Dumas met Charles Nodier, who invited him to his salon; there the young Dumas met the great figures of the French Romantic movement—Hugo and Lamartine, Honoré de Balzac, Alfred de Musset, Prosper Mérimée, Alfred de Vigny, Eugène Delacroix, and others. He met them and he became one of them. Within a year or so he would become one of the most famous of them.

On February 10, 1829—with the duke of Orleans in the audience—Dumas achieved one of the greatest triumphs any French playwright had ever enjoyed. The audience gave a tumultuous reception to Dumas's *Henry III and His Court*, and the victory of Romanticism over classicism was on the way to being realized—and in the very citadel of classicism, the Théâtre Français. By morning, Dumas was the hero of the younger generation of Parisians and was hailed as one of the great talents of the age. Later that day, the manuscript sold for six thousand francs, and at last Dumas was relieved of financial worries.

In the revolution of 1830, Dumas, the son of Napoleon's commander in chief of the Army of the Western Pyrenees, sent for his gun and took to the streets. Hearing that the people were short of powder, Dumas wrote to Soissons, near his home village, where he knew a powder factory was located. He returned to Paris with more than thirty-five hundred pounds of powder. After the brief revolt that put the duke of Orleans on the throne, Dumas's career continued to develop. He produced *Antony* and several other successful dramas before May of 1832, at which time *La Tour de Nesle* premiered—to the thunderous applause of astonished playgoers who raised Dumas's reputation and fortune to incredible heights.

Dumas's financial success enabled him to travel widely, and travelogues are another large aspect of his literary production. His travels to other countries began in 1832, with a trip to Switzerland, and *Impressions de Voyage: En Suisse*, the first of his *impressions de voyage*, appeared the following year. In the next four years he toured Provence, Italy, Belgium, and Germany. After his marriage to the actress Ida Ferrier early in 1840, they spent most of the next two and a half years in Italy. In 1842, in the company of Prince Napoleon, Bonaparte's nephew, he visited the small island of Monte-Cristo. The name stuck in his memory.

During this decade of travel, Dumas continued to compose dramas for the theaters of Paris, and for some years he enjoyed considerable favor. When the string of successes with dramas ended in the late 1830's, he decided to write a five-act comedy, *The Lady of Belle Isle*. Although Dumas had written only one-act comedies before, his first full comedy was an instantaneous success. Dumas, anxious to capitalize on his success, soon provided two more full comedies: *A Marriage of Convenience* in 1841 and *The Ladies of Saint-Cyr* in 1843. Both enjoyed favorable reception, though they did not prove as lasting as their predecessor.

Dumas would continue to write plays and draw audiences until 1869, the year before he died, but by the early 1840's his greatest and most innovative dramas were behind him. After that time the best of his work would come in areas other than the theater.

Dumas had begun to write novels in 1838, and in 1839 he began to publish serial novels. In the early 1840's he devoted more and more of his tremendous literary energies to fiction. In 1844 he finished five novels; one of these was *The Three Musketeers*. He also started serializing a sixth novel; this was *The Count of Monte-Cristo*. These two magnificent novels added greatly to his fame and fortune. He purchased land at Port-Marly, on which he built at immense cost a huge mansion, the Château de Monte-Cristo.

Unfortunately, serious reversals began for Dumas in 1845, when he was charged with plagiarism by Eugène de Mirecourt. Although his accuser was found guilty of libel, irrevocable damage had been done, and troubles began to mount. In 1847, Dumas lost a lawsuit brought by publishers for whom he had failed to provide material that he had contracted to supply. In the next two years, his literary newspaper, his magazine, and his own theater failed. Dumas was

bankrupt. His magnificent home was seized by creditors, and Dumas went into exile in Belgium in 1851.

From Brussels he began publishing *Mes Mémoires* (*My Memoirs*, 1907-1909) in 1852. Before the end of 1853 he had settled with his creditors, had returned to Paris, and had begun to publish a newspaper, *Le Mousquetaire*, which folded in 1857. He then began a weekly magazine, *Le Monte-Cristo*, but it lasted only until 1860. In June of that year, he traveled to join Giuseppe Garibaldi, allowing his yacht to be used by the Italian insurgent and founding a political journal, *Indépendente*. Returning to Paris in 1864, he tried to publish other periodicals, but none survived for long. His career as a playwright came to an end in 1869 with *Les Blancs et les bleus* (the whites and the blues). In 1870, he suffered a stroke, which caused considerable paralysis. He was carried to his son's home in Puys on the coast of Normandy, where he died on December 5. His body was interred temporarily at Neuville-les-Pollets, but in 1872 it was transferred to Paris.

ANALYSIS

Alexandre Dumas, *père*, rose to fame through his dramatic works, although later generations best remember him for his novels. For a period of forty years, Dumas was a major force in French literature. In 1893, almost a quarter-century after his death, one critic called Dumas "a summit of art"; the critic was George Bernard Shaw.

HENRY III AND HIS COURT

In his first major success, *Henry III and His Court*, Dumas combined a plot of sexual intrigue with one of political intrigue. The play begins with the queen of France, Catherine de Medicis, informing an astrologer, Ruggieri, of her plans to use a woman to overcome Henri, the duke of Guise, whom she sees as the greatest threat to her son, King Henry III, and to her own power. She has learned of the love shared by the duke's wife and one of the king's favorites, Saint Mégrin, who is due to visit Ruggieri shortly. The queen has had the duchess drugged and secretly transported to Ruggieri's quarters, where Saint-Mégrin will find her, and where the queen plans for the duke of Guise to find both of them. The duke arrives too late to catch his wife in a compromising situation, but in her haste she has left behind a handkerchief, which he finds and correctly guesses is proof of a rendezvous between his wife and Saint-Mégrin. Dumas carefully drafted his curtain lines, and the first-act curtain falls to the duke's fierce cry for vengeance. On the next day, the duke forces his wife to write a letter inviting her lover to her chamber. When he appears, she tries to send him away, but he is wounded by the henchman of the duke, who, from his wife's window, throws down the handkerchief that he found the night before and speaks the famous curtain lines that instruct his men to stuff his wife's handkerchief down Saint-Mégrin's throat so that his death will be the sweeter. Then the duke adds that, now that he has taken care of the servant, he will take care of the master. This last line keeps the political conflict of the play—the power struggle between Henry III and the Guise—firmly in the audience's mind. The Guise desires to become head of the Catholic League, but he is thwarted in his ambitions by the king, who appoints himself to the position, thus causing the ominous fury of the duke's closing line.

Dumas did an excellent job of bringing separate historical accounts together to create a sense of unity in his play. History recorded that the duke once angrily confronted his wife with charges of infidelity and gave her a choice of means of suicide: a dagger or a cup of poison. The fear-stricken duchess drank from the cup, only to be informed some hours later that she had merely tasted soup. The actual story of a jealous husband's revenge against his wife's lover comes from the account of the death of Bussy d'Amboise, killed by order of the count of Montsoreau. By attaching Montsoreau's story to the life of the duke of Guise and having d'Amboise become Saint-Mégrin, a follower of the king, Dumas was able to frame the domestic plot within the larger plot of the power struggle involving the League.

CHRISTINE

Dumas's next production was *Christine*. This was a revised version of an earlier play that he had not been able to get produced. In his new play about the Swedish queen who had abdicated but then plotted to regain her throne, Dumas added a new character,

Paula, a young woman who greatly affects the motives for the later action. When Christina and Mondaleschi, an Italian nobleman, leave Stockholm, Paula, in love with Mondaleschi, follows in disguise. Later, in Fontainebleau, Mondaleschi turns against Christina, who discovers his treachery and orders him killed. Paula commits suicide. In the earlier draft, Mondaleschi's murder had been merely a political action; Paula's presence makes the murder seem in part an action by a disappointed lover. In the third major episode, in Rome much later, the dying Christina speaks of her regrets for her actions years earlier. For the most part, the play received a favorable response, but it is not a great play. Dumas wrote it in verse, and he had no great talent for poetry. The play lacks the psychological power to be considered a tragedy, and it lacks the energy and fire needed to be termed a drama. Dumas knew that he had not succeeded in accomplishing his purposes with this work.

NAPOLÉON BONAPARTE

Nor was he satisfied with his next play, *Napoléon Bonaparte*, even though it also received a generally favorable reception from its audiences. He had written the play only because the producer Félix Harel had insisted on it (Harel had actually locked him in a room and told him that he could not leave until he had finished). The play covered three decades in the life of Bonaparte, was nine thousand lines long, and was written in nine days. Dumas knew it was not good, but under the circumstances he was not upset by its weaknesses. In less than four months, he would produce a play that became such an immediate success that he could afford not to dwell on the difficulties of his two previous efforts. *Antony* would take Paris by storm.

ANTONY

Just as *Henry III and His Court* was the first *drame historique*, so *Antony* was the first *drame moderne*. Everything about *Antony* is modern; everything belongs to the 1830's. The hero, Antony, is a passionate young man, unwilling to let conventional morality restrict his pleasures; he will enjoy the married lady of high position that he has chosen to love—regardless of what happens to him or to her.

At the beginning of the play, Antony returns to Paris after an absence of three years to see Adèle, the woman with whom he had fallen in love before. Antony, as is revealed later, is illegitimate. Therefore, because he could not offer Adèle a name and a future, he had run away earlier. Now he has decided to pursue her at all costs, even though she has married and given birth to a daughter during his absence. Adèle tries to avoid him, but her horses bolt, and she is saved from a dangerous accident by Antony. Antony has been injured while stopping the runaway horses and is carried into her house, where a doctor orders him to stay until he is fully recovered. Uncertain of her power to resist Antony's advances, Adèle runs away to join her husband, Colonel d'Hervey, in Strasbourg. The farewell letter she leaves for Antony angers him. He rushes ahead of her, and when she stops at an inn, she finds herself confronted by Antony, who breaks a pane on the glass door, unlatches it, rushes in, stifles her screams with his handkerchief, and drags her toward the bed. Some months later, Adèle is present at a party to which Antony has also been invited. Adèle's virtue is viciously attacked by one of the ladies present; Antony defends her and furiously denounces Parisian society for its hypocrisy and false values. Adèle flees, followed by Antony, who has just been warned that Colonel d'Hervey is due home very soon. Antony arrives only shortly before the angry husband begins to pound at the door. Antony begs Adèle to flee with him, but she refuses because of what the disgrace would do to her husband and daughter. Filled with fear and shame, she begs Antony to kill her in order to put an end to her agony. Antony stabs her to death just as d'Hervey batters down the door; in one of the magnificent curtain lines for which Dumas is famous, Antony protects Adèle's name by shouting to the astonished husband: "She resisted me—I have killed her."

The ending came so suddenly, so unexpectedly, that it had an unprecedented shock effect on its audience. Adultery, an attack on the laws of society, and then an abrupt murder—the audience was dismayed; yet it was also powerfully impressed, and its applause was overwhelming. Dumas had created a new dramatic world. The modern play in prose, initiated by *Antony*, would eventually come to dominate the theater of Paris.

Structurally, *Antony* is probably Dumas's best play. The action is straightforward, each scene moves logically to the next, and there is nothing extraneous to draw attention away from the essential elements of characterization and theme.

The play has much of Dumas's own life in it: Antony, a foundling with no family, no name, no place in society—who refuses, therefore, to allow society to dictate what his behavior should be—is Dumas, the quadroon with obvious Negroid features. Adèle is Melanie Waldor, Dumas's mistress from 1827 to 1830, and Colonel d'Hervey is her husband, Captain Waldor. To Melanie, Dumas wrote some of his most impassioned love letters. Antony's agony had been Dumas's, and many of the lines of the play had previously appeared in love letters written by Dumas and Waldor.

CHARLES VII CHEZ SES GRANDS VASSAUX

Dumas did not immediately follow *Antony* with more *drames modernes*. Instead, he tried to duplicate elements from two of his earlier plays. Later in 1831 he wrote *Charles VII chez ses grands vassaux* (Charles VII and his great vassals): Like *Henry III and His Court*, it would be a *drame historique*; like *Christine*, it would be in verse. The play was an almost complete failure, partly because of the language and partly because of Dumas's difficulties with the acting.

RICHARD DARLINGTON

Dumas then returned to more *drames modernes*, plays of the time for the time. *Richard Darlington*, staged in December of 1831, was the first. Darlington, like Antony, is a foundling and a selfish egoist, but power rather than love is his ambition. Befriended by Dr. Grey of Darlington in England, the foundling grows up to marry the doctor's daughter, Jenny, thereby gaining political influence in Darlington. Later, he needs to be rid of Jenny so that he may arrange a more politically advantageous marriage. He kills Jenny, but is caught and executed. The executioner reveals his true identity to Darlington—he is the father who had deserted him years before.

TERESA

Teresa is the story of a young woman, recently married, who resumes an affair with a former lover, who is engaged to her new stepdaughter. Once her secret is discovered by her husband, her shame drives her to suicide. Many of the questions voiced in *Antony* about society appear again in *Teresa*.

LA TOUR DE NESLE

A melodrama, *La Tour de Nesle* was an even greater success than Dumas's previous great triumphs. Originally the conception of Frédéric Gaillardet (who later sued Dumas and fought a duel with him over the rights to the play), it had been almost totally rewritten by Dumas, who, even so, requested that his name not appear on the playbills. Under Dumas's reshaping, the story became a struggle between Marguerite, a queen, and Buridan, an adventurer—the one with rank and power, the other with genius.

La Tour de Nesle deals with the gruesome legends attached to the story of Margeurite of Bourgogne, the wife of Louis X, and her sisters Jeanne and Blanche. Nightly the three women were supposed to indulge in orgies within the walls of the Tower of Nesle, located just across the Seine from the Louvre. The legend has it that each morning the bodies of three handsome young noblemen—the three lovers of the cruel sisters from the night before—would wash ashore below the Tower. Although the legend was false, it provided a powerful stimulus to the imagination of Dumas. As he told his tale of lust, adultery, murder, incest, filicide, and revenge, the supreme melodrama of the age was created. *La Tour de Nesle* may have had more than eight hundred performances between 1832 and 1834.

In the story, Buridan knows the deadly secrets of Marguerite of Bourgogne—twenty years earlier she had become pregnant by a page in her father's castle; she had hired him to kill her father in order to protect her reputation. The twin sons she bore were ordered killed, but a sympathetic friend protected them. Twenty years later, all these characters appear in Paris. Buridan, imprisoned by Marguerite, reveals himself to be her lover of two decades earlier and threatens to tell her story to the king. Marguerite quickly arranges his release, but she sets a trap for Buridan, who finds out that one of the young lovers recently killed by Marguerite was her own son by Buridan and that the other son is going to the Tower for a rendezvous with the queen. Buridan rushes to the Tower to try to save his son, Gualtier, but in the ensuing action Gualtier, Buridan, and Marguerite all perish.

The play was melodramatic, but as always Dumas's energy and verve could create scenes that were memorable: In the first act, Buridan leaps from a window to save himself from the assassins who kill Philippe, as the voice of a watchman is heard in the distance announcing the time and adding that all is well. In the third act, Marguerite comes to the prison to gloat over the captured Buridan, who slowly, calmly begins to recite the details of her past sins. The play was melodrama *par excellence*.

ANGÈLE

Angèle contains Dumas's first Don Juan type, Alfred d'Alvimar, who seduces Angèle, then runs away with her mother, a widow who is still young enough and pretty enough to be of interest to d'Alvimar—for a while at least. Some months later the pregnant Angèle finds her mother in Paris, just as d'Alvimar is planning to desert her. As d'Alvimar tries to flee, he is challenged by a young doctor, Henri, who is in love with Angèle. Henri kills d'Alvimar in a duel and then marries Angèle to give her and the child a name, even though he knows he soon will die from a disease that his medical knowledge cannot cure. As a *drame moderne*, *Angèle* is generally considered a better play than *Teresa*.

CATHERINE HOWARD

Among the plays which followed, *Catherine Howard* was a huge success. Dumas termed the play "extrahistorical"; that is, he took the names of characters from history but the actions of the characters are purely imaginary. Catherine, already married at the time Henry VIII decides he wants her for his queen, is quite willing to leave one husband for another if the new one can give her the glory of a crown. Her first husband drinks a potion that places him in a deathlike trance, and thereby he is able to escape being murdered by the king. Later, when Catherine has fallen out of favor with Henry, her executioner is her first husband.

DON JUAN DE MARANA

Don Juan de Marana is a weak and hurried effort. It reminds the reader somewhat of a *mystère* by Pedro Calderón de la Barca as good spirits struggle with evil ones. Dumas lifted several situations from other plays, a fact that his critics did not allow to pass unnoticed. The play is one of the worst Dumas ever penned.

EDMUND KEAN

In 1836, with *Edmund Kean*, which deals with the life of the English actor Edmund Kean, who had recently died, Dumas wrote one of his deepest and most interesting plays. Kean is a lineal descendant of Antony; specifically, he is a study of a great artist set apart from his fellows by his talent. Born into the lower classes, his talent has gained for him the adulation of the upper classes, even of royalty. He can be an acquaintance of lords and princes, but only to a certain degree: He must keep his place; he must not presume too far. Rival to the prince of Wales for the affections of the same lady, Kean stops in the middle of his performance of *Romeo and Juliet* to hurl insults at his rival in the audience.

As always in Dumas's *drames modernes*, society defeats the individual. Kean is advised to leave England after his tirade against the prince, and the lady whom he loves decides that she cannot sacrifice her social station or her rewarding position as the mistress of the heir to the throne merely to become Kean's. Dumas called his play a comedy and arranged a happy ending: Kean leaves for America with Anna, a young woman who has been in love with him for a long time and the very woman whom he once saved from abduction by an English nobleman, one of those fine gentlemen who believes himself far above Kean in quality.

The subtitle, "Désordre et génie" (literally, "disorder and genius"), glances at Kean's excesses, alcohol and sex, and implies the question of whether the genius would have been the same without the disorder. It is tempting to read *Edmund Kean* as, in part, the autobiography of Dumas. Kean's attack of English critics expresses Dumas's view of many French critics. Moreover, Dumas knew that, in spite of his literary accomplishments, there were many doors in Paris that would never be open to him because he was one-fourth black.

(When Jean-Paul Sartre wrote his *Edmund Kean* in 1953, an adaptation of Dumas's play, he had Kean playing Othello in the famous scene in which Kean denounces the prince from the stage.)

THE LADY OF BELLE ISLE

Early in 1839, *Bathilde*, written with Auguste Maquet, received a fair reception, and in April Dumas had three new plays appear, not one of which was entirely his own work. The most significant of these was the sparkling comedy *The Lady of Belle Isle*, which clearly showed Dumas's considerable gift for comedy. The Duke de Richelieu wagers that he can seduce a young lady, Gabrielle, within twenty-four hours; unfortunately, for this hurried enterprise he enlists the aid of a former mistress, the Marquise de Prie, who, being more than a little upset, substitutes herself for Gabrielle in the darkness of the young lady's bedchamber after having sent Gabrielle away to effect the other main action of the play, the release of her father and brother from the Bastille. The play was criticized for the unrealistic substitution of the marquise as the conquest of the evening, but this has not kept audiences from making it Dumas's most popular comedy.

LATER PLAYS

In 1841 and 1843, two more comedies in the same eighteenth century vein enjoyed a measure of popularity and further showed Dumas's gift for witty dialogue. After these comedies, Dumas's great success as a writer of novels left him with less time for the theater. Among his later plays, *Le Comte Hermann* (Count Hermann), produced in 1849, is one that he valued highly. There were a few other good moments for Dumas in the theater, and some very unusual ones as well—*Le Vampire*, for example, in 1851. By this time, however, French Romanticism was dying, Dumas's career was in serious decline, and he would never again be a vital force in the theater of Paris.

OTHER MAJOR WORKS

LONG FICTION: *Acté*, 1838 (English translation, 1904); *Le Capitaine Paul*, 1838 (*Captain Paul*, 1848); *La Salle d'Armes*, 1838 (includes *Pauline* [English translation, 1844], *Pascal Bruno* [English translation, 1837], and *Murat* [English translation, 1896]); *La*

Comtesse de Salisbury, 1839; *Le Capitaine Pamphile*, 1840 (*Captain Pamphile*, 1850); *Othon l'Archer*, 1840 (*Otho the Archer*, 1860); *Aventures de Lyderic*, 1842 (*Lyderic, Count of Flanders*, 1903); *Le Chevalier d'Harmental*, 1843 (with Auguste Maquet; *The Chevalier d'Harmental*, 1856); *Ascanio*, 1843 (with Paul Meurice; English translation, 1849); *Georges*, 1843 (*George*, 1846); *Amaury*, 1844 (English translation, 1854); *Une Fille du Régent*, 1844 (with Maquet; *The Regent's Daughter*, 1845); *Les Frères corses*, 1844 (*The Corsican Brothers*, 1880); *Gabriel Lambert*, 1844 (*The Galley Slave*, 1849; also as *Gabriel Lambert*, 1904); *Sylvandire*, 1844 (*The Disputed Inheritance*, 1847; also as *Sylvandire*, 1897); *Les Trois Mousquetaires*, 1844 (*The Three Musketeers*, 1846); *Le Comte de Monte-Cristo*, 1844-1845 (*The Count of Monte-Cristo*, 1846); *La Reine Margot*, 1845 (with Maquet; *Marguerite de Navarre*, 1845; better known as *Marguerite de Valois*, 1846); *Vingt Ans après*, 1845 (with Maquet; *Twenty Years After*, 1846); *La Guerre des femmes*, 1845-1846 (*Nanon*, 1847; also as *The War of Women*, 1895); *Le Bâtard de Mauléon*, 1846 (*The Bastard of Mauléon*, 1848); *Le Chevalier de Maison-Rouge*, 1846 (with Maquet; *Marie Antoinette: Or, The Chevalier of the Red House*, 1846; also as *The Chevalier de Maison-Rouge*, 1893); *La Dame de Monsoreau*, 1846 (*Chicot the Jester*, 1857); *Les Deux Diane*, 1846 (with Meurice; *The Two Dianas*, 1857); *Mémoires d'un médecin*, 1846-1848 (also as *Joseph Balsamo*; with Maquet; *Memoirs of a Physician*, 1846); *Les Quarante-cinq*, 1848 (with Maquet; *The Forty-five Guardsmen*, 1847); *Le Vicomte de Bragelonne*, 1848-1850 (with Maquet; *The Vicomte de Bragelonne*, 1857; also as 3 volumes: *The Vicomte de Bragelonne*, 1893; *Louise de la Vallière*, 1893; and *The Man in the Iron Mask*, 1893); *La Véloce*, 1848-1851; *Le Collier de la reine*, 1849-1850 (with Maquet; *The Queen's Necklace*, 1855); *La Tulipe noire*, 1850 (with Maquet and Paul Lacroix; *The Black Tulip*, 1851); *Conscience l'Innocent*, 1852 (*Conscience*, 1905); *Ange Pitou*, 1851 (*Six Years Later*, 1851; also as *Ange Pitou*, 1859); *Olympe de Clèves*, 1852 (English translation, 1894); *Isaac Laquedem*, 1852-1853; *La Comtesse de Charny*, 1853-1855 (*The Countess of Charny*, 1858); *Catherine Blum*, 1854

(*The Foresters*, 1854; also as *Catherine Blum*, 1861); *Ingénue*, 1854 (English translation, 1855); *Le Page du Duc de Savoie*, 1854 (*Emmanuel Philibert*, 1854; also as *The Page of the Duke of Savoy*, 1861); *El Saltéador*, 1854 (*The Brigand*, 1897); *Les Mohicans de Paris*, 1854-1855, and *Salvator*, 1855-1859 (*The Mohicans of Paris*, 1875; abridged version); *Charles le Téméraire*, 1857 (*Charles the Bold*, 1860); *Les Compagnons de Jéhu*, 1857 (*Roland de Montrevel*, 1860; also as *The Companions of Jéhu*, 1895); *Les Meneurs de loups*, 1857 (*The Wolf Leader*, 1904); *Ainsi-soit-il!*, 1858 (also as *Madame de Chamblay*, 1862; *Madame de Chamblay*, 1869); *Le Capitaine Richard*, 1858 (*The Twin Captains*, 1861); *L'Horoscope*, 1858 (*The Horoscope*, 1897); *Le Chasseur de Sauvagine*, 1859 (*The Wild Duck Shooter*, 1906); *Histoire d'un cabanon et d'un chalet*, 1859 (*The Convict's Son*, 1905); *Les Louves de Machecoul*, 1859 (*The Last Vendée*, 1894; also as *The She Wolves of Machecoul*, 1895); *Le Médecin de Java*, 1859 (also as *L'Île de Feu*, 1870; *Doctor Basilius*, 1860); *La Maison de Glace*, 1860 (*The Russian Gipsy*, 1860); *Le Père la Ruine*, 1860 (*Père la Ruine*, 1905); *La San-Felice*, 1864-1865 (*The Lovely Lady Hamilton*, 1903); *Le Comte de Moret*, 1866 (*The Count of Moret*, 1868); *La Terreur prussienne*, 1867 (*The Prussian Terror*, 1915); *Les Blancs et les bleus*, 1867-1868 (*The Whites and the Blues*, 1895); *The Romances of Alexandre Dumas*, 1893-1897 (60 volumes); *The Novels of Alexandre Dumas*, 1903-1911 (56 volumes).

NONFICTION: *Gaule et France*, 1833 (*The Progress of Democracy*, 1841); *Impressions de voyage*, 1833, 1838, 1841, 1843 (*Travels in Switzerland*, 1958); *La Vendée et Madame*, 1833 (*The Duchess of Berri in La Vendée*, 1833); *Guelfes et Gibelins*, 1836; *Isabel de Bavière*, 1836 (*Isabel of Bavaria*, 1846); *Napoléon*, 1836 (English translation, 1874); *Quinze Jours au Sinaï*, 1838 (*Impressions of Travel in Egypt and Arabia Petraea*, 1839); *Crimes célèbres*, 1838-1840 (*Celebrated Crimes*, 1896); *Excursions sur les bords du Rhin*, 1841 (with Gérard de Nerval); *Le Midi de la France*, 1841 (*Pictures of Travel in the South of France*, 1852); *Chroniques du roi Pépin*, 1842 (*Pepin*, 1906); *Jehanne la Pucelle, 1429-1431*,

1842 (*Joan the Heroic Maiden*, 1847); *Le Spéronare*, 1842; *Le Corricolo*, 1843; *Mes mémoires*, 1852, 1853, 1854-1855 (*My Memoirs*, 1907-1909); *Souvenirs de 1830 à 1842*, 1854-1855; *Causeries*, 1860; *Les Garibaldiens*, 1861 (*The Garibaldians in Sicily*, 1861); *Histoires de mes bêtes*, 1868 (*My Pets*, 1909); *Souvenirs dramatiques*, 1868; *Grand Dictionnaire de cuisine*, 1873 (with Anatole France); *On Board the "Emma,"* 1929; *The Road to Monte-Cristo*, 1956.

TRANSLATION: *Mémoires de Garibaldi*, 1860 (of Giuseppe Garibaldi's *Memorie autobiografiche*).

CHILDREN'S LITERATURE: *La Bouillie de la Comtesse Berthe*, 1845 (*Good Lady Bertha's Honey Broth*, 1846); *Histoire d'un casse-noisette*, 1845 (*Story of a Nutcracker*, 1846); *Le Roi de Bohème*, 1853 (also as *La Jeunesse de Pierrot*, 1854; *When Pierrot Was Young*, 1924); *Le Sifflet enchanté*, 1859 (*The Enchanted Whistle*, 1894).

MISCELLANEOUS: *Œuvres complètes*, 1846-1877 (301 volumes); *Œuvres d'Alexandre Dumas*, 1962-1967 (38 volumes).

BIBLIOGRAPHY

Hemmings, F. W. J. *Alexandre Dumas, the King of Romance*. New York: Scribner, 1979. A general biography of Dumas, covering his life and works. Bibliography and index.

Maurois, André. *The Titans: A Three-Generation Biography of the Dumas*. 1957. Westport, Conn.: Greenwood Press, 1971. An examination of the Dumas family, from Alexandre Dumas, *père*, to Alexandre Dumas, *fils*, to Thomas Alexandre Dumas. Bibliography.

Ross, Michael. *Alexandre Dumas*. North Pomfret, Vt.: David & Charles, 1981. A biography of the nineteenth century novelist and dramatist. Bibliography and index.

Schopp, Claude. *Alexandre Dumas: Genius of Life*. New York: Franklin Watts, 1988. A general biography of the elder Dumas, translated from the French. Index.

Spurr, Harry A. *The Life and Writings of Alexander Dumas*. Rev. ed. New York: Haskell House, 1973. A biography of Dumas that covers his life and literary works. Bibliography and index.

Stowe, Richard S. *Alexandre Dumas (père)*. Boston: Twayne, 1976. A basic biography of the elder Dumas, covering his literary output as well as his life. Bibliography and index.

Howard L. Ford

WILLIAM DUNLAP

Born: Perth Amboy, New Jersey; February 19, 1766
Died: New York, New York; September 28, 1839

PRINCIPAL DRAMA

The Father: Or, American Shandyism, pr., pb. 1789 (revised as *The Father of an Only Child*, pb. 1806)

Fountainville Abbey, pr. 1795, pb. 1806

The Archers: Or, Mountaineers of Switzerland, pr., pb. 1796 (opera; music by Benjamin Carr)

The Man of Fortitude: Or, The Knight's Adventure, pr. 1797, pb. 1807

Tell Truth and Shame the Devil, pr., pb. 1797 (adaptation of A. L. B. Robineau's play *Jérome Pointu*)

André, pr., pb. 1798

False Shame: Or, The American Orphan in Germany, pr. 1798, pb. 1940 (adaptation of August von Kotzebue's play *Falsche Schaam*)

The Stranger, pr., pb. 1798 (adaptation of Kotzebue's play *Menschenhass und Reue*)

Don Carlos, pr. 1799 (adaptation of Friedrich Schiller's play *Don Carlos, Infant von Spanien*)

Lovers' Vows, pr. 1799, pb. 1814 (adaptation of Kotzebue's play *Das Kind der Liebe*)

The Italian Father, pr. 1799, pb. 1800

The Virgin of the Sun, pr., pb. 1800 (adaptation of Kotzebue's play *Die Sonnen Jungfrau*)

Pizzaro in Peru: Or, The Death of Rolla, pr., pb.
1800 (adaptation of Kotzebue's play *Die
Spanier in Peru: Oder, Rollas Tod*)

Fraternal Discord, pr. 1800, pb. 1809 (adaptation
of Kotzebue's play *Die Versöhnung*)

Abaellino, the Great Bandit, pr. 1801, pb. 1802
(adaptation of J. H. D. Zschokke's play
Abällino der Grosse Bandit)

The Glory of Columbia—Her Yeomanry!, pr. 1803,
pb. 1817 (adaptation of *André*)

Ribbemont: Or, The Feudal Baron, pr., pb. 1803
(originally as *The Mysterious Monk*, pr. 1796)

The Wife of Two Husbands, pr., pb. 1804
(adaptation of Guilbert de Pixérécourt's play *La
Femme à deux maris*)

Leicester, pb. 1806 (originally as *The Fatal
Deception: Or, The Progress of Guilt*, pr. 1794)

The Dramatic Works of William Dunlap, pb. 1806,
1816 (3 volumes)

Thirty Years: Or, The Life of a Gamester, pr. 1828,
pb. 1940 (adaptation of Prosper Goubaux and
Victor Ducange's play *Trente Ans*)

A Trip to Niagara: Or, Travellers in America, pr.
1828, pb. 1830

Four Plays, 1789-1812, pb. 1976

Adaptations of European Plays, pb. 1988

Five Plays, pb. 1991

More Plays of William Dunlap, pb. 1995

OTHER LITERARY FORMS

Many of William Dunlap's nondramatic works
have earned for him solid status among students of
literature and visual art. His biography of his contemporary Charles Brockden Brown, America's first major gothic novelist, remains a standard reference tool.
Dunlap's other biographical works—a shorter piece
on Brown, sketches of Gilbert Stuart and Thomas
Abthorpe Cooper, and a book on George Frederick
Cooke—are valuable portraits by one who was on the
scene for many of the events presented. Because of
his career as a painter, Dunlap's *A History of the Rise
and Progress of the Arts of Design in the United
States* (1834) also remains a work worth consulting
for this aspect of the early cultural history of the
United States.

Still more important is *A History of American
Theatre* (1832). Dunlap's account of the American
theater from the 1790's through the first third of
the nineteenth century is at times blurred by faulty
memory. Nevertheless, before the work of George O.
Seilhamer, George C. D. Odell, Arthur Hornblow,
and Arthur Hobson Quinn, Dunlap offered a rich history of American drama. His firsthand account also
furnishes an autobiography of its author, and altogether, it remains a classic in the annals of the American stage.

Dunlap also wrote verse, and several of his short
stories, published in periodicals during the final decade of his life, merit critical attention. Many of his
periodical pieces were unsigned, making definite at-
tribution difficult. Dunlap intended to bring out a collected edition of his plays, in ten volumes. Only three
volumes of *The Dramatic Works of William Dunlap*
appeared, however, the first in 1806, the following
two in 1816.

ACHIEVEMENTS

Customarily designated the "Father of American
Drama," William Dunlap lived a long life through a
period of extraordinary historical change in American culture. He was the first American playwright
who turned to writing plays and managing theaters
for a livelihood. His output of original plays and adaptations or translations from foreign dramas adds
up to more than fifty titles. He gained considerable
fame, as well as the love of many who were connected with early American theater, during his management of playhouses in Philadelphia and New
York. Dunlap also deserves praise for his interest in
and knowledge of German language and literature, as
a result of which he was able to bring plays by August von Kotzebue, Friedrich Schiller, and J. H. D.
Zschokke to the American stage at the turn of the
nineteenth century. Such fare continued to be popular
for many years. Dunlap also adapted from French
theater, particularly from the then fairly new melodrama. His own pleasure in melodramatic and sensational scenes informs many of his original productions; he adapted many sentimental-sensational plays
for his theaters because he well comprehended the

desires of his audiences. His striving in his writing and in his theaters for high standards of morality, however, countered common tendencies to cater mainly to less admirable impulses of audiences eager for thrills and sexually suggestive titillation. At times, too, Dunlap's intense patriotism, centered on his admiration for George Washington, saved his own plays from running overmuch into sleazy melodramatics. On the other hand, that overt patriotism emphatically dates these plays and limits their appeal today, except as valuable literary history.

Dunlap as dramatist furnishes a curiosity in the accounts of anthologists and scholars of our national literature, in that most collections of eighteenth and early nineteenth century American plays have featured only *André*. Richard Moody, however, in his anthology *Dramas from the American Theatre, 1762-1909* (1966), provides other specimens from Dunlap's canon, *The Glory of Columbia—Her Yeomanry!* and *A Trip to Niagara*. The first is a reworking of *André*; the second demonstrates Dunlap's experimental combination of dramatic and visual-arts techniques. Dunlap's interests as playwright and painter make such a blending understandable.

Dunlap's decided inclination toward the gothic, obvious in *Leicester, Fountainville Abbey*, and other plays and clearly coursing through works in which other concerns are primary, has been sadly neglected, although this interest led to some of Dunlap's outstanding achievements. The early historians of American literature tended to follow too closely in the footsteps of Ralph Waldo Emerson, championing a distinctly national literary art. As a result, they generally regarded gothicism as a product of European decadence, a genre not conducive to the production of a genuinely indigenous American literature. Dunlap himself recognized the excesses to which literary gothicism was prone, as is evident in his short stories: There, as often as not, such exaggerations were subjected to hoax treatment. In the manner of Washington Irving and Edgar Allan Poe, Dunlap deftly mingled horror and humor.

Dunlap's partiality toward the gothic has not been the only aspect of his work to be noted unfavorably by critics and historians. Dunlap's twin interests, the theater and painting, have often been used against him by those who believe that he achieved slightly less than greatness in either, simply because he was engaged in two careers. Partly as a result of such prejudices, Dunlap's work as a playwright has been undervalued. At a time when bombast clouded much of American literature, Dunlap experimented with vernacular speech on the stage. He managed to effect compelling characters by such means. His practical experience of theater management gave him a command of his medium that many of his contemporaries did not enjoy, as, for example, the career of James Nelson Barker reveals. All his limitations notwithstanding, Dunlap merits greater attention than he has received from students of American drama.

BIOGRAPHY

William Dunlap, the only child of Samuel and Margaret Sargeant Dunlap, spent his early years in Perth Amboy, New Jersey, where he was born. The wealth of his father, a merchant specializing in the china and looking-glass trade, enabled the boy to receive a fine education. He was particularly fortunate in studying classical literature with the elderly Thomas Bartow, whose store of learning in the classics enriched the mind of his young friend. In the spring of 1777, Samuel Dunlap, whose sympathies were Loyalist, moved his family to New York City, where William was first introduced to stage drama. This interest was to continue throughout his life, and although reverses in fortune later dogged Dunlap, he never lost his enthusiasm for any aspect of the stage. In 1783, after the close of the Revolutionary War, the Dunlaps returned to Perth Amboy. Shortly thereafter, during the convening of Congress at Princeton, Dunlap first saw George Washington, and during the winter of 1783-1784, the young man painted a portrait of his hero.

From 1784 to August, 1787, Dunlap spent time in London, studying painting with Benjamin West and increasing his acquaintance with playgoing and with theater personages. Richard Brinsley Sheridan's plays were among his favorites. Returning to the United States, Dunlap tried to establish himself as a portrait painter, but the theater soon came to be uppermost in his mind and work. The success of Royall

Tyler's *The Contrast* (pr. 1787) inspired Dunlap to create his own first play, a comedy entitled "The Modest Soldier: Or, Love in New York," which was accepted by the American Company but never performed; the young playwright had failed to fashion parts suitable for the manager and his wife. Correcting that circumstance in his next work, *The Father*, written in 1788 and performed in 1789, Dunlap launched himself on a career as a dramatist that lasted for the next thirty years and made him famous. His experiments with numerous dramatic forms, his introduction of Kotzebue and other European playwrights to the American stage, and his career as a manager in Philadelphia and New York, as well as his ventures into painting (most notably portraits) and into other forms of writing, filled his life.

Dogged by financial misfortunes after he lost his fortune as a theater manager, Dunlap maintained a good temper, as well as the respect and love of a wide circle of friends. His marriage, in 1789, to Nabby Woolsey, of an old New York family, brought him into contact with many well-known figures of his day, including Timothy Dwight, his wife's brother-in-law, who was to become president of Yale University. Always a social being, Dunlap also maintained connections with several literary clubs. The Friendly Club numbered among its members, in addition to Dunlap, many who shaped the cultural history of the United States during its early national period. Dunlap died in New York on September 28, 1839, after suffering a stroke.

ANALYSIS

Possibly more than any other playwright of his age, William Dunlap has come down through chronicles of American drama, such as those of Arthur Hobson Quinn, Montrose J. Moses, and Oral Sumner Coad, as the author of a single play, *André*, although Quinn's account in his history of early American drama does reveal other facets of Dunlap's work. However, a number of Dunlap's other works merit discussion.

THE FATHER

The Father was Dunlap's first play to be performed; it was also the second comedy by an Ameri-

can playwright to enjoy public notice. As such, it deserves examination as a follow-up to Tyler's *The Contrast*. *The Father* still can entertain readers; its comic misunderstandings and mishaps, its portraiture of the typical Yankee character, and its lively dialogue retain their power to amuse.

The marriage of the Rackets has entered the doldrums; Mr. Racket believes that solace will come in the arms of country-bred Susannah, a pert household maid, while Mrs. Racket hopes to intensify her husband's love by inciting him to jealousy of their friend, Ranter. Ranter, however, has designs on her sister, Caroline. At an inopportune moment, Colonel Duncan, guardian to the sisters, enters and discovers Mrs. Racket fainting into Ranter's arms—and suspects the worst. The colonel and his servant, Cartridge, function, as Cartridge observes, like Laurence Sterne's Mr. Toby Shandy and Corporal Trim from the novel *The Life and Opinions of Tristram Shandy, Gent.* (1759-1767), a tale abounding in comic high jinks such as Dunlap tries to approximate with American characters. Ultimately, a solid reunion of the Rackets is effected by means of the exposure of Ranter's rascalities, the revelation that Caroline's lover, the long-lost son of Colonel Duncan, is alive, and the proper disposition of Susannah to Dr. Quiescent, a comic figure who has provided relief to tempestuous or grave incidents.

THE FATHER OF AN ONLY CHILD

Dunlap deftly revised this play into *The Father of an Only Child*, which was possibly never performed, although it certainly reads well and could be a lively performance piece. A more distinctly American tinge is emphasized by means of comic reference to the *American Monthly Magazine*, in the vernacular speech of some of the characters, principally the maid Susannah, and in diminishing the Latinate names (Dr. Quiescent becomes Dr. Tattle). The Rackets are still the bibulous Irishman who has an eye for the ladies, and the long-suffering, determined wife who wrongheadedly tries to use jealousy to regain her husband's affections. The Colonel, renamed Campbell (his aide is renamed Platoon), with his concern for the only son he left to others long ago, gives the new title to the play. The background (the recent adoption of the United States Constitution) provides plausibility for the drunken revelry at the opening of the play. The menial, Jacob, adds to the cast a comic "Dutch" character, soon to become a stereotype in American plays. The outcome of this play is similar to that of *The Father*, except that Susannah is destined for Platoon.

Susannah's speeches in particular are noteworthy for their colloquial flavor, as when she repulses Racket's advances: "I'm a poor Yankee girl, and you are a rich town gentleman, and I'm sartin sich are no more fit to go together than a *pumpkin* and a pine-apple. New mister Platoon don't go for higher than a good ripe ear of Indian corn, and a pumpkin needn't be ashamed of coming upon the same table any day." She remarks at this same juncture that "a body ought to keep company with a body's likes. Some folk's place is the keeping-room, and some folk's place is the stirring-room." Along with Platoon's praise for Colonel Campbell freeing his slaves (Dunlap's own action on his father's death), such speeches serve to add homey, American touches to *The Father of an Only Child*. The exposure of the villainous servant's machinations against his master—the long-lost lover of Mrs. Racket's sister—in both versions suggests that European villainy is more vicious than the rather tame misdoings of Americans (the Rackets are new Americans). Ranter-Marsh-Rushport has his disguise stripped from him, and the revelation that he is the ne'er-do-well son whose misdeeds killed his clergy-man father and whose ring is that of Caroline's be-trothed recalls the confusions of identity, duplicitous and otherwise, characteristic of the gothic romance so much in vogue at that time.

A TRIP TO NIAGARA

Similar comedies wherein misapprehension of motives furnishes the dramatic conflict are *False Shame*, adapted from Kotzebue, *Thirty Years*, adapted from Goubaux and Ducange, and Dunlap's original *A Trip to Niagara*. In this last play, Dunlap put together suitable dramatic action to enhance a diorama or re-volving set of scenery that moves the audience from New York Harbor to Catskill Landing, during which action the merits of the United States, as Dunlap's au-dience knew it, were debated—to the final yielding to

its excellences by the British antagonist. Too easily dismissed by critics, *A Trip to Niagara* is not poor dramatic art. The dialogue is spirited, the situation—of Amelia Wentworth's lover having to win her brother to things American in order to marry her—is good comic material, and the portraiture of comic stage types (French, Irish, Yankee) is compelling. The dialects, especially the American colloquial (al-though John Bull, Amelia's lover, merely impersonates a familiar Yankee figure), are well handled. Dunlap also presented the first serious portraiture of a black character of the American stage in Job Jerry-son, who is a far cry from the amusing black minstrel who became a popular stage type during the nine-teenth century. Despite Dunlap's apparent writing of this play on commission, he managed to create a comedy of no mean order.

LEICESTER

Dunlap's tragic muse also inspired him to write several plays of high quality; these tragedies often de-rive from gothic tradition. *Leicester*, *Fountainville Abbey*, *Ribbemont* (originally staged as *The Mysteri-ous Monk* in 1796), and *The Man of Fortitude* abound in eerie scenery; foreboding characters and settings in equally mysterious situations; intense, emotion-filled scenes; and death—with accompanying moral lofti-ness triumphing. Derivative as it is from William Shakespeare's *Macbeth* (pr. 1606)—itself an inspira-tion for gothic fiction—*Leicester* conveys splendidly the tensions of characters motivated by ambition, thwarted or illicit passion, and murderous impulses. The shifts in scenes, physical and psychological, through numerous shadows and glooms or fears and hysteria artistically support the strained verbal inter-changes among the *dramatis personae*.

FOUNTAINVILLE ABBEY

Fountainville Abbey, even more literary than his-torical in inspiration, was founded on Ann Radcliffe's famous gothic novel, *The Romance of the Forest* (1791), and a play that was based on it, by the British dramatist James Boaden, *Fountainville Forest* (pr. 1794). Dunlap's play, first performed in 1795, is an-other of his works that has been neglected in favor of historical-patriotic creation, although Elihu Hubbard Smith, thoroughly knowledgeable in cultural currents at the time, pronounced it the best tragedy he had seen in twenty years, adding that if Dunlap fulfilled his promise, he might well become the most respected dramatist of his time.

In Dunlap's hands, the British sources are transmuted into exceptional verse drama. Fleeing creditors, La Motte, his wife, and his servant, old Peter, along with Adeline, a girl mysteriously brought along by La Motte, find shelter in abandoned Fountainville Abbey. The darkness and obscurity of that locale blend well with a seeming ghost—who in the end turns out to be old Peter harmlessly going to and fro—to produce a rational supernaturalism, after the manner of Radcliffe and akin to what Dunlap's contemporary, the novelist Charles Brockden Brown, would soon purvey in his fiction. (Dunlap, however, should be credited with being the first American gothicist.) The wicked Marquis de Montalt, whom La Motte had attempted to rob, soon appears on the scene, lusts after Adeline, and then tries to browbeat La Motte into murdering the girl when he discovers that she is his niece, daughter of the brother and rightful marquis, whom he had murdered. In the end, justice and virtue triumph, but that happy conclusion occurs only after moments of great trauma. Adeline is restored to her rightful status, and with her wealth she will bring good fortune to La Motte as well. The Marquis unsuccessfully tries to commit suicide—and thus departs from his origins in Radcliffe and Boaden, wherein he does kill himself. La Motte, a man dogged by guilt, finally, and symbolically, is brought from darkness, in setting and spirit, to light and salvation. The backdrops are functional in enhancing the psychic upsets (more significant than physical action) in *Fountainville Abbey*.

RIBBEMONT

Dunlap's poetic heights in *Fountainville Abbey* are not matched in *Ribbemont*. Reminiscent of the *Romeo and Juliet* situation of poisoning, this play of apparently illicit love and murder is marred by too many overstrained speeches and too little action.

ADAPTATIONS

The Man of Fortitude, *The Stranger*, *The Italian Father*, *Don Carlos*, and *Abaellino, the Great Bandit*—adaptations from older English or from German

plays—contain fine scenes. They are interesting in that they exemplify types of stage fare, such as the gothic, the robber play, or the sentimental, much sought in the period of Dunlap's career. Overall, however, these works do not measure up to the high standards achieved in dramas such as *Leicester* or *Fountainville Abbey*.

ANDRÉ

André, Dunlap's best-known drama, though unsuccessful in its 1798 performance, reaches heights of psychological tension that are matched only in the gothic plays written shortly before, in the 1790's. It has also appealed to those whose tastes in early American drama turn decidedly toward the patriotic. The plot is simple: Major John André, en route to Benedict Arnold, is captured and sentenced to hang as a spy against the American cause during the Revolution. He ultimately goes off to die after successive emotionally charged attempts to save him fail. The dramatic interest centers on delineating the psychological workings of those who argue for André's life. Even George Washington finds admirable traits in André's personality, although he realizes that to pardon him would be to encourage treason. The action of young Bland, André's great friend, in throwing down his cockade before Washington, was hissed by the American audience on the opening-night performance, but his subsequent repentance of his rashness toned down the suggestion of treason in his anger. Dunlap did not observe strict historical accuracy in creating his play—only one, but the best, of several on the popular André theme. Documents reveal that the love affair between André and Honora, who in Dunlap's play appears to plead for him, was romanticized by the playwright. He also invented the Blands, a mother and son who, in their pleadings, doubtless appealed to an American audience's love of sentimentality.

THE GLORY OF COLUMBIA—HER YEOMANRY!

The André theme is reworked in *The Glory of Columbia—Her Yeomanry!*, nine of the fifteen scenes of which were taken from *André*, but to no great advantage. As the title change suggests, the center of interest shifts from André, who in both plays recalls the villain-hero of many tragedies, to the common people of the United States. Dunlap's handling of colloquial idiom is the single positive feature in this otherwise too fervently patriotic play, so blatantly calculated to wring the nationalistic hearts of American playgoers. Nevertheless, *The Glory of Columbia—Her Yeomanry!* was for some time revived each year to celebrate the Fourth of July.

OTHER MAJOR WORKS

NONFICTION: *Memoirs of the Life of George Frederick Cooke*, 1813 (2 volumes), 1815 (revised as *The Life of Cooke*); *The Life of Charles Brockden Brown*, 1815 (2 volumes); *A History of American Theatre*, 1832; *A History of the Rise and Progress of the Arts of Design in the United States*, 1834 (2 volumes); *Thirty Years Ago: Or, The Memoirs of a Water Drinker*, 1836 (as *Memoirs of a Water Drinker*, 1837); *A History of New York for Schools*, 1837 (2 volumes); *Diary of William Dunlap*, 1931, 1969 (Dorothy C. Barck, editor).

BIBLIOGRAPHY

Argetsinger, Gerald S. "Dunlap's *André*: The Beginning of American Tragedy." *Players* 49 (Spring, 1974): 62-64. Argetsinger demonstrates how *André* established Dunlap as the first major American dramatist and how it stands alone as the representative eighteenth century American tragedy.

Canary, Robert H. *William Dunlap*. New York: Twayne, 1970. Canary's biography of Dunlap charts his emergence as representative of the artists who made a place for the arts in the new nation. Dunlap's most important works are described together with the personal and critical principles that governed his work. Notes, references, and annotated bibliography.

Richards, Jeffrey H. *Early American Drama*. New York: Penguin Books, 1997. Richards presents selected early American plays, including Dunlap's *André*, along with an introduction and bibliography for each.

Rinehart, Lucy. "Manly Exercises." *Early American Literature* 36, no.2 (2001): 263-293. Johnson examines the intergenerational conflicts experienced by Dunlap and his contemporaries, children of the revolution. Includes analysis of several plays.

Benjamin Fisher,
updated by Gerald S. Argetsinger

LORD DUNSANY
Edward John Moreton Drax Plunkett

Born: London, England; July 24, 1878
Died: Dublin, Ireland; October 25, 1957

PRINCIPAL DRAMA

The Glittering Gate, pr. 1909, pb. 1914
King Argimenes and the Unknown Warrior, pr. 1911, pb. 1914
The Gods of the Mountain, pr. 1911, pb. 1914
The Golden Doom, pr. 1912, pb. 1914
The Lost Silk Hat, pr. 1913, pb. 1914
Five Plays, pb. 1914
The Tents of the Arabs, pr. 1914, pb. 1917
A Night at an Inn, pr., pb. 1916 (one act)
The Queen's Enemies, pr. 1916, pb. 1917
The Laughter of the Gods, pb. 1917, pr. 1919
Plays of Gods and Men, pb. 1917
If, pr., pb. 1921
Cheezo, pr. 1921, pb. 1922
Plays of Near and Far, pb. 1922
Lord Adrian, pr. 1923, pb. 1933
Alexander, pb. 1925, pr. 1938
Mr. Faithful, pr. 1927, pb. 1935
Seven Modern Comedies, pb. 1928
The Old Folk of the Centuries, pb. 1930
Plays for Earth and Air, pb. 1937

OTHER LITERARY FORMS

Lord Dunsany did not limit himself to a particular literary format; his prolific output consisted of novels, short stories, poems, translations, extensive periodical publication, and a wide range of literary and social criticism presented as lectures. Although his drama is historically significant, he is best remembered for his short tales and stories, which are still available in various reprints and anthologies. In these works, his fertile imagination best combined with a natural style to produce an appropriate single effect. Dunsany made little attempt to develop character or to probe the nuances of an individual mind. Instead, he created self-contained mythological worlds that depend on plot and highly stylized language to move the action to its inevitable conclusion. Dunsany's novels suffer from an excess of invention without a firm grounding in reality or psychological depth; as a remarkable curiosity of verbal ingenuity and fantasy, however, *The King of Elfland's Daughter* (1924) remains a classic. The critical reception of his poetry has been kind, but his work in this genre has never been considered anything but minor. Distinguished by an enviable range of interest in all aspects of art, Dunsany believed that the task of the artist is to create or reveal beauty; for him, the beauty evoked by the written word could be expressed in any form.

ACHIEVEMENTS

Lord Dunsany's first play, *The Glittering Gate*, was commissioned by William Butler Yeats for production at the Abbey Theatre, Dublin, in 1909. Having read Dunsany's earlier tales, Yeats thought him a genius and wished to include his work as part of the Irish Renaissance. Although public response to the play did not equal the furor provoked by John Millington Synge's *The Playboy of the Western World* (pr. 1907), Dunsany's delineation of the capriciousness of the gods and the emptiness of Heaven on the other side of the gate nevertheless raised a minor disturbance which seemed to ensure Dunsany a place in the group.

Yeats, however, was interested in developing a literature that was purely Irish in tone and subject matter, and his desire to include Dunsany as part of this movement seems to have been based on a misperception of Dunsany's point of view. While Dunsany may have been technically Irish, his was not the mystical outlook of Yeats or James Stephens but rather the sensibility of a certain type of Englishman, in the same strain as Rudyard Kipling, John Buchan, or J. R. R. Tolkien, a direct inheritor of the Romantic tradition of Lord Byron and Samuel Taylor Coleridge. In his youth, Dunsany's imagination was fueled more by the Brothers Grimm, Hans Christian Andersen, Edgar Allan Poe, and the Greek writers of the Golden Age than by Irish legends. His closest affinity to Ireland came through his appreciation of the lush beauty of its landscape, evoked with power and mystery in the best of his works.

His early plays were well received, the English casts often featuring respected actors such as Claude Rains (in *The Gods of the Mountain* and *The Golden Doom*), Cathleen Nesbit (in *The Queen's Enemies*), and Gladys Cooper (in *If*). *The Laughter of the Gods* was translated into Czech (as *Smich Boha*) and was

Lord Dunsany (Library of Congress)

also performed at the Moscow Art Theatre. Another of his early plays, *The Lost Silk Hat*, was produced in Russia, in 1915, and, even more unexpectedly, in China, at the end of World War I. Americans were his most admiring audiences, however, responding to the initial production of *A Night at an Inn*, according to *The New York Times*, "half-hysterical with excitement for the play is stirring beyond belief." His American biographer Edward Hale Bierstadt declared, "The three great contemporary dramatic poets of Ireland are Synge, Dunsany and Yeats."

Although Dunsany's literary influence has not been widespread, it has been important to the minor fictional area of fantasy. His successful Billiards Club series, for example—stories related by a retired adventurer to his cronies at the club—is echoed in Arthur C. Clarke's *Tales of the White Hart* (1957) and also in the Gavigan's Bar stories of Fletcher Pratt and L. Sprague de Camp. Both C. S. Lewis and H. P. Lovecraft were directly indebted to him, and today many of their followers, although not familiar with Dunsany's work at first hand, pursue the same tradition.

Dunsany was a fellow of the Royal Literary Society and of the Royal Geographical Society as well as president of the Authors' Society. He won the Harmsworth Award and was accorded an honorary doctor of letters degree, in 1939, from Dublin University.

BIOGRAPHY

Lord Dunsany was born Edward John Morton Drax Plunkett, becoming eighteenth baron Dunsany on the death of his father in 1899. He spent his early boyhood at Dunstall Priory in Kent, but in later years his principal residence was Dunsany Castle in Meath, Ireland. The influence of the Irish side of his heritage was muted greatly by political connections to England, his grandfather being seated in the House of Lords and his father and two uncles holding seats in the House of Commons. Dunsany himself stood as Conservative candidate for the Commons but lost in a local election.

Educated in England at Eton, Cambridge, and Sandhurst Military Academy, Dunsany accepted his role in the conventional upper-class life and adopted most of the attitudes and habits current among his peers. While writing was important to him, he gave every evidence of pursuing his literary career in a gentlemanly fashion, claiming that it engaged no more than 3 percent of his time.

In the spirit of the country gentleman, Dunsany led an active life as a sportsman, enjoying fishing, horseback riding, cricket, and hunting. He was a crack shot and became pistol-shooting champion of Ireland. A yearning for adventure led him to more serious pursuits in the military, and he first saw action at age twenty in the Coldstream Guards, fighting for the British in the Boer War. While in South Africa, he met Rudyard Kipling, a man similar in temperament and outlook, who was to remain his friend for life. Like Kipling, Dunsany was preoccupied with the conflict between the instinctive, primitive nature of human beings and the rational, respectable façade of civilization.

After leaving the army and experiencing the disappointments of political life, Dunsany married Lady Beatrice Villiers, the daughter of the earl and countess of Jersey, in 1904. Two years later, the Dunsanys' only child, Randall, was born. During this period, Dunsany wrote three volumes of stories, beginning with *The Gods of Pegāna* (1905). In these early tales, Dunsany set the tone for much of his later writing, evoking magical worlds of his own creation with great originality and humor. The language in which they are presented is poetic and biblical. They stress the beauty of the land, the power of fate, and the impotence of human intellect.

Dunsany's first play, commissioned by Yeats, was received with some acclaim by Abbey Theatre audiences, but when his second opened there, it was given little notice. He offered at least two other plays, *The Golden Doom* and *The Tents of the Arabs*, to Yeats and the Abbey Theatre and was rather hurt when they were rejected as "unsuitable." Because of this rejection, their differing views of the purpose of "Irish drama," and an awkward social situation created when Dunsany learned of some rather malicious remarks made about him, Dunsany's friendship with Yeats and Lady Augusta Gregory cooled and he severed his relationship with their group.

Many of the great and near-great of his time did like Dunsany, however, including writers Padraic Colum, George Russell (Æ), George Moore, Oliver St. John Gogarty, and H. G. Wells, as well as members of the nobility. His position on political affairs, particularly the Irish question, was hard to categorize. As a landlord in Ireland, Dunsany regarded the Sinn Féin as rebels and traitors. On the other hand, the reviews of his novel *Up in the Hills* (1935), a good-natured satire on the Troubles, were as enthusiastic in Ireland as in England.

Dunsany's brief flirtation with the Irish National Theatre at least induced him to continue writing plays, and from 1909 to 1922 he produced drama of interest, including *King Argimenes and the Unknown Warrior*, *The Gods of the Mountain*, *A Night at an Inn*, *The Tents of the Arabs*, and *If*. These plays often reached the stage in Britain and the United States, but with the return of realism in the 1920's, they were judged to be dated and facile.

Dunsany was thirty-six when World War I began in 1914. He enlisted in the National Volunteers and, shortly after, joined the Royal Inniskilling Fusiliers. After seeing action in France, Dunsany was wounded in Dublin during the Easter Rebellion in 1916. While out on a weekend pass, he was shot in the face and spent a week in a rebel hospital before his release. Subsequently, Dunsany joined the War Office to write propaganda.

Between the two world wars, Dunsany wrote with extraordinary energy and, although unsuccessful as a playwright, enjoyed popular acclaim for such novels as *The King of Elfland's Daughter* and *The Blessing of Pan* (1927), for his collections of poetry, and for the tales of his most ambitiously rendered character, Mr. Joseph Jorkens. The demand for Jorkens, the boastful, Dickensian drunk of the fictional Billiards Club, became so extraordinary that Dunsany was forced to write four more volumes to satisfy his growing public. Ever restless in his creativity, Dunsany also took up painting as a hobby and perfected his chess game enough to reign as Irish champion. His victories led to friendship with the famed world chess master José Raul Capablanca, who became a regular visitor at Dunsany Castle. Dunsany's taste for a fight did not diminish, either; at the age of sixty-two, he joined the Local Defence Volunteers in preparation for a possible Nazi invasion. When this service proved uneventful, he accepted an invitation from the British Council to take the Byron Chair of English Literature at the university in Athens and set off for that city in 1940, an experience that culminated in *Guerrilla* (1944), a novel about the war of resistance in Greece. One of his few semirealistic books, this novel demonstrated that he could control conventional fiction and also receive favorable response from tough-minded modern critics.

From 1945 to the end of his life, Dunsany's inventiveness never failed, but old age moderated his productivity. Eccentric, but no longer embittered by the brave new world's lack of appreciation for his work, Dunsany lived contentedly until his death after an appendix operation in 1957.

ANALYSIS

Lord Dunsany's writing consists of many elements found in his early reading of the tales of the Brothers Grimm, of Hans Christian Andersen, and of Greek mythology. His religious temperament was formed intuitively by the beauty and terror of mysterious fictional worlds rather than by formal theology. Dreamlands of mystery and mythology, filled with marvels and the exotic, confrontations between gods and heroes—or mere mortals—these were the center of most of his works. He found such subjects attractive in part because without them, life was less fun, less exciting, less colorful. While he managed to retain a childlike wonder at the vastness of the universe and the power of external forces which people disregard at their own peril, Dunsany was also a well-educated, sophisticated man of the world, and this dichotomy shows through. Just when his work seems ready to lapse into sentimentality, irony, satire, or an unexpected twist is encountered. Instead of bemoaning the dimness of the Celtic Twilight, Dunsany celebrated the adventuresome spirit of humankind. He continually pointed out that the dawning of the Age of Reason may have been announced, that worship of industrialization and technology may have swept the earth, but whenever humans become too confident in themselves and think they have safely pigeonholed the universe, the universe will surprise them by upsetting their pet ideas.

In his essay on playwriting, "Carving the Ivory" (1928), Dunsany claims that, as a playwright, he follows no formal rules of dramatic composition. He merely carves the play, "the ivory block," as a sculptor carves his material. The result is a finished shape which assumes a natural form, refined to its fruition as if no authorial hand were implicated in its making. Dunsany wrote quickly, with little revision—*A Night at an Inn*, for example, was completed between his noon meal and teatime—but his preoccupation with the mysteries of aesthetic romanticism is quite deceptive. The poetic language of his plays, often delivered in perfect hexameters, and their effective rhetorical devices reveal a thoughtful and cunning artist at work, adept at rendering a limpid style.

It may always be difficult to evaluate Dunsany's work fairly, since it is an admixture of so many strains. Audiences conditioned by the work of filmmakers George Lucas and Steven Spielberg may not object to the speaking statues or the ominous laughter of the gods, and audiences accustomed to Samuel Beckett, Eugène Ionesco, and T. S. Eliot may enjoy the stylized soft-edge mysticism—unfortunately, the two types rarely overlap.

In his search for eternal values in imaginative expression, Dunsany produced a body of work of considerable diversity and quality. His private mythological universe may seem too arcane for today's taste, but it is one of surprising richness and beauty. Dunsany's provocative plays are models of sophistication and verbal precision and certainly deserve more recognition than they have been afforded.

THE GLITTERING GATE

The Glittering Gate, which Dunsany said he had written chiefly to please Yeats, is not characteristic of Dunsany's work. It opens in a lonely place of rock suspended in an abyss hung with stars. Close to the landscape littered with thousands of beer bottles is a golden gate hinged in a wall of granite. Jim, a thief hanged for crimes on earth, wearily and cynically uncorks the bottles, but none of them contains beer. He is joined by Bill, formerly his student of burglary,

who has died from a gunshot wound while attempting to break into a house. At various points, there is faint and unpleasant laughter in the background. Bill is convinced that his jemmy, his "old nutcracker" burglary tool, can open the heavenly gate. Beyond it, he hopes to find angels, gold, apples, and his mother. Jim has a moment of astonishment as Bill succeeds in prying the door ajar. As they look out at the emptiness, cruel, violent laughter rises.

Dunsany's cynicism is apparent in this play, and although many critics downplay this quality in him, it is not uncharacteristic of his work. The case against the gods is one-sided in that the reader or viewer is not allowed to see what eventually happens to "good people"—unless, in ultimate cynicism, Dunsany wishes to indicate that even the best of humankind is, to the gods, no better than Jim or Bill. Each of the characters pays for his actions in the world and is abandoned to a form of punishment particularly suited to him: Jim will be perpetually thirsty, possibly more for hope than for beer, and Bill will never see his mother again. Even in the afterlife, each continues to be true to his criminal nature. Instead of feeling remorse, they seek a way out; they do not give in to the gods any more than the gods give in to them.

The play has parallels to the myth of Sisyphus. Like Sisyphus, forever rolling his stone up the mountainside only to have it roll back down again, Jim opens his beer bottles to find them empty. He knows he will not find beer, but he hopes that, if only once, the gods' trick might not work. His placid statement at the end, as he looks into nothingness, is that it is characteristic of the gods to have arranged such an anticlimax. In a similar way, Sisyphus understands his predicament but must nevertheless repeat the cycle of his condemnation. Jim's monologue on the meaninglessness of the years and the futility of confinement with Bill is also reminiscent of Jean-Paul Sartre's *Huis clos* (pr. 1944; *In Camera*, 1946, better known as *No Exit*, 1947).

THE GODS OF THE MOUNTAIN

Two closely related plays, *The Gods of the Mountain* and *A Night at an Inn*, clearly illustrate Dunsany's major theme of the arrogance of men provoking retribution at the hands of intransigent gods. In

The Gods of the Mountain, set somewhere in the East, a group of beggars, led by Agmar, wish to enter the city to seek riches at a time when the gods seem to be asleep and the divine in humankind seems to be dead. The beggars suggest posing as lords or kings, but Agmar insists that they impersonate gods. Disguised as the seven green jade idols of Marma, they fool a skeptical populace through the will and intellect of Agmar. Dunsany's admiration of Friedrich Nietzsche's *Thus Spake Zarathustra* (1883-1885) is reflected in the characterization of Agmar. Agmar dismisses the idea of subservience to anyone, but when the real gods enter to seek vengeance on the usurpers, Agmar's genius fails, and all the beggars are turned to stone.

A NIGHT AT AN INN

A Night at an Inn, a slighter play, demonstrates that human pride is as dangerous close to home as it is in the mysterious East. Three merchant sailors and their leader, A. E. Scott (the Toff), steal the ruby eye from a green idol, Klesh. The Toff remains aloof and calm on hearing that the priests of Klesh are following them. He says that they will not come until he is ready to receive them. After all, he says, he is able to see into the future. When the three priests appear, the Toff formulates and carries out a clever plan to murder them. The blind idol, however, claims his ruby eye and leaves the inn. Offstage, a seductive voice calls the names of the sailors, and, against their will, they exit into the darkness. On his way out, the Toff comments in despair that he did not foresee this conclusion.

These two works read better than they play. Unlike *The Glittering Gate*, both melodramas call for the physical presence of the gods, which lessens the mystery considerably in a staged version: The problem for Dunsany was to make the audience believe that an abstraction could operate on the material level; the attention commanded by the idols leaves the message out of focus and depersonalized. In reading, at least, each individual can create his own image of the idols.

OTHER MAJOR WORKS

LONG FICTION: *The Chronicles of Rodriguez*, 1922; *The King of Elfland's Daughter*, 1924; *The Char-* *woman's Shadow*, 1926; *The Blessing of Pan*, 1927; *The Curse of the Wise Woman*, 1933; *Up in the Hills*, 1935; *My Talks with Dean Spanley*, 1936; *Rory and Bran*, 1936; *The Story of Mona Sheehy*, 1939; *Guerrilla*, 1944; *The Strange Journeys of Colonel Polders*, 1950; *The Last Revolution*, 1951; *His Fellow Men*, 1952.

SHORT FICTION: *The Gods of Pegāna*, 1905; *Time and the Gods*, 1906; *The Sword of Welleran and Other Stories*, 1908; *A Dreamer's Tales*, 1910; *The Book of Wonder*, 1912; *Fifty-one Tales*, 1915; *The Last Book of Wonder*, 1916 (pb. in England as *Tales of Wonder*); *Tales of War*, 1918; *Tales of Three Hemispheres*, 1919; *The Travel Tales of Mr. Joseph Jorkens*, 1931; *Jorkens Remembers Africa*, 1934; *Jorkens Has a Large Whiskey*, 1940; *The Man Who Ate the Phoenix*, 1947; *The Fourth Book of Jorkens*, 1948; *The Little Tales of Smethers*, 1952; *Jorkens Borrows Another Whiskey*, 1954; *The Food of Death: Fifty-one Tales*, 1974.

POETRY: *Fifty Poems*, 1929; *Mirage Water*, 1938; *War Poems*, 1941; *Wandering Songs*, 1943; *The Year*, 1946; *To Awaken Pegasus and Other Poems*, 1949.

NONFICTION: *If I Were Dictator: The Pronouncement of the Grand Macaroni*, 1934; *My Ireland*, 1937; *Patches of Sunlight*, 1938; *While the Sirens Slept*, 1944; *The Sirens Wake*, 1945; *A Glimpse from a Watch Tower*, 1946.

TRANSLATION: *The Odes of Horace*, 1947.

BIBLIOGRAPHY

Amory, Mark. *Biography of Lord Dunsany*. London: Collins, 1972. A biography of Lord Dunsany, describing his life and analyzing his works.

Joshi, S. T. *Lord Dunsany: Master of the Anglo-Irish Imagination*. Westport, Conn.: Greenwood, 1995. A look at the writings of Dunsany, with particular attention to those writings that might be described as fantasy. Bibliography and index.

Joshi, S. T., and Darrell Schweitzer. *Lord Dunsany: A Bibliography*. Metuchen, N.J.: Scarecrow Press, 1993. A bibliography on the literature describing Lord Dunsany's life and works. Indexes.

James C. MacDonald,
updated by Frank Day

CHRISTOPHER DURANG

Born: Montclair, New Jersey; January 2, 1949

PRINCIPAL DRAMA

The Greatest Musical Ever Sung, pr. 1971

The Nature and Purpose of the Universe, wr. 1971, pr. 1975 (radio play), pr. 1979 (staged), pb. 1979

Better Dead than Sorry, pr. 1972 (libretto, music by Jack Feldman)

I Don't Generally Like Poetry but Have You Read "Trees"?, pr. 1972 (with Albert Innaurato)

The Life Story of Mitzi Gaynor: Or, Gyp, pr. 1973 (with Innaurato)

The Marriage of Bette and Boo, pr. 1973, pb. 1976, revised pr. 1979, pb. 1985

The Idiots Karamazov, pr., pb. 1974, augmented pb. 1981 (with Innaurato, music by Feldman)

Titanic, pr. 1974, pb. 1983

Death Comes to Us All, Mary Agnes, pr. 1975, pr. 1979

When Dinah Shore Ruled the Earth, pr. 1975 (with Wendy Wasserstein)

'dentity Crisis, pr. 1975, pb. 1979

Das Lusitania Songspiel, pr. 1976 (with Sigourney Weaver, music by Mel Marvin and Jack Gaughan)

A History of the American Film, pr. 1976, pb. 1978

The Vietnamization of New Jersey (An American Tragedy), pr. 1976, pb. 1978

Three Short Plays, pb. 1979

Sister Mary Ignatius Explains It All for You, pr. 1979, pb. 1980

The Actor's Nightmare, pr., pb. 1981

Beyond Therapy, pr. 1981, pb. 1983

Christopher Durang Explains It All for You, pb. 1983

Baby with the Bathwater, pr., pb. 1983

Sloth, pr. 1985

Laughing Wild, pr. 1987, pb. 1988

Naomi in the Living Room, pr. 1991, pb. 1998

Media Amok, pr. 1992

Durang/Durang, pr. 1994, pb. 1996 (6 short plays; *Mrs. Sorken, For Whom the Belle Tolls, A Stye of the Eye, Nina in the Morning, Wanda's Visit*, and *Business Lunch at the Russian Tea Room*)

Collected Works, pb. 1995-1997 (2 volumes; volume 1, *Twenty-seven Short Plays*; volume 2, *Complete Full-length Plays, 1975-1995*)

Sex and Longing, pr. 1996

Betty's Summer Vacation, pr. 1998, pb. 2000

OTHER LITERARY FORMS

Although Christopher Durang is known primarily for his plays, he has written a screenplay, *Beyond Therapy* (1987).

ACHIEVEMENTS

Christopher Durang belongs to a tradition of black humorists and fabulists who first emerged in the 1950's with the novelists Joseph Heller, Kurt Vonnegut, and Thomas Berger. His plays are ridiculous comedies that agitate the audience without propagating a particular political viewpoint, attacking every "great idea" of Western literature and philosophy merely because it is assailable. His writing centers on the enduring questions of human suffering and authority. His most popular play, *Sister Mary Ignatius Explains It All for You*, was hotly debated by theologians and theater critics alike and won an Obie Award as the best new Off-Broadway play of 1980. His other honors include grants from the Rockefeller Foundation and the Lecomte du Nuoy Foundation, fellowships from Guggenheim and the Columbia Broadcasting System, a Tony nomination for his musical *A History of the American Film*, the Sidney Kingsley Playwriting Award, and an Obie Award for distinguished playwriting for *Betty's Summer Vacation*. He co-chairs the playwriting program at the Julliard School of Manhattan. His work is characterized by energy and a sense of the ridiculous in life and art, sustained by anger and despair. The targets of his abusive wit are the sacred cows of contemporary American society: religion, family life, hero worship, law and order, and success.

Christopher Durang in 1984. (AP/Wide World Photos)

BIOGRAPHY

Christopher Ferdinand Durang was born in Montclair, New Jersey, on January 2, 1949. A humorous autobiographical sketch is given in the introduction to his plays in *Christopher Durang Explains It All for You*, beginning with his conception and ending with the reviews of *Beyond Therapy*. His parents, Francis Ferdinand and Patricia Elizabeth Durang, were devout Catholics who fought constantly until they were divorced, when Durang was still in grade school. Durang's interest in theater and playwriting became evident early in life. He wrote his first play while in the second grade in a Catholic elementary school. He subsequently attended a Catholic preparatory high school run by Benedictine priests. He continued to write plays, and though a fairly conservative and conventional student, he often inserted hints of sex for their shock effect. In high school, Durang was overcome with religious zeal and the desire to enter a monastery after graduation, but soon afterward he lost his faith and his interest in the Roman Catholic religion.

He attended Harvard University with the hope and expectation of discovering a more intellectual and less conservative dimension of Catholicism but was disappointed. In his second year at Harvard, he entered psychoanalysis with a priest. He became obsessed with motion pictures and neglected his academic studies. Although he had been a prodigious writer in high school, he wrote almost nothing in college until his senior year, when he wrote (as a form of therapy for his feeling of religious guilt) a musical-comedy version of the life of Christ called *The Greatest Musical Ever Sung*, which included such irreverent show-tune lampoons as "The Dove That Done Me Wrong" and "Everything's Coming up Moses." The play stirred up a local religious controversy but was well received by audiences, encouraging the young playwright to write more. His next effort, the ambitiously titled *The Nature and Purpose of the Universe*, was eventually produced in New York and, following Durang's graduation from Harvard in 1971, was submitted as part of his application to the Yale School of Drama.

At Yale, Durang met and worked with a number of actors and playwrights who were, along with him, to make their marks in the American theater. Among his classmates were Albert Innaurato (with whom Durang collaborated on several plays), Meryl Streep (who appeared in a Durang play in college), Wendy Wasserstein (with whom Durang wrote *When Dinah Shore Ruled the Earth*), and Sigourney Weaver (who appeared in several Durang plays in New York and with whom he wrote *Das Lusitania Songspiel*). His chief supporter at Yale and later in New York was Robert Brustein, who was dean of the drama school while Durang was enrolled there and artistic director of the Yale Repertory Theater. Durang received his M.F.A. in 1974 but remained in New Haven for an extra year, performing and writing at Yale, teaching drama at the Southern Connecticut College in New Haven, and working as a typist at the medical school.

Durang moved to New York in 1975. *Titanic*, which he wrote for a class at Yale, and *The Nature and Purpose of the Universe* were produced in Off-Broadway theaters. In 1976, his musical play *A History of the American Film* was produced in Water-ford, Connecticut, as part of the Eugene O'Neill Playwrights Conference, and in 1977 it was produced simultaneously on both coasts at the Hartford Stage Company in Connecticut, the Mark Taper Forum in Los Angeles, California, and the Arena Stage in Washington, D.C. In 1978, the play opened on Broadway at the American National Theatre. The play's subsequent failure on Broadway precipitated a period of depression that climaxed with the death of Durang's mother in March, 1979. Watching his mother die of incurable bone cancer and reassessing his Catholic upbringing, Durang started writing the play on which his reputation as a playwright would be secured, *Sister Mary Ignatius Explains It All for You*. The play was first produced in December, 1979, by Curt Dempster's Ensemble Studio Theatre in New York, along with one-act plays by David Mamet, Marsha Norman, and Tennessee Williams. Two years later, Andre Bishop's Playwrights Horizons produced the play Off-Broadway with two members of the original cast of six, along with Durang's *The Actor's Nightmare*, which he wrote as a curtain raiser. In 2000, the play was adapted for cable television under the title *Sister Mary Explains It All*, with Diane Keaton in the title role.

Sister Mary Ignatius Explains It All for You brought Durang to the public's attention, not only through the show's popularity but also through several battles against censorship when various Catholic organizations attempted to close down the play. The Phoenix Theatre commissioned Durang to write *Beyond Therapy*, which opened in 1981 and then, almost a year and a half later, was rewritten and produced on Broadway at the Brooks Atkinson Theater. Later, Durang revised and expanded two plays he originally wrote at Yale, *Baby with the Bathwater* and *The Marriage of Bette and Boo*, which also were produced in New York. A 1987 film version of *Beyond Therapy* directed by Robert Altman was a box-office failure, and Durang expressed his unhappiness with the experience. Nevertheless, he subsequently expressed his disenchantment with the New York theater scene and his intention to pursue work in film, which, he stated, offers more permanence and reaches a larger audience than live drama.

ANALYSIS

Christopher Durang belongs to the postmodernist wave of American playwrights who emerged during the 1970's, including A. R. Gurney, Jr., Tina Howe, and Sam Shepard. These writers fused the experimental techniques of the structuralist theater experiments of the 1960's with the "traditional" domestic drama of the early twentieth century American realists, creating a new form of theater that is simultaneously naturalistic and self-consciously theatrical. Evolving as it did from collegiate travesties and comedy sketches, Durang's drama violates many of the established principles of the well-made play. However sloppily constructed and politically unsophisticated his plays may be, Durang's genius is to create comedies out of existential anger and to infuse them with energy, thought, and an unbounded sense of liberty.

Durang's plays are remarkable for their absurdist approach to the important questions of modern philosophy, for their hilarious disregard for social conventions and traditional sexual roles, and for their uncompromisingly bleak assessment of human politics and society. As early as the satirical travesties he produced in college, Durang's abiding themes have been suffering and paternalism. The cutting edge of his humor is his insistence on the commonplaceness of suffering in the world. His plays are populated by archetypal sadists and victims, and the comedy is usually cruel (as the audience is made to laugh at the exaggerated and grotesque misery of the characters) and nearly always violent; death, suicide, disaster, and murder are never too far away in typical Durang slapstick. In a note accompanying the publication of *The Nature and Purpose of the Universe*, the writer explains that the violence of the play must appear simultaneously vicious and funny, demanding that performers make the audience sympathize with the victim and yet feel sufficiently "alienated" (in the sense of Bertolt Brecht's "alienation effect") from the theatrical action to be able to laugh at it. Presiding over the sufferers is a figure of authority, always coldly detached and frequently insane, who "explains" the suffering with banal truisms taken from philosophy, religion, and pop psychology, while in fact he or she acts as the instrument of the oppression and mindless malice.

Fear and insecurity are the principal components of Durang's comedy of paranoia. While his plays are repeatedly criticized for not being positive and for not suggesting any remedy to the problem of human evil, they are in fact relentlessly moral, fueled by a profound sense of outrage at the crimes against human dignity. Like Eugène Ionesco, Joe Orton, and Lenny Bruce, Durang attempts to shock the audience out of its complacency through the use of vulgarity, blasphemy, violence, and other forms of extremism. If his endings seem less than perfectly conclusive, and if his characters seem to be no more than cartoons, still, underneath all the madcap and sophomoric nonsense is a serious and humane plea for tolerance, diversity, and individual liberty. The object of the writer's most satirical attacks is the incompetent guardian, a sometimes well-intentioned but always destructive figure of patriarchal authority who appears in many different guises: parent, husband, teacher, analyst, hero, nanny, doctor, author, and even deity. This figure embodies for Durang all the evil elements of human nature and social hierarchy.

The Idiots Karamazov

Durang's drama of the mid-1970's, the plays that grew out of his college exercises at Yale, is chiefly parodic and yet contains kernels of the preoccupation with suffering characteristic of his later works. *The Idiots Karamazov*, which he wrote with Innaurato, is a musical-comedy travesty of the great Russian novelists of suffering, Fyodor Dostoevski and Leo Tolstoy. The principal character, Constance Garnett, is the translator, an older woman who uses a wheelchair and is attended by a suicidal manservant, Ernest. In Durang and Innaurato's version of Dostoevski's *The Brothers Karamazov*, the holy innocent and idiot savant Alyosha becomes a pop music star, and the "Great Books," along with other academic pretensions to cultural importance, are thus trivialized as commodities in a money-and-glitter-oriented enterprise.

A History of the American Film

Durang ridiculed Hollywood and motion pictures in *A History of the American Film*, a 1976 musical that opened on Broadway in 1978. The five principal characters are caricatures based on familiar Hollywood types. Loretta (as in Loretta Young) is the long-suffering and lovingly innocent heroine. Jimmy (as in James Cagney) is the tough guy, part hoodlum and part romantic hero. Bette (as in Bette Davis) is the vamp, a vindictive but seductive figure who enjoys nothing more than making Loretta suffer. Hank (as in Henry Fonda) is the strong and silent all-American good guy, who eventually turns psychotic. Eve (as in Eve Arden) is the ever-present true friend, who covers up her own sexual frustration with dry witticisms and hard-boiled mottoes. True to its title, the play satirizes the gamut of Hollywood kitsch, including jabs at *Birth of a Nation* (1915), *The Grapes of Wrath* (1940), *The Best Years of Our Lives* (1946), *Psycho* (1960), *Who's Afraid of Virginia Woolf?* (1966), and *Earthquake* (1974). On a deeper level, the play exposes the American film industry as a manufacturer of glamorous façades for real-life misery and fear.

The Vietnamization of New Jersey

In *The Vietnamization of New Jersey*, Durang takes on the legitimate theater itself. Using David Rabe's controversial Vietnam-era satire *Sticks and Bones* (pr. 1969, pb. 1972) as a starting place, Durang makes the social and political pretensions of "serious theater" seem silly, while castigating the various "isms" of contemporary culture: liberalism, consumerism, racism, militarism, and sexism. The play treats the horrors of war, mental illness, inflation, unemployment, and suicide with chilling comedy.

'dentity Crisis

In the late 1970's, when Durang wrote *'dentity Crisis, The Nature and Purpose of the Universe*, and the phenomenally successful *Sister Mary Ignatius Explains It All for You*, the playwright challenged the idea of authority or expertise itself. Inspired by R. D. Laing's controversial theories about schizophrenia, *'dentity Crisis* is an oddly moving comedy in one act and two scenes. The action centers on a young, depressed woman named Jane and her mother, Edith. The play opens as Edith returns from the dry cleaner with Jane's bloodstained dress, which has been ruined after an unsuccessful suicide attempt. Despite the initial impression, it soon appears that Jane is the only character in the play who is "sane." Edith manufactures and discards versions of reality with breathless speed, and Robert, the other occupant of the house, manifests four distinct personalities, alternately Jane's brother, father, and grandfather, as well as the Count de Rochelay, a foreign suitor of the perversely promiscuous Edith. Even Jane's psychoanalyst, Mr. Summers, is bizarrely inconsistent. In scene 1, the role is played by a man, and in scene 2, after a sex-change operation, by a woman (the actor who plays Mr. Summers in the first scene plays his wife in the second). Jane reveals the motive behind her suicide attempt in a poignant and surrealistic monologue concerning a production of *Peter Pan* she had seen as a girl. Life is not worth continuing, she says, if it only leads to death in the end. The play ends with the daughter's loss of her identity, but the audience's sympathy remains with her because it has entered her version of reality and regards the others as mad.

THE NATURE AND PURPOSE OF THE UNIVERSE

The authoritative Mr. and Mrs. Summers in *'dentity Crisis* are remarkably similar to Ronald and Elaine May Alcott, the two "agents of God" who borrow various guises in *The Nature and Purpose of the Universe*. Like its glib title, the play pokes fun at those who would offer easy explanations of the mysteries of existence and evil. It is a play in thirteen "chapters," each chronicling a different aspect of the tragicomic downfall of the hapless Eleanor Mann. Presiding over the events of the drama are Ronald and Elaine, who pretend to render meaningful the random catastrophes that they inflict on the Job-like Eleanor. Every now and then they enter the action of the play, purportedly to offer heavenly guidance and solace but actually to intensify the poor woman's suffering. Durang's comedy springs from the characters' absurdly cool responses to horror. When Eleanor is knocked to the kitchen floor and kicked by her drug-peddling son, her husband chides the boy, saying, "Donald, have a little patience with your mother." The play ends as, in a parody of Old Testament piety, Ronald and Elaine bind and gag Eleanor and sacrifice her to a distant and passively vicious God.

SISTER MARY IGNATIUS EXPLAINS IT ALL FOR YOU

Sister Mary Ignatius, teacher at Our Lady of Perpetual Sorrow and the menacingly maternal protagonist of *Sister Mary Ignatius Explains It All for You*, is the writer's classic realization of the banality and willful ignorance of human evil. The play falls into three sections. In the first, Sister Mary catechizes the audience on basic doctrines and practices of the Roman Catholic Church. As Durang noted in several interviews, the humor of this section stems from the unexaggerated reportage of the irrational but devoutly held beliefs of certain Christians: the existence of Heaven, Hell, and Purgatory within the physical universe; the supernatural births of Jesus Christ and Mary; the efficacy of Christ's suffering and death on a cross; the exclusively procreative function of sex; and God's everlasting vengeance against wrongdoers such as Zsa Zsa Gabor, Brooke Shields, and David Bowie. Repeatedly, however, Sister Mary dodges the more interesting issue of God's responsibility for the existence of evil and suffering in the world. The second section presents a Nativity play performed by four of Sister Mary's former students. More than anything else, the play demonstrates the triumph of dogma over narrative in traditional Christianity and portrays an absurdly abbreviated life of Christ. With only three characters, Mary, Joseph, and Misty the camel (two actors impersonate separate humps), and a doll as the infant Jesus, the play spans the time from the Immaculate Conception (of Mary) to the Ascension (of Jesus, Mary, Joseph, and Misty). The third section of the play involves the Nativity-scene actors' disclosure to Sister Mary of the courses their lives have taken after leaving Our Lady of Perpetual Sorrow. Philomena (Misty's front end) has borne a daughter out of wedlock. Aloysius (Misty's back end) has become a suicidal alcoholic who regularly beats his wife. Gary (Joseph) has had homosexual relationships. Diane (Mary), whom Sister Mary especially detests, has had two abortions. Diane engineers the climactic confrontation in order to embarrass Sister Mary and then reveals her intention to kill her, much to the surprise of her three cohorts. Victorious in the end, Sister Mary whips out a gun and kills Diane; then, after assuring herself that he has made a recent confession of his sexual sins, she kills Gary as well. The play ends with a recitation of the catechism by Thomas, a boy currently enrolled in the parochial school.

Beyond Therapy

In the 1980's, Durang turned his attention to other kinds of oppression in society, specifically the normalization of sexuality and family relationships. In *Beyond Therapy*, he again attacks psychoanalysis from a Laingian perspective, portraying the analysts in the play as more bizarre versions of Mr. Summers and his wife in *'dentity Crisis*. Their clients are a heterosexual woman and a bisexual man who meet through an advertisement in the personals column of a newspaper. The complex relationship they form is played mainly for laughs, but the butt of most of the jokes is pop psychology, as well as the notion of anyone's being an expert about how other people ought to live their lives.

Baby with the Bathwater and The Marriage of Bette and Boo

Both *Baby with the Bathwater* and *The Marriage of Bette and Boo* have their origins in plays Durang wrote while in college and pertain to American family life. *Baby with the Bathwater* is a grim but humorous indictment of the science of child-rearing. Born as a boy but reared as a girl, Daisy, the baby of the title, is the victim of two inept parents and a manipulative nanny. In the last act he appears in his analyst's office wearing a dress, clearly suffering from a sexual identity crisis. *The Marriage of Bette and Boo* takes the form of a college student's memories of his parents, both of whom are emotionally unbalanced and (for their son Matt, the narrator) unbalancing. The play is a parody of the family dramas of American dramatists Thornton Wilder and Eugene O'Neill. The mother, Bette, idolizes babies but is able to produce only one living descendant because her blood type is incompatible with her husband's. The several stillborn infants she produces she names after animal characters in Winnie the Pooh storybooks. The father, Boo, is an alcoholic whose life is a cycle of a reformation and backsliding. Though a comedy, the play touches on serious philosophical questions concerning God, suffering, death, the absurdity of life, and

the meaning of love. It is also the most autobiographical of Durang's plays.

Later plays

In the late 1980's, tired of New York and the theater, Durang began touring as a cabaret act, Chris Durang and Dawne. He soon returned to the theater, however, with *Media Amok*, a satire on the sensationalism of television talk shows. *Durang/Durang* contained six sketches lampooning playwrights Tennessee Williams, Sam Shepard, and David Mamet, with titles such as *For Whom the Belle Tolls*. A more serious and disturbing play followed. *Sex and Longing* tells of Lulu, a nymphomaniac whose roommate is a sexually compulsive homosexual. Lulu is attacked by a serial killer; her savior, a fundamentalist preacher, first converts her, then later rapes her.

Betty's Summer Vacation

Betty's Summer Vacation begins as a comedic farce, but soon spins out of control to an explosive ending. Betty is spending her vacation at a time-share by the beach with five bizarre strangers, one of whom is a serial killer. The American fascination with sensationalism on television is a theme again, with such targets as Fox network specials and coverage of the trials of Lorena Bobbit and O. J. Simpson.

Other major work

SCREENPLAY: *Beyond Therapy*, 1987.

Bibliography

Brustein, Robert. "The Crack in the Chimney: Reflections on Contemporary American Playwriting." *Theater* 9 (Spring, 1978): 21-29. A discussion of *The Vietnamization of New Jersey*, set against the more serious examination of the work of David Rabe, in *Sticks and Bones*.

Durang, Christopher. Introduction to *Christopher Durang Explains It All for You*. New York: Grove Weidenfeld, 1990. The introduction to this collection of six plays is a tongue-in-cheek autobiography, written in 1982, that includes anecdotes about playwriting classes under Howard Stein and Jules Feiffer and early psychiatric counseling.

_____. "Suspending Disbelief: An Interview with the Playwright by Himself." *American Theater* 16, no. 10 (December 1999): 37. A sardonic "interview" in which Durang discusses the writing of *Betty's Summer Vacation*, recurrent themes in his work, and future plans. Includes the full text of *Betty's Summer Vacation*.

Flippo, Chet. "Is Broadway Ready for Christopher Durang?" *New York* 15 (March 15, 1982): 40-43. "I was very depressed about how depressed I got," says Durang in this chatty, readable conversation. Discusses his early revues at Harvard University and cabaret pieces for the Yale School of Drama, his collaboration with Sigourney Weaver, and his development as a "fearless satirist." Demures on describing his vision of the world. Three photographs.

Savran, David. *In Their Own Words: Contemporary American Playwrights*. New York: Theatre Communications Group, 1988. A brief overview is followed by a protracted interview, centering on biographical history, the development of *The Marriage of Bette and Boo*, and Durang's writing habits. Durang sees advantages to filmmaking (if the playwright's script is not desecrated as with *Beyond Therapy*), including reaching a larger audience and enjoying more permanence.

Weales, Gerald. "American Theater Watch, 1981-1982." *The Georgia Review* 36 (Fall, 1982): 517-526. Weales offers insightful comments on Durang's comic style, but he is not impressed by his structure or depth. Drawn from interviews in *The New York Times*, this article summarizes critics' first reactions to this new voice.

Joseph Marohl,
updated by Thomas J. Taylor and
Irene Struthers Rush

MARGUERITE DURAS

Born: Gia Dinh, Indochina (now Vietnam); April 4, 1914

Died: Paris, France; March 3, 1996

PRINCIPAL DRAMA

Le Square, pr. 1957, pb. 1965 (*The Square*, 1967)

Les Viaducs de la Seine-et-Oise, pr., pb. 1960 (*The Viaducts of Seine-et-Oise*, 1967)

Les Papiers d'Aspern, pr. 1961, pb. 1970 (with Robert Antelme; adaptation of Michael Redgrave's adaptation of Henry James's novella *The Aspern Papers*)

La Bête dans la jungle, pr. 1962, pb. 1984 (with James Lord; adaptation of James's story "The Beast in the Jungle")

Miracle en Alabama, pr. 1962, pb. 1963 (with Gérard Jarlot; adaptation of William Gibson's play *The Miracle Worker*)

Les Eaux et forêts, pr., pb. 1965 (*The Rivers and Forests*, 1965)

La Musica, pr., pb. 1965 (*The Music*, 1967)

Des Journées entières dans les arbres, pr. 1965, pb. 1966 (*Days in the Trees*, 1967)

Théâtre I, pb. 1965 (includes *Les Eaux et forêts*, *Le Square*, and *La Musica*)

Three Plays, pb. 1967 (includes *The Square*, *Days in the Trees*, and *The Viaducts of Seine-et-Oise*)

Théâtre II, pb. 1968 (includes *Suzanna Andler* [English translation, 1973], *Des Journées entières dans les arbres*, *Yes, peut-être*, *Le Shaga*, and *Un homme est venu me voir*)

L'Amante anglaise, pr., pb. 1968 (*A Place Without Doors*, 1970)

Un Homme est venu me voir, pr., pb. 1968

La Danse de mort, pr. 1970, pb. 1984 (adaptation of August Strindberg's play *Dödsdansen, andra delen*)

Home, pb. 1973 (adaptation of David Storey's play)

India Song: Texte-théâtre-film, pb. 1973 (English translation, 1976)

L'Éden Cinéma, pr., pb. 1977 (*The Eden Cinema*, 1986)

Agatha, pb. 1981, pr. 1984 (English translation, 1992)

Savannah Bay, pr., pb. 1982 (English translation, 1992)

Théâtre III, pb. 1984 (includes *La Bête dans la jungle*, *Les Papiers d'Aspern*, and *La Danse de mort*)

La Mouette, pb. 1985 (adaptation of Anton Chekhov's play *The Seagull*)

La Musica, deuxième, pr., pb. 1985

Four Plays, pb. 1992 (includes *La Musica*, *The Eden Cinema*, *Savannah Bay*, and *India Song*)

Théâtre IV, pb. 1999 (includes *Véra Baxter*, *L'Éden cinema*, *L'Amante anglaise*, *Home*, and *La Mouette*)

OTHER LITERARY FORMS

Marguerite Duras began her writing career as a journalist and novelist and later moved on to motion pictures and the theater. It is difficult to distinguish Duras's dramatic output from the rest of her literary production. Characters and situations in her novels, films, and plays tend to reappear in later works, and her style remains constant throughout all genres. Duras's novels are filled with dramatic dialogue, and the stage directions of her screenplays are usually longer than the spoken text. *India Song: Texte-théâtre-film* does not consist of three different treatments of the same theme, as its subtitle might suggest. It is one comprehensive text, to be treated differently by readers, performers, and directors.

ACHIEVEMENTS

Marguerite Duras had already published several novels when she first achieved an international audience with the scenario of director Alain Resnais's *Hiroshima mon amour* (1959; *Hiroshima mon amour: Text by Marguerite Duras for the Film by Alain Resnais*, 1961). In 1984, she was awarded the coveted Prix Goncourt for her novel *L'Amant* (1984; *The Lover*, 1985).

The importance that Duras gave to the reader or spectator in her work, her search for "inner realism," and her systematic use of ellipsis bring her close to writers such as Nathalie Sarraute, Alain Robbe-Grillet, Claude Simon, Robert Pinget, and Michel Butor. Unlike these writers, however, she never felt the need to define a literary theory of any kind. To Duras, any preestablished formula seemed an instrusion into the freedom of the reader or spectator, an attempt to control his or her response. In this respect, she came close to realizing Gustave Flaubert's ideal of perfectly transparent prose. Duras also differed from the so-called New Novel/New Theater group in that she was politically committed to individual causes in which she believed and about which she was highly vocal. Here again, however, she did not fit under any label. Duras was expelled from the French Communist Party in 1950 and never again joined a political party. She did not like to be labeled a feminist either, although virtually all of her literary output addresses, in one way or another, the problem of feminine identity. Thus, Duras cannot be pinned to any literary or political school of thought. Instead, she developed her own original style and, deeply committed to the defense of human values, she became a controversial figure in France. Duras also attained recognition abroad, and many of her works have been translated into English. Within and beyond France, critical articles and doctoral dissertations are written on various aspects of her work. Her plays are performed throughout the world.

BIOGRAPHY

Marguerite Donnadieu was born on April 4, 1914, in Gia Dinh, in what was then Indochina and is now Vietnam. Her parents, who were teachers, had moved to Vietnam from the north of France. Widowed while her children (two sons and a daughter) were still young, Marguerite's mother tried to support the family by farming on land granted by the government. Unfortunately, the land was frequently flooded, and Marguerite's mother tried against all odds to reclaim it. This futile battle, Marguerite's difficult relationship with her feisty mother, whom she perceived as domineering, and Marguerite's attachment to her

Marguerite Duras in 1955 (New Press)

brother, are collectively the starting point of *The Eden Cinema*. Adding a definite sensual dimension to her work, the exotic landscape in which she grew up, with its steamy, hot climate and its luxuriant vegetation, is usually the setting for her plays. At the *lycée* in Saigon, Marguerite studied both Vietnamese and French and after receiving her *baccalauréat* (high school diploma), she continued her education in Paris, initially studying mathematics and finally getting her *licence* (undergraduate degree) in law in 1935.

Marguerite Donnadieu was married to Rober Antelme, a member of the Communist Party to which she herself belonged. She later was divorced from him and met another fellow Communist, Dionys Mascolo, with whom she had a son. After leaving the Ministère des Colonies in 1941, she went to work for the publisher Gallimard and began to write novels. At Gallimard, writer and editor Raymond Queneau was supportive of her first writing efforts, and subse-

quently most of her works appeared under the firm's imprint. With the publication of her first novel in 1943, she adopted her nom de plume Duras (the name of a village in Gascony).

On the request of actor-director Claude Martin, Duras adapted her novel *Le Square* (1955; *The Square*, 1959) for the stage and continued writing plays or adapting foreign plays for the French stage. Four of her early novels were made into motion pictures by René Clément, Peter Brook, Jules Dassin, and Tony Richardson, respectively. In 1960, Duras won international fame with her script for Alain Resnais's film *Hiroshima mon amour*. The critical and popular success of her novel *The Lover* and of its controversial film adaptation (1991) by Jean-Jacques Annaul once again catapulted Duras into the limelight. Ironically, her dissatisfaction with Annaud's treatment led to her rewriting her own versions of the screenplay as the cinematic novel *L'Amant de la Chine du Nord* (1991;

The North China Lover, 1992). Until late in her life, she remained actively engaged in writing for the theater and motion pictures, often closely following the rehearsals or shooting and sometimes directing them herself.

In her work as a journalist, Duras contributed both to newspapers and to television. She was a crime reporter for a time and maintained a fascination with crime, which she saw as a desperate way of making a statement. Her unique blend of politics and aesthetics marked her as one of the most original, visible, and controversial literary figures of twentieth century France.

ANALYSIS

Marguerite Duras was fond of saying that she did not come to theater, but that theater came to her when she was asked by the actor-director Claude Martin to rewrite her novel *The Square* for the stage. The theater was certainly a most appropriate medium for her because she aims at communicating the intensity of the moment. Although motion pictures offer more possibilities for the evocation of atmosphere, and the novel—if penned by a magician of style of Duras's caliber—can leave much more to the individual imagination, in theater, the audience participates in the "happening."

Ironically, this spontaneity is partially occasioned by Duras's elaborate stage directions, in which the audience is often mentioned as having already (or not yet) seen or heard or even smelled what the characters have already (or not yet) noticed. This creates a unique sense of immediacy for the audience. In Duras's plays, there is always a feeling that what is happening might not happen, that something else might happen instead. Most of the time, nothing happens at all, and everyone is kept in a state of expectation with no conclusion offered.

For Duras, writing a play did not consist of placing characters in an unfolding action with a beginning, a middle, and an end. She was not interested in individual psychology or in the resolution of a plot. Rather, she was in search of the absolute as revealed in the intensity of an instant. Duras once overheard someone describing the land he had just bought, and

she placed this description at the beginning of her novel *L'Après-midi de Monsieur Andesmas* (1962; *The Afternoon of Monsieur Andesmas*, 1964): "Here, there are instants of absolute light, revealing everything, polyvalent and at the same time precise, relentlessly bearing down on a single object." Duras brings that kind of light—polyvalent, precise, and merciless—to her subject, aiming at the absolute truth of the instant.

The sensual element was extremely important for Duras. She provided extensive details for sets, costumes, lighting, sounds or music, actors' movements, which are nearly choreographed, and even vocal intonations. Her prose is deceptively simple; easy to parody but difficult to imitate, it is sparse, disconnected, obsessive, and subtly effective.

Duras undertook nothing less than to establish a new type of communication between people. She refused any complicity with the reader or spectator; she refused to catalog things, to allow the audience to take anything for granted. Duras sought instead "a collective conspiracy" in order to come closer to reality. In the process, a comfortable sense of clear meaning is sacrificed. "Clarity is a disease of the French," said Duras. "They believe in it, it is everywhere!" With complex and subtle narrative techniques, Duras attempted to destroy memory, culture, and clarity, to arrive at a *tabula rasa* on which to build. She moved toward greater sobriety and complexity.

THE SQUARE

Duras's first play, *The Square*, is a conversation in a public garden between a young maid and a middle-aged traveling salesman. These two strangers leading uneventful lives try to break free of their solitude and to define their identities, as if talking to someone should help them to do so. Nothing happens, not even a hint of a flirtation. Their dialogue resembles two parallel monologues. It could go on forever if the public garden, *le square*, did not close. They part without having really met.

THE VIADUCTS OF SEINE-ET-OISE

The starting point of *The Viaducts of Seine-et-Oise* is an actual crime that Duras covered as a journalist: An aging couple had inexplicably murdered a deaf-mute relative who had been keeping house for them for a long time. After cutting up the body, they had disposed of the pieces by dropping them in the cars of freight trains as they passed under the Epinay viaduct. They were then arrested. In the play, two old people retrace the successive stages of their crime and finally confess it publicly in a café. The structure of the play, Duras's second, is still relatively traditional. About a decade later, with *L'Amante anglaise*, Duras would use the same story in a very different play, devoid of any realistic representation and with absurdist overtones.

THE RIVERS AND FORESTS

The Rivers and Forests is Duras's only comic play and also the one in which Eugène Ionesco's influence is felt most strongly. Despite its bucolic title, it actually takes place on a crosswalk where a man and two women engage in banal conversation; a dog belonging to one of them has bitten the man. In its tangential relation to the play's action, Duras's title recalls Ionesco's *La Cantatrice chauve* (1950; *The Bald Soprano*, 1956): The man may or may not be employed by Les Eaux et Forêts, a sort of government agency. The characters have names, but in the course of the conversation, the names are constantly interchanged, as in the case of the name Bobby Watson in *The Bald Soprano*. Meanwhile, in talking, the characters try to define their identities, but there is no truth in what they are saying, and they display a total inability to give or to receive.

THE MUSIC

In *The Music*, a man and a woman who have just been divorced meet for the last time in a hotel in Evreux. They talk, and talk, and talk. "I make them talk for hours just for the sake of talking," the author once said in a very characteristic statement. Present memory of things past has very little to do with whatever reality things may have had at one time. Twenty years after writing the original, Duras saw fit (or felt compelled) to add a second act to *The Music: La Musica, deuxième*. The sequel consists of more talk: The couple now realize that they are still in love, but they are already divorced.

THE EDEN CINEMA

The Eden Cinema brings to the stage the story of *The Sea Wall*. Suzanne and her brother are reminisc-

ing while their mother is swinging on a rocking chair between them. The static dialogue is interrupted by *intermèdes* in which the events talked about are enacted. Monsieur Jo also appears, courting Suzanne. In the Ubu repertory production, Oriental music contributed to the atmosphere.

INDIA SONG

India Song is one of the most interesting of Duras's plays. As has been noted before, the same text is presented as *texte-théâtre-film*. A few general remarks are offered at the beginning: for example, that all geographical references are incorrect and that geographical names are used "primarily in a musical sense." In *India Song*, as in the screenplay *La Femme du Gange* (1973; the woman of the Ganges), voices outside the narrative provide the means of exploration, revelation. These voices do not address the audience; they speak among themselves without knowing that they are overheard. They make it "possible to let the narrative be forgotten and put at the disposal of memories other than that of the author. Memories that distort. That create." There are characters, and some have names. They move around against lights, music, the voices, in the sultry atmosphere of the monsoon, with leprosy lurking about. Yet they seldom talk; they are talked about, indirectly, by the voices. Roland Barthes pointed out the resemblance of these scenes to the Greek theater: In both there is an organic alternation between what is being interrogated (the action, the setting, the dramatic dialogue) and man interrogating (the chorus, the commentary, the lyricism). The play is the result of this dialectical tension between the scene and the voices that are talking about it. Yet never do the voices *describe* the scene; there is no mimesis. The voices are totally disembodied, representative of pure memory. They all have known of this love story, directly or indirectly, and while none of them remembers it completely, some remember it better than others; their only identity is in the way they remember.

The story itself is that of Duras's novel *Le Vice-consul*, 1966 (*The Vice-Consul*, 1968), but Duras insisted that the play is not merely an adaptation of the novel. The characters, she said, have been "projected into new narrative regions." When an occasional episode has been transposed, "it has to be seen, read, differently."

The major components of Duras's magic seem to be combined in *India Song*: romantic sensibility carried by modern aesthetics. It is so subtle as to go unnoticed, but the main voices as well as the occasional voices of the party guests actually place the reader or the spectator in the disorienting situation of being a complete outsider (but not a voyeur) in a closed circle (here an embassy in a French colony in India), and of being caught at the same time in an unbound passion (that of the Vice-Consul for Anne-Marie Stretter, the ambassador's wife). Such passion is always a disconcerting experience, even in much less formal circles. Everywhere else, the tension is just as strong. The town, plagued by famine and leprosy in the warm humidity of the monsoon, is immobilized in a stillness ready to explode. Anne-Marie Stretter is the only detached person; she has been dead for some time and moves around gracefully indifferent to her surroundings. Then comes the climax, the paroxysm, the disturbing, the unacceptable, the unbearable: In desperation, "so that something should happen between us," the Vice-Consul shouts his love to Anne-Marie Stretter: "I have never loved anyone but her." Remarks a man's voice: "We are sorry but you are the kind of man who only interests us when you are not here." The commotion is soon over; as darkness falls, a piece of Ludwig van Beethoven is heard on the piano. The Vice-Consul knows the futility of his extreme act when he speculates: "They'll feel uncomfortable for half an hour. Then they'll start talking again."

Agatha

In *Agatha*, Duras evoked the memory of one of the key relationships of her childhood in Indochina, that with her long-dead younger brother Paulo. The play involves only two characters, sister and brother, both dressed in white, who variously close their eyes or look away from each other in order to avoid acknowledging and thus succumbing to the incestuous desires they once felt and still feel.

Savannah Bay

In *Savannah Bay*, Duras once again used an attenuated but haunting Southeast Asian setting. Two char-

acters, an aging actress named Madeleine and her granddaughter, identified only as Young Woman, strive to recount and reconstruct the story of Savannah. Herself a young woman of sixteen, Savannah had an affair with an older man and drowned herself in the waters of the Gulf of Siam shortly after the birth of their daughter. Madeleine and Young Woman, who may respectively be Savannah's mother and daughter, circle endlessly but unsuccessfully around the event.

The language of Duras's theater is at once vivid and elliptical, proceeding by allusions with the single-word sentences that are a distinctive feature of her style. Indeed, perhaps her most significant contribution to literature lies in her emphasis on the immediacy of the senses; nothing, to Duras, was merely intellectual. She did not try to convince; she provided favorable conditions for experience. Seldom has a writer left so much freedom to the audience.

Duras devoted great care to the staging of her plays. She favored simple aural and visual effects, preferring sets that could be progressively discovered, piece by piece. In *Savannah Bay* she made ironic use of the Michel Rivgauche/ Charles Dumont song "Les mots d'amour" ("The Words of Love") as sung by Edith Piaf. Appropriately enough, her stage directions for the same play call for two sets, a very small one in the foreground in which her two characters conduct their verbal inquest, and a larger, formally framed set—separate, stark, and looking out on an empty sea—in which the unresolved and apparently unknowable story of Savannah takes place.

Other major works

LONG FICTION: *Les Impudents*, 1943; *La Vie tranquille*, 1944; *Un Barrage contre le Pacifique*, 1950 (*The Sea Wall*, 1952; also known as *A Sea of Troubles*, 1953); *Le Marin de Gibraltar*, 1952 (*The Sailor from Gibraltar*, 1966); *Les Petits Chevaux de Tarquinia*, 1953 (*The Little Horses of Tarquinia*, 1960); *Le Square*, 1955 (*The Square*, 1959); *Moderato Cantabile*, 1958 (English translation, 1960); *Dix Heures et demie du soir en été*, 1960 (*Ten-Thirty on a Summer Night*, 1962); *L'Après-midi de Monsieur Andesmas*, 1962 (*The Afternoon of Monsieur Andes-*

mas, 1964); *Le Ravissement de Lol V. Stein*, 1964 (*The Ravishing of Lol Stein*, 1966); *Le Vice-consul*, 1966 (*The Vice-Consul*, 1968); *L'Amante anglaise*, 1967 (English translation, 1968); *Détruire, dit-elle*, 1969 (*Destroy, She Said*, 1970); *Abahn Sabana David*, 1970; *L'Amour*, 1971; *India Song: Texte-théâtre-film*, 1973 (English translation, 1976); *La Maladie de la morte*, 1982 (*The Malady of Death*, 1986); *L'Amant*, 1984 (*The Lover*, 1985); *Les Yeux bleus, cheveux noirs*, 1987 (*Blue Eyes, Black Hair*, 1987); *Emily L.*, 1987 (English translation, 1989); *La pluie d'été*, 1990 (*Summer Rain*, 1992); *L'Amant de la Chine du Nord*, 1991 (*The North China Lover*, 1992); *Yann Andrea Steiner*, 1992 (*Yann Andrea Steiner: A Memoir*, 1993).

SHORT FICTION: *Des Journées entières dans les arbres*, 1954 (*Days in the Trees*, 1967); *L'Homme assis dans le couloir*, 1980 (*The Man Sitting in the Corridor*, 1991); *L'Homme atlantique*, 1982 (*The Atlantic Man*, 1993); *La Pute de la côte Normande*, 1986 (*The Slut of the Normandy Coast*, 1993); *Two by Duras*, 1993 (includes *The Slut of the Normandy Coast* and *The Atlantic Man*).

SCREENPLAYS: *Hiroshima mon amour*, 1959 (*Hiroshima mon amour: Text by Marguerite Duras for the Film by Alain Resnais*, 1961); *Une Aussi longue absence*, 1961 (with Gérard Jarlot; English translation, 1966); *La Musica*, 1966 (with Paul Seban); *Détruire, dit-elle*, 1969; *Nathalie Granger*, 1972; *La Femme du Gange*, 1973; *India Song: Texte-théâtre-film*, 1973; *Baxter, Véra Baxter*, 1976; *Des Journées entières dans les arbres*, 1976; *Son nom de Venise dans Calcutta désert*, 1976; *Le Camion*, 1977; *Le Navire "Night,"* 1978; *Cesarée*, 1979; *Les Mains négatives*, 1979; *Aurélia Steiner*, 1979; *Agatha: Ou, Les Lectures illisibles*, 1982; *L'Homme atlantique*, 1982.

NONFICTION: *Les Parleuses*, 1974 (*Woman to Woman*, 1987); *Les Lieux de Marguerite Duras*, 1977; *Outside, papiers d'un jour*, 1981 (*Outside: Selected Writings*, 1986); *La Douleur*, 1985 (*The War: A Memoir*, 1986); *La Vie matérielle*, 1987 (*Practicalities: Marguerite Duras Speaks to Jérôme Beaujour*,

1990); *Les Yeux verts*, 1987 (*Green Eyes*, 1990); *Ecrire*, 1993 (*Writing*, 1998); *Outside II: Le Monde extérieur*, 1993; *C'est tout*, 1995 (*No More*, 1998).

BIBLIOGRAPHY

Adler, Laure. *Marguerite Duras: A Life*. Chicago: University of Chicago Press, 2000. An exhaustive biography, written with the full cooperation of its subject, by a journalist and historian who befriended Duras during her final years. Although Adler admits to leaving many "gaps" in Duras's dramatic life unfilled, hers is the standard biography in English.

Cody, Gabrielle H. *Impossible Performances: Duras as Dramatist*. New York: Peter Lang, 2000. Treats Duras as one of the most important dramatists of the century, a feminist and postcolonialist whose plays operate against what Cody identifies as the masculine ideals of representational, realistic theater.

Schuster, Marilyn R. *Marguerite Duras Revisited*. New York: Twayne, 1993. The best introduction in English to Duras, although it considers her drama as only a small portion of her extensive body of work. Concludes with useful primary and secondary bibliographies.

Vircondelet, Alain. *Duras: A Biography*. Normal, Ill.: Dalkey Archive, 1994. The first full-length biography, originally published in 1991 and updated for this English edition. Vircondelet was one of Duras's earliest critics, but his rhetorical style sometimes obscures rather than clarifies the events of his subject's life.

Winston, Jane Bradley. *Postcolonial Duras: Cultural Memory in Postwar France*. New York: Palgrave, 2002. An examination of Duras's role as an intellectual force in a colonizing power, particularly valuable in light of her early life in French Indochina and her continued use of the region as a setting.

Claire Brandicourt Saint-Léon,
updated by Grove Koger

FRIEDRICH DÜRRENMATT

Born: Konolfingen, Switzerland; January 5, 1921
Died: Neuchâtel, Switzerland; December 14, 1990

PRINCIPAL DRAMA

Es steht geschrieben, pr., pb. 1947 (revised as *Die
    Wiedertäufer*, pr., pb. 1967; *The Anabaptists*,
    1967)
Der Blinde, pr. 1948, pb. 1960
Romulus der Grosse, pr. 1949, second version pr.
    1957, pb. 1958, third version pb. 1961 (*Romulus
    the Great*, 1961)
Die Ehe des Herrn Mississippi, pr., pb. 1952,
    second version pb. 1957 (*The Marriage of Mr.
    Mississippi*, 1958)
Ein Engel kommt nach Babylon, pr. 1953, pb.
    1954, second version pb. 1957 (*An Angel
    Comes to Babylon*, 1962)
Herkulus und der Stall des Angias, wr. 1954, pr.,
    pb. 1959 (radio play), pr., pb. 1963 (staged;
    Hercules and the Augean Stables, 1966)
Der Besuch der alten Dame, pr., pb. 1956 (*The
    Visit*, 1958)
Komödien I-III, pb. 1957-1972 (3 volumes)
Frank der Fünfte: Opera einer Privatbank, pr.
    1959, pb. 1960 (libretto; music by Paul
    Burkhard)
Die Physiker, pr., pb. 1962 (*The Physicists*,
    1963)
Four Plays, pb. 1964
Der Meteor, pr., pb. 1966 (*The Meteor*, 1966)
König Johann, pr., pb. 1968 (adaptation of
    William Shakespeare's play *King John*)
*Play Strindberg: Totentanz nach August
    Strindberg*, pr., pb. 1969 (adaptation of August
    Strindberg's play *The Dance of Death*; *Play
    Strindberg: The Dance of Death*, 1971)
Porträt eines Planeten, pr. 1970, revised version
    pr., pb. 1971 (*Portrait of a Planet*, 1973)
Titus Andronicus, pr., pb. 1970 (adaptation of
    Shakespeare's play)
Urfaust, pr., pb. 1970 (adaptation of Johann
    Wolfgang von Goethe's play)
Der Mitmacher, pr. 1973, pb. 1976 (*The
    Conformer*, 1975)
Die Frist, pr., pb. 1977
Achterloo, pr., pb. 1983

OTHER LITERARY FORMS

Friedrich Dürrenmatt was a versatile and prolific
writer. In addition to his dramas, he wrote radio plays,
stories, novels, detective novels, prose sketches, film
scripts, and essays on dramatic theory and on a variety of literary, political, and social topics. He also
adapted plays by William Shakespeare, Johann Wolfgang von Goethe, and Georg Büchner.

ACHIEVEMENTS

Friedrich Dürrenmatt was the best-known dramatist writing in the German language of his day. In productions of German-language playwrights in West
Germany, Austria, and Switzerland, his plays were
consistently among the most frequently performed.
They have also been widely translated and are a standard part of the repertoire in theaters in the United
States and in the other countries of Western Europe.
Dürrenmatt was awarded many prizes for his works,
including the literature prize of the city of Bern in
1954, the Schiller Prize in 1959, and the Grillparzer
Prize of the Austrian Academy of Sciences in 1968.
He received honorary doctorates from Temple University, Philadelphia, in 1969, from the University of
Nice in 1977, and from the Hebrew University in Jerusalem in 1977. A thirty-volume German-language
edition of his works was published in 1980 by Dioge-
nes in Zürich. Dürrenmatt helped to compile this edition, for which he also wrote new versions of some of
his plays.

BIOGRAPHY

Friedrich Dürrenmatt was born in Konolfingen in
the Canton of Bern, Switzerland, on January 5, 1921.
His father, Reinhold, was a Protestant minister. In
1935, the family moved to Bern, where Dürrenmatt
was graduated from the Humboldtianum (a high

school) in 1941. In 1941 and 1942, Dürrenmatt studied philosophy, literature, and the natural sciences at thè universities of Zürich and Bern, but he did not complete his studies. At this time, he wanted to be a painter, not a writer. During these years, Dürrenmatt read works by Franz Kafka (whose influence is evident in Dürrenmatt's early works) and Søren Kierkegaard. He says that his greatest literary experience was reading Aristophanes, whose comedies helped shape Dürrenmatt's own views of comedy. In 1946, Dürrenmatt moved to Basel; he married the actress Lotte Geissler in 1947. For a time, he tried to earn his living as a theater critic for the Bern newspaper *Die Nation* and later, between 1951 and 1953, for the *Zürcher Weltwoche*. In 1948, Dürrenmatt and his family moved to Ligerz on Lake Biel, where they stayed until 1952, when Dürrenmatt bought a house in Neuchâtel and settled there with his family. He died there on December 14, 1990.

ANALYSIS

The world in Friedrich Dürrenmatt's plays is an enigma, peopled by executioners and victims, tyrants and the oppressed, and persecutors and the perse-

Friedrich Dürrenmatt (© Miriam Berkley)

cuted. It defies all rational attempts to change it and is dominated by accident and chance. Dürrenmatt believed that the world is indeed ruled by chance—a chance short circuit could launch the nuclear weapons that would destroy the world. The individual feels helpless: Those individuals in Dürrenmatt's works who do try to change the world are doomed to failure. Dürrenmatt was preoccupied with the question of justice (hence his fascination with the detective novel), but justice in his works is an unattainable, distant ideal.

Dürrenmatt believed that comedy is the only form of drama that can express adequately the situation of modern humanity; it alone can reproduce the formless contemporary world. Like his model, Aristophanes, Dürrenmatt was attracted to the social criticism inherent in the comic form. (Satire, he believed, is the only weapon that those in power fear.) In the essay *Theaterprobleme* (1955; *Problems of the Theater*, 1958), he writes that tragedy is no longer possible because it needs a fixed, moral order that does not exist today. In the modern world, tragedy is produced, in Dürrenmatt's view, by universal butchers and acted out by mincing machines. Tragedy presupposes acceptance of responsibility for guilt, without personal responsibility there can be no tragedy. Today, he said, people are no longer individually guilty; rather, they are collectively guilty. Dürrenmatt wrote, however, that the tragic is still possible within comedy; a comic plot for him was concluded only when it has taken the worst possible turn.

Through his comedies, Dürrenmatt lures the audience into confronting reality. He did not provide answers to the problems he depicted in the plays. Instead, he likened his role to that of a midwife—that is, he helps people find their own answers. In his comedies, Dürrenmatt emphasized *Einfälle* (ingenious plots). His plays are not intended to be faithful representations of reality. In all his plays, even when they are set in the past, the focus is on modern-day problems. Dürrenmatt believed that comedy creates the distance that enables people to view the present objectively. An essential part of his comedies is the grotesque. Dürrenmatt said that the logical contradiction of the grotesque makes the spectator laugh, while its ethical contradiction outrages him. He used the grotesque to portray the monstrous, the abyss concealed beneath the veneer of civilization.

Despite his gloomy view of the world, Dürrenmatt always stressed the importance of humor. His plays abound in grotesque and absurd situations, puns, slapstick, gags, verbal ingenuity, and parodies, all of which reflect his vital comic imagination. Humor, according to the playwright, does not mean to approve of the world, but rather to accept it for what it is, as something dubious, and not to despair; it means to accept this dubiousness and carry on.

In "Dramaturgische Überlegungen zu den *Wiedertäufern*" (1967; "Dramaturgical Considerations to *The Anabaptists*"), Dürrenmatt gives possible models of how the English antarctic explorer Robert Scott could be portrayed, and these models aptly summarize his theories of the drama. William Shakespeare, he said, would have shown Scott's downfall to be caused by a tragic flaw in his character. Ambition would have made him blind to the dangers of the region, and jealousy and betrayal by the other members of the expedition would have done the rest to bring about the catastrophe. Bertolt Brecht would have shown the expedition failing because of economic reasons and class thinking. An English education would have prevented Scott from making use of huskies, and in a style befitting his social class, he would have used ponies. Because of the higher cost of the ponies, he would have had to save on the rest of the equipment, which would have caused his downfall. Samuel Beckett would have concentrated only on the end. Changed into a block of ice, Scott would be sitting opposite other blocks of ice, talking without getting an answer from his comrades, not even sure whether he could be heard. Another possibility, which Dürrenmatt would prefer, would be to show Scott buying provisions for the expedition. While putting the provisions into the cold storage chamber, he would be locked in accidentally, where he would freeze to death. Scott dying far from all help among the glaciers of the Antarctic is a tragic figure; Scott locked into a cold storage chamber through mishap and dying in the middle of a city only a few yards from a busy street is transformed into a comic figure.

Dürrenmatt concluded that the worst possible turn that a story can take is the turn to comedy.

Although Dürrenmatt's comedies depict a world ruled by chance in which the individual is powerless, they are not utterly despairing. There are still courageous individuals such as Romulus and Graf Bodo von Übelohe-Zabernsee who try to change the world, even though they ultimately fail. As Dürrenmatt writes in *Problems of the Theater*, one has to accept the world for what it is and keep on living, refusing to give up. His vital comic imagination, evident in all his plays, alleviated his otherwise gloomy view of the world. In an interview with Horst Bienek in 1961, Dürrenmatt stressed the importance of humor in his plays; he said that he can be understood only from the point of view of humor taken seriously.

Common to most of Dürrenmatt's essays on dramatic theory is an emphasis on the practical problems of the theater. He was rarely satisfied with his plays, as the various versions of the plays demonstrate. Each time one of his plays was produced, he said, he saw new possibilities. Many of the problems he encountered in writing his plays could be solved only when he saw his play on the stage. Dürrenmatt protested against dramatic rules formulated by critics; such rules, he said, are of no use to the artist. He wanted his plays to be judged by their theatrical quality, not by how well they fit into some theory of drama.

ROMULUS THE GREAT

Dürrenmatt's belief that the individual is powerless to change events is shown clearly in *Romulus the Great*, his first Swiss success, which had its premiere on April 25, 1949, in the Stadttheater in Basel. There are five versions of the play. The major change occurs in the second version and is kept in the remaining versions. In the first version, Romulus is portrayed as a cunning, successful politician who realizes his goals. In the subsequent versions, he is no longer victor but victim, a failed and tragic figure who sees that his life has been senseless.

The play depicts the destruction of the Roman Empire by the Germans. The time is the Ides of March, 476 C.E. (another change from the first version), by which Dürrenmatt parodies Shakespeare's *Julius Caesar* (pr. c. 1599-1600) and mocks heroic ideals. The action takes place on Romulus's chicken farm, a grotesque incongruity, because the spectator has entirely different expectations of what the Roman court should be like. Dürrenmatt employs the classical dramatic unities as an ironic contrast to the chaotic world of hens on the stage. The play is called an "unhistorical-historical comedy." The real Romulus was sixteen when he became emperor and was seventeen when he was forced to abdicate. Dürrenmatt's Romulus is an older man. The many anachronisms in the play—the capitalist Cäsar Rupf, for example, who manufactures trousers—show that Dürrenmatt is using the fall of the Roman Empire to analyze modern problems.

Initially, Romulus appears to be lazy and disagreeable. Instead of trying to defend his empire, he sits comfortably eating and drinking. His only concern appears to be the fate of his beloved chickens, whom he has named after different Roman emperors. Yet there are indications that he is not as foolish and despicable as he appears. When Cäsar Rupf demands his daughter Rea's hand as the price for saving Rome, Romulus is the only one who refuses to sell off his daughter in this way. Romulus is also fully aware of the hopelessness of the situation. He deduces that the Germans will conquer Rome because the chicken named after the German leader Odoaker lays a lot of eggs. Only in the third act does Romulus appear as a wise man who is passionately concerned with justice and humaneness. He has become Emperor of Rome only to liquidate his empire. His role, as he sees it, is to judge Rome: Rome has been tyrannical and brutal, and Romulus intends to punish it for its crimes by destroying it. His plan to punish Rome and thereby make the world more humane rests on a delusion: He assumes that the Germans are more humane than the Romans, yet the future ruler Theoderich is just as brutal as the Romans, if not more so. Odoaker, Theoderich's uncle (a man who, like Romulus, is a passionate chicken-raiser), did not come to conquer Rome but to surrender to Romulus in order to save the world from his nephew. Despite their well-intentioned plans, Romulus and Odoaker are helpless; they cannot prevent the rise of another brutal empire under Theoderich.

Most of the other characters are comic figures. They swear that they will fight to the last drop of blood, but they actually flee in haste once the Germans approach. The empress Julia speaks of heroism and sacrifice, but when she flees she is concerned only with saving the imperial dinner service. Her marriage to Romulus has been loveless, since they only married each other for political reasons, to become emperor and empress. Their daughter Rea draws her notions of heroism from the tragic roles she rehearses under the guidance of the actor Phylax, notions that are far removed from the real world. The cynical art dealer Apollyon has no respect for art; for him it only means money. Cäsar Rupf parodies the political and economic power of the capitalist in the modern world (ironically, the capitalist, not the emperor, is called Caesar, an indication that the capitalist is the real power in the state). Zeno, the Byzantine emperor, is a would-be Machiavelli who has even intrigued against his own family. He is the only one who does not drown during the flight from the Germans: types such as Zeno, Dürrenmatt believed, are indestructible. Only Ämilian, Rea's fiancé, is not a comic figure. Ämilian is captured by the Germans and suffers from their brutality; Romulus sympathizes with him but thinks that his patriotism, heroism, and readiness to sacrifice himself for Rome are senseless. Romulus is suspicious of all such concepts, since they can be so easily misused by the state to encourage people to commit crimes.

The play is a mixture of tragic and comic elements. The comic aspects include the setting, plot, and characterizations. Dürrenmatt also uses sight gags, such as the chickens that are always underfoot and the comical hiding places of the plotters who want to murder Romulus. Dürrenmatt's mixture of different levels of language—jargon, mercantile language, empty clichés, slang, and extremely formal diction—also has a comic effect. The tragic part of the play is the conclusion. With the best intentions in the world, Romulus has dedicated his life to trying to make the world more just and humane. He believes that he can change the course of history and is willing to sacrifice his own life for this illusion, yet the world under Theoderich will be just as repressive as the Roman Empire, if not more so. At the end, Romulus is not even allowed to die but is pensioned off, thus forced to live with the bitter realization that his whole life has been senseless.

THE MARRIAGE OF MR. MISSISSIPPI

In *The Marriage of Mr. Mississippi*, Dürrenmatt shows his distrust of all ideologies. The play, which had its premiere in the Münchner Kammer-spiele on March 26, 1952, contributed significantly to establishing Dürrenmatt's reputation in Germany. Like *Romulus the Great*, the play has gone through five versions, and it has also been filmed. The main difference between the first version and subsequent versions is that the earliest version is more surrealistic and contains more religious symbolism while the later versions are more political.

The play takes place in one room. Through one window, a southern landscape with a temple and a cypress tree can be seen; through the other, a northern landscape with a Gothic cathedral and an apple tree. This indicates that Western culture has not managed to synthesize its classical and Christian heritage. The room contains a hodgepodge of furniture from different periods and thereby parodies Western culture. The play (which is structured epically) is not divided into acts and scenes but is broken up by the monologues spoken by the protagonists, who step out of their roles and address the audience. Dürrenmatt uses many exaggerated alienation effects (the characters even step out of their roles to comment on their own behavior). These alienation effects contribute to the play's comic effect and also suggest a parody of Bertolt Brecht. The circular structure of the play (which actually begins with the last scene) indicates that nobody has learned anything—future ideologists will be just as fanatical as the present-day ones.

Three of the main characters represent particular ideologies. The state prosecutor Mississippi believes in absolute justice, which he thinks he has found in the law of Moses (he tries to reintroduce this law in the twentieth century). He is a fanatical reformer who in his search for justice has had 350 executions carried out. Because Mississippi's first wife committed adultery, he poisoned her—a just punishment, he believes, according to Mosaic law. He then sentences

himself (as he says) to marry Anastasia, who has poisoned her husband, who was having an affair with Mississippi's wife. Through this loveless marriage, Mississippi hopes to change Anastasia for the better. To accomplish this, he forces her to attend executions. At the end of the play, he wants to know whether she has become a better person; his marriage to her would otherwise be senseless. Through her lie that she has been faithful to him, he is able to preserve his conviction that punishment improves people. Like Mississippi, Saint-Claude is idealistic and fanatical. He wants to change the world through Marxism, but he is liquidated because his communism differs so radically from the party dogma. Like Mississippi, Saint-Claude believes that the end justifies the means—he does not even know how many people he has killed in his search for a better world. The third ideologist is Graf Bodo von Übelohe-Zabernsee, who is a Christian. To help people, he has sacrificed his fortune and become a beggar. Although his goals of changing the world are praise-worthy, he is a laughable figure: Everything he tries to do fails. At the end of the play, he appears as Don Quixote, who fights senselessly, if courageously, against the windmills; he refuses, despite his failures, to give up his search for a better world.

In contrast to these ideologues, Anastasia and the politician Diego are pragmatic opportunists. Dürrenmatt said that Anastasia is supposed to symbolize the world. She has no morals or ideals, and she adapts easily to any situation. If it is to her advantage, she cold-bloodedly betrays her lovers. Through her, Dürrenmatt mocks the protagonists' attempts to change the world; like Anastasia, the world is impervious to change. Diego, who adeptly gains power during the play, is a cunning opportunist, like most of the politicians in Dürrenmatt's works.

Dürrenmatt's characteristic humor is especially evident in this play, which is filled with satiric depictions of murders and revolutions. The characters are exaggerated caricatures; through them, Dürrenmatt ridicules ideologies. In addition to the action, setting, and characterizations, Dürrenmatt employs other devices for comic effect. The language of the play is bombastic, and the betrayed husband is a staple of comedy. As in his other plays, Dürrenmatt delights here in using gags: A character jumps suddenly out of a grandfather clock; there is the frequent ritual of coffee drinking, and one never knows whether the coffee is poisoned. Sudden surprises, such as Mississippi's unexpected marriage proposal to Anastasia, also contribute to the comic effects.

Despite the comic elements, the atmosphere of the play is basically gloomy. At the end, Mississippi and Anastasia die (they have poisoned each other's coffee) and Saint-Claude is killed by the party. Yet they all rise up from the dead, and the play could start over again. As in *Romulus the Great* human life is depicted as a senseless, repetitive cycle that can never be changed.

THE VISIT

The central theme of *The Visit* is the problem of justice. Considered to be Dürrenmatt's masterpiece, *The Visit* had its premiere on January 29, 1956, at the Zürich Schauspielhaus. It is Dürrenmatt's most frequently performed play, and it established his reputation in the United States. *The Visit* takes place in the small town of Güllen (in Swiss dialect, *Güllen* means liquid manure); the time is the present. The town has stagnated economically: The local industries are ruined, the town is bankrupt, and the citizens live on welfare, while the neighboring towns are flourishing. The townspeople blame their misfortunes on Jews, Freemasons, Communists—on anyone but themselves. Their town has a cultural heritage, they think, because Goethe stayed the night there, Johannes Brahms composed a quartet there, and Berthold Schwarz invented gunpowder there. For them, culture is merely a series of clichés.

As the play opens, the community is hoping that Claire Zachanassian, the richest woman on earth, who used to live in Güllen, will help them. The festivities to welcome her are, however, hypocritical. When she lived in the town forty-five years ago, they despised her; now their exaggerated praise of her is calculated to manipulate her into giving the town money. Her former lover Alfred Ill is designated to appeal discreetly for her charity; as a reward for this job, he will be made the next mayor. Because Claire comes early, the effects of the welcome are

lost. The mayor's speech at the railroad station is drowned by the noise of the trains, and the choir has to be assembled hurriedly. At the dinner, the mayor's speech shows that he knows nothing whatsoever about Claire. Ill must keep on correcting him and, at the end of the speech, even Claire points out that he is wrong.

Claire is a grotesque figure whose right arm and left leg are prostheses to replace the limbs that she lost in accidents. Her retinue is equally grotesque: It consists of her butler; Toby and Roby, gumchewing gangsters whom she has saved from the electric chair; Koby and Loby, who are blind eunuchs; her seventh husband (she marries two more during the play); a black panther in a cage; a large amount of luggage; and a coffin. When she arrives, she asks strange and chilling questions: She asks the gymnast whether he has strangled anyone, the doctor whether he prepares death certificates, the policeman whether he can close his eyes, and the priest whether he consoles those who are condemned to death. At the meal in her honor, she drops her bombshell: She will give five hundred million to the town and five hundred million to be divided evenly among the town's families, on one condition: Someone must kill Alfred Ill. She has come, she says, to buy justice. Forty-five years before, she was expecting Ill's child. Ill refused to acknowledge that he was the father; instead, he bribed two witnesses with schnapps to say that they had slept with her. Claire was forced to leave Güllen; she then became a prostitute, and her child died. Becoming a prostitute, however, made Claire rich because it was in the brothel that she met Zachanassian, a rich oilman. Ill did not want to marry Claire because she was poor; instead, he married Mathilde because she owned a store. Claire's retinue consists, in part, of those connected with the paternity suit; the butler is the former judge, and Koby and Loby are the witnesses who committed perjury, whom she has relentlessly tracked down and then blinded and castrated. Claire is an emotional cripple whose life has been dedicated to revenge (the local teacher likens her to Medea). It turns out that Claire is responsible for the town's misfortunes: She has bought everything and let it stagnate. The mayor proudly refuses her money. He declares that the community is humane, that it is better to be poor than stained with blood. Claire knows better: She sits on her balcony and waits.

As she expects, the Gülleners cannot withstand temptation. All of them, including the leaders of the community to whom Ill vainly appeals for help, begin to spend freely and incur debts. They all buy yellow shoes; the policeman has a new gold tooth, the mayor a new typewriter; and even the priest has bought a new church bell. The priest tells Ill to flee so that he does not lead them into temptation. Even Ill's family joins in the spending spree: His wife buys a fur coat, his son a new car, and his daughter new clothes. His daughter also starts taking English and French lessons and plays tennis. The townspeople incur debts thoughtlessly, but as their debts mount, their attitude toward Ill changes. They no longer think of him as the most beloved member of the community, as they did when they thought he could persuade Claire to give the town money. Instead, they say that he is guilty of the crime and deserves punishment. When Claire's black panther escapes (Claire used to call Ill her panther), the citizens hunt and kill it, a foreshadowing of Ill's death.

Inevitably, they decide that Ill must die for the "well-being" of the community. A town meeting is called to decide Ill's fate. Before the meeting, the mayor tries to convince Ill that he should commit suicide out of love for his community and thus spare the town the guilt of his death. Ill refuses. He says that he has been through hell, watching the debts of the community grow; if they had spared him this fear, he might have killed himself for them. On the surface, the town meeting seems a model of democracy (the press enthusiastically interprets it in that way). The teacher speaks of justice and honor; his noble words are used to mask the common agreement to kill Ill. At the end of the meeting, Ill is killed, presumably by the most muscular member of the gym club in the midst of the Gülleners. His death is termed a heart attack caused by the joy of learning about Claire's gift. The Gülleners refuse to accept the fact that they killed Ill for money; instead, they see his death as just punishment for his earlier crime.

The townspeople are not particularly evil—they had intended to protect Ill. As the teacher notes, however, the temptation was too great. The teacher himself tries hard to resist, yet he tells Ill that he feels himself turning into a murderer; his humanistic training cannot avert this. At the end, Claire has her revenge on the town whose citizens had looked on coldly when she was forced to leave in the midst of winter, forty-five years ago.

During the play, Alfred Ill grows in stature until he almost becomes a tragic figure. At the outset, he is not concerned in the least about his former treatment of Claire. When he is confronted with his past behavior, he begins to see that he was wrong. He gradually accepts his guilt and realizes that he has made Claire what she is. Dürrenmatt remarked that Ill becomes great through his death. He noted that Ill's death is both meaningful and meaningless: Meaningful, because Ill accepts his guilt and grows as a human being; meaningless, because it achieves no moral redemption for the community. In a tragedy by Sophocles, Dürrenmatt said, such a death would have saved the community from the plague. In Güllen, however, Ill's death marks the beginning of the plague—that is, of moral corruption.

Dürrenmatt called his play a tragic comedy. The comedy stems in part from the characters and their actions (the hypocritical welcome prepared for Claire, and the way in which the press misunderstands the town meeting, for example). Dürrenmatt mocked religious and cultural clichés. He satirized the manner in which language disguises meaning (the press thinks that the teacher's speech shows "moral greatness" when in reality the teacher is justifying Ill's murder). The "romantic" meeting of Claire and Ill in the forest parodies German romanticism (the townspeople play the part of trees, and the noise of the woodpecker is made by a citizen tapping on his pipe with a rusty key). Dürrenmatt's parody of the Greek chorus at the end shows his conviction that tragedy is no longer possible.

There are, however, tragic elements in the play. Ill's fate is tragic. He is made into a scapegoat and is sacrificed for money. Dürrenmatt depicts vividly the moral and spiritual corruption of a community in which everything, including "justice," can be bought. The Gülleners do not accept responsibility for Ill's death but enjoy their new wealth, undisturbed by a guilty conscience. In his notes to the play, Dürrenmatt stresses that the Gülleners are people like all of humankind, who would, he implies, act as they did.

OTHER MAJOR WORKS

LONG FICTION: *Der Richter und sein Henker*, 1950 (*The Judge and His Hangman*, 1954); *Der Verdacht*, 1953 (*The Quarry*, 1961); *Grieche sucht Griechin*, 1955 (*Once a Greek . . .* , 1965); *Die Panne*, 1956 (*Traps*, 1960, pb. in England as *A Dangerous Game*); *Das Versprechen: Requiem auf den Kriminalroman*, 1958 (*The Pledge: Requiem for the Detective Novel*, 1959); *Der Sturz*, 1971; *Justiz*, 1985 (*The Execution of Justice*, 1989).

SHORT FICTION: *Die Stadt*, 1952; *Der Auftrag*, 1986 (*The Assignment*, 1988).

RADIO PLAYS: *Der Doppelgänger*, wr. 1946, 1961; *Der Prozess um des Esels Schatten*, wr. 1951, 1958 (based on Christoph Martin Wieland's *Die Abderiten*; *The Jackass*, 1960); *Stranitzky und der Nationalheld*, 1952; *Das Unternehmen der Wega*, 1955; *Die Panne*, 1956 (adaptation of his novel, *The Deadly Game*, 1963); *Gesammelte Hörspiele*, 1961.

NONFICTION: *Theaterprobleme*, 1955 (*Problems of the Theater*, 1958); *Theater-Schriften und Reden*, 1966 (*Writings on Theatre and Drama*, 1976).

MISCELLANEOUS: *Stoffe I-III*, 1981; *Werkausgabe in 30 Bänden*, 1982 (30 volumes); *Plays and Essays*, 1982.

BIBLIOGRAPHY

Arnold, Armin. *Friedrich Dürrenmatt*. New York: F. Ungar, 1972. A biography of Dürrenmatt, covering his life and works. Bibliography.

Chick, Edson M. *Dances of Death: Wedekind, Brecht, Dürrenmatt, and the Satiric Tradition*. Columbia, S.C.: Camden House, 1984. A study of satire in German drama, focusing on the works of Dürrenmatt, Bertolt Brecht, and Frank Wedekind. Bibliography and index.

Crockett, Roger A. *Understanding Friedrich Dürrenmatt*. Columbia: University of South Carolina Press, 1998. A biography and critical analysis of Dürrenmatt that includes analysis of his dramatic works. Bibliography and index.

Jenny, Urs. *Dürrenmatt: A Study of His Plays*. London: Eyre Methuen, 1978. A profile of the dramatist along with critical analyses of his plays. Index.

Tiusanen, Timo. *Dürrenmatt: A Study in Plays, Prose, Theory*. Princeton, N.J.: Princeton University Press, 1977. A critical study of the works and theory of Dürrenmatt. Bibliography and index.

Whitton, Kenneth S. *Dürrenmatt: Reinterpretation in Retrospect*. New York: St. Martin's Press, 1990. An examination of the works and life of Dürrenmatt. Bibliography and indexes.

_____. *The Theater of Friedrich Dürrenmatt: A Study in the Possibility of Freedom*. Atlantic Highlands, N.J.: Humanities Press, 1980. An analysis of the dramatic works of Dürrenmatt, with special emphasis on the subject of liberty. Bibliography and index.

Jennifer Michaels

E

JOSÉ ECHEGARAY Y EIZAGUIRRE

Born: Madrid, Spain; April 19, 1832
Died: Madrid, Spain; September 15, 1916

PRINCIPAL DRAMA

El libro talonario, pr., pb. 1874
La esposo del vengador, pr., pb. 1874
En el puño de la espada, pr., pb. 1875
La última noche, pr., pb. 1875
Cómo empieza y cómo acaba, pr., pb. 1876
O locura o santidad, pr., pb. 1877 (*Folly or Saintliness*, 1895)
El gran Galeoto, pr., pb. 1881 (verse play; *The Great Galeoto*, 1895)
Vida alegre y muerte triste, pr. 1885
El hijo de Don Juan, pr., pb. 1892 (*The Son of Don Juan*, 1895)
Mariana, pr., pb. 1892 (English translation, 1895)
El loco Dios, pr. 1902 (*The Madman Divine*, 1908)

OTHER LITERARY FORMS

In addition to his dramatic work, José Echegaray y Eizaguirre also wrote critical articles and essays on the nature of drama, some of which were collected in 1894 in his book *Algunas reflexiones generales sobre la crítica y el arte literario*. In 1912, he published a small collection of short stories, *Cuentos*, and wrote *Recuerdos*, an autobiography in three volumes, which was published posthumously in 1917. His true claim to literary importance, however, resides in the seventy-four dramas, satiric comedies, and one-act plays that he produced between 1874 and 1905.

ACHIEVEMENTS

Undoubtedly the most successful Spanish dramatist of the late nineteenth century, José Echegaray y Eizaguirre ruled as undisputed king of the stage from 1874, with the appearance of his first play, *El libro talonario* (the checkbook), until shortly after the turn of the twentieth century. Highly imaginative and prolific, Echegaray produced two or more successful plays a year throughout his dramatic career. The public response to his dramas, tragedies, and satiric comedies was, with a few notable exceptions, always enthusiastic. Each premiere was received with acclaim, and his works were nearly always judged popular successes before the curtain went up. Echegaray was also the first modern Spanish playwright to enjoy ample recognition and popularity outside Spain; his best plays, *The Great Galeoto*, *Folly or Saintliness*, *The Son of Don Juan*, and *Mariana*, were translated into several European languages and successfully staged in Europe and in the United States. Echegaray was elected to the Royal Spanish Academy in 1894 and was formally inducted in 1896. In 1904, he became the first Spaniard to be awarded the Nobel Prize in Literature (which he shared with the Provençal poet Frédéric Mistral).

Echegaray has not fared well, however, at the hands of twentieth century critics. The young intellectuals and writers of the Generation of 1898 strongly criticized the extreme sentiment and exaggerated style of his drama. For them, his plays were hopelessly dated romantic melodramas, reminiscent of the Romantic movement. More modern and contemporary criticism, no more merciful in its appraisal of Echegaray's theater, has pointed out, often justly, some of his shortcomings: his fondness for complicated plots and violent passions; his weakness in psychology and in character delineation; his histrionics, often resorting to sensationalism and bombast to conceal the weakness of his plots; and his almost inevitable concern with outdated romantic themes and devices—honor, duty, adultery, and the role of fate.

In spite of his faults, which critics have been almost too quick to emphasize, Echegaray has to be credited with lifting the Spanish stage from the state of neglect and prostration in which he found it. His lively imagination and fecundity of invention delighted the public. He was a master craftsman with a keen sense of tragedy and an unusual talent for developing theatrical situations. Above all, Echegaray was the first modern Spanish dramatist to break the bonds of myopic nationalism by introducing to the Spanish stage the dominant literary trends of his time. Strongly influenced by Henrik Ibsen and by the increasingly popular European thesis or problem play, he turned to social drama and the modern realistic theater of ideas. Thus, Echegaray's plays served to bridge the gap between the old-fashioned Spanish theater of the early nineteenth century and the more contemporary theater staged by Jacinto Benavente y Martínez and the Generation of 1898 at the beginning of the twentieth century. In this respect, he can be considered a dramatist of transition, and his contribution to the Spanish stage quite significant.

BIOGRAPHY

José Echegaray y Eizaguirre was born in Madrid, Spain, on April 19, 1832, to a middle-class family of Basque ancestry. When he was an infant, his father moved the family to Murcia, where Echegaray lived the first fourteen years of his life. The boy received a superior education in Murcia, excelling in mathematics and the sciences. In 1846, he returned to Madrid to enter the School of Engineering, where he was graduated first in his class with a degree in civil engineering. Immediately after graduation, he was hired by the Department of Public Works as an engineer in the building of roads in Almería and Granada. Not satisfied with practical work of this kind, Echegaray returned to Madrid in 1858 to become a professor of calculus at his alma mater, a position he held until the Revolution of 1868. Meanwhile, he perfected his knowledge of mathematics and physics and became the most eminent man in Spain in those disciplines. In 1866, at the young age of thirty-four, he was elected to the Academy of Exact Sciences of Madrid.

His second career as a politician and statesman began in 1868 when political conspiracy ended the rule of Isabel II. Echegaray, who had written a few articles criticizing Isabel's economic policies, was appointed director of public works and secretary of commerce in 1868. A year later, he was elected deputy to parliament, and, at various times, he held the important posts of secretary of the interior and of the treasury. Echegaray's political activities, however, virtually ended in 1874 with the change in government and the restoration of the Bourbon dynasty.

It was not until Echegaray was forty-two that he produced his first play, *El libro talonario*, staged in Madrid in 1874. Previously, Echegaray had shown no indication of being interested in the theater or in any other literary activity. As he wrote in his memoirs, the motivating factor in his decision to become a dramatist was a desire to emulate the successful career

José Echegaray y Eizaguirre (© The Nobel Foundation)

of his younger brother, Miguel, who was at that time the author of several comedies and zarzuelas (light musical plays). For the next thirty years, Echegaray devoted himself to the theater with his customary vigor, becoming the favorite of public and critics alike. After the 1900's, when he saw the popularity of his plays wane, Echegaray retired from public life, returning to the spotlight only on one occasion, when he was honored by his countrymen for having received the Nobel Prize. Echegaray died in Madrid on September 15, 1916.

ANALYSIS

José Echegaray y Eizaguirre's literary reputation has steadily declined in the last seventy-five years. Surely he was not the dramatist of genius that many of his contemporaries sought to make him out to be, and no modern critic would insist that Echegaray was "the greatest dramatist that Spain has produced for two hundred years," as Elizabeth R. Hunt stated in her 1914 introduction to Hannah Lynch's translation of *The Great Galeoto*. Yet *Folly or Saintliness*, *The Great Galeoto*, and *The Son of Don Juan*, by virtue of technique and scope, bear comparison with anything written in Europe during the last twenty-five years of the nineteenth century. They secure for Echegaray a rightful place in a critical survey of world drama.

Echegaray's success derived from his sensitivity to audiences' tastes and his ability to create a theater that satisfied their expectations. Generally considered a belated romantic, he resurrected the melodramatic plots and the florid language popular in the earlier part of the nineteenth century. Aware of the public's receptivity to highly emotional plays, he set as his goal a theater based on "weeping, grief, and death." Although the tone of his dramas can be considered anachronistic, he achieved a degree of modernity and originality in his works through the introduction of contemporary settings and social problems and by gradually discarding legendary settings and the use of verse.

Echegaray's dramas present the paradox of rigid theatrical logic applied to situations loaded with melodrama. In the execution, development, and conclusion there is an infallible, mathematical clarity.

Yet deep down the situation impresses one as being false and often strained; all the characters, it seems, are saints, demons, or freaks, harassed by some passion, *idée fixe*, or fate that drives them mad or kills them and also brings death and madness to other characters. It is evident that in such theater the flesh-and-bone human being, with all his complexities, rarely appears. Echegaray's dramas are the dramas of exceptional people in conflict with exceptional circumstances in which fate plays an important role. In the preface to his first social drama, *Cómo empieza y cómo acaba* (the beginning and the end), produced in 1876, Echegaray explains that his play is determined by the "logic of fatality" that "dominates when moral liberty surrenders to passion its place in the human soul." A close look at his scores of plays, however, shows clearly that fate as Echegaray conceives it is purely a social phenomenon, the familiar and inevitable opposition of society to the desires of the individual. Echegaray's plots generally revolve around two central points: honor and a strict sense of duty (*imperativo de conciencia*). He places his characters in agonizing situations in which they are torn apart by conflict between two duties or a conflict between duty and passion. His concept of honor, the traditional Spanish *punto de honor*, which involves men's passionate defense of women's chastity, is borrowed from Pedro Calderón de la Barca and Romanticism. Echegaray's concern with conflicts of conscience seems to be inspired by Ibsen or by some ill-defined Christian ethics, but the writer was also a man of his time and very often (particularly after 1880) mixed his basic themes with social and philosophical motifs such as the effects of heredity and environment, and psychological abnormalities, taken from the positivist and naturalistic schools of thought of the late nineteenth century.

Like other dramatists of his generation, Echegaray began by writing traditional romantic dramas such as *La esposo del vengador* (the avenger's wife) and *En el puño de la espada* (at the hilt of the sword); Echegaray, however, soon began to intersperse his historical dramas with others of contemporary setting. As early as 1875, he attempted modern realistic drama with *La última noche* (the last night), portraying the repentance of a libertine at the end of his life, but it was not until he composed his play *Folly or Saintliness* that Echegaray was able to produce a piece of work of high dramatic quality.

FOLLY OR SAINTLINESS

In *Folly or Saintliness*, a prose drama in three acts, Echegaray portrays a man with high ideals and an exaggerated sense of duty that run counter to every worldly consideration, creating a conflict that finally determines his fate. The drama begins when Don Lorenzo de Avendaño, the protagonist, discovers that his old nurse, Juana, is really his mother and that his alleged mother had claimed him as her child in order to secure an inheritance. Lorenzo decides to relinquish his name and fortune because they are not his own. Tension arises when his ideas and his concept of himself conflict with the materialistic interests of his wife, Angela, and his daughter Inéz, who is planning to marry Eduardo, the son of the Duchess of Almonte. Unable to understand Lorenzo's honesty and self-denial, they truly believe that he is insane and begin to plot his confinement to a mental institution. Even the dying nurse, his real mother, arriving at the same conclusion, burns the letter, the only evidence of the truth regarding his parentage. The crisis occurs when Lorenzo opens the envelope and finds a blank sheet of paper that Juana has substituted for the original. Profoundly disturbed, harassed by being continuously watched, unable to distinguish right from wrong anymore, Lorenzo acts as a madman and turns violently on his wife and daughter, whom he considers responsible for his misfortune. Lorenzo's behavior, along with his continued refusal to compromise, confirms the suspicions of the family and friends that he is mentally ill. The drama concludes when Lorenzo is taken to a mental institution, where he will spend the rest of his life.

Folly or Saintliness is a powerful drama. The tension that it generates between the worldly materialism of society on the one hand, and the high ideals and strict sense of duty of the protagonist on the other, has great dramatic value, which Echegaray skillfully exploits, creating suspense by moving the action in a wavelike motion—it advances, and then coils back on itself—as Lorenzo struggles many times with

himself and fights against the claim of his family and friends. As the action progresses, suspense mounts as the spectator or reader anxiously awaits an answer to the following questions: What course will Lorenzo take? Will Lorenzo yield to a reasonable appeal? Will he yield to threats? Echegaray's portrait of Don Lorenzo is unforgettable. The passion of the honor-loving Lorenzo and his obsession with the idea of living according to principles of absolute truth and justice regardless of the consequences are admirably set forth by the dramatist. His dilemma, however quixotic, is painfully perplexing. Don Lorenzo is an honorable man who scorns doing anything less than his utmost to realize his ideal. His family may be threatened with poverty, his daughter with an unhappy life, but he will not compromise. As with the character Brand in Ibsen's drama *Brand* (1866; English translation, 1891), "all or nothing" is Lorenzo's infallible test. Although this is basically a drama of one character— so overpowering is Lorenzo's personality—the antagonists, his wife Angela, his daughter Inéz, and particularly his skeptical friend Tomás, are developed by Echegaray with unerring skill. In the interplay of characters they represent the troll voices of narrow-minded egotism, hypocrisy, and deceit. It is not until the drama's conclusion, after Lorenzo has lost the struggle and finally been committed, that the puzzled reader asks himself: Was Lorenzo a fool, a madman, or a saint, insisting so much on his principles? Which is the dominant trait of Lorenzo? Or is it, perhaps, as Echegaray seems ironically to imply, that in this harsh world honesty is not the best policy because society considers the truly honest man to be insane?

As suggested above, *Folly or Saintliness* presents many analogies to Ibsen's *Brand*, which may have inspired the Spaniard in his first signal effort. Although the two dramas are clearly different in form, content, and style, in both, conflict arises from the fact that the protagonist is obsessed with living according to his principles and in doing so ruins his own life as well as the lives of those he loves. It is worth noting, however, that Lorenzo speaks of his idealism as having sprung from the reading of Miguel de Cervantes' *El ingenioso hidalgo don Quixote de la Mancha* (1605, 1615; *The History of the Valorous and Wittie Knight-*

Errant, Don Quixote of the Mancha, 1612-1620; better known as *Don Quixote de la Mancha*), and, in his very first appearance in the play, he foreshadows his quixotic trait by reading aloud a long passage of the novel and comparing himself to "the immortal hero of the immortal Cervantes."

THE GREAT GALEOTO

Echegaray achieved his most extraordinary and lasting success with *The Great Galeoto*, which has been regarded by many critics not only as the author's masterpiece but also as worthy for inclusion in the repertory of world drama. Set in Madrid in modern times, the play relates the tragic story of Ernesto, Don Julián, and Teodora. Ernesto, a poor, young dramatist, has been befriended by the older Don Julián and lives with him and his beautiful wife, Teodora. Although Ernesto feels only brotherly affection for Teodora, Don Julián's relatives inform the old man that people in Madrid are gossiping about the intimacy between Teodora and Ernesto and that "they say" that the drama Ernesto is writing is really about himself and Teodora. Although Don Julián does not pay attention to the rumors, the gossip upsets Ernesto so much that he moves out of the house. Nevertheless, rumors persist, and when the Viscount of Nebreda slanders Teodora in Ernesto's presence, Ernesto challenges him to a duel. Teodora seeks out Ernesto at his apartment in an effort to prevent the duel, but Don Julián, informed by his nephew Pepito of the insult, fights the Viscount himself. Mortally wounded, he is brought to Ernesto's quarters where he finds Teodora and becomes convinced that the gossip was indeed true, making Ernesto and Teodora's attempts to explain their innocence to the dying man futile. They are insulted and assailed afresh by Don Julián's relatives and cursed by the old man in his final moment. Then, Ernesto and Teodora, driven together by society's malicious gossip, decide to stay together. Ernesto says in the final words of the play: "Let no one touch this woman. She is mine! The world has so desired it, and that decision I accept."

Few plays present such a dramatic, logical, and convincing study of gossip and slander and their evil consequences. In *The Great Galeoto*, the spirit of gossip and slander, sometimes malicious, more often thoughtless or frivolous, gradually assumes an active role in the drama, destroying Don Julián's household and marriage and finally causing his death; through the power of suggestion, it also creates a guilty passion in Teodora and Ernesto, a love that previously existed only in the minds of idle gossips. It is a "triangle" play, but unlike most of them, the three main characters act with honorable motives. There is no villain, no hero, no heroine—all are victims of a society that in itself means no harm. Therein lies the essence of the tragedy. Society, the antagonist, is represented in the play by Don Julián's brother Severo, his wife, Doña Mercedes, and their son Pepito, who busy themselves with all the tidbits of slander, echoing, intensifying, and transmitting them to the protagonists. They do not occupy the central position in the drama, but it is through them that the malicious voice of the town is heard. They indeed become a microcosm of Madrid's society, so keenly is their presence felt. The central theme of the drama and the reason for the play's title are ingenious and cleverly introduced by Echegaray in the prologue, a dialogue in prose, which serves as the exposition to the three acts in verse that follow. Using the dramatic device of the play-within-a-play, Echegaray shows Ernesto thinking about a theme for his new drama and taking the idea from reading in Dante's *La divina commedia* (c. 1320; *The Divine Comedy*, 1802) the story of Paolo and Francesca, whose perusal of the medieval tale of Lancelot and Guinevere united by the page Galehoult (in Spanish, Galeoto), incites them to love. Ernesto decides that the go-between, or Galeoto, in his own drama will be *todo el mundo* (everybody), the scandal-talking crowd, who will become the protagonist of the drama.

The treatment of the malignant effect of gossip in *The Great Galeoto* has been compared with plays such as Richard Brinsley Sheridan's *The School for Scandal* (pr. 1777) and William Shakespeare's *Othello, the Moor of Venice* (pr. 1604), although in Shakespeare's tragedy, it is the personal villainy of Iago, not the impersonal force of society, that leads to the tragedy.

THE SON OF DON JUAN

The influence of Émile Zola's naturalistic school and of Ibsen are evident in *The Son of Don Juan*, a drama in three acts and in prose. In this play, Echegaray dramatizes the effects of inherited disease and the fearful results of libertinage. The drama opens when Don Juan, in spite of his dissolute past, has become an honorable man who anticipates an honorable and brilliant future for his son Lazarus. His son, he declares, shall inherit only his own finer aspirations. He will shine as a writer and marry his best friend's daughter. Meanwhile Lazarus, who was sent to France by his mother Dolores in order to escape the immoral influence of his father, returns to Madrid distraught and suddenly ill. When the family seeks the help of a famous physician, Dr. Bermudez, they find out the truth: Lazarus is cursed by an insidious disease, the result of his father's excesses; madness or idiocy inexorably awaits him. The situation arrives at a climactic point at the end of act 2, when Lazarus, feeling compassion for the girl he is to marry, rejects her at the betrothal ceremony. In the third act, Lazarus's health starts to deteriorate bit by bit before the eyes of the family; he is also going through an inner struggle caused by his love for Carmen: Should he marry her, knowing that his moral duty is not to do so? Must he then give up his only hope for happiness? At the end he decides to marry the girl regardless. It is then that the remorseful Don Juan steps in to prevent the wedding. The drama reaches its final crisis and conclusion when Lazarus in a frenzy clings to Carmen and collapses after begging his mother with pathetic insistence: "The Sun!. . . Mother, give me the Sun!" Already his mind has given way.

Several critics have suggested, and Echegaray openly admitted in his prologue to the English version of the drama, that Ibsen's *Gengangere* (pb. 1881; *Ghosts*, 1885) was the source of his inspiration for *The Son of Don Juan*. Lazarus, like Oswald Alving, is young, cursed with a congenital disease, and doomed from conception, and slowly loses his wits as the play goes on. Finally, the two collapse at the end asking for the sun. Despite the obvious similarities, *The Son of Don Juan* shows originality in its treatment of the story and in its point of view. Whereas Ibsen's *Ghosts* shifts the blame to the society that forces Mrs. Alving to stay with her sick husband, Echegaray's drama

lays all the blame on Don Juan's shoulders. It was also immaterial to Ibsen whether such a character as Captain Alving paid for his sins or not, but the Spaniard went back to traditional morality and made certain Don Juan paid the penalty for his transgression. George Bernard Shaw considered Echegaray "extremely readable" and praised *The Son of Don Juan* for its "original treatment" of Ibsen's theme. Through this association, *The Son of Don Juan* has become one of the best-known of Echegaray's dramas outside Spain.

MARIANA

In the same year that *The Son of Don Juan* premiered, Echegaray also produced *Mariana*, a four-act play in prose. The author dramatizes the story of a young and attractive woman, Mariana, who at the beginning flirts with Daniel Montoya, the man who courts her, but ends up falling deeply in love with him. The conflict arises from her discovery that Daniel's father had dishonored her mother, bringing about her unhappiness and premature death. Mariana is distraught because of her internal struggle, torn between her love for Daniel and an intense desire to avenge her mother's death by punishing the son of the aggressor. Honor preceding love, Mariana rejects Daniel and marries an old general, who she knows would kill her should she ever give in to the amorous attentions of the young man. In the last act, when Daniel asks her to leave Don Pablo and go away with him, she is unable to resist the temptation, and, in a scene of ultimate sacrifice, she screams for her husband to kill her and avenge his honor. Don Pablo shoots her and then challenges Daniel to a duel, the latter sensing that he will be reunited with Mariana in death.

Mariana would be a traditional honor play, with its typical love triangle, if it were not for Echegaray's magnificent psychological study of the female protagonist. Mariana's personality, marked by internal struggles, contradictions, and vacillations, is perfectly delineated. Except for an expected Echegarayan ending, *Mariana* is also comparatively free from the tense and melodramatic tone of many other works; regarding the solution of the problem presented here, however, the author looks back to the barbarous conception of honor associated with Calderón's dramas of the type of *El médico de su honra* (pb. 1637; *The Surgeon of His Honor*, 1853).

OTHER MAJOR WORKS

SHORT FICTION: *Cuentos*, 1912.

NONFICTION: *Algunas reflexiones generales sobre la crítica y el arte literario*, 1894; *Recuerdos*, 1917 (3 volumes).

BIBLIOGRAPHY

Gies, David Thatcher. *The Theatre in Nineteenth Century Spain*. New York: Cambridge University Press, 1994. Provides an overview of the theater in

Spain during the time in which Echegaray wrote. Bibliography and index.

Gregersen, Halfdan. *Ibsen and Spain: A Study in Comparative Drama*. 1936. Reprint. New York, Kraus Reprint, 1966. A study of Henrik Ibsen's influence on Spanish writers including Echegaray. Bibliography.

Ríos-Font, Wadda C. *Rewriting Melodrama: The Hidden Paradigm in Modern Spanish Theater*. Cranbury, N.J.: Associated University Presses, 1997. An analysis of Echegaray's use of melodrama and his influence on the dramatists who followed. Bibliography and index.

Gastón F. Fernández

LONNE ELDER III

Born: Americus, Georgia; December 26, 1931
Died: Woodland Hills, California; June 11, 1996

PRINCIPAL DRAMA

Ceremonies in Dark Old Men, pr. 1965, pb. 1969
Charades on East Fourth Street, pr. 1967, pb. 1971 (one act)
Splendid Mummer, pr. 1988

OTHER LITERARY FORMS

Lonne Elder III also wrote screenplays and television scripts. His screenplays include *Melinda* (1972), *Sounder, Part Two* (1976), and *Bustin' Loose* (1981), with Roger L. Simon and Richard Pryor. Among his teleplays are *Ceremonies in Dark Old Men* (1975), based on his play of the same title, and *A Woman Called Moses* (1978), based on a book by Marcy Heidish.

ACHIEVEMENTS

Lonne Elder III's playwriting reputation rests solidly on the drama *Ceremonies in Dark Old Men*, not because his formidable theatrical talents faltered after he created this early work but because he turned from the stage to write for film and television. *Ceremonies*

in Dark Old Men interweaves psychological and social themes in describing an African American family. Elder presents a careful dissection of the love and power relations within that family, while also, looked at more broadly, showing the adverse situation of African Americans living in a racially torn nation. Though his themes are somber, Elder injects his work with humor and affection, carefully balancing his audience's sympathy for the disparate characters. Although the play ends tragically, presenting the family's partial dissolution, it carries a positive undercurrent insofar as it charts the family's heroic resistance against difficult circumstances and portrays how a number of characters mature during the struggle.

Elder has received numerous awards, including the American National Theatre Academy Award (1967), the Outer Circle Award (1970), the Vernon Rice Award (1970), and the Stella Holt Memorial Playwrights Award (1970).

BIOGRAPHY

Lonne Elder III was born in Americus, Georgia, on December 26, 1931, to Lonne Elder II and Quincy Elder. While he was still an infant, his family moved to New York and New Jersey. He was orphaned at the age of ten and ended up living with relatives on a New Jersey farm. Rural life, however, was not for him, and, after he ran away a few times, he was sent to live with his uncle, a numbers runner, in Jersey City.

In 1949, Elder entered New Jersey State Teachers College, where he stayed less than a year. He then moved to New York City and took courses at the Jefferson School and the New School for Social Research, while becoming involved in the movement for social equality for black people. In 1952, he was drafted into the United States Army. While stationed near Fisk University, in Nashville, Tennessee, he met the poet and playwright Robert Hayden, who encouraged Elder with his writing.

Back in New York City in 1953, Elder shared an apartment with the aspiring playwright Douglas Turner Ward and began studying acting. Supporting himself through jobs as a dockworker, waiter, and poker dealer, among other things, he pursued his acting career, appearing on Broadway in 1959 in *A Raisin in the Sun* and with the Negro Ensemble Company (cofounded by Ward) in Ward's play *Day of Absence* (pr. 1965). During this time, he met such prominent black writers as Lorraine Hansberry and John Oliver Killens, married Betty Gross (in 1963), and wrote his first play. This work, "A Hysterical Turtle in a Rabbit Race," written in 1961 but never performed or published, broached Elder's favored topic of how a black family can be pulled apart by prejudice and false standards.

In 1965, his masterpiece, *Ceremonies in Dark Old Men*, was performed, earning for him fame and critical success. Along with his other ventures, such as writing television scripts for such shows as *N.Y.P.D.* and *McCloud*, it netted for him a number of awards and honors, including a fellowship to the Yale School of Drama in 1966-1967. His next play to be produced was the one-act *Charades on East Fourth Street*, which did not have the impact of his previous drama. It was performed in 1967.

In 1970, sick of New York City, Elder moved with his second wife, Judith Ann Johnson, whom he had married in 1969, to California. He was hoping to im-

prove the depiction of African Americans in Hollywood productions, and he did just that in his screenplay *Sounder* in 1972. After the critical success of this film, he continued working in the industry, producing more serious work about black life and tradition, such as his follow-up television script *Sounder, Part Two* (1976) and his television presentation about Harriet Ross Tubman, *A Woman Called Moses* (1978), as well as writing an occasional comedy, such as the 1981 Richard Pryor film *Bustin' Loose*.

In 1988, Elder returned briefly to the theater with *Splendid Mummer*, a historical play about a black expatriate actor who left the United States in the 1820's to practice his art in Europe. The play was liked by critics but was not a popular success and was not published. Elder continued to be primarily devoted to his goal of working in television and film to provide a positive and realistic view of African American life until his death in 1996.

ANALYSIS

In all Lonne Elder III's writings, such as his screenplay *Sounder*, his depictions of family life have been outstanding for their realism, compassion, and penetration, while those works that do not describe family connections, such as his play *Charades on East Fourth Street*, have been notably lacking in inspiration.

CEREMONIES IN DARK OLD MEN

His major play, *Ceremonies in Dark Old Men*, deals with the survival of the black family under duress. For Elder, the family is not a collection of autonomous individuals but a dynamic set of relationships. In *Ceremonies in Dark Old Men*, Elder focuses on how each family member's decisions crucially hinge on the words and actions of each other member. The playwright indicates, moreover, that under stressful conditions, the equilibrium of such a black family is a fragile thing, because the family is a working unit in a larger society that is controlled by white people to the disadvantage of black persons. The drama records how, under increasing pressure, the family disintegrates in some ways while it grows in others. Thus, Elder combines social criticism with a subtle look at the inner workings of families.

In much of post-World War II American theater, including such works as Arthur Miller's *Death of a Salesman* (pr., pb. 1949) and Tennessee Williams' *The Glass Menagerie* (pr. 1944, pb. 1945), the family is portrayed as entrapping and destructive of individualism. The family may stifle a son by forcing him to support it, as in Williams's play, or it may ruin his life by giving him false views, as happens to Biff in Miller's work; in either case, however, the family is inimical to self-reliance. By contrast, in *Ceremonies in Dark Old Men*, each family member has a role that is both constricting and sustaining, while each member either grows or diminishes as a result of the family's overall adaptation to the outside world.

At first sight, the family in Elder's play is organized in stereotypical "culture of poverty" fashion, with a female, the daughter Adele, being the de facto head of the house, since she supports the other, male family members. The two sons with the father, the nominal ruler of the house, are shiftless characters; the father, Russell, presides over a defunct barbershop, while his elder son, Theo, is a hapless loser, and the younger one, Bobby, a sneak thief. As the story develops, however, the audience learns that the three are not as parasitical as they first appeared. The father, for example, had been the mainstay of the family, earning a living as a professional dancer until his legs failed and he was unceremoniously dropped from his place. When viewers see the father returning from a day of job-hunting humiliation, they also learn that, as an over-the-hill black man, he has little hope of finding work.

The thrust of the play, however, is not to exonerate any individual but to show that the current operation of the family is, given the way the odds are stacked against prosperity for minority group members, probably the best possible. This view is shown by the simple, but fundamental, device of ending the first act with the beginning of a basic change in the household arrangements (as Theo sets up a viable, if illegal, business) and then jumping ahead a few months for the second act. In this way, in the second act, the audience can see how Theo's changed status, as he takes on a more manly role in the family and supports the others by working long hours, affects the personalities and actions of each of the others, often adversely. Adele, for example, no longer having to bear tremendous responsibility, lets herself go, running around with a notorious skirt chaser. Bobby, who never felt threatened by his brother, since Theo was as ambitionless as he was, now begins sullenly competing with him, becoming a big-time hoodlum.

This is not to say that, because there is more tension in the family after Theo begins working than previously, the old organization was better. Rather, Elder indicates—especially toward the end of the second act, when the family begins to calm down and Adele gives up her playboy boyfriend—that each set of family relationships is highly interdependent and serves as an essential means to help the members orient themselves to the outside world. Elder also indicates that each transition between different familial "steady states" will involve special periods of stress.

In his plays, it is clear that Elder is critical of the position that black persons are forced to occupy in the American economy, and it also may be evident that his anger is more latent than expressed. Rather than have his characters complain about the system, he makes the audience experience the constant feeling of failure that hovers over a family whose members are not fully employed, especially when, to a large degree, their unemployment is not their fault. In relation to one character, however, Elder's social criticism is less oblique. This character, Blue Haven, is a self-styled black activist, who, curiously, is not interested in fighting injustice and oppression through protests and political action; rather, he prefers to steal the clients of white people's liquor and gambling establishments by setting up bootleg and numbers operations of his own. In this portrayal, Elder reveals a satirical side to his talent and shows that he is as critical of black persons as he is of white ones, insofar as he shows that black residents of Harlem are more interested in supporting Blue Haven's "enterprises" than the businesses run by more bona fide progressives.

Elder's treatment of this character also reveals another point about his methods. Throughout most of the play, Blue Haven obtains little sympathy from the audience, being not only a sharper but also a hypocrite. Yet in a powerful monologue that he delivers in a confrontation with Theo, who accuses Blue Haven of exploiting him, Blue Haven presents his own tortured dreams, showing that he is capable of much deeper feeling than it would have been thought possible. This emotional monologue lifts him in the audience's estimation and establishes Elder's goal of giving every character his or her due.

The generosity in Elder's treatment of his characters, seen not only in the way he allows each to develop a voice but also in his mutualistic conception of the family, does have certain drawbacks. As none of the characters is larger than the others, none, in this tale of wrecked hopes, gains the type of tragic stature obtained by the leading characters in the Williams and Miller plays mentioned above. That is to say, none has the broken splendor of a Willy Loman, because, as each family member's choices are heavily dependent on others' situations, no character ever has to face the anxiety of bearing total responsibility for his or her actions. Thus, a character can never rise to the grandeur associated with an acceptance of such responsibility. Furthermore, as a number of critics have noted, Elder's evenhandedness sometimes hints at a distance between him and his creations, since his equal treatment of each problem reveals that he was not aroused by any of his characters' tribulations. Such an attitude can lead to the pathos and power of a given dramatic situation not being fully asserted.

One compensation for these drawbacks is compassion. Elder refuses to make any of his characterizations, even of such comic figures as Blue Haven, into caricatures. He extends to each a measure of respect and understanding. Further, Elder's undistorted, accepting view of his characters and their world matches their general realism. His characters are aware of their own and others' limitations and are largely accustomed to, though hurt by, their social inferiority. The family members tend to treat each new vicissitude with relatively good humor. Thus, near the end of the first act, when everyone is momentarily glum about future prospects, the father, having leeringly accepted Theo's proposal that he work with Blue Haven but being none too happy about it, engages in a little tap dancing. Although his steps are clumsy, the boys cheer him on, caught up in their infectious attempt to celebrate a dubious alliance. The frequent joking of the father and sons works to this same end, lightening the burdens they must bear.

CHARADES ON EAST FOURTH STREET

Elder's ability to create a multisided situation is found in his other published drama, *Charades on East Fourth Street*. This play belongs to a genre, delved into by black playwrights of the 1960's, that might be called "ritual drama." Ritual dramas were a component of the rebellious Black Arts movement that emphasized theater as a social ritual, such as the Catholic Mass, that worked to renew symbolically a society's cohesion. These works provided a way of going back to the sources of theater, as is evident in such dramas as the medieval mystery plays. Ritual dramas retold the story of Christ's passion, and, as the centerpiece of a worldview, its reenactment served to rededicate viewers to a common purpose as they reempathized with their binding social myth. Numerous modern authors, such as T. S. Eliot, have turned back to the roots of drama, but African American writers often gave this turn a perverse twist. Undoubtedly, one of the most brilliant of the black writers' ritual dramas was *Dutchman* (pr., pb. 1964) by LeRoi Jones (who later changed his name to Amiri Baraka). In this play, a black college student flirts with an initially willing white woman on a subway, but the game turns ugly, and she stabs him. All the other white passengers join her in disposing of the corpse. The ritual, then, is the sacrifice of a young African American male, portrayed as the glue holding together white society. Thus, *Dutchman*, pretending to reveal white America's ideological foundations, actually serves up an indictment of how, it claims, the United States can unite only by scapegoating its minorities.

It may be surmised from this plot recapitulation that such plays could easily become shrill. Although this is not the case with *Dutchman*, because of the author's use of three-dimensional characters, with the woman becoming a fury only in the last minutes, the same cannot be said for Elder's *Charades on East Fourth Street*. At points, his characters grow strident when they lecture one another about police brutality.

This short play revolves around the actions of a band of black youths who have kidnapped a white policeman who they believe is guilty of raping a teenage girl. Then, in keeping with the title, *Charades on East Fourth Street*, the youths force the officer to act out a series of degrading scenes. For example, they strip him and put him in bed with a teenage girl, saying that they will send photographs to his wife. It can be seen that in this sexual charade, he is acting out the same part that he supposedly plays in his oppression of the African American community.

As the play progresses, it grows more complex. It turns out, for example, that the gang has grabbed the wrong police officer. Furthermore, the audience learns that the majority of these black teenagers are not convinced of the utility of this kidnapping and are involved in it only because they have been pressured into acting by their leader. In a short (one-act) play such as this one, however, there is no room for excessive ambiguity. The fact that Elder does not give his black revolutionaries much conviction—the kind of fanaticism that Baraka's characters often display—takes the wind out of the story's sails. Without the time to develop the gang's interplay or the anger to make the play an indictment, Elder heroically fails at a genre for which he has no aptitude.

It could be said that Elder's lack of success at agitational drama indicates that, for him, to write well he must follow his bent, which comes from depicting the complexity of characters and the networks they form. His defense of the African American family in his most important play, *Ceremonies in Dark Old Men*, does not rest on any encomiums of individual family members' virtues but on an insistence on the value of the family as a mechanism offering support and solidarity in the face of a hostile society. The worth of Elder's works lies in the evocative power of his affirmation, which itself rests on a sophisticated analysis of how a family functions as one, composed of the relationships of people rather than of people standing alone.

OTHER MAJOR WORKS

SCREENPLAYS: *Melinda*, 1972; *Sounder*, 1972 (adaptation of William H. Armstrong's novel); *Sounder,*

Part Two, 1976; *Bustin' Loose*, 1981 (with Richard Pryor and Roger L. Simon; adaptation of a story by Pryor).

TELEPLAYS: *Camera Three*, 1963 season; *The Terrible Veil*, 1963; *N.Y.P.D.*, 1967-1968 season; *McCloud*, 1970-1971; *Ceremonies in Dark Old Men*, 1975; *A Woman Called Moses,* 1978 (miniseries based on Marcy Heidish's book); *The Negro Ensemble Company*, 1987.

NONFICTION: "Comment: Rambled Thoughts," in *Black Creation*, 1973; "Lorraine Hansberry: Social Consciousness and the Will," in *Freedomways*, 1979.

BIBLIOGRAPHY

Arkatov, Janice. "'Ceremonies' Marks Tribute to Black History Month: Judyann Elder Directs Husband's Classic Play that Offers Sad but Hopeful Statement." *Los Angeles Times*, February 5, 1988, p. 12. An interview with Elder's wife, Judyann Elder, on her directing of a revival of *Ceremonies in Dark Old Men* for Black History Month. She discusses the African American experience, contrasting the conditions in 1969 with those in 1988.

Eckstein, George. "Softened Voices in the Black Theater." *Dissent* 23 (Summer, 1976): 306-308. Eckstein analyzes the changes through which black drama has gone, from the heady, often outspokenly nationalist and/or revolutionary drama of the mid-1960's to the more reserved drama of the mid-1970's, which puts a greater stress on mere survival and family values. He chooses the works of Elder, as they have evolved in the transition from stage to screen, to signal these changes.

Harrison, Paul Carter. *The Drama of Nommo*. New York: Grove Press, 1972. This highly original look at black drama studies it within categories developed from African aesthetics. Harrison discusses *Ceremonies in Dark Old Men*, finding the play weak because it does not sufficiently bring to light the characters' own recognition of the moral implications of their actions.

Jeffers, Lance. "Bullins, Baraka, and Elder: The Dawn of Grandeur in Black Drama." *CLA Journal* 16 (September, 1972): 32-48. Looking at *Ceremonies in Dark Old Men*, Jeffers points to the resilience of the characters as they face oppressive circumstances. He states that one of Elder's themes is "that the genius and energy of young black America are thwarted and trampled upon, but they remain alive."

Oliver, Myrna. "Lonne Elder II: Award-Winning Writer." *Los Angeles Times*, June 14, 1996, p. 28. This obituary sums up Elder's life and touches on his works for the theater, television, and screen.

James Feast

T. S. ELIOT

Born: St. Louis, Missouri; September 26, 1888
Died: London, England; January 4, 1965

PRINCIPAL DRAMA

Sweeney Agonistes, pb. 1932, pr. 1933 (fragment)
The Rock: A Pageant Play, pr., pb. 1934
Murder in the Cathedral, pr., pb. 1935
The Family Reunion, pr., pb. 1939
The Cocktail Party, pr. 1949, pb. 1950
The Confidential Clerk, pr. 1953, pb. 1954
The Elder Statesman, pr. 1958, pb. 1959
Collected Plays, pb. 1962

OTHER LITERARY FORMS

In addition to being a successful liturgical dramatist, T. S. Eliot was an editor, an essayist, and a poet of great distinction. He became assistant editor of *The Egoist* in 1917 and founded *The Criterion* in 1922, serving as editor of the latter from then until its demise in 1939. As an essayist, Eliot explored the place of modern literature with regard to tradition, discussed the relationship between literature and ethics, and emphasized the need for a modern idiom. Among his extremely influential collections of essays are *The Sacred Wood* (1920) and *After Strange Gods* (1934), both dealing with the individual's debt to tradition, the latter propounding a moral standpoint; *The Use of Poetry and the Use of Criticism* (1933); and *On Poetry and Poets* (1957). In *For Lancelot Andrewes* (1928) and *The Idea of a Christian Society* (1939), the impact of his 1927 confirmation in the Church of England on his life and letters is particularly evident.

Eliot's poetry has had a greater influence, not only in England and the United States but also in world literature, than that of any of his contemporaries. *Prufrock and Other Observations* (1917), *Poems* (1919; printed by Leonard and Virginia Woolf), and *The Waste Land* (1922) illustrate his growing despair over personal problems as well as modern social trends. *Ash Wednesday* (1930) and *Four Quartets* (1943), produced following his confirmation, are meditations concerning spiritual illumination. In *Old Possum's Book of Practical Cats* (1939), Eliot demonstrated his talent for writing comic verse with equal success. That work has been reprinted widely in many formats and even, in 1983, provided the basis for a Tony Award winning musical, *Cats*.

ACHIEVEMENTS

Any assessment of T. S. Eliot's achievements as a dramatist must be made in the light of his own comments about the relationship between past and present, between "tradition and the individual talent." For Eliot, a new work of art causes a rearrangement of the ideal, preexisting order. As Carol Smith points out, his comments about "historical perspective" are not innovative; what is new is his idea that the "given" order defines the artist, whose chief responsibility is to subsume his individual talent as part of the progress of literary history. Eliot's dramatic works are therefore "classical" in the altered sense of his attempting to employ a modern idiom in the service of the imperatives of history, both literary and religious.

One of Eliot's achievements was the presentation of liturgical drama on the modern stage to a commer-

T. S. Eliot (© The Nobel Foundation)

cial audience. His endeavor in this regard began with his writing both a pageant, *The Rock*, and a ritual drama, *Murder in the Cathedral*, for the limited audiences provided respectively by a benefit to promote church building in London and the Canterbury Festival, audiences preconditioned to dramas of redemption. (*Sweeney Agonistes*, an experimental fragment, was not produced until 1933.) With his later plays, however, Eliot undertook the task of convincing secular audiences that traditional ideas about redemption were viable within a modern framework. *The Family Reunion*, his first full-length experiment in turning drawing-room comedy into religious fable, was not immediately successful; as his close friend and adviser Elliott Martin Browne reports, critics found the work mixed—the most negative reviews said that the play was characterized by "lifeless smoothness" and "difficulty" and was guaranteed to leave the audience

"vexed and exhausted." Some modern critics, however, such as Eliot's biographer T. S. Matthews, find the play "extraordinary, . . . far superior to his later, 'better made' plays." *The Cocktail Party*, on the other hand, was better received; even those who wrote negative reviews acknowledged that the production bordered on greatness. Browne notes that similar comments were made about *The Confidential Clerk*, although critical reception was influenced by the general belief that Eliot's attempt "to combine the esoteric with the entertaining" was no longer innovative. *The Elder Statesman*, Browne believes, was overinterpreted by gossipmongers intent on reading the play in the light of Eliot's marriage to his secretary, Valerie Fletcher, the previous year.

Quite aside from their mixed commercial appeal, Eliot's plays illustrate his critical theories not only about the connection between drama and poetry but also about the failure of realistic theater. As C. L. Barber notes, Eliot's Aristotelian viewpoint prompted him to criticize modern drama for its lack of rhythm. For Eliot, poetry was more than a distraction, more than an attempt to prettify dramatic diction. Never extrinsic to the action, poetry provides an underlying musical pattern that strengthens the audience's response. The presence of such an abstract pattern suggests, as Eliot says in "Four Elizabethan Dramatists" (written in 1924), that the great vice in English drama is realism, for it detracts from the unity of the play. As his large essay *Poetry and Drama* (1951) makes clear, such unity is more than a technical matter of form and content, for the literary is handmaiden to the religious. Eliot's ideal vision of verse drama is one in which "a design of human action and of words" is perpetuated in such a way that the connection between the everyday world and the universal design is illustrated; such a drama, Eliot believed, would provide the proper feeling of "reconciliation" to lead the audience to a spiritual awakening.

BIOGRAPHY

Thomas Stearns Eliot was born on September 26, 1888, in St. Louis, Missouri. His celebrated statement of his allegiances in *For Lancelot Andrewes*—"classicist in literature, royalist in politics, and Anglo-

Catholic in religion"—ran counter to the family tradition of Unitarianism; his grandfather, William Greenleaf Eliot, descendant of a pastor of Boston's Old North Church, established the Unitarian Church of the Messiah in St. Louis. Eliot's father himself was a renegade, refusing the ministry for what was eventually the presidency of the Hydraulic-Press Brick Company. His mother, Charlotte Stearns, was a descendant of one of the judges in the Salem witch trials. An intellectual woman, Stearns began a career as a schoolteacher and eventually became active in children's causes.

As Matthews notes, the family saying "*Tace et fac* ('Shut up and get on with it')" suggests a household in which indulgence gave way to duty. As a child, Eliot was considered delicate but precocious. At Smith Academy, he took the Latin prize and excelled in English. Deemed too young at seventeen to enter Harvard, he was sent first to Milton Academy. At Harvard, he was conservative and studious. He became an editor of the *Advocate*, a literary magazine, but his decision to accelerate his undergraduate work to pursue a master's degree left him small leisure for friends, such as Conrad Aiken. Important influences during his college years included his discovery of Arthur Symons's *The Symbolist Movement in Literature* (1899), a book that led him to imitate the verse of Jules Laforgue; his love for Elizabethan drama; and, finally, his acquaintance with Irving Babbitt, the leader of the New Humanism, an anti-Romantic movement that stressed the ethical nature of experience. Certainly, Babbitt's influence led Eliot to spend one of his graduate years in France, where, resisting the attractive Bohemianism open to a writer of his talents, he decided to pursue a degree in philosophy at Harvard, where he came under the influence of Bertrand Russell.

The fellowship that Harvard awarded Eliot in 1914 proved to alter the course of his life. Enrolled in Merton College, at Oxford, he began his long friendship with Ezra Pound, under whose aegis Eliot published "The Love Song of J. Alfred Prufrock" in *Poetry* magazine in 1915. In England, Eliot met and married his first wife, Vivienne Haigh-Wood. Described as a beautiful and entrancing individual, she nevertheless suffered from a nervous disability that had devastating emotional effects. In increasing financial difficulty, Eliot worked as an usher at a boys' school, an employee at Lloyd's Bank, a freelance journalist, and an assistant editor of *The Egoist*.

Eliot enjoyed many fruitful friendships, among them those with Bertrand Russell, Virginia Woolf, and I. A. Richards. From 1921 to 1925, when he was publishing reviews in the *Times Literary Supplement*, Eliot's health deteriorated; the unforeseen result of an enforced vacation was *The Waste Land*. In 1922, he founded *The Criterion*, a literary quarterly that was sponsored financially by Lady Rothermere. After a long period of ill health and self-doubt, he joined the Anglican Church. His biographer suggests a number of reasons for the decision, including certain social and "aesthetic" attractions of this particular denomination, the authoritarian cast of the Church, and the long Church "pedigree" that satisfied Eliot's belief in the importance of tradition. His decision to become a British citizen followed soon thereafter, partly, Matthews believes, because Eliot felt that in the United States "the aristocratic tradition of culture was dead."

Eliot's 1932 return to his native land was, like his first journey away, a new start, for it began his separation from Vivienne, for whom he had become more nurse than husband. To be sure, the attempt to escape from her neurotic persecution made his middle years unhappy ones, years complicated further by the exigencies of World War II. Despite such distractions, however, these were the years in which Eliot began his career as a playwright.

Quite clearly, Eliot's religious conversion provided the themes not only for his poetry but also for his plays. Events in Eliot's personal life, including the death of his estranged wife in 1947, are also reflected in his plays. Conceivably, his sense of alienation and guilt found its way into the portrait of Harry, the putative wife-killer in *The Family Reunion*, as well as into the depiction of the dreary marriage faced by the Chamberlaynes in *The Cocktail Party*. Other elements are identifiable, such as the figure of Agatha in *The Family Reunion*; the only one to understand Harry's spiritual search thoroughly, Agatha is said to be based on Emily Hale, Eliot's longtime friend, who had been a schoolmistress at Scripps College, Smith College, and Abbot Academy. Emily was as shocked by Eliot's second, clandestine, marriage as she was by his first; at the age of sixty-nine, Eliot married Valerie Fletcher, his secretary.

Before the arrival of that emotional security, however, Eliot had achieved other triumphs. He was awarded the Nobel Prize in 1948, and, in the same year, received the British Empire's Order of Merit. While he was drafting *The Cocktail Party*, he traveled to Princeton, New Jersey, to accept a fellowship at the Institute for Advanced Study. His last two plays— *The Confidential Clerk* and *The Elder Statesman*— were not as popular as *The Cocktail Party*; they do, however, show an increasing understanding of the way in which human relationships may be ameliorated. Indeed, in *The Elder Statesman*, the love experienced by Monica and Charles seems a reflection of the happiness that Eliot himself found with his second wife. For the first time in his dramatic writing, the possibility of redemption through human love is adequately broached. Indeed, for the first time, human love seems a model of divine love rather than, as Celia observes in *The Cocktail Party*, a distraction or a second-best choice.

On January 4, 1965, Eliot died in London. At his request, his ashes repose at East Coker, the birthplace of his ancestors and the titular locale of one of the *Four Quartets*; the memorial plaque in the Poets' Corner at Westminster Abbey was placed on January 4, 1967.

ANALYSIS

T. S. Eliot's conservative dramaturgy is clearly expressed in his 1928 essay "Dialogue on Dramatic Poetry" in which, as C. L. Barber notes, he suggests that "genuine drama" displays "a tension between liturgy and realism." To be sure, Eliot differed sharply from the advocates of Ibsenite realism, maintaining throughout his career that untrammeled realism operating outside the limitations of art did not produce classic harmony. In consequence, Eliot relied on a number of traditional forms, including the Mass and Greek drama. On the other hand, he created new verse forms, convinced that traditional forms such as Shakespearean blank verse would be inadequate to express modern experience. In *Sweeney Agonistes*, he made use of the rhythms of vaudeville, believing that such robust entertainment contained the seeds of a popular drama of high artistic quality, comparable to the achievements of the great Elizabethan and Jacobean playwrights.

Modern religious drama, Eliot believed, "should be able to hold the interest, to arouse the excitement, of people who are not religious." Redemption is the theme of all of his plays, a theme explored on different levels. For example, Becket's understanding, in *Murder in the Cathedral*, that salvation is a willing submission to a larger pattern is developed and tempered in the later social comedies.

In almost all of his plays, Eliot presents characters on a continuum of spiritual understanding, including the martyr or saint figure, the "guardians" (the spiritual advisers), the common folk (capable of limited perception or at least of accommodation), and the uncomprehending. In *The Family Reunion* and *The Cocktail Party*, respectively, Harry and Celia experience a sense of having sinned and the desire to atone. Celia's illumination is also characterized by a sense of having failed another person. Her martyrdom is correspondingly more moving, not because it is graphically described, but because it seems inexorable.

In *The Confidential Clerk*, Colby, whose search for a human father parallels his desire for a divine one, experiences his *éclaircissement* as a private moment in a garden and works out his salvation as an organist. In the aforementioned plays, guardian figures abound. Agatha councils Harry to follow attendant Eumenides if he wishes to expiate the family curse; Julia, Alex, and Reilly not only show Celia the way to enlightenment but reinstate the Chamberlaynes' marriage; the retired valet Eggerson offers Colby a job as an organist and predicts his eventual entry into holy orders. Eliot's last play, *The Elder Statesman*, is the only one in which human love is an adequate guide to divine love; in that sense, Monica, in her affection for her fiancé and in her unwavering love for her father despite his faults, is a guardian figure.

A development in the characterization of the common people may be seen as well. Because of their foolishness or their attempt to dominate, all of Harry's relatives seem lost to perceptiveness, except, perhaps, for his Uncle Charles, who begins to feel "That there is something I *could* understand, if I were told it." A wider hope is held out in *The Cocktail Party*, for while not all may follow Celia's path, the Chamberlaynes learn to accept the "good life" that is available to them, and even Peter, in love with Celia, may learn to "see" through the same qualities that make him a film producer. Again, while Colby withdraws from the family circle, those who remain—no matter how superficially mismatched—engage in a communion characterized most of all by a desire to understand and to love. Finally, in *The Elder Statesman*, Eliot achieves a balance in his continuum of characters, for he presents the salvation of the Calvertons by love as well as the possibility that, through Monica, Michael might return to find his self-identity, while both Gomez and Mrs. Carghill become lost souls as they pursue their revenge.

MURDER IN THE CATHEDRAL

Although originally produced for the Canterbury Festival, *Murder in the Cathedral* has achieved the most lasting interest of all Eliot's plays. It is a psychological and historical exploration of martyrdom that, as David R. Clark points out, speaks directly not only to current disputes about the interconnection between church and state but also to the ever-present contemporary threat of assassination. It is Eliot's most successful attempt to adapt verse forms to drama, particularly in the speeches of the Chorus, whose function, Eliot believed, was to interpret the action to the viewers and to strengthen the impact of the action by reflecting its effects. In the speeches of the Knights and Tempters (characters doubled when the play is staged) as well, attitudes are mirrored by poetic cadence—a fine example of form following content. As Grover Smith notes, the title itself, while commercially attractive, is somewhat misleading, as were other possibilities Eliot considered, among them "The Archbishop Murder Case" and "Fear in the Way," for *Murder in the Cathedral* is less a whodunit than an attempt to startle the unimpassioned be-

liever into percipience and the nonbeliever into understanding.

Like Eliot's first venture into ritualistic drama, *The Rock*, *Murder in the Cathedral* is based on an actual event, the martyrdom of Thomas à Becket in the year 1170 in the chapel of Saint Benedict in Canterbury Cathedral. Unlike *The Rock*, however, which is a spectacle play delineating the history of the Church, *Murder in the Cathedral* is focused on a dramatic event of great intensity. The play traces the spiritual education of Thomas, whose greatest temptation is self-aggrandizement; the education of the Chorus, who seek to escape both suffering and salvation; and the education of the Knights and the audience, whose worldliness implicates them jointly in the assassination.

Eliot's addition of a Fourth Tempter to Becket's "trial" in part 1 is crucial. The first three tempters are expected and easily rejected. The first, who offers sensual pleasures, resigns Becket to "the pleasures of [his] higher vices." One such vice is offered by the Second Tempter: "Temporal power, to build a good world," power that requires submission to secular law. Becket, who rejects this exercise in intelligent self-interest, also rejects the Third Tempter's offer of a coalition with the barons to overthrow the King; such an action would bestialize Becket, make him "a wolf among wolves."

The Fourth Tempter is, however, not so easily answered, for he brings the temptation of spiritual power through martyrdom. Counseling the Archbishop to seek death, he offers as its rewards the joy of wielding power over eternal life and death, the adulation of the masses, the richness of heavenly grandeur, and, finally, the sweetness of revenge, for Becket will then be able to look down and see his "persecutors, in timeless torment."

For Becket, the only way to escape the damning effects of his own spiritual pride is to give up self-will so that he may become part of a larger pattern. As Grover Smith notes, the counsel that Becket gives to the Chorus (ironically quoted to him by the Fourth Tempter) has its roots in Aristotle's image of the still point—on a wheel, for example—as the source of action:

You know and do not know, that acting is suffering,
And suffering action. Neither does the actor suffer
Nor the patient act. But both are fixed
In an eternal action, an eternal patience
To which all must consent that it may be willed
And which all must suffer that they may will it,
That the pattern may subsist, that the wheel may
    turn and still
Be forever still.

In theological terms, Eliot is suggesting that the nature of the relationship between action and suffering depends on the conception of God as the first mover, just as the still point is centered in the wheel. Becket, in willing martyrdom, has substituted his will for God's will. When he understands that he was doing the right deed for the wrong reason, he enters the ideal relationship between human beings and God—one of submission, of a person's consent to be an instrument. In that condition of bringing one's will into conformity with that of God, one paradoxically does not suffer, for one acts as an instrument; neither does one act, for one gives up will. Both Grover Smith and David E. Jones explore the extension of this idea from Aristotle to Dante to clarify the sources of Eliot's vision.

For the women whose barren lives are spent among small deeds, Becket becomes a new center; with their wills in conformity to his, they too become the instruments of God's will, even as the Knights are in the murder of Becket. For Grover Smith, whereas Becket's language is abstract and passionless, his decision hidden in difficult, paradoxical words, that of the women is overtly sensual; for Carol Smith, such language shows that the women have accepted their "Christian responsibility." The women's unwilling participation in the event is a violent disturbance of their willed attitude of noninterference; through Becket, they are touched not only by life but also by death. The key is in the homily delivered by Becket as an interlude in the play, a sermon in which he speaks of an attitude of mourning and rejoicing in martyrdom. Before his death, he warns the women that their joy will come only "when the figure of God's purpose is made complete"—when, in other words, they understand that his martyrdom is the answer to their despair.

The prose in which the Knights speak after the murder has taken place is to some critics jarring, but Eliot deliberately made it so; a far graver criticism is that it is either amusing, or, as Grover Smith suggests, misleading, insofar as the emphasis on the "contest . . . between brute power and resigned holiness" is shifted to an argument about Church and State. Jones disagrees; for him, the prose shakes the audience's sanctimonious complacency. The arguments offered by the Knights are familiar rationalizations. The Second Knight pleads disinterested duty as his reason for the murder, the Third that "violence is the only way in which social justice can be secured," and the Fourth that, since Becket's overweening egotism prompted the murder, the correct "verdict" is "Suicide while of Unsound Mind." The final words of the Chorus, spoken to a Te Deum in the background, serve as a corrective to any distorted view, for they, the "type of common man," not only accept responsibility for "the sin of the world" but also acknowledge that human consciousness is an affirmation of the ultimate design, of which they have willingly become a part.

THE FAMILY REUNION

Produced in March, 1939, *The Family Reunion* was considerably less successful than Eliot's first full-length play, partly because he was attempting to appeal to a secular audience; moreover, his evocation of the Aeschylean Eumenides—the Furies—as a group of well-dressed aunts and uncles and his deliberate blurring of the hero's motives and fate contribute to the weakness of the play. Various critics have traced the antecedents of *The Family Reunion*, including Henry James's "The Jolly Corner," William Shakespeare's *Hamlet, Prince of Denmark* (pr. c. 1600-1601), and Aeschylus's *Oresteia* (458 B.C.E.; English translation, 1777), sources discussed thoroughly by Grover Smith and David Jones. Eliot attempted to wed the classical and the modern, believing that poetry brought into the audience's world would help to heal social disintegration.

The two levels of the play—the realistic and the spiritual—are not always mutually illuminating. On the surface, the play depicts the homecoming of Harry, Lord Monchensey, to Wishwood, the family mansion that his mother, Amy, has maintained, unchanged, for his benefit. Harry, convinced that he murdered his wife a year ago, is unable to agree with the conventional wishes of his mother or of his featherheaded aunts, Ivy and Violet, or of his blundering uncles, Gerald and Charles. On another level, he arrives convinced that he is pursued by the Furies, only to learn from his Aunt Agatha that to *follow* the "bright angels" is the way to redemption through suffering.

The Family Reunion reflects Eliot's recurring preoccupation with original sin. Although Harry's own uncertainty about his responsibility for his wife's death may be unsettling to the audience, the point is surely that for Eliot the *fact* is irrelevant; what is important is that Harry (and Eliot, because of his own marital situation) feels guilty about the wish itself. Indeed, Harry seems to be burdened with a family curse that he must expiate. As Agatha tells him, his father wanted to murder Harry's mother but was prevented from doing so by Agatha, who loved him; Harry has lived to reenact his father's will. Harry's guilt thus is shifted to the larger framework of the *felix culpa*, or fortunate fall.

Again, Harry's character is so unappealing that to call him, as Agatha does, "the consciousness of your unhappy family,/ Its bird sent flying through the purgatorial fire," is not acceptable on the metaphoric level. His rudeness and abrupt repudiation of his mother (which leads to her death) conspire against the suggestion that he is to become a Christian mystic or saint—that, as Agatha says, he is destined for "broken stones/ That lie, fang up" or that, as he says, he is headed for "A stony sanctuary and a primitive altar" or "A care over lives of humble people."

The transformation of the Eumenides from "hounds of hell" to "bright angels" is justified not only by the *Oresteia* of Aeschylus but also by the idea, developed in *Murder in the Cathedral*, that suffering precedes atonement; on a psychological level, however, the idea poses problems. As the evocation of the watchful eyes possessed by both mother and wife, the Eumenides suggest a developing Oedipus complex; interpreted by Agatha as helpful guardians, they suggest a childish transference of affection to Agatha, an affec-

tion that is at once incestuous and spiritual. As both Barber and Grover Smith point out, Mary, Harry's childhood sweetheart, simply presents the desired but now impossible fulfillment of human love. For Agatha, however, and eventually for Harry, the Eumenides posit a frontier beyond which all experience is private, save that it is a confrontation between the human spirit and the divine, a purgatorial confrontation under "the judicial sun/ Of the final eye."

In the final analysis, the play is not a triumph of comedy—or of tragedy. With Amy dead, Harry's father has ironically gotten his wish; Wishwood is to be ceded to Harry's brother John, about whom Harry says brutally, "A minor trouble like a concussion/ Cannot make very much difference to John." In the ritualistic chorus performed by Agatha and Mary at the end of the play, Eliot emphasizes the inexorability of the curse around which he has built his plot as well as the possibility of salvation. What is lacking is an explanation of the nature of expiation.

THE COCKTAIL PARTY

First produced for the 1949 Edinburgh Festival, *The Cocktail Party* is, like *The Family Reunion*, an attempt to express modern concerns in the guise of ritualistic drama. In this case, however, Eliot depends on Euripides' *Alkēstis* (438 B.C.E.; *Alcestis*, 1781) as his classical antecedent, wisely eliminating the embodiment of the Furies that proved to be so dramatically disruptive. In one view, he effectively reproduced the sophisticated patois of cocktail-party chatter to distract his secular audience from what Grover Smith calls the play's theological "underpattern." Other critics, among them Barber and Carol Smith, suggest that the comic approach was a deliberate attempt at a reversal in which "surfaces" become "depths" and the comic resolution an indication of divine order.

A number of this play's themes are taken from Eliot's earlier plays. There is a reunion, although not in the sense of Harry Monchensey's mythopoeic experience, for the Chamberlaynes literally as well as figuratively re-create their marriage; again, there is the figure of the mystic, this time, however, a more convincing one, in Celia; moreover, there is a guardian, Reilly, who achieves expressed validity in his role as a psychologist. Finally, and perhaps most im portant, there is a sense that spiritual illumination is not restricted, except in its intensity, to martyr figures.

Superficially, the plot is familiar drawing-room comedy, entailing a series of love affairs. Edward's wife, Lavinia, has inexplicably left him; Peter Quilpe, a filmmaker, is in love with Celia Coplestone, Edward's mistress, while Lavinia is in love with Peter. Comic relief is provided by the scatter-brained Julia Shuttlethwaite, the peripatetic Alexander MacColgie Gibbs, and Sir Henry Harcourt-Reilly, an enigmatic, gin-swilling psychologist. As in the well-made play, the plot revolves around a secret: Julia and Alex have conspired with Reilly to reinvigorate the Chamberlaynes' marriage, in an association called variously "the Christian conspiracy" or, as Jones puts it, "the Community of Christians."

The marital difficulties would be familiar to the audience, but not Eliot's interpretation of them. Having confused desire with affection in his attachment to Celia, Edward must face the fact that he is essentially unloving, whereas Lavinia is by nature unlovable: Thus, Eliot suggests, they are perfectly matched. In addition, Edward, who is indecisive, must learn to face the consequences of making a decision—in this case, the decision that Lavinia should return to him. What he realizes is that her return is tantamount to inviting the angel of destruction into his life.

Possessed by the belief that he is suffering "the death of the spirit," that he can live neither with the role Lavinia imposes on him nor without it, Edward goes to Reilly for help. The language that this counselor uses indicates his role of spiritual guardianship. He speaks of Edward's "long journey" but refuses to send him to his "sanatorium," for to do so would be to abandon him to the "devils" that feast on the "shadow of desires of desires." Instead, he brings him face to face with Lavinia to convince him that the unloving and the unlovable should make the best of a bad job—or, in terms of the blessing he administers, must "work out [their] salvation with diligence." Carol Smith's review of Christian mysticism as a background to the play makes clear that Reilly encourages the Chamberlaynes to follow the "Affirmative Way," in which "all created things are to be accepted in love as images of the Divine," rather than the "Negative Way," which is characterized by detachment from "the love of all things."

Reilly's interview with Celia is substantially different, for while she, like Edward, complains of an awareness of solitude, she focuses less on herself than on a perception that loneliness is the human condition and that communication is therefore illusory. She also complains, unlike Edward, of a sense of sin, of a feeling that she must atone for having failed "someone, or something, outside." She attributes her failure to a self-willed fantasy: In Edward, she loved only a figment of her imagination. Unlike Edward, she has had a vision of the Godhead, an ecstatic exaltation "of loving in the spirit." It is this vision that she chooses to follow, although Reilly emphasizes that it is an unknown way, a blind journey, a way to being "transhumanized," the "way of illumination." Her way, the "Negative Way" of mysticism, culminates in her crucifixion "very near an ant-hill" in the jungles of Kinkanja.

What Eliot offers in *The Cocktail Party* is a series of gradations of spiritual understanding, gradations that were not presented adequately in *The Family Reunion*. Celia's way of illumination is undoubtedly more believable because her developing perceptions are not expressed in sibylline pronouncements; likewise, the guardians are given authenticity by the comic role their very eccentricity engenders. The common way, represented by the Chamberlaynes, is not appealing but understandable, and, as Reilly says, "In a world of lunacy,/ Violence, stupidity, greed . . . it is a good life." Finally, Peter Quilpe, shocked by the news of Celia's death, comes to understand that he had been loving only the image he had created of her. As Grover Smith comments, "the kind of comedy Eliot devised has been compared generically by some critics to Dante's *Commedia*, for in it the characters either fulfill their greatest potentialities or else are set firmly on the way toward doing so."

THE CONFIDENTIAL CLERK

In Eliot's fourth play, *The Confidential Clerk*, the theme of redemption is again explored, this time through a dependence on Euripides' *Iōn* (c. 411 B.C.E.; *Ion*, 1781), a play that deals with hidden paternity.

Eliot examines the sense of aloneness expressed so effectively by Celia, and the human penchant for re-creating other individuals to conform with one's own desires. In addition, Eliot shows the path that a mystical vocation may take.

Denis Donoghue pertinently remarks that Eliot solved the "false tone" occasioned by Celia's death by shifting his terms: Illumination becomes Art, and the worldly way, Commerce, both terms that avoid doctrinal problems. Metaphorically, an escape into Art (illumination) becomes an escape into a garden, one in which real communication is possible. So it is for the musical Colby Simpkins, about whom Lucasta Angel, Sir Claude Mulhammer's illegitimate daughter, notes that he has his "own world." Taken in by Sir Claude as his presumptive son, Colby is immediately claimed by Lady Elizabeth Mulhammer, a fashionable reincarnation of Julia Shuttlethwaite, as the lost son of her former lover, a poet. Each imagines Colby in terms of personal wish-fulfillment. To Colby, the failed musician, Sir Claude reveals his early yearnings to be a sculptor and his decision to follow in the family business. For Sir Claude, the act of creation is "a world where the form is the reality" and an "escape into living" from an illusory world. Indeed, for Sir Claude, life is a constant compromise, just as it is for the Chamberlaynes, a constant coping with two worlds, neither of which offers perfect fulfillment. It is, as he says, a substitute for religion.

Despite this analogy, Colby is unwilling to accept Sir Claude as a father. Colby expresses his yearning for an ideal father in words that may be read for their religious connotation. He wishes, as he says, to have a father "Whom I had never known and wouldn't know now/ . . . whom I could get to know/ Only by report, by documents," a father, he continues, "whose life I could in some way perpetuate/ By being the person he would have liked to be." The analogues to Christ are unmistakable. The revelation that Colby is actually the son of Herbert Guzzard, a "disappointed musician," suggesting a harmony between the mystical and the commonplace that is seldom achieved in *The Family Reunion*, adds to the success of *The Confidential Clerk*.

Like Celia, Colby chooses a life of service, if one more prosaic than joining a nursing order and perishing in Kinkanja. He acknowledges his inheritance by becoming the organist at a small church (rather than continuing to live on Sir Claude's generosity, for Sir Claude is eager to think of Colby as one with whom he shared disillusionment); Eggerson, the retired confidential clerk—who, as Jones notes, was for Eliot "'the only *developed* Christian in the play'"—suggests that Colby will enter the ministry.

As Barber points out, the play presents a succession of individuals who are reaching out after Colby, essentially as a way of gratifying their own expectations. It is only, however, when the audience knows the secret of Colby's birth that many of the early conversations make sense; consequently, Barber suggests, the play is weak in its early acts. Despite this criticism, *The Confidential Clerk* offered Eliot's most convincing and optimistic treatment to that time of the possibility of human communion, pointing the way to his hopeful treatment of human love in his last play, *The Elder Statesman*. It seems less important that Lady Elizabeth's up-to-date spiritualism, her substitute for religion, fails her in her perception that Colby is her son than that she is willing to accept as her real offspring B. Kaghan, a brash, successful businessman, a diamond in the rough. Again, it seems less important that Sir Claude has lost his desired son than that, in the end, he emotionally accepts Lucasta as a daughter. Indeed, the note that Eliot strikes—that, as the Mulhammers say, they are "to try to understand our children" and that both Lucasta and B. Kaghan desire to "mean something" to their new-found parents—is exceptionally conciliatory and suggestive of greater amelioration in the "good life" than is posited in the earlier plays.

THE ELDER STATESMAN

Eliot's final play, *The Elder Statesman*, is an extension not only of the idea that one must come to terms with his past, just as Harry Monchensey and the Mulhammers attempt to do, but also that this is, indeed, the only way to redemption. Such atonement on the part of Lord Claverton is presented in words that are less mystical than prosaic; indeed, his past is populated by the blackmailers Federico Gomez, who seeks to capitalize on his knowledge that Lord Calverton had run over a dead man after a drinking party, and Mrs. Carghill, who, as the actress Maisie Montjoy, possesses incriminating love letters. Certainly Calverton's immediate problem—that of being a terminally ill, newly retired man of consequence, suffering from the loneliness of "sitting in an empty waiting room"—is one with which the audience can quickly identify. As Jones points out, *The Elder Statesman* has a "naturalistic surface": The more plays Eliot wrote, the more muted the spiritual enlightenment became, so that eventually the social relationships became primary. Carol Smith, on the other hand, sees the play as a culmination of Eliot's development of the "dramatic fable" that serves as a "transparent mask" for permanent, religious meanings.

The corollary to Calverton's loneliness takes on sinister (and existential) connotations when it is present in Gomez, who has adopted a new name and new country after a prison sentence. As he says, he has returned to face Lord Calverton in order to find the self he left behind. Gomez charges Calverton with "creating him," with engineering his tastes and altering his career. In revenge, he threatens to make others see Calverton for what he really is—a murderer and a hypocrite. Calverton, in fact, has created his own ghosts by dominating the lives of others. The lesson that he must take responsibility for meddling in others' lives is reinforced by his realization that he is no better than those he created. Both Jones and Carol Smith point out that Calverton's and Gomez's careers parallel each other in that their ethical standards merely mirror the society of which they are a part and in that both have changed identities, the "statesman" Dick Ferry having adopted his wife's name for its impressiveness and the Oxford student having changed his name to blend into his new country. Gomez's desire to amalgamate his two personalities and his desire for revenge are satisfied when he meets Calverton's ne'er-do-well son Michael, to whom he offers the lure of easy money and a new identity. Gomez is, in short, reenacting Calverton's earlier role of tempter.

The other ghost that Calverton must face—Maisie Montjoy, known as Mrs. Carghill—has also been "created" by him. As his mistress, who sued him for breach of promise, she was irrevocably affected by his offer of and withdrawal of love. Indeed, their relationship is a parody of the fruitful, redeeming love that comes to Monica Calverton and Charles Hemington. Like Gomez, Mrs. Carghill has gone through a series of name changes reflecting a progressive confusion in identity. Like him, she resorts to blackmail to gain companionship, insisting on what Jones calls the "uncomfortable Christian conception of a man and a woman becoming the inseparable unity of 'one flesh,'" and like him, she seeks revenge by encouraging the weak-willed Michael to emigrate to South America.

The cure that Eliot proposes for Calverton's loneliness, for his series of facades, and for his discomfort with the past—love—also exorcises his ghosts by allowing him to face them. Accompanying that love is the relinquishment of power; understanding that Michael is a free agent, Calverton recognizes that he has been trying to dominate his son's choice of friends, lifestyle, and career. If Michael is a free agent, then Gomez and Carghill's revenge has lost its sting, because Calverton is no longer responsible for his son's actions. The model for the cure is the love shared by Monica and Charles, a love that creates a new, viable personage out of the you and the me. Unlike the kind of false images projected by Calverton's desire to dominate, the new individual is created by a submission of wills, a voluntary merging of the selves. It is, in short, a model of divine love. Eliot thus points to an achievable salvation unspoiled by artificial dramatic techniques such as the evocation of the Eumenides or the awkward ritualistic libation in *The Cocktail Party*.

Although Jones notes that for one reviewer, at least, the language of the lovers is abstract and lacking in evocative details, Calverton's illumination is clearly expressed: As Calverton says, if an individual is willing to confess everything to even one person—willing, that is, to appear without his mask—"Then he loves that person, and his love will save him." Calverton further realizes that his wish to dominate his children arises not from love but from the desire to foist on them an image so that he "could believe in

[his] own pretences." At peace with himself and with Monica, who has promised to remember Michael as he really is so that he may one day shed his mask and return to his real self, Calverton approaches death with serenity: "It is worth dying," he says, "to find out what life is."

OTHER MAJOR WORKS

POETRY: "The Love Song of J. Alfred Prufrock," 1915; *Prufrock and Other Observations*, 1917; *Poems*, 1919; *Ara Vos Prec*, 1920; *The Waste Land*, 1922; *Poems, 1909-1925*, 1925; *Ash Wednesday*, 1930; *Triumphal March*, 1931; *Sweeney Agonistes*, 1932; *Words for Music*, 1934; *Collected Poems, 1909-1935*, 1936; *Old Possum's Book of Practical Cats*, 1939; *Four Quartets*, 1943; *The Cultivation of Christmas Trees*, 1954; *Collected Poems, 1909-1962*, 1963; *Poems Written in Early Youth*, 1967; *The Complete Poems and Plays*, 1969.

NONFICTION: *Ezra Pound: His Metric and Poetry*, 1917; *The Sacred Wood*, 1920; *Homage to John Dryden*, 1924; *Shakespeare and the Stoicism of Seneca*, 1927; *For Lancelot Andrewes*, 1928; *Dante*, 1929; *Thoughts After Lambeth*, 1931; *Charles Whibley: A Memoir*, 1931; *John Dryden: The Poet, the Dramatist, the Critic*, 1932; *Selected Essays*, 1932, new edition 1950; *The Use of Poetry and the Use of Criticism*, 1933; *After Strange Gods*, 1934; *Elizabethan Essays*, 1934; *Essays Ancient and Modern*, 1936; *The Idea of a Christian Society*, 1939; *The Music of Poetry*, 1942; *The Classics and the Man of Letters*, 1942; *Notes Toward the Definition of Culture*, 1948; *Poetry and Drama*, 1951; *The Three Voices of Poetry*, 1953; *Religious Drama: Medieval and Modern*, 1954; *The Literature of Politics*, 1955; *The Frontiers of Criticism*, 1956; *On Poetry and Poets*, 1957; *Knowledge and Experience in the Philosophy of F. H. Bradley*, 1964; *To Criticize the Critic*, 1965; *The Letters of T. S. Eliot: Volume I, 1898-1922*, 1988.

BIBLIOGRAPHY

Childs, Donald J. *From Philosophy to Poetry: T. S. Eliot's Study of Knowledge and Experience*. London: Athalone Press, 2001. Childs analyzes Eliot's literary works with emphasis on how he expressed his philosophy through his poetry. Bibliography and index.

Davidson, Harriet, ed. *T. S. Eliot*. New York: Longman, 1999. A collection of literary criticism regarding Eliot and his works. Bibliography and index.

Donoghue, Denis. *Words Alone: The Poet T. S. Eliot*. New Haven, Conn.: Yale University Press, 2000. Donoghue, having discovered Eliot's poetry in 1946 when he left his native Warrenpoint to attend University College in Dublin, writes autobiographically about the experience and offers a close reading of Eliot's major poems and essays.

Gordon, Lyndall. *T. S. Eliot: An Imperfect Life*. New York: W. W. Norton, 1999. A heavily revised and updated edition of the two-volume biography that made Gordon one of Eliot's most sensitive interpreters.

Habib, Rafey. *The Early T. S. Eliot and Western Philosophy*. New York: Cambridge University Press, 1999. A look at the philosophical beliefs held by Eliot and how they found their way into his literary works. Bibliography and index.

Malamud, Randy. *T. S. Eliot's Drama: A Research and Production Sourcebook*. New York: Greenwood Press, 1992. A close look at the production of Eliot's dramatic works. Bibliography and indexes.

_____. *Where the Words Are Valid: T. S. Eliot's Communities of Drama*. Westport, Conn.: Greenwood Press, 1994. A critical analysis and interpretation of Eliot's plays. Bibliography and index.

Moody, A. David, ed. *The Cambridge Companion to T. S. Eliot*. New York: Cambridge University Press, 1994. A comprehensive reference work dedicated to Eliot's life, work, and times. Bibliography and index.

Schuchard, Ronald. *Eliot's Dark Angel: Intersections of Life and Art*. New York: Oxford University Press, 1999. An analysis of Eliot's work from a psychological perspective. Bibliography and index.

Patricia Marks,
updated by John R. Holmes

JUAN DEL ENCINA

Born: Salamanca, Spain; July 12, 1468?
Died: León, Spain; 1529?

PRINCIPAL DRAMA

Égloga representada en la noche de la natifidad (I), pr. c. 1494-1513

Égloga representada en la mesma noche de la navidad (II), pr. c. 1494-1513

Representación a la muy bendita pasión (III), pr. c. 1494-1513

Representación a la santíssima resurrección (IV), pr. c. 1494-1513

Égloga representada en la noche postrera de carnal (V), pr. c. 1494-1513

Égloga representada en la mesma noche de antruejo (VI), pr. c. 1494-1513

Égloga representada en reqüesta de unos amores (VII), pr. c. 1494-1513

Égloga representada por las mesmas personas (VIII), pr. c. 1494-1513

Égloga de las grandes lluvias (IX), pr. c. 1494-1513

El triunfo del amor (X), pr. c. 1494-1513

Égloga de los tres pastores (XII), pr. c. 1494-1513

Aucto del repelón (XIII), pr. c. 1494-1513

Cancionero: Égloga de Cristino y Febea (XI), pr. c. 1494-1513, pb. c. 1497-1512

Cancionero de las obras de Juan del Enzina, pb. 1496 (includes eclogues I-VIII), 4th edition pb. 1507 (includes eclogues I-X), 5th edition pb. 1509 (includes eclogues I-X, XII, and XIII)

Égloga de Plácida y Vitoriano (XIV), pr. 1513, pb. 1514

Églogas completas de Juan del Enzina, pb. 1968 (includes eclogues I-XIV; Humberto López-Morales, editor)

OTHER LITERARY FORMS

In addition to his dramatic works, Juan del Encina wrote numerous learned poems, amatory lyrics, jocose-satiric verses, and *villancicos* (carols), all published in the different editions of his *Cancionero*.

Arte de poesia castellana (1496; the art of Castilian poetry) is a treatise on the theory of poetry. *Églogas de Virgilio* (1496) is a paraphrase of the pastoral dialogues of Vergil's *Eclogues* (43-37 B.C.E.; also known as *Bucolics*; English translation, 1575). *Trivagia* (1521; journey to Jerusalem), Encina's last work, is an extensive poem offering an account of the journey to Jerusalem that Encina undertook in July, 1519, and from which he returned in 1521.

ACHIEVEMENTS

Juan del Encina has been called the patriarch, or father, of the Spanish theater. On the other hand, a number of literary historians have generally referred to Encina's dramatic productions as *los primeros balbuceos* (the first babbles) of the Spanish theater. This somewhat irreverent qualification was doubtless inspired by the unfavorable comparison of Encina's first dramatic essays with the perfection this new literary genre was later to reach in the Spanish *comedia* of the Golden Age.

In Spain there is no well-documented, gradual evolution from a medieval liturgical tradition to the formation of a secular drama, as has been the case in other Western European countries, such as France, England, and Germany. The only existing text of a vernacular drama is the *Aucto de los Reyes Magos*, dated around 1150. There is no textual support for the existence of a liturgical dramatic tradition in medieval Spain between 1150 and 1450. Encina established the drama as a literary genre in Spain and, indeed, fully deserves the distinction of being called the father of the Spanish theater.

Encina's dramatic universe is made up of pastoral poetry, and the *dramatis personae* of both his religious and his secular plays are shepherds. The influence of Vergil's *Bucolics*, which Encina translated and adapted, thus makes itself felt not only in the mere adoption of the term *Égloga*, which the Salamancan used for all his plays, but also in a much deeper sense: Encina's shepherds, like Vergil's, appear in a rustic setting and are, at least in Encina's secular plays, all subjected to the torments and pains of love. Love is the main theme of Encina's secular drama. His plays represent the gradual evolution and refinement of a theory of love in the incipient Spanish theater. This evolution can be clearly traced from Eclogues VII, VIII, and X, all the way through the last great Eclogues, XI, XII, and XIV. The dialects of love as developed in Encina's dramatic work were to be adopted almost without modifications by all the great dramatists of the Spanish Golden Age. Herein lies one of the most innovative contributions Encina brought to the establishment of the dramatic genre in Spain's Golden Age.

Encina was also a gifted musician and composer. More than sixty of his compositions have been preserved in the *Cancionero musical de palacio*, published by Barbieri in 1890. Twelve of Encina's eclogues terminate with a *villancico* (carol), the music of which was composed by the playwright himself. These musical finales must have added a special delight to the pleasure with which these first dramatic essays of the Spanish theater were relished by the dukes of Alba, together with the numerous members of their court in the palace of Alba de Tormes, where these plays were staged and performed during the last decade of the fifteenth century.

BIOGRAPHY

Juan del Encina was one of the many children of a humble shoemaker in Salamanca named Juan de Fermoselle. His mother's name probably was Encina. There is documental evidence that by 1490 Juan had changed his name from Fermoselle to Encina. This change of name was not an unusual practice among the humanists and artists of the Spanish Renaissance.

In 1484, Encina became a chorister in the Cathedral of Salamanca. Besides music, Encina studied law, Latin, and Greek at the university of Salamanca. At that early age, he also took minor orders, but only many years later, in 1519, was he finally ordained a priest. After the termination of his university studies, around 1492, Encina entered the household of the duke of Alba as a kind of program director for the entertainment presented on specific religious festivals and special occasions. The years Encina spent at the

ducal palace of Alba de Tormes, a provincial town near Salamanca, until his departure in 1498 or 1499 mark the crucial period of his greatest literary and musical creations. It was also during this period that Encina's professional and literary activities became closely connected with those of his great imitator, and possibly rival, Lucas Fernández, who in 1495 also had become part of the duke's household, probably as a part-time actor serving on programs directed by Encina. The importance of Fernández's role as cofounder of Spain's secular drama has been borne out by most recent research on the origins of Spanish theater. Although very little documental evidence is available to shed light on the personal relationship between Encina and Fernández during those years in Alba de Tormes, the direct and immediate dependence of Fernández's *farsas* and *comedias* on Encina's eclogues, as well as the new dramatic ingredients that the former incorporated in his plays, have made modern students of early Spanish theater more aware of the fact that the dramatic productions of both playwrights during that crucial period of their associated activities at the ducal palace are so closely linked as to be almost inseparable. In effect, if Fernández's dramatic production is conditioned to a great extent by that of Encina, it constitutes at the same time a short but decisive step away from the theatrical art of Encina. Fernández and not Encina seems to be the concrete point of departure for the next phase of development of Spain's early drama.

The ducal palace and court in Alba de Tormes provided an ideal environment not only for Encina's artistic development but also for his search for social recognition. Encina is regarded by most of his critics as a social climber. One cannot, in effect, help but wonder how this humble shoemaker's son could have risen so fast to the prominent social position he occupied, first in the palace of the dukes of Alba and later in Rome, where his musical and literary talents earned for him the favors and protection of very influential patrons, such as Popes Alexander VI, Julius II, and Leo X.

Encina's departure from Alba de Tormes in 1498 or 1499 signaled the end of his most productive period. With the exception of *Égloga de Plácida y*

Vitoriano, his whole dramatic œuvre was already complete. From the point of view of literary creativity, the following phase in Encina's life was of far less importance than the preceding one. In 1499 he set out for his first trip to Rome, where he stayed until 1510. Three other journeys followed: 1512-1513, 1514-1516, and the last one probably from 1517 to 1521. During these various stays in the Holy City, Encina was very successful in obtaining all kinds of papal favors, which were bestowed on him in the form of appointments to lucrative ecclesiastic positions in the Church of Salamanca, the Cathedral of Málaga, and the Cathedral of León. Then, in 1519, Encina, finally ordained priest, undertook a pilgrimage to the Holy Land and celebrated his first Mass on Mount Zion. An account of this journey is found in his *Trivagia*, a mediocre composition of some two hundred verses. Back in Spain in 1521, Encina spent the final years of his restless life in León, where he died toward the end of 1529. His mortal remains were transferred from León to Salamanca around 1534.

Encina's biography, incomplete and fragmentary as it is in many respects, like that of many other Spanish medieval and Renaissance writers, has been viewed by most Encina students as of paramount importance for an understanding of his literary work. Many details of Encina's biography easily lend themselves to be construed in such a way that the driving forces behind Encina's life and work can be identified as a relentless search for social prestige. The man who most consistently has pursued this line of critical approach is J. Richard Andrews in his important book *Juan del Encina: Prometheus in Search of Prestige* (1959). Other critics, however, pointing at the scarcity of identifiable biographical material in Encina's plays, argue against this approach. For them, the life and the work of Encina are two separate entities, equally enigmatic. Nothing of Encina's vital experience as a man of the Renaissance, close to the centers of power and cultural prestige, seems to be reflected in his dramatic work. A third direction in Encina scholarship is followed by those who have posited the thesis of Encina's Jewish ancestry. For them, Encina was a *Converso* (converted Jew), who, during his

whole life, sought the company and the protection of powerful patrons as a guarantee against those who could cause irreparable harm to his reputation and to his very existence by revealing and making public this "shameful" condition.

ANALYSIS

Literary historians generally agree that the secular eclogues of Juan del Encina are of far greater importance than his religious playlets. The latter were written to be performed as part of the yearly festivities that were organized in the palace of the duke and duchess of Alba on Christmas Eve, on Good Friday, and at the beginning of Carnival and Lent.

The entire dramatic output of Encina is written in verse form, presenting the prosodic variety that is characteristic of early Renaissance versification in Spain. All of Encina's eclogues are one-act plays with no scenic divisions. The only exception may be *Égloga de Plácida y Vitoriano*, in which the *villancico*, beginning at line 1192, clearly divides the eclogue into two parts or two acts.

The dramatic universe created by Encina in his secular plays is brief but at the same time profoundly enigmatic. In his pastoral world, where lovelorn shepherds express their afflictions and tribulations caused by love, no clues are provided for explaining these extreme emotional reactions other than in terms of an already established conventionalized pattern of affective behavior. This cultural-literary pattern, which was familiar to the contemporary audience of the early Spanish theater, is to be found in the lyric tradition of fifteenth century *cancionero* poetry. The brief dramatic universe created by Encina is carved out of the huge poetic metacontext of the *cancioneros*. The greatest contribution of Encina to the formation of the Spanish theater consists precisely of the fact that he adapted for the theatrical genre the theory of courtly love as it had already been worked out in the extensive love poetry of the fifteenth century—that is to say, in the thousands of amatory compositions brought together in the voluminous collections of poems that are called *cancioneros*. Encina himself has included in his *cancionero* many of this type of amorous poems. The forms and contents of these compositions are in absolute conformity with those found in other *cancioneros*. Thus, as a poet, Encina contributed to the lyric elaboration of a theory of courtly love that, as a dramatist, he adapted to the specific needs of the new genre he was creating at the same time. To a great extent, Encina's theatrical production is purely and simply *cancionero* poetry cast in the mold of dramatic dialogue.

An essential characteristic of the Spanish conception of courtly love is the wide range of religious ideas that are associated with this concept. The poetic inspiration that runs through the amatory lyrics of the fifteenth century is guided by the intent to reconcile courtly love with Christian doctrine. In the Spanish concept of courtly love as a literary theme, the medieval idea that woman is the instrument through which the devil causes man's perdition may still be strongly felt. This idea becomes combined in the imagination of the *cancionero* poets with the representation of woman as a depository of all the attributes and powers of the God of love: Woman incarnates love's power, a power which, on an allegorical plane, functions in the guise of the God of love. The only way man can preserve his freedom of will and the use of his rational faculties is to flee from the omnipotent power of love. In the Encinian drama this flight from love, inspired by the negative conception of love as a force inimical to man, is the main theme in his three great eclogues: *Égloga de los tres pastores*, *Égloga de Cristino y Febea*, and *Égloga de Plácida y Vitoriano*.

ÉGLOGA REPRESENTADA EN REQÜESTA DE UNOS AMORES

In *Égloga representada en reqüesta de unos amores* (eclogue acted in a dispute over love), Pascuala, a pretty shepherdess, is courted by the shepherd Mingo, who is married to Menga. He tells Pascuala that for the love of her, he is prepared to leave his wife, and as token of his love, he gives her a rose. At this point, an *escudero* (squire) enters who immediately falls in love with Pascuala, declaring his feelings for her in the lofty language of courtly love. The rustic shepherd and the noble suitor now compete for the love of the shepherdess in a dispute of country versus city dwellers. The comic contrast between the two styles of courtship is enhanced by Mingo's use of Sayagués, a rustic dialect spoken in the northwestern region of Sayago, to express his love for Pascuala. In the end, the two competitors agree to abide by the decision Pascuala will make. She chooses the squire, on condition that he pledge to become a shepherd.

This very short Eclogue VII, of only 253 lines, including the *villancico* at the end, is a *pastourelle*, a poetic genre that was abundantly cultivated in Provence and Portugal but much less popular in Castile. Its only precedents are to be found in the *serranillas* ("mountain-lass" poems) of Juan Ruiz, and in a few compositions of the marquess of Santillana.

ÉGLOGA REPRESENTADA POR LAS MESMAS PERSONAS

The same theme, as well as all the characters of *Égloga representada en reqüesta de unos amores*, reappears in Eclogue VIII, *Égloga representada por las mesmas personas* (eclogue acted by the same persons), which was performed in the hall of the Alba palace one year after the preceding eclogue. The dramatic action of Eclogue VIII takes place one year later. The squire-shepherd, now called Gil, has married his Pascuala and has adopted the dialectal speech of his fellow shepherds, but the monotony of the pastoral existence has begun to lower his spirits. He misses the palace and the pleasures of courtly life. He urges Pascuala to leave everything behind and go with him to the court. He also induces his former rival, Mingo, who has become his friend, and Menga to join them in this change of life. First Pascuala and then Mingo and Menga shed their rustic attire and help one another dress in fine robes, according to the courtly fashion. They marvel at the ennobling effect of this transformation brought about by the power of love. All four of them set out for their new life at the *villa y corte*. From the rustic shepherds they once were, they have been transformed into truly refined characters, eager to initiate themselves further, under the guidance of the squire (who has reverted again to standard Spanish), into the art of courtly life. In the final part of the eclogue, Gil exhorts his former fellow shepherds with the words: "*A la criança nos demos*" ("Let's dedicate ourselves to the courtly education or training").

As in the other secular plays of Encina, love is the predominant theme of Eclogues VII and VIII. What sets these two eclogues apart from the others, however, is the absence of any allegorical representation of love as a divine power. The interplay between the two male and the two female characters unfolds in a real human environment, depicted, to be sure, in the conventional colors of an idyllic Arcadian world, but without the allegorical intervention of the god of love, as happens in Eclogue X, *El triunfo del amor*.

While reading these two eclogues, one should remember that they were first performed, as were the rest of Encina's plays (with the exception of *Égloga de Plácida y Vitoriano*), in the aristocratic setting of the ducal palace of Alba, before the duke and duchess, their noble family and friends, and the undoubtedly larger plebeian part of the audience, which consisted of an extensive domestic staff of servants and other personnel attached to the duke's household and domains. Add to this peculiar composition of the first audience of Encina's dramas the circumstance that the role Mingo seems to have been played by Encina himself and that the other actors as well were probably equally well-known to this mixed audience, and one can easily imagine the unique nature of the interactions that took place between public and *dramatis personae* during these first theatrical performances of Encina's plays. Much autobiographical material has been woven into these plays under the guise of allusions, hints, and *sous-entendus*. Students of Encina have displayed great ingenuity and erudition in uncovering and interpreting these hidden aspects of Encinian drama, and these efforts have contributed considerably to scholars' insight into the personal relationship that existed between Encina and his dramatic creations, between the man and his work. The importance of the work itself, however, reaches far beyond the individual destiny of the man who created it.

EL TRIUNFO DEL AMOR

The tenth eclogue, *El triunfo del amor* (the triumph of love), presents, with the preceding Eclogues, VII and VIII, a fundamental thematic relationship that is most revealing for the evolution of the theatrical art of Encina.

At first sight, this tenth eclogue seems a regression to a more primitive phase in the dramatic craftmanship of Encina. Love enters here in allegorical form as a handsome youth. Armed with bow and arrow, Cupid boasts about the irresistible power of love. Pelayo, an ignorant shepherd, then enters. He foolishly incurs Cupid's wrath by his disrespectful admonishments to the *garçón de bel mirar* (pretty-eyed youth) that he is hunting on forbidden territory. Cupid, infuriated, wounds him with one of his arrows and departs, leaving the hapless shepherd behind in great agony. Pelayo is found by two other shepherds, Bras and Juanillo, to whom he reports the terrifying details of his encounter with the cruel hunter. The two immediately realize that the simpleminded Pelayo has dared to challenge the power of Cupid himself. Pelayo, overcome by pain, loses consciousness. Greatly alarmed, Bras and Juanillo, with the help of a squire who happens to pass by, try to identify the cause of the ailment that holds Pelayo prostrate on the ground. They decide it must be love. This elicits some skeptical comments from the squire, who believes that the sufferings of love can be experienced—and expressed—only by people of noble birth, not by rustic shepherds. When Bras mentions the name of Marinilla, Pelayo suddenly regains consciousness and recognizes that the secret malady from which he is suffering is his love for Marinilla.

Despite the awkwardly primitive dramatic form of this play, it possesses a consistently developed dramatic motive of great interest for the understanding of the theatrical theme of courtly love as introduced by Encina. What one witnesses in Eclogue X is a process of initiation in the art of courtly love. Pelayo's total unawareness of the presence and the power of love in his life is remedied by the teachings of Bras and Juanillo, who are more informed in these matters than Pelayo, and by those of noble character, represented by the squire, who represents a higher level of insight into the manifestations and effects of the power of love. This process of initiation, this kind of apprenticeship in the art of courtly love, lies also at the thematic core of the two preceding eclogues, VII and VIII, and therefore constitutes the unifying motif that links these three plays.

At this point, it becomes possible to define what seems to stand out as the single most distinctive feature of the whole Encinian drama. The theory of courtly love, as found in *cancionero* poetry, before being cast by Encina in the theatrical mold of his secular plays, went through an ideological revision in which noble birth was no longer considered to be the *conditio sine qua non* for the ability to experience and to express the sufferings and exaltations caused by love. In the Encinian drama, it is the nobility and loftiness of the sentiments experienced by the lover, whether he be noble or plebeian, which make him worthy to be included in the courtly cultus. Encina's aristocratic characters initially may express surprise at the claims of rustic shepherds who insist that they, as well as the aristocratic lovers, are capable of feeling and expressing the painful but ennobling effects of the power of love, but—after closer scrutiny—the noble characters end up recognizing that these claims on the part of the plebeian characters are, indeed, legitimate.

ÉGLOGA DE CRISTINO Y FEBEA

Cristino, the protagonist in *Égloga de Cristino y Febea* (XI), portrays the courtly features of this type of shepherd as worked out in the preceding eclogues, VII, VIII, and X. In the past, Cristino has always been a faithful servant of love, but now, disillusioned and weary of the ephemeral pleasures of love, he decides to run away from this sinful way of life and become a hermit. His friend Justino, although impressed by Cristino's saintly intentions, advises against such a radical change of life. In view of his friend's former lifestyle, Justino doubts that Cristino is strong enough to endure the hardships and the deprivations of the life of a hermit. Cristino, however, is not moved by Justino's objections and goes off to his self-imposed exile from the sinful world. Love then enters and, on hearing from Justino that Cristino has dared to flee from his omnipotent power, is inflamed with anger. He sends his nymph Febea to Cristino to entice the hermit to abandon his ascetic life, to return to the world, and to become again a faithful servant of Love. When later the god appears before Cristino and holds out the promise to grant him the love of Febea, Cristino no longer can resist these temptations

and yields to the overwhelming power of love. Still mortified by the humiliation of his defeat and fearful of what the people in the village may think of his apostasy, Cristino returns to the world.

There is great complexity and even confusion in the ways the various themes of this play are combined as well as opposed to each other in the dramatic action. The service of God, represented in the old medieval ideal of the ascetic life, and the service of love are pitched against each other in the polemical forms of a debate between the old and the new, between the medieval religious ideal and the Renaissance worldly cult of love. The radical character of this opposition, however, is mitigated to a great extent by the high degree of spirituality of Encina's love concept with its deliberate exclusion of the carnal intent. The fundamental impulse that impels the Encinian characters to flee from love's servitude and sufferings acquires in this play a fuller and more articulated expression than in any preceding eclogue.

ÉGLOGA DE LOS TRES PASTORES

The main interest of Eclogue XII, *Égloga de los tres pastores* (eclogue of the three shepherds), consists of the fact that it is yet another dramatization of this same impulse on the part of the protagonist, Fileno, to free himself from the intolerable tyranny of the amorous passion. The pathos and rhetoric of Fileno's laments, which resound throughout the entire eclogue, are in the purest tradition of fifteenth century courtly poetry. The few interventions on behalf of the two other shepherds, Zambardo and more especially Cardonio, who try in vain to comfort their friend, fail to dispel the essentially static character of this eclogue. In the end, Fileno kills himself and is declared a martyr of love by Cardonio and Zambardo. With even greater insistence than in Encina's other plays, love is depicted in this eclogue as an inimical force that implacably persecutes, torments, and finally kills its victim. Whereas Cristino's attempt, in Eclogue XII, to flee love's power fails, Fileno's flight from love is tragically successful.

ÉGLOGA DE PLÁCIDA Y VITORIANO

The plot of Encina's last eclogue, *Égloga de Plácida y Vitoriano*, is rather simple. The complexity of this play, just as of the preceding one, and even more so of *Égloga de Cristino y Febea*, lies in the complicated interplay between the various theatrical concepts and motives that Encina, guided by his highly eclectic genius, has drawn together here into the dramatic constitution of his main characters.

The eclogue begins with a long soliloquy of Plácida, a noble lady, in which she reveals her consuming passion for Vitoriano and at the same time her despair caused by her lover's absence. She fears that he is unfaithful to her. She is tempted by the idea of suicide because, without her lover, life seems intolerable to her. She decides to leave and to seek solace in the wild. From this early stage to the very last part of the eclogue, where, after committing suicide, she is found by Vitoriano, Plácida reappears only once, to utter another soliloquy of some hundred verses in the middle of the play.

The play's dramatic action revolves around events directly or indirectly related to Vitoriano's inner conflict and its final solution. Vitoriano is torn between two counteracting forces: his love for Plácida and his desire to flee love's bondage because of the suffering and loss of freedom it entails. He seeks the advice of Suplicio, a good friend, who recommends the cure of another love. This strategy in the battle of love, already found in Ovid's *Remedia amoris* (before 8 C.E.; *Cure for Love*, 1600), is cynically referred to by Suplicio as "to remove one stuck nail with another." Suplicio leads his friend to the house of Flugencia, a young prostitute whom Vitoriano courts as if she were a lady. At this point in the play, Encina also introduces Eritea, an old procuress, who is a close imitation of the famous character Celestina, created by Fernando de Rojas a dozen years before in his *Comedia de Calisto y Melibea* (1499, rev. ed. 1502 as *Tragicomedia de Calisto y Melibea*; commonly known as *La Celestina*; first English translation, *Celestina*, 1631).

The conversation between Flugencia and Eritea, full of piquant details about the obscene and infamous practices of the go-between and the prostitute, constitutes a long digression completely dislocated from the main theme of the play. It soon becomes apparent, however, that Flugencia's mercenary favors are unable to mitigate Vitoriano's longing for Plácida.

He sets out to look for her and, following the indications of some shepherds, finds her corpse in a desolate place. She has killed herself with Vitoriano's dagger. In a long interlude, the despairing lover expresses his laments for the loss of his beloved. He wants to kill himself, but Venus stays his hand, and, on her request, Mercury intervenes to bring Plácida back to life. The two reunited lovers realize—and this is an important last innovation in Encina's love concept—that the love they now feel for each other is free from the uncertainties and torments they suffered before. This transformation signals, at least in the work of Encina, the final rejection of the theory of courtly love.

This last eclogue illustrates as no other before the tentative, experimental nature of Encina's mastery of the dramatist's crafts, with its indisputable gains and often inexplicable setbacks. Encina's irremediable eclecticism, which was perhaps considered with more indulgence in his own time than it is today, is no doubt responsible for the lack of cohesion in large portions of the dramatic action. What is impressive, however, is the consistency of his inspiration in pursuing, up to this eclogue, the development of what is undoubtedly his main dramatic motif: the flight from love. The dramatic form chosen by Encina to represent this flight in his last play is Vitoriano's failed attempt to seek refuge from love's omnipotence in adopting the hedonistic lifestyle as practiced and preached by his friend Suplicio.

OTHER MAJOR WORKS

POETRY: *Arte de poesia castellana*, 1496; *Églogas de Virgilio*, 1496; *Trivagia*, 1521.

MUSIC: *Cancionero musical de palacio*, 1890.

BIBLIOGRAPHY

Andrews, J. Richard. *Juan del Encina: Prometheus in Search of Prestige*. Berkeley: University of California Press, 1959. A classic study of the works of Encina. Bibliography and index.

Hathaway, Robert L. *Love in the Early Spanish Theatre*. Madrid: Playor, 1975. A look at the topic of love in the first Spanish dramas, including those of Encina.

Kidd, Michael. "Myth, Desire, and the Play of Inversion: The Fourteenth Eclogue of Juan del Encina." *Hispanic Review* 65, no. 2 (Spring, 1997): 217-236. Kidd looks at the *Égloga de Plácida y Vitoriano*, which he sees as a dramatization of sexual desire.

Sullivan, Henry W. *Juan del Encina*. Boston: Twayne, 1976. A basic biography of Encina that covers his life and works. Bibliography and index.

Antony van Beysterveldt

QUINTUS ENNIUS

Born: Rudiae, Calabria; 239 B.C.E.
Died: Rome; 169 B.C.E.?

PRINCIPAL DRAMA

Achilles, c. 204-169 B.C.E.
Aiax, c. 204-169 B.C.E. (*Ajax*, 1935)
Alcmeo, c. 204-169 B.C.E.
Alexander, c. 204-169 B.C.E.
Andromacha, c. 204-169 B.C.E. (*Andromache*, 1935)
Andromeda, c. 204-169 B.C.E.
Athamas, c. 204-169 B.C.E.
Cresphontes, c. 204-169 B.C.E.
Erechtheus, c. 204-169 B.C.E.
Eumenides, c. 204-169 B.C.E.
Hectoris lytra, c. 204-169 B.C.E. (*The Ransom of Hector*, 1935)
Hecuba, c. 204-169 B.C.E.
Iphigenia, c. 204-169 B.C.E.
Medea, c. 204-169 B.C.E.
Melanippa, c. 204-169 B.C.E. (*Melanippe*, 1935)
Nemea, c. 204-169 B.C.E.
Phoenix, c. 204-169 B.C.E.
Telamo, c. 204-169 B.C.E. (*Telemon*, 1935)
Telephus, c. 204-169 B.C.E.
Thyestes, c. 204-169 B.C.E.

OTHER LITERARY FORMS

Quintus Ennius is best known as an analyst historian. His now fragmentary poem *Annales* (c. 204-169 B.C.E., *Annals*, 1935), originally written in eighteen books, spanned the legendary period of Aeneas to his own day. He also wrote the *Saturae* (c. 204-169 B.C.E.; *Miscellanies*, 1935), a collection of miscellaneous poems in various meters on everything from Pythagorean philosophy (*Epicharmus*) and Pythagorean mythology (*Euhemerus*) to gastronomy (*Hedyphagetica; The Art of Dining*, 1935). The *Saturae* also are fragmentary. Ennius wrote epigrams as well; those on Scipio Africanus and on himself are the best known.

ACHIEVEMENTS

Quintus Ennius believed that his greatest achievement was the ability to speak three languages: Greek, Latin, and Oscan. He was fond of saying that he "possessed three hearts." Significantly, these are the three languages of ancient drama. In his own time Ennius was considered the Latin Homer because of his *Annals*. Apparently he was not considered a dramatist of stature equal to either Pacuvius or Accius in tragedy. Volcacius Sedigitus, who in the second century B.C.E. drew up a list of the ten best comic poets, places Ennius tenth and notes that he includes him only because of his early date.

Ennius's achievements were not only literary; he also served with distinction as a centurion in the Roman army in Sardinia. It was during this period that Cato, who was then quaestor in Sardinia, taught him Greek. Ennius also served on the staff of the general Fulvius Nobilior during the Roman campaign in Aetolia. In 184 B.C.E., Fulvius's son, with approval of the people, awarded Ennius a lot among the Triumviri Coloniae Deducenrae, thus constituting him a Roman citizen, although none of these honors brought him personal wealth.

Ennius's military career brought him the acquaintance of wealthy and powerful Romans, and when he came to Rome in 204 B.C.E., he quickly established himself as an effective teacher and began the literary career that would win him further renown. His *Annals* were praised in his own time, both because they extended the Latin language into areas that had been previously reserved for Greek and because they dealt with explaining Roman origins, a theme that repeatedly appears in Latin literature. His *Saturae* further demonstrated his versatility and contained poems on Pythagoreanism (his knowledge in this area probably was acquired through his residence in southern Italy) and even Greek gastronomy. No doubt he knew the Greek towns of southern Italy as well, for he was in every sense a Hellenized Roman, the Roman historian Suetonius having coined the word "semi-Graecus" to describe him.

The greatest achievement of Ennius's dramatic production was his ability to imitate in Latin the style of the Greek tragic poets. Probably his most successful efforts here were imitations of Euripides, though some of the titles indicate that he adapted Aeschylus and Sophocles as well.

BIOGRAPHY

Information concerning Quintus Ennius's life comes largely through references in his own works. For this reason it is probably reliable, as it could easily have been contradicted by his contemporaries given the wide circulation his works had during his lifetime. His Calabrian origins were humble, and even after he came to Rome and established himself on the Aventine he lived simply, with a single servant.

Though he served in the Second Punic War and held the post of centurion in Sardinia, his experience in the military served mainly to introduce him to Cato, Scipio Africanus, and Fulvius Nobilior, who would further his interests after he came to Rome. According to tradition, a bust of Ennius was placed beside Scipio's tomb.

Roman teachers required recommendations to advance their careers, and Ennius certainly had these, though it may well be that the death of the dramatist Livius Andronicus and subsequent retirement of

Ganeus Naevius helped advance Ennius's literary career after 204 B.C.E. Indeed, Ennius saw himself in roles that were to some extent contradictory—as a free spirit and innovator, a sophisticated Grecophile, on the one hand, and, on the other, a Roman citizen intensely proud of his adopted city, enamored of its origins and concerned with propagandizing them.

Ennius's literary career increasingly preoccupied him in his middle years, and indications are that the *Annals*, which eventually filled eighteen books, probably were circulated in successive parts of three books each. They were immediately accepted into the school curriculum, and their praise of Rome won for Ennius a wide audience. The longest extant passages from this collection are the "Dream of Ilia" (the daughter of Aeneas) and the "Auspices of Romulus and Remus." Each of these is about ten lines long. It may be that wide acceptance of the *Annals* inspired Ennius to write a *praetexta* (historical drama) called *Sabinae*, on the rape of the Sabine women, and perhaps another entitled *Ambracia*, in praise of the achievements of Fulvius, though the authorship of these works is open to question.

Though always poor, Ennius enjoyed living well, and personal references in his works attest his long-time sufferings with gout. Despite such mundane reflections and evidence of stilted versification, Ennius provided a source of inspiration traceable throughout the subsequent history of Roman literature. Lucretius, Vergil, Horace, and others owe him a substantial debt.

ANALYSIS

Only about four hundred lines of Quintus Ennius's twenty plays remain extant. A few lines remain from the *Sabinae* and the *Ambracia*, the two *praetextae* (historical dramas) regularly attributed to him. Nothing except the titles *Cupuncula* and *Pancratiastes* survives of his comedies, and even his authorship of these depends on the testimony of the literary historian Volcacius Sedigitus, whose list of Roman comedians has been preserved in the *Noctes Atticae* (c. 180 C.E.; *Attic Nights*, 1927) of Aulus Gellius. Even these meager remains would probably not have survived if Ennius had not been so frequently quoted by subsequent Roman writers. That Varro and Cicero quote so frequently from Ennius testifies to the importance he had for classical Latin authors.

EURIPIDES AND ENNIUS

Euripides' plays especially attracted Ennius. Their modern and adventuresome qualities no doubt appealed to Ennius's own free spirit. Most contemporary critics agree that more than half his plays derive from Euripides. Sufficient material survives from *Hecuba*, *Iphigenia*, and *Medea* to compare the fragments with the Euripidean originals. *Eumenides*, the third play of Aeschylus's *Oresteia* (458 B.C.E.; English translation, 1777), probably inspired Ennius's *Eumenides*, and Aristarchus was probably the source of his *Achilles*. The historian Cicero reports that Homer inspired Ennius, though any direct translation is unlikely, based on the evidence that is available. In any case, it appears to have been the established practice of Roman dramatists to base their plays directly on a given Greek tragedy or comedy.

In his *De finibus bonorum et malorum* (45 B.C.E.; *On the Definitions of Good and Evil*, 1702), Cicero reports that all the Roman tragedians translated their works verbatim from the Greek originals. This, indeed, seems to have been the case, for the Ennian fragments can almost always be compared with a Greek original when that play itself exists. Still, Gellius maintained that there was nothing in Euripides' *Iphigenia* to compare with the choral ode he quotes from Ennius's play. In Euripides' play, the chorus is composed of Chalcian women who have come to Aulis to witness the arrival of the Greek fleet. Moreover, they influence the play's action very little, and their songs are lengthy, oblique, and sometimes obscure. Ennius, however, had made his chorus a group of soldiers and gives them a song on idleness that anticipates Plautine patter. Clearly, Ennius departed from his Greek original when he believed that he could improve dramatic structure or where the Greek became too abstruse to translate directly. Even here, though, such conclusions have to be tentative. Ennius may have maintained the Euripidean chorus and introduced the soldiers on his own as an excuse to present a piece of his own poetry.

Very strong Euripidean influence appears in Ennius's *Eumenides*. All the fragments correspond to Euripides' play. It is strange that this play, so important to Athenians because of its praise of the Areopagus, the ancient murder court, would find popularity before a Roman audience without Ennian equivalents of the dramatically compelling *Agamemnōn* (*Agamemnon*, 1777) and *Choēphoroi* (*Libation Bearers*, 1777) that were part of Aeschylus's *Oresteia*. There might have been such plays, though only logic could argue for their existence.

In any case, Ennius's meters are completely his own. In *Medea*, he freely turns Greek iambs into Latin trochees in Medea's interview with Jason and, perhaps to the drama's detriment, lightens the impact of Medea's final words by altering Greek trimeter. He similarly adopts trochaics in his version of the Euripidean choral ode, which begins at line 1251.

STYLISTIC ELEGANCE

One must bear in mind that Roman audiences of the first century B.C.E. would not have considered verbatim translation mere plagiarism. On the contrary, Ennius's ability to transfer Greek stylistic elegance to the Latin language (a tongue that even many Romans viewed as primitive) was seen as an indication of his virtuosity and patriotism. At times these translations are especially elegant. For example, the phrase in Euripides' *Hecuba* that introduces Hecuba's dream concerning Troy's fall corresponds to one of Ennius's fragments. Hecuba invokes the dwellings of the gods, which are "mingled with the shining stars" ("*commixta stellis splendidis*"). Gellius found the fragments in which Hecuba tells Ulysses that he will prevail over Troy even as he recognizes that his cause is unjust to be noteworthy for their diction, thought, and economy.

One of the best examples of Ennian stylistic elegance is the lament of Cassandra over Hector's body in *Alexander*. This passage, which begins "O light of Troy, my brother Hector" ("*O lux Troiae, germane Hector*"), was adapted by Vergil in the *Aeneid* (c. 29-19 B.C.E.; English translation, 1553) and quoted by Macrobius in *Saturnalia* (date unknown; English translation, 1969).

Iphigenia, whose source is certainly Euripides, is the most consistently rhetorical of Ennius's plays, based on the extant fragments. Ennius makes the repartee of Agamemnon and Menelaus even more rapid and more elegant through his use of alliteration and assonance, as in Agamemnon's words, "Am I taunted because you do wrong? Because you go astray, am I brought to task?" ("*Ego proiector quod tu precas? Tu delinquis, ego arguor?*").

PLOTS OF THE PLAYS

It is difficult to make worthwhile comments concerning the plot lines of the tragedies, given their fragmentary state. Some critics argue of *Achilles* that Homer's *Iliad* (c. 800 B.C.E.; English translation, 1616) rather than the work of Aristarchus (a contemporary of Euripides) is Ennius's primary source or that Ennius wrote two plays on Achilles, but most now agree on an Aristarchan exemplar and discount the double title as a scribal addition. One can assume, given the relatively close resemblance of the fragments to the originals, that Ennian plots were similar in all essential details.

Similar plots still allowed certain changes in emphasis and structure. Ennius appears to have relied less on the chorus in most of his plays than did Euripides. Often he assigns it poetry that could stand separate from the plot, verse that could be classified as "cantica" because of its lyric quality. These songs were performed with minimal musical accompaniment and always staged in an area apart from that used by the actors. Correspondingly, Ennius's plays lacked elaborate dancing like that found in presentations of the Greek originals. (Plautine comedy, with the single exception of *Rudens*, date unknown; *The Rope*, 1694, would abolish the chorus altogether.) Metrical complexity replaces music, and Ennian drama demonstrates a consistent reliance on rhetorical effect. Mythic characters debating like court lawyers was an alteration designed specifically for Roman taste. The wrangling of Agamemnon and Menelaus in the *Iphigenia* has the tone of the Senate of the Forum about it.

What seems jarring to a classically trained Latinist was probably appreciated by an audience of Ennius's time. Cassandra's passionate alliteration as she prophesies to Hecuba the destruction Alexander will bring to Troy—"Mother, better by far than the best of women, I was driven by superstitious prophecies" ("*Mater optumarum multo mulier melior mulierum/ missa sum supsititiosis hariolationibus*"; Alexander)—hardly sounds Euripidean. Jason's words *amoris* and *honoris* jangle against each other in the interview with Medea: "You saved me more for love's sake than for honor's" ("*Tu me amoris magis quam honoris servavisti gratis*"; Medea). Such effects reflect taste. They appeal to a preoccupation with immediate effect achieved at the expense of dramatic substance, but they also reflect experimentation with the extent to which literary Latin diction, then in its infancy, could be taken. Ennius was never the equal of his Greek predecessors; he may not even have achieved the level of his successor tragedians Pacuvius and Accius. What is clear is that he inspired generations of Roman writers and advanced the development of the Latin language.

OTHER MAJOR WORKS

POETRY: *Annales*, c. 204-169 B.C.E. (*Annals*, 1935); *Saturae*, c. 204-169 B.C.E. (*Miscellanies*, 1935).

BIBLIOGRAPHY

Brooks, Robert Angus. *Ennius and Roman Tragedy.* 1981. Reprint. Salem, N.H.: Ayer, 1984. An examination of Ennius and his dramatic works. Includes bibliography.

Jocelyn, H. D. *The Tragedies of Ennius.* Cambridge, England: Cambridge University Press, 1993. Jocelyn presents a scholarly examination of Ennius's tragedies.

Warmington, E. H. *Remains of Old Latin.* Cambridge, Mass.: Harvard University Press, 1987. Translations and literary criticism of fragments from Latin writers, including Ennius.

Robert J. Forman

PAUL ERNST

Born: Elbingerode, Saxony (now in Germany);
   March 7, 1866
Died: St. Georgen, Austria; May 13, 1933

PRINCIPAL DRAMA

Lumpenbagasch, pr., pb. 1898
Im Chambre séparée, pb. 1898, pr. 1899
Die schnelle Verlobung, pr., pb. 1899
Wenn die Blätter fallen, pr. 1899, pb. 1900
Demetrios, pb. 1905 pr. 1910
Das Gold, pb. 1906
Der Hulla, pb. 1906, pr. 1907
Canossa, pb. 1908, pr. 1918
Brunhild, pb. 1909, pr. 1911
Ninon de Lenclos, pb. 1910, pr. 1911
Ariadne auf Naxos, pb. 1912, pr. 1914
Die heilige Crispin, pb. 1913, pr. 1927
Manfred und Beatrice, pb. 1913, pr. 1918
Preussengeist, pr., pb. 1915
Kassandra, pb. 1918, pr. 1931
Yorck, pb. 1918, pr. 1933
Chriemhild, pb. 1922, pr. 1924

OTHER LITERARY FORMS

During the early 1890's, Paul Ernst was editor of the Marxist *Berliner Volkstribüne* (Berlin people's tribune), but he left politics and journalism in 1896 to pursue a career as a poet, philosopher, and literary critic. He was a prolific writer. In addition to drama, he wrote poetry, a number of novels—as well as a popular autobiography—a large corpus of epic verse, numerous short stories, and hundreds of essays on economic, philosophical, and literary issues.

ACHIEVEMENTS

Paul Ernst, like many thinkers of the late nineteenth and early twentieth centuries, was deeply troubled by the growing pessimism and cultural skepticism of his times. Worried that this spiritual malaise—in his eyes, the result of the dehumanizing effects of the modern industrial world—was draining Western civilization of its vital strength, Ernst felt compelled to take ac-

tion. He turned first to politics. Soon disappointed by the failure of the German Social Democratic movement to effect any lasting change at the turn of the twentieth century, he then turned to theater. For him, drama—the "highest" form of all art—held the key to modern people's spiritual rejuvenation because it, like all art, was in principle capable of rising above what he called the "tyrannies" of socioeconomic determination. Unlike other human institutions, drama thus enjoyed a certain autonomy, which, when cultivated, could present humanity with an inspiring vision of the ultimate value and freedom of the human spirit.

To this end, he strove to articulate a modern, "neo-classical," form of drama that, contrary to the tastes of the time, harkened back to the strict form and structure of classical Greek drama to impart its timeless message about the heroic and idealistic human spirit. Because matters of plot and action were, however, ultimately subordinate to the dictates of refined form and dramatic conflict, Ernst's exalted idealism failed to move audiences. Though inspired and noble in conception, Ernst's dramas proved all too often to be little more than thinly veiled platforms for his personal crusade.

In an essay of 1916 written in honor of Ernst's fiftieth birthday, the influential Hungarian literary critic and political philosopher Georg Lukács characterized Ernst as a great writer and thinker whose dramas were nevertheless doomed to be excluded from the canons of the literary establishment. Though Lukács was later to recant his praise of Ernst, these early remarks proved to be prophetic: With the exception of one brief period, Ernst's dramatic works never enjoyed wide recognition. His talents, literary historians are quick to point out, were of a more philosophical than artistic nature. Indeed, Ernst was himself painfully aware of the crippling discrepancy between his theoretical program and his artistic production, and though he made repeated attempts to bridge the gap between theory and practice, he never really succeeded in translating his philosophical idealism into artistic creativity.

It is ironic that the only period in which Ernst's drama enjoyed positive critical acclaim was posthumously, during the National Socialist era. This ill-fated recognition—Nazi purveyors of German cultural supremacy hailed him as the misunderstood prophet of the new German society—dealt his reputation the final deathblow. Except for a few literary historians who have sought to understand his relation to cultural and aesthetic revolutions of the early twentieth century, Ernst's dramatic works have attracted little critical attention since the fall of the Third Reich.

BIOGRAPHY

In 1866, Paul Karl Friedrich Ernst was born in Elbingerode, a small town in the Harz Mountains of central Germany. The son of a miner who valued education and learning, the young Ernst was encouraged to pursue his early interests in literature and philosophy. These interests, combined with his generally brooding temperament, earned for him the nickname Philosopher from his schoolmates. In 1885, he began his university training at Göttingen and, complying with the wishes of his parents, took up the study of theology. In the following year, after a semester at Tübingen, he transferred to Berlin, where his interest in literature brought him into contact with Gerhart Hauptmann, Arno Holz, and Johannes Schlaf, the leading figures of the naturalist movement in Germany. Through his close association with these politically engaged writers, he developed an intense concern for the plight of the exploited working class, and shortly after his arrival in Berlin he joined the Social Democratic Party. Having abandoned theology to devote himself to the study of political science and economics, Ernst felt obliged to forgo the financial support of his parents. For the next twelve years, until he married into the financially secure von Berda family, he supported himself as a freelance journalist, writing emotionally charged essays on a wide range of subjects, from politics and social reform to literary criticism.

During this period—from the late 1880's to the early 1890's—Ernst put political activism above everything else in his life because, as a confirmed Marxist, he believed that the revolutionary Social Democratic movement was capable of altering the socioeconomic structure and achieving social equality. Though he was drawn to great works of literature, especially the monumental works of Fyodor Dostoevski, he felt no compelling inner need to take up the literary pen himself. By the mid-1890's, however, he began to realize that the social reform he sought was unattainable by political means. Bitterly disillusioned by the lack of progress made by the Social Democrats, indeed by political activism in general, he left politics for good in 1896, channeling his revolutionary zeal into literary production. Literature, he had come to believe, must strive to achieve that which is unattainable in the political arena.

Though his early one-act plays *Lumpenbagasch* and *Im Chambre séparée* won the praise of his naturalist contemporaries, Ernst harbored serious doubts about the ultimate success of the naturalist project, which, in focusing attention on the abject conditions of the downtrodden working class, was supposed to bring about social reform. These doubts crystallized in 1898 in his critique of naturalism found in the essay "Modern Drama." Here Ernst begins to articulate ideas that form the mainstay of his neoclassical theory of drama. Naturalist drama, he argued, was doomed to failure because its dismal portrayal of modern humanity as a powerless victim of social and economic forces was, in the final analysis, too pessimistic. Humanity is more than a will-less product of its milieu, Ernst argued, because there is something noble and idealistic in individuals that will always struggle to resist the tyrannical forces of reality.

During the next five years—a period that he later described as a "veritable hell"—Ernst produced a series of theoretical tracts and a small amount of fiction—including his first novel, *Der schmale Weg zum Gluck* (published 1904)—but no drama. In 1903, he moved to Weimar, where he hoped to become the first director of a newly forming theater company. Though the proposed company did not materialize, Ernst found in Weimar support and encouragement from a small circle of like-minded neoclassicists (most notably Samuel Lublinski and Wilhelm von Scholz), and in that same year he completed his first neoclassical tragedy, *Demetrios*. The next few years found Ernst at the apex of his career as a dramatist. Within the span of three years, he produced, in addition to a large corpus of dramaturgical writings, no fewer than six dramas. The year 1905 seemed to Ernst to be particularly auspicious. Having accepted a position as chief artist-in-residence at the prestigious Düsseldorf Playhouse, Ernst believed that he and his movement were at long last on the verge of lasting success. This, however, did not prove to be the case; his hopes of making the Düsseldorf theater into a kind of center for neoclassicism, like his planned periodical, *Form*, were short-lived. Ernst's high-minded theater project, like his dramas themselves, were met with a crushing indifference. Within a year of arriving in Düsseldorf, he returned, bitter and discouraged, to Weimar.

After his disappointing engagement in Düsseldorf, Ernst became increasingly cynical, conservative, and reclusive. Despite the repeated failure of his work, he nevertheless continued to write plays for another decade. By 1918, however, he was all but convinced that the true artist has no place in the modern world; having completed that year his last drama, he took leave of society and retired to Sonnenhof, his Bavarian country estate. There, he refocused his intellectual energies, and in 1918, as World War I was reaching its devastating end, he published his well-timed collections of essays, *Der Zusammenbruch des deutschen Idealismus* (the collapse of idealism) and *Der Zusammenbruch des Marxismus* (the collapse of Marxism). In these books, marked by a resentful spirit of resignation, he attempted to understand and then articulate why not only idealistic philosophy and literature but also Marxist political theory had failed to halt the destructive advance of European capitalism and the cultural-spiritual bankruptcy that, he thought, had followed in its wake.

In the final period of his life, Ernst devoted himself to prose, to autobiographical writing, and to the monumental task of creating three volumes of a verse epic. Shortly before his death in 1933, he returned to Germany from Austria, where he had been living since 1925, and was shocked by the new nationalistic

regime that had begun to sing his praises. Sad and disoriented, he left Germany and died a few months later at his isolated castle in St. Georgen, Austria. In a sonnet composed in final days, he lamented: "The world is such, that I cannot live."

ANALYSIS

Paul Ernst's dramatic work falls into three major periods: his early, naturalistic period; his late, redemption drama period; and his middle, neoclassical period, for which he is best known. Though his work underwent significant changes in theme and style, one aspect remained constant throughout his career: All his dramas depict humanity struggling for freedom—and, ultimately, ethical ideals—in an overpowering world of rigid necessities. In his early naturalistic plays *Lumpenbagasch* and *Im Chambre séparée*, which attempted to reflect in the crassest terms the sordid milieu of the degenerate and oppressed lower class, these necessities are manifest in the theme of social determinism. In the plays of his middle and late periods, beginning with his first neoclassical tragedy, *Demetrios*, Ernst moved from the explicitly social sphere to, in his view, the higher and more universally valid realm of fate. By reactivating and modernizing the classical Greek notion of an incomprehensible fate, which he saw as analogous to the bewilderingly complex and unintelligible socioeconomic forces at play in the modern industrial world, Ernst attempted to create dramatic situations that would reawaken people's ethical and idealistic spirit.

With the exception of five one-act plays written during his early period, all of Ernst's eighteen dramas are set in either a historical or a mythical past. This distance from the realities of the present, Ernst believed, was a necessary condition for presenting "eternally" valid dramatic conflict. In thereby avoiding the relativism of the naturalist milieu drama and the self-indulgent excesses of *fin de siècle* impressionism, Ernst hoped to free his drama from temporal and subjective limitations so that he could concentrate on what he called the objective "requirements of form." For Ernst, successful drama—that is, drama capable of countering the pessimism of the times and of extolling the inherent value and dignity of humanity's struggle for existence—could be produced only by an artist who willingly submitted to certain timeless principles. His five-act tragedy *Demetrios*, written in 1903 and 1904, was his first attempt to put into practice the universally valid principles of dramatic construction that he had painstakingly elaborated in his theoretical writings of the preceding six years. *Demetrios* is written in a somber and refined blank verse, a form that he perfected in his later work, but this stylistic virtuosity was perhaps unsuited to the turbulent crisis years of the early twentieth century.

The tragedy *Demetrios* is the closest Ernst ever came to putting his neoclassical theory into practice. In viewing the protagonist's struggle with insurmountable sociopolitical forces—his inexorable fate—the audience was supposed to be inspired by his valiant but tragic demise. In *Canossa*, however, written only four years later, Ernst had already begun to deviate from his strict neoclassical theory of tragedy, and though the hero also suffers a defeat at the hands of political intrigue, the outcome of the play is less tragic: The malevolent antagonist, who is transformed by his opponent's demise, promises to change his evil ways in the end. Written four years after *Canossa*, *Ariadne auf Naxos*—his most popular drama—marks the turning point in his career. No longer a tragedy, this redemption play ends with a—quite literally—*deus ex machina* resolution, in which the heros are rewarded for their suffering. Ernst's missionary zeal and creative energy waned after *Ariadne auf Naxos*. Nevertheless, one of Ernst's (dubiously) best-known works, the redemption drama *Preussengeist*, was written during this last period of productivity.

Though Ernst's move from tragedy to redemption drama demonstrates an attempt to loosen his rigid neoclassical stance to convey his message about humanity's ethical-idealistic being, he never succeeded in making the necessary connection with audiences. His overly formalistic conception of drama invariably yielded one-dimensional characters and improbable situations, which far too clearly bore the stamp of his abstract notions and thus failed to elicit the sympathy of the public. This failure was compounded by Ernst's unabashed intellectual elitism, which effec-

tively prevented the playwright from taking into account the pragmatic considerations of public reception. Rather than addressing the real needs and expectations of his audience, he became increasingly cynical, ultimately blaming the failure of his works on the modern public's general ignorance and increasing preoccupation with the material concerns of daily life.

DEMETRIOS

Inspired by a conversation with Wilhelm von Scholz, Ernst decided to take on the difficult Demetrios theme, which had defeated in the preceding century such renowned German dramatists as Friedrich Hebbel and Friedrich Schiller. Therefore, after a series of no fewer than fifteen failed attempts—if the playwright can be taken at his word—he finally succeeded in writing a classical drama whose tragic but idealistic hero was to serve weak-kneed modern human beings as a paragon of strength and ethical virtue. Culling from Hebbel's fragment the story of the rise and fall of a pretender to the Russian throne, Ernst removed his drama from seventeenth century historical Russia to the mythical past of ancient Sparta.

Demetrios begins with a love triangle in which the slave Pytheus, hopelessly in love with his master's daughter, kills her arrogantly aristocratic suitor. For this crime he must pay with his life. As Pytheus is about to be crucified, however, it is discovered that he has always worn the token of Apollo, a royal insignia. Pytheus, it turns out, is really Demetrios, the only surviving heir to the throne. His noble identity is then confirmed by Tritäa, the slave woman who reared him. She claims that, in the confusion of an insurrection through which the tyrant Nabis ascended to the throne, she had mistakenly saved the noble child instead of her own. Believing now that he is the rightful king, Demetrios, with the support of the Spartan nobility, overthrows Nabis and becomes the new ruler of the city-state. His reign, however, is neither long nor secure: He is forced by political realities to be as tyrannical as his predecessor, and unrest begins to mount among his subjects. To make matters worse, Demetrios now learns from Tritäa that he is really the former king's illegitimate son and that she is, after all, his real mother. Half slave and half king, Demetrios-Pytheus stands tragically between two worlds—he is at once both tyrant and victim. Unable to conceal his illegitimacy from his plotting enemies, he is publicly accused of deception and given an ultimatum: Kill Tritäa, thereby proving that she is not his real mother or be killed. In noble exasperation, he cries out, "I am Pytheus, son of a slave," and is struck down by a man who a short time before had helped him gain the throne. By confessing his humble slave side, he signs his own death warrant, but in so doing he also reveals that his true nobility is of spirit and not of birth. True to Ernstian theory, Demetrios-Pytheus is a hero who stands at the crossing of two divergent but inescapable necessities; in choosing one, he is destroyed by the other. Nevertheless, although Pytheus the individual must perish, his idealism lives on.

From a formal standpoint, the *Demetrios* tragedy is almost flawlessly executed. The work is a unified structure in which every scene contributes with near mathematical precision to the inevitable and necessary tragic outcome. Yet because the characters are more like functional parts of a fugue than real-life people of flesh and blood, their actions seem wooden and contrived. Rather than identifying with Demetrios and then being uplifted by his doomed yet heroic struggle with fate, Ernst's audience, like the reader today, remained unmoved. One cannot help but wonder how such an impossible predicament and truly dismal outcome—Ernst's noble intentions notwithstanding—could ever have been expected to impart a sense of joy and optimism.

CANOSSA

The theme of the helplessly isolated ruler at the mercy of political intrigue is taken up again in Ernst's monumental and highly symmetrical tragedy *Canossa*. This time Ernst turns to the medieval power struggle between Pope Gregor VII and the German emperor of the Holy Roman Empire, Heinrich IV. Juxtaposing two men and two realms, the settings of the first four acts alternate between Rome and Germany. All action culminates in the fifth act when, on Christmas Day in 1077, the two men meet face to face at Canossa.

In the first act, the audience learns that Gregor, born Hildebrand, never aspired to the papacy and that he once actually vowed to the German emperor never to become pope. To remain a monk, however, is not to be his fate. Forced by the absence of any clerical leader capable of saving the papacy from the evils of secular power looming in Germany, Gregor breaks his vow and becomes pope. Like the character Demetrios-Pytheus in Ernst's first tragedy, he is forced by political expediency to compromise his convictions and rule with an iron hand. When visiting their pious son, his parents are horrified to discover that the evil world has forced Gregor to commit perjury and murder to carry out his holy mission.

Heinrich, on the other hand, knows nothing higher than his own egocentric needs and desires. He is a man without scruples who thrives on power. Hearing, in the second act, that the high-minded and influential monk Hildebrand has become pope, he sets out to depose the papal reformer. His plans, however, do not materialize, for as he is about to leave for Rome, the news breaks that righteous Gregor has excommunicated him. Deprived of the holy sanction of Rome, Heinrich's once faithful dukes, wherein his real power lay, renounce their allegiance.

The scene is now set for the fifth act's fateful confrontation at Canossa. Unfortunately, and to the detriment of the play, the audience must endure two more acts of melodramatic buildup before witnessing the inevitable and tragic conflict. Ernst, holding true to the tragedy's balanced structural schema, artfully fills these two interim acts with intrigues and counterintrigues. Even the secondary characters evince a symmetry in word and action.

The action of act five, though predictable in the main, does have an interesting twist. Heinrich is approaching Canossa. Not knowing that the emperor comes as a penitent to seek absolution from his ban, Gregor believes that he will have to submit to the secular ruler and therefore prepares to die a martyr. To his surprise, Heinrich appears wearing the hair shirt of a penitent. It is obvious to all involved that lust for power and not contrition motivates Heinrich's action; an excommunicated emperor is a powerless ruler. Still, the pope is faced with a no-win situation;

like Demetrios, he is caught between necessities. If he receives Heinrich's confession and lifts the ban, as the law of the Church—the will of God—dictates, he will restore the emperor to his former power and, in effect, clear the way for Heinrich to carry out his evil plans. If he refuses to hear the confession, he, as God's highest earthly representative, will fail to fulfill his God-ordained duty. After a lengthy and impassioned exchange with Heinrich, Gregor realizes that he has no choice but to accept the confession, which he does. Feeling forsaken both by God and by the world, Gregor shakes his fists at Heaven and curses: "Because I loved right and hated wrong, I must therefore, God, die in exile." Seeing and hearing the utterly dejected pope curse God, Heinrich has a miraculous, if not improbable, change of heart: As the curtain falls, he promises to mend his ways, to forget himself, and to serve humankind. Far from convincing, Heinrich's sudden and anticlimactic change, in stark contrast to the arrantly deceitful, scheming, and power-crazed character developed thus far, undermines the dramatic effect that has been building throughout the play. In view of Heinrich's transformation, Gregor's defeat loses its tragic impact; his work and suffering, it appears, have not been in vain. The play *Canossa*, therefore, ceases in the closing lines to be a tragedy. Sensing that spectators might not grasp the full implications of Gregor's inspiring demise, Ernst seems to have deviated from his own theory of neoclassical tragedy to present the audience with a role model to follow.

ARIADNE AUF NAXOS

Ernst's first redemption drama, *Ariadne auf Naxos*, dramatizes the Greek mythological love story of Ariadne and Theseus. Shorter than his neoclassical tragedies, this three-act play is probably his most successful work; unlike his other dramas, it enjoyed an extended run—at the Kleines Theater unter den Linden in Berlin during World War I. Its success was attributable, in part at least, to the sense of hope that its decidedly positive outcome brought to war-weary German audiences.

Like Ernst's tragedies, *Ariadne auf Naxos* is written in blank verse. Because it begins, true to its classical origins, *in medias res*, it presupposes a certain knowledge of Greek mythology. The play takes place on the beautiful Aegean island of Naxos, where Ariadne, the daughter of King Minos of Crete, has just arrived with Theseus, who had gone to Crete to destroy Minos's monster, the Minotaur. Ariadne, who fell in love with Theseus while on Crete, helped him to slay the Minotaur and was thus forced to flee with her lover from the wrath of her tyrannical father.

Ernst, however, makes one slight but significant change in the story: To set up a potentially tragic sequence of events, he has Ariadne poison her father to save her lover. This fact she has managed to keep secret from her inflexibly idealistic Theseus, who, believing in the superiority of good over all evil in the world, believes that it is his calling to found a new, ethical society on the island of Naxos. The first act finds Ariadne tormented by guilt and the fear that righteous Theseus will discover her evil patricidal deed and cast her out. Mysteriously, in the midst of her despair, the god Dionysus appears and cryptically assures her that she, like all human beings, must suffer to live.

In the second act, the inevitable happens; news of Minos's murder reaches the shores of Naxos, and even as Theseus tries to cheer up his inexplicably disconsolate lover, a priest arrives bearing the fateful tidings. Just as Ariadne had feared, Theseus is incapable of understanding her deed, but before he can cast her aside, the priest informs the couple that the people of Naxos, believing Theseus to be her accomplice, are outraged by his apparent hypocrisy. Realizing now that their destinies have been united by the murder, Theseus resolves to defend her to the end, and as the second act closes, he goes off to confront the angry mob.

In the relatively short third act, Dionysus returns to redeem the hopelessly despairing Ariadne. In an exalted speech, Dionysus tells her that through her selfless suffering she has risen above the narrow good-versus-evil schema that enslaves ordinary mortals (Theseus being a prime example). Immediately before she is carried off by Dionysus into the shining heavens, delivered from all earthly care and woe, the mortally wounded and anguishing Theseus returns in the arms of the priest. Suddenly, in the presence of the divine, he sees the grander scheme of things and his incomprehensible and undeserved fate becomes clear to him. He realizes, as death approaches, that the true value of human existence lies not in specific moral precepts or lofty ideals but rather in humanity's eternal suffering and striving for those ideals, be they right or wrong.

In the redemption drama *Ariadne auf Naxos*, a religious-metaphysical theme supplants the sociopolitical dimension of Ernst's earlier plays. Though Aridane and Theseus, like Demetrios and Gregor, are victims of their inexorable fates, they are not tragic heroes. In the end, they are not so much destroyed by the necessities of the world (by equally destructive unavoidable choices) but transfigured by them. Rather than dying in despair, they are, as Ernst wished his audience to be, exalted by their quasi-mystical revelation.

PREUSSENGEIST

Ernst's last dramatic work of note, *Preussengeist*, though not as overtly religious as *Ariadne auf Naxos*, carries a similar message about the value of sacrifice and suffering in life. Written at the outbreak of World War I, this redemption drama is unfortunately weakened by its at times excessively nationalistic tone. Set in mid-seventeenth century Prussia, the play is based on an incident from Frederick the Great's youth. Wishing to escape an arranged marriage and the future responsibilities of the crown, Ernst's eighteen-year-old protagonist, Crown Prince Friedrich, makes plans to flee the country with his friend, Lieutenant von Katte. Even though their plan is discovered before they can carry it out, Friedrich's father, the king, views their intended flight as desertion and has them court-martialed. Von Katte is sentenced to death, while the king himself must determine the fate of his son. Having resolved to have Friedrich executed as well, the king changes his mind at the last minute when he sees the transformation that takes place in his son after he witnesses his friend's execution. In the moment of truth, young Friedrich professes his revelation that his life belongs not to him but to the

fatherland. Interpreting this as a sign from God, analogous to the biblical story of Abraham and Isaac, the king spares his son. As in *Ariadne auf Naxos*, tragedy is averted by invoking a higher, metaphysical order that stands above human law. Because duty, obedience, and fatherland are implicitly linked to divine providence in this play, it is easy to see why the National Socialists saw in Ernst the harbinger of the new German society.

OTHER MAJOR WORKS

LONG FICTION: *Der schmale Weg zum Glück*, 1904; *Saat auf Hoffnung*, 1916; *Der Schatz im Morgenbrotsaal*, 1926; *Jugenderinnerungen*, 1930; *Das Glück von Lautenthal*, 1933; *Grün aus Trümmern*, 1933.

SHORT FICTION: *Die Hochzeit*, 1913; *Die Taufe*, 1916; *Der Nobelpreis*, 1919; *Kommödianten und Spitzbubengeschicten*, 1920; *Geschicten von deutscher Art*, 1928.

POETRY: *Das Kaiserbuch*, 1923-1928 (3 volumes); *Der Heiland*, 1930.

NONFICTION: *Der Weg zur Form*, 1906; *Der Zusammenbruch des deutschen Idealismus*, 1918; *Der Zusammenbruch des Marxismus*, 1919; *Erdachte Gespräche*, 1921.

BIBLIOGRAPHY

Bucquet-Radczewski, Jutta. *Die neuklassische Tragödie bei Paul Ernst (1900-1920)*. Würzburg, Germany: Königshausen & Neumann, 1993. An examination of the dramatic works of Ernst. In German. Bibliography.

Jelavich, Peter. "Paul Ernst." In *World Drama*, compiled by Oscar G. Brocket and Mark Rape. New York: Holt, Rinehart, and Winston, 1984. A concise overview of the life and works of Ernst.

Pierson, Stanley. *Marxist Intellectuals and the Working-Class Mentality in Germany, 1887-1912*. Cambridge, Mass.: Harvard University Press, 1993. Contains a discussion of Ernst's disillusionment with Marxism and subsequent pursuit of a better society through other means.

Eric Williams

ST. JOHN ERVINE

Born: Belfast, Northern Ireland; December 28, 1883
Died: London, England; January 24, 1971

PRINCIPAL DRAMA

The Magnanimous Lover, wr. 1907, pr., pb. 1912
   (one act)
Mixed Marriage, pr., pb. 1911
Jane Clegg, pr. 1913, pb. 1914
John Ferguson, pr., pb. 1915
The Ship, pr., pb. 1922
The Lady of Belmont, pb. 1923, pr. 1924
Anthony and Anna, pb. 1925, pr. 1926
The First Mrs. Fraser, pr., pb. 1929
Boyd's Shop, pr., pb. 1936
Robert's Wife, pr. 1937, pb. 1938
William John Mawhinney, pr. 1940 (also as
   Ballyfarland's Festival, pr. 1953)
Friends and Relations, pr. 1941, pb. 1947
Private Enterprise, pr. 1947, pb. 1948
My Brother Tom, pr., pb. 1952
Esperanza, pr. 1957
Selected Plays of St. John Ervine, pb. 1988

OTHER LITERARY FORMS

St. John Ervine was the author of several novels that were highly regarded in their day. His novels, such as *Mrs. Martin's Man* (1914) and *The Foolish Lovers* (1920), display the same strengths as the best of his plays—realism and clarity of design and structure. Ervine also wrote abrasive and controversial drama criticism for several newspapers. Finally, he was the author of several opinionated biographies of literary and public figures, including Oscar Wilde and George Bernard Shaw.

ACHIEVEMENTS

St. John Ervine holds an honorable place in the Irish Literary Renaissance; as such, he is aligned with William Butler Yeats, Lady Augusta Gregory, and the Abbey Theatre. His greatest achievements are his early Irish plays, two of which, *Jane Clegg* and *John Ferguson*, have long been recognized as minor clas-

sics. After a brief time as manager of the Abbey Theatre followed by wartime military service, Ervine settled in England and was chosen as a member of the Irish Academy. He served as professor of dramatic literature for the Royal Society of Literature from 1933 through 1936. His critical theory supports his practice in his early plays: Dramatic value resides in the author's attempt to present real people dealing with believable human situations. Though he turned from playwriting to novels, criticism, and political and biographical essays, Ervine is best remembered as a spokesperson for and practitioner of dramatic realism. His influence on a later generation of Irish playwrights, while indirect, may be seen in the continuation of the realistic tradition. Ervine serves as an exemplar of honest, realistic, economically plotted, straightforward playwriting.

BIOGRAPHY

St. John Greer Ervine was born in Belfast in Northern Ireland on December 28, 1883. He did not take a university degree but was writing plays by age twenty-four. In 1911, he married Leonora Mary Davis and became associated with the Abbey Theatre in Dublin. He served for a brief time as manager of the Abbey Theatre and, in that capacity, produced his best play, *John Ferguson*. His British sympathies caused an estrangement between him and the theater players, and on May 29, 1916, the actors declared their unwillingness to work under Ervine's direction. The resultant break with the Abbey Theatre, combined with the escalation of World War I, led Ervine to turn away from Ireland and exclusively Irish subject matter. His service in a regiment of the British Household Battalion and, later, with the Royal Dublin Fusiliers ended in 1918, when he was severely wounded and suffered the loss of a leg.

After the war, Ervine settled in London. His first London success was in 1929, when his play, *The First Mrs. Fraser*, enjoyed an extended run. That success was repeated the next year in New York. His career expanded to include novels, essays on political and ethical subjects, drama criticism, and biographies. He was drama critic for *The Sunday Observer* of London, and in 1929, he was guest drama critic for *The World* in New York. His criticism was controversial, which is usually attributed to Ervine's plainspoken, even harsh criticism of American plays. His reputation for acerbity rests additionally on his style. Abandoning his polished, sophisticated prose, he wrote in an approximation of a "Broadway" dialect; this caused at least as much outrage as his astringent critical judgments. Indeed, this choice of dialect seems to have been a mistake. As dialect, it is not accurate, and its use seems patronizing, even if that was not Ervine's intent.

After his return to London, Ervine served for three years as professor of dramatic literature for the Royal Society of Literature. His later plays, written after he left Ireland, are less serious than his early work. These later plays, written for a British audience, are sophisticated comedies of manners that rely on wit and topicality for their very considerable effect. Ervine's biographical subjects included men of letters such as Shaw and Wilde; William Booth, founder and General of the Salvation Army; and Lord Craigavon, the first prime minister of Ulster. His biographies reflect his literary, ethical, and political interests. They are partisan rather than objective, polemical rather than scholarly.

With the production of *William John Mawhinney* in 1940, Ervine renewed his association with the Abbey Theatre; one of his next plays, *Friends and Relations*, was produced at the Abbey Theatre in 1941. These were the last of Ervine's works to premiere at the Abbey Theatre, however, and in 1957, Ervine completed his theatrical career with the production of *Esperanza*. Ervine died in 1971, at the age of eighty-seven.

ANALYSIS

St. John Ervine's early plays are good plays, strong and believable in their economy and in characters who force the viewer to accept plots that have become clichés. The deliberate simplicity of construction, the unity of tone and theme, the absolutely vital characters, make Ervine an important playwright. His plays are not complex or difficult to understand; their value lies precisely in their accessibility and believability.

Ervine's early Irish plays are his finest, displaying the strengths characteristic of his best work in all genres. *Mixed Marriage*, *Jane Clegg*, *John Ferguson*, and *The Ship* are uniformly serious in plot and theme, realistic in subject matter, and economical in structure. Ervine's virtues as a playwright are traditional ones; each play has a single, unified plot and an unambiguous, uncomplicated theme. Each play displays great economy of construction and a modest level of aspiration, and within this deliberately simple, unassuming framework, it succeeds because of certain very real strengths of structure and characterization.

ECONOMY

In his drama criticism, Ervine's touchstone is economy. In every important way, the early plays illustrate that Ervine believed in and followed his own theory. Economy is not a negative value of limiting, cutting, and leaving out; it is, rather, a positive principle. Good theater, to Ervine, is that which exhibits restraint and simplicity in cast size, subject matter, plot line, dialogue, and characterization.

The casts, for example, are uniformly small. *John Ferguson* has the largest cast; there are eleven characters. *Jane Clegg* has seven; *The Ship*, eight; and *Mixed Marriage*, six. There are simply no minor characters whose dramatic function may be described as merely decorative. Every character is important and necessary to the development of the action of the play.

The action of each play is also dictated in part by Ervine's rule of economy. On a superficial level, his plays are devoid of luxuries such as tableau scenes, offstage voices, and unnecessary dramatic business. There is a minimum of exposition; for the most part, each play consists only of those events that are seen by the audience. The exposition in *John Ferguson*, for example, is limited to the information that the Fergusons are going to lose their farm unless they manage to pay the mortgage; the audience learns of the successive trials of John Ferguson's faith in a just God as Ferguson himself experiences them. The exposition in *Jane Clegg* is limited to the information that Henry Clegg has been unfaithful to his wife in the past. This immediacy of action is present in all the early plays. Nothing *has* happened; everything happens onstage during the course of the play.

The plays are all limited to a single plot, which is usually a familiar one and which is uniformly serious. Each of the long plays consists of a single story whose content is that of everyday life. *Jane Clegg* deals with the failure of a marriage, *John Ferguson* with the loss of a farm and the destruction of a family through violence. *The Ship* is a study of the lack of communication between a strong-willed father and his son. *Mixed Marriage* deals with the public forces that destroy the private romance of a Protestant boy and a Catholic girl. The stories are familiar ones, and Ervine does not alter his material so that it appears to be anything other than what it essentially is—newspaper realism, known territory to everyone. At the same time, there is always a single sustained idea that informs and illuminates the play.

The dialogue of Ervine's plays also exhibits his characteristic economy. The language of all the early plays is simple and easily understood and has as its function the furthering of the plot and the revelation of character. Dialogue, Ervine believed, should sound artlessly natural but should actually be an artful construct. None of Ervine's characters chatters aimlessly; no one repeats himself or leaves a sentence or thought unfinished. Ervine eliminates those parts of ordinary talk that would produce conversation rather than dialogue. Even when his characters are supposed to be merely making conversation, there is no excess. Each seemingly meaningless sentence is working to establish character. Again, the principle of economy is used as a positive force to shape an element of Ervine's plays.

The characters in Ervine's plays are, like his plots, familiar and instantly recognizable types, yet they are also extremely believable and vital. The character of Jane Clegg is strong and able to bear suffering; Rainey of *Mixed Marriage* and John Thurlow of *The Ship* are egotists. In each character, there is a single, prevailing element of personality, and each character becomes real and believable within his own "humor." The characters are drawn with little internal complexity; they are not cowardly *and* brave, but rather cowardly *or* brave. Like his dialogue, Ervine's characters appear to be natural but are in fact artful constructs.

PLOT

One can appreciate Ervine's art most fully by examining the elements of plot and character in his early plays. In general, the plot is the weakest element of each play. All the plays have plots associated with melodrama. *John Ferguson* is the story of a family whose farm is lost to the evil landlord who forecloses, rapes the daughter, and is murdered by the son. *Jane Clegg* is the story of the strong, long-suffering wife who holds her family together while her husband loses her money, embezzles company funds, and finally runs away with a younger woman. *Mixed Marriage* deals with young lovers surrounded by the chaos of a strike that rapidly becomes a religious war; ultimately, the lovers are destroyed by the religious bigotry of the Protestant father. *The Ship* is the story of a strong-willed father who builds a ship that "God couldn't sink" and forces his son to sail on her maiden voyage. The son, who has refused to enter the family business, dies when the ship is sunk after colliding with an iceberg. The plots are both melodramatic and highly conventional. There are no surprising turns, no innovative twists in the action.

An important technique that Ervine used to control the response of the audience is one that is closely related to satire. Within the structure of the plot, there is always an explicit norm with which the audience can identify. The plots of the early plays make, in some way, an attack on stupidity, and there is usually a character who explicitly represents the sane, moral position of playwright and audience. Jane Clegg, John Ferguson, Old Mrs. Thurlow, and Mrs. Rainey are articulate spokespersons for the standards of good sense and morality. One recognizes the standard they offer and judges the other characters and the plot development by this explicit norm.

The plots of the four plays hinge on dramatic irony of the simplest, most basic sort. John Ferguson's family is destroyed because his brother forgot to mail the money that would have saved the farm; Jack Thurlow dies because his father asks him to sail with the ship just this once. John Rainey loses his children because his religious prejudice is stronger than his desire to unite the Protestant and Catholic strikers.

Although the plots of these plays are simple and melodramatic, this is not a serious weakness in Ervine's art. Perhaps a playwright cannot create great drama from this material, but he can create great theater. Ervine asks his audience to respond in a rather uncomplicated, unsophisticated manner; he manages to get an audience, conditioned to dismiss plots of this nature as slight and hackneyed, to believe implicitly in his stories. The audience understands the familiar, unambiguous plots and themes, applauds the hero and hisses the villain, but not with the self-conscious condescension that one would bring to minstrel-show melodrama. The audience reacts in an unsophisticated way to the plays, but it reacts sincerely.

CHARACTERS

In large part, this response can be attributed to the vitality of Ervine's characters. His best characters are universal types: The audience recognizes the villainous landlord or the foolish, irritating mother-in-law with a shock of pleasure. Each character is also, within his or her type, absolutely individual.

Ervine is particularly good with certain types of characters. His villains are all lifelike and effective. They are of two types: The first is the unpleasant little vermin, such as Jimmy Caesar in *John Ferguson*; Henry Clegg and the racing tout, Munce, in *Jane Clegg*; and Captain Cornelius in *The Ship*. The second type is the monster of evil, such as Witherow in *John Ferguson*. The villain Witherow has no redeeming qualities; he is unalterably evil. He is a brilliantly drawn one-dimensional character; the audience hates him and is appeased by his death.

Jimmy Caesar and the other little villains are villainous because they are weak and mean-spirited. They are more satisfactory characters than is Witherow because they are more complex, and the audience is able to despise them as well as hate them. They are all incapable of anything as large and important as a foreclosure or a rape. Their villainies are secret and unsavory; they are all cowards. Captain Cornelius is willing to accept money from John Thurlow in return for ruining Jack's farm; Munce is quite willing to ruin

lives to get his money from Henry Clegg; Henry himself leaves his wife, children, and mother penniless for another woman and cannot understand why no one is terribly sorry to see him go. Jimmy Caesar, the most vividly drawn of the weak villains, is the unsavory suitor of Hannah Ferguson; he grovels at Witherow's feet, nauseates Hannah when he tries to kiss her, goes home to bed when he is supposedly avenging her honor, eats a hearty breakfast while he confesses his cowardice, and offers to marry Hannah even though her rape has made her "unworthy" of him.

In Mrs. Rainey, Old Mrs. Thurlow, and John Ferguson, Ervine creates strong, sympathetic moral characters. John Ferguson, for example, is uniformly good without being unrealistic. He is devout, gentle, and forgiving, yet, unlike many virtuous characters, absolutely convincing. His moments of doubt are canceled by his monumental Christian goodness and faith. He is a truly decent man who keeps his faith in a just God even as he mourns his ruined son and daughter. Like John Ferguson, Mrs. Rainey in *Mixed Marriage* is consistently good, tender and protective toward her sons, sensible and tolerant toward Michael O'Hara, their Catholic friend, and gentle with Nora, Hugh's girlfriend. Most important, she manages to love her husband even though she has no respect for him and disapproves of his tenaciously held prejudices. Mrs. Rainey, Old Mrs. Thurlow, and John Ferguson are all voices of sanity in situations that have suddenly gone insane. Mrs. Rainey pleads for religious tolerance in the middle of a religious war; John Ferguson tries to love and protect the man who has taken his farm and raped his daughter; Old Mrs. Thurlow of *The Ship* tries to reconcile her son and grandson, and when Jack dies in his father's place, she comforts and encourages John Thurlow to continue to live with unchanged goals even though she believes him to be wrong.

OTHER MAJOR WORKS

LONG FICTION: *Francis Place, the Tailor of Charing Cross*, 1912; *Mrs. Martin's Man*, 1914; *Alice and a Family*, 1915; *The Foolish Lovers*, 1920; *The First Mrs. Fraser*, 1931 (novelization of his play).

NONFICTION: *The Organized Theatre: A Plea in Civics*, 1924; *Parnell*, 1925; *How to Write a Play*, 1928; *God's Soldier: General William Booth*, 1934; *The Christian and the New Morality*, 1940; *Oscar Wilde*, 1951; *Bernard Shaw: His Life, Work and Friends*, 1956.

BIBLIOGRAPHY

Bell, Sam Hanna. *The Theatre in Ulster*. Totowa, N.J.: Rowman and Littlefield, 1972. Bell considers Ervine as an Ulster dramatist and compares his work with that of other playwrights of his generation from Northern Ireland. Discusses briefly productions of Ervine's works and mentions their main social and cultural features, though the brevity of this study's overview limits discussion.

Cronin, John. Introduction to *Selected Plays of St. John Ervine*. Washington, D.C.: Catholic University of America Press, 1988. Contains *Mixed Marriage*, *Jane Clegg*, *John Ferguson*, *Boyd's Shop*, and *Friends and Relations*. The introduction provides biographical information and establishes a cultural context for Ervine's work. Includes extracts from Ervine's dramaturgical writings and a bibliography of Ervine's dramatic and numerous other works.

Hogan, Robert, and James Kilroy. *The Modern Irish Drama: A Documentary History*. 6 vols. Atlantic Highlands, N.J.: Humanities Press, 1975-1992. A multivolume history of Irish drama, including dramatists such as Ervine.

Hunt, Hugh. *The Abbey: Ireland's National Theatre, 1904-1978*. New York: Columbia University Press, 1979. This historical narrative deals in passing with Ervine's plays. Provides a more detailed description of the playwright's sojourn as manager of the Abbey Theatre and assesses its effects. Includes a full list of productions at the Abbey from the theater's foundation, facilitating a preliminary chronology of Ervine's dramatic career there.

Maxwell, D. E. S. *A Critical History of Modern Irish Drama, 1891-1980*. Cambridge, England: Cambridge University Press, 1984. Locates Ervine's drama in the context of developments in realism in the Irish theater and provides a critical analysis of his most noteworthy plays. Draws attention to the Ulster origins of much of Ervine's dramatic material. Contains a bibliography and a chronology of Irish theater.

Elizabeth Buckmaster,
updated by George O'Brien

SIR GEORGE ETHEREGE

Born: Maidenhead(?), England; c. 1635
Died: Paris(?), France; c. May 10, 1691

PRINCIPAL DRAMA

The Comical Revenge: Or, Love in a Tub, pr., pb. 1664

She Would if She Could, pr., pb. 1668

The Man of Mode: Or, Sir Fopling Flutter, pr., pb. 1676

OTHER LITERARY FORMS

In addition to his drama, Sir George Etherege wrote poetry, collected and published posthumously in *Poems* (1963). His correspondence is collected in *The Letterbook of Sir George Etherege* (1928) and *Letters of Sir George Etherege* (1973).

ACHIEVEMENTS

In the amazingly vital and varied drama that developed, flourished, and faded in London within a few decades after the restoration of Charles II to the throne in 1660, the most important type was the so-called comedy of manners. The comedy of manners was characterized by strong contemporary realism, by resolution of the main plot in marriage, and by pairs of characters arranged in a hierarchy of wit, from the most witty down to the most foolish. In the Restoration drama, wit is determined in part by the ability of individuals to get their own way and in part by their social grace, best exemplified in the witty (meaning comic, ingenious, and psychologically astute) verbal duels with which the plays abound. It was Sir George Etherege's achievement to develop and define this distinctive Restoration form in *The Comical Revenge* and *She Would if She Could* and to bring it to full maturity in *The Man of Mode*.

BIOGRAPHY

Sir George Etherege's life resembled those of the wits, courtiers, and rakes who populate his plays. When he was born, his father had a small place at court. In 1644, during the civil war, when the queen escaped to France, Etherege's father followed her into exile, where he died in 1650. Etherege himself was probably reared by his grandfather in England, obtaining along the way a good education and an excellent knowledge of French. In 1654, he was appointed a clerk to George Goswold, an attorney at Beaconsfield. In 1668, *The Comical Revenge*, Etherege's first play, was performed at Lincoln's Inn Fields. It was well received, and Etherege's reputation was at once established. His next play, *She Would if She Could*, was performed at Lincoln's Inn Fields in 1668. Although a better play than the first, it was poorly rehearsed and badly performed, and it fared very poorly. By this time, Etherege was a member of the circle of courtiers and wits that included Sir Charles Sedley and the earl of Rochester. He was made a gentleman of the Privy Chamber and went, as secretary to the ambassador, to Constantinople. Etherege returned to London in 1671, and for the next few years he, along with the earl of Rochester, was mixed up in several wild and rather unsavory scrapes, resulting in at least one death.

In 1676, *The Man of Mode* was performed at the Duke's Theatre in Dorset Garden. Remembering his earlier failure, Etherege was careful to have a first-class performance, with the top actors of the period playing the principal parts, particularly Thomas Betterton, the most famous actor of his time, who took the role of Dorimant. This major play was, as it de-

served to be, an enormous success. During this period, Etherege was knighted and then married a rich old widow, daughter of a London merchant. By 1683, he was rapidly squandering his wife's wealth on cards and dice at Locket's, a popular coffeehouse. He was offered a minor diplomatic post, under King James II, at the Diet of the Holy Roman Empire in Regensburg, Bavaria. He gladly accepted the appointment, possibly escaping heavy gambling debts in London and certainly leaving his unloved wife behind. He outraged and antagonized the staid and pompous German ministers there with his informal behavior. During this period, he carried on widespread correspondence. Almost four hundred letters have been preserved, which give the best existing portrait of the life and thoughts of a Restoration playwright and wit. When James II was deposed in 1689, Etherege left his post to try to join him in France. Etherege died, possibly first converting to Roman Catholicism, in 1691.

ANALYSIS

Sir George Etherege developed and refined the comedy of manners with his dramatic works. The developmental process is evident in his first work, *The Comical Revenge*, and the fruition of his efforts is revealed in his *The Man of Mode*.

THE COMICAL REVENGE

Etherege's first play, *The Comical Revenge*, has no discernible main plot. Rather, it has four more or less unconnected subplots. Three of the plots are derivative of earlier drama; the fourth constitutes Etherege's real contribution to dramatic form. The first of the derivative plots is the "heroic" plot, based no doubt on the romantic plays of Francis Beaumont and John Fletcher (still very popular during this period) and of Sir William Davenant. When the characters of this plot, with their characteristically romantic names, come onstage, the play's usual prose dialogue shifts to rhyming verse. The action in this subplot revolves around highly stylized conflicts between love and honor. Graciana and Lord Beaufort are madly in love. By mischance, however, Graciana's brother has told his best friend, Colonel Bruce, that Graciana will marry him. Colonel Bruce does not care particularly about Graciana, whom he has not met, but would like to be connected to the family of his best friend. Secretly, Graciana's sister Aurelia is madly in love with Bruce but out of honor cannot tell him. When Colonel Bruce discovers that Beaufort might be his rival for Graciana, he fights a duel with him, is disarmed but is magnanimously given his life by Beaufort. Not to be outdone in honor, Bruce falls on his sword. As he lies grievously wounded, Graciana feels honor-bound to pretend to Beaufort that she never loved him but only led him on to test Bruce's love for her. She pledges to Bruce that if he survives she will marry him; if he dies, she will remain forever a virgin. At the last minute, everybody accidentally overhears everybody else confessing his and her true thoughts. All are overcome by how honorable all the rest are, and the right couples get together and live happily ever after.

The second plot is low farcical comedy of a kind to delight those who guffaw at dialect jokes and pratfalls. The humor is meant to come in part from the nearly unintelligible French accent of the servant, Dufoy ("Begar me vil havé de revengé"), and in part from his situation. He looks pale and unhealthy, and when people ask the cause, he claims he is languishing from unrequited love for Betty, a waiting woman. Actually, it soon comes out, he is languishing from a venereal disease. Betty, highly indignant when she discovers that he has been pretending to love her, locks him up in a washtub (the "comical revenge," or "love in a tub" of the title), providing opportunities for various farcical jokes. In the "happy ending," it appears that Dufoy and Betty actually *are* to get married. It is difficult to guess how boisterously audiences may have responded to this kind of comedy.

The third plot seems to derive from the comedy of Ben Jonson, or perhaps of Thomas Middleton. It involves Sir Nicholas Cully, who, as his name suggests, is a gull waiting to be swindled. He falls into the clutches of Wheadle and Palmer, two con artists; thinking all the time that he is the one who is doing the swindling, Cully gets the treatment he deserves. What separates this plot from the first two is its astonishing, almost documentary realism: The

language of the street plays against the absurdly elevated "torments" and "despair" of the heroic scenes and the theatrically conventional burlesque French accent of Dufoy. For example, Wheadle and Palmer, having maneuvered Cully into a tavern to play cards, want to shift from the public table where they are seated to a back-room table, where they can cheat their victim in private. Finding a pretext for this move, one of them says, "this table is so wet, there's no playing upon it." That may be the first time in the history of the drama that a character mentions something so homely and realistic as the wetness of a table that has had several glasses and bottles sitting on it.

The fourth plot, which in the play gets no more emphasis than the other three, constitutes Etherege's major contribution to Restoration drama and was to become the central plot of his two comedies to follow. It involves Sir Frederick Frollick, a young rake and gallant and wit about town. Audiences were no doubt accustomed to the nonspecific, timeless settings of William Shakespeare and to the remote and imaginary settings of the romantic plays of Beaumont and Fletcher. Suddenly, Sir Frederick walks in off the very London streets the playgoers themselves have just quitted to see this play. The language he speaks is their language, and the class to which he belongs is theirs. His conversation is topical. He is indeed a sad young rake, keeping his wench, intriguing with dozens of women, drinking, carousing, fighting, breaking windows, and otherwise tearing about. He is also, at least to a degree, witty, fashionable, and genteel. As the wealthy widow he is chasing throughout the play admits, he is "the prettiest, wittiest, wildest gentleman about the town." Having gone through his fortune, he must court and wed the widow to mend his estate, as Etherege himself was to do a few years later.

The play as a whole is not memorable. Except for the moments of fine realism in the swindling scenes, the motivation for actions and the conflicts to be overcome are all weakly contrived. The four plots are but faintly connected. At the end, all the players—servants, whores, swindlers, rakes, and romantic lovers—are improbably brought onstage together in a mass marriage ceremony. With the exception of this unlikely event, they could as easily have been in separate plays.

Still, the play contained important innovations, and Etherege, shrewdly observing his audience, must have seen their delight and response to his contemporary rake speaking their language and frequenting the same places of pleasure as they did. He must also have recognized his facility in rendering such a character (so like himself) and his witty language. He made such characters the center of his subsequent plays, wisely phasing out the other subplots or rather disguising, shifting, and transforming them until they were no longer recognizable, serving instead as underpinnings to his main plot.

SHE WOULD IF SHE COULD

Etherege's second play, *She Would if She Could*, is a considerable refinement on *The Comical Revenge*. The structure is clearer, simpler, and the actions more logically motivated. Three plot lines are discernible, but one of these is clearly the major plot, and the two minor plots are closely integrated with it, supporting its actions and commenting on it thematically. Most important, in the play as a whole, the contrast between the Truewit and the Witwoud, or would-be wit, has become central, setting the pattern for the great comedies of manners of the period.

The Witwouds are at the center of the two minor plots. In one subplot, Sir Oliver Cockwood is a "country knight." In the social geography of the Restoration stage, the courtiers, rakes, and the stylish and witty women all live in the "town," the fashionable West End of London. The "city" is the commercial part of London, where the "cits," the much despised middle class, live. Worst of all, however, is the country. For the wits, the chief pleasures in life were found in association with town and court: the coffeehouses, the playhouses, the pleasure resorts, the fashionable clothing. The severest penance, therefore, would be to live in the country, where everything is several years out of date, where the only diversion is going for long walks. Witty young people forced to live in the country by cruel parents who do not trust them among the seductions of London are justified in using any means to escape to the town. Older people from the country are automatically assumed to be foolish and out of fashion.

Sir Oliver Cockwood is typical of the country knights. His name, to begin with, is appropriate (the "wood" having the sense of "would-be"), since his annoyed wife charges that he is impotent. If he stayed in the country, got drunk every night, and hunted foxes during the day, no one would object to him. His fault is that he has come to town to act like a young rake and to boast of all of his amorous adventures. He spends most of his time running away from his wife to make ineffectual dates with prostitutes. He becomes a comic butt because of his pretensions to being a man of honor (that is, a duelist and a lover) when he is actually timid and impotent.

In the other subplot, his wife, Lady Cockwood, is equally well named, though with an opposite signification. She tries to make assignations with any young man who will look at her. The problem is that she also wants to maintain her reputation for honor and virtue. She becomes a comic butt because of her pretensions to being modest and chaste, when it is obvious to everyone that she would readily be unchaste if she could. Interestingly, Lady Cockwood's language is a burlesqued echo of the heroic or romantic scenes of *The Comical Revenge*. Her dialogue is filled with such words as "honor," "ruined," "undone," "betrayed," and "false," but with the meanings comically reversed. If a young rake fails to keep his assignation with her, he is "wicked." If he finally does show up to commit adultery with her, "truly he is a person of much worth and honor."

The subplots in which these foolish persons partake, by giving examples of Witwouds—failed Truewits— provide a backdrop against which the Truewits of the main plot can be measured. These Truewits are the young men Courtall and Freeman and the young women Gatty and Ariana. The young men are considerable refinements on Sir Frederick Frollick of *The Comical Revenge*. For example, Frollick's idea of courtship is to get drunk and go to his lady's window in the wee hours of the morning to shout out ribald suggestions to her. He marries at the end a wealthy widow, behavior that Etherege himself was not above. Courtall is above it. He is much more self-assured than Frollick and has his drives, emotions, and true feelings absolutely under control—an important sign of the Truewit. Losing control, however, and thus putting himself at the mercy of others, is the unmistakable sign of the Witwoud. Courtall needs to marry a rich heiress but will not consider a widow. His wife, in addition to being rich, must also be young, beautiful, as witty as he, and untouched by other men.

Of particular interest in this play are the roles of the female characters. Lady Cockwood is an archetypal character—the lustful woman—who has appeared in both comedy and tragedy from the classical drama onward. Etherege, however, makes specific Restoration uses of her. She is made comic by her pretension to heroic virtue and by the fact that she has so little control of her emotions that she gives herself away at every word. By the lights of the Restoration society, she is not wrong in wishing to have a reputation for chastity, for without such a reputation a woman was lost (with the exception of mistresses of high royalty). At the same time, she was not wrong to possess sexual desire, for women, in this realistic society, were allowed to have at least moderate appetites. She was wrong, and therefore comic, in her extreme pretension of virtue, in her extreme libidinousness, and in her consequent inability to control herself. Control of self was highly valued in Restoration theater because only through self-control, so it was believed, could one's external world be controlled. The world of Restoration theater is one in which a person must control himself or be controlled. Courtall, for example, by pretending to be interested in her, used Lady Cockwood in order to gain access to Gatty and Ariana, who are staying in her house, and then uses her desire to save her reputation to fend her off. He fends her off, interestingly, because her overeagerness has rendered her undesirable.

Gatty and Ariana represent the feminine witty ideal. Envious of the men for their freedom (which the women cannot have, for reputation is important), they decide, while resolving "to be mighty honest" to have as much fun as circumstances will allow. They put on masks (very popular at the time) to disguise their identities and go strolling in the fashionable Mulberry Garden in hopes of flirting innocently with some handsome and witty men. Though the men whom they encounter (Courtall and Freeman) are tremendously attractive to them, the women easily fend them off with witty conversation and a dissembling of their emotions. This response does not mean that they lack emotions, for in private they admit to each other how much the men tempt them. As Gatty says to Ariana: "I hate to dissemble when I need not. 'Twould look as affected in us to be reserved now we're alone as for a player to maintain the character she acts in the tiring [dressing] room." The scene is in direct contrast with the scene in which Lady Cockwood sends out her maid to pimp for her and then scolds her (even though they are in private) for doing so.

She Would if She Could, in short, is a didactic play, suggesting which emotions, which pretenses, which modes of behavior are proper—that is, witty—and which are not. The modern theatergoer, losing sight of this and responding to the play as simply a realistic social document, can misinterpret it in certain ways, seeing cruelty, for example, where a Restoration theatergoer would see a didactic point being made.

The finest thing of all in *She Would if She Could* is the witty love dialogue between Courtall and Freeman and the two women. Their first encounter is quite delightful. The girls, in their masks, are strolling through the Mulberry Garden. When Courtall and Freeman see them, they immediately set out after them, planning to engage them in witty repartee, but the women, who have been brought up in the country, are such swift walkers that the men are soon panting and puffing, quite unable to overtake them. Freeman says, "Whatever faults they have, they cannot be broken-winded."

When the men finally do catch up, the women are equally nimble verbally. When the men insist on kissing their hands, Ariana says, "Well, I am not the first unfortunate woman that has been forced to give her hand where she never intends to bestow her heart." They part, agreeing to meet again the next day, each side immensely pleased with the other (though of course the women have not admitted their feelings). The jealous Lady Cockwood, hoping to win the two men for herself, starts a rumor that the men have spoken slightly of Gatty's and Ariana's honor. The next time Gatty and Ariana meet with the innocent and unsuspecting men, their witty banter suddenly has real bite and sting to it. The men, puzzled by the shift in tone, scarcely know how to reply. The dialogue is wonderfully witty; at the same time, it is subtly and dramatically revelatory of the inner states of the characters.

THE MAN OF MODE

Etherege's last play, *The Man of Mode*, is in every respect a major work and remains the central document of Restoration comedy. The brilliant opening act is so relaxed and casual as to seem like a slice of life rather than the first act of a tightly constructed play. A minor poet of the time even alluded to Etherege as "one that does presume to say,/ A plot's too gross for any play." Such an impression is deceptive, however, for every word in the first act carefully defines characters and sets up the complex chain of events to follow. On the surface, the first act is a very naturalistic presentation of Dorimant (whose name suggests "the gift of love") in the morning. He is composing a letter to his current mistress, whose suggestive name is Loveit. When his friend Medley drops in on him, it emerges in conversation between them that he is tired of Loveit and wants to break off with her so he can begin with a new girl, Bellinda. He plans to use Bellinda in his plot to break with Loveit, who is passionately jealous; Bellinda will call on her just before Dorimant is expected to arrive, and she will insinuate that Dorimant has been seeing someone else. Dorimant will walk in, and Loveit, who has no control of her emotions, will fall on him in a passion; he will then instantly break with her and stalk out. While Dorimant is recounting his plot to Medley, an old woman selling fruit arrives at his door. She is, in addition, a bawd who keeps a watchful eye out for young women in whom young men might be interested. She brings information to Dorimant that an extremely beautiful and wealthy heiress has come to town and has seen Dorimant and is attracted to him. The woman's name is Harriet, and she has been brought to town from the country by her mother, Lady Woodvill. Dorimant immediately begins plot-

ting to get to know her. Young Bellair, another friend, drops in, and Medley and Dorimant begin teasing him about his coming marriage to Emilia. Marriage, to the young rakes, is nearly equivalent to suicide, as it means the end of their bachelor freedom and a limitation on their openly chasing after new mistresses. Young Bellair is in love and takes their teasing lightly. Then they discuss Sir Fopling Flutter, newly arrived in town from a long stay in Paris. Fopling wants desperately to be a true-wit, but he is in every way the opposite of Dorimant. Where Dorimant dresses well, Fopling dresses extravagantly. Where Dorimant has several affairs, Fopling strives only for the reputation of having several affairs. Where Dorimant is casually witty and literate, Fopling works hard to achieve these graces, even affecting a French accent (the last lingering echo of Dufoy in *The Comical Revenge*) to let everyone know he has been abroad. Dorimant decides to use him in his plot to break with Loveit: He will pretend to be jealous himself and charge her with chasing after Fopling.

At this point, a messenger calls Young Bellair outside the room, and while he is out, Dorimant confesses to Medley that he has encouraged Young Bellair to marry Emilia. Dorimant has tried in the past to seduce her, with no luck. He thinks that once she is married and no longer needs to worry about her maidenhood, she will be more accessible to him. Young Bellair comes back in with the news that his father, Old Bellair, is in town. The father, not knowing anything about Emilia, has conspired with Lady Woodvill to arrange a marriage between Young Bellair and Harriet. If Young Bellair does not agree to the marriage, he will lose his inheritance. Young Bellair leaves in distress. As a last bit of business in the act, before Dorimant and Medley go off to dine, Dorimant receives a note from a former girlfriend fallen on hard times and sends her some money.

No brief summary can hope to render the quality of this act, one of the finest things in Restoration drama. The witty repartee, the different levels of language, the naturalness, all make it a virtuoso performance, but one should not lose sight of the function of the act in terms of the unfolding action of the play. First, it has introduced Dorimant, the main character.

He is witty, relaxed, capable of dealing with all social classes on their own terms, shamefully indulgent of his servants, most of whom have not yet got out of bed by the end of the act. At the same time, he is the supreme gallant, with, as Medley says of him, "more mistresses now depending" than the most eminent lawyer in England has cases. The audience sees abundant proof of this. In the course of one morning, he is forming plans to cast off one mistress, Loveit, as he begins to close with a new one, Bellinda, and tries to get Emilia married off in hopes that matrimony will make her more vulnerable to him. At the same time, he is already beginning to think ahead to Harriet, whom he has not even met and, at last, sends money to a girlfriend from sometime in the past. The audience also gets an insight into Dorimant's modus operandi. He thinks in terms of power plays and manipulation. People, to him, are to be used: He employs the fruiterer to bring him information on new beauties come to town. He uses his mistress-to-be to help him break off with Loveit, and Young Bellair to make Emilia more accessible. He also plans to use Fopling in his plot to rid himself of Loveit. He states his attitude more baldly in a later scene: "You mistake the use of fools, they are designed for properties and not for friends." In this respect, almost all are fools to Dorimant.

In addition to Dorimant, the first act introduces the audience to two other major characters, Medley and Young Bellair, and gives capsule profiles to prepare the audience in advance for seeing the other important characters: Loveit, Fopling, Old Bellair, Lady Woodvill, and Harriet. Finally, the groundwork is laid for the main action of the play, Dorimant's pursuit of Harriet, and for the four subplots: Dorimant's breaking off with Loveit; his coming to terms with his new mistress, Bellinda; Young Bellair's attempt to marry the woman he loves without being disinherited; and the fun they will all have with the foolish Sir Fopling Flutter, especially when Dorimant tries to foist him off on Loveit.

The play now unrolls quickly. Old Bellair meets Emilia and, not knowing she is his son's fiancée, begins chasing her himself. She humors him in his infatuation, hoping it will help later when she confesses her love for his son. In the meantime, Young Bellair has met Harriet. Harriet has no intention of marrying him but has only pretended to go along with the match as an excuse to get out of the country and come to London. She and Young Bellair act out a courtship for the sake of their parents, in order to buy time. At the proper moment, Young Bellair and Emilia sneak off and get married. They fall on their knees before Old Bellair, and he is prevailed on to give them his blessing. He cannot say his son has made a bad choice, as it was the choice he was thinking of making himself.

In the meantime, Dorimant's plans go off almost but not quite perfectly. Loveit rages at him jealously, and he storms off, charging her with chasing after Fopling. Bellinda is timid but at last submits to a meeting with him in his room, but Loveit is suspicious and almost catches Bellinda in the act, so that Bellinda would have lost her reputation on her very first fall from grace. She cleverly talks her way out of being discovered but vows never to take such a chance again. Dorimant, though charging Loveit with receiving Fopling's advances (as an excuse for dropping her), still wants her to spurn Fopling publicly, thus showing that he holds complete power even over a cast-off mistress. He even brings Medley along to be a witness to Fopling's discomfiture. Loveit, however, realizing that Dorimant is using her, greets Fopling with open arms and walks off with him. Medley jibes: "Would you had brought some more of your friends, Dorimant, to have been witnesses of Sir Fopling's disgrace and your triumph." Dorimant begs Medley not to tell everyone for a few days, to give him a chance to make amends. He wants his reputation as a perfect manipulator of women to remain intact. In the meantime, Dorimant has met Harriet, and they have a duel of brilliant repartee, almost like the love song of two wary but amorous birds of prey.

The final scene shows Dorimant in high gear, running from woman to woman, keeping all bridges unburned. First, he convinces Loveit that he is courting Harriet only for her fortune, as he has gone through his own inheritance, and that he will come back to her as soon as he can. She is sufficiently satisfied to snub Fopling publicly the next time he enters—and Medley declares Dorimant's reputation clear. Dorimant convinces Bellinda that she should take another chance with him, keeps his lines of communication open with Emilia, and gains permission from Lady Woodvill to pay his court to Harriet. A marriage seems in the offing, but it has not happened by the end of the play, and Dorimant is still free to go in any direction he chooses.

It is a play, then, in which a vain, arrogant man, renowned for his deceptions, seductions, cruel manipulations, and constant infidelities, has by the end achieved the admiration of all the men, has all the women at his beck, and has the prospect of a rich, witty, beautiful young girl's hand in marriage. It may seem a considerable leap to maintain that *The Man of Mode* is a didactic play (even liberated modern audiences have difficulty with the morality of the play), but such it is. Although courtship is at the center of Restoration drama, *The Man of Mode* and similar masterpieces of the period are not romantic works; on the contrary, they are cynically realistic. The plays abound with cautionary examples of bad marriages—marriages inappropriately arranged by parents, resulting in spouses who detest each other, are rude to each other in public, and betray each other at every chance—or, at the other extreme, "love" matches in which neither partner has any money, condemned to sink into sordidness. The appropriate marriage is one in which at least one of the partners has enough money to make them both comfortable for life (because a gentleman, by definition, does not work for a living) and the partners are so perfectly matched in wit and attractiveness that they can continue to be interesting and exciting to each other even after the novelty of the chase is over. It is a serious and realistic business, and a misstep has the lifetime repercussion of an unhappy marriage. That is why this drama can be so ruthless and competitive. The stakes are high. The good-natured, trusting person is the one who will be exploited; the shrewd, perceptive person has the best chance of winning.

Because accurate judgment of one's partner is of the utmost importance in this dangerous game, part of the didactic purpose of the play is to serve as a sort of field guide to help the audience tell true wit from would-be wit—and, of course, through poking fun at the fools and fops, to laugh members of the audience out of any foolishness or foppery they may have acquired. With these practical purposes in mind, the Restoration comedy of manners, by its end, will have arranged the characters into a hierarchy from the most witty—in other words, most desirable (if most dangerous)—down to the least witty (or most to be reviled and mocked).

An examination of the hierarchy of wit in *The Man of Mode* will demonstrate how complex and subtle this ranking can be. The characters are divided, first, into young characters and old characters, and the audience is asked to judge each character according to the behavior appropriate to his or her station in life. Dorimant is obviously at the top of the pecking order among the young men. He is the cleverest and wittiest in speech, he dresses in perfect taste, he is the most perceptive in judging the motives and the weaknesses of others yet the most astute in concealing his own. Another essential quality is his "malice." His pleasure in manipulating others and triumphing over them—which can seem so ugly to modern audiences—is the very quality that gives him the competitive edge over others.

Young Bellair is next in the pecking order. He is attractive and clever, and some modern audiences prefer him to Dorimant. That is to miss the point. In Dorimant's accurate summation: "He's handsome, well-bred, and by much the most tolerable of all the young men that do not abound in wit." Young Bellair's crippling defect is that he has not as much malice as Dorimant, so he does not disguise his emotions, being genuinely in love with Emilia. Because of his lack of malice, he is unsuspicious of malice in others, and Dorimant, pretending friendship, is using him. In the play's most cruel—if most realistic and psychologically astute—line, Dorimant says that, because he has been unable to seduce Emilia, he is encouraging the marriage between her and Young Bellair because "I have known many women make a difficulty of losing a maidenhead, who have afterwards made none of making a cuckold."

Sir Fopling Flutter obviously finishes last. With his Frenchified language and excessively fashionable clothing, he is the laughingstock of the town. He attempts to maintain a reputation as a lover, but all the characters easily see through him, and correctly so, for underneath, he appears to be all but sexless. Dorimant has an easy time making Fopling a tool in his plot to cast off Loveit.

Harriet is at the top of the pecking order of the young women. She is the wittiest in dialogue, the most handsomely yet naturally dressed, and as the characters admiringly point out, she is as full of malice—of pleasure in using and abusing others—as Dorimant. Although she has been described and discussed throughout the play, Etherege, for dramatic effect, does not allow her to appear onstage until the third act. That act is a replay of the first act, as Harriet rises in the morning, the scene almost point for point paralleling the first, to underline what an even and perfect match Dorimant and Harriet are. She is constantly on guard against him, and so she is the only female who can resist him, meaning, at the end, the only one who might possibly get him in marriage.

Emilia, Young Bellair's fiancée, is next in line. Like Young Bellair, her single failing is that she has not enough malice, and for that reason, she is not suspicious enough of it in others. Like Young Bellair, she is sufficiently clever to make use of Old Bellair and Lady Woodvill to get them into a position to agree to the marriage between her and Young Bellair, but again like Young Bellair, she is no match for Dorimant. She is second in the pecking order because, by play's end, she still has not been seduced by Dorimant, but she is clearly in danger. When Bellinda tries to warn her that Dorimant is not to be trusted, she innocently disputes this, saying he is a completely good, trustworthy man—thus indicating that she has her guard down.

Bellinda is third, because she has let Dorimant seduce her. Still, she is shrewd, clever, and witty enough to keep herself from being found out by the others, so she has, for the time being, preserved her reputation. Loveit is last because, unable to control her jealous passions, she has let everyone in town know that she is having an affair with Dorimant. It is her lack of self-control that has allowed Dorimant

to work his will on her to begin with, and to continue triumphing over her even after he has cast her off. An outward sign of her lack of wit is in her language. Instead of the repartee of the others, she speaks in the exaggerated tones of the heroic lovers of *The Comical Revenge*: "Traitor! . . . Ingrateful perjured man!"

What is the proper role for the older characters, who are beyond the courtship stage of their lives? Medley and Lady Townley are good examples. They do not come forward and obtrude their advice where it is not wanted but help out the young lovers when they are asked and generally provide the gracious and civilized background against which the young people play out their courtship. They also—somewhat like a Greek chorus—keep track of the young people's reputations and make judgments (which young ladies' reputations are unblemished, which are in danger, which young men are the most perfect gallants with women). The negative examples of the older characters are Old Bellair and Lady Woodvill, who both feel that they can choose marriage partners for their children and yet whose language immediately marks them as so far behind the times, so out of touch socially, that they would make disastrous choices. Luckily, however, they are also so socially inept that the young people manipulate them easily.

The Man of Mode suggests that self-interest—Dorimant's "malice"—is necessary to the successful functioning of society. In a reaction against this Restoration worldview in the eighteenth century, later playwrights left out the cruelty and malice in their dramas of courtship. The result was sentimental theater, frankly unrealistic. If Dorimant and Harriet are removed from the play, Young Bellair and Emilia will come to the top of the pecking order. Like them, the sentimental dramas of the eighteenth century are "tolerable" but do not "abound with wit."

OTHER MAJOR WORKS

POETRY: *The New Academy of Complements*, 1669; *A Collection of Poems, Written upon Several Occasions*, 1673; *Restoration Carnival*, 1954 (V. De Sola Pinto, editor); *Poems*, 1963 (James Thorpe, editor).

NONFICTION: *The Letterbook of Sir George Etherege*, 1928 (Sybil Rosenfeld, editor); *Letters of Sir George Etherege*, 1973.

MISCELLANEOUS: *The Works of Sir George Etherege: Containing His Plays and Poems*, 1704; *The Works of Sir George Etherege: Plays and Poems*, 1888 (A. Wilson Verity, editor).

BIBLIOGRAPHY

Gill, Pat. *Interpreting Ladies: Women, Wit, and Morality in the Restoration Comedy of Manners*. Athens: University of Georgia Press, 1995. This study of women in Restoration comedies examines Etherege's *The Man of Mode* as well as works by William Wycherley and William Congreve.

Huseboe, Arthur R. *Sir George Etherege*. Boston: Twayne, 1987. This introduction to Etherege includes a chronology, a biographical chapter incorporating later research, separate chapters on the three plays and the minor works, a valuable annotated bibliography, and notes. The epilogue summarizes the course of Etherege scholarship. Index.

Jantz, Ursula. *Targets of Satire in the Comedies of Etherege, Wycherley, and Congreve*. Slazburg, Switzerland: University of Salzburg Press, 1978. A look at the role of satire in the works of Etherege, William Wycherley, and William Congreve. Bibliography.

Mann, David D. *Sir George Etherege: A Reference Guide*. Boston: G. K. Hall, 1981. This work dedicated to Etherege scholarship is designed to help scholars find their way in Restoration drama. Although it needs to be supplemented with bibliographies of recent work, this guide is extremely useful for the period it covers.

Markley, Robert. *Two-edg'd Weapons: Style and Ideology in the Comedies of Etherege, Wycherley, and Congreve*. New York: Oxford University Press, 1988. A critical analysis of the works of three Restoration dramatists: Etherege, William Wycherley, and William Congreve. Bibliography and index.

Young, Douglas M. *The Feminist Voices in Restoration Comedy: The Virtuous Women in the Play-world of Etherege, Wycherley, and Congreve*. Lanham, Md.: University Press of America, 1997. An examination of the female characters in the comedies of Etherege, William Wycherley, and William Congreve. Bibliography and index.

Norman Lavers,
updated by Frank Day

EURIPIDES

Born: Phlya, Greece; c. 485 B.C.E.
Died: Macedonia, Greece; 406 B.C.E.

PRINCIPAL DRAMA

Of the 66 tragedies and 22 satyr plays Euripides wrote, the following survive:

Alkēstis, 438 B.C.E. (*Alcestis*, 1781)
Mēdeia, 431 B.C.E. (*Medea*, 1781)
Hērakleidai, c. 430 B.C.E. (*The Children of Herakles*, 1781)
Hippolytos, 428 B.C.E. (revision of an earlier play; *Hippolytus*, 1781)
Andromachē, c. 426 B.C.E. (*Andromache*, 1782)
Heklabē, 425 B.C.E. (*Hecuba*, 1782)

Hiketides, c. 423 B.C.E. (*The Suppliants*, 1781)
Kyklōps, c. 421 B.C.E. (*Cyclops*, 1782)
Hērakles, c. 420 B.C.E. (*Heracles*, 1781)
Trōiades, 415 B.C.E. (*The Trojan Women*, 1782)
Iphigeneia ē en Taurois, c. 414 B.C.E. (*Iphigenia in Tauris*, 1782)
Ēlektra, 413 B.C.E. (*Electra*, 1782)
Helenē, 412 B.C.E. (*Helen*, 1782)
Iōn, c. 411 B.C.E. (*Ion*, 1781)
Phoinissai, 409 B.C.E. (*The Phoenician Women*, 1781)
Orestēs, 408 B.C.E. (*Orestes*, 1782)
Bakchai, 405 B.C.E. (*The Bacchae*, 1781)
Iphigeneia ē en Aulidi, 405 B.C.E. (*Iphigenia in Aulis*, 1782)

OTHER LITERARY FORMS

Like Aeschylus and Sophocles, Euripides wrote elegies and lyric poems, none of which has survived intact. The poet is said to have been commissioned by his fellow Athenians to write a funeral epitaph for the dead at Syracuse in 413 B.C.E., but the lines handed down in Plutarch's *Life of Nicias* (in *Bioi paralleloi*, c. 105-115 C.E.; *Parallel Lives*, 1579) are not usually accepted as Euripidean. Several lines exist of an epinician, or victory, ode said to have been dedicated by Euripides to the Athenian politician Alcibiades after an Olympic victory, but even in antiquity, this ode was attributed to others as well.

ACHIEVEMENTS

The ancient *Bios Euripidou* (third century B.C.E.; life of Euripides) by Satyrus assigns to the playwright innovations in the following areas: prologues, scientific dissertations on nature, oratorical pieces, and recognitions. This vague statement requires considerable qualification. Although the extant plays show little of the interest in natural science suggested by the anonymous author of the *Life of Euripides* and confirmed by several fragments from lost plays, Euripides' dramatic application of set speeches and rhetorical devices is a common feature of his plays, as in the legal debate between Hecuba and Helen in *The Trojan Women*. These scientific and rhetorical features reveal Euripides' place in the intellectual mainstream of late fifth century B.C.E. Athens, a position that it is difficult for a modern reader to appreciate fully because so much of the existing nondramatic evidence is fragmentary. Euripides very well may have been the first tragedian to highlight these contemporary trends in his drama.

Euripides certainly did not invent anagnorisis, or recognition, which existed in Greek literature as early as Homer's *Odyssey* (c. 800 B.C.E.; English translation, 1616) and in drama as early as Aeschylus's *Choēphoroi* (458 B.C.E.; *Libation Bearers*, 1777), but Euripides uses these recognition scenes frequently and with a novelty and skill much admired by Aristotle in his *De poetica* (c. 334-323 B.C.E.; *Poetics*, 1705). Indeed, it is Euripides' focus on recognition and intrigue in his later dramas, such as *Ion*, *Helen*,

Euripides (Library of Congress)

and *Iphigenia in Tauris*, that has led him to be called a father of the New Greek Comedy of Menander in the late fourth century B.C.E. Although these recognition dramas were technically produced by Euripides as tragedies, they are not necessarily "tragic" in the modern sense, but are more "tragicomic" and have sometimes been labeled as *tyche* dramas, or dramas of "chance."

Alcestis deserves special mention. Technically not a tragedy, it is rather a pro-satyr play because it was produced in place of a satyr play. Euripides is known to have experimented with such pro-satyr plays several other times, and the pro-satyr play may have been a Euripidean innovation. Knowledge of the Greek satyr play tradition is generally scanty as Euripides' *Cyclops* is the only complete drama of this type to survive, along with significant papyrus fragments of two Sophoclean satyr plays, but two special features of satyr plays were known to have been choruses of satyrs and scenes of buffoonery. While *Alcestis* lacks the former, its links with the satyr play can be seen in the comic scene with Heracles. Euripides' *Alcestis* and his *tyche* dramas thus serve as a caution against making general statements about the genre of Greek "tragedy" or about "Euripidean tragedy" in particular. The definition of "tragedy" in fifth century B.C.E. Athens was clearly much broader than it is today.

The *Life of Euripides* notwithstanding, Euripides definitely did not invent the tragic prologue, which, by Aristotelian definition in *Poetics* was "that part of a tragedy which precedes the parodos or chorus's entrance song." Several extant plays of Aeschylus have such prologues, but Euripides, like Sophocles, added his own distinctive feature: a scene, often called expository, in which a character, usually a mortal but sometimes a god, identifies himself and outlines the characters and background of the plot. Every extant Euripidean tragedy has such an expository prologue, which cannot always be dismissed as a mere nondramatic playbill. The expositions spoken by gods (in *Alcestis*, *Hippolytus*, *The Trojan Women*, *Ion*, and *The Bacchae*) are particularly significant in that the dramatic events generally do not evolve exactly as predicted by the gods in the prologues. In each of these five prologues, the playwright makes his deity more or less misleading as to subsequent dramatic events. At the least, such "deceptive" prologues serve to create interest in the story without giving away the plot. At the same time, such prologues may reveal the gods' inability to control human action and to move it along their preordained plans.

The expository prologue has also been called an archaizing element in Euripidean drama, but too little is known of Greek tragedy in its infancy to say with certainty that such scenes were a common early feature. Euripides' plays, however, do exhibit several traits that could be labeled archaisms in that they can be traced back to Aeschylean elements. The dramas of Aeschylus, first produced in Euripides' youth and revived throughout his lifetime, seem to have been a particular source of dramatic inspiration to the younger playwright. Euripidean imitation of Aeschylean techniques can be seen in several areas: Euripides' altar scenes, such as those in *The Suppliants* and *Ion*, may be based on similar scenes in such plays as Aeschylus's *Hiketides* (463 B.C.E.?; *The Suppliants*,

1777) and *Eumenides* (458 B.C.E.; English translation, 1777). Luring speeches, such as those in *Hecuba* and *Electra*, are probably derived from the carpet scene in Aeschylus's *Agamemnōn* (458 B.C.E.; *Agamemnon*, 1777). The pathetic ghost of Polydorus in *Hecuba* can be traced back to the ghosts in *Persai* (472 B.C.E.; *The Persians*, 1777) and *Eumenides*. The mad scene of *Heracles* may possibly be modeled on the last scene of *Libation Bearers*. Aeschylus's *Eumenides* and *The Suppliants* are the probable prototypes for Euripides' subsidiary choruses in *Hippolytus* and *The Suppliants*, and Euripides' *The Suppliants* is almost certainly following its predecessor in the use of the chorus as the main character. It has also been suggested that the model for the "bad women" of Euripides, such as Medea and Phaedra, was Aeschylus's Clytemnestra, and that Euripides' "unhappy women," such as Hecuba, were modeled on Aeschylus's Atossa.

Also like Aeschylus, Euripides was a master of stage machinery, including the *eccyclema*, a device used to show interiors, which Euripides employs in daring ways in *Alcestis*, *Hippolytus*, and other plays. For Euripides, however, stage machinery means especially the *mechane*, a crane used to swing an actor into the orchestra. Euripides has a *mechane*, which is the origin of the term *deus ex machina*, at the end of ten of his extant plays, almost always to enable a god to make an appearance and resolve dramatic difficulties. By contrast, the *mechane* is used in only one of Sophocles' surviving plays, *Philoktētēs* (409 B.C.E.; *Philoctetes*, 1729), and in none of Aeschylus's, except perhaps *Prometheus desmōtēs* (date unknown; *Prometheus Bound*, 1777). Euripides himself makes brilliant original use of the technique in *Medea*, in which it is Medea herself who escapes in a crane dramatically transformed into the magic chariot of the sun.

A final Aeschylean dramatic feature that is often linked with Euripides is the connected trilogy. T. B L. Webster is the most prominent proponent of this view, which has had remarkable tenacity despite meager evidence. The most that can be said about the possibility of Euripidean-connected trilogies is that neither of the most likely trilogic candidates, Euripides' production of 415 B.C.E. (including the lost *Alexander* and *Palamedes*, as well as the surviving *The Trojan Women*), often called his "Trojan Trilogy"; his production of c. 410-409 B.C.E. (*Antiope* and *Hypsipyle*, now lost, and *The Phoenician Women*), a "Theban Trilogy," appear to have been connected in the closely knit thematic and chronological way that is notable in the *Oresteia* (458 B.C.E.; English translation, 1777), Aeschylus's only surviving trilogy. It is possible that Euripides may have linked plays within a dramatic group through a sort of meaningful variation, but such connections do not necessarily make a trilogy. Like his contemporary, Sophocles, Euripides was an artistic master of the single play rather than of the connected trilogy.

Euripides was an acknowledged virtuoso of Greek tragic language in all its forms. In the iambic or spoken portions of his plays, his elaborate agons, or debates, and his carefully detailed messenger speeches, such as the famous report of Hippolytus's death in *Hippolytus* are particularly noteworthy. In the lyric, or sung, portions of his plays, Euripides was in the vanguard of the late fifth century B.C.E. trend toward more song by actors and less by the chorus alone. Thus, Euripidean plays tend to have more monodies, or solo songs by actors, and *kommoi*, or duets between the chorus and one or more actors, as well as fewer and shorter choral odes than in earlier tragedy. *Kommostic parodoi*, or choral entrance songs sung by both chorus and actor(s), are a special favorite of Euripides (as in *Medea* and *The Trojan Women*).

Under the influence of the contemporary poet Timotheus of Miletus, Euripides also moved in his later plays toward a New Lyric form marked especially by astrophic, or stanzaless, songs and *polymetria*, or the use of more than one meter in a single song (as in *Iphigenia in Tauris*, *Helen*, and *The Phoenician Women*). Late Euripidean tragedy only sporadically reflects another trend of New Lyric, that toward choral odes that are apparently unconnected to dramatic events. In general, even such a well-known Euripidean ode as the "Demeter Ode" (in *Helen*), which is difficult to relate to the plot, is not so much detached from the play as it is a more indirect, mythological exemplum of dramatic events.

New Lyric, connected, as it was, with a new school of emotional music, was an ideal medium for Euripides' dramatic art, which is preeminently a study of human psychology and emotion. The playwright, noted for his studies of the feminine psyche in such diverse characters as Alcestis, Medea, Phaedra, and Hecuba, created character studies filled with psychological insight. Unlike the Sophoclean hero, who never changes or loses his resolve, the Euripidean character is more unstable. Like Medea or Phaedra, the character may waver at length between several courses of action or, like Ion, who is transformed in the course of the action from a boy into a man, may exhibit significant growth of personality. The persona of Euripides often lacks that nobility of character that Aristotle believed to be essential to real tragedy, and which the seventeenth century French dramatist Jean Racine tried to restore in his imitation of Euripides' characters. Euripides' contemporary, Sophocles, demonstrated uncanny insight when he stated that he "made men as they ought to be; Euripides as they are."

Euripides' innovations in the mythical background to his plays are often the result of his realistic psychology as well as his desire for dramatic shock effect. His most noteworthy mythical changes are the marriage of Electra, the reversal of the traditional sequence of Heracles' madness and the hero's labors, and, probably, the murder of her own children by Medea. Euripides may also have been the inventor of scenes of voluntary self-sacrifice, of which the "Cassandra scene" of *The Trojan Women* is a noteworthy example. Other such scenes can be found in *Iphigenia in Aulis*, *The Children of Herakles*, *Hecuba*, and *The Phoenician Women*.

It is the rare Euripidean play that does not include at least one deity among its *dramatis personae*, but these divine appearances are generally restricted to the prologues and *exodoi*, or last scenes, and serve as a frame for the central, "human" part of the drama. Much has been read into Euripides' beliefs from the role of the gods in his plays, but it is also significant to note that the Euripidean gods serve an important dramatic function as causes of events independent of human motivation. In general, the gods place Euripides' psychological studies in their appropriate mythical background.

BIOGRAPHY

The manuscript tradition of Euripides contains an ancient *Life of Euripides*, clearly a composite of several sources, including Philochorus, a fourth century B.C.E. Attic historian, and Satyros, a third century Peripatetic biographer, fragments of whose own *Life of Euripides* exist on papyrus. Unfortunately, however, much of the ancient biographical tradition about Euripides is derived from ancient comedy, especially from that of Aristophanes, whose *Thesmophoriazousai* (411 B.C.E.; *Thesmophoriazusae*, 1837) and *Batrachoi* (405 B.C.E.; *The Frogs*, 1780) both contain caricatures of Euripides and who is therefore suspect as a historical source.

The problem of source reliability starts with Euripides' parentage. The comic tradition that Euripides' father, Mnesarchus (or Mnesarchides), was a shopkeeper and his mother, Clito, a greengrocer, is apparently contradicted by ancient statements that Euripides' mother belonged to a noble family and that Euripides himself was granted honors worthy of high rank, including those of dancing at Athens in the sacred dance to Delian Apollo and of being a fire bearer in another cult of Apollo. Euripides is said to have been born on the island of Salamis, but he was a member of the Athenian deme of Phlya, where he may have held a local priesthood of Zeus. His date of birth is variously given as either 485 or 480 B.C.E., the later date being based on the persistent ancient tradition that the playwright was born on Salamis on the very day of the battle in which Aeschylus may have fought and after which Sophocles as a youth is said to have danced in the victory celebration. Apparently, Euripides' ties with Salamis were strong, for he is said to have composed many of his plays in a solitary cave on the island.

The ancient *Life of Euripides* states that, as a youth, Euripides studied painting and was trained as an athlete because of a misinterpretation of an oracle stating that he would someday win "crowns in contests at Athens." Although Euripides may, as some sources suggest, have won some early athletic victo-ries at Athens, his real victories were to be won in the dramatic competitions at Athens' Greater Dionysia.

Euripides is linked intellectually with many of the great thinkers of his day. The ancient *Life of Euripides* lists among his teachers Anaxagoras, whose doctrines can be seen in *Hippolytus*, *The Trojan Women*, and elsewhere; Protagoras, who is said to have read his treatise "On the Gods" in Euripides' house; the Sophist Prodicus; and even Socrates, who was at least fifteen years Euripides' junior and whom Aristophanes called a collaborator in Euripides' dramatic compositions. As a fifth century B.C.E. Athenian, Euripides certainly came in contact with all these men, but none of them is likely to have a formal student-teacher relationship with Euripides. The influence of the tragedian Aeschylus and the poet Timotheus on Euripides' dramatic development has already been mentioned. The poet may also have had some connections with the historian Thucydides. A memorial inscription dedicated to Euripides is ascribed to Thucydides, although it is sometimes attributed to Timotheus.

The story of Euripides' two unhappy marriages, first to Melito and then to a Choerile or Choerine, daughter of Mnesilochus, is too clearly entangled in comic tradition to be historical. According to the *Life of Euripides*, the second wife committed adultery with a certain Cephisophon, who is described both as a house slave and as a literary collaborator with Euripides. The playwright is said to have written his scandalous first *Hippolytus* in reaction to his wife's infidelity. Actually, both unhappy marriages and his traditional misogyny may be a comic exaggeration of Euripides' depiction of evil women in such plays as the first *Hippolytus* and *Medea*.

Euripides had three sons: Mnesarchides, a merchant; Mnesilochus, an actor; and Euripides the younger, a tragic poet who produced *Iphigenia in Aulis* and *The Bacchae* posthumously for his father.

Euripides appears to have led a very quiet life except for his dramatic career. The only public duty attributed to him, an ambassadorship to Syracuse, is generally discounted today. Euripides may have been friendly with the Athenian politician Alcibiades. An epinician ode to Alcibiades is perhaps attributable to the dramatist, and unmistakable strains of Athenian patriotism are notable in such plays as *Medea* and *The Suppliants*, in which the Athenian heroes Aegeus and Theseus are used as symbols of Athens's role as savior of the oppressed. On the other hand, intense hatred of war can be seen in such plays as *Hecuba* and *The Trojan Women*, and much of the exotic in late Euripidean plays such as *Helen* and *Iphigenia in Tauris* can be explained as dramatic escapism from the horrors of the Peloponnesian War. Criticism of the Athenian massacre of the Melians, described by Thucydides, can be read into Euripides' *The Trojan Women*, produced in 415 B.C.E., the year after the massacre. More specific political allusions have been sought in the extant corpus but are very difficult to document.

Euripides' first dramatic competition was in 455 B.C.E., when he placed with *Peliades*, now lost. He did not win a first prize until 442 or 441. In contrast to Sophocles' numerous dramatic victories, Euripides won first prize only five times (including one posthumous victory) out of twenty-two productions. Although Euripides' dramatic career began in 455, he produced very few plays in the next twenty-five years. Only six Euripidean productions are known before 431 B.C.E. The remaining sixteen productions fall in the period 431-406 B.C.E., roughly coinciding with the Peloponnesian War. In the last decade of the poet's life, 415-406 B.C.E., he competed every year but two.

In 438 B.C.E., Euripides placed second to Sophocles with a group composed of the lost tragedies *Cretan Women*, *Alcmaeon at Psophis*, and *Telephus* and the extant pro-satyr play *Alcestis*. Sometime in the period 437-432 B.C.E., Euripides produced a *Hippolytus*, later identified by the subtitle *Kalyptomenos*, or "veiled," to distinguish it from the extant play on the same theme, *Hippolytus Stephanophoros*, or "Hippolytus the wreath-bearer." Apparently, this first *Hippolytus*, now lost, received harsh criticism for its depiction of a scandalous Phaedra, who revealed her love to her stepson. In his revised *Hippolytus*, produced in 428 B.C.E., Euripides was more careful to preserve Phaedra's reputation and was awarded first prize over the tragedians Iophon, son of Sophocles, and Ion. *Medea*, produced in 431 B.C.E. with the lost

Philoctetes and *Dictys*, was beaten by the works of both Euphorion, son of Aeschylus, and Sophocles. *Andromache*, while not firmly datable, is significant in that the play apparently was not performed at Athens, but the actual place of production is unknown. Euripides is said to have made several other productions outside Athens. In 415 B.C.E., Euripides came in second place to a certain Xenocles with his lost *Alexander* and *Palamedes* and the surviving *The Trojan Women*.

In 408 B.C.E., after the production of *Orestes* in Athens, the septuagenarian Euripides left his native city, never to return. The poet went first to Magnesia, where he received several honors, and then to Macedonia, to the court of Archelaus, whose patronage of the arts also attracted the tragic poet Agathon and Euripides' friend, the poet Timotheus. In Macedonia, Euripides produced *Archelaus*, now lost, which was a play about an ancestor of his royal host, and wrote the extant *Iphigenia in Aulis* and *The Bacchae* and the lost *Alcmaeon in Corinth*, which were produced posthumously in Athens by Euripides' son of the same name and which won first prize.

After Euripides' death in Macedonia in early 406, Sophocles dressed a chorus in mourning for his fellow tragedian at the *proagon*, or preview, to the Greater Dionysia of that year. That Euripides died by *sparagmos*—that is, by being torn apart either accidentally by Archelaus's hunting dogs or by women angered by the poet's depiction of their sex—must be dismissed as comic apocrypha because of the legend's similarity to the fate of Pentheus in *The Bacchae*.

The most disturbing result of all these biographical data tarnished by the comic tradition is the cloud that has enveloped Euripides' popularity in fifth century B.C.E. Athens. Like his contemporary, Socrates, Euripides was a favorite butt of comedy, both while he was alive (as in Aristophanes' *Thesmophoriazusae*) and after his death (as in Aristophanes' *The Frogs* of 405 B.C.E.), and according to the ancient *Life of Euripides*, this comic ridicule was so intense that it was the cause of Euripides' departure from Athens in 408 B.C.E. There are also several noncomic hints of Euripides' unpopularity: the failure of the first *Hippolytus*, as well as the small number of first prizes that he won. On the other hand, this tradition of unpopularity may be the result of comic exaggeration misunderstood by later critics.

That Euripides was a prolific playwright, with sixteen productions in the last twenty-five years of his life, is itself strong evidence for sustained contemporary enthusiasm for his plays, as competition for permission to perform at the Greater Dionysia was stiff, and only three poets were chosen annually. There is also an attractive notice in Plutarch's *Life of Nicias* that some Athenian prisoners in Sicily were granted better treatment by their captors if they could recite Euripides' poetry, which was held in great esteem by the Sicilian Greeks. Nor must Euripides' sojourn in Macedonia be interpreted, as it is in the ancient *Life of Euripides*, as only a self-imposed exile from his Athenian critics. Rather, it may also be seen as the result of the attraction that royal patrons often held toward ancient Greek poets, including Anacreon and Ibycus to the court of the Samian tyrant Polycrates, Aeschylus and Pindar to the court of Hieron in Sicily, and Agathon and Timotheus to the court of Archelaus.

A more likely interpretation of the evidence is that Euripides' plays were often controversial in his lifetime because of their depiction of realistic characters in a traditional myth but were still generally admired for their dramatic and poetic force. As time passed, the sensationalism of Euripides' character development has worn off, and the poet has come to be admired for his masterful studies of human psychology, so that the funeral inscription written in Euripides' memory by either the historian Thucydides or the poet Timotheus is even more valid today than it was in the fifth century B.C.E.

> All Greece is the tomb of Euripides, whose bones rest
> In Macedonia where he met his end.
> His native city, Athens, is the Greece of Greece
> And he has earned much praise for the delights of his
>   Muse.

Euripides' plays were certainly in demand after his death. Revivals of Euripidean plays occurred throughout the fourth century B.C.E. (a performance of *Orestes* is documented in 341 B.C.E.) and were a direct influence on the New Comedy of Menander (late fourth century B.C.E.) and, through Greek New Comedy, on Roman Comedy, including Plautus and Terence (second century B.C.E.). Enthusiasm for Euripides was maintained throughout antiquity, as is evidenced by the larger number of plays that survive and by the great number of papyrus fragments of Euripides that have been discovered in Egypt and that are second in quantity only to Homeric papyri. Adaptations of Euripidean plays include Seneca's *Phaedra* (c. 40-50 C.E.; English translation, 1581), modeled on Euripides' first *Hippolytus*; Racine's *Phèdre* (pr., pb. 1677; *Phaedra*, 1701), a seventeenth century version of *Hippolytus*; Eugene O'Neill's twentieth century version of *Mourning Becomes Electra* (pr., pb. 1931); and the contemporary Nigerian playwright Wole Soyinka's unique adaptation of *The Bacchae* (pr., pb. 1973), with its blending of Dionysus with the Yoruba deity Ogun.

ANALYSIS

Euripides wrote eighty-eight dramas, including sixty-six tragedies and twenty-two satyr plays. Nineteen plays survive in the manuscript tradition, but one of these, the tragedy *Rhesus* (written sometime between 455 and 441 B.C.E.), is generally considered to be spurious. *Cyclops*, the only complete extant satyr play, is not precisely datable. In addition to the pro-satyr play *Alcestis*, seven tragedies are securely dated: *Medea, Hippolytus, The Trojan Women, Helen, Orestes, Iphigenia in Aulis*, and *The Bacchae*, these last two produced posthumously. The other tragedies can be only approximately dated, based on metrical evidence and contemporary allusions. In addition, considerable fragments from lost plays survive on papyrus.

The large number of extant Euripidean plays (compared to only seven each for Aeschylus and Sophocles) is attributable to a combination of conscious selection and chance. When the Athenian orator Lycurgus established the texts of Aeschylus and Sophocles in the late fourth century B.C.E., he also made the first edition of Euripides, but not before numerous actors' interpolations had crept into the text. The number of plays contained in the Lycurgan edition is unknown, but only seventy-eight dramas, including four considered apocryphal by the editor, were included in the definitive Alexandrian edition by Aristophanes of Byzantium in the second century B.C.E. Another important edition was made by Didymus of Chalcedon in the first century B.C.E. Didymus's edition included scholia, or marginal notes, on which are based the scholia in the surviving manuscripts.

Sometime after the second century C.E., school anthologies were made of the plays of Aeschylus, Sophocles, and Euripides, but although only seven each were chosen for Aeschylus and Sophocles, Euripides' great popularity in antiquity caused ten plays to be included in his selection: *Hecuba, Orestes, The Phoenician Women, Hippolytus, Medea, Alcestis, Andromache, Rhesus, The Trojan Women,* and *The Bacchae.* Although this school group was narrowed in the Byzantine period to *Hecuba, Orestes,* and *The Phoenician Women,* all ten plays of the original selection reached the West in the fourteenth century, together with a group of nine other Euripidean plays, preserved by chance from an edition (perhaps that of Aristophanes) arranged alphabetically: *The Suppliants, Cyclops, The Children of Herakles, Heracles, Helen, Ion, Iphigenia in Tauris, Iphigenia in Aulis,* and *Electra.* The first printed edition of Euripides was the Aldine edition of Venice, 1503.

Although certain dramatic features, such as the expository prologue and the appearance of a god in the *mechane,* tend to recur in play after play of Euripides, the overall impression made by his corpus, when viewed as a whole, is one of remarkable diversity. Euripides is a poet of stark contradictions. A single production, such as *Hippolytus,* can display both bitter misogyny and a sensitive portrayal of a woman such as Phaedra. One play, such as *Medea,* may sink to the depths of tragedy; another, such as *Ion,* will float from those depths, buoyed on comic resolution. Certain plays, it is true, can be said to form subgroups, such as the so-called political plays, including *The Children of Herakles, The Suppliants,* and *Andromache,* or the *tyche* dramas *Ion, Helen,* and *Iphigenia in Tauris,* but the dramatic gulf that spans a career including *Alcestis, Hippolytus, Ion,* and *The Bacchae* cannot be easily bridged.

There are too few neat generalizations comparable to the Aeschylean concept of justice or the Sophoclean hero on which to establish a poetic or intellectual unity within the Euripidean corpus. Perhaps if as many plays of Aeschylus and Sophocles had survived, more variety would be found in those dramatists as well, but one has the impression after reading Euripides that for this playwright, at least, variety is almost an organizing feature. Most often, generalizations about Euripides have centered on his portrayal of the gods and his apparent disbelief in Greek deities and traditional myths, but then one is forced by *The Bacchae,* with its intense religious mood, either to see the play as an end-of-life palinode, a refutation of the earlier works, or to put aside the generalization entirely. Variety within the Euripidean corpus is caused, to a great extent, by the playwright's focus on the particular psychology of each character.

Like the Sophists of his age, who operated on an ethical system of amoral pragmatism, Euripides is a practical stage manager who is willing to thwart theatrical convention and traditional beliefs for dramatic effect. In general, the goal of Euripidean drama is not the development of a theological system or an ideal code of conduct, but rather the depiction of human emotions under strain. The dramas of Euripides are thus not really concerned with the gods or superheroes, but with ordinary people trying to deal, in their own personal ways, with real-life situations including love, jealousy, divorce, and death. This is the source of Euripides' diversity and of his appeal. His psychological studies, as diverse and as complex as the human mind itself, are at the heart of his plays, which fluctuate in form, mood, and tone to suit particular dramatic and psychological situations. Unlike Sophocles, who depicted people as they ought to be, Euripides depicted people as they are (according to Aristotle's *Poetics*). This Euripidean realism accounts for the differences among *Alcestis, Medea, Hippolytus, Ion, The Bacchae,* and his other plays. Euripidean tragedy is, above all, a drama of life itself.

ALCESTIS

In *Alcestis,* Euripides presents a study of the loyal, self-sacrificing wife. That Alcestis would die for her husband, Admetus, is easy to accept after Alcestis's touching and revealing speech in the second episode, but the character of Admetus is more difficult to understand and easier to condemn as selfish and self-centered. Interpretation of his character and of the play as a whole is widely debated, but Admetus's salvation, if it occurs at all, must be sought in *xenia*, the ancient Greek custom of guestfriendship. *Xenia* is Admetus's chief—and perhaps his only—virtue.

In the typically Euripidean expository prologue, the god Apollo explains how he will save Admetus's life because the latter was a good host to him while he, Apollo, was on earth, and, in the central portion of the fourth episode, Heracles is willing to get Alcestis back from Death because of the hospitality his friend Admetus has shown to him even at a time of deep mourning. The Third Choral Ode is filled with glowing praise for Admetus's *xenia*. On the other hand, Admetus comes off quite badly both in an agon with his father Pheres, in which the aged father explains his refusal to die for his selfish son, and in the exodos, in which Admetus accepts in marriage an unidentified woman from Heracles, despite his earlier promise to the dying Alcestis never to remarry, even before it becomes clear that the veiled woman might be Alcestis. Perhaps some of this play's difficulty is attributable to its position as a pro-satyr play, a fact that helps explain the pathetic comedy of the drunken scene with Heracles and especially the tragicomic ambiguity of the exodos. Through it all, however, Euripides' depiction of Alcestis as a loving wife and mother is a constant on which the variables of Admetus's character and the play's denouement are based. Whether Admetus in the exodos is rewarded for his virtuous *xenia* or punished for his selfishness, neither could have occurred without the remarkable and loving selflessness of his wife. Euripides' emphasis on a human situation and human emotion is paramount.

MEDEA

Medea is one of the few extant plays of Euripides that function without the gods. Instead, Euripides has taken two superhuman figures from Greek mythology, Medea and Jason, and placed them in a very human situation: the breakdown of a marriage. Especially in their bitter agon in the second episode, Medea is clearly the wronged woman who has sacrificed everything for her husband and does not want the divorce, and Jason is shown to be heartless, calculating, and ambitious. Euripides achieves his most brilliant dramatic stroke, however, by complicating his psychological study of Medea with an emphasis on the exotic side of her character. Not only is she depicted in her traditional role as a witch and as a foreigner and therefore a barbarian, but there is an implicit suggestion that Medea is also unnatural because of her love for Jason, because of her uncontrollable passion. Medea's emotional imbalance, caused by Jason's desertion, is therefore the heart of the play and leads inevitably to her murder of Jason's intended second wife and then of her own children, whose death, she realizes, will wound Jason more than would any other act of revenge.

Yet Medea is not completely unnatural; she is rather a woman caught between her jealous passion for Jason and her maternal instincts. That she does not lose all her sympathy by yielding in the end to her passion speaks highly of Euripides' character development of his heroine. The chorus is particularly significant in the play for this reason. From their arrival, the women of the chorus are sympathetic to Medea and convinced that she has been wronged by Jason. Their First Ode is a bitter condemnation of the perfidy of men toward women, and during Medea's intrigue, the chorus actually serve as Medea's confidante. The Fifth Choral Ode is about the sorrows of childbearing, and the chorus's last song is a terrified prayer to the Sun, Medea's grandfather, to stop Medea's unnatural act. The chorus members therefore are an important dramatic foil to Medea. As women, they are sympathetic to Medea, but they cannot understand or condone the murder of her own children. The chorus are a psychological scale by which Medea's passion is measured and found imbalanced.

Compared to the tragicomedy *Alcestis*, the dramatic effect of *Medea* can be nothing less than complete emotional exhaustion. In a memorable section of *Poetics*, Aristotle criticizes the emotional effect of

Medea as *miaron*, moral revulsion, which inhibits the development of a true tragic feeling for Medea, who, fully conscious of the horrors of her act, murders her children. Yet this awareness that she is caught between Jason and her children is the emotional key to Medea's psychology and enables her to construe her act as both revenge against Jason and protection against further harm for her children. In *Medea*, Euripides has developed the illogical conclusions of a mind crazed by spurned love.

HIPPOLYTUS

Passion is also the subject of *Hippolytus*, but here, the heroine Phaedra struggles in vain to control her illicit love for her stepson Hippolytus. The gods play a much a greater role in this play. In the prologue, Aphrodite announces that she has caused Phaedra's love in vengeance against Hippolytus, who scorns her worship, and Artemis appears in the exodos to restore the good name of her dying devotee Hippolytus. This drama, often praised for its structural and thematic balance between Aphrodite and Artemis, between Phaedra and Hippolytus, between passion and chastity, is another brilliant Euripidean study of emotional stress, of Phaedra striving desperately to maintain her good name, first by keeping secret her uncontrollable love and then by accusing Hippolytus of rape and committing suicide, and of Hippolytus, at first horrified when he learns of Phaedra's infatuation and then nobly faithful to his oaths of secrecy even when falsely accused of violating his stepmother. The tension between the two sides is maintained by well-developed hunting and sea imagery, which Euripides manipulates for meaningful character development. For example, Hippolytus's "untouched meadows" can be applied not only to nature and to the speaker's virtuous chastity but also to a sense of spiritual smugness, a holier-than-thou attitude against which Hippolytus is warned by his own servant. Phaedra's wish to "drink fresh water from a running spring" is a repressed sexual desire, especially when she couples this desire with one to "lie in the grassy meadow."

It would have been a useful guide for an interpretation of this play to know exactly how these characterizations of Hippolytus and Phaedra compared with those in Euripides' unsuccessful first version of the theme. How much less virtuous was the first Phaedra? Was the first Hippolytus as spiritually superior or as bitterly misogynistic? Satisfactory answers to these questions can probably never be found, however, and the extant *Hippolytus* must be interpreted on its own evidence. As such, *Hippolytus* can be seen to depict a passion that neither Phaedra nor Hippolytus is able to control. Both are engulfed in a powerful force, which, in this play at least, with its appearance of Aphrodite in the prologue, is more than human; it is divine. The Second Choral Ode, poised dramatically between Phaedra's accidental confession of love to the nurse in the second episode and the nurse's disastrous conversation with Hippolytus in the third episode, is a lyric statement of love's power in which the chorus describe love's destructive force and add the stories of Deianira and Semele as mythological exempla. Although violent passions are the subjects of both *Medea* and *Hippolytus*, the former play is perhaps more devoted to the depiction of the horrible effects of Medea's passion. *Hippolytus* places more emphasis on the inevitability not only of Phaedra's love, which Euripides expresses in theological, mythological, and, above all, human terms, but also of Hippolytus's intractable, passionless nature, which is developed in the same powerful terms as Phaedra's. In *Hippolytus*, Euripides thus demonstrates an astute awareness of the complexities of human psychology.

ION

Ion is one of several Euripidean dramas that revolve around anagnorisis, or recognition. This play, in fact, has two recognitions: a false recognition by Xuthus, king of Athens, that Ion is his son, and a true recognition by Creusa, Xuthus's wife, that Ion is really her son, conceived by the god Apollo and abandoned in infancy. Ion was reared as an orphan at Apollo's temple at Delphi, where the action of the drama takes place. Although the major *dramatis personae* are all illustrious figures from the Athenian past, the events that they experience were not that extraordinary in fifth century B.C.E. Greece. Many Athenians would have gone to Delphi, as Xuthus and Creusa did, to consult the oracle and to visit Apollo's temple, which the chorus as sightseers describe in the parodos. The rituals preceding a request for a Delphic oracle would also have been familiar to Euripides' audience. Further, the reliability of Apollo's shrine as an oracular seat is an issue that haunts Ion and that very much concerned Euripides' contemporaries. Apollo's reputation in this play is especially tarnished by Creusa's claim that the god raped and then abandoned her to deal alone with an unwanted pregnancy. These concerns about Apollo are directed toward the character of Ion, whose idealistic view of Apollo at the beginning of the play is repeatedly challenged, first by Creusa's story of Apollo's rape and later by the story of his true identity.

The inevitable result of these intellectual challenges is Ion's transformation from a simpleminded boy into an intelligent, questioning adult. In the end, Ion accepts Apollo's story on trust, but this leap of faith, Ion's statement of implicit faith and trust in the god, can also be interpreted as ironic, as a cynical acceptance of his fate to be the son of Xuthus "by gift" and of Creusa "by Apollo." On an understanding of Ion's intent hinges the interpretation not only of Ion's character development but also an understanding of the play itself. On the one hand, if Ion is transformed into a skeptic, the play becomes a serious condemnation of Apollo. On the other hand, if Ion's belief in Apollo matures from childlike acceptance into the faith of an adult, the play is a more optimistic statement concerning the role of deity in human life. There is no answer to this ambiguity, just as there is none for the ambiguity of *Alcestis*. It is perhaps significant, however, that Athena's appearance in the *mechane* occurs, not at the very tense dramatic moment when Ion nearly kills Creusa without knowing that she is his real mother, but rather at the point when Ion turns to ask the truth of his identity from Apollo in an oracle. Athena prevents Ion from querying the oracle because Ion is searching for a direct answer to a question that cannot be answered directly. Rather, he must be content with the ambiguity of the situation, with the contradiction that he is the son both of Xuthus and of Apollo. The dramatic emphasis is thus on Ion's intellectual growth rather than on the veracity of Apollo.

The dramatic tone of *Ion* is in strong contrast to that of *Medea* or *Hippolytus*. The horrid deaths of the earlier plays are avoided in this drama. Both Creusa and Ion are brought in the play to the point of committing the crime of Oedipus—that of unwittingly killing a blood relation—but both murders are thwarted by the dramatic circumstances. This is a tragicomedy, a *tyche* drama, in which Euripides has approached the human situation and human psychology from a completely different, and less serious, direction.

THE BACCHAE

The Bacchae is, in several ways, Euripides' most unusual work. It is the only extant Greek tragedy based on a Dionysian story, despite the cultic association of Greek tragedy with that god. Unlike many of Euripides' works, *The Bacchae* displays a religious intensity that complicates any discussion of the gods in Euripides. Further, this religious fervor is most completely developed by the chorus of bacchants, who achieve in this play a dramatic centrality lacking in other choruses, even those, such as the chorus in Euripides' *The Suppliants*, which are meant to be main characters. Even more than Dionysus himself, who is one of the *dramatis personae*, his chorus of female followers project the meaning of the Dionysian religion and its complete psychological dependence on the god. The parodos is an especially vivid example of such Dionysiac ecstasy.

However, there are important points of intersection between *The Bacchae* and Euripides' earlier plays. Most notable are the expository prologue, spoken by Dionysus, with its deceptive features; the bawdy scene between Teiresias and Cadmus in the first episode; the vivid messenger speeches; and the appearance of Dionysus in the *mechane* in the exodos.

The Bacchae is not simply about Dionysus and his religion; it also concerns Pentheus, king of Thebes, and his opposition to the new religion. The conflict between Dionysus and Pentheus and the eventual death of Pentheus at the hands of the gods' followers make possible another superb Euripidean psychological study, this one of a human mind in deterioration. Dramatic events depict the progressive insanity of Pentheus, which, on a religious level, is imposed as a punishment for opposing Dionysus. On the level of imagery, the chorus emphasize Pentheus's irrationality by describing the king as a "wild beast" in the Second Choral Ode.

BIBLIOGRAPHY

Allan, William. *The "Andromache" and Euripedean Tragedy.* Oxford, England: Oxford University Press, 2000. A thorough analysis of the play, which the author asserts deserves a greater degree of critical appreciation than it has received historically.

Bloom, Harold, ed. *Euripides.* Philadelphia: Chelsea House, 2001. Part of a series on dramatists meant for secondary school students, this book contains essays examining the work and life of Euripides. Includes a bibliography and index.

Croally, N. T. *Euripidean Polemic: The Trojan Women and the Function of Tragedy.* New York: Cambridge University Press, 1994. Croally argues that the function of Greek tragedy was didactic and that *The Trojan Women* educated by discussing Athenian ideology. He also looks at Euripides' relation with the Sophists.

Dunn, Francis M. *Tragedy's End: Closure and Innovation in Euripidean Drama.* New York: Oxford University Press, 1996. In this study of closure in Euripides' works, Dunn argues that the playwright's innovative endings opened up the form of tragedy although his artificial endings disallowed an authoritative reading of his plays.

Gounaridou, Kiki. *Euripides and "Alcestis": Speculations, Simulations, and Stories of Love in the Athenian Culture.* Lanham, Md.: University Press of America, 1998. Gounaridou examines the ambiguity and indeterminancy in *Alcestis*, analyzing about eighty scholarly attempts to interpret the play and adding her own interpretation.

Lloyd, Michael. *The Agon in Euripides.* New York: Oxford University Press, 1992. Lloyd examines the works of Euripides, focusing on the concept of agon.

Rabinowitz, Nancy Sorkin. *Anxiety Veiled: Euripides and the Traffic in Women.* Ithaca, N.Y.: Cornell University Press, 1993. Rabinowitz looks at the prominence of women in Euripides' plays and concludes that he was neither a misogynist nor a feminist. She sees him establishing male dominance while attributing strength to women.

Sullivan, Shirley Darcus. *Euripides' Use of Psychological Terminology.* Montreal: McGill-Queen's University Press, 2000. Sullivan uses psychology to dissect the works of Euripides.

Thomas J. Sienkewicz

NIKOLAI EVREINOV

Born: St. Petersburg, Russia; February 26, 1879
Died: Paris, France; February 7, 1953

PRINCIPAL DRAMA

Fundament schastya, pr. 1905
Styopik i Manyurochka, pr. 1905
Krasivy despot, pr. 1906 (*The Beautiful Despot,* 1916)
Dramaticheskiye sochineniya, pb. 1907-1923 (3 volumes)
Takaya zhenshchina, pr. 1908

Vesyolaya smert, pr. 1909 (*A Merry Death,* 1916)
Predstavlenie lyubvi, pb. 1910
Revizor, pr. 1912 (*The Inspector General,* 1984; based on Nikolai Gogol's play)
V kulisakh dushi, pr. 1912 (*The Theatre of the Soul,* 1915)
Chetvyortaya stena, pr. 1915 (*The Fourth Wall,* 1983)
Vzyatiye zimnego dvorsta, pr. 1920
Samoe glavnoe, pr., pb. 1921 (*The Main Thing,* 1926)

Korabl pravednykh, wr. 1924, pr. in Polish 1925
   (*The Ship of the Righteous*, 1970)
Teatr vechnoy voyny, pb. 1928, pr. 1929 (*The
   Unmasked Ball*, 1973)
Chemu nyet imeni: Bednoy devuchke snilos, pb.
   1965
Life as Theatre: Five Modern Plays, pb. 1973

OTHER LITERARY FORMS

Nikolai Evreinov's theories on drama are presented in *Vvedenie v monodramu* (1909; an introduction to monodrama), *Teatr kak takovoy* (1913; the theater as such), and the three-volume *Teatr dlya sebya* (1915-1917; *The Theater in Life*, 1927). A summary of these theoretical writings is available in English in *The Theater in Life*, reissued in 1970. Evreinov also wrote articles and books on various dramatic topics, such as Spanish actors of the sixteenth and seventeenth centuries, serf actors, theatrical invention, the origin of drama, Semitic and German drama, and the Russian theater. His own and other plays staged by him at The Crooked Mirror were published under his editorship in the three-volume *Dramaticheskiye sochineniya* (1907-1923).

ACHIEVEMENTS

Nikolai Evreinov belongs to those avant-garde playwright-directors who revitalized the Russian stage in the first decades of the twentieth century. After Anton Chekhov's death in 1904, these writers, among them Vsevolod Meyerhold, experimented with new forms and ideas, all of which represented a reaction to the realism and naturalism that had dominated the stage throughout the nineteenth century. Evreinov's contributions to this period of innovation in Russian theater are several. He strove to eliminate the barriers between audience and stage through a number of devices, including prologues that exposed the tricks of the trade by exhibiting props, explaining set arrangement and function, and changing scenery in view of the audience. His highly exotic settings incorporated grotesque placards, carnival paraphernalia, and dances and music. He brought back the stock characters of the *commedia dell'arte* and adopted its practice of giving the actors wide scope to improvise.

Evreinov developed a type of "short play," a sophisticated version of the humorous sketch found in cabaret, and staged this genre at The Crooked Mirror, the intimate St. Petersburg theater under his direction from 1910 to 1917. These skits subsequently became very popular in Russia and entered the general repertory as a standard feature. Evreinov's desire to focus attention on the theatrical aspects of performance caused him to make prominent use of the play-within-a-play, which is present in all his major dramas. Evreinov's assertions that "life is theater," that life must be theatricalized, and that art influences life also occupy him in his theoretical writings. In these works, he expounds on his belief that the theatrical instinct is basic to human nature, causing the human personality to play parts, mask intents, and project images constantly. The drama, according to Evreinov, must give expression to this urge by stressing the theatrical side of its enterprise and by involving the audience.

Evreinov's efforts to increase dramatic tension led him to expand on the monodrama. Whereas previously the term had designated a single actor, Evreinov split this individual into several parts, representing competing psychological tendencies. Luigi Pirandello valued Evreinov's originality so highly that he produced *The Main Thing* in his own theater in 1924. The play's Italian success prompted several American companies to mount productions, and in 1926, the Theater Guild engaged Evreinov to assist in a New York staging. Though American audiences found the intricate work strange, critics generally paid tribute to its uniqueness and recognized the potential of its new dramatic form. Evreinov's plays are not frequently performed in the United States, nor is his name widely known in the West. He also finds very little recognition on the Soviet stage, given his émigré status: the Great Soviet Encyclopedia does not even list him. Many of his innovations, however, have become permanent features of modern performance the world over.

BIOGRAPHY

Nikolai Nikolayevich Evreinov was from birth immersed in the cultural graces of the aristocratic St.

Petersburg family into which he was born on February 26, 1879. His love for the theater began in his childhood, which saw his first attempts at directing, staging, and writing. His versatility, too, was apparent early. In 1901, he was graduated from the Imperial Law Institute and embarked on a civil service career. At the same time, he developed his musical talents under Nikolai Rimsky-Korsakov and took a degree at the conservatory. Socially, he impressed others by his interests in and knowledge of art and by his sophisticated humor and improvisations. He took his government service in St. Petersburg lightly, devoting his energies to working out new forms for the stage. During the 1907-1908 season, he started directing at the St. Petersburg Starinnyi Teatr (Theater of Antiquity), where he began to apply his theories. His overriding interest in the theater soon led him to give up his legal work altogether.

In 1908, Evreinov replaced Meyerhold at the Kommissarzhevskaya Theater. Evreinov's insistence on "theatricalization," however, clashed with the conventions of the Kommissarzhevskaya, and he searched for a more suitable niche. This he found in 1910, when he took over as regisseur of Krivoye Zerkalo (The Crooked Mirror), a theater of "small forms" that was not imperially subsidized and was open to experimentation and improvisation. The position as head regisseur combined the duties of director, business manager, stage manager, and general overseer, so that he had a completely free hand in determining the course of a production. He remained at The Crooked Mirror until the Revolution, in 1917, and his activity there included presentation of his own shorter pieces.

After the Revolution, Evreinov turned his full attention to writing plays. A stay in the Caucasus during the civil war saw the completion of his major work *The Main Thing*. On his return to Petrograd (the former St. Petersburg) in 1920, he found a changed artistic climate. The Bolshevik regime called for grandiose popular spectacles with political themes. In the beginning, this orientation caught Evreinov's fancy because it coincided with his own emphasis on theatricality. In November, 1920, he staged *Vzyatiye zimnego dvorsta* (the taking of the Winter Palace), re-

joicing in the large-scale participation of some eight thousand players, a five-hundred musician orchestra, and the warship *Aurora*. The event drew an estimated 150,000 spectators. The production of this revolutionary festival gave Evreinov a chance to develop the striking visual effects that he favored. His fee, in these times when money was worthless and goods scarce, consisted of a much-needed winter coat and food.

His participation in the festival also paved the way for approval of the nonpolitical *The Main Thing* at The Free Comedy Theater in February, 1921. Despite censorial grumbling that the play lacked the desired ideological dimension, *The Main Thing* had an enthusiastic reception and continued performance through several seasons. The play was also successful in the West, and the fame it brought the author led him to consider emigration. Soviet censorship in general restrained his experimental activity and endeavored to limit him to ostentatious festival pieces with revolutionary topics. After Evreinov's mother died in 1923, he carried out his plan and settled with his talented actress-author wife, Anna Kashina, in Paris in 1925.

Before his departure, while his wife recuperated in the South of Russia, Evreinov wrote *The Ship of the Righteous*, which is dedicated to her. Although he inserted a superficial political dimension, the censors refused to allow production of the play, thereby strengthening Evreinov's resolve to leave his homeland. The Warsaw Teatr Polski performed *The Ship of the Righteous* in 1925 to great acclaim, but the playwright himself was rejected as a Bolshevik sympathizer because of his part in revolutionary theater. His last major play, *The Unmasked Ball*, was first produced in Milan in 1929, and went on to become a European success.

In exile, Evreinov turned his attention to books and essays on the history of theater. He remained a dynamic personality, was famous for his unconventional productions of Russian operas, and was in great demand as an intelligent conversationalist. His dramatic triumphs, however, were closely linked to his staging experiments in prerevolutionary Russia, and these he was not able to repeat abroad. He died in Paris on February 7, 1953.

ANALYSIS

Nikolai Evreinov's contributions to twentieth century drama are several. He developed his own form of epic theater, independent of Bertolt Brecht and Pirandello. His multiple talents as director, writer, and musician (he composed his own music for *A Merry Death* and *The Ship of the Righteous*) combined to produce some of the most provocative staging and sets to be found anywhere. He pioneered approaches to actor-audience interaction and to making theater theatrical. Most important, he transformed his own theories on the function of illusion into highly unusual, sophisticated dramas.

The idea that life is theater, which is at the base of Evreinov's theoretical writings, takes its cue from William Shakespeare's "all the world is a stage." Each of Evreinov's dramas in one way or another, incorporates this notion. His innovations developed from a reaction against the dramatic realism that characterized nineteenth century Russian theater. He also believed that Chekhov, genius though he was, had dominated the Russian stage to the exclusion of all others. As staged by Konstantin Stanislavsky, the Chekhov drama tended toward stark naturalism, and this was in direct opposition to Evreinov's view of the purpose of theater. For Evreinov, to strive for verisimilitude constituted only a cardboard faithfulness to reality, a vulgar pretension. Instead, he endeavored to appeal to the theatrical instincts of the public, to the role-playing in which everyone engaged in daily life. This necessitated the disclosure of dramatic devices, an emphasis on the theatrical properties of theater through striking visual effects and exotic nonrepresentational staging, and interaction, or at least identification, between public and players.

Toward this end, Evreinov devoted as much effort to staging as to writing. His first professional theater activity, the production of medieval mystery plays at the Theater of Antiquity immediately reflected his novel ideas. In 1907, for a Latin-language mystery play based on the Three Magi theme, he composed a prologue in Russian that revealed to the spectators the props to be used, the staging devices, and other behind-the-scenes information. He used his tenure at The Crooked Mirror to perfect his own version of the monodrama, or single-act play. In *The Theatre of the Soul*, his creative staging is designed to focus audience attention on the props. The character of the Professor, in a long prologue, uses blackboard drawings to explain the parts of the personality that the performers act out. Evreinov requires large, colorful displays for the parts of the body. Heart and lungs beat rhythmically in time to background music, speeding up or slowing down to reflect the mood of the central character, who never appears onstage. The suicide of the latter is signaled through a sudden gaping hole in the heart, which disgorges rolls of red ribbons.

Evreinov's early piece *A Merry Death* gives full expression to his preference for *commedia dell'arte* characters. The practice of *commedia dell'arte* according to which the same persons portrayed Harlequin, Pierrot, Columbine, and the Doctor for long periods, resulting in identification of actor with role, appealed greatly to Evreinov's dramatic ideas. He also liked the Harlequin actors' freedom to improvise and their informal interaction with the audience. At the conclusion of *A Merry Death*, Pierrot discusses with the audience the extent of the actors' obligation to the playwright. The use of harlequinade sequences also permitted Evreinov to forgo a traditional conclusion. Instead, a carnivalistic flourish, often including Harlequin and his group, emphasizes that human existence has no neat solutions, that nothing in life, as Pierrot says in *A Merry Death*, is worth taking seriously.

Another technique that Evreinov frequently employed was a play-within-a-play. This device allowed Evreinov to focus on the mechanics of the production, as the performers prepare for their parts, construct the set-within-the-set, and rehearse their roles. In all cases, however, the content of the inserted playlet is a comment on the theme of the entire piece. In *The Main Thing*, a rehearsal of *Quo Vadis* reveals the tensions attending a production, shows that the actors' personal perceptions continuously affect their acting, and demonstrates that the stage is a most artificial and unsuitable place for actors. Their failure onstage is redeemed by successful performances in "living roles" offstage, enriching the lives of several unhappy people. In *The Ship of the Righteous*, the tragicomic play-within-a-play "Ham Versus Noah," in which the actors don animal masks to portray the ark, foreshadows the abandonment of the two central characters in their search for a seafaring utopia. In *The Unmasked Ball*, the playlet takes the form of an "unmasked ball," in which the performers are to express their opinions honestly. The resulting disillusionment proves that role playing is far superior to naked truth in human relationships.

Evreinov also made frequent use of direct address to the audience to ensure public involvement. In *A Merry Death*, Pierrot greets his listeners with a long monologue and keeps up a continuous chatter with them. In *The Theatre of the Soul*, the Professor gives a scientific explanation of the ego, id, and superego before the actors appear. *The Main Thing* brings the director and regisseur onstage in order to force Harlequin to finish the performance, so that the spectators will not miss the last streetcar. All of Evreinov's plays, in the end, illustrate the author's viewpoint that life and theater are closely interwoven.

EARLY WORKS

Even those of Evreinov's humorous and grotesque satires written while he still pursued a civil service career contain the seeds of his later technique. *Fundament schastya* (the foundation of happiness) features a dream, humor directed at the audience, an undertaker who cheerfully tyrannizes his family, and a fantastic conclusion. *Styopik i Manyurochka* reveals the follies of the title characters to the audience bit by bit. The hero of *The Beautiful Despot*, vaguely resembling Luigi Pirandello's *Enrico IV* (pr., pb. 1922; *Henry IV*, 1923), plays the role of an enigmatic landowner who charms a group of rurals into submitting to his tyranny. From these popular but artistically far-from-novel skits, Evreinov moved to the proper one-act play.

A MERRY DEATH

Evreinov's first experiment in this form, *A Merry Death*, turned into an international success as American, French, and Italian performances followed the Russian premiere in 1909. The four characters are the stock figures from the *commedia dell'arte*, who basically play their traditional parts embellished by Evreinov's modern touches. The piece serves as a

good illustration of how Evreinov used the harlequinade. Pierrot's contact is primarily with the audience. He is delighted to have delayed the appointed midnight death of his friend Harlequin by two hours. Harlequin himself is determined to live his last evening to the fullest by spending it in intimate caresses with Pierrot's willing wife, Columbine. Interludes with the Doctor show off Harlequin's witty tongue and his *carpe diem* philosophy. As the kissing intensifies, Pierrot is torn between sympathy for his dying friend and jealousy. As these conflicting sentiments have no resolution in life, Evreinov resorts to the destruction of dramatic illusion that is so typical of his later work. Pierrot brings down the curtain and blames the "nonending" on the playwright. His own pitiful situation he ascribes to identification with the traditional Pierrot. He admonishes the spectators not to take the play seriously and assures them that Harlequin is not dead but a fellow actor waiting for his curtain call.

PREDSTAVLENIE LYUBVI

Evreinov next completed another one-act piece, *Predstavlenie lyubvi* (the play of love), labeled a monodrama. He failed to find a producer, despite the fact that the play already displayed the staging methods of his major drama. A central character, "I," interacts with his inner voice, with a female, and with a rival. Each change in mood is signaled by a change in setting, and the latter is brought about through creative lighting techniques.

THE THEATRE OF THE SOUL

The author fared much better with a similar work, *The Theatre of the Soul*, which is still a universal favorite. Its continuing appeal is attributable both to imaginative staging and to Evreinov's modern view of the complexity of human motives. Multicolored chalks trace a complicated network of veins and nerves, the latter represented by taut musical strings, whose sounds accompany the action. Heart and lungs loom garishly large; the head is absent, its function fulfilled by a yellow telephone. The primary confrontation is between the rational and emotional selves of an alcoholic clerk, who tries to regenerate his drab life by mentally transforming an aging songstress into a siren. The two selves conjure up correspondingly clashing images of the mistress, as well as diametrically opposed images of the wife, one a loving mother, the other a sharp-tongued hag. As the idealizations struggle with each other, the immense parts of the body, which dominate the stage, are in continuous motion and music. When the singer abandons the penniless clerk, the emotional self conquers its rational counterpart and signals, via the telephone, that it is time for the pistol. The suicide is depicted through images representing the disgorging of blood by the trembling mechanism. In conclusion, a third, inactive, subconscious self, vaguely alluding to a soul, is led off the stage (that is, out of the body) by a lantern-carrying conductor. This highly experimental piece was immediately popular and remained in the Soviet repertory even after Evreinov's emigration. It fared equally well abroad.

THE MAIN THING

Evreinov's success as a director kept him occupied in that capacity until the Revolution closed many theaters for ideological review. When he resumed writing, he found the full-length play a better format. *The Main Thing* is Evreinov's first and most successful major play, fully illustrating his favorite ideas and techniques. The central character, Paraclete, plays many parts. His name, signifying the third member of the Trinity, the Holy Spirit, suggests a religious dimension, which is sustained through several guises, until it is abandoned at the finale, as the monk changes into Harlequin, the trickster. Paraclete's first role is that of Lady Fortune Teller, on the lookout for unhappy clients. She chooses two groups to demonstrate the benefits of role-playing on "the world's stage": boardinghouse tenants with problems, and dissatisfied actors. Paraclete, in his second guise as "theater of life" producer, witnesses the pitiful efforts of the troupe to rehearse *Quo Vadis* and engages the major performers to resolve the tenants' difficulties by playing roles suited to the tenants' needs. Paraclete himself oversees "The Boarding House Play" in the role of the "savior" Schmid. The living theater prospers as the romantic lead woos a lonely, unattractive typist and transforms her into a more self-assured woman. His wife, the dancer, now a maid, gains the confidence and love of a suicidal student, whom she

helps to cope with his situation. The comic's assignment is to provide a romantic interest for an embittered, unpleasant old woman.

As always in Evreinov's plays, the actors' own private tensions and other outside influences intrude, resulting in a blending of life and dramatization. When the tenants discover the masquerade, ambiguity enters. On the one hand, they have benefited from the encounter, the memory of which is to sustain them. On the other hand, they may backslide, bereft of their emotional support as the actors leave. Paraclete himself loses control. He has been in the habit of marrying unhappy women to provide them with a short span of joy, but when confronted by charges of polygamy, he takes refuge in more role-playing. First, he tries a monk's disguise, emphasizing his religico-ethical motivation. When that fails, he abandons any attempt at resolution and concludes the play with a carousing carnival, himself a scheming Harlequin, while the romantic lead, the dancer, and the comic are transformed into Pierrot, Columbine, and the Doctor, respectively. The players rush to mingle with the spectators, while the directors try to find a suitable finish for the performance. The various references to the title suggest that "the main thing" in life is whatever people designate as such at any given moment. This unusual piece premiered the same year as Pirandello's *Sei personaggi in cerca d'autore* (pr., pb. 1921; *Six Characters in Search of an Author*, 1922), with which it has much in common in theme and treatment. *The Main Thing* went on to be performed in twenty-five languages, including a screen version in 1942.

THE SHIP OF THE RIGHTEOUS

Evreinov called *The Ship of the Righteous* a "dramatic epopee." It deals with the efforts of two radical idealists, named Madman and Dream, to form a morally righteous commune aboard ship, which is to cruise eternally to avoid contamination with evil (represented by land). The basic plot elements are akin to those of *The Main Thing*. The recruited group hopes to leave its various personal problems behind, onshore, as it embarks on a new life with all good intentions. Initially, the escape seems successful. The passengers try to be "good." All the difficulties and tensions of past life, however, surface during the course of the play. A stowaway former lover disrupts the newly established purity of relationships; jealousies masquerade under cover of ethical outrage; and a play-within-a-play gives evidence of revolt against the leaders of the "ark." Intrigues are unmasked, villains revealed, and illusions destroyed as the passengers, one after another, return to normal life on land. The central dreamers appeal to the audience to support them in their lonely struggle against evil, but the final image is one of disbelief in such a venture. Once again, Evreinov used a setting in which people seek to be good, only to discover that the dynamics of life are not so one-sided. Soviet censors, sensing that Evreinov was attacking their socialist utopia, refused permission to stage the drama. *The Ship of the Righteous* has not been widely performed anywhere, though the Virginia Theater Wagon staged it in 1970 to a good reception.

THE UNMASKED BALL

Evreinov considered his three major dramas a trilogy, with each work a different manifestation of the theater of life. *The Unmasked Ball*, his last major play, which was initially successful though not widely performed, is more explicit in delineating the role of illusion. The setting is a school in which students learn to dramatize all human relationships. The play suggests that survival depends on successful presentation of the proper mask at the proper time. The true self must be hidden, masquerades of deceit are encouraged, and the general impression is that life is a battlefield, ready to devour the uncamouflaged self. Hypocrisy is so commonplace that truth-telling is staged as a special event, an "unmasked ball." The result is deeply discouraging. Honest opinions and actions mercilessly undo the network of deceptive masking that permits people to cope. The final cry is for a return to blissful illusion, where betrayal and grief cannot employ their mutilating edge.

OTHER MAJOR WORKS

NONFICTION: *Vvedenie v monodramu*, 1909; *Krepostnye aktyory*, 1911; *Ispanski aktyor XVI-XVII vekov*, 1911; *Teatr kak takovoy*, 1913; *Teatr dlya sebya*, 1915-1917 (*The Theater in Life*, 1927); *Chto takoe teatr*, 1921; *Teatralnye inventsii*, 1922; *Azazel i Dionis*, 1924; *Teatr v Rossii do 1946 goda*, 1946; *Istoriya russkogo teatra*, 1947; *Istoriya russkogo teatra v drevneishikh vremyon do 1917 goda*, 1955.

BIBLIOGRAPHY

Carnicke, Sharon Marie. *The Theatrical Instinct: Nikolai Evreinov and the Russian Theatre of the Early Twentieth Century*. New York: Peter Lang, 1989. Carnicke examines Evreinov's drama within the larger context of early twentieth century Russian theater. Bibliography and index.

Golub, Spencer. *Evreinov: The Theater of Paradox and Transformation*. Ann Arbor, Mich.: UMI Research Press, 1984. An analysis of the theater art created by Evreinov. Bibliography and index.

Moody, C. "Nikolai Nikolaevich Evreinov, 1879-1953." *Russian Literature Triquarterly* 13 (1975): 659-695. A concise overview of the life and works of Evreinov.

Proffer, Ellendea, ed. *Evreinov: A Pictorial Biography*. Ann Arbor, Mich.: Ardis, 1981. A photobiography of Evreinov that provides useful information on his life.

Margot K. Frank

F

GEORGE FARQUHAR

Born: Londonderry, Ireland; 1677 or 1678
Died: London, England; late May, 1707

PRINCIPAL DRAMA

Love and a Bottle, pr. 1698, pb. 1699
The Constant Couple: Or, A Trip to the Jubilee, pr. 1699, pb. 1700
Sir Harry Wildair, Being the Sequel of a Trip to the Jubilee, pr., pb. 1701
The Inconstant: Or, The Way to Win Him, pr., pb. 1702 (adaptation of John Fletcher's play *The Wild Goose Chase*)
The Twin Rivals, pr. 1702, pb. 1703
The Stage Coach, pr., pb. 1704 (with Peter Anthony Motteux; adaptation of Jean de La Chapelle's play *Les Carosses d'Orléans*)
The Recruiting Officer, pr., pb. 1706
The Beaux' Stratagem, pr., pb. 1707

OTHER LITERARY FORMS

George Farquhar wrote a few short poems, one long occasional poem entitled *Barcellona* (1710), numerous prologues and epilogues for plays, a short novel called *The Adventures of Covent Garden* (1698), and one miscellany entitled *Love and Business* (1702), besides contributing letters to two other miscellanies.

ACHIEVEMENTS

George Farquhar was one of the most popular dramatists at the end of the Restoration period. His success is illustrated by the number of prologues and epilogues he was asked to write for other plays and by his contributions to popular miscellanies such as *Familiar and Courtly Letters* (1700) and *Letters of Wit, Politicks, and Morality* (1701). The popularity of his plays with actors, particularly *The Beaux' Stratagem* and *The Recruiting Officer*, accounted in no small measure for their survival during the eighteenth century and has played a large part in their continued visibility in modern times.

Farquhar's skill in modifying typical Restoration themes and characters accounted for much of the success of his work. He reintroduced a significant degree of realism into drama and used topical issues for comic effect. Although classed among the Restoration playwrights, he stands somewhat apart from them in his craftsmanship and his philosophy of drama, showing greater variety of plot and depth of feeling. In his later work, he sought to reconcile the liberal sexual attitudes of early comedy of manners with the more severe, increasingly moralistic tone of the early eighteenth century. He thus produced a type of comedy that stands between the traditional Restoration comedy of wit and the later sentimental comedy.

The influence of Farquhar's approach to comedy is most apparent not in the work of succeeding dramatists (although Oliver Goldsmith reveals an indebtedness to Farquhar, particularly in *She Stoops to Conquer*, pr., pb. 1773), but in the novels of Henry Fielding, in both terms of sense of humor and breadth of social milieu. Oddly enough, Farquhar was to exert a considerable influence on the development of eighteenth century German drama, mainly as a result of Gotthold Ephraim Lessing's great enthusiasm for him. His continued influence on the history of German theater is displayed in the work of a major twentieth century dramatist, Bertolt Brecht.

BIOGRAPHY

Many traditions and legends have developed around the sparse facts known about the life of George Farquhar. The earliest documented evidence is contained in the records of Trinity College, which list him as entering in July, 1694, at the age of seventeen, establishing his year of birth as either 1677 or 1678.

These records also note Londonderry, Ireland, as his place of birth, and Walker as the name of his previous teacher. Farquhar entered Trinity College, presumably to study for the Church, with a sizarship that entitled him to an allowance of bread and ale in return for serving duties. He won a scholarship less than a year after entering. This four pounds a year was suspended for a time, however, because of his riotous behavior at the Donnybrook Fair. Sometime after February, 1696, he left Trinity without taking a degree.

Not long after, Farquhar became an actor at the Smock Alley Theatre, the only theater in Dublin. His not particularly successful career as an actor ended after he wounded a fellow player in a duel scene, having forgotten to use a blunted foil. It was supposedly on the advice of his friend Robert Wilks, who was later to become one of the most popular actors on the London stage, that Farquhar went to London, probably in 1697, to write plays. *Love and a Bottle*, his first play, was produced at the Theatre Royal in Drury Lane in December, 1698. It reportedly ran for nine nights, a successful debut for the young playwright. That same month, a pamphlet entitled *The Adventures of Covent Garden* appeared anonymously. It has been attributed with some certainty to Farquhar on the basis of hints in the preface, the technique of the writer, and the fact that one of the poems appears in a later text, this time signed by Farquhar.

About a year later, again at Drury Lane, *The Constant Couple* was performed, which Farquhar later described as drawing some fifty audiences in a five-month period. Robert Wilks, who had probably joined the company at Farquhar's request, was immensely popular as Sir Harry, and another actor gained the lifelong nickname of "Jubilee Dicky" as a result of the play. Suddenly, Farquhar had become the most popular dramatist in London.

Between 1700 and 1703, three more plays appeared, all relatively unsuccessful: *Sir Harry Wildair*, a sequel to *The Constant Couple*; *The Inconstant*, an adaptation of John Fletcher's *The Wild Goose Chase* (pr. 1621, pb. 1652); and *The Twin Rivals*. Sometime between the fall of 1700 and the spring of 1702, a date earlier than the once-proposed 1704, Farquhar—in collaboration with Peter Anthony Motteux—adapted Jean de La Chapelle's *Les Carosses d'Orléans* into a farce entitled *The Stage Coach*. The authors probably did not make much money from it because one-act plays could not stand alone on a program. Adding to his increasing financial difficulties, Farquhar was married, probably in 1703, to Margaret Pemell, a widow by whom he was to have two daughters. Knowing that Farquhar needed money, Pemell tricked him into marriage by having rumors spread that she was an heiress.

During the period from 1704 to 1706, Farquhar did not stage any plays. In 1704, he received a lieutenancy from the earl of Orrery's Regiment of Foot, which was sent for service in Ireland. This commission assured him of a small yearly income of about fifty pounds. He was soon sent into western England on a recruiting campaign. In 1705, he wrote his poem *Barcellona* on the occasion of the taking of that city by the earl of Peterborough; the poem was not published until after his death. It was also in 1705, supposedly during a stay at the Raven Inn while recruiting at Shrewsbury, that *The Recruiting Officer* was written. In the spring of 1706, this play was an overwhelming success, first at Drury Lane, then at the Queen's Theatre when some of the Drury Lane players moved to the new rival company.

Despite this success, Farquhar still seems to have had financial difficulties. In the fall or winter of 1706, he sold his commission to pay his debts, reportedly after a promise by the duke of Ormonde that he would obtain for him another commission. This promise apparently came to nothing. In the meantime, Farquhar became ill. Wilks, seeking him out after an absence from the theater, advised him to write a new play and loaned him twenty guineas. The result was *The Beaux' Stratagem*, written in six weeks during his continued illness. The new play, produced in March, 1707, proved to be another success.

The register of St. Martin's in the Fields lists Farquhar's funeral, paid for by Wilks, on May 23, 1707, although his death must have occurred a few days earlier, rather than on the traditionally accepted date, that of the third performance of *The Beaux' Stratagem* in April. He may have died of tuberculosis.

ANALYSIS

In general, past criticism of George Farquhar's plays has centered on two basic areas: finding possible autobiographical references in both characters and settings and comparing Farquhar's moral attitudes to those of previous Restoration dramatists. In fact, many critics view Farquhar as the harbinger of the eighteenth century sentimental comedy. Both these views fail to deal adequately with Farquhar's artistic development of comedy. Unlike the writers of previous Restoration drama and subsequent sentimental comedy, Farquhar presents a balanced view of humanity and an equal appeal to the intellect and the emotions. His notion of the proper function of comedy, as expressed in a letter entitled "A Discourse upon Comedy" from *Love and Business*, includes the responsibility to portray the times accurately. The playwright's diversions must be realistic if he is also to carry out his task of instruction. Following these ideas, Farquhar produced drama that rests at some point of balance between the earlier cynical, witty comedy of manners and the later melodramatic sentimental comedy. Thematic development, dramatic conflict, and sources of comedy in Farquhar's three most popular plays—*The Constant Couple, The Recruiting Officer*, and *The Beaux' Stratagem*—illustrate his philosophy of comedy.

In these three plays, the treatment of theme, dramatic conflict, and sources of comedy contributes to an increased realism. The stiff, artificial characters of early Restoration drama have no place in Farquhar's theater. The audience at the turn of the eighteenth century was mainly a middle-class audience with an awakening sense of social consciousness.

Farquhar opened the window to a blast of fresh air for English comedy. By placing his characters in the world of innkeepers, military recruits, and highwaymen, Farquhar directed attention to humor rather than wit, and, in so doing, broadened the scope for comedy. His plays may well be less sharp-tongued than those of the dramatists who preceded him, but his work displays a greater naturalness and a deeper sense of life. His is the more human view of the world.

THE CONSTANT COUPLE

The Constant Couple is characterized by a light, often farcical atmosphere centered on situational comedy that instructs both by positive and by negative example. The efforts of several of the characters to attend the Jubilee in Rome gave the play a topical flavor.

Farquhar's habit of sustaining dramatic tension by action rather than by dialogue is a primary characteristic of *The Constant Couple*. The main actions center on Lady Lurewell, Colonel Standard, Sir Harry Wildair, and Angelica Darling, whose names alone suggest positive and negative examples. Angelica virtuously rejects a hypocritical suitor in the beginning, quickly establishing her character. In revenge, this suitor, appropriately named Vizard, tells Sir Harry that Angelica is a prostitute. Sir Harry, who has followed Lady Lurewell from Europe in hopes of a conquest, makes several humorous attempts to solicit Angelica's services; the best he can do is to look foolish and to hum when he discovers his mistake. Meanwhile, Lady Lurewell is involved in making all of her would-be lovers pay for the trickery of a man who seduced her at a young age. Her revenge takes the form of getting her suitors into foolish, farcical situations. Sir Harry finally abandons his wooing of Lady Lurewell to marry Angelica, and Standard is revealed as Lady Lurewell's seducer, who has been faithful to his previous engagement with her. All potentially sentimental situations, such as the reconciliation of Lady Lurewell and Standard, are short and factual rather than long and emotional.

Another aspect of *The Constant Couple* that is typical of Farquhar's plays is his modification of the usual Restoration characters. Sir Harry is not the stereotyped rake, cool and polished, living by his wit alone. Above all, he is good-natured and full of contradictions. He has been a good soldier, but he avoids a duel. He loves fashion as well as French phrases.

THE RECRUITING OFFICER

In *The Recruiting Officer*, typical Restoration characters and themes are similarly modified. The action centers on recruiting antics and the difficulties of the relationships of two couples: Plume and Silvia, and Worthy and Melinda. At the play's end, both couples plan to be married. This theme of marriage, a typical Restoration theme, is a common motif in the play, but marriage is no longer a loveless relationship with both parties finding pleasure in affairs. Much of the play is devoted to the growing companionship between Plume and Silvia. This marriage, unlike the marriages in earlier Restoration drama, is not for money alone.

Farquhar's characters are also modified from the previous extremes of the Restoration. Farquhar's fop figure, Brazen, who has hopes of marrying Melinda, represents a fragmentation of the usual Restoration fop. Brazen has none of the typical clothes and affectations of the Restoration fop and much less of the foolish gullibility. Farquhar instead takes the social qualities of a fop, exaggerates them, and fits them into a military atmosphere. Brazen's bragging, traditional for the fop, encompasses the world of battle and the world of the beau. The social memory and name-dropping tendency of a fop are exaggerated. It is precisely these characteristics of Brazen that leave him open to ridicule by other characters within the play.

The rake figure also undergoes modification in *The Recruiting Officer*. Plume asks the country girl, Rose, to his lodging not to debauch her but to get her to aid in his recruiting, his main area of manipulation. Plume has a definite share of kindness and good nature. He provides for the subsistence of his bastard and provides a husband for the mother. He releases the disguised Silvia from her enlistment because he values an obligation to her father above money. Plume's dialogue has its share of wit, but it also reveals his fundamentally kind nature.

Although wit is used to produce comedy in *The Recruiting Officer*, the dialogue also features puns, farce, and comical treatment of social issues. The greater use of the latter as one of the major sources of comedy distinguishes Farquhar from other Restoration dramatists. The recruiting issue underlies a large part of the comedy in *The Recruiting Officer* and often provides for major dramatic conflict. The light atmosphere is set in the prologue, when the action is foretold and ironically compared to heroic times. The recruiting tricks of Kite play on possibilities, however improbable, of military advancement and even on the superstitions of the people when he dons his fortune-telling disguise. Less gentle is the comedy of Plume's entering his bastard as a recruit and wanting no one in his company who can write or who is a gentleman.

The Beaux' Stratagem

In Farquhar's *The Beaux' Stratagem*, social issues and modification of traditional Restoration themes and characters again play a prominent role. *The Beaux' Stratagem* is regarded by most critics as Farquhar's finest achievement. Its great sense of naturalness, of fidelity to life, continues to make it a great favorite with actors and audiences alike. The action centers on Aimwell's courtship of Dorinda, first of all for her money but later for love. Archer, Aimwell's friend disguised as a servant, also courts Cherry, the innkeeper's daughter, and Mrs. Sullen, an unhappily married woman. In the meantime, a series of scenes alternates between the inn, whose owner is a highwayman, and the manor, in which a robbery and a midnight love scene occur.

Farquhar's use of the social issue of the recent war against France and the resulting anti-French sentiment pervades all levels of the play. In the inn, Frenchmen pay double the regular fee. Scrub, Mr. Sullen's servant, parodies the French, while Aimwell quips that he would not like a woman who was fond of a Frenchman. Count Bellair, Mrs. Sullen's suitor, and Foigard, Bellair's chaplain, both come in for a large portion of the anti-French comedy.

The concept of social equality also becomes a major source for comedy, including the financial inequality created by primogeniture. Gibbet, the highwayman, excuses himself because he is a younger brother. Aimwell initiates dramatic conflict because of his status as a younger brother. In *The Beaux' Stratagem*, Farquhar stresses the fact that class differences do not correspond to levels of virtue. He achieves this emphasis by showing the same goodness in Cherry and Lady Bountiful, and the same corruption in Boniface and Sullen. In the robbery scene, Archer himself is cleverly associated with the thieves by Mrs. Sullen's cry of "Thieves, Murder." The same fundamental human qualities are thus shown to exist both in the inn and in the country mansion.

As in *The Recruiting Officer*, the plot of *The Beaux' Stratagem* deals with a modified marriage theme. The subject of marriage is not discussed using the common gaming imagery of the earlier Restoration drama, and the only slave imagery is used to describe Mrs. Sullen's marriage. In this instance, the marriage conflict is a conflict between law and nature. Sullen lies with his wife because of the law, and the natural differences between them do not come within the bounds of divorce law. In the conclusion, however, the maxim of nature as the first lawgiver is upheld.

The roster of traditional figures, as in *The Recruiting Officer*, is again modified. Count Bellair in *The Beaux' Stratagem* is a different variety of fop. He is obviously less foolish than the traditional fop because Mrs. Sullen chooses the Count to be part of her manipulations. Bellair shows extraordinary intelligence, for a fop, in initiating his own manipulation to get into Mrs. Sullen's closet. In creating Count Bellair, Farquhar took one aspect of the traditional fop, the beau, and exaggerated it. Bellair functions exceedingly well in this role, but he is also ridiculed because of his French qualities and becomes emblematic of the deeper conflict of social ideas in Farquhar.

OTHER MAJOR WORKS

SHORT FICTION: *The Adventures of Covent Garden*, 1698.

POETRY: *Barcellona*, 1710.

MISCELLANEOUS: *Love and Business*, 1702; *The Complete Works of George Farquhar*, 1930 (Charles Stonehill, editor); *The Works of George Farquhar*, 1988 (Shirley Strum Kenny, editor).

BIBLIOGRAPHY

Bull, John. *Vanbrugh and Farquhar*. New York: St. Martin's Press, 1998. Bull compares and contrasts the comic dramatists Sir John Vanbrugh and George Farquhar. Includes bibliography and index.

James, Eugene Nelson. *The Development of George Farquhar as a Comic Dramatist*. The Hague: Mouton, 1972. After a brief introduction, "The Traditions in Farquhar Criticism," James marches through the plays a chapter at a time. *The Recruiting Officer* is judged "climactic" for its form, and *The Beaux' Stratagem* is the "fulfillment of a promise." Rich source notes.

Milhous, Judith, and Robert D. Hume. *Producible Interpretation: Eight English Plays, 1675-1707*. Carbondale: Southern Illinois University Press, 1985. "By 'producible interpretation' we mean a critical reading that a director could communicate to an audience in performance," the authors note. *The Beaux' Stratagem* is "an effective stage vehicle," and the authors devote twenty-seven pages to discussing possibilities of stage interpretation. An insightful essay.

Rothstein, Eric. *George Farquhar*. New York: Twayne, 1967. This volume in the Twayne series is an excellent introduction to and overview of both Farquhar's life and his work.

Stafford-Clark, Max. *Letters to George: The Account of a Rehearsal*. 1990. Reprint. London: N. Hern Books, 1997. These letters look at Farquhar's *Recruiting Officer* and the production of Farquhar's dramas. Includes bibliography.

Eril Barnett Hughes,
updated by Frank Day

EDNA FERBER

Born: Kalamazoo, Michigan; August 15, 1885
Died: New York, New York; April 16, 1968

PRINCIPAL DRAMA

Our Mrs. McChesney, pr., pb. 1915 (with George V. Hobart)

$1200 a Year, pr., pb. 1920 (with Newman A. Levy)

Minick, pr., pb. 1924 (with George S. Kaufman)

The Royal Family, pr. 1927, pb. 1928 (with Kaufman)

Dinner at Eight, pr., pb. 1932 (with Kaufman)

Stage Door, pr., pb. 1936 (with Kaufman)
The Land Is Bright, pr., pb. 1941 (with Kaufman)
Bravo!, pr. 1948, pb. 1949 (with Kaufman)

OTHER LITERARY FORMS

Edna Ferber hoped she would be remembered as a playwright, but even during her lifetime, she was considered primarily a novelist and writer of short stories; nevertheless, the ease with which several of her major novels, among them *Show Boat* (1926), *Saratoga Trunk* (1941), and *Giant* (1952), have been adapted to musical theater and film proves that memorable characterization is the greatest strength her works possess. Strong characterization appears even in her first novel, *Dawn O'Hara: The Girl Who Laughed* (1911), and Ferber achieved national success with the Emma McChesney stories, which were published originally in *American* and *Cosmopolitan* magazines, quickly reprinted as collections from 1913 to 1915, and finally distilled as Ferber's first dramatic collaboration, *Our Mrs. McChesney*.

Ferber's works were perfectly attuned to American popular taste. This was especially true of the novels and short stories written in the years between the two world wars, when her career was at its height. Her first venture in autobiography, *A Peculiar Treasure* (1939), written just before the outbreak of World War II, appropriately finishes this period. This work especially shows Ferber's identification with European Jewry suffering under Nazi persecution and ominously foreshadows the horrors of the Holocaust.

Giant was Ferber's last successful major novel, and it appears that even as she wrote her somewhat anticlimactic second autobiographical volume, *A Kind of Magic* (1963), she was aware that her popularity had waned. She continued to write until her death, however, managing to sell film rights to her unsuccessful last novel, *Ice Palace* (1958), even before its publication.

ACHIEVEMENTS

Edna Ferber's reputation as a novelist and writer of short stories made possible her ventures into drama and autobiography. Paradoxically, the adaptation of several of her major novels to musical theater

(*Show Boat*), film (*Saratoga Trunk, So Big, Giant, Ice Palace*), and even television (*Cimarron*, 1930) served to reduce public recognition of the novels from which the adaptations were derived. Correspondingly, two substantial autobiographies, coupled with a biography by Ferber's great-niece Julie Goldsmith Gilbert, discouraged scholarly research.

Ferber's novels are large in scope yet regional in character, and Ferber considered it an accomplishment that she was able to write with apparent ease about so many locations in which she had never lived, describing not only the Midwest, where she was reared, but the South, the West, and even the Arctic. She rightly believed that her strength lay in the ability to isolate the distinctive character of each region and describe it in terms appropriate to the popular imagination.

The Midwest of Emma McChesney, the South of *Show Boat*, even the Texas of *Giant* no longer exist, however, and this has served to make some of Ferber's finest works period pieces. Stronger, more contemporary statements have been made about the plight of minorities; anonymous corporate greed has exceeded that of individual families; and novels of manners are generally out of favor. The works of Willa Cather and William Faulkner, although also regional, can survive on the universal applicability of the situations they describe, but Ferber's work cannot.

Ferber's greatest popularity came in the nostalgic period between the two world wars and during the Depression, when Americans sought escape from overwhelming reality. *So Big* (1924) won the Pulitzer Prize in 1925, and this led to a flurry of publication that slowed only after 1941. Today, most of her works are out of print, even some of her best-known books—books that sold thousands of copies before the advent of the paperback and that won the unsolicited plaudits of Rudyard Kipling and both Theodore and Franklin D. Roosevelt.

The situation is even more dismal in the case of Ferber's plays, this despite her often brilliant collaborations with George S. Kaufman. When *The Royal Family, Dinner at Eight*, or *Stage Door* is mentioned, a glimmer of recognition comes to the eye of a well-read person, but even these works are not generally associated with Ferber's name. Sometimes they are remembered as Kaufman's work, perhaps because his name always preceded Ferber's on the title page and in billing, but they are as likely to be recalled only as films.

Ferber was adept at female characterization, and strong women, who were also usually amiable, fill the pages of her works. This was considered by many an innovation that made Ferber in her own time a popular counterweight to Ernest Hemingway, but it has not continued to save her literary reputation.

BIOGRAPHY

Edna Ferber considered her earliest years turbulent and unhappy, particularly the time before her family's move to Appleton, Wisconsin. This unhappiness had essentially two causes: awareness that as the child of middle-class Jewish merchants, she was often not accepted by rough-edged Midwestern farmers, and her recognition of the isolated and difficult nature of plains life in the last quarter of the nineteenth century. Her parents, Jacob and Julia, made several moves, evidently seeking a more comfortable life for the family, and Edna was born in Kalamazoo, Michigan, on August 15, 1885. (Ferber, perhaps from the vanity to which she confesses in her autobiography, gave the date as 1887, and this was the year published in *The New York Times* obituary.) By 1888, Jacob, though he seems to have prospered moderately in Kalamazoo, moved his family to Chicago, where his wife, Julia Neumann Ferber, had been reared, and the Ferbers lived for a year in the large Neumann house on Calumet Avenue. Jacob's desire for independence, as well as his idea that his dry goods business would be more successful in an isolated town, prompted him to move the family again, this time to Ottumwa, Iowa, and the Ferbers lived in this farming and coal-mining town from 1890 to 1897. Edna Ferber always considered the place brutal and crude; it was a struggle to maintain even a modicum of comfort in this primitive town, which quite often was openly anti-Semitic. Jacob's progressive blindness was first diagnosed in the Ottumwa years, and this served to place more business and family responsibilities on Julia. A successful lawsuit for slander brought by a

Edna Ferber (Hulton Archive by Getty Images)

fired employee cost the Ferbers several thousand dollars and hastened their move to Wisconsin.

Appleton provided more congenial surroundings. There was a small Jewish community there, good schools, and the pleasant atmosphere of a Midwestern college town. Ferber excelled in declamation and debate for Ryan High School's Forum Debating Society, and her first prize at a statewide declamation contest paved the way at age seventeen for her position as reporter on the Appleton *Daily Crescent*, the town's newspaper. Ferber, like Willa Cather, planned a career in journalism, and in 1905, she accepted an offer to work on the *Milwaukee Journal*.

Milwaukee proved a big change for the nineteen-year-old Ferber. She was suddenly on her own, living in a boardinghouse whose principal tenants were German-speaking engineers employed in the steelworks and engineering plants in and around the city. She drew on this experience for her first novel, *Dawn O'Hara*, a few years later. Milwaukee also provided more chances than ever to attend the theater, and some of Ferber's earliest writings were drama and music reviews published in both the *Milwaukee Journal* and the *Daily Crescent*. Her health suffered, however, and forced her return to Appleton after three years.

Though Ferber had planned to return to Milwaukee after recovering her strength in Appleton, she never did. On a secondhand typewriter, she wrote an essay entitled "Why I Lost My Job," entered it in a contest sponsored by the *Chicago Tribune*, and won first prize. Encouraged by this success, she began to write *Dawn O'Hara*. On Jacob's death in 1909, Julia returned to Chicago with Edna and her older sister Fannie (the Fannie Fox who wrote the famous cookbook). This was the beginning of Ferber's Chicago period, and for the next thirteen years, she lived in hotels and furnished apartments. She continued to write freelance articles for the *Tribune*, but she directed her energies primarily toward fiction.

Short stories in the style of O. Henry poured from her typewriter, and her 1911 success with *Dawn O'Hara* enabled her to publish much of this material. Good reviews for *Buttered Side Down* (1912) continued the momentum, but it was the McChesney stories, which were published in nationally circulated magazines, that brought her popular success. They introduced an admirable and determined traveling saleswoman named Emma McChesney, a character derived from Ferber's mercantile and Midwestern background. These successes led Ferber to divide her time, somewhat awkwardly, between Chicago and New York. She was able to use her training in journalism to cover the 1912 Republican and Democratic National Conventions for the Franklin P. Adams syndicate. It was at this time that she met William Allen White, who would remain a friend and confidant for the rest of her life. The dramatic rights to the McChesney stories were sold to Joseph Brooks at the end of 1913, and in 1915 they appeared as the play *Our Mrs. McChesney*, a difficult collaboration with George V. Hobart. Ethel Barrymore, as Emma McChesney, saved this mediocre play, although Ferber always maintained that Barrymore had been miscast.

Although Ferber could have allowed her reputation to rest on the McChesney character alone, she wisely sought new literary horizons. Returning by ship from a European holiday, she met a young Chicago lawyer, Newman A. Levy, who was a playwright and artist by avocation, and this meeting resulted in the play *$1200 a Year*. Although a dismal failure, the play anticipated the direction her future works in drama would take and led to more successful collaborations with George S. Kaufman. *The Royal Family*, *Dinner at Eight*, and *Stage Door* remain minor classics, although they stand more effectively as literature than as revivals. Her novel *Fanny Herself* (1917), which enjoyed only moderate success, enabled Ferber to see that her greatest abilities lay in the novel, the direction her career would ultimately take.

So Big, *Show Boat*, and *Cimarron* appeared in quick succession during the post-World War I years, and Ferber was firmly established as a New York-based writer and a popular success. She frequented the Algonquin Round Table and met Marc Connelly, Robert E. Sherwood, Deems Taylor, Alexander Woollcott, George Oppenheimer, and other literary notables in that circle. These were her most productive years.

Ferber's move to Connecticut and Treasure Hill, the country home she built there in the late 1930's, continued to feed her muse. Her autobiography *A Peculiar Treasure* was written while her house was being built, and *Nobody's in Town* (1938), a collection of short stories, also appeared at this time. The onset of World War II, however, reduced her literary output considerably, and it was only at the war's end that her novel *Great Son* (1945) appeared. It was not until 1952 that *Giant*, her novel on life among the oil-rich families of Texas, brought her new acclaim.

In the early 1960's, Doubleday, the publisher with which Ferber had enjoyed such a successful association, encouraged her to write a novel that she had been planning on the American Indian, tentatively entitled "The Squaw." Ferber was doing research for this projected work even as she was suffering from a painful facial nerve disease and finally from the stomach cancer that eventually took her life. She carried on gallantly to the last, dining regally at her favorite restaurants and enjoying the company of her sister's family. She had never married.

ANALYSIS

"Stagestruck" Edna Ferber, as she described herself, could not help writing plays, though she never attempted to do this alone. It appears, from a reading of those she wrote with George S. Kaufman, that she relied on Kaufman's skill for timing and dialogue but that the characterizations are essentially her own. A consistent development in Ferber's dramatic skills can be traced, beginning with her collaboration with Newman A. Levy, *$1200 a Year.*

$1200 A YEAR

Ferber wrote *$1200 a Year* with Levy during 1920, which was a transitional year in her life. Still living in Chicago but contemplating a permanent move to New York, she was at once attracted and repelled by city life and the large sums of money that could be earned there. She wrote to William Allen White that she hated the play even as she and Levy were writing it, that everyone but she seemed to be earning $100,000 a year, and that she was eager to work on her novel *The Girls* (1921). She describes the multiple coats of "paint" and "varnish" that she and Levy were applying to the play in an effort to make it stageworthy. This less than enthusiastic approach to the task may well have been one of the reasons for the play's dismal failure. Sam Harris, who had agreed to produce the play, closed it after a week of Baltimore tryouts. Nevertheless, *$1200 a Year* reveals a good deal about Ferber as a developing playwright.

Broadly drawn characterizations and stereotypes developed through hyperbole appear throughout the work. The once-moneyed Massachusetts aristocracy, represented by the appropriately named Winthrop family, contrasts with the prosperous immigrant Cyrus McClure, the Scot who built the Wickley, Pennsylvania, steel mill, which supports most of the town's affluent working class. These personalities, in turn, contrast with those of the mill workers, recent immigrants who have supplied the brawn that the system demands and so have prospered. Paul Stoddard, the protagonist, is a professor of economics at Dinsmore, the university maintained by McClure's money. Stoddard teaches his students, among them McClure's son Steven, the mysteries of political economy, and although he understands theoretically how to make great

sums of money, he struggles to survive on his meager professor's salary of twelve hundred dollars a year.

Stoddard's lectures and research have dealt with the growth of fifteenth century English trade guilds. This has angered Cyrus McClure, who is a member of the Dinsmore Board of Trustees and who fears that the mill workers' children attending the university will convince their parents to agitate for the establishment of unions at the mill.

When Stoddard first appears, McClure and the other trustees have already issued an ultimatum that the young professor delete this potentially inflammatory material from his lectures. Stoddard has met these demands by submitting his resignation. He decides to leave the threadbare aristocracy of college life and apply for a worker's job at McClure's mill. He completes the transformation to worker by living among the workers of the mill district.

Six months later, he has acquired all the material things he and his wife, Jean, have always wanted and has acquired as well a new group of friends, among whom is mill hand Chris Zsupnik. In his free time, Stoddard lectures to receptive audiences, outlining his theories on the potential power of workers, and his words soon have an effect. Significantly, the effect is most pronounced among American academics and other underpaid professionals who flock to join the ranks of unskilled laborers. These new workers create such an imbalance in the labor supply that colleges and universities all over the United States begin to close. What is more, factory and mill owners such as McClure threaten to cut wages to absorb the new supply of workers and maintain a market for the goods they produce. Another group of casualties includes academics who cannot make the transition to the working class. Jean's older brother, Henry Adams Winthrop, who knows little of any historical event that has occurred since the Peloponnesian War, is now utterly unemployable.

Of necessity, a reversal now occurs. Stoddard's fellow workers become convinced that the academic is merely doing a form of practical research and attempting to see if his theories really work. Jean is never comfortable with her working-class neighbors, even though she does like what Stoddard's higher salary can buy. Jean is a characteristic Ferber heroine: She takes decisive action and bargains with McClure on her own. McClure shrewdly uses his interview with Jean to convince his mill workers that he, and not Stoddard, is their true friend.

The play is now at an impasse, which can be solved only by *deus ex machina*, which arrives in the form of Cleveland Welch, talent scout for the Mastodon Art-Film Company. He offers Stoddard five thousand dollars a week to play the lead in a great new heartthrob film to be entitled *Brains and Brawn*. The film will be the life story of Paul Stoddard, who has put theory to practice in order to conquer the illiterate tyrant Cyrus McClure. When McClure hears Welch's offer, he asks what Stoddard would consider a fair salary for a university professor. The audience never hears Stoddard's reply, for the curtain descends just as he is about to name a figure.

Ferber's first autobiographical memoir, *A Peculiar Treasure*, describes the special affection she had for immigrants to the United States, an affection apparent in the sympathetic portrait of the Zsupnik family in *$1200 a Year*. Her father's background and her life in Appleton and Milwaukee provided inspiration for many of these characters in her comedy.

Although a failure, *$1200 a Year* foreshadows themes that would be developed in subsequent Ferber plays. Topics such as socialism in the United States following the Russian Revolution, immigration, unfair distribution of wealth, the advancing labor movement, and how the United States chooses its heroes provide the play's background. Still, *$1200 a Year* never becomes a diatribe on American life. Hyperbole allows the audience to see absurdity where it exists and to draw the obvious conclusion that the common interest is served only by fair dealing; anything else is merely a short-term advantage.

DINNER AT EIGHT

Dinner at Eight was successful in its first production and shows a more mature development of similar themes. In this play, Ferber and Kaufman explore American classes and manners against the background of New York during the Depression. The changed circumstances in which many Americans found themselves in 1932 are obviously at the root of the play's

action, but once again, the audience is allowed to discover this on its own. The Jordan family, described in terms Ferber had earlier used for the Winthrops, represents the Yankee aristocracy. Oliver Jordan has come to realize that the family shipping line, which had always seemed a sure source of continuing income, is threatened with bankruptcy. His wife, Millicent, seems blissfully unaware of this. Her greatest concern is planning a pretheater dinner for Lord and Lady Ferncliffe, who have just arrived in town.

The guest list is planned to combine business and social requirements. Don Packard, whose manners still betray his Western mining days, and his Passaic-born wife, Kitty, receive Millicent's invitation only through Oliver's urgent petition. Oliver hopes to enlist Dan's aid to rescue the Jordan line. One of Oliver's old flames, Carlotta Vance, an apparently wealthy but faded actress, also receives an invitation; Larry Renault, an equally faded actor, is to be her dinner companion. Oliver's physician, J. Wayne Talbot, and his wife, Lucy, will complete the guest list. (Kaufman worried that the social complications that the play relates would invite comparisons with *The Grand Hotel*, which had been produced the same year; this was indeed the case, for *Dinner at Eight* rivaled *The Grand Hotel* in complexity.)

As the dinner preparations continue, the audience learns that Oliver, struggling to keep the Jordan Line afloat, has an incurable heart disease; that Carlotta has sold her Jordan stock, thereby making Oliver's business problems more acute; that Dan has been maneuvering behind the scenes to acquire control of the Jordan company; that Kitty has been having an affair with Wayne Talbot; and that the Jordans' daughter Paula, though engaged, has been enjoying her own liaison with the alcoholic actor Larry Renault. Ironically, the Ferncliffes, who leave New York for Florida at the last moment, never appear at the party in their honor, and their place is filled, somewhat unwillingly, by Millicent's sister Hattie and her husband, Ed. Larry Renault never appears either, for he commits suicide after learning that he cannot get even a supporting part in an upcoming play.

As usual in Ferber's plays, external events influence the action but are never incorporated into the play. The audience recognizes that the Depression is the fundamental cause of much of what happens, but beyond an occasional reference to difficult times, no one mentions it. Each of the characters has brought on personal disaster by some individual failing: Oliver through lack of diligent management, Dan because of his preoccupation with money making, Larry by his alcoholism, and Talbot through his womanizing. This allows Ferber to maintain her fundamentally optimistic view of American life. The seeds of decadence are present, and a few succumb to them, but others, such as Hattie and Ed, retain the common sense and attachment to simple pleasures that allow them to avoid the disasters that afflict the major characters.

STAGE DOOR

In *Stage Door*, her next play after *Dinner at Eight*, Ferber introduces a large cast of characters to portray manners and emphasize conflict. This 1936 collaboration with Kaufman features thirty-two actors, each of whom plays a character with a remarkably different personality. Even the minor characters become essential to advance the play's action.

The plot is relatively simple. There is only one scene, at the Footlights Club, a boardinghouse for aspiring actresses. Life at the club is one of genteel and somewhat Bohemian poverty. The young women are without jobs more often than with them. They discreetly jockey for position and sometimes grant their favors to assorted "stage-door-Johnnys," writers, producers, and movie moguls.

Terry Randall is the single exception. She refuses a film offer made through David Kingsley, a Broadway producer who has sought greener pastures in Hollywood. She encourages an idealistic writer named Keith Burgess but does not criticize his decision to write screenplays for Hollywood. She resents, though silently, Jean Maitland's exploitation of the Footlights Club to publicize an already successful film career. Rather than rely on the financial support of her father, she works at Macy's department store and seeks auditions during her lunch hour. In short, Terry remains in control of her life throughout the play and never sacrifices her idealism. Inspired by her example, Kingsley decides to return to Broadway

as the producer of a play that he rescues from the clutches of movie executive Adolph Gretzl, who had planned to use the play only to publicize Maitland's latest film. *Stage Door* concludes with idealism triumphant. Terry will star in the rescued play and will marry Kingsley, the man whom she has rescued from the dangers of materialism.

THE ROYAL FAMILY

It is interesting that Julie Cavendish, in the Ferber-Kaufman collaboration *The Royal Family*, best sums up the way Ferber saw her relationship to the theater. (Indeed, Ferber's single experience as an actress was her portrayal of Julie in a 1940 revival of the play staged in Maplewood, New Jersey.) Julie, a character based on Ethel Barrymore, Ferber's girlhood stage heroine, sees her life as a grand drama. Like Ferber, she is a woman who wants all that life can offer. Ferber, however, had infinitely more common sense and considerably more business acumen than Julie possessed. Her popular appeal made possible the unquestioned success that she enjoyed during her lifetime, even if it has not assured her immortality as a writer.

OTHER MAJOR WORKS

LONG FICTION: *Dawn O'Hara: The Girl Who Laughed*, 1911; *Funny Herself*, 1917; *The Girls*, 1921; *So Big*, 1924; *Show Boat*, 1926; *Cimarron*, 1930; *American Beauty*, 1931; *Come and Get It*, 1935; *Saratoga Trunk*, 1941; *Great Son*, 1945; *Giant*, 1952; *Ice Palace*, 1958.

SHORT FICTION: *Buttered Side Down*, 1912; *Roast Beef Medium*, 1913; *Personality Plus*, 1914; *Emma McChesney and Co.*, 1915; *Cheerful—By Request*, 1918; *Half Portions*, 1919; *Gigolo*, 1922; *Mother Knows Best*, 1927; *They Brought Their Women*, 1933; *Nobody's in Town*, 1938 (includes *Nobody's in Town* and *Trees Die at the Top*); *One Basket*, 1947.

NONFICTION: *A Peculiar Treasure*, 1939, revised 1960 (with new introduction); *A Kind of Magic*, 1963.

BIBLIOGRAPHY

Antler, Joyce. *The Journey Home: Jewish Women and the American Century*. New York: Free Press, 1997. This overview of the lives of a selection of

American Jewish women beginning in 1890 contains a portrait of Ferber.

Batker, Carol. "Literary Reformers: Crossing Class and Ethnic Boundaries in Jewish Women's Fiction of the 1920's." *MELUS* 25, no.1 (Spring, 2000): 81-104. Ferber's work is examined in the context of Jewish women's fiction, along with that of Anzia Yezierska and Fannie Hurst.

Bloom, Harold, ed. *Jewish Women Fiction Writers*. Women Writers of English and Their Works series. Philadelphia, Pa.: Chelsea House, 1998. This collection of critical essays contains a discussion of Ferber with a bibliography of her work.

Gilbert, Julie Goldsmith. *Ferber: A Biography*. 1978. Reprint. New York: Applause, 1999. Gilbert describes, with style and wit, Ferber's life and work. She calls Ferber a romantic realist, not opposed to working with the system, yet creating her own unique niche within it. Rather than proceeding chronologically, Gilbert begins her narrative with Ferber's death and moves through the major turning points in her life. Illustrated.

Goldstein, Malcolm. *George S. Kaufman: His Life, His Theatre*. New York: Oxford University Press, 1979. In addition to rendering an insightful account of the man, this work is considered a standard source on the theater of the period. Details Kaufman's collaborations with many dramatists, including Ferber.

Mordden, Ethan. *The American Theatre*. New York: Oxford University Press, 1981. In this insightful investigation of what is peculiarly American in American theater, the author writes a straight chronicle, following the evolution of the American stage as art and industry from its beginnings to 1980. His discussion of Ferber focuses on the play *The Royal Family*. Contains a useful guide for further reading.

Robert J. Forman,
updated by Genevieve Slomski

ANTÓNIO FERREIRA

Born: Lisbon, Portugal; 1528
Died: Lisbon, Portugal; November 29, 1569

PRINCIPAL DRAMA

Bristo, pr. 1552-1553, pb. 1562 (*The Comedy of Bristo: Or, The Pimp*, 1990)

A Castro, pr. 1553-1556, pb. 1587 (*Ignez de Castro*, 1825)

Cioso, pr. 1554-1555. pb. 1622 (English translation, 1825)

OTHER LITERARY FORMS

In addition to two comedies and one tragedy, António Ferreira wrote and published in various poetic forms—sonnets, odes, eclogues, epigrams, and epitaphs—as well as writing letters and a history. In most of these works, Ferreira shows the great influence that Greek, Latin, and Renaissance Italian authors had on him, especially Horace, Vergil, and Petrarch.

ACHIEVEMENTS

António Ferreira was indisputably the best-educated poet and dramatist in sixteenth century Portugal; as such, his knowledge of the classics was both extensive and profound. In his many odes and particularly in his letters, Ferreira the humanist stands forth clearly. Indeed, he may be considered the greatest theorist of humanistic values—especially in the realm of literary art—in the Portugal of his time. Having been the student, at the university in Coimbra, of the renowned humanists George Buchanan and Nicolau Grouchy, Ferreira came to view his career as a mission for spreading Christian, humanistic, and classical values and ideals to contemporary as well as to future generations of writers, artists, and critics.

A proponent of the theory that reason is the dominant force among humankind and that terrestrial happiness will result from constant application of reason over passions, illusions, and impulses, Ferreira was against the pursuit of warfare as a noble endeavor, finding physical courage of inferior status to reason. He even went so far as to remind influential aristocrats that they too were heirs to the human condition, and that the aristocracy of knowledge and intelligence was far more desirable than that of inherited bloodlines.

The impact that Ferreira had on fellow writers and other important persons in the area of humanism was equaled if not surpassed by his impact on the Portuguese language. He has been compared to the great French poet and linguist Joachim Du Bellay, whose *Défense et illustration de la langue française* (1549) became the manifesto for the invigoration of French as a literary language at least equal to Latin, and he was deeply interested in all aspects of Portuguese, including the medieval forms. Ferreira was especially bold in his opposition to the seeming dominance of Castilian among his contemporary poets in Portugal; in fact, he was possibly the only major Portuguese poet of his day who never wrote a single verse in the Castilian dialect. His linguistic chauvinism is evident even in the title of his collected works *Poemas lusitanos* (1598; Portuguese poems).

As a classicist, Ferreira had a tremendous effect on other writers of his time, as well as of succeeding generations. Taking Horace as his principal model and tutor, he unceasingly promoted the typical precepts of the classical school: the primacy of study and hard work over inspiration; the necessity of a profound and broad knowledge of the classics as well as imitation of them; the need for criticism and self-criticism, for a feeling for proper balance and proportion; and the proscription of virtually all peninsular medieval inheritance (of Spain in particular). He also hoped and worked for the eventual creation of a Portuguese national epic poem—one based not so much on heroic deeds in war and on crusades, but rather one that would be a monument to the people and culture of his native land, one that would, above all, ennoble the Portuguese language. His contemporary, the great Luís de Camões, would indeed follow many of Ferreira's dictates in his epic poem *Os Lusíadas* (1572; *The Lusiad*, 1655).

In his own work, Ferreira was true to the precepts that he dictated for others. He was opposed to the Baroque, and in his writing he attempted to create a modern language free of archaisms, colloquialisms, and overly picturesque speech. At the same time, he encouraged a freedom of expression based on Latin syntax as well as a vitality in the best French tradition. It has been said that, between the days of antiquity and the present, Ferreira represents the high point of classical and humanistic ideals in Portuguese literature.

BIOGRAPHY

António Ferreira was born in 1528 in Lisbon, a city he would soon come to love above all others and about which he would frequently write flowery and often majestic verses that reveal an innate sincerity. Ferreira was proud of his family name, and with ample reason. His was a noble family of ancient origin going as far back as King Arthur, from whom it was claimed that they were descended, as well as from Ferrabac, the first Norman king. The Ferreira name probably was associated with the craft of ironworking—one of the few trades that the nobility was allowed to practice in the Middle Ages. The poet's father, Martim Ferreira, was a Knight of the Order of Saint James and was attached to the household of the duke of Coimbra; his mother, Mexia Froes Varella, who was descended from the first kings and queens of Castile, probably died when Ferreira was a child. He had one brother, Garcia Fróis, who at one time was in the service of the queen of Portugal, Catherine of Austria, in the middle of the sixteenth century.

Ferreira spent his childhood and part of his adolescence in Lisbon, but when it came time to take up his studies, he moved to Coimbra, where the king, John III, had transferred the university in 1537. The period from 1543 to 1556, which he spent almost entirely in Coimbra, was the most prolific period of his life. It was during this time that he accomplished his extensive studies, discovered love, and wrote most of his works. On July 16, 1551, Ferreira received his first diploma, or "bachelor's" degree; some four years later, on July 14, 1555, he was awarded the doctorate. Comfortable but by no means wealthy, Ferreira was apparently well liked by his fellow students. It was during this period also that he became acquainted with the great Portuguese poet Francisco de Sá de Miranda, whose son, a classmate of his, was tragically killed in battle in 1553.

The death of Prince John, son of John III, on January 2, 1554, was a particular blow to Ferreira, who had dedicated his first comedy, *The Comedy of Bristo*, written in 1552, to the young prince. Ferreira's professors had been instrumental, indirectly, in encouraging him to write this play. Coming not only from Portugal but also from Italy, France, Scotland, Spain, and Greece, the humanistic faculty had quickly recognized talent in the young scholar.

It is evident from the poetry that he composed during his university days that Ferreira had several different amorous liaisons of varying intensity. In early 1554, he fell in love with his future wife, Maria Pimentel.

His studies completed, Ferreira left Coimbra in 1556 for Lisbon. Frustrated in his many attempts to obtain a comfortable governmental position and unhappy at the delay of his marriage, Ferreira continued studying law through 1557. Finally, in the second half of that same year, he was named a magistrate and was finally married. His wedded bliss was soon to end, however, with the premature death of Maria in 1560. His immense sadness at her death was gradually put to rest only through the compassionate sympathy and encouragement of his friends, to whom he expressed gratitude through poems and letters.

Following his recovery from the death of his wife, Ferreira grew in importance as a magistrate and became the intimate of many highly placed personages. Sometime around 1564, he found and married a new love, Maria Leite. From this marriage was born their son, Miguel Leite Ferreira, who would later collect his father's writings in the posthumous anthology *Poemas lusitanos*.

Continuing in his service as magistrate, Ferreira also continued his literary pursuits up until his death. It is thought, in fact, that he was planning to compose an epic poem about his beloved fellow countrymen when he was struck down by the plague on November 29, 1569. His sepulcher was originally located in the Gothic Convent of Carmel in Lisbon, specifically in the transept, where numerous epitaphs from friends and admirers could also be found. His death was considered a sad loss, and he was mourned by many. Today, nothing remains of the sepulcher, yet the writings of António Ferreira ensure his immortality, for, after all, as he wrote in one of his elegies, "Mausoleums give not life to the dead."

ANALYSIS

Apart from the many poems and letters that he wrote, António Ferreira is known as the author of three plays: *The Comedy of Bristo*, *Cioso*, and *Ignez de Castro*, the first two being comedies, the last a tragedy. It was common in the Middle Ages and the Renaissance for university students, on holidays, to produce comedies and tragedies—especially those of Seneca, Plautus, and Terence—in the original Latin. With interest in antiquity flourishing throughout the fourteenth, fifteenth, and sixteenth centuries in Europe, many revivals, as well as translations and imitations, of classical authors were popular. The central theme of comedies of the Greek type is almost always that of a young man who, with the aid of a sympathetic servant or friend, attains the love a beautiful slave girl, who, it turns out, is actually of noble birth and who as a child or youth was lost at sea or captured by pirates. So popular had the presentation of plays by students on holidays become that they were declared mandatory in 1546 by John III at the university of Coimbra. The first original Portuguese comedy would seem to be *Os estrangeiros* (c. 1527; foreigners), by Sá de Miranda, in which the typical intrigues are played out.

THE COMEDY OF BRISTO

The first comedy written by Ferreira, *The Comedy of Bristo*, also known as *Fanchono*, is the earliest remaining example of those student-produced comedies from the mid-sixteenth century in Portugal. The comic element consists primarily in the rivalry and reciprocal trickery between two boastful young men-about-town, as well as in their competition in love. The plot is eventually resolved through the devices, common to such Greek-style comedies, of recognitions and unexpected, outlandish marriages.

CIOSO

Cioso (jealousy) is Ferreira's only other comedy, and it was written during the same period as was *The Comedy of Bristo*. The story unfolds much like a tale by Giovanni Boccaccio: Júlio, a jealous husband who is madly in love with the courtesan Faustina, ends up being doubly caught in the web of his own treachery and her tricks. More serious, perhaps, than *The Comedy of Bristo*, *Cioso* tends to present a moral character. These two works, much like many of the comedies in the same style, offer little to interest the modern reader, and they remain far inferior to similar plays by Italian dramatists. The action seems to become lost in the midst of many monologues, which appear to have no sequential place in the play, and is reduced usually to dry explanations between accomplices. The many coincidences (unexpected recognition scenes between relatives and friends, other nearly miraculous episodes) and the *deus ex machina* weaken plays in a genre that was already, at the time of their composition, nearly exhausted of possible originality.

IGNEZ DE CASTRO

If Ferreira's comedies are forgettable, his attempt to introduce classical tragedy into the Portuguese theater was a great success. In all Western Europe, Ferreira's play *Ignez de Castro* constitutes one of the greatest contributions to the resurrection of Greek tragedy during the sixteenth century. Beginning with the production of the Italian Giambattista Giraldi Cinthio's play *Orbecche* in 1541 and continuing through the tragedies presented in the second half of the sixteenth century by the French playwrights Étienne Jodelle and Robert Garnier, as well as those of the Elizabethans in England, culminating finally in the seventeenth century in the classical dramas of Pierre Corneille and Jean Racine, the classical movement played a major role in the history of the theater in Europe.

In Portugal, many translations and adaptations in Portuguese were staged during the first half of the sixteenth century. Among these were also Latin versions of Greek tragedies, some of which were rendered by George Buchanan. Most probably the first original tragedy written in Portuguese was *Cleópatra*

(c. 1550) by Sá de Miranda, of which unfortunately only a few verses remain. Undoubtedly under the influence of his teachers, Ferreira composed his one tragedy, *Ignez de Castro*, between 1553 and 1556; it was published posthumously in 1587. In 1577, Jerónimo Bermudez published a Castilian version of the same play, and this fact has led to some disputes over the originality of Ferreira's version. Evidence unearthed in the twentieth century, however, has convinced most critics of the authenticity of the work by Ferreira.

The story of Dom Pedro and Ignez de Castro had previously been published in the "Trovas à morte de D. Inês" (ballads on the death of Doña Inês) by Garcia de Resende in the *Cancioneiro genéral* (1516; general book of songs). In typical classical tradition, the principal characters reveal themselves successively through dialogues with their counselors/confidants.

In act 1, Ignez expresses to her nurse her great joy over her reciprocated love for the prince, Dom Pedro. Two scenes later, Pedro and his counselor have a long conversation concerning the fatal dilemma of the story: Pedro, the successor to the throne, is in love with Ignez but is promised to another by his father, the king. The counselor argues that it is imperative, for the good of the state and the people, that Pedro give up Ignez and marry his betrothed. At the end of the scene, the chorus intervenes and discourses on various aspects of love.

In act 2, King Alphonse IV is advised by his counselors that, given the intensity of Pedro's love for Ignez, the only solution is to kill Ignez. When the king protests against such a harsh, immoral act, his counselors argue that as he rules by divine right, he is acting in God's behalf and thus would not be committing a sin by ordering her death. The counselors assert their willingness to die for their actions at the hand of Pedro; it will be a fitting sacrifice, they maintain, for the future good of the people. The counselors depart and the king prays for guidance. In a stirring monologue, he decries the notions of divine rule that make a king more a slave to his kingdom than are any of his subjects. The chorus then reminds the king that fortune is the master of all people, even members of royalty.

In act 3, Ignez has just awakened from a dream—a nightmare, really—which has put her in a state of extreme agitation. She relates the dream to her nurse: In it, a lion approaches her menacingly, only to retreat at the last moment, immediately after which three wolves attack and kill her. Yet Ignez's anguish over her death is caused by how miserable she imagines Pedro will be after she is gone. The nurse attempts to reassure and comfort her, and the act closes when the chorus enters to foretell the death of Ignez and subsequently of Pedro. The chorus then apostrophizes Pedro, imploring him to come to the rescue of his beloved.

In act 4, Ignez goes to King Alphonse IV to beg for her life. Having decided to allow his counselors to kill Ignez, he now breaks down under the weight of her imploring and relents, giving her back her life. The counselors enter and argue strongly against his new decision. Finally, in an action reminiscent of Pontius Pilate, the king washes his hands of the whole problem, telling the counselors that he will not order it but that if they insist on the assassination, they may do it themselves. The murder is accomplished, although not onstage (in the true classical manner); at the end of the act, the chorus enters to announce Ignez's death, noting that her name, however, will never die.

Act 5 opens with a long monologue by Pedro to the absent Ignez, in which he wonders at the everlasting nature of their love. His philosophizing is brutally cut short in the next and last scene of the play, when a messenger arrives to announce the death of Ignez. Predictably, he reacts with disbelief, then remorse and rage; the curtain drops on Pedro swearing vengeance against those who killed his beloved Ignez.

Ferreira's dramatic version of the fourteenth century story of Pedro and Ignez de Castro follows historical events rather closely. In his play, the political complexities surrounding the motives of the king's counselors are, happily, omitted. In the true story, which is perhaps the most famous romance in a land whose history can boast of a rich variety of romantic stories, Pedro was still married to his wife, a Spanish princess, when he fell in love with Ignez, one of her ladies-in-waiting. Though the princess tried to halt the affair, their mutual love continued, and, after Pedro's wife died, he installed Ignez as his mistress, without,

however, trying to make her his princess. They had several children, whose existence would later complicate the question of royal succession. While Ignez apparently had little or no ambition, being content merely to keep her beloved Pedro happy, those around her soon began intriguing against her to the old king, Alphonse IV. Warning that Ignez and her brood sought the throne for themselves, they eventually persuaded the king to allow her assassination. When she learned of the plot against her, however, she begged him for her life, which he granted. Once removed from her presence, however, the king was convinced by the courtiers of the soundness of their arguments, whereupon he left her fate up to them. (It is at this point that Ferreira's play comes to an end.)

On hearing of her murder, Pedro broke into rebellion. Realizing that his father had acted on the advice of others, he reconciled with him. In 1357, Alphonse died and Pedro succeeded him to the throne. He at once began a campaign of vengeance against those responsible for Ignez's death, most of whom had fled to Castile. Pedro managed to have them extradited to Portugal, and when they were delivered to him he showed no mercy, having them brutally tortured and killed. The story of King Pedro's having the body of Ignez exhumed, set on the throne, and crowned his queen is undoubtedly untrue, for Pedro was no madman but was considered a wise and just king for the short time that he reigned (1357-1367).

Ferreira's play *Ignez de Castro* may be considered the first important literary rendering of the story of the doomed love of Pedro and Ignez, and as such it was an influential drama. The impact of the play was basically twofold: First, firmly grounded in the Greek style of tragedy, *Ignez de Castro* would take its place among the several substantial classical tragedies in European literature of the Renaissance and later; second, the play would inspire other contemporary poets and dramatists, as well as future writers, to use the story to their own literary devices.

The basic philosophical problem presented in *Ignez de Castro* is whether the end justifies the means—a theme with which artists and writers have grappled throughout the ages. The main character in the play, and certainly the most interesting, is not Pedro or

Ignez but Alphonse IV, whose internal conflict, misery, and eventual indecisiveness could easily provide literary grist for a modern-day existentialist's mill.

Aside from the imitation of *Ignez de Castro* done by Bermudez (as noted above), the first prominent retelling was by Luís de Camões, a contemporary of Ferreira, in his justly famous epic poem, *The Lusiad*. In 1606, Juan Suárez de Alarcón retold the story in a poem entitled *La infanta coronada* (the crowned infanta), which was followed in 1612 by an adaptation by Mexía de la Cerda, *Tragedia famosa de doña Inés de Castro*. Other Spanish versions were made, as well as English versions and translations: There was a neoclassical tragedy by the Frenchman Houdart de la Motte in 1723, a Dutch version in 1793, another Portuguese retelling by Eugênio de Castro in 1900, and—perhaps the best-known depiction since that of Camões—*La Reine morte* (pr., pb. 1942; *Queen After Death*, 1915) by Henry de Montherlant. While it would be inaccurate to claim that all these writers had read and were inspired by the tragedy of Ferreira, nevertheless it is probably fair to give him a large share of the credit for the enduring nature of this much-told tale. For that alone, the name Ferreira deserves to be remembered.

OTHER MAJOR WORKS

MISCELLANEOUS: *Poemas lusitanos*, 1598 (poetry and 2 plays).

BIBLIOGRAPHY

Earle, T. F. *The Muse Reborn: The Poetry of António Ferreira*. New York: Oxford University Press, 1988. Although this work focuses on the poetry of Ferreira, it provides valuable insights into his dramas. Bibliography and index.

Martyn, John R. C. Introduction to *The Comedy of Bristo: Or, The Pimp*, by António Ferreira. Ottawa: Dovehouse Editions, 1990. In his introduction, Martyn provides information on Ferreira as well as on the play *The Comedy of Bristo*. Bibliography.

_____. Introduction to *The Tragedy of Ines de Castro*, by António Ferreira. Coimbra, Portugal: Universidade de Coimbra Press, 1987. This introduction to the English translation of *Ignez de Castro* presents information about Ferreira's life and writings, in addition to the translated play. Bibliography.

Christopher R. McRae

GEORGES FEYDEAU

Born: Paris, France; December 8, 1862
Died: Paris, France; June 5, 1921

PRINCIPAL DRAMA

Tailleur pour dames, pr. 1886, pb. 1888 (*A Gown for His Mistress*, 1969)

L'Affaire Édouard, pr., pb. 1889 (with Maurice Desvallières)

Monsieur chasse!, pr. 1892, pb. 1896 (*The Happy Hunter*, 1973)

Champignol malgré lui, pr., pb. 1892 (with Desvallières; *A Close Shave*, 1892)

Un Fil à la patte, pr. 1894, pb. 1899 (*Not by Bed Alone*, 1970)

L'Hôtel du Libre-Échange, pr. 1894, pb. 1928 (with Desvallières; *Hotel Paradiso*, 1957)

Le Dindon, pr. 1896, pb. 1949 (*There Is One in Every Marriage*, 1970)

La Dame de chez Maxim, pr. 1899, pb. 1914 (*The Lady from Maxim's*, 1899)

La Duchesse des Folies-Bergère, pr. 1902, pb. 1955

La Main passe!, pr. 1904, pb. 1906 (*Chemin de Fer*, 1968)

Le Bourgeon, pr. 1906, pb. 1907

La Puce à l'oreille, pr. 1907, pb. 1909 (*A Flea in Her Ear*, 1966)

Occupe-toi d'Amélie, pr. 1908, pb. 1911 (*Keep an Eye on Amélie*, 1958)

Feu la mère de Madame, pr. 1908, pb. 1923 (*Better Late*, 1973)

On purge bébé, pr., pb. 1910 (*Going to Pot*, 1970)

"Mais n'te promène donc pas toute nue!," pr. 1911, pb. 1912 (*Don't Run Around in the Nude*, 1987)

Léonie est en avance: Ou, Le Mal Joli, pr. 1911, pb. 1919 (*The Pregnant Pause: Or, Love's Labor Lost*, 1985)

Hortense a dit: "Je m'en fous!," pr. 1916, pb. 1948 (*Tooth and Consequences*, 1976)

Théâtre complet, pb. 1948-1956 (9 volumes)

Four Farces by Georges Feydeau, pb. 1970

Five by Feydeau, pb. 1994

OTHER LITERARY FORMS

Georges Feydeau wrote more than twenty monologues over the years, but he is best known for his comedies.

ACHIEVEMENTS

Marcel Achard, a good playwright himself and a knowledgeable man of the theater, opens his introduction to Georges Feydeau's *Théâtre complet* with the assertion that Feydeau is the greatest French comic dramatist after Molière. He may well be one of the most performed as well. The records kept by the Société des Auteurs Dramatiques indicate that Feydeau's plays are performed each month of the year in about seventy different theaters the world over, from Japan to Turkey, from Europe to North America.

The name Feydeau is immediately associated with the boulevard theater of the *belle époque*, the twenty-odd years between the World's Fair of 1889 and the eve of World War I—a period that worshiped wealth and sought pleasure and immediate gratification; a period identified with frivolity, gaiety, and high living; a period reproduced brilliantly in Feydeau's plays. He is also remembered as the best exponent of the well-made play, the creator of labyrinthine and precision-made plots, and, above all, the undisputed master of the bedroom farce, the king of vaudeville.

By the time Feydeau was ready to join the ranks of the *vaudevillistes*, vaudeville, though outwardly still as popular as it had ever been, was already in an advanced state of decline. The influential theater critic Francisque Sarcey had predicted its imminent demise as early as 1880. This condition had not escaped young Feydeau. Though Feydeau would devote two full years to learning his craft by studying the masters of the genre—Eugène Scribe, Eugène Labiche, Henri Meilhac, and Alfred Hennequin—he also knew that vaudeville had become calcified, too dependent on traditional mechanical devices.

Feydeau also thought that characters had ceased to behave as human beings and had become caricatures of earlier, more successfully created, rounder characters. He often said that in order to create a good vaudeville the playwright must take the most tragic situation possible, a situation capable of touching even the caretaker in a morgue, and try to extract from it its ludicrous side. According to him, characters are not necessarily comical in and of themselves; the situation in which they are plunged, and the words they are made to utter, are. From this discrepancy stems the incongruity out of which laughter is born. Yet Feydeau wanted to do more than rejuvenate obsolete plots and create credible, living, and distinct characters. His mission was to revive the whole concept behind vaudeville. That he achieved his goal is evidenced by the universal and lasting popularity of his plays.

BIOGRAPHY

On December 8, 1862, Georges-Léon-Jules-Marie Feydeau was born in Paris to Ernest Feydeau, a man of many and varied occupations, and to Lodzia Zelewska, a young Polish woman whose extraordinary beauty had attracted many eminent suitors before she agreed to marry the much older Ernest. In fact, rumor had it that Georges's real father was the Emperor Louis-Napoleon himself. From all accounts, the type of life the Feydeaus led and the kind of acquaintances they entertained may have provided young Georges with more than mere inspiration for his famous bedroom farces. It is perhaps relevant that the first thing Feydeau ever wrote, when still a child, was a play about a king, a queen, and her young lover—and how they learn to live happily ever after in a *ménage à trois*.

Feydeau made his debut in 1880 with a verse monologue. His first real success, however, came with his first full-length play, *A Gown for His Mis-*

tress, in 1886. After a series of flops and a two-year hiatus during which he went back to the basics and to study the works of his predecessors, he returned to the stage with a vengeance. On April 23, 1892, *The Happy Hunter* opened at the Palais Royal to critical and public acclaim. On November 5 of the same year, *A Close Shave* premiered at the Nouveautés with resounding success. From this year on, every play this Midas of the theater wrote turned into gold.

Ironically, there seemed to be an inverse correlation between Feydeau's professional and domestic life. The more successes he accumulated, the worse his private life became. His rather unusual daily routine did not help matters. His bohemian life was legendary: He did not get up until past midday, and then worked until around seven or eight, after which began a nocturnal pilgrimage that took him from one of the several choice cafés popular among artists and literary people to the famous and glamorous restaurant Maxim's, his laboratory of human behavior.

Feydeau's nocturnal escapades exacerbated the tensions already present in his marriage. Finally, in September, 1909, after an unusually violent quarrel, Feydeau left his home, never to return. For the next ten years, the Hotel Terminus became his home, where he lived surrounded by piles of books, paintings, perfume bottles, and a large suit of armor.

The creator of hilarious comedies, Feydeau was actually a retiring and sad man who never laughed and was uncomfortable with the attention he drew. He dreaded small talk and felt an aversion to extended conversation. Yet his fear of solitude forced him to seek out the company of whatever acquaintance happened to be present and awake at the early hours of the morning.

By 1916, when Feydeau obtained a divorce from his wife, his proverbial imagination and inventiveness ran dry. Although he was only in his early fifties, he seemed much older. He had contracted a serious venereal disease that led in rapid stages to his end. Feydeau, the comic genius who had made people all over the world laugh at the madness he created, had himself become a victim of madness. The king of vaudeville died in a mental institution on June 5, 1921, and with him ended the era of modern farce.

ANALYSIS

To explain the nature of Georges Feydeau's lasting popularity is to analyze the sum of the many different parts that constitute the whole of his drama. Feydeau's plays contain those farcical qualities that seldom fail to delight audiences: apparitions, cataclysmic encounters, ludicrous duels, falls, booby-trapped bedrooms, and, above all, embarrassing mishaps, all which are played with breathtaking rapidity. Yet his theater also possesses other characteristics that provide delight and release. Like Feydeau's original audiences, modern audiences of Feydeau's plays watch their own repressed desires acted out before them as they observe Feydeau's hero/victims, who, in their attempts to circumvent society's laws and to extricate themselves from embarrassing or compromising situations, find themselves struggling desperately but hilariously against unknown and overwhelming external forces.

At the same time, Feydeau is a social critic whose plays reveal the emerging cracks in the social edifice of *belle époque* France and the moral, psychological, and emotional deficiencies of its inhabitants. In fact, even the happy endings bring only temporary happiness and raise more doubts than they resolve. Pervasive pessimism hides behind the mask of comedy. In the world that Feydeau creates, servants are abused by their employers; army officers are depicted as dehumanized despots, robots that behave by reflex action; doctors, lawyers, and businessmen lack ethical principles; and the aristocracy is shown in an advanced state of moral decay. Patience, forgiveness, charity, and decency are seldom found in Feydeau's characters. Envy, hate, and cruelty occur far more naturally. Even friendship and love seem meaningless. Not surprisingly, marriage is invariably hell on earth; children are odious and a source of conjugal disharmony; relatives are always inconvenient; and family life is an unmitigated calvary.

The lives of individuals in Feydeau's world are no better. Their frenzied searches for happiness and pleasure rarely succeed. Though they constantly talk, they seldom communicate. Ultimately, Feydeau's characters become the victims of their own doing and end up imprisoned within their own selfishness.

Feydeau's theater also appeals to the modern taste for the gratuitous, the extravagant, and the irrational. Anticipating the Theater of the Absurd, he placed onstage a series of characters who, as they stop laughing and come to rest after their dizzying adventures, come face-to-face with what appears to be an inexorable and absurd world.

Feydeau's theater is not, by and large, a theater of ideas. His main objective was to entertain, to make audiences laugh, uncontrollably if possible. His comedy is above all a comedy of situation. The main line of his plots is initially quite simple, but imbroglios, countless inopportune and near-catastrophic encounters, missed or delayed confrontations, chases, and incredible inventiveness and improvisation on the part of would-be adulterers soon render the simplest and most innocent situation diabolically complex.

Feydeau's first acts are marvels of preparation. Stealthily and unobtrusively, he weaves a complex fabric in which all subplots are not only interrelated but also inseparable from the main plot, so that nothing happens to anyone without affecting the others. Every detail is carefully and meticulously orchestrated so that almost all characters introduced in the first act have a good, often inevitable reason for being where they will encounter the person or persons they least expect or wish to see.

Consequently, all of Feydeau's second acts present situations that rebound on each other, characters who behave like possessed individuals as the wheels of their fate spin faster, and a general tempo that shifts into a madder pace, making the inconceivable acceptable and inevitable. Feydeau creates an impression of chaos and progressive madness that ensnares all involved as farce takes over and hilarity overcomes the audience.

Feydeau approaches his concluding acts with the same concern for naturalness and action. He may well begin to unravel some of the threads of the subplots, but in most plays, the action continues to mount as the main plot grows still more complex. The denouement does not actually occur until the last few scenes.

Feydeau's theatrical production can be easily divided into three distinct cycles. The most enduring plays in the first cycle are *The Happy Hunter* (Fey-

deau's favorite play), *Hotel Paradiso*, *There Is One in Every Marriage*, *Chemin de Fer*, and *A Flea in Her Ear*. In most of the plays of this cycle, Feydeau portrays what apparently were his favorite female characters: *femmes du monde*, society women of impeccable bourgeois upbringing. These bourgeoises are housewives with few pleasures and interests, plenty of free time, few female friends, and husbands whose attentions are reserved for their mistresses. As Feydeau once said, these women "breathe virtue, but they are easily out of breath."

Despite their impeccable upbringing and professed honesty, most of these wives have already picked a lover whom they keep "on ice," so to speak, should their husbands transgress. They are quick to retaliate when they have proof of their husbands' infidelity. It must be quickly added, however, that most of the husbands hardly deserve better treatment. Unfaithful, vain, and self-congratulating, they are usually blind to the dangers they run by ignoring their wives and by giving them ample opportunity to fall into adulterous temptations.

A Flea in Her Ear

Feydeau's plays are purely theatrical: They must be seen onstage; they must be experienced. The hilarity that they elicit in performance evaporates when reduced to summary. Nevertheless, a brief summary of the best known of these plays, *A Flea in Her Ear*, provides a good yardstick for measuring the craftsmanship and comedic talent of its author.

Chandebise, a loving husband, has recently been unable to fulfill his conjugal obligations, and the more he worries, the worse his condition gets. Raymonde, his wife, suspects him of infidelity. One day, Raymonde "mistakenly" opens a package addressed to Chandebise from the Hôtel du Minet-Galant. It contains her husband's suspenders. She now has the evidence she needs. What she does not know is that, following Dr. Finache's advice, and in an attempt to find a cure for his affliction, Chandebise has changed the style of his suspenders and has given the old ones to his nephew, Camille, who left them at the hotel the last time he took his lover Antoinette there.

Raymonde wastes no time in setting up a trap to catch her husband in the act. She convinces her friend Lucienne Homénidès to write a love letter to Chandebise begging him to meet her at the Hôtel du Minet-Galant. Raymonde will be waiting for him there. When Chandebise receives the letter, he is convinced that there must be an error. The woman must have mistaken him for his best friend, Tournel, a handsome man notorious for his powers of seduction and Raymonde Chandebise's lover-in-waiting. Tournel is more than eager to keep the rendezvous.

In the meantime, however, flattered by the interest he has awakened in a woman, Chandebise shows off the love letter to his client, Homénidès. On recognizing his wife's handwriting, Homénidès draws a huge revolver, and Chandebise barely escapes death by telling the homicidally jealous Homénidès that Tournel is the one meeting Lucienne. As act 1 comes to a close, Chandebise sends his servant Émile, Antoinette's husband, to warn Tournel while he sets off to warn Lucienne.

In his usual fashion, Feydeau arranges events quite realistically to ensure that all those who should not meet will turn up in the same place. The proprietor of the Hôtel du Minet-Galant, knowing his clientele, has built a room with a bed attached to a revolving wall. In case of emergency, by pushing a button on the wall the amorous couple can disappear into the adjacent room as the bed permanently occupied by Baptistin, the hotel owner's uncle, comes to take the place of the original bed. The first to arrive at the hotel is Raymonde, who, hidden behind the curtain, receives Tournel, whom she mistakes for her husband, with a monumental slap. When she recognizes her error, and Tournel explains, she wants to run to Chandebise. Tournel, however, has been waiting far too long to let such a moment go to waste. As he goes to lock the door, Raymonde, frightened, pushes the button next to the bed to call for help. She is transported into the next room, and when Tournel leaps onto the bed, it is Baptistin whom he covers with kisses.

Together once again, Raymonde and Tournel are about to leave when they come on Chandebise, "disguised" as a hotel clerk. They kneel down, implore his forgiveness, and insist that he demonstrate it by kissing them both. The hotel clerk, who happens to look exactly like Chandebise, does as he is told,

though he insists that he is Poche. Raymonde and Tournel are successively shocked, disgusted, and relieved when they learn of Poche's real identity. They are again about to leave when they see Chandebise's nephew and Antoinette arrive. They must hide again—and so must Camille and Antoinette when they spot Poche, whom they mistake for Chandebise. In the confusion, Antoinette goes into the room of a man called Rugby, a violent sex maniac who proceeds to undress her; at the same time, Antoinette's husband, Émile, walks in. Émile suffers the same fate Camille did when he tried to come to Antoinette's rescue: He receives a severe thrashing at the hands of the barbaric Rugby. At one point or another, everyone ends up in the room of this violent Englishman, with similar results.

As this is going on, Lucienne comes to meet Raymonde. She is followed by Chandebise and Homénidès. The pace becomes frantic as everyone is trying desperately to escape from the homicidal Homénidès, from the brutal Rugby, and from Chandebise, who, inexplicably to them, seems to be everywhere. Raymonde and Tournel are speechless when Chandebise, who has been brutally forced to put on Poche's uniform by the proprietor of the hotel, wants to strangle Tournel when he sees him with his wife. Like Raymonde's, Lucienne's efforts to escape from her husband fail. While she is being comforted in Baptistin's room by Poche, Homénidès storms into the neighboring room and, frustrated at finding it empty, shoots at the button. To everyone's surprise, the wall begins to move, bringing into full view Lucienne and Poche. Homénidès runs after Poche, whom he takes for Chandebise. The act ends in total chaos as everyone races out of the hotel.

Feydeau waits until the last possible moment to resolve most of the misunderstandings and reveal the main *quid pro quo*. Antoinette returns home first. She bribes the concierge into swearing to her husband that she has been home all day long. She is followed by Raymonde, Lucienne, and Tournel. All await the arrival of Chandebise with trepidation. It is Poche, however, who comes next. He wants to return Chandebise's coat and retrieve his uniform. Thinking that Poche is Chandebise and that he is obviously ill and drunk, they put him to bed. While a reluctant Poche is put to bed, Chandebise arrives, followed immediately by the hotel proprietor, who, on seeing his "clerk" far from his job, starts kicking his posterior to the chagrin and humiliation of the master of the house. In a desperate attempt to escape this brutal man, he runs into Homénidès, who threatens him with his gun. He thinks he is going out of his mind when he sees "himself" in his own bed. When Poche comes out, he is forced to jump out the window to avoid being killed by the mad Spaniard. At the last minute, all misunderstandings and mistaken identities are clarified logically and naturally. Both aggrieved husbands forgive their wives. Chandebise promises to show his wife that he has regained his amorous ardor.

Nowhere in Feydeau's works is the expression invented to describe Alfred Hennequin's theater, "theater of a hundred doors," more applicable than in *A Flea in Her Ear*. As Feydeau masterfully acquired the equilibrium of a tightrope walker in balancing the myriad aspects of his tightly wrought imbroglios, the movement of characters in and out of doors—and windows on occasion—increased perceptibly. In *A Flea in Her Ear*, there are 274 comings and goings. This is perhaps the most physical of his plays. The pace, particularly in the second act, is literally breathtaking. Spectators are subjected to viewing so much chaos, so much movement, so many complications, so many encounters, so many breakneck chases, so many gasping and panting characters, that at the end they are themselves left breathless and physically exhausted.

Though Feydeau believed that situations, not characters, elicit laughter, he did create comical characters. Camille, for instance, has a physical impairment that never fails to generate an enormous amount of laughter. He suffers from a severe cleft palate and can enunciate only vowels, making his speech comprehensible only to those initiated.

Foreigners always provide some of the most humorous moments in Feydeau. Rugby's inability to speak French and insistence on speaking English make for some exploitable situations. Perhaps the most amusing character is Carlos Homénidès de Histangua, whose French is atrocious. His violent

jealousy also renders him quite ingenious. He decides to insure his wife's life with the Boston Life Company, but not wanting any man to see or touch her, he takes the required physical checkup himself. When Chandebise becomes aware of the situation and insists that the rules necessitate that Lucienne undergo medical examination, Homénidès stubbornly refuses. Having taken a urine test himself, he adds bluntly and vulgarly, "Rules, I break them; I already peesed for her."

Always one to provide variations on the central theme of his theater, Feydeau offers a play in which neither wife nor husband is even seriously contemplating adultery. Yet it is *suspected* adultery that sets Feydeau's infernal machine in motion. Raymonde's reason for even considering taking a lover is as curious as it is illogical. According to her own account, her life with Chandebise has been a "continuous love," a "constant Spring." Yet the lack of "clouds"—obstacles or worries of any kind—makes it all so monotonous that she seriously considers turning to Tournel. Equally illogical is her behavior at the hotel. The happier she becomes about learning of Chandebise's innocence, the more she kisses Tournel and allows herself to be kissed by him. Yet she is indignant when Tournel maneuvers her closer to the bed. She truly believes that a lover would be satisfied with the gift of her mind and heart. She does not realize that Tournel is after other parts of her anatomy.

The comical elements in *A Flea in Her Ear* hide its dark side. Spectators are made to laugh so much that they hardly have time to realize that the objects of their hilarity are in fact victims—often innocent victims—of an infernal machine, a capricious destiny that buffets them about at random. For Chandebise, whose only flaw is to have temporarily failed, through no fault of his own, in his conjugal duties, the punishment is utterly out of proportion. For this minor fault, he is driven to the brink of insanity. An adoring husband, he is sent on a nightmarish journey during which he is manhandled, brutalized, tormented, humiliated, kicked in the rear, threatened with death, accused of alcoholism, made to swallow foul-tasting medicines, and forced to question his own identity. Many other characters find themselves in difficult and incomprehensible situations, but few suffer as much unwarranted punishment as Chandebise. Like a character out of a play by Franz Kafka, he is assailed by unknown forces for incomprehensible reasons. It is the structure of Feydeau's plays that best responds to his vision of the modern world, at once perfectly logical and perfectly illogical.

THE *COCOTTE*

The second cycle of Feydeau's career offers a very distinct type of leading lady. The second type is the *cocotte*, the woman of easy virtue. A traditional character in vaudeville, the *cocotte* was almost always given a minor role by Feydeau's predecessors, but Feydeau soon envisioned the potential comedic richness inherent in such women and elevated them to the rank of leading ladies.

Feydeau's originality shines brightest with his creation of three major characters, namely, Lucette Gautier in *Not by Bed Alone*, Môme Crevette in *The Lady from Maxim*'s and later in *La Duchesse des Folies-Bergère*, and Amélie d'Avranches in *Keep an Eye on Amélie*. The pronounced and charismatic personality of these women, their spontaneous and impulsive nature, their picturesque and idiosyncratic speech patterns and social manners, their general lack of standards of value, their marginal social position, their propensity for pleasure and riches, and their malicious playfulness count among Feydeau's greatest accomplishments. These *cocottes*, prone to all kinds of madness, are inherently comical and function as instigators and creators of countless humorous situations and imbroglios. They also permit Feydeau to enter, observe, and depict the exotic, illicit, and picturesque demimonde where social barriers and rank dissolve in the common pursuit of pleasure.

NOT BY BED ALONE

Not by Bed Alone is perhaps the most representative play of this cycle, and as such it is worth discussing in greater detail. Bois d'Enghien, a type well represented in vaudeville, is a pleasure-seeker whose time has come to marry well. His designs, however, are burdened by an affair. When the play starts, he has three goals in mind: to break with Lucette, to marry Viviane Duverger, and to make sure that the two never meet. In Feydeau's hands, these simple ambitions turn into a nightmare.

The wedding contract is to be signed at the house of Baronne Duverger. Yet Bois d'Enghien's efforts to break the news to Lucette have met with failure as she showers him with love and threats of suicide should he ever leave her for another. One by one, all the guests that come to visit Lucette bring a copy of *Le Figaro* that features a laudatory article on her singing. Next to it, to Bois d'Enghien's dismay, appears the announcement of his engagement. As copies of the newspaper proliferate, the behavior of Bois d'Enghien becomes increasingly bizarre, a fact observed by the guests.

While dinner in honor of Bois d'Enghien is in progress, two people arrive: the Baronne Duverger, who comes to solicit Lucette's professional services for the contract ceremony, and Bouzin, a notary clerk and composer of ridiculous songs, who has come to ask Lucette's opinion about a song that he has composed with her in mind. While waiting, Bouzin sees the servant bring a beautiful and anonymous bouquet of flowers and, surreptitiously, places his calling card among the flowers. Before Lucette has a chance to see the bouquet, Bouzin is thrown out of the house for composing such horrendous songs. She feels remorse, however, when she discovers the card and an extremely expensive ring hidden among the flowers. Could she have mistaken Bouzin's talent? When the timid and fearful composer returns to retrieve his umbrella, she welcomes him with great effusion.

While Bouzin goes back home to fetch his song, Irrigua, an exiled Latin American general, arrives. In a comical series of exchanges it becomes clear that the general, not Bouzin, is responsible for the generous gift. It takes Irrigua only a few minutes to display his irascible nature, his fiery temperament, and his jealous rage. When Lucette, faithful to Bois d'Enghien, informs him that she loves another man and will love him until he dies, Irrigua makes no secret that this can be easily arranged. When Bois d'Enghien discovers Irrigua's intentions, he cravenly tells the general that Bouzin is his man. As could be expected, Bouzin comes back with his song and is savagely attacked by Irrigua before being thrown out of Lucette's house again.

The second act takes place at the home of Baronne Duverger, where, naturally, all the characters turn up again with predictable consequences. The play comes to a happy resolution when Vivianne Duverger, whom the scandal has made madly in love with Bois d'Enghien, convinces her mother that she has been compromised and must be joined in marriage to the man who has faulted her.

The success of this play depends largely on the characters Feydeau creates and on the peculiar characteristics he bestows on them. Fontanet, for example, otherwise a charming man, is afflicted by a serious case of bad breath, an affliction that Feydeau drains of all its potential comedy. General Irrigua is, however, the single most comical character in the entire play. His personality is the prime source of his comedic appeal. A former minister of war sentenced to death in his country, he is of unequal humor, savagely frank, exceedingly passionate, excessively effusive, and inordinately jealous. He spends most of the play chasing rivals, real or imaginary, and challenging them to duels. He threatens to kill at the slightest provocation and knows no compromise. Incapable of subtlety, his social graces are as polished as his French, which he tortures and mutilates at the turn of each phrase. He mixes French and Spanish continually. Colloquial expressions become unrecognizable in his mouth. What is most ironic and comical is that before he joined the army, this man was a professor who supplemented his meager salary by giving private lessons in French.

Feydeau's mastery of the technical and structural aspects is accompanied by a growing delicacy of touch in characterization and social commentary. To some extent the first act of this play could be termed a tableau of manners in which Feydeau first introduces the spectator to the demimonde, the world in which *cocottes* reign supreme.

As in *A Flea in Her Ear*, the comedy of his situation underscores the gratuitous nature of Bouzin's disproportionate sufferings. There is no doubt that he is somewhat fatuous and that he has committed one small indiscretion. For this he is booted ignominiously out of a house, chased about and threatened with death by a mad general, stripped and robbed of his pants, and carted to jail for indecent exposure. Cruelty was beginning to creep into Feydeau's world.

CRUELTY

Cruelty is what characterizes the plays that make up Feydeau's third and final cycle. Feydeau grouped *Better Late*, *Going to Pot*, *Don't Run Around in the Nude*, *The Pregnant Pause*, and *Tooth and Consequences* under the collective title "From Marriage to Divorce." Such grouping attests the unity of his inspiration. Feydeau's own family recognized Mme Feydeau as the main model for all five of the leading ladies. This explains why Yvonne, Julie, Clarisse, Léonie, and Marcelle, the female protagonists of these five comedies, resemble one another and differ much less in personality than in the salient negative traits that particularize them.

These new female lead characters possess few redeeming qualities. They are exasperating, obstinate, indiscreet, ignorant, vain, vulgar, and illogical women, and they make imposing enemies for their husbands. These poor men can never win an argument as they are confronted with a baffling system of female reasoning that challenges both rationality and logic. If they attempt to impose themselves, domestic life is but a continual nightmarish struggle; if, to find peace, they relent, they incur the wrath and scorn of wives who despise weakness. The husband is no longer the king of his castle. He has abdicated his authority and his dignity. He is totally subjugated, psychologically castrated.

GOING TO POT

In *Going to Pot*, for example, Julie is ignorant, illogical, cruel, nagging, and exasperating. She receives her husband's prospective business partners in her nightgown, in curlers, her stockings rolled down and hanging over the heels of her house slippers. Wherever she goes, she carries with her a bucket full of filthy water. Her only concern is to get Toto, their son, "to go potty." In quick succession, she manages to ruin her husband's chances of a lucrative contract with the Ministry of War, insults the ministry's purchaser by alluding to his cuckoldry, gets him into a duel with his wife's lover, and, to top it all, forces him to be a good example to Toto by taking a laxative, even though Follavoine has repeatedly pleaded that he is extremely allergic to laxatives. As everything collapses around Follavoine, Julie still manages to add salt to his wounds by telling him that it is all his fault.

THE PREGNANT PAUSE

The Pregnant Pause offers further vignettes that chronicle the incompatibility of the sexes and its inevitable consequences. Toudoux is unable to please his pregnant wife, Léonie. Whatever he does is criticized. The arrival of Léonie's mother exacerbates his alleged clumsiness and insignificance. Suddenly Léonie has a wish: She wants her husband to wear the expected baby's chamber pot as if it were a top hat. His refusals are condemned by wife and mother-in-law. When, overwhelmed by the avalanche of arguments, he finally succumbs, his wife chases him with scorn for looking so ridiculous. His wife's parents blame him for the baby's premature arrival. When it turns out that Léonie's was no more than a "hysterical pregnancy," Toudoux is accused of incompetence: What can be expected from a man who is willing to wear a chamber pot on his head? Unable to take any more abuse, Toudoux takes the chamber pot, places it on his father-in-law's head, and storms out of the house.

The five plays in his last cycle offer a mosaic of domestic situations that, though hardly tragic in Aristotelian terms, do show human tragedy in a minor key. For the men in these plays, discontent yields to unhappiness, and torment gives way to torture. Marriage as seen by Feydeau is a sordid battleground in which there are no victors. Well before Eugène

Ionesco, Samuel Beckett, and Edward Albee—and in similar fashion—Feydeau underlines the absurdity of social institutions, the stupidity of ordinary speech and small talk, the impossibility of true communication despite constant talking, the incompatibility of the sexes, and the ultimate isolation of the individual. Feydeau is a modern writer.

BIBLIOGRAPHY

Baker, Stuart E. *Georges Feydeau and the Aesthetics of Farce*. Ann Arbor, Mich.: UMI Research Press, 1981. A scholarly study of the farces of Feydeau. Index.

Esteban, Manuel A. *Georges Feydeau*. Boston: Twayne, 1983. A basic biography of Feydeau that covers his life and works. Bibliography and index.

Marcous, J. Paul. Introduction to *Georges Feydeau, Three Farces*. Lanham, Md.: University Press of America, 1986. The introduction to three farces by Feydeau provides insight into his life and works.

Pronko, Leonard C. *Eugene Labiche and Georges Feydeau*. New York: Grove Press, 1982. An examination of the lives and works of Eugene Labiche and Feydeau. Bibliography and index.

_____. *Georges Feydeau*. New York: Ungar, 1975. A basic biography covering the life and works of Feydeau. Bibliography and index.

Manuel A. Esteban

HENRY FIELDING

Born: Sharpham Park, Somersetshire, England; April 22, 1707
Died: Lisbon, Portugal; October 8, 1754

PRINCIPAL DRAMA
Love in Several Masques, pr., pb. 1728
The Temple Beau, pr., pb. 1730
The Author's Farce, and The Pleasures of the Town, pr., pb. 1730
Tom Thumb: A Tragedy, pr., pb. 1730 (revised as

The Tragedy of Tragedies, pr., pb. 1731)
Rape upon Rape: Or, Justice Caught in His Own Trap, pr., pb. 1730 (also known as *The Coffee-House Politician*)
The Letter-Writers: Or, A New Way to Keep a Wife at Home, pr., pb. 1731
The Welsh Opera: Or, The Grey Mare the Better Horse, pr., pb. 1731 (revised as *The Grub-Street Opera*, pb. 1731)
The Lottery, pr., pb. 1732

The Modern Husband, pr., pb. 1732 (five acts)

The Old Debauchees, pr., pb. 1732

The Covent Garden Tragedy, pr., pb. 1732

The Mock Doctor: Or, The Dumb Lady Cur'd, pr.,
  pb. 1732 (adaptation of Molière's *Le Medecin
  malgré lui*)

The Miser, pr., pb. 1733 (adaptation of Molière's
  L'Avare)

Don Quixote in England, pr., pb. 1734

The Intriguing Chambermaid, pr., pb. 1734
  (adaptation of Jean-François Regnard's *Le
  Retour imprévu*)

*An Old Man Taught Wisdom: Or, The Virgin
  Unmask'd*, pr., pb. 1735

*The Universal Gallant: Or, The Different
  Husbands*, pr., pb. 1735 (five acts)

Pasquin: Or, A Dramatic Satire on the Times, pr.,
  pb. 1736

Tumble-Down Dick: Or, Phaeton in the Suds, pr.,
  pb. 1736

Eurydice: Or, The Devil's Henpeck'd, pr. 1737, pb.
  1743 (one act)

Eurydice Hiss'd: Or, A Word to the Wise, pr., pb.
  1737

The Historical Register for the Year 1736, pr., pb.
  1737 (three acts)

Miss Lucy in Town, pr., pb. 1742 (one act)

The Wedding-Day, pr., pb. 1743 (five acts; also
  known as *The Virgin Unmask'd*)

The Dramatic Works of Henry Fielding, Esq., pb.
  1755 (3 volumes)

The Fathers: Or, The Good-Natured Man, pr., pb.
  1778 (revised for posthumous production by
  David Garrick)

OTHER LITERARY FORMS

The focus of Henry Fielding's work progressed
from drama to satire to the novel to legal inquiries
and proposals, with some overlap and with a nearly
constant overlay of critical and political journalism.
Among his novels, his masterpiece *Tom Jones* (1749)
is a monument of English literature, though *Joseph
Andrews* (1742) is highly regarded and *Amelia* (1751)
was his own favorite. *An Apology for the Life of Mrs.
Shamela Andrews* (1741) burlesques Samuel Richardson's novel *Pamela* (1740-1741), and the strongly
satiric *The History of the Adventures of Joseph Andrews, and of His Friend Mr. Abraham Adams* (1743)
attacks the contemporary prime minister of England,
Sir Robert Walpole. Political satire formed the staple
of *The Champion*, a thrice-weekly journal in which
Fielding was a leading partner in 1739 and 1740, but
social commentary and drama criticism played a large
role in *The Covent-Garden Journal*, which came out
during 1752. In the early 1750's, Fielding authored
several influential tracts aimed at reforming his country's criminal and poor laws, and in 1754 he wrote a
moving and contemplative travel book, *The Journal
of a Voyage to Lisbon* (1755).

ACHIEVEMENTS

Henry Fielding was a central figure in the theatrical world of the 1730's, and he continued to be influential as a literary and social critic almost up to his
death in 1754. He wrote in popular and established
forms, but his cleverness and vigor raised his work
well above the level set by his contemporaries.
Fielding exploited the ballad opera, a form originated by John Gay, with particular success. By add-

Henry Fielding (Library of Congress)

ing broad farce and often surreal fantasy to Gay's inspiration of setting satiric lyrics to popular tunes sung in operatic style, Fielding produced one of his best plays, *The Author's Farce*. He combined farce, burlesque, and fantasy to create *The Tragedy of Tragedies*, another masterpiece. Both plays, often classified as dramatic satires, were hugely popular by the standards of the time.

Beyond his contribution as a playwright, Fielding's management of the Little Theatre in the Haymarket set a dangerously bold pace in terms of showmanship and satire. He attacked the shortcomings of society in general and of the theater in particular but found his chief target in the Whig government of Robert Walpole. Fielding's popularity, his influence in the theater, and the potency of his satire are usually credited with bringing on the Licensing Act of 1737, an instrument of political censorship that limited the staging of plays to a select list of theaters and required the Lord Chamberlain's approval before a new play could be staged or an old one altered. The Licensing Act ended Fielding's theatrical career on an ironic note; he had made the stage at once so lively and so central to England's political life that its control and suppression had become a political necessity.

Shorn of topical relevance and their original sense of daring, only two or three of his plays are still performed. They have wit and pace, and they certainly repay the discriminating reader, but they no longer exert the tremendous popular appeal that was Fielding's first goal. As a contributor to dramatic tradition, Fielding presents another irony; he was restless within the forms he chose, but his experimentation forced and complicated those forms rather than breaking through and extending them. Had his career as a playwright not ended so early—in part through his own doing—he might well have made a more substantial contribution to the genre. As it was, his interest turned to the novel, and he joined Daniel Defoe and Richardson in establishing a great new English literary tradition.

BIOGRAPHY

Born on April 22, 1707, Henry Fielding grew up quietly in Somerset and Dorset. When he was eleven, however, his mother died, and after a year of turmoil,

during which his father remarried and quarreled violently with his mother's relatives, young Henry was sent to Eton. After making as much as possible of the excellent if strict and structured education offered by this famous school, Fielding chose, about 1724, to enjoy life in London rather than enter a university.

In 1728, his comedy *Love in Several Masques* was staged at the Theatre Royal. Instead of pursuing a stage career at once, however, Fielding enrolled at the University of Leyden, where he remained for a year, probably studying classical literature. In 1729, Fielding returned to England, where his second play, *The Temple Beau*, was accepted by the theater in Goodman's Fields. This coup inaugurated ten years of immersion in the London theater world, a brilliant career in the course of which Fielding became both widely known and respected and widely disparaged and attacked. His third play, a ballad opera called *The Author's Farce*, opened at a more prestigious theater, the Little Theatre in the Haymarket, where it met with great success; it was followed immediately by *Tom Thumb*, a minor masterpiece that Fielding reworked the following year as *The Tragedy of Tragedies*. This satire on Robert Walpole, a parody of heroic tragedy, is today Fielding's most widely known dramatic production.

After his spectacular initial success, Fielding's ability to please the public became less certain. *Rape upon Rape* was found only acceptable, and its afterpiece, *The Letter-Writers*, had to be withdrawn. A new and highly political afterpiece, however, *The Welsh Opera*, played to enthusiastic houses. Already the government was aware of Fielding; the play's even more outspoken revision, *The Grub-Street Opera*, was suppressed before it could open.

In 1732, Fielding continued to increase the pressure he had caused by his inflammatory satire with *The Lottery*, an attack on the combination of financial corruption and public foolishness represented by lottery-ticket jobbers. This play did well, but *The Modern Husband*, a strong satire on public—rather than political or financial—morals, had a mixed reception, as did *The Old Debauchees*, which is a much darker work than Fielding's lighthearted style usually produced. The afterpiece for *The Old Debauchees*,

The Covent Garden Tragedy, was a flat failure and had to be replaced by *The Mock Doctor*. This ballad opera was the first of Fielding's two successful adaptations of Molière. The second, a highly successful farce entitled *The Miser*, was produced the following year, followed by another ballad opera, *The Intriguing Chambermaid*.

Fielding was now well established as a popular London playwright, a figure to be reckoned with among his literary peers, and a man well able to earn a decent, if uneven, income through his art. At the same time, he had already made enemies among both politicians and literary critics and had himself been the butt of sharp satiric comment.

At this juncture, late in 1734, Fielding married. For information about how he lived, passed his days, dealt with his necessities, and satisfied his tastes—whatever these were—one must rely on generalizations about the period. No Fielding diaries have been found, and very little of his correspondence exists. He and his new wife, the former Charlotte Cradock, lived in the heart of London while he opened *An Old Man Taught Wisdom*, a successful ballad opera/farce, and *The Universal Gallant*, a comedy that failed emphatically.

The death of Fielding's mother-in-law, which came soon after this failure, left his wife with a small estate. After dealing with financial matters related to the estate, the couple managed to spend a good deal of the year 1735 at Fielding's family home in East Stour, but Fielding apparently did not take well to rural life. By the time he was back in London for the fall season, he had succeeded in gaining control of the Little Theatre, where he organized a group of young actors referred to as the Great Mogul's Company of Comedians. *Pasquin*, a dramatic satire, which was more specific in its personal reference than any of Fielding's other works, made the new company's name. This was followed with a farce, *Tumble-Down Dick*, which was aimed at his theatrical compatriots.

Fielding continued to provide competition and stimulation to the new theatrical season with a provoking and innovative schedule at the Little Theatre, also offering a short farce of his own, *Eurydice*, to Drury Lane, a rival house. *Eurydice* failed, giving Fielding the opportunity to rework it (twice), ending up with

Eurydice Hiss'd, a short farce that played for more than a month as a popular afterpiece to *The Historical Register for the Year 1736*. The latter, while it provides the broad social satire suggested by its title and takes aim at the theatrical world as well, is largely a political allegory to which Walpole's government, hard-pressed and near its end, was sensitive. Fielding's next offering, a play called *The Fall of Bob, Alias Gin* (now lost), apparently did much to end his career in the theater, although after his works had lost some of their notoriety, he did produce a few minor pieces.

The Licensing Act of 1737 closed the Little Theatre as well as those in Lincoln's Inn Fields and Goodman's Fields. Moreover, it closed all stages to Fielding, whose development as a dramatist had increasingly led him to the kind of material that would never pass a government censor. Fielding's engagement in anything with which he was involved had been intensely energetic and provocative; he was always searching, pushing, and trying something new. Faced with chains and muzzles, he simply shifted his energies to two, or perhaps three, new careers.

Ostensibly, Fielding became a lawyer instead of a playwright. He resumed his formal education, studying at the Middle Temple, and was admitted to the bar in 1740. He practiced as a barrister, riding the Western Circuit and generally working hard for small financial reward. In 1748, however, he was made a justice of the peace for the city of Westminster, and for the next six years he served as a stern but sympathetic judge, concerned with discerning and remedying the causes of crime as well as reforming and improving the city's means of protecting itself, its rudimentary police force. During this period, Fielding continued to interest himself in politics and the drama through three journals, *The Champion* (1739-1741), *The Jacobite Journal* (1747-1748), and *The Covent-Garden Journal* (1752).

Not satisfied by law and journalism, Fielding channeled into prose fiction the creative powers cut off from the stage. In 1741, very soon after he abandoned *The Champion* and less than a year after he began to practice law, Fielding published *An Apology for the Life of Mrs. Shamela Andrews*, a parody of Richardson's *Pamela*. This led the next year to *The*

History of the Adventures of Joseph Andrews, and of His Friend Mr. Abraham Adams, the first of his three great novels. This work, published anonymously, begins as another attack on Richardson's ethical and moral vision but soon goes off in its own direction, a picaresque work—in the tradition of *Don Quixote de la Mancha*—which is centered on the inscrutable character of Parson Adams. Fielding next published his *Miscellanies* (1743), a collection of both old and new works that was especially notable for the inclusion of *The History of the Life of the Late Mr. Jonathan Wild the Great*. This intense and bitter satire equates political greatness with criminal notoriety, insisting that greed, ruthlessness, cunning, and singleness of vision propel men to success in crime and government alike. Six years later, *Tom Jones*, Fielding's masterpiece and one of the world's great novels, made original literary contributions, which the plays had not managed to produce. *Amelia*, which Fielding published at the end of 1751, lacks the robust spirit and characters of *Tom Jones* but sold well when it first appeared. Fielding himself favored the book and was disappointed with its critical reception.

By the time *Amelia* was published, Fielding was nearing the end of his life. Making do with the inadequate resources of the legal system, constantly exposed to the diseases of those brought before him in court, and fundamentally weakened, perhaps, by the pace of his own somewhat intemperate life, Fielding required constant medical attention. He did not, however, slow down until the summer of 1754, when he decided to travel to Portugal for his health. During the slow, uncomfortable journey, he wrote *The Journal of a Voyage to Lisbon*, a work of shrewd, humorous observation. It was his last effort. On October 8, 1754, Fielding died, widely mourned by friends who, however much they had valued him, were unlikely to appreciate the scope and variety of his achievements or grasp the extent of the contributions he had made in the forty-seven years of his life.

ANALYSIS

In a period of only nine years, Henry Fielding wrote and staged more than twenty plays. Such a sustained outburst recalls the careers of Elizabethan dramatists Thomas Dekker and John Fletcher, who in the early 1600's turned out three or four scripts a year to feed London's voracious appetite for new plays. The decade of the 1730's was another theatrically hungry period. Five theaters competed for reputation, audience, and income; their managers vied for the best authors, plays, and actors. The pressure of competition added farces, burlesques, operas, pantomime, and even puppet shows to the repertory of drama by standard playwrights. In the struggle to keep up and get ahead, authors and companies freely borrowed material from the French and Italian theaters and readily used singers, dancers, jugglers, and anything else that attracted customers. Innovative theater often brought quick profits, but it challenged many dramatic conventions (especially notions of genre) and often sacrificed dramatic quality to gain immediate impact.

Though Fielding's plays are diverse in method and form, they are alike in motivation. Fielding used the stage as early eighteenth century writers used every literary genre: as a forum for the discussion of current events. With journalistic promptness and intensity, Fielding (like other dramatists of the 1730's) built plays around current events in London: examples of private morality and immorality, political issues and personalities, and trends in the theater. Like a journalist, Fielding wrote rapidly. If a play succeeded, it was imitated or redone in a bigger and better version. If a play failed, it was pulled from the stage and replaced. Fielding was adept at writing quickly as well as ingeniously, whether reviving old material or concocting new combinations of dramatic staples. These "unshaped monsters of a wanton brain" could never bring Fielding the literary fame that successful five-act comedies would have brought, but several of them are masterpieces of the 1730's, one of the liveliest and most experimental eras of English theater.

A review of Fielding's plays shows that he attempted to work in one traditional dramatic style, the comedy of manners, but, more important, to cater to the popular taste for new dramatic entertainments. Fielding first tried his hand at five-act comedies in the style of William Congreve and Sir John Vanbrugh. When he met limited success with this form, Fielding turned to farce, one- and two-act plays designed as afterpieces to the main performance. These short plays, at which Fielding proved adept, emphasized broad characterization, limited plots, and busy stage action. If Fielding had worked only in these two styles, however, his modern reputation as a dramatist would be negligible. The theatrical rivalry of his era led Fielding to experiment with dramatic form and stage technique. He experimented both to find innovations that would please audiences and to poke fun at rival playwrights. His experimental dramas (which he once called the "unshaped monsters of a wanton brain") defy categorization because they mix freely and imaginatively elements of manners comedy, farce, burlesque, and ballad opera. Fielding's plays represent different levels of achievement. Skillful as he could be at following convention or manipulating it, Fielding often pursued thematic concerns at the expense of form. His themes are as numerous as the plays themselves: the moral state of London society, the political health of the nation under the administration of Prime Minister Robert Walpole, the condition of modern marriage, and the quality of contemporary theater.

The emphasis on theme made Fielding only a mediocre practitioner of the five-act comedy. His Congrevian comedies were progressively ill-received by audiences, and modern scholarship has devoted attention to them primarily because of Fielding's reputation in other genres. The thematic emphasis was more congenial in farce, where conventions were less firm, but at the same time, the form worked against any substantial thematic exploration or revelation. Fielding's "unshaped monsters," plays in which form is shaped almost organically as a means of expressing theme, are his major achievement. They are amusing, imaginative, and energetic. Even though two centuries have dulled some of the pointed satire, they are a delight to read. In the 1730's these experimental plays, mingling dramatic elements in unexpected ways for irreverent purposes, sometimes pleased and sometimes puzzled. Modern readers—accustomed to W. S. Gilbert and Sir Arthur Sullivan operettas, Marx Brothers films, and Monty Python skits—can easily visualize these works in performance. A term Fielding used for one of this group, "dramatic satire," might serve for all of them.

Tracing the sequence of Fielding's five-act comedies, one sees clearly how the conventions of the genre and Fielding's interests grew steadily. The Congrevian comedy of manners followed patterns that had codified during four decades of Restoration theater. The staple plot presents a witty hero in pursuit of love and fortune through fashionable London society. Love begins as a hunt for pleasure—like a fox hunt, a chase of elaborate ceremony—with the hunter well equipped by a solid inheritance. The hero, a skeptic about the virtues of marriage, enjoys the hunt until he meets a woman whose wit and intelligence match his own. Now the hero's pursuit changes: Love's quality matters more to him than variety, and his wealth enables him to avoid mindless conformity to society's customs. The lovers display their attractive characters and mutual affection in brilliant dialogue, and they overcome whatever obstacles arise: rival lovers, disagreeable guardians, legal complexities. By manipulating other characters, the lovers bring their courtship to a successful conclusion which sees deserving heads, hearts, and fortunes united. Although the dramatist might make, in the course of things, satiric points about contemporary values and attitudes, Congrevian comedy emphasizes the mutual attraction of the young lovers. John Loftis has called this celebration of attraction, as it matures from a physical desire to incorporate intellectual parity, the "gaiety of sex." Congrevian comedy entertains and improves by championing the pursuit of love.

LOVE IN SEVERAL MASQUES

Fielding's first two comedies, *Love in Several Masques* and *The Temple Beau*, remain faithful to the conventions and emphases of the type. In the first play, Merital seeks to win Helena, whose guardians, an aunt and uncle, wish to marry her to the foolish man-about-town, Apish. The aunt, Lady Trap, is an obstacle in another sense: She is trying to seduce Merital. The lovers elope after Merital pretends friendship with Apish to gain access to Helena. In the second play, Veromil, though defrauded of his inheritance by a rascally brother, pursues Bellaria because he loves her. His rival is a high-living rake and supposed law student, Henry Wilding, who courts Bellaria as a means of recouping his wasted fortune. The timely intervention of an old family servant exposes the fraud and secures social recognition for Veromil's marriage to Bellaria. Although the plays attack the contemporary feeling that money and concern for the family name are more important than love, their satire does not obscure the zesty pursuit of love.

This is not the case, however, in Fielding's other five-act comedies. Perhaps because comedy is a traditional vehicle for lashing vice and exposing folly, Fielding increasingly gave precedence to theme over conventions of character and plot. A moralist, like many eighteenth century authors, he could not help paying more attention to political, professional, and social corruption than he did to literary traditions. Though this emphasis weakened the public appeal of his five-act plays, it shows his thinking and underlies his growing sense of dramatic freedom.

RAPE UPON RAPE

Rape upon Rape, which claims to present contemporary life as any observer could remark it, is more a thesis play than a comedy. The title (which offended Fielding's contemporaries and had to be changed) both describes the literal action and also becomes a symbolic indictment of the English judicial system. Hilaret's plans to elope with Captain Constant are upset when she is accosted by the rakish Ramble. Her cry of "rape" causes Ramble to be apprehended, but he then charges her with swearing a false accusation. Both are hauled before Justice Squeezum, who solicits bribes from men and women alike: money from the former and sex from the latter. Managing to escape Squeezum's solicitations, Hilaret learns that Constant has been carried to the same court on a false rape charge. Although Hilaret and Constant are true lovers, who proceed to expose Squeezum's corruption and manage to marry, little attention is paid to celebrating their mutual attraction. The play offers some amusing moments, but there is, not surprisingly, little gaiety in the themes of pandering, attempted rape, and injustice.

THE MODERN HUSBAND AND
THE UNIVERSAL GALLANT

Fielding's subsequent five-act comedies move even further from the model. There are courting lovers in *The Modern Husband*, but they are not the central couple; there are no unmarried lovers in *The Universal Gallant*, nor are the married people especially attractive people in either play. The main action of *The Modern Husband* is a strong indictment of aristocratic power and middle-class groveling: Lord Richly awards power and prestige to men who prostitute their wives to him and then uses those couples to seduce others. The play shows Richly attempting to use Mr. and Mrs. Modern to bring Mr. and Mrs. Bellamant within his circle. Fortunately, the Bellamants are faithful to each other and clever enough to thwart Richly's design. *The Universal Gallant* contrasts the overly suspicious Sir Simon Raffler, whose wife is faithful, with the trusting Colonel Raffler, whose wife is regularly unfaithful. Entangled with these couples are Captain Spark, who boasts (without justification) of numerous conquests, and the beau Mondish, who goes quietly about several amours. Sex abounds in both plays, but, again, little of it is lighthearted. The Bellamants and the Simon Rafflers find only distress in love; the couples endure, but with little sense of celebration.

THE LOTTERY

Fielding found farce a better medium than comedy for exaggerated characterization and pointed satire. Eighteenth century farce did not have as many conventions as manners comedy, but its assumptions were well understood. In the prologue to *The Lottery*, Fielding comments on two important differences between the types. First, while "Comedy delights to punish the fool,/ Farce challenges the vulgar as her prize"; that is, the characters satirized in farce are more mean-spirited than self-deluded (and probably of a low social class). Second, farce identifies and attacks its targets by a "magnifying right/ To raise the object still larger to the sight"; that is, it allows exaggeration, hyperbole, and caricature. Formally, farce differs from comedy by dispensing with subplot, speeding up the pace, and emphasizing humor rather than wit in dialogue.

The Lottery is a good example of the latitude that farce gave Fielding's interests. The play exposes the foolishness of those who literally mortgage their futures to a one-in-ten-thousand chance and deplores the corruption of those who capitalize on foolish hopes. Mr. Stocks, who sells lottery tickets, knows "what an abundance of rich men will one month reduce to their former poverty." The brief plot follows the rocky love affair of Mr. Stock's younger brother Jack, who has no inheritance and whose beloved puts all their hopes for a happy married life on winning a ten-thousand-pound first prize. Fortunately, the lovers' natural affection survives the inevitable disappointment when their ticket does not win.

EURYDICE

Eurydice shows a more imaginative use of farce's freewheeling style. The play depicts the visit of Orpheus to the Underworld in pursuit of his wife, Eurydice. Orpheus, singing ballad opera instead of strumming the lyre, charms Pluto, god of the Underworld, into granting permission for Eurydice to return to earth. Eurydice, however, is reluctant to return to modern London, where married love is accorded little respect. If Orpheus is like other modern husbands, he will soon lose interest in her. She wonders if she is not better off in a kingdom where she is free to govern herself. After much singing about the advantages and disadvantages of either choice, Eurydice finally decides to stay, and Orpheus departs alone, warning other husbands to appreciate their wives while they have them. *Eurydice* was not well received by its first audience, which took an unexpected dislike to one character, the ghost of an army beau. This reception led Fielding to write a sequel, *Eurydice Hiss'd*, about an author whose play, though imperfect, is unjustly scorned by theatergoers.

FRENCH FARCES

The Lottery and *Eurydice* are typical English farces, with a certain zaniness that results from making the plot fit the satiric theme. There was another tradition of farce, however, that Fielding explored in the 1730's. This other tradition was French; its major practitioner was Molière. Its satire is general (the incompetence of doctors, the social vanity of the nouveau riche), its structure built on the traditional devices of fast-paced action, intrigue, and disguise rather than on ludicrous situations. One might call it the "well-made farce": The plot leaves no loose ends. Such plays demand especially skillful actors; Fielding, who was always aware of how much a play's success

depended on its cast, twice adapted material from the French to match the talent of a specific actress—in *The Intriguing Chambermaid* and *The Mock Doctor*. Taking stock situations such as the clever servant who outwits a master and the couple for whom marital life and marital strife are synonymous, these farces move briskly to unfold, develop, and tie together the action. *The Intriguing Chambermaid* and *The Mock Doctor*, both successful pieces, show that Fielding could adapt as well as be original in the art of farce.

Fielding, like many of his contemporaries, spoke slightingly of farce because it was without classical precedent and therefore less literary: "The stage . . . was not for low farce designed/ But to divert, instruct, and mend mankind" through comedy. Fielding moved progressively away from comedy, however, as his own interests and theatrical developments in the 1730's did more to shape his drama than did the desire to succeed as a regular dramatist. Fielding found two vehicles, ballad opera and burlesque, ideal for presenting satire in drama. Ballad opera combined farce, music, and ingenious paralleling; it originated with John Gay's *The Beggar's Opera* (pr. 1728), a tale of London's underworld in which thieves and prostitutes sing arias (set to native English tunes) about their lives, which show embarrassing similarities to those of the rich and powerful. Burlesque exaggerated theatrical conventions in order to poke fun at them and to indict a public taste for such inferior entertainment. (Sometimes, however, "inferior" meant only "what was currently successful at a rival theater.")

DRAMATIC SATIRES

Fielding never wrote pure burlesque or ballad opera, preferring to draw on these forms for devices which, when mixed with elements of comedy and farce, could produce ingenious and distinctive plays. As suggested earlier, Fielding's alternative title for *Pasquin*, which was *A Dramatic Satire on the Times*, may be the most useful way of describing these plays. "Satire" comes from the Latin *satura*, which means a medley; Fielding's dramatic satires are indeed medleys for the stage, collections of parts and techniques and themes which the critical purist may find offensive but which the responsive reader often finds delightful. Fielding, never able to give up hope of becoming famous for his five-act comedies, often apologized for the dramatic satires, calling them products of "his unskilled muse," because they pleased the fancy more than the judgment. Those who read the dramatic satires today could hardly disagree more. Written to "combat the follies of the town," these plays do suffer somewhat because some contemporary allusions are lost, but Fielding is one of the great detectors of human folly, and the truth of his observations is not limited to any time, any place, or any social class.

THE TRAGEDY OF TRAGEDIES

Four plays—*The Tragedy of Tragedies*, *The Author's Farce*, *Pasquin*, and *The Historical Register for the Year 1736*—are Fielding's masterpieces in dramatic satire. They demonstrate his inventiveness, his versatility, his wit, and his thematic concerns. *The Tragedy of Tragedies* (a three-act version of the two-act afterpiece *Tom Thumb*) is a fantastic burlesque of heroic tragedy. The court of King Arthur and Queen Dollalolla is attacked by a race of warriors led by the giantess Glumdalca. The invaders are defeated by Arthur's champion, Tom Thumb, a knight as big as the digit whose name he bears. In reward, Tom is allowed to marry the Princess Huncamunca, but the proposed union causes much jealousy. Lord Grizzle, who loves Huncamunca, refuses to see her wed to one "fitter for [her] pocket than [her] bed." The queen and Glumdalca despair because they both love Tom. The giantess must forsake Tom because of their physical difference, and the queen's marriage vows intrude, although Dollalolla finds that in Cupid's scale, "Tom Thumb is heavier than my Virtue."

While Tom celebrates his engagement by murdering two bailiffs who arrest his courtier friends for debt, Grizzle attempts to woo Huncamunca. He succeeds quickly, but only because the princess is ready to marry either man—or any man. Grizzle vows to kill Tom by leading a rebellion. Meanwhile, King Arthur is visited by a ghost who prophesies Tom's death. When the loyal army confronts the rebels, Grizzle kills Glumdalca, but Tom slays Grizzle. The celebration at court is spoiled, however, when news comes that on meeting the victors in their march home, "a Cow, of larger size than usual/ . . . in a Moment swallowed up Tom Thumb."

As farce, *The Tragedy of Tragedies* is humorous, but as burlesque it is brilliant. As he exaggerates tragic conventions, Fielding also mocks their language by mimicking it. Inflated rhetoric, overblown metaphor, inappropriate diction, and ironic simile provide an aural equivalent of the visual farce. The king inquires thus about Dollalolla's health: "What wrinkled Sorrow,/ Hangs, sits, lies, frowns upon thy knitted brow?" Huncamunca describes pining for Tom: "For him I've sighed, I've wept, I've gnawed my Sheets." The parson prays for the fruitfulness of Tom's marriage: "So when the Cheshire Cheese a Maggot breeds,/ . . . By thousands, and ten thousands they increase,/ Till one continued Maggot fills the rotten Cheese." Glumdalca laments the emotional storm raised in her by the sight of Tom: "I'm all within a Hurricane, as if/ The World's four winds were pent within my Carcass." A giantess filled with one wind to expel is awesome; the notion of four winds pent within her is catastrophic.

The printed text of the play adds another target to the burlesque: It is a mock scholarly edition with critical apparatus. Fielding names his editor H. Scriblerus *Secundus* in the tradition of Martinus Scriblerus, whom Alexander Pope and Jonathan Swift had created to satirize pedantic scholarship. In a preface filled with Latin tags and authoritative references, Scriblerus argues that *The Tragedy of Tragedies*, conforming perfectly to classical precedent, is renowned throughout Europe. The footnotes increase the fun. Fielding had borrowed lines from actual plays (sometimes crucially altered, sometimes not) for his burlesque; the footnotes invert the procedure by demonstrating that *The Tragedy of Tragedies* was actually written in Elizabethan times and has itself been borrowed from and pillaged by all subsequent dramatists.

THE AUTHOR'S FARCE

The Author's Farce also ridicules, in a somewhat freer form than *The Tragedy of Tragedies*, theatrical tastes of the day. It tells of a struggling playwright named Luckless who is having great difficulty getting his piece performed or published. Luckless is sure the work is just the thing to please contemporary audiences: a puppet show, called *The Pleasures of the Town*, which uses live actors. The inversion is typically Fielding; he teases the current rage for puppet actors performing cut-down standard plays by positing live actors performing Punch-and-Joan (as Judy was universally known then) antics.

The play is not pure burlesque but a mixture of comic traditions. Act 1 is traditional manners comedy. It shows Luckless unable to pay his rent because he is unable to sell his play. Witty though impoverished, Luckless fends off the financial and amorous demands of his landlady, Mrs. Moneywood, because he is really in love with her daughter, Harriot. Luckless's friend Witmore aids him in his battles against dunning creditors and stingy booksellers. When Witmore pays off the back rent, the ingenious Luckless dupes Moneywood into turning the cash over to him. When the publisher Bookweight refuses Luckless an advance, Bookweight is abused and thrown out of the apartment. At least Luckless gains some emotional satisfaction, and he possesses the pluck, the hauteur, and the quick-wittedness of the Congrevian hero.

Act 2 is closer to farce. Ten rapid scenes show Luckless trying to get his puppet show staged immediately. Two theater managers (representing Colley Cibber and Robert Wilks of Drury Lane) turn the play down because the author has no "interest"—that is, no standing within the ruling theatrical clique. Taking his case directly to other managers and to the actors, Luckless arranges for a performance that very night. Bookweight, discovered at his shop overseeing instant dedications and rapid translations written by his stable of hacks, now willingly listens to Luckless because he has "interest." A crier advertises the performance, "in which will be shown the whole Court of Dullness with abundance of singing and dancing and several other entertainments . . . to be performed by living figures, some of them six foot high."

The third act, the actual performance of Luckless's play, combines farce and burlesque. *The Pleasures of the Town* opens with a scene of the archetypal feuding couple, Punch and Joan; the arguing, singing, and dancing please popular taste but in no way relate to what follows. The next scene introduces a deceased poet on his way to the Goddess of Nonsense's Underworld court; the poet meets several other travelers fresh from London who are on the same route. There is Don Tragedio, who died after one performance; Sir Farcical Comic, who was hissed to death; Mr. Pantomime, whose neck the audience wrung; and Madam Novel, who went unread. Preeminent among these victims of shifting audience taste is Don Opera, who was so overwhelmed with the audience's approbation and his own dying aria that he swooned to death. Don Opera has been chosen as the fittest spouse for the Goddess of Nonsense. After an irrelevant scene presenting a card game among four shrieking harridans, the stage is set for the wedding. At this moment, *The Pleasures of the Town* turns into a ballad opera and emotional outbursts are rendered in song. There is plenty of passionate carrying-on: Nonsense discovers that Opera is already wed to Novel, and Opera protests that death has freed him from his vows. Unconvinced, Nonsense invites wooing from Farcical, Pantomime, and the others. Spurned, Opera proclaims his undying affection for Novel.

This dramatic moment is interrupted by Parson Murdertext, who has brought Constable to arrest Luckless for staging a sacrilegious play. The characters in the puppet show argue with Murdertext and Constable, thus blurring the line between play and play-within-the-play. That line grows even fainter as Harriot and Witmore enter with the ambassador from the Javanese kingdom of Bantom. The newcomer proclaims Luckless as the long-lost heir to Bantom's throne. A messenger enters to announce that the old Javanese king has just died, and Luckless is immediately proclaimed Henry I of Bantom. He appoints all the characters (not the actors) in the puppet-show to important government posts. Punch returns to identify himself as Harriot's lost brother, and Moneywood proclaims herself the impoverished Queen of Brentford. The play concludes with a dance.

Without a well-annotated text, modern readers will miss many of the in-jokes, yet none will miss Fielding's general indictment of the foolishness that passes as entertainment. Sudden reversals of fortune, reliance on spectacle in place of development, and heavy use of coincidence are all marks of amateurishness or incompetence that mar drama, whether their victim is an eighteenth century play, a Hollywood movie, or a television sitcom.

PASQUIN

Pasquin, a dramatic satire that shows Fielding's seemingly limitless inventiveness, follows one of the few traditions for a satiric play: a rehearsal of another play. George Villiers's *The Rehearsal* (pr. 1671, pb. 1672), which mocked the heroic plays of John Dryden and Robert Howard, originated the form, which became standard in the self-conscious theater of the late seventeenth and early eighteenth centuries. Fielding's twist on the formula is to include two rehearsals—one of a comedy and one of a tragedy—in the same play. For two and a half acts, *Pasquin* shows Trapwit leading the actors through a comedy about how to win an election; for another two and a half acts, *Pasquin* presents Fustian taking the cast through his tragedy on the death of Queen Commonsense.

There is much comment and satire in *Pasquin* on now-familiar theatrical topics: the plight of actors and actresses, the looming specter of debtor's prison for authors and performers, hasty production of plays, scenes written by formula, reliance in dialogue on bombast and innuendo (Trapwit, for example, protests that "except about a dozen, or a score, or so, there is not an impure joke" in his comedy), and production opportunity allowed only to already-successful authors. Fielding's main target in *Pasquin*, however, is not the theater; his subjects are political and intellectual. *Pasquin* has more in common with Swift's *Gulliver's Travels* (1726) and Pope's *The Dunciad* (1728-1743) than it does with other plays of the period. Trapwit's comedy is a merciless exposure of election campaigning, and Fustian's tragedy is an indictment of three professions: law, medicine, and religion. The play's title suggests the wide-ranging assault: Pasquin was the name of a Roman statue that was annually festooned with satiric epigrams and verses.

Like Swift, Fielding shows that people get the politicians they deserve. Trapwit's comedy observes the conduct of a contemporary election. Lord Place and Colonel Promise, the court's candidates (representing the Whig party of Sir Robert Walpole), vie for seats in Parliament with Sir Henry Foxchase and Squire Tankard, the country candidates (representing the Tory party). As the Mayor and aldermen sit in a tavern discussing the election, Place and Promise arrive and begin campaigning; they simply bribe each voter. In contrast to this method, which Trapwit calls "direct bribing," Foxchase and Tankard engage in indirect bribing: They buy meat and drink freely for the tavern crowd, patronize the merchants with prodigious orders for silks and clothing, and lament the corruption of courtiers who openly buy votes. The Mayor and aldermen rally for a moment to the newcomers and their slogan of "Liberty, property, and no excise."

Meanwhile, Place and Promise have been active among the ladies of the town, filling their ears with stories about the masquerades and fashionable gowns that could be theirs if the Court candidates win. Mrs. Mayoress and Miss Mayoress conclude that the lord and the colonel are "the finest men . . . the prettiest men . . . the sweetest men" and that the Mayor must vote for them. Miss Mayoress also persuades Miss Stitch, by the gift of a fan, to seek her beau's vote for the Court. The ladies carry the day with the Mayor, and when Foxchase and Tankard win the election, the Mayor is much chagrined that he has supported the losing party. Unable to give up her dreams of Court preferment, Mrs. Mayoress convinces her husband to certify that the losers are really the victors. As she announces this startling development to the surprised courtiers, she encourages them, "when we have returned you so [that is, duly elected] it will be your fault if you don't prove yourself so." Mrs. Mayoress refers to the wonderful knack of eighteenth century incumbents, especially Walpole's supporters, for keeping their seats by parliamentary maneuvering—regardless of an election's outcome.

Fustian's play, more allegorical than Trapwit's, is set at the court of Queen Commonsense in the days when she ruled England. Three of her chief ministers—Law, Physic, and Firebrand (who stands for religion)—are unhappy because the reign of logic and reason in the land has diminished their power. For example, when two men suing each other over property lose it to their own lawyers, the queen is ready to reform the legal system, but Law sees only a decline in his authority and income. When news comes that Queen Ignorance, with an army of "singers, fiddlers, tumblers, and rope-dancers," has invaded the island, the disgruntled courtiers threaten to join the rebels unless Commonsense yields them more power. Nevertheless, the queen bravely contends:

> Religion, law, and physic were designed
> By Heaven, the greatest blessings of mankind;
> But priests and lawyers and physicians made
> These general goods to each a private trade;
> With each they rob, with each they fill their purses,
> And turn our benefits into our curses.

Commonsense's refusal to surrender brings on a battle. Gradually, her followers are slain until only a poet remains. His support of Commonsense has been so weak of late that he readily goes over to the enemy. Firebrand stabs Commonsense, and the reign of Ignorance is established. Only the ghost of Commonsense remains to harass Ignorance's minions on occasion. The play ends, like Pope's *The Dunciad*, with universal darkness covering just about all.

In neither *The Author's Farce* nor *Pasquin* is Fielding's satire subtle. No characters are fully realized, plots jump as need be, and the dialogue has more sarcasm than wit. Fielding's ingenuity is in the juxtaposition of diverse and eclectic elements; the plays please through surprise and bluntness.

THE HISTORICAL REGISTER FOR THE YEAR 1736

The Historical Register for the Year 1736 is less imaginative in its theatrical technique but more daring in its political attack. It, too, is cast as a rehearsal, this time of the playwright Medley's work about the previous year's events on the island kingdom of Corsica (which is obviously a symbol of Walpolian England). Medley's play alternates comments on the theater and on the nation because "There is a ministry in the latter as well as the former, and I believe as weak a ministry as any poor kingdom could boast of." In linking the two worlds of the prime minister and the theater manager, Medley observes that "though

the public damn both, yet while they [the ministers] receive their pay, they laugh at the public behind the scenes." Through Medley's play, Fielding takes the audience behind the scenes.

Act 1 begins by assembling some observers of the rehearsal and showing what kind of reception Medley might expect. Medley and the actors, happy merely to have a script to perform and a stage to use, convene. The critic Sourwit joins them, immediately damning whatever he sees. Lord Dapper looks on, so weak-brained that the most obvious satire must be explained to him. As the rehearsal commences, Medley reads a prologue, an ode to the New Year (with immortal lines such as "This is a day in days of yore/ Our fathers never saw before"), which burlesques the vapid verse of the poet laureate and theater manager Colley Cibber. The first scene displays a cabal of politicians who respond to financial crisis by voting another tax. Finding everything already taxed, one politico proposes a tax on learning, but another counters, "I think we had better lay it on Ignorance," which "will take in most of the great fortunes in the Kingdom." Lord Dapper is present proof that the speaker is right. Fielding manages to abuse both politicians and, through them, the masters they serve.

Act 2 continues the assault with an opening scene in which fashionable ladies (formula comedies always open the second act with fashionable ladies) adore the latest opera singer, whose performances currently pack the theaters. They display their enthusiasm by carrying his "babies" (little wax dolls in his image), certainly an ironic tribute to a castrato. Because these dolls are more valuable than lapdogs or spouses, one lady protests, "If my husband was to make any objection to my having 'em, I'd run away from him and take the dear babies with me." In the next scene, the women attend an auction (the current faddish pastime), where the satire turns political. Up for sale are items such as a cloth remnant of political honesty, a piece of patriotism big enough to show off but too small to hold attention, a few grains of modesty, and an unopened bottle of courage; the buyers disparage the goods. Fielding's comment is twofold: There is only enough virtue in political society to give the illusion of honesty, and even that little claims no great market. The act ends with the entrance of the madman Pistol, who claims the title of Prime Minister Theatrical. When a mob hisses, he takes the sound as a sign of approbation. Pistol is a caricature of Theophilus Cibber, who, like his father, Colley, aspired to this title by hearing applause in a round of catcalls.

The third act dramatizes Medley's thesis that in the contemporary world "a man of parts, learning, and virtue is fit for no employment whatever . . . that honesty is the only sort of folly for which a man ought to be utterly neglected and condemned." The theatrical and political implications of this view are worked out as a modern-day Apollo casts the players for a performance of William Shakespeare's *King John* (pr., c. 1596-1597) with little regard for their competency. Like the theater managers of *The Author's Farce*, the god makes his decisions on the basis of "interest," the auditioner's relationship to someone in power. The consequences of such thinking are dramatized as Pistol becomes Prime Minister Theatrical by usurping his father and as Quidam, the model of a modern politician, bilks five citizens of the little money with which he had bribed them at election time. Quidam's fraud is accomplished through a pantomime dance that demonstrates that politics is nothing but theater; Pistol's accession shows how political theater is. The dance concludes the play, yet it is not a proper dramatic ending, simply one that caters to the people's taste. If the actors laugh while they dance, the target of their laughter is clear.

OTHER MAJOR WORKS

LONG FICTION: *An Apology for the Life of Mrs. Shamela Andrews*, 1741; *The History of the Adventures of Joseph Andrews, and of His Friend Mr. Abraham Adams*, 1742 (commonly known as *Joseph Andrews*); *The History of the Life of the Late Mr. Jonathan Wild the Great*, 1743, 1754; *The History of Tom Jones, a Foundling*, 1749 (commonly known as *Tom Jones*); *Amelia*, 1751.

NONFICTION: *The Journal of a Voyage to Lisbon*, 1755.

TRANSLATION: *The Military History of Charles XII King of Sweden*, 1740.

MISCELLANEOUS: *Miscellanies*, 1743 (3 volumes).

BIBLIOGRAPHY

Battestin, Martin C. *A Henry Fielding Companion.* Westport, Conn.: Greenwood, 2000. A comprehensive reference work covering the life and writings of Fielding. Includes sections on where he lived, his family, significant historical figures and literary influences, his works, themes, and characters. Bibliography and index.

Bertelsen, Lance. *Henry Fielding at Work: Magistrate, Businessman, Writer.* New York: Palgrave, 2000. An analysis of Fielding in his roles as writer, magistrate, and businessman. Bibliography and index.

Campbell, Jill. *Natural Masques: Gender and Identity in Fielding's Plays and Novels.* Stanford, Calif.: Stanford University Press, 1995. A look at gender and identity issues in the works of Fielding. Bibliography and index.

Michie, Allen. *Richardson and Fielding: The Dynamics of a Critical Rivalry.* Lewisburg, Pa.: Bucknell University Press, 1999. A study of the relationship between Fielding and Samuel Richardson. Bibliography and index.

Pagliaro, Harold E. *Henry Fielding: A Literary Life.* New York: St. Martin's Press, 1998. A presentation of the life of Fielding, with emphasis on his role as writer. Bibliography and indexes.

Paulson, Ronald. *The Life of Henry Fielding: A Critical Biography.* Malden, Mass.: Blackwell, 2000. Paulson examines how Fielding's literary works— plays, essays, and novels—all contained autobiographical elements. Bibliography and index.

Rivero, Albert J. *The Plays of Henry Fielding: A Critical Study of His Dramatic Career.* Charlottesville: University Press of Virginia, 1989. Rivero offers a detailed critique of ten representative plays. Discusses dramatic technique, construction, and themes and provides some historical context to the plays.

Uglow, Jennifer S. *Henry Fielding.* Plymouth, England: Northcote House, 1995. An examination of the life and works of Fielding. Bibliography and index.

Robert M. Otten and Richard N. Ramsey, updated by Genevieve Slomski

HARVEY FIERSTEIN

Born: Brooklyn, New York; June 6, 1954

PRINCIPAL DRAMA

In Search of the Cobra Jewels, pr. 1972

Freaky Pussy, pr. 1973

Cannibals Just Don't Know Better, pr. 1974

Flatbush Tosca, pr. 1975

Torch Song Trilogy, pr. 1978-1979, pb. 1979
(includes *The International Stud*, *Fugue in a Nursery*, and *Widows and Children First!*)

Spookhouse, pr. 1982

La Cage aux folles, pr. 1983 (libretto; music and lyrics by Jerry Herman)

Safe Sex, pr., pb. 1987 (trilogy; includes *Manny and Jake*, *Safe Sex*, and *On Tidy Endings*)

Forget Him, pr., pb. 1988

Legs Diamond, pr. 1988 (libretto; music and lyrics by Peter Allen)

OTHER LITERARY FORMS

Harvey Fierstein writes for both stage and screen. He based his screenplay *Torch Song Trilogy* (1988) on the three one-act plays published under the same name, and his teleplay *Tidy Endings* (1988) was a screen adaptation of the third play of his *Safe Sex* trilogy. He also wrote the teleplay *Kaddish and Old Men* (1987).

ACHIEVEMENTS

Harvey Fierstein has received numerous awards for his writing and for his acting, both on stage and screen. He received a Special Citation Obie in 1981-1982 for his play *Torch Song Trilogy*. The following year, he won two Tony Awards (Best Play and Best Actor) for *Torch Song Trilogy*, and in 1984, *La Cage aux folles* received the Tony Award for Best Musical. In 1988 he received the Fennecus Award for his adapted screenplay *Torch Song Trilogy* and for his performances of the songs "Love for Sale" and "Svelte" in that film. In 1989 he was presented with the Independent Spirit Award for his leading role in the film *Torch Song Trilogy*. He won Fennecus

Awards for his acting in *Mrs. Doubtfire* in 1993 and in *Bullets Over Broadway* in 1994, Apex Awards for Actor in a Supporting Role in *Mrs. Doubtfire* in 1993 and *Independence Day* in 1996, a GLAAD Award for visibility in 1994, and the Humanitas Prize in children's animation for *The Sissy Duckling* in 2000. He has received awards and other honors from Theater World, Oppenheimer, the Dramatists Guild, Hull/Warriner, Drama Desk, and the Los Angeles Drama Critics Circle, and he was honored with a plaque on Brooklyn's Walk of Fame. He has received grants from the Ford and Rockefeller foundations.

His distinctive voice has made him a popular reader of audio books as well as the voice for characters in animated films such as *Mulan* (1998). He narrated the Academy Award-winning documentary *The Times of Harvey Milk* (1984). He wrote and starred in the multiple Ace Award-winning Home Box Office (HBO) Showcase production *Tidy Endings*. His performance album *This Is Not Going to Be Pretty* is destined, according to some reviewers, to become "a classic in the vein of Lenny Bruce and George Carlin."

BIOGRAPHY

Harvey Fierstein was born in Brooklyn, New York, to a linen manufacturer and a librarian. He got his start in acting at age eleven when he became one of the founding actors in the Gallery Players Community Theater in Brooklyn. In 1973 he graduated with a bachelor of fine arts degree from Pratt Institute.

In 1971 Fierstein appeared in Andy Warhol's play *Pork*, at La Mama E.T.C. Since then, he has acted in numerous stage productions. He has appeared on television programs such as *Murder She Wrote*, *Miami Vice*, *Cheers*, *Daddy's Girl*, and the soap opera *Loving* and on talk shows such as *The Tonight Show*, *David Letterman*, *Arsenio Hall*, and *Politically Incorrect*. His film credits include *Garbo Talks* (1984), *Mrs. Doubtfire*, and *Independence Day*.

Between 1976 and 1979, he wrote his best-known work, *Torch Song Trilogy*, which he later adapted for the big screen. The plays were first produced in small theaters. In 1981 Fierstein starred in an Off-Broadway production of the *Torch Song Trilogy*, which he later took to Broadway. He was the first person to win a Tony Award for both Best Actor and Best Play for the same production. The film appeared, receiving its own awards, in 1988.

In both his public and private life, Fierstein is a gay rights activist. He has characterized himself as having been the first "real live and out-of-the-closet queer on Broadway." Homosexuality is the source of much of his comedy as well as the source of much of the tragedy of his drama. In 1998 he spoke at the Matthew Shepard Memorial March and Rally of his emotions at hearing of the student's death, saying "rage tore through my body nearly shredding my heart." In his plays and in his public appearances, he has demonstrated his hope that the "struggle for freedom" for the gay and lesbian community may be won.

ANALYSIS

The feelings experienced by Harvey Fierstein when learning of the death of student Matthew Shepard are expressed in his plays. In his speech at the memorial, he gave voice to a theme that is at the center of his dramatic works: Because politicians and moral leaders—and thus society—assault the "dignity and humanity" of the gay and lesbian community, its members "must take hold of [their] own destinies." The characters in his plays display their pain, their dignity, and their humanity as they show how capable, or at least how determined, they are to be masters of their own destinies.

Fierstein's drama is New Wave in its expression of his personal viewpoints and experiences. It is expressionistic in its frequent depiction of experience in a way that distorts reality in order to present psychological truths. It is existential in that it emphasizes the individual's freedom of choice and the distortion of society's role in its seeking to inhibit the choice of so many of its constituents.

TORCH SONG TRILOGY

In adapting his three one-act dramas for the screen, Fierstein had to eliminate some of his expressionistic techniques. This is most obvious when in a compari-

son of the stage and screen versions of *Fugue in a Nursery*. In the stage version of *Fugue in a Nursery*, there is little action: Four actors appear in a large bed with light focused on the speaker who reveals unseen aspects of the action or the drama to the audience or on speakers whose conversation carries the essence of the present dramatic moment. In the film, the action and emotional development are presented in linear fashion, and scene changes are frequent. Fierstein has bemoaned the loss of many good jokes in the transfer from stage to screen. However, his writing as well as his acting in both versions of *Torch Song Trilogy* have been widely appreciated.

THE INTERNATIONAL STUD

The difficulty of being a homosexual in the second half of the twentieth century is poignantly rendered in this first play of the *Torch Song Trilogy*. Ed Reiss is a boyish-looking thirty-five-year-old man who cannot commit to drag queen Arnold Beckoff, the trilogy's main character, because he is ashamed to

Harvey Fierstein (Hulton Archive by Getty Images)

admit that he is gay. The two men, Ed and Arnold, come to care deeply for each other, but Ed stops seeing Arnold and forces himself to spend time only with Laurel, who is not shown in this play but is featured in the second play of the trilogy.

Other evidence of Ed's ambivalence can be found in his avoidance of Arnold while Ed's parents are in town. When they leave, he turns once more to Arnold. Fearing the displeasure of his parents and society, Ed tries to conform to the standards they have set, but the denial of his true self is deadly. His return to Arnold is a plea for salvation.

In the final scene of *The International Stud*, Ed appears in Arnold's backstage dressing room after an absence of several months. He tells Arnold that he and Laurel are engaged. He also tells him that he has had a dream, which he can discuss with no one but Arnold. In his dream, Ed searches his father's workroom for a rag and turpentine. He takes the rag soaked in turpentine and a plastic bag to his bed. When Laurel calls, he wakes to find the soaked rag and the bag actually beside him on his pillow.

The grand finale of *The International Stud* leaves the audience with a heartbreaking image of what society's impact on its offspring can be. Ed, a young, appealing teacher, has been driven to the point of suicide by the demands placed on him by a society that reviles him. Arnold confesses that he still loves Ed. However, in this context of societal pressure and imposed self-hatred, Arnold's final question "Is love enough?" rings loudly in the ears and hearts of audience members.

FUGUE IN A NURSERY

Ed has told Arnold that Arnold's boudoir is the place that has offered him the most comfort in his life. In *Fugue in a Nursery*, each of the four occupants of a large bed are searching for the comfort of a nursery. Ed, who had found comfort with Arnold, is trying, still, to find comfort in the life that society favors. Laurel, Ed's fiancée, wants the comfort she hopes that Ed's seeing Arnold with Alan will bring to her relationship with Ed. Alan wants the comfort he hopes that Arnold's seeing Ed with Laurel will bring to his relationship with Arnold. Arnold, comfortable with himself and with his relationship with Alan,

wants only to return to the comfort of the home that he and Alan have made together. In all of this comfort seeking, of course, there has to be—and is—an added conflict: Ed and Alan create a fleeting partnership of their own. It is this final complication that sets up the framework for the third play of the trilogy.

WIDOWS AND CHILDREN FIRST!

The crucial need for self-acceptance of *The International Stud* leads logically to the seeking and vulnerability in *Fugue in a Nursery*. The final drama of this trilogy presents another variation of the family/nursery theme by tying together the threads of rejection and acceptance. Once more there is familial disapproval, this time onstage as Arnold's mother pays him a visit. In contrast to this negative image of family, however, *Widows and Children First!* offers a positive image, that of Arnold as a foster father to a fifteen-year-old boy, David.

David's new family is warm and loving. Arnold is both loving father and mother to him, and Ed has moved in temporarily (perhaps) as he is newly separated from his wife. They are a happy threesome. Discord arrives with Arnold's mother, Mrs. Beckoff. The negative and positive family images intertwine when Mrs. Beckoff worries that her son will be a bad role model for his foster son and Arnold informs her that David is gay and that he has been entrusted to Arnold's care because of the positive role model that Arnold will be. Arnold, a gay man who has a very real sense of his dignity as a human being, is giving to David what he has had to fight so hard for and what Ed is still fighting for: the comfort of self-acceptance.

As Arnold and his mother argue—as she again and again shows her disapproval of what he is—Arnold tells her that it is parents with attitudes like hers who teach their children that it is all right to take baseball bats and beat gay men to death, as someone had done to Alan. Through a comparison of his mother's and his own loss of partners, Arnold convinces his mother that a loving partnership is every bit as meaningful to gay partners as it is to heterosexual partners. Initially, when Arnold compares his grief at losing Alan to hers on the loss of her husband, Mrs. Beckoff takes it as an insult, but when Arnold demonstrates that he experienced the same lone-liness at the breakfast table as she had and the same grief at disposing of the departed's belongings as she had, she becomes convinced that she has never known enough about her son. She backs down from her disapproving stance, and after giving him a brief motherly lesson in grieving, she leaves.

In their conversations during the play, Arnold tells his mother that he has taught himself to do everything for himself so that he can rely solely on himself. Of any accepted associate, he says, he demands love and respect. He wins, finally, the grudging respect of his mother, and he has already won the love and respect of his foster son. Ed, who is finding comfort in Arnold's home, is learning to show his ungrudging love and respect for its members.

At the end of the play, the audience is left to imagine that there will be a renewed relationship between Arnold and Ed and to feel almost certain that Arnold's application for adoption of David will be approved. The play closes on the note of comfort sought in the other plays of the trilogy.

Fierstein's point is obvious but poignant—both on its own merits and because of its context. The society that has nearly killed Ed has killed Alan. Arnold has survived by not depending on that society and by not yet encountering children with baseball bats. Arnold's demands are Fierstein's demands: that each human being show if not love, then respect for others. *Torch Song Trilogy* brings the audience into Arnold's home and into his life, demonstrating his absolute humanity. The trilogy shows that the judgments passed by society have been passed because of ignorance. In speaking about gay and lesbian rights, Fierstein has said that no uninvited guest belongs in his bedroom. His trilogy makes the point that those who castigate homosexuals and homosexuality are indeed placing themselves in the bedrooms of others and asks who among these people would invite others into their bedrooms to be judged solely on their private activities therein.

MANNY AND JAKE

This first of the three plays of the *Safe Sex* trilogy is built on a single line. The line "Can you kiss?" is the source of humor and the source of the ultimate pathos of the play. In *Manny and Jake*, two attractive young gay men confront, on a level at once simple and profound, the emotional frustration of life in the age of AIDS (acquired immunodeficiency syndrome).

Manny's "Can you kiss?" elicits a no-complaints line from Jake. Manny, shown meditating throughout the play, leads Jake and the audience to the conclusion that this most simple and spontaneous act of affection is curtailed by the dread disease. Denied the sweetness of the kiss, Manny (who has found that he is HIV positive) has decided to live his life alone—in meditation.

SAFE SEX

Fierstein the comedian is more evident in this play than in the others of the *Safe Sex* trilogy. However, the basis for the play's humor, AIDS, is anything but funny. Although *Manny and Jake* focuses on spontaneity, this second play about Ghee and his partner focuses on protection as it makes the lack of spontaneity the source of its humor.

Ghee has an obsessive-compulsive personality. One of his obsessions is "the list." He cannot respond in any way to his partner without first checking the list. Once the contents of this list are established, other lists are introduced. The most significant list is one that consists of the names of the disease's victims. Throughout the play, Ghee and his partner converse while balancing on a teeter-totter. The balancing act of gay men in a sick society is thus set visually as well as conversationally before the eye and the mind of the audience from the play's beginning to end.

ON TIDY ENDINGS

The *Safe Sex* trilogy closes, as does its predecessor, on the idea of family. It also features two bereaved halves of a couple and a child. As did *Widows and Children First!*, this play dramatizes the inevitability of the breakup of a family in which one of the partners denies his true identity as a homosexual. In *On Tidy Endings*, the two "widows" are the two partners, male and female, of the same man. During the course of the play, the man's child is brought to a better understanding of his father's final relationship and of his father's partner. The child's mother comes to admit her respect for the man who took sole responsibility for her former husband during his debilitating illness. Both mother and son, finally, express admiration for the play's third surviving character.

The ending of the play is tidy, as the three come together to "tidy up" after the passing of the beloved partner and father.

OTHER MAJOR WORKS

SCREENPLAY: *Torch Song Trilogy*, 1988 (adaptation of his play).

TELEPLAYS: *Kaddish and Old Men*, 1987; *Tidy Endings*, 1988 (adaptation of his play *On Tidy Endings*).

CHILDREN'S LITERATURE: *The Sissy Duckling*, 2002.

BIBLIOGRAPHY

Connema, Richard. "San Francisco's Torch Song." *Talkin' Broadway's Regional News: San Francisco Reviews*, June 27, 2000. Presents a history of *Torch Song Trilogy* and a study of the drama itself as well as a review of a 2000 theater production. Connema calls the play, which he also saw in the 1980's, "the best gay play written at the time; far superior to *Boys in the Band*."

Ebert, Roger. "*Torch Song Trilogy*." *Chicago Sun-Times*, December 23, 1988. Offers insight into the ideas behind the film and praises Fierstein's on-screen portrayal of the character he had initially created for the stage. Ebert calls the film "more intimate and intense" than the play; and in saying that the main character is more comfortable with his sexuality than with other facets of himself, he concludes that "homosexuality is not his problem—it is the arena for his problems."

Hungerford, Jason. "My Reaction to *Torch Song Trilogy*." *Pflag-Talk*, January 19, 1997. Offers a response to the film that addresses and underlines the reality with which the stage and screen version of Fierstein's *Torch Song Trilogy* deals. Hungerford is inspired by Fierstein's film to say that "it's because of the kids who live on the streets, and the innocent children disowned by their parents, and the people who have lost their respectable jobs, and the people who have died senseless deaths, it's because of all of them that I do what I do."

Judith K. Taylor

CLYDE FITCH

Born: Elmira, New York; May 2, 1865
Died: Châlons-sur-Marne, France; September 4, 1909

PRINCIPAL DRAMA

Beau Brummell, pr. 1890, pb. 1908
Frederick Lemaître, pr. 1890, pb. 1933 (one act)
Betty's Finish, pr. 1890
Pamela's Prodigy, pr. 1891, pb. 1893
A Modern Match, pr. 1892
The Masked Ball, pr. 1892 (adaptation of Alexandre Bisson and Albert Carré's play *Le Veglione*)
The Social Swim, pr. 1893 (adaptation of Victorien Sardou's play *Maison neuve*)
The Harvest, pr. 1893
April Weather, pr. 1893

A Shattered Idol, pr. 1893 (adaptation of Honoré de Balzac's novel *Le Père Goriot*)
An American Duchess, pr. 1893 (adaptation of Henri Lavedan's play *Le Prince d'Aurec*)
Mrs. Grundy, Jr., pb. 1893
His Grace de Grammont, pr. 1894
Lovers' Lane, wr. 1894, pr. 1901, pb. 1915
Gossip, pr. 1895 (with Leo Ditrichstein; adaptation of Jules Claretie's play)
Mistress Betty, pr. 1895
Bohemia, pr. 1896 (adaptation of Henri Murger's novel *Scènes de la vie de Bohème*)
The Liar, pr. 1896 (adaptation of Bisson's play)
The Superfluous Husband, pr. 1897 (with Ditrichstein; adaptation of Ludwig Fulda's play)
Nathan Hale, pr. 1898, pb. 1899

The Moth and the Flame, pr. 1898, pb. 1908
   (revision of *The Harvest*)
The Head of the Family, pr. 1898 (adaptation of
   Adolf L'Arronge's play *Hasemanns Töchter*)
The Cowboy and the Lady, pr. 1899, pb. 1908
Barbara Frietchie, pr. 1899, pb. 1900
Sapho, pr. 1899 (adaptation of scenes by Alphonse
   Daudet and Adolphe Belot and adaptation of
   Daudet's novel)
Captain Jinks of the Horse Marines, pr. 1901, pb.
   1902
The Climbers, pr. 1901, pb. 1906
The Last of the Dandies, pr. 1901
The Marriage Game, pr. 1901 (adaptation of Émile
   Augier's play *Le Mariage d'Olympe*)
The Way of the World, pr. 1901
The Girl and the Judge, pr. 1901
The Stubbornness of Geraldine, pr. 1902, pb. 1906
The Girl with the Green Eyes, pr. 1902, pb. 1905
The Bird in the Cage, pr. 1903 (adaptation of Ernst
   von Wildenbruch's play *Die Haubenlerche*)
The Frisky Mrs. Johnson, pr. 1903, pb. 1908
   (adaptation of Paul Gavault and Georges Berr's
   play *Madame Flirt*)
Her Own Way, pr. 1903, pb. 1907
Major André, pr. 1903
Glad of It, pr. 1903
The Coronet of the Duchess, pr. 1904
Granny, pr. 1904 (adaptation of Michel Georges-
   Michel's novel *L'Aïeule*)
Cousin Billy, pr. 1905 (adaptation of Eugène
   Labiche and Édouard Martin's play *Le Voyage
   de M. Perrichon*)
The Woman in the Case, pr. 1905, pb. 1915
Her Great Match, pr. 1905, pb. 1916
The Toast of the Town, pr. 1905 (revision of
   Mistress Betty)
Wolfville, pr. 1905 (with Willis Steell; adaptation
   of Alfred Henry Lewis's stories)
The Girl Who Has Everything, pr. 1906
Toddles, pr. 1906 (adaptation of André Godfernaux
   and Tristan Bernard's play *Triplepatte*)
The House of Mirth, pr. 1906, pb. 1981 (with Edith
   Wharton; adaptation of Wharton's novel)
The Straight Road, pr. 1906

The Truth, pr. 1906, pb. 1907
Her Sister, pr. 1907
Girls, pr. 1908 (adaptation of Alexander Engel and
   Julius Horst's play *Die Welt ohne Männer*)
The Blue Mouse, pr. 1908
A Happy Marriage, pr. 1909
The Bachelor, pr. 1909
The City, pr. 1909, pb. 1915
Plays, pb. 1915 (4 volumes)

OTHER LITERARY FORMS

Clyde Fitch's nondramatic works have never been
collected. He wrote one novel, *A Wave of Life*, which
appeared in *Lippincott's* magazine in February, 1891,
and which was later published by Mitchell Kennerley,
with a foreword by Montrose J. Moses. Before the
novel was published, Fitch had served his literary apprenticeship by writing short stories for a variety of
commercial and church-related magazines. In 1889
alone, *The Independent*, *The Christian Union*, *The
Churchman*, *Puck*, *Life*, and the children's magazine
Young Hearts had accepted his stories, and in 1891,
Fitch gathered a number of his vignettes of childhood
into a volume entitled *The Knighting of the Twins*,
which was published by Roberts Brothers in Boston;
one of the stories, "An Unchronicled Miracle," was
dedicated to Walter Pater. Known for his association
with the Pre-Raphaelite movement, that author of
Studies in the History of the Renaissance (1873) answered Fitch's whimsical verse that suggested that
"even a cat may look on a king" with a pleasant, congratulatory note. *Some Correspondence and Six Conversations* (1896) and *The Smart Set* (1897), both collections of letters and discussions, were published by
Stone and Kimball in Chicago. Fitch's nondramatic
works are out of print and difficult to obtain; some of
the short stories in such magazines as *Puck* and *Life*
have not been identified.

ACHIEVEMENTS

Although Clyde Fitch was awarded no prizes or
honors, he deserves mention as one of the first American playwrights to achieve popular success on his
home ground. Indeed, the theatrical climate was ripe
for his combination of romance and realism with

purely American settings; most Broadway plays were either comedies of manners imported from England or farces translated from the French or German. Fitch wrote, then, when many serious as well as satiric publications were concerned not only with "Anglomania" but also with the development of a national literature. Given such a receptive audience, Fitch frequently produced a number of plays within one season.

To be sure, he was criticized for his "artificial" plotting, for tailoring his plays to available actresses, and for both borrowing from successful foreign plays and taking poetic license with history. Nevertheless, his development from farce to drama was sure and steady, and his careful attention to scenic detail and acting method earmarked him as a major influence on the realistic stage. Fitch's later experimentation, notably in *The City*, would make him memorable.

Fitch's works generally met with wildly enthusiastic responses from audiences but were often less generously received by critics, many of whom felt that his mechanical, well-made plots were indicative of a superficial point of view. Others, however, believed that his carefully tailored dramatic structures were foils for a social consciousness that would not be accepted in an undisguised form. In one sense, at least, such negative criticism was justified. The lighthearted *Captain Jinks of the Horse Marines*, starring Ethel Barrymore as the enterprising and charming Bronxite who pretends to be an Italian soprano, was resoundingly successful; the more serious *The Truth*, treating the marital consequences of inveterate lying, was not—at least in the United States. Marie Tempest made the play one of the first American successes throughout Europe, but at home, reception was cool, perhaps because the title betokened a more serious treatment than the public wished. Certainly, *The Climbers* had similar trouble, refused by all the New York producers because of what they believed to be a twin disability: a death and a suicide. The producers were wrong: Fitch's audience, which was both nurtured on the new realism of Theodore Dreiser and Stephen Crane and rooted in the nostalgia of the nineteenth century, appeared in droves, not only to witness the January-May marriage of the widowed Mrs. Hunter and the wealthy, socially inept Johnny Trotter,

but also to hear about the self-denying love between Blanche Sterling and Edward Warden.

Critics and audiences agreed that Fitch excelled in the details of his settings. Producers were content to give him free rein, knowing that the playwright who worked almost eighteen hours a day and who was concerned in *Barbara Frietchie*, for example, that a fan failed to blow the curtains realistically enough to simulate a Maryland breeze, would mount a production with the finest attention to detail. Such attention came from his own aesthetic predilections: Once he achieved financial success, he traveled to Europe every spring, collecting the Della Robbias, the Louis IV furniture, the rare books, and the Watteaus that spilled over in his New York salon.

For Fitch, the collection of such paraphernalia, which might be regarded as mere affectation, was much in concert with his immersion in the theater. Without family attachments, he saw his work as defining his life; in words reminiscent of Henry James, Fitch wrote that he spent his time "studying and observing life" and that he had one goal—"to develop always." Praised for his "psychology," ideas, and theatrical savvy abroad, he failed to win serious critical acclaim at home, yet a modern reassessment suggests that his enthusiastic audiences were wiser than the savants. Fitch is important, not simply as one of the first American playwrights to achieve solid popularity but also as a transitional figure between nineteenth century melodrama and twentieth century realism.

Biography

Born in Elmira, New York, on May 2, 1865, William Clyde Fitch was the first of five children and the only son of Alice Maud Clark of Hagerstown, Maryland, and William Goodwin Fitch, a staff member to General Heintzelsman during the Civil War. When he was four, the family moved to Schenectady, where he later joined with friends to form the Amateur Club and the Hookey Club and edited *The Rising Sun*, the pages of which express Fitch's early verve and vitality. His childhood frailty and love of beauty, learned from his charming, vivacious mother and sisters, made him an anomaly as he grew older; preferring the company of girls, to whom he wrote precocious love notes, and affecting individualistic aesthetic costumes, he marked himself as an original as early as his attendance at the Hartford Public High School.

Fitch's reputation followed him through preparatory school in Holderness, New Hampshire, and to Amherst College, where his classmates and Chi Psi fraternity brothers found his picturesque appearance no deterrent to his good humor and inventiveness. In fact, his first dramatic effort was a second act to a *Harper's* operetta, *Il Jacobi*, written in haste to complete an evening program for his fraternity. During his college years, he acted, produced, and painted scenery, frequently transposing effects from, for example, Daly's theater in New York, where he was an avid visitor. His college acting career included performances in Oliver Goldsmith's *She Stoops to Conquer* (pr. 1773) and in Richard Brinsley Sheridan's *The Rivals* (pr. 1775).

After graduating from Amherst College in 1886, Fitch went to New York, attempting both journalism and tutoring—which he disliked—to support himself. His novel *A Wave of Life* and short stories for *The Churchman* were written at a boardinghouse on West Fifty-third Street. The beginnings of his successful career can be traced to two experiences: He presented a letter of introduction to E. A. Dithmars, the drama critic for *The Times*, who provided the entrée to opening nights; and he spent some time in Paris with his mother in 1888, where he composed and read the one-act original play *Frederick Lemaître*.

By 1889, Fitch had established himself in New York and increased his circle of acquaintances to include such artists and writers as Oliver Herford of *Life* and William Dean Howells. His old friend Dithmars spurred Fitch's dramatic career by introducing the young playwright to the actor Richard Mansfield, who wanted a tailor-made play about Beau Brummell. After several false starts, including an argument with Mansfield about the ending, the play opened on a shoestring budget on May 17, 1890, at the Madison Square Theatre, where it was a huge success. Five months later, Felix Morris produced *Frederick Lemaître* in Chicago with the Rosina Vokes Company.

Soon before Fitch went to London to work on the unsuccessful comedy *Pamela's Prodigy*, he countered the critic William Winter's charges that Mansfield's kindness had made him only the titular author of *Beau Brummell*. His apprenticeship years, from 1890 to 1892, were devoted to adapting and rewriting, commissions appearing at financially opportune times. Of his works in this period, his adaptation of *The Masked Ball* from Bisson and Carré's French play *Le Veglione* proved the most important, catapulting John Drew and Maude Adams to stardom and assuring the reputation of Charles Frohman.

Fitch's output of plays produced between 1891 and 1898 testifies to his unremitting industry, broken only by his lavish entertainment for his growing circle of theatrical acquaintances and his frequent trips abroad. His two biggest successes during this time were *Nathan Hale*, which opened at Hooley's Theatre in Chicago, and *The Moth and the Flame*, first produced in Philadelphia. He became, in fact, one of the first commercially successful American dramatists; Frohman, who had looked to the British playwrights Arthur Wing Pinero and Henry Arthur Jones for his productions, tapped the young playwright. *Barbara Frietchie*, which opened at the Philadelphia Broad Street Theater on October 10, 1899, surpassed even *Nathan Hale* in popularity, bringing in ten thousand dollars in a single week. Inspired by a photograph of Fitch's mother as a girl and written for Julia Marlowe, the play, a romanticized version of the events surrounding the American revolutionary war hero, evoked an ongoing discussion about poetic license. His next major success was *The Cowboy and the Lady*, which was well received on the circuit and in New York in 1899, but it was criticized because of the swearing, which Fitch, who had never been West, employed as local color. Clearly, Fitch proved himself a master of versatility. As the year 1901 opened, no fewer than three Fitch plays, aside from *Barbara Frietchie*, were on the boards in New York: *The Climbers*, a comedy of manners; *Lovers' Lane*, a rural romance; and *Captain Jinks of the Horse Marines*, described as a "fantastic comedy."

Indeed, Fitch frequently had more than one play running at the same time. His Greenwich, Connecticut, homesite, purchased in March, 1902, and christened Quiet Corner, was to alleviate some of the intense pressure under which he worked in his studio in New York, a studio crammed with keepsakes and theatrical books, flowers, and memoirs—and guests. In addition, Fitch traveled some six months of the year, sometimes taking a "cure" such as the one at Parma, Italy, where he met actress Lily Langtry. Throughout all, he continued to write; in 1902, suffering from illness and exhaustion, he produced both *The Stubbornness of Geraldine* in November and *The Girl with the Green Eyes* in December, both with the same attention to fine detail that fostered his reputation as a realist.

The composition and rehearsal of the less than successful *The Coronet of the Duchess* in 1904 were typical of Fitch's work habits at Quiet Corner, where he and his menagerie of pets entertained a constant flow of visitors and where he composed his plays under a favorite apple tree, his birdcages hanging above him and his company chattering around him. After the next year, in which *Her Great Match*, *Wolfville*, and *The Toast of the Town* were produced, Fitch gave a series of lectures in Philadelphia and New York at Yale and Harvard, in an attempt to educate the public, as he put it, about their responsibility: "Hardened theater" was the result, he believed, of a constant and unhealthy cry for novelty and a refusal to take the drama seriously.

In one sense Fitch heeded his own words when, in 1906, in the midst of *Toddles*, *The House of Mirth* (produced with the cooperation of Edith Wharton), and *The Girl Who Has Everything*, he began to write *The Truth* for Clara Bloodgood. This play, which depicts the effect of inveterate lying, seems to be an oblique commentary on the falseness of the theatergoing public itself, which *prefers* to trivialize the truth into melodrama, just as the heroine *prefers* to jeopardize a happy marriage for the sake of fibbing and flirtation. Perhaps not surprisingly, the initial reception was not as enthusiastic as that of *The Straight Road*, opening the same night. Reviewers became more warm in their praise, however, even comparing Fitch to Henrik Ibsen; the French wildly applauded Marie Tempest in the foreign presentation of the play.

Fitch's years of overwork began to take their toll.

Suffering from perpetual indigestion and a weak heart, he virtually retired to Katonah, New York, in 1907. The last year of his life found him writing *The City*, a play that justifies his self-assessment as a major contributor to the American drama. Indeed, his last reading of the play, five days before he left for his last trip to Europe, left him exhausted. His continued illness on the trip ended in his death in Châlons-sur-Marne on September 4, 1909.

ANALYSIS

Although many of Clyde Fitch's plays were written while he was traveling—as, for example, was *Her Own Way*, written for Maxine Elliott partly in Florence and read aloud to friends in London—Fitch's plays are thoroughly American, a fact recognized by William Dean Howells, who favorably reviewed *Glad of It* in *Harper's Weekly* early in 1904. In a letter of thanks to Howells, Fitch acknowledged the novelist's influence, writing that, although he himself was lost in the midst of "shams," Howells's name was a signpost to the true path.

BEAU BRUMMELL

Fitch's generally undeserved reputation as a playwright who wrote exclusively for star performers gained currency with his first success *Beau Brummell*, written at the request of Richard Mansfield through the influence of the reviewer E. A. Dithmars. Mansfield, unhappy with Blanchard Jerrold's version, was initially pleased with Fitch's script. With the play in rehearsal at Palmer's Theatre in January, 1890, Mansfield suddenly withdrew the play, then decided to go ahead at the Madison Square Theatre in May. Even then, the production was fraught with problems; Mansfield, financially overdrawn, was forced to cut corners. Costumes were at a premium, borrowed or provided out of the actors' own trunks. In addition, actor and playwright argued over the last act, Mansfield insisting on a happy ending. Fitch's compromise—bringing back the king and Brummell's old friends at the very moment of the Beau's death—made the play a success.

Based on the life of the eighteenth century dandy George Bryan Brummell, the friend of the prince regent George IV, the play is a potpourri of romance, wit, and nostalgia that does, nevertheless, depict enough character development in Beau to gain the audience's sympathy when he finally dies impoverished in France. His first-act appearance is characterized by superficial wit, polished manners, and exquisite sensibility as contrasted with the bluff, natural mien of his nephew, Reginald Courtenay. The romantic interest involves Reginald's clandestine love for an unnamed woman whose father refuses consent, and Beau's financially motivated proposal to Mariana Vincent, Reginald's beloved.

While Beau's mistaken identification of Mr. Vincent as a merchant peddler and his difficulty in disentangling himself from his mistress, Mrs. St. Aubyn, provide comic relief, the second act presents Brummell in a more ennobling light as he confesses to Mariana that, although he proposed because of her wealth, he finds that he loves her in her own right. His quarrel with the prince regent is occasioned by his attempt to protect her father. Flustered by having his flirtation with Mrs. St. Aubyn exposed to public scrutiny by the clumsiness of Mr. Vincent, the prince is offended by Brummell's familiarity.

Again, in act 3, Brummell becomes more humanized as Mariana, convinced that he has saved her father's honor by snubbing the prince regent, refuses to give up her engagement at the urging of Mrs. St. Aubyn, who, out of jealousy, offers to intercede with the prince if Mariana will not marry. Knowing that her wealth can save Beau from his creditors, Mariana agrees to marry him; then she meets Reginald, whose letters have been stopped by connivance between the servants. Beau, in a self-sacrificing gesture, releases her from her engagement and is led away by the bailiffs.

Beau, with his "glory gone," is depicted in the fourth act in abject poverty, his faithful servant Mortimer having pawned all his possessions. Fitch's melodramatic genius created the act in which Brummell sees his old friends in a vision, Mortimer assisting as he goes through the empty formalities of greeting his nonexistent guests. That the guests actually return to play their parts at the end of the play satisfied both Mansfield's desire for a happy ending and Fitch's realization that no happy ending was possible.

THE TRUTH

The Truth began as a casual remark in 1906 to Fitch's business agent about a character who could not avoid telling lies. He elaborated the plot in less than two hours after being asked to write a play for the actress Clara Bloodgood and was convinced that the result was "psychologically and technically" his best work. Initially, the critics were less convinced; reviews after the first night, on which he also opened *The Straight Road*, were unenthusiastic. As the record shows, however, the second tour of the play, in October, 1907, was very successful. In addition, European audiences and reviewers were extraordinarily enthusiastic over the performance of Marie Tempest, whom Fitch met at Versailles. Indeed, her success abroad was the indirect cause of the suicide of Bloodgood, depressed over the lack of American response.

Becky Warder, the play's protagonist, seems to lie for the sheer inventiveness and challenge of juggling varieties of truth. Perhaps if Fitch had been a greater playwright, he would have explored, as the twentieth century playwright Luigi Pirandello did, the existential ramifications of such a condition. Fitch, however, concentrated on the effects of Becky's lying on her marriage. Like his later play *The City, The Truth* ends with a reconciliation based on self-knowledge.

Act 1 is reminiscent of the eighteenth century comedy of manners. Becky carries on a flirtation with Lindon, under the pretext of reconciling him with his wife, Eve, and she entertains his wife between his visits. She deceives her husband not only about Lindon but also about the price of a bonnet and about money sent to her sponging father. Through it all, she protests that she loves her husband. The audience can judge that she does indeed try to convince Lindon to return to Eve; nevertheless, she cannot stop lying.

The converse, that a sincere man can awaken a woman to good, is only suggested, not underscored, because it is the character of Becky that is emphasized, not that of Warder. Indeed, the sudden appearance of Becky's father and Mrs. Crespigny—the landlady with whom he has been living, from whom he has been borrowing, and whom he has been refusing to marry—interrupts the theme. Mrs. Crespigny, both comic and sincere in her awe at the Warders' residence, is a variation of the "prostitute with the heart of gold," yet she encourages Roland in his profligate habits rather than helping him. The act seems to fall into two halves: Tom Warder confronts his wife with the detectives' evidence that Eve has gathered against Lindon and Becky, and Roland and Mrs. Crespigny arrive to ask for money. Warder, who discovers that Becky has lied about sending money to her father and that she has indeed seen Lindon, no longer trusts her when she does tell the truth concerning her refusal to give in to Lindon's propositioning.

The function of the Crespigny subplot becomes clear when the third act opens: Becky decides to live with her father once Tom has left her, and the act takes place at the landlady's cheap boardinghouse. In this play as in *The City*, Fitch merely touches on the effect of upbringing and heredity in shaping character. Becky's father himself is a consummate liar—in fact, his scheme to reconcile Becky and her husband is based on a lie. Its double function—to save him from a second marriage and to resume his lifestyle without Becky's interference—is predicated on her agreeing to play a charade. His telegram to Tom that Becky is seriously ill brings Tom to the boardinghouse; Becky is to play the part of an invalid and so evoke her husband's pity.

At the final moment, Becky cannot play the game. "If I can't win his love back by the truth I'll never be able to keep it, so what's the use of getting it back at all?" she asks. In a scene reminiscent of the one with which Fitch ends *The City*, Tom forgives Becky—not because she is without fault, but because she has finally learned to be herself without shamming. "We don't love people because they are perfect," he says. "We love them because they are themselves."

In the final analysis, the play presents a problem that borders on the tragic; thus, the denouement seems too easy, although Fitch made an effort not to provide a *deus ex machina*, a solution achieved by external means, but rather one brought about by character change. The change in Becky wrought by her father's confession of his own propensity for lying and by the disagreeable surroundings of the boardinghouse seems, however, temporary at best.

THE CITY

Fitch's last play, *The City*, produced posthumously in New York in 1909, was conceived while he was at work on an English adaptation of a German farce, *The Blue Mouse*. *The City* is said to contain the best and the worst of Fitch: While it is a thesis play—arguing that the city is a crucible that reveals a person's essential strengths and weaknesses—it is also a melodrama, and while the dialogue is witty, it calls attention to itself at the expense of the plot. The play displays Fitch's gifts as a distinctively American playwright, dealing with a theme that is one of the staples of modern American literature: urbanization and its consequences.

Fitch was convinced that he had written his best play, and modern assessments agree. As usual, he read the script to a circle of friends in Katonah. The reading, which took place only five days before he sailed on his annual trip to Europe, lasted until two o'clock in the morning, during which time Fitch rewrote and removed scenes as he read. Although the play was not produced until December, 1909, some three months after his death, his production notes were clear, and his company, under the direction of stage manager John Emerson, attempted to reproduce Fitch's directions. Perhaps encouraged by the death of a favorite playwright, the audience's mood of expectation reportedly became hysterical at the end of the play. For once, the critics agreed with the audience, and *The City* finally earned for Fitch the critical acceptance that he had wanted.

In part, the play is an examination of the secret tensions that underlie an average American home and therefore may be seen within the context of Ibsen's realism. Like Ibsen, Fitch was not reluctant to confront, onstage, matters such as incest, adultery, and suicide. Fitch was considerably more conventional than Ibsen, however, and so even *The City* presents the audience with a satisfying "happy" ending.

In the opening act, the tension in the Rand family, comfortably established in Middleburg, seems to lie between the security of the small town and the lure of the city. The father, a successful banker, opposes the social aspirations of his wife and daughters, Teresa and Cicely, and the professional ambitions of his son

George, Jr., all of whom want to move to New York. Underlying that tension, however, is the idea that to stay in Middleburg, or in any small town, for that matter, is not to be "safe." George Rand, the pillar of the community, has engineered illegal bank deals; moreover, he is being blackmailed by George Frederick Hannock, his illegitimate son. Before the close of the act, Rand falls dead, a victim of a heart attack apparently precipitated by another demand from Hannock and the necessity of confessing his hypocrisy to his son George.

For the family, the death means release to go to the city, where George establishes himself as a financier and political aspirant. Fitch does more, however, than simply show that Rand was wrong to force his family to stay in Middleburg or that the city offers unlimited opportunity. George, it is revealed, copies his father's suspect business practices by gambling with his partner's investment and selling at a favorable time; Hannock threatens to publicize the deal, which could send George to prison.

With every event, George is put to the test: Honesty will lose for him not only the nomination but also his fiancé, as plain dealing would have lost him money. His political success is threatened by Teresa's pending divorce and by Hannock's drug addiction and dubious associates. The realistic depiction of family problems becomes melodrama, however, when George tries to tell Cicely that in her secret marriage to Hannock, she has committed incest; Hannock shoots Cicely to prevent her knowing the truth. Fitch piles incident on incident. George's final test in the second act is whether to allow Hannock to kill himself before the police arrive. Hiding his shady financial dealings protected his reputation; likewise, he has made a deal with Teresa: To save his nomination, she will live in apparent harmony with her husband. Hannock's death, which might be passed off as an accident, would hide the worst of the story of incest and crime and salvage George's own engagement to Eleanor, a woman who, as her father says, must "look up to" the man she marries.

The brief third act opens with George's confession to his fiancé's father and his old friend and political supporter. His determination is not to return to Middleburg, a decision that underlines Fitch's refusal to draw the conventional good/bad distinction between country and city. In perhaps the best speech in the play, George defends the city:

> *She* gives the man his opportunity; it is up to *him* what he makes of it! A man can live in a small town all his life, and deceive the whole place and *himself* into thinking he's got all the virtues, when at heart he's a hypocrite! . . . *But the City!* . . . there she strips him naked of all his disguises—and all his hypocrisies . . . and then she says to him, Make good if you can, or to Hell with you! And what is in him comes out to clothe his nakedness, and to the City he can't lie! *I know*, because *I tried*!

His truth-telling has an immediate effect on others: Teresa and her husband drop their twin divorce suits, convinced that unselfish consideration of their children is more rewarding than personal gratification.

George's more difficult confession is to Eleanor, to whom he says that he disguised lying and cheating as "business diplomacy" and as "the commercial code." His excuse—that he simply patterned himself on others around him—is, he says, finally no excuse at all because, as a grown man, he was in possession of his own judgment. Eleanor's response, that someone who makes a fresh start because "it is the right thing to do" and because "he *had to be honest with himself*" is "twice the man" he was the day before, provides the kind of satisfying ending that Fitch's audiences enjoyed.

Fitch is noteworthy, then, in giving the theme of the city a new twist: As the small town is no guarantor of virtue—not only because it does not provide a test but also because it allows one to deceive oneself with the approval of one's neighbors—so the city is no guarantor of vice. Indeed, for George Rand, it is a place where, in the midst of millions of people, he has learned to live with himself.

OTHER MAJOR WORKS

LONG FICTION: *A Wave of Life*, 1891.

NONFICTION: *Some Correspondence and Six Conversations*, 1896; *The Smart Set*, 1897; *Clyde Fitch and His Letters*, 1924 (Montrose J. Moses and Virginia Gerson, editors).

CHILDREN'S LITERATURE: *The Knighting of the Twins*, 1891.

BIBLIOGRAPHY

Andrews, Peter. "More Sock and Less Buskin: In the Hands of a Rococo Yankee Named Clyde Fitch the American Stage Came of Age with a Gasp of Scandalized Shock." *American Heritage* 23 (April, 1972): 48-57. Written for the general public, this essay follows a chronological order in describing the playwright's role in the American theater. Photographs of the flamboyant Fitch and some of the stars he directed make the work appealing.

Mordden, Ethan. "Clyde Fitch, Mrs. Fiske, Shaw, and Barrie." In *The American Theatre*. New York: Oxford University Press, 1981. This historical survey attempts to identify the American characteristics of Fitch's theater. In the chapter on comedy from 1900-1915, Mordden examines the plays and contrasts them to those of George Bernard Shaw. He also compares Fitch to Eugene O'Neill and provides an informative chapter on satire.

Wattenberg, Richard. "Taming the Frontier Myth: Clyde Fitch's *The Cowboy and the Lady*." *Journal of American Culture* 16, no. 2 (Summer, 1993): 77. An examination of Fitch's portrayal of the West and the frontier in *The Cowboy and the Lady*.

Patricia Marks,
updated by Irene Gnarra

MARIELUISE FLEISSER

Born: Ingolstadt, Germany; November 23, 1901
Died: Ingolstadt, West Germany; February 2, 1974

PRINCIPAL DRAMA

Fegefeuer in Ingolstadt, pr. 1926, revised pr. 1971, both versions pb. 1972

Pioniere in Ingolstadt, first version pr. 1928, second version pr. 1929, pb. 1972, third version pb. 1968, pr. 1970

Der Tiefseefisch, wr. 1929-1930, enlarged pb. 1972, pr. 1980

Karl Stuart, wr. 1938-1945, pb. 1946

Der starke Stamm, first (dialect) version wr. 1944-1945, second (dialect) version pr. 1950, third version wr. after 1950, fourth version pb. 1972, pr. 1974

OTHER LITERARY FORMS

In addition to her plays, Marieluise Fleisser wrote a novel and more than thirty short stories as well as literary essays and autobiographical articles. Most of these writings are included in volumes 2 and 3 of the *Gesammelte Werke* (1972), edited by Günther Rühle.

The only omission of consequence is a key essay on the dramatist Heinrich vo4n Kleist, reprinted in *Schriftsteller über Kleist* (1976; writers on Kleist), edited by Peter Goldammer.

ACHIEVEMENTS

Until five years before her death in 1974, Marieluise Fleisser was considered to be a minor writer of the Weimar Republic, worthy of honorable mention in a footnote embellishing the biography of Bertolt Brecht, probably the most formidable German dramatist and director of the twentieth century. From 1924 until her break with him in 1929, Fleisser succumbed totally to the spell cast by his genius and served, off and on, as his lover, his confidante, and his collaborator. Brecht directed her second play, *Pioniere in Ingolstadt* (combat engineers in Ingolstadt), in such a way as to precipitate Germany's biggest theatrical scandal between the wars and to secure for both Fleisser and himself a prominent place in the history of literary censorship. The ensuing furor over the play was the first clear indication Germans were given of the ugly policy toward culture that the Nazis would institute when they came to power. *Pioniere in Ingolstadt* also holds the distinction of being the only drama authored by someone other than Brecht to have played an important part in the development of the epic theater. Apart from the depiction of a character based on Brecht in Lion Feuchtwanger's novel *Erfolg* (1930; *Success*, 1930), the only literary portrait of him during the Weimar period is in Fleisser's third play, *Der Tiefseefisch* (the deep-sea fish), an ironic exposé of Brecht's working techniques, including the crafty manipulation of his assistants. Both this play and Fleisser's heavily autobiographical story "Avantgarde" (1963; "Avant-Garde") remain the sole critical accounts of the private side of Brecht by a member of his inner circle and anticipate the more detailed revelations in the biographical studies of Klaus Völker (*Bertolt Brecht: Eine Biographie*, 1976) and James K. Lyon (*Brecht in America*, 1980).

In her last years, Fleisser was able to move out from under Brecht's shadow and become one of the most celebrated writers of the 1970's in Germany. There were three reasons for this. In the late 1960's, a number of young Bavarian playwrights began taking an unsparing look at life in the provinces against the background of a highly industrialized and capitalized West Germany. They took as their model two rather obscure dramatists of the late Weimar period, the Austrian-Hungarian Ödön von Horváth and Fleisser, who were credited with the simultaneous independent discovery of the politically and socially oriented *Volksstück*, or folk play. This literary form deviated sharply from the uncritical celebrations of earthy peasant or small-town life that had characterized the genre heretofore and that had reached their high point in Carl Zuckmayer's *Der fröliche Weinberg* (1925; the merry vineyard), one of the most popular theatrical successes of the Weimar Republic. The three leading practitioners of the new critical realism, Franz Xaver Kroetz, Martin Sperr, and the late Rainer Werner Fassbinder, have explicitly acknowledged their indebtedness to Fleisser. Fassbinder went so far as to say that he decided to become a writer only after he had read *Pioniere in Ingolstadt*. The "boom" in the production of Fleisser's plays initiated by these playwrights did not show signs of abating until the early

1980's. In turn, the rediscovery of Fleisser was in large measure responsible for their own breakthrough.

Fleisser has also acquired a reputation as a major force in feminist literature. Unlike most of the leading German women writers who emancipated themselves through the act of writing, Fleisser's depiction of what she was wont to describe as the central thread tying together all her works—the relations (or better, the lack of relations) between men and women—stems from a real-life failure to free herself from the strictures imposed by a male-oriented world. In four of her five plays, and in her best short stories (especially the ones written in the middle 1920's), her emphasis is on the feminine search for release from loneliness and insecurity and for equal partnership based on the mutual recognition of personality. The quest is forever frustrated by the innate "motherliness" of the female, which renders her vulnerable to the brutality inherent in the male of the species. Fleisser's greatest strength here is a naïve style that is based on a concrete relationship to reality and obviates even the hint of a preachment. Another strong point is a remarkable sense of fairness, a capacity to see the world through the eyes of her male antagonists. Nowhere is this done with greater effectiveness than in her only novel, *Mehlreisende Frieda Geier: Roman vom Rauchen, Sporteln, Lieben, und Verkaufen* (1931; Frieda Geier, traveling saleswoman in flour: a novel about smoking, sporting, loving, and selling), which deals with the unsettling intrusion of a (for the moment) financially independent woman into the patriarchal world of a German town.

Probably Fleisser's most lasting literary achievement is the first play she wrote, *Fegefeuer in Ingolstadt* (purgatory in Ingolstadt), long forgotten and then finally revived in four highly individualistic stagings shortly before her death. It has come to be regarded by many commentators as one of the most fascinating, enigmatic, and prophetic plays of the century, and certainly the best play by a German woman. Written before Brecht's literary influence made itself felt, the drama treats a tragically timeless topic: the warping of the human spirit through a loveless ideology. In its depiction of the spiritual provincialism of small-town pseudo-Christianity, the play foreshadows the frightening racial provincialism of the Nazis. Interestingly enough, the theme of cultural alienation is also central to the work, which launched the critico-realistic folk theater, Martin Sperr's *Jagdszenen aus Niederbayern* (1966; hunting scenes from Lower Bavaria), a devastating look at Fascistic attitudes in the Germany of the Currency Reform of 1948.

Perhaps to justify to some extent their part in the underestimation of Fleisser's stature, which began with the burning of her books by the Nazis and continued for almost forty years, some observers of the literary scene have warned of the danger of overestimating her importance. It is a warning that, for now at least, can go unheeded.

BIOGRAPHY

For Marieluise Fleisser, born on November 23, 1901, in the Lower Bavarian city of Ingolstadt, both biology and the place of her birth became her destiny. Three men would play a major and sometimes deleterious role in her life. The first has been described as a genius, the second as a screwball, and the third as a clod. What is certain is that all of them were male chauvinists of the first rank. Her native town had a venerable ecclesiastical tradition and enjoyed its reputation as the number-one military city of Bavaria before the Treaty of Versailles compelled the sorely resented evacuation of the garrison of the five thousand combat engineers located there. Fleisser would write two plays about Ingolstadt, one of which, using the military ambience, was to make her overnight the most notorious and maligned woman in the Weimar Republic, and the other of which, exploiting the provincial Catholicism of the city, was to secure a reputation as a minor classic of the German stage almost half a century after she completed it and not long before her death.

Fleisser's father, a stolid ironmonger and jewelry maker who ran a hardware business in town, recognized her talents and set his heart on her becoming a high school teacher. She was the only one of his four daughters encouraged to enter the gymnasium, or academic high school. Unfortunately, coeducational

gymnasiums were still quite rare in Germany, and Fleisser had to attend the convent school in Regensburg, some two hours away by train. For five years, from 1914 to 1919, she received a prim and proper education in the patriarchal mold, which left her ill-equipped to stand on her own two feet and compete in a man's world. On graduation, she matriculated at the University of Munich and began studying drama and "theatrical science" under the innovative and influential Professor Arthur Kutscher. At a carnival party, she met the well-known novelist and dramatist Feuchtwanger, who gave her some solid avuncular advice on how to write: not in the shopworn expressionist manner, but in the up-and-coming style of neorealism. She destroyed everything she had written and began anew. Through Feuchtwanger, she was introduced to the plays of Brecht and eventually, in 1924, to Brecht himself.

Hurled into the world of the Munich *Boheme*, Fleisser experienced a profound cultural shock, the literary outcome of which was her first play, *Fegefeuer in Ingolstadt*. Through connections, Brecht and Feuchtwanger were able to get Fleisser's short fiction published in newspapers. She was beginning to make a name for herself. At the same time, she fell totally under the spell of Brecht's genius, becoming both his companion and his literary collaborator. In 1926, Brecht arranged for a matinee performance of *Fegefeuer in Ingolstadt*. Although the reviews were mixed, what counted was the fact that the two most influential Berlin critics, arch-rivals who rarely agreed on anything, praised Fleisser as a fledgling dramatist of tremendous potential.

Fleisser's next play was written on assignment from Brecht. Practically dictating the plot, he dispatched her to Ingolstadt to observe at first hand the temporary return of the combat engineers to the town and to record in dramatic fashion the "human" effects of this invasion on the populace. Brecht was pleased with the epic structure, the naïvely realistic style, and the sociological bias of the new play, all of which corresponded to his own experiments in the direction of an anti-Aristotelian theater. He had been uncomfortable with the seemingly murky metaphysics of Fleisser's first drama. With the more down-to-earth

Pioniere in Ingolstadt, he had a play into which he could sink his director's teeth. At its premiere in Dresden in 1928, a staging with which Brecht had nothing to do, the reception had been lukewarm. Brecht arranged for a Berlin opening at the Theater am Schiffbauerdamm, where his word was law because the sensational run of *Die Dreigroschenoper* (pr. 1928; *The Threepenny Opera*, 1949) had made it the most celebrated theater in the German capital. He wanted to ensure the play's success and at the same time conduct a "sociological experiment" that would expose, as he saw it, the intolerance and philistinism lurking beneath the veneer of liberalism and enlightenment of the typical bourgeois theatergoer. To achieve this, the recently converted Communist playwright-director exaggerated the fairly tepid antimilitarism of the original and injected a number of sensational sexual elements.

The play no longer seemed to belong to Fleisser; she even stayed away from the final rehearsals. Brecht reveled in the ensuing national scandal, but Fleisser bore the brunt of vicious criticism from nationalist circles as well as from her fellow townspeople in Ingolstadt. For writing the lowest sort of "Jewish-Bolshevist-gutter-trash," she was accused of betraying and perverting her German womanhood. Fleisser broke with Brecht. He had made her one of several mistresses in his harem, he had demanded the surrender of her talents to his genius as one of a number of "collaborators," and he had callously brought about her separation from family and friends through public disgrace (her libel suit against the mayor of Ingolstadt for defamation of character, which she finally won, dragged on for three years).

In her isolation and defenselessness, Fleisser sought love and a sense of security from a writer who was Brecht's diametric opposite in every respect except one. Hellmuth Draws-Tychsen was a one-woman-at-a-time man, a very unsuccessful playwright, a mystic poet of little talent, a hater of the big city and a lover of nature, and an arch-conservative. Like Brecht, however, he had a knack for exploiting women. He became engaged to Fleisser because he thought her reputation as an important playwright could add some luster to his lackluster career and because he took it

for granted that she would support him and his relatives financially. Some of the whims and neuroticisms she had to endure are recorded in her third play, *Der Tiefseefisch*, which contrasts the rival literary cliques centered on Draws-Tychsen and Brecht. Fleisser had been unable to follow Brecht into Marxism; with the advent to power of the Nazis, she was unwilling to write the kind of thing that would be accepted by a state-controlled press that regarded her as tainted by her former leftist connections (Brecht had been one of the first to flee Germany and to have his books burned). A woman who could not earn *his* keep was of no use to Draws-Tychsen; separation ensued, but not before Fleisser attempted suicide.

Fleisser returned to her hometown, at best shunned by her neighbors, at worst threatened and reviled. In 1935, when she married Joseph Haindl, a former sweetheart, the fiction of her only novel, *Mehlreisende Frieda Geier*, was twisted into a grim reality. In the novel, the hero, like Haindl the owner of a tobacco business and a local athletic celebrity, falls in love with an "emancipated" businesswoman. She refuses to marry him because he insists that she spend the rest of her life behind the counter of his store. The marriage meant the practical end of Fleisser's literary career. Her husband, well-intentioned but an incorrigible philistine, insisted that she devote all of her time to both household and business. In 1938, she suffered a nervous breakdown and spent three months in a sanatorium.

Luckily for Fleisser, the doctor in charge of the hospital was an understanding and compassionate man (among other things, he was harboring Jews) who made it clear to her husband that she could not tolerate the strains of business life. In 1943, however, she was pressed into national service for nearly a year despite her delicate health. In the research section of a local armaments plant, she was never allowed to forget that she had once authored a scurrilously unpatriotic play. By the time her husband was able to secure a medical discharge for her, she had already ruined her eyesight. At the end of the war, she was falsely accused of blackmarketing in tobacco and jailed by the victorious Americans. Although she was released a short time after her arrest, her husband's store of tobacco, with which he hoped to start up the business again after the war, was confiscated. He blamed his wife for the loss and, until his death in 1958, their life together was not very pleasant, or for that matter, easy.

Haindl's deteriorating health made it necessary to find a business partner, but this move led to bankruptcy. In 1955, in an act of desperation, an anguished Fleisser appealed to Brecht in East Berlin for help. They had resumed relations in 1950, when Fleisser visited the renowned playwright during rehearsals for the West German premiere of *Mutter Courage und ihre Kinder* (pr. 1941; *Mother Courage and Her Children*, 1948) in Munich. He had, shortly thereafter, arranged for the premiere of her most recent play, *Der starke Stamm* (of sturdy stock), a Bavarian comedy of folk manners that she had somehow managed to write in the last months of the war. Now Brecht was able to offer her a "sinecure" in East Germany, provided, of course, that she work within a dramatists' collective that he had established under the aegis of the Academy of Arts. In the end, Fleisser rejected the offer. She could not bring herself to leave her ailing and fairly helpless husband, and her reconversion to Catholicism, she believed, would have led to ideological unpleasantness in a Communist country.

Five days after her husband's death, Fleisser suffered a near-fatal heart attack that put her in the hospital for three months. It took another year to liquidate the business. She was now "free" to write for the first time in almost thirty years. Having been out of the mainstream of literary events for so long, she was artistically depleted. Instead of trying to catch up, Fleisser delved into her own past and in the last decade of life came up with four stories that rivaled in quality if not in quantity the short fiction she had turned out in the middle and later 1920's under Brecht's inspiration: "Avant-Garde," a revealing insight into the character of the early Brecht; "Die im Dunkeln" (1965; those in the darkness), based on the events surrounding her mental breakdown; "Eine ganz gewöhnliche Vorhölle" (1972; a very ordinary limbo), concerning her life as a forced laborer; and "Der Rauch" (1964; smoke), which recounts her last

days under Adolf Hitler and her first under the Americans.

Toward the end of the 1960's, Fleisser began revising some of her prewar works, concentrating on clarifications of language and style and emphasizing more strongly those aspects that anticipated a Fascist takeover in Germany. A number of factors combined to bring about her rediscovery: the cultural predominance of the New Left, the sudden interest in the socioeconomics of Fascism and in the literature and culture of the Weimar Republic, the displacement of the Theater of the Absurd and the documentary theater of Rolf Hochhuth and Peter Weiss by a group of playwrights who emphasized the political life of the provinces, and the hunt for antecedents by these same writers, which led initially to the rediscovery of the long-forgotten Austrian-Hungarian folk-dramatist Horváth and then to his German counterpart, Fleisser. The Fleisser "boom" commenced in 1968 with a Rainer Werner Fassbinder collage based on *Pioniere in Ingolstadt* and entitled *Zum Beispiel Ingolstadt* (for example, Ingolstadt). It reached its apex three years later, with the publication of her collected works by one of German's most prestigious publishing houses and the brilliant Berlin staging of the original version of *Fegefeuer in Ingolstadt* by Peter Stein. Before her death some thirteen months later, Fleisser was being discussed by critics as the peer of Horváth and the early Brecht.

ANALYSIS

Marieluise Fleisser observed on a number of occasions that it was impossible for her to create out of thin air and on demand. Nearly everything she wrote was based on a combination of personal experience and observation of her immediate surroundings. In other words, she was subject to the impulses and urges of an extremely autobiographical writer. There is no significant development in her work as a dramatist; there is, however, a definite difference in literary approach—and arguably in quality—between her first play and the other four.

What accounts for this dichotomy in Fleisser's career both as a playwright and as a writer of prose fiction is, in a word, Brecht. Not long before her death, she told an interviewer that he had destroyed something in her. To be convinced of this, she said, one had simply to compare the earlier *Fegefeuer in Ingolstadt* with the later *Pioniere in Ingolstadt*. Her first play was written in secret, free of the influence of Brecht's theorizing and of his overwhelming and often overbearing personality. For Fleisser, the writing of *Fegefeuer in Ingolstadt* was an existential necessity, born of the mental anguish caused by the sudden clash of opposite worlds. One was the confining, rigid, and narrowly moralistic world of a Gretchen, reared in the provinces and educated by sheltering nuns. The other world was the wide-open, liberating, and neopagan world of the big city of the Roaring Twenties, where Gretchen encountered Mephisto (Feuchtwanger), who in turn introduced her to the genius of Faust (the works of Brecht; later, *after* the completion of her play, to the man himself).

Brecht was more impressed by Fleisser's talent than by her play. When he succeeded in having it staged, he did everything he could to downgrade the religious atmosphere, which Fleisser herself believed was one of the elements on which the life of the play depended. Brecht much preferred *Pioniere in Ingolstadt*, which he had practically commissioned Fleisser to write. When the scandal provoked by Brecht's staging of the play in Berlin in 1929 erupted, Fleisser finally faced up to the fact that if she were to save her writer's soul, she would have to make a clean break with him. She was constitutionally opposed to his insistence that an author should sacrifice his or her uniqueness to the collective production of socially significant literature. In cutting herself off from Brecht, Fleisser hoped to regain her independence as a writer, but she could not cut herself off from his influence. In this regard, she gained much, but she lost even more. After Brecht, one finds her autobiographical bent reinforced by a sharper sense of naturalness or naïveté. There is also a greater openness to the sociological side of human existence. These elements account for much of the strength of her one novel. Their presence in her last play, *Der starke Stamm*, helps explain why, after resuming relations with Fleisser in 1950, Brecht went out of his way to secure a world premiere. As for the deficit

side of her relations with Brecht, something which Günther Rühle, the editor of her collected works, calls her "original substance" was "broken." Gone was the impulse or perhaps the ability to capture the world beyond the senses in fantasies and symbols, to come to grips with the abstractions of religion and myth, to make concrete the irrational realm of the psyche—in other words, to write something as fascinatingly elusive and shattering as her first play. Only in two haunting short stories, written four years after World War II, was Fleisser able to put her "original" self together again: "Das Pferd und die Jungfer" (1952; the horse and the spinster) and "Er hätte besser alles verschlafen" (1963; better if he had slept through it all).

FEGENFEUER IN INGOLSTADT

Fleisser's first play, *Fegenfuer in Ingolstadt*, is a milieu study of a Catholic town in the Germany of the early 1920's, and, at the same time, an intuitive portrayal of certain realities that made possible Hitler's great election victories in the provinces. It focuses on a small band of high school students who are the exemplars of the milieu at large. Actually, this group within a group can be described in terms of a pack or a gang, for it is characterized by mean-spiritedness and narrow-mindedness. Its members reflect the ugliness of life in a small town that, to borrow the words of the West German theater critic Benjamin Henrichs, is caught between a clerical past and a Fascistic future. The young people of Fleisser's play are trapped in their own vicious world of hatred and envy, of spying and extortion, of humiliation and oppression, of excruciating loneliness and emptiness that cries out for a redeemer. This redeemer can only be somebody who will appeal to the baser side of their nature.

The type of Christianity practiced by these young people (and, behind the scenes, their elders) is actually a perversion of religion because it excludes its most essential component—love. The negative Catholicism of the play puts its emphasis on a harsh God eager to pounce on sinners, on rigid commandments, stern moral principles, and endless prohibitions. In the process, self-esteem is torn down and the personality deformed; the major concern is with one's own sins and salvation rather than the liberation of the neighbor from oppression. The central sacrament of this negative Catholicism is penance; the central sin is impurity. All morality tends to become equated with sexual morality; as a result, the social, political, and economic aspects of life are excluded from the moral sphere or relegated to its outer fringes. The religion of the milieu fosters a spirit of exclusivity that makes it easy to look inward and hard to look outward. Unwilling to reach out to the "otherness" of the neighbor, the milieu concentrates almost exclusively on its own survival and on parochial issues, on questions of dogma and morality connected with its myopic view of the world.

In her tersest description of the plot content of *Fegenfeuer in Ingolstadt*, Fleisser said simply that it is "a play about the law of the herd and about those forcefully excluded from it." Postwar studies have confirmed the existence of this "law of the herd," or Catholicism of negation, and its disastrous consequences. Scholars such as Carl Amery, Guenther Lewy, and Gordon Zahn have demonstrated that the religion of the milieu brought on "that moral collapse of German Catholicism which made possible the successful realization of the policies of National Socialism" (Amery). Many Catholics welcomed Hitler as a staunch ally in the fight against indecency in general and pornography and homosexuality in particular, while exploiting this kinship as an excuse to overlook the immorality of his ideology and the criminality of his politics. On "house" issues, such as euthanasia, sterilization, and the removal of crucifixes from the schools, milieu Catholicism bravely stood up to and bested Hitler. On the issue of the "excluded neighbor," the Church suffered its greatest moral defeat: There was never a public utterance of protest against the incarceration of gypsies, Jehovah's Witnesses, socialists, and pacifists, or against the extermination of the Jews.

In anticipating the failure of the Church to respond actively to Christ's summons to love God in and through one's neighbor, Fleisser's play becomes one of the most remarkably prophetic literary documents of the century. Equally remarkable is the way in which she chose to approach her subject matter. The so-called reality of everyday life in Ingolstadt is combined with a spiritual dimension that in no way betrays the world of the senses. This intertwining of the psychosocial and metaphysical is complemented by a highly stylized form of dialogue unique in its fascinating and untranslatable mixture of High German, Bavarian dialect, and slang spoken by youngsters who talk past one another, who at times sound like their grandfathers, and who are not permitted by Fleisser to distinguish between important and unimportant words.

At the heart of the play is a struggle between the forces of good and evil in which the former are overwhelmed. The human capacity for love is embodied in a Christ figure who is driven to insanity. Fleisser's point is made startlingly clear: Not even Jesus Christ would stand a chance against the hellishness that pervades Ingolstadt. An atmosphere of terror and fright, based on the fear of Hell and the Devil and relentlessly sustained throughout the four acts of the play, serves as the backdrop for a hierarchy of evildoers. At its helm is the terrestrial counterpart of Satan, a certain Dr. Hähnle. Engaged in conducting scientific experiments on people, he is reminiscent of the infamous doctor of Georg Büchner's *Woyzeck* (wr. 1836, pb. 1879; English translation, 1927). Fleisser created her character without having read a line of Büchner, yet both doctors are a frightening portent of Dr. Joseph Mengele and Auschwitz, of the first massive application in history of science and technology to genocide.

Directly below Dr. Hähnle in the hierarchy of evil are his two assistants, Gervase and Protase, correlatives of the fallen spirits the Devil assigns to individual humans to offset the influence of their guardian angels. They seem almost nonhuman, if not antihuman, in their ability to dart in and out of the play at will, always appearing out of nowhere to do their dirty work for the doctor, which consists mostly in spying out the sins and weaknesses of others. They are a major factor in creating an ambience that smacks of the police state with its system of block wardens and neighborhood denunciations, even within the bosom of one's own family. They introduce themselves as bloodless humans—which means not only that they associate themselves with the spirit world but also, and more important, that they see themselves as direct antagonists of the Christ figure, Roelle, and his spiritual twin, Olga, as well as of the Gospel of Love that these two try so very hard to promote.

The point is sharply illustrated in the last act, when the audience learns that Protase "happened" to be a disinterested (bloodless) spectator during Olga's attempt at suicide by drowning in the Danube. Roelle, on the other hand, overcomes his morbid fear of water and risks his life in a successful effort to rescue the girl. The inaction of Protase and the action of Roelle represent, respectively, the negation and affirmation of the supreme test of neighborliness as set up by Christ shortly before his death on the Cross on behalf of *all* humankind: "This is my commandment: love one another, as I have loved you. A man can have no greater love than to lay down his life for his friends." Fleisser borrowed the names of her human devils from Saint Gervase and Saint Protase, early martyrs celebrated for their fraternal love for each other and for the Christ in whose name they laid down their lives. Because in Fleisser's topsy-turvy world the pious are really the wicked, the saints can readily serve as examples of how the Christians of Ingolstadt hate, rather than love, one another. These Christians, populating the bottom level of the hierarchy, constitute the pack or gang. When their leader Crusius, as the last gang-member to appear onstage, explains and excuses his past injustices to Roelle *as an experiment*, the audience is abruptly brought back to the top level of the hierarchy. It becomes very easy to visualize Crusius as an SS doctor in a concentration camp some ten or fifteen years hence.

The forces of evil in Fleisser's play are straightforward and relentless. The forces of good are marked by ambiguity and equivocation, for their arch-representative, Roelle, has been fashioned into a Christ figure defiled by the stench of his environment. One of the most complex monsters ever to appear on a German stage, Roelle becomes a liar, a thief, and a blackmailer in a world in which the best are made the worst. Robbed of his self-esteem and suffering from a tremendous inferiority complex, Fleisser's hero tries to reclaim his dignity in sadomasochistic ways. At times he evinces a desire to be punished for the sins that are weighing on his scrupulous conscience. At

other times, there is the urge to lash out at those around him: hence the act of cruelty perpetrated on a dog by sticking its eyes full of needles as an outlet for the agony in Roelle's soul; hence, too, his willingness to humiliate in public the girl he loves after he has been humiliated by her. His religious mania is psychologically connected with his attempts at self-assertion. By becoming a holy man, he hopes to solve his chief problems: inability to win the affections of Olga because of a warped and twisted sexuality, and a need for recognition. As a religious leader, he can win the love of Olga on a sublimated level (he in fact dubs her his Saint John, the disciple whom Jesus loved the most), and he can secure the reverence and respect of the common herd.

There is, however, much more to Roelle than can be provided by an analysis à la Freud. Fleisser's main concern is not with her hero's inability to have normal sex and the problems attendant on this. Her focus is, rather, on the metaphysical aspects of Roelle's capacity and need to love. As one dimension of human love, sex is subsumed in charity. This is something Herbert Ihering, one of the most perspicacious theater critics of the Weimar Republic, sensed when he observed that the decisive element in the play is the fact that "behind all the bigotry lie the roots of a very deep piety, behind the urge to dissemble lies the urge to truth, and . . . within these fettered human beings there is clearly a spiritual potential for creative liberation." The deepest piety is love of God and neighbor, a total love that liberates one from narrowness and provincialism. Roelle's desire to perfect and spread this love is central to his role as a Christ figure, as is evident from the symbolism most obviously tied in with his outsider status. Everybody makes fun of his bloated neck, which he can stretch a good distance in wormlike fashion as he aspires to reach a higher and better world (at one point his neck is called "spiritual"). His hydrophobia, too, is notorious. Roelle must overcome his horror of water if he is to be liberated.

Fleisser makes it very clear that she is using water as a symbol of healthy sexual contact with a woman. At the moment when he is about to be stripped and bathed and shortly before his relationship with Olga will suffer a grievous breakdown (in a spiritual as well as a physical sense), Roelle is told by one of his teenage tormentors, in a play on Genesis 3:15: "And let there be enmity between you and the water." More important, however, water is also a sign of the ultimate spiritual (and therefore human) redemption, as attested by the frequently cited words of Jesus to Nicodemus: "I tell you most solemnly, unless a man is born through water and the spirit, he cannot enter the kingdom of God." Roelle enters this kingdom for an all-too-brief period of time when he overcomes his dread of water and rescues Olga from the deep. However deformed his religiosity, however mixed his motives, it is his most Christlike action. Ironically, it takes place just before his destruction by the establishment.

It seems clear that Roelle is a fictionalized transfiguration of Jesus. Events as set down in the New Testament prefigure the action of the play, through not in chronological sequence. The correspondences between Jesus and Roelle can be divided into two groups, the first of which relates to the person and mission of Christ and the second of which relates to analogues of His Passion and death. Some additional items that do not fall into either category are also readily associated with a literary Christ figure: the fact that the original title of the play, "Die Fusswaschung" (the washing of feet), is based on an occurrence in the Gospel of John; the fact that Roelle has physical characteristics that set him apart (a bloated neck, previously discussed, and epilepsy—the latter an exploitation by Fleisser of the venerable belief that divine truth and madness are somehow linked); and the fact that the halo, the arch-symbol of transfiguration, is conferred on her hero. As for the correspondences, those relating to the characteristics and mission of Christ are far more numerous than those concerning His Passion and death (and also far too numerous to mention here).

From a structural standpoint, however, the analogues to the Passion, which are vital for the establishment of Roelle as a modern-day savior, dominate the play. The second act, during which the hero is getting ready to suffer and die, is modeled on events in the Garden of Gethsemane. Act 3, the setting of which is a wine party in the home of Olga's father, is

Roelle's Last Supper, the last time in life he will be together with his teenage friends and followers. The act culminates in the foot-washing scene from which the play derived its original title. It is significant that Fleisser found her inspiration in John's account of the Last Supper, rather than those of the Synoptics. Her focal point is not the institution of the Eucharist, but rather Christ's message of the love of God through love for the neighbor, concretely dramatized in the washing of his disciples' feet. This act of humility and service is transmuted into an act of spiteful humiliation, as a terror-stricken Roelle is stripped naked and washed by his would-be friends, highlighting the central theme of communal lovelessness.

The final scene relates to the events surrounding the Crucifixion. Among other things, Roelle is betrayed by a thief (Crusius) just as Christ was (by Judas). He is also accused of being a thief; Christ himself was crucified between two robbers. At the end, Roelle's sense of abandonment assumes Christ-like dimensions, and his destruction—whether by derangement alone or coupled with suicide (the text permits either interpretation)—is an acceptable modern equivalent of a no longer fashionable death by crucifixion, especially when the anguish that precedes it is taken into account. Roelle's final words and actions are a recapitulation of the three incidents of the Passion on which the second, third, and fourth acts are largely modeled. As Christ did at Gethsemane, so, too, Roelle takes on the burden of humankind's sins. He consumes the piece of paper on which he was wont to jot down the sins committed since his last good confession. Significantly, Roelle's memory-aid includes not only his own transgressions but also a list of the seven capital sins, the source of all and every wrongdoing in the world. The slip of paper is at the same time transformed into the Eucharist, the sacrament instututed at the Last Supper, the consumption of which confers eternal life: "Anyone who eats this bread will live forever, and the bread that I shall give is my flesh, for the life of the world." Unfortunately, the actions and intentions of Roelle are those of a lunatic. In this fact lies Roelle's glory—he has given his "flesh" in the form of his conscious life—as well as his great defeat. In the real world, Ingolstadt sought and found its redeemer on a different plane of existence some nine years after Fleisser's play was written.

There are those who contend that with the clear exception of *Dantons Tod* (pb. 1835; *Danton's Death*, 1927) by George Büchner, no *first* play in the history of German drama has been more provocative, more prognostic, and ultimately more powerful than *Purgatory in Ingolstadt*.

PIONIERE IN INGOLSTADT

Of the four plays written after her personal encounter with Brecht, *Pioniere in Ingolstadt* is probably Fleisser's best. Set in a representative provincial city of the 1920's, it depicts the effects of a hierarchically structured society on the lives of ordinary people. The catalyst is the sudden appearance in Ingolstadt of a company of combat engineers assigned to build a bridge over a tributary of the Danube. In a series of loosely connected scenes, Fleisser establishes a pecking order, at the bottom of which are servant girls seeking emancipation from a dreary present and an even drabber future and soldiers seeking release from the disciplinary rigors of their profession. Officers put pressure on NCO's, and sergeants made sadistic by the system take it out on the enlisted men; in turn, the soldiers, trained to be aggressive and at the same time to obey, vent their frustrations on the hapless female of the moment. Both the soldiers and the servant girls are also victims of the civilian world, the former as cheap labor for the city, the latter as objects of financial and sexual exploitation by their at best whimsical, and at worst tyrannical, employers.

The epic structure of the play is held together by the love stories of two maids. Alma takes the realistic low road in a society in which everything has its price and in which, under prevailing conditions (the shortage of men after World War I), women are at a distinct disadvantage. She sells her body for social gain and ultimately latches on to a solid burgher. Berta embarks on the romantic high road of "true" but blinding love ("I am *not* like any of the other girls"), only to sacrifice her treasured virginity to a loveless prince charming, the soldier Korl ("I *am* like all the other soldiers"). When at the urging of Brecht's widow, Helen Weigel, the play was revised in 1967-1968, Fleisser made considerable changes, almost doubling its length, in an attempt to reinforce the antimilitary and anticapitalistic tendencies. That the dialogue between Korl and Anna was left practically untouched is a clear indication that Fleisser regarded their relationship as the heart and soul of her play. She was no doubt right, because, as Henrichs aptly pointed out after seeing the world premiere of the revised version in 1970, the story of Korl and Anna is more genuine, more bitter, and more unsentimental than any of the love relationships created by her archrival, Horváth. Whereas the latter invariably sided with his female protagonists, Fleisser could penetrate the world of the male as well. She was able to show that on the objective level, both Korl and Anna are doomed to remain strangers to each other, not because of their personal "philosophies of life" (his belief in the wickedness of humankind, her conviction that the human being is essentially decent), but because they are the ignorant victims of the prevailing social system.

A second element of the play that still fascinates after more than half a century is Fleisser's ability to create in the simplest language possible stage models of irreducible dimensions that concretely define abstractions such as poverty and oppression. Ironically, however, the postwar revisions in the direction of greater social relevance in the spirit of Brecht have served only to compound the problem of the play's historicity. The consistently mixed reception accorded the various revivals since 1971 may in large measure be attributable to the fact that the play is too closely tied to its era. The social realities Fleisser uses to illustrate her ideological biases are no longer very topical in a country in which house servants are at a premium and soldiers can clamor for a trade union to represent their interests.

DER TIEFSEEFISCH

In Fleisser's next play, *Der Tiefseefisch*, there is a drop in dramatic effectiveness. *Der Tiefseefisch* was written in the main shortly after the break with Brecht in 1929; a fourth act was added in 1972. What little plot there is concerns the efforts of two rival literary cliques to retain or regain, respectively, the loyalty and services of a prominent woman writer named Gesine (actually Fleisser in real life). One clique is led by a poet called Laurenz, closely modeled on the writer Draws-Tychsen, the egomaniacal oddball of little artistic talent whose protection and affection Fleisser felt she urgently needed after leaving Brecht. The other clique is dictatorially run by a certain Tütü (Brecht). The only real "action" takes place offstage, when a literary evening featuring the reading of Gesine's works is sabotaged by the release of a swarm of white mice.

The first two acts concentrate on the personal relationship between Gesine and Laurenz. The price of his love is the total subordination of soul, talents, and earning power to his self-proclaimed genius. Because he supposedly has mystical qualities that enable him to penetrate regions forever barred to ordinary mortals (he compares himself to the deep-sea fish that is privy to the most profound mysteries—hence the title of the play), and because such qualities are the stuff of poets of the highest rank, of geniuses normally forced to go unrecognized in their own lifetime, everybody, and especially Gesine, owes him a living. Unfortunately, it is never made quite clear by Fleisser why Laurenz is able to exert so much power over her heroine. Despite herself, Fleisser was really convinced at the time that Draws-Tychsen was the foremost lyric poet of his day, a conviction that any audience has to take on faith. What it sees, however, is an obnoxious and selfish neurotic whose male chauvinism taxes credulity.

The third act, the dramaturgical excuse for which is Tütü's efforts to get Laurenz to join his literary group and in this way to regain control over Gesine, is actually a devastatingly satiric exposé of the inner operations of the "Brecht Circle." Tütü's "writer factory" represents the application of rationalized or "American" methods of production to the realm of aesthetics in order to turn out socially relevant works. The producer is nothing, the end-product everything. Tütü runs his factory along military lines. Echelon "A" comprises the more talented coworkers, who are on occasion allowed to produce something in their own right, as long as it conforms to collectivist guidelines. (Fleisser was in this group.) Echelon "B" is staffed by the not-so-gifted, mostly females, whose only reason for existence is to accommodate Echelon

"A" and who, after being thoroughly exploited and debilitated, can be discarded with impunity. (Supersecretarial collaborators of Brecht in this category included Elisabeth Hauptmann, Margarete Steffen, and Ruth Berlau.) The third act is thus a settling of accounts with Brecht, who successfully applied pressure to prevent the one and only performance of the play planned in Fleisser's lifetime.

Unfortunately, Fleisser's exposé created an unbridgeable dichotomy in the dramatic structure of the play, compounded some forty years later when she added a fourth act that resumed the Gesine-Laurenz relationship in an unsatisfactory attempt to provide a denouement. Somehow, Gesine finds the strength to leave her tyrannical lover at the moment of her greatest dependence and abasement, for the Nazis have suddenly come to power (although there is no mention of them in the first three acts), and only her connection with the ultra-rightist Laurenz can save her from her leftist past. The price she must pay for this security is the writing of works that will earn enough to support Laurenz and will be to the liking of the Nazis; thus, she must prostitute her artistic soul. The three elements that make the play historically interesting—the insights into Fleisser's life, the Brecht circle, and the life of the Berlin intelligentsia during the last days of Weimar—also give it the lack of cohesiveness that discouraged any and all attempts at staging it until 1980. Surprisingly, some five months after its dismal world premiere in Vienna, an astute production successfully mounted in Berlin by Thomas Reichert suggested previously hidden possibilities. The director downgraded the last two acts and concentrated on making psychologically plausible the tragedy of two totally incompatible people who desperately need each other's love.

At the time of her death, Fleisser was making plans to expand *Der Tiefseefisch* into an autobiographical account starting with her entry into the world of Brecht and the Roaring Twenties and ending with her total disappearance from the public eye in the Nazi era as the wife of a small-town tobacconist. The play was to be rechristened "Ehe in Ingolstadt" (marriage in Ingolstadt), and the last act was to show a Gesine cut off both by decree of the Nazis and by order of her business-minded husband from the world of art that had given her life its meaning. Literally the prisoner of a government and a city that could not let her forget that she had besmirched the honor of Germany and her fellow townspeople, she would nevertheless refuse to conform to the system and would somehow manage to endure to the end.

KARL STUART

In fact, Fleisser's perseverance as a human being and an artist was closely connected with the play that followed *Der Tiefseefisch*. *Karl Stuart* was the only play she would bring to conclusion under the Nazis. In 1935, a contemporary portrait of Charles I of England, the first king in modern times to be executed by order of a legislative body, caught her eye because of the extremely melancholy look on the face of the monarch. Haunted by the "saddest picture" she had ever seen, she began a study of the luckless king, and by 1938 she was engaged in writing a play about him. The task, which took seven years, became for Fleisser an act of existential necessity, for she identified her quiet disavowal of the system with the king's refusal to sell his royal soul to Oliver Cromwell in exchange for his life. At the end of the play, a battered but unbowed Charles ascends the scaffold, the symbol of an indestructible inner freedom.

Karl Stuart holds a unique position in Fleisser's oeuvre because it is her only play that is not strictly autobiographical. Further, its uniqueness also accounts for the critical consensus that it is her weakest play. In attempting a historical tragedy, Fleisser was out of her element. She was unfamiliar with the politics and customs of the British, and the elevated language her nobles speak is at best wooden and stilted, in sharp contrast to the marvelously stylized and practically untranslatable Bavarian that characterizes her best dramas. The play is also ultraconventional in structure. In *Karl Stuart*, Fleisser stuck more or less meticulously to the techniques of playwriting elaborated by Gustav Freytag in a "classically popular" handbook already dated when it appeared in 1863. Her dramaturgy here was a far cry from the heady epic experimentation of *Pioniere in Ingolstadt*. Perhaps the clearest indication that the isolated artist in her was frantically reaching out to Brecht is the fact

that there is a startling resemblance between the relation of Charles to Lord Strafford and the king to Gaveston in *Leben Eduards des Zweiten von England* (pr., pb. 1924; *Edward II*, 1926), the play by Brecht (and Feuchtwanger), which happened to be the first great theatrical experience of Fleisser's life. In both works, the downfall of the king is precipitated by stubborn loyalty to a highly unpopular favorite. Unfortunately, further comparison with Brecht's play reveals the extent of the deleterious effect on her artistry wrought by the Nazi years. *Karl Stuart* is devoid of the erotic passion, the depth, sparkle, movement, and tension that mark *Edward II*. What has to count in the last analysis is not that Fleisser wrote a weak play but that she wrote a play at all, a personal document affirming her link to the civilized community.

DER STARKE STAMM

With *Karl Stuart*, Fleisser had sought refuge in a past that was unfamiliar to her. On its completion in the last and worst year of the war, the playwright sought sustenance by turning to her familial roots. It was, she stated later, "an act of sheer self-defence, an act of self-assertion in the interests of survival." If *Karl Stuart* had enabled her to survive artistically, the writing of her next play, *Der starke Stamm*, was an act of physical and mental survival, a game of life "that the imagination plays with uncles and fathers and sons, and with a womanliness that will never die out." Destined to become Fleisser's most popular work, *Der starke Stamm* celebrates the irrepressible life cycle of the "little man" (the first act opens with a funeral and the last closes with the approaching birth of a baby legitimatized through an October-June wedding). The male protagonist, Leonhard Bitterwolf, a saddlemaker in a small Bavarian town, is modeled on Fleisser's grandfather and father, who between them wore out five wives. Unlike the idealized figures of run-of-the-mill folk plays, the characters are depicted with unsparing realism, as lusty, greedy, malicious, yet very human beings who must cope in a world where money usually takes precedence over love and happy endings are a pipe dream.

The theme of greed versus love was reinforced by Fleisser five years after the war in a way that gave the play contemporary relevance. As a result of a major revision probably inspired by Brecht (he and Fleisser resumed relations in 1950), *Der starke Stamm* became the first play to depict the effects on provincial Germany of the "economic miracle" rendered possible by currency reform and American aid. In her criticism of an encroaching capitalism that reduces morality and friendship to a question of who owns how much, Fleisser thus anticipated by some fifteen years the emergence (or reemergence, if one takes into account the Weimar plays of Fleisser and Horváth) of the sociocritical folk play. The play itself exerted a considerable direct influence on Martin Sperr, who was one of the most talented of the socially conscious young playwrights of the postwar era.

From a dramaturgical standpoint, *Der starke Stamm* holds up well—first, because Fleisser succeeded in balancing her comic and satiric intentions, so that the spectator is neither put off nor taken in completely by the characters. He or she can enjoy, so to speak, the best of both worlds. (Unfortunately, a number of directors have been unable to transfer Fleisser's delicate balancing act to the stage.) Further, in the person of Balbina Buhleller, the long-widowed sister-in-law of Bitterwolf, Fleisser fashioned one of the richest female roles in the postwar German theater. The struggle to compete as a woman alone in a universe controlled, if not constructed, by the male of the species has made her hard, bitter, and tough without destroying her delicious sense of humor or repressing her vitality. In her pursuit of security and the good life on the premise that unless one rises one will surely sink, she suffers one defeat after another (losing out to a rapacious maid in her quest for Bitterwolf's hand; going bankrupt when her slot-machine business—a reflection of the American influence on the German economy—folds; being disinherited by a capricious rich uncle). At play's end, an undaunted Balbina is more than willing to renounce her (unprofitable) venture into the pornographic picture-postcard business so that she can cash in on the pious excitement generated by the reputed appearance of the Virgin Mary in a village far away from any public transportation. Some critics have seen fit to put Balbina in the company of the two most finely wrought (and most sturdy) female protagonists of the modern Ger-

man stage, Frau Wolf of Gerhart Hauptmann's *Der Biberpelz* (pr., pb. 1893; *The Beaver Coat*, 1912) and the eponymous heroine of Brecht's *Mother Courage and Her Children*. If it is true that, as Rainer Maria Rilke wrote, enduring is everything, then this tribute to Fleisser's craftsmanship becomes at the same time a strong nod to her humanity, for Balbina's irrepressible nature is also the playwright's.

OTHER MAJOR WORKS

LONG FICTION: *Mehlreisende Frieda Geier: Roman vom Rauchen, Sporteln, Lieben, und Verkaufen*, 1931, revised 1972 (as *Eine Zierde für den Verein*).

SHORT FICTION: *Ein Pfund Orangen und neun andere Geschichten der Marieluise Fleisser aus Ingolstadt*, 1929; *Avantgarde*, 1963; *Abenteuer aus dem englischen Garten*, 1969.

NONFICTION: *Andorranische Abenteuer*, 1932.

MISCELLANEOUS: *Gesammelte Werke*, 1972.

BIBLIOGRAPHY

Hoffmeister, Donna L. *The Theater of Confinement: Language and Survival in the Milieu Plays of Marieluise Fleisser and Franz Xaver Kroetz*. Columbia, S.C.: Camden House, 1983. Hoffmeister compares and contrasts the dramatic works of Fleisser and Franz Xaver Kroetz. She pays special attention to the language used by the two authors.

Joeres, Ruth-Ellen B. "Records of Survival: The Autobiographical Writings of Marieluise Fleisser and Marie Luise Kaschnitz." In *Faith of a (Woman) Writer*, edited by Alice Kessler-Harris Joeres and William McBrien. Westport, Conn.: Greenwood Press, 1988. This essay examines the autobiographical tendencies exhibited by Fleisser and Marie Luise Kaschnitz in their writings.

Kord, Susanne. "Fading Out: Invisible Women in Marieluise Fleisser's Early Dramas." In *Women in German Yearbook: Feminist Studies and German Culture*, edited by Jeanette Clausen and Helen Cafferty. Lanham, Md.: University Press of America, 1989. An examination of the role of women in Fleisser's early plays.

Ley, Ralph. "Beyond 1984: Provocation and Prognosis in Marieluise Fleisser's *Purgatory in Ingol-*

stadt." *Modern Drama* 31 (September, 1988): 340-351. Ley examines the political overtones in Fleisser's *Purgatory in Ingolstadt*.

_____. "Liberation from Brecht: Marieluise Fleisser in Her Own Right." *Modern Language Studies* 16 (Spring, 1986): 54-61. Ley discusses the relationship between Bertolt Brecht and Fleisser and her writing when separated from Brecht.

_____. "Outsidership and Irredemption in the Twentieth Century: Marieluise Fleisser's Play *Fegefeuer in Ingolstadt*." *University of Dayton Review* 19 (Summer, 1988): 3-41. Ley looks at the role of the outsider, a role that Fleisser would later play, in her drama *Fegefeuer in Ingolstadt*.

Ralph Ley

JOHN FLETCHER

Born: Rye, Sussex, England; December, 1579
Died: London, England; August, 1625

PRINCIPAL DRAMA

The Woman's Prize: Or, The Tamer Tamed, pr. c. 1604, pb. 1647

The Woman Hater, pr. c. 1606, pb. 1607 (with Francis Beaumont)

The Faithful Shepherdess, pr. c. 1608-1609, pb. 1629

The Coxcomb, pr. c. 1608-1610, pb. 1647 (with Beaumont)

Philaster: Or, Love Lies A-Bleeding, pr. c. 1609, pb. 1620 (with Beaumont)

The Captain, pr. c. 1609-1612, pb. 1647 (with Beaumont)

Bonduca, pr. 1609-1614, pb. 1647

Valentinian, pr. 1610-1614, pb. 1647

Monsieur Thomas, pr. 1610-1616, pb. 1639

The Maid's Tragedy, pr. c. 1611, pb. 1619 (with Beaumont)

A King and No King, pr. 1611, pb. 1619 (with Beaumont)

The Night Walker: Or, The Little Thief, pr. c. 1611, pb. 1640

Cupid's Revenge, pr. 1612, pb. 1615 (with Beaumont)

Four Plays, or Moral Representations, in One, pr. c. 1612, pb. 1647 (commonly known as *Four Plays in One*; with Beaumont)

The Two Noble Kinsmen, pr. c. 1612-1613, pb. 1634 (with William Shakespeare)

The Masque of the Inner Temple and Grayes Inn, pr., pb. 1613 (masque; with Beaumont)

Henry VIII, pr. 1613, pb. 1623 (with Shakespeare)

Wit Without Money, pr. c. 1614, pb. 1639

The Scornful Lady, pr. c. 1615-1616, pb. 1616 (with Beaumont)

The Nice Valour: Or, The Passionate Madman, pr. 1616 (?), pb. 1649

The Mad Lover, pr. 1616(?), pb. 1647

Love's Pilgrimage, pr. 1616(?), pb. 1647

The Queen of Corinth, pr. 1616-1617, pb. 1647

The Knight of Malta, pr. 1616-1618, pb. 1647

The Tragedy of Thierry, King of France, and His Brother Theodoret, pr. 1617(?), pb. 1621 (commonly known as *Thierry and Theodoret*; with Beaumont)

The Chances, pr. c. 1617, pb. 1647

The Loyal Subject, pr. 1618, pb. 1647

Sir John van Olden Barnavelt, pr. 1619, pb. 1883 (with Philip Massinger)

The Humorous Lieutenant, pr. 1619, pb. 1647

The Custom of the Country, pr. c. 1619-1620, pb. 1647 (with Massinger)

The Little French Lawyer, pr. 1619-1623, pb. 1647 (with Massinger)

Women Pleased, wr. 1619-1623, pb. 1647

The Island Princess: Or, The Generous Portugal, pr. 1619-1621, pb. 1647

The False One, pr. c. 1620, pb. 1647 (with
Massinger)

The Double Marriage, pr. c. 1621, pb. 1647 (with
Massinger)

The Wild Goose Chase, pr. 1621, pb. 1652

The Pilgrim, pr. 1621, pb. 1647

The Beggars' Bush, pr. before 1622, pb. 1647 (with
Massinger)

The Prophetess, pr. 1622, pb. 1647 (with Massinger)

The Sea Voyage, pr. 1622, pb. 1647

The Spanish Curate, pr. 1622, pb. 1647

The Maid in the Mill, pr. 1623, pb. 1647 (with
William Rowley)

The Lover's Progress, pr. 1623, pb. 1647 (revised
by Massinger, 1634)

A Wife for a Month, pr. 1624, pb. 1647

Rule a Wife and Have a Wife, pr. 1624, pb. 1647

The Elder Brother, pr. 1625(?), pb. 1637 (with
Massinger)

The Fair Maid of the Inn, pr. 1626, pb. 1647 (with
Massinger?)

Wit at Several Weapons, pb. 1647 (with
Beaumont?)

*The Dramatic Works in the Beaumont and Fletcher
Canon*, pb. 1966-1985 (6 volumes)

OTHER LITERARY FORMS

John Fletcher apparently wrote very little or no
poetry. He may have collaborated with other playwrights in the composition of court masques, but no
direct evidence has been introduced identifying his
hand in entertainments of that kind.

ACHIEVEMENTS

Although John Fletcher wrote many plays alone,
he is best known for those he composed in collaboration with Francis Beaumont. In fact, much of the criticism of these playwrights' work regards them as an
inseparable team. This practice has tended to obscure
the technical brilliance of Fletcher's own plays, many
of which were revived successfully on the Restoration stage. In their collaboration, however, the two
dramatists came to be recognized as the inventors and
chief practitioners of a style of drama, tragicomedy,
that won enthusiastic applause from audiences at the

Jacobean public theaters. Fletcher published a definition of the new genre in the preface to one of his earliest plays, *The Faithful Shepherdess:*

> A tragi-comedy is not so called in respect of mirth and
> killing, but in respect it wants deaths, which is inough
> to make it no tragedie, yet brings some neere it, which
> is inough to make it no comedie: which must be a rep-
> resentation of familiar people, with such kinde of
> trouble as no life be questioned, so that a God is as
> lawfull in this as in a Tragedie, and meane people as a
> comedie.

Although the play to which this preface was ap-
pended proved unpopular with its audience, Fletcher,
with the older Beaumont, went on to instant success
in *Philaster*, one of his first collaborative efforts in
the new form. This event was also notable because it
cemented the playwrights' connection with William
Shakespeare's company, the King's Men. Beaumont
and Fletcher continued to write for that company for
the rest of their careers.

What attracted Jacobean playgoers to *Philaster*
was its complicated but relatively fresh plot (no
sources have been identified), romantic setting, and
suspenseful denouement: The heroic prince discovers
that the page who has served him faithfully throughout the play is in fact a woman—a woman who is
deeply in love with him. The happy ending, however,
leaves the audience with a sense of having been manipulated; Beaumont and Fletcher take little care to
develop their characters or to motivate action. Even
so, *Philaster* won the playwrights a reputation with
the gentlemen and ladies who increasingly made up
the audience at the Blackfriars playhouse.

Before Beaumont's retirement in 1613, he and
Fletcher worked together on several other plays, only
a few of which were in fact tragicomedies. Other than
Philaster, *A King and No King* is probably the best
example of the genre. *A King and No King*, like many
Jacobean plays, depends on the frisson of an incestuous love: The hero believes that he has engaged in intercourse with his sister. As it turns out, the two are
not in fact brother and sister, the hero's parentage
having been misrepresented by a deceitful queen. Despite this happy evasion of tragedy, the purpose of tit-

illating the viewers was deftly accomplished. The dramatic rhythm of relaxation and sudden surprise is reinforced by a style of verse that alternates between realistic conversation and high-flown rhetoric. This characteristic of the verse (informal talk that suddenly gives way to elevated poetry) was widely admired by the audiences of Beaumont and Fletcher's era and by Restoration audiences, for whom the plays became regular revival fare. Indeed, their tragicomedies were staged more frequently in the period from 1660 to 1700 than were the works of William Shakespeare, who was judged too rough-edged, or Ben Jonson, who was regarded as too satiric.

Beaumont and Fletcher also composed tragedies— *Cupid's Revenge*, *The Maid's Tragedy*—and witty comedies—*The Coxcomb*, *The Scornful Lady*—in the Jonsonian vein. These plays demonstrate the versatility and range of these playwrights, but they helped propel the Jacobean stage into decadence. The dominant scene in *The Maid's Tragedy*, for example, contains a wedding-night confession by the heroine to her warrior-hero husband that she has been and intends to continue to be the king's mistress. This situation brings the style and tone of *The Maid's Tragedy* perilously close to the realm of soap opera.

After Beaumont's death, Fletcher continued to work in collaboration, primarily with Philip Massinger and William Shakespeare. The plays produced during this period were largely tragedies and tragicomedies that responded to the audience's desire for spectacular entertainment. The teaming of Fletcher and Shakespeare likewise suggests that the style of tragicomedy developed by Fletcher strongly influenced Shakespeare's own play production. Romances such as *Pericles, Prince of Tyre* (pr. c. 1607-1608), *The Winter's Tale* (pr. c. 1610-1611), and *The Tempest* (pr. 1611) display the same fascination for plot turns, type characters, exotic settings, and elevated verse found in Beaumont and Fletcher's tragicomedies. When left to his own devices, however, Fletcher also turned his hand to comedy that explored the manners of upper-class Englishmen. Most of these plays are distinguished by complicated plots, humorous characters, and witty dialogue. His ease in writing comedy has led many critics to conclude that Fletcher

John Fletcher (Library of Congress)

was the author of the comic scenes in the tragicomedies, while Beaumont was responsible for the tragic scenes and characters. Fletcher's comedies, with their themes of youthful love and sexual combat, caught the fancy of Stuart courtiers and helped to lay the groundwork for the Restoration comedies of manners.

Although he ended his career by composing sophisticated comedies, Fletcher has been recognized by commentators on the Jacobean stage as the innovator of tragicomedy and as the period's foremost dramatic collaborator. His name seems destined to be linked with that of Beaumont or Massinger in future critical analyses as well. The body of work turned out by Fletcher with his fellow playwrights is truly impressive: some fifty plays in the Second Folio (1679). Considerable time and print have been spent in attempts to determine the relative contributions of each playwright to the comedies, tragedies, and tragicomedies printed in the First and Second Folios—a task that is still going on and may never be satisfactorily completed. As a result, much valuable criticism of the style and content of the individual plays still remains to be done.

BIOGRAPHY

John Fletcher was born in Rye, Sussex, where he was baptized on December 20, 1579. His father, Richard, was a clergyman who attended Cambridge and was later made president of Corpus Christi College, Cambridge, dean of Peterborough, and eventually bishop of London. Elizabeth I reportedly admired his talent as a scholar and bestowed special favor on him. John Fletcher's uncles, Giles and Phineas Fletcher, were poets with respected reputations, and their successes added honors to the family name. These conditions of birth and social standing were somewhat unusual among playwrights of the age and doubtless helped to reinforce Fletcher's reputation as an entertainer of gentlemen.

Although Fletcher no doubt attended lectures at his father's alma mater, he may have been forced to leave Cambridge in 1596 when, perhaps in part because of an ill-advised second marriage, Bishop Fletcher was suspended by the queen. Later in that same year, he died, and Fletcher was probably taken under the wing of his uncle Giles, who may have helped to pay off the family's large debts. Just when Fletcher began writing plays is not known, but it is certain that he was hard at work in collaboration with Beaumont early in the first decade of the seventeenth century. After Beaumont left the profession in 1613, Fletcher continued as the chief playwright for the King's Men, working alone or with Philip Massinger, William Shakespeare (on *The Two Noble Kinsmen* and *Henry VIII*), and several others. Fletcher's death in August, 1625, was caused by the plague; he was buried in St. Saviours Church, Southwark, the district in which he had resided throughout his career in London.

ANALYSIS

The rich legacy of John Fletcher's work, and that of his collaborators, was warmly received in the Restoration. It appears that the complex and suddenly turning plots, remote but familiar settings, effectively imitated manners, and high-flown rhetoric of the

tragicomedies accurately reflected the taste of the age. Fletcher was also skilled at capturing the rhythm and diction of elevated conversation, which clearly contributed to his talents as a writer of comedy. "Sophistication" is a word that recurs in critical commentary on the comedies and tragicomedies, while assessments of the tragedies written alone and in collaboration often employ the words "facile" or "extravagant." That Fletcher was an innovator cannot be denied, but he (along with Beaumont and Massinger) was also an entertainer. He was to some extent lucky in sensing the taste of the age and in devising plays to indulge that taste. Even though one rarely finds a Fletcher play in theatrical repertories today, many of the comedies and some of the seriocomic pieces one sees on the modern stage feature scenes and characters that trace their lineage back to the theatrical genius of Fletcher.

THE FAITHFUL SHEPHERDESS

Although only five plays in the tragicomic genre are accepted as bearing the stamp of the mutual authorship of Beaumont and Fletcher, their names are so closely linked with tragicomedy as to be nearly synonymous with the genre, and recent critical assessments have largely continued this association. Certainly, there are good reasons for the tenacity of the popular view, including the fact that Fletcher named and defined the genre in the preface to one of his earliest plays, *The Faithful Shepherdess*. They play may have been inspired by Battista Guarini's *Il pastor fido* (pb. 1590, pr. 1596; *The Faithful Shepherd*, 1602), but it bears little resemblance to the realistic "sad shepherd" plays, marked by dancing and festivity, with which the English audience of that day was familiar. In fact, with its shepherd and shepherdess lovers poeticizing about passion and lust, *The Faithful Shepherdess* more nearly approximates the prose romances of Edmund Spenser and Sir Philip Sidney.

Set in Thessaly, the play introduces the virgin shepherdess Clorin who, having vowed to purge all passion from her heart in memory of her dead lover, lives beside his grave and dispenses healing herbs to those wounded by love or lust. This devotion sets the standard against which one is to judge the behavior of all the other characters—especially the central couple, Perigot and Amoret, pastoral lovers who vow to exchange only chaste kisses. The comedy of errors that develops tests this resolve, and their love. Amarillis, Amoret's rival, wantonly pursues Perigot, who dutifully rejects her. She vows to gain revenge against Amoret by magically transforming herself into Amoret's double. Despite her altered appearance and her use of every conceivable weapon of seduction, Amarillis finds Perigot unable to love in any but a chaste fashion. As might be expected, when Perigot next encounters the true Amoret, he is so incensed by what he believes is her blatant cynicism that he strikes her with his sword. Later, Amarillis takes pity on the grieving Perigot, who believes he has killed his true love. She admits to disguising herself as Amoret and offers to do so again to prove her case. When the real Amoret reappears, seeking to reassure Perigot of her love, he believes she is intentionally deceiving him and once again wounds her with his sword. Through the good offices of Clorin, however, the two lovers are finally reconciled and Amarillis, along with two other unchaste lovers, is cured of her affliction.

In the main plot and in subplots involving other pastoral characters (among them, a satyr, a river god, and the Caliban-like Sullen Shepherd), Fletcher sets up moral and ethical contrasts: He disguises vice as virtue and virtue as vice in an attempt to dramatize conflicts between essentially one-dimensional characters. Although the action is occasionally brought to the brink of tragedy only to be saved by some intervention of fortune, the plot depends on a kind of mechanical alteration of moods. Almost more an exercise in poetic composition—with impressive variations in sound effects and imagery, for example, used to indicate subtle differences between characters—the play's style has been nicely characterized by Eugene Waith as "the product of refined sensationalism." Whether because the contemporary audiences perceived this flaw or were simply unprepared to believe or care about the rather stylized figures delivering, in long poems of closely rhymed verse, explanations for their attitudes and desires, the play proved a failure on the stage.

CUPID'S REVENGE

As did *The Faithful Shepherdess*, *Cupid's Revenge* turns on the contrast between lust and love. Princess Hidaspes, a virtuous woman who recalls Clorin, is given one wish on her birthday, and she wishes for the destruction of Cupid's altars. When this occurs, a vengeful Cupid forces Hidaspes to fall in love with the court dwarf, who is later killed by the king. Hidaspes then expires from a broken heart. In a second story, Prince Leucippus, Hidaspes' brother, falls in love with Bacha, an unchaste woman who has wooed both the prince and the king (Leontius) by means of a mask of chastity. Thus, male and female members of the royal household are made to suffer because of love—degradation (in the case of Leucippus and Leontius) and death (Hidaspes). Like *The Faithful Shepherdess*, *Cupid's Revenge* is filled not with well-motivated dramatic characterizations but rather with representations of the moral dimensions of love.

PHILASTER

An incident inserted in *Cupid's Revenge* primarily to play on the sympathies of the viewers concerns Urania, daughter to Bacha, who loves Leucippus and disguises herself as a page in order to be near him after his banishment. She is murdered when she rushes between her lover and a messenger sent by Bacha to kill him. Leucippus's discovery of Urania's true identity provides the occasion for a melodramatic statement on the fortunes of true love. This situation was repeated by Fletcher and Beaumont in the popular and dramatically fresh *Philaster*. The hero, a disinterested prince who has been compared by many critics to Hamlet, finds himself living in the court of an evil king, usurper of his throne. Philaster falls in love with Arethusa, the king's daughter, but is informed by Megra, a scheming, lascivious lady of the court, that his beloved has deceived him with Bellario, a young page who has served as their messenger. Aroused to a sudden anger, Philaster attacks Bellario and Arethusa but is quickly arrested by the usurping king. After a revolt by the people helps Philaster win back his throne, his marriage to Arethusa is made public. Megra revives the old charge against Arethusa, and Philaster orders Bellario stripped and beaten. Only then is the page revealed to be Euphrasia, a noble's daughter who is hopelessly in love with Philaster; the revelation results in the banishment of Megra. Hero and heroine live happily ever after, although the continued presence of Philaster's "loyal" servant (often compared to Viola in *Twelfth Night*) seems to strike a melancholy note.

Philaster carries on the debates about love and lust, loyalty and deceit, that were a part of Fletcher's earlier work. By setting the action in a distant time not associated with the pastoral, Beaumont and Fletcher managed to avoid much of the confusion that resulted from a pastoral setting. The characters here are types—the lover, the lustful lady, the usurper—whose actions are not carefully motivated; they behave in a manner required by the situation. There can be little doubt that the poetry spoken by these characters, which is often refined and beautiful, helped considerably in holding the contemporary playgoer's attention. More than any other element, however, the scenes depicting Philaster striking his loyal servant and Bellario disclosing her true identity are typical of Beaumont and Fletcher's successful plays. They are suspenseful and surprising; they wrench potentially tragic situations into the realm of romantic happiness, usually at the last possible moment.

A KING AND NO KING

A somewhat different, more serious tone prevails in *A King and No King*. As in *Philaster*, King Arbaces faces a romantic dilemma, but unlike Philaster, he falls in love with his sister—when they meet after a long separation. Although promised to Arbaces' rival Tigranes, the captured king of Armenia, Panthea returns her brother's love, thereby setting the stage for what appears to be an incestuous affair. The shock of this situation is created through dubious maneuvering, but one can readily see that it is the type of dilemma requiring the radical, even sensational resolution typical of Beaumont and Fletcher's tragicomic style.

Just as Arbaces concludes that the only course for a sinner like him is suicide, he learns that his real father is the Lord-Protector, who had helped the queen "produce" an heir, allowing her to present his newborn infant as her own son. Panthea emerges as the true heir to the throne, thereby legitimating Arbaces' love for her. The two are married, Tigranes finds Spaconia to be his true love, and the terrible atmosphere of evil that dominates the play in its earlier stages seems banished like a bad dream. The audience has followed the hero and heroine to the brink of tragedy, but once again, through a miraculous discovery, a happy ending has been imposed. What gives this play greater weight than even *Philaster* is the way in which Arbaces' struggle with his emotions has been thoroughly explored. He emerges as more than a type, although his flaws, which have seemed so real throughout the body of the play, seem to disappear with the discovery and resolution. Arbaces emerges in this regard as a "problem" character similar to Shakespeare's Angelo (*Measure for Measure*, pr. 1604) and Bertram (*All's Well That Ends Well*, pr. c. 1602-1603).

THE MAID'S TRAGEDY

Although the central dilemma of *The Maid's Tragedy*—what a worthy man should do after learning that his bride is the king's mistress—could have been resolved through the devices of tragicomedy, Beaumont and Fletcher chose instead to make the play into a tragedy. The result is a compelling, artful play. Amintor is persuaded to marry Evadne by the predictably evil king; in order to do so, Amintor breaks off his engagement with Aspatia—and breaks her heart. When Evadne informs Amintor that their marriage is only a cover-up, he swears vengeance, but when he learns he has been cuckolded by the king, he decides against taking revenge because of his strong feeling of loyalty toward the throne. Amintor does divulge his awful secret to his fellow warrior Melantius, who also happens to be Evadne's brother. Melantius confronts his sister with the truth and says that she must repair the damage to her marriage—and to the country—by murdering the king: "All the gods require it." In another of those contrived but riveting scenes so typical of Beaumont and Fletcher plots, Evadne comes to Amintor, her hands covered with the king's blood, to ask his forgiveness, only to find him weeping over the body of Aspatia. Aspatia, despairing of happiness, had disguised herself as a man (a favorite convention in the tragicomedies) and provoked a duel with Amintor, falling on his sword and killing herself. When Amintor realizes when Evadne has done, he rejects her, in blank verse that rivals Shakespeare's in sheer dramatic strength. Evadne cannot withstand his rebuke and soon commits suicide. Finally, Amintor, struck by the horrible sight of these women who died for him, likewise gives up the struggle.

Despite the tragic impact of this final scene, it is difficult to describe either Amintor or Aspatia as characters with the capacity for suffering of a Hamlet or Ophelia. Both are sentimental figures. Whether, as one critic has observed, Aspatia represents the pure heroine of the Elizabethan period brought down by the sophisticated and corrupt Jacobean heroine is a matter for debate. She certainly traces her origins back to the disguised page characters of the earlier tragicomedies. The regular introduction of debates over honor and loyalty, the sudden twists of plot, the prominence of an intriguing and vengeful figure such as Melantius, and the almost operatic verse style are all elements that look ahead to the heroic drama of John Dryden and Sir William Davenant. Other than *A King and No King*, *The Maid's Tragedy* is probably the most carefully constructed and emotionally rich of the plays written by Beaumont and Fletcher.

THE SCORNFUL LADY

In addition to tragicomedy and tragedy, the two playwrights also worked together on a number of comedies. Two of the best of these are *The Scornful Lady* and *The Coxcomb*. In *The Scornful Lady*, a play originally written for the Queen's Revels Children, two pairs of male lovers woo different ladies. The brothers Loveless, the older a sober fellow who engages in combats of wit with the Lady and the younger a prodigal who woos and wins a rich widow, are the comic heroes of this comedy of manners. The main action concerns Elder Loveless's attempt to purge the humor of the Lady, who longs for her lover when he is away but abuses and mocks him when he is present; he vies for her favor with the good-looking Walford, who, on losing the contest, settles for the Lady's sister. In this situation one can clearly see the influence of Jonson on Fletcher; the humor scheme is

worked in similar fashion in Jonson's *Epicoene: Or, The Silent Woman* (pr. 1609, pb. 1616). Young Loveless also woos a lady, a beautiful and wealthy widow, but in a style that is considerably more boisterous than that of his brother, and he, too, faces a rival—Morecraft, a moneylender who had previously fleeced him. Young Loveless might be called a "playboy" in modern usage, and he and his companions nearly drive the steward of his beloved's house mad with their drinking and carousing. Although his speech lacks the verbal pyrotechnics to be found in the dialogue of Restoration comedy, Young Loveless does stand for the power of revelry and good fun, and the stratagems and spicy wit that finally bring him and his brother their desired prizes were a model for subsequent playwrights.

THE COXCOMB

Like *The Scornful Lady*, *The Coxcomb* follows a dual plot structure and depends somewhat heavily on the humor scheme for its effects. Antonio, the coxcomb or cuckold, proves to be so generous that the moment he learns of his friend Mercury's love for his wife (Maria), he literally forces her into Mercury's arms. Antonio even resorts to a disguise to bring the two together for what appears to be a lust-satisfying tryst. To the end, however, Antonio apologizes profusely for his wife's "excessive" virtue. The subplot (really a second story) concerns Viola, a fair maid who is scorned by her lover Ricardo. Forced to wander the countryside alone, Viola is robbed and nearly raped by an oversexed "gentleman." She is finally befriended by two milkmaids, a circumstance that allows her to praise the inherent virtues of country life. Her short verse encomium provides an effective contrast to the rough-and-tumble prose speech of the rustic characters. When Ricardo is finally reunited with Viola, he begs forgiveness for the wanton behavior that led him to scorn her. How this romantic tale relates to the more tragicomic one involving Antonio, Maria, and Mercury, however, remains unclear. Both heroes might be viewed as humor types who are, because of their blindness, susceptible to being cuckolded. Despite its disjointed plot, *The Coxcomb* is a comedy of lively contrast between city and country life, urban and rustic foolery.

WIT AT SEVERAL WEAPONS

A similar farce, *Wit at Several Weapons*, has been variously attributed to Fletcher alone, to Beaumont and Fletcher, and even to such revisers as Middleton. It is the story of Sir Perfidious Oldcraft, who strives to make his son, Wittypate, less of a dunce. After a complicated series of intrigues, the father discovers that Wittypate has been deceiving him from the beginning and, in fact, truly does possess wit. This recognition makes Oldcraft so happy that he immediately gives the boy a large allowance. In the subplot, a character named Sir Gregory Fop also finds himself the victim of trickery, but the result is a happy one: marriage to an attractive heiress. Even though the action, with its emphasis on intrigue and duping, smacks of Jonson, Beaumont and Fletcher do not intrude the element of keen satire here. Indeed, the mood is one of high spirits, involving stock character speaking humorous but not ingenious verse.

BONDUCA

When Beaumont retired from the stage in 1613, Fletcher continued to write plays on his own and in collaboration with others. He had become a valued member of the King's Men, recognized as a skilled and popular creator of tragicomedies, tragedies, and comedies. Indeed, there is convincing evidence that Fletcher was composing successful plays on his own even during the period of his collaboration with Beaumont. *Bonduca* and *Valentinian* are two tragedies written by Fletcher that appealed to the Globe and Blackfriars audiences. *Bonduca* dramatizes events related to the wars between Britons and Romans, and it may have been inspired by Shakespeare's *Cymbeline* (pr. c. 1609-1610). Although the play is named after the English queen Bonduca, she has very little part in it. The tragic hero is a brave lad named Hengo, who is deceitfully killed by the Roman Judas. Caratach, a courageous old soldier who is the other major figure in the play, avenges the murder by slaying Judas. The death scene, with its rhapsodizing about Britain and youthful death, smacks of the kind of pathos that Fletcher achieves in the verse of the tragicomedies. Whether Caratach was intended as a dramatic copy of Sir Walter Raleigh, at that time a prisoner in the Tower and widely regarded as a cham-

pion of the good old cause, is difficult to determine. There can be no doubt, however, that *Bonduca* was intended to be a play about English patriotism and loyalty.

VALENTINIAN

Valentinian achieves a greater tragic impact than does *Bonduca*, primarily because its villain is the Roman emperor who rapes Lucina, the honest wife of a brave soldier named Maximus. Fletcher spins out the action by means of contrast between the brave and loyal army captains and the dissolute world of the court, with the emperor Valentinian announcing to the prostrate Lucina: "Justice shall never hear you; I am justice." Here is the mood and style of a work such as *The Maid's Tragedy*, with its helpless victims and seemingly omnipotent villains. When Lucina dies, Maximus, instead of seeking direct revenge against Valentinian, becomes a Machiavellian intriguer who employs servants to taunt and then poison the villain, betraying his own friend Aecius as one step toward this end. After Maximus marries the emperor's widow, he foolishly tells her of his deeds, and she proceeds to poison him in turn, by crowning him with a poisoned wreath. This serpentine plotting corrupts the tragic mood of *Valentinian*, which is also marred by special effects and what one critic has called "Fletcher's flamboyant declamation."

THE FALSE ONE

Fletcher's chief collaborator after Beaumont was Philip Massinger. The two men produced at least ten plays together, most of them tragedies and comedies. *The False One* and *Sir John van Olden Barnavelt* are two representative examples of this collaboration. The former tragedy depicts Caesar's affair with Cleopatra in Egypt, although the title does not refer to the queen but to a Roman named Septimius, who is responsible for the murder of his old general, Pompey. In a bold move, Septimius vows to murder Caesar, and much of the action concerns the intrigues against him. In the end, however, Caesar outwits and defeats his enemies, which makes it difficult to regard the ending as tragic. Massinger was probably responsible for the opening and closing scenes of the play, while Fletcher depicted the love scenes involving Caesar and Cleopatra and invented the breathtaking masque of Nilus. Honor and nobility are at stake throughout, but the action and characters do not achieve the heights or complexity found in Shakespeare's play dealing with similar materials.

SIR JOHN VAN OLDEN BARNAVELT

Sir John van Olden Barnavelt deals with a contemporary rather than an ancient event in history—the downfall and death of the well-known Dutch statesman in May, 1619. There are also allusions in this tragedy to the execution of Sir Walter Raleigh, which had taken place the previous year, making it difficult to understand how the play was allowed on the stage (it was not published until 1883). Massinger's interest in political themes and foreign policy (see his *Believe as You List*, pr. 1631) is evident in this aspect of the play, while Fletcher no doubt wrote the scenes that deal with Barnavelt's emotional side. The play suffers from hasty composition: It was written and put into production within three months of Barnavelt's death. Of particular importance, however, is the fact that Fletcher lent his talent to a play dealing with the topic of absolutism. He is no doubt the author of a sensational scene in which three executioners throw dice to decide who will carry out the beheading.

HENRY VIII AND THE TWO NOBLE KINSMEN

Besides Massinger, Fletcher was also working with Shakespeare during this period (1613-1620), and *Henry VIII* and *The Two Noble Kinsmen* bear the mark of Fletcher's hand. In *Henry VIII*, the spectacular celebrations and the episodic plot are reminiscent of the style of *A King and No King* and *Thierry and Theodoret*. Little attention is given to Henry himself, the best speeches and scenes going to Wolsey (whose famous farewell may indeed have been written by Fletcher) and Cranmer. The same emphasis on spectacle, especially scenes of pageantry, can be seen in *The Two Noble Kinsmen*.

LATER WORKS

Although Fletcher collaborated with other playwrights after 1616, the main body of his work in this period was in his own hand and in his favorite genres: comedy and tragicomedy. Tragicomedy was apparently more attractive for him than tragedy because he was either incapable of or uninterested in exploring internal conflict by means of the soliloquy.

THE MAD LOVER

A few tragicomedies from Fletcher's later works should suffice to illustrate his dramatic style at this stage in his career. In some ways, Fletcher's interests reveal a return to the themes and characters of his earliest plays. *The Mad Lover* features a hero named Memnon, who leaves his career as a vainglorious warrior to woo the beautiful Princess Calis. This rejection of war in favor of love was a subject treated in earlier tragicomedies, such as *Philaster* and *A King and No King*. Memnon, however, follows a rigid code of honor in his love that is mocked by other characters in the court of Paphos, where a cynical view of romance prevails. His chief rival for Calis's hand turns out to be his own brother, Polydor, who wins the princess's heart even as he tells her she must love his brother. In a spectacular denouement typical of Fletcher, Polydor has himself sent to Calis in a coffin, bearing a will that directs her to marry Memnon. When Memnon enters, however, he sees his apparently dead brother and declares his intention to follow him to the grave. At this point, Polydor arises, still pleading for his brother as suitor. Memnon, however, perceives the truth—that Calis loves Polydor deeply—and decides to return to war. This heroic gesture places Memnon in the first order of heroic lovers that will come to dominate the Restoration stage. He also qualifies as one of Fletcher's most memorable tragicomic figures, changing from an essentially foolish soldier to a romantic Platonist.

THE LOYAL SUBJECT

In *The Loyal Subject*, Fletcher likewise gives the action coherence by organizing it around the theme of duty to self and sovereign. Based on an earlier play by Thomas Heywood (*The Royal King and Loyal Subject*, pr. 1602?, pb. 1637), Fletcher's tragicomedy concerns the staunch loyalty of the general Archas to the weak and easily flattered duke of Moscow. That devotion is contrasted to the Machiavellianism of Boroskie, who seeks to widen a rift that has resulted in Archas's resignation. Archas is then subjected to exile, imprisonment, and torture, but at every instance of national crisis, he acts to aid his country. Only after Archas's daughters are able to convince the duke of their father's loyalty is he allowed to live.

Before this happens, Archas is brought to a point at which he threatens to kill his son Theodore for speaking out against the cruel duke and Boroskie. This disaster is deftly avoided by a general resolution in which Archas is forced to relent when his youngest son is threatened with death. The resolution allows Archas to remain true to his personal and political codes of honor. It also has suggested to certain critics that Fletcher meant his audience to be thinking about the fate—and principled character—of Sir Walter Raleigh as it listened to Archas's declamations (particularly when added to numerous contemporary references related to Raleigh). Certainly the extravagant rhetoric, overwrought scenes of conflict, and surprising convolutions of plot serve to place the play squarely in the Fletcher canon.

THE ISLAND PRINCESS

One final tragicomedy gives some sense of the range of Fletcher's last plays. *The Island Princess* has as its central character a woman, the Princess Quisara, who offers her hand to any suitor brave enough to rescue her brother, the King of Sidore, from captivity. When the Portuguese captain Armusia manages the release, it appears as if a joyous marriage will follow. The king, however, fears the Portuguese will attempt to take over his island and requires that Armusia change his religion before he marries Quisara. Armusia refuses and is thrown in prison, where Quisara, moved by her love's defiance, decides to join him. They are soon rescued by friends of Armusia, who also manage to unmask a priest responsible for poisoning the king's mind against Armusia. (He turns out to be the enemy king who held Quisara's brother captive at the opening of the action.) The king now welcomes his new brother-in-law, declaring that he is "half-persuaded" to become a Christian. As this happy resolution takes place, it becomes clear that the play has not really concerned religion or the conflict of East and West. The exotic setting proves to be only the backdrop for a tragicomic study of honor. It should also be added that *The Island Princess* looks forward to such Restoration plays as John Dryden's *The Indian Emperor* (pr. 1665), where the setting provides the occasion for spectacle and heroic flights of rhetoric. Fletcher's late comedies, in particular *The Chances*, *The Wild Goose Chase*, and *Rule a Wife and Have a Wife*, likewise foreshadowed the comedy of manners, which was to prove so popular during the Restoration.

BIBLIOGRAPHY

Clark, Sandra. *The Plays of Beaumont and Fletcher: Sexual Themes and Dramatic Representation.* New York: Harvester Wheatsheaf, 1994. A look at the plays of Beaumont and Fletcher in regard to their treatment of sex. Bibliography and index.

Finkelpearl, Philip J. *Court and Country Politics in the Plays of Beaumont and Fletcher.* Princeton, N.J.: Princeton University Press, 1990. Considers the plays in connection with the author's three worlds: the country, the playhouse, and the Mermaid Tavern. Analyzes eight plays in depth for their political relevance. Among the themes discussed are the Anti-Prince, corruption of royal power, and tyrannicide.

Frey, Charles H., ed. *Shakespeare, Fletcher, and "The Two Noble Kinsmen."* Columbia: University of Missouri Press, 1989. A look at the authorship of *The Two Noble Kinsmen*, an apparent collaboration of William Shakespeare and Fletcher. Bibliography and index.

Gossett, Suzanne. *The Influence of the Jacobean Masque on the Plays of Beaumont and Fletcher.* New York: Garland, 1988. An analysis of the Jacobean masque and its influence on the dramas of Beaumont and Fletcher. Bibliography and index.

McMullan, Gordon. *The Politics of Unease in the Plays of John Fletcher.* Amherst: University of Massachusetts Press, 1994. A look at the political and social views held by Fletcher as they manifested themselves in his plays. Bibliography and index.

Squier, Charles L. *John Fletcher.* Boston: Twayne, 1986. A general study that contains individual chapters on the tragicomedies, the tragedies, and the comedies. Includes a section on Fletcher's critical reputation in the last two centuries and on stylistic idiosyncrasies. Annotated bibliography.

Robert F. Willson, Jr., updated by Howard L. Ford

DARIO FO

Born: San Giano, Italy; March 24, 1926

PRINCIPAL DRAMA

Poer nano, pr. 1951 (radio play), pr. 1952 (staged)

Il dito nell' occhio, pr. 1953 (with Franco Parenti and Giustino Durano)

I sani da legare, pr. 1954 (with Parenti and Durano)

Ladri, manichini, e donne nude, pr. 1958, pb. 1962 (includes *L'uomo nudo e l'uomo in frack* [*One Was Nude and One Wore Tails*, 1985], *I cadaveri si spediscono le donne si spogliano*, *Gli imbianchini non hanno ricordi*, and *Non tutti i ladri vengono per nuocere* [*The Virtuous Burglars*, 1992])

Comica finale, pr. 1959, pb. 1962 (includes *Quando sarai povero sarai re*, *La Marcolfa*, *Un morto da vendere*, and *I tre bravi*)

Gli arcangeli non giocano a flipper, pr. 1959, pb. 1966 (*Archangels Don't Play Pinball*, 1987)

Aveva due pistole con gli occhi bianchi e neri, pr., pb. 1960

Chi ruba un piede è fortunato in amore, pr., pb. 1961

Isabella, tre caravelle e un cacciaballe, pr., pb. 1963

Settimo: Ruba un po' meno, pr., pb. 1964

La colpa è sempre del diavolo, pr., pb. 1965

La signora è da buttare, pr., pb. 1967

Grande pantomima con bandiere e pupazzi piccoli e medi, pr. 1968, pb. 1975

La fine del mondo, pr. 1969

Mistero buffo: Giullarata popolare, pr. 1969, pb. 1970 (*Mistero Buffo: Comic Mysteries*, 1983)

Legami pure che tanto spacco tutto lo stesso, pr. 1969, pb. 1975 (includes *Il telaio* and *Il funerale del padrone*)

L'operaio conosce trecento parole, il padrone mille: Per questo lui è il padrone, pr. 1969, pb. 1970 (*The Worker Knows Three Hundred Words, the Boss Knows a Thousand: That's Why He's the Boss*, 1983)

Morte accidentale di un anarchico, pr., pb. 1970 (*Accidental Death of an Anarchist*, 1979)

Vorrei morire anche stasera se dovessi pensare che non è servito a niente, pr., pb. 1970

Tutti uniti! Tutti insieme! Ma scusa, quello non è il padrone?, pr., pb. 1971

Fedayn, pr., pb. 1972

Oridine per DIO.000.000!, pr., pb. 1972

Pum, pum! Chi è? La Polizia!, pb. 1972, pr. 1973

Guerra di popolo in Cile, pr., pb. 1973

Le commedie di Dario Fo, pb. 1974-1998 (13 volumes)

Non si paga! Non si paga!, pr., pb. 1974 (*We Can't Pay! We Won't Pay!*, 1978)

Il Fanfani rapito, pr., pb. 1975

La giullarata, pb. 1975, pr. 1976

La marijuana della mama è la più bella, pr., pb. 1976

Parliamo di donne, pr. 1977 (with Franca Rame; televised)

Tutta casa, letto e chiesa, pr., pb. 1978 (with Rame; adapted as *Female Parts*, 1981; also known as *Orgasmo Adulto Escapes from the Zoo*)

La storia della tigre, pr. 1978, pb. 1980 (*The Tale of a Tiger*, 1984)

La storia di un soldato, (libretto by C. F. Ramuz; adaptation of Igor Stravinsky's opera *The Soldier's Tale*)

La tragedia di Aldo Moro, pr. 1979

Clacson, trombette e pernacchi, pr. 1981 (*Trumpets and Raspberries*, 1981; also as *About Face*, 1983)

L'opera dello sghignazzo, pr. 1981 (music by Kurt Weill; adaptation of Bertolt Brecht's play *The Threepenny Opera* and John Gay's play *The Beggar's Opera*)

Il fabulazzo osceno, pr., pb. 1982

Patapumfete, pr., pb. 1982

Coppia aperta, quasi spalancata, pr. 1983 (with Rame; *An Open Couple—Very Open*, 1985)

Elisabetta: Quasi per caso una donna, pr. 1984 (*Almost by Chance a Woman, Elizabeth*, 1987)

Dio li fa e poi li accoppa, pb. 1986

Hellequin, Arlekin, Arlecchino, pr. 1986

Il ratto della Francesca, pr., pb. 1986

Parti femminili, pr. 1987 (with Rame; includes revised version of *Coppia aperta* [*An Open Couple*, 1990] and *Una giornata qualunque* [*An Ordinary Day*, 1990])

Papa e la strega, pr. 1989, pb. 1994 (*The Pope and the Witch*, 1992)

Zitti! Stiamo precipitando!, pr. 1990, pb. 1998

Johan Padan a la descoverta de la Americhe, pb. 1992, pr. 1998 (*Johan Padan and the Discovery of the Americas*, 2001)

Plays, pb. 1992-1993 (2 volumes)

Dario Fo incontra Ruzzante, pr. 1993, revised pr. 1995 as *Dario Fo recita Ruzzante*

Mamma! I Sanculotti!, pr. 1993, pb. 1998

Sesso? Grazie, tanto per gradire, pr. 1994, pb. 1998 (with Rame)

Il diavolo con le zinne, pr. 1997, pb. 1998 (*The Devil in Drag*, 1999)

We Can't Pay! We Won't Pay! and Other Plays, pb. 2001

OTHER LITERARY FORMS

Dario Fo's songs and poems are collected in *Ballate e canzoni* (1974; ballads and songs). He has also designed sets and written scripts for several films, including Carlo Lizzani's *Lo Svitato* (1956). *Ci ragiono è canto* (1966), *Ci ragiono è canto No. 2* (1969), and *Ci ragiono è canto No. 3* (1973)—which can be translated as "I think things out and sing about them," numbers one, two, and three—are spectacles based on Italian folk and traditional songs. Fo also has written plays and programs for television and numerous monologues, often with Franca Rame.

ACHIEVEMENTS

Dario Fo is concerned above all with reviving a tradition of "popular" theater, presenting a satirical critique of modern society, especially of authority and the powers that be, and highlighting corruption and injustice. He is deeply involved in contemporary issues, and his texts remain flexible so as to reflect current changes (some plays—for example, *Acciden-*

tal Death of an Anarchist—present the critic with at least three, sometimes more, versions, differing slightly from one another, as the situation that engendered them changed and developed). Fo himself traces his inspiration back to the medieval *giullare*, the joker, who performed at fairs and in marketplaces, entertaining the people, expressing their complaints and grievances in a popular form of political satire (for which he was not infrequently persecuted or even executed by the authorities). In spite of the political content of his plays, however, Fo stresses the fact that he does not belong to any communist or Marxist party, because bureaucracy, in whatever guise, is "destructive." As a modern-day *giullare*, beyond political commentary and satire, Fo aims at all times to entertain his audience, to make people laugh, "because laughter activates intelligence." The label most often applied to Fo is that of "clown": not so much a circus clown, although clownish antics often form part of his act, but a farcical Chaplinesque clown, with a sharp bite behind the laughter. Fo is a virtuoso performer of immense skill and dynamism, described as a superstar by enthusiastic reviewers. With the serious popular tradition of the *giullare*, he has combined the stage antics and tricks of the *commedia dell'arte*, along with its tradition of improvisation.

In what is a close working partnership with his wife, Franca Rame, he takes his theater to the working class, performing in labor halls, workers' cooperatives, factories, and market squares. With his wife and members of his company, he has traveled widely abroad, arousing both enthusiasm and polemic. In 1981, he was awarded the Danish Sonnig Prize, and in 1987, he won an Obie Award. Nominated for the Nobel Prize in 1977, he won the Nobel Prize in Literature in 1997. According to Tony Kushner in *The Nation*, "Fo deserves to win the Nobel Prize for his life of theatrical activism, yes, his dedication to progressive politics. . . . Fo deserves to win because, as the Vatican . . . put it, he writes *debatable* texts. He has dedicated his genius to making everything he touches debatable."

BIOGRAPHY

Dario Fo was born in 1926, in San Giano, Italy, a small town in Lombardy on the shores of Lake

Dario Fo in Milan, Italy, in 1995. (AP/Wide World Photos)

Maggiore, near the Swiss border. His father was a railway worker who enjoyed acting in an amateur theater company, and his mother came from a peasant family. As a boy, Dario was very much influenced by the *fabulatori* and *cantastorie*, traveling storytellers and ballad singers who wandered around the shores of the lake entertaining the local fishermen. As a youth, he went to Milan, where he studied painting at the Brera Academy and architecture at the Polytechnic Institute, abandoning his studies when he was close to obtaining his degree. When he suffered a nervous breakdown in the late 1940's, he was advised to pursue what he found most enjoyable, and he thereafter turned more and more to theater. During the 1950's, Fo tried his hand at radio, revues, and films. During the period between 1958 and 1959, he wrote, produced, directed, and performed in one-act farces and short comic pieces, inspired by theatrical traditions ranging from the *commedia dell'arte* to the "French Farce" of Ernest Feydeau. "These farces

were a very important exercise for me in understanding how to write a theatrical text. I learned how to dismantle and re-assemble the mechanisms of comedy," Fo has said. "I also realized how many antiquated, useless things there were in many plays which belong to the theatre of words."

In 1954, Fo married actress Franca Rame, a member of a popular touring theater family. (Their son, Jacopo, in 1977 provided the illustrations for two scenarios from *Poer Nano*, which were published in cartoon form.) In 1959, the Fos formed their own company, La Compagnia Dario Fo-Franca Rame, in Milan.

The years 1959 to 1968 are usually described as Fo's "bourgeois period," because the company performed mainly before middle-class audiences, working in traditional boulevard or Broadway-type commercial theaters. The plays had consistent plot lines and character development, but they all satirized and criticized the government and existing political and social conditions in Italy. "Having accepted this circuit and these audiences," Fo recalls, "we had to put across political and social truths under the guise of satiric licence."

In 1959, Fo and Rame were invited to present some of their farces on the government-controlled national television, RAI-TV. In 1962, they worked in a popular Italian television series, *Canzonissima*. Fo's sketches, highly satirical and explicitly political, were censored, causing Fo and Rame to resign in protest. The Fos were then sued by RAI and effectively excluded from Italian television for some fourteen years. *Ci ragiono è canto* was an uneasy collaboration with a musical group interested in reviving peasant and working-class songs. Fo directed the show and rewrote some of the songs.

The Paris revolts in May, 1968, the protests against the Vietnam War, the cultural revolution in China, and revolts in Latin America and Africa all helped to influence Fo's decision to break away from establishment, mainstream, bourgeois theater and lend his voice to the class struggle and to political revolt. He declared that he no longer wanted to be "the court jester of the bourgeoisie," preferring instead to serve as the "the jester of the proletariat."

The year 1968 also witnessed the dissolution of La Compagnia Dario Fo-Franca Rame, to be replaced by the Associazione Nuova Scena, a cooperative theater company, organized under the auspices of Associazione Ricreativa Culturale Italiana (ARCI), the cultural and recreational organization of the Italian Communist Party (PCI). Yet Fo's refusal to toe any party line and his indiscriminate satirical attacks on bureaucracy soon brought him into conflict with the PCI, leading to their boycott of the group's performances. In 1970, after internal debates and conflicts, Fo and Rame withdrew from Nuova Scena and founded Il Collettivo Teatrale "La Comune," an independent, self-supporting political theater group allied to organizations of the extraparliamentary Left.

Rame was abducted and tortured by a fascist group in 1973. In a separate incident later that year, Fo was arrested and briefly imprisoned in Sassari (Sardinia) but was released after his company organized a demonstration outside the police station.

After a highly successful tour of *Mistero Buffo* in France, in 1974, the reorganized Il Collettivo Teatrale "La Comune" set about finding itself a permanent location. The group finally occupied an abandoned building, the Palazzina Liberty, close to the center of Milan. This led to a struggle with the authorities, which developed into a major national issue, but eventually the group was given temporary permission to remain. The painter Matta was closely involved and painted murals in the Palazzina.

The decade of the 1970's saw the beginning of Fo's and Rame's extensive trips and performances abroad, although the United States denied them visas in 1980 and again in 1984, a denial based on the "ideological exclusionary clauses" of the McCarthy-era immigration law. Not until 1985 were Fo and Rame allowed to enter the United States, and then for less than a week, to attend final rehearsals and previews of a Broadway production of *Accidental Death of an Anarchist*. In 1986, however, they were allowed to visit the United States for a six-week performance tour; they returned again in 1987.

In 1977, Fo performed *Mistero Buffo* on Italian television, arousing bitter protests from the Roman Catholic Church and government. In the same year, collaborating for the first time with Rame, he wrote *Female Parts*, a series of monologues dealing with the condition of women, which she subsequently performed. Other monologues followed, dealing with the frustration of women at their role of second-class citizens, or "sub-proletariat."

Mistero Buffo was presented at the Berlin International Festival in 1978. There was something of a return to the bourgeois theater in that year, with the touring of *The Tale of a Tiger* around Italy. For the 1978-1979 season at the world-famous La Scala opera theater, Fo directed a politically oriented adaptation of Igor Stravinsky's *The Soldier's Tale* (1918), to the disgust of opera connoisseurs. Fo's collaboration with La Scala was short-lived.

Eviction from the Palazzina Liberty was followed by further tours abroad for Fo and Rame, who were ever more in demand. Since the loss of the Palazzina Liberty, Fo and Rame have had no permanent base in Italy, although from time to time they have made a provisional home in the Teatro Cristallo in Milan, a former music hall. Abroad, however, theater locations have never been a problem. Fo's plays have been produced in so many countries and translated into so many languages that he has been described as the most widely performed living Italian dramatist.

Internationally acclaimed political playwright Fo's work has won critical praise and popular success for its content, its skillful improvisation, comedic techniques, and its satirical perspective. With his wife and collaborator Rame, Fo has been active in the Italian and European theater for more than forty years, performing in many countries to many groups. Yet only in the 1980's did his work come to the attention of English-speaking audiences. Fo's life and work display his credo that the theater can be not only an instrument of entertainment but also one of political illumination.

ANALYSIS

One of the problems that faces agitprop theater is that of combining a militant political message with a powerful dramatic and artistic effect because each may tend to weaken the other. Dario Fo's theater successfully maintains a balance between the two. Although the intensity and actuality of the political message, being too close to the bone, have created problems for the Fos in their own country, the effectiveness of their theater has contributed much to their popularity abroad, where the political implications are less specific. Fo's theater is not nihilistic: It aims at making people think, and it does this chiefly through laughter because, as Rame says, when one laughs, one's mind is suddenly opened to be "pierced by the nails of reason." Fo's laughter is the uneasy kind that goes naturally "with a degree of cynicism" that satire induces, or "a kind of *grand guignol* scream," resulting from those "nails of reason" piercing one's head.

It is sometimes asked whether, and to what extent, Fo's statements, being so closely rooted in contemporary events, can be expected to retain their interest. Certain of Fo's plays had somewhat fallen from favor by the beginning of the twenty-first century, but since this happens often in the case of plays that are never published, it is difficult to judge the possible reasons for the public's loss of interest. Much of Fo's theater continues to play to an ever-growing following. The recurring themes in his work, his protest against injustice and oppression, are at once contemporary expressions and universal concerns. Built on a series of contradictions, drawing together and carefully balancing disparate elements such as comedy and tragedy, farce, and political back-benching, Fo's forcefully committed theater also emerges at all times as highly successful entertainment.

ARCHANGELS DON'T PLAY PINBALL

After various one-act farces and playlets, *Archangels Don't Play Pinball*, a three-act play with music and a traditional structure that approximates that of the well-made play, introduced Fo's bourgeois period. As its title page notes, one of the main incidents is inspired by a short story by Augusto Frassineti, but the treatment is Fo's own. Through a complex plot of farcical twists and reversals, surrealistic dream sequences, and stylized, balletlike stage business, Fo attacks the stupidity and narrow-mindedness of Italian bureaucratic red tape and the inefficiency and corruption of government ministers. The starting point of the play is a group of petty criminals, "good-natured,

sulphuric louts, a kind of proletariat of the outer suburbs who survive on expedients." They are responsible for introducing the main character, Lanky, to the girl of his dreams, the Blonde, through the elaborate theatrical practical joke they construct. Theater within theater, and a fusion to the point of confusion of theatricality and reality, are elements that would continue to run through Fo's plays. Interesting also is the mention, for the first time in a Fo drama, of the *giullare* tradition, which would play such a dominant role in the development of his theater.

AVEVA DUE PISTOLE CON GLI OCCHI BIANCHI E NERI

The underworld returned, but with gangsters, in Fo's next play, *Aveva due pistole con gli occhi bianchi e neri* (he had two pistols with white and black eyes). The plot remains farcical, based on a "double" and a series of mistaken identities, and the play is again interspersed with musical numbers. The political satire is predominant, however, and in an interview Fo described the company's difficulties with censorship (not for the last time in Fo's career). Problems of madness and psychiatry, themes that recur in Fo's theater, here make a brief appearance, as the main character struggles with amnesia and with the difficulty of establishing his identity in a psychiatric hospital. The influence of Bertolt Brecht can be clearly sensed in this play—an influence that causes Fo to refer to certain aspects of his drama as "epic."

ISABELLA, TRE CARAVELLE E UN CACCIABALLE

This influence can be found, too, in *Isabella, tre caravelle e un cacciaballe* (Isabella, three sailing ships, and a con man), a play in two acts and an interlude, which has certain similarities to Brecht's *Leben des Galileo* (pr. 1943, revised 1947-1957; *Life of Galileo*, 1947), which had enjoyed a memorable production in Milan in the same season, although the way Fo's Columbus comes into conflict with the established political powers differs from that of Brecht's hero. *Isabella, tre caravelle e un cacciaballe* is a historical play that relies on detachment and distancing of the audience. Fo's aim was to "dismantle a character who had been embalmed as a hero in school history books"; the critique of a Columbus, who is at once an intellectual and a political opportunist, a "sailor" and an "adventurer," is developed in a highly satirical vein through a play-within-the-play. A recurring figure throughout Fo's theater, that of the madman, or simple fool, is embodied in this play in Isabella's daughter, Giovanna la Pazza (Joanna the Mad). Fo's use of songs differs from Brecht's, inasmuch as they are more strongly a means of political or social comment rather than part of the action.

MISTERO BUFFO

Mistero Buffo: Comic Mysteries is among the best-known and most popular of Fo's works outside Italy. It has been described as the culmination of Fo's research into popular culture. It consists of a series of texts developed over several years and divided into two sections. To the first part belong sketches such as "Bonifacio VIII," a merciless satire of Pope Boniface VIII, attacked by Dante in the *Inferno*, but Fo also alludes to Pope John Paul II. "La resurrezione di Lazzaro" is presented from the point of view of the crowd as a once-in-a-lifetime spectacle not to be missed; "La nascita del giullare" describes how a victimized, downtrodden peasant, about to hang himself, is stopped by Christ, who praises him for resisting the tyranny of the authorities and gives him the gift of telling stories so that he may share his experiences with others and encourage them also to resistance and revolt.

The second part comprises sketches such as "Maria viene a conoscere della condanna imposta al figlio," in which the Virgin Mary learns that the joyful crowds that she thought might be going to a wedding are in fact going to her son's crucifixion; "Gioco del matto sotto la croce" is a gruesomely comic sketch dealing with the difficulties of driving in the nails at the Crucifixion, and an aborted attempt by the madman to rescue Jesus from the Cross. The historical aspect of these *giullarate* is emphasized by Fo's introductions, complete with reproductions of ancient manuscripts or paintings; the contemporary message, on the other hand, is stressed by topical allusions that may change, if not always from one night to the next, at least over a period of weeks or months. The text is never definitive; it remains fluid. Fo is always responsive and flexible to dynamic interaction and intimate rapport with his audience.

Most of the texts are in a language that Fo describes as "fifteenth century Padano," an amalgam of various Northern Italian dialects. Fo adapts these dialects, sometimes modernizes them, and invents words, so that the language functions as a codified system of sounds. Furthermore, it was in *Mistero Buffo*, in some of the sketches, that Fo introduced what he calls "grammelot," a mainly invented language that uses some real or recognizable words. Thus, he has developed a French grammelot, an American grammelot, and so on. Although some of the grammelot sketches, such as "Il sogno dello Zanni" ("Johnny's dream," but also "the Zanni's dream," the Italian title meaning either or both), are among Fo's most famous performance pieces, they have been found to defy transcription or publication, as opposed to those sketches in dialect, which are published side by side with a translation into modern Italian. Fo ascribes the use of an amalgam of dialects, or of grammelot, as deriving from the itinerant nature of the *giullare*, who had to be understood by all the people wherever he went and who could not learn an unlimited number of dialects. Yet grammelot has the advantage of providing legal protection, inasmuch as it is, strictly speaking, a nonlanguage. In all of his plays, Fo makes use of nonverbal noises: In *Mistero Buffo*, belches, farts, and other uncouth sounds become an integral part of the text. The Chinese-inspired *The Tale of a Tiger*, *La giullarata* (which includes an essay concerning the origin of the *giullare*), and *Il fabulazzo osceno*, which is based on fabliaux, continue along the lines of *Mistero Buffo*.

ACCIDENTAL DEATH OF AN ANARCHIST

Almost equally well-known and popular in the English-speaking world is *Accidental Death of an Anarchist*, directly inspired by a headline event: the death, accidental or otherwise, of the anarchist Giuseppe Pinelli, supposedly responsible for the bombing of a bank in Milan in 1969 in which sixteen people were killed and some one hundred injured. Ostensibly, the play treats of the death, in 1921, of the anarchist, Salsedo, who "fell" out of a window while being interrogated by the police in New York, although characters within the play refer on more than one occasion to the "transposition": A character will confuse Milan and New York, Rome and Washington, then correct himself, excusing himself for having forgotten that the story has been "transposed." The central character is a madman (somewhat inaccurately translated into English as "maniac"), a favorite figure with Fo, since a madman, or simpleton, or fool, can speak unpalatable truths with impunity. Having been arrested for impersonation and taking money under false pretenses, the Madman proceeds to impersonate various figures of high authority, not only turning the police station topsy-turvy in the best farcical tradition but also bringing to light the corruption and the dishonesty of the authorities. This play, along with *Mistero Buffo*, is one of the best examples of Fo's flexible, living text, since the play developed and changed to keep up with the investigation into Pinelli's death. The various published versions of the play (three in Italian and two in English) reveal differences, some more significant than others. Although strongly political, the play is also highly farcical. Fo explains this in a postword to the 1974 Italian publication: "So painfully grotesque" did he and his company find the actions of the authorities, from the documents of the inquiry they were allowed to see. On the other hand, Fo has also criticized English-speaking productions for being so slapstick that the political element was lost in the madcap farce. The exact, careful balance of the two opposing elements of farce and political criticism lies at the heart of Fo's genius and artistic achievement.

WE CAN'T PAY! WE WON'T PAY!

Some of the themes of *Mistero Buffo*, such as hunger, poverty, and oppression, return in an updated setting in *We Can't Pay! We Won't Pay!* The play is based on happenings in Italy in 1974, when in various cities working people refused to pay rising prices in supermarkets, public transport, utility bills, and so on, limiting themselves to paying only what they considered a fair price. The structure is farcical, based on plot complications and reversals of situation. It has been described as Fo's "first feminine comedy" for the prominence it gives to the two women characters and the sympathetic treatment of the problems working women face while trying to run a household successfully and smoothly in the face of low wages and

rising prices. Stolen goods hidden under the women's skirts or inside a coffin, along with an unconscious constable stashed into a closet together with stolen loot, are among the farcical elements that provide the laughter in the play.

FO AND RAME COLLABORATIONS

Collaboration between Fo and Rame produced various monologues that she performed, collected under the title *Parliamo di donne*, produced for television in 1977, and *Female Parts* the following year. To some extent, these might be described as feminine *giullarate*, paralleling Fo's monologues. The Fos have also collaborated on a one-act play *An Open Couple—Very Open*, somewhat reminiscent of Edward Albee's *Who's Afraid of Virginia Woolf?* (pr., pb. 1962) in the tensions and conflicts that separate and draw together a husband and wife, although the problems involved are quite different. The two quarrel, insult each other, attack each other verbally and physically, and relapse into tenderness. Unlike Albee's play, however, that of Fo and Rame is basically a farce, although once again Fo has expressed dissatisfaction with foreign productions that stress the comedy element to the detriment of the tragedy, upsetting his own carefully contrived balance.

ABOUT FACE

About Face is based on the farcical device of mistaken identity. In dealing with the issues of terrorism and its possible connections with high finance and the Italian government, this play, more than others, shows a tendency to lengthy speeches and lectures. In spite of this weakness, as forceful political theater the play drew large audiences in Milan and has attracted a certain amount of attention abroad (in "adaptations," which have usually made a number of cuts).

L'OPERA DELLO SGHIGNAZZO

In 1981, Fo was invited by the Berliner Ensemble to adapt Brecht's *The Threepenny Opera* (1928) for a modern public. His version, however, proved to be too original and was rejected by those who had commissioned it. Fo himself claimed that he was following Brecht in spirit by showing disrespect for a "classic." At another time, he explained that Brecht utilized cabaret theater because it was linked to the

German popular tradition, stressing that any "epic" theater bases itself on its own popular tradition. As for what has become *L'opera dello sghignazzo*, Fo admitted that his play owes more to the original *The Beggar's Opera* (pr., pb. 1728) by John Gay than to Brecht's adaptation of it. Fo introduced many of his own concerns and preoccupations into the work. Peachum, for example, deals with visas for people from Africa and Asia and specializes in sickness benefits for false cripples and false drug addicts, while Mackie is an Italian Mafia-style gangster. Fo also introduces some of his own songs.

DIO LI FA E POI LI ACCOPPA

Terrorism, allied to corruption in high places, reappears in *Dio li fa e poi li accoppa* (God makes them and then kills them), in which an eminent surgeon, Professor Bernari, a drug addict, appropriator of government grants, and leader of one clique or band, has organized the terrorist-style assassination of another eminent doctor, a neurologist, leader of a rival organization, not knowing that there is a third rival organization trying to get him. Echoes of *An Open Couple—Very Open* return as the Professor's wife, rebelling against his jealousy, tries to affirm that what is sauce for the goose is sauce for the gander. The farce in this play derives from a slapstick operation onstage, as the Professor tries to deal with one of the hired killers who has been shot in the stomach; from a series of impersonations; and from a wild exchange of roles and personages. The political criticism is filtered through the farcical situation but is emphasized at the end, when most of the characters are about to murder one another, as the characters step briefly outside their roles to discuss what was or was not in the script, and which of them are worth saving.

THE POPE AND THE WITCH

In the 1990's Fo continued to satirically attack sacred cows in his monologues and plays. The church, the judiciary, authorities in power, and the government do not escape being targets. The nameless Pope in *The Pope and the Witch* sends for a specialist to cure him of his fear of children. With the specialist arrives a witch posing as a missionary nun who cures the Pope's phobia but not his arthritis. When the Pope is subjected to an overdose by drug dealers, he puts out an Encyclical urging the distribution of drugs at reasonable prices by all national governments with comic anarchy and Vatican confusion resulting. A political play imbued with anticlericalism, it essentially deals with the social problem of drugs and the question of whether solutions lie in police action or more enlightened policies that address the social causes of addiction and the needs of addicts. The Italian production was more successful than those in England and the United States.

MAMMA! I SANCULOTTI!

In *Mamma! I Sanculotti!*, Fo uses the French Revolution to draw a parallel between the eighteenth and twentieth centuries. On an operating table set up like a banquet table, a corrupt medical supervisor has authorized fearful doctors to operate. What ensues is a carousel of investigations conducted by both corrupt and respectable judges that dredges up allusions to the real perpetrators of state massacres, the obsessive collusion of the Mafia and terrorists with the Secret Service, and the disquieting political events of modern time. At the play's center is a characteristic Fo theme: the judiciary in conflict with the mendacity of those in power. Winning some critical approval, the play proved to be an inventive farce based on misunderstandings treating transvestism, absurd operations involving animal organ transplants, and significant political commentary.

THE DEVIL IN DRAG

In 1997 *The Devil in Drag* used situations from the comic theater of the Renaissance to evaluate the present from a historical perspective. A sixteenth century progressive magistrate investigates arson in a cathedral only to stumble on a sacrilegious theft that neither church authorities or prominent citizens wish examined. To discredit the honest magistrate, influential citizens employ devils to enter the magistrate to corrupt him. Misunderstanding, one devil enters the body of the magistrate's elderly housekeeper, transforming her into a delectable, busty lady who gets her drunken master into bed. There he is purposefully discovered *flagrante delicto* by authorities and put on trial for immorality but acquitted thanks to the aid of the she-devil. However, in a subsequent trial, he is accused of heresy and condemned to become a galley slave. Although critical reception was reserved, the drama farcically projected a Fo theme, the equation of corruption with power. Fo continues to be an internationally acclaimed political playwright whose widely performed plays use characteristics of traditional Italian theater to treat topical issues satirically. "My plays," says Fo, "are provocations, like catalysts in a chemical solution. When you want to know what elements a particular liquid is composed of, you put in another liquid, and perhaps the mixture turns blue, or it boils, or it changes. . . . I put some drops of absurdity in this calm and tranquil liquid, which is society, and the reactions reveal things that were hidden before the absurdity brought them out into the open."

OTHER MAJOR WORKS

POETRY: *Ballate e canzoni*, 1974.
SCREENPLAY: *Lo Svitato*, 1956.
NONFICTION: *Manuale minimo dell'attore*, 1987 (*The Tricks of the Trade*, 1991).

BIBLIOGRAPHY

Behan, Tom. *Dario Fo: Revolutionary Theatre*. Sterling, Va.: Pluto Press, 2000. Analysis and criticism of Fo's theatrical works. Bibliography and index.

Farrell, Joseph. *Dario Fo and Franca Rame: Harlequins of the Revolution*. London, Methuen, 2001. An examination of the collaboration between Fo and Rame, with emphasis on their political activities. Bibliography and index.

Farrell, Joseph, and Antonio Scuderi, eds. *Dario Fo: Stage, Text, and Tradition*. Carbondale: Southern Illinois University Press, 2000. Contains a comprehensive introduction and eleven well-selected essays treating the man and his work by respected Fo scholars. Particularly interesting are Bent Holm's discussion of Fo's plays and performances from 1957 to 1967, Walter Valeri's view of Fo as actor-playwright, and Antonio Scuderi's insight into Fo's use of adapting principles and techniques of ancient and medieval Italian comedy to a contemporary context. Includes photographs of Fo, three of his sketches, and an informative index.

Jenkins, Ronald Scott. *Dario Fo and Franca Rame: Artful Laughter*. New York: Aperture, 2001. A look at Fo and Rame as dramatists and the state of theater during the twentieth century in Italy. Bibliography.

Kushner, Tony. "Fo's Last Laugh—I, Fo's Last Laugh—II." *The Nation*, November 3, 1997: 4-5. Kushner rejects Vatican disdain for Fo as a Nobel Prize winner, finds Fo most worthy of the Nobel award, and praises his life of courageous political activism. Fo's stature as a performer, researcher, and playwright is specially admired.

Mitchell, Tony. *Dario Fo: People's Court Jester*. Rev. ed. London: Methuen, 1999. An examination of Fo's drama with emphasis on his political views. Contains a stage history, bibliography, and index.

Ada Coe,
updated by Christian H. Moe

DENIS IVANOVICH FONVIZIN

Born: Moscow, Russia; April 3, 1745
Died: St. Petersburg, Russia; December 1, 1792

PRINCIPAL DRAMA

Korion, pr. 1764, pb. 1769 (adaptation of Jean-Baptiste Gresset's play *Sidnei*)

Brigadir, wr. 1769, pr. 1780, pb. 1790 (*The Brigadier*, 1967)
Nedorosl, pr. 1782, pb. 1783 (*The Minor*, 1933)
Vybor guvernera, wr. 1790-1792, pb. 1830, pr. 1892 (*The Choice of a Tutor*, 1916)
Dramatic Works of D. I. Fonvizin, pb. 1974

OTHER LITERARY FORMS

In addition to his dramatic works, Denis Ivanovich Fonvizin produced letters, essays, and translations.

ACHIEVEMENTS

Denis Ivanovich Fonvizin's *The Minor* was, at its premiere, recognized as the first authentically Russian comic masterpiece in drama, and the play has never left the repertoire. It satirizes the ignorance of Russian country nobility, presenting Fonvizin's abiding convictions about a close connection between education, honest people, and good government. The playwright's earlier *The Brigadier* was the first Russian comedy of note to include realistic depiction of character and dialogue while transforming the conventional masks of neoclassical French comedy into Russian images satirizing social ills. The play also exposed to scorn the Frenchified Russians, victims of the pervasive mania for the Gallic of the late eighteenth century—a favorite topic of other Russian writers of the time. Fonvizin's active participation in Catherine's civil service made his attacks on stupid and brutal serf-owners resonate to the policy of the empress. Both *The Brigadier* and *The Minor* pleased the court of Catherine II with their didactic purpose while entertaining the audience with slapstick and wit adapted to the Russian scene and character.

Fonvizin contributed to the formation of the literary language of his time. While attacking the superficial French copied by Russian nobility in their subservience to French culture, he nevertheless incorporated French constructions into Russian speech, in the mouths of the educated characters in his plays. The names of these characters themselves brought into the language words drawn from French philosophy and cultural ideals. Fonvizin's language drew also from Church Slavic and from the diction of the court, and he contributed to an early dictionary of the Russian literary language, the *Academy Dictionary*. Quite apart from his impact on the literary language, Fonvizin contributed through his plays new words in Russian: A "Mitrofan" is still recognized in Russian as a lazy lout, and a "Prostakova" is still a word for a brutal shrew.

While Fonvizin's influence on Russian drama and theater was direct and strong in the last years of the eighteenth century, his continuing influence is more general in form. At the beginning of the nineteenth century, Alexander Pushkin admired Fonvizin but saw him as already a part of literary history. According to Charles A. Moser and K. V. Pigarev, the image of the man of intellect frustrated by the stupidity of the society that he tries to correct persists in Alexander Griboyedov's *Gore ot uma* (wr. 1824, uncensored pr. 1831, pb. 1861; *The Mischief of Being Clever*, 1857) in the character of Chatsky. These critics see Nikolai Gogol's setting and satiric approach to Russian small-town bureaucracy in *Revizor* (pr., pb. 1836; *The Inspector General*, 1892) as similar to Fonvizin's attack on country nobility. Critic Alexander Slonimsky sees more than a casual parallel in the mixture of farce and pity in treatment of character by these two playwrights.

Fyodor Dostoevski's rejection of the Western self-assurance of superiority mirrors Fonvizin's attitude in questioning in his plays the Russian self-abasement before European culture. The nineteenth century critic especially beloved in the Soviet period, Vissarion Belinsky, praised the lifelike reality of Fonvizin's work. Soviet critics of Fonvizin have emphasized the "critical realism" and the progressive tendency of his plays, as many nineteenth century critics focused on the satire of Francomania. The playwright elicited good biographies and critical works in the Soviet period. The interest in creating a new Soviet satire encouraged careful consideration of this indigenous Russian satirist.

BIOGRAPHY

Denis Ivanovich Fonvizin was born in 1745 into a family of middle nobility. His father, having retired from military service as a major, had a modest civil position in Moscow; Fonvizin's mother was from an older noble family. The Fonvizin family had entered Russia from Germany during the mid-sixteenth century and was thoroughly Russian by the time of Catherine, when Denis lived; he had to learn German in school. Unlike many Russian nobles, he learned French only as a young adult.

When he was ten, Fonvizin was one of the first admitted to the newly opened Moscow University, apparently at a preparatory level required to produce students ready for university education. His education gave him a taste for literature and equipped him for the government service he was to enter when he found a patron. An early trip to St. Petersburg (1760) took him to the imperial theater, where he saw a play by the Danish dramatist Ludvig Holberg. The experience triggered his enduring interest in drama; in 1761, he published a translation of a selection of moral fables by Holberg. The didactic element was in Fonvizin's work from the start. The writer improved his Russian literary style and his command of French and German with a variety of translation projects for university journals.

At seventeen, a common age for the sons of the nobility to enter service, Fonvizin got his first job in the civil service of the newly crowned Empress Catherine as a translator in the foreign office. Catherine's court was at the time briefly in Moscow, but when it returned to St. Petersburg in 1763, Fonvizin followed. Provided with personal servants for the first time, he read the work of the satirist Antiokh Kantemir, whose work, though written earlier, was published only in 1762. Under this influence, Fonvizin decided to write a humorous letter to his three servants. "Poslaniye k slugam moim Shumilovu, Vanke i Petrushka" (1763-1764; epistle to my servants Shumilov, Vanke, and Petrushka) was the result and circulated widely among freethinkers in St. Petersburg. It contained some of the first realistic and satiric observation of ordinary reality that appeared later in the playwright's major plays.

In October, 1763, Fonvizin obtained a patron in Ivan Perfilevich Yelagin, a supporter of Catherine and a man with literary and theatrical interests. In Yelagin's service, Fonvizin found himself in competition with Vladimir Lukin, a playwright of considerable talent. Lukin pressed for a thoroughly national drama; he put on stage some realistic Russian characters—a pawnbroker, for example—but he never achieved realistic speech for them. No love was lost between the two writers, and the young Fonvizin meanwhile cultivated friends among actors and actresses, especially the famous Ivan Dmitrevskii, who played in Aleksandr Sumarokov's tragedies. Fonvizin's duties with Yelagin allowed him, during the 1760's, to experiment with poetry and with further literary translations. He tried a verse translation of Voltaire's *Alzire* (pr., pb. 1736; English translation, 1763) but did not publish it, discovering that though he wished to write tragedy, his natural talent was for wit and satire.

The young man saw at this time productions of the neoclassical tragedies and comedies of Sumarokov, and he saw numerous productions of the lightweight French comedies translated by young noblemen of the capital. Fonvizin also translated such a play, *Sid nei*, by Jean-Baptiste Gresset; he called his Russian version *Korion*. Though moved to a Russian setting, the characters kept their French names. The play was staged in November, 1764, at the court theater, without much success. A brief scene between the valet Andrei and a peasant messenger had the breath of reality about it, but it was otherwise still in the Sumarokov style.

Fonvizin's life in fashionable St. Petersburg at this time gave him a world of observation that eventually found its way into his plays. His own upbringing had made Fonvizin dislike pretense, and he disliked the French-speaking Petersburg fops, with their blind adulation of French language and fashion and their contempt for anything Russian. Fonvizin, on the contrary, found much to admire in Russian life—for example, the intellectuals Mikhail V. Lamonosov and V. N. Titishchev. His father's influence gave him a strong sense of duty to his country. Encouraged by the theatrical interests of his superior, Yelagin, he decided to satirize these fops in a comedy. He would add figures that had not yet appeared on any Russian stage, the crude and petty nobility who lived in small towns and on their own estates, people of little education who had served mindlessly in the rigidly disciplined military until they retired with perhaps the rank of brigadier. Their wives were a match for them, barely literate, not knowing anything beyond household management. Fonvizin would add judicial bribe-takers to the satire, of whom he knew much from his father's experience as an honest judge among the dishonest. The comedy *The Brigadier* was the result.

Fonvizin read the play at Yelagin's house, and then in June, 1769, at Peterhof for the empress, who enjoyed the play. The twenty-four-year-old Fonvizin impressed everyone with the authenticity of his Russians on the stage.

It was at Peterhof that Fonvizin met Count Nikita I. Panin, head of Catherine's foreign office and the man entrusted with the education of Paul, Catherine's son, the heir apparent. Panin took this work with deep seriousness, hoping to mold the next tsar into an enlightened autocrat. He saw the relation of education to good government, and Fonvizin, in his work with Panin, added to his own already enthusiastic views on the importance of education. Panin chose Fonvizin as secretary, and the young man quickly became a close and valued associate.

One of the most powerful influences at Catherine's court, Panin was, however, already past the time of his greatest power when Fonvizin joined him. Panin's views on government coincided with and developed those that the young Fonvizin had been formulating, and the relationship with Panin colors all of Fonvizin's political views thereafter. Panin thought, for example, that the power of an autocratic ruler should be limited by law and by the advice of the most notable courtiers. Fonvizin served with Panin for fourteen years.

With the outbreak of war with Turkey in 1768, Panin's policies had come into doubt. As a result, Fonvizin, on beginning work with Panin, had no time for literature. The early 1770's involved peace negotiations with Turkey and the partition of Poland. Paul, the tsar-to-be, fell ill in 1772; on his recovery Fonvizin wrote a discourse on his recovery, asserting that all Russia rejoiced. In 1773, year of the Pugachev Rebellion so ruthlessly put down by Catherine, Panin lost his position as tutor to Paul, now legally of age and married. Catherine, as exit honors, gave Panin many gifts, and Panin shared her largesse with his assistants. Fonvizin received an estate in Byelorussia with 1,180 serfs, making him financially secure for many years. He never apparently became an ideal estate owner, however, and the estate was woefully mismanaged for Fonvizin as absentee landlord. The Pugachev Rebellion nevertheless had a big effect on Fonvizin's later work, influencing his darkest satire of the cruelty of landowners against peasants.

In 1774, Fonvizin married Ekaterina Ivanovna Khlopova, a former neighbor of the Fonvizins in Moscow. The couple lived well in St. Petersburg, began to collect art, and traveled abroad (1777-1778) for her health. They went to Germany and France, being entertained at Russian embassies but making a great effort to observe the local customs. In letters home, Fonvizin gave vivid accounts of his impressions. The letters provide, with real literary merit, his views on Europe. He was no blind admirer; he saw suffering and stupidity there as at home. His patriotism is apparent even when he is most impressed with the cultural achievements of the West.

Influenced by Panin, Fonvizin's other writing of this period directed itself more toward politics than literature. *Pokhvalnoye slovo Marku* (eulogy of Marcus Aurelius) in 1777, for example, his translation of a work by Antoine Thomas on how a ruler should rule, anticipates ideas that Pravdin uses in *The Minor*.

In the fall of 1778, Fonvizin, home briefly in Moscow, began to write *The Minor*. Russian theater had developed richly in the years since the writer had seen his first play; there were now two theaters in St. Petersburg and a permanent theater with a Russian troupe in Moscow. Sentimental dramas were becoming popular, and they required a more natural acting style than had been used in the declamatory work of Sumarokov's day. Comic operas, light musical plays with dancing such as those of Mikhail Matinskii, held the interest of the court audience with satiric images of merchants and others in everyday life—though no images of the nobility. Peasants onstage were ordinarily idealized; no one had as yet shown the crudity and cruelty of the provincial landowners.

The values Fonvizin had developed in Panin's service gave him more ideas and characterizations for his play. In 1779 the playwright translated *Ta-Gio* (*Ta-Hsueh: Or, That Great Learning Which Comprises Higher Chinese Philosophy*, 1966), a Chinese Confucian classic. (Fonvizin used a translation into French as the basis for his own work.) *Ta-Hsueh* argues that virtue is the root of all good and that there is no difference between a sovereign and the most humble of his subjects in the pursuit of virtue. The theme is that promulgated by Starodum in the play, which Fonvizin finished in 1782, having retired from government service. He read the play aloud in St. Petersburg noble houses, and Dmitrevskii, the longtime actor friend of the playwright, staged it and acted the role of Starodum. The performance took place in a private theater and was very successful with the audience; nevertheless, a production in Moscow was delayed by the Moscow censor until May, 1783.

Panin died in 1783. His former student, Paul, on taking the throne, seemed a real despot, ignoring Panin's enlightened instruction. Before his death, Panin, with Fonvizin's help, wrote but did not finish a statement of the changes he thought needed to be made in Russia. Fonvizin hid the manuscript, and this *rassuzhdeniye* (discourse) or *zaveshchaniye* (testament) circulated from hand to hand for many years and was printed only after the Revolution of 1905. Fonvizin retired in the spring of 1783, three weeks after Panin's death.

Ready to turn again to literature, Fonvizin began to contribute to the literary phenomenon of satiric literary journals, which began to appear in Moscow at this time. One was sponsored by Catherine herself; another, by N. I. Novikov, had already suffered censorship in 1770. A new journal, *Sobesednik lyubitel'yei rossiiskogo slova* (interlocutor of lovers of the Russian word), appeared. Fonvizin wrote for it witty Russian synonym studies with satiric thrusts. Catherine contributed to this journal anonymously. Aware of the imperial participation, Fonvizin had the idea to address a series of bold questions to the anonymous columnist. Catherine, as an enlightened despot, did not censor the questions but answered them in such a way as to preclude such questions in the future. Fonvizin wrote other satiric literary and linguistic papers during this period, including a bitter satire of flattery at the court, "Vseobshchaya pridvornaya grammatika" (1783-1784; "Universal Courtiers's Grammar," 1947). He also wrote an appreciative *Sokrashchennoye opisaniye zhitiya grafa N. I. Panina* (1784; a brief description of the life of Count N. I. Panin). The praise of his fallen hero was published anonymously, first in French in London and two years later in Russian.

The Fonvizins took a second trip abroad, this time to Italy, hoping to improve his health; he had long suffered from severe headaches. He needed money and planned to buy paintings and sell them on his return. This plan did not work out, and these years were full of financial as well as other troubles. His letters home again contained close observation of both the beauties and the deficiencies of Europe. He suffered a severe illness in Rome, recovered sufficiently to make the return trip, but in Moscow had a stroke that paralyzed his arm and leg and affected his speech. He never fully recovered. He made two further trips abroad for his health (1786-1787 and 1789). He attempted to start a new journal in 1788, but the police forbade its publication and it never appeared. He attempted a collection of his works, but that, too, was never realized. *The Choice of a Tutor*, another partially finished comedy, had little of his former strength. Aware that he was dying, he began a frank memoir, *Chistoserdechnoye priznaniye v delakh moikh i pomyshleniyakh* (1790-1792; a candid confession of my deeds and thoughts), but as he wrote, the work became a simple and vivid account of events and people who had meant much to him in his youth. The manuscript remained uncompleted, and Fonvizin died, only forty-seven years old, at the house of the poet G. R. Derzhavin on December 1, 1792.

ANALYSIS

Only *The Brigadier* and *The Minor* deserve systematic analysis here; Denis Ivanovich Fonvizin's main work in life as a diplomatic secretary in Catherine II's foreign office and the polemical writing emerging from that experience contributed to the content of the plays but limited his dramatic output. Some mention can be made of the unfinished third play, *The Choice of a Tutor*.

Fonvizin's plays were the first to present native Russian customs and speech successfully, a process that began in the eighteenth century to transform the common dramatic fare of the time, mainly French neoclassical drama. The transformation continued for a century. Earlier Russian dramatists in both tragedy and comedy had modeled their plays on neoclassical principles, often retaining French names for the characters, even when they had changed the setting to Russia.

The didactic impulse of eighteenth century comedy in France was very much a part of audience expectation and dramatic practice when Fonvizin wrote his plays. The characters were types—young lovers, the domineering father, the buffoon—deriving from earlier French drama and from still earlier Italian and Latin plays. The convention of the *raisonneur*, a wise character who comments on the implication of the dramatic events and states explicitly the message of the author, operated in these plays, too. Elements of the emerging sentimentalism found their way into the plays as well.

THE BRIGADIER

The Brigadier, written when Fonvizin was twenty-four years old, manipulates a situation comedy for plot but breaks new ground in its conception of character and in the speech of its *dramatis personae*. The action and characters satirize the Francomania of the Russian petty nobility, the brutality of military life, the stupidity of people without any real education, and the shallowness of morality among the country gentry. The play begins in a conventional setting of the provincial nobility: The Brigadier and his wife have brought their son, Ivan, to visit the family of Sofya, the girl they have arranged for him to marry. They intend to set the date for the wedding, but the course of the action becomes clear in the second line, with Ivan's response, in French, to this effort: "Hé-las!" No wedding between the two will take place, but crudely hilarious love intrigues must run their course before that happy ending can occur.

The Brigadier pursues the Councilor's wife, with whom he falls in love because she is so cultivated and intelligent compared with his own wife; and the Councilor pursues the Brigadier's wife because he is so impressed by her household economy. Ivan, however, also pursues the Councilor's wife rather than his intended fiancé, Sofya, because the Councilor's wife speaks French—and rhapsodizes over anyone who has ever lived in Paris. (Ivan has just returned.) The Brigadier, caught in the act of pursuing the wife of his host, is shocked to discover that his son is his rival for the boy's mother-in-law to be. In a roundly comic scene, the Councilor cannot make clear to the Brigadier's wife his proposal to have an affair with her, partly because she is so thickheaded and partly because she is in fact virtuous and unable to imagine herself as an object of desire.

Unlikely as the emotions of these people are, they set in motion scenes that keep the laughter of the audience ringing. Meanwhile, the conventional love interest between the heroine Sofya and her goodhearted officer Dobrolyubov makes good progress when they interrupt a love scene between Ivan and the Councilor's wife. Revelations all around resolve the dramatic problem; so many sins cancel each other out, and the visitors leave in shame—and disgust. Sofya's match with Ivan is broken off and Dobrolyubov gets his girl, especially since the legal problems holding up his inheritance have been settled. The speed with which the play moves gives the audience no time to think about how unlikely the action is.

The revelation of character in this merry-go-round, however, transforms the comedy. These are no sophisticated French couples frivolously pursuing amours. In accounting for the appetites they raise in each other, Fonvizin cuts deep, satirizing their distinctively Russian failings.

The Brigadier has been brutalized by his military life. The Councilor says of him, "Sometimes he loves his horse more than his wife." The rank of which he is so proud gives him control over his peasants, and his usual mode of communication is violent. He disciplines his wife with his fists, and that good lady recalls a Captain Gvozdilov's wife beaten more often than she. Tenderhearted Sofya asks her to stop telling about the wife beating. She answers, "You don't want to even hear about it, but what was it like for the Captain's wife who had to bear it?" Dostoevski later used the name Gvozdilov to refer to this kind of brutality.

The Councilor, a retired bribe-taking judge, grieves for the good old days when children obeyed their parents, not so many people were literate, and cases could be settled according to how much the judge was paid. He is a man willing to sacrifice his daughter's happiness for the property he expects to get from the marriage agreement. He loves the Brigadier's wife because she is as stingy with the peasants they own as he is with his. When he discovers that his wife is untrue, he swears not that he will beat Ivan for tempting her but that he will sue him for his last kopek.

The Councilor's idle, vacuous wife gets perhaps the worst of Fonvizin's scorn for the Frenchified Russian. When her Ivanushka tells her his only unhappiness is that she is Russian, she agrees, "That, my angel, is pure perdition for me!" Fonvizin's love of country underlies the contempt he pours on her. Ivan, as empty as she, is in fact a suitable mate for her; their pleasure in imitating the superficialities of French life is absurd to those, like Fonvizin, who have come to hate the Frenchified dandies of St. Petersburg who waste the proceeds of Russian labor on imported luxuries that are sent from France.

The force of the play lies especially in the language. First is the satire of the Russian use of French. Ivan and the Councilor's wife speak an amusing pastiche of Russian and French; they know only the small coin of the language. Second is the mispronunciation and failure to understand French by the Brigadier, and the total rejection of it by the Brigadier's wife. What the earliest audience of the play enjoyed most, however, was the richness of the Russian colloquial speech, tailored to the speaker, that the truly Russian characters speak. Russian proverbs abound; set phrases and pet turns of phrase mark the speaker. The Brigadier's wife's sympathetic, practical-minded innocence is caught perfectly in her language, for example. Fonvizin begins here the task of making natural Russian a dramatic language, a task to be mastered a century and a half later by Alexander Ostrovsky and, later still, by Anton Chekhov.

For all its excellence, *The Brigadier* nevertheless is psychologically shallow and unbelievable. These people would not in real life act the way they do onstage. Authentic members of the Russian lower nobility are caught in a trivial French plot, and they must be found inappropriate there, once the audience stops laughing. The positive characters lack shading to make them more believable. That is doubtless why

The Brigadier has had fewer productions than the second work of its author, *The Minor*.

THE MINOR

The Minor catches eighteenth century Russian culture at its worst and best, in all its bestiality side by side with its commitment to enlightenment and the honor of an "honest man," Fonvizin's measure of what a human being should be. Fonvizin's characters were designed to satirize the unenlightened country nobility and to encourage patriotism, the rule of law in the treatment of dependents, and the relation of education to virtue and the right use of authority, and their names have become part of the Russian language. For example, "Mitrofans" are ignorant boobies; "Skotinins" are men too swinelike to qualify as human; and "Prostakovas" are the virulent shrews who are nevertheless tender mothers, a lasting contradiction that appeals to the best and the beast in human beings everywhere.

The play is structurally very different from *The Brigadier*. The plot arises from actions that would become patterns in melodrama in the nineteenth century: the marrying off of an heiress, the return of a long-lost rich uncle, the maltreatment of an orphan, the timely arrival of the hero to save the heroine. The punishment of the villains comes about through the offices of a figure Gogol used later in *The Inspector General*, a government inspector secretly observing the action.

The ostensible main action is an eighteenth century cliché: arranging the marriage of the heroine. Barely motivated coincidence brings characters together at the moment they are needed. The whole is arranged with small care for conventional suspense because the inspector announces his presence (though not to the villains) in the first act, the hero gets the girl in a scene well before the end of the play, and the uncle makes his agency for good abundantly clear from the start.

All this matters little, however, because the real center of the action is the undoing of the villain, Prostakova, a domestic tyrant, a shrew, a brutal mistress—and the loving mother of her Mitrofanushka. This line of action has its ups and downs, but its movement nevertheless is not the focus of interest for

Fonvizin because the dramatist interrupts the main action repeatedly with long conversations that in fact are his main interest. The interest in theme can best be understood in a discussion of the characters.

The characterizations are the source of this play's greatness. The benighted ignorance and beastliness of Prostakova and her brother Skotinin come to symbolize the brutality of the unenlightened country nobility, the main subject of Fonvizin's satire. Both characters, while hilarious caricatures of human beings, cut deeply with their merciless self-interest and inhumanity displayed toward those in their power. They make the audience laugh, but they represent Fonvizin's didactic message more profoundly than the long and wise conversations between Starodum, Provdin, Milon, and Sofya, in which the message comes out directly.

Prostakova's confident verbal and physical abuse of everyone around her except her beloved son and those from whom she hopes to benefit brands her as a villain. Yet as Starodum points out, she is motivated by the single-minded love for her son, and when he, too, deserts her at the end of the play, one cannot help but feel pity. Her name, meaning "simpleton," allows for the contradiction. This ambiguity, and the very vigor of her personality, make her one of the great characters in Russian drama. Her husband is a mere postscript to her, a nonentity of a henpecked husband who has no opinion of his own, not even on whether his son's new coat is too big or too small. Little sympathy can be wasted on him.

Her brother Skotinin, perhaps the grossest caricature, and certainly the grossest character, carries farthest Fonvizin's attack on the beastliness of the unenlightened. Skotinin, whose name means "beastly," is a monomaniac about hogs. As he says himself, "men and women try to show me how clever they are, but among my pigs I am the cleverest one." He is interested in marrying Sofya solely to acquire more pigs. When it is suggested that he would not provide well for his wife, he indignantly makes clear that she would have as good a pen as any of his pigs.

Mitrofan (the name means "mother's son") is the petted darling of his profoundly ignorant mother; he becomes the symbol of the kind of human being that results from a pampered and unenlightened upbringing. Lazy, self-willed, and hostile to the education his mother has arranged for him, he has no principles, but lives solely for physical pleasures. He is greedy at table and, as the "minor"—a young man supposed to be studying to take on adult responsibility—he says, "I don't want to study; I want to marry."

Yeremeyevna, Mitrofan's old nurse, is a potent symbol of the victimization the Skotinins and Prostakovs practice. Held in constant fear by physical punishment—she gets "five roubles a year and five slaps a day"—she is nevertheless fiercely loyal to her charge, her loyalty repaid with contemptuous abuse. Her dignity as a human being hangs in the mind long after the comedy is over.

The qualities of the three incompetent tutors—Kuteikin, Cipherkin, and Vralman—summarize what Fonvizin wishes to criticize in the miseducation of the country nobility. Cipherkin is perhaps the best of the three, an "honest man," a retired soldier who has the barest knowledge of arithmetic; his knowledge is nevertheless far above Mitrofan's capacity to learn. In Kuteikin, an unsuccessful seminarist, Fonvizin satirizes the demi-educated churchman. Pious Church Slavonicisms permeate Kuteikin's speech, creating a comic effect onstage. His grasping nature and essential dishonesty are revealed when he pads his bill as Pravdin intends to pay him what the Prostakovs owe him. Vralman (liar) does Mitrofan's and Prostakova's will in frustrating the meager efforts of the other two tutors to educate Mitrofan, and he is a fraud, besides. A coachman in want of a job, he has convinced the Prostakovs that he is a learned and wise man. They are incompetent to recognize an authentic man of learning. As a teacher, he is a competent coachman, and Fonvizin allows him to return to his trade at the end of the play.

The positive characters voice the recommendations Fonvizin had to make to the court and responsible Russian nobility, the message based on his lifetime of service in government. In long, undramatic speeches, they simply stand and make the pleas for Russia's inprovement that Fonvizin had formulated over the years, especially under Count Panin's tutelage. Pravdin, the government inspector, brings the czar's justice to the brutal landlord Prostakova, in the rule of law. Starodum (old wisdom) praises patriotic duty and personal virtue even above education, though he makes clear that the virtuous man will also be educated. Sofya is a somewhat sickeningly sweet young woman who looks to her admired uncle for guidance, as a good ward should. She is obedient, capable of true love, generous in spirit. To modern ears, her echoing of the sentiments her uncle expresses is mildly repellent, but her forgiving spirit toward the Prostakovs when she gets free of them is winning. Milon, the young noble officer who wins her love, is not a credible character but an instrument Fonvizin uses to state his views on civil and military valor, as distinguished from mere courage in service to the fatherland. While all these speeches may have held the interest of contemporaries, and they often state values in memorable ways, these representatives of Fonvizin's ideals need strong acting to hold their own with the negative characters.

Fonvizin's themes are clear: Children should be obedient, and they should be educated with an eye to encouraging their virtue. Parents and rulers should be responsible, loving, and just. Teachers should be competent. Men and women should marry for love and accept their responsibilities. Flattery should not be the means by which people should acquire wealth. Justice should be done by the rule of enlightened law. Generosity of spirit should pervade human relations, and education should enlighten the rule of law. True nobility is of character, not birth or wealth. *The Minor* is the fruit of all Fonvizin's experience in Russian government and society, all that he wished to improve in a country he loved and deplored. It is a masterpiece not in its explicit messages, however, but in its richly comic caricatures of human evils as they appear in eighteenth century Russian guise.

THE CHOICE OF A TUTOR

The Choice of a Tutor, a three-act comedy of which the second act is incomplete, is one of Fonvizin's last works, written after his severe illness and partial paralysis. The play continues the dramatist's exploration of the importance of education and the satire of efforts by ignorant Russians to secure proper education for their children. The satire also directs itself to

ward pride in lineage preferred to true nobility. Prince and Princess Slaboumov (weak-minded) seek a tutor to encourage in their child a sense of their own self-importance because of their lineage. The choice includes an honest retired Russian officer, but the parents choose instead a fraudulent Frenchman, in fact a fugitive medical orderly. The traditional inauthenticity of Russian tutors persists. Long discussions between a sound local marshal of the nobility and the retired officer assess the impact of the French Revolution and reject the possibility of the social equality it supposes. The play was produced a century after it was written, in St. Petersburg, on the occasion of the centenary of Fonvizin's death.

OTHER MAJOR WORKS

NONFICTION: "Poslaniye k slugam moim Shumilovu, Vanke i Petrushka," c. 1763-1764; "Rassuzhdeniye o nepremennykh gosudarstvennykh zakonakh," c. 1780 ("A Discourse on Permanent Laws of State," 1966); "Vseobshchaya pridvornaya grammatika," 1783-1784 ("Universal Courtiers's Grammar," 1947); *Sokrashchennoye opisaniye zhitiya grafa N. I. Panina*, 1784; *Chistoserdechnoye priznaniye v delakh moikh i pomyshleniyakh*, 1790-1792; "Letters to Count P. I. Panin During His First Journey Abroad (Excerpts)," 1902; "Letters from My Second Journey Abroad," 1967; "Letters from My Third Journey Abroad," 1967.

TRANSLATIONS: *Basni nravouchitelnyya gospodina barona Golberga*, 1761 (of moral fables by Ludvig Holberg); *Pokhvalnoye slovo Marku*, 1777 (of Antoine Thomas's eulogy of Marcus Aurelius); *Ta-Gio*, 1779 (*Ta-Hsueh: Or, That Great Learning Which Comprises Higher Chinese Philosophy*, 1966).

MISCELLANEOUS: *Sobraniye sochinenii*, 1959 (2 volumes).

BIBLIOGRAPHY

Gleason, Walter. Introduction to *The Political and Legal Writings of Denis Fonvizin*. Ann Arbor, Mich.: Ardis Publishers, 1985. In this introduction to some of Fonvizin's prose works, Gleason describes the life of the Russian dramatist and his political and social views, which permeated his writings. Bibliography.

Kochetkova, Natal'ia Dmitrievna. "Denis Ivanovich Fonvizin." In *Early Modern Russian Writers, Late Seventeenth and Eighteenth Centuries*. Vol. 150 in *Dictionary of Literary Biography*, edited by Marcus C. Levitt. Detroit, Mich.: The Gale Group, 1995. A concise overview of the life and works of Fonvizin.

Moser, Charles A. *Denis Fonvizin*. Boston: Twayne, 1979. A basic biography of Fonvizin that covers his life and works. Bibliography and index.

_____. *Fonvizin, Russia, and Europe*. Washington, D.C.: Kennan Institute for Advanced Russian Studies, 1978. An examination of Fonvizin and Russia and Europe during the time in which he lived. Bibliography.

Offord, Derek. "Beware the Garden of Earthly Delights: Fonvizin and Dostoevskii on Life in France." *The Slavonic and East European Review* 78, no. 4 (October, 2000): 625-642. Offord takes the view that Fonvizin and Fyodor Dostoevski represent a continuous literary tradition and examines how each depicted France.

Martha Manheim

HORTON FOOTE

Born: Wharton, Texas; March 14, 1916

PRINCIPAL DRAMA

Wharton Dance, pr. 1939

Texas Town, pr. 1941

Out of My House, pr. 1942

Only the Heart, pr. 1942, pb. 1944

Homecoming, pr. 1944

The Chase, pr., pb. 1952

The Trip to Bountiful, pr. 1953, pb. 1954

The Traveling Lady, pr. 1954, pb. 1955

Horton Foote: Three Plays, pb. 1962

Gone with the Wind, pr. 1972 (based on Margaret Mitchell's novel)

The Orphans' Home, pr. 1977-1997, pb. 1987-1988 (a cycle of nine plays)

Night Seasons, pr. 1978, pb. 1993

Harrison, Texas, pr. 1985 (three one-act plays: *The One-Armed Man*, *The Prisoner's Song*, and *Blind Date*)

The Habitation of Dragons, pr. 1988, pb. 1993

Dividing the Estate, pr. 1989

Selected One-Act Plays of Horton Foote, pb. 1989

Four New Plays, pb. 1993

The Young Man from Atlanta, pr., pb. 1995

Laura Dennis, pr. 1995, pb. 1996

Collected Plays, pb. 1996

Getting Frankie Married—And Afterwards, pb. 1998, pr. 2002

"Getting Frankie Married—And Afterwards" and Other Plays, pb. 1998

The Last of the Thorntons, pr., pb. 2000

The Carpetbagger's Children, pr. 2001

OTHER LITERARY FORMS

Horton Foote's best-known works are the screenplays for such successful films as *To Kill a Mockingbird* (1962), *Tender Mercies* (1983), and *The Trip to Bountiful* (1985). Beginning in the early fifties, he also wrote numerous scripts for various television programs. His novel *The Chase* came out in 1956. In 1999, he published *Farewell: A Memoir of a Texas Childhood*, which was followed in 2001 by a sequel, *Beginnings: A Memoir*.

ACHIEVEMENTS

Along with the Academy Awards he received for his screenplays of *To Kill a Mockingbird* and *Tender Mercies*, Horton Foote won a Pulitzer Prize for his play *The Young Man from Atlanta* (1995). He was also nominated for an Oscar for his screenplay of *The Trip to Bountiful* and received an Emmy in 1997 for his adaptation of the William Faulkner story *Old Man.* His work has received numerous other awards, and in 1996, Foote was named to the Theater Hall of Fame.

BIOGRAPHY

Albert Horton Foote, Jr., was born in Wharton, Texas, on March 14, 1916. His family had significant connections in Texas history, his great-great-grandfather having been the first elected lieutenant governor of Texas. While attending high school in Wharton, Foote developed an interest in drama and played parts in several school plays. He decided to study acting, and though the Depression was well under way, he was given enough assistance by members of his family to take classes at an acting school in Dallas, and a year later, his father sent him to California to study at the Pasadena Playhouse. During his two years in Pasadena, he worked on his acting skills, and after seeing Eva Le Gallienne in a memorable performance of Henrik Ibsen's *Hedda Gabler* (pb. 1890; English translation, 1891), Foote resolved to pursue a career in the theater. After completing his second year in Pasadena, he accepted a friend's offer of summer work associated with a drama company in Martha's Vineyard, Massachusetts. After two months in Massachusetts, Foote moved to New York City, where he survived by getting occasional acting parts. A chance encounter with an old acquaintance led to his meeting Tamara Daykarhanova, Andrius Jilinsky, and Vera Soloviova, Russian exiles who taught acting, and from whom Foote began taking classes. Later, Foote joined several other students in forming the American Actors Company.

In 1939, Agnes de Mille suggested to Foote that he write a play. He wrote a one-act play titled *Gulf Storm,* which was produced as *Wharton Dance* by the American Actors Company and favorably reviewed by Robert Coleman. This production marks a significant mile-

stone in the career of Foote, whose career as playwright was to last more than sixty years and to include, by his own estimate, some sixty plays. He continued to play various theatrical parts with the American Actors and wherever else he could find work, but as his desire to write plays grew, his desire to act in plays diminished. He had already realized that in writing drama he could combine the world of his own past with the cosmopolitan world of the theater, and it is significant that he went home to Wharton, Texas, to write his second play *Texas Town.*

Shortly after the Japanese attack on Pearl Harbor in December, 1941, Foote's third play *Out of My House* was produced, and Foote prepared himself for the military draft. Somewhat to his shock, he was found by the medical examiners to have a hernia, which disqualified him. Foote found a job as a night-shift elevator attendant, which gave him time to

Horton Foote receives the National Medal of Arts from President Bill Clinton in 2000. (AP/Wide World Photos)

write. His play *Only the Heart* was produced in both 1942 and 1943. While working as manager of a bookstore, he met his future wife, Lillian Vallish, and the two were married in 1945. Foote continued to write, and, in the year of his marriage, he moved to Washington, D.C., where he was a principal figure in the formation of a new acting school and theater company. While in Washington, Foote taught drama and directed four of his own new plays, and he directed plays by Ibsen, Federico García Lorca, and Tennessee Williams. By 1949, however, he came to realize that he preferred to write as he had done before going to Washington. As he explains in *Beginnings*, "I felt I was a storyteller, and that I wanted to write plays simply and directly." In the fall of 1949, Horton and his wife returned to New York, where he found a position teaching at the American Theater Wing.

By this time, the development of television was producing new opportunities for actors and writers, and Foote's growing reputation led to his employment as writer for the new medium. He began writing for *The Gabby Hayes Show* in 1950 and soon was asked to write nine one-hour plays for television. He remained a writer of stage plays during this period. In 1956, he completed his first screenplay, an adaptation of Clinton Seeley's novel *Storm Fear*, and the film appeared that same year. Also in 1956, the Footes moved to Nyack, New York.

Although Foote remained busy in the 1950's, his next major career achievement was his successful screen adaptation of Harper Lee's novel *To Kill a Mockingbird* (1960), which had won a Pulitzer Prize. When the film was released in 1962, it won Oscars for both leading actor Gregory Peck and for Foote.

In 1971, Foote's stage adaptation of Margaret Mitchell's novel *Gone with the Wind* was produced in London. By 1974, he had begun the composition of what would eventually be a nine-play cycle collectively titled *The Orphans' Home*. By the late 1970's, Foote was again fully engaged with the stage, and though he wrote two television adaptations of short stories by Flannery O'Connor ("The Displaced Person") and William Faulkner ("Barn Burning") during this time, he was also teaching, directing, and writing. In the early 1980's, his plays continued to be pro-

duced, and Foote won his second Academy Award for his screenplay of *Tender Mercies* (1983). His 1985 screenplay for *The Trip to Bountiful* was also nominated for an Oscar. Foote began producing independent films based on some of his earlier plays, with *1918* appearing in 1985, *On Valentine's Day* in 1986, and *Courtship* in 1987. In 1988, he directed *The Habitation of Dragons* in its first version, with his daughter Hallie and his son Horton, Jr., among the cast.

Foote remained productive and professionally active through the 1990's, despite the death in 1992 of his beloved wife. In 1995, he not only received a Pulitzer Prize for his play *The Young Man from Atlanta*, but he was also honored by Brigham Young University, which held a festival of his works.

In 1999, he published his first volume of memoirs, dealing mainly with his family's past, the local history of Wharton, Texas, and the events that led to his departure to Pasadena to study acting. The second volume, which describes his life in Pasadena, New York, and Washington, appeared in 2001. Also in 2001, Foote's play *The Carpetbagger's Children*, with Jean Stapleton, Hallie Foote, and Roberta Maxwell, had its world premiere in Houston, Texas.

ANALYSIS

Like fellow southern fiction writers William Faulkner and Flannery O'Connor, Horton Foote derived much of his inspiration from his strong identification with a region he knew intimately. Also like Faulkner and O'Connor, Foote drew from his knowledge of local information a powerful sense of larger truths, particularly that of the human potential for spiritual nobility in the face of suffering. Unlike these authors, however, Foote does not allow the intensity of his perception to shape his art into the macabre, and he achieves his best effects with a certain lightness of touch that never reduces his work to triviality but instead magnifies the significance of casual things. Foote's mastery of the rhythms of conversation must be to some extent a product of his years of studying the art of acting, but many of those rhythms come from the endless conversations of his Wharton childhood. Because most of Foote's plays are set in Harrison, Texas, a fictional version of Wharton, the playwright's preoccupation with the past constitutes a significant element of his dramaturgic vision. A descendant of families who had established themselves in Texas in the nineteenth century, Foote was thirteen when the Great Depression struck. His father, a diehard Democrat, became an ardent supporter of Franklin Roosevelt, who was one of the principal advocates of political reform. Thus Foote, who, given his ancestry, might have joined many of his fellow southerners in resisting change, saw in his father an example of openness to change. His experience in California and in New York also gave him a better sense of some of the less laudable aspects of southern life in the middle third of the century. Combined with this wider perspective, however, was an abiding sympathy for the ordinary people who live in a town whose economy is at the mercy of the notoriously unreliable cotton harvest. Always important to Foote is the relation of the individual to family, to the community, to hardship, and to death.

ONLY THE HEART

Originally titled *Mamie Borden*, this play explores the relationships among the members of the Borden family. Mamie Borden, the central character, copes with life by controlling others, orchestrating a marriage for her daughter so as to maintain power over her. Mamie's machinations, however, only estrange Julia, who departs with her new spouse. Because Mamie's schemes of power have already alienated her husband, who has become unfaithful to her, Mamie finds herself finally isolated. This play bears an odd resemblance to Sophocles' *Antigonē* (441 B.C.E.; *Antigone*, 1729), if one considers the similarity of Mamie and Creon, each of whom allows a domineering spirit to annihilate the possible effect of good intentions. Foote's play, however, emphasizes the danger of dissociation of heart and mind in personal relationships.

THE TRIP TO BOUNTIFUL

An early play that Foote later adapted for the screen, *The Trip to Bountiful* embodies many of the themes and qualities essential to his best writing. The main character is Mrs. Watts, who lives with her son and his wife in an apartment in Houston. Her son, Ludie, is a hangdog loser who loves his mother but is dominated by his selfish and rude wife, who only tolerates her mother-in-law's presence because of her pension check. Mrs. Watts's dream is to escape to her old home place at Bountiful, a few miles from Harrison. The dynamics of this household are disturbing. Mrs. Watts shows occasional ominous signs of losing mental clarity, suggesting that the days of her life (and pension check) are numbered. Ludie realizes that he needs to make more money, but his helplessness is not promising. He cannot even defend his mother from the abusive comments of his wife. Jessie Mae herself would like to see Ludie bring in more money, but she is generally satisfied with the situation because she controls the pension check once it arrives. Her complaints mainly have to do with the inconvenience of having Mrs. Watts around. She particularly dislikes Mrs. Watts's habit of singing hymns.

When Mrs. Watts, who has hidden the month's pension check away for the purpose, escapes on the bus to Harrison, she finds that the friend with whom she has planned to stay, and who was the last person living in Bountiful, has died. The sheriff arrives, having received word of Mrs. Watts's escape from her family, and, moved by her despair, eventually drives her to her old home, where they await the arrival of Ludie and Jessie Mae from Houston. When the two arrive in a car Ludie has borrowed from a friend, Mrs. Watts and her son reminisce privately in front of the house. At first Mrs. Watts is made desperate by the imminent prospect of returning to Houston, but as she looks into her son's agonized face she puts her own grief aside, telling him: "I've found my dignity and my strength." Calmly accepting Jessie Mae's new rules for her future behavior, Mrs. Watts quietly says good-bye to Bountiful and walks away.

In this final scene, a number of themes come together. Ludie (whose name suggests that he is something of a joke) is the last of the family, and the play strongly suggests that he and his wife are to have no children. The neglected old family home, it is noted, will soon fall into the river. Ludie's predicament, like that of the house and of his mother, results from the country's shift from a rural, agricultural economy to the industrial economy of the city, where car brakes squeal at all hours and country people have trouble sleeping. Yet compassion exists, and Mrs. Watts's love for her son is still such that she renounces her own claims to happiness to end his suffering. In addition, there is the compassion of the sheriff, and that of Thelma, the young woman with whom Mrs. Watts rides the bus from Houston to Harrison.

Despite the annihilation of Mrs. Watts's fantasy of a return to the past, the end of the play finds her with a new resolve that makes her more admirable than the confused and desperate person she was earlier in the play, and it can even be argued that Ludie, who has after all come up with the gumption to ask for a raise and to borrow a car, is showing signs of resolve, particularly when he speaks very firmly to Jessie Mae at the end of the play.

THE ORPHANS' HOME

This cycle of nine plays represents Foote's engagement of creative imagination with the specific history of his family and region. Resulting to some extent from his meditations on the deaths of his parents, this cycle of plays explores and develops various dimensions of the cycle of birth and death, elaborating, as always, the potential of personal relationships to fulfil or frustrate those involved in them. *Roots in a Parched Ground*, the first in the sequence, had been written before Foote decided to write the cycle, but the other plays were written in what seems to be an expanded variation of the early Athenian trilogy or the Shakespearian tetralogy.

OTHER MAJOR WORKS

LONG FICTION: *The Chase*, 1956 (adptation of his play).

SCREENPLAYS: *Storm Fear*, 1956 (adaptation of Clinton Seeley's novel); *To Kill a Mockingbird*, 1962 (adaptation of Harper Lee's novel); *Tomorrow*, 1972 (adaptation of William Faulkner's short story); *Tender Mercies*, 1983; *The Trip to Bountiful*, 1985 (adaptation of his play); *Of Mice and Men*, 1992 (adaptation of John Steinbeck's novel).

NONFICTION: *Farewell: A Memoir of a Texas Childhood*, 1999; *Beginnings: A Memoir*, 2001.

BIBLIOGRAPHY

Briley, Rebecca. *You Can Go Home Again: The Focus on Family in the Works of Horton Foote*. New York: Peter Lang, 1993. Based on Briley's 1990 doctoral dissertation from the University of Kentucky, this study provides useful information about the importance of family in Foote's plays. However, Briley was not able to obtain access to some important resources that are now available, and her work, though helpful, suffers somewhat from excessive reiteration of her thesis.

Moore, Barbara, and David G. Yellin, eds. *Horton Foote's Three Trips to Bountiful*. Dallas: Southern Methodist University Press, 1993. This work compares the alterations and revisions made in the successive versions of *The Trip to Bountiful* between the first 1953 version and the film version of 1985. Changes in the texts are set forth in a chart, and there is a useful bibliography.

Porter, Laurin R. "An Interview with Horton Foote." *Studies in American Drama, 1945-Present* 6, no. 2 (1991): 177-194. A 1988 interview with Foote, covering his tastes in literature, his development and training as actor and playwright, and the background of *The Orphans' Home* cycle. This interview gives the reader a good sense of Foote's conversational style, his humor, and his modesty.

Wood, Gerald C. *Horton Foote and the Theater of Intimacy*. Baton Rouge: Louisiana State University Press, 1999. Wood argues that Foote's dramas reflect his characters' struggles against fear, struggles that are often made victorious by the achievement of a personal intimacy made possible by a spiritual feminine presence. Well written and persuasive, this work also includes a splendid bibliographical appendix of materials for those working on Foote's plays, screenplays, and teleplays.

Wood, Gerald C., ed. *Horton Foote: A Casebook*. New York: Garland, 1998. Contains twelve articles by various critics, divided into three main categories: "Biographical/Contextual Essays," "Perspectives on Style/Themes," and "The Signature Theater Series." Includes a chronology of Foote's life, a bibliography of his works, an annotated critical biography, and an index.

Robert W. Haynes

SAMUEL FOOTE

Born: Truro, England; January 27, 1720 (baptized)
Died: Dover, England; October 21, 1777

PRINCIPAL DRAMA

The Diversions of the Morning, pr. 1747-1754
   (series of vaudeville sketches)
The Auction of Pictures, pr. 1748
The Knights, pr. 1749 (revised, pr., pb. 1754)
Taste, pr., pb. 1752
The Englishman in Paris, pr., pb. 1753
The Englishman Returned from Paris, pr., pb. 1756
The Author, pr., pb. 1757
The Minor, pr., pb. 1760
The Liar, pr. 1762, pb. 1764
The Orators, pr., pb. 1762
The Mayor of Garratt, pr., pb. 1763
The Patron, pr., pb. 1764
The Commissary, pr., pb. 1765
The Tailors, pr. 1767, pb. 1778
The Devil upon Two Sticks, pr., pb. 1768
The Lame Lover, pr., pb. 1770
The Maid of Bath, pr., pb. 1771
The Nabob, pr. 1772, pb. 1778
The Handsome Housemaid: Or, Piety in Pattens,
   pr. 1773 (as *Piety in Pattens*)
Primitive Puppet Shew, pr. 1773
The Bankrupt, pr. 1773, pb. 1776
The Cozeners, pr. 1774, pb. 1778
The Trip to Calais, pr. 1775, pb. 1778
The Capuchin, pr. 1776, pb. 1778 (revision of *The
   Trip to Calais* with new last half)
Dramatic Works, pb. 1929 (M. M. Belden, editor)

OTHER LITERARY FORMS

Although Samuel Foote is known chiefly for his dramatic works, he wrote several critical essays and letters and translated a French comedy. His *The Roman and English Comedy Consider'd and Compar'd* (1747) and *A Treatise on the Passions* (1747) are well written and sound, but they are short and reflect traditional, conservative Augustan literary and dramatic criticism. *A Letter from Mr. Foote, to the Reverend*

Author of the *"Remarks, Critical and Christian,"* on *"The Minor"* (1760) and *Apology for "The Minor"* (1771) are significant because in them Foote delineates his critical ideas concerning affectation, hypocrisy, comedy, farce, the humorist, and the man of humor. Foote's thinking as presented in these two essays is strikingly similar to Henry Fielding's ideas on these topics as stated in the famous preface to *Joseph Andrews* (1742). Several of Foote's prologues and prefaces, such as the preface to *Taste* and the preface to *The Minor*, are critically important for their discussions of the aims and purposes of his satires. (The prologue to *Taste* that was written and spoken by actor David Garrick seems also to present some of Foote's views.) Foote's *The Comic Theatre, Being a Free Translation of All the Best French Comedies, by Samuel Foote and Others* (1762) was an ambitious undertaking, and although he wrote the preface for it, he translated only one play, *The Young Hypocrite*, leaving "the others" to translate the remainder of the five volumes.

ACHIEVEMENTS

In his time, Samuel Foote was known as the English Aristophanes, a sobriquet originally used by the opposition in a libel suit but one that stuck because of Foote's dramatic satires of living persons and of contemporary scandals. G. H. Nettleton has described Foote as Henry Fielding's direct descendant, because he fully developed the latter's personalities, localized mimicry, and contemporary satire. In formulating his comic theory, Foote emphasized the corrective purpose of comedy, whose ridicule he considered to be more effective than law or reason in combating folly and vice. There were indeed times when Foote's satire achieved this purpose. When Foote played Lady Pentweazel in his comedy *Taste*, for example, he wore a huge headdress made with large, loose feathers that fell off his head to litter the stage throughout the play. His ridicule of the absurd hats then in vogue was credited with reforming this extreme fashion.

Perhaps Foote's greatest achievement was breaking the monopoly of Drury Lane and Covent Garden, the only two theaters in London that had official permission to produce plays and that did so primarily during the winter, when the social season was at his height. Foote made significant strides in breaking this monopoly when he evaded the 1737 Stage Licensing Act by advertising his performances not as drama but as entertainments, scheduling them for early in the day, and describing them under various names such as *The Diversions of the Morning*, *The Auction of Pictures*, "a dish of chocolate," or "an invitation to a dish of tea." None of these had a set content but instead contained combinations of successful old material, reworked material, and new material based on the latest social and political gossip. The result of Foote's "diversions," according to Simon Trefman (in his 1971 book on Foote), was the first theatrical matinee.

Foote finally broke the monopoly when the king awarded him a summer patent to the Haymarket Theatre that allowed him to operate between May fifteenth and September fifteenth of each year. Foote's resourcefulness and energy were tremendous, and so was his success. He wrote, produced, and directed his plays and, for most of the season, played the leading roles in them. Most of his plays enjoyed long runs, commanding large audiences not only at his establishment but elsewhere. *The Englishman in Paris*, for example, became part of the repertoire at Drury Lane and Covent Garden and was regularly played for more than twenty years. In addition, Foote was able to give steady employment to almost fifty actors during each season and to run his performances for fifty to sixty nights. Trefman claims that no one else in the history of English theater had ever drawn such crowds by the sheer power of satiric invention.

Foote was interested in new and experimental theatrical devices. The framing techniques he used in *Taste* and *The Orators* provided both unity for the segments that made up the pieces and a plausible explanation for poor and inexperienced performers, with whom they might be staged. He also experimented with puppets in his *Primitive Puppet Shew*. Foote's performances were successful not only in England but also in Ireland and Scotland.

Biography

Samuel Foote, although he receives very little attention today, was one of the leading playwrights, actors, and theater managers in mid-eighteenth century England. Foote's father was an attorney and magistrate who served as mayor in Truro, Cornwall, as Member of Parliament for Tiverton, as commissioner of the Prize Office, and receiver of fines. His mother was Eleanor Dinely Goodere, the daughter of baronet Sir Edward Goodere of Hereford.

Samuel was the youngest of three sons. The oldest son, Edward, was trained as a clergyman but was unable to support himself financially and depended on Samuel. There is very little recorded about the second son, John.

Foote attended Truro Grammar School and, in 1737, entered Worcester College, Oxford, whose founder, Sir Thomas Cookes, was related to the Foote family. During his tenure at Oxford, Foote is said to have become a competent Greek and Latin scholar. He was an undisciplined student, however, and his frequent unauthorized absences led the College to disenroll him on January 28, 1740.

After leaving Oxford, Foote entered London's Inner Temple to study law, but he soon left to replenish his depleted fortune. On January 10, 1741, he married Mary Hicks, an old acquaintance from Truro. After spending her dowry, Foote neglected and deserted her. This marriage produced no children, but Foote's will mentions two sons, Francis and George. Scholar Trefman suggests that these children were the result of a short-lived liaison between Foote and one of his servants.

Foote made his first appearance as a professional actor on February 6, 1744, at the Haymarket Theatre in the role of Othello. Foote's forte, however, was not tragedy but comedy and impersonation. Foote mimicked many of the luminaries of his day, including Charles Macklin, Thomas Sheridan (father of playwright Richard Brinsley Sheridan), David Garrick, Arthur Murphy, and Henry Fielding. This comedic flair marked his private life as well, and he was a noted conversationalist. Even Samuel Johnson found Foote's humor attractive, observing "He has wit too, and is not deficient in ideas, or in fertility and variety

Samuel Foote (Library of Congress)

of imagery . . . he never lets truth stand between him and a jest, and he is sometimes mighty coarse."

Foote had friends at court, including the duke of York, although these relationships often seemed to be troublesome rather than advantageous. His lifelong connection with wealthy, handsome, socialite Francis Blake Delaval, for example, did lead to many high times at Delaval's family seat. However, when Delaval commissioned Foote to facilitate the marriage between a supposedly wealthy elderly widow, Lady Isabella Pawlett, and Delaval, the result was strikingly similar to a stage farce: legal battles, social scandal, and very little money for either Foote or Delaval—most of Lady Isabella's wealth proving to be part of an irrevocable trust for her daughter. Another scheme—in which Foote and some demimondaines were to accompany Delaval and Sir Richard Atkins on a yacht trip to Corsica and help Delaval secure the vacant throne of that country—ended in the death of Sir Richard.

The temptations of high-living friends with money to waste led to other problems for Foote. Although he worked hard, was a prolific playwright, and was much in demand as an actor, debts plagued him for most of his life. A low point was reached in 1742, when he was imprisoned for nonpayment of debts, having been charged by creditors ranging from his mother to Lady Viscountess Castlecoma. The passage of a bill for the relief of insolvent debtors led to Foote's release, but although his economic difficulties were never to become that acute again, they never entirely disappeared.

Foote traveled often for both work and recreation. It became habitual for him to travel to Dublin and Edinburgh to act, and he regularly spent his holidays in Paris. His trips to Paris inspired *The Englishman in Paris* and *The Englishman Returned from Paris.*

Foote's strongest competition as a theater manager came from the licensed winter theaters, Drury Lane and Covent Garden. In order to make a living, Foote rented and managed the Little Theatre in the Haymarket during the summer months—an insecure undertaking because he did not have legal permission to operate his theater. There he began what came to be a wildly popular form of entertainment consisting of imitations of various actors and celebrities and satiric sketches loosely grouped in programs that were commonly called *The Diversions of the Morning.*

This situation changed in 1765 as a result of a sad accident. While visiting the aristocratic Lord and Lady Mexborough, Foote's friends teased him into claiming that he was a good horseman. In backing up this false claim, Foote mounted the duke of York's spirited horse and was thrown immediately. The hard fall shattered Foote's leg in several places and the duke's personal physician had to amputate it. Feeling guilty for his role in this affair, the duke used his influence to obtain for Foote the summer patent rights to the theater, a patent good for the remainder of Foote's life.

In 1767, Foote bought and refurbished the Haymarket Theatre. He successfully managed it and played most of the lead roles or acted in the afterpieces until 1776, when George Colman was finally able to rent the patent from him. Several times before this, Foote had contemplated retiring and leasing his theater rights, but his reluctance to give up his extremely favorable position in the theater world had always made him reconsider. He only gave the lease to

Colman because of the mounting pressure of a battle Foote was waging against the duchess of Kingston, the last and perhaps most disastrous lawsuit resulting from Foote's habit of satirizing persons involved in contemporary scandals. (An earlier lawsuit over Foote's lampoon in *The Orators* of the one-legged Dublin printer George Faulkner had been won by Faulkner.)

The duchess of Kingston, the one-time countess of Bristol, had begun life as Elizabeth Chudleigh. While Chudleigh was maid of honor to the princess of Wales, she met and married the heir to the earl of Bristol—in secret, so that her standing at Court was not jeopardized. A few years later, she found a man she preferred, the wealthy and elderly duke of Kingston. Becoming the duchess involved a series of shady legal maneuvers, but the transfer was accomplished; after the duke's death, however, the duchess was indicted for bigamy and her trial became the focus for gossip in the highest social circles.

Almost inevitably, Foote made the duchess's greed and hypocrisy the subject of a satire, *The Trip to Calais*, enraging the duchess. She retaliated by using her connections to prohibit the play's continued production. Foote did rewrite the play, with a new second act, as *The Capuchin*, but the duchess and her supporters were not appeased. A newspaper war ensued. One of Chudleigh's hangers-on, William Jackson, editor of *The Public Ledger*, bribed a servant whom Foote had discharged, John Sangster, to sue Foote for homosexual assault, and covered the matter extensively in his scandal sheet.

When the matter finally came to trial, the charge was found to be totally unsubstantiated, and Foote was acquitted. Although Foote appeared in forty-nine mainpieces and twenty-six afterpieces while awaiting trial, the most acting he had done since the loss of his leg, after the verdict was rendered he began to suffer from recurring seizures. In order to rebuild his health, Foote started for Paris, but he died en route at the Ship Inn at Dover. On October 27, 1777, his friends buried him in Westminster Abbey.

ANALYSIS

Samuel Foote developed his theory of comedy over a fifteen-year period in several critical works.

According to Foote, the main purpose of comedy is to correct vice and folly by ridiculing them while pleasing and delighting the imagination. By representing fashionable foibles and extravagant humors, comedy teaches people to avoid folly. Foote's comic design was to amend the heart, improve the understanding, and please the imagination. In his *A Letter from Mr. Foote*, Foote outlined the requirements of comedy: Comedy should be true to nature; it must represent exactly the peculiar manners of a people; it must faithfully imitate singular absurdities and particular follies. Comic imitation and representation provide an example to the entire community.

Foote himself likened his comic-satiric method to that employed by Aristophanes, William Shakespeare, Molière, John Dryden, Alexander Pope, Jean de La Bruyère, and Nicolas Boileau. For Foote, character was the greatest comic requisite, and his definitions of two comic character types—the "humorist" and the "man of humor"—constitute his major contribution to comic theory. According to Foote, the humorist possesses some internal disposition that makes him say or do absurd and ridiculous things while firmly convinced that his actions are correct and acceptable. Foote's man of humor is the pleasant person who enjoys the humorist's eccentricities or affectations and exposes them.

TASTE

Foote's plays *Taste* and *The Orators* exemplify his comic method, although an analysis of any of Foote's plays must necessarily be incomplete since it depends on the printed version, while almost every performance was different. *Taste* was first produced at Drury Lane on January 11, 1752. Foote's target in this play was the booming art market of the time, the notoriously ignorant and gullible society poseurs who craved antiques and works of old masters only because of the current fad, and the dishonesty of dealers and auctioneers who preyed on them. The play, staged only five times during the 1752 season, was a failure because, according to the critical judgment of the day, the audience lacked taste and did not understand the method or objectives of Foote's satire. Foote's satiric approach was high burlesque. In order to appreciate high burlesque, an audience must be aware of certain standards of true taste and judgment and therefore be able to recognize the discrepancy between these standards and the pretensions of the characters in the play. Audiences who were devoted to a similar mad pursuit of trends were unlikely to appreciate Foote's humor on the subject.

Foote's theory of taste is similar to the theories of the leading formulators of a standard of taste in the eighteenth century such as David Hume, Edmund Burke, Sir Joshua Reynolds, James Beattie, Oliver Goldsmith, and Joseph Addison. All held the same fundamental requisites to a standard of taste: sensibility, imagination, judgment, education, common sense, morality, and objectivity. In *Taste*, Foote develops these principles by exhibiting the follies of people who lack these requisites. Foote's "connoisseurs," Lord Dupe, Novice, Lady Pentweazel, Squander, and Sir Positive Bubble, are so overcome by the fashionable craze for mutilated objects that are promoted as antiques, for foreign artworks, and for foreign artists that what little intellect they may have suspends operation.

Foote, in the preface to *Taste*, presents his views on education and morality as necessary to a standard of taste. He says that he is determined to satirize the barbarians who have prostituted the study of antiquity to trifling superficiality, who have blasted the progress of the elegant arts by unpardonable frauds and absurd prejudices, and who have vitiated the minds and morals of youth by persuading them that what serves only to illustrate literature is true knowledge and that active idleness is real business.

In the context of the play itself, the virtuosi do not know art. Lady Pentweazel thinks that the *Mary de Medicis* and the *Venus de Medicis* were sisters in the Medici family instead of paintings. Novice and Dupe think that they can evaluate the age and worth of a coin or medal by tasting it. Puff, the auctioneer, is able to convince Dupe, Novice, and Sir Positive that broken statuary and china are more valuable than perfect pieces. Lord Dupe demonstrates a complete lack of common sense when he purchases a canvas that has all the paint scraped off it. Carmine, Puff, and their associates even convince the dupes that a head from Herculaneum dates from before the biblical account of the Creation.

Satire is invariably based on human foibles evident in the time in which it is written, but in good satire, such as that of Aristophanes, the point being made is more widely applicable. *Taste* reflects conditions that existed in Foote's day, but its humor is generalizable not merely to any era in which works of art are bought and sold by fashionable and ignorant collectors; it also has something to say about the way in which people come to be so easily misled, no matter what the issue or era.

THE ORATORS

The Orators, a three-act comedy that presented different aspects of another currently fashionable preoccupation, was first produced on Wednesday, April 28, 1762, in Foote's Haymarket Theatre. Unlike *Taste*, *The Orators* was highly successful, appearing thirty-nine times in the first year.

The Orators is a framed play. In the printed version (as was the case with many of Foote's plays, the staged version varied from one performance to the next), this play consists of three parts. The first is a long satire on oratory, the second is a mock trial of the Cock-Lane ghost (introduced so that students at Foote's onstage oratory class could practice judicial oratory in the trial of a currently notorious apparition), and the third features amateur debating clubs such as the Robin Hood Society. The parts are united by the four or five principal characters that appear in each, not by plot, because there is none—even within the individual parts.

Originally advertised as "A Course of Comic Lectures on English Oratory," the play is set in a theater. Harry Scamper and Will Tirehack, two Oxford dandies looking for amusement, enter, seat themselves in a side box, and after questioning the candle-snuffer about what the lectures will contain, call for the theater's manager, Mr. Foote, played by the author himself. They want him to assure them that they will be amused. From a box on the other side of the stage, Ephraim Suds, a soap-boiler, wants reassurance that the lectures will be educational—that he will learn to give speeches. Foote declares that both needs will be met. In the course of his explanation, it is revealed that Foote operates a school of oratory guaranteed to train even the most burr-tongued Scotsman to be a golden-throated speaker. This prepares the way for the introduction of the other major character, Donald, a young Scot with a broad accent.

After the opening lecture on the principles of oratory, Foote allows his "students" to practice what they have learned in various professions and situations. This framework provides not only unity but also an excuse for poor performers. In one scene, the actors are merely beginning students, in another they are rehearsing. This device enabled Foote to use a series of less skilled (and less expensive) actors and to vary lines on short notice without in any way diminishing the humor of the play.

Foote wrote *The Orators* primarily to satirize the British Elocutionary Movement and its leader, Thomas Sheridan, whose success as an actor gave weight to his pronouncements on delivery. From the days of the early Greeks, rhetoric had been regarded as possessing five aspects: *inventio, dispositio, elocutio, pronuntiatio,* and *memoria* (or discovery of a thesis, arrangement of argument, style, delivery, and memory). It was the belief of more conservative rhetoricians of Foote's day that Sheridan had devalued rhetoric by extending Cicero's definition of *pronuntiatio* and making it seem that it was the whole of the art of ancient rhetoric rather than merely one of five parts, and a lesser one at that.

Foote gives a good picture, though satirized and therefore exaggerated, of the tenets of Sheridan's elocutionary theory in act 1 of *The Orators*. At the beginning of his lecture, he refers to Sheridan's *Lectures on Elocution* (1762), which delineates Sheridan's plan "to revive the long-lost art of oratory, and to correct, ascertain, and fix the English language." To achieve these goals, Sheridan wanted to establish an academy, but the institution had to be structured on his plan alone. Foote ridicules Sheridan's egocentrism by saying that he (Foote) wants to be made perpetual professor of his own academy.

Foote mimics Sheridan's intention to "correct, ascertain, and fix the English language" in the character of Ephraim Suds, who has just finished taking Sheridan's course of oratory. Suds has learned little from Sheridan's teaching, for he mispronounces words, such as "empharis" for "emphasis," and speaks ungrammatical English.

Sheridan not only believed his academy could perfect the English language but also envisioned his school as an Irish center for the study of correct English speech, and he thought that students would flock to it from Scotland, Wales, America, and the other British colonies abroad, in order to correct provincialisms in speech. Foote satirizes these ideas by demonstrating the effects of Sheridan's education on Donald, a Scottish orator who has studied for one year under Sheridan and six weeks under Foote. Donald continues to speak with a heavy Scottish accent and uses dialectal diction that Scamper and Tirehack cannot understand.

Foote also uses Donald to satirize Sheridan's emphasis on pronunciation—his belief that a good orator could, by following proper accents, read a work he did not understand. In an exaggerated paraphrase of Sheridan's discussion of pronunciation, Donald contradicts the ancient rhetoricians Demosthenes and Cicero, who called delivery the fourth rather than the first part of oratory. Scamper and Tirehack notice the contradiction and complain. Again, Foote attacks Sheridan and the Elocutionists for their emphasis on voice and gesture to the exclusion of the other four major procedures in rhetoric.

Donald becomes furious at Scamper and Tirehack's correction, and they tell him that he must tell the truth. Donald replies that he can tell the truth "logically," satirizing internal or artistic proofs which are based not on empirical evidence but on probability. The Elocutionists wanted to persuade and to win debates through a grandiloquent style, and they did not care about truth; they excluded from rhetoric considerations of subject matter and arrangement of argument and thereby reduced it to style, voice, and gesture alone.

Foote suggests a motto for a treatise that Sheridan planned to write. He adds, however, that Sheridan is probably already well provided with an apt Latin or a Greek one. Here, Foote's comment is most likely a strike at Sheridan's greatest shortcoming, his total inability to understand the Greek and Latin rhetoricians from whom he quoted so often, and the consequential diminishing of ancient oratory.

Although today his work is known only to specialists, Foote's colorful and successful theatrical career offers rich insights concerning the practical exigencies and the underlying values of the eighteenth century English style.

OTHER MAJOR WORKS

NONFICTION: *The Roman and English Comedy Consider'd and Compar'd*, 1747; *A Treatise on the Passions*, 1747; *A Letter from Mr. Foote, to the Reverend Author of the "Remarks, Critical and Christian," on "The Minor,"* 1760; *Apology for "The Minor,"* 1771.

TRANSLATION: *The Comic Theatre, Being a Free Translation of All the Best French Comedies, by Samuel Foote and Others*, 1762 (with others).

BIBLIOGRAPHY

Chatten, Elizabeth N. *Samuel Foote.* Boston: Twayne, 1980. Chatten focuses on a discussion of Foote's dramatic works and essays on drama, evaluating them in the light of social history. She describes him as a witty social satirist who resides firmly within eighteenth century literary tradition. Chronology, annotated bibliography, and index.

Freeman, Terence M. "Best Foote Forward." *Studies in English Literature, 1500-1900* 29, no. 3 (Summer, 1989): 563. A personal profile of Foote, emphasizing his importance as an ironic satirist.

Kinservik, Matthew J. "The Censorship of Samuel Foote's *The Minor* (1760): Stage Controversy in the Mid-eighteenth Century." *Studies in the Literary Imagination* 32, no. 2 (Fall, 1999): 89-104. Kinservik argues that Foote benefited from the censorship of *The Minor*, a satiric anti-Methodist play.

Lamb, Susan. "The Popular Theater of Samuel Foote and British National Identity." *Comparative Drama* 30, no. 2 (Summer, 1996): 245. Lamb relates Foote's satires in his plays to the changes that were taking place in the England of the time. Examines *The Englishman in Paris* and *The Englishman Returned from Paris*, among others.

Murphy, Mary C. *Samuel Foote's "Taste" and "The Orators": A Modern Edition with Five Essays.* Annapolis, Md.: U.S. Naval Academy, 1982. In the essays that accompany's Foote's *Taste* and *The Orators*, Murphy provides information on Foote's life and these two works. Bibliography.

Singh, Jyotsna G. *Colonial Narratives/Cultural Dialogues: "Discoveries" of India in the Language of Colonialism.* London: Routledge, 1996. Contains a discussion of Foote's *The Nabob* for its depiction of relations between the British and the Indians.

Trefman, Simon. *Foote, Comedian, 1720-1777.* New York: New York University Press, 1971. An examination of Foote's works and life.

Mary C. Murphy,
updated by Gerald S. Argetsinger

JOHN FORD

Born: Near Ilsington, England; April 17, 1586 (baptized)
Died: Place unknown; after 1639

PRINCIPAL DRAMA

The Witch of Edmonton, pr. 1621, pb. 1658 (with Thomas Dekker and William Rowley)
Perkin Warbeck, pr. c. 1622-1632, pb. 1634

The Sun's Darling, pr. 1624, pb. 1656 (with Dekker)
The Broken Heart, pr. c. 1627-1631, pb. 1633
The Lover's Melancholy, pr. 1628, pb. 1629
'Tis Pity She's a Whore, pr. 1629(?)-1633, pb. 1633
The Fancies Chaste and Noble, pr. 1631(?) or 1635-1636(?), pb. 1638
Love's Sacrifice, pr. 1632(?), pb. 1633

The Lady's Trial, pr. 1638, pb. 1639
The Queen: Or, The Excellency of Her Sex, pb. 1653

OTHER LITERARY FORMS

In addition to his plays, John Ford published two long poems and three prose pamphlets. *Fame's Memorial: Or, The Earl of Devonshire Deceased* (1606) is an elegy praising Charles Blount, who had married Penelope Devereux (on whom Sir Philip Sidney based his Stella) after her divorce from Lord Rich. *Christ's Bloody Sweat: Or, The Son of God in His Agony* (1613) is a religious poem on the efficacy of repentance. *Honor Triumphant: Or, The Peer's Challenge* (1606) argues four propositions in mock style; *The Golden Mean* (1613) praises Stoicism; and *A Line of Life* (1620) describes the Stoic conduct of a man, a public man, and a good man.

ACHIEVEMENTS

Many critics have acclaimed John Ford as the outstanding dramatist of the Caroline Age (1625-1649), and his plays give ample evidence of the justice of this claim. Today, almost any full-year course on the drama surrounding William Shakespeare will include *The Broken Heart*, *'Tis Pity She's a Whore*, and *Perkin Warbeck*. These plays are being produced and evoke a positive response from modern audiences. Although he is not known for innovation, Ford creatively employed such common forms of the age as tragicomedy, revenge tragedy, and the visual elements of the masque. His plays are rich in resonances from other dramatists of the period (particularly Shakespeare, Ben Jonson, and John Webster), but what he borrows, he transforms for his own use. In no way is Ford a surface dramatist. He was deeply interested in Burtonian psychology, but he was never a slave to its formulas. In his drama, he was continually probing into the depths of personality, and he was particularly interested in exploring the human psyche in relationship to or confrontation with other human beings.

BIOGRAPHY

Very little is known about John Ford's life other than a few isolated facts. He was baptized on April 17, 1586, the second son of a Devonshire country gentleman. He was admitted to Middle Temple in 1602, expelled for not paying a board bill in 1606, readmitted in 1608, and involved in a dispute over the wearing of hats in 1617. His father died in 1610, leaving Ford a paltry ten pounds, and six years later, his income was increased by a bequest of twenty pounds a year from his elder brother's estate. Nothing is known of his style of life—whether he was ever married or engaged in a profession—and no record has yet been found of his death.

ANALYSIS

John Ford's fascination with the psychology of love in its many-faceted applications to social life is evident in his earliest produced play, *The Witch of Edmonton*, which he wrote in collaboration with Thomas Dekker and William Rowley. Here also is evident Ford's propensity to the sensational as well as the association of love with death, which was to reappear in many of his subsequent plays.

THE WITCH OF EDMONTON

In the first scene, Frank Thorney has just been married to Sir Arthur Clarington's serving maid, Winnifride, who is with child. The marriage is to be kept in the dark until Frank can secure his inheritance. Sir Arthur abets this deception by writing a letter certifying that no marriage has taken place, even though he is frustrated in his hopes of maintaining a relationship with Winnifride, who takes her marriage and her new status most seriously. The reason for the secrecy becomes gradually yet shockingly apparent as the audience realizes that Frank, who seems to have a strong and genuine love for his bride, nevertheless intends to secure his inheritance through a bigamous marriage with his longtime neighbor Susan Carter. There is irony throughout the scene of his second courtship, but particularly in Susan's outburst of hymeneal joy at having her heart settled with her one true love and winning the right to dismiss her unwanted suitors. Frank, who seems to like Susan well enough, blames his situation on fate—an ever-present force in Ford's dramas.

The violent outcome of this wedding is predicted in the imagery as Susan's father remembers a proverb relating weddings with hangings. One of her former suitors remarks on the unity of the newly married couple, but with an undesirable cutting edge as he compares them with a "new pair of Sheffield knives, fitted both to one sheath." To Susan as to Ford, real love involves unity and the sharing of souls, and she is disturbed to discover that Frank is unable to share with her the source of his obvious discontent. In a pleading not unlike Portia's to Brutus in Shakespeare's *Julius Caesar* (pr. c. 1599-1600), she coaxes him to display his mind: "You shall not shut me from partaking/ The least dislike that grieves you; I'm all yours. . . . I must know/ The ground of your disturbance." Frank assures Susan that the cause has nothing to do with her, blaming his unrest on "the poison'd leeches twist about my heart." He comes close to revealing his bigamy, telling of a palmist who predicted that he should have two wives, but Susan naturally assumes that the second will appear only after her death and, with saintly humility, wishes that "fate" might give him a second wife to outmatch his first—that is, herself.

Frank's two wives are brought together for a brief scene in which Frank is leaving on a journey with his first wife, dressed as a page for the occasion, and stops to say a farewell to Susan. Winnifride, apprised of the situation, is horrified at Frank's lawlessness and callousness in committing bigamy for money, but she has little choice but to follow his lead, and her love for him seems to survive. Susan, in ignorance of the situation, ironically pleads with Frank's "page" to be servant, friend, and wife to him on their journey. Susan contrives to bid farewell to Frank privately; she delays their parting as long as possible, exacerbating Frank's impatience until a white dog enters the scene and Frank suddenly murders Susan, wounds himself, ties himself up (with the dog's help), and cries out "murder." In the supernatural scenes of the play, from which it gets its title and which are generally ascribed to Dekker, the dog is both the witch's familiar and the representative of the Devil himself. In the scenes by Ford, such as this, the dog almost seems to be a bodily representation of the force of fate, tainted as it is in this play with more than a touch of evil.

Later, in Frank's sickroom, where he is recovering from his wound, the dog enters just as Susan's sister discovers the incriminating knife. When she leaves, Frank is visited by the ghost of Susan and by a very live Winnifride before the authorities enter, and both Frank and his remaining wife are carted off to jail. In the final scene of the play, Winnifride is free but faints under the heaviness of her emotion and the weight of her continuing love for her condemned husband. A wave of pity for the bigamist-murderer seems to come over the crowd—a pity that Ford would evidently induce in his audience. This is strengthened by Frank's final speech on his way to execution. In deep penitence, he comments on the rightness of his own death, asks for forgiveness, and seeks to obtain financial security for Winnifride, whom he has never ceased to love, though his ways of demonstrating that love are aberrant in the extreme. Ford's obvious sympathy for the murderer, who planned the bigamy long before any "dog" urged him to go further, is an indication of a moral ambiguity that many critics have found in his plays, but it is also an empathetic examination of a kind of love, pure on the part of both Susan and Winnifride and tainted on Frank's, that can survive in spite of circumstances and a society that would threaten to smother it completely.

THE SUN'S DARLING

Dekker also collaborated with Ford on another early play (it is almost impossible to date Ford's plays precisely), a delightful marriage of morality play and masque entitled *The Sun's Darling*. Raybright, an Everyman figure who is the offspring of the Sun, travels through the domains of the four seasons, each of which attempts to entice him to stay, while his companion, Humour, enlists counterforces to lure him on to the next segment of the year. Each act, representing a season, is a masque in its own right, and each introduces separate masquelike episodes, with songs, dances, and poetic combats presenting various virtues and vices. The most insidious vice of the play is undoubtedly the Spanish confectioner in Spring's entourage, who brags that he "can teach sugar to slip down your throat a thousand ways." Perhaps the most outlandish is the personified Detraction, who claims that scholars are merely "petty penmen [who] covet/ Fame by Folly." The production ends with a final masque performed by the four elements and the four humors, after which the Sun itself descends to make its comments on health and harmony in the perfect interaction of these eight dancers.

There is much about love in the play, as each of the seasons courts Raybright, but he discerns that much of what is presented as love is merely an attempt to buy him with the various gifts the seasons offer. In Autumn and Winter, the season-acts most often ascribed to Ford on the basis of style, it is interesting to note that the ideas of love grow more complex. There is mutuality in the love offered by Autumn, who recognizes that Raybright, in representing the Sun, has as much to offer the season as Autumn has to offer him. "Let us be twins in heart," she suggests, after which Humour and her companion Folly have a harder time convincing Raybright to leave. He does leave eventually, and as he approaches Winter, the love imagery of the play becomes theological if not downright messianic. Raybright, the son of the Sun, is the "excellently good" one for whom they have been waiting. He comes with justice and impartial law. The clowns who oppose his coming are waging "war against heaven" and thereby subject themselves to the "thunder-stroke" that is able to cast them "From heaven's sublime height to the depth of hell." In terms of the Book of Revelation, Raybright will appear like a star, and "Night shall be chang'd into perpetual day."

The Lover's Melancholy

The Lover's Melancholy, which is probably the first play Ford wrote without a collaborator, examines love in what is almost a clinical study. The play opens with a veritable symphony of frustration. When Menaphon returns from a year's trip abroad, he is met by his soul-friend Amethus, who laments that his loved Cleophila (a kinswoman of Menaphon) has remained cold to him, because she cares only for her aging and infirm father. Menaphon, in return, discovers that his love, Thamasta, who also happens to be Amethus's sister, is still "intermured with ice"—absence having done nothing to make her heart grow fond. The illness of Cleophila's father, Meleander, is related to love, because its genesis was the disappearance of his loved daughter, Eroclea. The classic case of love mel-

ancholy, however, is that of Palador, the Prince of Cyprus, whose kingdom has been in a sharp decline since Eroclea's departure. She had been promised to him in marriage by his tyrant father, but only as a trick to lure her to court, where she was to be raped by lecherous courtiers—a fate from which she had been saved by her father, who was promptly dismissed from court as his reward. This was certainly a factor in producing his melancholy state.

The sickness suffered by the prince has descended through him to the state. Ford presents this on the stage via another returned traveler, Rhetias, who determines to play the role of court railer. His soliloquy against court foolery at the beginning of the second scene of the play is aided by the entrance of two court sycophants, Pelias and Cuculus, who provide excellent targets for his barrage of satire. At the end of the scene, Rhetias finds a partner in raillery in Corax, the physician who has been called into court to heal the prince's malady. The description of a sick court is enhanced by Meleander himself, as, in beautifully mad poetry, he pictures the decadence perpetrated by the former tyrant, moans over the futility of court life, and pleads for a funeral without pomp, ceremony, or expense. Even Thamasta shows a side of love melancholy as she conceives of herself in love with the youth, Parthenophill, whom Menaphon has brought back from his travels. "Love is a tyrant/ Resisted," she proclaims—a complaint that might have come from any one of the multifarious treatises on melancholy produced in the sixteenth and seventeenth centuries. This aberrant love, however, is easily treated when she discovers at the end of one particularly well-wrought scene that the object of her misguided affection is indeed a woman. "Cupid," Parthenophill points out, "Comes to make sport between us with no weapon."

The presence of a physician in the court, and hence in the play, gives Ford his chance to examine love melancholy as a form of diseased love. When Prince Palador enters like the melancholy Hamlet, reading a book, Corax caustically reminds him that he had prescribed exercise, not sonnets. Later, two court counselors open the door for a lecture by asking Corax to explain the nature of melancholy, which he does fairly directly out of Robert Burton's *The Anatomy of Melancholy* (1621). Being a master of stagecraft, Ford, through Corax, arranges for a "masque of melancholy" to be presented before the prince, in which Burtonian characters of Lycanthropia, Hydrophobia, Delirium, Phrenitis, Hypochondriacal Melancholy (including a delightful poem against tobacco), and Wanton Melancholy all make their appearance on the stage with appropriate speeches. Prince Palador perhaps assumes that he is getting off lightly because love melancholy is not among the characters. However, thus relaxed (as Claudius perhaps relaxed after the dumb show), he is an easy target for Corax, who, claiming that the condition is too serious and complex to be presented by art (art versus nature being one of the concerns of the play), describes love melancholy to him and suggests that Parthenophill, pale and wan for a lad, is a *living* example of the disease. As visibly moved as Claudius, Palador abruptly dismisses the gathering, and Corax has his diagnosis confirmed: "Love . . . will be seen." Corax's cure is surely made easier by the fact that Parthenophill is in truth Eroclea, who had been in Athens under the care of Rhetias and opportunely found a way to return with Menaphon after the death of Palador's tyrannical father. Even so, the prince has to be prepared for her return with a closely paralleled parable, and he accepts her actual presence only very slowly, thinking it might be some trick—perhaps Parthenophill disguised as Eroclea. Ford fashions their meeting with another demonstration of the mutuality necessary for real love. When she enters the scene, she finishes his speech as if she were privy to the thoughts of his mind, and she also reveals that she has been carrying his picture next to her breast in exactly the same fashion that, it has been earlier revealed, he has been carrying hers.

In addition, the healing of Meleander is carefully wrought by the scholar-physician Corax. He first prepares Meleander (who enters raging, with a poleax) by staring him down, having donned a frightful mask. He then tries to establish empathy with him by claiming that he, Corax, has a daughter who has been snatched away, leaving him with a crazed head and an acute lack of sleep. It works; Meleander does thereaf-

ter claim a special affinity for Corax, admitting "I hug my afflictions," and fetches Cleophila to praise her virtues and compare them with those of the lost Eroclea. In the final scene of the play, Meleander is reached with another court device, perhaps even more dramatic than the masque of melancholy. Meleander has been drugged, delivered to a barber to have his four-years' beard removed, and carted to a tailor to fit him with fresh clothes. When he wakes to the sound of music, he is met with a procession of messengers. First, Aretus, the court tutor, announces that all of Meleander's honors have been restored, and Amethus then presents him with a staff of office, indicating a healing to take place in the state as well as in the individual. Sophronos, Meleander's brother and the father of Menaphon, hands him the picture of Eroclea that Palador had worn next to his heart and that he no longer needs, further announcing that the prince is ready to address Meleander as father. When Cleophila enters with her sister, the meeting of father and daughter is natural and joyful as the story of her disappearance is related. When Prince Palador finally enters, he joyfully greets Meleander as father with the "prince's sweetness," which completes his cure. He makes all necessary explanations and arranges for the marriages, bringing the comedy to a healthy close.

THE BROKEN HEART

In many ways, *The Broken Heart* is a study in courtship and marriage. The play opens with Orgilus discussing his relationship with his betrothed, Penthea, which has been thwarted by, to use his words, a "poisonous stalk/ Of aconite" in the person of Penthea's brother, Ithocles, who, in spite of the betrothal, has compelled Penthea to marry Bassanes, an older and richer, though hardly wiser, nobleman. At first, Orgilus, who is later referred to as a married bachelor, seems to show some real concern for Penthea as he informs his father, Crotolon, that he is leaving Sparta for Athens not only to escape from the jealousies of Bassanes and to ease the pain he feels in Penthea's presence but also to free her "from a hell on earth," caught between her present husband and her former lover. All of this, however, turns out to be little more than subterfuge, of which Orgilus is a master. He soon returns in disguise as a scholar, spies on her in an unconscionable way, continually describes his love for her in terms bordering on the lascivious, and, in one painful scene, even tries by psychological pressure to force her to violate her marriage vows, claiming that their prior betrothal was the more valid contract. His attempts on her honor fall little short of attempted rape, and her resistance serves but to whet his already sharp appetite for revenge.

Orgilus's lack of integrity is also manifest in his extraction of a promise from his own sister, Euphrania, that she will never marry without his consent. In doing this, Orgilus is taking control of his sister's marriage in the same way that Ithocles had manipulated Penthea's. Euphrania's love for Prophilus seems genuine, pure, and controlled throughout. It outlasts the delay imposed on them by having to wait for permission from the supposedly absent Orgilus, and it survives his close examination of the relationship, disguised as student who by accident becomes the messenger by whom they exchange letters while their love is still secret. Because Prophilus is a close friend of the hated Ithocles, Orgilus's permission is wrenched from him only with the greatest difficulty, although once it is given, his rancor seems to be forgotten if not totally dissipated.

The marriage between Penthea and Bassanes is indeed a hellish affair. Orgilus deems it a "monster-love" because she had been previously betrothed to him, but surely it is monstrous in its own right. The cliché of an older man's fear of cuckoldry when married to a young, attractive woman comes to life on the stage. In the audience's first glimpse into their home, Bassanes is arranging for a mason to have the front window "dammed up" lest it afford passersby a glimpse of Penthea's beauty. She is continually spied on by Brausis, a delightfully doughty old woman described in the *dramatis personae* as her overseer. Bassanes is even jealous of Penthea's brother, but perhaps this is not untoward in a Ford play. In spite of this oppressive picture of his personality, there is also a note of pathos in it. Although he was the benefactor of Ithocles' pandering, he did not devise it. The court he describes is indeed a dangerous place for an attractive woman, and his appreciation of her beauty has a numinous quality to it. At her first entrance, he ex-

claims: "She comes, she comes! So shoots the morning forth,/ Spangled with pearls of transparent dew." His own intoxication with her beauty justifies his belief that others might be equally affected.

The mad jealousy of Bassanes is dramatically revealed to all when he breaks in on a conference between his wife and her brother and imagines their incest. Ithocles, long since repentant of this marriage that he forced on his sister, now takes decisive steps to remove her from the oppression of this home and put her under his own protection. The shock of public horror at his behavior and the losing of his wife bring Bassanes to a sudden but believable repentance, and he genuinely laments the loss of a love he was not fit to enjoy. Ironically, his repentance comes too late to transform him into a fit husband at the same moment that Ithocles, through painful repentance, has belatedly become a fit brother.

In this state, Ithocles earnestly attempts to elicit his sister's forgiveness, but every opening gesture he makes is met with scornful barbs forged in the deep center of pain that Penthea feels from having been wrenched from her betrothed love and forced into a relationship that she therefore considers adulterous. She relents only when, sensitized to the psychological conditions of impossible love, she senses the nature of her brother's recent illness and evokes from him a confession of his love for Calantha, the daughter of his king, who is at the moment being newly courted by Nearchus, prince of neighboring Argos. Penthea recovers from her bitterness to visit Calantha, in the guise of asking her to be the executrix of her will. Using a familiar Renaissance form, she prettily bequeaths her youth to chaste wives who marry "for ties of love,/ Rather than ranging of their blood"; then her fame is left to memory and truth. Calantha is beginning to enjoy the game, when suddenly Penthea shatters the tradition and unexpectedly leaves Ithocles her brother to Calantha. The princess is irate at the presumption of this suggestion but withholds any comment on the suggestion itself. In the next scene, however, Calantha takes a ring that has been given to her by Nearchus and rejects it by tossing it to Ithocles, suggesting that he "give it at next meeting to a mistress." It is Ithocles' turn for presumption now, as he returns the ring to the princess herself, causing some resentment among the supporters of Nearchus. The love between Calantha and Ithocles is evidently genuine and reciprocal, and Nearchus, making a chorus-like comment on the theme of marriage, shows genuine humility and understanding.

By the next scene, Calantha and Ithocles have courted and grown mature in their love, and she asks her dying father, the king, for permission to marry, which is readily granted. Ithocles has proved himself worthy on the battlefield and in the court and through repentance has cleansed himself of his earlier inclinations to control the lives of others. Calantha is a magnificent woman, a queen, knowing herself and her own love and managing to keep love, passion, and will in perfect balance. Unfortunately, however, their love is to be consummated only in death. Ithocles dies magnificently under the revenger's dagger as Orgilus first catches him fast in a trick chair and then coolly deprives him of life. Calantha is leading the festivities at the wedding celebration for Euphrania and Prophilus when, on successive changes of the dance, she hears of the deaths of her father, her best friend Penthea, and her betrothed. Giving no evidence of the shock she feels at the news brought by successive messengers, she continues the dance to its conclusion. As the reigning queen, she comments on Penthea's death; provides for the continuing rule of her country in a wedding contract with Nearchus, which, as Bassanes comments, is actually her will and testament. Then, placing her mother's wedding ring on Ithocles' lifeless finger as a symbol of the consummation of a timeless love, she dies, indeed of a "broken heart."

LOVE'S SACRIFICE

In *Love's Sacrifice*, Ford is concerned with human relationships between the sexes in which no fulfillment is possible. The play opens with the banishment of Roseilli, an honest courtier, from the court. The only explanation he can surmise for his banishment is that somewhere behind the action is Fiormonda, the woman he has been unsuccessfully wooing for some time and who wants only to be rid of him.

When the duke enters with his duchess, Bianca, it at first seems as if they are a well-mated pair. Their entrance is announced by courtiers praising the duke for choosing Bianca not because of family or connections but simply because of her beauty, to which Fernando adds virtue. Onstage, the duke affirms that he values only two things: his duchess and his trusted friend Fernando. Intimations of things to come present themselves shortly after their departure, however, when the trusted Fernando laments his all-consuming love for the duchess. He is hardly through with this speech when Fiormonda enters to court him. He deftly puts her off by praising not only her beauty but also her loyalty to her dead husband; however, this serves only as a cue for Fiormonda to produce the ring that her husband instructed her to give to the one she could love as much as she had loved him. The scene is interrupted (a blessing to Fernando and a curse to Fiormonda) by the entrance of Bianca, asking Fernando's help in convincing the duke to recall Roseilli, the man Fiormonda had just succeeded in getting out of her way.

The intrigue does not stop here. The beginning of the second act discloses still another courtier enamored of Fiormonda, and the court gets a good laugh as, from the upper stage, it overhears and sees Mauruccio practicing ridiculous speeches, designing outlandish costumes, and devising foolish gifts as he outlines his assault on his beloved—the only member of the court who is not in stitches at the entire proceeding. Thus, the audience is introduced to a court with its love triangles, quadrangles, and octangles, none of which promises to produce anything but pain.

The unhealthy quality of the love in this play is underscored by a quantity of disease imagery, with love referred to as a leprosy at least three times. The center of this disease in the court is the duke's new counselor, Ferentes, who initiates an intriguing scene in which two young ladies and one older one all discover they are pregnant, having been bribed into bed with a promise of marriage from the same man. This source of the disease is effectively purged, however, in a scene reminiscent of dramatist Thomas Kyd, in which Ferentes is stabbed by all three of the women in a court masque presented in honor of a visiting abbot (Bianca's uncle). To justify this action, each woman displays her newborn infant.

The primary love business of the play, between Fernando and Bianca, is strong, poignant, and confusing. At his first opportunity, Fernando speaks most eloquently of his love, evidently for the third time, and is put down with equal force and eloquence by a diatribe on chastity from Bianca, who takes her marriage vows seriously. In spite of being charged never to speak of love again, on pain of exposure and certain death, Fernando cannot contain himself, and once more pleads his plight. The situation is ominous. D'Avolos has noted Fernando's passion and, by means of displaying a pair of pictures, has trapped him into disclosing the object of his desire. With the duke away, Fiormonda has maneuvered the couple into a chess game (fraught with double entendre) and then, pleading sickness, has managed to leave them alone except for D'Avolos, who is sent back to spy on them. The situation is too much for Fernando; even though warned, he is soon on his knees declaring his love. Again he is chastely humbled by Bianca, who deplores his "bestial dalliance" and warns that if he opens his "leprous mouth" again on the subject, it will mean "the forfeit of thy life." Fernando agrees to silence, but with Donne-like eloquence declares that if his heart is ripped open at his death, there the observer will read "Bianca's name carv'd out in bloody lines." From his observation post, D'Avolos completely misreads this scene and reports to Fiormonda that the couple are on their way to bed, to which she, playing the role of a good revenger, vows "to stir up tragedies as black as brave."

This misreading is the only preparation that exists in the play for the next turn in the relationship, which surprises the reader in the very next scene. Bianca suddenly becomes the initiator in the game of love, appears in Fernando's bedroom while he is fast asleep, and wakes him with her declaration of mutual love. Even though she comes with "shame and passion," caught up by the "tyranny" of love, there is also an invitation in her words: "If thou tempt'st/ My bosom to thy pleasures, I will yield." Her invitation, however, has a barb in it; though she is torn by the passion of her love, she is also constant to her "vow to live a constant wife." Her impossible solution to this dilemma is to follow her passion in offering herself to

Fernando but also to follow her conscience in declaring that, should he accept, "Ere yet the morning shall new-christen day,/ I'll kill myself." Fernando at first hopes this is some jest, but finally takes her at her word, vowing to master his passion and sublimate their love into a spiritual relationship, though he is still uneasy enough to ask if she will later laugh at him for refusing the wondrous gift. At the end of the scene, she echoes Fernando's own avowal of constancy.

The reader is never quite sure of her mood after this. In one scene she contrives, in public, to wipe Fernando's lips and adds in an aside, "Speak, shall I steal a kiss? believe me, my lord, I long." There is something too coquettish in these lines coming from the woman vowed to death should her lover go beyond the kiss. Furthermore, in the final scenes of the play, she confesses to the duke, her husband, that she desired Fernando madly, tried her best to seduce him, but was unable to overcome his scruples. Perhaps she wanted both Fernando and death; this would not, certainly, be beyond the scope of Ford's imagination. Perhaps, in this scene, she was merely trying to save his life in the face of the revenge-fury that Fiormonda had worked up in the duke. The latter seems most likely, in that she attributes Fernando's technical chastity not to the concern for her life but rather to his constant loyalty to the duke himself—an idea that, as far as the audience can tell, never entered Fernando's head, though perhaps it should have.

Typical of Ford's plays, the love that is impossible in life finds its consummation in death, as has been foreshadowed throughout the play. There is something noble about the way in which Bianca bravely bares her breast to receive death from her husband's dagger. She may be seeking death as the only way out of her dilemma, using her cruel and seemingly needless taunting of the duke (by proclaiming Fernando's superiority) as a device to be sure he is angry enough to complete the deed. She warns him that he will suffer when he comes to accept the validity of her physical chastity, but he cannot believe this, and his one moment of relenting is quickly overcome by the urging of Fiormonda, the real revenger, from the upper stage. The duke's anger is inflamed, and the murder committed.

When the duke, again at Fiormonda's urging, approaches Fernando to complete his revenge, he finds him armed and unhesitatingly challenges him to a duel to the death. Fernando, however, on hearing that Bianca is dead, drops his sword and bares his breast, willing to be sacrificed in the same manner that she had been, thus joining her in a death union symbolically apparent on the stage. He is denied this symmetry, however, for the duke, finally convinced of his wife's chastity if not her constancy, tries to stab himself, though he is stopped before completing his self-immolation. Instead, he arranges for a coffin and a funeral procession for his wife's body, and the abbot returns in time to add his dignity and pomp to the occasion. After an eloquent tribute to his dead wife, the duke opens the burial vault, only to find Fernando there ahead of him, still quite alive but dressed in his winding sheet. He answers the duke's attempt to drag him out by gulping poison to join his Bianca. The bliss of their union in death (assuming that such is possible) is, however, short-lived. The duke proclaims that after he dies, he would like to be buried in one monument with his wife and friend, then makes the waiting time short by stabbing himself to join them. The love triangle presumably moves from the human stage into an eternal tension.

Whether Ford is trying to say that all attempts at a solution by means of death are in vain or is quietly mocking himself, the situation suggests that there is neither glory nor promise nor fulfillment in love's sacrifice, which seeks to find on the other side of the grave what it is denied in life. On this side of the tomb, life goes on. The dukedom is perpetuated when Fiormonda, the sole surviving heir, offers the dukedom along with herself to Roselli, who seems to be worthy of the post and establishes justice by consigning D'Avolos to the hangman. Fiormonda, however, who is the real source of evil in the play, lives to become the new duchess. Roselli vows to live a celibate life within marriage. This, given his love for her, punishes him almost as much as it does Fiormonda, but it also reiterates the theme of the play, which is dominated by love, or at least by passion, without fulfillment.

'TIS PITY SHE'S A WHORE

The play widely regarded as Ford's best, *'Tis Pity She's a Whore*, is a study of a single but hopelessly tainted love—that between Giovanni and his sister Annabella. The other loves that emerge serve but to cast light on the central pair of lovers.

In the opening speech of the play, the friar is in the process of urging young Giovanni to abandon love. For several lines, Ford artistically delays revealing the nature of the friar's objection until Giovanni reveals the state of his psyche by genuinely asking a question, the answer to which is totally obvious both to the friar and to the play's audience: "Shall then, for that I am her brother born,/ My joys be ever banish'd from her bed?" What Giovanni wants from the friar is some means of justifying his love and of consummating it, but what he gets is a formula for exorcising the "leprosy of lust/ That rots thy soul," as the friar describes his condition. Giovanni agrees to the regime, even though it seems obvious that it will not succeed, and the scene ends by introducing two powerful forces at work within the play: revenge and fate.

Undoubtedly the greatest critical problem in this play is the simple fact that although Giovanni's passion is by common definition a sick love, it is by far the healthiest love in the play. Giovanni and Annabella join strengths, not weaknesses; they augment each other's personalities through giving, never by preying on each other. Giovanni is praised for his "government, behaviour, learning, speech,/ Sweetness, and all that could make up a man," and Annabella's virtues are lauded throughout the play as she is courted by at least three others and described by father, brother, and nurse. The quality most conducive to a genuine love in Ford's plays is mutuality, and this brother-sister love abounds with it. Giovanni justifies his love to the friar by describing their unity, and it is the primary mark of their first love scene when it is discovered that Annabella has long had the same feeling for her brother but has not dared to speak it. In this scene, both brother and sister seem to be free from a sense of guilt. Their mutual vows, "love me or kill me," speak of the strength of their love in the face of the opposition of the world, not a mutual guilt. By their next meeting, their love has been consummated, and the poetry of their union marks it as complete. When Giovanni tries to rationalize his love to the friar in terms of school principles, it turns out to be mere sophistry, but the real and convincing argument is her beauty, in which almost every cliché of Renaissance poetry is created anew.

It is also in the presence of the friar that some hint of division comes between Giovanni and Annabella. Although little noted by critics, it is surely her pregnancy that brings Annabella to her knees, weeping in contrition before the friar, who responds by offering her a fine condensation of Dante's *Inferno*. The means to salvation, he suggests, is for her to marry her suitor, Soranzo, not only to cover her pregnancy but also to live totally loyal to him all her days. The marriage is easily achieved, and that very day Annabella and Soranzo exchange vows. Loyalty and commitment, however, are harder to muster, and when Soranzo discovers the pregnancy and excoriates her as a common whore engaging in "belly sports," she taunts him with high praise of her former lover, a man whom Soranzo could never match. He ought to be proud, she insists, to "have the glory/ To father what so brave a father got." Though she is hardly an obedient wife (evidently continuing her relations with Giovanni), Annabella does grow in penitence, wishing in love, like John Milton's Eve, to take the penalty due Giovanni on herself. When the friar enters in the middle of her soliloquy, he is delighted and agrees to deliver a letter to Giovanni, both suggesting that he join her in repentance and also warning him against the revenge-fury of Soranzo.

The change in Giovanni is subtler, but there is a definite shift in his attitude from love of a woman to love of the pleasure itself. Ford has underlined this in the structure of his play, for just as the friar interrupted Annabella's soliloquy of repentance, he enters in the middle of Giovanni's soliloquy glorying that even after her marriage, he finds "no change/ Of pleasure in this formal law of sports." Annabella was once more than a sport, and though he can still speak of "united hearts" and a love to the death, the emphasis is on the pleasure. In their final meeting, "lying on a bed," Giovanni is upset at Annabella's sudden resolve to "be honest," and certainly his anger and re-

sentment at being denied his pleasure contributes to the impetus to murder. Even after he is convinced that their end is near and the talk turns to eschatology and life after death, his mind is on pleasure: "May we kiss one another, prate or laugh,/ Or do as we do here?" Annabella, however, does not know the answer, but Giovanni, convinced that death is on the way and that only after death is there any possibility for their love, frustrates Soranzo's elaborate plans for revenge by sacrificing his love on his own dagger. Like William Shakespeare's Othello, he exacts three kisses from her, finally resolving to "kill thee in a kiss" as she begs heaven to forgive him and cries for mercy. The final scene of the play, in which Giovanni, quietly and rationally demented, enters the banquet scene carrying her bleeding heart on the tip of his dagger, is one that few can forget.

It is not only the sensationalism of this final scene nor the disturbingly sympathetic treatment of an incestuous love that makes this play memorable but also the poetry, which is of a consistently high caliber, forming a mirror of the souls of the characters. Recurring motifs, particularly of music and the full and ebbing sea, bind the play together. The pervasive resounding of love associated with death, accentuated by images of piercing and ripping, artistically creates a unified tone and foreshadows the end. Further, Ford's masterful use of the irony inherent in the situation, in which only the audience and the friar know of the clandestine love, adds enjoyment and understanding to the experience of the play.

This work also receives Ford's most complete examination of the role fate plays in life, a topic that obsessed him. In the very first scene of the play, Giovanni is convinced that he is compelled into his love by a force beyond him, not by what the friar describes as his "wilful flames." When Giovanni resolves to tell his sister of his love, he proclaims (perhaps protesting too much), "'tis not, I know,/ My lust, but 'tis my fate that leads me on." He uses the idea of fate in pleading his love, insisting, "'tis my destiny/ That you must either love, or I must die," and fate justifies the incest: "Wise nature first in your creation meant/ To make you mine; else't had been sin and foul." Annabella also uses fate to justify her actions, as she unconvincingly tries to convince Soranzo that he should accept an impregnated bride: "Why, 'tis thy fate." Later, in soliloquy, she echoes an earlier pair of star-crossed lovers as, regarding Giovanni, she laments: "Would thou hadst been less subject to those stars/ That luckless reign'd at my nativity." The friar tries to make a distinction between fate as nature's dictates and the destiny that is the will of heaven. Both of the minor, bungling revengers, Richardetto and Hippolita, indicate that they are trying to control fate, and against this background, it is interesting that Giovanni also, as he begins to assume the role of avenger, changes from a victim of destiny to one who would manufacture his own fate. He does not, however, outlive his revenges, and a sword in the fist of Vasques deals him the final blow, which otherwise he had determined to inflict on himself. He dies declaring the irrelevance of mercy in the fact of the justice he has met, and wishing to "enjoy this grace,/ Freely to view my Annabella's face."

PERKIN WARBECK

Perkin Warbeck has been termed a tragedy by some critics and a history play by most. It is about a legitimate king and an infamous claimant to the throne, yet it has no villain, unless it be Margaret of Burgundy, who never appears in the play, although her murky influence is felt behind Warbeck's claim to the throne. Henry himself is presented as an efficient king who rules well, with both foresight and insight, keeping always the good of his kingdom as his first goal and using mercy and goodness whenever they coincide with his major purpose. James of Scotland joins forces with Perkin Warbeck, out of a genuine though misguided sense of right. He is a weak but not a sinister character. He quickly takes the expedient course when he perceives that no English forces are rising to back Warbeck and when the forces of Spain and the empire are discovered to be totally behind the current English king. Warbeck himself is not without dignity in the play. Totally convinced that he is the duke who should rightfully have inherited the throne of England, he behaves in all respects like a king. Ford heightens his sense of nobility in the closing act of the play by contrasting him with Lambert Simnel, a previous pretender to the throne who is presented

on the stage as a tempter of Warbeck. Simnel has bought his life by accepting the abject position of the king's falconer, and it is made plain that a similar choice is open to Warbeck. Convinced that he is indeed of royal blood, however, he will have none of it. In a conventional but moving speech on the nobility of death, he is taken off to his own in royal dignity, a genuine, almost heroic figure who has almost persuaded the audience.

Interested as Ford is in the proper rules of succession and in affirming the legitimacy of the Tudor and Stuart lines, the play is just as much concerned with the quality of love, the dominant theme in his plays. In *Perkin Warbeck*, there are two examples of deep spiritual love of man for man. One instance is King Henry's attachment to his counselor, Lord Stanley. When Clifford reveals Stanley's complicity in the Warbeck plot, the king is shaken. Stanley had saved Henry's life on the battlefield and placed the crown on his head. Since that time, there had been nothing the king would not have done for him. The king's feelings for Stanley are poignantly evident in the scene of Stanley's condemnation. The king confides to his couselors that his heart would pardon Stanley, that there is "a chancery of pity in our bosom," but his better sense (awakened by a few strong words from his advisers) knows that this is impossible. Even so, he absents himself from the trial, fearing his own strong emotions. Stanley himself seems to underline the strength of their relationship as he responds to his sentence: "O the king,/ Next to my soul, shall be the nearest subject/ Of my last prayers!" In the face of this love, the reasons for his complicity in the plot remain a mystery.

Even stronger than this relationship is that between the Scots' Lord Huntley and Daliell, the suitor for his daughter Katherine's hand. Because she is an attractive girl with royal blood flowing in her veins, her father feels that she might well be a fit choice for King James himself, yet he is so fond of Daliell that he finally agrees to give his blessing to the match if Katherine should answer Daliell's plea with proper passion, though he does not agree to recommend the match to her. When Kate shatters the dreams of both men by turning her passion toward Warbeck, whom her father sees as a mere impostor, the relationship between Huntley and Daliell deepens and the older man invites Daliell to "Come with me, for I feel thy griefs as full/ As mine; let's steal away and cry together." This friendship is deepened at the wedding feast, where the music sounds to Huntley "Like to so many choristers of Bedlam/ Trolling a catch." In spite of a good nature that has learned to make light of hardships and a determination to be merry in a court in which flattery keeps him secure, there is a touch of bitterness in Huntley's resignation to kings who are "earthly gods" with "anointed bodies" and in the renunciation of his child, who has chosen a "dukeling mushroom" for a husband. Daliell cuts through this mood of the older man, and with a more humble, continuing, and faithful love adds a tincture of consolation to their meeting. When Huntley asks for pardon for slighting Daliell's suit, the younger man offers him "a love, a service,/ A friendship to posterity," and Huntley expresses his gratitude for "some ease,/ A partner in affliction," after which the two men together endure the remainder of the wedding feast. They next appear after Warbeck has been rejected by King James, and although they enter together, they leave separately. Huntley, after a moving farewell to his daughter, returns to Scotland, but Daliell, in an act of faithfulness resembling that of Lear's Kent, asks permission to join Katherine and her husband in their sojourn to Cornwall. When Huntley appears for a brief moment at the end of the play, he does not converse with Daliell, but the two men are obviously united in their attitudes toward Katherine.

The major examination of love in the play involves Katherine. Although when Daliell begins to address her, Huntley suspects that an arrangement has already been made between them, the passion that he supposed to exist is the one thing lacking. Instead of responding to his suit, Katherine pleads duty to her father as an excuse to say no. Highly appreciative of his virtues, she gently and coolly suggests a Platonic courtly-love relationship. In sharp contrast with this is Katherine's first response to Warbeck. She merely watches his arrival in court from the sidelines, when the Countess of Crawford, observing her, remarks, "Madam, y'are passionate." To this passion is added

the press of duty to accept Warbeck for a husband, but it is not duty to her father. In spite of Huntley's vociferous objections to the match, King James himself has insisted on it, claiming an "Instinct of Sovereignty" to authenticate his choice. Katherine is nothing loath to accept this higher authority. She must be hurt deeply, however, when her father refuses his blessing on the match and goes off to commiserate with Daliell.

From this point on, Katherine's love is a blend of commitment, duty, and faithfulness marked by a desire to share every life experience with her husband. She begs to go off to war with him, and when she is denied this, she extracts from him a promise that he will never again leave without her. Later, when Warbeck is dismissed by King James, his first reaction is not concern for his kingdom but a fear that James will find a way to retract the marriage and separate him from his new wife. Kate affirms her faithfulness to her husband. With bravery and courage, she is ready for what amounts to exile, exhibiting no bitterness toward the king, who commanded her into the marriage. She evinces a majestic sense of pride, vowing that she will not return as long as Warbeck is banished from the king's presence.

At the end of the play, Katherine is not allowed to share Warbeck's death, but she does share the humiliation that he has already turned into triumph by royally refusing to capitulate either to the king's taunts or to Lambert Simnel's demeaning compromise. In a magnificent bit of stagecraft, characteristic of Ford, Katherine climbs up onto the stocks in which he has been fixed. Though the Earl of Oxford is shocked and angered by the indignity, Katherine answers him with an affirmation of her marriage vows and her intention to live or die with her husband. Fate, however, which plays an important part in this play, as it does in Ford's others, decrees otherwise, and Perkin is taken off to his death, while Katherine is escorted to her apartment, her true love thwarted by a tragic misconception of birth and role.

THE LADY'S TRIAL

The question of love is again examined in *The Lady's Trial*, and this time it is social: Is it possible for love and marriage to succeed across socioeconomic lines? The well-born Auria has married Spinella with no dowry except her youth and beauty. His bosom friend, Aurelio, had warned him against this move, and indeed, shortly after the marriage, Auria is forced to leave Genoa to seek his fortune in the desperate arena of fighting Turkish pirates—not without an "I told you so" from Aurelio. Spinella's real dowry is faithfulness, honor, and an inner nobility. With humility and scorn, she spurns the suit of the ranking lord, Adurni, who, in her husband's absence, has trapped her into a bedroom replete with seductive music and a full banquet spread for the two of them. Aurelio, who discovers them together, threatens to expose her infamy. Although by hiding at Auria's return, she evinces some doubt of his willingness to believe her innocence, a mutual, perfect trust is reestablished at the close of the play, and all is well.

The theme is perhaps even more expressly considered in the subplots of the play. Levidolche has married beneath her station one Benatzi, whom her uncle, Martino, has designated a mere "trencher-waiter." The upper ranks of society beckon, however, and after becoming the mistress of Adurni, she divorces her husband, whose fortunes then degenerate until he becomes a galley slave to the Turks. When Adurni's affections begin to cool (as he plans his seduction of Spinella), Levidolche writes a passionate letter seeking to enter into a relationship with Malfato, a lowly gentleman of the court, Spinella's uncle and ward. She confides her thoughts on rank to Futelli, whom she has hired to deliver the letter (and who betrays her by bringing it to Adurni first). "The properest men," she states, "should be preferr'd to fortune." Futelli leads her to admit that Adurni is not a man she admires by suggesting that "The title of a lord was not enough/ For absolute perfection," which she answers by describing the real perfections of Malfato. He, however, scorns her letter completely and publicly, mistakenly believing that Adurni was behind the solicitation, seeking to dupe Malfato into a marriage that would serve as both a cover-up for and pregnancy insurance against Adurni's own illicit relationship with the woman he would marry off.

Infuriated at her betrayal by the two men, Levidolche seeks an avenger and hires Benatzi, who has been freed from the Turks by Auria and is now in disguise as a returned soldier and outlaw. His fee, however, is not money but marriage, and he insists on a wedding before the commission is fulfilled. She confesses her adultery and looseness, but he affirms his faith in her ability to reform. As he leaves, Levidolche smiles, confiding to the audience that "Love is sharp-sighted,/ And can pierce through the cunning of disguises./ False pleasures, I cashier ye; fair truth, welcome!"

This change of heart and life, induced by trust, is evidently genuine and lasting. When Levidolche's uncle, Martino, first sees her with this disheveled, disreputable piece of man-flesh, he accuses her of going public in her whoredom, setting up shop and crying "A market open; to't and welcome," but when he is informed of the marriage and let in on her secret that this creature is in reality her former husband, to whom she now intends absolute fidelity, her uncle is won over and convinced of her ability to achieve faithfulness. In the final scene of the play, Levidolche proclaims her new lifestyle to the entire court, and they, too, believe, accepting her fully into their society. She blushes to face Malfato but is forgiven by him, and she is supported financially in her new start by Adurni, Spinella, and her sister Castanna. This is indeed what Robert Grams Hunter would call "comedy of forgiveness."

The theme is reiterated on still another level of society, in which it approaches farce. Amoretta has a fixation: Although lacking social status herself, she refuses to marry anyone less than a count and believes that she is really fit for a duke. Futelli and his friend Piero plot to cure her of this disease by having her courted by one Guzman, in the disguise of a Spanish grandee, and by Fulgoso, one of the newly rich who has devised for himself a long and honorable family tree. In four long and delightful pages, Futelli coaches Guzman on the proper method to approach Amoretta, describing correct courtship in terms of military strategy. When Piero enters, counseling Fulgoso, the two would-be lovers challenge each other to a bloody resolution of their rivalry, but when they discover their mutual gluttony, they decide to have a sumptuous dinner together instead. In the wooing scene, in which Amoretta's heavy lisp adds to the foolishness, both Guzman and Fulgoso plead their cases by giving long and hilarious recitations of their family ancestries, and eventually they become so ridiculous that they are literally kicked off the stage with a cruelty reminiscent of Ben Jonson. Amoretta is cured and readily agrees to accept the mate of her father's choice, who later turns out to be Futelli.

Although there may be no such genre, this play can be best classified as a revenge comedy. It is almost as if Ford looked at his earlier tragedies and asked what psychological factors might have kept the blood from the stage. Many elements of revenge tragedy are present. There is an age discrepancy between Auria and Spinella, and when Auria leaves court, he warns his young wife not to give even the slightest appearance of infidelity, charging her to remember "whose wife thou art." Against this charge, Aurelio, who has the innate potential to become an Iago figure, is commissioned to watch her. His love for Auria, which is twice mentioned in the play, is enough to create jealousy. He has warned Auria that his wife's youth and beauty are "baits for dishonour," and he would naturally like to prove his forebodings justified. Further motivation is provided in that Auria has made Aurelio his heir, to inherit all of his assets except "Some fit deduction for a worthy widow/ Allow'd, with caution she be like to prove so." In addition to this, Aurelio is provided with "occular proof," which seems totally convincing to him when he finds Spinella locked in the bedroom with Adurni. His threat to inform his newly returned friend of this infidelity is ominous, and it is little wonder, remembering Auria's departing charge, that Spinella chooses to hide rather than to face her husband after he has heard Aurelio's accusations. Hiding, however, could well be interpreted as an admission of guilt, adding one more bit of evidence to the already convincing testimony.

What is the psychological ambience that resolves all of these elements into comedy rather than tragedy? The answer is in the quality of love in the play. Auria answers Aurelio's accusations with common sense and a luminous sense of trust in his wife, a quality that is completely absent in revenge tragedy.

The evidence against her is circumstantial, he explains to Aurelio, and other interpretations are equally satisfactory. It is Auria's relationship with his friend that is threatened, not that with his wife. What a refreshing current this is in the murky waters of Renaissance drama: One can trust the person one loves; accusations dissolve into nothing in the clear, binding matrix of love. The one thing that hurts Auria is that Spinella's absence seems to say she did not trust him to have faith in her. His dealing with this seems a bit cruel, for on their meeting, he pretends not to recognize her. Spinella retains her dignity and is eloquent against both liars and those who believe them. To this, Aurelio confesses that his accusations were engendered more by his suspicions than knowledge, but Auria then suggests the disparity in their ages as a possible cause of her dissatisfaction, to which she answers that there was none. Adurni, who had previously confessed to Auria that his confrontation with Spinella had changed his entire attitude toward women, convincing him that good women exist, enters to ask pardon of Spinella. When Auria seems not to accept even this as evidence of her innocence, Spinella strikes at the heart of their relationship: "You can suspect?/ So reconciliation, then, is needless." To allay Auria's suspicions would be irrelevant; if he has suspicions, the relationship is already beyond salvation. The reader, however, knows that he has none, but is worried about *her* suspicions of him. This worry removed, their relationship of mutual trust is reaffirmed. The real "lady's trial," then, appears not to be the obvious external assault on her virtue, portrayed in the first half of the drama, but the inward trial of the mutual trust, the real basis of love and marriage—the kind that makes tragedy impossible.

The other strain in which the play skirts on tragedy is in Levidolche's cry for revenge, which seems genuine and threatening. Her method of hiring a revenger is also typical of revenge tragedy, as she drops a purse with a note in it from a second-story window in the dark of night, so that it appears mysterious to all those on the lower stage. Benatzi, disguised as Parado, is certainly a fit instrument for revenge. Like Bosola, he has been both a soldier and a galley slave, and he makes a ragged appearance on the stage—an outsider to society. It is only when her renewed love for him proves to be genuine and permanent that the audience knows the revenge will not take place, though some suspense is maintained right up to the moment that he is disarmed in court. The play ends in merriment as Futelli is to wed Amoretta, Adurni is betrothed to Spinella's sister Castanna, and Fulgoso and Guzman enter to make their final foolish speeches before Auria dismisses all to attend the revels celebrating both marriages and his own promotions.

OTHER MAJOR WORKS

POETRY: *Fame's Memorial: Or, The Earl of Devonshire Deceased*, 1606; *Christ's Bloody Sweat: Or, The Son of God in His Agony*, 1613.

NONFICTION: *Honor Triumphant: Or, The Peer's Challenge*, 1606; *The Golden Mean*, 1613; *A Line of Life*, 1620.

MISCELLANEOUS: *The Works of John Ford*, 1869 (Alexander Dyce, editor; includes previously uncollected poetry); *The Nondramatic Works of John Ford*, 1991 (L. E. Stock et al., editors).

BIBLIOGRAPHY

Anderson, Donald K., Jr., ed. *"Concord in Discord": The Plays of John Ford, 1586-1986*. New York: AMS Press, 1987. The first book of essays on Ford, this collection presents the work of thirteen scholars and includes many useful discussions: Robert Heilman on the perverse in Ford's plays, Eugene Waith on the staging and spectacle of Ford's concluding scenes, David Bergeron on brother-sister relationships, Larry Champion on Ford's early works as a precursor of his later tragedies, Richard Ide and Mark Stavig both on aspects of *'Tis Pity She's a Whore*, and Anderson on Ford's manipulation of the audience in *The Fancies Chaste and Noble*.

_____. *John Ford*. New York: Twayne, 1972. Rich in insights into Ford's dramaturgy and imagery, this well-written study provides a sensitive, balanced understanding of all Ford's plays and poems. To judge by the numerous references to this work by others, Anderson's book has had a strong influence on Ford studies. The work includes the chapters "Ford and His Age" and "Ford and the Critics" as well as an annotated bibliography.

Clark, Ira. *Professional Playwrights: Massinger, Ford, Shirley, and Brome*. Lexington: University Press of Kentucky, 1992. Clark examines the works of Ford as well as those of Philip Massinger, James Shirley, and Richard Brome. Includes bibliography and index.

Farr, Dorothy. *John Ford and the Caroline Theatre*. London: Macmillan, 1979. Farr studies Ford's plays and their suitability for the specific theaters where they were first staged, but such a narrow-sounding topic should not deter the general reader. Farr writes effectively about many aspects of Ford's art, and not incidentally, her remarks about the indoor, private theaters of the time of Charles I provide an informative supplement to most readers' greater knowledge of the open-air, public theaters of the Elizabethan age.

Neill, Michael, ed. *John Ford: Critical Re-Visions*. Cambridge, England: Cambridge University Press, 1988. Eleven essays cover topics such as stage history, imagery, use of melodrama, the question of decadence, metatheater in *Love's Sacrifice*, and gender in *Perkin Warbeck*.

Sanders, Julie. *Caroline Drama: The Plays of Massinger, Ford, Shirley, and Brome*. Plymouth, England: Northcote House, in association with the British Council, 1999. Sanders examines the works of Caroline Age dramatists Philip Massinger, James Shirley, Richard Brome, and Ford. Includes bibliography and index.

Howard C. Adams,
updated by Glenn Hopp

RICHARD FOREMAN

Born: New York, New York; June 10, 1937

PRINCIPAL DRAMA

Angelface, pr. 1968, pb. 1976

Elephant-Steps, pr. 1968 (libretto; music by
  Stanley Silverman)

Ida-Eyed, pr. 1969

Real Magic in New York, pr. 1970

Total Recall: Or, Sophia = (Wisdom) Part II, pr.
  1970, pb. 1976

Dream Tantras for Western Massachusetts, pr.
  1971 (libretto; music by Silverman)

HCohtienla: Or, Hotel China: Parts I and II, pr.,
  pb. 1972

Dr. Selavy's Magic Theatre, pr. 1972 (libretto;
  music by Silverman, lyrics by Thomas Hendry)

Evidence, pr. 1972

Sophia = (Wisdom) Part III: The Cliffs, pr. 1972,
  pb. 1973

Honor, pr. 1973

Particle Theory, pr. 1973

Une Semaine sous l'influence de . . ., pr. 1973, pb.
  1976 (pr. in U.S. as *Classical Therapy: Or, A
  Week Under the Influence*)

*Pain(t), and Vertical Mobility: Sophia = (Wisdom)
  Part IV*, pr. 1974, pb. 1976

Pandering to the Masses: A Misrepresentation, pr.
  1975, pb. 1977

Hotel for Criminals, pr. 1975, pb. 1991 (libretto;
  music by Silverman)

Rhoda in Potatoland (Her Fall-starts), pr. 1975, pb.
  1976

Livre de splendeurs (Part I), pr., pb. 1976 (pb. as
  Book of Splendors: Part I, 1985)

Plays and Manifestos of Richard Foreman, pb.
  1976

Book of Splendors: Part II, pr. 1977, pb. 1985

Boulevard de Paris, pr. 1977, pb. 1985

*Madness and Tranquility (My Head Was a
  Sledgehammer)*, pr. 1979

Luogo + Bersaglio, pr. 1979, pb. 1985 (as *Place +
  Target*)

Penguin Touquet, pr. 1980, pb. 1985

Madame Adare, pr. 1980 (libretto; music by
  Silverman)

Café Amerique, pr. 1981, pb. 1985

Egyptology (My Head Was a Sledgehammer), pr.
  1983, pb. 1985

La Robe de chambre de Georges Bataille, pr. 1983

The Golem, pr. 1984

Miss Universal Happiness, pr. 1985

Birth of the Poet, pr. 1985 (with Kathy Acker)

Reverberation Machines: Later Plays and Essays,
  pb. 1985

The Cure, pr. 1986, pb. 1992

Film Is Evil: Radio Is Good, pr., pb. 1987

Symphony of Rats, pr. 1988, pb. 1992

What Did He See?, pr. 1988, pb. 1992

Lava, pr. 1989, pb. 1992

Eddie Goes to Poetry City: Part I, pr. 1990, pb.
  1995

Eddie Goes to Poetry City: Part II, pr. 1991, pb.
  1995

Love and Science: Selected Librettos, pb. 1991

The Mind King, pr. 1992, pb. 1995

Unbalancing Acts: Foundations for a Theater, pb.
  1992

Samuel's Major Problems, pr. 1993, pb. 1995

My Head Was a Sledgehammer, pr. 1994, pb. 1995

I've Got the Shakes, pr., pb. 1995

The Universe, pr. 1996, pb. 2001

Permanent Brain Damage, pr. 1996, pb. 2001

Pearls for Pigs, pr. 1996, pb. 2001

Benita Canova, pr. 1997, pb. 2001

Paradise Hotel, pr. 1998, pb. 2001

Bad Boy Nietzsche, pr. 2000

*Now That Communism Is Dead, My Life Feels
  Empty*, pr. 2001

Maria Del Bosco, pr. 2002

OTHER LITERARY FORMS

Richard Foreman has been involved in all aspects
of theater. In addition to his plays, he has written several manifestos and essays that explain the genesis of

his theater work from a philosophical point of view, and he has also directed several plays and produced numerous videos. He has also published selected librettos and a novel, *No-Body* (1996).

ACHIEVEMENTS

Richard Foreman is one of the founders of the contemporary American theatrical avant-garde. His Ontological-Hysteric Theatre—for which Foreman acted as the sole playwright, director, and designer—is influenced by the theories of Bertolt Brecht and Gertrude Stein. Foreman's intent is to distance the audience from their normal expectations of a pleasurable theater experience and to make spectators aware of the process of perception. To force this awareness, he often obscures the stage picture with bright lights; leaves his scripts meaningless, nonnarrative, and nonlinear; and uses loud sounds to unsettle the spectator from passive complacency. Foreman has also applied his avant-garde aesthetic to texts by other writers, and even as a director, his signature remains unmistakable. Foreman's style was the harbinger of the postmodern theater work of artists such as the Wooster Group and John Jesurun. Foreman has received nine *Village Voice* Obies (including three for best play, and one for lifetime achievement), two New York State Creative Artists Public Service Awards, a Rockefeller Foundation playwrights grant, a Guggenheim Fellowship, and a Ford Foundation playwrights grant. He has also received the PEN/Laura Pels Master American Playwright Award, the MacArthur fellowship (1995-2000), the Edwin Booth Award for Theatrical Achievement, American Academy and Institute of Arts and Letters Award in literature; National Endowment for the Arts (NEA) Distinguished Artist Fellowship for lifetime achievement in theater, and two NEA Playwriting fellowships.

BIOGRAPHY

Richard Foreman was born in New York City on June 10, 1937, and was reared in Scarsdale, an affluent New York suburb in Westchester County. He became interested in theater as an adolescent, encouraged by an indulgent high school teacher who allowed him to express his already iconoclastic vision in inappropriately surreal set designs for school plays. During this time, Foreman studied the writings of Brecht, whose theories permeated Foreman's thought and would later profoundly influence his theater work. At Brown University, from which he was graduated magna cum laude in 1959, Foreman became interested first in film and then in playwriting, and was introduced to the writings of José Ortega y Gasset, which also influenced his later, rigorous style. Foreman studied with John Gassner at Yale University, from which he received his M.F.A. in 1962.

Foreman married his high school friend Amy Taubin in 1962. They moved to New York City, where Taubin pursued an acting career and Foreman joined the playwriting unit of the Actors Studio, writing conventional plays in the style of Clifford Odets and Arthur Miller. From 1962 to 1967, Foreman and Taubin immersed themselves in the New American Cinema movement evolving in lower Manhattan and became captivated by the avant-garde work of filmmakers Ken Jacobs, Michael Snow, and Jack Smith. Foreman gradually began applying the avant-garde film aesthetic to his own playwriting, leaving gaps and rough spots where he had once sought closure and polish. He presented *Angelface*, his first Ontological-Hysteric Theatre production, in 1968, at the Cinematheque on Wooster Street in Manhattan's SoHo district, and began collaborating with musician Stanley Silverman on experimental musical productions for the Music Theatre Group/Lenox Art Center.

Foreman dislodged his productions from his Wooster Street loft in 1976 and began working occasionally in Europe through the early 1980's. He spent most of this period either in Paris or touring to different performance spaces in Europe, such as Teatro Nuovo in Turin, Italy, and the Mickery Theatre in Amsterdam, Holland. Some of Foreman's later works were first performed in Europe: *Livre de splendeurs* was first shown in Paris, and *Luogo + Bersaglio* was first performed, in Italian, in Rome. During the 1990's and early twenty-first century, Foreman went on to have many plays produced in Europe, including *Paradise Hotel, Maria Del Bosco, Now That Communism Is Dead, My Life Feels Empty*; and *Bad Boy Nietzsche*.

In 1982, Foreman began directing occasional productions for Joseph Papp's New York Shakespeare Festival, where he mounted Botho Strauss's *Trilogie des Wiedersehens* (pr. 1975; *Three Acts of Recognition*, 1982) and Molière's *Don Juan: Ou, Le Festin de Pierre* (pr. 1655; *Don Juan*, 1755) in 1982, H. Leivick's *Der Golem* (1921; *The Golem*, 1966) in 1984, and Václav Havel's *Largo Desolato* (pb. 1985; English translation, 1985) in 1986. He has also directed productions of *Don Juan* for the Guthrie Theatre in Minneapolis, Minnesota (1981), and Arthur Kopit's *End of the World* (pr., pb. 1984) for the American Repertory Theatre (1987) in Cambridge, Massachusetts. Foreman married Kate Mannheim in 1990, and in 1992 he made the historic St. Mark's Church in New York City's East Village his home base. He has continued to write, design, and direct his own productions. He rehearses and produces one of his new plays each year, and each play is performed for sixteen weeks every winter.

ANALYSIS

Richard Foreman began his theater career as a playwright and progressed toward international recognition as one of the most influential auteurs of the contemporary American avant-garde. Foreman's writing style helped to establish what has come to be called the postmodern aesthetic, in which character no longer exists as a theatrical element, and the Theater of Images, in which aural and visual elements of a production become more important than the literary. His scripts for the Ontological-Hysteric Theatre represent only the workings of his mind while he writes them.

As a designer, Foreman constructs a playing space jumbled with objects and sensory input, which he then obscures from the spectator by shining blinding white lights into their eyes. Although he still presents Ontological-Hysteric Theatre productions, over which he maintains absolute control, Foreman has begun to direct other classic and contemporary plays, yet his unique directorial style is always apparent in his work.

Foreman established his Ontological-Hysteric Theatre in 1968, in a long, narrow loft that he converted into a performance space in the SoHo neighborhood of Manhattan. The name Ontological-Hysteric, although chosen rather capriciously, has come to symbolize many of Foreman's preoccupations. In both his playwriting and his subsequent staging of his own texts and those of other playwrights, Foreman's goal is to materialize the workings of consciousness and to make spectators aware of how they perceive their world.

Foreman sees consciousness as a perceptual mechanism that filters the world through the senses, and he believes that habit has taught people to limit their sensory input. To free them to explore their perceptual potential, Foreman constructs a rigorous attack on habitual ways of seeing the world and seeing art. Foreman's early Ontological-Hysteric Theatre works, such as *Sophia = (Wisdom) Part III*, *Pain(t)*, and *Vertical Mobility*, *Pandering to the Masses*, and *Rhoda in Potatoland (Her Fall-starts)*, insistently aimed to reshape spectators' perceptions by focusing on form and structure. He created a perceptually challenging environment that forced the audience to participate actively in constructing the theater experience.

In contrast with realistic theater (which strives to provide catharsis and to resolve its ambiguities and questions in a happy conclusion), Foreman's art avoids moral issues and the linear development of traditional plots. He forces spectators to expend their energies on "blasting" themselves into productions in which the entire framework of traditional theater—plot, characterization, and settings—has been discarded. The required perceptual work replaces the usual theater experience, in which the audience passively awaits catharsis through identification with a hero.

Foreman was considerably influenced by the theories of Brecht, whose alienation effect forced spectators into critical contemplation of the actions presented in his epic dramas. Brecht discouraged the identification processes of more realistic theater, which he believed rendered spectators passive and unable to move toward political change. Brecht's stagings were presentational. He used placards to announce his drama's episodes, intentionally interrupting the seductive narrative flow. His performers were taught to present quoted characterizations that maintained the separation between actor and character and gave the spectators room to contemplate the play's meanings.

Where Brecht encouraged critical distance in order to allow political self-determination, Foreman, however, was emphatically apolitical: He wanted his spectators to contemplate purely perceptual concerns. His work, moreover, departs from traditional Brechtian techniques. Particularly in his early Ontological-Hysteric Theatre pieces, preferring to work with nonactors, he discouraged his performers from acting as anyone other than themselves, and he directed them to deliver their lines in a flat monotone. Sometimes, performers' dialogue was recorded on tape and played back during performance, dissociating them from their voices. The performers moved through a series of complex, carefully choreographed movements and tasks. Actors in Foreman's early productions were merely demonstrators for his perceptual experiments.

Foreman established his unique style while other artists were also disrupting the conventions of traditional theater. In the late 1960's and early 1970's, the Performance Group, the Living Theatre, and the Open Theatre staged their productions environmentally, using the whole theater instead of only the stage behind the proscenium. All three encouraged their performers to interact physically with the audience and created texts that were often didactic, reflecting the radical political sentiment of the era.

Foreman, a staunch formalist, was at that time diametrically opposed to what he called such "expressionistic" theater. He maintained the proscenium/spectator arrangement, carefully orchestrating his stage pictures in static or slow-moving tableaux behind the proscenium frame; he prohibited his actors from interacting with spectators and maintained the fourth wall convention, in which spectators expect to feel as though they are looking into a world from which they cannot be seen; and he offered no didactic meanings for his spectators to consider from a political perspective. Within these conventional outlines, however, Foreman's theater was revolutionary in other ways.

Along with Robert Wilson and Lee Breuer, Foreman's work helped coin the term Theater of Images. Despite his theoretical concern with language, Foreman's theater is distinctly nonliterary. The Theater of Images increases the value of its visual and aural elements, displacing the text's primacy as the motivating principle. As a result, plot and character lose their places as the predominant bearers of meaning. Because the Theater of Images is dominated by sights and sounds that occur in space and time, within the immediate theater experience, sense impressions and the present-tense manipulation of perception become primary.

It is impossible to understand the full impact of a Foreman play by reading it on a page, because the experience of time and space is so important to his work. The atomization of movement and motion allows spectators' minds to roam freely, considering each part of the stage picture. The carefully constructed tableaux allow theatrical time to pause or even slow to a standstill, so that the spectator can choose which elements of the complex picture to relish visually and which objects to connect with others placed around the space.

Foreman takes a phenomenological approach to the stage space and his props. His aesthetic is similar to Gertrude Stein's, whose notion of a "continuous present" informed her landscape plays, which also stripped things to their essences. Wrenched out of context, objects become things without associations that impose meaning. To this end, Foreman constructs his scenography to render the ordinary extraordinary. Potatoes in *Rhoda in Potatoland (Her Fall-starts)* become larger-than-life. Clocks, such as the grandfather clock in *Sophia = (Wisdom) Part III*, become animate objects that enter the playing space. People become objects related to other objects. The potatoes that come crashing through windows in *Rhoda in Potatoland (Her Fall-starts)* are as much performers as the human beings inhabiting Foreman's cerebral landscape.

Spectators are also kept from finding meaning in Foreman's plays by the intentionally disorienting, uncomfortable process of perceiving the work. Lights shine directly in the spectators' eyes, making it difficult to see the stage. Loud noises startle the spectators out of passive contemplation, jolting them back into full awareness. The texts constantly comment on Foreman's process of creating them, calling attention to the arbitrary nature of words themselves. Snatches of familiar music are used to seduce the spectator into a feeling of ease, then are abruptly curtailed.

Foreman's scripts are plotless, self-reflective meditations on the act of writing. Although nothing ever happens in the conventional sense of action and linear narrative in a Foreman play, his scripts are often humorous and ironic, and they invite spectators to share in their witty investigations of how meaning is being created or withheld in the present theatrical moment. Where Brecht's writing was episodic, Foreman's is atomistic, a succession of brief, discrete moments intended to replicate the workings of his mind in the process of writing his plays.

Although there are no carefully crafted, fictional characters in Foreman's work, each person onstage represents a part of Foreman's consciousness. In his early work, a group of characters reappeared in different productions over several years. His works from this early period resembled something of a soap opera, in that the plotless productions never gave spectators the pleasure of a satisfactory ending. The character Max, whom some critics saw as Foreman's fictional counterpart, was a kind of artist figure constantly defining himself intellectually in relation to Rhoda. Rhoda, who was always played by Foreman's lover, Kate Mannheim, and who had a direct influence on his writing and staging, represented the archetypal woman. She symbolized the dark continent of sexuality and repressed psychology that could not be explained by rational male intellect. These strict gender dichotomies, which some feminist critics find misogynous, are very apparent in Foreman's early work and, despite minor alterations, operate throughout his oeuvre.

Although Foreman's theater is clearly ontological because of its obsession with questions of consciousness and being, his theater is aptly named "hysteric" in that it also deals with a more surrealist world of dreams, sexual desire, and anxieties. Foreman uses the ubiquitous Max and Rhoda to represent his consciousness and fears. Rhoda, in particular, represents Foreman grappling with the nature of sexuality and a more irrational world not easily explained by his otherwise rampant intellect.

Foreman's scenography further illustrates his theoretical and philosophical preoccupations. Foreman's sets are distinguished by their jumble of outsized objects, the strings stretched in a maze across the performance space that carves it into geometric patterns, the words or phrases of language decorating the space as though they, too, were objects, and the brightly colored streamers and other fanciful or bizarre props and materials that make for something of a carnivalesque atmosphere. Foreman's scenography is intended to force the eye to scan the stage picture. No one object or person is more important than another, and the taut strings are used to move the eye around the playing space. Miscellaneous words often dangle from the strings in Foreman's design, inviting the spectators to read the stage in a careful, perceptive way.

Foreman is preoccupied with the mechanisms of perception, which his scenography continually challenges. The hallmark of Foreman's productions are the bright white lights turned to shine in spectators' eyes, obscuring often tantalizing images within the stage picture; loud, irritating buzzers that interrupt the dialogue; bells that determine the beginning and the end of bits of action; and taped voices that dissociate the performers from their bodies or order them around. During productions at his Wooster Street loft, Foreman would sit at a table directly in front of the playing space, controlling the lights and the sound. Because many of the performers' cues were on an audiotape, he could change a performance's pace by adjusting the speed of the tape.

After spending a period from the late 1970's to the early 1980's in Europe, where his Ontological-Hysteric Theatre preoccupations were translated into French and toured avant-garde performance spaces, Foreman returned to the United States and began to focus on directing. Because he brings his own unique aesthetic to any play he undertakes, Foreman is often accused of "trashing" classical texts. His unusual scenography and presentational directing style might indeed seem out of place in plays such as Václav Havel's *Largo Desolato*, which has its own internal meanings that some critics believed were obscured by Foreman's external devices. His treatments of Molière's *Don Juan* and the classic folktale *The Golem*, however, were applauded for rejuvenating these texts from a new, contemporary perspective.

MISS UNIVERSAL HAPPINESS

Still, Foreman's most exciting directorial work seems to be accomplished on the fringes of established theater, in conjunction with avant-garde performance groups. Foreman's *Miss Universal Happiness*, for example, was a collaboration with the Wooster Group at the Performing Garage in SoHo. The Wooster Group's performances for this piece were physical and presentational, in the post-Brechtian style that is the Group's hallmark.

Miss Universal Happiness was purportedly a political piece, although Foreman is avowedly apolitical. The *mise en scène* had revolutionary overtones: The men wore combat clothes, the women dressed in rags and ripped stockings, and all the performers wore sombreros, vaguely referring to Third World revolutions and political strife. Yet more than revolutionary struggle, the performance was a self-reflexive commentary on how meaning is produced in theater. A teenage boy, the youngest member of the Wooster Group, began the piece by displaying his "lead lined" raincoat, which "protects you from ambiguities and obscurities" in the script. The remark was a wry warning to spectators that they should not try hard to look for meaning.

In the mid-1980's, Foreman departed from the slow, static tableaux that had once characterized his style. The stage images in *Miss Universal Happiness*, for example, were created by manic direction. The performers played musical chairs, but every time the music stopped, there was one chair too many, and another player was added to, instead of subtracted from, the game. Miss Universal Happiness, a parody of the Statue of Liberty, ran about the space dressed in black, wearing a black crown, and holding a tennis racket instead of a flame. Foreman did, however, maintain the artifice of his trademark scenography. A man in a rabbit suit appeared with two oversize oblong objects that could have been either missiles or cold capsules. Two big painted eyes were set up on easels in the back of the space, to watch *Miss Universal Happiness* progress.

BIRTH OF THE POET

Foreman's piece *Birth of the Poet*, with a script by Kathy Acker, was presented in Rotterdam, Holland, and then at the Brooklyn Academy of Music's Next Wave Festival in 1985. Acker's text was as disjunctive and fragmented as Foreman's. There were no characters in *Birth of the Poet*, which consisted of many long, rambling speeches about workers, productivity, and nuclear energy, delivered along with aggressively pornographic imagery and language. To emphasize the technological theme, the performers maneuvered golf carts around the space and moved manically among huge set pieces by sculptor David Salle.

Each of the three production elements—script, set, and music by Peter Gordon—were conceived individually, then brought together by Foreman's direction, a method that echoed the chance performances of composer John Cage. Foreman's signature devices were missing from this production. There were no strings pulled taut across the stage, and Foreman's usually witty, ironic text was replaced by Acker's pornographic script, which the performers shouted through microphones worn like headsets. Yet Foreman's concerns were still in evidence. Part of Foreman's theatrical project is to expose the process of creating performance. In *Birth of the Poet*, the battery packs that feed the microphones the performers wore were visibly strapped to their waists, and the dissociation of their voices from their source through amplification was intentional.

Foreman's concern with language was still clear in *Birth of the Poet*. A tubular steel structure hung from the flies with colorful cloth banners stretched from end to end. For the first hour or so of performance, one word—"talent"—and fragments of other words were on view. These fragments were meaningless until later in the performance. When the structure was moved offstage—by stagehands whose presence also emphasized the process of creating performance normally hidden from the audience's view—complementary word fragments at other angles formed complete words.

Foreman's trademark bright lights were present, but obscuring the spectators' view was meaningless in *Birth of the Poet*, since little happened onstage.

The space looked empty and disinterested, despite designer David Salle's unusual images: gigantic, two-dimensional ears of corn, a full-stage human body made of steel tubing and purple cloth, a giant steel hand that becomes a cage, a giant steel vagina, and expressionistic painted backdrops of a man's head, a dog's head, and a woman bent over at the waist peering through her legs at the audience.

THE CURE

After *Miss Universal Happiness*, Foreman shifted gears, moving away from the frenzied acting so amenable to the style of the Wooster Group. His next plays, beginning with *The Cure*, maintained a calmer and meditative pace conducive to greater reflection. Instead of a large number of actors, there were only three in *The Cure*. Although all three wore radio microphones, they spoke softly to elicit an intimate glimpse into more interior states. For Foreman, this was also the beginning of a greater interest in developing more psychologically based acting while retaining the structural and perceptual dynamics of his earlier work. *The Cure* is poetic both in structure and in tone, and more coherent than previous plays.

FILM IS EVIL: RADIO IS GOOD

Film Is Evil: Radio Is Good is striking in its move toward considering the ethical consequences of the manipulation of perceptual processes. It demonstrates that cinematic images seduce viewers to the point of confusion about the nature of material reality, deliberately using the second commandment—prohibiting graven images—as a point of departure. Set as an old-fashioned radio studio and using New York University theater students as a chorus, the play examines the critical freedom that hearing language involves versus the authoritarian imposition of images of film, combined with its narcissistic allure, that denies critical distance. Yet there is a deep ambivalence evident, given Foreman's own relation to the visual, that is demonstrated by the central use of a film, *Radio Rick in Heaven and Radio Richard in Hell*, in which Foreman appears as an authoritarian figure, but who magically disappears after prostrating himself before the camera.

SYMPHONY OF RATS

This socially conscious extension of his own theo-ries of perception reaches a political level in *Symphony of Rats*. Ron Vawter of the Wooster Group plays the president of the United States, whose judgments are guided by voices from "outer space," which in theatrical terms mean the words of Foreman as author. Foreman represents this connection even more by the appearance of his face on video monitors serving as the heads of two giant "spacemen" flanking the stage. This meditation on the social source of language that confuses the nature of internally and externally produced thought is derived in part from French poststructuralist theory. Reflection on the social origins of thought and perception resulted in Foreman's reassessing his early work as also being "political," but not in the sense of the exposition of ideological positions. His direction of Vawter's acting as riding the line between external and internal questioning showed, again, his movement toward the use of psychological technique.

WHAT DID HE SEE? AND LAVA

What Did He See? and *Lava* entail Foreman's further self-assessment of earlier work. *What Did He See?* involves questioning the nature of hermetic, possibly solipsistic, experimentation as a form of escapism, while *Lava* involves moving through conceptual categories of cognitive processes. Category One is the logical use of language and gesture in defining reality, common to conventional drama. Category Two is the random use of language and gesture, characteristic of Foreman's earlier plays. Category Three represents the space between these two, the gaps in understanding that defy conceptualization and that indicate a more spiritual form of experience. *What Did He See?* also saw the origination of a playing space that became an important part of Foreman's style. Installing a plexiglass screen that separates the actors from the spectators, thus forbidding any interaction with the viewers, this screen also creates the effect of a display window in which viewers see their reflecting images while also being seen from behind it as outsiders passively looking in on the action. Creating this aesthetic and emotional distance allowed the audience to view the play in a less conventionally empathic way, instead inviting a more vigilant, analytic reaction to the dream-like spectacle before them.

SAMUEL'S MAJOR PROBLEMS

Foreman continued to use this clear plastic screen in almost all his subsequent productions, beginning with *Samuel's Major Problems* in 1993. Continuing Foreman's interest in psychological acting and in bringing to life his characters' consciousness, *Samuel's Major Problems* reveals the principal character's fright in a nightmarish battle in which a devilish couple (a man and a woman) inflict both physical and mental stress on the character. Samuel, the principal character, a bedeviled hunchback, is stabbed, following a New Year's Eve party, by the woman, who at times represents the Devil and at others Death. The tormented Samuel finds that he is on his own, cannot get medical help, and is trapped in his nightmare and hallucinations, in an eerie play that is masterfully manipulated by Foreman.

PERMANENT BRAIN DAMAGE

Although Foreman's early plays were intent upon exemplifying the atomistic processes of perception, Foreman's plays after *The Cure* show a tendency toward more coherent dialogue *about* the nature of perception, while never eliminating exemplification entirely. What remains are scenic, gestural, and aural techniques that prevent simple empathic responses from the audience and that indicate that Foreman's theater remains a theater of the mind. As Foreman continued to write plays toward and beyond the millennium, he continued in this idiom. Many of these plays featured a protagonist who symbolized a principle of intellect or consciousness, troubled by a variety of tormentors who undermined him. In *Permanent Brain Damage*, for example, strange creatures, notably a sadistic man and a seductive woman, mock and torment a lonely and confused "egghead."

BAD BOY NIETZSCHE

This figure of a timid intellectual beleaguered by a cruel man and a beautiful woman returns in one of Foreman's major works of this period, *Bad Boy Nietzsche*, which takes as its subject the seminal German philosopher Friedrich Nietzsche as he descends into madness and death. Nietzsche fits perfectly into Foreman's gallery of cerebral men enmeshed in all that is irrational and disreputable, but the binary opposition between the thinking man and his opponents is con-stantly subverted, as is always the case in Foreman's plays. As a result, the ultimate meaning of the conflict is deliberately made indeterminate and paradoxical.

NOW THAT COMMUNISM IS DEAD, MY LIFE FEELS EMPTY AND PARADISE HOTEL

Another play of this period that features male protagonists involved in maddening contradictions is *Now That Communism Is Dead, My Life Feels Empty*. This play features two characters who must face the death of the idealistic, utopian dreams of the 1960's that had shaped their lives. That sense of disillusionment is also apparent in *Paradise Hotel*, a major play that explores another utopian experiment, namely the movement for sexual liberation associated with the 1960's. However, in contrast with a utopic image of sexuality as redemptive and liberating, *Paradise Hotel* creates a sobering picture of sexuality that is relentlessly crude and comical. That the Paradise Hotel seems to morph into the crass, pornographic Hotel Fuck, or, occasionally, into the absurdly sentimental Hotel Beautiful Roses, makes the journey all the more unstable and disorienting.

BENITA CANOVA

Two other important pieces from this period feature female protagonists reminiscent of Foreman's earlier Rhoda character. In *Benita Canova*, the protagonist of the same name is preoccupied with metaphysical problems. However, as she ponders the nature of reality, Benita Canova is subjected to absurd and degrading aggressive and sexual advances in a brothel-like setting. Like Foreman's male protagonists, the character of Benita Canova stands for the conscious intellect enmeshed in a paradoxical relationship with various inner and outer demons.

MARIA DEL BOSCO

In 2002, Foreman returned with another female protagonist in *Maria del Bosco*, a satiric indictment of the commercial society that has replaced the utopian dreams of the 1960's. Foreman here also returned to recorded layers of simultaneous language, using a text that consists only of forty-four statements repeated in varying patterns. On a philosophic level, Foreman is raising the issue of whether people are all trapped inside language patterns from which they can never escape, and in general, this play suggests dark and inescapable realities that dominate the characters' lives in a totalitarian way. The major character, the Countess Maria Del Bosco, personifies beauty and success but seems to also be complicit with and utterly subject to a world of brutality and ugliness. That the situation of the Countess indicates a contemporary society overwhelmingly informed by false and depraved values is reinforced by a giant sign that slides on repeatedly with the urgent advice to "Resist the Present." Although Foreman is suggesting that the world does not have to be the way it seems to be, it is important to realize that the Countess is contemporary but also timeless. In addition, she is both false and true, risible and beautiful, profane and holy. The Countess is trapped within a materialistic present but also transcends it and indicates a reality that suggests the sacred. The ambiguity of the Countess perpetuates a typically Foremanesque picture of human personality that is endlessly contradictory. This and other plays of Foreman's tenure at St. Mark's suggest that Foreman is not only continuing to interrogate many of the various ideological and social movements and trends that have affected American society in modern times but is continuing as well to explore the paradoxes in the human personality and in the nature of existence itself.

OTHER MAJOR WORK

LONG FICTION: *No-Body*, 1996.

BIBLIOGRAPHY

Bigsby, C. W. E. *Beyond Broadway.* Vol. 3 in *A Critical Introduction to Twentieth Century American Drama.* New York: Cambridge University Press, 1985. Bigsby's chapter on Foreman is at once explanatory and critical, analyzing Foreman's manifestos and early plays. He points to the inconsistencies and shortcomings of some of Foreman's theories within actual theater practice and its reception. He also connects the work with that of the absurdists and the novels of Alain Robbe-Grillet.

Davy, Kate. *Richard Foreman and the Ontological-Hysteric Theatre.* Ann Arbor, Mich.: UMI Research Press, 1981. This in-depth book details Foreman's working methods as writer, director, scenographer, and composer. It is also invaluable as an analysis of the dramatic theories of Bertolt Brecht and Gertrude Stein insofar as they have influenced Foreman's theory and practice.

Foreman, Richard. "A Conversation with Richard Foreman." Interview by Charles Bernstein. *The Drama Review* 36 (Fall, 1992): 103-130. In this interview, Foreman describes developments and shifts in his working methods and philosophy. He also reveals his literary and philosophical influences as well as the types of theater against which he is reacting—Jerzy Grotowski's, in particular.

Halstead, Jack. "Re-Viewing Richard Foreman and Theater of Images." *Journal of Dramatic Theory and Criticism* 4 (Spring, 1992). Halstead elaborates on Foreman's earlier Ontological-Hysteric Theatre practice in terms of mimesis and writing, viewing these issues from the standpoint of post-structuralist theory. He draws clear parallels between Foreman's work and the ideas of Roland Barthes and Jacques Derrida.

Munk, Erika. "Film Is Ego, Radio Is God: Richard Foreman and the Arts of Control." *The Drama Review* 31 (Winter, 1987): 125-135. This review-essay on *Film Is Evil: Radio Is Good* contemplates how far Foreman has pushed reflection about his own authority by concentrating on a medium—film—that inevitably reinforces his authority. Munk surmises that technological forms throw one back on a self that finds it increasingly difficult to recognize itself.

Rabkin, Gerald, ed. *Richard Foreman.* Baltimore, Md.: The Johns Hopkins University Press, 1999. Wide-ranging anthology includes reviews, interviews, essays and a selection of Foreman's writings. Detailed chronology of Foreman's career, bibliography, and nineteen photographs.

Robinson, Marc. *The Other American Drama.* Cambridge, England: Cambridge University Press, 1994. Study of alternative American drama beginning with Gertrude Stein concludes its survey with a chapter on Foreman.

Jill Dolan,
updated by Jon Erickson
and Margaret Boe Birns